MW01534656

Justice John Marshall Harlan II Dissents

Edited by Robert Dittmer

Text Copyright © 2018 Robert Dittmer
All Rights Reserved

Note on the text: most italics and bold has been removed.

Acknowledgements

Websites (in no particular order):

www.law.cornell.edu   supreme.justia.com   caselaw.findlaw.com
Public.Resource.Org   Openjurist.org   scholar.google.com
en.wikipedia.org

"I think, moreover, in the context of a statute so broad as the one before us, churches may properly receive an exemption even though they do not themselves sponsor the secular-type activities mentioned in the statute but exist merely for the convenience of their interested members. As long as the breadth of exemption includes groups that pursue cultural, moral, or spiritual improvement in multifarious secular ways, including, I would suppose, groups whose avowed tenets may be antitheological, atheistic, or agnostic, I can see no lack of neutrality in extending the benefit of the exemption to organized religious groups."

-Justice Harlan's concurrence in Walz v. Tax Comm'n NYC (May 4, 1970)

Table of Contents

Justice Harlan's dissent in Emspak v. US (May 23, 1955)

MR. JUSTICE HARLAN, dissenting.

A valid claim of privilege against self-incrimination under the Fifth Amendment has two requisites: (1) the privilege must be adequately invoked, and (2) a possible answer to the question against which the privilege is asserted must have some tendency to incriminate the person to whom the question is addressed. Although Emspak's invocation of the privilege left much to be desired, I agree with the majority's view that it was adequate, and that Emspak at no time abandoned his claim. But I must dissent from the Court's holding that all of the questions involved in the indictment called for possibly incriminatory answers.

The Court also holds, as an alternative ground for reversing Emspak's conviction for contempt of the House Subcommittee, that Emspak was not sufficiently apprised of the fact that the Subcommittee, notwithstanding the claim of privilege, was insisting upon answers to the questions put to him. From this holding I must also dissent.

My disagreement with the Court on both scores goes to the first 58 counts of the indictment.[1] As the Court's opinion recognizes, the upholding of Emspak's conviction on any one count of the indictment would require affirmance of the judgment below, because the general sentence imposed on all counts was less than the maximum allowable on any single count. See Sinclair v. United States, 279 U. S. 263, 299 (1929).

I.

AS TO THE INCRIMINATORY CHARACTER OF THE 58 QUESTIONS.

It is quite true, as the majority observes, that this issue was not dealt with by either of the courts below. The District Court and the Court of Appeals did not have to reach the problem because of their conclusion that Emspak's claim of privilege was inadequate. And for some reason the Government has not pressed the point. This, however, does not foreclose this Court from considering it. See Swift & Co. v. Hocking Valley R. Co., 243 U. S. 281, 289 (1917). And perhaps it is due that I should explain why I think we should deal with it. My reason is twofold: first, because to hold, as the Court does, that the questions involved in Counts 1 to 58 of the indictment were of an incriminatory character seems to me to verge on an abandonment of the rule that a valid claim of privilege exists only as to incriminatory questions; and second, because the more recent decisions of this Court appear to me to leave the standard for determining whether a question is incriminatory in great confusion. For example, the Court of Appeals for the Third Circuit had occasion not so long ago to manifest its bewilderment as to where this aspect of the privilege against self-incrimination now stands in light of recent decisions of this Court. See United States v. Coffey, 198 F. 2d 438 (1952). In short, I think the standard for judging the character of a question against which the Fifth Amendment privilege is asserted needs both rehabilitation and restatement.

(1) The standard.

The concept of an incriminating answer includes not only those answers which constitute an admission of guilt, but also those which may furnish evidence of guilt or merely supply a lead to obtaining such evidence. Counselman v. Hitchcock, 142 U. S. 547 (1892).

The answer to almost any question a witness is asked could be regarded as being useful as evidence, or as furnishing a lead to evidence, in support of some conceivable criminal charge against the person to whom the question is addressed. But unlike a defendant in a criminal case, a witness in a grand jury or other judicial or legislative proceeding has never been allowed, by claiming his privilege, to refuse to answer any questions at all. That would completely subordinate the public interest in the conduct of such proceedings. Accordingly, lest claims of the Fifth Amendment privilege be used as a cover for a person refusing to perform his duty to co-operate in such proceedings, reasonable bounds have been put upon the exercise of the privilege. Those bounds were stated as long ago as 1861 by the English Court of Queen's Bench in The Queen v. Boyes, 1 B. & S. 311, 330-331, in language which this Court has adopted as the basis for the rule in this country. See Brown v. Walker, 161 U. S. 591, 599-600 (1896); Mason v. United States, 244 U. S. 362, 365-366 (1917). In the Boyes case, Cockburn, C. J., said:

"Further than this, we are of opinion that the danger to be apprehended must be real and appreciable, with reference to the ordinary operation of law in the ordinary course of things—not a danger of an imaginary and unsubstantial character, having reference to some extraordinary and barely possible contingency, so improbable that no reasonable man would suffer it to influence his conduct. We think that a merely remote and naked possibility, out of the ordinary course of the law and such as no reasonable man would be affected by, should not be suffered to obstruct the administration of justice.

The object of the law is to afford to a party, called upon to give evidence in a proceeding inter alios, protection against being brought by means of his own evidence within the penalties of the law. But it would be to convert a salutary protection into a means of abuse if it were to be held that a mere imaginary possibility of danger, however remote and improbable, was sufficient to justify the withholding of evidence essential to the ends of justice."

Throughout the course of its decisions this Court has consistently stated that the "real danger v. imaginary possibility" test is the proper standard to be applied in deciding whether particular questions are subject to a valid Fifth Amendment claim. See Brown v. Walker, supra; Heike v. United States, 227 U. S. 131, 144 (1913); Mason v. United States, supra; Rogers v. United States, 340 U. S. 367 (1951); Blau v. United States, 340 U. S. 159, 161 (1950); Hoffman v. United States, 341 U. S. 479, 486 (1951). But in recent per curiam reversals of contempt convictions this Court seems to have indicated a tendency to stray from the application of this traditional standard.[2] And I shall presently show that it has departed from that standard in this case.

(2) Application of the standard to questions innocent on their face.

The next question requiring consideration is: How should this standard be applied in a case where the questions appear on their face to call only for innocent answers? In

United States v. Weisman, 111 F. 2d 260 (1940), the Court of Appeals for the Second Circuit had before it a claim of the Fifth Amendment privilege to a question in substantially the following form: "Did you know anyone who visited or lived in Shanghai between 1934 and 1939?" On the surface of things—had nothing more appeared—the possible answers to this question— "Yes," "No" or "I don't know"—would all appear innocent. A situation could be imagined in which one of these answers would have tended to incriminate, but this possibility by itself would not be enough to justify the claim of privilege. Additional facts appeared, however, which showed the question to be part of an incriminatory pattern: the witness was a New York night club proprietor, unlikely to be acquainted with Shanghai residents or visitors, and he had engaged in transactions looking suspiciously like importations of narcotics from China. Because of these and other facts, a real danger of incrimination from answering the question was held to exist by the court, through Judge Learned Hand. It may be argued that the admission sought was not sufficiently implicating to justify the invocation of the privilege, see Wigmore, Evidence, §§ 2260-2261; but for present purposes we may assume that the result is a correct one.

Of course, in some cases the background facts making an apparently innocent question dangerous may not be known to the court. Then the choice must be made between requiring the court to accept the witness' word that facts exist which would make his answer incriminating, and requiring the witness to explain the circumstances which justify his claim of privilege. To be sure, the second alternative involves the danger that the witness will have to reveal some incriminatory evidence in order to show why he should not be required to answer. Nevertheless, traditionally the witness has not been allowed to be sole judge of the character of the questions objected to; he is required to open the door wide enough for the court to see that there is substance to his claim. United States v. Weisman, supra. If the background facts are known or suspected to exist, this problem disappears, for all the witness has to do is point to such facts or suspicions.

(3) Application of the standard to dangerous questions.

It seems to me that the "real danger v. imaginary possibility" standard ought to be applied in the same fashion to dangerous questions. Such questions include those which call for an admission of a crime or a necessary element of a crime, or a fact which, while innocent on its face, is dangerous in the light of other facts already developed.

In all such cases other facts may appear which serve to cast an innocent aspect upon the question. Suppose two men are suspected of having conspired to steal cash from a bank one day during business hours. Each is asked whether he saw the other on the day of the theft, and each pleads his privilege. But facts already developed in the investigation show that both men are tellers in this bank and have worked in the same cage for ten years. Certainly, in these circumstances, the fact of each having seen the other cannot rationally be said to have any tendency to establish their guilt, or, in any realistic sense, to aid the prosecution in discovering evidence against them, since the prosecution already would be expected to have independent evidence of their presence in the bank on that day. In other words, if background facts can make an innocent question dangerous, they can also make a dangerous question innocent. And in deciding whether the privilege is available, we must take into account all the facts—not just those tending to make the question dangerous.

I do not suggest that in a trial for contempt a Fifth Amendment defense should be set at naught whenever the prosecution is able to offer an exculpatory explanation for an otherwise incriminating answer. What I do submit is that the privilege should not be available when the facts have been sufficiently developed at the time the claim of privilege is made so that it is plain that no possible answer to the question put to the witness could rationally tend to prove his guilt or supply the prosecution with leads to evidence against him. In such circumstances there is no real danger of harm to the witness to be apprehended from his answering the question.

(4) Application of the standard to this case.

I come finally to the issue as to how the "real danger v. imaginary possibility" standard should be applied to the questions involved in the first 58 counts of the indictment.[3] Typical of these questions were the following: "Are you acquainted with Joseph Persily?"; "Is Max Helford at the present time a field organizer for the UE?"

On their face, and without more, these questions were certainly innocent enough. And therefore the first issue confronting us is whether other existing background facts and circumstances made the questions incriminatory. We start from these premises: From the announced purposes of the Subcommittee and the pattern of its questioning of witnesses, it is a fair inference that one of the Subcommittee's objectives was to show that communists held positions of responsibility in this Union. This in turn might be the starting point for prosecutions for filing false noncommunist affidavits under the Taft-Hartley Act[4] or for violations of the Smith Act.[5] The conclusion also seems justified that most, if not all, of the persons referred to in the 58 questions put to Emspak, and Emspak himself, were suspected of being communists or of having communist affiliations. Indeed, the Government on the oral argument conceded as much. Had Emspak admitted knowing any of these people, this might tend to show association with communists. While the decisions of this Court do not establish that these factors would have sufficed to make those questions incriminatory, lower courts have gone far in this direction. See Kasinowitz v. United States, 181 F. 2d 632 (1950); United States v. Raley, 96 F. Supp. 495 (1951); see also Falknor, Self-Crimination Privilege: "Links in the Chain," 5 Vand. L. Rev. 479, 485-489 (1952).

But there were also other background facts and circumstances. Emspak had told the Subcommittee that he was Secretary of the Union. He was asked if other named individuals held positions in the same Union, and with respect to some of them, whether he knew them personally. These things being so, it is difficult to see how the fact that Emspak knew some of these people or what position each held in the Union can rationally be said to support even an inference that he knew of their alleged communist affiliations, much less tend to prove that he himself had taken part in a conspiracy to advocate the forcible overthrow of the Government or had falsely sworn that he was not a communist.

Nor could the answers to the questions have been of material assistance in providing leads to evidence to be used against him. Investigators presumably would already know that the Secretary of the Union knew other Union officials. Thus, in light of Emspak's admitted position, the questions appear proper.

This conclusion is not affected by the additional possibility that Emspak's answers might have been admissible against him in a later criminal trial. If the answers were admissible, this fact should not of itself make the questions incriminatory, even though the answers might have been utilized by the prosecutor to show Emspak's acquaintance with these other persons as a first step in proving conspiracy, and the prosecutor would thus have been spared the necessity of proving this acquaintance by independent evidence. But in fact Emspak's answers would not have been admissible against him in such a trial. For at the time Emspak testified before the Sub-committee, a federal statute prevented the use of any of his testimony before that body as evidence against him in any later criminal proceedings, except a prosecution for perjury in the giving of the testimony.[6] Thus, to the extent that the incriminatory character of these questions depends solely upon the admissibility of Emspak's answers in evidence against him in a later criminal trial, there could hardly be a valid objection to them on this score.

In the last analysis, the Court's holding seems to rest on the premise that the questions put to Emspak became automatically incriminatory once it was shown that he and those about whom he was interrogated were under suspicion of communism. This is painting with too broad a brush.

It is true that under the rule as it exists a witness may sometimes have to walk a tightrope between waiver of his privilege, if he answers a question later held to be incriminatory, and contempt, if he refuses to answer a question later held to be nonincriminatory. And it may be that in some circumstances the privilege should be held to extend to questions which are not in themselves incriminatory, but which seem likely to lead to other questions which are. But in my view any such doctrine should be regarded as an exception to the general rule and should be confined to cases where special circumstances exist which make it unfair to apply the ordinary rule, such as where the witness is without counsel, is ignorant or confused, and the like. Some of the decisions of lower courts seem to suggest that in proceedings obviously designed to develop a case against a particular witness, the witness may be allowed to invoke the privilege as to all questions, as may a defendant in a criminal case. See Marcello v. United States, 196 F. 2d 437 (1952); Maffie v. United States, 209 F. 2d 225 (1954). I think, however, that such a view is too sweeping, and also that where there is room for the application of an exception to the ordinary rule, it should be done openly, and not under the guise of holding nonincriminatory questions incriminatory. No circumstances are shown here which would call for the application of any such exception. Emspak was represented by counsel and was obviously an intelligent and shrewd witness. The inference most readily drawn from the record is that Emspak did not want to "stool pigeon" against his associates. While such a motive would not, in my opinion, vitiate an otherwise valid claim of the privilege, it certainly furnished no legal excuse for refusing to answer nonincriminatory questions.

II.

AS TO EMSPAK'S KNOWLEDGE THAT THE SUBCOMMITTEE WANTED ITS QUESTIONS ANSWERED.

The majority holds that whenever a witness objects to a question there is no violation of 2 U. S. C. § 192 until he is clearly apprised that the Committee demands his answer, notwithstanding his objection. Until then, so the Court holds, the witness has not evidenced the requisite criminal intent, that is, a deliberate refusal to answer. The Court elaborates this thesis in the Quinn case, ante, p. 155, decided today, and applies it in this case and in the Bart case, post, p. 219, also decided today.

I am unable to accept the Court's holding on this score, and agree with MR. JUSTICE REED'S criticism of it in his two dissenting opinions in these three cases. I consider it desirable, however, to elaborate somewhat upon what MR. JUSTICE REED has said.

Section 192 speaks only of refusal to answer. "Refusal" implies simply recognition of what the Committee is after and failure either to supply it or to explain an inability to supply it. It only confuses the matter to say that the "refusal" must be "intentional" or "deliberate" or that it must manifest a "criminal intent." Indeed, Sinclair v. United States, 279 U. S. 263, 299 (1929), upon which the Court relies, was later discussed in United States v. Murdock, 290 U. S. 389, 396, 397 (1933), and the Court there pointed out that § 192 does not make a bad purpose or evil intent an ingredient of the crime of refusing to answer a question pertinent to the matter under inquiry.

Beyond this, I see no reason for thinking that when a witness couples an objection with a refusal to answer, his refusal becomes any the less "deliberate" or "intentional." The Court holds that if the objection were accepted by the Committee, the requirement of "deliberateness" would not have been met. For my part, the proper analysis of such a situation is rather that there has been a "refusal to answer," and thus at least a prima facie violation of the statute, but the Committee has chosen not to press the matter further. What the Committee does after the witness makes his objection should not be held to have any bearing on the question whether there was a refusal, or on the question whether it was "deliberate," if that connotes anything more. Those questions must be determined as of the time the witness speaks.

Thus I do not see how the Court's result can be hinged to any language in the statute. Perhaps a privilege to object could be derived, however, from what must be taken to be the statute's over-all purpose: to enable committees to obtain the information they wish without at the same time treating witnesses unfairly. Thus, a witness might be held privileged to refuse to answer a question, for the purpose of presenting, at reasonable length, a colorable objection to the propriety of the question. But this privilege would terminate when it became reasonably apparent to the witness that the objection was not acceptable to the Committee. Then the witness would have to choose between answering and standing on the validity of his objection.

If this is the standard which the Court's construction establishes, I would quarrel only with its application here. But in requiring that a witness who objects be "clearly apprised" that his objection is unsatisfactory and that the Committee wishes his answer, the Court may have meant to go further. If that is so, then I would question the standard itself. Moreover, I think that even this more lenient standard would have been met in this case. For surely the record shows that Emspak was clearly apprised that, despite his objections, the Committee wanted answers to the 58 questions, so that there is a violation of the statute under either standard. After Emspak had answered a number of preliminary questions concerning the organization of his Union, the following discussion took place between him, Congressman Moulder, and Mr. Tavenner, the Committee Counsel:

"Mr. Tavenner. Mr. Emspak, are you acquainted with Joseph Persily?

"Mr. Emspak. Mr. Chairman, I would like to say something at this point.

"Mr. Moulder. You mean in response to the question?

"Mr. Emspak. I will answer the question; yes, in response to the question and as a statement of position.

"What I say revolves around two points, one organizationally and another as an individual. Organizationally, my job as an officer of this union is to represent the interest of the membership as they determine it at the annual conventions and at other means they have of getting together and expressing themselves. My job is to administer that aspect to the best of my ability, using one very simple measuring stick, and that is: Does a given policy or action contribute to the well-being of the membership, individually and collectively?

"As an individual I would like to say one thing, and that is this: The line of questioning that counsel is developing now is a line that has been used on numerous occasions by this committee and other congressional committees in an attempt to harass the union, its leadership, and its members. It is a line of questioning that goes against my grain as an American. I was born in this country. Everything I am—

"Mr. Moulder. How long will this statement take, Mr. Emspak?

"Mr. Emspak. About two or three more minutes.

"Mr. Moulder. Proceed.

"Mr. Emspak. Everything I am, I owe to the rich heritage and tradition of this country. I do not believe that a committee of this kind, especially in view of the recent record of this committee where it stooped to interfere in the partisan affairs of a local union, or any congressional committee, because of the rich tradition of this country which, if not perverted, will lead to a greater and better country—I don't think a committee like this or any subcommittee has a right to go into any question of my beliefs, my associations, or anything else. I have a couple of kids. They have a stake in this country, too.

"Mr. Moulder. I want to give you full opportunity to express yourself in answer to the question, but you are making an oration now.

"Mr. Emspak. It is not an oration. It happens to be a very profound personal feeling.

"Mr. Moulder. What is the question?

"Mr. Tavenner. The question is: Are you acquainted with Joseph Persily.

"Mr. Moulder. How do you spell that?

"Mr. Tavenner. P-e-r-s-i-l-y.

"Mr. Emspak. Because I have a stake in this country—

"Mr. Moulder. You are not answering the question. He asked you if you are acquainted with this man.

"Mr. Emspak. I will answer it.

"Mr. Moulder. Are you or not?

"Mr. Emspak. I was on the verge of answering it.

"Mr. Moulder. If you have any explanation to make you will be permitted to do so after you answer the question.

"Mr. Emspak. Because of my interest in what is going on these days, because of the activities of this committee—

"Mr. Moulder. Are you going to answer the question?

"Mr. Emspak. Because of the hysteria, I think it is my duty to endeavor to protect the rights guaranteed under the Constitution, primarily the first amendment, supplemented by the fifth. This committee will corrupt those rights.

"Mr. Moulder. Do you think it corrupts you to answer the question?

"Mr. Emspak. I certainly do.

"Mr. Moulder. Why does it corrupt you?

"Mr. Emspak. Your activities are designed to harm the working people of this country. Every action this committee has ever taken has done that. You interfered last summer in the election of a local union at the request of a priest. You know that. You dragged down the prestige of this country.

"Mr. Moulder. You are not going to take over this committee.

"Mr. Emspak. I don't want to.

"Mr. Moulder. And your statements are pre-posterous. The purpose of this committee is to expose communism as it exists in this country. What is the question?

"Mr. Tavenner. Are you acquainted with Joseph Persily?

"Mr. Emspak. For the reasons I stated before, I answered it.

"Mr. Moulder. Then you refuse to answer the question?

"Mr. Emspak. No. I answered it.

"Mr. Tavenner. Are you or are you not acquainted with Joseph Persily?

"Mr. Emspak. I answered the question.

"Mr. Tavenner. Your replies are a refusal to comply with the request to answer it?

"(Witness confers with his counsel.)

"Mr. Moulder. The record will reveal that you have not answered the question.

"Mr. Emspak. I have answered it to the best of my ability under the circumstances.

"Mr. Moulder. Any further questions?

"Mr. Tavenner. Yes. In what capacity is Joseph Persily associated with the UE at this time?

"Mr. Emspak. It is the same question over again. I will give the same answer.

"Mr. Tavenner. Is he an organizer in the UE?

"Mr. Emspak. Mr. Chairman, it is the same question.

"Mr. Tavenner. You refuse to answer that?

"Mr. Emspak. I answered it."

Following this, Emspak was asked 55 questions of exactly the same character as those relating to Persily, to each of which he reiterated, with minor variations: "Same answer." This was obviously, on this record, nothing other than a formula for refusing to answer without appearing to do so. In the face of such a record, I find it impossible to understand how the Court can conclude that Emspak was not clearly apprised of the fact that the Subcommittee wanted his answers.

Were this opinion being written for the Court, it would be necessary, before affirming this conviction, to deal with the other points Emspak urges for reversal. Since the Court, under its view of the case, did not reach any of them, I think it would not be appropriate for me to discuss them. I am therefore content to say that I find none of those points tenable on this record.

I would affirm the judgment of conviction.

Notes

[1] However, I do agree with the Court that the privilege was available as to the questions involved in Counts 59 through 68 of the indictment, since, under the circumstances shown by the record, each of those questions did call for a possibly incriminatory answer. Because this would in any event require reversal of the conviction on those counts, as to them I need not reach the issue of whether Emspak was adequately apprised that the Subcommittee was insisting upon his answers, despite the claim of privilege.

[2] See Greenberg v. United States, 341 U. S. 944 (1951), 343 U. S. 918 (1952); Singleton v. United States, 343 U. S. 944 (1952), and the discussion of the Court of Appeals for the Third Circuit in United States v. Coffey, supra.

[3] I consider that the 10 questions involved in Counts 59-68 of the indictment qualified, in the circumstances of this case, as incriminatory questions under the "real danger v. imaginary possibility" standard.

[4] 61 Stat. 146, 29 U. S. C. § 159 (h).

[5] 18 U. S. C. § 2385.

[6] R. S. § 859, 18 U. S. C. (1952 ed.) § 3486: "No testimony given by a witness before either House, or before any committee of either House, or before any joint committee established by a joint or concurrent resolution of the two Houses of Congress, shall be used as evidence in any criminal proceeding against him in any court, except in a

prosecution for perjury committed in giving such testimony. But an official paper or record produced by him is not within the said privilege." This statute, falling short of a complete grant of immunity to the witness from prosecution on account of testimony given by him, would not have been effective to compel testimony over a valid claim of privilege, but it was effective to prevent the use of such testimony against the witness in a subsequent criminal prosecution. See Adams v. Maryland, 347 U. S. 179, 182-183 (1954). This statute was in effect until August 20, 1954, when it was superseded by 68 Stat. 745. The supersession would not affect the inadmissibility of testimony given while the old statute was in effect. See Cameron v. United States, 231 U. S. 710 (1914).

The possibility that a witness might commit perjury in answering a question has never been regarded as justification for invoking the privilege to the question. See Noonan, Inferences from the Invocation of the Privilege Against Self-Incrimination, 41 Va. L. Rev. 311, 321-322 (1955).

Justice Harlan's dissent in Bart v. US (May 23, 1955)

MR. JUSTICE HARLAN, dissenting.

I would affirm the judgment of conviction in this case, on the reasoning stated in part II of my dissenting opinion in the Emspak case, ante, p. 203, at p. 213, decided this day. To what is said there I should add what follows.

Even under the Court's standard of "apprisal," the record in this case is convincing that Bart must have understood that the Subcommittee was insisting on his answers to the questions involved in the indictment. I need only refer to the fact that four of the counts of the indictment charge Bart with refusing to answer what was in substance the same question, namely, what Bart's name had been before he changed it. As to these questions the record shows the following:

"Mr. Case [Committee Member]. What was your name at the time you came to the United States?

"Mr. Bart. I have already answered this question.

"Mr. Walter [Committee Chairman]. What was it?

"Mr. Unger [Bart's Counsel]. Mr. Chairman, I think we are spending a good deal of time, with all due respect to the Chair, on a point that has absolutely no bearing on any issue here.

"Mr. Walter. That is only your opinion.

"Mr. Unger. I said that was my opinion.

"Mr. Case. Mr. Chairman, I don't know what the question will lead up to, but it certainly has been customary, when we have been interrogating witnesses who have come to the United States from other countries, to know when they came to the United States, and to know under what name they came, and to know the name shown on the passport. There is nothing improper or out of the way in asking such a question. I think we should have an answer to the question of the name he had when he came to the United States.

"Mr. Unger. Are you suggesting the inquiry has to do with what this man did when he was 10 years old? You are talking about a 10-year-old boy.

"Mr. Walter. Just a moment. I think Mr. Tavenner should be able to proceed, and after his questions, Mr. Case, you may ask such questions as you may desire. May I suggest, Mr. Tavenner, that you refresh the witness' recollection by telling him what his name was before he assumed his present name? Proceed.

"Mr. Tavenner [Committee Counsel]. You are a naturalized American citizen?

"Mr. Bart. Yes.

"Mr. Tavenner. How did you become naturalized?

"Mr. Bart. Through process of my father.

"Mr. Tavenner. What was your father's name?

"Mr. Bart. I have already dealt with this question.

"Mr. Tavenner. When was your father naturalized?

"Mr. Bart. I do not remember.

"Mr. Unger. Just a minute.

"(Witness confers with his counsel.)

"Mr. Bart. About 30 years ago.

"Mr. Tavenner. Do you refuse to tell the committee your father's name?

"Mr. Unger. Mr. Tavenner, he doesn't refuse to tell the committee. He is trying to tell the committee that this line of inquiry is a highly improper one.

"Mr. Walter. That is not within his province. The committee determines what is proper and what is not proper, and it is not up to you to determine that.

"Mr. Unger. That is true.

"Mr. Case. Mr. Chairman, it seems to me the counsel should advise his client and not the committee.

"Mr. Unger. I am not trying to advise the committee. I tried to respectfully point out why it is an improper question. He is not ashamed of his father's name or his mother's name. What difference can it possibly make what his name was when he came here?

"Mr. Walter. We are not going to have you arguing with the committee or giving us your legal opinion, which may or may not be worth anything.

"Mr. Unger. I have no further comment on the question.

"Mr. Walter. All right.

"Mr. Bart, you claim citizenship by virtue of your father's citizenship; is that right?

"Mr. Bart. That is right.

"Mr. Walter. Under what name did your father become a citizen of the United States?

"Mr. Bart. Under his own name.

"Mr. Walter. What was that name?

"Mr. Bart. I have already stated my reply to this question as far as I am concerned.

"Mr. Walter. How can you claim citizenship by virtue of your father's citizenship if you don't know what name your father used when he became a citizen?

"Mr. Unger. Mr. Chairman—

"Mr. Walter. Let the witness answer the question. You may advise your client.

"Mr. Bart. I have answered I am a citizen by virtue of that fact, and that this is my legal name by which I vote and am registered and am known.

"Mr. Walter. When did you legally change your name?

"Mr. Bart. Many years ago.

"Mr. Walter. Where?

"Mr. Bart. In the city of New York.

"Mr. Walter. Did you have your name changed in court?

"Mr. Bart. Yes; about 15 years ago.

"Mr. Unger. His answer is about 15 years ago.

"Mr. Walter. I understand. What name did you change your name from?

"Mr. Bart. I have already stated my reply to this question.

"Mr. Harrison [Committee Member]. I understand you refuse to answer the chairman's question?

"Mr. Bart. My answer is that I have answered what my name is here, which is the only question pertaining to the inquiry, it seems to me.

"Mr. Walter. Of course all of this is a matter of public record?

"Mr. Bart. Correct.

"Mr. Walter. And then I suppose you know that under the law a question innocent on its face can't be arbitrarily ignored. You can't refuse to answer such a question without running the risk of the consequences.

"Mr. Unger. I think, again, Mr. Chairman, Mr. Bart has indicated very plainly he has not been contumacious in any regard. He states his name has been Philip Bart for a large number of years.

"Mr. Walter. Don't argue with the committee. You advise your client as you see fit.

"Mr. Case. Mr. Chairman, it seems to me the witness should be advised of the possibilities of contempt when he fails to answer a question as simple and as proper as your question as to what his name was before it was changed.

"Mr. Walter. No. He has counsel. Counsel knows that is the law. Proceed, Mr. Tavenner."[*]

The very fact that the same answer was sought in four different ways must have impressed upon a man of Bart's intelligence that the Committee considered his objections unfounded, and wished him to answer.

For the reasons stated in my Emspak dissent, I do not deal with any of the petitioner's other contentions, save to say that on this record I consider them all untenable.

I would affirm the judgment of conviction.

[*] The Court attaches importance to the colloquy between Mr. Case and Mr. Walter shown in the last two paragraphs quoted above, and to Mr. Walter's later rejoinder to Mr. Unger: "Of course, you know there are many preliminary questions asked witnesses, leading up to some point. As they are propounded you will readily learn what the purpose is. Just advise your client and don't argue with the committee, because we don't rule on objections." (Italics supplied by the Court.) Read in context, these excerpts indicate to me nothing more than that the committee was expressing its impatience with interruptions by counsel. I am unable to read the record, as the Court seems to have done, as indicating that the Subcommittee was avoiding taking a position on Bart's objections.

Justice Harlan's concurrence in Bernhardt v. Polygraphic Co. of America (Jan 16, 1956)

MR. JUSTICE HARLAN, concurring.

I concur in the opinion of the Court except insofar as it undertakes to review and affirm the District Court's interpretation of Vermont law. I agree with MR. JUSTICE FRANKFURTER that the review of questions of state law should ordinarily be left to the Courts of Appeals and would remand the case to the Court of Appeals for that purpose.

Justice Harlan's dissent in Slochower v. Board of Higher Ed. of NYC (April 9, 1956)

MR. JUSTICE HARLAN, dissenting.

I dissent because I think the Court has misconceived the nature of § 903 as construed and applied by the New York Court of Appeals, and has unduly circumscribed the power of the State to ensure the qualifications of its teachers.

As I understand MR. JUSTICE CLARK'S opinion, the Court regards § 903 as raising some sort of presumption of guilt from Dr. Slochower's claim of privilege. That is not the way the Court of Appeals construed the statute. On the contrary, that Court said: "we do not presume, of course, that these petitioners [one of whom was Dr. Slochower] by their action have shown cause to be discharged under the Feinberg Law (L. 1949, ch. 360) since no inference of membership in the Communist party may be drawn from the assertion of one's privilege against self incrimination."[1] Since § 903 is inoperative if even incriminating answers are given, it is apparent that it is the exercise of the privilege itself which is the basis for the discharge, quite apart from any inference of guilt. Thus the Court of Appeals could say that "The assertion of the privilege against self incrimination is equivalent to a resignation."[2] It is also clear that the Board of Education's discharge of Dr. Slochower was on this same premise. The question this case presents, therefore, is not whether any inferences can constitutionally be drawn from a claim of privilege, but whether a State violates due process when it makes a claim of privilege grounds for discharge.

In effect, what New York has done is to say that it will not employ teachers who refuse to cooperate with public authorities when asked questions relating to official conduct. Does such a statute bear a reasonable relation to New York's interest in ensuring the qualifications of its teachers? The majority seems to decide that it does not. This Court has already held, however, that a State may properly make knowing membership in an organization dedicated to the overthrow of the Government by force a ground for disqualification from public school teaching. Adler v. Board of Education, 342 U. S. 485. A requirement that public school teachers shall furnish information as to their past or present membership in the Communist Party is a relevant step in the implementation of such a state policy, and a teacher may be discharged for refusing to comply with that requirement. Garner v. Los Angeles Board, 341 U. S. 716. Moreover, I think that a State may justifiably consider that teachers who refuse to answer questions concerning their official conduct are no longer qualified for public school teaching, on the ground that their refusal to answer jeopardizes the confidence that the public should have in its school system. On either view of the statute. I think Dr. Slochower's discharge did not violate due process.

It makes no difference that the question which Dr. Slochower refused to answer was put to him by a federal rather than a state body. The authority of the subcommittee to ask the question is not controverted. While as an original matter I would be doubtful whether § 903 was intended to apply to federal investigations, the Court of Appeals has ruled otherwise, and its interpretation is binding on us. Dr. Slochower cannot discriminate between forums in deciding whether or not to answer a proper and relevant question, if the State requires him to answer before every lawfully constituted body. Here, the information sought to be elicited from Dr. Slochower could have been considered by state authorities in reviewing Dr. Slochower's qualifications, and the effect of his claim of privilege on the public confidence in its school system was at least as great as it would have been had his refusal to answer been before a state legislative committee.

There is some evidence that Dr. Slochower had already answered, before a state committee, the same question which he refused to answer before the congressional subcommittee.[3] Even assuming that New York already had the information, I cannot see how that would prevent New York from constitutionally applying § 903 to this claim of privilege. Apart from other considerations, who can tell whether Dr. Slochower would have answered the question the same way as he had before?

On this record I would affirm the decision of the Court of Appeals. A different question would be presented under the Privileges and Immunities Clause of the Fourteenth Amendment. But that question was not raised below, and is therefore not open here. Dewey v. Des Moines, 173 U. S. 193.

Notes

[1] 306 N. Y. 532, 538, 119 N. E. 2d 373, 377.

[2] Ibid.

[3] At the Senate subcommittee hearing, in response to Senator Ferguson's inquiry whether or not Dr. Slochower had "ever" answered a question concerning Communist Party membership in 1940 or 1941, Dr. Slochower replied: "Yes, I did answer it."

Justice Harlan's dissent in Griffin v. Illinois (April 23, 1956)

MR. JUSTICE HARLAN, dissenting.

Much as I would prefer to see free transcripts furnished to indigent defendants in all felony cases, I find myself unable to join in the Court's holding that the Fourteenth Amendment requires a State to do so or to furnish indigents with equivalent means of exercising a right to appeal. The importance of the question decided by the Court justifies adding to what MR. JUSTICE BURTON and MR. JUSTICE MINTON have written my further grounds for dissenting and the reasons why I find the majority opinions unsatisfying.

1. Inadequacy of the Record.—I would decline to decide the constitutional question tendered by petitioners because the record does not present it in that "clean-cut," "concrete," and "unclouded" form usually demanded for a decision of constitutional issues. Rescue Army v. Municipal Court of Los Angeles, 331 U. S. 549, 584. In my judgment the case should be remanded to the Illinois courts for further proceedings so that we might know the precise nature of petitioners' claim before passing on it.

The record contains nothing more definite than the allegation that "petitioners are poor persons with no means of paying the necessary fees to acquire the Transcript and Court Records needed to prosecute an appeal from their convictions." For my part I cannot tell whether petitioners' claim is that a transcript was "needed" because (a) under Illinois law a transcript is a prerequisite to appellate review of trial errors,[1] or (b) as a factual matter petitioners could not prepare an adequate bill of exceptions short of having a transcript.

If the claim is that a transcript was legally necessary, it is based on an erroneous view of Illinois law. The Illinois cases cited by the petitioners establish only that trial errors cannot be reviewed in the absence of a bill of exceptions, and not that a transcript is essential to the preparation of such a bill.[2] To the contrary, an unbroken line of Illinois cases establishes that a bill of exceptions may consist simply of a narrative account of the trial proceedings prepared from any available sources—for example, from the notes or memory of the trial judge, counsel, the defendant, or bystanders—and that the trial judge must either certify such a bill as accurate or point out the corrections to be made.[3] Viewed in the light of these cases, the only constitutional question presented by petitioners' bare allegation that they were unable to purchase a transcript would be: Is an indigent defendant, who has not shown that he is unable to obtain full appellate review of his conviction by a narrative bill of exceptions, constitutionally entitled to the added advantage of a free transcript of the trial proceedings for use as a bill of exceptions? I need hardly pause to suggest that such a claim would present no substantial constitutional question.

The Court, however, either takes judicial notice that as a practical matter the alternative methods of preparing a bill of exceptions are inadequate or finds in petitioners' claims an allegation of fact that their circumstances were such as to prevent them from utilizing the alternative methods. But even accepting this reading of the pleadings, the constitutional question tendered should not be decided without knowing the circumstances underlying the conclusory allegation of "need." Petitioners' indigence, the only underlying "fact" alleged, did not in itself necessarily preclude them from preparing a narrative bill of exceptions, and we are told nothing as to the other circumstances which prevented them from doing so. The record does not even disclose whether petitioners were incarcerated during the period in which the bill of exceptions had to be filed, or whether they were represented by counsel at the trial. We are left to speculate on the nature of the alleged trial errors and the scope of the bill of exceptions needed to present them. Who can say that if we knew the facts we might not have before us a much narrower constitutional question than the one decided today, or perhaps no such question at all. In these circumstances, I would follow the salutary policy "of avoiding constitutional decisions until the issues are presented with clarity, precision and certainty," Rescue Army v. Municipal Court of Los Angeles, supra, at p. 576, and would refuse to decide the constitutional question in the abstract form in which it has been presented here.

According to petitioners' tabulation, no more than 29 States provide free transcripts as of right to indigents convicted of non-capital crimes. Thus the sweeping constitutional pronouncement made by the Court today will touch the laws of at least 19 States[4] and will create a host of problems affecting the status of an unknown multitude of indigent convicts. A decision having such wide impact should not be made upon a record as obscure as this, especially where there are means ready at hand to have clarified the issue sought to be presented.

However, since I stand alone in my view that the Court should refrain from deciding the broad question urged upon us until the necessity for such a decision becomes manifest, I deem it appropriate also to note my disagreement with the Court's decision of that question. Inasmuch as the Court's decision is not—and on this record cannot be— based on any facts peculiar to this case, I consider that question to be: Is an indigent defendant who "needs" a transcript in order to appeal constitutionally entitled, regardless of the nature of the circumstances producing that need, to have the State either furnish a free transcript or take some other action to assure that he does in fact obtain full appellate review?

2. Equal Protection.—In finding an answer to that question in the Equal Protection Clause, the Court has painted with a broad brush. It is said that a State cannot discriminate between the "rich" and the "poor" in its system of criminal appeals. That statement of course commands support, but it hardly sheds light on the true character of

the problem confronting us here. Illinois has not imposed any arbitrary conditions upon the exercise of the right of appeal nor any requirements unnecessary to the effective working of its appellate system. Trial errors cannot be reviewed without an appropriate record of the proceedings below; if a transcript is used, it is surely not unreasonable to require the appellant to bear its cost; and Illinois has not foreclosed any other feasible means of preparing such a record. Nor is this a case where the State's own action has prevented a defendant from appealing. Cf. Dowd v. United States ex rel. Cook, 340 U. S. 206; Cochran v. Kansas, 316 U. S. 255. All that Illinois has done is to fail to alleviate the consequences of differences in economic circumstances that exist wholly apart from any state action.

The Court thus holds that, at least in this area of criminal appeals, the Equal Protection Clause imposes on the States an affirmative duty to life the handicaps flowing from differences in economic circumstances. That holding produces the anomalous result that a constitutional admonition to the States to treat all persons equally means in this instance that Illinois must give to some what it requires others to pay for. Granting that such a classification would be reasonable, it does not follow that a State's failure to make it can be regarded as discrimination.

It may as accurately be said that the real issue in this case is not whether Illinois has discriminated but whether it has a duty to discriminate.

I do not understand the Court to dispute either the necessity for a bill of exceptions or the reasonableness of the general requirement that the trial transcript, if used in its preparation, be paid for by the appealing party. The Court finds in the operation of these requirements, however, an invidious classification between the "rich" and the "poor." But no economic burden attendant upon the exercise of a privilege bears equally upon all, and in other circumstances the resulting differentiation is not treated as an invidious classification by the State, even though discrimination against "indigents" by name would be unconstitutional. Thus, while the exclusion of "indigents" from a free state university would deny them equal protection, requiring the payment of tuition fees surely would not, despite the resulting exclusion of those who could not afford to pay the fees. And if imposing a condition of payment is not the equivalent of a classification by the State in one case, I fail to see why it should be so regarded in another. Thus if requiring defendants in felony cases to pay for a transcript constitutes a discriminatory denial to indigents of the right of appeal available to others, why is it not a similar denial in misdemeanor cases or, for that matter, civil cases?

It is no answer to say that equal protection is not an absolute, and that in other than criminal cases the differentiation is "reasonable." The resulting classification would be invidious in all cases, and an invidious classification offends equal protection regardless of the seriousness of the consequences. Hence it must be that the differences are "reasonable" in other cases not because the "classification" is reasonable but simply because it is not unreasonable in those cases for the State to fail to relieve indigents of the economic burden. That is, the issue here is not the typical equal protection question of the reasonableness of a "classification" on the basis of which the State has imposed legal disabilities, but rather the reasonableness of the State's failure to remove natural disabilities. The Court holds that the failure of the State to do so is constitutionally unreasonable in this case although it might not be in others. I submit that the basis for that holding is simply an unarticulated conclusion that it violates "fundamental fairness" for a State which provides for appellate review, and thus apparently considers such review necessary to assure justice, not to see to it that such appeals are in fact available to those it would imprison for serious crimes. That of course is the traditional language of due process, see Betts v. Brady, 316 U. S. 455, 462, and I see no reason to import new substance into the concept of equal protection to dispose of the case, especially when to do so gives rise to the all-too-easy opportunity to ignore the real issue and solve the problem simply by labeling the Illinois practice as invidious "discrimination."

3. Due Process.—Has there been a violation of the Due Process Clause? The majority of the Court concedes that the Fourteenth Amendment does not require the States to provide for any kind of appellate review. Nevertheless, Illinois, in the forefront among the States, established writs of error in criminal cases as early as 1827.[5] In 1887, it provided for official court reporters, thereby relieving defendants of the burden of hiring reporters in order to obtain a transcript.[6] In 1927, it provided that for indigents sentenced to death "all necessary costs and expenses" incident to a writ of error, including the cost of a transcript, would be paid by the counties.[7] And in 1953, free transcripts were authorized for the presentation of constitutional claims.[8] Thus Illinois has steadily expanded the protection afforded defendants in criminal cases, and in recent years has made substantial strides towards alleviating the natural disadvantages of indigents. Can it be that, while it was not unconstitutional for Illinois to afford no appeals, its steady progress in increasing the safeguards against erroneous convictions has resulted in a constitutional decline?

Of course the fact that appeals are not constitutionally required does not mean that a State is free of constitutional restraints in establishing the terms upon which appeals will be allowed. It does mean, however, that there is no "right" to an appeal in the same sense that there is a right to a trial.[9] Rather the constitutional right under the Due Process Clause is simply the right not to be denied an appeal for arbitrary or capricious reasons. Nothing of that kind, however, can be found in any of the steps by which Illinois has established its appellate system.

We are all agreed that no objection of substance can be made to the provisions for free transcripts in capital and constitutional cases. The due process challenge must therefore be directed to the basic step of permitting appeals at all without also providing an in forma pauperis procedure. But whatever else may be said of Illinois' reluctance to expend public funds in perfecting appeals for indigents, it can hardly be said to be arbitrary. A policy of economy may be unenlightened, but it is certainly not capricious. And that it has never generally been so regarded is evidenced by the fact that our attention has been called to no State in which in forma pauperis appeals were established contemporaneously with the right of appeal. I can find nothing in the past decisions of this Court justifying a holding that the Fourteenth Amendment confines the States to a choice between allowing no appeals at all or undertaking to bear the cost of appeals for indigents, which is what the Court in effect now holds.

It is argued finally that, even if it cannot be said to be "arbitrary," the failure of Illinois to provide petitioners with the means of exercising the right of appeal that others are able to exercise is simply so "unfair" as to be a denial of due process. I have some question whether the non-arbitrary denial of a right that the State may withhold altogether could ever be so characterized. In any event, however, to so hold it is not enough that we consider free transcripts for indigents to be a desirable policy or that we would weigh the competing social values in favor of such a policy were it our function to distribute Illinois' public funds among alternative uses. Rather the question is whether some method of assuring that an indigent is able to exercise his right of appeal is "implicit in the concept of ordered liberty," Palko v. Connecticut, 302 U. S. 319, 325, so that the failure of a State so to provide constitutes a "denial of fundamental fairness, shocking to the universal sense of justice," Betts v. Brady, supra, at 462. Such an equivalence between persons in the means with which to exercise a right of appeal has not, however, traditionally been regarded as an essential of "fundamental fairness," and the reforms extending such aid to indigents have only recently gained widespread acceptance. Indeed, it was not until an Act of Congress in 1944 that defendants in federal criminal cases became entitled to free transcripts,[10] and to date approximately one-third of the States still have not taken that step. With due regard for the constitutional limitations upon the power of this Court to intervene in State matters, I am unable to bring myself to say that Illinois' failure to furnish free transcripts to indigents in all criminal cases is "shocking to the universal sense of justice."

As I view this case, it contains none of the elements hitherto regarded as essential to justify action by this Court under the Fourteenth Amendment. In truth what we have here is but the failure of Illinois to adopt as promptly as other States a desirable reform in its criminal procedure. Whatever might be said were this a question of procedure in the federal courts, regard for our system of federalism requires that matters such as this be left to the States. However strong may be one's inclination to hasten the day when in forma pauperis criminal procedures will be universal among the States, I think it is beyond the province of this Court to tell Illinois that it must provide such procedures.

Notes

[1] The Illinois Supreme Court may have interpreted the pleadings in this manner. It described the petitioners' "sole contention" as being that they were "unable to purchase a bill of exceptions and were, therefore, unable to obtain a complete review by this Court." This suggests that the state court construed the claim to be that an appeal was necessarily precluded by the lack of a transcript, not that the petitioners' particular circumstances produced that result. If that is what the Illinois court meant, its construction, having a

reasonable basis, would be binding on this Court and would constitute an adequate state ground for the denial of any claim premised on the existence of particular circumstances preventing the petitioners from pursuing other available methods of review.

[2] E. g., People v. Johns, 388 Ill. 212, 57 N. E. 2d 895; People v. Loftus, 400 Ill. 432, 81 N. E. 2d 495; People v. O'Connell, 411 Ill. 591, 104 N. E. 2d 825.

[3] Weatherford v. Wilson, 3 Ill. (2 Scam.) 253 (1840); People ex rel. Maher v. Williams, 91 Ill. 87 (1878); People ex rel. Munson v. Gary, 105 Ill. 264 (1883); People ex rel. Hall v. Holdom, 193 Ill. 319, 61 N. E. 1014 (1901); 162 East Ohio Street Hotel Corp. v. Lindheimer, 368 Ill. 294, 13 N. E. 2d 970 (1938); Weber v. Sneeringer, 247 Ill. App. 294 (1928); Merkle v. Kegerreis, 350 Ill. App. 103, 112 N. E. 2d 175 (1953); see also People ex rel. North American Restaurant v. Chetlain, 219 Ill. 248, 76 N. E. 364 (1906); Mayville v. French, 246 Ill. 434, 92 N. E. 919 (1910); People ex rel. Simus v. Donoghue, 377 Ill. 122, 35 N. E. 2d 371 (1941). This line of cases was reaffirmed by the Illinois Supreme Court in 1953, just three months before the petitioners were convicted, in People v. Joyce, 1 Ill. 2d 225, 230, 115 N. E. 2d 262, 264-265, in which the Williams, Gary, Holdom and Lindheimer cases, supra, were cited with approval for the proposition that trial errors may be presented on a writ of error by a "constructed or `bystander's' bill of exceptions." The holding of that case was that a defendant to whom these alternative methods were not available "as a practical matter" because of his indigence and incarceration did not, by failing to seek direct review of his conviction, "waive" the right given him by the Illinois Post-Conviction Hearing Act to assert his constitutional claims in a collateral proceeding. Accord: People v. La Frana, 4 Ill. 2d 261, 266, 122 N. E. 2d 583, 585-586. That holding does not, of course, detract from the court's affirmation that a transcript is not legally required for appellate review of trial errors. It is equally clear that Illinois' recognition of "practicalities" in not applying a strict doctrine of waiver to the remedial Post-Conviction Hearing Act does not necessarily mean that the alternative methods of obtaining review are not sufficiently "available" to satisfy any supposed constitutional requirements. That question would depend upon the facts of the particular case—of which we have not been informed here—and upon the evaluation of them for constitutional purposes.

[4] Of these 19 at least 5 have, however, expressly given the trial courts discretionary power to order free transcripts in non-capital cases. Mass. Ann. Laws, c. 278, § 33A, as amended by Acts 1955, c. 352 ("by order of the court"); N. D. Rev. Code, 1943, § 27-0606 (when "there is reasonable cause therefor"); Ore. Rev. Stat., 1953, § 21.470 (if "justice will be thereby promoted"); S. D. Code, 1939, § 34.3903 (if "essential to the protection of the substantial rights of the defendant"); Wash. Rev. Code, 1951, § 2.32.240 (if "justice will thereby be promoted"). The Rhode Island Supreme Court has reached a similar result by interpretation of a statute authorizing reimbursement for expenditures of appointed counsel. State v. Hudson, 55 R. I. 141, 179 A. 130 (1935) ("sound discretion. . . to be exercised with great circumspection and only for serious cause"). In addition, petitioners' brief refers to a letter from the Chief Justice of the Connecticut Supreme Court of Errors which states that free transcripts may be furnished in the discretion of the court

in non-capital cases.

[5] Ill. Rev. L. 1827, Crim. Code, §§ 186, 187; Ill. Rev. Stat., 1955, c. 38, § 769.1.

[6] Ill. Laws 1887, p. 159; Ill. Rev. Stat., 1955, c. 37, § 163b.

[7] Ill. Laws 1927, p. 400, § 1 1/2; Ill. Rev. Stat., 1955, c. 38, § 769a.

[8] Ill. Laws 1953, p. 859; Ill. Rev. Stat., 1955, c. 37, § 163f.

[9] This difference makes of dubious validity any analogy between a condition imposed upon the right to defend oneself and a condition imposed upon the right to appeal.

[10] 58 Stat. 5, 28 U. S. C. §§ 753 (f), 1915 (a). On the prior federal practice, see, e. g., Estabrook v. King, 119 F. 2d 607, 610 (C.A. 8th Cir.); United States v. Fair, 235 F. 1015 (D. C. N. D. Calif.).

Justice Harlan's concurrence and dissent in US v. Storer Broadcasting (May 21, 1956)

MR. JUSTICE HARLAN, concurring in part and dissenting in part.

The Court has properly deemed it necessary to question sua sponte the jurisdiction of the Court of Appeals to entertain this case,[1] but I am unable to agree with its decision that such jurisdiction existed. In my view, Storer was not a "party aggrieved by a final order" of the Commission, within the meaning of 5 U. S. C. § 1034, and hence was not entitled to invoke the jurisdiction of the Court of Appeals. Accordingly, I would vacate the judgment below and remand the case to the Court of Appeals with directions to dismiss the petition for lack of jurisdiction.

1. These regulations do not, in my view, constitute an "order" within the meaning of § 1034. They simply establish certain standards to be followed by the Commission in the future exercise of its licensing powers; they do not require any licensee to do or to refrain from doing anything, attach no consequences to his action or inaction, and determine no questions as to his legal status. As such they are quite unlike the Chain Broadcasting regulations which were held to be a reviewable "order" in Columbia Broadcasting System v. United States, 316 U. S. 407, in a proceeding comparable to this one. Those regulations were held reviewable, not because every Commission action in the form of a regulation was considered to be an "order," but for the specific reason that they proscribed certain kinds of contracts between licensees and the national networks and, by prescribing the sanction of license cancellation for noncompliance, operated to coerce action by the licensees and to determine the legal status of the networks' contracts. Of their own force and with no further administrative action being taken, the regulations induced licensees to cancel existing network contracts and deterred them from entering into new ones. That coercive effect of the regulations on present conduct, the very characteristic which led the Court to regard the Chain Broadcasting regulations as an "order" despite their form, is totally lacking here.[2]

2. A second obstacle to review of the regulations here is that, even if they be

deemed an "order," Storer has not shown that it is "aggrieved" by them.

In assessing the character of Storer's grievance, we must put aside the Commission's order, made simultaneously with its promulgation of the challenged regulations, which denied a pending application by Storer for a sixth television license. That order was reviewable only by a direct appeal within 30 days under 47 U. S. C. § 402 (b), (c), Federal Communications Comm'n v. Columbia Broadcasting System, 311 U. S. 132, and became final and conclusive upon Storer's failure to appeal from it. Since that order cannot be reviewed, and no relief from it may be granted in this proceeding, it is only of the prospective effect of the regulations, not their past application, that Storer may complain. And it is by that effect that Storer must show it is "aggrieved."

In its petition for review, Storer alleged that it was aggrieved by the regulations in that:

"(a) Storer is denied the right of a full and fair hearing to determine whether its ownership of an interest in more than seven (7) standard radio and five (5) television broadcast stations, in light of and upon a showing of all material circumstances, will thereby serve the public interest, convenience and necessity.

"(b) The acquisition of Storer's voting stock by the public under circumstances beyond the control of Storer, may and could be violative of the Multiple Ownership rules, as amended, and result in a forfeiture of licenses now held by Storer, with resultant loss and injury to Storer and to all other Storer stockholders."

However these allegations are read, they assert no more than that the Commission may in the future take action pursuant to the regulations to deny or revoke a license. Of course, if such action should ever be taken, Storer would then be "aggrieved." But by the same token it would then have a complete remedy through a direct appeal from such action under § 402 (b). Until such time as the regulations are applied to it, however, Storer will not have been "aggrieved" and hence will not be entitled to review. Indeed, in this case we do not even reach the often difficult problem whether an alleged injury is sufficient or of such a nature as to entitle the complaining party to review; here we have that rare case in which no present injury of any kind is even alleged.

It is said, however, that the regulations "now operate to control the business affairs of Storer," despite the absence of any such allegation by Storer. Since the regulations do not have any coercive effect, I take that to mean only that Storer, if it exercises prudent business judgment, will take into account the announced policy of the Commission in deciding whether or not to apply for an additional license. No doubt that is true, but I fail to see how Storer has been "aggrieved" by being told in advance one of the factors that will govern the disposition of any future license application on its part. If anything, Storer is now able to make a more enlightened judgment as to the probabilities of success in obtaining a further license.

3. So clear is it, in fact, that Storer has not been "aggrieved" by the mere issuance of the regulations, that the Court's grant of review in this case must be premised not upon the effect of the regulations themselves, but simply upon Storer's interest in knowing

whether or not a future application of them would be valid. The result is that the statutory procedure for obtaining relief from a present injury caused by an order has been converted into something quite different—namely, a procedure for obtaining a declaratory judgment as to the validity of a future application of new regulations. Not only is such a proceeding not authorized by the statute, however, but Storer would not have standing to invoke it even if it were.

That declaratory relief from future orders is not contemplated by § 1034 seems clear. That section authorizes review only of an "order," only if the order is "final," and only at the instance of one aggrieved "by" the challenged order itself. The regulations here are not an "order"; if they were it would not be "final" since further administrative action must be taken before Storer will be affected; and Storer's grievance, if any, will be caused not "by" the regulations but only by their future application. Moreover, quite apart from these obstacles, the procedure provided for by § 1034 is inappropriate for anticipatory equitable relief. That section requires, for example, that petitions for review be filed within 60 days after the order is issued. While such a time limitation is clearly appropriate to a procedure for relief from an injury already suffered, there seems no justification for so limiting the availability of declaratory relief from future action. Why should declaratory relief be denied as the threat of the future injury becomes more imminent, or be granted to those who have a sufficient interest to seek review immediately while being denied to those who later acquire a similar or even greater interest? Finally, no reason is apparent why existing procedures for declaratory judgments are not adequate; to construe § 1034 as an alternative declaratory judgment procedure simply produces the incongruous result of authorizing declaratory relief in the Courts of Appeals within 60 days after the order is issued and in the District Courts thereafter.

In the second place, even if § 1034 is to be construed as authorizing declaratory relief, I see no reason why the usual requirements for invoking equity jurisdiction should not be as applicable to such a proceeding as they are to an ordinary declaratory judgment action or to a proceeding to set aside a Commission order under the Urgent Deficiencies Act, the predecessor to § 1034 under which the CBS case arose. In that case, CBS's right to equitable relief in advance of the application of the regulations was expressly based on the irreparable injury it would suffer—the wholesale cancellation of its contracts with licensees—before any further administrative action was taken and for which there was no other adequate remedy. Unless these requirements for equitable relief are to be abandoned, there can be no right to relief here, for Storer alleges no threatened injury of any kind, other than the possibility of future administrative action for which there would be a complete remedy by appeal.

It is said, however—again without support of any allegations by Storer—that Storer "cannot cogently plan its present or future operations" unless it is advised whether or not the regulations are valid. But plans for expansion of communications facilities have always had to be made subject to the contingency that the Commission might refuse to grant the necessary license for any one of a number of reasons. Storer's position in this respect is now no different than it was before the regulations were issued: any plan to acquire a new station must simply take into account, among the several contingencies, the likelihood that a denial of a license under the regulations would be upheld on appeal. What this argument comes down to, therefore, is that Storer needs to know whether or not it can validly be denied a license under the regulations so that, if it can, it need not make an application. That is, the injury that Storer will have suffered if the decision on the validity of the regulations is postponed until Storer in fact applies for a license is the expense of making that very application, the same injury that is suffered by all unsuccessful license applicants. Until today, I should not have thought argument was necessary to reject such a basis for declaratory relief. Declaratory relief has been denied persons whose only alternative was to risk both dismissal from public employment and the imposition of criminal penalties, United Public Workers v. Mitchell, 330 U. S. 75, yet it is granted here to relieve Storer of the mere burden of making an application for a license.[3]

4. The holding of the Court today amounts to this: that regulations which impose no duty and determine no rights may be reviewed at the instance of a person who alleges no injury, to settle whether a future application of the regulations that may never occur would be valid. The lack of support for this decision is disclosed by the Court's primary reliance on CBS,[4] a case which in my view not only fails to support the Court's conclusion but is persuasive, if not controlling, authority for precisely the opposite result.[5] In my opinion, the implications of the decision undermine much of the settled law on reviewability of administrative action, and it is the more unfortunate because made without the benefit of briefs or argument by the parties. I cannot concur in that part of the Court's opinion.

The Court having decided, however, that the Court of Appeals had jurisdiction, I concur with the Court on the merits.

Notes

[1] Although the question of reviewability was not raised below or argued here, there can be no doubt of the power of the Court to consider the issue sua sponte, since it goes to the jurisdiction of the Court of Appeals and of this Court. Cf. Federal Communications Comm'n v. National Broadcasting Co., 319 U. S. 239, 246; Rochester Telephone Corp. v. United States, 307 U. S. 125, 128, n. 3; American Federation of Labor v. Labor Board, 308 U. S. 401, 404. The jurisdiction of the Courts of Appeals to review orders of the Federal Communications Commission, other than those granting or denying licenses, is granted by the Act of December 29, 1950, 64 Stat. 1129, 5 U. S. C. §§ 1031-1042. Section 1032, which confers the jurisdiction, provides that "Such jurisdiction shall be invoked by the filing of a petition as provided in section 1034." Section 1034, in turn, provides that "Any party aggrieved by a final order . . . may, within sixty days after entry of such order, file in the court of appeals . . . a petition to review such order." In short, the court's jurisdiction may be invoked only upon the petition of a "party aggrieved by a final order."

[2] Insofar as the Multiple Ownership regulations provide for the revocation of existing licenses upon the purchase by a licensee of a stock interest in more than the maximum number of stations, they could arguably be deemed an "order" forbidding licensees, under pain of license revocation, to engage in stock transactions the result of which would violate the numerical limitations. Storer is not complaining, however, of any such deterrent effect of the regulations and does not allege that it desires either to buy or to sell stock in any licensee. It objects only to the possibility of a future loss of a license should persons beyond its control—and, by hypothesis, not deterred by the regulations—purchase its stock. See paragraph (b) of Storer's allegations, p. 208, infra.

[3] The recent holding of this Court in East Texas Motor Freight Lines, Inc. v. Frozen Food Express, ante, p. 49, does not support the result reached here. In that case the declaratory interpretation of the Interstate Commerce Act—sought by way of review of the Commission's interpretative regulations in a proceeding under the Urgent Deficiencies Act—was considered justified because of the possibility of criminal penalties being imposed for violations of the Act and the risk of loss of substantial investments in operations that might subsequently be enjoined by the Commission. No such necessity for declaratory relief is even alleged here; there is no threat of criminal prosecutions and, since a license is always a condition precedent to acquisition of a new station, there is no danger of the loss of investments to be made prior to the future administrative action.

[4] Of the other cases cited by the Court, only Federal Communications Comm'n v. American Broadcasting Co., 347 U. S. 284, involved a similar situation, and there the jurisdictional problem was neither raised by the parties nor noted by the Court.

[5] Throughout the opinion in the CBS case, the Court emphasized the exceptional circumstances which justified immediate review of the Chain Broadcasting regulations and distinguished them from regulations of the sort here involved. See, e. g., 316 U. S., at 424-425:

"We need not stop to discuss here the great variety of administrative rulings which, unlike this one, are not reviewable—either because they do not adjudicate rights or declare them legislatively, or because there are adequate administrative remedies which must be pursued before resorting to judicial remedies, or because there is no occasion to resort to equitable remedies. But we should not for that reason fail to discriminate between them and this case in which, because of its peculiar circumstances, all the elements prerequisite to judicial review are present. The ultimate test of reviewability is not to be found in an overrefined technique, but in the need of the review to protect from the irreparable injury threatened in the exceptional case by administrative rulings which attach legal consequences to action taken in advance of other hearings and adjudications that may follow, the results of which the regulations purport to control."

Justice Harlan's dissent in US v. McKesson & Robbins, Inc. (June 11, 1956)

MR. JUSTICE HARLAN, whom MR. JUSTICE FRANKFURTER and MR.

JUSTICE BURTON join, dissenting.

Lack of sympathy with an Act of Congress does not justify giving to it a construction that cannot be rationalized in terms of any policy reasonably attributable to Congress. Rather our duty, as always, is to seek out the policy underlying the Act and, if possible, give effect to it. In this instance, I think the Court has departed from that rule by giving the Miller-Tydings and McGuire Acts an artificial construction which produces results that could hardly have been intended by Congress.

The purpose of the state fair-trade laws is to allow the manufacturer of a brand-named product to protect the goodwill his name enjoys by controlling the prices at which his branded products are resold. Old Dearborn Distributing Co. v. Seagram-Distillers Corp., 299 U. S. 183, 193-194. The necessary result—indeed, the very object—is to permit the elimination of price competition in the branded product among those who sell it. Congress has sanctioned those laws in the Miller-Tydings and McGuire Acts, considering them not to be offensive to federal antitrust policy.[1] Sufficient protection to the public interest was deemed to be afforded by the competition among different brands, a safeguard made express by the provision of the Miller-Tydings and McGuire Acts denying fair-trade contracts exemption from the antitrust laws unless the fair-traded product is "in free and open competition with commodities of the same general class." In short, the very purpose of the Acts is to permit a manufacturer to set the resale price for his own products while preserving competition between brands—that is, between the fair-traded item and similar items produced by other manufacturers.

If we accept the legislative judgment implicit in the Acts that resale price maintenance is necessary and desirable to protect the goodwill attached to a brand name, there is no meaningful distinction between the fair-trade contracts of integrated and non-integrated manufacturers. Certainly the integrated manufacturer has as strong a claim to protection of his goodwill as a non-integrated manufacturer, and the economic effect of the contracts is the same. In both cases price competition in the resale of the branded product is eliminated, and in neither case does the price fixing extend beyond the manufacturer's own product. While the Government concedes the right of a non-integrated manufacturer to eliminate price competition in his products between wholesalers, it finds a vice not contemplated by the Acts when one of the "wholesalers" is also the manufacturer, for then the contracts eliminate competition between the very parties to the contracts. But, in either case, all price competition is eliminated, and I am unable to see what difference it makes between whom the eliminated competition would have existed had it not been eliminated. The other bases of distinction suggested by the Government are equally tenuous and reflect a subtlety of analysis for which there is no support in either the Acts or their history.

So unsatisfactory, indeed, are the Government's attempts to rationalize the result contended for, that the Court chooses not to rely upon them, finding the language of the provisos so clear as to make it unnecessary even to hypothesize a consistent rationale attributable to Congress that might justify the discrimination against integrated producers. Indeed, not even the fact that the only legislative history directly in point is squarely opposed to the Court's reading of the statute (see note 17 of the Court's opinion, pp. 313-315) prompts enough doubt in the Court to require an inquiry into the purpose of the Acts. The Court's reasoning is this: the provisos except from the Acts contracts "between whole-salers" or "between persons, firms, or corporations in competition with each other"; McKesson is a "wholesaler" as well as a manufacturer and is also "in competition with" independent wholesalers; its contracts with independent wholesalers are therefore forbidden contracts "between wholesalers" and between "corporations in competition with each other." This verbalistic argument can be answered by the equally verbalistic one that the fair-trade contracts, being made in connection with the sale of its own branded products, were made by McKesson in its capacity as a "manufacturer" rather than as a competing "wholesaler." Neither argument being more conclusive than the other, the answer to the problem can be found only by looking to the purpose of the provisos and its relation to the basic policy of permitting resale price maintenance of branded goods.

As noted above, the Acts necessarily contemplate the elimination of price competition in the resale of a particular branded product and rely for protection of the public interest upon competition between brands. Viewed in the light of this purpose, the provisos become readily understandable. The vice of price-fixing agreements between those in competition with each other, whether at the manufacturing, wholesaling, or retailing level, is that they can be utilized to eliminate competition between brands. Thus manufacturers might agree to fix the resale prices of their competing brands in relation to each other; the same result, on an even broader scale, could be achieved by agreements between whole-salers or retailers. Further, agreements initiated by anyone other than the owner of the brand name are unnecessary to the protection of goodwill, the very justification for permitting fair-trade contracts. Thus an agreement between wholesalers to fix the price of a product bearing the trade name of neither would serve no purpose other than the elimination of competition. Interpreting the provisos in the light of these considerations, I conclude that an integrated manufacturer selling its products under fair-trade contracts to independent wholesalers should be deemed to be acting as a "manufacturer" rather than as a "wholesaler." This interpretation of the provisos fits with their terms and produces, rather than an arbitrary discrimination hardly intended by Congress, a result fully in harmony with the policy of the Acts to permit manufacturers to maintain the resale prices of their branded products while preserving competition between brands.[2]

For these reasons, therefore, I would hold McKesson's contracts to be within the Miller-Tydings and McGuire Acts and would affirm the judgment below.

Notes

[1] The Court refers to the Miller-Tydings Act as having been "passed as a rider to a District of Columbia revenue bill." It is pertinent to note that, in passing the later McGuire Act, Congress not only reaffirmed the policy of the Miller-Tydings Act but also

eliminated the restrictive effect of this Court's decision in Schwegmann Bros. v. Calvert Distillers Corp., 341 U. S. 384, as regards "non-signers" of fair-trade contracts.

[2] The Federal Trade Commission, the administrative agency specially charged with administering the McGuire Act, has reached like conclusions. See Eastman Kodak Co., 3 CCH Trade Reg. Rep. (10th ed.), par. 25, 291.

Justice Harlan's dissent in Mesarosh v. US (Oct 10, 1956, delivered Nov 5, 1956)

MR. JUSTICE HARLAN, with whom MR. JUSTICE FRANKFURTER and MR. JUSTICE BURTON join, dissenting.

When the Court's order denying the Government's motion to remand, and granting the petitioners a new trial, was announced by THE CHIEF JUSTICE on October 10, MR. JUSTICE FRANKFURTER, MR. JUSTICE BURTON and I dissented.[1] We reserved our right to file an opinion stating our reasons for thinking that the Government's motion should have been granted. This is that opinion.

On August 20, 1953, after a lengthy jury trial, petitioners were convicted of violating the Smith Act and the general federal conspiracy statute, 54 Stat. 670, 671, 18 U. S. C. §§ 2385, 371, by conspiring to advocate the overthrow of the United States Government by force and violence. The Court of Appeals for the Third Circuit, sitting en banc, affirmed by a divided vote.[2] This Court granted certiorari.[3]

On September 27, 1956, about two weeks before the case was scheduled for argument, the Solicitor General filed a motion asking us to remand the case to the District Court for a hearing as to the truthfulness and credibility of one Mazzei, a government informant and witness at the trial. The occasion for this motion was that the Solicitor General's office, some ten days before, had come into possession of information which led it seriously to doubt the correctness of certain testimony given by Mazzei in various independent proceedings, all but one of which occurred after the trial, as to his relations with Communists and the Federal Bureau of Investigation.[4]

In its motion papers the Government stated that while it still believed that Mazzei's testimony at the trial had been "entirely truthful and credible," his post-trial testimony in these other proceedings was such as to "lead us to suggest that the issue of his truthfulness at the trial of these petitioners should now be determined by the District Court after a hearing." Petitioners' answer to this motion was that, while they considered themselves entitled to a judgment of acquittal or a new trial on the basis of the Government's disclosures, disposition of the Government's motion should nevertheless await this Court's decision on the issues brought here by the writ of certiorari.

On October 8, the Court directed that the Government's motion be heard orally at the threshold of the main case. My brother FRANKFURTER, who felt that the motion should have been granted forthwith, filed a dissenting memorandum.[5] When the matter was heard by the Court on October 10, the positions taken by the Government and the defense were as follows: The Government was not yet prepared to say that Mazzei had committed perjury either at the trial or in any of the collateral proceedings.[6] Conceivably, the Solicitor General thought, it might turn out that Mazzei was a psychiatric case. The Solicitor General pointed out that the petitioners had not previously moved for a new trial on the grounds relied upon in the Government's motion, although much of the later information as to Mazzei was known to them at the time of their motion for reargument in the Court of Appeals. Even so, the Solicitor General felt that in the broader interests of justice it was his duty to pursue the matter as soon as it came to his knowledge that a cloud was cast upon Mazzei's truthfulness or credibility.[7] If he had been satisfied that Mazzei was a perjurer, the Solicitor General stated, he would have recommended that this Court reverse the convictions of two of the petitioners (Careathers and Dolsen). Since he was not so satisfied, he thought the proper procedure was to remand the case to the District Court for full exploration of the truthfulness and credibility of this witness.[8] As to the other three petitioners, the Solicitor General regarded Mazzei's trial testimony of so little importance that the trial court, even if it found Mazzei was a perjurer, would have to review the entire case against them before ordering a new trial. Petitioners' position was that if this Court was unwilling to hear the main case on the merits, it should, without more, deny the Government's motion and reverse the convictions with directions for acquittal or at least a new trial. At the conclusion of the oral argument on the motion to remand, the Court recessed to consider the matter, following which its decision denying the Government's motion was announced from the bench.

We are in full agreement that the Court properly refused to pass on the merits of the case until this cloud upon the integrity of the convictions had been dissolved. Communist Party v. Subversive Activities Control Board, 351 U. S. 115. What we object to is that this Court itself should have undertaken to deal with the subtle and complicated issues presented by the Government's motion instead of sending the case back to the District Court for the determination of these issues after a full investigation. It is fitting that we state our reasons for this view.

1. We believe that the reversal of these convictions represents an unprecedented and dangerous departure from sound principles of judicial administration. The Court has overturned the results of a complex, protracted, and expensive trial before any investigation has been made of the suspicions which the Solicitor General brought to the attention of the Court promptly after the facts giving rise to them came to his notice. We find the Court's justification of its summary action unconvincing.

The basic justification given is that "either this Court or the District Court should accept the statements of the Solicitor General as indicating the unreliability of this Government witness." In effect, the Court has treated the case as if the Solicitor General had conceded the untrustworthiness of Mazzei's testimony at the trial. To us this reflects a misunderstanding of the Solicitor General's position. As to Mazzei's trial testimony, the Solicitor General—whose forthrightness and candor no one could doubt, and whose conduct in this situation has been commended by this Court—represented that the

Government did not consider it yet had sufficient basis for regarding such testimony as untruthful. As to Mazzei's testimony in collateral proceedings, the Solicitor General, while stating his personal belief that some of it was untruthful, represented that he could not responsibly say whether such testimony involved perjury rather than psychopathic imbalance, and, if the latter, when that condition first arose or whether it was of such a character as to affect Mazzei's competency as a witness. In short, we think it abundantly clear that the Solicitor General conceded no more than that the situation was one that called for a thorough investigation.

We also observe that the Court finds that "no other conclusion is possible" than that "Mazzei's credibility has been wholly discredited," and that some parts of his post-trial testimony have been "positively established as untrue." We do not see how these conclusions can be reached in the face of the Government's representation that it still believes Mazzei's trial testimony to have been "entirely truthful and credible," and without the production of any evidence, or the examination and cross-examination of Mazzei and those who contradicted him, as to the post-trial episodes which have been called in question. Nor can we agree with the manner in which the Court has dealt with the Solicitor General's contentions as to petitioners Mesarosh, Albertson and Weissman. The Court simply says that Mazzei's testimony against Careathers and Dolsen was of such a character that, having been admitted against all defendants, it tainted the whole trial. But we cannot understand how this can be said short of a painstaking appraisal of the entire record which the Court acknowledges it has not read. The Court was quite right not to read the record, for in our view this was not the business of this Court, but that of the District Court; but by the same token, we think, the decision as to whether a new trial was justified was also, in the first instance, the business of the District Court.

In the Communist Party case, supra, where there were undenied charges of perjury, we did not undertake to resolve those charges here, but instead sent the case back to the Board for exploration. We think a similar course should have been followed in this case. The Court suggests that the situation presented here differs from that in the Communist Party case, in that there the Board was the trier of the facts, whereas here it was for the jury, not the court, to weigh the truthfulness and credibility of Mazzei's trial testimony. This, however, overlooks the fact that as a preliminary to a new trial it must first be determined whether any of Mazzei's collateral testimony, now drawn in question, so reflects upon the truthfulness or credibility of his trial testimony as to warrant submission of the case to a new jury. That preliminary determination has always been recognized as the function of the trial court. United States v. Johnson, 327 U. S. 106; United States v. Troche, 213 F. 2d 401; United States v. Rutkin, 208 F. 2d 647; Gordon v. United States, 178 F. 2d 896, cert. denied, 339 U. S. 935.[9]

Finally, the Court suggests that a different result might have been required if it were dealing with a defense motion for a new trial. However, we fail to see why the Government's motion, which was prompted by a desire to ascertain the true facts in all their ramifications, and which is aimed at the possibility of a new trial, calls for a different result or procedure than a defense motion for a new trial based on similar suspicions.

2. The District Court was the proper forum for the kind of investigation which should have been conducted here. This Court, and for that matter the Courts of Appeals, are ill-equipped for such a task. We need say no more than that appellate courts have no facilities for the examination of witnesses; nor in the nature of things can they have that intimate knowledge of the evidence and "feel" of the trial scene, which are so essential to sound judgment upon matters of such complexity and subtlety as those involved here, and which are possessed by the trial court alone.

3. Certainly there is no room for doubting the Solicitor General's good faith in this matter, or for supposing that the conduct of the further proceedings below would fall short of the highest standards of criminal justice. We have the Solicitor General's assurance that all of the Government's information bearing upon Mazzei's truthfulness and credibility would be made available to the defense, subject to appropriate safeguards.[10] As to the end result, the Solicitor General stated that in his view the trial court would have to acquit petitioners Careathers and Dolsen if it found that Mazzei had perjured himself at the trial or had then been incompetent to testify, and as to the other petitioners might have to order a new trial.[11] We need not consider at this time whether the Solicitor General's statement exhausts all of the factors that might require a new trial. Suffice it to say that we regard the Solicitor General's approach to this difficult situation as unexceptionable; and it is hardly to be assumed that the District Court would not do its full duty or would fall into error. We need only add that had the Government's motion been granted this Court would no doubt have accompanied its remand with appropriate instructions to guide the District Court in coping with this complicated problem. And surely the fact that this case has been long-drawn-out does not justify short-circuiting normal and orderly judicial procedures. The procedure adopted in United States v. Flynn, 130 F. Supp. 412, 131 F. Supp. 742, commends itself to us as a proper means of dealing with problems such as those raised by the Solicitor General's motion. We do not, of course, even remotely imply that we give any tolerance to the notion that a criminal conviction found to be infected by tainted testimony should be allowed to stand. We do say that ascertainment of where the truth lies here requires the kind of probing that is beyond the facilities and practices of this Court.

For the foregoing reasons we dissent. We think that the Government's motion to remand should have been granted.

Notes

[1] 352 U. S. 862.

[2] 223 F. 2d 449.

[3] 350 U. S. 922.

[4] One of these episodes took place before the Senate Permanent Subcommittee on Investigations, in Washington, D. C., on June 18, 1953 (while the trial was still in progress). There Mazzei had testified that at a meeting of the Civil Rights Congress on December 4, 1952, one Louis Bortz (an alleged Communist Party functionary) told him

that he, Bortz, had been "selected by the Communist Party to do a job in the liquidation of Senator Joseph McCarthy." On the oral argument the Solicitor General told us that the Government was not prepared at the time of the trial to regard this testimony of Mazzei as a fabrication, because Bortz when questioned on this subject before the Senate Committee had pleaded his privilege, stating that the answers to the questions "would" incriminate him. It appears that Mazzei's Senate testimony was brought to the attention of the trial judge and that it was the basis of an unsuccessful defense motion for a mistrial. The Solicitor General further stated that it was not until the recent discovery of Mazzei's later testimony in the other post-trial collateral proceedings—particularly that given in certain Florida disbarment proceedings on July 2, 1956—that his department began to have serious doubts as to Mazzei's truthfulness or credibility.

[5] 352 U. S. 808.

[6] As to Mazzei's trial testimony, the Solicitor General stated: "Before the witness [Mazzei] was presented to the [trial] court, his testimony was carefully appraised as to whether or not it was supported by any other material the Department had, and he was not contradicted. Although witnesses took the stand in behalf of the defendants his testimony was not contradicted at all, and that was one of the factors that bothered the Government in connection with these subsequent events that have caused us to conclude that this man's testimony should be carefully reexamined by the lower court in regard to validity at the time of the trial, because of what has occurred since, which, ordinarily, even though there was actual perjury, would not determine the validity of the testimony at the trial, depending upon what the circumstances were."

As to Mazzei's testimony in the collateral proceedings, the Solicitor General stated: "We believe that his [1953 Senate] testimony in that regard [the McCarthy incident] was not credible in light of what happened later [in the Florida disbarment proceedings]. We do not know at this point whether or not there is something psychiatric about this situation. We are disturbed about that." The Solicitor General further stated that, while his "personal belief is he [Mazzei] was not truthful" in his testimony as to the McCarthy episode, "I don't want it left on the record that I believe this man to be a perjurer, because I think in order to commit perjury you have to have the intent, and that is what disturbs me about this whole situation. I can't accept his testimony, over all these events [referring to Mazzei's Senate and Florida testimony], as being valid. But whether or not he knowingly does it with the intent [to commit perjury] is something else and that is what I can't follow through."

As to the possibility of Mazzei's being a psychopath: The Government's motion papers showed that in 1952 Mazzei had pleaded guilty to charges of adultery and bastardy in a Pennsylvania state court, and that this fact had been brought out at petitioners' trial. They further showed that in 1953, after petitioners' trial had ended, Mazzei had moved in the Pennsylvania court to set aside his former plea, alleging that he "was not guilty of the charge to which he was induced to plead . . . but did so only in his official capacity (as a Government informant) at the insistence of his superior in the FBI to avoid testifying."

These allegations, the Government informs us, were denied under oath by the F. B. I. and Mazzei's application to set aside his plea was denied by the Pennsylvania court. Further, the Government's motion papers here show that in the 1956 Florida disbarment proceedings Mazzei testified that the F. B. I. had arranged to get him into the Army so that he could watch a certain Communist Party member, whereas in fact Mazzei was drafted into the Army, and the F. B. I. had nothing to do with it. The Government states that in the same proceedings Mazzei testified that the F. B. I. paid him about $1,000 a month for expenses, whereas over the entire period from 1942 to 1952 the F. B. I. had paid him total expense money of only $172.05; and that Mazzei testified he had never been arrested, whereas in fact he had been arrested several times. As to these episodes the Solicitor General stated at the oral argument: "It certainly seems to me that that is a very peculiar action, and that he [Mazzei] should have anticipated, even if he wanted to lie about it, that the FBI agent would be there promptly testifying to the facts. And so it is very unusual to me that a person normally, wanting to falsify, would do such a thing. But, I think the trial courts have examined into competency a good many times, and do it every day, and should be able to determine whether or not he was competent at the time." The Solicitor General also stated that he was "disturbed about whether it [a psychopathic condition] occurred even back at the trial [of these petitioners], and I think the court should examine into that carefully." (The above, and similar quotations, are taken from the tape recording of the Solicitor General's oral argument before this Court, the writer's interpolations being indicated by brackets.)

[7] As to this the Solicitor General stated: "If I may say one word more in regard to that [the failure of the defense to move for a new trial], I feel that the obligation of the Government in a situation of this kind reaches far beyond the rights of these particular defendants, and it is its duty to this Court, and to the country, and it is our obligation in a situation of this kind, to try and see that justice is done. . . . We may be criticized for being too late, but I think it is never too late, to try to do justice. Having come to that conclusion [that the validity of this testimony is open to doubt], I think we should come before the courts, whichever one is proper, and try to get a correction of the wrong, if there is one."

[8] The Solicitor General stated: "Well, we would have recommended that [reversal] to the Court if we had been satisfied ourselves that Mazzei's testimony at the time of trial—which we think was the determining point in the proper conduct of judicial proceedings—[was untruthful], . . . because we feel at least as to these two defendants [petitioners Careathers and Dolsen] there was no [other] basis for their conviction. But it is possible that something has happened to this man [Mazzei], that his uncontradicted testimony was valid at the time of trial, and it seemed to us that with a long case tried like this and the jury involved and the trial court and the courts of appeal, and so on, the proper thing to do was to send it back to the trial court for its examination carefully into this question to determine what the fact is, and then assume that he [the trial court] would do his duty, which I think he will, and have the case handled properly at the point."

[9] Whatever may be the differences between the rules governing a motion for a

new trial based upon recantation of trial testimony or other types of "newly discovered" evidence, ante, p. 12, n. 6, certainly none of those differences suggest that the trial court is not the proper tribunal for resolution of the issues presented by such a motion.

[10] In response to a question as to whether the defense would be furnished with all of the Government's information bearing on the truth of Mazzei's Senate testimony relating to the McCarthy incident, the Solicitor General stated: "Well, that would depend on what the trial court thought should be done, I think, in the conduct of the case. The only reason I suggest that possibly it should not be made available to them is that in this whole problem there are several people involved who might get hurt by a public airing of their connection with this matter. And it would be too bad, and very unfortunate, if it wasn't handled so as not to injure those people when it isn't necessary to the proper handling of this problem. . . . We will do whatever this Court thinks we should do, but what I had in mind was to lay before the judge all of the information the Government has about the entire matter, and then he can sort out and protect the various innocent persons, who are described in the files, and should not be hurt in such a proceeding, and yet give them [the defendants] the benefit of the full and complete protection in such a proceeding as to what the facts are in this matter. . . . I had in mind that certain portions the judge would handle in camera so as to protect innocent people. And all others, that would reach into the merits of the situation, would certainly be handled by the court in such a way as to give all the parties an adequate opportunity to present their defense."

[11] The Solicitor General stated: "Yes, without his [Mazzei's] testimony as to those defendants [Careathers and Dolsen], I do not think they could have been convicted. I think the court would have had to direct a verdict in their favor, at least. As to the other three defendants, there is practically no testimony by this witness. It is very slight. I could give it to the Court. . . . [It] seems to me the lower court would have to examine the situation and see . . . whether or not it [Mazzei's testimony] had an effect on the conviction of every one of the defendants. . . . It would seem to me that . . . the trial court could determine the extent of the effect that this witness might have had on the other defendants, because there was a large volume of testimony in regard to the other defendants that bore directly upon their participation in the conspiracy, and their overt acts; and the testimony of this witness was so limited as to even a reference—he said that they solicited money from him, two of them—and is so slight as to any direct connection with it, that it seems to me the court would have to weigh whether or not, under that situation, he would decide that there is a doubt in his mind, in which case I am sure he would [direct a new trial]." In the absence of an exhaustive examination of the voluminous record, we are unable to understand how any adequate evaluation could be made of these considerations as to the petitioners Mesarosh, Albertson, and Weissman. When he was asked to "assume" that the trial court would find Mazzei to have been a perjurer, and his trial testimony to have been of importance in the conviction of these three petitioners, the Solicitor General promptly stated that he was "satisfied" that the court would set aside their convictions "if he came to these conclusions."

Justice Harlan's dissent in Putnam v. Commissioner (Dec 3, 1956)

MR. JUSTICE HARLAN, dissenting.

Being unreconciled to the Court's decision, which settles a conflict on this tax question among the Courts of Appeals and thus has an impact beyond the confines of this particular case, I must regretfully dissent.

The Court's approval of the Commissioner's treatment of petitioner's loss as one arising from a "nonbusiness debt," within the meaning of § 23 (k) (4) of the Internal Revenue Code of 1939,[1] instead of as a loss incurred in a "transaction entered into for profit," under § 23 (e) (2),[2] rests on what is, in my opinion, a strained application of the equitable doctrine of subrogation. No one contends that petitioner acquired the Company's debt to the lending Bank when he entered into the agreement guaranteeing payment of that indebtedness. Rather, the Government's basic argument, as taken from its brief, is this:

"The principle is well established, both generally and in the State of Iowa [where the guaranty was executed and performed], that a guarantor who is required to make payment under his guaranty contract succeeds to the rights of the creditor by subrogation. The law implies a promise on the part of the principal debtor to reimburse the guarantor, and the guarantor's payment is treated not as extinguishing the debt but as merely substituting the guarantor for the creditor. . . . Accordingly, while a guarantor by entering into the guaranty contract and making payment thereunder puts himself in a position where he may sustain a loss, it is only if, and to the extent that, the debt which he acquires by subrogation is worthless that he actually sustains a loss. Thus, if the guarantor, having made payment under his guaranty contract, is able to recover in full from the principal debtor, he clearly suffers no loss at all. It follows, therefore, that any loss, the existence and extent of which is wholly and directly dependent upon the worthlessness of a debt, should be attributed to the worthlessness of that debt, i. e., should be considered a bad debt loss."

The Government then adds this footnote: "So long as payment of a debt is guaranteed by a solvent guarantor, the insolvency of the principal debtor obviously does not render the debt worthless. Consequently, if the debt which a guarantor acquires by subrogation becomes worthless, it necessarily becomes worthless in the hands of the guarantor rather than in the hands of the original creditor."

Upon analysis, the Government's argument comes down to this: when the petitioner honored his guaranty obligation his payment was offset by the acquisition of the creditor Bank's rights against the Company on its indebtedness; in the Bank's hands those rights were worth full value, since the Company's indebtedness was secured by the guaranty; therefore petitioner's loss should be attributed to the subrogation debt, which became worthless in his hands because no longer so secured.

This argument would have substance in a case where the principal debtor was not insolvent at the time the guaranty was fulfilled; for in such a case it could be said that the acquired debt was not without value in the guarantor's hands, and hence he should not be allowed a tax deduction until the debt turns out to be worthless. But when, as here, the debtor is insolvent at the very time the guarantor meets his obligation, it defies reality to attribute the guarantor's loss to anything other than the discharge of his guaranty obligation. To attribute that loss to the acquired debt in such a case requires one to conceive of the debt as having value at the moment of acquisition, but as withering to worthlessness the moment the guarantor touches it. That the same debt in the same millisecond can have both of these antagonistic characteristics is, for me, too esoteric a concept to carry legal consequences, even in the field of taxation.

It was this departure from reality which first led the Court of Appeals for the Second Circuit to reject the Commissioner's theory, as applied to a loss incurred by a widow upon a guaranty of her husband's brokerage account which she was called upon to honor long after his death and the winding up of his insolvent estate. Fox v. Commissioner, 190 F. 2d 101. In that case the court, after referring to the "illusory character" of the subrogation claim which, the Tax Court held, she had acquired against her late husband upon her payment of the guaranty, went on to say, at pp. 103-104:

"She [the widow] argues that the court's theory of a debt against her husband's estate amounts to a subrogation forced upon her, contrary to the equitable spirit of the doctrine, to yield her an utterly worthless claim and a very real tax liability.... [W]e think her argument persuasive.... Clearly ... the [guaranty] transaction was not then one involving a bad debt, since she had not even made the payment which alone would give rise to a claim in her favor. Nor could payment ten years later create a debt out of something less than even the proverbial stone. It is utterly unrealistic to consider the payment as one made in any expectation of recovery over of any legal claim for collection. Actually it was merely the fulfillment of her contractual obligation of the earlier date. The baddebt provision thus had no direct application; only by straining the statutory language can we erect here a disembodied debt against an insolvent and long dead debtor."

Being unable to differentiate the worthlessness of a subrogation debt claim against a nonexistent individual debtor from such a claim against an existent, but insolvent, corporate debtor, the Courts of Appeals, until the present case,[3] have consistently applied the reasoning of the Fox case to losses incurred on individual guaranties of corporate indebtedness where the corporation, though still in existence, was insolvent at the time the guaranty was honored. Pollak v. Commissioner, 209 F. 2d 57;[4] Edwards v. Allen, 216 F. 2d 794;[5] Cudlip v. Commissioner, 220 F. 2d 565;[6] see also Ansley v. Commissioner, 217 F. 2d 252.[7] The rationale of these four Courts of Appeals is, in my opinion, more convincing than that of the Commissioner, and I think this Court should have approved and followed it here by holding that this taxpayer's loss was fully deductible under § 23 (e) (2) as a loss on a "transaction entered into for profit," instead of regarding it as a "nonbusiness debt" loss, subject to capital loss treatment under § 23 (k) (4).

I cannot agree with the Court that either the circumstances under which § 23 (k)

(4) was enacted in 1942, or the provisions of § 166 (f) of the Internal Revenue Code of 1954,[8] point to an opposite conclusion. Section 23 (k) (4) created a new category of debt losses, namely, "nonbusiness debt" losses, which were thenceforth to be given capital loss treatment instead of the full loss deduction theretofore accorded them.[9] The Court finds the "objectives sought to be achieved by the Congress," through the enactment of this section, "persuasive that § 23 (k) (4) applies to a guarantor's nonbusiness debt losses," in that the "section was part of the comprehensive tax program enacted by the Revenue Act of 1942 to increase the national revenue," in connection with World War II, and "was suited to put nonbusiness investments in the form of loans on a footing with other nonbusiness investments." But it seems to me that the House Ways and Means Committee Report on the bill shows that § 23 (k) (4) was aimed at a specific narrow objective, namely, that of reducing revenue loss from the deduction of "family" or "friendly" loans which were in reality gifts. The Report states:

"C. Nonbusiness Bad Debts.

"The present law gives the same tax treatment to bad debts incurred in nonbusiness transactions as it allows to business bad debts. An example of a nonbusiness bad debt would be an unrepaid loan to a friend or relative, while business bad debts arise in the course of the taxpayer's trade or business. This liberal allowance for nonbusiness bad debts has suffered considerable abuse through taxpayers making loans which they do not expect to be repaid. This practice is particularly prevalent in the case of loans to persons with respect to whom the taxpayer is not entitled to a credit for dependents. This situation has presented serious administrative difficulties because of the requirement of proof.

"The bill treats the loss from nonbusiness bad debts as a short-term capital loss. The effect of this provision is to take the loss fully into account, but to allow it to be used only to reduce capital gains. Like any other capital loss, however, the amount of such bad debt losses may be taken to the extent of $1,000 against ordinary income and the 5-year carryover provision applies."[10]

I am unable to find in this, or in any of the other legislative history to which the Court refers, any clear intimation of a broad policy to analogize generally all types of nonbusiness loans to other forms of capital investment,[11] still less anything which indicates that guarantors' losses were considered as falling within the new section.[12]

Likewise I think that the Court's reliance on § 166 (f) of the 1954 Code is misplaced. That section provides that an individual taxpayer's guaranty payment discharging the obligation of a noncorporate debtor "shall be treated as a debt becoming worthless within such taxable year," and shall be deductible in full if (a) the proceeds of the guaranteed obligation were used "in the trade or business of the borrower," and (b) that obligation was worthless at the time the guarantor made payment.[13] The Court says that by enacting this section Congress confirmed the administrative practice of treating guarantors' losses as bad debt losses, at least so far as guaranties of certain noncorporate obligations are concerned. I cannot agree, for again I think this section had a specific and limited purpose, which did not include the thrust which the Court now gives the section. That purpose, I think, was simply to permit deduction of certain guaranty payments that were not deductible at all under the 1939 Code. Payments now deductible under § 166 (f) need not be made in the course of the guarantor's "trade or business," nor need they be attributable to a transaction "entered into for profit." They are deductible, it would seem, so long as the guarantor had some expectation of being repaid—so long, in other words, as the transaction was not a gift. Under prior law, such payments would not have been deductible as "business" debts, under § 23 (k) (1),[14] or as losses on transactions "entered into for profit," under § 23 (e) (2), or even as "nonbusiness" debts under § 23 (k) (4), since the Fox line of cases held that such payments do not give rise to "debts." However, here again, as with the enactment of the § 23 (k) (4) "nonbusiness debt" provision in 1942, Congress was concerned with fending against allowance of this type of deduction in cases of fictitious "family" or "friendly" guaranties. Hence it was unwilling to allow the deduction to all guarantors of individual borrowings. Considering guaranties of loans sought for business purposes to be free of such infirmities, Congress attempted to obviate abuse of § 166 (f) by limiting its application to guaranties of loans the proceeds of which "were used in the trade or business of the borrower."

In light of what seems to have been the particular congressional purpose, I think it strains § 166 (f) to read it as broadly confirming the treatment of guaranty losses as bad debt losses.[15] Congress presumably knew of the Fox line of cases, supra, which had refused "debt" treatment to guarantors' losses, and it is not without significance that the Senate Report on § 166 (f) stated: "If the requirements of this section are not met, the taxpayer will, as under present law, be treated taxwise under whatever provisions of the code are applicable in the factual situation."[16] It is true that § 166 (f) provides that any payment included therein "shall be treated as a debt"; but of more significance is the fact that the person claiming the deduction need not show that he in fact owned a "debt" or that such debt had "become worthless during the taxable year"—the requirement for deductibility of both business and nonbusiness bad debts under § 23 (k) (1) and (4)—since "for purposes of this section" (§ 166 (f)) the guarantor's loss is "treated as" a debt "becoming worthless within such taxable year" as the loss occurs. In other words, though assimilated to a "debt" loss, the loss arising from the guaranty payment in fact need have none of the attributes of a debt loss in order to be deductible. The primary thrust of § 166 (f) was to make deductible some kinds of losses which were theretofore not deductible, and I think that drawing from the language of the Section a definitive characterization of such losses as "debts" involves a misplacing of emphasis.

Of still greater significance is the fact that § 166 (f) losses are deductible in full. This, it seems to me, is more consistent with the view that Congress did not intend to disturb the line of cases which, following Fox, gave a full deduction under § 23 (e) (2) to losses on guaranties of corporate obligations, than it is with the Court's view that § 166 (f) confirms Congress' intent that such losses should be only partially deductible as nonbusiness bad debts under § 23 (k) (4). Otherwise we would have the anomalous result that under the 1954 Code individual guarantors of noncorporate obligations are given better treatment than those guaranteeing corporate obligations, even though the basic limitation which Congress imposed upon the deductibility of § 166 (f) losses, namely, that the proceeds of the guaranteed obligation "were used in the trade or business of the borrower," is always present in the case of a guaranty of a corporate obligation.

In short, I think that when the purposes and provisions of § 166 (f) are taken together, it is quite evident that the section was intended to complement the decisions of these four Courts of Appeals,[17] and not to override them.

Finally, the Government suggests that giving guarantors' losses the same capital loss treatment as nonbusiness debt losses would make for a better tax structure, since, it is argued, both kinds of losses are comparable to losses from investments, which receive capital loss treatment under both the 1939 and 1954 Codes.[18] Even if that be so, this would be a matter for Congress. Our duty is to take the statute as we find it. I would reverse.

Notes

[1] "[§ 23 (k)] (4) NON-BUSINESS DEBTS.

"In the case of a taxpayer, other than a corporation, if a nonbusiness debt becomes worthless within the taxable year, the loss resulting therefrom shall be considered a loss from the sale or exchange, during the taxable year, of a capital asset held for not more than 6 months. The term `non-business debt' means a debt other than a debt evidenced by a security as defined in paragraph (3) and other than a debt the loss from the worthlessness of which is incurred in the taxpayer's trade or business."

[2] "§ 23. DEDUCTIONS FROM GROSS INCOME.

"In computing net income there shall be allowed as deductions:

.....

"(e) LOSSES BY INDIVIDUALS.

"In the case of an individual, losses sustained during the taxable year and not compensated for by insurance or otherwise—

.....

"(2) if incurred in any transaction entered into for profit, though not connected with the trade or business . . . ."

[3] 224 F. 2d 947.

[4] Third Circuit.

[5] Fifth Circuit.

[6] Sixth Circuit.

[7] Third Circuit.

[8] "[§ 166] (f) GUARANTOR OF CERTAIN NONCORPORATE OBLIGATIONS. — A payment by the taxpayer (other than a corporation) in discharge of part or all of his obligation as a guarantor, endorser, or indemnitor of a noncorporate obligation the proceeds of which were used in the trade or business of the borrower shall be treated as a

debt becoming worthless within such taxable year for purposes of this section (except that subsection (d) shall not apply), but only if the obligation of the borrower to the person to whom such payment was made was worthless (without regard to such guaranty, endorsement, or indemnity) at the time of such payment."

[9] I. R. C., 1939, § 23 (k) (1), 53 Stat. 13, 26 U. S. C. (1940 ed.) § 23 (k) (1).

[10] H. R. Rep. No. 2333, 77th Cong., 2d Sess. 45.

[11] Had this been the congressional purpose, it could have been accomplished simply by subjecting nonbusiness debt losses to the provisions of the statute dealing with worthless securities. See § 23 (g) (2)-(4) of the Internal Revenue Code of 1939.

[12] When it enacted § 23 (k) (4) Congress left undisturbed § 23 (e) (2) relating to the deductibility of losses on "any transaction entered into for profit," and that section was subsequently re-enacted, unchanged, as § 165 (c) (2) of the Internal Revenue Code of 1954.

[13] See note 8, supra.

[14] "§ 23. DEDUCTIONS FROM GROSS INCOME.

"In computing net income there shall be allowed as deductions:

.....

"(k) BAD DEBTS.

"(1) GENERAL RULE.

"Debts which become worthless within the taxable year . . . . This paragraph shall not apply in the case of a taxpayer, other than a corporation, with respect to a non-business debt, as defined in paragraph (4) of this subsection."

[15] The Senate Report on § 166 (f) simply states: "Your committee also provided that business bad debt treatment will be available where a noncorporate taxpayer, who was the endorser (or guarantor or indemnitor) of the obligation of another, is required to pay the other's debt (and cannot collect it from the debtor). However, this treatment is to be available only where the debt represents money used in the other person's trade or business. Your committee believes that this treatment should be available in such cases since in most cases debts of this type usually are incurred because of business relationships." S. Rep. No. 1622, 83d Cong., 2d Sess. 24-25.

[16] S. Rep. No. 1622, 83d Cong., 2d Sess. 200. (Italics supplied.)

[17] Ante, p. 97.

[18] I. R. C., 1939, § 23 (g) (2)-(4); I. R. C., 1954, § 165 (g).

Justice Harlan's concurrence in Mass. Bonding v. US (Dec 10, 1956)

MR. JUSTICE HARLAN, concurring.

Although I join in the Court's opinion in this case, the importance of the question impels me to add a word to what MR. JUSTICE DOUGLAS has written. The problem is not an easy one, and I do not think that inquiry can stop with a literal reading of the terms of the statute, plain though they may appear to be. Taking, as I think we should, § 2674 (2) within the wider context of the purpose of the Tort Claims Act as a whole, I am still not convinced that Congress intended the $20,000 limitation in the Massachusetts punitive statute to apply to recoveries under the Tort Claims Act.

In applying that limitation, the underlying reasoning of the Court of Appeals was that § 2674 (2) must not be read as subverting the overriding philosophy of the Tort Claims Act, that is, that the Government should be liable "in the same manner and to the same extent" as a private individual under state law would be liable. It therefore argued that although § 2674 (2) departed from this philosophy when it made recovery compensatory rather than punitive in instances where the state remedy was punitive, the section in every other respect should be construed harmoniously with this philosophy, and that therefore maxima in state statutes should apply to recoveries against the Government as well as private individuals, even though such a statute is punitive.

But it seems to me that the whole purpose and reason for the enactment of § 2674 (2) was to differentiate between the Government and private defendants in the "manner" and "extent" of recovery in the particular cases where it applied, and I can find no good reason for giving the section only partial effect. In no case in Alabama or Massachusetts will a plaintiff recover from the Government "in the same manner" as he would against an individual defendant, and in no case, except by fortuitous circumstance, will he recover to "the same extent." In both of these States if a highly culpable defendant causes small pecuniary injury, he will be "punished" at a high figure, whereas the Government will merely pay the small amount of compensation. Or if a merely careless defendant causes high pecuniary damage, he is punished at a low figure under state law, while the Government must pay for the heavy damage done. In both cases, the effect of the statute is to make the Government liable in a different manner and to a different extent than a private individual under the same circumstances; this, indeed, was the very purpose of the amendment. I therefore do not see why this purposeful differentiation in "manner" and "extent" of recovery should stop at the problem of maximum recoveries. Since the Government is by the very statute made liable on a different basis than a private individual and will in every case pay a different amount than would a private individual, why does it offend the philosophy of the Act to make the Government liable for more than a private individual would pay? Thus, while it is true that in general the Tort Claims Act makes the United States pro tanto a private defendant, the very purpose of § 2674 (2) was to prevent this assimilation in States where recovery is punitive. It seems to me, therefore, that there is no reason to re-establish the assimilation on this one matter of maximum allowable recovery.

Furthermore, I find it unlikely that Congress would have intended to subject plaintiffs to a maximum which was established for reasons of policy irrelevant to litigation under the Tort Claims Act. Massachusetts has decided that for reasons of policy—possibly because of the danger of excessive jury verdicts in "punitive" cases— recovery under its punitive statute should be limited to $20,000. The statute being penal, it embodies the judgment of the legislature that the highest punishment that should be imposed for nonhomicidal death is this figure. But as soon as punishment has nothing to do with the lawsuit—as it does not in suits under § 2674 (2)—and as soon as recovery is for compensation of the victim rather than punishment, then the policy reasons on which the $20,000 limit are based vanish. Massachusetts might, of course, impose a limit on compensatory recoveries as well. It did so for a short time, but then repealed the statute. But it is clear that the limit embodied in this statute has nothing to do with a compensatory suit; the factors which led to the imposition of this maximum are irrelevant when damages are not punitive. It would therefore seem to me just as artificial to take the $20,000 limit of this statute and impose it on a Tort Claims Act recovery as it would be to use as a limit a maximum figure taken from a state criminal statute imposing a fine for negligent homicide. The limitation in the Massachusetts penal statute was arrived at under penal concepts, and should not be artificially imposed on a recovery from which penal considerations have been eliminated by congressional mandate.

The Court of Appeals suggests that if the Massachusetts "punitive" maximum were not applicable, the Government would be put at a unique disadvantage in Massachusetts, since the death statutes of some twelve other States place limitations on recovery which concededly would be applicable to the United States under the provisions of the Tort Claims Act. But the limitations in these other States all relate to compensation statutes, and I do not, of course, suggest that such a limitation in Massachusetts would not also apply to the Government. The resulting lack of symmetry in the operation of the Act as between Massachusetts and the other States having death recovery maxima, seems to me no greater than it is as between such States and those which impose no monetary limitation on death recoveries. Moreover, symmetry in the first aspect can only be achieved at the expense of offending "the general scheme of the Tort Claims Act to refer questions of liability of the United States to the provisions of `the law of the place where the act or omission complained of occurred,' "[*] since Massachusetts does not recognize compensatory actions.

I think, therefore, that recovery of actual compensatory damages is, in this case, in full accord with the philosophy of the Tort Claims Act.

[*] 227 F. 2d 385, 391.

Justice Harlan's concurrence and dissent in NLRB v. Lion Oil (Jan 22, 1957)

MR. JUSTICE HARLAN, concurring in part and dissenting in part.

I join in so much of the Court's opinion as relates to the construction of § 8 (d), agreeing with THE CHIEF JUSTICE'S reasoning and MR. JUSTICE FRANKFURTER'S further amplification of that problem. But I dissent from that part of the Court's opinion which dismisses respondent's breach of contract defense. That question was never passed on by the Court of Appeals, and I think that our remand should leave it open for the Court of Appeals to decide in the first instance. Further, I find the Court's opinion unclear as to whether the Court of Appeals is likewise foreclosed from now dealing with the sufficiency of the evidence as to the unfair labor practice charge against respondent—a question which the Court of Appeals also did not reach because of its views on § 8 (d)—and I think that question, too, should be left open for the Court of Appeals on remand.

This is the fourth time this Term that the Court has passed on questions which the court below never reached. See Mesarosh v. United States, 352 U. S. 1;[1] Thompson v. Coastal Oil Co., 352 U. S. 862;[2] Gibson v. Phillips Petroleum Co., 352 U. S. 874.[3] I think this practice is an unfortunate one, depriving this Court, as it does, of the considered views of the lower courts. Its dangers are particularly apparent in the present case. As my brother FRANKFURTER points out, there is at least some question as to whether respondent ever raised its breach of contract defense before the National Labor Relations Board. And on the merits the question is an unusual one because of the atypical nature of this contract, and surely requires for its reliable adjudication much sharper consideration than it is possible for this Court to give it here as an original matter. Indeed, the nature of the question is such that the Court of Appeals might well conclude that the issue should be referred to the Board for its expert views in the first instance.

This kind of original adjudication by this Court is not what litigants have a right to expect. Moreover, to decide questions which, as here, have not been raised in the petition for certiorari offends our own rules.[4] There will no doubt be cases where remand is not justified because the questions left open by the lower court are manifestly insubstantial. It seems to me that in such instances this Court should state that it is not remanding for that reason, instead of proceeding as a matter of course to decide the questions itself, either expressly or sub silentio. The latter procedure can only have a tendency to lead this Court, as here, to decide questions which it should not pass upon in the first instance, and in my opinion represents unsound judicial administration.

Notes

[1] This Court granted the defendants a new trial on the ground that their conviction was tainted by prosecution evidence suspected to be perjurious. Neither the trial court nor the Court of Appeals had passed on this question, and there had been no investigation as to the reliability of the testimony or its precise bearing on the case.

[2] The Court of Appeals reversed a judgment for the plaintiff in an unseaworthiness case on the ground that plaintiff had signed a valid release. This Court reversed, holding the release invalid, and reinstated the judgment of the District Court. The Court of Appeals therefore never had an opportunity to pass on the other points raised by the defendant on its appeal, mainly the question whether there was sufficient evidence for the finding that the vessel was unseaworthy.

[3] The Court of Appeals had held that as a matter of Texas law plaintiff was barred from recovery by his own contributory negligence. This Court reversed and reinstated the judgment of the District Court. Again, the Court of Appeals had no opportunity to pass on alleged errors of the trial court in instructing the jury, that court not having reached those questions on the initial appeal.

[4] Rule 23, 1 (e), Revised Rules.

Justice Harlan's dissent in Radovich v. NFL (Feb 25, 1957)

MR. JUSTICE HARLAN, with whom MR. JUSTICE BRENNAN joins, dissenting.

What was foreshadowed by United States v. International Boxing Club, 348 U. S. 236, has now come to pass. The Court, in holding that professional football is subject to the antitrust laws, now says in effect that professional baseball is sui generis so far as those laws are concerned, and that therefore Federal Base Ball Club v. National League, 259 U. S. 200, and Toolson v. New York Yankees, Inc., 346 U. S. 356, do not control football by reason of stare decisis. Since I am unable to distinguish football from baseball under the rationale of Federal Base Ball and Toolson, and can find no basis for attributing to Congress a purpose to put baseball in a class by itself, I would adhere to the rule of stare decisis and affirm the judgment below.

If the situation resulting from the baseball decisions is to be changed, I think it far better to leave it to be dealt with by Congress than for this Court to becloud the situation further, either by making untenable distinctions between baseball and other professional sports, or by discriminatory fiat in favor of baseball.

Justice Harlan's concurrence and dissent in Ferguson v. Moore-McCormack Lines, Inc. (Feb 25, 1957)

MR. JUSTICE HARLAN, concurring in No. 46 and dissenting in Nos. 28, 42 and 59.[*]

I.

I am in full agreement with what my Brother FRANKFURTER has written in criticism of the Court's recurring willingness to grant certiorari in cases of this type. For the reasons he has given, I think the Court should not have heard any of these four cases. Nevertheless, the cases having been taken, I have conceived it to be my duty to consider them on their merits, because I cannot reconcile voting to dismiss the writs as "improvidently granted" with the Court's "rule of four." In my opinion due adherence to that rule requires that once certiorari has been granted a case should be disposed of on the premise that it is properly here, in the absence of considerations appearing which were not manifest or fully apprehended at the time certiorari was granted. In these instances I am unable to say that such considerations exist, even though I do think that the arguments on the merits underscored the views of those of us who originally felt that the cases should not be taken because they involved only issues of fact, and presented nothing of sufficient general importance to warrant this substantial expenditure of the Court's time.

I do not think that, in the absence of the considerations mentioned, voting to dismiss a writ after it has been granted can be justified on the basis of an inherent right of dissent. In the case of a petition for certiorari that right, it seems to me—again without the presence of intervening factors—is exhausted once the petition has been granted and the cause set for argument.[1] Otherwise the "rule of four" surely becomes a meaningless thing in more than one respect. First, notwithstanding the "rule of four," five objecting Justices could undo the grant by voting, after the case has been heard, to dismiss the writ as improvidently granted—a course which would hardly be fair to litigants who have expended time, effort, and money on the assumption that their cases would be heard and decided on the merits. While in the nature of things litigants must assume the risk of "improvidently granted" dismissals because of factors not fully apprehended when the petition for certiorari was under consideration, short of that it seems to me that the Court would stultify its own rule if it were permissible for a writ of certiorari to be annulled by the later vote of five objecting Justices. Indeed, if that were proper, it would be preferable to have the vote of annulment come into play the moment after the petition for certiorari has been granted, since then at least the litigants would be spared useless effort in briefing and preparing for the argument of their cases. Second, permitting the grant of a writ to be thus undone would undermine the whole philosophy of the "rule of four," which is that any case warranting consideration in the opinion of such a substantial minority of the Court will be taken and disposed of. It appears to me that such a practice would accomplish just the contrary of what representatives of this Court stated to Congress as to the "rule of four" at the time the Court's certiorari jurisdiction was enlarged by the Judiciary Act of 1925.[2] In effect the "rule of four" would, by indirection, become a "rule of five." Third, such a practice would, in my opinion, be inconsistent with the long-standing and desirable custom of not announcing the Conference vote on petitions for certiorari. For in the absence of the intervening circumstances which may cause a Justice to vote to dismiss a writ as improvidently granted, such a disposition of the case on his part is almost bound to be taken as reflecting his original Conference vote on the petition. And if such a practice is permissible, then by the same token I do not see how those who voted in favor of the petition can reasonably be expected to refrain from announcing their Conference votes at the time the petition is acted on.

My Brother FRANKFURTER states that the course he advocates will not result in making of the "rule of four" an empty thing, suggesting that in individual cases "a doubting Justice" will normally respect "the judgment of his brethren that the case does concern issues important enough for the Court's consideration and adjudication," and that it is only "when a class of cases is systematically taken for review" that such a Justice "cannot forego his duty to voice his dissent to the Court's action." However, it seems to me that it is precisely in that type of situation where the exercise of the right of dissent may well result in nullification of the "rule of four" by the action of five Justices. For differences of view as to the desirability of the Court's taking particular "classes" of cases—the situation we have here—are prone to lead to more or less definite lines of cleavage among the Justices, which past experience has shown may well involve an alignment of four Justices who favor granting certiorari in such cases and five who do not. If in such situations it becomes the duty of one Justice among the disagreeing five not to "forego" his right to dissent, then I do not see why it is not equally the duty of the remaining four, resulting in the "rule of four" being set at naught. I thus see no basis in the circumstance that a case is an "individual" one rather than one of a "class" for distinctions in what may be done by an individual Justice who disapproves of the Court's action in granting certiorari.

Although I feel strongly that cases of this kind do not belong in this Court, I can see no other course, consistent with the "rule of four," but to continue our Conference debates, with the hope that persuasion or the mounting calendars of the Court will eventually bring our differing brethren to another point of view.

II.

Since I can find no intervening circumstances which would justify my voting now to dismiss the writs in these cases as improvidently granted, I turn to the merits of the four cases before us. I agree with, and join in, the Court's opinion in No. 46. I dissent in Nos. 28, 42 and 59. No doubt the evidence in the latter three cases can be viewed both as the three courts below did and as this Court does. So far as I can see all this Court has done is to substitute its views on the evidence for those of the Missouri Supreme Court and the two Courts of Appeals, and that is my first reason for dissenting. In my view we should not interfere with the decisions of these three courts in the absence of clear legal error, or some capricious or unreasonable action on their part. Nothing of that kind has been shown here. I would apply to cases of this type the reasoning of the Court in Labor Board v. Pittsburgh Steamship Co., 340 U. S. 498, 502-503, dealing with review of decisions of the National Labor Relations Board by the Courts of Appeals:

"Were we called upon to pass on the Board's conclusions in the first instance or to make an independent review of the review by the Court of Appeals, we might well support the Board's conclusion and reject that of the court below. But Congress has charged the Courts of Appeals and not this Court with [that] normal and primary responsibility . . . . The same considerations that should lead us to leave undisturbed, by denying certiorari, decisions of Courts of Appeals involving solely a fair assessment of a record on the issue of unsubstantiality, ought to lead us to do no more than decide that there was such a fair assessment when the case is here . . . .

"This is not the place to review a conflict of evidence nor to reverse a Court of Appeals because were we in its place we would find the record tilting one way rather than the other, though fair-minded judges could find it tilting either way."

For my part, to overturn the judgments below simply involves second-guessing the Missouri Supreme Court, the Court of Appeals for the Seventh Circuit, and the Court of Appeals for the Second Circuit, on questions of fact on which they brought to bear judgments neither capricious nor unreasonable, and on which they made a "fair assessment of a record."

I dissent also for another reason. No scientific or precise yardstick can be devised to test the sufficiency of the evidence in a negligence case. The problem has always been one of judgment, to be applied in view of the purposes of the statute. It has, however, been common ground that a verdict must be based on evidence—not on a scintilla of evidence but evidence sufficient to enable a reasoning man to infer both negligence and causation by reasoning from the evidence. Moore v. Chesapeake & O. R. Co., 340 U. S. 573. And it has always been the function of the court to see to it that jury verdicts stay within that boundary, that they be arrived at by reason and not by will or sheer speculation. Neither the Seventh Amendment nor the Federal Employers' Liability Act lifted that duty from the courts. However, in judging these cases, the Court appears to me to have departed from these long-established standards, for, as I read these opinions, the implication seems to be that the question, at least as to the element of causation, is not whether the evidence is sufficient to convince a reasoning man, but whether there is any scintilla of evidence at all to justify the jury verdicts. I cannot agree with such a standard, for I consider it a departure from a wise rule of law, not justified either by the provision of the FELA making employers liable for injuries resulting "in whole or in part" from their negligence, or by anything else in the Act or its history, which evinces no purpose to depart in these respects from common-law rules.

For these reasons I think the judgments in Nos. 28, 42 and 59, as well as that in No. 46, should be affirmed.

Notes

[1] In some instances where the Court has granted certiorari and simultaneously summarily disposed of the case on the merits, individual Justices (including the writer) have merely noted their dissent to the grant without reaching the merits. See, e. g., Anderson v. Atlantic Coast Line R. Co., 350 U. S. 807; Cahill v. New York, N. H. & H. R. Co., 350 U. S. 898. Even here, I am bound to say, it would probably be better practice for a Justice, who has unsuccessfully opposed certiorari, to face the merits, and to dissent from the summary disposition rather than from the grant of certiorari if he is not prepared to reach the merits without full-dress argument.

[2] See Burton, Judging Is Also Administration, 21 Temple Law Quarterly 77, 84-85, and n. 23 (1947).

Justice Harlan's dissent in Automobile Club of Mich. v. Comm'r (April 22, 1957)

MR. JUSTICE HARLAN, dissenting.

I think collection of the 1943 and 1944 taxes, based on the Commissioner's retroactive revocation of his 1934 and 1938 exemption rulings, was barred by the three-year statute of limitations.[1] I would hold that the limitations period began to run when the taxpayer, relying on the exemption ruling, duly filed its Form 990 returns[2] for the years 1943 and 1944. I see no reason why we should strain to construe "return" in § 275 (a) as excluding an information return when such a return was the only one required of this taxpayer, exempt from taxation at the time, and especially when that construction produces the inequitable consequences which have resulted here. Section 275 (a) should be construed in conjunction with § 276 (a),[3] which provides that an assessment may be made without regard to the statute of limitations in "the case of a false or fraudulent return with intent to evade tax or of a failure to file a return . . . ." In my judgment, a taxpayer who files a return on one form rather than another because the Commissioner directs him to do so cannot be charged with the "failure" contemplated by the statute. See Stockstrom v. Commissioner, 88 U. S. App. D. C. 286, 190 F. 2d 283; Balkan Nat. Ins. Co. v. Commissioner, 101 F. 2d 75. Commissioner v. Lane-Wells Co., 321 U. S. 219, cited by the Court, is inapposite because the taxpayer there was required by applicable statutes and regulations to file two returns and had filed only one. Compare Germantown Trust Co. v. Commissioner, 309 U. S. 304. Under the decision of the Court, the Commissioner may revoke his rulings retroactively so long as his action does not constitute an "abuse of discretion." I see no reason why that power should not also be subjected to the three-year limit established by Congress.

I also disagree with the Court's holding that the Commissioner may properly tax in the year of receipt the full amount of petitioner's prepaid membership dues. The Commissioner seeks to justify that course under the "claim of right" doctrine announced in North American Oil v. Burnet, 286 U. S. 417. However, that doctrine, it seems to me, comes into play only in determining whether the treatment of an item of income should be influenced by the fact that the right to receive or keep it is in dispute; it does not relate to the entirely different question whether items that admittedly belong to the taxpayer may be attributed to a taxable year other than that of receipt in accordance with principles of accrual accounting. See Brown v. Helvering, 291 U. S. 193, where these two problems were involved and were treated as distinct. The collection of taxes clearly should not be made to depend on the vicissitudes of litigation with third parties in which the taxpayer may be engaged. That is quite a different thing, however, from holding that the Commissioner may force taxpayers to abandon reasonable and accurate methods of accounting simply because they do not reflect advance receipts as income in the year received. Under § 41 of the Internal Revenue Code of 1939,[4] the income of the taxpayer is to be determined "in accordance with the method of accounting regularly employed in keeping the [taxpayer's] books," unless "the method employed does not clearly reflect" the taxpayer's income. Under § 42,[5] items of gross income need not be reported in the taxable year in which received by the taxpayer if, "under methods of accounting permitted under section 41, any such amounts are to be properly accounted for as of a different period." And it is clear that accrual methods of accounting may be employed. United States v. Anderson, 269 U. S. 422. The Commissioner's own regulations authorize the deferral of income in some instances.[6]

The Court, however, now by-passes the Commissioner's "claim of right" argument, and rests its decision instead on the ground that the "pro rata allocation of the membership dues in monthly amounts is purely artificial and bears no relation to the services which petitioner may in fact be called upon to render for the member," so that it cannot say that in doing what he did the Commissioner exceeded the limits of his discretion. I do not understand this, because the Commissioner does not deny—as, indeed, he could not—that the method of accounting used by the taxpayer reflects its net earnings with considerably greater accuracy than the method he proposes. Nor does he urge that the taxpayer's accounting system defers income in a manner or to an extent that would make the Government unreasonably dependent on the continued solvency of the taxpayer's business. And no other circumstances have been shown which would justify application of the statutory exception.

On both of these grounds I would reverse the judgment below.

Notes
[1] 53 Stat. 86, 26 U. S. C. § 275 (a).
[2] 58 Stat. 36, 26 U. S. C. § 54 (f).
[3] 53 Stat. 87, 26 U. S. C. § 276 (a).
[4] 53 Stat. 24, 26 U. S. C. § 41.
[5] 53 Stat. 24, 26 U. S. C. § 42.
[6] Regulations 111, §§ 29.22 (a)-17 (2) (a) (bond premiums), 29.42-4 (long-term contracts). See also I. T. 3369, 1940-1 Cum. Bull. 46 (prepaid subscriptions to periodicals); I. T. 2080, III-2 Cum. Bull. 48 (1924) (advance receipts from sales of tickets for tourist cruises).

Justice Harlan's dissent in Arnold v. Panhandle & Santa Fe R. (May 13, 1957)

MR. JUSTICE HARLAN, whom MR. JUSTICE BURTON and MR. JUSTICE WHITTAKER join, dissenting.

As this case presents a different situation from that involved in other negligence cases which, in increasing numbers I regret to say, have been passed on by this Court during the current Term,[1] I am constrained to write a few words in explanation of my dissent, beyond the views expressed in my dissenting opinion in Rogers v. Missouri Pac. R. Co., 352 U. S. 500, 559.

This case involves more than the problem of the sufficiency of the evidence to support a jury verdict. Under Texas procedure, the trial court in this case required the jury to bring in a general verdict on the issue of whether the respondent had negligently failed to furnish petitioner with a safe place to work, and, if so, whether such failure was a contributing cause to the accident. The jury was also asked to make findings on special issues put to it by the court. The jury's general verdict was favorable to the petitioner, but its findings on the special issues were in favor of the respondent, and, as I see them, were wholly inconsistent with the general verdict.[2] In these circumstances the state appellate court, applying Texas law, held that the general verdict must yield to the inconsistent findings on the special issues, and that the trial court should have entered judgment for the respondent.

I am unable to see any valid basis for this Court's action in upsetting this state judgment. Clearly, it seems to me, the Texas procedural rule which the Court of Civil Appeals applied in resolving the head-on collision in the jury's verdict did not subvert assertion of the federal rights established by the Federal Employers' Liability Act. Compare Brown v. Western R. Co., 338 U. S. 294. Nor, in my opinion, can it be said that resolving these inconsistencies, in accordance with this local rule of practice, deprived the petitioner of any substantive right given him by the federal statute. Compare Dice v. Akron, C. & Y. R. Co., 342 U. S. 359. Indeed, the procedural rule applied by the Texas court is identical with that which would have been applicable, in the same circumstances, had this case been tried in a federal court. See Fed. Rules Civ. Proc., 49 (b).

I would affirm.

Notes

[1] Rogers v. Missouri Pac. R. Co., 352 U. S. 500; Webb v. Illinois Central R. Co., 352 U. S. 512; Herdman v. Pennsylvania R. Co., 352 U. S. 518; Ferguson v. Moore-McCormack Lines, Inc., 352 U. S. 521; Gibson v. Phillips Petroleum Co., 352 U. S. 874; Johnson v. Union Pac. R. Co., 352 U. S. 957; Shaw v. Atlantic Coast Line R. Co., 353 U. S. 920; Futrelle v. Atlantic Coast Line R. Co., 353 U. S. 920; Deen v. Gulf, C. & S. F. R. Co., 353 U. S. 925; Thomson v. Texas & Pac. R. Co., 353 U. S. 926.

[2] Petitioner, respondent's car inspector, sued to recover for injuries sustained while he was inspecting railroad cars in a passageway ten feet wide, having been struck by a truck backing into the same passageway. He alleged that the respondent had negligently failed to provide him with a safe place to work by (1) not warning petitioner of the truck; (2) not protecting petitioner while he was working in the passageway; (3) allowing the truck to be driven into the passageway; and (4) failing to see that the truck was not driven negligently. As to the special issues the jury found: (1) there was no negligence in failing to warn the petitioner of the truck; (2) there was no negligence in allowing the truck to be driven onto the passageway while the petitioner was working there; (3) there was no negligent failure on the part of the respondent to keep a proper lookout; (4) there was no negligent failure on the part of the truck driver to keep a proper lookout; (5) there was no negligence in failing to give a warning before backing up the truck; (6) there was no negligence in backing the truck into the passageway; (7) the truck did not back too close to the tracks, did not back up too fast, and was not negligently driven without adequate visibility; (8) petitioner did not move into the path of the truck "when such movement could not be made with safety"; and (9) petitioner failed to keep a proper lookout for the truck, and this failure was a cause of the accident, though not the sole cause.

I do not understand how it could be claimed that these findings were not inconsistent with the general verdict. Indeed, every specific allegation of negligence set forth in petitioner's complaint was rejected by the jury. And, as I see it, every factual basis on which a finding could be based that respondent had negligently failed to provide petitioner with a safe place to work was rejected by the jury. All that remains to show that the passageway was a dangerous spot is the fact that the accident occurred there—

something which, until now, I have never supposed could be equated with negligence.

Justice Harlan's concurrence in Reid v. Covert (June 10, 1957) [Excerpt]

MR. JUSTICE HARLAN, concurring in the result.

I concur in the result, on the narrow ground that where the offense is capital, Article 2 (11)[1] cannot constitutionally be applied to the trial of civilian dependents of members of the armed forces overseas in times of peace. [. . .]

I have since concluded that this analysis was not sound, for two reasons:

(1) The underlying premise of the prior opinion, it seems to me, is that under the Constitution the mere absence of a prohibition against an asserted power, plus the abstract reasonableness of its use, is enough to establish the existence of the power. I think this is erroneous. The powers of Congress, unlike those of the English Parliament, are constitutionally circumscribed. Under the Constitution Congress has only such powers as are expressly granted or those that are implied as reasonably necessary and proper to carry out the granted powers. [. . .]

I come then to the question whether this court-martial jurisdiction can be justified as an exercise of Congress' Article I power to regulate the armed forces.

At the outset, I cannot accept the implication of my brother BLACK'S opinion that this Article I power was intended to be unmodified by the Necessary and Proper Clause of the Constitution,[4] and that therefore this power is incapable of expansion under changing circumstances. The historical evidence, in fact, shows quite the opposite. True, the records of the time indicate that the Founders shared a deep fear of an unchecked military branch. But what they feared was a military branch unchecked by the legislature, and susceptible of use by an arbitrary executive power.[5] So far as I know, there is no evidence at all that the Founders intended to limit the power of the people, as embodied in the legislature, to make such laws in the regulation of the land and naval forces as are necessary to the proper functioning of those forces. In other words, there is no indication that any special limitation on the power of Congress, as opposed to the power of the executive, was subsumed in the grant of power to govern the land and naval forces. Alexander Hamilton, indeed, stated exactly the opposite:[6]

"The authorities essential to the common defense are these: to raise armies; to build and equip fleets; to prescribe rules for the government of both; to direct their operations; to provide for their support. These powers ought to exist without limitation, because it is impossible to foresee or define the extent and variety of national exigencies, or the correspondent extent and variety of the means which may be necessary to satisfy them. The circumstances that endanger the safety of nations are infinite, and for this reason no constitutional shackles can wisely be imposed on the power to which the care of it is committed. This power ought to be coextensive with all the possible combinations of such circumstances; and ought to be under the direction of the same councils which are appointed to preside over the common defense.

.....

". . . Shall the Union be constituted the guardian of the common safety? Are fleets and armies and revenues necessary to this purpose? The government of the Union must be empowered to pass all laws, and to make all regulations which have relation to them. . . .

.....

"Every view we may take of the subject, as candid inquirers after truth, will serve to convince us, that it is both unwise and dangerous to deny the federal government an unconfined authority, as to all those objects which are intrusted to its management.. . . A government, the constitution of which renders it unfit to be trusted with all the powers which a free people ought to delegate to any government, would be an unsafe and improper depositary of the national interests. Wherever these can with propriety be confided, the coincident powers may safely accompany them." [. . .]

On this basis, I cannot agree with the sweeping proposition that a full Article III trial, with indictment and trial by jury, is required in every case for the trial of a civilian dependent of a serviceman overseas. The Government, it seems to me, has made an impressive showing that at least for the run-of-the-mill offenses committed by dependents overseas, such a requirement would be as impractical and as anomalous as it would have been to require jury trial for Balzac in Porto Rico.[12] Again, I need not go into details, beyond stating that except for capital offenses, such as we have here, to which, in my opinion, special considerations apply, I am by no means ready to say that Congress' power to provide for trial by court-martial of civilian dependents overseas is limited by Article III and the Fifth and Sixth Amendments.

Where, if at all, the dividing line should be drawn among cases not capital, need not now be decided. We are confronted here with capital offenses alone; and it seems to me particularly unwise now to decide more than we have to. Our far-flung foreign military establishments are a new phenomenon in our national life, and I think it would be unfortunate were we unnecessarily to foreclose, as my four brothers would do, our future consideration of the broad questions involved in maintaining the effectiveness of these national outposts, in the light of continuing experience with these problems.

So far as capital cases are concerned, I think they stand on quite a different footing than other offenses. In such cases the law is especially sensitive to demands for that procedural fairness which inheres in a civilian trial where the judge and trier of fact are not responsive to the command of the convening authority. I do not concede that whatever process is "due" an offender faced with a fine or a prison sentence necessarily satisfies the requirements of the Constitution in a capital case. The distinction is by no means novel, compare Powell v. Alabama, 287 U. S. 45, with Betts v. Brady, 316 U. S. 455; nor is it negligible, being literally that between life and death. And, under what I deem to be the correct view of Ross and the Insular Cases, it is precisely the kind of distinction which plays a large role in the process of weighing the competing considerations which lead to sound judgment upon the question whether certain safeguards of the Constitution should be given effect in the trial of an American citizen abroad. In fact, the Government itself has conceded that one grave offense, treason, presents a special case: "The gravity of this offense is such that we can well assume that, whatever difficulties may be involved in trial far from the scene of the offense . . . the trial should be in our courts." I see no reason for not applying the same principle to any case where a civilian dependent stands trial on pain of life itself. The number of such cases would appear to be so negligible that the practical problems of affording the defendant a civilian trial would not present insuperable problems.

On this narrow ground I concur in the result in these cases.

Justice Harlan's dissent in Vanderbilt v. Vanderbilt (June 24, 1957)

MR. JUSTICE HARLAN, dissenting.

The Court holds today, as I understand its opinion, that Nevada, lacking personal jurisdiction over Mrs. Vanderbilt, had no power to adjudicate the question of support, and that any divorce decree purporting so to do is to that extent wholly void—presumably in Nevada as well as in New York—under the Due Process Clause of the Fourteenth Amendment, pursuant to the doctrine of Pennoyer v. Neff, 95 U. S. 714.

I cannot agree with such a holding. In the first place, as I see this case, there is no necessity to pass on this question at all. Our problem should be, initially at least, not whether this decree, insofar as it affects property, is "void" for lack of due process, but whether it binds New York under the Full Faith and Credit Clause. In other words, we need not, in the first instance, decide what the Due Process Clause forbids Nevada to do, but merely what the Full Faith and Credit Clause compels New York to do. One of the wisest of our constitutional commentators has warned us to beware the "constricting necessitarianism" of deeming the two questions to be one and the same:

"In a problem so fraught with infelicities whatever mediation is devised, there is wisdom in confining pronouncements closely to what is imperative in the particular case. It is not logically necessary to deny Nevada's mastery within her own boundaries in order to deny her power of projection beyond them. Freedom of home manufacture and consumption does not necessarily entail freedom of export. Only if it is inexorable that what is meant by `jurisdiction' must be either wholly absent or wholly unlimited need frailty in sister states be conditioned on total impotence at home." T. R. Powell, And Repent at Leisure, 58 Harv. L. Rev. 930, 936.

Were we compelled to reach the question, I would by no means be ready to hold that Nevada, in connection with a valid divorce proceeding, had no power to adjudicate an incident so inextricably knit to the marriage status as is support. I would agree with Judge Fuld, dissenting below, that the denial of power to Nevada rests on the "erroneous premise that a mere incident of the marital status, which `in itself furnishes no foundation for a cause of action' . . . is the equivalent of an independent right."[1] Nor does it help to label Mrs. Vanderbilt's claim to support a "property" right and therefore an in personam, rather than an in rem, matter. If it is due process for Nevada to adjudicate the marriage status of a domiciliary without personal service over the absent spouse (as it clearly is, see Williams v. North Carolina, I, 317 U. S. 287), I see no reason why Nevada cannot, at least for the purposes of her own law, also adjudicate the incidents of that status.

I do not think, however, that this forecloses the issue before us. I revert, therefore, to what, for me, is the real question in this case: must New York respect Nevada's decree insofar as it purports to adjudicate the question of support? The answer to this question, I think, turns squarely on an issue of New York law, namely, whether Mrs. Vanderbilt was domiciled in New York at the time of the divorce.

If Mrs. Vanderbilt was a New York domiciliary at the time of the divorce, the situation would seem to me to be as follows: New York's law and policy is that the right of a married woman domiciled in New York to support survives an ex parte divorce, whether obtained in New York or elsewhere. The only question under the Full Faith and Credit Clause is whether New York is compelled to disregard her own law and policy in favor of the law of Nevada on the question of the survival of support rights subsequent to an ex parte divorce. My answer to this question is "no." The interest of New York in her domiciliaries seems to me to be of sufficient weight to justify allowing her to apply her own policy on the question of what effect ex parte divorces will be given as against the surviving support rights of her own domiciliaries. In my view it does not follow automatically that merely because New York must recognize the validity of Nevada's ex parte divorce, she must also recognize the effect Nevada would give to that divorce in connection with the wife's rights to support. The two questions are governed by different considerations. I quote again from Professor Powell:

"The `irreconcilable conflict' between two states on the question of marital status is not so insuperable in dealing with matters of money. It is less irksome to support two wives than to go to jail because of them. Though with respect to status one state or the other must yield, with respect to maintenance such yielding is not necessary.

". . . `The problem under the full faith and credit clause is to accommodate as fully as possible the conflicting interests of the two States.' The solution is a matter of judgment in each case, judgment based not only on the particularities of the individual case or type of case but upon the desirability of as much generality and predictability as is consistent with a fair degree of control by a state over the conduct and the relationships of persons who in every substantial sense are its own home folks. . . .

.....

"[It is argued] that the state where the stay-behind spouse has long been domiciled has an interest in making a quondam husband continue a prior obligation to support her, and that this interest is stronger and more meritorious than any possible opposing interest to prevent it that can be accredited to the state which gave him a divorce after being blindly satisfied that he intended an indefinite stay there. This seems so sensible that it should be obvious to any one who had never become confused by studying law." Powell, supra, at 952, 954-955.

In effect, the situation before us seems to me to be analogous to dower. If New York law should provide that the dower rights of her domiciliaries survive ex parte divorces, I would suppose that New York could give effect to that policy in spite of an ex parte Nevada divorce which purported to cut off the right to dower. The problem in each case is to weigh the policy of giving an ex parte judgment uniform effect throughout the nation, against the interest of a particular State in a particular local policy. Where status is concerned, this Court held that the interest in certainty as to whether one is married or single outweighs the interest of home States in the marital status of their domiciliaries, so that North Carolina was forced to swallow Nevada's views as to what is sufficient cause for divorce even though the North Carolina wife had not appeared in the Nevada proceeding. Williams, I, supra. But I see no reason why we should extend that, for me, already somewhat unpalatable mediation to the limits of its logic in order to hold that Nevada's views as to support as well as divorce must be forced onto other States, and that Nevada can not only compel wives domiciled elsewhere to become single against their will, but to be pauperized against their will as well. Of course, the reason for the distinction is not that the wife's right to support is "worth" more than her interest in remaining a wife. But the interest of the wife in not becoming single and penniless is greater than her interest in not becoming single. In other words, merely because it is held that the wife must be deprived of one benefit ex parte, in the interest of national uniformity, does not compel us to hold that the other benefit must vanish with it, where the interest in national uniformity is not as compelling.[2]

In deciding this case we must always remember that the reason why the Nevada ex parte divorce has the effect of a judgment in New York even on the question of status is because this Court found, in measuring the competing interests, that uniformity should prevail. It will not do, therefore, to say that once that is done the Court is foreclosed from weighing competing interests in determining the effect of the Nevada adjudication as to questions other than status. One cannot rest on the inexorability that the Nevada decree is a "judgment" and eliminate the fact that it was held to be a judgment outside Nevada as to status for reasons which do not necessarily apply to the question of support, any more than one can solve the problem by labeling support as a "property" right.[3]

Quite a different case is presented, it seems to me, where a wife becomes a domiciliary of New York after the ex parte divorce and is then granted support. In such a case New York could not pretend to be assuring the wife the mere survival of a pre-existing right, because the wife could have had no pre-divorce rights in New York at all. New York would merely be granting the wife a marital right in the teeth of a valid Nevada adjudication that there is no marriage. And, of course, at the time of the divorce New York would have had no interest in the situation of any kind. In such a case, therefore, it seems to me that the Full Faith and Credit Clause would require New York to respect the Nevada judgment as to support rights. Furthermore, even aside from the judgment, as a matter of choice of law I should think New York would be forced to look to the law of a State which had a substantial contact with these parties at the time of the divorce in determining the effect to be given to the divorce decree. It seems to me unfortunate that this Court should permit spouses divorced by valid decrees to comb the country, after the divorce, in search of any State where the divorcing spouse has property and which has favorable support laws, in order there to obtain alimony. I would therefore by no means hold the Nevada adjudication "void" and therefore of no effect in any State.[4]

Thus decision here, as I see it, turns on the domicile of Mrs. Vanderbilt at the time of the divorce. On this question I am left in some doubt. Section 1165-a of the New York Civil Practice Act makes one year's residence necessary to suits for support. This is amenable to the interpretation that New York would not recognize Mrs. Vanderbilt as domiciled in that State until the lapse of a year, that is, after the decree of divorce here involved. See de Meli v. de Meli, 120 N. Y. 485, 24 N. E. 996. On the other hand, the opinion below intimates that the one-year residency can be regarded as merely a procedural prerequisite to filing suit under § 1170-b, and does not affect Mrs. Vanderbilt's status as a domiciliary of New York ab initio.[5] In view of this uncertainty in the state law, I would remand to the state court for reconsideration in light of the above-stated principles.

Notes
[1] N. Y. 2d 342, 357, 135 N. E. 2d 553, 561.
[2] "It is easier to have a flat rule than to make distinctions based on judgment. Yet, from the standpoint of partitioning power among the several states, there may well be wisdom in having a gap between what due process will not forbid and what full faith and credit will not require. Certainly in suits over property and money there may be grounds that are thought good enough to justify a state in exerting its power so far as it relies wholly on its own strength and yet not so good that other states should be bound to lend a hand." Powell, supra, at 936; and see id., n. 14.
[3] For the most compendious exposition of the many situations where this Court has held that the Full Faith and Credit Clause does not demand automatic respect in a sister State for a judgment valid in the State where rendered, see the dissent of Mr. Justice Stone and Mr. Justice Cardozo in Yarborough v. Yarborough, 290 U. S. 202, 213. There can hardly be dispute over the proposition that "in the assertion of rights, defined by a judgment of one state, within the territory of another, there is often an inescapable conflict of interest of the two states, and there comes a point beyond which the imposition of the will of one state beyond its own borders involves a forbidden infringement of some legitimate domestic interest of the other. That point may vary with the circumstances of the case; and in the absence of provisions more specific than the general terms of the congressional enactment this Court must determine for itself the extent to which one state may qualify or deny rights claimed under proceedings or records of other states." Id., at 215 (footnotes omitted).
[4] See Morris, Divisible Divorce, 64 Harv. L. Rev. 1287.
[5] I draw that implication from the following passage in the opinion of the Court

of Appeals: "But when the husband, abandoning his wife, left their California domicile to establish a Nevada domicile for his own purposes, the abandoned wife had a right to set up a New York domicile for herself and bring the matrimonial domicile to New York with her . . . . That right she exercised in this instance before the Nevada judgment was entered and she satisfied New York's residence requirements before suing for a separation. . . . We need not decide whether she would have the same right to come into New York, even after a foreign-State divorce, to take advantage of section 1170-b." 1 N. Y. 2d, at 351, 135 N. E. 2d, at 558.

Justice Harlan's dissent in Rowoldt v. Perfetto (Dec 9, 1957) [Appendix omitted]

MR. JUSTICE HARLAN, whom MR. JUSTICE BURTON, MR. JUSTICE CLARK and MR. JUSTICE WHITTAKER join, dissenting.

I regret my inability to join the Court's opinion, for its effort to find a way out from the rigors of a severe statute has alluring appeal. The difficulty is that in order to reach its result the Court has had to take impermissible liberties with the statute and the record upon which this case is based.

Section 22 of the Internal Security Act of 1950, under which these proceedings were brought, provides for the deportation of aliens who at the time of entry into the United States, or thereafter, were "members of or affiliated with . . . the Communist Party of the United States . . . ."[1] In this case there is no dispute that the petitioner was a dues-paying member of the Communist Party for about a year after he entered the United States. The Court, however, finds the record insufficient to establish that petitioner's membership was "the kind of meaningful association required by the alleviating Amendment of 1951," and suggests that "the dominating impulse to his `affiliation' with the Communist Party may well have been wholly devoid of any `political' implications."

This holding is derived from the Act of March 28, 1951, which amended the Internal Security Act by exempting from the broad sweep of the membership provision those persons who joined the Party "(a) when under sixteen years of age, (b) by operation of law, or (c) for purposes of obtaining employment, food rations, or other essentials of living, and where necessary for such purposes."[2] The Court does not rely here upon any of these exemptions as such, but rests its decision on its finding in Galvan v. Press, 347 U. S. 522, 527, that the legislative discussion of these exemptions indicates that the membership provision of the 1950 Act should be read benignly.

The Court's holding as to the insufficiency of this record may be interpreted in one of two ways, either (a) that petitioner was not shown to have joined the Communist Party conscious of its character as a political organization, or (b) that if he did so join, his membership was nonetheless excusable under the 1950 Act because it was predominantly motivated by economic necessity.

Under either view of the Court's opinion I think that the setting aside of this deportation order cannot be reconciled with the holding in Galvan v. Press, supra. There the Court, in rejecting the contention that the statute should be interpreted as not reaching persons who joined or remained members of the Communist Party without knowledge of its tenets of force and violence,[3] said, p. 528: "It is enough that the alien joined the Party, aware that he was joining an organization known as the Communist Party which operates as a distinct and active political organization, and that he did so of his own free will." I need not retrace the reasoning which inescapably led the Court to that decision,[4] save to note one point not alluded to in the Galvan opinion, namely, that the ameliorating amendment of the 1951 Act, on whose "spirit" the Court here relies, was motivated solely by the problems of aliens who were being excluded from entry into the United States because they had joined totalitarian organizations in foreign countries.[5]

Under the first possible view of the Court's opinion it is plain that the petitioner is deportable, for in my judgment the record leaves no room for the conclusion that he was unaware that the Communist Party was "a distinct and active political organization." The petitioner has freely admitted that he was a member of the Party for about a year; that he paid Party dues; that he attended Party meetings; and that he worked, without pay, in the Party bookstore, which he recognized as "an official outlet for communist literature." Beyond this, petitioner's testimony betrayed considerable, albeit rudimentary, knowledge of Communist history and philosophy. To be sure, he disclaimed belief in the forcible overthrow of government, but that, as Galvan holds, is immaterial under this statute.

Perhaps it should be added that I do not understand the Court to suggest that, although petitioner joined the Communist Party aware that it was a political organization, his activities in the Party were too slight to constitute him a "member" within the meaning of the 1950 Act. The Court's reaffirmation of the Galvan definition of membership would seem to preclude such an interpretation of the opinion. Moreover, that interpretation would do violence to the sweeping and unequivocal language of the Act itself.

The Court says that the "differences on the facts between Galvan v. Press . . . and this case are too obvious to be detailed." But, in respect to the crucial question whether conscious membership in the Communist Party as a political organization was sufficiently shown, I submit that this record is at least as strong as that in Galvan. A "detailing" of the record before us will demonstrate this, and I have therefore liberally quoted from it in the Appendix to this opinion, post, p. 127.

The second possible ground of the Court's decision is equally foreclosed by Galvan. For if the record shows, as I believe it plainly does, that the petitioner joined the Communist Party of the United States of his own free will, and knowing it to be "a distinct and active political organization," the 1950 Act makes his economic motives for joining just as irrelevant as the absence of proof that he did not believe in the violent overthrow of government.

The Court's action in this case calls to mind what Mr. Justice Cardozo said in Anderson v. Wilson, 289 U. S. 20, 27: "We do not pause to consider whether a statute differently conceived and framed would yield results more consonant with fairness and reason. We take the statute as we find it." Again, with specific reference to the statute here involved, this Court said in Galvan, p. 528: "A fair reading of the legislation requires that this scope [see ante, p. 122] be given to what Congress enacted in 1950, however severe the consequences and whatever view one may have of the wisdom of the means which Congress employed to meet its desired end." I fear that the Court has departed from those wise precepts in this instance.

My view of this case would require us to deal with petitioner's contention that the statute, as applied to him, is unconstitutional. Since the Court does not reach that question, no extended discussion of it seems appropriate in a dissenting opinion. It is enough to say that I regard petitioner's constitutional argument foreclosed by Galvan v. Press, supra, Harisiades v. Shaughnessy, 342 U. S. 580, and by the considerations and long line of authorities to which those cases refer. Whatever may be the scope of the limitations of the Fifth Amendment upon the deportation power (see Galvan, at pp. 530-531) —a question as to which I reserve the right to speak when occasion arises—I think that there is no constitutional bar to the statute as applied in this case.

For the foregoing reasons I would affirm the judgment below.

Notes

[1] 64 Stat. 987, 1006, 1008.

[2] 65 Stat. 28.

[3] "It must be concluded, therefore, that support, or even demonstrated knowledge, of the Communist Party's advocacy of violence was not intended to be a prerequisite to deportation." 347 U. S., at 528.

[4] The result reached in Galvan was thoroughly consistent both with the judicial and administrative decisions interpreting the predecessors of the 1950 Act, and with the purpose of that Act to "strengthen" the provisions of the law relating "to the exclusion and deportation. . . of subversive aliens." See H. R. Rep. No. 3112, 81st Cong., 2d Sess., p. 54. Compare the exhaustive treatment in Latva v. Nicolls, 106 F. Supp. 658, where Judge Wyzanski reached the same conclusion as to the meaning of the 1950 Act.

[5] This conclusion is compelled by the legislative history. The House of Representatives Report on the bill embodying the amendment stated:

"The attention of the Committees on the Judiciary of both Houses has been directed to the increasing number of cases in which nonimmigrant and immigrant visas have been withheld or admission into this country denied to aliens on the basis of regulations issued pursuant to the act of October 16, 1918, as amended. The majority of the cases brought to the attention of the committees involve spouses of servicemen, close relatives of American citizens, permanent residents previously admitted into the United States and returning from abroad to their unrelinquished domiciles with appropriate documentation, such as reentry permits, etc.

"The reason most frequently given for the denial of visas or the denial of admission appears to be the applicant's past membership of [sic], or affiliation with, certain totalitarian youth, national labor, or professional student, or similar organizations, or the alien's service in the German or Italian Armies, or his involuntary membership in totalitarian parties or their affiliates and auxiliaries, including those cases where it was shown that such membership or affiliation occurred by operation of law or edict, or for purposes of obtaining or preserving employment, food rations, or other essentials of living.

.....

"The bill makes clear the intent of Congress that aliens who are, or were, voluntary members of . . . totalitarian parties or organizations are to be excluded, but aliens who were involuntary members. . . are not to be considered ipso facto as members of, or affiliated with, the . . . organizations within the meaning of the act of October 16, 1918, as amended." H. R. Rep. No. 118, 82d Cong., 1st Sess., pp. 1-2. (Italics added.)

The debates on the floor of both Houses of Congress provide additional evidence on this score. In the Senate, where the major discussion took place, every specific reference to the scope of the proposed amendment discloses that its purpose was to assist individuals who were being denied admission into the United States because of their prior membership in totalitarian organizations in their homeland. For example, Senator Smith inquired at one point: "Would the pending bill exclude, for instance, a Ukrainian who lived in the Soviet Union and who was forced to belong to a Kulak farm cooperative in order to obtain work? Would such a man be excluded?" 97 Cong. Rec. 2369. And Senator McCarran, the chief author of the amendment, described its three subsections in revealing detail. With respect to each he emphasized that many "spouses of members of the United States Armed Forces" were included. The first class, he said, consisted of persons "who during infancy where [sic] members of the Hitler Youth, Fascist Youth, and similar organizations where the child's education and welfare were made dependent upon membership . . . ." The second class embraced "aliens who unwittingly, and without their knowledge or consent, were impressed into the various labor fronts and professional unions and organizations; aliens who served in the German and Italian Armies; and aliens who . . . by law or decree became members of or affiliated with subsidiary totalitarian organizations." And the third class, as described by Senator McCarran, consisted of "aliens who were forced to become members of totalitarian organizations in order to obtain food ration cards, housing, employment, and other essentials of living." 97 Cong. Rec. 2370-2371.

The inference that Congress intended to aid only persons being denied admission to the United States rather than persons subject to deportation for membership which took place in this country is substantially reinforced by the fact that when the Immigration and Nationality Act of 1952 repealed the ameliorating amendment, 66 Stat. 163, 280, its substance was re-enacted as far as exclusions were concerned, 66 Stat. 186, but not with respect to deportation.

Justice Harlan's dissent in Sinkler v. Missouri Pacific R. Co. (April 28, 1958)

MR. JUSTICE HARLAN, whom MR. JUSTICE FRANKFURTER joins, dissenting.

This case is a further step in a course of decisions through which the Court has been rapidly converting the Federal Employers' Liability Act, 35 Stat. 65, as amended, 45 U. S. C. §§ 51-60 (and the Jones Act, which incorporates the FELA, 41 Stat. 1007, 46 U. S. C. § 688), into what amounts to a workmen's compensation statute.

This process recently gained marked momentum with Rogers v. Missouri Pacific R. Co., 352 U. S. 500, 524, 559, decided at the 1956 Term, where the Court in effect established a "scintilla" rule in these cases for judging the sufficiency of the evidence on the issue of "causation." In subsequent decisions that rule has been extended, sub silentio, to cover also the issue of "negligence."[1] More recently in Kernan v. American Dredging Co., 355 U. S. 426, decided a few months ago, the Court still further expanded these enactments to embrace a concept of absolute liability for violation of any statutory duty occasioning injury to one entitled to sue under them. And today we are told that ". . . when a railroad employee's injury is caused in whole or in part by the fault of others performing, under contract, operational activities of his employer, such others are `agents' of the employer within the meaning of § 1 of FELA." This is held to be so even though it has long been customary in railroading for carriers to delegate to others activities such as the switching operation here, see Fort Worth Belt R. Co. v. United States, 22 F. 2d 795, and notwithstanding that under traditional common-law concepts those performing such specialized activities would be regarded as independent contractors.[2] See, e. g., Brady v. Chicago & G. W. R. Co., 114 F. 100, 108-112; Moleton v. Union Pacific R. Co., 118 Utah 107, 114-115, 219 P. 2d 1080, 1084.

In light of the FELA and its legislative history it is difficult to regard any of these developments as other than the products of freewheeling. The FELA ". . . is founded on common-law concepts of negligence and injury, subject to such qualifications as Congress has imported into those terms." Urie v. Thompson, 337 U. S. 163, 182. See also dissenting opinions in Rogers v. Missouri Pacific R. Co., supra, at 524, 538-539, 559, 563-564; and in Kernan v. American Dredging Co., supra, at 441, 451-452. The only such qualifications which Congress has yet seen fit to enact are those effected by §§ 3 and 4 of the Act, modifying or abolishing the common-law defenses of contributory negligence and assumption of risk. 35 Stat. 66, 45 U. S. C. § 53; 35 Stat. 66, as amended, 45 U. S. C. § 54. More particularly, when a well-known legal term like "agents" is used in legislation, it should be taken as carrying its ordinary meaning unless the statute indicates the contrary. Cf. Hull v. Philadelphia & R. R. Co., 252 U. S. 475, 479. The principle of "accommodating scope" to which the Court resorts for justification of the expansive meaning now given that term is, as applied here, a new rule of statutory construction of which I have not been aware until today.

I must dissent.

Notes

[1] Webb v. Illinois Central R. Co., 352 U. S. 512; Ferguson v. Moore-McCormack Lines, Inc., 352 U. S. 521; Shaw v. Atlantic Coast Line R. Co., 353 U. S. 920; Futrelle v. Atlantic Coast Line R. Co., 353 U. S. 920; Deen v. Gulf, Colorado & S. F. R. Co., 353 U. S. 925; Thomson v. Texas & P. R. Co., 353 U. S. 926; Ringhiser v. Chesapeake & O. R. Co., 354 U. S. 901; McBride v. Toledo Terminal R. Co., 354 U. S. 517; Gibson v. Thompson, 355 U. S. 18; Stinson v. Atlantic Coast Line R. Co., 355 U. S. 62; Honeycutt v. Wabash R. Co., 355 U. S. 424; Ferguson v. St. Louis-San Francisco R. Co., 356 U. S. 41; Butler v. Whiteman, 356 U. S. 271.

[2] Although the Court in footnote 2 of its opinion refers to the jury's special finding that Belt Railway was under the "control and supervision" of respondent, I do not understand that any reliance is placed upon that finding here. It seems enough to say that this finding was without support in the evidence, as the state appellate court held.

Justice Harlan's concurrence and dissent in NLRB v. Wooster Div. of Borg-Warner Corp. (May 5, 1958)

MR. JUSTICE HARLAN, whom MR. JUSTICE CLARK and MR. JUSTICE WHITTAKER join, concurring in part and dissenting in part.

I agree that the company's insistence on the "recognition" clause constituted an unfair labor practice, but reach that conclusion by a different route from that taken by the Court. However, in light of the finding below that the company bargained in "good faith," I dissent from the view that its insistence on the "ballot" clause can support the charge of an unfair labor practice.

Over twenty years ago this Court said in its first decision under the Wagner Act: "The theory of the Act is that free opportunity for negotiation with accredited representatives of employees is likely to promote industrial peace and may bring about the adjustments and agreements which the Act in itself does not attempt to compel." Labor Board v. Jones & Laughlin Steel Corp., 301 U. S. 1, 45. (Italics added.) Today's decision proceeds on assumptions which I deem incompatible with this basic philosophy of the original labor Act, which has retained its vitality under the amendments effected by the Taft-Hartley Act. See Labor Board v. American National Insurance Co., 343 U. S. 395, 401-404. I fear that the decision may open the door to an intrusion by the Board into the substantive aspects of the bargaining process which goes beyond anything contemplated by the National Labor Relations Act or suggested in this Court's prior decisions under it.

The Court considers both the "ballot" and "recognition" clauses to be outside the scope of the mandatory bargaining provisions of § 8 (d) of the Act, which in connection with §§ 8 (a) (5) and 8 (b) (3) imposes an obligation on an employer and a union to ". . . confer in good faith with respect to wages, hours, and other terms and conditions of employment. . . ." From this conclusion it is said to follow that although the company was free to "propose" these clauses and "bargain" over them, it could not "insist" on their inclusion in the collective bargaining contract as the price of agreement, and that such insistence was a per se unfair labor practice because it was tantamount to a refusal to bargain on "mandatory" subjects. At the same time the Court accepts the Trial Examiner's unchallenged finding that the company had bargained in "good faith," both with reference to these clauses and all other subjects, and holds that the clauses are lawful in themselves and ". . . would be enforceable if agreed to by the unions."

Preliminarily, I must state that I am unable to grasp a concept of "bargaining" which enables one to "propose" a particular point, but not to "insist" on it as a condition to agreement. The right to bargain becomes illusory if one is not free to press a proposal in good faith to the point of insistence. Surely adoption of so inherently vague and fluid a standard is apt to inhibit the entire bargaining process because of a party's fear that strenuous argument might shade into forbidden insistence and thereby produce a charge of an unfair labor practice. This watered-down notion of "bargaining" which the Court imports into the Act with reference to matters not within the scope of § 8 (d) appears as foreign to the labor field as it would be to the commercial world. To me all of this adds up to saying that the Act limits effective "bargaining" to subjects within the three fields referred to in § 8 (d), that is "wages, hours, and other terms and conditions of employment," even though the Court expressly disclaims so holding.

I shall discuss my difficulties with the Court's opinion in terms of the "ballot" clause. The "recognition" clause is subject in my view to different considerations.

I

At the start, I question the Court's conclusion that the "ballot" clause does not come within the "other terms and conditions of employment" provision of § 8 (d). The phrase is inherently vague and prior to this decision has been accorded by the Board and courts an expansive rather than a grudging interpretation. Many matters which might have been thought to be the sole concern of management are now dealt with as compulsory bargaining topics. E. g., Labor Board v. J. H. Allison & Co., 165 F. 2d 766 (merit increases). And since a "no-strike" clause is something about which an employer can concededly bargain to the point of insistence, see Shell Oil Co., 77 N. L. R. B. 1306, I find it difficult to understand even under the Court's analysis of this problem why the "ballot" clause should not be considered within the area of bargaining described in § 8 (d). It affects the employer-employee relationship in much the same way, in that it may determine the timing of strikes or even whether a strike will occur by requiring a vote to ascertain the employees' sentiment prior to the union's decision.

Nonetheless I shall accept the Court's holding that this clause is not a condition of employment, for even though the union would accordingly not be obliged under § 8 (d) to bargain over it, in my view it does not follow that the company was prohibited from insisting on its inclusion in the collective bargaining agreement. In other words, I think the clause was a permissible, even if not an obligatory, subject of good faith bargaining.

The legislative history behind the Wagner and Taft-Hartley Acts persuasively indicates that the Board was never intended to have power to prevent good faith bargaining as to any subject not violative of the provisions or policies of those Acts. As a leading proponent for the Wagner Act explained:

"When the employees have chosen their organization, when they have selected their representatives, all the bill proposes to do is to escort them to the door of their employer and say, `Here they are, the legal representatives of your employees.' What happens behind those doors is not inquired into, and the bill does not seek to inquire into it." 79 Cong. Rec. 7660.

The Wagner Act did not contain the "good faith" qualification now written into the bargaining requirements of § 8 (d), although this lack was remedied by early judicial interpretation which implied from former § 8 (5), 49 Stat. 453, the requirement that an employer bargain in good faith. E. g., Labor Board v. Griswold Mfg. Co., 106 F. 2d 713. But apart from this essential check on the bargaining process, the Board possessed no statutory authority to regulate the substantive scope of the bargaining process insofar as lawful demands of the parties were concerned. Nevertheless, the Board engaged occasionally in the practice of determining that certain contract terms urged by unions were conditions of employment and thereby imposing on employers an affirmative duty to bargain as to such terms rather than insist upon their unilateral determination, e. g., Singer Mfg. Co., 24 N. L. R. B. 444, or conversely of determining that certain clauses were not conditions of employment and thereby prohibiting an employer from bargaining over them. E. g., Jasper Blackburn Products Corp., 21 N. L. R. B. 1240.

These early intrusions of the Board into the substantive aspects of the bargaining process became a matter of concern to Congress, and in the 1947 Taft-Hartley amendments to the Wagner Act, Congress took steps to curtail them by writing into § 8 (d) the particular fields as to which it considered bargaining should be required. The bill originally passed by the House of Representatives contained a definition of the term "collective bargaining" which restricted the area of compulsory negotiation to specified subjects, such as wages, hours, discharge or seniority provisions, safety conditions, and vacations. § 2 (11), H. R. 3020, 80th Cong., 1st Sess. The House Report on this bill, submitted by its sponsor, noted that the suggested provision would require unions and employers to bargain collectively as to specified topics and would limit that area ". . . to matters of interest to the employer and to the individual man at work." H. R. Rep. No. 245, 80th Cong., 1st Sess. 7. In explaining the need for specifying the topics over which bargaining was mandatory, and thereby establishing "objective standards" for the Board to follow, the Report continues:

". . . [T]he present Board has gone very far, in the guise of determining whether or not employers had bargained in good faith, in setting itself up as the judge of what concessions an employer must make and of the proposals and counterproposals that he may or may not make. . . . [Discussion of Board cases.]

. . . . .

"These cases show that unless Congress writes into the law guides for the Board to follow, the Board may attempt to carry this process still further and seek to control more and more the terms of collective-bargaining agreements." Id., at 19-20.

The Senate amendment to the House bill recast these provisions to read in substantially the form of present § 8 (d). That is, the Senate provisions contained no elaboration of compulsory bargaining topics, but used the general phrase: "wages, hours, and other terms and conditions of employment." In commenting on these changes, the managers of the House Conference appended a statement to the House Conference Report which observed:

". . . [T]he Senate amendment, while it did not prescribe a purely objective test of what constituted collective bargaining, as did the House bill, had to a very substantial extent the same effects as the House bill in this regard, since it rejected, as a factor in determining good faith, the test of making a concession and thus prevented the Board from determining the merits of the positions of the parties." H. R. Conf. Rep. No. 510, 80th Cong., 1st Sess. 34.

The foregoing history evinces a clear congressional purpose to assure the parties to a proposed collective bargaining agreement the greatest degree of freedom in their negotiations, and to require the Board to remain as aloof as possible from regulation of the bargaining process in its substantive aspects.

The decision of this Court in 1952 in Labor Board v. American National Insurance Co., supra, was fully in accord with this legislative background in holding that the Board lacked power to order an employer to cease bargaining over a particular clause because such bargaining under the Board's view, entirely apart from a showing of bad faith, constituted per se an unfair labor practice. There an employer insisted during negotiations upon the union's acceptance of a "management functions" clause which would vest exclusively in management during the period of the collective bargaining agreement the right to select, hire, and promote employees, to discharge for cause and maintain discipline, and to determine work schedules. The arguments advanced by the Board in that case in support of its conclusion that the employer had committed an unfair labor practice through its insistence on this clause were strikingly similar to those before us here. It was said that such a clause was "in derogation of" statutory rights to bargain given to the employees, and that insistence upon it was tantamount to refusal to bargain as to all statutory subjects covered by it.

But this Court, in reversing the Board, emphasized that flexibility was an essential characteristic of the process of collective bargaining, and that whether the topics contained in the disputed clause should be allocated exclusively to management or decided jointly by management and union ". . . is an issue for determination across the bargaining table, not by the Board." 343 U. S., at 409. It is true that the disputed clause related to matters which concededly were "terms and conditions of employment," but the broad rationale of the Court's opinion undercuts an attempt to distinguish the case on any such ground. "Congress provided expressly that the Board should not pass upon the desirability of the substantive terms of labor agreements. . . . The duty to bargain collectively is to be enforced by application of the good faith bargaining standards of Section 8 (d) to the facts of each case . . . ." 343 U. S., at 408-409.

I therefore cannot escape the view that today's decision is deeply inconsistent with legislative intention and this Court's precedents. The Act sought to compel management and labor to meet and bargain in good faith as to certain topics. This is the affirmative requirement of § 8 (d) which the Board is specifically empowered to enforce, but I see no warrant for inferring from it any power in the Board to prohibit bargaining in good faith as to lawful matters not included in § 8 (d). The Court reasons that such conduct on the part of the employer, when carried to the point of insistence, is in substance equivalent to a refusal to bargain as to the statutory subjects, but I cannot understand how this can be said over the Trial Examiner's unequivocal finding that the employer did in fact bargain in "good faith," not only over the disputed clauses but also over the statutory subjects.

It must not be forgotten that the Act requires bargaining, not agreement, for the obligation to bargain ". . . does not compel either party to agree to a proposal or require the making of a concession." § 8 (d). Here the employer concededly bargained but simply refused to agree until the union would accept what the Court holds would have been a lawful contract provision. It may be that an employer or union, by adamant insistence in good faith upon a provision which is not a statutory subject under § 8 (d), does in fact require the other party to bargain over it. But this effect is traceable to the economic power of the employer or union in the circumstances of a given situation and should not affect our construction of the Act. If one thing is clear, it is that the Board was not viewed by Congress as an agency which should exercise its powers to aid a party to collective bargaining which was in an economically disadvantageous position.

The most cursory view of decisions of the Board and the circuit courts under the National Labor Relations Act reveals the unsettled and evolving character of collective bargaining agreements. Provisions which two decades ago might have been thought to be the exclusive concern of labor or management are today commonplace in such agreements.[1] The bargaining process should be left fluid, free from intervention of the Board leading to premature crystallization of labor agreements into any one pattern of contract provisions, so that these agreements can be adapted through collective bargaining to the changing needs of our society and to the changing concepts of the responsibilities of labor and management. What the Court does today may impede this evolutionary process. Under the facts of this case, an employer is precluded from attempting to limit the likelihood of a strike. But by the same token it would seem to follow that unions which bargain in good faith would be precluded from insisting upon contract clauses which might not be deemed statutory subjects within § 8 (d).

As unqualifiedly stated in Labor Board v. American National Insurance Co., supra, p. 357, it is through the "good faith" requirement of § 8 (d) that the Board is to enforce the bargaining provisions of § 8. A determination that a party bargained as to statutory or nonstatutory subjects in good or bad faith must depend upon an evaluation of the total circumstances surrounding any given situation. I do not deny that there may be instances where unyielding insistence on a particular item may be a relevant consideration in the over-all picture in determining "good faith," for the demands of a party might in the context of a particular industry be so extreme as to constitute some evidence of an unwillingness to bargain. But no such situation is presented in this instance by the "ballot" clause. "No-strike" clauses, and other provisions analogous to the "ballot" clause limiting the right to strike, are hardly novel to labor agreements.[2] And in any event the uncontested finding of "good faith" by the Trial Examiner forecloses that issue here.

Of course an employer or union cannot insist upon a clause which would be illegal under the Act's provisions, Labor Board v. National Maritime Union, 175 F. 2d 686, or conduct itself so as to contravene specific requirements of the Act. Medo Photo Supply Corp. v. Labor Board, 321 U. S. 678. But here the Court recognizes, as it must, that the clause is lawful under the Act,[3] and I think it clear that the company's insistence upon it violated no statutory duty to which it was subject. The fact that the employer here did bargain with the union over the inclusion of the "ballot" clause in the proposed agreement distinguishes this case from the situation involved in the Medo Photo Supply Corp. case, supra, where an employer, without the sanction of a labor agreement contemplating such action, negotiated directly with its employees in reference to wages. This Court upheld the finding of an unfair labor practice, observing that the Act ". . . makes it the duty of the employer to bargain collectively with the chosen representatives of his employees. The obligation being exclusive . . . , it exacts 'the negative duty to treat with no other.' " 321 U. S., at 683-684. (Italics added.) Bargaining directly with employees ". . . would be subversive of the mode of collective bargaining which the statute has ordained . . . ." 321 U. S., at 684. The important consideration is that the Act does not purport to define the terms of an agreement but simply secures the representative status of the union for purposes of bargaining. The controlling distinction from Medo Photo is that the employer here has not sought to bargain with anyone else over the terms of the agreement being negotiated.

II.

The company's insistence on the "recognition" clause, which had the effect of excluding the International Union as a party signatory to agreement and making Local 1239 the sole contracting party on the union side, presents a different problem. In my opinion the company's action in this regard did constitute an unfair labor practice since it contravened specific requirements of the Act.

Section 8 (a) (5) makes it an unfair labor practice for an employer not to bargain collectively "with the representatives of his employees." Such representatives are those who have been chosen by a majority of the employees of the appropriate unit, and they constitute ". . . the exclusive representatives of all the employees in such unit for the purposes of collective bargaining. . . ." § 9 (a). The Board under § 9 (c) is authorized to direct a representation election and certify its results. The employer's duty to bargain with the representatives includes not merely the obligation to confer in good faith, but also ". . . the execution of a written contract incorporating any agreement reached if requested . . ." by the employees' representatives. § 8 (d). I think it hardly debatable that this language must be read to require the company, if so requested, to sign any agreement reached with the same representative with which it is required to bargain. By conditioning agreement upon a change in signatory from the certified exclusive bargaining representative, the company here in effect violated this duty.

I would affirm the judgment of the Court of Appeals in both cases and require the Board to modify its cease and desist order so as to allow the company to bargain over the "ballot" clause.

Notes

[1] A variety of topics have been held to be subjects over which an employer must bargain. E. g., Inland Steel Co. v. Labor Board, 170 F. 2d 247 (pension and retirement plans); Union Mfg. Co., 76 N. L. R. B. 322 (bonuses).

[2] It was stipulated by the parties during hearing on the charge of unfair labor practices that collective bargaining agreements between several unions and companies have incorporated clauses requiring, in one form or another, secret ballots of employees before the union is able to call a strike. The clauses varied in defining employees to include only union members or all those working in the unit represented by the union and gave varying effect to the employee vote. The clause here involved does not purport to make the vote of the employees binding on the union.

[3] I find no merit in the union's position that the "ballot" clause is unlawful under the Act since in derogation of the representative status of the union. The statute and its legislative background undermine any such argument, for the Taft-Hartley Act incorporates in two sections provisions for a pre-strike ballot of employees and earlier drafts of the Act would have made an employee ballot mandatory as a condition precedent to all strikes.

The Hartley bill, as passed by the House, provided that employees should be informed in writing of issues in dispute and that a secret ballot of employees should be held on the employer's last offer of settlement and on the question of a strike. Only if the employees rejected the last offer and voted to strike could the union authorize a strike. § 2 (11), H. R. 3020, 80th Cong., 1st Sess. The Report on the bill states that ". . . at least the more irresponsible strikes . . . will be greatly reduced by requiring strike votes after each side has had an opportunity to state its position and to urge its fairness upon those called upon to do the striking." H. R. Rep. No. 245, 80th Cong., 1st Sess. 22.

These mandatory provisions were later discarded, and in their place Congress enacted § 203 (c) in Title II of the Taft-Hartley Act, 61 Stat. 154, 29 U. S. C. § 173 (c), under which the Director of the Federal Mediation and Conciliation Service is in certain situations to seek to induce the parties in dispute to agree voluntarily to an employee vote on the employer's last offer prior to a strike. In commenting on this change, the managers of the House Conference stated: "While the vote on the employer's last offer by secret ballot is not compulsory as it was in the House bill, it is expected that this procedure will be extensively used and that it will have the effect of preventing many strikes which might otherwise take place." H. R. Conf. Rep. No. 510, 80th Cong., 1st Sess. 63. The inescapable conclusion in view of this legislative history is that Congress, instead of making the pre-strike ballot mandatory, intended to leave such ballot clauses to the decision of the parties to a labor agreement to be arrived at through the normal collective bargaining process. Cf. § 201 (c) of Title II, 61 Stat. 152, 29 U. S. C. § 171 (c). There is a further provision for a pre-strike ballot in § 209 (b) of Title II, 61 Stat. 156, 29 U. S. C. § 179 (b), which relates to disputes which imperil national health or safety.

Justice Harlan's dissent in Federal Maritime Bd. v. Isbrandtsen (May 19, 1958)

MR. JUSTICE HARLAN, dissenting.

Except in one respect, I agree with the dissenting opinion of MR. JUSTICE FRANKFURTER. I do not think that this Court's decisions in United States Navigation Co. v. Cunard Steamship Co., 284 U. S. 474, and Far East Conference v. United States, 342 U. S. 570, have the effect which that opinion attributes to them. Despite the logic of the argument flowing from the doctrine of primary jurisdiction, and the lack of any substantial factual distinction between the agreements in those cases and in this one, I am unable to read Cunard and Far East Conference as having determined, without any discussion, the far-reaching question which has been decided today. See especially Cunard, 284 U. S., at 483-484, 487. On the merits, however, I dissent for the reasons set forth in MR. JUSTICE FRANKFURTER'S opinion.

Justice Harlan's dissent in Byrd v. Blue Ridge Rural Elec. Coop. (May 19, 1958)

MR. JUSTICE HARLAN, dissenting.

I join in MR. JUSTICE FRANKFURTER'S dissenting opinion, but desire to add two further reasons why I believe the judgment of the Court of Appeals should be affirmed. As I read that court's opinion, it held that under South Carolina law the construction of facilities needed to transmit electric power was necessarily a part of the business of furnishing power, whether such construction was performed by the respondent itself or let out to others, and that in either case respondent would be liable to petitioner for compensation as his statutory employer. Since there is no dispute that respondent at the time of the accident was engaged in the business of furnishing power and that petitioner was injured while engaged in construction in furtherance of that business, I do not perceive how any further evidence which might be adduced by petitioner could change the result reached by the Court of Appeals. In any event, in the circumstances disclosed by the record before us, we should at the very least require petitioner to make some showing here of the character of the further evidence he expects to introduce before we disturb the judgment below.

Justice Harlan's dissent in Chicago v. Atchison, T. & SFR Co. (June 16, 1958)

MR. JUSTICE HARLAN, whom MR. JUSTICE FRANKFURTER and MR. JUSTICE BURTON join, dissenting.

In my opinion the Court has acted prematurely in striking down this Chicago ordinance as it relates to Transfer. I accept the premise that the railroads have the right to choose whom they please to perform the transfer services, subject only to the City's right to regulate how transfer vehicles shall be operated. Nevertheless, the validity of the ordinance should not be determined until Transfer has applied to Chicago for a "terminal" license and the local authorities have had an opportunity to act on the application. Not until then will it be known whether the ordinance, as it may be applied to Transfer's operations, trespasses upon paramount federal concerns. Proper regard for the City's legitimate interests in enforcing this local enactment entitles Chicago to that opportunity. Cf. Public Utilities Comm'n of California v. United States, 355 U. S. 534, 546 (dissenting opinion).

No provision of the Interstate Commerce Act purports to pre-empt Chicago's power to apply its ordinance to one in the position of Transfer. This is therefore not a case where particular provisions of federal and local legislation conflict in such a way that they cannot logically or practically stand together, cf. Cloverleaf Butter Co. v. Patterson, 315 U. S. 148; First Iowa Hydro-Electric Cooperative v. Federal Power Comm'n, 328 U. S. 152, nor one where there is such overall similarity between federal and state regulation that a congressional purpose to displace state action in its entirety can fairly be deduced. Cf. Hines v. Davidowitz, 312 U. S. 52; Pennsylvania v. Nelson, 350 U. S. 497. And because Transfer does not hold a certificate of necessity from the Interstate Commerce Commission, and seemingly cannot get one, see Status of Parmelee Transportation Co., 288 I. C. C. 95, no conflict appears between federal and local regulatory policies respecting those performing transfer services. Cf. Castle v. Hayes Freight Lines, Inc., 348 U. S. 61. The sole question is thus whether the ordinance must be struck down, when applied to Transfer's operations, as "inconsistent" with the policy of the Interstate Commerce Act to foster efficient interstate transportation.

In determining whether Chicago's ordinance should now be annulled it must be borne in mind that local authorities are not foreclosed from regulating matters of local concern merely because there may be some incidental, but not burdensome, effect on interstate commerce. At least since Cooley v. Board of Wardens, 12 How. 299, it has been recognized that because regulation of local incidents of interstate transportation is, as a practical matter, beyond the effective reach of Congress, there would frequently be an undesirable absence of needed regulation unless States and municipalities were free to act. See California v. Thompson, 313 U. S. 109; see also H. P. Welch Co. v. New Hampshire, 306 U. S. 79; Eichholz v. Public Service Comm'n of Missouri, 306 U. S. 268. So much indeed is recognized by the Court today when it says that Chicago, as part of its "considerable authority" to regulate the operation of transfer vehicles, may exact fees for their use of the city streets and may require them to meet with safety regulations and to be registered with the City. And, of course, the Court's examples do not exhaust the scope of local regulatory power to insure safe transportation. Nor can I perceive why the City should not be permitted to exercise such power before permitting unlicensed vehicles to travel on its streets. On the other hand, I would agree that Chicago, under the guise of promoting safe and proper transportation, could not validly limit on "economic" grounds those with whom the railroads may contract to carry its interstate passengers through the City. Cf. Buck v. Kuykendall, 267 U. S. 307.

We do not yet know how Chicago will apply the ordinance. If it should grant Transfer a license, that will end the present controversy. If a license is denied, it will then be time enough to determine whether the basis for denial runs afoul of federal transportation policy. It is true that the ordinance gives the City broad authority, but that does not justify the assumption that such authority will be exercised beyond permissible bounds, especially since Chicago has acknowledged that it could not properly withhold a license "solely or even primarily" because existing transfer facilities were adequate or because additional licenses would adversely affect the competitive situation. Only by refraining from passing on the ordinance until Chicago has had a chance to act under it, do we respect the long-standing tradition of this Court not to interfere prematurely with the administration of state and local enactments. See, e. g., Alabama Federation of Labor v. McAdory, 325 U. S. 450; Public Service Comm'n of Utah v. Wycoff Co., 344 U. S. 237. Cf. Spector Motor Service, Inc., v. McLaughlin, 323 U. S. 101.

The fact that this course of action would involve some further delay and expense does not, in my judgment, justify by-passing the municipal authorities. Transfer accepted the risk of such a result when it failed to apply for a license in the first instance. And if it is said that this course will expose the transfer operations to hazards in the interval, the answer is that the Federal District Court in Chicago possesses ample authority to prevent any interference with Transfer's activities pending final adjudication of the matters in controversy.

Some years ago, in a situation closely analogous to the one before us, this Court approved the decision of a three-judge District Court declining to entertain a complaint attacking the constitutionality of a Missouri statute which prohibited interstate carriers from using state highways without obtaining a permit from the State, on the ground that the complainant had not applied for such a permit. Columbia Terminals Co. v. Lambert, 30 F. Supp. 28; 309 U. S. 620. I believe that Columbia Terminals provides the guiding principle for the appropriate disposition of premature challenges to the validity of local ordinances. However, in view of the posture of the present litigation, I would follow a somewhat different course here, and would vacate the judgment of the Court of Appeals and remand the case to the District Court. Our mandate should enable the District Court to stay the operation of Chicago's ordinance and to retain jurisdiction over this case, pending Transfer's prompt steps to initiate license proceedings before the local authorities and the outcome of such proceedings.

Justice Harlan's dissent in US v. Central Eureka Mining Co. (June 16, 1958)

Mr. Justice HARLAN, dissenting.

I dissent because I believe that the Fifth Amendment to the Constitution requires the Government to pay just compensation to the respondents for the temporary 'taking' of their property accomplished by WPB Order L—208.

The Court views L—208 as a normal regulatory measure of the WPB, which had authority to allocate critical materials during the late war. It holds that this was the character of the administrative Order even though the Court of Claims found that L 208 was actually designed to cause a shift of gold miners to other nonferrous metal mines, rather than to control the allocation of mining equipment in short supply, as the Order on its face purported to do. In so holding, the Court emphasizes that the 'manpower' objective was simply one of the purposes of L—208. I am unable to reconcile the Court's conclusions with the findings of the Court of Claims. Finding 46 of the Court of Claims states that reallocation of gold miners by forced closure of the gold mines was 'The dominant consideration * * * in the issuance of * * * L—208.' (Italics supplied.) That this finding reflected the conclusion that the 'manpower' purpose was the sole objective of the Order seems clear from the fact that the Court of Claims struck from this finding, as submitted to it by the hearing officer, the following two sentences:

'Another consideration in the issuance of the order was as stated in the preamble that the fulfillment of requirements for the defense of the United States had created a shortage in the supply of critical materials which had been used in the maintenance and operation of gold mines.

'Both objectives (the other being 'manpower') were in some measure accomplished with the closing of the plaintiffs' gold mines pursuant to the order.'

On the basis of its findings, the Court of Claims concluded in its opinion:

'From the language of the order itself (L—208) and from the circumstances surrounding its promulgation, it is apparent that its only purpose was to deprive the gold mine owners and operators of their right to make use of their mining properties.'

These conclusions, which seem to me to be convincingly supported by the evidence in the record, require that L—208 be regarded as having no other purpose than to effect the closing of respondents' mines in order to free gold mine labor for essential war work. The Government acknowledges that during the war it lacked any legal authority to order the transfer of civilian manpower.

Viewing L—208 in this light, I cannot agree with the Court's conclusion that the Order was simply a 'regulation' incident to which respondents happened to suffer financial loss. Instead, I believe that L—208 effected a temporary 'taking' of the respondents' right to mine gold which is compensable under the Fifth Amendment.

L—208 was the only order promulgated during World War II which by its terms required a lawful and productive industry to shut down at a severe economic cost. See S.Rep. No. 1605, 82d Cong., 2d Sess. 3. As a result of the Order the respondents were totally deprived of the beneficial use of their property. Any suggestion that the mines could have been used in such a way (that is, other than to mine gold) so as to remove them from the scope of the Order would be chimerical. Not only were the respondents completely prevented from making profitable use of their property, but the Government acquired all that it wanted from the mines their complete immobilization and the resulting discharge of the hardrock miners. It is plain that as a practical matter the Order led to consequences no different from those that would have followed the temporary acquisition of physical possession of these mines by the United States.

In these circumstances making the respondents' right to compensation turn on whether the Government took the ceremonial step of planting the American flag on the mining premises, cf. United States v. Pewee Coal Co., 341 U.S. 114, 116, 71 S.Ct. 670, 671, 95 L.Ed. 809, is surely to permit technicalities of form to dictate consequences of substance. In my judgment the present case should be viewed precisely as if the United States, in order to accomplish its purpose of freeing gold miners for essential work, had taken possession of the gold mines and allowed them to lie fallow for the duration of the war. Had the Government adopted the latter course it is hardly debatable that respondents would have been entitled to compensation. See United States v. Pewee Coal Co., supra.

As the Court recognizes, governmental action in the form of regulation which severely diminishes the value of property may constitute a 'taking.' See United States v. Kansas City Life Ins. Co., 339 U.S. 799, 70 S.Ct. 885, 94 L.Ed. 1277; United States v. Causby, 328 U.S. 256, 66 S.Ct. 1062, 90 L.Ed. 1206; Richards v. Washington Terminal Co., 233 U.S. 546. 'The general rule at least is, that while property may be regulated to a certain extent, if regulation goes too far it will be recognized as a taking.' Pennsylvania Coal Co. v. Mahon, 260 U.S. 393, 415, 43 S.Ct. 158, 160, 67 L.Ed. 322. In my opinion application of this principle calls here for the conclusion that there was a 'taking,' for it is difficult to conceive of a greater impairment of the use of property by a regulatory measure than that suffered by the respondents as a result of L—208.

None of the cases relied on by the Government precludes our acknowledging the confiscatory nature of L—208 and according respondents just compensation. Except in the extraordinary situation where private property is destroyed by American armed forces to meet the exigencies of the military situation in a theatre of war, see United States v. Caltex (Philippines), Inc., 344 U.S. 149, 73 S.Ct. 200, 97 L.Ed. 157, no case in this Court has held that the Government is excused from providing compensation when property has been 'taken' from its owners during wartime in the interest of the common good. Cases such as Yakus v. United States, 321 U.S. 414, 64 S.Ct. 660, 88 L.Ed. 834; Bowles v. Willingham, 321 U.S. 503, 64 S.Ct. 641, 88 L.Ed. 892; Lichter v. United States, 334 U.S. 742, 68 S.Ct. 1294, 92 L.Ed. 1694, involving the wartime regulation of prices, rents, and profits, are wide of the mark. In all of them the Government was administering a nationwide regulatory system rather than a narrowly confined order directed to a small, singled-out category of individual concerns. Furthermore, none of the regulations involved in those cases prohibited the profitable exploitation of a legal business. And in none of them did the Government, following issuance of its edict, stand virtually in the position of one in physical possession of the property.

Also beside the point are the wartime prohibition cases. Hamilton v. Kentucky Distilleries & Warehouse Co., 251 U.S. 146, 40 S.Ct. 106, 64 L.Ed. 194, dealt with the consequences of the Act of November 21, 1918, 40 Stat. 1045, 1046, which placed upon the property owners a burden not nearly so onerous as the one imposed on respondents by L—208. That Act permitted unrestricted sale of liquor for more than seven months from the date of its passage, and even after that time there was no restriction on sale for export or on local sale for other than beverage purposes. Moreover, the prohibition cases arose only after congressional action dealing specifically with the sale of liquor, and the Court in Hamilton particularly adverted to the fact that Congress might properly conclude that such sale should be halted 'in order to guard and promote the efficiency' of the armed forces and defense workers. Hamilton v. Kentucky Distilleries & Warehouse Co., supra, 251 U.S. at page 155, 40 S.Ct. at page 107. This latter factor was also the premise of Jacob Ruppert, Inc., v. Caffey, 251 U.S. 264, 40 S.Ct. 141, 64 L.Ed. 260. Not only has there been no comparable congressional finding that gold mining was injurious, but the Senate Committee on the Judiciary, which conducted a thorough analysis of the operation of L—208, recognized that 'Issuance of the order was an administrative error * * * and may, furthermore, have been illegal.' S.Rep. No. 1605, 82d Cong., 2d Sess. 3.

The question whether there has been a taking cannot of course be resolved by general formulae, but must turn on the circumstances of each particular case. As I have shown, the present case is plainly outside the run of past decisions. In those cases the Court was rightfully reluctant to sanction compensation for losses resulting from wartime regulatory measures which, under conditions of total mobilization, have ramifications touching everyone in one degree or another. But where the Government proceeds by indirection, and accomplishes by regulation what is the equivalent of outright physical seizure of private property, courts should guard themselves against permitting formalities to obscure actualities. As Mr. Justice Holmes observed in Pennsylvania Coal Co. v. Mahon, supra, 260 U.S. at page 416, 43 S.Ct. at page 160: 'We are in danger of forgetting that a strong public desire to improve the public condition is not enough to warrant achieving the desire by a shorter cut than the constitutional way of paying for the change.'

We should treat L—208 as being what in every realistic sense it was, a temporary confiscation of respondents' property. The Government is not absolved from providing just compensation here because the WPB may have lacked authority to 'take' respondents' mines in order to free the miners for essential work in other mines. See International Paper Co. v. United States, 282 U.S. 399, 406, 51 S.Ct. 176, 177, 75 L.Ed. 410; cf. Hatahley v. United States, 351 U.S. 173, 76 S.Ct. 745, 100 L.Ed. 1065. I need hardly add that we should not be deterred from according respondents their due because their claims and those of others similarly situated may run into sizable amounts. The Court of Claims, certainly not given to the easy allowance of demands upon the public treasury, faced up to what the Constitution plainly requires in this instance. We should affirm its judgment.

Justice Harlan's dissent in FHA v. The Darlington, Inc. (Nov 24, 1958)

MR. JUSTICE HARLAN, whom MR. JUSTICE FRANKFURTER and MR. JUSTICE WHITTAKER join, dissenting.

The question in this case is whether appellee Darlington is entitled to rent to transients (that is, so far as this case is concerned, for periods of less than 30 days) a small number of apartments in its building, which is covered by a mortgage insured by the FHA. Darlington's FHA mortgage was consummated and insured in December 1949. At that time neither the controlling statute, § 608 of the National Housing Act, 56 Stat. 303, as amended, 12 U. S. C. § 1743, nor the regulations issued thereunder, 24 CFR § 280 et seq., contained any provision prohibiting rentals to transients. Such provisions are found for the first time in § 513 of the Housing Act of 1954, 68 Stat. 610, 12 U. S. C. (Supp. V) § 1731b, passed some five years after this mortgage was made.

A three-judge District Court, largely adopting the findings and conclusions of the single district judge before whom this case was originally heard, held that as the law stood in 1949, when the mortgage here involved was issued, Darlington was not forbidden to make occasional transient rentals, and that the Federal Housing Administrator may not now prohibit such rentals since that would involve an unconstitutional retroactive application of the relevant provisions of the Housing Act of 1954.[1] This Court now holds that under the statute and regulations as they stood in 1949 Darlington was never entitled to make any transient rentals, and that in any event the prohibitory provisions of the 1954 Act may be applied to prevent such rentals. From these holdings I must dissent.

In construing the earlier statute the Court, in my opinion, has proceeded on an erroneous premise. The Court holds that "no right or privilege to rent to transients is expressly included in the [pre-1954] Act nor fairly implied." In my view, however, the true issue is not whether the statute under which Darlington's mortgage was insured gave the right to an FHA-insured mortgagor to make such rentals, but rather whether it prohibited such a mortgagor from making them. Given this as the issue, it seems to me that the record is compelling against the Court's conclusion as to § 608, that the provisions of the 1954 Act cannot be applied to one in Darlington's position, and that the decision below was clearly right.

1. As already noted, § 608 and the regulations implementing it were barren of any provision excluding rentals to transients at the time Darlington's mortgage was insured by the FHA.

2. The District Court found that (1) Darlington's rentals to transients even at the height of Charleston's transient season constituted no more than ten percent of the building's total available occupancy; (2) "no person entitled to priority has ever been rejected, and no one desiring so-called `permanent' occupancy of an apartment has been required to wait any time to obtain same"; and (3) Darlington "does not advertise as a hotel, has no license as such, and no signs appear indicating its willingness to accept

transients." 142 F. Supp., at 349. According the utmost effect to the conceded purpose of § 608 to provide housing for World War II veterans and their families, and to the recitals in the regulations to the effect that property subject to FHA mortgages shall be "designed principally for residential use" (italics supplied), I am unable to understand why Darlington's practices, as found by the lower court, should be regarded as violative of either the letter or spirit of these statutory or regulatory provisions. Not until the passage of the 1954 Act do we find any suggestion that the words "designed principally for residential use" were, in the language of the Court, "evidently used so as not to preclude some commercial [as distinguished from transient] rentals."

3. As the FHA conceded and the District Court found, nothing in Darlington's charter, bylaws, mortgage, or mortgage note, all of which were subject to the FHA's advance approval, expressly restricted its right "to lease apartments in its project for periods of less than thirty (30) days." The only period of rental limitation appearing in any of these instruments was the following, contained in Darlington's charter: "Dwelling accommodations of the [appellee] shall not be rented for a period in excess of three years . . . ." 142 F. Supp., at 346. It is too much to attribute to the word "dwelling," as the Court now in effect does, an implied prohibition of less-than-30-days rentals.

4. The FHA had in a number of instances before 1954 actually given specific approval to less-than-30-days rentals by insured mortgagors where veteran demand for housing had fallen off, and when in 1955 Darlington inquired of the FHA the basis of its position that less-than-30-days rentals by such mortgagors were not permissible the agency simply referred appellee to the provisions of the Housing Act of 1954. These events conclusively show that the Housing Administration did not construe the statute or regulations before 1954 to prohibit transient rentals altogether.

5. There is nothing in this record to indicate that Darlington was engaged in any kind of a scheme to subvert the purposes of this federal housing legislation. Its occasional transient rentals seem to have been nothing more than an effort to plug the gap in its revenues left by a falling off of the demand for long-term apartment space, and do not depict a sub rosa hotel operation.

Upon these undisputed facts, which are reinforced by other factors detailed in the two opinions below, I can find no basis for impugning the soundness of the District Court's holding that under the law as it existed at the time Darlington embarked upon this project nothing prohibited it from making the occasional transient rentals shown by this record. The 1954 Act was new, and not merely confirmatory, legislation.

Hence I consider that the FHA's position in this case must stand or fall on whether the less-than-30-days rental provision of the 1954 Act, which in terms applies to mortgagors insured before as well as after the Act's effective date (see 12 U. S. C. (Supp. V) § 1731b (b)), can be given application to Darlington to increase the obligations assumed by it under its 1949 contract with the United States. I do not think it can. As the District Court correctly put it: "When the United States enters into contractual relations, its rights and duties therein are governed generally by the law applicable to contracts between private individuals." 142 F. Supp., at 351. See Lynch v. United States, 292 U. S. 571; Sinking-Fund Cases, 99 U. S. 700, 718. What was said in the Lynch case as to contracts of war-risk insurance applies here: "As Congress had the power . . . to issue them, the due process clause prohibits the United States from annulling them, unless, indeed, the action taken falls within the federal police power or some other paramount power." 292 U. S., at 579. I do not understand the Housing Administration to contend that the United States possesses general regulatory power over appellee outside the contractual relationship, and the Court has pointed to no such "paramount power" by which the imposition of the 1954 Act's prohibitions might be justified in this case. Under these circumstances I see no reason for disregarding the principles set forth in the cases cited, particularly when the District Court with ample justification found that "the 1954 Act is designed to afford relief for private interests, as distinguished from public purposes . . . ." 142 F. Supp., at 353.[2] Indeed the Court's treatment of this case seems to reinforce my view about the 1954 Act; else why all this straining to bring the matter under the pre-1954 statute?

I would affirm.

Notes

[1] The opinion of the district judge who first heard this case is reported at 142 F. Supp. 341. Subsequent references to the decision below are to that opinion.

The three-judge District Court's opinion is reported at 154 F. Supp. 411. Its decree imposed on Darlington (plaintiff) the following conditions:

"(a) The plaintiff shall not lease, or make available for leasing, for terms of less than thirty days more than 15% of the total number of apartments in the project.

"(b) The plaintiff shall not increase its schedule of rents and charges now in effect for rentals of apartments for less than thirty days and for furnishings and other incidentals offered or supplied in connection therewith.

"(c) The plaintiff shall not advertise itself as a `hotel', nor shall it through the use of any advertising medium, the circulation of letters, the maintenance of signs, or otherwise solicit the business of transients for less than thirty days occupancy, or advise the general public of its willingness to provide accommodations for transients for periods of less than thirty days occupancy.

"(d) The plaintiff shall not provide occupants of its project with food or beverage room service, or maintain regular bell boy service."

The District Court retained jurisdiction of the cause for the purpose of effectuating its decree.

[2] This fact is demonstrated by the rather unusual provision of the 1954 Act which gives hotel operators and owners the right to seek federal court injunctions against violations of the transient rental prohibition of the statute. 68 Stat. 611, 12 U. S. C. (Supp. V) § 1731b (i). See also the testimony of Arthur J. Packard and Earl M. Johnson, respectively Chairman of the Board and Treasurer of the American Hotel Association, before the congressional committees considering the bills which became the Housing Act

of 1954. Hearings before the Senate Committee on Banking and Currency, 83d Cong., 2d Sess., on S. 2889, S. 2938, S. 2949, pp. 654-661; Hearings before the House Committee on Banking and Currency, 83d Cong., 2d Sess., on H. R. 7839, pp. 507-515.

Justice Harlan's dissent in Lee v. Madigan (Jan 12, 1959)

MR. JUSTICE HARLAN, whom MR. JUSTICE CLARK joins, dissenting.

The Court today holds that on June 10, 1949, the date of this capital offense, this country was "in time of peace" within the meaning of Article of War 92, 10 U. S. C. (1946 ed., Supp. IV) § 1564, and therefore that the court-martial before which petitioner was tried was without statutory jurisdiction to entertain the proceeding. Believing that the ground upon which the Court nullifies petitioner's conviction has long been settled squarely to the contrary, and that a de novo examination of the question also requires the conclusion that the United States, on June 10, 1949, was not "in time of peace" within the meaning of Article 92, I respectfully dissent.

In Kahn v. Anderson, 255 U. S. 1, 10, this Court unanimously held that the term "in time of peace" in Article 92 "signifies peace in the complete sense, officially declared." See also Givens v. Zerbst, 255 U. S. 11, 21. The Court now dismisses this square holding as "dictum" and as "quite unnecessary for the decision," pointing out that the statement of facts in Kahn shows that the capital offense for which petitioner there was tried was committed before the Armistice which resulted in the termination of active hostilities in World War I, and that the court-martial which tried him was also convened before the Armistice. I think that Kahn can hardly be dismissed so lightly. The conclusion there as to the meaning of "in time of peace" might have been regarded as unnecessary to decision only had the Court, proceeding on a theory entirely different from that which it actually adopted, relied on the date of the offense or of the beginning of trial as dispositive. But plainly the Court did not proceed on any such basis. Rather, it accepted at least arguendo petitioner's contention that the court-martial which had tried him did not have jurisdiction to continue "in time of peace" even a trial previously begun. It is thus not sound to say that the holding that "peace" in Article 92 "signifies peace in the complete sense, officially declared," was unnecessary to the decision in Kahn. Given the ground upon which the Court chose to decide the case it was quite indispensable. The idea that the ground on which a court actually decides a case becomes dictum because the case might have been decided on another ground is novel doctrine to me.

I think that Congress, and the military authorities charged with the implementation and enforcement of the Articles of War, should be able to rely on a construction given one of those Articles by a unanimous decision of this Court. The conclusion in Kahn was not reached lightly without full consideration, as is shown by the fact that nearly two pages of the summary of counsels' argument contained in the report of the case are devoted to a discussion of the question, and another two pages to the Court's expression of the reasoning underlying its decision on the point. In 1948, 27 years after

Kahn and a single year before the prosecution here involved. Congress re-enacted Article 92 without change in the relevant language. The Court now holds that between 1921 and 1949 the meaning of the statute underwent an inexplicable change, and that the authority under the statute then confirmed must now be denied. I see no warrant for thus speculating anew as to the motives of Congress in enacting and re-enacting the phrase "in time of peace" in Article 92.[1]

Entirely apart from Kahn, I think today's decision is demonstrably wrong. This Court has consistently for nearly 100 years recognized, in many contexts, that a cessation of active hostilities does not denote the end of "war" or the beginning of "peace" as those or similar terms have been used from time to time by Congress in legislation. In McElrath v. United States, 102 U. S. 426, there was before the Court a statute of Congress prohibiting summary dismissal by the President of military officers "in time of peace." Although I venture to say that almost as many reasons could be conjured up for construing the term loosely in that context as in that now before us, the Court unanimously held that July 1866 was not "in time of peace" although active hostilities between North and South had long since ceased, and that "peace, in contemplation of law" did not exist until the Presidential Proclamation of August 20, 1866. See also United States v. Anderson, 9 Wall. 56. In Ludecke v. Watkins, 335 U. S. 160, 168-169, this Court in construing a statute recognized that " `The state of war' may be terminated by treaty or legislation or Presidential proclamation. Whatever the mode, its termination is a political act." See also Woods v. Miller Co., 333 U. S. 138; Knauff v. Shaughnessy, 338 U. S. 537, both expressly recognizing that the state of war between this country and the Axis powers was not terminated by either the Presidential Proclamation of 1946 or the Joint Resolution of July 1947.

The Court says that "Congress in drafting laws may decide that the Nation may be `at war' for one purpose, and `at peace' for another." Of course it may. But the Court points to no case, and I know of none, which has construed statutory language similar to that found in Article 92 to mean anything but "peace in the complete sense, officially declared." Under these circumstances, and given McElrath and Kahn, the conclusion seems to me unmistakable that Congress intended that "peace" in Article 92 mean what we have always, until today, held it meant in this and other congressional legislation. When Congress has wished to define "war" or "peace" in particular statutes as meaning something else, it has explicitly done so. See, e. g., War Brides Act, 59 Stat. 659: "For the purpose of this Act, the Second World War shall be deemed to have commenced on December 7, 1941, and to have ceased upon the termination of hostilities as declared by the President or by a joint resolution of Congress."

Today's decision casts a cloud upon the meaning of all federal legislation the impact of which depends upon the existence of "peace" or "war." Hitherto legislation of this sort has been construed according to well-defined principles, the Court looking to "treaty or legislation or Presidential proclamation," Ludecke v. Watkins, 335 U. S., at 168, to ascertain whether a "state of war" exists. The Court, in an effort to make a "more particularized and discriminating analysis," has apparently jettisoned these principles. It is far from clear to me just what has taken their place.[2]

The Court does not reach petitioner's contention that he could not constitutionally be tried by court-martial because he was not a member of the armed forces at the time this offense was committed. It is sufficient to say that this contention is also squarely foreclosed by Kahn v. Anderson, supra, and that in my opinion nothing in Toth v. Quarles, 350 U. S. 11, or in Reid v. Covert, 354 U. S. 1, impairs the authority of Kahn on this score.

I would affirm.

Notes

[1] The Court's heavy reliance in construing the statute here involved on its attribution to Congress of "a purpose to guard jealously against the dilution of the liberties of the citizen that would result if the jurisdiction of military tribunals were enlarged at the expense of civil courts" is rendered somewhat suspect, to say the least, by the fact that under the Uniform Code of Military Justice, 64 Stat. 108, 10 U. S. C. (Supp. V) § 801, enacted May 5, 1950, Congress has apparently chosen to give courts-martial jurisdiction over capital crimes committed in this country in time of peace as well as in time of war. See 10 U. S. C. (Supp. V) §§ 918, 920.

[2] The Court does not say when the "peace" which it finds to have existed in June 1949 came into being. It may be noted that the Presidential Proclamation of December 31, 1946, proclaiming the cessation of hostilities, specifically announced that "a state of war still exists," and that Senate Joint Resolution 123, 61 Stat. 449 (effective July 25, 1947), which repealed or rendered inoperative a selected group of wartime measures (not including Article 92), was obviously an expression of a conscious and deliberate decision by Congress that the time had not yet come to end the state of war. It was not until October 19, 1951, that Congress, by joint resolution, declared that "the state of war declared to exist between the United States and the Government of Germany by the joint resolution of Congress approved December 11, 1941, is hereby terminated," 65 Stat. 451, and not until April 28, 1952, the effective date of the Japanese Peace Treaty, that peace with Japan was proclaimed by the President, 66 Stat. c31.

Justice Harlan's dissent in International Boxing Club v. US (Jan 12, 1959)

MR. JUSTICE HARLAN, whom MR. JUSTICE FRANKFURTER and MR. JUSTICE WHITTAKER join, dissenting in part.

I am unable to subscribe to the Court's approval of those parts of the decree below which ordered (1) the divestiture of the stockholdings of Norris and Wirtz in Madison Square Garden Corporation and (2) the dissolution of the New York and Illinois International Boxing Clubs. On the other aspects of the case I agree with the results the Court has reached.

DIVESTITURE.

As a starting point I accept the conclusion of the District Court that competition in the promotion and exhibition of professional championship boxing could not be effectively restored so long as Norris and Wirtz remained in control of Madison Square Garden's activities in this field. Because of the pre-eminence of the Garden as a site for boxing contests, the District Court found that its control by Norris and Wirtz constituted the fulcrum of the antitrust violations which were adjudged. That finding is supported by the evidence, and in turn justifies the court's conclusion that the elimination of their influence in the Garden was prerequisite to restoring competition.

It by no means follows, however, that the order divesting Norris and Wirtz of their Garden stockholdings was an appropriate method of accomplishing that objective in the circumstances of this case. Unless past pronouncements of this Court cautioning against the indiscriminate use of divestiture as a remedy in antitrust cases, see Timken Co. v. United States, 341 U. S. 593, are to be taken less seriously than they should be, it seems to me that the Court has too lightly given approval to the use of that drastic measure here.

First. It is not at all clear to me just why the District Court, which in the early stages of the hearings on relief expressed itself strongly against divestiture, ultimately reached the conclusion that such a course was necessary. Indeed the record can be read as indicating the court's belief that the five-year trusteeship of the stock, though designed to alleviate some of the hardships of a forced sale, would at the same time effectively remove Norris and Wirtz from control over the Garden's affairs and therefore in conjunction with the other provisions of the decree result in restoring competitive conditions, whether or not the correlative requirement of sale was carried out within the five-year period.[1] The decree itself supports this reading. For despite the evident realization that the stock might not be sold within five years, the provisions of the decree especially aimed at opening up competition for the use of the Garden are all geared to this period. If in fact the District Court though this five-year insulation of Norris and Wirtz from managerial and policy-making activities at the Garden would combine with the other restrictions to restore competition, justification for divestiture must then be found in a purpose to prevent a relapse into noncompetitive conditions after the five years have elapsed, something which the District Court quite properly considered to be a function of the decree. On this premise I am at a loss to see why continuance of the trusteeship, and, if necessary, the concomitant restrictions on the Garden's activities, should not have been considered adequate to serve that end.

Second. If I am mistaken in thus divining the thinking of the District Court, I still consider that in the circumstances of this case divestiture was at least ordered prematurely. Determination whether that drastic remedy was required should have been postponed until the expiration of the trusteeship period so that the necessity for its application could then be judged in light of the effectiveness of the other sanctions of the decree. I recognize that various contingencies can be conjured up to support the view that divestiture, rather than trusteeship, holds the more solid promise of assuring the preservation of competition. Nevertheless I think that rejection of a continuance of the trusteeship in favor of divestiture should, in the peculiar setting of this case, be based on experience rather than speculative apprehension.

Three factors seem to me especially compelling toward such a course. In the first place, this cannot properly be considered a case of reprehensible immoral conduct or willful lawbreaking.[2] Not until January 31, 1955, when this Court handed down its opinion in United States v. International Boxing Club, 348 U. S. 236, did it become known that professional boxing was even subject to the federal antitrust laws. In view of this Court's earlier decisions in the baseball cases, Federal Baseball Club v. National League, 259 U. S. 200, and Toolson v. New York Yankees, Inc., 346 U. S. 356, I think it reasonable to say that in 1949 when this alleged conspiracy began most well-informed lawyers believed that professional boxing, like professional baseball, was beyond antitrust stricture. Hence the appellants had every reason to believe their actions were innocent when taken. Putting the matter somewhat differently, we should be slow in lending approval to the use of such a drastic remedy as this in a case where the appellants have never had the opportunity to demonstrate their willingness to comply with the law once they have learned that it applies to their activities. In my opinion, the thrust of this factor is not blunted by arguing, as the Court does, that appellants should voluntarily have done something to unscramble their relationships during the two and a half years that elapsed between the Court's decision in the original International Boxing case and the entry of the present decree. That sort of squeeze play should not be expected of those already involved in a lawsuit.

Further, divestiture here is brought to bear upon a large investment much of which was acquired long before the conduct charged in this case began, and the balance of which was obtained prior to the announcement of the International Boxing decision. The "unlawful fruits" doctrine accordingly offers no justification for this divestiture. Although recognizing this to be true, the Court states that the Garden stock was nonetheless utilized as means of accomplishing the antitrust violations. But this is just another way of saying that divestiture is a necessary element of effective relief; it affords no independent justification for the employment of that remedy.

Lastly, the divestiture order reaches far beyond the subject matter of the action. It permanently removes Norris and Wirtz from all interest in the Garden, over 90% of whose activities are entirely unrelated to professional boxing.

Third. It is true, of course, that the trial court's considered judgment on what is necessary to dissipate the effects and prevent recurrence of an adjudged antitrust violation is entitled to much deference from this Court. But by the same token this Court, before it is asked to put its stamp of approval on such a drastic remedy as divestiture, is entitled to have a clear and unambiguous expression of the district court's reasoning in choosing such a course. Especially is this so where, as here, this Court is the sole reviewing authority and in consequence has not had the benefit of an intermediate review of the issues by a Court of Appeals. In my opinion this record leaves much to be desired in this regard. The most I can make of it, taking the case for divestiture most favorably to the Government, is that the District Court would have been justified in reserving that issue for consideration at the time the five-year trusteeship of the Norris and Wirtz stock expired. Certainly no adequate case for a present order of divestiture has been made out. In this view of the matter it becomes unnecessary to discuss at this time the various "options" alternative to divestiture which were rejected by the District Court.

DISSOLUTION.

I can find no adequate basis for the order dissolving the two International Boxing Clubs. My difficulty with this aspect of the relief is sufficiently shown by the fact that, as I read the record, it would be permissible for Madison Square Garden and the Norris and Wirtz interests in Chicago to create new corporations carrying exactly the same name as the two present organizations. The only justification offered by the Government for this aspect of the decree is that the two clubs were instrumentalities of the antitrust conspiracy and that their dissolution was but an expedient for insuring that all of their illegal agreements had been put to an end. But since all such agreements, both written and oral, are already canceled by other provisions of the decree, and since there is no suggestion that the sweeping relief granted by the District Court has any loopholes which would permit these organizations to function improperly, this justification is hardly convincing. In these circumstances dissolution appears to me to be not only punitive but futile, something not promotive of sound antitrust law enforcement.

I would remand the case to the District Court with instructions to modify its decree by striking the provisions for compulsory sale of the Norris and Wirtz stock in the Madison Square Garden Corporation, reserving the issue of divestiture for further proceedings at the end of the five-year trusteeship period, and eliminating the requirement of dissolution of the two International Boxing Clubs.

Notes

[1] Apart from its divestiture and dissolution provisions, the decree imposes wide-ranging and pervasive restrictions on appellants' activities in boxing promotion and exhibition. It renders void all exclusive contracts which they may presently have with boxers. It prohibits the making of new exclusive contracts, with the exception that, after five years, exclusive provision may be made for return bouts. Similarly, exclusive leases with stadia not owned by appellants are proscribed. So, too, are such arrangements with television and radio broadcasters. Further, appellants are restrained, for a period of five years, from promoting more than four championship boxing programs annually, two by Madison Square Garden and two, cumulatively, by Norris and Wirtz. During that five-year period also, the compulsory leasing provisions discussed in the Court's opinion are to be in effect. Finally, the decree removes Norris and Wirtz as officers and directors of Madison Square Garden, and enjoins them from holding such positions in the future.

[2] The District Court put the matter in this way: "I don't charge them [Norris and Wirtz] with malicious intentional and moral wrong doing, nor do I proceed to formulate the decree on such a basis. They are guilty, if anything, of a moral, prohibitive wrong

which was in doubt as to whether it was even prohibitive at the time some of these acts were done, and serious doubt, but most people held it was not."

Justice Harlan's dissent in SEC v. Variable Annuity Life Ins. (March 23, 1959)

MR. JUSTICE HARLAN, whom MR. JUSTICE FRANKFURTER, MR. JUSTICE CLARK and MR. JUSTICE WHITTAKER join, dissenting.

The issue in these cases is whether Variable Annuity Life Insurance Company of America (VALIC) and The Equity Annuity Life Insurance Company (EALIC) are subject to regulation by the Securities and Exchange Commission under the Securities Act of 1933 and the Investment Company Act of 1940 with respect to their variable annuity business.

Section 3 (a) (8) of the Securities Act, 48 Stat. 74, 76, 15 U. S. C. § 77c (a) (8), provides that the statute shall not apply to:

"Any insurance or endowment policy or annuity contract or optional annuity contract, issued by a corporation subject to the supervision of the insurance commissioner, bank commissioner, or any agency or officer performing like functions, of any State or Territory of the United States or the District of Columbia."

Section 3 (c) (3) of the Investment Company Act, 54 Stat. 789, 798, 15 U. S. C. § 80a-3 (c) (3), puts outside the coverage of the Act "[a]ny . . . insurance company," and § 2 (a) (17), 54 Stat. 789, 793, 15 U. S. C. § 80a-2 (a) (17), defines an insurance company as:

"a company which is organized as an insurance company, whose primary and predominant business activity is the writing of insurance or the reinsuring of risks underwritten by insurance companies, and which is subject to supervision by the insurance commissioner or a similar official or agency of a State; or any receiver or similar official or any liquidating agent for such a company, in his capacity as such."

These two insurance companies are organized under the Life Insurance Act of the District of Columbia, 35 D. C. Code, 1951, §§ 35-301 to 35-803, and are subject to regulation by the Superintendent of Insurance of the District of Columbia, who has approved the annuity policies written by them. At the time of trial VALIC had also qualified to do business in Arkansas, Kentucky, and West Virginia, and its annuity policies had likewise been approved by the insurance departments of those States.[1] Both companies in the District of Columbia, and VALIC in the other States, offer their policies to the public only through insurance agents duly licensed by the local insurance authority.

Variable annuity policies are a recent development in the insurance business designed to meet inflationary trends in the economy by substituting for annuity payments in fixed-dollar amounts payments in fluctuating amounts, measured ultimately by the company's success in investing the premium payments received from annuitants. One of the early pioneers in this field was Teachers Insurance and Annuity Association, a New York regulated life insurance organization engaged in selling annuities to college personnel. The Association in 1950 made exhaustive studies into the feasibility and soundness of variable annuities. Two years later, it incorporated College Retirement

Equities Fund, a companion company under joint management with Teachers Insurance, which, subject to regulation under the New York Insurance Law, commenced offering such annuity contracts in the teaching profession.[2] The first life insurance company to offer such contracts generally appears to have been the Participating Annuity Life Insurance Company, which since 1954 has been selling variable annuity policies under the supervision of the Arkansas insurance authorities. VALIC and EALIC entered the field in 1955 and 1956 respectively.

The characteristics of a typical variable annuity contract have been adumbrated by the majority. It is sufficient to note here that, as the majority concludes, as the two lower courts found, and as the SEC itself recognizes, it may fairly be said that variable annuity contracts contain both "insurance" and "securities" features. It is certainly beyond question that the "mortality" aspect of these annuities—that is the assumption by the company of the entire risk of longevity—involves nothing other than classic insurance concepts and procedures, and I do not understand how that feature can be said to be "not substantial," determining as it does, apart from options, the commencement and duration of annuity payments to the policyholder. On the other hand it cannot be denied that the investment policies underlying these annuities, and the stake of the annuitants in their success or failure, place the insurance company in a position closely resembling that of a company issuing certificates in a periodic payment investment plan. Even so, analysis by fragmentization is at best a hazardous business, and in this instance has, in my opinion, led the Court to unsound legal conclusions. It is important to keep in mind that these are not cases where the label "annuity" has simply been attached to a securities scheme, or where the offering companies are traveling under false colors, in an effort to avoid federal regulation. The bona fides of this new development in the field of insurance is beyond dispute.

The Court's holding that these two companies are subject to SEC regulation stems from its preoccupation with a constricted "color matching" approach to the construction of the relevant federal statutes which fails to take adequate account of the historic congressional policy of leaving regulation of the business of insurance entirely to the States. It would be carrying coals to Newcastle to re-examine here the history of that policy which was fully canvassed in the several opinions of the Justices in United States v. South-Eastern Underwriters Assn., 322 U. S. 533, and which was again implicitly recognized by this Court as recently as last Term when, in Federal Trade Comm'n v. National Casualty Co., 357 U. S. 560, we declined to give a niggardly construction to the McCarran Act. Suffice it to say that in consequence of this Court's decision 90 years ago in Paul v. Virginia, 8 Wall. 168, and the many cases following it,[3] there had come to be "widespread doubt" prior to the time the Securities and Investment Company Acts were passed "that the Federal Government could enter the field [of insurance regulation] at all." Wilburn Boat Co. v. Fireman's Fund Ins. Co., 348 U. S. 310, 318; see also Prudential Ins. Co. v. Benjamin, 328 U. S. 408, 414.

I can find nothing in the history of the Securities Act of 1933 which savors in the slightest degree of a purpose to depart from or dilute this traditional federal "hands off" policy respecting insurance regulation. On the contrary, the exemption of insurance from that Act, which is couched in the broadest terms, reflected not merely adherence to tradition but also compliance with a supposed command of the Constitution. In a study of the proposed Act, the Department of Commerce concluded that the legislation could be bottomed on the federal power over commerce because securities did have the independent general commercial existence and value which the Paul decision had found lacking in insurance policies. See A Study of the Economic and Legal Aspects of the Proposed Federal Securities Act, reprinted in Hearings before Senate Committee on Banking and Currency on S. 875, 73d Cong., 1st Sess. 312, at 330, and in Hearings before House Committee on Interstate and Foreign Commerce on H. R. 4314, 73d Cong., 1st Sess. 87, at 105. This distinction between securities and insurance, mistaken or not, underlay the passage of the final bill. When the proposed act was considered by the Senate and House Committees, it did not contain an express exemption of insurance. The House Committee explained that the exemption in the final bill (§ 3 (a) (8) of the Act):

"makes clear what is already implied in the act, namely, that insurance policies are not to be regarded as securities subject to the provisions of the act. The insurance policy and like contracts are not regarded in the commercial world as securities offered to the public for investment purposes. The entire tenor of the act would lead, even without this specific exemption, to the exclusion of insurance policies from the provisions of the act, but the specific exemption is included to make misinterpretation impossible." H. R. Rep. No. 85, 73d Cong., 1st Sess. 15.

That this distinction stemmed from the feared implications of the Paul decision appears from the House debates. See 73d Cong., 1st Sess., 77 Cong. Rec. 2936, 2937, 2938, 2946. Moreover, two days after the Senate began consideration of the proposed act, Senator Robinson introduced a resolution (S. J. Res. 51) calling for a constitutional amendment because, in his view, "the National Government at present has no authority whatever over insurance companies." 73d Cong., 1st Sess., 77 Cong. Rec. 3109.

Similarly, I can find nothing in the history of the Investment Company Act of 1940 which points in any way to a change in federal policy on this score. Here tradition, perhaps more than constitutional doubt, explains the exemption of insurance companies from the Act. In hearings before the House Committee, Commissioner Healy of the SEC discussed the "face-amount installment certificates" issued by certain investment companies and often "sold on the basis of the comparison with savings bank deposits and insurance policies." The major factor appearing to distinguish these investment companies from insurance companies for purposes of federal control was the strict state regulation present over insurance policies but absent over investment certificates. Hearings before House Committee on Interstate and Foreign Commerce on H. R. 10065, 76th Cong., 3d Sess. 61-62. Likewise, in the Senate debates, preservation of state regulation over insurance companies appears as the crucial factor distinguishing them from investment trusts. 76th Cong., 3d Sess., 86 Cong. Rec. 10070. Stating that "the bill has nothing to do with the regulation of insurance companies," Senator Byrnes went on to say: "The platforms of both political parties have urged supervision of insurance by the several States, but not regulation by the Federal Government." Id., at 10071. See also United States v. South-Eastern Underwriters Assn., supra, at 584, 591-592, n. 12 (dissenting opinion).

In 1944, this Court removed the supposed constitutional basis for exemption of insurance by holding, in United States v. South-Eastern Underwriters Assn., supra, that the business of insurance was subject to federal regulation under the commerce power. Congress was quick to respond. It forthwith enacted the McCarran Act, 59 Stat. 33, 15 U. S. C. §§ 1011-1015, which on its face demonstrates the purpose "broadly to give support to the existing and future state systems for regulating and taxing the business of insurance," Prudential Ins. Co. v. Benjamin, supra, at 429, and "to assure that existing state power to regulate insurance would continue." Wilburn Boat Co. v. Fireman's Fund Ins. Co., supra, at 319. Thus, rather than encouraging Congress to enter the field of insurance, the South-Eastern decision spurred reiteration of its undeviating policy of abstention.

In this framework of history the course for us in these cases seems to me plain. We should decline to admit the SEC into this traditionally state regulatory domain.

Admittedly the variable annuity was not in the picture when the Securities and Investment Company Acts were passed. It is a new development combining both substantial insurance and securities features in an experiment designed to accommodate annuity insurance coverage to contingencies of the present day economic climate.[4] This, however, should not be allowed to obscure the fact that Congress intended when it enacted these statutes to leave the future regulation of the business of insurance wholly with the States. This intent, repeatedly expressed in a history of which the Securities and Investment Company Acts were only a part, in my view demands that bona fide experiments in the insurance field, even though a particular development may also have securities aspects, be classed within the federal exemption of insurance, and not within the federal regulation of securities.[5] Certainly these statutes breathe no notion of concurrent regulation by the SEC and state insurance authorities. The fact that they do not serves to reinforce the view that the congressional exemption of insurance was but another manifestation of the historic federal policy leaving regulation of the business of insurance exclusively to the States.[6]

It is asserted that state regulation, as it existed when the Securities and Investment Company Acts were passed, was inadequate to protect annuitants against the risks inherent in the variable annuity and that therefore such contracts should be considered within the orbit of SEC regulation. The Court is agreed that we should not "freeze" the concept of insurance as it then existed. By the same token we should not proceed on the assumption that the thrust of state regulation is frozen. As the insurance business develops new concepts the States adjust and develop their controls. This is in the tradition of state regulation and federal abstention. If the innovation of federal control is nevertheless to be desired, it is for the Congress, not this Court, to effect.

I would affirm.

Notes

[1] Since the trial VALIC has also qualified in Alabama and New Mexico, and EALIC in North Dakota.

[2] By the end of 1956 the College Retirement Fund had issued such annuities to more than 31,000 individuals, and the value of its annuity units had increased from $10 to $18.51.

[3] The cases are collected in United States v. South-Eastern Underwriters Assn., supra, at 544, n. 18.

[4] See Morrissey, Dispute Over the Variable Annuity, 35 Harv. Bus. Rev. 75 (1957).

[5] It is worth observing that in reporting the proposed Securities Act of 1933 the House Committee stated that insurance policies "and like contracts" were to be exempt from federal regulation. See ante, p. 98.

[6] In contrast, § 18 of the Securities Act, 48 Stat. 74, 85, 15 U. S. C. § 77r, provides that the Act shall not affect the jurisdiction of state securities commissions, thus recognizing a system of dual regulation where the exemptive provisions are not applicable. The Investment Company Act has a similar provision, § 50. 54 Stat. 789, 846, 15 U. S. C. § 80a-49.

Justice Harlan's dissent in The Monrosa v. Carbon Black Export, Inc. (March 30, 1959)

MR. JUSTICE HARLAN, whom MR. JUSTICE FRANKFURTER, MR. JUSTICE WHITTAKER, and MR. JUSTICE STEWART join, dissenting.

I cannot agree with the Court's view that Clause 27 of the bill of lading, fixing Genoa, Italy, as the forum for legal proceedings in respect of loss or damage to the goods shipped, applies only to actions in personam, and not to actions in rem. The Court's reading of the clause imputes to the parties the drawing of a distinction the purpose of which is impossible to grasp. As this Court said in Consumers Import Co. v. Kabushiki Kaisha Kawasaki Zosenjo, 320 U. S. 249, 253, in referring to an earlier case, "The Court said that `To say that an owner is not liable. but that his vessel is liable, seems to us like talking in riddles.' The riddle after more than half a century repeated to us in different context does not appear to us to have improved with age."

Apart from this, however, I see no justification for our not reaching the question of the validity of Clause 27 with respect to in personam actions, an issue which still remains in the case even on the Court's view that the clause does not embrace in rem proceedings. That question, of course, presents no constitutional issue which we should strive to avoid, but is only one of ordinary commercial admiralty law. It is the only question which led us to take this case for review. And the issue has been fully briefed and argued by the parties. To be sure, it is possible that this question is not of great importance to the litigants if the in rem action can in any case go forward in Texas. But the very fact that respondent chose to institute and continue actions both in personam and in rem shows that it was not content to rely solely on the vessel's surety, and cautions against our now gratuitously treating the in personam action as purely academic. Moreover, review by certiorari, as Chief Justice Hughes once put it, is "in the interest of the law, its appropriate exposition and enforcement, not in the mere interest of the litigants."[*]

Furthermore, I do not think this can be called a case where the circumstances presently confronting us "were not manifest or fully apprehended at the time certiorari was granted." See Ferguson v. Moore-McCormack Lines, Inc., 352 U. S. 521, 559 (separate opinion). The question of the construction of the clause, and that of its validity, were both fully discussed by the parties in their certiorari papers. Indeed, it was apparent on the surface of things that we might find ourselves in the very position we now are, since the Court of Appeals had itself found Clause 27 inapplicable to in rem proceedings and had then gone on to consider the validity of the clause as related to in personam actions.

Avoidance of decision now on a question which is obviously bound to recur seems to me to be both unsatisfactory and unsound judicial administration. The course which the Court has taken serves only to leave the lower federal courts in confusion and uncertainty and to make it necessary for us to mortgage our future and constantly mounting calendars with a question which we could and should decide today. As the Court has not spoken on that question it would be inappropriate for me to express my own view upon it.

[*] S. Rep. No. 711, 75th Cong., 1st Sess., p. 39.

Justice Harlan's dissent in Magenau v. Aetna Freight Lines (June 15, 1959)

MR. JUSTICE HARLAN, whom MR. JUSTICE STEWART joins, dissenting.

Plenary consideration of this case, and indeed the opinion of the majority of this Court, have made it clear that the Court of Appeals dealt with the factual issues involved on the basis of a concession by the respondent and the jury's answer to Interrogatory No. 1. It is therefore now apparent that this case presents no question concerning the classification of these issues as for the court or for the jury under the decision in Byrd v. Blue Ridge Rural Cooperative, Inc., 356 U. S. 525, and that the premise on which we granted certiorari was accordingly a mistaken one. And whether or not the Court of Appeals in acting as it did was correct in its assessment of the trial record is certainly not a matter justifying the exercise of our certiorari power within the criteria of Rule 19. I therefore agree with my Brother FRANKFURTER that the writ of certiorari should be dismissed as improvidently granted, and join in his dissenting opinion.

Even if a Byrd issue could be considered as properly presented, the most that should be done is to remand the case to the Court of Appeals for further consideration in light of that decision. A retrial of this case would be justified under Byrd only if the Pennsylvania practice treating factual issues under § 104 of the Workmen's Compensation Act as for the court, instead of for the jury, see Persing v. Citizens Traction Co., 294 Pa.

230, 144 A. 97; Vescio v. Pennsylvania Electric Co., 336 Pa. 502, 9 A. 2d 546, is merely a "form and mode" of procedure rather than "an integral part" of the rights created by the Act. Before deciding such a difficult and subtle question of local law, this Court should have the aid of the Court of Appeals whose members are more competent than we to speak on Pennsylvania law.

Justice Harlan's dissent in Harris v. Pennsylvania R. (Oct 19, 1959)

MR. JUSTICE HARLAN, whom MR. JUSTICE WHITTAKER joins, dissenting.

The opening of a new Term that confronts the Court with the usual volume of important and exacting business impels me to reiterate the view that cases involving only factual issues and which are of no general importance have no legitimate demands upon our energies, already taxed to the utmost. See Rogers v. Missouri Pacific R. Co., 352 U. S. 500, 524, 559 (dissenting opinions). The extreme character of the adjudication which has been made in this case also deserves something more than merely noting my dissent on the merits, for I do not think that the reversal of this judgment is to be justified even under the philosophy of Rogers.

Petitioner was injured while engaged, as a member of a "wreck train crew," in retracking two derailed boxcars on the line of another railroad during the early morning of a "sleety, wet and sloppy" day. The operation involved the use on each car of a derrick and four outriggers. Each outrigger was supported from beneath by wooden blocks. The first derailed car was successfully retracked. The equipment then had to be moved for a similar operation on the second car. In this process petitioner wrenched his back while attempting to remove one of the wooden blocks which had become embedded in mud. Being unable to brace his right foot on the narrow surface of the ground between the block and one of the railroad crossties, petitioner placed that foot on the tie itself. In answer to interrogatories the jury found that respondent had been negligent in that "the tie of the track [petitioner] was required to walk was elevated a substantial distance above the ground level and was covered with grease or oil, thereby affording unstable footing." A verdict in the sum of $25,000 was returned, which on review was set aside by the Ohio Supreme Court.

The Court does not reach the question as to the applicability of the Ohio rule that this specification of negligence excluded appellate consideration of any others asserted by petitioner. I can hardly believe that the Court quarrels with the state court's ruling that as a matter of law the "position of the crosstie, slightly elevated above the roadbed" could not support the jury's finding of negligence because such state of affairs was a common and notorious one. Hence justification for the overturning of this judgment must rest upon what the record shows as to the presence of grease on the crosstie and as to the respondent's culpability for that alleged condition.

Unless liability in FELA cases may be predicated upon mere conjecture, this record for me is manifestly deficient. The only evidence that there was grease on the crosstie was petitioner's statement on cross-examination that he found some grease on the sole of the shoe of his right foot, and the testimony of a section foreman of the other railroad that grease was used on that railroad's switches, which were customarily lubricated at least twice a week. Petitioner had not mentioned on direct examination, in his pre-trial deposition, or in a written account of the accident made shortly after it occurred, that he had encountered grease at any stage of the operation, and even on cross-examination did not claim that he had seen grease anywhere in the vicinity, still less on the particular crosstie where his foot had rested. With respect to the foreman's testimony, there is no evidence at all in the record before us as to the position of any of the switches in relation to the crosstie in question—whether any of them were adjacent to it or far removed.

But even if this evidence be considered as justifying the jury's conclusion that there was grease on this particular crosstie, there was, in the words of the Ohio court, no evidence whatever that respondent "placed it there, knew about it, or, in the exercise of ordinary care, should have known about it." Evidence as to how long the alleged greasy condition of this crosstie had existed was wholly lacking. The tie on the day in question was covered with mud. And the section foreman of the other railroad testified that there was nothing untoward about the condition of the area when he inspected it the next morning. How in these circumstances it could "with reason" be said that the respondent failed in some duty of inspection is beyond me.

I cannot understand how on this record even the "scintilla" rule of Rogers and its progeny, see dissenting opinion in Sinkler v. Missouri Pacific R. Co., 356 U. S. 326, 332, can be thought to justify the overturning of this judgment. I fear that this decision confirms my growing suspicion that the real but unarticulated meaning of Rogers is that in FELA cases anything that a jury says goes, with the consequence that all meaningful judicial supervision over jury verdicts in such cases has been put at an end. See separate memorandum in Gibson v. Thompson, 355 U. S. 18, 19. If so, I think the time has come when the Court should frankly say so. If not, then the Court should at least give expression to the standards by which the lower courts are to be guided in these cases. Continuance of the present unsatisfactory state of affairs can only lead to much waste motion on the part of lower courts and defense lawyers.

I would affirm.

Justice Harlan's concurrence and dissent in Kinsella v. US ex rel. Singleton (Jan 18, 1960)

MR. JUSTICE HARLAN, whom MR. JUSTICE FRANKFURTER joins, dissenting in Nos. 22, 21, and 37, and concurring in No. 58.[*]

Within the compass of "any treaty or agreement to which the United States is or may be a party" and "any accepted rule of international law," Article 2 (11) of the Uniform Code of Military Justice makes subject to the Code, and therefore prosecutable by courts-martial for offenses committed abroad, all "persons serving with, employed by, or accompanying the armed forces" outside the United States and certain other areas.[1]

These four cases, involving persons and crimes concededly covered by the Military Code, bring before us the constitutionality of Article 2 (11) as applied to (1) civilian service dependents charged with noncapital offenses (No. 22); (2) civilian service employees, also charged with noncapital offenses (Nos. 21 and 37);[2] and (3) civilian service employees charged with capital offenses (No. 58). In each instance the Court holds the Act unconstitutional. While I agree with the judgment in No. 58, which involves a capital offense. I cannot agree with the judgments in Nos. 22, 21 and 37, in each of which the conviction was for a noncapital offense.

The effect of these decisions is to deny to Congress the power to give the military services, when the United States is not actually at war, criminal jurisdiction over noncapital offenses committed by nonmilitary personnel while accompanying or serving with our armed forces abroad. I consider this a much too narrow conception of the constitutional power of Congress and the result particularly unfortunate in the setting of the present-day international scene. To put what the Court has decided in proper context, some review of the past fate of Article 2 (11) in this Court is desirable.

At the 1955 Term there came before the Court in Kinsella v. Krueger, 351 U. S. 470, and Reid v. Covert, 351 U. S. 487, the question whether two army wives could be constitutionally convicted, under Article 2 (11), of the capital offense of first degree murder, committed while stationed with their husbands at military bases abroad. Initially a divided Court, in two opinions which I joined, upheld the convictions.[3] In so holding the Court relied not upon the constitutional power of Congress "To make Rules for the Government and Regulation of the land and naval Forces," Art. I, § 8, cl. 14, but upon In re Ross, 140 U. S. 453, the so-called Insular Cases, e. g., Balzac v. Porto Rico, 258 U. S. 298, and Art. IV, § 3, of the Constitution, respecting congressional power over Territories. These factors, in combination, led the Court to conclude that the constitutional guarantees of Article III and the Fifth and Sixth Amendments did not apply to criminal trials of Americans abroad before legislatively established tribunals; that it was permissible for Congress to conclude that persons circumstanced as those women were should be tried before a court-martial, rather than a civil tribunal; and that such trials did not offend the fundamentals of due process.

The decisions in these cases were reached under the pressures of the closing days of the Term. See 351 U. S., at 483-486. Having become convinced over the summer that the grounds on which they rested were untenable, I moved at the opening of the 1956 Term that the cases be reheard, being joined by the four Justices who had been in the minority. See 352 U. S. 901, 354 U. S. 1, 65-67.[4]

Upon a consolidated rehearing of the cases, the Court's original opinions and the judgments of conviction were set aside, a majority of the Court then holding that whether the convictions should stand or fall depended solely on the Art. I, § 8, cl. 14 power, and that such power could not be constitutionally applied in those cases. Reid v. Covert, 354 U. S. 1. There was, however, no opinion for the Court. Four Justices joined in an opinion broadly holding that "civilians" can never be criminally tried by military courts in times of peace, id., at 3-41.[5] Two Justices concurred specially in the result, on the narrow ground that Article 2 (11) could not be so applied to civilian service dependents charged with capital offenses, explicitly reserving judgment, however, as to whether nonmilitary personnel charged with other than capital offenses could be subjected to such trials.[6] Id., at 41-64, 65-78. Two Justices dissented, adhering to the grounds expressed in the earlier majority opinions.[7] Id., at 78. And one Justice did not participate in the cases.[8]

Thus the only issue that second Covert actually decided was that Article 2 (11) could not be constitutionally applied to civilian service dependents charged with capital offenses. Nevertheless, despite the wide differences of views by which this particular result was reached— none of which commanded the assent of a majority of the Court—Covert is now regarded as establishing that nonmilitary personnel are never within the reach of the Article I power in times of peace. On this faulty view of the case, it is considered that Covert controls the issues presently before us. Apart from that view I think it fair to say different results might well have been reached in the three noncapital cases now under consideration. Without needlessly traversing ground already covered in my separate opinion in Covert, id., at 67-78, I shall give my reasons for believing that while the result reached by the Court in the capital case is right, its decisions in the noncapital cases are wrong.

First. The Court's view of the effect of Covert in these noncapital cases stems from the basic premise that only persons occupying a military "status" are within the scope of the Art. I. § 8. cl. 14 power. The judgment in Covert having decided that civilian service dependents were not within the reach of that power in capital cases, it is said to follow that such dependents, and presumably all other "civilians," may also not be tried by courts-martial in noncapital cases; this because neither the statute nor Article I makes exercise of the power turn upon the nature of the offense involved.

I think the "status" premise on which the Court has proceeded is unsound. Article I. § 8. cl. 14. speaks not in narrow terms of soldiers and sailors, but broadly gives Congress power to prescribe "Rules for the Government and Regulation of the land and naval Forces."[9] This power must be read in connection with Clause 18 of the same Article, authorizing Congress

"To make all Laws which shall be necessary and proper for carrying into Execution the foregoing Powers, and all other Powers vested by this Constitution in the Government of the United States, or in any Department or Officer thereof."

Thus read, the power respecting the land and naval forces encompasses, in my opinion, all that Congress may appropriately deem "necessary" for their good order. It does not automatically exclude the regulation of non-military personnel.

I think it impermissible to conclude, as some of my brethren have indicated on an earlier occasion (see second Covert, supra, at 20-22), and as the Court now holds, ante, p. 248, that the Necessary and Proper Clause may not be resorted to in judging constitutionality in cases of this type. The clause, itself a part of Art. I. § 8, in which the power to regulate the armed forces is also found, applies no less to that power than it does to the other § 8 congressional powers, and indeed is to be read "as an integral part of each" such power. Second Covert, supra, at 43 (concurring opinion of FRANKFURTER, J.). As Mr. Justice Brandeis put it in Jacob Ruppert v. Caffey, 251 U. S. 264, at 300-301:

> "Whether it be for purposes of national defense, or for the purpose of establishing post offices and post roads or for the purpose of regulating commerce among the several States Congress has the power `to make all laws which shall be necessary and proper for carrying into execution' the duty so reposed in the Federal Government. While this is a Government of enumerated powers it has full attributes of sovereignty within the limits of those powers. In re Debs, 158 U. S. 564. Some confusion of thought might perhaps have been avoided, if, instead of distinguishing between powers by the terms express and implied, the terms specific and general had been used. For the power conferred by clause 18 of § 8 `to make all laws which shall be necessary and proper for carrying into execution' powers specifically enumerated is also an express power . . . ."

See also United States v. Classic, 313 U. S. 299, 320.

Of course, the Necessary and Proper Clause cannot be used to "expand" powers which are otherwise constitutionally limited, but that is only to say that when an asserted power is not appropriate to the exercise of an express power, to which all "necessary and proper" powers must relate, the asserted power is not a "proper" one. But to say, as the Court does now, that the Necessary and Proper Clause "is not itself a grant of power" is to disregard Clause 18 as one of the enumerated powers of § 8 of Art. I.

Viewing Congress' power to provide for the governing of the armed forces in connection with the Necessary and Proper Clause, it becomes apparent, I believe, that a person's "status" with reference to the military establishment is but one, and not alone the determinative, factor in judging the constitutionality of a particular exercise of that power. By the same token, the major premise on which the Court ascribes to Covert a controlling effect in these noncapital cases disappears.

Second. It is further suggested that the difference between capital and noncapital offenses is not constitutionally significant, and that if Article 2 (11) of the Military Code, as applied to nonmilitary persons, is unconstitutional in one case, it equally is so in the other. I think this passes over too lightly the awesome finality of a capital case, a factor which in other instances has been reflected both in the constitutional adjudications of this Court and in the special procedural safeguards which have been thrown around those charged with such crimes.

Thus, this Court has held that the Fourteenth Amendment requires a State to appoint counsel for an indigent defendant in a capital case, Powell v. Alabama, 287 U. S. 45, whereas in noncapital cases a defendant has no such absolute right to counsel, Betts v. Brady, 316 U. S. 455. Again, the Congress in first degree murder cases has in effect put infliction of the death penalty in the hands of the jury, rather than the judge, 18 U. S. C. § 1111 (b); see also 60 Stat. 766, as amended, 42 U. S. C. § 2274 (a), and various States have similar statutes.[10] Further illustrations of the same concern about capital cases are the prohibition on acceptance of pleas of guilty in such cases,[11] and, in the appellate field, provisions for mandatory or automatic appeals from such convictions.[12]

In my Covert opinion I pointed out that the Government itself had in effect acknowledged that because of the gravity of the offense, a treason case against a nonsoldier in time of peace could not constitutionally be held to be within the otherwise unlimited scope of Article 2 (11); and I expressed the view that the same constitutional limitation should obtain whenever the death penalty is involved. 354 U. S., at 77. I see no reason for retreating from that conclusion. The view that we must hold that nonmilitary personnel abroad are subject to peace-time court-martial jurisdiction either for all offenses, or for none at all, represents an inexorable approach to constitutional adjudication to which I cannot subscribe.

It is one thing to hold that nonmilitary personnel situated at our foreign bases may be tried abroad by courts-martial in times of peace for noncapital offenses, but quite another to say that they may be so tried where life is at stake. In the latter situation I do not believe that the Necessary and Proper Clause, which alone in cases like this brings the exceptional Article I jurisdiction into play, can properly be taken as justifying the trial of nonmilitary personnel without the full protections of an Article III court. See 354 U. S., at 77. Before the constitutional existence of such a power can be found, for me a much more persuasive showing would be required that Congress had good reason for concluding that such a course is necessary to the proper maintenance of our military establishment abroad than has been made in any of the cases of this kind which have thus far come before the Court.

Third. I revert to the Court's "status" approach to the power of Congress to make rules for governing the armed forces. How little of substance that view holds appears when it is pointed out that had those involved in these cases been inducted into the army, though otherwise maintaining their same capacities, it would presumably have been held that they were all fully subject to Article 2 (11). Yet except for this formality their real "status" would have remained the same.

Although it was recognized in the second Covert case that a person might be subject to Article 2 (11) "even though he had not formally been inducted into the military or did not wear a uniform," 354 U. S., at 23, I think that drawing a line of demarcation between those who are constitutionally subject to the Art. I, § 8, cl. 14 power, and those who are not, defies definition in terms of military "status." I believe that the true issue on this aspect of all such cases concerns the closeness or remoteness of the relationship between the person affected and the military establishment. Is that relationship close enough so that Congress may, in light of all the factors involved, appropriately deem it "necessary" that the military be given jurisdiction to deal with offenses committed by such persons?

I think that such relationship here was close enough, and in this respect can draw no constitutional distinction between the army wife in No. 22 and the civilian service employees in the other cases. Though their presence at these army overseas bases was for different reasons and purposes, the relationship of both to the military community was such as to render them constitutionally amenable to the Article 2 (11) jurisdiction. By the same token, being of the view that the constitutional existence of such jurisdiction has not been shown as to civilian service dependents charged with capital offenses, I am equally of the opinion that it cannot be found with respect to civilian service employees similarly charged. For these reasons I concur in the judgment of the Court in No. 58.

Fourth. The other factors which must be weighed in judging the constitutionality of Article 2 (11) as applied to noncapital cases have, in my opinion, been adequately satisfied. I need not add to what was said in my concurring opinion in Covert, 354 U. S., at 70-73, 76-77, with reference to the matters which originally were adumbrated by my Brother CLARK in his dissent in the same case. Id., at 83-88. Nothing in the supplemental historical data respecting courts-martial which have been presented in these cases persuades me that we would be justified in holding that Congress' exercise of its constitutional powers in this area was without a rational and appropriate basis, so far as noncapital cases are concerned. Although it is now suggested that the problem with which Congress sought to deal in Article 2 (11) may be met in other ways. I submit that once it is shown that Congress' choice was not excluded by a rational judgment concerned with the problem it is beyond our competence to find constitutional command for other procedures.

I think it unfortunate that this Court should have found the Constitution lacking in enabling Congress to cope effectively with matters which are so intertwined with broader problems that have been engendered by present disturbed world conditions. Those problems are fraught with many factors that this Court is ill-equipped to assess, and involve important national concerns into which we should be reluctant to enter except under the clearest sort of constitutional compulsion. That such compulsion is lacking here has been amply demonstrated by the chequered history of the past cases of this kind in the Court. Today's decisions are the more regrettable because they are bound to disturb delicate arrangements with many foreign countries, and may result in our having to relinquish to other nations where United States forces are stationed a substantial part of the jurisdiction now retained over American personnel under the Status of Forces Agreements.

I would reverse in Nos. 22, 21, and 58, and affirm in No. 37.

Notes

[1] To wit: "that part of Alaska east of longitude 172 degrees west, the Canal Zone, the main group of the Hawaiian Islands, Puerto Rico, and the Virgin Islands."

[2] In No. 37 the Government, alternatively, relies on the "War Power," the offense having been committed in the American Occupied Zone of West Berlin. Cf. Madsen v. Kinsella, 343 U. S. 341. Apart from whether or not the contention is available in light of the course of the proceedings below, I do not reach that issue.

[3] In addition to myself, the majority opinions, written by MR. JUSTICE CLARK,

were joined by JUSTICE REED, BURTON and MINTON, 351 U. S. 470 and 487. THE CHIEF JUSTICE and JUSTICE BLACK and DOUGLAS dissented. Id., at 485. MR. JUSTICE FRANKFURTER filed a Reservation. Id., at 481.

[4] The three remaining members of the original majority were in dissent, 352 U. S., at 902, MR. JUSTICE MINTON having meanwhile retired. MR. JUSTICE BRENNAN, his successor, did not participate on the motion.

[5] THE CHIEF JUSTICE, MR. JUSTICE BLACK (the writer of the opinion), and JUSTICES DOUGLAS and BRENNAN.

[6] MR. JUSTICE FRANKFURTER and myself.

[7] JUSTICE CLARK and BURTON.

[8] MR. JUSTICE WHITTAKER, succeeding MR. JUSTICE REED who had meanwhile retired.

[9] The Fifth Amendment excepts from its protection "cases arising," not persons, "in the land or naval forces."

[10] E. g., Mass. Gen. Laws Ann., c. 265, § 2; Miss. Code Ann., § 2536; N. H. Rev. Stat. Ann., c. 585, § 4.

[11] E. g., N. Y. Code Crim. Proc., § 332.

[12] E. g., Cal. Penal Code. § 1239 (b); Ore, Rev. Stat., § 138.810.

Justice Harlan's dissent in Hess v. US (Jan 18, 1960) [Notes omitted]

MR. JUSTICE HARLAN, whom MR. JUSTICE FRANKFURTER joins, dissenting.

Since The Hamilton, 207 U. S. 398, it has been settled law that an action in personam for wrongful death occurring on navigable waters, not available under maritime law, The Harrisburg, 119 U. S. 199, may be brought under a state wrongful death statute. In The Tungus v. Skovgaard, 358 U. S. 588, decided last Term, we held that such an action could be maintained only in accordance with the limitations placed upon it by state law. This case presents the further question, not involved in The Tungus, namely, whether such an action lies when the conduct said to give rise to liability is measured under state law by greater substantive standards of duty than those which would have governed the same conduct under maritime law had death not occurred.[1]

The Court, if I read its opinion aright, holds that when a victim of a maritime tort dies as a result of such conduct the law of the State whose wrongful death statute is invoked wholly governs liability.[2] At the same time the Court leaves open the question whether a state wrongful death act might contain "provisions so offensive to traditional principles of maritime law that the admiralty would decline to enforce them," finding that this Oregon statute "presents no such problem."

I cannot agree with the view that wrongful death actions growing out of maritime torts are so pervasively controlled by state law, or with the conclusion that this state statute in its substantive provisions is, in any event, not offensive to maritime law. Nor can I subscribe to the intimation that the question which the Court reserves is seriously open to debate. Because of the importance of the issue, a fuller statement of my views is justified than might be appropriate in a case of lesser general concern.

I.

It is surely beyond dispute that the Oregon Employers' Liability Law, Ore. Rev. Stat. § 654.305, imposes a stricter standard of duty than that imposed by maritime law. Under maritime law the basis of liability in cases like this is the failure to use reasonable care in light of the attendant circumstances, that is, negligence. See Kermarec v. Compagnie Generale, 358 U. S. 625, 630, 632. The state statute, on the other hand, imposes the duty to use—

"every device, care and precaution which it is practicable to use for the protection and safety of life and limb, limited only by the necessity for preserving the efficiency of the . . . device, and without regard to the additional cost of suitable material or safety appliance [sic] and devices." Ore. Rev. Stat. § 654.305.

Oregon itself has recognized that this statute imposes a "much higher degree of care," Hoffman v. Broadway Hazelwood, 139 Ore. 519, 524, 10 P. 2d 349, 351, 11 P. 2d 814, than that generally required of defendants in accident cases. See Camenzind v. Freeland Furniture Co., 89 Ore. 158, 172-173, 174 P. 139, 144. So much indeed I do not understand the Court to deny.

II.

Had this accident resulted in injuries short of death, it is clear that the United States could not have been held liable except in accordance with the standards of duty imposed by maritime law. This follows from the general constitutional doctrine of federal supremacy in maritime affairs, and more particularly from the rule first unmistakably announced in Chelentis v. Luckenbach S. S. Co., 247 U. S. 372, which rejected the notion that the "saving clause" of § 9 of the Judiciary Act of 1789, 1 Stat. 77, permitted the application in maritime tort cases of state substantive rules in derogation of maritime law.[3] That case was a maritime tort action brought in a state court by a seaman, seeking compensatory damages for injuries claimed to have been caused by the negligence of his employer. Historically, maritime law recognized no such cause of action. The duty of a shipowner to an injured crewman was only to provide for his maintenance and cure, and that irrespective of negligence; full indemnity was owing only for breach of the warranty of seaworthiness.[4] The Court held, first, that § 20 of the Merchant Marine Act of 1915, 38 Stat. 1185,[5] notwithstanding, such was still the rule. This being so, a state court was not free to apply any other rule to a maritime tort:

"Plainly, we think, under the saving clause a right sanctioned by the maritime law may be enforced through any appropriate remedy recognized at common law; but we find nothing therein which reveals an intention to give the complaining party an election to determine whether the defendant's liability shall be measured by common-law standards rather than those of the maritime law. Under the circumstances here presented, without regard to the court where he might ask relief, petitioner's rights were those recognized by the law of the sea." Id., at 384.

This rule was soon reiterated in two subsequent cases. The first was Carlisle Packing Co. v. Sandanger, 259 U. S. 255, which, like Chelentis, was a state court action by a crew member against the shipowner. Injury was allegedly caused by mislabeling of a can of gasoline and by the negligent failure to stock a life preserver on board. A judgment for plaintiff was affirmed, but on the ground that the vessel was unseaworthy in the respects named; the existence of a cause of action for negligence was denied. "The general rules of the maritime law apply whether the proceeding be instituted in an admiralty or common-law court." Id., at 259. The second case was Robins Dry Dock Co. v. Dahl, 266 U. S. 449, where the action, again in a state court for negligence, was by an employee of an independent contractor against his employer for a shipboard injury. Such a right of action existed in admiralty, Atlantic Transport Co. v. Imbrovek, 234 U. S. 52, and the question was as to the scope of the defendant's duty. Here too the same principle of federal supremacy was upheld. An instruction permitting the jury to consider the requirements of a state safety statute on the issue of negligence was held erroneous. "The rights and liabilities of the parties arose out of and depended upon the general maritime law and could not be enlarged or impaired by the state statute." 266 U. S., at 457.

Largely owing to the passage of the Jones Act, 46 U. S. C. § 688,[6] which bound nonadmiralty as well as admiralty courts,[7] the issue was not again raised in litigation here for several decades. Garrett v. Moore-McCormack Co., 317 U. S. 239, however, demonstrates the pervasive scope given to the same principle of federal supremacy in the application of that Act. There a State was denied power, by characterizing the matter as "procedural," to apply its own rules to the question of burden of proof of fraud in the obtaining of a release from an injured seaman. Rather the state court was required to apply the rule adopted by federal maritime law. The case thus manifests the continued vitality of the supremacy principle in this area. 317 U. S., at 244, n. 10.

It remained for Pope & Talbot, Inc., v. Hawn, 346 U. S. 406, unmistakably to demonstrate that the principle embodied in the Chelentis, Sandanger, and Robins Dry Dock decisions had not withered with time. There a shore-based carpenter, employed by an independent contractor, sought a recovery against a shipowner based on negligence[8] and unseaworthiness. The Court held that under federal law a right of action was available on both grounds, and that under the maritime rule the effect of plaintiff's contributory negligence was to diminish, but not wholly defeat, his recovery. This being so, a State was debarred from applying another rule.

Finally, when, only last Term, the Court came to consider, in Kermarec v. Compagnie Generale, 358 U. S. 625, the scope of a shipowner's duty of care toward a social guest of a crew member, it had no hesitation about the proposition that federal law must govern an action within the jurisdiction of admiralty.

"The District Court was in error in ruling that the governing law in this case was that of the State of New York. Kermarec was injured aboard a ship upon navigable waters. It was there that the conduct of which he complained occurred. The legal rights and liabilities arising from that conduct were therefore within the full reach of the admiralty jurisdiction and measurable by the standards of maritime law. . . . If this action had been brought in a state court, reference to admiralty law would have been necessary to determine the rights and liabilities of the parties. Carlisle Packing Co. v. Sandanger, 259 U. S. 255, 259. Where the plaintiff exercises the right conferred by diversity of citizenship to choose a federal forum, the result is no different, even though he exercise the further right to a jury trial. Whatever doubt may once have existed on that score was effectively laid to rest by Pope & Talbot, Inc., v. Hawn, 346 U. S. 406, 410-11." Id., at 628.

I think it is clear, then, that the supremacy principle established by this line of cases may not be shrugged off as a discredited relic of an earlier day.[9] Indeed, the Court's total disregard of that principle in the present case is not grounded on the view that it is no longer generally viable. Rather, the Court appears to consider it inapplicable in an action for wrongful death. For reasons now to be discussed I think this is a mistaken view.

III.

What I shall address myself to at this point is the reason why maritime law permits resort to state wrongful death statutes.[10] For it is only through an understanding of that reason that light can be shed on the pivotal issue in this case.

Unfortunately such rationalization as has been made of the problem in the wrongful death cases in this Court does not carry us very far. Mr. Justice Holmes in The Hamilton was content to say no more than that permitting state death statutes to be used would not produce "any lamentable lack of uniformity" in the maritime law. 207 U. S., at 406. Mr. Justice McReynolds in Western Fuel Co. v. Garcia, 257 U. S. 233, simply observed that the use of such statutes was "the logical result of prior decisions," that "[t]he subject is maritime and local in character," and that the innovation "will not work material prejudice to the characteristic features of the general maritime law, nor interfere with the proper harmony and uniformity of that law in its international and interstate relations." Id., at 242.[11]

Other rationalizations of the subject leave much to be desired. It has been said that the application of state wrongful death statutes is permitted to "fill a void" in maritime law. See, e. g., 41 Va. L. Rev. 251, 252; 34 B. U. L. Rev. 365, 366; cf. The Tungus, supra, at 592. But there is a "void" only in the sense that there is an absence of a right of action in such cases; admiralty does not lack a rule on the subject. It has also been suggested that the Court permits the application of state death acts because it regards such statutes as wiser in this respect than maritime law, although it deems itself unable to alter the disfavored federal rule. See, e. g., Note, 73 Harv. L. Rev. 84, 148, 149. But if the rule of The Harrisburg is so firmly established that legislation is the only available means of reform, cf. The Tungus, supra, at 590, 599, it is scarcely legitimate to turn, for that very reason, to state law.

I think the fault with such explanations lies in the emphasis given to admiralty's endeavor to find in state law a supplement to its own shortcomings, something which federal power has always been fully competent to remedy internally on its own account.

Instead, the proper point of departure is, I believe, to recognize that in permitting use of wrongful death statutes admiralty is endeavoring to accommodate itself to state policies represented by such statutes. That indeed appears to have been the approach of Congress in enacting the Death on the High Seas Act, for as was said in The Tungus the legislative history of that Act "discloses a clear congressional purpose to leave `unimpaired the rights under State statutes as to deaths on waters within the territorial jurisdiction of the States' " and "reflects deep concern that the power of the States to create actions for wrongful death in no way be affected by enactment of the federal law." 358 U. S., at 593. At the same time there was no suggestion that Congress contemplated that the supremacy of admiralty law should be yielded to the States in maritime death cases. Cf. id., at 607-608, separate opinion.

It only confuses things to say, as has sometimes been loosely remarked, that in maritime wrongful death cases admiralty absorbs state law, or that the States have embraced maritime law. State and maritime systems of law stand separately, even though the two may not always be mutually exclusive, and when a conflict arises the latter yields to the former only in face of a superior state interest. This, I think, is what Mr. Justice McReynolds had in mind when he stated in Garcia that a wrongful death statute is a subject both "maritime and local in character." The true inquiry thus becomes one involving the nature of the state interest in a wrongful death statute, the extent to which such interest intrudes upon federal concerns, and the basis of the reasoning that led Mr. Justice Holmes to state summarily in The Hamilton that resort to such statutes would not result in "any lamentable lack of uniformity" in maritime law.

What no lesser authority in admiralty matters than Judge Addison Brown said many years ago in The City of Norwalk, 55 F. 98,[12] is highly illuminating. He gave these reasons for permitting a state death statute to apply to a maritime tort:

"(1) It is a general law of personal rights, not specially directed to commerce or navigation, but applying alike on sea or shore; (2) it is within the police power; for it is `a statute intended to protect life,' (Huntington v. Attrill, 146 U. S. 657. 675 . . .) through one of the most effectual of all sanctions, viz. by imposing on the offender a liability to pay a pecuniary indemnity; while in the interest of the public, it also tends to avert the dependency or pauperism of the survivors by shifting the burden of their support, in part at least, from the community to the authors of the wrong; (3) it is local in its scope and interferes in no way with any needful uniformity in the general law of the seas, or with international or interstate interests." Id., at 108.

Where tortious conduct causes death, the decision of a State to provide a right of action in favor of the victim's estate or beneficiaries represents a response to considerations peculiarly within traditional state competence: providing for the victim's family, and preventing pauperism by shifting what would otherwise be a public responsibility to those who committed the wrong. These are matters intimately concerned with the State's interest in regulating familial relationships. Moreover, where the injury is wrongful under maritime law, this is the predominant, if indeed not the sole, purpose of the statute. In such instances the State is not legislating in order to affect the defendant's conduct, since by hypothesis a federally imposed duty already exists. For merely because no federal action lies for wrongful death, one can hardly say that there is no duty not to kill through negligence, but there is a duty not to injure. The tortious conduct is the same in either case, and wrongful under federal law. The state statute therefore makes no meaningful inroads on federal interests. To quote further from Judge Brown:

"The state statute does not create the cause of action. It does, indeed, create a new right, and liability; but it does not create a single one of the elements that make up the fundamental cause of action, that is, the essential grounds of the demand. All these elements exist independently of the statute, and are not in the least affected by it. It no more creates the wrong, or the damage, than it creates the negligence or the death; nor does it, as in the pilotage and double wharfage cases, add anything to the damages sustained. It authorizes no recovery except for `the pecuniary damages' already existing. It is apparent, therefore, that, as suggested by Mr. Justice Clifford in Steamboat Co. v. Chase, 16 Wall. 532, the statute does no more than `take the case out of the operation of the common-law maxim that an action for death dies with the person.' " 55 F., at 109.

"Before the statute, the case was damnum absque injuria; by the statute, it became at once a tort in the full legal sense, and a marine tort by reason of its place, its nature, and its circumstances . . . ." Id., at 110.

Thus, where the duty imposed by a state death act is no greater than that already existing under federal law, the application of the statute is solely, or nearly so, a reaction to strong, localized state interests, and there is no real encroachment on federal interests.[13]

Far different is the case when a State purports, as here, to impose a duty which under federal law a person does not bear. Then it can hardly be said that the State is not seeking to regulate conduct within federal maritime jurisdiction. The very purpose of a statute like the one here invoked is to induce those to whom it applies to take the precautions required by it. In such a case, the mere fact that it is a death act which imposes the duty cannot be thought to render the import of the matter of "local" concern only. The state interests given expression no longer are predominantly those peculiarly within state concern. By the same token the intrusion into federally regulated interests is no longer minimal.

I can find no justification, consistent with the course of adjudication in this Court, for upholding state power here, without so much as even suggesting the need for an inquiry as to the extent of federal interest in the activity in question.[14]

IV.

Nothing in the wrongful death cases on which the Court relies calls for today's holding. None of them involved, as here, the assertion of any local rules of substantive law going beyond those applicable under federal standards.[15]

The essential failing in the Court's use of these cases is its view that, because rights asserted under a state death statute are manifestly rights created by the State, no federal element is involved in their assertion. The truth is, however, that, where the tort is maritime and the action is brought under the "saving clause," state-created rights may be asserted only by federal permission. That is the premise on which The Hamilton, and its offspring, proceeded. When such a right is asserted, the plaintiff must, however, show more than that a State can give him a right to recover; he must also show that it has done so. Thus, if a State has chosen not to provide a right of action to one who does not sue within a stated period, The Harrisburg, supra; Western Fuel Co. v. Garcia, supra; Levinson v. Deupree, 345 U. S. 648, 651-652; to one who does not have a stated relationship to the decedent, id., at 651; to one whose decedent's negligence contributed to the fatal injury, United Pilots Assn. v. Halecki, 358 U. S. 613, 615; or to one whose right of action is based on breach of the uniquely maritime duty to provide a seaworthy ship, The Tungus v. Skovgaard, supra, there can be no right of recovery, for neither federal nor state law affords it.[16] For this reason, when asking whether a plaintiff has made out a cause of action under a state death act, the Court approaches the statute "as it would one originating in any foreign jurisdiction," Levinson v. Deupree, supra, at 652, in an "endeavor to determine the issues in accordance with the substantive law of the State," Garrett v. Moore-McCormack Co., 317 U. S., at 245. This, because the State having created the right, one must look to state law to "determine the circumstances under which that right exists." The Tungus, supra, at 594.

But none of these cases is apposite when the question is not whether a federally permitted state right of action has in fact been conferred by the State, but whether federal maritime law permits the State to create an asserted right of action. It is surely fallacious to reason that, because the principle of the supremacy of federal maritime law has been held not to bar a right of action for death caused by a defendant's failure to take reasonable precautions to avoid exposing those to whom the duty is owed to an undue risk of harm, it follows that such principle does not bar a right of action for death caused by failure to "use every device, care and precaution which it is practicable to use," Ore. Rev. Stat. § 654.305. When the Court, in The Hamilton and its successors, held that the federal supremacy principle did not prevent a State from giving any right of action for wrongful death caused by a maritime tort, it did not thereby eschew forever all federal limits on the content of substantive obligations appearing in statutes bearing the label "wrongful death act."

It may be that the Court does not intend to go so far. It asserts, albeit almost as an afterthought, that some state doctrines might be constitutionally inapplicable to maritime torts, notwithstanding that they are embodied in a death statute.[17] It then summarily finds the possible reservation inapplicable in this instance on the ground that other provisions of the Oregon Employers' Liability Law, not here involved, resemble some admiralty doctrines, with which also we are not now concerned, more than do comparable provisions in the State's general wrongful death statute, which presumably can be constitutionally applied to a maritime tort. With all deference, I must say that the total irrelevance of that fact seems plain. We are not reviewing the general constitutionality of the Employers' Liability Law; we are concerned only with the constitutionality of the standard-of-care provisions of that law, as applied to an employee of an independent contractor injured on navigable waters and seeking to impose liability upon the owner and operator of a dam. The Court does not find that the federal interest in regulating the conduct of the dam owner is so minimal —whether by reason of the fixed situs of the dam or on some other ground—that the federal supremacy principle may reasonably be found inapplicable. Neither does the Court assert, for it could scarcely do so, that the standard of care required by this statute is not significantly greater than that imposed by federal law. Thus, if the principle of the supremacy of maritime law calls for anything more than an empty nod, it calls for a result contrary to that reached today.

It is suggested that a contrary decision will lack "even-handedness," apparently for the reason that, since those invoking state death statutes must sometimes bear the burden of comparatively unfavorable provisions, it is only fair that, when more favorable provisions obtain, they be able to enjoy the benefits of such rules. But, as the Court points out, "[w]e are concerned with constitutional adjudication, not with reaching particular results in given cases." Such unevenhandedness as there may be in this area is the consequence of the rule of The Harrisburg, to which this Court has steadfastly adhered for nearly 75 years,[18] and which Congress, when it enacted the Death on the High Seas Act, saw fit to change only in a limited way. See The Tungus, supra, at 592-593. When federal law permits the application of state death acts, those on whom the state statute confers a right of action may escape the harsh consequences of that rule. Those whom the state law has declined to benefit are left as they were. Certainly we should not, in the name of "evenhandedness," permit a State to exceed constitutional limitations merely because in some instances it may have chosen not to do all it might under the Constitution.[19]

I would affirm.

Justice Harlan's dissent in Davis v. Virginian R. Co. (Jan 25, 1960)

MR. JUSTICE HARLAN, dissenting.

From the point of view of the functions of this Court, this decision provides another example of the futility of continuing to bring here for review cases of this kind. So long as jury verdicts remain subject to some degree of judicial supervision, cf. Harris v. Pennsylvania R. Co., 361 U. S. 15, 27-28 (dissenting opinion), whether or not the evidence is sufficient to warrant removing a particular case from consideration of the jury is a question which will doubtless continue to divide equally conscientious judges in all except the clearest instances. As to the issue upon which the judgment below is now reversed,[*] a majority of the Court disagrees with the unanimous view of the record taken by the two state courts. My Brother WHITTAKER, in dissent, takes a different view from that of the majority. And I, also in dissent, take still a different view from either approach.

As I read the record and the briefs, petitioner's theory was that this accident would not have happened had he not been forced to work on top of the cars, instead of on the ground where he usually worked, in consequence of (1) the company's instructions to perform the car-shifting operation in unusually short order, and (2) its failure to supply him with experienced helpers. Under the Rogers "rule of reason," 352 U. S. 500, I suppose it could be said that there was an issue for the jury on both scores, in light of the not unequivocal testimony of the petitioner, quoted in my Brother WHITTAKER'S opinion, and the other matters referred to in the Court's opinion. Even so, this makes out no case for the jury, unless there is evidence that one or both of these factors contributed to increase the normal hazards of petitioner's employment. I think there is no such evidence.

The record is barren of anything showing why this accident occurred. There was no evidence whatever that either the car or the ladder from which the petitioner fell was faulty. Petitioner admitted to being an experienced railroad worker whose duties had at times carried him up and down ladders, and on the tops of railroad cars. At the time of his fall the cars had stopped moving, or nearly so. When asked by the trial court to explain how he happened to fall, all petitioner could say was "it might have been grease or anything on my shoe"; and this was pure conjecture, as the record shows. More especially, petitioner did not say that he fell because he was "rushed."

In these circumstances, to hold that the jury might have found that what respondent did contributed to enhance the normal hazards of petitioner's employment is, in my opinion, to say in effect that the jury should have been allowed to substitute atmosphere for evidence and speculation for reason.

On the basis of the criteria governing our certiorari jurisdiction, this case has not been profitable business for this Court.

I would affirm.

Justice Harlan's dissent in US v. Parke, Davis & Co. (Feb 29, 1960)

MR. JUSTICE HARLAN, whom MR. JUSTICE FRANKFURTER and MR. JUSTICE WHITTAKER join, dissenting.

The Court's opinion reaches much further than at once may meet the eye, and justifies fuller discussion than otherwise might appear warranted. Scrutiny of the opinion will reveal that the Court has done no less than send to its demise the Colgate doctrine which has been a basic part of antitrust law concepts since it was first announced in 1919 in United States v. Colgate, 250 U. S. 300.

I begin with that doctrine and how it was applied by the District Court in this case. In the words of the Court's opinion, Colgate held that in the absence of a monopolistic setting, "a manufacturer, having announced a price maintenance policy, may bring about adherence to it by refusing to deal with customers who do not observe that policy." "And," as said in Colgate (at 307), "of course, he may announce in advance the circumstances under which he will refuse to sell."

The Government's complaint, seeking to enjoin alleged violations of §§ 1 and 3 of the Sherman Act,[1] in substance charged Parke Davis with having combined and conspired with wholesalers and retailers of its products in the District of Columbia and

Virginia, in four respects: (1) with retailers, to fix retail prices; (2) with retailers, to suppress advertising of cut prices; (3) with wholesalers, to fix wholesale prices; and (4) with wholesalers, to boycott retail price cutters. The Company's defense was that the activities complained of simply constituted a legitimate exercise of its rights under the Colgate doctrine. The detailed findings of the District Court are epitomized in its opinion as follows:

(1) Parke Davis "had well-established policies concerning the prices at which [its] products were to be sold by wholesalers and retailers, and the type of retailers to whom the wholesalers could re-sell";[2]

(2) Parke Davis' "representatives . . . notified retailers concerning the policy under which its goods must be sold, but the retailers were free either to do without such goods or sell them in accordance with defendant's policy";

(3) Parke Davis' "representatives likewise contacted wholesalers, notifying them of its policy and the wholesalers were likewise free to refuse to comply and thus risk being cut off by the defendant";

(4) "every visit made by the representatives to the retailers and wholesalers was, to each of them, separate and apart from all others";

(5) "[t]he evidence is clear that both wholesalers and retailers valued [Parke Davis'] business so highly that they acceded to its policy";

(6) "there was no coercion by defendant and no agreement with [wholesaler or retailer] co-conspirators as alleged in the Complaint";

(7) as to the Government's contention that proof of the alleged conspiracy "is implicit in (1) defendant's calling the attention of both retailers and wholesalers to its policy, and (2) the distributors' acquiescence to the policy . . . [t]he Court cannot agree to such a nebulous deduction from the record before it.

On these premises the District Court concluded: "Clearly, the actions of defendant were properly unilateral and sanctioned by law under the doctrine laid down in the case of United States v. Colgate & Co., 250 U. S. 300. . . ."

The Court appears to recognize that as the Colgate doctrine was originally understood, the District Court's findings would require affirmance of its judgment here. It is said, however, that reversal is required because Federal Trade Comm'n v. Beech-Nut Packing Co., 257 U. S. 441, and United States v. Bausch & Lomb Optical Co., 321 U. S. 707, subsequently "narrowly limited" the Colgate rule. The claim is that whereas prior to Beech-Nut it was considered that, fair trade laws apart, resale price maintenance came within the ban of the Sherman Act only if it was brought about by express or implied agreement between the parties—which the Court says meant "contractual arrangements"—Beech-Nut, which was carried forward by Bausch & Lomb, later established that such agreements or contractual arrangements need not be shown. Recognizing that §§ 1 and 3 of the Sherman Act explicitly require a "contract, combination . . . or conspiracy," the Court says this requirement is satisfied by conduct which falls short of express or implied agreement, if it goes beyond the seller's mere announcement of terms and his refusal to deal with those who will not comply with them. Concluding that the District Court in the present case mistakenly proceeded solely on the "agreement" view of Colgate, it is then said that its findings of fact are not binding on us because they were based on an erroneous legal standard, and that therefore "Rule 52 has no application here."[3]

I think this reasoning not only misconceives the Beech-Nut and Bausch & Lomb cases, but also mistakes the premises on which the District Court decided this case, and its actual findings of fact.

First. I cannot read Beech-Nut or Bausch & Lomb as introducing a new narrowing concept into the Colgate doctrine. Until today I had not supposed that any informed antitrust practitioner or judge would have had to await Beech-Nut to know that the concerted action proscribed by the Sherman Act need not amount to a contractual agreement. But neither do I think it would have been supposed that the Sherman Act does not require concerted action in some form. In Beech-Nut itself the Court stated the rule to be that a seller may not restrain trade "by contracts or combinations, express or implied," and there found suppression of competition "by methods in which the company secures the cooperation of its distributors and customers, which are quite as effectual as agreements express or implied intended to accomplish the same purpose." 257 U. S., at 453, 455. It is obvious that the "methods" thus referred to were the "cooperative methods" which the Federal Trade Commission had found to exist, for the Court expressly limited the Commission's order to the granting of relief against such methods. Id., 455-456. Far from announcing that no concerted action need be shown, the Court accepted the Commission's factual determination that such action did exist.

Similarly, in Bausch & Lomb, the District Court had found that Soft-Lite had entered into "agreements with wholesale customers" to fix prices and boycott unlicensed retailers. 321 U. S., at 717. This Court held that the facts "all amply support indeed require, the inference of the trial court that a conspiracy to maintain prices down the distribution system existed between the wholesalers and Soft-Lite." Id., 720. The Court reiterated that resale price maintenance could not be achieved "by agreement, express or implied." Id., 721. In rejecting the applicability of the Colgate doctrine, it said that none of the cases applying the doctrine "involve, as the present case does, an agreement between the seller and purchaser to maintain resale prices." Ibid. It justified the finding of concerted action on the ground that "[t]he wholesalers accepted Soft-Lite's proffer of a plan of distribution by cooperating in prices, limitation of sales to and approval of retail licensees." Id., 723.

The results in Beech-Nut and Bausch & Lomb, as in all Sherman Act cases, turned on the application of established standards of concerted action to the full sweep of the particular facts in those cases, and not upon any new meaning given to the words "contract, combination . . . or conspiracy." The Court now says that the seller runs afoul of the Sherman Act when he goes beyond mere announcement of his policy and refusal to sell, not because the bare announcement and refusal fall outside the statutory phrase, but because any additional step removes a "countervailing consideration" in favor of permitting a seller to choose his customers. But we are left wholly in the dark as to what the purported new standard is for establishing a "contract, combination . . . or conspiracy."

Second. The Court is mistaken in attributing to the District Court the limited view that Parke Davis' activities should, under Colgate, be upheld unless they involved some express or implied "contractual arrangement" with wholesalers or retailers. The Government's complaint specifically charged a "combination and conspiracy" between Parke Davis and its wholesale and retail customers in the areas involved, comprising a "continuing agreement, understanding and concert of action" in the four aspects already noted. Ante, p. 50. In its 31 detailed findings of fact the District Court repeatedly emphasized that Parke Davis did not have an "agreement or understanding of any kind" with its distributors, and it concluded that the evidence as a whole did not support the Government's allegations. It determined with respect to each of the four facets of the alleged conspiracy that "there was no coercion" and that "Parke, Davis did not combine, conspire or enter into an agreement, understanding or concert of action" with the wholesalers, retailers, or anyone else. I cannot detect in the record any indication that the District Court in making these findings applied anything other than the standard which has always been understood to govern prosecutions based on §§ 1 and 3 of the Sherman Act.

Third. Bearing down heavily on the statement in Beech-Nut that the conduct there involved showed more than "the simple refusal to sell," 257 U. S., at 454 (see also Bausch & Lomb, supra, at 722), the Court finds that Parke Davis' conduct exceeded the permissible limits of Colgate in two respects. The first is that Parke Davis announced that it would, and did, cut off wholesalers who continued to sell to price-cutting retailers. The second is that the Company in at least one instance reported its talks with one or more retailers to other retailers; that in "this manner Parke Davis sought assurances of compliance and got them"; and that it "was only by actively bringing about substantial unanimity among the competitors that Parke Davis was able to gain adherence to its policy."

There are two difficulties with the Court's analysis on these scores. The first is the findings of the District Court. As to refusals to sell to wholesalers, the lower court found that such conduct did not involve any concert of action, but was wholly unilateral on Parke Davis' part. And I cannot see how such unilateral action, permissible in itself, becomes any less unilateral because it is taken simultaneously with similar unilateral action at the retail level. As to the other respect in which the Court holds Parke Davis' conduct was illegal, the District Court found that the Company did not make "the enforcement of its policies as to any one wholesaler or retailer dependent upon the action of any other wholesaler or retailer." And it further stated that the "evidence is clear that both wholesalers and retailers valued defendant's business so highly that they acceded to its policy," and that such acquiescence was not brought about by "coercion" or "agreement". Even if this were not true, so that concerted action among the retailers at the "horizontal" level might be inferred, as the Court indicates, under the principles of Interstate Circuit, Inc., v. United States, 306 U. S. 208, I do not see how that itself would justify an inference that concerted action at the "vertical" level existed between Parke Davis and the retailers or wholesalers.

The second difficulty with the Court's analysis is that even reviewing the District Court's findings only as a matter of law, as the Court purports to do, the cases do not justify overturning the lower court's resulting conclusions. Beech-Nut did not say that refusals to sell to wholesalers who persisted in selling to cut-price retailers— conduct which was present in that case (257 U. S., at 448)—was a per se infraction of the Colgate rule, but only that it was offensive if it was the result of cooperative group action. While the Court in Beech-Nut and Bausch & Lomb inferred from the aggressive, widespread, highly organized, and successful merchandising programs involved there that such concerted action existed in those cases, the defensive, limited, unorganized, and unsuccessful effort of Parke Davis to maintain its resale price policy[4] does not justify our disregarding the District Court's finding to the contrary in this case.[5]

In light of the whole history of the Colgate doctrine, it is surely this Court, and not the District Court, that has proceeded on erroneous premises in deciding this case. Unless there is to be attributed to the Court a purpose to overturn the findings of fact of the District Court—something which its opinion not only expressly disclaims doing, but which would also be in plain defiance of the Federal Rules of Civil Procedure, Rule 52 (a), and principles announced in past cases (see, e. g., United States v. Yellow Cab Co., 338 U. S. 338, 341-342; International Boxing Club of New York, Inc., v. United States, 358 U. S. 242, 252)—I think that what the Court has really done here is to throw the Colgate doctrine into discard.

To be sure, the Government has explicitly stated that it does not ask us to overrule Colgate, and the Court professes not to do so. But contrary to the long understanding of bench and bar, the Court treats Colgate as turning not on the absence of the concerted action explicitly required by §§ 1 and 3 of the Sherman Act, but upon the Court's notion of "countervailing" social policies. I can regard the Court's profession as no more than a bow to the fact that Colgate, decided more than 40 years ago, has become part of the economic regime of the country upon which the commercial community and the lawyers who advise it have justifiably relied.

If the principle for which Colgate stands is to be reversed, it is, as the Government's position plainly indicates, something that should be left to the Congress. It is surely the emptiest of formalisms to profess respect for Colgate and eviscerate it in application.

I would affirm.

Notes

[1] These are the "restraint of trade," not the "monopoly," provisions of the Sherman Act. See Note 1 of the Court's opinion.

[2] Those "authorized by law to fill or dispense prescriptions."

[3] Rule 52 (a), Fed. Rules Civ. Proc. provides in relevant part: "Findings of fact shall not be set aside unless clearly erroneous, and due regard shall be given to the

opportunity of the trial court to judge of the credibility of the witnesses."

[4] The District Court found, among other things, that the efforts of Parke Davis in the District of Columbia and Virginia came about only after some of its competitors had engaged in damaging local "deep price cutting" on Parke Davis products (Fdg. 12); that Parke Davis' sales in those areas constituted less than 5% of the total pharmaceutical sales therein (Fdg. 3); that these efforts followed the legal advice previously given by the Company's counsel (Fdg. 12); that Parke Davis did not have "any regularized or systematic machinery for maintaining its suggested minimum prices as to either retailers or wholesalers" (Fdg. 10); that the entire episode lasted only from July to the fall of 1956, when the Company "in good faith" abandoned all further such efforts (Fdgs. 12, 27); and that since that time retailers in these areas "have continuously sold and advertised Parke, Davis products at cut prices, and have been able to obtain those products from both the wholesalers and/or Parke, Davis itself." (Fdg. 27.)

[5] It may be observed that the facts found by the District Court militate more strongly against violation of the Sherman Act than those which formed the basis of the charge held erroneous by this Court in Cudahy, 256 U. S., at 210-211. Although the Court now repudiates what was said in Cudahy in this respect, I submit that there is nothing in Beech-Nut, Bausch & Lomb, or any other case in this Court which justifies this.

Justice Harlan's dissent in FTC v. Travelers Health Assn. (March 28, 1960)

MR. JUSTICE HARLAN, whom MR. JUSTICE FRANKFURTER and MR. JUSTICE WHITTAKER join, dissenting.

This case marks the second time within a year that the Court has made inroads upon the policy of the McCarran-Ferguson Act by which Congress pervasively restored to the States the regulation of the business of insurance, a function which until this Court's decision in United States v. South-Eastern Underwriters Association, 322 U. S. 533, traditionally had been considered to be exclusively theirs. Last Term the Court held variable annuity policies, sold across state lines, subject to regulation by the Securities and Exchange Commission. See Securities & Exchange Comm'n v. Variable Annuity Co., 359 U. S. 65, 93-101 (dissenting opinion). Today it holds that advertising materials mailed into other States by a health insurance company, already regulated under the laws of its own State with respect to the out-of-state transmission of such materials, are subject also to regulation by the Federal Trade Commission, at least to the extent that such advertising matter is unregulated by the laws of the State into which it is sent.

The Court's holding is based upon its conclusion "that when Congress provided [in § 2 (b) of the McCarran-Ferguson Act] that the Federal Trade Commission Act would be displaced to the extent that the insurance business was `regulated' by state law, it referred only to regulation by the State where the business activities have their operative force." I think the data on which the Court relies is much too meagre to justify this conclusion, and believe, as the Court of Appeals did, that Nebraska's regulation of these activities of the respondent foreclosed Federal Trade Commission jurisdiction.

What is referred to in the majority opinion as "specific legislative history" on the issue before us seems to me to fall far short of being persuasive towards the Court's view of the statute. The report on the original House bill, on which so much store is placed, was directed, as I read it, not to differentiating between the kinds of state insurance regulation which would, after the moratorium period provided in the statute had ended,[1] exempt from federal regulation and control the business of insurance in all but limited aspects,[2] but to the general proposition that the new statute would not enlarge or narrow state regulatory power as it had existed before this Court's decision in the South-Eastern Underwriters case, supra. That no more than this can be got out of the report on the original House bill is made manifest by Senator McCarran's explanation of the conference bill when he presented it to the Senate—an episode to which the Court refers. Quoting from the report, the Senator said: "That expression [meaning the report] should be made a part of this explanation. In other words, we give to the States no more powers than those they previously had, and we take none from them."[3] 91 Cong. Rec. 1442.

I believe that the fragments from the ensuing Senate debate, on which the Court further relies, indicate no more than does the report.[4] The same is true, in my opinion, of expressions made during the debate relating to the desirability of leaving insurance regulation to local authorities because they were, so to speak, on the ground, expressions which, the Court correctly observes, reflected "a basic motivating policy behind the legislative movement that culminated in the enactment of the McCarran-Ferguson Act." And since the Court very gingerly throws out possible constitutional questions, I think it appropriate to say that the right of Nebraska to police its own insurance company domiciliaries, with respect to their advertising sent from Nebraska into other States, is not seriously open to constitutional doubt. See Hammond Packing Co. v. Arkansas, 212 U. S. 322; Sligh v. Kirkwood, 237 U. S. 52. There is certainly nothing in Alaska Packers Assn. v. Commission, 294 U. S. 532, which points to the contrary.

The temptation is strong, no doubt, to ask the Court to innovate with respect to the McCarran-Ferguson Act when state regulation may be thought to have fallen short. Two years ago we declined to do so when invited by the Federal Trade Commission in the National Casualty case, supra, at 564-565. I think it unwise for us now to yield to this encore on the part of the Commission. One innovation with the Act is apt to lead to another, and may ultimately result in a hybrid scheme of insurance regulation, bringing about uncertainties and possible duplications which should be avoided.

"Obviously Congress' purpose was broadly to give support to the existing and future state systems for regulating and taxing the business of insurance. This was done in two ways. One was by removing obstructions which might be thought to flow from its own power, whether dormant or exercised, except as otherwise expressly provided in the Act itself or in future legislation. The other was by declaring expressly and affirmatively that continued state regulation and taxation of this business is in the public interest and that the business and all who engage in it `shall be subject to' the laws of the several states in these respects.

"Moreover, in taking this action Congress must have had full knowledge of the nation-wide existence of state systems of regulation and taxation; of the fact that they differ greatly in the scope and character of the regulations imposed and of the taxes exacted; and of the further fact that many, if not all, include features which, to some extent, have not been applied generally to other interstate business. Congress could not have been unacquainted with these facts and its purpose was evidently to throw the whole weight of its power behind the state systems, notwithstanding these variations." Prudential Ins. Co. v. Benjamin, 328 U. S. 408, 429-430.

See also Wilburn Boat Co. v. Fireman's Ins. Co., 348 U. S. 310, 318-321; Securities & Exchange Comm'n v. Variable Annuity Co., supra, at 68-69, and dissenting opinion at 93 et seq.

If innovations in the policy of the McCarran-Ferguson Act are thought desirable, they should be made by Congress, not by us.

I would affirm.

Notes

[1] In addition to § 2 (b) set forth in note 1 of the Court's opinion, ante, p. 295, § 3 (a) of the Act provides: "Until June 30, 1948, the Act of July 2, 1890, as amended, known as the Sherman Act, and the Act of October 15, 1914, as amended, known as the Clayton Act, and the Act of September 26, 1914, known as the Federal Trade Commission Act, as amended, and the Act of June 19, 1936, known as the Robinson-Patman Antidiscrimination Act, shall not apply to the business of insurance or to acts in the conduct thereof."

[2] Section 3 (b) of the Act provides: "Nothing contained in this Act shall render the said Sherman Act inapplicable to any agreement to boycott, coerce, or intimidate, or act of boycott, coercion, or intimidation."

[3] Senator McCarran's reading of the report on the original House bill stopped short of the last clause (following the citation of cases) quoted in the Court's opinion. Ante, p. 301.

[4] It is worth observing that one of the hypothetical questions put to Senator Ferguson by Senator Pepper of Florida, an opponent of the bill, related to whether the bill would permit Florida, in disregard of the federal antitrust laws, to authorize the sale in Florida of insurance at rates fixed by an out-of-state insurance rating bureau, and that Senator Ferguson replied in the affirmative. 91 Cong. Rec. 1481. Yet the Court now finds it offensive to the concept of the statute to consider that other States may be content to rely on Nebraska's regulation of advertising material mailed to their citizens by Nebraska insurance companies. The Court reserves "for what they are worth" the questions that would arise were such other States to legislate against the out-of-state mailing of insurance advertising into their jurisdictions. Yet even if such legislation proved abortive as a practical matter, because of a foreign insurance company having no office, agents, or

assets within the State so legislating, such legislation would nonetheless presumably exclude Federal Trade Commission jurisdiction, unless we were to depart from our holding in Federal Trade Comm'n v. National Casualty Co., 357 U. S. 560, to the effect that it is the existence of state regulatory legislation, and not the effectiveness of such regulation, that is the controlling factor. The distinction between such a case as that, and the one before us, seems to me to be one without a difference.

Justice Harlan's dissent in Miller Music v. Charles N. Daniels (April 18, 1960)

MR. JUSTICE HARLAN, whom MR. JUSTICE FRANKFURTER, MR. JUSTICE WHITTAKER, and MR. JUSTICE STEWART join, dissenting.

I cannot agree to this decision, by which the assignee of an author's renewal rights in a copyrighted work is deprived of the fruits of his purchase—a purchase which, we must assume, was made in good faith and for a consideration fairly agreed upon.[1] While, for all that appears, the author in this case may not have contemplated the defeat of his assignment, the effect of the decision is to enable an author who has sold his renewal rights during his lifetime to defeat the transaction by a deliberate subsequent bequest of those rights to others in his will.

An assignee of renewal rights inter vivos cannot of course protect himself from such an unjust result by obtaining an assignment from the author's executor, who acquires his status as such only upon the author's death. Nor can he with any assurance of success seek to secure assignments from everyone who might be expected to be the fortunate legatee. In consequence, the efficacy of a good-faith attempt to accomplish a lasting conveyance of renewal rights may hereafter depend on whether a particular transaction, under the law of whichever State may ultimately govern the matter, will be deemed a contract to make a will and given effect as such. The resulting uncertainties as to construction, validity, and mode of enforcement of such transactions under the laws of the various States need hardly be spelled out. A result so unjust and unsettling, and which indeed may impair the marketability of an author's renewal rights, should be reached only if clear statutory language or evident legislative purpose fairly compels it. Far from resting on such considerations, this decision is supported only by a parlaying of an ill-considered "concession" of counsel with an exaltation of literal "symmetry and logic" (ante, p. 378) over what it seems to me a more penetrating inquiry into congressional aims would have revealed.

For convenience I quote the Copyright Act, 17 U. S. C. § 24, again:

"That . . . the author of such work, if still living, or the widow, widower, or children of the author, if the author be not living, or if such author, widow, widower, or children be not living, then the author's executors, or in the absence of a will, his next of kin shall be entitled to a renewal and extension of the copyright in such work for a further term of twenty-eight years when application for such renewal and extension shall have been made to the copyright office and duly registered therein within one year prior to the expiration of the original term of copyright."

On its face, the section manifests no intention to deal with the problem of priority of rights as between an assignee and the persons named in the section. The discussion in the House Report quoted by the Court, ante, p. 377, likewise shows no advertence to the question, and we are referred to no other significant legislative history on this score. Hence, we must resolve the matter in light of the purpose disclosed by the structure of the provision.

On this basis we do not write upon a clean slate. In Fisher Co. v. Witmark & Sons, 318 U. S. 643, it was argued that the renewal provisions of the statute demonstrated a congressional determination "to treat the author as though he were the beneficiary of a spendthrift trust." Brief for petitioners, No. 327, O. T. 1942, p. 36. The Court, finding no support in the evolutionary history of the legislation and its structure, rejected that view, and held that an author could, during the original term of his copyright, validly assign his right to apply for the renewal, and that having done so he could not, upon the arrival of the renewal year, himself claim that right. The Court seems to regard that case as entirely inapplicable in a situation where, as here, the author has not survived the beginning of the renewal year. But had the statute conferred renewal rights on "the author, if still living, or if the author be not living, on his executors or administrators," I have little doubt that the Fisher decision would control this case and require its reversal. The important question, then, is to determine the extent to which Congress has seen fit to depart from the ordinary rules of succession. In reaching its conclusion, the Court has, I think, overlooked critical distinctions between the different clauses of the statute.

The evolution of § 24 was exhaustively described and analyzed in Fisher, and need not be recanvassed here. See also De Sylva v. Ballentine, 351 U. S. 570, 574-576.

Briefly, the clause regarding widows, widowers, and children originated with the 1831 Act, 4 Stat. 436, while that dealing with executors and next of kin was added in 1909, 35 Stat. 1081. The retention, at that latter date, of the provision for widows, widowers, and children, and its position in the amended statute, can only be taken as expressive of a desire to regard them, in the words of the Court, as a "preferred class," and to ensure that the author could not by bequest confer on another the benefits of the renewal term. Cf. De Sylva v. Ballentine, supra, at 582. For it would indeed be anomalous to say that an author could convey for a consideration during his lifetime what he is not permitted to bequeath at death. Hence I agree that the provision for a "compulsory bequest," ibid., to the author's widow and children should be held to bar effective assignment of renewal rights as against them.

But I cannot perceive the applicability of this reasoning to the executor. There is simply no warrant for regarding him as in any way one of a "preferred class." The executor himself manifestly could not have been the object of such congressional solicitude, since he takes nothing beneficially, but only as a fiduciary for those benefited by the will. As to the latter, a legatee can be any person, corporation, or association capable of taking property by bequest. Surely we cannot infer legislative concern over the protection of the interest of whosoever, of the large indeterminate class of potential legatees, should prove in fact to be chosen by the author. The evident purpose of the clause regarding executors was merely "to permit the author who had no wife or children to bequeath by will the right to apply for the renewal." H. R. Rep. No. 2222, 60th Cong., 2d Sess., p. 15. The Court gave full effect to that purpose in Fox Film Corp. v. Knowles, 261 U. S. 326, when it held that an executor acquired the right to apply for renewal, even though the author's death occurred prior to the renewal year, when the author himself first could have renewed his copyright. It goes beyond that purpose, and beyond anything at issue in Fox Film, to read into the statute a desire to protect legatees from the claims of an assignee of the author.

The Court's treatment of the rights of an author's next of kin is especially curious. With no more authority than what appears to me to have been a demonstrably unnecessary "concession" of counsel,[2] the Court regards it as "clear" that the next of kin take over an assignee. From this dubious premise, the Court reasons that the executor, being thus surrounded in the "hierarchy of people granted renewal rights" by persons whose rights are superior to those of an assignee, must be "placed in the same preferred position." This reasoning, I submit, ignores the legislative purpose evidenced by the statute. There is no basis whatever for supposing that next of kin were sought to be protected from loss of rights arising out of the author's acts, in the sense that widows and children were. For the obvious fact is that under the statute next of kin, though related— albeit often distantly[3]—to the author, may be deprived of any interest in the renewal rights by a bequest of those rights by the author to another—even to one who is a total stranger.

It is thus apparent that Congress had no intention of protecting next of kin from defeasance of their expectancy.

Its purpose was more limited. Having determined that, despite an author's death without a surviving spouse or child prior to the renewal year, his work should not pass into the public domain, Congress sought to ensure that the failure of the author to leave a will would not bring this result about. The decision to give the renewal rights directly to the next of kin, rather than to an administrator, may well have been due to a desire to save authors' estates—which not infrequently might contain no other asset of substance—the expense of going through administration. Be that as it may, it seems to me abundantly clear that the result now reached by the Court was never intended.

To construe the statute as I have is not to "refashion" it, but only to appraise the competing claims of the author's assignee and those named in § 24 in light of the policy indicated by the manner in which the various interests involved are dealt with by the statute. The "symmetry and logic" of the provision is a dynamic, not a static or syntactical, symmetry and logic. Consistently with Fisher, the assignment is given effect as against those whose claims must rest on the voluntary decision of the author to benefit them; as to the surviving spouse and children, however, the legislative care taken to make their rights independent of the author's desires leads to a contrary result. It is only to that extent that Congress has departed from the ordinary rules of succession, in accord, it may be noted, with modern legislative trends precluding disinheritance of widows and children. We should not, by failing to heed the limits of that departure, foster an unjust and disruptive result. By undermining the sales value of renewal rights at the expense of the author and his immediate family this decision impinges on the very interests which the Copyright Act was designed to protect.

I would reverse.

Notes

[1] Today even less than when Fisher Co. v. Witmark & Sons, 318 U. S. 643, was decided, "can we be unmindful of the fact that authors have themselves devised means of safeguarding their interests." Id., at 657. More particularly there is no suggestion in this case that the sale of these renewal rights was in any way improvident.

[2] It is not difficult to understand why a publisher would be content with a rule preferring the next of kin—who can ordinarily be determined with reasonable accuracy during the assignor's lifetime, and from whom an assignment can often be purchased, as indeed was done in this instance—and at the same time regard application of a similar principle to the executor as unworkable. Yet it need hardly be said that such practical considerations do not relieve this Court of the duty of construing the statute for itself.

[3] Our reference in the De Sylva case, supra, at 582, to the "family" of the author was of course to the immediate family, the spouse and children, and not to all those related, however remotely, to the author.

Justice Harlan's dissent in Mitchell v. Trawler Racer, Inc. (May 16, 1960)

MR. JUSTICE HARLAN, whom MR. JUSTICE FRANKFURTER and MR. JUSTICE WHITTAKER join, dissenting.

In joining my Brother FRANKFURTER'S dissent, I wish to add a few words. I believe the Court's decision not only finds no support in the past cases, but also is unjustified in principle, and is directed at ends not appropriately within our domain. The Second Circuit's decision in Poignant v. United States, 225 F. 2d 595, provides a useful point of departure for what I have to say.

In Poignant the libellant, a crew member, slipped on a small piece of garbage lying in a passageway of the ship. The vessel lacked garbage chutes, and the garbage was pulled, in cans, through the passageway to a railing, where it was jettisoned. The Court of Appeals first expressed the view that any unseaworthy condition which existed had in all probability arisen after the voyage had commenced. It said, much as the Court now holds, that Alaska Steamship Co. v. Petterson, 347 U. S. 396, required it to apply a rule of absolute liability nonetheless. It then put, as the critical issue, the question whether the presence of some garbage in a public passageway constituted an unseaworthy condition, and, finding the matter to turn on an issue of fact, remanded the case for trial. However, it is important to note the manner in which the court dealt with the problem. Although at the outset of the opinion the allegedly unseaworthy condition was assumed to be the presence of garbage in a passageway, 225 F. 2d, at 597, the remand was in fact directed to the question whether the absence of garbage chutes rendered the vessel not reasonably fit for the voyage, and therefore unseaworthy. Id., at 598. This, of course, would be a condition going to the proper outfitting of the vessel for sea travel, and a clear case of initial unseaworthiness. In such event, the injury would have been the proximate result of that unseaworthiness, for it was by reason of the lack of chutes that garbage was carried through the passageways at all.

For me this approach indicates the rule which should govern the case before us. Had the petitioner contended and proved that a properly outfitted trawler of this type should have had a particular device for unloading fish, or an alternative means of facilitating petitioner's egress from the vessel, so that either the railing would not have been slippery or the petitioner would not have been required to use the railing in debarking, the case would have been governed by the absolute liability rule of Sandanger and its successors, and respondent's opportunity to remove the spawn from the rail would properly be held immaterial. As the case is decided, however, we are told that even though there is no claim that the vessel should have made different provisions for the unloading of its catch or the debarking of its crew, the shipowner is liable for an injury caused by a temporary unsafe condition arising from the normal operation of the vessel, not the result of fault or mismanagement of anyone on board, and which no one had a reasonable opportunity to remedy. Had there been negligence, either in permitting the spawn to accumulate or in failing to remove it, the admiralty principles developed in the cargo cases, and taken over into personal injury cases, would warrant an imposition of liability, although as to cargo damage the Harter Act and the Carriage of Goods by Sea Act would, of course, bar recovery. The Silvia, 171 U. S. 462. But where, as here, there is neither a claim that the vessel was initially unseaworthy, nor any showing of negligence, the imposition of liability seems to me, borrowing from Judge Magruder, a "hard doctrine," "startlingly opposed to principle." 265 F. 2d, at 432.

The Court is not fashioning a rule designed to protect life, cf. Bullard v. Roger Williams Ins. Co., 4 Fed. Cas. 643, No. 2,122, at 646, for there appears no real basis for expectation that today's decision will promote the taking of greater precautions at sea. See, dissenting opinion of FRANKFURTER, J., ante, p. 557. The respondent is held liable, without being told that there was something left undone which should have been done, for petitioner is not asked to show, as was the libellant in Poignant, that the vessel ought to have been outfitted differently, that is, in a fashion which would have prevented the dangerous condition from arising at all. Nor is the respondent permitted to show that such condition was not due to its fault.

The sole interest served by the Court's decision is compensation. Such an interest is, of course, equally present in the case of an undoubted accident, where under the Court's ruling no right of recovery is bestowed, as it is in the present case. But, because of the Court's inherent incapacity to deal with the problem in the comprehensive and integrated manner which would doubtless characterize its legislative treatment, cf. Dixon v. United States, 219 F. 2d 10, 15, this arbitrary limitation is preserved. This internal contradiction in the rule which the Court has established only serves to highlight a more central point: it is not for a court, even a court of admiralty, to fashion a tort rule solely in response to considerations which underlie workmen's compensation legislation, weighty as such considerations doubtless are as a legislative matter. Citation is not needed to remind one of the readiness of Congress to deal with felt deficiencies in judicial protection of the interests of those who go to sea. We should heed the limitations on our own capacity and authority. See Halcyon Lines v. Haenn Ship Corp., 342 U. S. 282, 285-287.

I would affirm.

Justice Harlan's dissent in US v. Florida (May 31, 1960)

MR. JUSTICE HARLAN, dissenting.

It is with regret that I find myself unable to agree that Florida has made a case for "three-league" rights under the Submerged Lands Act. As shown in the Court's opinion relating to the other States involved in the litigation (ante, pp. 16-36), a state seaward boundary satisfying the requirements of the Submerged Lands Act must be one which by virtue of Congressional action would have been legally effective to carry, as between State and Nation, submerged land rights under the Pollard rule, as Congress conceived that rule to have been prior to this Court's decision in the California case, 332 U. S. 19. That test supplies the meaning and content not only of the phrase "boundaries . . . as they existed at the time such State became a member of the Union," but also of the phrase "boundaries . . . as heretofore approved by Congress," contained in § 2 of the Submerged Lands Act (ante, p. 9, note 7). Florida must satisfy that test if it is to prevail in this case.

The Court's Florida opinion conceives the issue to be whether Congress in 1868 made a "general scrutiny of all the provisions of" Florida's Constitution, and states that the Submerged Lands Act requires only that it have been "examined and approved as a whole." The concurring opinion asserts that the relevant inquiry is "whether congressional approval of the new Florida Constitution . . . amounted to an approval of the three-league boundary which that constitution explicitly set forth." In my view, neither formulation adequately characterizes the nature of the question left by the Submerged Lands Act to this Court. It may be conceded that Congress scrutinized all the provisions of Florida's Constitution and that by accepting the Constitution it, in an abstract sense, approved the boundary provision. The further and controlling inquiry that must be made is whether the legal effect of such action was to establish a valid three-league boundary for Florida. If not, Florida would not have owned the submerged lands to that distance under Congress' concept of the Pollard rule, and it would therefore be entitled to no better rights under the Submerged Lands Act. On neither branch of its claims do I believe that Florida's showing measures up to that standard.

I.

My difficulty with Florida's "readmission" claim begins with the proposition that a State relying on a readmission boundary stands on quite a different legal footing than one relying on an original admission boundary. In the latter instance the fixing of a boundary is a necessary incident of Congress' power to admit new States. A newly admitted State, in the absence of an express fixation of its boundary by the Congressional act of admission or an articulated rejection of its preadmission boundary, may, I think, rely on a presumed Congressional purpose to adopt whatever boundary the political entity had immediately prior to its admission as a State.[1] That would seem to be the effect of New Mexico v. Colorado, 267 U. S. 30, and New Mexico v. Texas, 275 U. S. 279, 276 U. S. 557.[2]

Different considerations, however, obtain in the case of a State readmitted to "representation in Congress" after the Civil War. Such a State renounced the Union with boundaries already fixed by Congress at the time of original admission. When it was restored to full participation in the Union, there is no reason to suppose its territorial limits would not remain the same. So much indeed finds sound support in the constitutional doctrines evolved in the so-called reconstruction cases, even though they related to different problems arising out of the Civil War. See Texas v. White, 7 Wall. 700, 726; White v. Hart, 13 Wall. 646, 649-652; Gunn v. Barry, 15 Wall. 610, 623; Keith v. Clark, 97 U. S. 454, 461. Since, as will be shown later (post, pp. 140-141), Florida renounced the Union with a seaward boundary no greater than three miles, the issue here is whether upon readmission Congress changed that boundary to three leagues. Unlike the situation at original admission, where the necessity of fixing some boundary for a newly admitted State leads readily to the presumption of Congressional approval of a tendered preadmission boundary, no similar presumption arises in connection with an alleged change in a state boundary already fixed by Congress.

After a painstaking examination of the legislative materials I can find no evidence whatever that the Congress intended to change Florida's seaward boundary from one not in excess of three miles to one of three leagues when the State was readmitted to representation in 1868. Certainly the Act of readmission (Act of June 25, 1868, 15 Stat. 73), upon which Florida relies, affords no basis for a claim that Congress expressly approved the State's three-league boundary provision.[3] The statute refers in no way to boundaries; it does not even undertake to approve Florida's Constitution, let alone the boundaries described therein; and it is entitled merely as "An Act to admit . . . Florida, to Representation in Congress," not as an act to admit it to the Union. Cf. White v. Hart, supra, at 652.[4]

Nor can I find any basis in the legislative record for a conclusion that Congress impliedly changed Florida's boundary. The Congressional debates and reports may be searched in vain for a single reference—even a casual one—to the boundaries of any of the readmitted States. The preamble of the Act of June 25, 1868, and the Congressional debates affirmatively show that all with which Congress was concerned was whether the constitutions of the readmitted States had been validly adopted and were republican in structure, and, in a few instances, whether they contained provisions in palpable violation of the Federal Constitution.[5] No territorial questions at all appear to have figured in the debates. In these circumstances the case of Virginia v. Tennessee, 148 U. S. 503, upon which Florida relies in support of its argument as to implied approval, is quite inapposite. There the two States had made a compact with respect to the boundary between them. Subsequently Congress adopted the line so established in setting up districts for judicial, revenue, election, and appointive purposes. It was held that Congress had thereby impliedly approved the interstate compact. Id., 521-522. In the present instance we have no affirmative action by Congress respecting the 1868 proffered Florida boundary in any way comparable to that in this earlier case.

Nor can a purpose to change Florida's boundary be inferred from the bare context of the Congressional action. The constitutional area in which the Congress was moving in 1868 should not be forgotten. Congress was not undertaking to exercise its power to fix state boundaries incident to the admission of new States. Rather, it was engaged in "re-establishing the broken relations of the State[s] with the Union," and in satisfying itself that the constitutions of the States lately in rebellion had been validly adopted and were republican in form, all pursuant to Congress' constitutional obligation to guarantee to each State a republican form of government. See Texas v. White, supra, 727-728. This is not to say that Congress could not at the same time have changed any State's original admission boundary, but only to raise the question whether it in fact did so. While the exercise of a particular constitutional power does not of course preclude resort to others, the nature of the power exerted in 1868 does seem to me to negative the idea that Congress also purported to exercise its power to change Florida's boundary.[6]

In the last analysis I think that Florida's claim here could only be sustained on the view that Congress was under a duty to speak with reference to the State's boundary provision, failing which Congress' silence should as a matter of law be deemed the equivalent of acceptance of the provision. In light of factors already adverted to I cannot perceive how such a duty could be found to exist. To uphold Florida's claim on any such theory would be novel doctrine indeed, particularly where property rights of the United States are involved. Cf. United States v. California, supra, at 39-40. Moreover, to say that such a duty existed seems to me to misconceive the nature of the "approval" of the constitutions of the seceded States contemplated by the reconstruction statutes. Such approval was not of the sort involved in the case of a constitution submitted to a constitutional convention for adoption or ratification, where the failure to reject a particular provision would be equivalent to its acceptance. Instead, the whole tenor of the reconstruction debates clearly shows that all that was meant by "approval" was that before any seceded State was restored to representation, Congress must be satisfied that its constitution had been properly adopted and was republican in its general structure. That kind of a requirement of "approval" does not lend itself to the conclusion that this Court would be attributing to the 1868 Congress a "deceptive subtlety" unless it regards silence upon Florida's boundary provision as tantamount to its acceptance. Especially so, when that provision was quite outside the realm of matters upon which Congress had been called upon to act. "Great acts of State" these events of the reconstruction period were indeed, but I do not think they can now be taken as having encompassed acceptance of the territorial pretensions of any particular State.

In sum, I believe the conclusion inescapable that all that Congress can properly be taken to have done in readmitting Florida was to declare that nothing in the State's new constitution disqualified its Senators and Representatives from taking their seats in Congress. While such action may in some abstract sense have constituted "approval" of Florida's boundary provision, since it was included in its constitution, in my opinion it did not represent the sort of advertent, affirmative Congressional action which legally would have been necessary to effectuate an actual change in Florida's original admission boundary. It therefore did not "approve" Florida's three-league boundary within the only sense contemplated by the Submerged Lands Act.

II.

It is clear that the State fares no better on its alternative claim, based upon its original admission boundary. Since the Court does not reach this claim, it will be enough to state briefly the reasons which require its rejection.

The territory which now comprises the State of Florida was originally acquired by England from France and Spain by the Treaty of Paris of February 10, 1763.[7] By the proclamation of October 7, 1763,[8] King George III divided the acquired territory into East and West Florida. East Florida was declared to be "bounded to the westward by the Gulf of Mexico and the Apalachicola river . . . and to the east and south by the Atlantic ocean and the gulf of Florida, including all islands within six leagues of the sea coast." West Florida was declared to be "bounded to the southward by the gulf of Mexico, including all islands within six leagues of the coast, from the river Apalachicola to Lake Pontchartrain . . . ."

By the Treaty of Versailles of September 3, 1783, England ceded to Spain the territory described merely as "East Florida, as also West Florida."[9] By the Treaty of Amity, Settlement, and Limits of February 22, 1819, Spain ceded to the United States "all the territories which belong to [Spain], situated to the eastward of the Mississippi, known by the name of East and West Florida."[10] Both the Act establishing Florida as a Territory,[11] and the Act admitting it to the Union,[12] describe it in terms of the territories of East and West Florida ceded by the Treaty of 1819.

Florida contends that the provision in King George's proclamation relating to all islands within six leagues of the coast was an assertion of a territorial boundary at that distance along the entire coast, and that subsequent conveyances necessarily incorporated that description. The opinion of the Court relating to Louisiana, Mississippi, and Alabama disposes of that contention (ante, pp. 66-82), and what has been said there need not be repeated here.

Florida also relies on many of the same treaties as does Louisiana to show that this country's predecessors in title claimed large amounts of territorial sea. Without elaborating on what has already been said (ante, pp. 73-74), it is sufficient to point out here that these treaties did not constitute territorial assertions, but merely established obligations between the parties of a special and limited nature, and varied so widely in the distances specified as not to be of any value whatever in showing a uniform practice.

I would grant the Government's motion for judgment as to Florida.

Notes

[1] More is required of Texas in this case because of the manner in which the Joint Resolution admitting Texas to the Union was drawn. See the Court's opinion relating to the other States, ante, pp. 44-47.

[2] In both cases, the description of the boundary fixed for the State by the event of admission was agreed upon—the 37th parallel in the Texas case, and the middle of the channel of the Rio Grande in the Colorado case. The actual physical location of those respective boundaries, however, was in dispute. In the former, the Court held that the location of the boundary was fixed by the event of admission in accordance with a survey of the 37th parallel which had been theretofore made, even though it might not have been a correct survey. In the latter case, it held that since the location of the Rio Grande's channel in 1850 had been continuously accepted as the location of New Mexico's boundary prior to statehood, and had been so specified in its constitution when admitted to the Union, that became the location of the State's boundary.

[3] In pertinent part the Act reads:

"WHEREAS the people of North Carolina, South Carolina, Louisiana, Georgia, Alabama, and Florida have, in pursuance of the provisions of an act entitled `An act for the more efficient government of the rebel States,' passed March second, eighteen hundred and sixtyseven, and the acts supplementary thereto [see note 4, post], framed constitutions of State government which are republican, and have adopted said constitutions by large majorities of the votes cast at the elections held for the ratification or rejection of the same: Therefore,

"Be it enacted by the Senate and House of Representatives of the United States of America in Congress assembled, That each of the States of North Carolina, South Carolina, Louisiana, Georgia, Alabama, and Florida, shall be entitled and admitted to representation in Congress as a State of the Union when the legislature of such State shall have duly ratified the amendment to the Constitution of the United States proposed by the Thirty-ninth Congress, and known as article fourteen, upon the following fundamental conditions: That the constitutions of neither of said States shall ever be so amended or changed as to deprive any citizen or class of citizens of the United States of the right to vote in said State, who are entitled to vote by the constitution thereof herein recognized, except as a punishment for such crimes as are now felonies at common law, whereof they shall have been duly convicted under laws equally applicable to all the inhabitants of said State: Provided, That any alteration of said constitution may be made with regard to the time and place of residence of voters; and the State of Georgia shall only be entitled and admitted to representation upon this further fundamental condition: that the first and third subdivisions of section seventeen of the fifth article of the constitution of said State, except the proviso to the first subdivision, shall be null and void, and that the general assembly of said State by solemn public act shall declare the assent of the State to the foregoing fundamental condition."

[4] Reliance is placed on the Act of March 2, 1867, 14 Stat. 428, providing for a State's readmission when, among other things, its "constitution shall have been submitted to Congress for examination and approval, and Congress shall have approved the same . . . ." I find nothing in this provision, or in those of any of the other so-called reconstruction legislation, Act of March 23, 1867, 15 Stat. 2; Act of July 19, 1867, 15 Stat. 14; Act of March 11, 1868, 15 Stat. 41, which warrants the conclusion that the constitutions of the readmitted States were to be "approved" by Congress, except in the sense that Congress must be satisfied that they had been duly adopted and were republican in form.

[5] The following excerpts from the Congressional debates are typical of many others: "Now, sir, what is the particular question we are considering? Five or six States have had submitted to them the question of forming constitutions for their own government. They have voluntarily formed such constitutions, under the direction of the Government of the United States. They have sent those constitutions here . . . . We have looked at them; we have pronounced them republican in form; and all we propose to require is that they shall remain so forever. Subject to this requirement, we are willing to admit them into the Union." Representative Stevens of Pennsylvania, Cong. Globe, 40th Cong., 2d Sess. 2465.

"All previous fundamental conditions imposed upon a State being admitted into the Union have been upon one of two grounds, either that the clause in the State constitution objected to was in violation of the Constitution of the United States, or that it affected some great, material right, without which the government would not be republican in form. . . .

.....

"When we go beyond securing the enforcement of the guaranty of republican government, which we have the power to do, when we undertake to legislate for them upon matters on which they have passed, we transcend our bounds." Senator Sherman of Ohio, Cong. Globe, 40th Cong., 2d Sess. 2968, 2969.

[6] In passing the Submerged Lands Act, Congress seems to have assumed that it has always had the power so to change a State's boundary, provided the State consents. For purposes of this case, we need not stop to inquire as to the source of the assumed power. It is sufficient to say that, whatever may be the power of Congress to change boundaries as a general matter, Congress clearly has the power to change boundaries, with a State's consent, to the extent that such a change affects only the exercise of property rights as between State and Nation.

[7] 15 Parliamentary History of England 1291, 1296, 1301.

[8] 2 White, A New Collection of Laws, Charters and Local Ordinances of Great Britain, France and Spain (1839), 292.

[9] 39 Journal of the House of Commons 722, 723.

[10] 8 Stat. 252, 254. The Treaty also provided: "The adjacent islands dependent on said provinces, all public lots and squares, vacant lands, public edifices, fortifications, barracks, and other buildings, which are not private property, archives and documents, which relate directly to the property and sovereignty of said provinces, are included in this article."

[11] 3 Stat. 654.

[12] 5 Stat. 742.

Justice Harlan's dissent in Aquilino v. US (June 20, 1960)

MR. JUSTICE HARLAN, dissenting in Nos. 1 and 23.[*]

I am unable to subscribe to the reasoning which underlies the Court's disposition of these cases. By holding that they both turn on whether the taxpayer had "property" under state law to which the Government's lien could attach, the Court has sanctioned a result consistently prohibited by us in a line of cases dealing with the priority of federal tax liens.[1]

In both cases, the delinquent taxpayer is a defaulting general contractor whose subcontractors remain unpaid. The Government's lien is asserted against the chose in action which the general contractor allegedly holds against the owner of the real estate on which the improvements were made, in respect of amounts due from the owner under the construction contract. If the subcontractors had sought to enforce their claims by imposing a lien on that chose in action, there is no question that the Government's lien would prevail. Under the decisions of this Court cited in note 1, supra, a federal tax lien asserted against a taxpayer's property under §§ 3670 and 3671 of the Internal Revenue Code of 1939[2] prevails over all other claims against such property except (1) those which attach and become "choate" before the federal lien attaches, and (2) those specifically protected by § 3672 (a).[3] It is conceded that the interests of the subcontractors in the present cases are not protected by § 3672 (a) and would not be considered choate under the applicable decisions. See United States v. Kings County Iron Works, 224 F. 2d 232 (C. A. 2d Cir. 1955).

The Court believes, however, that the present cases are different, because under state law, the general contractor in Aquilino held his claim against the owner in trust for the subcontractors to the extent of their claims, and because the subcontractors in Durham Lumber were given, to the extent of their claims, a direct right of action against the owner in respect of his debt to the general contractor, and that in these circumstances the rights of the subcontractors in the owner's debt are superior to those of the general contractor. It is said that, to the extent of the subcontractors' claims, the general contractor, under state law, thus had no "property" interest in the amounts due him from the owner, and that under the principles enunciated in United States v. Bess, 357 U. S. 51, a federal tax lien can attach only to a property interest which exists under state law.

I cannot see how it makes any difference, for purposes of the federal tax-lien statute, whether state law purports to prefer subcontractors over the general contractor and parties claiming through him by giving the subcontractors a lien on the general contractor's right of action against the owner or by giving them a prior right to collect the debt itself. In both instances, the owner is under a contractual duty to pay the general contractor and the latter is under a contractual duty to pay the subcontractors. In both instances, the subcontractors are attempting to satisfy their claims against the general contractor. And in both instances, they are seeking to satisfy themselves by claiming precisely the same thing—a prior right in the proceeds of the debt which arises by virtue of the contractual relationship between the owner and the general contractor.[4] In neither instance can the subcontractors collect more than that to which the subcontract entitles them, and in neither can the owner be required to pay more than that to which the main contract obligates him. If federal law requires that subordination of the general contractor's interest be ignored in the one instance, it does so equally in the other.

The Bess case does not require a contrary conclusion. That case held only that while a federal tax lien attached to the cash surrender value of a life insurance policy owned by the taxpayer, it did not attach to the proceeds paid on his death, because under state law he had no right to such proceeds during his life. There was no reason under those circumstances why state property concepts should not control. To read that case as standing for the proposition that such concepts must also be controlling in cases such as these defeats the rule that "[t]he relative priority of the lien of the United States for unpaid taxes is . . . always a federal question to be determined finally by the federal courts." United States v. Acri, 348 U. S. 211, 213. It is one thing to say, as the Court did in Bess, that the federal interest in uniform application of federal tax liens does not require, as a general rule, that state property concepts be disregarded. It is quite another to permit such concepts to control the extent of a federal lien's application in situations indistinguishable from those where the Court has in fact, rightly or wrongly, enforced a uniform federal rule. Given federal supremacy in this field, it surely cannot be that the federal courts may not appraise for themselves the true impact of state-created rights upon the priority of federal tax liens within the criteria established by this Court. Cf. Carpenter v. Shaw, 280 U. S. 363, 367; City of Detroit v. Murray Corporation, 355 U. S. 489, 492. To recognize the substantial equivalence of the situations is not to create a new rule of federal property law but to require an evenhanded application of an already established one. It seems to me that Judge Fuld of the New York Court of Appeals was quite right in holding in the Aquilino case that New York could not, consistently with the past decisions of our Court, defeat the otherwise superior federal lien upon the owner's debt to the general contractor by converting the debt into a trust for the benefit of the subcontractor.[5]

To read Bess as the Court does can only lead to confusion in the administration of the federal tax-lien statute. A taxpayer's property in a debt is surely diminished by the imposition of a lien on his interest, for he has no right to collect the liened portion nor to alienate it. Yet in precisely this situation, we have held that the federal tax lien is not affected by such diminution. United States v. Liverpool & London Globe Ins. Co., 348 U. S. 215. If this holding is to be preserved after today's decision, subsequent cases must turn on the elusive distinction between diminishing a greater property interest and initially conferring a lesser one.[6] The very difficulty which this Court experiences in trying to determine whether under New York law the general contractor really holds only a bare legal title in trust for the subcontractors or has full ownership of the debt subject to a lien in favor of the subcontractors demonstrates the futility of attempting to draw such distinctions for federal purposes. I venture to suggest that on remand, the Court of Appeals can with equal facility label the subcontractors' interests "property" or a "lien," the relevant incidents of the relationship being the same in either case. Why should not that court and the legislatures of other States readily respond in choosing the former alternative?

I would affirm the judgment in No. 1, and would reverse in No. 23 on the ground that North Carolina can under no circumstances accord subcontractors a right in the proceeds of the debt arising from the construction contract superior to the Government's lien without satisfying one of the two requirements laid down by federal law. If the federal standard of choateness is thought to be an undesirable restriction on the States' freedom to regulate property relationships, the cases establishing that standard should be expressly overruled and not emasculated by dubious distinctions.

MR. JUSTICE BLACK, while adhering to the dissenting views expressed by him in Commissioner v. Stern, 357 U. S. 39, 47, and United States v. Bess, 357 U. S. 51, 59, concurs in this opinion.

Notes

[*] [No. 23 is United States v. Durham Lumber Co. et al., post, p. 522.]

[1] United States v. Security Trust & Savings Bank, 340 U. S. 47 (1950); United States v. City of New Britain, 347 U. S. 81 (1954); United States v. Acri, 348 U. S. 211 (1955); United States v. Liverpool & London Globe Ins. Co., Ltd., 348 U. S. 215 (1955); United States v. Scovil, 348 U. S. 218 (1955); United States v. Colotta, 350 U. S. 808 (1955); United States v. White Bear Brewing Co., 350 U. S. 1010 (1956); United States v. Vorreiter, 355 U. S. 15 (1957); United States v. Ball Construction Co., Inc., 355 U. S. 587 (1958); United States v. Hulley, 358 U. S. 66 (1958).

[2] The text of these sections, applicable in the Aquilino case, are set forth in note 1 of the Court's opinion in No. 1, ante, p. 511. The comparable provisions of the Internal Revenue Code of 1954, §§ 6321 and 6322, applicable in the Durham Lumber case, are printed in notes 1 and 2 of the Court's opinion in No. 23, post, p. 524.

[3] That section, as amended, provides: "Such lien shall not be valid as against any mortgagee, pledgee, purchaser, or judgment creditor until notice thereof has been filed by the collector . . . ." 53 Stat. 882. The comparable provision of the Internal Revenue Code of 1954 is § 6323 (a).

[4] It is noteworthy that the North Carolina law involved in the Durham Lumber

case requires the general contractor to furnish the owner with a statement of subcontractors' claims "before receiving any part of the contract price, as it may become due," and that it is thereafter the duty of the owner to retain an appropriate amount "from the money then due the contractor." N. C. Gen. Stat., 1950, § 44-8. (Emphasis added.) Although this section indicates that the general contractor has no right to collect the proceeds of the main contract until the statutory conditions are satisfied, it obviously recognizes the owner's contractual obligation as the real basis of the transaction and the source of the subcontractors' rights. The subcontractors' claims are thus not akin to liens on the owner's real estate, as this Court suggests, but are asserted solely in respect of the monetary claim held by the general contractor against the owner.

[5] "It is, by now, exceedingly well settled that no state-created rule may defeat the paramount right of the United States to levy and collect taxes uniformly throughout the land. (See United States v. Vorreiter, 355 U. S. 15, revg. 134 Col. 543; United States v. White Bear Brewing Co., 350 U. S. 1010, revg. 227 F. 2d 359; United States v. Colotta, supra, 350 U. S. 808, revg. 224 Miss. 33; United States v. Scovil, supra, 348 U. S. 218, 220-221; United States v. New Britain, supra, 347 U. S. 81, 84-87; United States v. Kings County Iron Works, supra, 224 F. 2d 232, 237). That being so, it follows that the provision in this state's Lien Law, to which respondents point—that funds received by a contractor from the owner for the improvement of real property shall be deemed `trust funds' for the payment of subcontractors (§ 36-a; § 13, subd. [7])—may not be construed to affect the rights of the government or the priority of its tax lien." 3 N. Y. 2d, at 516, 146 N. E. 2d, at 777-778.

[6] It will not do to distinguish the present type of case from the lien-priority cases on the ground that in the latter cases the taxpayer remains the owner in a very real sense and can continue to enjoy the property if he discharges the debt it secures. In both instances, the taxpayer is temporarily deprived of certain incidents of ownership as a device for securing the payment of a debt, and is restored to the full enjoyment of the property only when the debt is discharged. And it is illusory to say that ownership of a debt which can be neither collected nor alienated is any more "real" than the ownership of no debt at all. Whether the diminution of the taxpayer's interest is sufficiently definite and complete to conclude the federal lien is precisely the question on which this Court has held federal law must control. It is admitted that, if the federal standard of "choateness" developed by this Court in the lien-priority cases is applied, the incidents of ownership retained by the taxpayers here must in fact be deemed greater than those retained by taxpayers in cases where state-created liens imposed on their interests have prevailed over the Government's lien.

Justice Harlan's dissent in US v. American-Foreign SS (June 20, 1960)

MR. JUSTICE HARLAN, whom MR. JUSTICE FRANKFURTER and MR. JUSTICE BRENNAN join, dissenting.

I can find nothing in 28 U. S. C. § 46 (c) which requires the decision the Court has made, and nothing in the decision which commends itself to considerations of sound judicial administration. For convenience I again quote § 46 (c):

"Cases and controversies shall be heard and determined by a court or division of not more than three judges, unless a hearing or rehearing before the court in banc is ordered by a majority of the circuit judges of the circuit who are in active service. A court in banc shall consist of all active circuit judges of the circuit."

The statute need hardly be read, as the Court now holds it should be, as saying that a case in an en banc court shall be "heard and determined" by the active circuit judges; still less does it say that a case is not "determined" until the decision of it is announced. The statute says no more than that ordinarily lawsuits before the Courts of Appeals are to be "heard and determined" before a panel of not more than three judges, but that a majority of the judges in active service may order that a case be set for "hearing or rehearing" before a court consisting of all the active circuit judges of the circuit sitting en banc.

The "heard and determined" clause on which the Court relies appears in a sentence whose purposes were simply to codify the doctrine that a Court of Appeals had power to sit en banc, Textile Mills Corp. v. Commissioner, 314 U. S. 326, while making clear that the usual procedure was to be decision by a three-judge panel.[1] It is not an unknown phenomenon in federal adjudication that a case, though heard by less than the entire tribunal, may be decided according to the majority vote of all. Cf. I. R. C., § 7460; see 2 Casey, Federal Tax Practice, 274-280. The traditional term, "heard and determined," in my view was designed to do no more than reflect the obvious inappropriateness of such a procedure to the deliberations of the Court of Appeals. There is no necessity for finding in that term, in light of the context in which it appears, any Congressional direction regarding the constitution of an en banc court.

The requirements governing the composition of an en banc court are found in the last sentence of § 46 (c). All it provides is that such a court shall not include retired circuit judges. The reason for such a provision is not hard to discern. Congress would hardly have required a retired circuit judge to return to the bench to attend at an en banc hearing and, as between leaving the matter to the discretion of the individual judge and limiting the court to active judges, it is not surprising—in view of the varying degrees of judicial activity of the retired judges, and the administrative undesirability of having, for these purposes, a court of unpredictable size and complement— that Congress should have chosen the latter course.

The language and context, then, of § 46 (c) are given full effect by holding, as I would, that the statute requires no more than that the members of an en banc court be in active status at the time the case is argued or submitted. Such a construction, for a court which decided the Textile Mills case, supra, should not be difficult to reach. The issue there was whether the predecessor of § 46 (c), conferring appellate jurisdiction on circuit courts consisting of three judges, prevented adjudication by a circuit court composed of five judges, constituting all the active circuit judges of the particular circuit there involved. In holding that it did not, the Court, making a wise "sacrifice of literalness for common sense," 314 U. S., at 334, found no difficulty in rising above the arithmetic of the predecessor of § 46 (c) so as to achieve a sensible result. Still less should there be difficulty here in accommodating § 46 (c) to the needs of sound judicial administration. So construed, the statute was complied with here.[2]

But even were I to accept the Court's premises—a reading into the en banc procedure of a requirement that only active judges may participate in the "determination" of such cases, and a view of § 46 (c) as expressing a Congressional policy against participation by retired judges in decisions setting the "major doctrinal trends" of a court— I could not agree that they justify this decision. Choice of the date of announcement of a decision as the date of "determination" of the cause may provide a touchstone which a disappointed litigant searching for grounds for reversal can easily apply. However, it seems a singularly infelicitous construction of this particular legislative language.[3] "[L]aws are not abstract propositions. They are expressions of policy arising out of specific situations and addressed to the attainment of particular ends." Frankfurter, Some Reflections on the Reading of Statutes, 47 Col. L. Rev. 527, 533. The exact point of time when a case is "determined" is, as all informed lawyers know, a question whose answer varies from case to case, and which is known in a particular instance only to the judges themselves. Certainly, if an opinion—all argument, reflection, deliberation, and explication having been completed by a court composed of active judges only—is filed with the clerk of the court on the morning following the retirement of one of its members, no policy remotely discernible in § 46 (c) can justify a requirement that his vote in the case should not be counted. If any such policy can be thought to be reflected in the en banc statute, it should not be taken as requiring more than that a judge, whose retirement comes at a time when meaningful things in the process of adjudication still remain to be done, must withdraw from further participation. But where such is not the case, the statute should not be thought to require a precipitous termination of judicial affairs and the undoing of adjudications properly made. In the nature of things the effectuation of such a policy should be left with the various Courts of Appeals, if indeed not to the conscience and good taste of the particular circuit judge concerned, as in most instances of individual disqualification for other reasons. Cf. 28 U. S. C. § 455.

It is not a ground for objection that such a construction would provide no test which an outsider, whether litigant or reviewing court, could apply.[4] As this Court has observed: "In our view, § 46 (c) is not addressed to litigants. It is addressed to the Court of Appeals." Western Pacific Railroad Case, 345 U. S. 247, 250. On its view of the statute the Court should not have hesitated to adopt that construction of the "heard and determined" clause which most faithfully reflects its purpose merely because those with whom the statute is not concerned are thereby hampered in voicing their own objections.

Indeed, while I need express no definite view on the question, since I regard the claim of noncompliance with § 46 (c) as untenable, I must say that the Court's opinion presents no substantial reason for permitting a litigant to overturn a judgment of the Court of Appeals through this sort of collateral attack on the competence of one of its members to sit. Had Judge Medina found in § 46 (c), as the Court holds he should have found, a statutory direction to withdraw from further participation in this lawsuit, petitioner and not respondents would have prevailed on the appeal, since that would have resulted in the affirmance, by an equally divided Court of Appeals, of the District Court's judgment in favor of the Government. Of course, to a litigant, there is no greater injury than to lose a case, but I have difficulty understanding just what legal error has been committed against petitioner, such as to warrant vacation by this Court of the judgment below, thus giving the Government an opportunity to retrieve its original loss in the en banc Court of Appeals. Clearly, Judge Medina was not a mere interloper, or a usurper. He was, and is, a circuit judge of the United States, bearing a commission signed by the President. Abstractions about "competence" only becloud the matter. All that has happened is that Judge Medina has exercised the right conferred by Congress (28 U. S. C. § 371 (b)) to retire from active service. Nothing in that action, or in what the Court has said concerning the scope of § 46 (c), renders the judgment of the court below vulnerable to attack. The cases cited by the Court dealt with disqualifications based on policy grounds the effectuation of which called for a vacation of the judgments rendered there.[5] No reason has been given why that is so here.

I would affirm.

Notes

[1] The Reviser's Note to § 46 shows this to be true. "This section preserves the interpretation established by the Textile Mills case but provides in subsection (c) that cases shall be heard by a court of not more than three judges unless the court has provided for hearing in banc. This provision continues the tradition of a three-judge appellate court and makes the decision of a division, the decision of the court, unless rehearing in banc is ordered. It makes judges available for other assignments, and permits a rotation of judges in such manner as to give to each a maximum of time for the preparation of opinions."

[2] The order granting the respondents' petition for rehearing en banc required that the case be submitted on written briefs, to be filed by Jan. 8, 1958. Judge Medina retired on Mar. 1, 1958. The action of the Judicial Conference in 1959, to which the Court refers (ante, p. 690, note 7), does not of course bear upon the narrow issue before us. That action was broadly directed to permitting retired circuit judges to sit on en banc courts in instances where they had sat on the panel originally deciding the case. Indeed, the recommendation of the Judicial Conference goes far to dilute the force of the Court's attribution to Congress of a design to leave in the hands of active circuit judges alone the setting of the "major doctrinal trends" of their courts.

[3] In construing a statute far more amenable to a technical approach, we recently rejected an analogous construction of the word "determined." United States v. Price, 361 U. S. 304, 307.

[4] In this case, one cannot say that such a standard was not followed. Although the decision was not announced until nearly five months after his retirement (265 F. 2d 136, 144), Judge Medina had sat on the panel which originally heard the case, and the briefs on reargument were submitted almost three months prior to his retirement. He did not write an opinion in the case.

[5] In Frad v. Kelly, 302 U. S. 312, a motion for discharge from probation was entertained and granted by a judge not of the district where sentence had been imposed. The evident purpose of the statute limiting consideration of such matters to judges of the sentencing court was to permit those judges to develop an integrated policy governing probation. Id., at 318. To give effect to that policy, the order of discharge was vacated. The dictum in American Construction Co. v. Jacksonville, T. & K. W. R. Co., 148 U. S. 372, 387, concerned a violation by a judge of the requirement that he not sit on an appeal from a judgment or order which he had entered. It hardly needs elucidation to recognize that disregard of such a policy infects the judgment rendered.

Justice Harlan's concurrence and dissent in Massey Motors v. US (June 27, 1960)

MR. JUSTICE HARLAN, whom MR. JUSTICE WHITTAKER, and MR. JUSTICE STEWART join, dissenting in Nos. 141 and 143, and concurring in the judgment in No. 283.[*]

This is one of those situations where what may be thought to be an appealing practical position on the part of the Government has obscured the weaknesses of its legal position, at least in Nos. 141 and 143.

The position which the Commissioner takes in these cases with respect to the basic issue of "useful life" is that contained in the regulations promulgated by him in 1956 under the Internal Revenue Code of 1954, which define the useful life of a depreciable asset as the

"period over which the asset may reasonably be expected to be useful to the taxpayer in his trade or business . . . ."[1]

In No. 283 the Commissioner seeks to apply this regulatory definition to the returns of the taxpayer with respect to the taxable years ended March 31, 1954, 1955, and 1956.

In Nos. 141 and 143 he seeks in effect to apply the same definition to the taxable years 1950 and 1951, both of which were of course long before the enactment of the 1954 Code. See 264 F. 2d, at 506.

I agree that these regulations represent a reasonable method for calculating depreciation within the meaning of the 1954 Code, and that they are valid as applied prospectively. But since I believe that as to "useful life" they are wholly inconsistent with the position uniformly taken by the Commissioner in the past, I do not think they can be applied retrospectively in all instances. While I consider that the regulations may be so applied in No. 283, in my opinion that is not so in Nos. 141 and 143.

I.

It is first important to understand the precise nature of the issues before the Court. Both the method of depreciation contended for by the taxpayers and that urged by the Government purport to allocate an appropriate portion of an asset's total cost to each of the years during which the taxpayer holds it. Both methods define the total cost to be so allocated as the original cost of the asset less its salvage value at the end of its useful life. And under both methods, the total cost to be allocated is divided by the number of years in the useful life and the resulting figure is deducted from the taxpayer's income each year he holds the asset. As the Court correctly notes, the practical difference in the end results of the two methods involves the extent to which a taxpayer may be able to obtain capital-gains treatment for assets sold at or before the end of their useful life for amounts realized in excess of their remaining undepreciated cost.

The difference between the two methods from a theoretical standpoint is simply this: The taxpayers define useful life as the estimated physical life of the asset, while the Government defines the term as the period during which the taxpayer anticipates actually retaining the asset in his business. Thus, under the taxpayers' system, the total cost to be allocated is original cost less the salvage or junk value of the asset at the end of its physical life. This figure is divided by the number of years of estimated physical life, and the quotient is subtracted from income each year the taxpayer holds the asset. Under the Government's method, the total cost to be allocated is original cost less the "salvage" value at the end of the asset's actual use in the business, that is, less the price anticipated on its resale at that time, even though the asset may not be in fact physically exhausted. This figure is divided by the number of years in the holding period, and the quotient is subtracted from income each year the taxpayer holds the asset.

If an asset is held until it is physically exhausted, both methods produce exactly the same result. Similarly, both methods can result in inaccuracies if predictions of useful life and salvage value turn out to be wrong. The Government, however, contends that where it can be predicted with reasonable certainty that an asset will be disposed of before the end of its physical life, its method of depreciation is more likely to reflect the true cost of the asset to the particular business. This is said to be so because the true cost to the business, in the end, is the asset's original cost less the amount recovered on its resale, and the Government's method starts from an estimate of that amount, which is then allocated among the years involved. The taxpayers' method on the other hand, starts from an estimate of the end cost of the asset in the general business world, and will accurately reflect such cost to the taxpayer's business only if the decline in market value at the time of resale can be expected to correspond roughly to the portion of the asset's general business end cost which has been theretofore depreciated. In many cases that may be true, but in the present cases, there is in fact a great disparity between actual decline in market value at the time of resale and the portion of cost theretofore depreciated under taxpayers' method.

It need not be decided whether, as an abstract matter, one method or the other is deemed preferable in accounting practice. Apparently there is a split of authority on that very question.[2] It is sufficient to note that in most instances either method seems to give satisfactory results. Assuming that because of the unusual case, such as we have here, the Government's method on the whole may more accurately reflect the cost to a particular taxpayer's business, the question for me is whether the Commissioner has nevertheless established a practice to the contrary upon which taxpayers were entitled to rely until changed by him. I turn now to the examination of that question.

II.

The Court relies on the wording of certain revenue statutes and regulations to show that the period during which depreciable assets are employed in the taxpayer's business, as opposed to the period of their physical life, has always been regarded as useful life for purposes of depreciation. Concededly, the term useful life did not appear in the statute until the Internal Revenue Code of 1954, and though it had appeared in the regulations as early as 1919, Treas. Reg. 45, Art. 161, was never defined therein until 1956, ante, p. 107, when the Commissioner took the position he now asserts. The Court seizes on language which was not directed to the present problem and which could equally be read to support the Government's or the taxpayers' contention. The situation before 1956 was as follows:

The Act of Oct. 3, 1913, permitted a reasonable allowance for "wear and tear of property arising out of its use or employment in the business."[3] It is certainly true, as the Court says, that this means that "the wear and tear to the property must arise from its use in the business of the taxpayer." But it does not follow at all that the formula for calculating that wear and tear must be based on a useful life equal to the period the asset is held in the business. For, as noted above, a formula based on the physical life of the asset also results in an estimate of the portion of the asset's total cost attributable to its use in the business, and may in some circumstances yield the same tax consequences as a "holding-period" formula.

Treasury Regulations 45, Art. 161, promulgated in 1919 and continued in substantially the same form until 1942, provided that the taxpayer should set aside each year an amount such that "the aggregate of such amounts for the useful life of the property in the business will suffice, with the salvage value, at the end of such useful life to provide in place of the property its cost . . . ." In 1942, the statute was amended to permit depreciation, not only, as before, on property used in the trade or business, but also on property held for the production of income. Accordingly, the regulation was revised to delete the words "property in the business" and substitute therefor "the depreciable property." Reg. 111, § 29.23 (l)-1. The Court says that the deleted term could not have been meant to define the type of property subject to the depreciation allowance, since that function was already performed by another section of the regulation. That may be true, but it does not show that the language was meant to define the period of useful life. If it had been so meant, the Commissioner would hardly have simply substituted "useful life of the depreciable property" for "useful life of the property in the business," but would have inserted appropriate language, such as "useful life of the property while used in the business or held for the production of income." It is quite evident that the question of a holding period different from the physical life of the property was never adverted to, and that the term "property in the business," while not an affirmative definition of the type of property subject to depreciation, simply referred to that definition in connection with useful life because it was apparently assumed that assets were generally held in a taxpayer's business until worn out.

In light of the above, the Government's reliance on cases such as United States v. Ludey, 274 U. S. 295, 300-301, and Detroit Edison Co. v. Commissioner, 319 U. S. 98, 101, is wide of the mark. The language relied upon in Ludey is virtually identical to that contained in the pre-1942 regulations, and that in Detroit Edison merely says that the purpose of depreciation is to recover, by the time of an asset's retirement, the original investment therein. As noted above, depreciation based on either definition of useful life is dedicated to that end. The Government's reliance on Bulletin "F" is also misplaced. The Court refers to a statement on page 2 of the Bulletin which merely lifts from the regulation the phrase "useful life of the property in the business." The Court also relies on a statement appearing on page 7, defining salvage as "the amount realizable from the sale . . . when property has become no longer useful in the taxpayer's business and is demolished, dismantled, or retired from service." (Emphasis added.) The italicized language again reveals the assumption that assets were generally intended for use in the business until their physical exhaustion. The present question was never adverted to.

I believe, therefore, that the statute and regulations are wholly inconclusive, and that the Commissioner's position can be gleaned only from the stand he has taken in litigated cases. I turn now to those cases. Contrary to the picture of uncertainty which the Court draws from them, I believe they leave little room for doubt but that the Commissioner's pre-1956 position on "useful life" was flatly opposed to that which he now takes.

III.

In examining the cases, it must be borne in mind that even the Commissioner does not contend that a taxpayer who happens to dispose of some asset before its physical exhaustion must depreciate it on a useful life equal to the time it was actually held. It is only when the asset "may reasonably be expected" to be disposed of prior to the end of its physical life that the taxpayer must base depreciation on the shorter period. Reg. § 1.167 (a)-1 (b). Therefore, the only cases relevant in this regard are those in which the taxpayer's past experience indicated that assets would be disposed of prior to becoming junk, thus presenting the issue whether the shorter or longer period should control for purposes of depreciation.[4]

In four such cases, involving tax years prior to 1942, the taxpayer had a practice of disposing of assets substantially prior to their physical exhaustion. In Merkle Broom Co., 3 B. T. A. 1084, the taxpayer customarily disposed of its automobiles after two years. It attempted to depreciate them over a three-year useful life; the Commissioner asserted a five-year useful life; and the court allowed four years.

In Kurtz, 8 B. T. A. 679, the taxpayers customarily sold their automobiles after two or three years at substantial values. They depreciated on a four-year useful life; the Commissioner asserted a five-year life; and the court agreed.

In Sanford Cotton Mills, 14 B. T. A. 1210, the taxpayer customarily disposed of its motor trucks after two and one-half years. It claimed a three-year useful life; the Commissioner asserted a five-year useful life; and the court found that four years was reasonable.

In General Securities Co., 1942 P-H BTA-TC Mem. Dec. ¶ 42,219, the taxpayer sold its automobiles after one or two years. The court held that a reasonable useful life was three years.

It is apparent from these cases that both the Commissioner and the courts were thinking solely in terms of the physical life of the asset, despite the fact that the taxpayer customarily held the assets for a substantially shorter period. In at least some of the cases, it would have made a very real difference had depreciation been calculated on the basis that the useful life of the asset meant its holding period. For example, in the Sanford case, taxpayer's trucks were sold after two and one-half years at less than one-seventh of their original cost. Given the five-year useful life proposed by the Commissioner, taxpayer would have had, at the time of resale, an undepreciated basis equal to half the original cost, while the proceeds of resale would have brought it only one-seventh of original cost, thus giving rise to a loss of the difference. If the Government's present position had been applied, the difference between original cost and resale value would have been depreciated over two and one-half years, giving rise to no gain or loss at the end of that time. Similarly, in the General Securities case, given a three-year useful life, the taxpayer's automobiles, when traded in after one year, had an undepreciated basis of two-thirds of original cost, yet their resale brought only one-half to one-third of their original cost, again resulting in a substantial loss which would have been avoided under the Government's present method.

It is true that the only tax distortion present in these cases was a shift of ordinary deductions from the years in which the property was used in the business to the final year of its disposition. It is also true that had the situation been reversed, so that depreciation on a physical-life basis outran decline in market value, the resulting gain in the year of disposition would have been ordinary income, since capital-gains treatment for disposition of property used in the trade or business was not accorded by Congress until 1942.[5] However, it is significant that the Commissioner's adherence to a physical-life method did result in a distortion of income by shifting deductions among various tax years, which often entails serious revenue consequences, and that by 1942 physical life seems to have been uniformly accepted as the proper definition of useful life.

In light of these circumstances, four cases involving tax years subsequent to 1942 acquire special significance. In Pilot Freight Carriers, Inc., 15 CCH T. C. Mem. 1027, the taxpayer disposed of its tractors after an average of 38 months and its trailers after an average of 32.6 months. It claimed depreciation on a four-year useful life with 10% or less salvage value. The Commissioner asserted useful lives of five and six years for the tractors and trailers, respectively, and the court found that four and five years, respectively, was reasonable. It is to be noted that upon resale, taxpayer received, because of wartime inflation, amounts substantially in excess of undepreciated cost, resulting in large capital gains. Yet the Commissioner, in attempting to correct this disparity, asserted only that useful life should be increased to reflect more accurately the physical exhaustion of the assets, not that it should be equated with the holding period.

In Lynch-Davidson Motors, Inc., v. Tomlinson, 58-2 U. S. T. C. ¶ 9738, an automobile dealer disposed of company cars each year when new models were brought out, yet depreciated on a three-year useful life with salvage value of $50. The Commissioner did not dispute this method of depreciation and the court held it to be proper. In the companion case of Davidson v. Tomlinson, 58-2 U. S. T. C. ¶ 9739, taxpayers were in the automobile rental business, and kept their automobiles only one year. They also were permitted to depreciate on a useful life of three years with $50 salvage value. The striking similarity between the facts of these two cases and those of the present ones need not be elaborated.

Finally, as late as 1959, in Hillard, 31 T. C. 961, the Commissioner took the position that the taxpayer, who operated a car rental business, and who disposed of his cars after one year, should depreciate them on the basis of a four-year useful life rather than the three years contended for by taxpayer.

Thus in all these cases, as in the cases before us, the problem of offsetting depreciation deductions by capital gains existed; nevertheless the Commissioner consistently adhered to the position, adopted long prior to 1942, that physical life controlled.

The Court, however, seems to believe that the effect of these cases is vitiated by several cases dealing with "salvage" value. In three of such cases,[6] the assets were apparently held by the taxpayer until at or near the end of their physical lives, and the only issue was whether the taxpayer had erroneously calculated the salvage value at the end of that time. Thus they are of no significance for present purposes.

The Court's view fares no better under any other of these cases. In Bolta Co., 4 CCH T. C. Mem. 1067, involving a 1941 tax year, the taxpayer disposed of several machines after they had ceased to be useful in its business but while they were still useful in other businesses. It projected an average holding period of five years and assumed no salvage value. The Commissioner acquiesced in the five-year useful life but contended that the taxpayer could reasonably have anticipated a salvage value equal to 25% of original cost. The court agreed.

In Koelling v. United States, 57-1 U. S. T. C. ¶ 9453, taxpayers disposed of cattle after they were no longer useful for breeding, and depreciated them on a useful life equal to that period, making no allowance for salvage value. The Commissioner found that it was unreasonable thus to deduct the entire cost of the animals over their breeding life, and required the taxpayers to deduct as salvage value their predicted resale price.

In Cohn v. United States, 259 F. 2d 371, taxpayers had established flying schools during 1941 and 1942 under contract with the Army Air Corps. The arrangement was expected to last only until the end of 1944, and the useful life of property used in the business was calculated on that basis, with no allowance for salvage value. The Commissioner asserted various longer useful lives for the property, varying from five to ten years. The court permitted the taxpayers to use the shorter useful life, but required them to deduct the reasonable salvage value of the equipment which would be realized at the end of that period. The Government did not appeal from the useful-life ruling and the only dispute was over the correct amount of salvage value.

Thus in two of the relevant salvage-value cases, Bolta and Koelling, the taxpayer himself proposed a useful life equivalent to holding period but employed a hybrid version by failing to adopt the corresponding concept of salvage value. The Commissioner merely took the position that if the holding-period method was to be used, it must be used consistently by deducting the appropriate salvage value. In the third, Cohn, the Commissioner actually rejected the taxpayers' attempt to employ the holding period and merely acquiesced when the court permitted the taxpayers to do so, provided the corresponding salvage value was deducted. However, in no case, until the present ones, does it appear that the Commissioner has ever sought to require the taxpayer to use the holding-period method where the taxpayer has attempted to use physical life. And I do not understand the Government to controvert this. To the contrary, the Commissioner has not infrequently required the taxpayer to depreciate on the basis of physical life where the taxpayer had attempted to employ a shorter period, even in instances where significant capital-gains consequences turned on the difference. Indeed, as the Lynch-Davidson, Davidson, and Hillard cases, supra, indicate, the Commissioner, until quite recently, has adhered to the physical-life concept in automobile cases virtually indistinguishable from the present ones. In the past the Commissioner, unsuccessfully, has merely sought to curb the capital-gains possibilities in such instances by contending that the automobiles involved were not depreciable assets subject to capital-gains treatment under § 117 (j) of the Internal Revenue Code of 1939. Having conceded that the property involved in the present cases is subject to the depreciation deduction, I do not think the Commissioner should now be permitted to defeat his own position as regards the meaning of "useful life"—a position consistently maintained by him over a period of 33 years from 1926 to 1959 in every litigated case to which our attention has been called—by requiring these taxpayers, in respect of taxable years not subject to the provisions of the 1954 Code, to adopt a holding-period formula for useful life in depreciating the assets in question. Cf. Helvering v. R. J. Reynolds Tobacco Co., 306 U. S. 110, and Helvering v. Griffiths, 318 U. S. 371. In the application of this salutary principle it should make no difference that the Commissioner's earlier different practice was not embodied in a formal regulation. Cf. Helvering v. Reynolds, 313 U. S. 428, 432; Higgins v. Commissioner, 312 U. S. 212, 216.

Accordingly, I would reverse in No. 141 and affirm in No. 143.

IV.

The situation presented in No. 283 is, however, different. The taxable years in question there are those terminating on March 31, 1954, 1955, and 1956, respectively. All the taxable years thus ended before the promulgation of the new depreciation regulations on June 11, 1956.[7] The Government concedes that Congress did not change the concept of useful life when it enacted the 1954 Code. Therefore, the question here is whether the Commissioner can, by a formal regulation, change his position retroactive only to the effective date of the statute under which it is promulgated.

Petitioner, relying on Helvering v. R. J. Reynolds Tobacco Co. and Helvering v. Griffiths, supra, asserts that where a regulation interpreting a statute has been in force for some time and has survived the re-enactment of the statute, the Commissioner cannot retroactively change that interpretation by a new regulation. However, here the Commissioner's earlier adherence to the physical-life concept of useful life was expressed not in the regulations —which did not refer to the problem—but in his own administrative practice. Therefore, the present case is more like Helvering v. Reynolds, 313 U. S. 428, wherein this Court permitted the Commissioner to apply a regulation retroactive to the effective date of the statute under which it was promulgated, where his previous contrary position had been expressed only by informal administrative practice, even though the statute had been re-enacted in the interim. Application of this principle in the present case is the more called for, since Congress, in the 1954 Code, has for the first time used the term "useful life" and has made the availability of certain new accelerated methods of depreciation—among them the so-called "declining balance method," used by the taxpayer here—dependent upon its definition. It is appropriate therefore to permit the Treasury maximum discretion in integrating the concept of useful life into the new provisions and in doing so from the effective date of the statute forward.

Since the statute permits use of the declining-balance method only as to property with a useful life of three years or more, it follows that the Commissioner properly disallowed use of the declining-balance method as to Hertz' automobiles, whose useful life under the new regulation was less than three years. As to its trucks, admittedly held for more than three years, the only remaining question is whether Hertz should be allowed to depreciate them below what the Commissioner considers to be a reasonable salvage value. Given the fact that the Commissioner's definition of salvage value as resale price on disposition of the asset at the end of its holding period is validly applicable to Hertz, it becomes important that the declining-balance method not be construed to defeat that concept. Were there no "salvage stop" in connection with declining-balance depreciation, it is clear that taxpayers who held assets for relatively short periods of time might be able to depreciate far below anticipated resale price, since the declining-balance rate is applied against the entire cost of the asset undiminished by salvage. Since the legislative history of the statute in this regard is ambiguous at best, and since there is no prior statute or administrative interpretation to becloud the issue, the Commissioner's construction should be allowed to stand. Accordingly, I concur in the Court's judgment affirming No. 283.

[*] [This opinion applies also to No. 283, Hertz Corporation v. United States, post, p. 122.]

Notes

[1] Treasury Regulations on Depreciation, § 1.167 (a)-1 (b), T. D. 6182, 1956-1 Cum. Bull. 98, June 11, 1956.

[2] At the trials below, taxpayers' expert witnesses testified that depreciation based on physical life was the commonly accepted accounting standard. Several textbooks, cited by the Court, ante. p. 106, take the contrary view.

[3] 38 Stat. 114, 167.

[4] Three cases cited by the Court, West Virginia & Pennsylvania Coal & Coke Co., 1 B. T. A. 790; James, 2 B. T. A. 1071; and Whitman-Douglas Co., 8 B. T. A. 694, involved isolated dispositions of assets prior to their physical exhaustion, and there was no evidence indicating a consistent practice by the taxpayer in this regard.

[5] Revenue Act of 1942 § 151, 56 Stat. 846.

[6] Wier Long Leaf Lumber Co., 9 T. C. 990; W. H. Norris Lumber Co., 7 CCH T. C. Mem. 728; Davidson, 12 CCH T. C. Mem. 1080. In the Wier case, it is not clear whether some of the assets might have been useful for some additional period in other businesses.

[7] T. D. 6182, 1956-1 Cum. Bull. 98. Prior to that time the regulations under the 1939 Code were continued in force. T. D. 6091, 1954-2 Cum. Bull. 47.

Justice Harlan's dissent in Sunray Mid-Continent Oil v. FPC (June 27, 1960)

MR. JUSTICE HARLAN, whom MR. JUSTICE FRANKFURTER, MR. JUSTICE WHITTAKER, and MR. JUSTICE STEWART join, dissenting.[*]

The basic issue presented by these two cases is essentially this: When an independent producer of natural gas enters into a contract for the sale of his gas in interstate commerce for resale, and seeks a certificate from the Federal Power Commission to carry out that contract, may the Commission issue a certificate of unlimited duration not limited to the term of the contract, in the absence of a special showing that the public convenience and necessity require the certificate to be perpetual? In holding that it may, I believe the Court has strained the provisions of the Natural Gas Act beyond permissible limits in order to reach a result which it deems more appropriate to effective regulation. In my opinion, neither will the Act bear the meaning the Court attributes to it, nor will a contrary interpretation bring about the practical evils which the Court imagines.

I.

In my view the Court's conclusions are attributable at bottom to its failure to take into account the basic distinction between an interstate pipeline and an independent producer of natural gas. A pipeline performs a service akin to those traditionally performed by public utilities. The independent producer, on the other hand, is unique among the objects of public-utility regulation because it is not engaged in rendering a service to the public in the conventional sense of that concept, but rather simply in selling a commodity which it owns. The Court's basic error, it seems to me, is its notion that the petitioners are rendering a continuing service to the public in the same sense as a pipeline or other conventional utility, to which the usual modes of utility regulation are equally applicable.

I think that the Natural Gas Act, particularly as construed by the Court in Phillips Petroleum Co. v. Wisconsin, 347 U. S. 672, recognizes this important distinction. The basic jurisdictional framework of the Natural Gas Act is found in § 1 (b) which provides:

"The provisions of this chapter shall apply to the transportation of natural gas in interstate commerce, to the sale in interstate commerce of natural gas for resale . . . , and to natural-gas companies engaged in such transportation or sale, but shall not apply to . . . the production or gathering of natural gas." (Emphasis added.)

In Phillips the application of this provision to independent producers, such as the petitioners in these cases, was considered. Phillips there contended that it was not subject to the Act because it did not engage in the interstate transmission of gas and was not affiliated with any interstate pipeline company, and that to regulate its prices would be to control the "production or gathering" of natural gas, which is specifically exempted by § 1 (b). The Court rejected that argument, holding that Phillips' sales, which were unquestionably made "in interstate commerce . . . for resale," were subject to the Commission's jurisdiction. It recognized that the Act creates two separate and distinct bases of jurisdiction—transportation and sale; that an independent producer engages solely in the latter; and that because of the production and gathering exemption, it is only the act of sale itself, which occurs at the very end of the production and gathering process, to which the Commission's jurisdiction attaches. It is thus evident that the Court recognized that, as to independent producers, the Act envisaged only a limited scheme of regulation, namely control over the prices and the other terms of sale of their natural gas. The blurring of this distinction respecting the scope of the regulatory scheme of the Act as between independent producers and others can only lead to confusion when, as here, the Court is faced with deciding the proper scope of the operative provisions of the statute.

The operative provisions of the Act consistently reflect their more limited reach as regards independent producers than with respect to others. Section 7 (c) requires certification in order to

"engage in the transportation or sale of natural gas, subject to the jurisdiction of the Commission, or undertake the construction or extension of any facilities therefor, or acquire or operate any such facilities or extensions thereof . . . ."

Thus three distinct categories of jurisdictional acts are subject to certification: (1) transportation, (2) sale, and (3) maintenance of jurisdictional facilities. A pipeline must necessarily secure authorization for both transportation and maintenance of jurisdictional facilities, acts which by their nature are continuing services. But I do not understand the Court to contend that petitioners, as independent producers, have engaged in any jurisdictional act other than a sale.

The word "sale," in its ordinary sense, signifies a transaction limited in duration and amount. Section 7 (c) requires certification of a sale, and there is nothing in the Act which suggests that the certification is to be broader than the jurisdictional act which it authorizes. On the contrary, § 7 (e), infra, p. 163, directs the Commission to issue a certificate authorizing "the . . . sale . . . covered by the application." The Court suggests that a perpetual certificate does in fact authorize the specific sale proposed, and that to say that the Commission can authorize no more than that is to "load" the statutory language with a negative implication which was never intended. However, authorizing a producer to sell in perpetuity is certainly something different from authorizing him to make a specific sale. It could hardly be contended that a statutory direction to the Commission to authorize "the . . . sale . . . covered by the application" permits it to authorize some different sale.

The Court's assumption that a perpetual certificate authorizes nothing different than what the producer has in effect applied for can in the end be justified only by its view, alluded to before, that what is involved is not a "sale" at all, but a "service" consisting of the perpetual movement of gas in interstate commerce. However, as already mentioned, this flouts the industrial realities. The independent producer does not perform a service; he owns and sells a commodity. Since he need not dedicate his gas supply to the interstate market at all, surely he may propose the amount he will dedicate. The Commission of course need not accept the proposal. But neither can it in effect require acceptance of a certificate authorizing something more, on pain of denying the applicant any certificate, without satisfying the requirements of § 7 (e), infra, for the imposition of conditions on certificates.

The Court, however, purports to find support in the statute for its notion that a sale is really a perpetual service. It relies primarily on § 7 (e), which provides in relevant part that

"a certificate shall be issued to any qualified applicant therefor, authorizing the whole or any part of the operation, sale, service, construction, extension, or acquisition covered by the application, if it is found that the applicant is able and willing properly to do the acts and to perform the service proposed, . . . and that the proposed service, sale, operation, construction, extension, or acquisition . . . will be required by the . . . public convenience and necessity. . . ." (Emphasis added.)

It would appear plain from the face of the very language quoted that, while the word "service" is used, it is used disjunctively with "sale" and several other words, so that a sale and a service are simply two different, and not synonymous, things the Commission is authorized to certificate. However, the Court reasons that "service" must refer back to "transportation or sale," for which § 7 (c) requires a certificate. But § 7 (c) requires a certificate for three separate categories of jurisdictional acts— transportation, sale, and maintenance of facilities. And § 7 (e), concededly referring back to those categories, lists six items—operation, sale, service, construction, extension, and acquisition. Why the term "service" in § 7 (e) should be thought to refer to "sale," the least apt of the three categories in § 7 (c) which it could describe, when it is immediately preceded in § 7 (e) by the word "sale" itself, is difficult to understand.

The Court further says that the provisions of §§ 4 (c)[1] and 7 (b)[2] present the same feature. In § 4 (c), the word "service" again appears as part of an omnibus definition which refers to a number of antecedents. Even assuming, as the Court does, that the only antecedent is "transportation or sale," there is no reason to suppose that "service" was meant to be taken as the equivalent of "sale" as well as of "transportation," or that it limits either. Section 7 (b) refers only to the abandonment of services "rendered by means of" jurisdictional facilities. There is not the slightest hint in the section that sales are considered to be such services.

Finally, the Court points to the requirement of § 7 (e), ante, p. 148, that the applicant for a certificate be willing and able "to do the acts and perform the service proposed." From this it infers that all the matters for which § 7 (c), ante, p. 149, requires a certificate "must be justified in terms of a `service' to which they relate." I should have thought it quite plain that an applicant is required to "perform the service proposed" only if a service is proposed. Perhaps it would have been more apt for Congress to have said "do the acts and/or perform the services proposed," but I cannot understand how the clause as written can be read as meaning that whatever the applicant proposes must be both an act and a service.

I must conclude that there is nothing in the statute which makes "sale" the equivalent of "service." On the contrary, the terms are always used disjunctively. A sale, as a jurisdictional ground distinct from either transportation or the maintenance of jurisdictional facilities (§ 1 (b) ante, p. 160) is a limited transaction. A certificate authorizing a sale authorizes no more and, in my view, must be regarded as expiring when the underlying sale terminates, except in a situation where the Commission has properly conditioned issuance on continuance of the certificate for a longer period. See post, p. 167. It is suggested that the Commission has consistently held that the obligation to provide service persists even after a particular contract terminates. See United Gas Pipe Line Co., 3 F. P. C. 3; Cabot Gas Corp., id., 357; Godfrey L. Cabot, Inc., id., 582; Panhandle Eastern Pipe Line Co., 11 F. P. C. 167, 172. All those cases, however, involved pipeline companies which were in fact providing a continuing service and which had facilities subject to the jurisdiction of the Commission regardless of the duration of a particular contract. They serve as no authority for the present quite different situation where an independent producer is subject to the Commission's jurisdiction only by virtue of his sales.

II.

The Court asserts that a construction of the statute contrary to the one it reaches will result in intolerable consequences, primarily in two respects. First, it says, producers and pipelines would be able to abandon their undertakings at the end of the contract term without a showing that the public convenience and necessity justify such abandonment, thus defeating the policy of § 7 (b) of the Act, and giving the industry a lever to avert regulation of any kind. Second, it concludes, producers would be able, at the expiration of their contracts, to file a higher price as an initial rate under a new certificate. This would force the Commission, it is said, to test the reasonableness of the rate under § 5 (a), ante, p. 144, where the Commission has the burden of proof and where experience has shown the procedure to be subject to great delays, and would avoid the rate-change procedures of § 4 (e), ante, p. 145, where the producer has the burden of proof and the effectiveness of the rate can be suspended pending investigation.

As to abandonment, the Court's view again rests on the erroneous notion that the Commission is charged with assuring continuity of "service" on the part of independent producers. However, § 7 (b), by its own terms, prohibits abandonment of only two things: jurisdictional facilities, and any service "rendered by means of" such facilities. The Court does not suggest that petitioners have any jurisdictional facilities. And there can be no apprehension about the pipelines, since they clearly provide a service by means of jurisdictional facilities and are certificated for an unlimited duration.

There is a more basic reason, however, why the evils which the Court imagines do not exist. The Commission is required to issue a certificate only if the applicant's proposal is required by the public convenience and necessity. The vast majority of sales are, of economic necessity, bona fide transactions of substantial duration (see United Gas Pipe Line Co. v. Mobile Gas Service Corp., 350 U. S. 332, at 344) and will, of course, be approved in ordinary course. But surely, if a proposal contains such disingenuous provisions as the Court suggests, its certification would not be in the public interest. The Court's fear that denial of the certificate under such circumstances would be overturned on review is the severest speculation, especially in an area where the Commission is entrusted with such wide discretion.

Furthermore, the Commission can tender a perpetual certificate under its § 7 (e) power to attach reasonable terms and conditions.[3] But in such a case, it would have to bear the burden of showing that the public convenience and necessity require such a condition. What the Court in effect permits the Commission to do here is simply to attach the condition without such a showing. If, as the Commission stoutly maintains, a limited certificate would constitute a serious threat to the public interest, then surely it is not too much to ask it to show that fact before tendering a producer a certificate different from the one he has requested. And where the Commission has fairly made such a showing, I cannot believe, with all deference to the Court's contrary intimation, that there is the slightest danger that its action would nonetheless be overturned on the theory it was attempting to accomplish indirectly that which it cannot do directly. Such a view assumes that a court will be blind to the conditioning power expressly given the Commission by statute, and ignores the fact that there is a very real difference between tendering an unlimited certificate when the Commission has made no affirmative showing of public need for a perpetual duration and tendering one when it has made such a showing. In the last analysis, that additional burden is the only consequence which turns on the outcome of these cases.

I would hold that where, as in No. 335, an independent producer applies for authority simply to engage in a sale transaction specifically limited in duration, the Commission has no authority to tender an unlimited certificate without bearing the burden of showing that such a departure from the proposal is required by the public convenience and necessity.

III.

The question remains whether petitioner in No. 321 proposed a sale transaction which was limited in duration and whether the Commission certificated no more than that sale. The term of the contract filed with the Commission was clearly limited to 10 years. Petitioner's application incorporated that contract by reference, and declared that "[t]his application is hereby made only for a certificate of public convenience and necessity authorizing the sale of natural gas in the circumstances above described." The Commission ordered that a certificate be "hereby issued . . . authorizing the sale by Applicant of natural gas . . . as more fully described in the application and exhibits in this proceeding. . . . The certificate. . . shall be effective only so long as Applicant continues the acts or operations hereby authorized in accordance with the provisions of the Natural Gas Act . . . ." I think the fair interpretation of all this is that what was authorized was the sale proposed, and that the certificate should therefore be taken as limited in duration to the term of the sale contract.

The Commission, however, contends that since, at the time petitioner's certificate was issued, it had taken the position in Sunray Oil Corp., 14 F. P. C. 877, that it had no power to issue a certificate specifically limited in duration, this certificate must be taken as one unlimited in duration. That position, however, was later reversed on appeal, Sunray Mid-Continent Oil Co. v. Federal Power Comm'n, 239 F. 2d 97, and the Commission acquiesced therein. But the Commission was more fundamentally wrong in believing that a certificate authorizing a sale is unlimited unless specifically otherwise conditioned. Therefore, when it tendered to petitioner a certificate without any limiting language, its erroneous belief that it was issuing a perpetual certificate could not bind petitioner. The Commission was authorized to issue only a certificate limited to the duration of the sale unless a condition were expressly imposed to the contrary, and what it issued purported to be no more than that. Petitioner cannot be taken to have acquiesced in a certificate authorizing something other than it requested, where the certificate gave no notice of that fact, simply because the Commission may have believed its effect to be otherwise.

I fear this is another instance where the Court has taken impermissible liberties with statutory language in order to remedy what it considers an undesirable deficiency in the way Congress has written the statute. Cf. United States v. Republic Steel Corp., 362 U. S. 482, 493 (dissenting opinion).

I would reverse the judgments in both cases.

Notes

[1] "(c) Under such rules and regulations as the Commission may prescribe, every natural-gas company shall file with the Commission, within such time (not less than sixty days from June 21, 1938) and in such form as the Commission may designate, and shall keep open in convenient form and place for public inspection, schedules showing all rates and charges for any transportation or sale subject to the jurisdiction of the Commission, and the classifications, practices, and regulations affecting such rates and charges, together with all contracts which in any manner affect or relate to such rates, charges, classifications, and services."

[2] "(b) No natural-gas company shall abandon all or any portion of its facilities subject to the jurisdiction of the Commission, or any service rendered by means of such facilities, without the permission and approval of the Commission first had and obtained, after due hearing, and a finding by the Commission that the available supply of natural gas is depleted to the extent that the continuance of service is unwarranted, or that the present or future public convenience or necessity permit such abandonment."

[3] "The Commission shall have the power to attach to the issuance of the certificate and to the exercise of the rights granted thereunder such reasonable terms and conditions as the public convenience and necessity may require."

Justice Harlan's dissent in US v. Mississippi Valley Co. (Jan 9, 1961)

MR. JUSTICE HARLAN, whom MR. JUSTICE WHITTAKER and MR. JUSTICE STEWART join, dissenting.

In a case like this controlling legal issues are apt to become blurred under the urge of vindicating a public policy whose importance no one will dispute. However, we sit here not as a committee on general business ethics, but as a court enforcing a specific piece of legislation.

While I am bound to say that the Government's defense to this claim for out-of-pocket expenses incurred in a matter that the Government was once anxious to explore, is far from ingratiating,[1] I must agree with the Court that Wenzell's government role in connection with the Mississippi Valley contract, though in the view of the Court of Claims it was quite peripheral, was sufficient to constitute him one who "acts as an officer or agent of the United States" within the meaning of 18 U. S. C. § 434,[2] and that if he was personally "indirectly interested" in that contract via First Boston the case must go for the Government. But in light of the findings of the Court of Claims I cannot agree that Wenzell was so interested, within the contemplation of § 434. In my opinion this Court's contrary conclusion rests upon too loose a view of the controlling statutory phrase.

Referring to the period of Wenzell's governmental service, the Court of Claims concluded:

"There is not a shadow of evidence that it [First Boston] had any agreement or commitment, written or oral, formal or informal, contingent or otherwise that, in the event that the proposal [of the Dixon-Yates group] which was in preparation when

Wenzell's Government employment ended should result in negotiations which should, in the course of events, result in a contract, First Boston would be given the opportunity to earn a commission by selling the bonds of the corporation [Mississippi Valley] which would be formed to sign and perform the contract. The evidence is perfectly plain that there was no such agreement or understanding." 175 F. Supp., at 518.

I do not understand the Court to take issue with this conclusion or with any of the findings of the Hearing Examiner on which it was based. It could not well do so, cf. Commissioner v. Duberstein, 363 U. S. 278; nor does the Government ask this. Rather, the Court finds the prohibited "indirect interest" to consist of Wenzell's expectation in the probability that First Boston, by virtue of its reputation in the field of private power financing and its having previously arranged the financing for a similar project, would eventually share in the financing of this venture.

I do not believe that such a probability alone gives rise to a contaminating interest under § 434. The fact that the probability eventuated into actuality after Wenzell's government service terminated can hardly be relevant, for what the Court, under its view of the statute, correctly says as to the immateriality of First Boston's later waiver of commissions must surely also work in reverse. Whether or not a prohibited interest exists must be determined as of the period during which an individual is acting for the Government. And when the asserted interest arises "indirectly" by way of a subcontract, its existence can, in my opinion, only be found in some commitment, arrangement, or understanding obtaining at that time between the prime contractor and subcontractor.[3] I believe this latter proposition is supported by persuasive considerations.

First. It fits the language of § 434, whereas the Court's view does not. The statute does not speak of the disqualifying factors in terms of expectations or probabilities, but imports a precise standard, that is, a present status or pecuniary interest arising from some existing relationship with the business entity contracting with the Government. Certainly this is true as to an "officer," "agent," or "member" of the contracting enterprise. It is equally true of one disqualified by reason of "being . . . directly . . . interested in the pecuniary profits or contracts" of such an entity. I can see no reason why it should not also be true as to one "indirectly" so interested, requiring in this instance proof of some then-existing arrangement between Mississippi Valley and First Boston. I do not mean to suggest that such an arrangement must be evidenced by a formal agreement, for of course any sort of tacit understanding or "gentlemen's agreement" will suffice. But here the Court of Claims has expressly found against the existence of any such thing.

Second. The view which I take of the matter also fits the purposes of § 434. The policy and rationale of the statute are clear: an individual who negotiates business for the Government should not be exposed to the temptation which might be created by a loyalty divided between the interest of the Government and his own self-interest; the risk that the Government will not be left with the best possible transaction is too great. In terms of these factors, a finding of some commitment, arrangement or understanding between the prime contractor and the subcontractor should be required when the contracting officer's adverse interest arises by way of a subcontract, since only where some such arrangement exists can the officer be taken to have known that any undue benefit he confers on the prime contractor will not eventually redound to the profit of some other competing subcontractor.

Here, for instance, it was found below that Mississippi Valley "a month after Wenzell's Government employment had terminated . . . felt perfectly free to give the bond-selling business to whomever it pleased." 175 F. Supp., at 518. Hence if Wenzell did in fact confer some undue benefit on Mississippi during the term of his government service (although none is suggested), he must have known that he was conferring that benefit at large, and that if First Boston later were to share in it this would only be the consequence of its having successfully competed against other investment bankers with similar qualifications. Furthermore, where the government officer's eventual indirect participation in the contract which he has negotiated (by hypothesis improperly) depends on the chance of competition after he has lost the leverage which his position gave, then it would be subject to the additional hazard that although the contractor has received a boon at his hands, all the subcontractor receives is such a normal subcontract as he might have had in any case.

Third. The Court's interpretation of § 434 introduces unnecessary and undesirable uncertainties into the statute. Instead of presenting the individual concerned or the trier of fact with a definite standard for determining whether a disqualifying interest of this kind is present— the existence vel non of a commitment or undertaking between the primary and secondary contractors—the question is left at large. The opinion in this case indeed highlights the matter. For after apparently agreeing that a "mere hope" that First Boston might share in the financing of the power contract would not be enough, the Court goes on to describe that eventuality in a variety of ways—that there was "a substantial probability" of it; that it was "probable"; that "it seemed likely"; that it "stood a good chance" of coming to pass; and that it might simply follow from the " `logic of circumstances' " as a " `substantial possibility.' "

Such uncertainty, inherent in the Court's view of the statute, is bound to cause future confusion in an area where the line of demarcation should be clear cut. As time goes on it will face many conscientious persons with the kind of close and subtle niceties which, as every judge and lawyer knows, often attend a matter of possible disqualification. Such illusive factors should not be imported into a statute governing the conduct primarily of laymen serving the Government.

Fourth. I think there is affirmative ground in the pattern of conflict-of-interest legislation for not attributing to Congress the purpose which the Court here does. The statute in question is the most general conflict-of-interest enactment, but there are other provisions of law, as well as federal regulations, which also deal with the subject. Particularly 5 U. S. C. § 99 and 18 U. S. C. § 284 indicate a different approach to the problem. The two statutes disqualify former officers and employees of governmental agencies or departments for a period of two years from prosecuting or aiding in any way in the prosecution of a claim which had been pending at the time of their employment. A similar approach is suggested by this Court's Rule 7 which prohibits clerks and secretaries from practicing before this Court for a period of two years after leaving the Court, and from participating in any way in a case which was before the Court during the term of their employment. Cf. Canon 36 of the Canons of Professional Ethics of the American Bar Association.

The interpretation which the Court today gives 18 U. S. C. § 434, if it is to be taken as more than a disposition of this particular controversy, will go a long way to assimilating that statute in practical effect to the absolute disqualification type of provision, for certainly where criminal sanctions are involved no prudent man will risk later acquiring an interest in a contract which he helped to negotiate during a previous term of government employment. Whether such a rigid rule, of a kind traditional in the legal profession, should also be regarded as one of general morality in the public service may, of course, well be debated. However, Congress did not, in my view, enact this precept into law in the present statute, and where it has enacted this policy it has done so with a clarity and precision which I feel the present reading of § 434 lacks.

I would affirm.

Notes

[1] Wenzell's superiors in the Government were fully aware of his connection with First Boston and of the possibility that First Boston might later figure in the financing of the contemplated private power project; and with such knowledge they affirmatively acquiesced, and indeed encouraged, his continuing in his consultative role. The power contract, which the Government recognizes was the product of hard bargaining and implicitly concedes was fair, was eventually terminated only because the Government had lost interest in it. The defense of illegality was raised for the first time in this suit, and only after a political storm had arisen over the public versus private power issue. Nevertheless I think the Court is right in considering that all these factors are rendered immaterial by the statute in question.

[2] "§ 434. Interested persons acting as Government agents.

"Whoever, being an officer, agent or member of, or directly or indirectly interested in the pecuniary profits or contracts of any corporation, joint-stock company, or association, or of any firm or partnership, or other business entity, is employed or acts as an officer or agent of the United States for the transaction of business with such business entity, shall be fined not more than $2,000 or imprisoned not more than two years, or both."

[3] Whether absence of knowledge of such an arrangement on the part of the individual concerned would be a defense is a matter not presented by this case.

Justice Harlan's concurrence in Monroe v. Pape (Feb 20, 1961) [Notes omitted]

MR. JUSTICE HARLAN, whom MR. JUSTICE STEWART joins, concurring.

Were this case here as one of first impression, I would find the "under color of any statute" issue very close indeed. However, in Classic[1] and Screws[2] this Court considered a substantially identical statutory phrase to have a meaning which, unless we now retreat from it, requires that issue to go for the petitioners here.

From my point of view, the policy of stare decisis, as it should be applied in matters of statutory construction, and, to a lesser extent, the indications of congressional acceptance of this Court's earlier interpretation, require that it appear beyond doubt from the legislative history of the 1871 statute that Classic and Screws misapprehended the meaning of the controlling provision,[3] before a departure from what was decided in those cases would be justified. Since I can find no such justifying indication in that legislative history, I join the opinion of the Court. However, what has been written on both sides of the matter makes some additional observations appropriate.

Those aspects of Congress' purpose which are quite clear in the earlier congressional debates, as quoted by my Brothers DOUGLAS and FRANKFURTER in turn, seem to me to be inherently ambiguous when applied to the case of an isolated abuse of state authority by an official. One can agree with the Court's opinion that:

"It is abundantly clear that one reason the legislation was passed was to afford a federal right in federal courts because, by reason of prejudice, passion, neglect, intolerance or otherwise, state laws might not be enforced and the claims of citizens to the enjoyment of rights, privileges, and immunities guaranteed by the Fourteenth Amendment might be denied by the state agencies. . . ."

without being certain that Congress meant to deal with anything other than abuses so recurrent as to amount to "custom, or usage." One can agree with my Brother FRANKFURTER, in dissent, that Congress had no intention of taking over the whole field of ordinary state torts and crimes, without being certain that the enacting Congress would not have regarded actions by an official, made possible by his position, as far more serious than an ordinary state tort, and therefore as a matter of federal concern. If attention is directed at the rare specific references to isolated abuses of state authority, one finds them neither so clear nor so disproportionately divided between favoring the positions of the majority or the dissent as to make either position seem plainly correct.[4]

Besides the inconclusiveness I find in the legislative history, it seems to me by no means evident that a position favoring departure from Classic and Screws fits better that with which the enacting Congress was concerned than does the position the Court adopted 20 years ago. There are apparent incongruities in the view of the dissent which may be more easily reconciled in terms of the earlier holding in Classic.

The dissent considers that the "under color of" provision of § 1983 distinguishes between unconstitutional actions taken without state authority, which only the State should remedy, and unconstitutional actions authorized by the State, which the Federal Act was to reach. If so, then the controlling difference for the enacting legislature must have been either that the state remedy was more adequate for unauthorized actions than for authorized ones or that there was, in some sense, greater harm from unconstitutional actions authorized by the full panoply of state power and approval than from unconstitutional actions not so authorized or acquiesced in by the State. I find less than compelling the evidence that either distinction was important to that Congress.

I.

If the state remedy was considered adequate when the official's unconstitutional act was unauthorized, why should it not be thought equally adequate when the unconstitutional act was authorized? For if one thing is very clear in the legislative history, it is that the Congress of 1871 was well aware that no action requiring state judicial enforcement could be taken in violation of the Fourteenth Amendment without that enforcement being declared void by this Court on direct review from the state courts. And presumably it must also have been understood that there would be Supreme Court review of the denial of a state damage remedy against an official on grounds of state authorization of the unconstitutional action. It therefore seems to me that the same state remedies would, with ultimate aid of Supreme Court review, furnish identical relief in the two situations. This is the point Senator Blair made when, having stated that the object of the Fourteenth Amendment was to prevent any discrimination by the law of any State, he argued that:

"This being forbidden by the Constitution of the United States, and all the judges, State and national, being sworn to support the Constitution of the United States, and the Supreme Court of the United States having power to supervise and correct the action of the State courts when they violated the Constitution of the United States, there could be no danger of the violation of the right of citizens under color of the laws of the States." Cong. Globe, 42d Cong., 1st Sess., at App. 231.

Since the suggested narrow construction of § 1983 presupposes that state measures were adequate to remedy unauthorized deprivations of constitutional rights and since the identical state relief could be obtained for state-authorized acts with the aid of Supreme Court review, this narrow construction would reduce the statute to having merely a jurisdictional function, shifting the load of federal supervision from the Supreme Court to the lower courts and providing a federal tribunal for fact findings in cases involving authorized action. Such a function could be justified on various grounds. It could, for example, be argued that the state courts would be less willing to find a constitutional violation in cases involving "authorized action" and that therefore the victim of such action would bear a greater burden in that he would more likely have to carry his case to this Court, and once here, might be bound by unfavorable state court findings. But the legislative debates do not disclose congressional concern about the burdens of litigation placed upon the victims of "authorized" constitutional violations contrasted to the victims of unauthorized violations. Neither did Congress indicate an interest in relieving the burden placed on this Court in reviewing such cases.

The statute becomes more than a jurisdictional provision only if one attributes to the enacting legislature the view that a deprivation of a constitutional right is significantly different from and more serious than a violation of a state right and therefore deserves a different remedy even though the same act may constitute both a state tort and the deprivation of a constitutional right. This view, by no means unrealistic as a common-sense matter,[5] is, I believe, more consistent with the flavor of the legislative history than is a view that the primary purpose of the statute was to grant a lower court forum for fact findings. For example, the tone is surely one of overflowing protection of constitutional rights, and there is not a hint of concern about the administrative burden on the Supreme Court, when Senator Frelinghuysen says:

"As to the civil remedies, for a violation of these privileges, we know that when the courts of a State violate the provisions of the Constitution or the law of the United States there is now relief afforded by a review in the Federal courts. And since the 14th Amendment forbids any State from making or enforcing any law abridging these privileges and immunities, as you cannot reach the Legislatures, the injured party should have an original action in our Federal courts, so that by injunction or by the recovery of damages he could have relief against the party who under color of such law is guilty of infringing his rights. As to the civil remedy no one, I think, can object." Id., at 501.

And Senator Carpenter reflected a similar belief that the protection granted by the statute was to be very different from the relief available on review of state proceedings:

"The prohibition in the old Constitution that no State should pass a law impairing the obligation of contracts was a negative prohibition laid upon the State. Congress was not authorized to interfere in case the State violated that provision. It is true that when private rights were affected by such a State law, and that was brought before the judiciary, either of the State or nation, it was the duty of the court to pronounce the act void; but there the matter ended. Under the present Constitution, however, in regard to those rights which are secured by the fourteenth amendment, they are not left as the right of the citizen in regard to laws impairing the obligation of contracts was left, to be disposed of by the courts as the cases should arise between man and man, but Congress is clothed with the affirmative power and jurisdiction to correct the evil.

"I think there is one of the fundamental, one of the great, the tremendous revolutions effected in our Government by that article of the Constitution. It gives Congress affirmative power to protect the rights of the citizen, whereas before no such right was given to save the citizen from the violation of any of his rights by State Legislatures, and the only remedy was a judicial one when the case arose." Id., at 577.

In my view, these considerations put in serious doubt the conclusion that § 1983 was limited to state-authorized unconstitutional acts, on the premise that state remedies respecting them were considered less adequate than those available for unauthorized acts.

II.

I think this limited interpretation of § 1983 fares no better when viewed from the other possible premise for it, namely that state-approved constitutional deprivations were considered more offensive than those not so approved. For one thing, the enacting

Congress was not unaware of the fact that there was a substantial overlap between the protections granted by state constitutional provisions and those granted by the Fourteenth Amendment. Indeed one opponent of the bill, Senator Trumbull, went so far as to state in a debate with Senators Carpenter and Edmunds that his research indicated a complete overlap in every State, at least as to the protections of the Due Process Clause.[6] Thus, in one very significant sense, there was no ultimate state approval of a large portion of otherwise authorized actions depriving a person of due-process rights. I hesitate to assume that the proponents of the present statute, who regarded it as necessary even though they knew that the provisions of the Fourteenth Amendment were self-executing, would have thought the remedies unnecessary whenever there were self-executing provisions of state constitutions also forbidding what the Fourteenth Amendment forbids. The only alternative is to disregard the possibility that a state court would find the action unauthorized on grounds of the state constitution. But if the defendant official is denied the right to defend in the federal court upon the ground that a state court would find his action unauthorized in the light of the state constitution, it is difficult to contend that it is the added harmfulness of state approval that justifies a different remedy for authorized than for unauthorized actions of state officers. Moreover, if indeed the legislature meant to distinguish between authorized and unauthorized acts and yet did not mean the statute to be inapplicable whenever there was a state constitutional provision which, reasonably interpreted, gave protection similar to that of a provision of the Fourteenth Amendment, would there not have been some explanation of this exception to the general rule? The fact that there is none in the legislative history at least makes more difficult a contention that these legislators were in fact making a distinction between use and misuse of state power.

There is a further basis for doubt that it was the additional force of state approval which justified a distinction between authorized and unauthorized actions. No one suggests that there is a difference in the showing the plaintiff must make to assert a claim under § 1983 depending upon whether he is asserting a denial of rights secured by the Equal Protection Clause or a denial of rights secured by the Due Process Clause of the Fourteenth Amendment. If the same Congress which passed what is now § 1983 also provided remedies against two or more nonofficials who conspire to prevent an official from granting equal protection of the laws, see 42 U. S. C. § 1985, then it would seem almost untenable to insist that this Congress would have hesitated, on the grounds of lack of full state approval of the official's act, to provide similar remedies against an official who, unauthorized, denied that equal protection of the laws on his own initiative. For there would be no likely state approval of or even acquiescence in a conspiracy to coerce a state official to deny equal protection. Indeed it is difficult to attribute to a Congress which forbade two private citizens from hindering an official's giving of equal protection an intent to leave that official free to deny equal protection of his own accord.[7]

We have not passed upon the question whether 42 U. S. C. § 1985,[8] which was passed as the second section of the Act that included § 1983, was intended to reach only the Ku Klux Klan or other substantially organized group activity, as distinguished from what its words seem to include, any conspiracy of two persons with "the purpose of preventing or hindering the constituted authorities of any State . . . from giving or securing to all persons within such State . . . the equal protection of the laws . . . ."[9] Without now deciding the question, I think it is sufficient to note that the legislative history is not without indications that what the words of the statute seem to state was in fact the meaning assumed by Congress.[10]

These difficulties in explaining the basis of a distinction between authorized and unauthorized deprivations of constitutional rights fortify my view that the legislative history does not bear the burden which stare decisis casts upon it. For this reason and for those stated in the opinion of the Court, I agree that we should not now depart from the holdings of the Classic and Screws cases.

Justice Harlan's dissent in Aro Mfg. Co. v. Convertible Top Replacement Co. (Feb 27, 1961)

MR. JUSTICE HARLAN, whom MR. JUSTICE FRANKFURTER and MR. JUSTICE STEWART join, dissenting.

For more than a hundred years it has been the law that the owner of a device covered by a combination patent can, without infringing, keep the device in good working order by replacing, either himself or through any source he wishes, unpatented parts, but that he may not, without rendering himself liable for infringement, reconstruct the device itself, whether because of its deterioration or for any other reason, and even though all of the component parts of the device are themselves unpatented. Wilson v. Simpson, 9 How. 109; Cotton-Tie Co. v. Simmons, 106 U. S. 89; Morgan Envelope Co. v. Albany Perforated Wrapping Paper Co., 152 U. S. 425; Leeds & Catlin Co. v. Victor Talking Machine Co., 213 U. S. 325; Heyer v. Duplicator Mfg. Co., 263 U. S. 100. The underlying rationale of the rule is of course that the owner's license to use the device carries with it an implied license to keep it fit for the use for which it was intended, but not to duplicate the invention itself. Correlatively, one who knowingly participates in an impermissible reconstruction of a patented combination is guilty of contributory infringement. "Direct" and "contributory" infringements are now codified in § 271 of the Patent Act of 1952. 35 U. S. C. § 271.[1]

In this case the District Court and the Court of Appeals upon full consideration have concurred in finding that Aro's replacement-supplying of the fabric portion of respondent's convertible automobile tops contributorily infringed the latter's territorial rights under the valid Mackie-Duluk combination patent, in that such activity constituted a deliberate participation on Aro's part in a forbidden reconstruction of the patented combination. In reversing, the Court holds that there can be no direct infringement (and hence, of course, no contributory infringement) of a combination patent by replacement of any of the components of the patented entity unless (1) such component is itself separately patented or (2) the entire entity is rebuilt at one time. Since the fabric cover component of the Mackie-Duluk top was not itself separately patented, and since it constituted but one part of the patented combination, the Court concludes that Aro's supplying of such covers for replacement on cars equipped with respondent's tops did not as a matter of law constitute contributory infringement.[2]

My Brother BRENNAN'S opinion, while disagreeing with that conclusion, would reverse because on its view of the record, untrammeled by the contrary findings and conclusions of the two lower courts, it is concluded that what here took place constituted "repair" and not "reconstruction" of the Mackie-Duluk tops.

I am unable to subscribe to either of these views.

I.

I believe that the narrow concept of what constitutes impermissible reconstruction, reflected in the opinion of the Court, departs from established principles— principles which, it will be shown, were approved by Congress when it enacted § 271 of the new Patent Act, over objections of the Department of Justice altogether comparable to the position which it now advances as amicus in the present case.

The all-important thing is to determine from the past decisions of this Court what the proper test of "reconstruction" is, for I agree that 35 U. S. C. § 271 (c) limits contributory infringement to that which would be direct infringement, and that § 271 (a), dealing with direct infringement, leaves intact the pre-existing case law. The cases cited above amply demonstrate that there is no single yardstick for determining whether particular substitutions of new for original unpatented parts of a patented combination amount to permissible repair or forbidden reconstruction. The matter is to be resolved "on principles of common sense applied to the specific facts" of a given case, Heyer, supra, at 102. The single simple rule of "reconstruction" which the Court finds in those cases can, in my view, only be divined at the expense of reconstructing the decisions themselves.

The leading case is Wilson v. Simpson, supra. There, in holding that the owner of a planing machine covered by a combination patent could replace from any source he desired the unpatented cutting knives thereof, the Court said, p. 125:

"The right of the assignee [the owner of the machine] to replace the cutter-knives is not because they are of perishable materials, but because the inventor of the machine has so arranged them as a part of its combination, that the machine could not be continued in use without a succession of knives at short intervals. Unless they were replaced, the invention would have been but of little use to the inventor or to others. The other constituent parts of this invention, though liable to be worn out, are not made with reference to any use of them which will require them to be replaced. These, without having a definite duration, are contemplated by the inventor to last so long as the materials of which they are formed can hold together in use in such a combination. No replacement of them at intermediate intervals is meant or is necessary. They may be repaired as the use may require. With such intentions, they are put into the structure. So it is understood by a purchaser, and beyond the duration of them a purchaser of the machine has not a longer use. But if another constituent part of the combination is meant to be only temporary in the use of the whole, and to be frequently replaced, because it will not last as long as the other parts of the combination, its inventor cannot complain, if he sells the use of his machine, that the purchaser uses it in the way the inventor meant it to be used, and in the only way in which the machine can be used."

In the Cotton-Tie case, supra, the question was whether combination patents for the making of ties for cotton bales, consisting of a metal buckle and band, were infringed by one who bought as scrap metal such ties and bands after severance from cotton bales, and resold them for further use as baling ties after piecing together several segments of the old bands and reconnecting the resulting single band with the original buckle. In holding that this was an impermissible reconstruction of the patented combination,[3] the Court said:

"Whatever right the defendants could acquire to the use of the old buckle, they acquired no right to combine it with a substantially new band, to make a cotton-bale tie. They so combined it when they combined it with a band made of the pieces of the old band in the way described. What the defendants did in piecing together the pieces of the old band was not a repair of the band or the tie, in any proper sense. The band was voluntarily severed by the consumer at the cotton-mill because the tie had performed its function of confining the bale of cotton in its transit from the plantation or the press to the mill. Its capacity for use as a tie was voluntarily destroyed. As it left the bale it could not be used again as a tie. As a tie the defendants reconstructed it, although they used the old buckle without repairing that. The case is not like putting new cutters into a planing-machine in place of those worn out by use, as in Wilson v. Simpson, 9 How. 109. The principle of that case was, that temporary parts wearing out in a machine might be replaced to preserve the machine, in accordance with the intention of the vendor, without amounting to a reconstruction of the machine." At 93-94.

In Morgan Envelope, supra, the Court found no contributory infringement on the part of one supplying toilet paper rolls specially designed for use in a patented combination, comprising a dispenser and the paper rolls themselves. Remarking (p. 433) that there "are doubtless many cases to the effect that the manufacture and sale of a single element of a combination, with intent that it shall be united to the other elements, and so complete the combination, is an infringement," the Court found the situation before it distinguishable in that "the element [paper roll] made by the alleged infringer is an article of manufacture perishable in its nature, which it is the object of the mechanism [the dispenser] to deliver, and which must be renewed periodically, whenever the device is put to use." Ibid. On similar grounds the Court in Heyer, supra, found no contributory infringement in the intentional supplying of unpatented gelatine bands for use in a duplicating machine covered by a combination patent, of which one element was the gelatine band.

On the other hand, in Leeds & Catlin, supra, the intentional supplying of phonograph records for use on respondent's talking machines, which were protected by a combination patent covering both machine and records, was held to be contributory infringement, it being found that records were the "operative ultimate tool of the invention," that respondent's records were not inherently "perishable" in nature, and that the supplying of the competitor's records was not to replace records "deteriorated by use" or which had suffered "breakage." (P. 336.)

These cases destroy the significance of two factors on which the Court heavily relies for its conclusion in the present case: first, that the fabric top was an unpatented element of the Mackie-Duluk invention, and, second, that Aro's tops constituted a replacement of but one part of the patented combination. For as was said in Leeds & Catlin (p. 333), "[i]t can make no difference as to the infringement or non-infringement of a combination that one of its elements or all of its elements are unpatented"; and in all of these cases the claimed infringing replacement involved only one of the elements of the patented combination. Further, the different results reached in the cases, two finding "reconstruction" and three only "repair," also vitiate the reasoning of the Court, in that they show that the issue of reconstruction vel non turns not upon any single factor, but depends instead upon a variety of circumstances, differing from case to case. The true rule was well put by this same Court of Appeals in its earlier decision in Goodyear Shoe Machinery Co. v. Jackson, 112 F. 146, 150:

"It is impracticable, as well as unwise, to attempt to lay down any rule on this subject, owing to the number and infinite variety of patented inventions. Each case, as it arises, must be decided in the light of all the facts and circumstances presented, and with an intelligent comprehension of the scope, nature, and purpose of the patented invention, and the fair and reasonable intention of the parties. Having clearly in mind the specification and claims of the patent, together with the condition of decay or destruction of the patented device or machine, the question whether its restoration to a sound state was legitimate repair, or a substantial reconstruction or reproduction of the patented invention, should be determined less by definitions or technical rules than by the exercise of sound common sense and an intelligent judgment."

More particularly, none of the past cases in this Court or in the lower federal courts remotely suggests that "reconstruction" can be found only in a situation where the patented combination has been rebuilt de novo from the ground up.[4]

The reference which the Court makes to the Mercoid cases, 320 U. S. 661, 320 U. S. 680, is, in my opinion, entirely inapposite, since those cases, as the Court recognizes, p. 344, n. 10, supra, dealt with the issue of patent misuse, an issue which specifically is not before the Court at this time.[5] I realize that some of the language in the first Mercoid case (320 U. S., at 667-669), and more particularly its disapproving remarks about Leeds & Catlin (id., 668), may be said to cast doubt on what it appears to me the contributory infringement cases plainly establish. Yet I cannot believe that Mercoid is properly to be read as throwing into discard all the teaching of the repair-reconstruction cases. What was said in Mercoid about contributory infringement must be read in the context of Mercoid's claim, found to have been established, that Mid-Continent had misused its combination patent by attempting in effect to wield it as a weapon to monopolize the sale of an unpatented element, a claim which is not here made.

I think it significant that in stating (p. 668) that the doctrine of the Leeds & Catlin case "must no longer prevail against the defense that a combination patent is being used to protect an unpatented part from competition," the Court went on to say, at 668-669:

"That result obtains here though we assume for the purposes of this case that Mercoid was a contributory infringer and that respondents could have enjoined the infringement had they not misused the patent for the purpose of monopolizing unpatented material. Inasmuch as their misuse of the patent would have precluded them from enjoining a direct infringement [citing the Morton Salt case] they cannot stand in any better position with respect to a contributory infringer. Where there is a collision between the principle of the Carbice case and the conventional rules governing either direct or contributory infringement, the former prevails." (Italics supplied.)

Thus Mercoid, far from modifying the doctrine of the Wilson line of cases as to what constitutes contributory infringement, assumed that doctrine and defined the special circumstances when the court would refuse to give a patentee the benefit of that doctrine.[6] Those circumstances are not present in this case.

As for my Brother BLACK'S opinion, the congressional action of 1952, reaffirming what I consider must be taken as the doctrine of the Wilson line of cases, also requires rejection of what he now conceives to be a more enlightened policy in this field of law.[7]

II.

My Brother BRENNAN'S opinion for reversal rests, as I understand it, not upon the view that the two courts below applied wrong legal standards in reaching their conclusion, but that " `repair' or `reconstruction' is so far a question of law as to relieve appellate review from the restraints of Federal Rule of Civil Procedure 52 (a)" and to allow the "making [of] an independent application of the proper standard" to the facts in this case. (Italics supplied.) For reasons larger than this particular litigation I cannot agree that it is either necessary or appropriate for us to substitute our particular judgment on this particular application of correct standards to the facts.

We do not sit in judgment on the decisions of the lower federal courts because we are endowed with some special measure of discernment, but because it is imperative that on matters of general concern, that is on matters of principle, there should be one authoritative and unifying expositor of federal law. I need not join issue on whether Rule 52 (a) serves to constrict appellate review in cases like this, cf. Graver Tank & Mfg. Co. v. Linde Air Products Co., 336 U. S. 271, 275, 279, for the rule which I believe should limit us is based on the purposes which this Court can and should fulfill.

In this case there is no question but that the two courts below adverted to all the relevant standards but, having done so, they concluded that on the facts before them there was contributory infringement. I cannot see what else my Brother BRENNAN is doing but reaching a different conclusion of his own. I cannot understand how such a conclusion, even were it accepted by a majority of the Court, could provide greater guidance to either courts or litigants than would a mere statement of approbation for the standards espoused by the courts below.

Because the question of "repair" or "reconstruction" must be a mixed question of law and fact, it does not follow that we should review other than gross misapplications (certainly not present here), when the legal ingredient of this mixture is concededly correct. In the analogous area of determining the issue of patentable novelty, Courts of Appeal have consistently deferred to the judgment of the District Court (see the excellent statement of Judge Fahy in Standard Oil Development Co. v. Marzall, 86 U. S. App. D. C. 210, 181 F. 2d 280, 283-284), and where they have departed from this judgment the reason has generally been because the District Court had failed to reach its conclusions by reference to correct standards. See Kwikset Locks, Inc., v. Hillgren, 210 F. 2d 483; cf. Great Atlantic & Pacific Tea Co. v. Supermarket Equipment Corp., 340 U. S. 147, 153, 154. Whether this practice be considered as compelled by the dictates of good sense or by Rule 52 (a), surely particular judgments fairly and reasonably reached in two lower courts in light of correct legal standards deserve at least that same deference from us.

I would affirm.

Notes

[1] "(a) Except as otherwise provided in this title, whoever without authority makes, uses or sells any patented invention, within the United States during the term of the patent therefor, infringes the patent.

"(b) Whoever actively induces infringement of a patent shall be liable as an infringer.

"(c) Whoever sells a component of a patented machine, manufacture, combination or composition, or a material or apparatus for use in practicing a patented process, constituting a material part of the invention, knowing the same to be especially made or especially adapted for use in an infringement of such patent, and not a staple article or commodity of commerce suitable for substantial noninfringing use, shall be liable as a contributory infringer."

[2] The Mackie-Duluk invention was described by the Court of Appeals as follows:

"Folding tops for vehicles consisting of bows of wood or metal covered with a flexible waterproof fabric . . . are, of course, as old as the automobile art which in the beginning only adopted with necessary modifications the much older art of collapsible tops for chaises, buggies and some other horse drawn vehicles. The rear panels of the folding tops of earlier days were fastened permanently at the bottom to the outside of the top of the rear portion of the body of the vehicle, and the quarters, the rear portions of the sides of the vehicle, if protected at all, were protected with flaps or curtains, sometimes integral with the top and sometimes not, fastened at the bottom to the outside of the top of the body with buttons, snaps or some equivalent means of fastening. Naturally, to prevent tearing, these quarter flaps had to be unfastened by hand when the top was lowered and when the top was put up fastened again by hand for neat appearance and also to prevent the entrance of rain. This manual fastening and unfastening of the bottoms of the quarter flaps presented no great problem until the advent of the so-called convertible automobile with a folding top operated mechanically rather than manually. The problem presented by the quarter flaps of tops of this kind was first partially solved by fastening the bottom of the flap to the outside of the top of the body of the vehicle with `releasable fastening means,' that is to say, with some sort of slide fastening device which would detach automatically when the top was lowered. The major part of the problem remained, however, for when the top was put up the flaps had to be fastened manually, which meant that the operator was required to get out of the car altogether, or at least to reach out, often, of course, in the rain. The object of the Mackie-Duluk patent was `to provide an automatic fastening and sealing means at the top and sides of the tonneau of the convertible' which `never has to be operated or touched by the driver of the car.' And, as we have already indicated, the District Court found that the patentees succeeded in attaining their object by devising a patentable combination of elements.

"The Mackie-Duluk device consisted of providing an elongated flap integral with the quarter sections of the fabric top adapted to be permanently fastened at the bottom deep within the body of the car, at or perhaps below, but certainly not in front, of the axis of rotation of the bows, to a trough welded to the body of the car and provided with a drain to carry off water entering between the flap and the car body. In addition, to minimize the entrance of water between the body and the flap, they provided a `wiper arm' so-called, which in effect acted as an additional, low rearward bow pressing the downwardly extending flap outwardly against the top of the body of the vehicle as the top is raised from its folded position to close, or substantially to close, any gap there might be between the inside of the top of the body of the car and the flap extending downward into the interior of the automobile body." 270 F. 2d, at 202-203.

The District Court said:

"Mackie-Duluk was a substantial and enlightened step, filling a long-felt want, in a field in which defendants have produced, with one exception, only paper patents, the most emphasized being foreign, which did not even purport to do what Mackie-Duluk accomplished." Id., at 201.

[3] While, as the Court remarks (ante, p. 343, n. 9), the Court there did refer to the fact that the original ties were stamped "Licensed to use once only," it is manifest that nothing really turned on that point.

[4] Compare note 7, infra.

[5] The District Court found against Aro's claim of patent misuse based on respondent's acquisition of territorial rights in the Mackie-Duluk patent. Aro did not appeal that finding.

[6] It seems clear from the legislative history of the 1952 Act that Congress intended (1) to reaffirm the doctrine of contributory infringement as laid down in Wilson v. Simpson and reasserted in cases like Leeds & Catlin, (2) to give that doctrine precedence against a claim of patent misuse as conceived in the Mercoid cases, at least where the misuse is said to inhere simply in assertion of patent rights. Both the proponents of the statute and the Department of Justice which opposed it assumed that contributory

infringement, as defined in the Wilson line of cases, was one thing, and misuse, as then most recently defined in Mercoid, another. See Hearings before Subcommittee of House Judiciary Committee on H. R. 3866, 81st Cong., 1st Sess. 53-59 (1949); Hearings before Subcommittee of House Judiciary Committee on H. R. 3760, 82d Cong., 1st Sess. 168-175 (1951). The opinion of the Court seems to reconfirm Mercoid to fuller effectiveness than it had even before the 1952 Act by treating it as if the test of whether there was contributory infringement at all was to be found in its language.

[7] This policy was before the Committee in the form of an objection to the proposed codification of the Wilson line of cases and its doctrine in the 1952 Act. Despite the objection Congress passed § 271 without amendment.

"Mr. CRUMPACKER: We have received protests from manufacturers of replacement parts for such things as automobiles, farm tractors, and the like, who evidently feel that the language used in this H. R. 3760 would make them contributory infringers of patents on the original article, the tractor or something of that sort.

.....

"Mr. RICH [who was the principal spokesman for the group which drafted the present statute]: Those were the most vociferous objectors to the old bills on the subject. Whether or not they would be liable would depend on the facts in each particular case. . . ." Hearings before Subcommittee of House Judiciary Committee on H. R. 3760, 82d Cong., 1st Sess., at p. 153 (1951).

Justice Harlan's dissent in Deutch v. US (June 12, 1961)

MR. JUSTICE HARLAN, whom MR. JUSTICE FRANKFURTER joins, dissenting.

There is, of course, no doubt that a showing of "pertinency" is an essential part of the Government's burden in a prosecution under 2 U. S. C. § 192. But the nature of this burden may differ, dependent upon what transpired at the Congressional inquiry giving rise to the prosecution.

In a case where the prosecution involves the defendant's refusal to answer a question whose pertinency was explained to him by the Congressional Committee before which he appeared as a witness—following his appropriate objection that the question was not pertinent to the matter "under inquiry," see Barenblatt v. United States, 360 U. S. 109, 123-124—the Government must stand or fall upon that explanation. For it would be obviously unfair to allow the Government at trial to prove pertinency on a different theory than was given to the defendant at the time he testified, and on the basis of which he presumably determined that he need not answer the question put.

Where, however, the defendant made no "pertinency" objection as a witness before the Congressional Committee, the Government at trial is left free to satisfy the requirement of pertinency in any way it may choose. The present case is such a one, for, as the Court's opinion recognizes, the petitioner here made no adequate pertinency objection before the House Un-American Activities Subcommittee.

I dissent because in my opinion the Court's holding that the Government failed to establish "pertinency" rests on a too niggardly view of both the issue and the record. Pertinency, which in the context of an investigatory proceeding is of course a term of wider import than "relevancy" in the context of a trial, is to be judged not in terms of the immediate probative significance of a particular question to the matter under authorized inquiry, but in light of its tendency to elicit information which might be a useful link in the investigatory chain. See Carroll v. United States, 16 F. 2d 951, 953. An investigation must proceed "step by step." Ibid.

Pertinency is found lacking here because (1) inquiry as to affairs relating to petitioner's student days at Cornell University, situated at Ithaca, N. Y., it is said, was not germane to the Subcommittee's investigation as to Communist activities in "the Albany area"; and (2) in any event, such investigation, the Court finds, related only to alleged Communist infiltration into labor unions and not as well to infiltration "at Cornell or in educational institutions generally." I can agree with neither facet of this holding.

It is quite true, as the Court says, that Ithaca is some 165 miles away from Albany, but it seems to me much too refined to say, as a matter of law, that the trial court could not reasonably determine that Ithaca was within the Subcommittee's terms of reference. Indeed, I think it fair to suggest that in common usage, at least among New Yorkers, "Albany area" would be regarded as aptly descriptive of "upstate" New York. In relation to "pertinency" the matter should not be judged as if it were one of technical jurisdiction or venue.

The other aspect of the Court's holding seems to me equally infirm. Accepting, as I shall, the Court's view that the trial record shows that the Subcommittee, at the relevant time, was investigating only alleged Communist "labor union," and not "educational," infiltration, it seems to me abundantly clear that the lower courts were justified in concluding that all of the questions with respect to which the petitioner was convicted[*] were pertinent to that matter.

Only shortly before it examined petitioner, the Subcommittee had interrogated two witnesses, Marqusee and Richardson, with respect to their Communist affiliations, their summer work with two labor unions in Schenectady and in Syracuse, and Communist infiltration into such unions, all while they were both students at Cornell. One of these witnesses, Richardson, had testified that during this period he had known the petitioner, and one Homer Owen (Count Four of the indictment), as Communists on the Cornell campus. I do not see why it should now be deemed either that the Subcommittee's interest in petitioner's testimony was confined to "educational infiltration," or that its preliminary questioning of him might not have led to developing information bearing on "labor union infiltration," possibly stemming from student Communist activity on the Cornell campus, had further inquiry not been blocked by petitioner's refusal to answer.

I cannot agree that the decision of this case has been made "within the conventional framework of the federal criminal law." For surely in judging the pertinency of a question put in the course of an otherwise valid Congressional inquiry, as this one is recognized to have been, we should not insist that the inquiring committee follow stricter rules than the courts themselves apply in determining, for example, the sufficiency of a plea of self-incrimination under the "link in the chain" rule, see, e. g., Blau v. United States, 340 U. S. 159, or in judging "materiality" in a perjury case, see, e. g., Carroll v. United States, supra. In reversing this conviction, I think the Court has strayed from the even course of decision.

I would affirm.

[*] Counts One, Two, Four, and Five of the indictment, set forth in note 5 of the Court's opinion. Ante, p. 461.

Justice Harlan's dissent in Culombe v. Connecticut (June 19, 1961)

MR. JUSTICE HARLAN, whom MR. JUSTICE CLARK and MR. JUSTICE WHITTAKER join, dissenting.

I agree to what my Brother FRANKFURTER has written in delineation of the general principles governing police interrogation of those suspected of, or under investigation in connection with, the commission of crime, and as to the factors which should guide federal judicial review of state action in this field. I think, however, that upon this record, which contains few of the hallmarks usually found in "coerced confession" cases, such considerations find their proper reflection in affirmance of this judgment.

With due regard to the medical and other evidence as to petitioner's history and subnormal mentality, I am unable to consider that it was constitutionally impermissible for the State to conclude that petitioner's "Wednesday" confessions were the product of a deliberate choice on his part to try to ameliorate his fate by making a clean breast of things, and not the consequence of improper police activity. To me, petitioner's supplemental confession on the following Saturday night, which as depicted by the record bears all the indicia of spontaneity, is especially persuasive against this Court's contrary view.

I should also add that I find no constitutional infirmity in the standards used by the Connecticut courts in evaluating the voluntariness of petitioner's confessions. Cf. Rogers v. Richmond, 365 U. S. 534.

I would affirm.

Justice Harlan's dissent in Mapp v. Ohio (June 19, 1961)

MR. JUSTICE HARLAN, whom MR. JUSTICE FRANKFURTER and MR. JUSTICE WHITTAKER join, dissenting.

In overruling the Wolf case, the Court, in my opinion, has forgotten the sense of judicial restraint which, with due regard for stare decisis, is one element that should enter into deciding whether a past decision of this Court should be overruled. Apart from that, I also believe that the Wolf rule represents sounder Constitutional doctrine than the new rule which now replaces it.

I

From the Court's statement of the case, one would gather that the central, if not controlling, issue on this appeal is whether illegally state-seized evidence is Constitutionally admissible in a state prosecution, an issue which would, of course, face us with the need for reexamining Wolf. However, such is not the situation. For, although that question was indeed raised here and below among appellant's subordinate points, the new and pivotal issue brought to the Court by this appeal is whether § 2905.34 of the Ohio Revised Code, making criminal the mere knowing possession or control of obscene material, [n1] and under which appellant has been convicted, is consistent with the rights of free thought and expression assured against state action by the Fourteenth Amendment. [n2] That was the principal issue which was decided by the Ohio Supreme Court, [n3] which was tendered by appellant's Jurisdictional Statement, [n4] and which was briefed [n5] and argued [n6] in this Court.

In this posture of things, I think it fair to say that five members of this Court have simply "reached out" to overrule Wolf. With all respect, for the views of the majority, and recognizing that stare decisis carries different weight in Constitutional adjudication than it does in nonconstitutional decision, I can perceive no justification for regarding this case as an appropriate occasion for reexamining Wolf.

The action of the Court finds no support in the rule that decision of Constitutional issues should be avoided wherever possible. For, in overruling Wolf, the Court, instead of passing upon the validity of Ohio's § 2905.34, has simply chosen between two Constitutional questions. Moreover, I submit that it has chosen the more difficult and less appropriate of the two questions. The Ohio statute which, as construed by the State Supreme Court, punishes knowing possession or control of obscene material, irrespective of the purposes of such possession or control (with exceptions not here applicable) [n7] and irrespective of whether the accused had any reasonable opportunity to rid himself of the material after discovering that it was obscene, [n8] surely presents a Constitutional question which is both simpler and less far-reaching than the question which the Court decides today. It seems to me that justice might well have been done in this case without overturning a decision on which the administration of criminal law in many of the States has long justifiably relied.

Since the demands of the case before us do not require us to reach the question of the validity of Wolf, I think this case furnishes a singularly inappropriate occasion for reconsideration of that decision, if reconsideration is indeed warranted. Even the most cursory examination will reveal that the doctrine of the Wolf case has been of continuing importance in the administration of state criminal law. Indeed, certainly as regards its "nonexclusionary" aspect, Wolf did no more than articulate the then existing assumption among the States that the federal cases enforcing the exclusionary rule

do not bind [the States], for they construe provisions of the Federal Constitution, the Fourth and Fifth Amendments, not applicable to the States.

People v. Defore, 242 N.Y. 13, 20, 150 N.E. 585, 587. Though, of course, not reflecting the full measure of this continuing reliance, I find that, during the last three Terms, for instance, the issue of the inadmissibility of illegally state-obtained evidence appears on an average of about fifteen times per Term just in the in forma pauperis cases summarily disposed of by us. This would indicate both that the issue which is now being decided may well have untoward practical ramifications respecting state cases long since disposed of in reliance on Wolf, and that were we determined to reexamine that doctrine, we would not lack future opportunity.

The occasion which the Court has taken here is in the context of a case where the question was briefed not at all and argued only extremely tangentially. The unwisdom of overruling Wolf without full-dress argument is aggravated by the circumstance that that decision is a comparatively recent one (1949) to which three members of the present majority have at one time or other expressly subscribed, one, to be sure, with explicit misgivings. [n9] I would think that our obligation to the States, on whom we impose this new rule, as well as the obligation of orderly adherence to our own processes would demand that we seek that aid which adequate briefing and argument lends to the determination of an important issue. It certainly has never been a postulate of judicial power that mere altered disposition, or subsequent membership on the Court, is sufficient warrant for overturning a deliberately decided rule of Constitutional law.

Thus, if the Court were bent on reconsidering Wolf, I think that there would soon have presented itself an appropriate opportunity in which we could have had the benefit of full briefing and argument. In any event, at the very least, the present case should have been set down for reargument, in view of the inadequate briefing and argument we have received on the Wolf point. To all intents and purpose,s the Court's present action amounts to a summary reversal of Wolf, without argument.

I am bound to say that what has been done is not likely to promote respect either for the Court's adjudicatory process or for the stability of its decisions. Having been unable, however, to persuade any of the majority to a different procedural course, I now turn to the merits of the present decision.

II

Essential to the majority's argument against Wolf is the proposition that the rule of Weeks v. United States, 232 U.S. 383, excluding in federal criminal trials the use of evidence obtained in violation of the Fourth Amendment, derives not from the "supervisory power" of this Court over the federal judicial system, but from Constitutional requirement. This is so because no one, I suppose, would suggest that this Court possesses any general supervisory power over the state courts. Although I entertain considerable doubt as to the soundness of this foundational proposition of the majority, cf. Wolf v. Colorado, 338 U.S. at 39-40 (concurring opinion), I shall assume, for present purposes, that the Weeks rule "is of constitutional origin."

At the heart of the majority's opinion in this case is the following syllogism: (1) the rule excluding in federal criminal trials evidence which is the product of an illegal search and seizure is "part and parcel" of the Fourth Amendment; (2) Wolf held that the "privacy" assured against federal action by the Fourth Amendment is also protected against state action by the Fourteenth Amendment, and (3) it is therefore "logically and constitutionally necessary" that the Weeks exclusionary rule should also be enforced against the States. [n10]

This reasoning ultimately rests on the unsound premise that, because Wolf carried into the States, as part of "the concept of ordered liberty" embodied in the Fourteenth Amendment, the principle of "privacy" underlying the Fourth Amendment (338 U.S. at 27), it must follow that whatever configurations of the Fourth Amendment have been developed in the particularizing federal precedents are likewise to be deemed a part of "ordered liberty," and as such are enforceable against the States. For me, this does not follow at all.

It cannot be too much emphasized that what was recognized in Wolf was not that the Fourth Amendment, as such, is enforceable against the States as a facet of due process, a view of the Fourteenth Amendment which, as Wolf itself pointed out (338 U.S. at 26), has long since been discredited, but the principle of privacy "which is at the core of the Fourth Amendment." (Id. at 27.) It would not be proper to expect or impose any precise equivalence, either as regards the scope of the right or the means of its implementation, between the requirements of the Fourth and Fourteenth Amendments. For the Fourth, unlike what was said in Wolf of the Fourteenth, does not state a general principle only; it is a particular command, having its setting in a preexisting legal context on which both interpreting decisions and enabling statutes must at least build.

Thus, even in a case which presented simply the question of whether a particular search and seizure was constitutionally "unreasonable" -- say in a tort action against state officers -- we would not be true to the Fourteenth Amendment were we merely to stretch the general principle of individual privacy on a Procrustean bed of federal precedents under the Fourth Amendment. But, in this instance, more than that is involved, for here we are reviewing not a determination that what the state police did was Constitutionally permissible (since the state court quite evidently assumed that it was not), but a determination that appellant was properly found guilty of conduct which, for present purposes, it is to be assumed the State could Constitutionally punish. Since there is not the slightest suggestion that Ohio's policy is "affirmatively to sanction . . . police incursion into privacy," (338 U.S. at 28), compare Marcus v. Search Warrants, post, p. 717, what the Court is now doing is to impose upon the States not only federal substantive standards of "search and seizure", but also the basic federal remedy for violation of those standards. For I think it entirely clear that the Weeks exclusionary rule is but a remedy which, by penalizing past official misconduct, is aimed at deterring such conduct in the future.

I would not impose upon the States this federal exclusionary remedy. The reasons given by the majority for now suddenly turning its back on Wolf seem to me notably unconvincing.

First, it is said that "the factual grounds upon which Wolf was based" have since changed, in that more States now follow the Weeks exclusionary rule than was so at the time Wolf was decided. While that is true, a recent survey indicates that, at present, one-half of the States still adhere to the common law non-exclusionary rule, and one, Maryland, retains the rule as to felonies. Berman and Oberst, Admissibility of Evidence Obtained by an Unconstitutional Search and Seizure, 55 N.W.L.Rev. 525, 532-533. But, in any case, surely all this is beside the point, as the majority itself indeed seems to recognize. Our concern here, as it was in Wolf, is not with the desirability of that rule, but only with the question whether the States are Constitutionally free to follow it or not as they may themselves determine, and the relevance of the disparity of views among the States on this point lies simply in the fact that the judgment involved is a debatable one. Moreover, the very fact on which the majority relies, instead of lending support to what is now being done, points away from the need of replacing voluntary state action with federal compulsion.

The preservation of a proper balance between state and federal responsibility in the administration of criminal justice demands patience on the part of those who might like to see things move faster among the States in this respect. Problems of criminal law enforcement vary widely from State to State. One State, in considering the totality of its legal picture, may conclude that the need for embracing the Weeks rule is pressing because other remedies are unavailable or inadequate to secure compliance with the substantive Constitutional principle involved. Another, though equally solicitous of Constitutional rights, may choose to pursue one purpose at a time, allowing all evidence relevant to guilt to be brought into a criminal trial, and dealing with Constitutional infractions by other means. Still another may consider the exclusionary rule too rough-and-ready a remedy, in that it reaches only unconstitutional intrusions which eventuate in criminal prosecution of the victims. Further, a State after experimenting with the Weeks rule for a time may, because of unsatisfactory experience with it, decide to revert to a non-exclusionary rule. And so on. From the standpoint of Constitutional permissibility in pointing a State in one direction or another, I do not see at all why "time has set its face against" the considerations which led Mr. Justice Cardozo, then chief judge of the New York Court of Appeals, to reject for New York in People v. Defore, 242 N.Y. 13, 150 N.E. 585, the Weeks exclusionary rule. For us, the question remains, as it has always been, one of state power, not one of passing judgment on the wisdom of one state course or another. In my view, this Court should continue to forbear from fettering the States with an adamant rule which may embarrass them in coping with their own peculiar problems in criminal law enforcement.

Further, we are told that imposition of the Weeks rule on the States makes "very good sense," in that it will promote recognition by state and federal officials of their "mutual obligation to respect the same fundamental criteria" in their approach to law enforcement, and will avoid "'needless conflict between state and federal courts.'" Indeed, the majority now finds an incongruity in Wolf's discriminating perception between the demands of "ordered liberty" as respects the basic right of "privacy" and the means of securing it among the States. That perception, resting both on a sensitive regard for our federal system and a sound recognition of this Court's remoteness from particular state problems, is, for me, the strength of that decision.

An approach which regards the issue as one of achieving procedural symmetry or of serving administrative convenience surely disfigures the boundaries of this Court's functions in relation to the state and federal courts. Our role in promulgating the Weeks rule and its extensions in such cases as Rea, Elkins, and Rios [n11] was quite a different one than it is here. There, in implementing the Fourth Amendment, we occupied the position of a tribunal having the ultimate responsibility for developing the standards and procedures of judicial administration within the judicial system over which it presides. Here, we review state procedures whose measure is to be taken not against the specific substantive commands of the Fourth Amendment, but under the flexible contours of the Due Process Clause. I do not believe that the Fourteenth Amendment empowers this Court to mould state remedies effectuating the right to freedom from "arbitrary intrusion by the police" to suit its own notions of how things should be done, as, for instance, the California Supreme Court did in People v. Cahan, 44 Cal.2d 434, 282 P.2d 905, with reference to procedures in the California courts, or as this Court did in Weeks for the lower federal courts.

A state conviction comes to us as the complete product of a sovereign judicial system. Typically, a case will have been tried in a trial court, tested in some final appellate court, and will go no further. In the comparatively rare instance when a conviction is reviewed by us on due process grounds, we deal then with a finished product in the creation of which we are allowed no hand, and our task, far from being one of over-all supervision, is, speaking generally, restricted to a determination of whether the prosecution was constitutionally fair. The specifics of trial procedure, which in every mature legal system will vary greatly in detail, are within the sole competence of the States. I do not see how it can be said that a trial becomes unfair simply because a State determines that evidence may be considered by the trier of fact, regardless of how it was obtained, if it is relevant to the one issue with which the trial is concerned, the guilt or innocence of the accused. Of course, a court may use its procedures as an incidental means of pursuing other ends than the correct resolution of the controversies before it. Such indeed is the Weeks rule, but if a State does not choose to use its courts in this way, I do not believe that this Court is empowered to impose this much-debated procedure on local courts, however efficacious we may consider the Weeks rule to be as a means of securing Constitutional rights.

Finally, it is said that the overruling of Wolf is supported by the established doctrine that the admission in evidence of an involuntary confession renders a state conviction constitutionally invalid. Since such a confession may often be entirely reliable, and therefore of the greatest relevance to the issue of the trial, the argument continues, this doctrine is ample warrant in precedent that the way evidence was obtained, and not just its relevance, is constitutionally significant to the fairness of a trial. I believe this analogy is not a true one. The "coerced confession" rule is certainly not a rule that any illegally obtained statements may not be used in evidence. I would suppose that a statement which is procured during a period of illegal detention, McNabb v. United States, 318 U.S. 332, is, as much as unlawfully seized evidence, illegally obtained, but this Court has consistently refused to reverse state convictions resting on the use of such statements. Indeed, it would seem the Court laid at rest the very argument now made by the majority when, in Lisenba v. California, 314 U.S. 219, a state-coerced confession case, it said (at 235):

It may be assumed [that the] treatment of the petitioner [by the police] . . . deprived him of his liberty without due process, and that the petitioner would have been afforded preventive relief if he could have gained access to a court to seek it.

But illegal acts, as such, committed in the course of obtaining a confession . . . do not furnish an answer to the constitutional question we must decide. . . . The gravamen of his complaint is the unfairness of the use of his confessions, and what occurred in their procurement is relevant only as it bears on that issue.

(Emphasis supplied.)

The point, then, must be that, in requiring exclusion of an involuntary statement of an accused, we are concerned not with an appropriate remedy for what the police have done, but with something which is regarded as going to the heart of our concepts of fairness in judicial procedure. The operative assumption of our procedural system is that

Ours is the accusatorial, as opposed to the inquisitorial system. Such has been the characteristic of Anglo-American criminal justice since it freed itself from practices borrowed by the Star Chamber from the Continent whereby the accused was interrogated in secret for hours on end.

Watts v. Indiana, 338 U.S. 49, 54. See Rogers v. Richmond, 365 U.S. 534, 541. The pressures brought to bear against an accused leading to a confession, unlike an unconstitutional violation of privacy, do not, apart from the use of the confession at trial, necessarily involve independent Constitutional violations. What is crucial is that the trial defense to which an accused is entitled should not be rendered an empty formality by reason of statements wrung from him, for then "a prisoner . . . [has been] made the deluded instrument of his own conviction." 2 Hawkins, Pleas of the Crown (8th ed., 1824), c. 46, § 34. That this is a procedural right, and that its violation occurs at the time his improperly obtained statement is admitted at trial, is manifest. For without this right, all the careful safeguards erected around the giving of testimony, whether by an accused or any other witness, would become empty formalities in a procedure where the most compelling possible evidence of guilt, a confession, would have already been obtained at the unsupervised pleasure of the police.

This, and not the disciplining of the police, as with illegally seized evidence, is surely the true basis for excluding a statement of the accused which was unconstitutionally obtained. In sum, I think the coerced confession analogy works strongly against what the

Court does today.

In conclusion, it should be noted that the majority opinion in this case is, in fact, an opinion only for the judgment overruling Wolf, and not for the basic rationale by which four members of the majority have reached that result. For my Brother BLACK is unwilling to subscribe to their view that the Weeks exclusionary rule derives from the Fourth Amendment itself (see ante, p. 661), but joins the majority opinion on the premise that its end result can be achieved by bringing the Fifth Amendment to the aid of the Fourth (see ante pp. 662-665). [n12] On that score I need only say that whatever the validity of the "Fourth-Fifth Amendment" correlation which the Boyd case (116 U.S. 616) found, see 8 Wigmore, Evidence (3d ed.1940), § 2184, we have only very recently again reiterated the long-established doctrine of this Court that the Fifth Amendment privilege against self-incrimination is not applicable to the States. See Cohen v. Hurley, 366 U.S. 117.

I regret that I find so unwise in principle and so inexpedient in policy a decision motivated by the high purpose of increasing respect for Constitutional rights. But, in the last analysis, I think this Court can increase respect for the Constitution only if it rigidly respects the limitations which the Constitution places upon it, and respects as well the principles inherent in its own processes. In the present case, I think we exceed both, and that our voice becomes only a voice of power, not of reason.

Notes

1. The material parts of that law are quoted in note 1 of the Court's opinion. Ante, p. 643.

2. In its note 3, ante, p. 646, the Court, it seems to me, has turned upside down the relative importance of appellant's reliance on the various points made by him on this appeal.

3. See 170 Ohio St. 427, 166 N.E.2d 387. Because of the unusual provision of the Ohio Constitution requiring "the concurrence of at least all but one of the judges" of the Ohio Supreme Court before a state law is held unconstitutional (except in the case of affirmance of a holding of unconstitutionality by the Ohio Court of Appeals), Ohio Const., Art. IV, § 2, the State Supreme Court was compelled to uphold the constitutionality of § 2905.34 despite the fact that four of its seven judges thought the statute offensive to the Fourteenth Amendment.

4. Respecting the "substantiality" of the federal questions tendered by this appeal, appellant's Jurisdictional Statement contained the following:

The Federal questions raised by this appeal are substantial for the following reasons:

The Ohio Statute under which the defendant was convicted violates one's sacred right to own and hold property, which has been held inviolate by the Federal Constitution. The right of the individual

to read, to believe or disbelieve, and to think without governmental supervision is one of our basic liberties, but to dictate to the mature adult what books he may have in his own private library seems to be a clear infringement of the constitutional rights of the individual

(Justice Herbert's dissenting Opinion, Appendix "A"). Many convictions have followed that of the defendant in the State Courts of Ohio based upon this very same statute. Unless this Honorable Court hears this matter and determines once and for all that the Statute is unconstitutional as defendant contends, there will be many such appeals. When Sections 2905.34, 2905.37 and 3767.01 of the Ohio Revised Code [the latter two Sections providing exceptions to the coverage of § 2905.34 and related provisions of Ohio's obscenity statutes] are read together, . . . they obviously contravene the Federal and State constitutional provisions; by being convicted under the Statute involved herein, and in the manner in which she was convicted, Defendant-Appellant has been denied due process of law; a sentence of from one (1) to seven (7) years in a penal institution for alleged violation of this unconstitutional section of the Ohio Revised Code deprives the defendant of her right to liberty and the pursuit of happiness, contrary to the Federal and State constitutional provisions, for circumstances which she herself did not put in motion, and is a cruel and unusual punishment inflicted upon her contrary to the State and Federal Constitutions.

5. The appellant's brief did not urge the overruling of Wolf. Indeed, it did not even cite the case. The brief of the appellee merely relied on Wolf in support of the State's contention that appellant's conviction was not vitiated by the admission in evidence of the fruits of the alleged unlawful search and seizure by the police. The brief of the American and Ohio Civil Liberties Unions, as amici, did, in one short concluding paragraph of its argument, "request" the Court to reexamine and overrule Wolf, but without argumentation. I quote in full this part of their brief:

This case presents the issue of whether evidence obtained in an illegal search and seizure can constitutionally be used in a State criminal proceeding. We are aware of the view that this Court has taken on this issue in Wolf v. Colorado, 338 U.S. 25. It is our purpose by this paragraph to respectfully request that this Court reexamine this issue and conclude that the ordered liberty concept guaranteed to persons by the due process clause of the Fourteenth Amendment necessarily requires that evidence illegally obtained in violation thereof, not be admissible in state criminal proceedings.

6. Counsel for appellant on oral argument, as in his brief, did not urge that Wolf be overruled. Indeed, when pressed by questioning from the bench whether he was not, in fact, urging us to overrule Wolf, counsel expressly disavowed any such purpose.

7. 2905.37 LEGITIMATE PUBLICATIONS NOT OBSCENE.

Sections 2905.33 to 2905.36, inclusive, of the Revised Code do not affect teaching in regularly chartered medical colleges, the publication of standard medical books, or regular practitioners of medicine or druggists in their legitimate business, nor do they affect the publication and distribution of bona fide works of art. No articles specified in sections 2905.33, 2905.34, and 2905.36 of the Revised Code shall be considered a work of art unless such article is made, published, and distributed by a bona fide association of artists or an association for the advancement of art whose demonstrated purpose does not contravene sections 2905.06 to 2905.44, inclusive, of the Revised Code, and which is not organized for profit.

§ 3767.01(c)

This section and sections 2905.34, . . . 2905.37 . . . of the Revised Code shall not affect . . . any newspaper, magazine, or other publication entered as second class matter by the post office department.

8. The Ohio Supreme Court, in its construction of § 2905.34, controlling upon us here, refused to import into it any other exceptions than those expressly provided by the statute. See note 7, supra. Instead, it held that "If anyone looks at a book and finds it lewd, he is forthwith, under this legislation, guilty. . . ."

9. See Wolf v. Colorado, 338 U.S. at 39-40; Irvine v. California, 347 U.S. 128, 133-134, and at 138-139. In the latter case, decided in 1954, Mr. Justice Jackson, writing for the majority, said (at p. 134): "We think that the Wolf decision should not be overruled, for the reasons so persuasively stated therein." Compare Schwartz v. Texas, 344 U.S. 199, and Stefanelli v. Minard, 342 U.S. 117, in which the Wolf case was discussed and in no way disapproved. And see Pugach v. Dollinger, 365 U.S. 458, which relied on Schwartz.

10. Actually, only four members of the majority support this reasoning. See pp. 685-686, infra.

11. Rea v. United States, 350 U.S. 214; Elkins v. United States, 364 U.S. 206; Rios v. United States, 364 U.S. 253.

12. My Brother STEWART concurs in the Court's judgment on grounds which have nothing to do with Wolf.

Justice Harlan's dissent to denial of certiorari in Poe v. Ullman (June 19, 1961)

MR. JUSTICE HARLAN, dissenting.

I am compelled, with all respect, to dissent from the dismissal of these appeals. In my view, the course which the Court has taken does violence to established concepts of "justiciability," and unjustifiably leaves these appellants under the threat of unconstitutional prosecution. Regrettably, an adequate exposition of my views calls for a dissenting opinion of unusual length.

Between them these suits seek declaratory relief against the threatened enforcement of Connecticut's anti-birth control laws making criminal the use of contraceptives, insofar as such laws relate to the use of contraceptives by married persons and the giving of advice to married persons in their use. [1] The appellants, a married couple, a married woman, and a doctor, ask that it be adjudged, contrary to what the Connecticut courts have held, that such laws, as threatened to be applied to them in circumstances described in the opinion announcing the judgment of the Court (ante, pp.

367 U. S. 498-500), violate the Fourteenth Amendment, in that they deprive appellants of life, liberty, or property without due process.

The plurality opinion of the Court gives, as the basis for dismissing the appeals, the reason that, as to the two married appellants, the lack of demonstrated enforcement of the Connecticut statute bespeaks an absence of exigent adversity which is posited as the condition for evoking adjudication from us, and, as to the doctor, that his compliance with the state statute is uncoerced by any "realistic fear of prosecution," giving due recognition to his "standing as a physician and to his personal sensitiveness." With these reasons it appears that the concurring opinion agrees.

In Alabama State Federation of Labor v. McAdory, 325 U. S. 450, 325 U. S. 462, it was said that

"declaratory judgment procedure may be resorted to only in the sound discretion of the Court and where the interests of justice will be advanced and an adequate and effective judgment may be rendered."

In my view of these cases, a present determination of the constitutional issues is the only course which will advance justice, and I can find no sound reason born of considerations as to the possible inadequacy or ineffectiveness of the judgment that might be rendered which justifies the Court's contrary disposition. While ordinarily I would not deem it appropriate to deal, in dissent, with constitutional issues which the Court has not reached, I shall do so here because such issues, as I see things, are entangled with the Court's conclusion as to the nonjusticiability of these appeals.

PART ONE

Justiciability

There can be no quarrel with the plurality opinion's statement that "Justiciability is, of course, not a legal concept with a fixed content or susceptible of scientific verification," but, with deference, the fact that justiciability is not precisely definable does not make it ineffable. Although a large number of cases are brought to bear on the conclusion that is reached, I think it is fairly demonstrable that the authorities fall far short of compelling dismissal of these appeals. [2] Even so, it is suggested that the cases do point the way to a "rigorous insistence on exigent adversity" and a "policy against premature constitutional decision," which, properly understood, does indeed demand that result.

The policy referred to is one to which I unreservedly subscribe. Without undertaking to be definitive, I would suppose it is a policy the wisdom of which is woven of several strands: (1) due regard for the fact that the source of the Court's power lies ultimately in its duty to decide, in conformity with the Constitution, the particular controversies which come to it, and does not arise from some generalized power of supervision over state and national legislatures; (2) therefore it should insist that litigants bring to the Court interests and rights which require present recognition and controversies demanding immediate resolution; (3) also it follows that the controversy must be one which is in truth and fact the litigant's own, so that the clash of adversary contest which is needed to sharpen and illuminate issues is present and gives that aid on which our adjudicatory system has come to rely; (4) finally, it is required that other means of redress for the particular right claimed be unavailable, so that the process of the Court may not become overburdened and conflicts with other courts or departments of government may not needlessly be created, which might come about if either those truly affected are not the ones demanding relief, or if the relief we can give is not truly needed.

In particularization of this composite policy, the Court, in the course of its decisions on matters of justiciability, has developed and given expression to a number of important limitations on the exercise of its jurisdiction, the presence or absence of which here should determine the justiciability of these appeals. Since all of them are referred to here in one way or another, it is well to proceed to a disclosure of those which are not involved in the present appeals, thereby focusing attention on the one factor on which reliance appears to be placed by both the plurality and concurring opinions in this instance.

First: it should by now be abundantly clear that the fact that only constitutional claims are presented in proceedings seeking anticipatory relief against state criminal statutes does not, for that reason alone, make the claims premature. See, e.g., Terrace v. Thompson, 263 U. S. 197; Pierce v. Society of Sisters, 268 U. S. 510; Euclid, Ohio v. Ambler Realty Co., 272 U. S. 365. Whatever general pronouncements may be found to the contrary must, in context, be seen to refer to considerations quite different from anything present in these cases.

Thus, in Alabama State Federation of Labor v. McAdory, supra, anticipatory relief was withheld for the precise reason that, normally, this Court ought not to consider the constitutionality of a state statute in the absence of a controlling interpretation of its meaning and effect by the state courts. To the same effect, see Parker v. Los Angeles County, 338 U. S. 327; Watson v. Buck, 313 U. S. 387; Beal v. Missouri Pacific R. Co., 312 U. S. 45. Indeed, without belaboring the point, the principle that anticipatory relief against state criminal statutes is not unavailable as a general matter may best be illustrated by several cases recently decided in this Court. In Harrison v. NAACP, 360 U. S. 167, the premise of our action was that anticipatory relief should be obtained, if possible -- with review here on certiorari or appeal -- in a state court which could then authoritatively construe a new and ambiguous state statute; only if such relief were unavailable should a Federal District Court exercise its statutory jurisdiction. And in our recent decisions upholding the constitutionality of state Sunday closing laws, 366 U. S. 366 U.S. 420 et seq., not one of the opinions paused even slightly over the appropriateness of anticipatory relief, although, in one case, that issue was argued, Gallagher v. Crown Kosher Super Market, 366 U. S. 617.

Hence, any language in the cases where the Court has abstained from exercising its jurisdiction to the effect that we should not "entertain constitutional questions in advance of the strictest necessity," Parker v. Los Angeles County, supra, at 338 U. S. 333, is not at all apposite in the present cases. For these appeals come to us from the highest court of Connecticut, thus affording us -- in company with previous state interpretations of the same statute -- a clear construction of the scope of the statute, thereby in effect assuring that our review constitutes no greater interference with state administration than the state procedures themselves allow.

Second: I do not think these appeals may be dismissed for want of "ripeness" as that concept has been understood in its "varied applications." [3] There is no lack of "ripeness" in the sense that is exemplified by cases such as Stearns v. Wood,236 U. S. 75; Electric Bond & Share Co. v. Securities & Exchange Comm'n, 303 U. S. 419; United Public Workers v. Mitchell, 330 U. S. 75; International Longshoremen's Union v. Boyd, 347 U. S. 222; and perhaps again Parker v. Los Angeles County, supra. In all of those cases, the lack of ripeness inhered in the fact that the need for some further procedure, some further contingency of application or interpretation, whether judicial, administrative or executive, or some further clarification of the intentions of the claimant, served to make remote the issue which was sought to be presented to the Court. Certainly the appellants have stated in their pleadings fully and unequivocally what it is that they intend to do; no clarifying or resolving contingency stands in their way before they may embark on that conduct. Thus there is no circumstance, besides that of detection or prosecution, to make remote the particular controversy. And it is clear beyond cavil that the mere fact that a controversy such as this is rendered still more unavoidable by an actual prosecution is not alone sufficient to make the case too remote, not ideally enough "ripe" for adjudication, at the prior stage of anticipatory relief.

Moreover, it follows from what has already been said that there is no such want of ripeness as was presented in Rescue Army v. Municipal Court, 331 U. S. 549, or in our recent decisions dismissing the appeals in Atlanta Newspapers, Inc. v. Grimes, 364 U. S. 290, and United States v. Fruehauf, 365 U. S. 146, where the records presented for adjudication a controversy so artificially truncated as to make the cases not susceptible to intelligent decision. I cannot see what further elaboration is required to enable us to decide the appellants' claims, and indeed neither the plurality opinion nor the concurring opinion -- notwithstanding the latter's characterization of this record as "skimpy" -- suggests what mere grist is needed before the judicial mill could turn.

Third: This is not a feigned, hypothetical, friendly or colorable suit such as discloses "a want of a truly adversary contest." Clearly, these cases are not analogous to Wood-Paper Co. v. Heft, 8 Wall. 333, or South Spring Hill Gold Mining Co. v. Amador Medean Gold Mining Co.,145 U. S. 300, where, prior to consideration, the controversy in effect became moot by the merger of the two contesting interests. Nor is there any question of collusion, as in Lord v. Veazie, 8 How. 251, or in United States v. Johnson, 319 U. S. 302. And there is nothing to suggest that the parties, by their conduct of this litigation, have cooperated to force an adjudication of a constitutional issue which -- were the parties interested solely in winning their cases, rather than obtaining a constitutional decision -- might not arise in an arm's-length contested proceeding. Such was the situation in Chicago & Grand Trunk R. Co. v. Wellman, 143 U. S. 339, where the parties sought a ruling as to whether a particular passenger rate was unconstitutionally confiscatory, having stipulated all the debatable and contingent facts which otherwise might have rendered a constitutional decision unnecessary.

In the present appeals, no more is alleged or conceded than is consistent with undisputed facts and with ordinary practice in deciding a case for anticipatory relief on demurrer. I think it is unjustifiably stretching things to assume that appellants are not deterred by the threat of prosecution from engaging in the conduct in which they assert a right to engage, or to assume that appellee's demurrer to the proposition that he asserts the right to enforce the statute against appellants at any time he chooses is anything but a candid one.

Indeed, as will be developed below, I think both the plurality and concurring opinions confuse on this score the predictive likelihood that, had they not brought themselves to appellee's attention, he would not enforce the statute against them, with some entirely suppositious "tacit agreement" not to prosecute, thereby ignoring the prosecutor's claim, asserted in these very proceedings, of a right, at his unbounded prosecutorial discretion, to enforce the statute.

Fourth: The doctrine of the cases dealing with a litigant's lack of standing to raise a constitutional claim is said to justify the dismissal of these appeals. The precedents put forward as examples of this doctrine, see the plurality opinion, note 5 as well as cases such as Frothingham v. Mellon and Massachusetts v. Mellon, 262 U. S. 447, and Texas v. Interstate Commerce Comm'n,258 U. S. 158, do indeed stand for the proposition that a legal claim will not be considered at the instance of one who has no real and concrete interest in its vindication. This is well in accord with the grounds for declining jurisdiction suggested above. But this doctrine, in turn, needs further particularization, lest it become a catchall for an unarticulated discretion on the part of this Court to decline to adjudicate appeals involving constitutional issues.

There is no question but that appellants here are asserting rights which are peculiarly their own, and which, if they are to be raised at all, may be raised most appropriately by them. Cf. Tileston v. Ullman, 318 U. S. 44; Texas v. Interstate Commerce Comm'n, supra; Yazoo & Mississippi Valley R. Co. v. Jackson Vinegar Co.,226 U. S. 217; Ashwander v. Tennessee Valley Authority,297 U. S. 288, 297 U. S. 341 (concurring opinion). Nor do I understand the argument to be that this is the sort of claim which is too remote ever to be pressed by anyone, because no one is ever sufficiently involved. Cf. Massachusetts v. Mellon, Frothingham v. Mellon, supra. Thus, in truth, it is not the parties pressing this claim, but the occasion chosen for pressing it, which is objected to. But, as has been shown, the fact that it is anticipatory relief which is asked cannot, of itself, make the occasion objectionable.

We are brought, then, to the precise failing in these proceedings which is said to justify refusal to exercise our mandatory appellate jurisdiction: that there has been but one recorded Connecticut case dealing with a prosecution under the statute. [4] The significance of this lack of recorded evidence of prosecutions is said to make the presentation of appellants' rights too remote, too contingent, too hypothetical for adjudication in the light of the policies already considered. See pp. 367 U. S. 526-530, supra. In my view, it is only as a result of misconceptions both about the purport of the record before us and about the nature of the rights appellants put forward that this conclusion can be reached.

As far as the record is concerned, I think it is pure conjecture, and indeed conjecture which to me seems contrary to realities, that an open violation of the statute by a doctor (or more obviously still by a birth control clinic) would not result in a substantial threat of prosecution. Crucial to the opposite conclusion is the description of the 1940 prosecution instituted in State v. Nelson, 126 Conn. 412, 11 A.2d 856, as a "test case" which, as it is viewed, scarcely even punctuates the uniform state practice of nonenforcement of this statute. I read the history of Connecticut enforcement in a very different light. The Nelson case, as appears from the state court's opinion, was a prosecution of two doctors and a nurse for aiding and abetting violations of this statute by married women in prescribing and advising the use of contraceptive materials by them. It is true that there is evidence of a customary unwillingness to enforce the statute prior to Nelson, for, in that case, the prosecutor stated to the trial court, in a later motion to discontinue the prosecutions, that,

"When this Waterbury clinic [operated by the defendants] was opened, there were in open operation elsewhere in the State at least eight other contraceptive clinics which had been in existence for a long period of time, and no questions as to their right to operate had been raised. . . . [5]"

What must also be noted is that the prosecutor followed this statement with an explanation that the primary purpose of the prosecution was to provide clear warning to all those who, like Nelson, might rely on this practice of nonenforcement. He stated that the purpose of the prosecution was:

"the establishment of the constitutional validity and efficacy of the statutes under which these accused are informed against. Henceforth any person, whether a physician or layman, who violates the provisions of these statutes must expect to be prosecuted and punished in accordance with the literal provisions of the law. [6] "

Thus, the respect in which Nelson was a test case is only that it was brought for the purpose of making entirely clear the State's power and willingness to enforce against "any person, whether a physician or layman" (emphasis supplied), the statute and to eliminate from future cases the very doubt about the existence of these elements which had resulted in eight open birth control clinics, and which would have made unfair the conviction of Nelson.

The plurality opinion now finds, and the concurring opinion must assume, that the only explanation of the absence of recorded prosecutions subsequent to the Nelson case is that Connecticut has renounced that intention to prosecute and punish "any person . . . in accordance with the literal provisions of the law" which it announced in Nelson. But if renunciation of the purposes of the Nelson prosecution is consistent with a lack of subsequent prosecutions, success of that purpose is no less consistent with this lack. I find it difficult to believe that doctors generally -- and not just those operating specialized clinics -- would continue openly to disseminate advice about contraceptives after Nelson in reliance on the State's supposed unwillingness to prosecute, or to consider that high-minded members of the profession would, in consequence of such inaction, deem themselves warranted in disrespecting this law so long as it is on the books. Nor can I regard as "chimerical" the fear of enforcement of these provisions that seems to have caused the disappearance of at least nine birth control clinics. [7] In short, I fear that the Court has indulged in a bit of sleight of hand to be rid of this case. It has treated the significance of the absence of prosecutions during the twenty years since Nelson as identical with that of the absence of prosecutions during the years before Nelson. It has ignored the fact that the very purpose of the Nelson prosecution was to change defiance into compliance. It has ignored the very possibility that this purpose may have been successful. [8] The result is to postulate a security from prosecution for open defiance of the statute which I do not believe the record supports. [9]

These considerations alone serve to bring appellants so squarely within the rule of Pierce v. Society of Sisters,268 U. S. 510, and Traux v. Raich,239 U. S. 33, that further demonstration would be pointless.

But even if Dr. Buxton were not in the litigation and appellants, the Poes and Doe, were seeking simply to use contraceptives without any need of consulting a physician beforehand -- which is not the case we have, although it is the case which the plurality opinion of the Court is primarily concerned to discuss -- even then, I think that it misconceives the concept of justiciability and the nature of these appellants' rights to say that the failure of the State to carry through any criminal prosecution requires dismissal of their appeals.

The Court's disposition assumes that to decide the case now, in the absence of any consummated prosecutions, is unwise, because it forces a difficult decision in advance of any exigent necessity therefor. Of course, it is abundantly clear that this requisite necessity can exist prior to any actual prosecution, for that is the theory of anticipatory relief, and is, by now, familiar law. What must be relied on, therefore, is that the historical absence of prosecutions in some way leaves these appellants free to violate the statute without fear of prosecution, whether or not the law is constitutional, and thus absolves us from the duty of deciding if it is. Despite the suggestion of a "tougher and truer law" of immunity from criminal prosecution, and despite speculation as to a "tacit agreement" that this law will not be enforced, there is, of course, no suggestion of an estoppel against the State if it should attempt to prosecute appellants. Neither the plurality nor the concurring opinion suggests that appellants have some legally cognizable right not to be prosecuted if the statute is constitutional. What is meant is simply that the appellants are more or less free to act without fear of prosecution because the prosecuting authorities of the State, in their discretion and at their whim, are, as a matter of prediction, unlikely to decide to prosecute.

Here is the core of my disagreement with the present disposition. As I will develop later in this opinion, the most substantial claim which these married persons press is their right to enjoy the privacy of their marital relations, free of the enquiry of the criminal law, whether it be in a prosecution of them or of a doctor whom they have consulted. And I cannot agreed that their enjoyment of this privacy is not substantially impinged upon when they are told that if they use contraceptives, indeed whether they do so or not, the only thing which stands between them and being forced to render criminal account of their marital privacy is the whim of the prosecutor. [10] Connecticut's highest court has told us in the clearest terms that, given proof, the prosecutor will succeed if he decides to bring a proceeding against one of the appellants for taking the precise actions appellants have announced they intend to take. The State Court does not agree that there has come into play a "tougher and truer law than the dead words of the written text," and, in the light of twelve unsuccessful attempts since 1943 to change this legislation, Poe v. Ullman, 147 Conn. 48, 56, note 2, 156 A.2d 508, 513, this position is not difficult to understand. Prosecution and conviction for the clearly spelled-out actions the appellants wish to take is not made unlikely by any fortuitous factor outside the control of the parties, nor is it made uncertain by possible variations in the actions appellants actually take from those the state courts have already passed upon. All that stands between the appellants and jail is the legally unfettered whim of the prosecutor and the constitutional issue this Court today refuses to decide.

If we revert again to the reasons underlying our reluctance to exercise a jurisdiction which technically we possess, and the concrete expression of those underlying reasons in our cases, see pp. 367 U. S. 526-531, supra, then I think it must become clear that there is no justification for failing to decide these married persons' appeals. The controversy awaits nothing but an actual prosecution, and, as will be shown, the substantial damage against which these appellants, Mrs. Doe and the Poes, are entitled to protection will be accomplished by such a prosecution, whatever its outcome in the state courts or here. By the present decision, although, as a general matter, the parties would be entitled to our review in an anticipatory proceeding which the State allowed to be instituted in its courts, these appellants are made to await actual prosecution before we will hear them. Indeed, it appears that, whereas appellants would surely have been entitled to review were this a new statute, see Harrison v. NAACP, supra, the State here is enabled to maintain at least some substantial measure of compliance with this statute and still obviate any review in this Court, by the device of purely discretionary prosecutorial inactivity. It seems to me to destroy the whole purpose of anticipatory relief to consider the prosecutor's discretion, once all legal and administrative channels have been cleared, as in any way analogous to those other contingencies which make remote a controversy presenting constitutional claims.

In this light, it is not surprising that the Court's position is without support in the precedents. [11] Indeed, it seems to me that Pierce v. Society of Sisters, 268 U. S. 510, provides very clear authority contrary to the position of the Court in this case, for there, a Court which included Justices Holmes, Brandeis, and Stone rejected a claim of prematureness and then passed upon and held unconstitutional a state statute whose sanctions were not even to become effective for more than seventeen months after the time the case was argued to this Court. The Court found allegations of present loss of business, caused by the threat of the statute's future enforcement against the Society's clientele, sufficient to make the injury to the Society "present and very real." 268 U.S. at 268 U. S. 536. I cannot regard as less present, or less real, the tendency to discourage the exercise of the liberties of these appellants, caused by reluctance to submit their freedoms from prosecution and conviction to the discretion of the Connecticut prosecuting authorities. I therefore think it incumbent on us to consider the merits of appellants' constitutional claims.

PART TWO

Constitutionality

I consider that this Connecticut legislation, as construed to apply to these appellants, violates the Fourteenth Amendment. I believe that a statute making it a criminal offense for married couples to use contraceptives is an intolerable and unjustifiable invasion of privacy in the conduct of the most intimate concerns of an individual's personal life. I reach this conclusion even though I find it difficult and unnecessary at this juncture to accept appellants' other argument that the judgment of policy behind the statute, so applied, is so arbitrary and unreasonable as to render the enactment invalid for that reason alone. Since both the contentions draw their basis from no explicit language of the Constitution, and have yet to find expression in any decision of this Court, I feel it desirable at the outset to state the framework of constitutional principles in which I think the issue must be judged.

I

In reviewing state legislation, whether considered to be in the exercise of the State's police powers or in provision for the health, safety, morals or welfare of its people, it is clear that what is concerned are "the powers of government inherent in every sovereignty." The License Cases, 5 How. 504, 46 U. S. 583. Only to the extent that the Constitution so requires may this Court interfere with the exercise of this plenary power of government. Barron v. Mayor of City of Baltimore, 7 Pet. 243. But precisely because it is the Constitution alone which warrants judicial interference in sovereign operations of the State, the basis of judgment as to the constitutionality of state action must be a rational one, approaching the text which is the only commission for our power not in a literalistic way, as if we had a tax statute before us, but as the basic charter of our society, setting out in spare but meaningful terms the principles of government. M'Culloch v. Maryland, 4 Wheat. 316. But as inescapable as is the rational process in constitutional adjudication in general, nowhere is it more so than in giving meaning to the prohibitions of the Fourteenth Amendment, and, where the Federal Government is involved, the Fifth Amendment, against the deprivation of life, liberty or property without due process of law.

It is but a truism to say that this provision of both Amendments is not self-explanatory. As to the Fourteenth, which is involved here, the history of the Amendment also sheds little light on the meaning of the provision. Fairman, Does the Fourteenth Amendment Incorporate the Bill of Rights, 2 Stan.L.Re v. 15. It is important to note, however, that two views of the Amendment have not been accepted by this Court as delineating its scope. One view, which was ably and insistently argued in response to what were felt to be abuses by this Court of its reviewing power, sought to limit the provision to a guarantee of procedural fairness. See Davidson v. City of New Orleans,96 U. S. 97, 96 U. S. 105; Brandeis, J., in Whitney v. California,274 U. S. 357, at 274 U. S. 373; Warren, The New "Liberty" under the 14th Amendment, 39 Harv.L.Re v. 431; Reeder, The Due Process Clauses and "The Substance of Individual Rights," 58 U.Pa.L.Re v. 191; Shattuck, The True Meaning of the Term "Liberty" in Those Clauses in the Federal and State Constitutions Which Protect "Life, Liberty, and Property," 4 Harv.L.Re v. 365. The other view which has been rejected would have it that the Fourteenth Amendment, whether by way of the Privileges and Immunities Clause or the Due Process Clause, applied against the States only and precisely those restraints which had, prior to the Amendment, been applicable merely to federal action. However, "due process," in the consistent view of this Court, has even been a broader concept than the first view, and more flexible than the second.

Were due process merely a procedural safeguard, it would fail to reach those situations where the deprivation of life, liberty or property was accomplished by legislation which by operating in the future could, given even the fairest possible procedure in application to individuals, nevertheless destroy the enjoyment of all three. Compare, e.g., Selective Draft Law Cases,245 U. S. 366; Butler v. Perry,240 U. S. 328; Korematsu v. United States, 323 U. S. 214. Thus the guaranties of due process, though having their roots in Magna Carta's "per legem terrae" and considered as procedural safeguards "against executive usurpation and tyranny," have in this country "become bulwarks also against arbitrary legislation." Hurtado v. California,110 U. S. 516, at 110 U. S. 532.

However, it is not the particular enumeration of rights in the first eight Amendments which spells out the reach of Fourteenth Amendment due process, but rather, as was suggested in another context long before the adoption of that Amendment, those concepts which are considered to embrace those rights "which are . . . fundamental; which belong . . . to the citizens of all free governments," Corfield v. Coryell, 4 Wash.C.C. 371, 380, for "the purposes (of securing) which men enter into society," Calder v. Bull, 3 Dall. 386, 3 U. S. 388. Again and again, this Court has resisted the notion that the Fourteenth Amendment is no more than a shorthand reference to what is explicitly set out elsewhere in the Bill of Rights. The Slaughter-House Cases, 16 Wall. 36; Walker v. Sauvinet,92 U. S. 90; Hurtado v. California,110 U. S. 516; Presser v. Illinois,116 U. S. 252; In re Kemmler,136 U. S. 436; Twining v. New Jersey,211 U. S. 78; Palko v. Connecticut, 302 U. S. 319. Indeed, the fact that an identical provision limiting federal action is found among the first eight Amendments, applying to the Federal Government, suggests that due process is a discrete concept which subsists as an independent guaranty of liberty and procedural fairness, more general and inclusive than the specific prohibitions. See Mormon Church v. United States, 136 U. S. 1; Downes v. Bidwell, 182 U. S. 244; Hawaii v.

Mankichi, 190 U. S. 197; Balzac v. Porto Rico, 258 U. S. 298; Farrington v. Tokushige, 273 U. S. 284; Bolling v. Sharpe, 347 U. S. 497.

Due process has not been reduced to any formula; its content cannot be determined by reference to any code. The best that can be said is that, through the course of this Court's decisions, it has represented the balance which our Nation, built upon postulates of respect for the liberty of the individual, has struck between that liberty and the demands of organized society. If the supplying of content to this constitutional concept has of necessity been a rational process, it certainly has not been one where judges have felt free to roam where unguided speculation might take them. The balance of which I speak is the balance struck by this country, having regard to what history teaches are the traditions from which it developed as well as the traditions from which it broke. That tradition is a living thing. A decision of this Court which radically departs from it could not long survive, while a decision which builds on what has survived is likely to be sound. No formula could serve as a substitute, in this area, for judgment and restraint.

It is this outlook which has led the Court continuingly to perceive distinctions in the imperative character of constitutional provisions, since that character must be discerned from a particular provision's larger context. And inasmuch as this context is one not of words, but of history and purposes, the full scope of the liberty guaranteed by the Due Process Clause cannot be found in or limited by the precise terms of the specific guarantees elsewhere provided in the Constitution. This "liberty" is not a series of isolated points pricked out in terms of the taking of property; the freedom of speech, press, and religion; the right to keep and bear arms; the freedom from unreasonable searches and seizures; and so on. It is a rational continuum which, broadly speaking, includes a freedom from all substantial arbitrary impositions and purposeless restraints, see Allgeyer v. Louisiana,165 U. S. 578; Holden v. Hardy,169 U. S. 366; Booth v. Illinois,184 U. S. 425; Nebbia v. New York,291 U. S. 502; Skinner v. Oklahoma, 316 U. S. 535, 544 (concurring opinion); Schware v. Board of Bar Examiners, 353 U. S. 232, and which also recognizes, what a reasonable and sensitive judgment must, that certain interests require particularly careful scrutiny of the state needs asserted to justify their abridgment. Cf. Skinner v. Oklahoma, supra; Bolling v. Sharpe, supra.

As was said in Meyer v. Nebraska,262 U. S. 390, 262 U. S. 399,

"this court has not attempted to define with exactness the liberty thus guaranteed. . . . Without doubt, it denotes, not merely freedom from bodily restraint. . . ."

Thus, for instance, when, in that case and in Pierce v. Society of Sisters,268 U. S. 510, the Court struck down laws which sought not to require what children must learn in schools, but to prescribe, in the first case, what they must not learn, and in the second, where they must acquire their learning, I do not think it was wrong to put those decisions on "the right of the individual to . . . establish a home and bring up children," Meyer v. Nebraska, ibid., or on the basis that

"The fundamental theory of liberty upon which all governments in this Union repose excludes any general power of the State to standardize its children by forcing them to accept instruction from public teachers only,"

Pierce v. Society of Sisters, 268 U.S. at 268 U. S. 535. I consider this so even though today those decisions would probably have gone by reference to the concepts of freedom of expression and conscience assured against state action by the Fourteenth Amendment, concepts that are derived from the explicit guarantees of the First Amendment against federal encroachment upon freedom of speech and belief. See West Virginia State Board of Education v. Barnette, 319 U. S. 624 and 319 U. S. 656 (dissenting opinion); Prince v. Massachusetts, 321 U. S. 158, 321 U. S. 166. For it is the purposes of those guarantees and not their text, the reasons for their statement by the Framers and not the statement itself, see Palko v. Connecticut, 302 U. S. 319, 302 U. S. 324-327; United States v. Carolene Products Co., 304 U. S. 144, 304 U. S. 152-153, which have led to their present status in the compendious notion of "liberty" embraced in the Fourteenth Amendment.

Each new claim to constitutional protection must be considered against a background of constitutional purposes, as they have been rationally perceived and historically developed. Though we exercise limited and sharply restrained judgment, yet there is no "mechanical yard-stick," no "mechanical answer." The decision of an apparently novel claim must depend on grounds which follow closely on well accepted principles and criteria. The new decision must take "its place in relation to what went before and further [cut] a channel for what is to come." Irvine v. California, 347 U. S. 128, 347 U. S. 147 (dissenting opinion). The matter was well put in Rochin v. California, 342 U. S. 165, 342 U. S. 170-171:

"The vague contours of the Due Process Clause do not leave judges at large. We may not draw on our merely personal and private notions and disregard the limits that bind judges in their judicial function. Even though the concept of due process of law is not final and fixed, these limits are derived from considerations that are fused in the whole nature of our judicial process. . . . These are considerations deeply rooted in reason and in the compelling traditions of the legal profession."

On these premises, I turn to the particular constitutional claim in this case.

II

Appellants contend that the Connecticut statute deprives them, as it unquestionably does, of a substantial measure of liberty in carrying on the most intimate of all personal relationships, and that it does so arbitrarily and without any rational, justifying purpose. The State, on the other hand, asserts that it is acting to protect the moral welfare of its citizenry, both directly, in that it considers the practice of contraception immoral in itself, and instrumentally, in that the availability of contraceptive materials tends to minimize "the disastrous consequence of dissolute action," that is fornication and adultery.

It is argued by appellants that the judgment, implicit in this statute -- that the use of contraceptives by married couples is immoral -- is an irrational one, that, in effect, it subjects them in a very important matter to the arbitrary whim of the legislature, and that it does so for no good purpose. Where, as here, we are dealing with what must be considered "a basic liberty," cf. Skinner v. Oklahoma, supra, at 316 U. S. 541, "[t]here are limits to the extent to which the presumption of constitutionality can be pressed," id., at 316 U. S. 544 (concurring opinion), and the mere assertion that the action of the State finds justification in the controversial realm of morals cannot justify alone any and every restriction it imposes. See Alberts v. California, 354 U. S. 476.

Yet the very inclusion of the category of morality among state concerns indicates that society is not limited in its objects only to the physical wellbeing of the community, but has traditionally concerned itself with the moral soundness of its people as well. Indeed, to attempt a line between public behavior and that which is purely consensual or solitary would be to withdraw from community concern a range of subjects with which every society in civilized times has found it necessary to deal. The laws regarding marriage which provide both when the sexual powers may be used and the legal and societal context in which children are born and brought up, as well as laws forbidding adultery, fornication and homosexual practices which express the negative of the proposition, confining sexuality to lawful marriage, form a pattern so deeply pressed into the substance of our social life that any constitutional doctrine in this area must build upon that basis. Compare McGowan v. Maryland, 366 U. S. 420.

It is in this area of sexual morality, which contains many proscriptions of consensual behavior having little or no direct impact on others, that the Connecticut has expressed its moral judgment that all use of contraceptives is improper. Appellants cite an impressive list of authorities who, from a great variety of points of view, commend the considered use of contraceptives by married couples. What they do not emphasize is that, not too long ago, the current of opinion was very probably quite the opposite, [12] and that, even today, the issue is not

free of controversy. Certainly, Connecticut's judgment is no more demonstrably correct or incorrect than are the varieties of judgment, expressed in law, on marriage and divorce, on adult consensual homosexuality, abortion, and sterilization, or euthanasia and suicide. If we had a case before us which required us to decide simply, and in abstraction, whether the moral judgment implicit in the application of the present statute to married couples was a sound one, the very controversial nature of these questions would, I think, require us to hesitate long before concluding that the Constitution precluded Connecticut from choosing as it has among these various views. Cf. Alberts v. California, 354 U. S. 476, 354 U. S. 500-503 (concurring opinion).

But, as might be expected, we are not presented simply with this moral judgment to be passed on as an abstract proposition. The secular state is not an examiner of consciences: it must operate in the realm of behavior, of overt actions, and where it does so operate, not only the underlying, moral purpose of its operations, but also the choice of means becomes relevant to any constitutional judgment on what is done. The moral presupposition on which appellants ask us to pass judgment could form the basis of a variety of legal rules and administrative choices, each presenting a different issue for adjudication. For example, one practical expression of the moral view propounded here might be the rule that a marriage in which only contraceptive relations had taken place had never been consummated, and could be annulled. Compare, e.g., 2 Bouscaren, Canon Law Digest, 307-313. Again, the use of contraceptives might be made a ground for divorce, or perhaps tax benefits and subsidies could be provided for large families. Other examples also readily suggest themselves.

III

Precisely what is involved here is this: the State is asserting the right to enforce its moral judgment by intruding upon the most intimate details of the marital relation with the full power of the criminal law. Potentially, this could allow the deployment of all the incidental machinery of the criminal law, arrests, searches and seizures; inevitably, it must mean, at the very least, the lodging of criminal charges, a public trial, and testimony as to the corpus delicti. Nor could any imaginable elaboration of presumptions, testimonial privileges, or other safeguards, alleviate the necessity for testimony as to the mode and manner of the married couples' sexual relations, or at least the opportunity for the accused to make denial of the charges. In sum, the statute allows the State to enquire into, prove and punish married people for the private use of their marital intimacy.

This, then, is the precise character of the enactment whose constitutional measure we must take. The statute must pass a more rigorous constitutional test than that going merely to the plausibility of its underlying rationale. See pp. 367 U. S. 542-545, supra. This enactment involves what, by common understanding throughout the English-speaking world, must be granted to be a most fundamental aspect of "liberty," the privacy of the home in its most basic sense, and it is this which requires that the statute be subjected to "strict scrutiny." Skinner v. Oklahoma, supra, at 316 U. S. 541.

That aspect of liberty which embraces the concept of the privacy of the home receives explicit constitutional protection at two places only. These are the Third Amendment, relating to the quartering of soldiers, [13] and the Fourth Amendment, prohibiting unreasonable searches and seizures. [14] While these Amendments reach only the Federal Government, this Court has held in the strongest terms, and today again confirms, that the concept of "privacy" embodied in the Fourth Amendment is part of the "ordered liberty" assured against state action by the Fourteenth Amendment. See Wolf v. Colorado, 338 U. S. 25; Mapp v. Ohio, 367 U. S. 643.

It is clear, of course, that this Connecticut statute does not invade the privacy of the home in the usual sense, since the invasion involved here may, and doubtless usually would, be accomplished without any physical intrusion whatever into the home. What the statute undertakes to do, however, is to create a crime which is grossly offensive to this privacy, while the Constitution refers only to methods of ferreting out substantive wrongs, and the procedure it requires presupposes that substantive offenses may be committed and sought out in the privacy of the home. But such an analysis forecloses any claim to constitutional protection against this form of deprivation of privacy, only if due process in this respect is limited to what is explicitly provided in the Constitution, divorced from the rational purposes, historical roots, and subsequent developments of the relevant provisions.

Perhaps the most comprehensive statement of the principle of liberty underlying these aspects of the Constitution was given by Mr. Justice Brandeis, dissenting in Olmstead v. United States,277 U. S. 438, at 277 U. S. 478:

"The protection guaranteed by the [Fourth and Fifth] Amendments is much broader in scope. The makers of our Constitution undertook to secure conditions favorable to the pursuit of happiness. They recognized the significance of man's spiritual nature, of his feelings and of his intellect. They knew that only a part of the pain, pleasure and satisfactions of life are to be found in material things. They sought to protect Americans in their beliefs, their thoughts, their emotions and their sensations. They conferred, as against the government, the right to be let alone -- the most comprehensive of rights and the right most valued by civilized men. To protect that right, every unjustifiable intrusion by the government upon the privacy of the individual, whatever the means employed, must be deemed a violation of the Fourth Amendment. . . ."

I think the sweep of the Court's decisions, under both the Fourth and Fourteenth Amendments amply shows that the Constitution protects the privacy of the home against all unreasonable intrusion of whatever character.

"[These] principles . . . affect the very essence of constitutional liberty and security. They reach farther than [a] concrete form of the case . . . before the court, with its adventitious circumstances; they apply to all invasions on the part of the government and its employees of the sanctity of a man's home and the privacies of life. . . ."

Boyd v. United States,116 U. S. 616, 116 U. S. 630.

"The security of one's privacy against arbitrary intrusion by the police -- which is at the core of the Fourth Amendment -- is basic to a free society."

Wolf v. Colorado, supra, at 338 U. S. 27. In addition, see, e.g., Davis v. United States, 328 U. S. 582, 328 U. S. 587; Oklahoma Press Pub. Co. v. Walling, 327 U. S. 186, 327 U. S. 202-203; Frank v. Maryland, 359 U. S. 360, 359 U. S. 365-366; Silverman v. United States, 365 U. S. 505, 365 U. S. 511.

It would surely be an extreme instance of sacrificing substance to form were it to be held that the constitutional principle of privacy against arbitrary official intrusion comprehends only physical invasions by the police. To be sure, the times presented the Framers with two particular threats to that principle, the general warrant, see Boyd v. United States, supra, and the quartering of soldiers in private homes. But though

"[l]egislation, both statutory and constitutional, is enacted . . . from an experience of evils . . ., its general language should not, therefore, be necessarily confined to the form that evil had theretofore taken. . . . [A] principle, to be vital, must be capable of wider application than the mischief which gave it birth."

Weems v. United States,217 U. S. 349, 217 U. S. 373.

Although the form of intrusion here -- the enactment of a substantive offense -- does not, in my opinion, preclude the making of a claim based on the right of privacy embraced in the "liberty" of the Due Process Clause, it must be acknowledged that there is another sense in which it could be argued that this intrusion on privacy differs from what the Fourth Amendment, and the similar concept of the Fourteenth, were intended to protect: here, we have not an intrusion into the home so much as on the life which characteristically has its place in the home. But, to my mind, such a distinction is so insubstantial as to be captious: if the physical curtilage of the home is protected, it is surely as a result of solicitude to protect the privacies of the life within. Certainly the safeguarding of the home does not follow merely from the sanctity of property rights. The home derives its preeminence as the seat of family life. And the integrity of that life is something so fundamental that it has been found to draw to its protection the principles of more than one explicitly granted constitutional right. Thus, Mr. Justice Brandeis, writing of a statute which made "it punishable to teach [pacifism] in any place [to] a single person . . ., no matter what the relation of the parties may be," found such a

"statute invades the privacy and freedom of the home. Father and mother may not follow the promptings of religious belief, of conscience or of conviction, and teach son or daughter the doctrine of pacifism. If they do, any police officer may summarily arrest them."

Gilbert v. Minnesota,254 U. S. 325, 254 U. S. 335-336 (dissenting opinion). This same principle is expressed in the Pierce and Meyer cases, supra. These decisions, as was said in Prince v. Massachusetts, 321 U. S. 158, at 321 U. S. 166, "have respected the private realm of family life which the state cannot enter."

Of this whole "private realm of family life," it is difficult to imagine what is more private or more intimate than a husband and wife's marital relations. We would indeed be straining at a gnat and swallowing a camel were we to show concern for the niceties of property law involved in our recent decision, under the Fourth Amendment, in Chapman v. United States, 365 U. S. 610, and yet fail at least to see any substantial claim here.

Of course, just as the requirement of a warrant is not inflexible in carrying out searches and seizures, see Abel v. United States, 362 U. S. 217; United States v. Rabinowitz, 339 U. S. 56, so there are countervailing considerations at this more fundamental aspect of the right involved. "[T]he family . . . is not beyond regulation," Prince v. Massachusetts, supra, and it would be an absurdity to suggest either that offenses may not be committed in the bosom of the family or that the home can be made a sanctuary for crime. The right of privacy most manifestly is not an absolute. Thus, I would not suggest that adultery, homosexuality, fornication, and incest are immune from criminal enquiry, however privately practiced. So much has been explicitly recognized in acknowledging the State's rightful concern for its people's moral welfare. See pp. 367 U. S. 545-548, supra. But not to discriminate between what is involved in this case and either the traditional offenses against good morals or crimes which, though they may be committed anywhere, happen to have been committed or concealed in the home would entirely misconceive the argument that is being made.

Adultery, homosexuality, and the like are sexual intimacies which the State forbids altogether, but the intimacy of husband and wife is necessarily an essential and accepted feature of the institution of marriage, an institution which the State not only must allow, but which, always and in every age, it has fostered and protected. It is one thing when the State exerts its power either to forbid extramarital sexuality altogether, or to say who may marry, but it is quite another when, having acknowledged a marriage and the intimacies inherent in it, it undertakes to regulate by means of the criminal law the details of that intimacy.

In sum, even though the State has determined that the use of contraceptives is as iniquitous as any act of extramarital sexual immorality, the intrusion of the whole machinery of the criminal law into the very heart of marital privacy, requiring husband and wife to render account before a criminal tribunal of their uses of that intimacy, is surely a very different thing indeed from punishing those who establish intimacies which the law has always forbidden and which can have no claim to social protection.

In my view, the appellants have presented a very pressing claim for constitutional protection. Such difficulty as the claim presents lies only in evaluating it against the State's countervailing contention that it be allowed to enforce, by whatever means it deems appropriate, its judgment of the immorality of the practice this law condemns.

In resolving this conflict, a number of factors compel me to conclude that the decision here must most emphatically be for the appellants. Since, as it appears to me, the statute marks an abridgment of important fundamental liberties protected by the Fourteenth Amendment, it will not do to urge in justification of that abridgment simply that the statute is rationally related to the effectuation of a proper state purpose. A closer scrutiny and stronger justification than that are required. See pp. 367 U. S. 542-545, supra.

Though the State has argued the constitutional permissibility of the moral judgment underlying this statute, neither its brief, nor its argument, nor anything in any of the opinions of its highest court in these or other cases even remotely suggests a justification for the obnoxiously intrusive means it has chosen to effectuate that policy. To me, the very circumstance that Connecticut has not chosen to press the enforcement of this statute against individual users, while it nevertheless persists in asserting its right to do so at any time -- in effect, a right to hold this statute as an imminent threat to the privacy of the households of the State -- conduces to the inference either that it does not consider the policy of the statute a very important one or that it does not regard the means it has chosen for its effectuation as appropriate or necessary.

But conclusive, in my view, is the utter novelty of this enactment. Although the Federal Government and many States have at one time or other had on their books statutes forbidding or regulating the distribution of contraceptives, none, so far as I can find, has made the use of contraceptives a crime. [15] Indeed, a diligent search has revealed that no nation, including several which quite evidently share Connecticut's moral policy, [16] has seen fit to effectuate that policy by the means presented here.

Though undoubtedly the States are and should be left free to reflect a wide variety of policies, and should be allowed broad scope in experimenting with various means of promoting those policies, I must agree with Mr. Justice Jackson that

"There are limits to the extent to which a legislatively represented majority may conduct . . . experiments at the expense of the dignity and personality"

of the individual. Skinner v. Oklahoma, supra. In this instance, these limits are, in my view, reached and passed.

I would adjudicate these appeals and hold this statute unconstitutional insofar as it purports to make criminal the conduct contemplated by these married women. It follows that if their conduct cannot be a crime, appellant Buxton cannot be an accomplice thereto. I would reverse the judgment in each of these cases.

Notes

[1] These statutes, Conn.Gen.Stat.Re v.1958, § 53-32 (forbidding the use of contraceptives), and Conn.Gen.Stat.Re v.1958, § 54-196 (the general accessory law), are set forth in note 2 of the plurality opinion, ante,367 U. S. 499.

[2] Only two cases are squarely relied on, CIO v. McAdory,325 U. S. 472, a companion case to Alabama State Federation of Labor v. McAdory, supra, discussed at pp. 367 U. S. 526-527, infra, and tendering the same issues, and Ex parte La Prade,289 U. S. 444. The appeal in the principal McAdory case was dismissed because the state statute there challenged had not yet been construed by the state courts, and it was thought that state construction might remove some constitutional doubts. In the companion McAdory case, the appeal was likewise dismissed, the State having

"agreed not to enforce § 7 of the Act (there challenged) until the final decision as to the section's validity by this Court in Alabama State Federation of Labor v. McAdory. . . ."

Id.,. at 325 U. S. 475. In the present appeals, there is no agreement not to prosecute, no companion case awaiting disposition, and no uncertainty about state law due to lack of state construction.

As to Ex parte La Prade, supra, seenote 11, infra.

[3] Manifestly, the type of ripeness found wanting in cases such as Massachusetts v. Mellon,262 U. S. 447; Texas v. Interstate Commerce Comm'n,258 U. S. 158; New Jersey v. Sargent,269 U. S. 328, and Arizona v. California,283 U. S. 423, is not lacking in the cases before us. For the recurrent theme of those cases, all of which challenge federal action as an encroachment on state sovereignty, is the fact that the mere existence of state sovereign powers and prerogatives which may bear generally upon individual rights raises no such concrete and practical issues as courts are accustomed to consider, so that adjudication upon their validity in such circumstances would take place in the most abstract kind of setting.

[4] Some support is sought to be drawn for the supposition of state acquiescence in violation of the statute from the case of State v. Certain Contraceptive Materials, 126 Conn. 428, 11 A.2d 863. But that case held no more than that contraceptive materials

could not be seized under the authority of a statute interpreted to deal with the seizure of gambling paraphernalia.

[5] The "circumstances" of the Nelson case may best be gathered from the remarks of the State's prosecuting attorney, Mr. Fitzgerald, seeking the approval of the trial judge for a nolle prosequi in that case after the decision of the State Supreme Court. In an affidavit accompanying a transcript of the proceedings on the State's motion, the attorney for the defendants stated that

"said criminal prosecutions were prosecutions instituted by the State upon complaint of a citizen and were instituted in no sense with the prior knowledge or approval of the accused and there was no pretrial acquiescence by the accused that said actions would be instituted to test the constitutionality of the statutes in question."

[6] This statement was made in the same proceedings referred to in note 5, supra.

[7] See Brief of Planned Parenthood Federation of America, Inc., as amicus curiae, p. 4, and Appendix f.

[8] The concurring opinion concludes, apparently on the basis of the Nelson episode, that the "true controversy in this case is over the opening of birth control clinics on a large scale. . . ." It should be said at once that, as to these appeals, this is an entirely unwarranted assumption. The amicus curiae in this case, the Planned Parenthood Federation of America, Inc., is indeed interested in such clinics, seenote 7, supra, but as to the actual parties here, there is not one word in the record or their briefs to suggest that their interest is anything other than they say it is. The Nelson prosecution, it is true, involved a doctor and nurses at a birth control clinic, but there is nothing about these statutes, as they have been authoritatively construed in this and previous cases, that limits their application to advice given by a doctor in a clinic of that sort, as opposed to advice given by a doctor in some less specialized clinic, a hospital or in his own office.

The only conceivable sense in which "[t]he true controversy in this case is over the opening of birth control clinics" must lie in the circumstance that, since the notorious and avowed purpose of such a clinic is the violation of these statutes, there would not be the same problem of detection or proof of violations as might otherwise present itself. The relevance, in turn, of this circumstance must be that, in the view of the concurring opinion, there is a present threat of enforcement against any such clinic -- which I too believe -- but coupled with a further assumption -- one shared by the plurality opinion, though lacking any factual warrant whatever -- that these statutes do not also deter members of the medical profession in general from violating these statutes. Furthermore, both opinions must share the assumption that the appellants may be required to hold what may be their constitutional rights at the whim and pleasure of the prosecutor. In sum, the strong implication of the concurring opinion that a suit for anticipatory relief brought by a birth control clinic (though it would raise no different issues and present a record no less "skimpy") would succeed in invoking our jurisdiction where these suits fail, exposes the fallacy underlying the Court's disposition: the unprecedented doctrine that a suit for anticipatory relief will be entertained at the instance of one who is forced to violate a statute flagrantly, but not at the urging of one who may violate it surreptitiously with a high probability of avoiding detection.

[9] In this regard, it is worth comparing the record of the Federal Communications Commission in enforcing its regulations by means of a threat of revocation of station licenses. The Commission has not, as is generally known, used this sanction much more readily than Connecticut has invoked criminal penalties to enforce the laws here in question, but no one would discount entirely the efficacy of the threat, or suggest that open defiance of Commission regulations is without substantial risks.

[10] It is suggested that prosecution is unlikely because of an interspousal testimonial privilege in Connecticut. Assuming that such a privilege exists and is applicable here, the testimony of either spouse is not necessary to a conviction. Furthermore, as will be argued, the real incursion here inheres in the institution of a prosecution in this matter at all, with the consequent need of an opportunity for the parties -- guilty or innocent -- to defend themselves against the charges. See p. 367 U. S. 548, infra.

[11] There is a much discredited dictum in Ex parte La Prade,289 U. S. 444, that, in an injunction action, there must be an allegation of threatened immediate enforcement of the statute. See 50 Yale L.J. 1278; Borchard, Challenging "Penal" Statutes by Declaratory Action, 52 Yale L.J. 445; 62 Harv.L.Re v. 870-871. But against this dictum (which, even in its context, was justified only as a natural consequence of the rule of Ex parte Young,209 U. S. 123, involving suits against state officers) one can array numerous cases in which proof of any such immediate threat was considered unnecessary, and the Court proceeded to a determination of the merits. See, e.g., Pennsylvania v. West Virginia,262 U. S. 553; Euclid, Ohio v. Ambler Realty Co.,272 U. S. 365; Carter v. Carter Coal Co.,298 U. S. 238; Currin v. Wallace,306 U. S. 1.

[12] The so-called Comstock Law, 17 Stat. 598, may be regarded as characteristic of the attitude of a large segment of public opinion on this matter through the end of the last century. It was only by judicial interpretation at a later date that the absolute prohibitions of the law were qualified to exclude professional medical use. Youngs Rubber Corp. v. C. I. Lee & Co., 45 F.2d 103; Davis v. United States, 62 F.2d 473; United States v. One Package, 86 F.2d 737; 50 Harv.L.Re v. 1312. However, the Comstock Law, in its original form, "started a fashion," and many States enacted similar legislation, some of which is still on the books. See Stone and Pilpel, The Social and Legal Status of Contraception, 22 N.C.L.Re v. 212; Legislation Note, 45 Harv.L.Re v. 723; Note, 6 U. of Chi.L.Re v. 260; Murray, America's Four Conspiracies, at 32-33, in Religion in America (Cogley ed.). Indeed the criticism of these measures assume that they represented general public opinion, though of a bygone day. See, e.g., Knopf, Various Aspects of Birth Control; Birth Control Clinical Research Bureau, Laws Relating to Birth Control in the United States and its Territories, foreword and introduction; Stone and Pilpel, supra; Hearings on H.R. 11082, 72d Cong., 1st Sess. See generally Broun and Leech, Anthony Comstock; Dennett, Birth Control Laws.

[13] "No Soldier shall, in time of peace be quartered in any house, without the consent of the Owner, nor in time of war, but in a manner to be prescribed by law."

[14] "The right of the people to be secure in their persons, houses, papers, and effects, against unreasonable searches and seizures, shall not be violated, and no Warrants shall issue, but upon probable cause, supported by Oath or affirmation, and particularly describing the place to be searched, and the persons or things to be seized."

[15] See tabulation of statutes in Birth Control Legislation, 9 Cleveland-Marshall Law Review, 245 (1960); Legislation Note, 45 Harv.L.Re v. 723 (1932); Birth Control Clinical Research Bureau, Laws Relating to Birth Control in the United States and its Territories (1938).

[16] Unqualified disapproval of contraception is implicit in the laws of Belgium, Droit Penal, § 383; France, Code Penal, Art. 317; Ireland, Censorship of Publications Act of 1929, §§ 16, 17, Criminal Law Amendment Act of 1935, § 17; Italy, Codice Penale, Arts. 553, 555; and Spain, Codigo Penal, Art. 416. Compare the more permissive legislation in Canada, Criminal Code, § 150; Germany, Strafgesetzbuch, § 184; Switzerland, Code Penal, Art. 211.

Justice Harlan's dissent in US v. Drum (Jan 15, 1962)

MR. JUSTICE HARLAN, whom MR. JUSTICE WHITTAKER joins, dissenting.

Were this an instance of a District Court substituting its judgment for that of the Interstate Commerce Commission on a matter which Congress had reserved for agency determination, I would be among the first to maintain that the Commission's action should be respected. Cf. I. C. C. v. J-T Transport Co., 368 U. S. 81, 126-130 (dissenting opinion). But the order entered by the Commission in the cases now before us is so utterly lacking in evidentiary support, so inconsistent with the uniform course of agency and court decisions, and so contrary to the regulatory plan embodied in the Motor Carrier Act of 1935 and its later amendments, that I cannot join in the judgment which reinstates that order. As I view this record what the Commission has done here amounts in effect to an exercise of power which it does not possess.

Under the Motor Carrier Act two things are indisputably clear: (1) Congress, in subjecting "private" motor carriage only to safety regulation, did not mean otherwise to regulate interstate transportation by persons of "their own goods in their own vehicles for commercial purposes" (79 Cong. Rec. 5651 (1935), remarks of Senator Wheeler, Chairman of the Senate Committee on Interstate Commerce);[1] (2) one engaged in the business of leasing motor vehicles for commercial carriage is not by that fact alone made a "contract carrier," subject to full Commission regulation; in other words, equipment rentals as such are not reached by the statute.[2] Under the plain terms of the Act and Commission rulings, economic regulation of such rentals comes into play only where "for-hire" motor carriage has been shown.[3]

This then is not a case like Labor Board v. Hearst Publications, Inc., 322 U. S. 111, where the construction of an inexplicitly defined term in a statute which was broadly remedial was left to the agency enforcing the law. Despite strong suggestions to the contrary,[4] Congress saw fit to exempt private carriers from economic regulation under the Motor Carrier Act. If we were to permit the Commission to exercise its discretion to sweep in a variety of arrangements which legitimately constitute private carriage, we would be authorizing disobedience of the legislative mandate as surely as if we allowed the agency to remove from regulation what clearly amounts to "for-hire" carriage.

Until late 1952, Oklahoma Furniture Company, a manufacturer of low-priced furniture, shipped its product to retail purchasers throughout the United States in company-owned tractors and trailers, driven by its own full-time salaried employees. Discovering that some of its drivers were misusing company credit cards, given them to enable their charging against the Company operating and living expenses while on the road. Oklahoma revamped its long-haul transportation system in such a way as to remove these temptations.[5] In essence the new arrangement involved, on the one hand, leasing from each of 11 of the Company's employee-drivers one of the tractors used in long-haul service,[6] and shifting to the driver the economic incidents of its maintenance and operation; and, on the other hand, preserving to the Company the exclusive use of the tractor in the conduct of its business, and keeping, in every practical sense, the employee relationship between the driver and the Company. The details of the arrangement and its operation are accurately summarized in the District Court's opinion.[7]

The process of reasoning by which the Commission reached the conclusion that this rearrangement changed to fully regulatable activity that which had therefore been subject to Commission jurisdiction only from the standpoint of safety, is at best obscure. However, the true measure of what the Court now sanctions is revealed by laying bare the extent to which the agency's conclusion involved a departure from the common-sense criteria that have heretofore entered into Commission determinations as to whether particular arrangements reflected "private" or "for-hire" motor carriage.[8]

The Court holds that the shifting of three economic burdens from the Company to the drivers justified the Commission's determination: (1) the substantial capital investments in the tractors, along with the risk of premature loss, were borne by the drivers;[9] (2) they undertook the costs of maintaining the vehicles and their own living expenses on the road; and (3) they bore the risk, as the Court envisages it, of "non-utilization of high-priced equipment" and of their own unemployment. These factors, either singly or in combination, do not, in my view, suffice to warrant the Commission's ruling. The first of them is the normal concomitant of any equipment rental; its presence cannot serve to change the character of a relationship which is not of itself subject to Commission regulation, except from the standpoint of safety (supra, p. 387, note 1). The costs of gas, repairs, and garaging are commonly also assumed by those leasing out motor vehicles for private use.[10] See, e. g., R. N. G. Commercial Auto Renters, Inc., 73 M. C. C. 665; Scott Bros., Inc., 32 M. C. C. 253; U-Drive-It Co. of Pennsylvania, 23 M. C. C. 799. The third factor, whatever may be its weight when supported by actuality, is, in the circumstances depicted in this record, no more than a pure abstraction (pp. 394-395, infra).

As the Court appears to recognize, the other provisions of the arrangement, relating to the cost of maintaining the leased equipment, all point to "private" carriage. Past cases in the Commission where "for-hire" carriage has been found, in the face of similar provisions, all involved other factors not present here. Under this arrangement, the Company was entitled to exclusive use of the tractors during the rental period (cf. Joseph A. Bisceglia, 34 M. C. C. 233); it loaded, dispatched, and routed the trucks (cf. William A. Shields, 41 M. C. C. 100);[11] it instructed the drivers as to details of service (cf. McKeown Transportation Co., 42 M. C. C. 792); it assumed the risk of loss or damage to the cargo (cf. Edward Allen Carroll, 1 M. C. C. 788); it paid for liability and property damage insurance (cf. Centre Trucking Co., 32 M. C. C. 313);[12] it undertook to inspect the tractors to insure compliance with safety regulations (cf. Driver Service, Inc., 77 M. C. C. 243); and it shipped the goods without bills of lading (cf. Jacobs Transfer Co., 46 M. C. C. 265).

Nor is the Commission's case strengthened by the circumstance that the appellees, in addition to supplying the vehicles, provided their own services as drivers. That factor would be significant only if the appellees furnished these services as independent contractors, for it is only then that the arrangement differs from an equipment rental in which the lessee mans the leased vehicle with his own employees. It would be strange indeed to attribute to Congress a purpose to classify as a "for-hire" carrier any employee who, as a condition of employment, is required to purchase a vehicle in which his employer's goods are to be transported.

All the standards by which the Commission has previously tested a purported "employment" relationship prove the existence of such a relationship here. The Company paid the drivers' wages (cf. Columbia Terminals Co., 18 M. C. C. 662);[13] deducted social security and federal income taxes (cf. Motor Haulage Co., 46 M. C. C. 107); retained drivers' trip logs and medical certificates (cf. Watson Mfg. Co., 51 M. C. C. 223); bargained with the drivers' labor union over conditions of employment (cf. R. N. G. Commercial Auto Renters, Inc., 73 M. C. C. 665); and reserved the right to engage and discharge (cf. John J. Casale, Inc., 49 M. C. C. 15). In Teamsters Union v. Oliver, 358 U. S. 283, we held that an agreement setting a minimum rental and other terms for the use of a lessor-driver's equipment was "within the scope of collective bargaining as defined by federal law." Id., at 293. In light of the dissenting opinion, id., at 297-298, it seems clear that the Court concluded that the lessor-drivers were employees, not independent contractors, for purposes of the National Labor Relations Act.

Despite the total supervision thus exercised by the Company, if the record revealed that these drivers really risked having no work at all, thus earning no wage, over any period of time, there might be room for argument that they were, in fact, independent contractors. Under the terms of their employment such a theoretical possibility exists, but the facts prove it could not happen.

The appellees were paid rental for their vehicles and wages for their services on a per-mile basis. But the testimony of the Company's truck superintendent shows that the Company deliberately attempted to distribute the work so as to assure to each driver weekly wages which were within limits acceptable both to the individual concerned and his labor union. Six tractors continued to be owned by the Company, and individual employees were assigned to these tractors, one to a vehicle, just as the appellees were in effect assigned by the Company to the tractors they owned. Those assigned to company-owned tractors were paid $50 a week plus two cents a mile, and they were dispatched on short hauls. The appellees were sent on long hauls, so that their total mileage would make up for the absence of any fixed wage.[14] In addition, if one of the appellees was sick, a driver usually assigned to a company-owned vehicle would be directed to operate the tractor belonging to the incapacitated man in order to assure him of at least the rental payment for his equipment. In short, there is nothing in the record which warrants a finding that the status of the appellees was anything other than that of bona fide employees, or that they in fact shouldered, or anticipated that they might have to bear, any of the economic burdens undertaken by independent contractors.

I am not unmindful that the Interstate Commerce Commission has, of late, been much concerned with the problem of drawing the line between legitimate equipment rentals, which it concedes to be "private carriage," and what it has come to call "pseudo-private carriage," i. e., contract carriage disguised as lease of equipment.[15]

Obviously the Commission must have the power to deal with schemes that have been devised to avoid regulation. No one would suppose that the Commission was acting beyond its authority if it pierced through the form assumed by a business enterprise purportedly engaged in providing equipment for "private" carriage and disclosed that it was really supplying "for-hire" carriage. Decisions of District Courts and Courts of Appeals have uniformly approved the application of the test of "substance" in such circumstances. E. g., Lamb v. I. C. C., 259 F. 2d 358; I. C. C. v. Isner, 92 F. Supp. 582; I. C. C. v. Gannoe, 100 F. Supp. 790. I disagree with the result reached here by the Court, not because the Commission has supplemented its earlier test of "control" with one of "substance,"[16] but because the application of the very test that is now urged persuades me that this was in reality an employment relationship with an employer engaged in private carriage, and not a "for-hire" carriage arrangement.

In sum, this is a case in which there is no allegation of subterfuge and no basis in the record for attributing a devious motive to the lessee; in which the economic risks transferred by the arrangement to the lessor are no more, and possibly even less, substantial[17] than those in the ordinary rental of equipment; and in which the actual conditions of hire disclose that the drivers are bona fide employees of the lessor and are protected by their union representatives against overreaching by the employer. The Commission's order is not saved by the "totality" test which the Court now brings to its aid. For however viewed, this record adds up to nothing more than a mere rearrangement of Oklahoma's private carriage activities in such a way as, and for no other purpose than, to protect the Company against being cheated by its long-haul driver-employees.

If it is within the range of the Commission's permissible discretion to classify these appellees as contract carriers— and thus subject them to the rigorous standards of financial fitness and suitability that the Commission's regulations require of such carriers—what has been thought of as the "gray" area becomes black, and, in truth, much of what has heretofore been taken for white is now gray. What, for example, would have been the result had title to these tractors remained with the Company under an arrangement whereby they were leased to the drivers and then subleased back to the Company, with the Company assuming the risk of catastrophic loss or destruction? Or what if the drivers had been guaranteed $50 a week in total rental and wages? Would either of these changed circumstances have ousted the Commission of authority to hold the contracts to be "for-hire" carriage?

Indeed, the Court's decision goes far to encourage the Commission to obliterate entirely the congressionally drawn distinction between private and contract carriage. It will be interesting to see as time goes on whether there will be an aftermath to this decision similar to that which followed the blurring of the line between common and contract motor carriers effected by the Court's decision in United States v. Contract Steel Carriers, 350 U. S. 409. See I. C. C. v. J-T Transport Co., supra, at 107-109 (dissenting opinion).

I would affirm.

Notes

[1] See also S. Doc. No. 152, 73d Cong., 2d Sess. 33 (1934); H. R. Doc. No. 89, 74th Cong., 1st Sess. 17 (1935); S. Rep. No. 482, 74th Cong., 1st Sess. 1 (1935); H. R. Rep. No. 1645, 74th Cong., 1st Sess. 4 (1935).

[2] There has been some equipment rental regulation by the States, whether it is also desirable as a matter of federal policy has yet to be determined by Congress. See Nutting and Kuhn, Motor Carrier Regulation—The Third Phase, 10 U. of Pitt. L. Rev. 477, 487-491 (1949); Note, 39 Ky. L. J. 338 (1951).

[3] The relevant statutory provisions are set forth in footnotes 1,2,3 and 5 of the Court's opinion. See also U-Drive-It Co. of Pennsylvania, 23 M. C. C. 799; Scott Bros., Inc., 32 M. C. C. 253. In Lease and Interchange of Vehicles by Motor Carriers, 51 M. C. C. 461, 521, the Commission did not premise its authority to regulate lease and interchange practices among common and contract carriers on any authority generally to control vehicles engaged in interstate commerce. The Commission rather infered from its authority to regulate the transportation offered by common and contract carriers the power to regulate, as well, "the procurement of transportation." This conclusion in no way suggests its authority to regulate the rental of vehicles by noncarriers from companies engaged solely in rental activities.

[4] See S. Doc. No. 152, 73d Cong., 2d Sess. 26 (1934); Hearings before Senate Committee on Interstate Commerce on the Motor Carrier Act of 1935, 74th Cong., 1st Sess. 333, 345, 347-350 (1935).

[5] Short hauls of company products in company-owned and driven equipment remained unaffected by the new arrangement, presumably because there was less opportunity for the misuse of company credit cards in connection with such hauls.

[6] The record does not show the terms on which the drivers acquired the tractors, whether they were bought from the Company or others, and if from the Company, what, if any, consideration was paid. The trailers drawn by these tractors continued to be owned by the Company.

[7] "The leases provide in substance as follows: (1) the Company shall pay the owner-operator 10¢ a mile for hauling single-axle trailers and 11¢ a mile for hauling tandem-axle trailers, plus an additional 3¢ a mile for back-haul of the Company's raw materials, (2) payments under the agreement shall be made weekly, (3) motor vehicles covered by the agreement shall be operated by an employee of the Company who shall be properly qualified and physically fit in accordance with state and federal regulations, (4) the owner-operator shall pay all operating costs arising from operation of said equipment (gasoline, oil, grease and parts) and shall pay cost of license plates, (5) the Company shall keep and maintain said equipment in first-class operating condition and in compliance with all safety rules and regulations of state and federal regulatory bodies, (6) if owner-operator fails to pay operating cost of equipment, the Company may cancel the agreement or at its option pay the necessary operating costs and charge same to owner-operator's account with the Company, (7) the Company shall have sole control, right of direction, and use of the leased equipment, all property transported by the leased vehicles shall belong to the Company and the Company will not sub-lease the equipment to any other person, firm or corporation, (8) the Company shall not be liable for wear, tear and depreciation nor for any damage caused to the leased equipment by accident, theft, fire or any other hazard or casualty, (9) the owner-operator shall not be responsible for loss to company equipment, property and cargo, (10) the Company will have the name of the owner-operator endorsed as an additional assured upon its policies of property damage and public liability insurance covering the operation of motor vehicles, (11) either party may cancel the lease upon giving 30 days' written notice to the other party, (12) the agreement shall remain in full force and effect for one year from date of execution and shall be automatically renewed for further periods of one year unless cancelled in accordance with provisions of the agreement, or terminated by operation of law.

"The Company also entered into a union contract as employer of its drivers. The contract covers both drivers of company-owned vehicles and the owner-operators who usually drive their own tractors and who are also treated by the Company as employees. Although all the drivers do not belong to the union, the terms of the contract apply equally to non-union employees. This contract provides, in pertinent part, as follows: (1) the Company may discharge any employee for cause, (2) the owner-operators shall be paid at the rate of 4.5 cents a mile for driving, 0.25 cents a mile for living expenses, and 0.25 cents a mile for labor in the maintenance of the truck, or a total of 5 cents a mile, and shall be paid 6 cents a mile for back-hauls of raw materials, (3) drivers of company-owned tractors shall receive a basic salary of $50 a week plus 2 cents a mile for driving, (4) owner-operators having driven 75,000 miles during a year in which the contract is in effect shall be entitled to vacation pay computed upon the rate of pay for driving and the average weekly mileage in the preceding year, (5) owner-operators shall maintain their trucks in good running condition at all times, (6) owner-operators shall pay their own living expenses while on the road, (7) the provision of the union contract which guarantees employees 6 hours work or pay if they report for work at their usual or regular time shall not apply to owner-operators.

"The record made before the Commission shows that the operations of the Company and the owner-operators are in substance carried on in accordance with the provisions of the lease agreements and the union contract, with one exception. The lease agreements provide that the Company shall maintain the tractors of the owner-operators and the union contract provides that the owner-operators shall maintain them. The testimony in the record supports the Commission's finding that the owner-operators in fact maintain their vehicles.

"The record also reveals the following: The owner-operators are not authorized by the Interstate Commerce Commission to engage in the transportation of property either as contract carriers or common carriers by motor vehicle in interstate commerce. The Company uses the 6 tractors which it owns chiefly for short hauls and these are usually driven by the salaried company drivers. The tractors leased by the Company are utilized chiefly for long hauls and are usually operated by the owner-operators, each driving his own tractor. It is the practice of the Company to assign the same driver to the same equipment, regardless of whether it is company-owned or leased. However, when necessity or convenience make it more feasible to do so, drivers who usually drive company-owned tractors are assigned to leased tractors and owner-operators to company-owned tractors. All trailers used in the Company's operations are owned by it. A supervisor employed by the Company oversees all drivers, assigns trips and checks to see that all equipment is properly maintained and repaired. Detailed routing instructions are issued to all drivers and compliance therewith is insured by manner of loading, e. g., last goods to come off are loaded first and the first to come off are loaded last. Prior to departure drivers are handed a truck bill manifest which differs from a bill of lading in that the drivers are not required to sign a receipt for the freight they transport. Each owner operator receives two weekly paychecks, one for rental of his tractor and the other for his service as a driver. The Company deducts from the paychecks of the owner-operators social security and withholding taxes, pays the employer's share of social security and provides workmen's compensation benefits for them. The Company maintains on file drivers' logs, physicians' certificates and vehicle inspection reports. Both company-owned tractors and leased tractors are garaged at the homes of their respective drivers. The Company has the right to hire and fire drivers independently of the lease agreement." 193 F. Supp., at 277-278.

[8] See generally O'Brien, Twenty-Five Years of Federal Motor Carrier Licensing—The Private Versus For-Hire Carrier Problem, 35 N. Y. U. L. Rev. 1150 (1960); Matthews,

Truck Leasing By Shippers and the Problem of the Dangling Instrumentalities, 27 I. C. C. Prac. J. 370 (1960); Porter, Federal Regulation of Private Carriers, 64 Harv. L. Rev. 896 (1951).

[9] But see note 6, supra.

[10] To the extent that this second "risk" concerns personal living expenses on the road, it would be unrealistic to consider it a "risk" at all, since the cost of it was assumed, albeit at a flat rate of one-fourth cent per mile, by the Company under the terms of a collective-bargaining agreement with the labor union representing the drivers.

[11] Compare Consolidated Trucking, Inc., 41 M. C. C. 737; Jacobs Transfer Co., 46 M. C. C. 265 (shippers' control over routing and dispatching held insufficient to constitute private carriage).

[12] Since some equipment rental firms pay for liability insurance, the financial burden assumed by the appellees here may even have been less than that assumed by equipment rental firms.

[13] The Commission does not consider itself bound by the form in which wage payments are made and occasionally considers who it is who actually bears the wage burden. See Roy Rittenhouse, 78 M. C. C. 389. But even this factor is not always determinative. Pacific Diesel Rental Co., 78 M. C. C. 161.

[14] The reasons for differentiating between long and short hauls, as respects the ownership of the tractors used in each type of service, have already been given. Supra, note 5

[15] E. g., 69 I. C. C. Ann. Rep. 99; 72 I. C. C. Ann. Rep. 43; 73 I. C. C. Ann. Rep. 51; 74 I. C. C. Ann. Rep. 57-58. A thorough study of the "gray area"—defined as "transport operations which lie between legitimate private carriage and the transportation authorized by Government regulatory bodies"—was recently submitted to the Senate Committee on Interstate and Foreign Commerce by the Commission's Bureau of Transport Economics and Statistics. It recognized that one major type of operation conducted in order to avoid regulation was the "shipper lease of vehicle with driver." I. C. C., Bureau of Transport Economics and Statistics, Gray Area of Transportation Operations (1960), 27-37.

[16] In a leading decision the Commission set down a rule whereby "in cases in which the question of the status created by a lease of equipment with drivers by a carrier to a shipper is presented, in the absence of a showing to the contrary, the presumption arises that the transportation is performed by the carrier for compensation, in other words is for-hire transportation and as such is subject to regulation." H. B. Church Truck Service, 27 M. C. C. 191, 196. I do not quarrel with the general validity of this presumption, although, until the present case, even the Commission thought it applicable only to leases by those who were otherwise "for-hire" carriers. John J. Casale, Inc., 44 M. C. C. 45, 52-53. It is only because the "showing to the contrary" in this instance is so overwhelming that I think it was impermissible for the Commission to apply that rule here.

[17] The Company here assumed the full cost of an unproductive back-haul, since it paid its drivers for their tractors and their services whether the trailer returned empty or

full. If the backhaul was productive, four cents per mile was added to the total payment, possibly as compensation for increased wear-and-tear and more rigorous duties. Although a lease of equipment may, under certain circumstances, require a lessee to return the vehicle to the location where it was first taken, large rental firms do provide for one-way leases at slightly increased rates. The Company might, therefore, well have been able to reduce its loss on an unproductive backhaul by leasing equipment on terms which would have permitted it to return the equipment at the destination.

Justice Harlan's concurrence in Oyler v. Boles (Feb 19, 1962)

MR. JUSTICE HARLAN, concurring.

I join the Court's opinion in Oyler v. Boles and Crabtree v. Boles, Nos. 56 and 57, and concur in the result in Chewning v. Cunningham, No. 63, ante, p. 368 U. S. 443.

In my view, the issues decided in Oyler and Crabtree, on the one hand, and in Chewning, on the other, represent opposite sides of the same coin. Since their interrelationship does not appear from the opinions of the Court, and since I cannot agree with the grounds of decision stated in Chewning, I file this separate opinion.

The statutes of both Virginia and West Virginia provide for enhanced punishment of multiple offenders. Apparently under the practice of neither State is the alleged recidivist given advance notice, either before the trial for his latest offense or after that trial but before sentencing, of the charges that are made in the multiple-offense accusation. It is not until he appears in open court and hears the prosecutor's information read to him that the accused learns on which convictions it is that the State relies in support of its demand for an increased sentence. And it is then and there that he must plead and state what his defense is, if he has any. This procedure was followed in each of the present cases.

For an individual unrepresented by counsel, this is surely too precipitous a procedure to satisfy the standards of fairness required of state courts by the Due Process Clause of the Fourteenth Amendment. In re Oliver, 333 U. S. 257, 333 U. S. 273; see Williams v. New York, 337 U. S. 241, 337 U. S. 245; Cole v. Arkansas, 333 U. S. 196, 333 U. S. 201. One who is untutored in the law cannot help but be bewildered by this sudden presentation of the charges against him and the demand for an immediate response. Without suggesting that advance notice of any particular duration must be afforded, still less that such notice must be given before trial or sentencing on the latest offense, had the petitioners in Oyler and Crabtree been without the aid of counsel at their multiple-offender hearings, I would entertain grave doubts as to the constitutionality of the procedure from which their increased sentences resulted.

But the records in these cases reveal that both Oyler and Crabtree had counsel at hand when the multiple-offender hearing was held and when they were asked to plead. Counsel could have requested a continuance in order to look into the validity of the previous convictions or other possible defenses to the recidivist charges, or, if there was any doubt, to establish the identities of the previous offenders. They chose not to do so, and I think this choice forecloses the petitioners' claims that they were not given adequate notice and opportunity to prepare a defense.

In Chewning, however, the petitioner had no counsel. He was taken from the state penitentiary without any warning of what was in store for him, and was accused in open court of having been convicted on three prior occasions. His allegations that he requested the assignment of counsel, and that such request was denied, are not controverted. [1]

The Court strikes down the enhanced sentence, despite the apparent similarity between this claim and the one rejected in Gryger v. Burke, 334 U. S. 728, because it holds that various defenses that were available to Chewning under Virginia law could not have been known to or presented by a layman. To me, the bare possibility that any of these improbable claims could have been asserted does not amount to the "exceptional circumstances" which, under existing law, e.g., Betts v. Brady, 316 U. S. 455, must be present before the Fourteenth Amendment imposes on the State a duty to provide counsel for an indigent accused in a noncapital case. Nor do I think that a decision on these grounds can be reconciled with the holding in Gryger, in which the Court rejected the proposition, made by able appointed counsel, that certain contentions, much like those here suggested by the Court, could have been offered had the petitioner in that case been provided with counsel for his multiple-offender hearing.

What does distinguish this case from Gryger, however, and persuades me that the failure to supply assistance of counsel amounted to a denial of the procedural fairness assured by the Fourteenth Amendment, is the want of adequate notice in advance of the hearing. In Gryger, a copy of the information listing the prior occasions on which the accused had been convicted was served upon him more than six and a half months before he was brought into court and asked to plead. This was more than ample time for him to engage an attorney, request assignment of counsel, or decide for himself what line of defense to take. [2] In the case before us now, Chewning was given no such opportunity. Hence, I agree that the least that fairness required was that he be provided with counsel so as to be advised of the courses available to him. With no opportunity to get such advice, I do not think that his own failure to ask for a continuance has any legal significance.

Notes

[1] Although petitioner did not allege in his habeas corpus petition that he was indigent at the time of the recidivist hearing, the state court apparently proceeded on the assumption that he had met the necessary poverty standard.

[2] It is true that a subsidiary claim in Gryger was that the petitioner had been denied access to legal materials which were necessary in the preparation of his defense. But he was at least able to reflect calmly on the factual accusation being made against him, and was able to plan in advance what plea to enter and how best to present his case.

Justice Harlan's dissent in Poller v. CBS (Feb 19, 1962)

MR. JUSTICE HARLAN, with whom MR. JUSTICE FRANKFURTER, MR. JUSTICE WHITTAKER and MR. JUSTICE STEWART join, dissenting.

As I see it, this is one of those cases, not unfamiliar in treble-damage litigation, where injury resulting from normal business hazards is sought to be made redressable by casting the affair in antitrust terms. I think that the antitrust laws do not fit this case, and that the courts below were quite correct in holding that the respondents were entitled to judgment as a matter of law.

The litigation arises out of CBS' cancellation of an affiliation arrangement with WCAN, a UHF television broadcasting station in Milwaukee, owned by Midwest Broadcasting Company of whose property Poller is assignee. CBS maintains that such cancellation was but the legitimate exercise of a contractual right. Poller says that it was part of a conspiracy to restrain and monopolize trade in the television broadcasting business, violative of §§ 1 and 2 of the Sherman Act. Suing under § 4 of the Clayton Act,[1] Poller seeks to recover as damages the trebled fair value of the WCAN station and equipment, whose sale to CBS at a distress price he claims was forced upon him in consequence of CBS' cancellation of the WCAN affiliation contract.

Poller asserts that CBS, joined by others as conspirators, wanted to put him out of business as the first step in a grand design to destroy UHF broadcasting in Milwaukee, if not indeed throughout the United States. It is said that CBS looked with disfavor upon the growth of UHF broadcasting, being itself already heavily committed to VHF. As subsidiary steps towards the effectuation of this plan, it is charged that CBS chilled prospective purchasers of WCAN; acquired the only then competing UHF station in Milwaukee, WOKY; and later closed that station down.[2] CBS' co-conspirators are said to have been CBS-Television, an unincorporated division of CBS; certain officers of CBS; Bartell, the then owner of WOKY; and Holt, a management consultant, who at CBS' behest obtained from Bartell an option to purchase WOKY.

I assume that Poller would be entitled to proceed to trial if the record before the District Court had left open a genuine question of fact as to whether the alleged conspiracy had as its object the elimination of all UHF stations in the Milwaukee area, or even if it appeared that petitioner might prove that the respondents entered upon this course in order to reduce the number of UHF stations in Milwaukee from two to one, which was to be owned outright by CBS.[3] But, for reasons given below, I think that the depositions and affidavits which were before the District Court disclosed to a practical certainty that such proof could not be made.

What did remain open to proof was an alleged arrangement among CBS, its television division, and its officers and agents whereby CBS canceled an affiliation with one UHF station and purchased the facilities of a competing station. Even if somewhere among those sought to be drawn into petitioner's net there can be found two independent actors whose meeting of minds would satisfy the usual conspiracy requirement of "plurality of parties,"[4] their agreement to carry out that design would not, in my view, of itself offend anything proscribed by §§ 1 or 2 of the Sherman Act.

    I.

In passing on the motion for summary judgment, the District Court had before it more than the four affidavits of interested parties to which the Court's opinion seems especially to refer (ante, pp. 468, 473). In the record was the testimony of four key witnesses taken by pretrial depositions. Petitioner's counsel had examined Frank Stanton, President of CBS; Richard Salant, a Vice-President of CBS; and Thad Holt, who acted for CBS in procuring the option on the Bartell station.[5] Petitioner's testimony was also in the record in the form of a deposition taken by respondents' counsel, and two affidavits submitted in opposition to the motion for summary judgment. In addition, the record contained the respondents' answers to written interrogatories put by the petitioner. It is in light of this far from meager pretrial discovery that the appropriateness of summary judgment must be evaluated.

Federal Rule of Civil Procedure 56 (c) authorizes a District Court to enter summary judgment

    "if the pleadings, depositions, and admissions on file, together with the affidavits, if any, show that there is no genuine issue as to any material fact and that the moving party is entitled to a judgment as a matter of law."

In so providing, the draftsmen of the Rule of course did not intend to cut off a litigant's right to a trial before the appropriate fact-finder if triable issues remained unresolved after the pleadings were closed and pretrial discovery had. Sartor v. Arkansas Natural Gas Corp., 321 U. S. 620, 627; Fountain v. Filson, 336 U. S. 681. On the other hand, it is equally clear that their purpose was to obviate trials which would serve no useful purpose. In administering the Rule, the availability of pretrial discovery, as well as matter actually discovered, is a factor to be considered in determining whether a "genuine issue as to any material fact" is open. E. g., Schneider v. McKesson & Robbins, Inc., 254 F. 2d 827, 831. Further, the Rule does not indicate that it is to be used any more "sparingly" in antitrust litigation (ante, p. 473) than in other kinds of litigation, or that its employment in antitrust cases is subject to more stringent criteria than in others. On the contrary, without reflecting in any way upon the good faith of this particular lawsuit, having regard for the special temptations that the statutory private antitrust remedy affords for the institution of vexatious litigation, and the inordinate amount of time that such cases sometimes demand of the trial courts, there is good reason for giving the summary judgment rule its full legitimate sweep in this field.

In this case petitioner, the party opposing the motion, had complete access by means of pretrial discovery to all the evidence he could marshal at a trial on the merits.[6] Neither his cross-examination of hostile witnesses nor his own direct testimony by way of deposition and affidavit produced any evidence which would indicate that the respondents sought to accomplish anything more than to purchase for CBS a UHF station in Milwaukee. As the Court's opinion seems to recognize, such a purchase (accompanied by a cancellation of petitioner's station affiliation) would be unlawful only if "conceived in a purpose to unreasonably restrain trade, control a market, or monopolize." (Ante, p. 469.) (Emphasis added.) In other words, unless a purpose to cancel petitioner's affiliation and purchase the Bartell station would, by itself, be unlawful, petitioner could prevail in this suit only if he proved that the respondents intended to stifle competition in, or monopolize, television broadcasting, either by closing down his station or, more broadly, by destroying the UHF business in whole or in part.[7]

This crucial issue, therefore, turns on proof of the respondents' motives. Had petitioner proceeded to trial and introduced no more evidence of motive than was revealed by the pretrial depositions and affidavits, the case, in my opinion, could not well have been permitted to go to the jury. There being no extrinsic evidence of an unlawful purpose, and CBS' executives having unequivocally denied any purpose to eliminate petitioner as a competitor, the jury would be left with no affirmative evidence of any intent to restrain trade. The possibility that the jury might disbelieve the respondents' assertions of innocence is not enough to forestall the entry of summary judgment in their favor. Dyer v. MacDougall, 201 F. 2d 265.

Despite the ample opportunity afforded him by the availability of pretrial discovery procedures, petitioner, as will be shown, was able to produce no evidence to support his charges that a conspiracy, narrow or far-reaching, had been hatched. He should not be permitted to proceed to trial just on the hope that in the more formal atmosphere of the courtroom witnesses will revise their testimony or that a clever trial tactic will produce helpful evidence. Courts do not exist to afford opportunities for such litigating gambles. See Radio City Music Hall Corp. v. United States, 135 F. 2d 715; Schneider v. McKesson & Robbins, Inc., supra; cf. Orvis v. Brickman, 90 U. S. App. D. C. 266, 270, 196 F. 2d 762, 765-766; Lavine v. Shapiro, 257 F. 2d 14, 20-21.

II.

I find nothing in this record to support a claim that CBS, in proceeding as it did, was actuated by a desire to restrain or monopolize trade.

It appears from questions asked of Stanton and Salant, two CBS officers, that petitioner sought to imply an unlawful motive to destroy competition from CBS' failure to negotiate with him in the first instance for the purchase of WCAN. Were it shown that respondents refused to consider purchasing petitioner's instead of Bartell's station, although the former was available on satisfactory terms, such a showing might be some evidence of an intent to eliminate petitioner as a competitor of the other station bought by CBS. But the record shows that respondents throughout insisted that their refusal to deal with petitioner was the result of information that he had placed an exorbitant price on his station. That insistence, which Poller did not controvert or himself impugn, is confirmed by his own computation of damages in this case, as well as by his deposition testimony which reveals that he valued the WCAN property at $2,000,000 and demanded that price of all interested purchasers. CBS bought the Bartell station, although to be sure it had substantially inferior facilities, for $335,000.

Nor is there any evidence in the record to indicate that the respondents anticipated petitioner's offer to sell his facilities to CBS. It is clear from the affidavits and depositions, and is, in fact, conceded in petitioner's brief before this Court, that it was petitioner who initiated the negotiations and "importuned CBS to take his equipment off his hands." Petitioner contends that the respondents knew he would have no use for the recently enlarged plant once his CBS affiliation was canceled, so that his offer of sale was a necessary consequence of the disaffiliation. But this proves only that petitioner's injury may as readily have been the result of CBS' lawful program of expansion as of an invidious scheme to restrain competition. It buttresses the conclusion reached by the Court of Appeals (109 U. S. App. D. C. 170, 173, 176, 284 F. 2d 599, 602, 605) that the diminution in the value of petitioner's property was attributable to petitioner's imprudent investment[8] rather than to any antitrust conspiracy by the respondents. In addition, petitioner's surmise that the respondents must have known that the cancellation of Poller's affiliation would result in his offering his equipment to CBS is hardly consistent with the fact, sworn to by Salant and never traversed, that CBS had its engineering department draw up complete plans as to how the Bartell facilities could be expanded to make them suitable for CBS' intended use.

Finally, it is entirely clear from the record that petitioner was unable to prove that the respondents' motive was to eliminate his station. It is undisputed that at the time Holt obtained the option on the Bartell station both the American Broadcasting and DuMont networks had no primary affiliates in the Milwaukee market. There is nothing to indicate that respondents should have anticipated at the birth of their alleged conspiracy that such affiliations would be unavailable to petitioner if the CBS tie were broken. Moreover, it is patent from the terms of the contract under which CBS purchased petitioner's equipment that petitioner represented to the respondents that he would continue broadcasting operations as an independent from the studio formerly occupied by Bartell.[9] It was only after this representation was made, albeit, as petitioner now claims, with only "about a 5 per cent hope" that he would be able to continue, that the exchange of facilities was consummated. The transaction was in all ways consistent with the parties' written intention to maintain two operating UHF stations in Milwaukee. For it was surely much more likely that petitioner could survive as an independent by using the smaller Bartell plant than by remaining in his enlarged studio, which had absorbed a large amount of capital that could not, at least immediately, be put to fruitful use.

In sum, the District Court had before it on this motion for summary judgment a record on which it was apparent that petitioner could prove only that CBS had undertaken to cancel its affiliation with petitioner's station and, with Holt's assistance, to purchase a competing UHF station. Only if such a "conspiracy" is prohibited by § 1 or § 2 of the Sherman Act should the petitioner have been permitted to proceed to trial.

III.

Respondents freely admit that the purchase of the Bartell station and the cancellation of petitioner's affiliation were parts of one course of action. They maintain, however, that their intention was to purchase a UHF station in Milwaukee as the first step in an incipient program of expansion into the UHF market, made possible by the Federal Communications Commission's then recently adopted "5-and-2" amendment to its multiple-ownership rule. By reason of this amendment, a single licensee was permitted to own two UHF stations in addition to the maximum five VHF stations theretofore allowed. I would hold that an arrangement to attain this objective did not, of itself, violate § 1 of the Sherman Act.

It must be obvious that the cancellation of an affiliation agreement by one network, not acting in concert with any other, does not alone give rise to a cause of action under the antitrust laws. Federal Broadcasting System, Inc., v. American Broadcasting Co., 167 F. 2d 349. A network is surely free to cut its ties to one station and affiliate with another in the same market. Such an act is analogous to a manufacturer's transfer of an exclusive distributorship from one dealer in the market to another. This freedom to choose with whom one deals is preserved under the antitrust laws not only because it is a unilateral decision, but because it does not amount to an unreasonable restraint of trade in any meaningful sense of the term, cf. Packard Motor Car Co. v. Webster Motor Car Co., 100 U. S. App. D. C. 161, 243 F. 2d 418; Fargo Glass & Paint Co. v. Globe American Corp., 201 F. 2d 534.

To overcome these apparent barriers to any holding that § 1 of the Sherman Act was here violated, petitioner suggests two theories under which respondents' conduct might constitute a forbidden restraint of trade: (1) That by reason of the "leverage of its network power" CBS was able to restrain trade among the independently owned UHF stations in the Milwaukee area; and (2) that CBS' purchase of a television station amounted, per se, to an unreasonable restraint of trade. How either of these alleged restraints, assuming they are unlawful, caused petitioner's alleged loss is left a mystery. Regardless of any question of causation, however, petitioner can prevail on neither theory.

To the extent that the "leverage" complained of charges CBS with monopolizing a market, petitioner's claim falls under § 2, a matter to which I will revert in a moment. Infra, pp. 485-486. Apart from monopoly power, the respondents could have violated the antitrust laws only by conspiring in some manner to use CBS' "leverage" to restrain trade. Clearly, the disaffiliation alone was not an unlawful use of the network's power. Having built up the value of his station substantially because of its CBS affiliation, petitioner is hardly in a position to claim that by depriving him, in the exercise of a contract right, of the benefit of such an affiliation CBS was unreasonably exercising its superior power to restrain trade. And there is no indication in the record that this "leverage" in any way affected the purchase price of petitioner's equipment, even were it to be assumed that the respondents foresaw that petitioner would be willing to sell. The charges here are unlike those in United States v. Radio Corporation of America, 158 F. Supp. 333, reversed, 358 U. S. 334, in which the Government sought to enjoin, as violating § 1, a network's attempt to coerce an independent owner into selling his station to the network under threat of canceling the network's affiliation with other stations under the same ownership. In this case there is no claim made that CBS conditioned the continuation of some network service upon petitioner's consent to sell his equipment, or on his willingness to reduce his price.

Nor can I agree that the contract whereby CBS became a station owner in the Milwaukee market was, in and of itself, a contract in restraint of trade. Petitioner is unable to point to any convincing differences between the vertical integration that is accomplished when a network purchases a station and that which results from an affiliation contract. Moreover, the very contention now being made here by the petitioner has repeatedly been presented to the Federal Communications Commission, and that agency has consistently adhered to the view that network ownership of stations, subject, of course, to the maximum-ownership limitation, is not contrary to the public interest. E. g., ABC-Paramount Merger, 8 Pike and Fischer Radio Reg. 541; St. Louis Telecast, Inc., 12 Pike and Fischer Radio Reg. 1289, 1372; National Broadcasting Co., 20 Pike and Fischer Radio Reg. 411, 419.

This Court has also been reluctant to hold that vertical expansion alone can amount to an unreasonable restraint prohibited by § 1 of the Sherman Act. United States v. Paramount Pictures, Inc., 334 U. S. 131, 173-174; United States v. Columbia Steel Co., 334 U. S. 495, 525. Without of course suggesting that the Federal Communications Commission has authority to alleviate an applicant for a station license from the requirements of the antitrust laws, United States v. Radio Corporation of America, 358 U. S. 334, in light of the uniform course of decisions by the agency familiar with the field, and in the absence of any indication that this particular purchase in fact restrained trade, I think it is clear that petitioner's injury, even if it be assumed partially attributable to CBS' purchase, may not be made the basis of a treble-damage action.

Petitioner's § 2 claim is if anything even more insubstantial. He contends that respondents conspired to monopolize the UHF market in Milwaukee, and perhaps across the country, and that they succeeded in their attempt, at least in Milwaukee. But it is undisputed that the television sets being produced and sold in the Milwaukee area at the time of the alleged conspiracy were all equipped to receive VHF broadcasts and could be adapted to receive UHF signals as well. Thus, any UHF station was necessarily in competition with all VHF stations in the market with respect to both the viewing and the advertising public. Indeed, as the record uncontrovertedly shows, the CBS station ultimately succumbed because the VHF competition was too strong. Since CBS was patently not a monopolist in the Milwaukee market (which included both UHF and VHF), and since there was no allegation that it approached monopoly power in any other market in which petitioner was a competitor, the entry of summary judgment in favor of the respondents on this claim too was eminently correct.

I have gone into this matter at some length because in my opinion the Court's encouragement of this sort of antitrust "enforcement" does disservice to the healthy observance of these laws. I would affirm.

Notes

[1] Under 15 U. S. C. § 15 "Any person who shall be injured in his business or property by reason of anything forbidden in the antitrust laws is given a private right of action."

[2] The last of these allegations was not included in the complaint since the station acquired by CBS did not cease operations until after this suit was brought. It was alleged, however, in petitioner's supplemental affidavit in response to the motion for summary judgment.

[3] If such issues of fact were open and petitioner could prove at the trial that respondents' motives were unlawful, I think it would still be incumbent upon him to prove that the disaffiliation of WCAN was part of the illegal scheme. There is evidence in the record, not contradicted, tending to show that CBS would have canceled that affiliation without regard to its purchase of the Bartell station. If so, much, if not all, of petitioner's alleged loss would have been incurred because of this unilateral act, and not "by reason of anything forbidden in the antitrust laws."

[4] While I do not reach respondents' contention that no consensual arrangement of any kind was shown, I must say that the Court has stretched very far in suggesting that Holt may have been a "conspirator." The record shows, beyond any real possibility of contradiction, that Holt was simply engaged by CBS to act for it, as undisclosed principal, in procuring from Bartell an option to purchase WOKY. So far as Bartell is concerned, it stands uncontroverted in the record that he never knew of CBS' interest in Holt's option until it was exercised by CBS.

[5] The record shows that the undisclosed employment of Holt was due to CBS' desire to keep its competitors, particularly the National Broadcasting Company, from knowledge of its intentions respecting WOKY. This is, of course, a perfectly normal business phenomenon.

[6] There is no suggestion that petitioner was not afforded opportunity to examine any witness he wanted, either before or after respondents made their motion for summary judgment.

[7] The assertion that respondents sought to destroy "the UHF industry . . . because of the enormous economic investment they had in VHF," upon which the Court relies (ante, p. 469), was not made in any of the papers filed with the District Court. It was first raised during oral argument on the motion for summary judgment. There is nothing in the record to support this charge except the hindsight inference arising from the fact that after four years of operating the UHF station in Milwaukee, CBS discontinued it, claiming that the VHF competition was too powerful.

The Court's opinion takes out of context certain statements in a CBS report and infers from them that CBS was intending to make only a short-term venture out of its UHF purchase. But a full reading of the report in question, which was appended to petitioner's affidavit in opposition to the motion for summary judgment, reveals that CBS rejected the suggestion that it purchase a UHF station in a market that was primarily VHF, for the very reason that it would have only short-term advantages. Moreover, the Court's construction of the passage on which it relies hardly reflects its real meaning. The central question on which the report focused was "the degree of short-term cost and inconvenience that is to be undergone in order to obtain the eventual gain" in the purchase of a UHF station. In this context, the report noted that CBS television programs, broadcast by a CBS affiliate in the area (i. e., WCAN), had already built up a UHF viewing market, so that the losses that might be expected at the outset of any such venture would be minimized. The inference is that it would be wise for CBS to capitalize on this headstart before it was cut into by more VHF stations, not that CBS should purchase the station and abandon it as soon as other VHF stations entered the market.

[8] The record shows that Poller from the beginning had unsuccessfully tried to persuade CBS to enlarge the term of his affiliation contract cancellation clause from six months to two years, and that, with eyes thus open, he nonetheless proceeded with his substantial equipment investment.

[9] One of the introductory clauses of the contract provided:

"WHEREAS, Midwest [petitioner] has represented to CBS that Midwest intends to continue the operation of WCAN and all business incidental thereto, and for that purpose CBS proposes to make the sale and transfers hereinafter set forth; . . ."

I find no persuasive basis in the record for petitioner's assertion that this was designed as a self-serving declaration to cloak CBS' alleged antitrust malefactions. By that same contract CBS sold to Poller the WOKY equipment, in part consideration for the purchase of his equipment, the thought quite evidently being that such equipment would suffice for his continued operations, while the superior WCAN equipment would relieve CBS from the necessity of completely re-equipping WOKY.

Justice Harlan's dissent in Public Affairs v. Rickover (March 5, 1962)

MR. JUSTICE HARLAN, dissenting.

The basic issue which brought these cases here was whether Admiral Rickover's speeches were copyrightable in light of the following provision of the Copyright Act: "No copyright shall subsist in . . . any publication of the United States Government." (17 U. S. C. § 8.) As I see it, decision of that issue turns not merely on whether such speeches were made by the Admiral in the "line of duty," but also, and in my view more fundamentally, on whether such speeches were in any event "publication[s] of the United States Government." In my opinion the record is sufficient to require adjudication on both aspects of that issue, and on this phase of the controversy I agree with the result reached by the Court of Appeals. I also agree with its determination as to the adequacy of the copyright notice affixed to speeches delivered after December 1, 1958.

However, I consider the record inadequate to justify adjudication as to whether Admiral Rickover's right to copyright was lost with respect to speeches delivered before December 1, 1958, by reason of their alleged entry into "the public domain."[*] As to that issue I would vacate the judgment of the Court of Appeals and remand the case to the

District Court for further proceedings. In all other respects I would affirm the judgment below.

[*] The stipulation states that with respect to 20 of the 22 speeches made before December 1, 1958, "Admiral Rickover mailed some to individuals who had requested copies or who Admiral Rickover believed would be interested in the subject. Some were sent by Admiral Rickover . . . to the sponsor of the speech to be made available to the press and others at the place where the speech was to be delivered." (Emphasis added.) It appears from the stipulation that no further distribution other than for press use was ever made. Whether the foregoing publications were general enough to amount to a dedication to the public of all or any of these speeches depends on more precise information than is afforded by the stipulation.

Justice Harlan's dissent in United Gas Pipe Line v. Ideal Cement (March 19, 1962)

MR. JUSTICE HARLAN, dissenting.

In my opinion none of the considerations underlying the doctrine of federal judicial abstention (see Harrison v. N. A. A. C. P., 360 U. S. 167, 176-177) call for its application here. There is no reasonable likelihood that a prior state construction of this License Code would either change the complexion of the constitutional issue or avoid the necessity of its eventual adjudication by this Court.

Even were this local enactment to be construed by the state courts to require a license of the appellant as a precondition of engaging in the distribution of natural gas within the City of Mobile, that of itself would not ordain the answer to the constitutional question. See Southern Natural Gas Corp. v. Alabama, 301 U. S. 148; East Ohio Gas Co. v. Tax Comm'n, 283 U. S. 465; see also Illinois Natural Gas Co. v. Central Illinois Pub. Serv. Co., 314 U. S. 498, 506. Cf. Northwestern States Portland Cement Co. v. Minnesota, 358 U. S. 450. Nor can I see how such a state adjudication would serve to illumine the nature of United's activities in Mobile.

As I view matters, nothing useful is to be accomplished by remitting the parties to the state courts, and I would adjudicate the constitutional issue now.

Justice Harlan's dissent in Rusk v. Cort (April 2, 1962) [Notes omitted]

MR. JUSTICE HARLAN, whom MR. JUSTICE FRANKFURTER and MR. JUSTICE CLARK join, dissenting.

The decision that the District Court had jurisdiction to entertain this declaratory judgment action, notwithstanding that the appellee is a foreign resident, seems to me manifestly wrong, in light of the governing statute and its legislative history which could hardly be more clear.

This issue depends upon § 360 of the 1952 Act. That section is entitled:

"Proceedings For Declaration of United States Nationality In The Event of [the administrative] Denial of Rights And Privileges as National." The provisions of the section set out in full in the margin,[1] may be summarized as follows:

(1) If the person whose rights as a national have been administratively denied "is within the United States," he may bring a declaratory judgment action under 28 U. S. C. § 2201 to establish his citizenship,[2] unless that issue was, or is, already involved in an "exclusion" proceeding. The action must be brought within five years after the final administrative denial, and in the district where such person resides or claims residence. (Subsection "(a).")

(2) If such person is "not within the United States," but had previously been "physically" there, or was born abroad of an American citizen parent and is under the age of 16, (i) he may apply abroad for a "certificate of identity" to enable him to seek admission to the United States (subsection "(b)"); and (ii) if admission at a port of entry is finally denied him by the Attorney General, he may have that determination judicially reviewed "in habeas corpus proceedings and not otherwise." If ultimately excluded from the United States, such person is made subject to all the provisions of the immigration law relating to the admission of aliens to the United States. (Subsection "(c).")

As will be shown later, these provisions of the 1952 Act, among other things, departed from the comparable procedural provisions of § 503 of the Nationality Act of 1940, 54 Stat. 1137, 1171-1172, which had expressly made declaratory relief available to all citizenship claimants, whether "within the United States or abroad," following an administrative denial of that status.[3] The purpose and effect of the new provisions are shown by the following extract from the Senate Judiciary Committee's report on the bill (S. 2550), § 360 of which, with only a minor addition and deletion,[4] now bears the same number in the 1952 Act:

"G. DECLARATORY JUDGMENT

"Under the provisions of section 503 of the Nationality Act of 1940 any person who claims a right or privilege as a national of the United States and who is denied such right or privilege by a governmental agency on the ground that he is not a national of the United States may institute an action in a district Federal court for a judgment declaring him to be a national of the United States. If such person is outside the United States and shall have instituted the action in court, he may obtain from a diplomatic or consular officer a certificate of identity and may be admitted to the United States with the certificate upon the condition that he shall be subject to deportation in case it shall be decided by the court that he is not a national of the United States.

"The bill modifies section 503 of the Nationality Act of 1940 by limiting the court action exclusively to persons who are within the United States, and prohibits the court action in any case if the issue of the person's status as a national of the United States (1) arose by reason of, or in connection with, any deportation or exclusion proceeding or (2) is an issue in any such deportation or exclusion proceeding. The reason for the modification is that the issue of citizenship is always germane in an exclusion and deportation proceeding, in which case an adjudication of nationality status can be appropriately made.

"The bill further provides that any person who has previously been physically present in the United States but who is not within the United States who claims a right or privilege as a national of the United States and is denied such right or privilege by any government agency may be issued a certificate of identity for the purpose of traveling to the United States and applying for admission to the United States. The net effect of this provision is to require that the determination of the nationality of such person shall be made in accordance with the normal immigration procedures. These procedures include review by habeas corpus proceedings where the issue of the nationality status of the person can be properly adjudicated." S. Rep. No. 1137, to accompany S. 2550, 82d Cong., 2d Sess., p. 50. (Emphasis added.)

The Court now holds, however, that under § 360 declaratory relief is still available to those "not within the United States" as well as those "within the United States," as was so under § 503 of the 1940 Act; that the certificate of identity procedure provided in subsections (b) and (c) of § 360 is not the exclusive remedy available to nonresident citizenship claimants; that Congress' "predominant concern" in enacting those subsections was to fend against possible misuse of certificates of identity in effecting fraudulent entry into this country; and that jurisdiction of this action accordingly lies under the Declaratory Judgment Act and the Administrative Procedure Act. These conclusions, which I believe are plainly inconsistent with the congressional purpose, as reflected on the fact of § 360 itself and in the foregoing Senate Judiciary Committee report, are refuted beyond any doubt by the background and legislative history of § 360.

Prior to 1940, immigration and nationality statutes were silent on the form and scope of judicial review in deportation, exclusion, and nationality cases. In 1905 this Court, in a habeas corpus proceeding involving an administrative denial of admission to this country of a nonresident citizenship claimant who had temporarily departed, held that due process did not require a judicial trial of the issue of citizenship; and that the courts could inquire into the administrative decision only within the conventional limits of habeas corpus review.[5] United States v. Ju Toy, 198 U. S. 253 (Holmes, J.). In 1922, however, the Court held that a resident claimant in a deportation proceeding was entitled to a judicial determination of his citizenship status, thus turning the availability of full judicial relief on the geographical location of the claimant. Ng Fung Ho v. White, 259 U. S. 276 (Brandeis, J.).

In 1934 the Declaratory Judgment Act was passed. 48 Stat. 955-956; 28 U. S. C. § 2201, as since amended.

In a case decided in 1939, this Court held that remedy applicable to resident citizenship claimants, see Perkins v. Elg, 307 U. S. 325. However, despite the Elg decision, and no doubt because of the Ju Toy and Ng Fung Ho cases, the continuing prevailing view prior to 1940 seems to have been that relief under the Declaratory Judgment Act was not available to nonresidents seeking a determination of their citizenship claims.

It was not until 1940 that Congress, in the Nationality Act of 1940, first specifically dealt with the availability of declaratory relief in nationality cases. Under that statute the requirements for citizenship were greatly tightened and the provisions for loss of citizenship expanded. During the debates concern was expressed lest under existing law some persons might not get their "day in court" with respect to claims to citizenship. 86 Cong. Rec. 13247. This led to the enactment of § 503 under which declaratory relief was made available to resident and nonresident claimants alike, and, in the case of the latter, authorizing, but not requiring, their provisional entry into the United States under certificates of identity, issuable in aid of a declaratory judgment suit already filed. Note 3, supra.

At the same time Congress recognized the possibility of abuse of this liberalized procedure on the part of nonresident claimants who might seek certificates of identity only to achieve entry into this country, without any thought of pressing their citizenship claims; and an attempt was made to guard against such abuse. Accordingly, the section was written to provide that certificates of identity should be furnished only upon "a sworn application showing that the claim of nationality presented in such [declaratory judgment] action is made in good faith and has a substantial basis"; it also authorized the Secretary of State, with the approval of the Attorney General, to prescribe regulations for the issuance of such certificates.[6] Note 3, supra.

Commencing soon after the close of World War II, and perhaps in part as a result of the then recent repeal of the Chinese Exclusion Act and continuing Communist successes in China, a large number of suits were filed in the federal courts by Chinese citizenship claimants. These carried in their wake consequences which Congress could hardly have fully anticipated when it enacted § 503. Such consequences were principally of three kinds. First, there was an increase in the volume of fraudulent entries into this country; many Chinese who had obtained certificates of identity incident to the institution of a declaratory judgment citizenship action would abandon the suit upon arrival here and disappear into the stream of the population. Second, the courts experienced difficulty in adjudicating "derivative" citizenship claims without the claimants having been first exposed to normal immigration screening; such claims were often based on the assertion that the claimant was the foreign-born child of an American citizen who had temporarily returned to China, an assertion frequently difficult to disprove. Third, the federal court dockets became cluttered with these suits. See, e. g., United States ex rel. Dong Wing Ott v. Shaughnessy, 116 F. Supp. 745, 751-752, aff'd, 220 F. 2d 537; Mar Gong v. McGranery, 109 F. Supp. 821, rev'd sub nom. Mar Gong v. Brownell, 209 F. 2d 448. By the end of 1952, 1,288 such cases had been instituted. See Ly Shew v. Acheson, 110 F. Supp. 50, 54-55, vacated and remanded sub nom. Ly Shew v. Dulles, 219 F. 2d 413; Annual Reports of the Attorney General for 1956 (pp. 111-113) and 1957 (pp. 121-123). This state of affairs contributed in no small degree to the revamping of § 503 by § 360 of the statute now before us, enacted after five years of investigation pursuant to a 1947 Senate Resolution authorizing a general study of the immigration laws. S. Res. No. 137, 80th Cong., 1st Sess.

(1947).

The first step in this direction occurred in 1950 when Senator McCarran introduced S. 3455, § 359 of which, entitled "Judicial Proceedings for Declaration of United States Nationality in the Event of Denial of Rights and Privileges as a National,"[7] was the earliest version of what ultimately became § 360 of the 1952 Act. Section 359 provided declaratory relief only for "any person in the United States." The Senate Report[8] accompanying that bill, after observing that § 503 of the 1940 Act permitted persons "within or without" the United States to file declaratory judgment suits, went on to say of proposed new § 359:

"In spite of the definite restrictions on the use and application of section 503 to bona fide cases [see supra, pp. 389-390], the subcommittee finds that the section had been subject to broad interpretation, and that it has been used, in a considerable number of cases, to gain entry into the United States where no such right existed. . . . The subcommittee therefore recommends that the provisions of section 503 as set out in the proposed bill be modified to limit the privilege to persons who are in the United States . . . ." (Emphasis added.)

Read in connection with this report it is surely beyond doubt that the § 503 "privilege" which was intended to be changed was not merely the right to a certificate of identity, which, under the existing statute, was an optional, not a necessary, appurtenance of a declaratory judgment suit, but the right of one abroad to maintain such a suit itself. Since a person "in" the United States had no need for a certificate of identity, the "privilege" limited by this bill to persons "in" the United States can only mean the privilege of bringing a declaratory suit. In other words, the new proposal did not view the "entry" problem as something that could be dealt with independently of the character of the judicial remedy to be afforded those administratively denied citizenship.[9] This, as will be seen, remained in the forefront of the subsequent legislative discussions.

Early in the following year three additional bills were placed before the Congress, one in the Senate and two in the House. S. 716,[10] a revision of the earlier McCarran bill, and H. R. 2379,[11] introduced by Representative Walter, both provided for "citizenship" declaratory relief only as to persons "within the United States." The third, H. R. 2816,[12] introduced by Representative Celler, afforded such relief to "any person" (making no reference to location), and in other respects was also substantially like existing § 503.

In the ensuing Joint Hearings on these bills[13] attention became sharply focused on the question of what, if any, judicial relief (other than habeas corpus) should be available to nonresident citizenship claimants. The most revealing points of view are found in the statements submitted on behalf of the Departments of State and Justice.[14] While both Departments took the position that some such relief should be afforded nonresidents,[15] their proposals were quite different. State suggested declaratory relief for persons abroad limited to those whose original citizenship status was not in doubt, but who were deemed to have lost it; and that certificates of identity should be made available to such persons, on an optional basis, to permit their coming to this country in aid of their suits.[16] Justice, on the other hand, recommended that all nonresidents whose claims to citizenship were not frivolous should be required to obtain a special certificate of identity, or its equivalent, so as to permit them to come to this country to test their claims in accordance with normal immigration procedures.[17]

However, it is evident that the proposals of both State and Justice were intended to fill the remedial gap in S. 716 respecting nonresidents; that they contemplated either limiting, or entirely doing away with, the unrestricted declaratory relief available to nonresidents under § 503 of the 1940 statute; that they were envisaged as constituting the exclusive remedy for those living abroad; and that they negative any idea that one so situated was to have the choice between such procedures and the general remedies provided by the Declaratory Judgment Act or the Administrative Procedure Act.

Following the Joint Hearings, the McCarran bill, S. 716, was redrawn as S. 2055,[18] and the Walter bill, H. R. 2379, was revised as H. R. 5678,[19] in consultation with representatives of the State and Justice Departments.[20] The revised McCarran bill adopted the Department of Justice proposals, in effect limiting the judicial remedy for testing nonresident citizenship claims to that afforded in connection with "exclusion" cases, that is habeas corpus.[21] The new Walter bill was in effect a combination of existing § 503 and the suggestions of the State Department.[22] That bill was eventually passed by the House.[23] The McCarran bill, except for two minor deletions,[24] was reported out by the Senate Judiciary Committee as S. 2550 and passed by the Senate. Supra, pp. 386-387.

Congress, thus squarely faced with making, or not making, declaratory relief available to nonresident citizenship claimants, chose the latter course. It accepted S. 2550,[25] the judicial remedy provisions of which became § 360 of the Immigration and Nationality Act of 1952. Note 1, supra.

In light of this unambiguous course of events, I do not understand how the Government's contention that the District Court lacked jurisdiction over this declaratory judgment action can be successfully challenged, the appellee at all relevant times having resided abroad. To say the least, the Court's contrary conclusion seems to me to rest on the most insecure kind of reasoning.

Certainly, the past cases in this Court lend no support to this decision. Perkins v. Elg, 307 U. S. 325, holding that a resident, threatened with deportation, could maintain a declaratory judgment action to establish citizenship, was of course quite in line with Ng Fung Ho v. White, supra. Moreover, the case was decided in 1939, before Congress, for the first time, addressed itself to the availability of declaratory relief in nationality cases. Supra, p. 389. McGrath v. Kristensen, 340 U. S. 162, is even more inapposite. The issue there was simply whether, in the circumstances involved, an alien then in this country was eligible for naturalization, so that the Attorney General had power to stay his deportation. The Court noted that § 503 of the 1940 Act was not available to the alien, since his citizenship status was not in issue. Incidentally, the Court did not reach the applicability of the Administrative Procedure Act. Flemming v. Nestor, 363 U. S. 603, involved a nonresident alien's right to social security benefits, not citizenship.[26]

   Shaughnessy v. Pedreiro, 349 U. S. 48, and Brownell v. Tom We Shung, 352 U. S. 180, the two cases relied on by the Court as supporting the applicability of the Administrative Procedure Act in this instance, were, respectively, simply straightforward deportation and exclusion cases, neither involving a citizenship claim. Unlike the sections in the 1952 Act relating to nationality, those governing deportation and exclusion then had no specific provisions dealing with judicial relief,[27] and unlike this case, the relief in those cases was sought only after the administrative process had run its full course, and a "final" determination had been made by the Attorney General.

   When it comes to § 360 itself and the legislative history of the section, the Court's analysis is, if anything, even more cursory and unpersuasive. The Court initially finds that the declaratory judgment provision respecting nonresidents, contained in the predecessor of § 360— § 503 of the 1940 Act—was understood "to be merely a confirmation of existing law, or at most a clarification of it." In this, the Court has overlooked the Ju Toy and Ng Fung Ho cases which of course indicate precisely the contrary. Supra, p. 388, and note 6.

   Proceeding from that premise, and despite the unequivocal directive in subsection (c) of § 360 that a final determination of the Attorney General denying admission to a citizenship claimant shall be subject to judicial review "in habeas corpus proceedings and not otherwise," the Court concludes that such is not indeed the exclusive remedy. This is said to be so because § 360 provides only that the claimant "may" apply abroad for a certificate of identity (subsection (b)), and upon arrival at our shores "may" apply for admission (subsection (c)). This conclusion is supported only by a quotation from the District Court's opinion in this very case. It cannot withstand the statute and legislative history already discussed.

   Finally, the Court considers that Congress' "predominate concern" in enacting subsections (b) and (c) of § 360 was with fraudulent entry, not judicial remedies. It is said that this "seems obvious" because the phrase "such person," contained in the extract quoted by the Court from the Judiciary Committee Report on S. 2550 (ante, pp. 378-379), refers grammatically only to those persons who had elected to pursue the certificate of identity procedure in prosecuting their citizenship claims. But this conclusion also will hardly stand up when the full text of the Judiciary Committee Report, especially the clause "The bill modifies section 503 of the Nationality Act of 1940 by limiting the court action exclusively to persons who are within the United States . . . ," is read (supra, p. 387), and the relevant legislative history is considered.

   In deciding the jurisdictional issue as it has, I fear that the Court has become the victim of the manner in which it has put that issue to itself:

   "More precisely stated, the question in this case is whether, despite the liberal provisions of the Administrative Procedure Act, Congress intended that a native of this country living abroad must travel thousands of miles, be arrested, and go to jail in order to attack an administrative finding that he is not a citizen of the United States."

   But to sustain the Government's position on this issue it is not necessary to find that Congress, in enacting § 360, suddenly became severe, irrational, or capricious. As a result of the unfavorable experience with § 503 of the 1940 Act, Congress simply restored, with some alleviations, what until 1940 had been the procedure in such cases—a procedure whose constitutionality had long since been upheld by this Court with the firm support of such men as Holmes and Brandeis, JJ. And in so doing Congress acted only after the fullest inquiry, debate, and deliberation.

I am unable to grasp how the Court could have reached the conclusion that the present declaratory action is not precluded by § 360, except by making its own wish father to the thought.[28]

Justice Harlan's dissent in Scholle v. Hare (April 23, 1962)

MR. JUSTICE HARLAN, dissenting.

The Court remands this case to the Supreme Court of Michigan "for further consideration in the light of Baker v. Carr, 369 U. S. 186." In my opinion nothing decided or said by the majority in Baker casts any light upon, still less controls, the only issue actually adjudicated by the Michigan Supreme Court in the present case. I think that either this appeal should be dismissed for want of a substantial federal question or probable jurisdiction should be noted and the case set for argument.

The sole and dispositive question decided by the Michigan Supreme Court was concisely put by Justice Edwards, speaking for four members of that eight-man court:

"Does the Fourteenth Amendment to the United States Constitution prohibit any State from enacting provisions for electoral districts for 1 house of its legislature [the State Senate] which result in substantial inequality of popular representation in that house?" Scholle v. Secretary of State, 360 Mich. 1, at 85, 104 N. W. 2d 63, at 107.

These four members of the state court concluded that nothing in the Fourteenth Amendment or in the decisions of this Court construing the Equal Protection Clause "prohibits a State from establishing senate electoral districts by geographic areas drawn generally along county lines which result in substantial inequality of voter representation favoring thinly populated areas as opposed to populous ones." 360 Mich., at 91, 104 N. W. 2d, at 110. Accordingly, the original petition for mandamus filed in the Supreme Court of Michigan was dismissed.[1] The opinion of the four judges did not so much as mention questions pertaining to the "jurisdiction" of the court, the "standing" of the appellant, or the "justiciability" of his claim.

Appellant filed a timely notice of appeal to this Court, and on docketing the record submitted a jurisdictional statement which set forth the questions presented for review.[2] These papers, along with the motion to dismiss or affirm, taken in light of the prevailing opinion in the Michigan Supreme Court, leave no room for doubt but that the precise and single issue in this case is the one presented as Question IV in the jurisdictional statement: "Do the 1952 amendments to Art. V, § 2 and § 4 of the Michigan Constitution, and the implementing legislation thereto, offend the Fourteenth Amendment to the U. S.

Constitution, including the due-process and equal protection clauses thereof?" That issue is the more precisely delineated by three circumstances: (1) the legislative branch with which this case is concerned is the State Senate (not the entire State Legislature, as in Baker v. Carr); (2) the challenged electoral apportionment reflects the desires of Michigan's citizenry, as expressed in a 1952 popular referendum (and is not, as in Baker v. Carr, the product of legislative inaction);[3] and (3) the present apportionment is prescribed by the Michigan Constitution (and is not in conflict with the State Constitution, as in Baker v. Carr).

Were there anything in this Court's recent decision in Baker v. Carr intimating that the constitutional question in this case ought to have been decided differently than it was by the Michigan Supreme Court, I would be content, for reasons given in my dissent in Baker (369 U. S. 186, 330), simply to note my dissent to the Court's failure to dismiss this appeal for want of a substantial federal question. But both the majority opinion in the Baker case and a separate concurrence written to dispel any "distressingly inaccurate impression of what the Court decides," 369 U. S., at 265, were at pains to warn that nothing more was decided than "(a) that the [federal district] court possessed jurisdiction of the subject matter; (b) that a justiciable cause of action is stated upon which appellants would be entitled to appropriate relief; and (c) . . . that the appellants have standing to challenge the Tennessee apportionment statutes." 369 U. S., at 197-198, 265. How any of the extensive discussion on these three subjects in the Baker majority opinion can be thought to shed light on the discrete federal constitutional question on which the present case turns—a question which was indeed studiously avoided in the majority opinion in Baker—is difficult to understand.

Moreover, the remand cannot be justified on the theory that Baker v. Carr for the first time suggests—albeit sub silentio—that an arbitrary or capricious state legislative apportionment may violate the Equal Protection Clause. For the Michigan Supreme Court assumed precisely that proposition and nonetheless said of the existing apportionment: "In the face of . . . history and . . . precedent, we find no way by which we can say that the classification we are concerned with herein is `wholly arbitrary,' and hence repugnant to the Fourteenth Amendment of the United States Constitution as the United States supreme court has construed it to this date." 360 Mich., at 106, 104 N. W. 2d, at 118.

With all respect, I consider that in thus remanding this case the Court has been less than forthright with the Michigan Supreme Court. That court is left in the uncomfortable position where it will have to choose between adhering to its present decision—in my view a faithful reflection of this Court's past cases—or treating the remand as an oblique invitation from this Court to hold that the Equal Protection Clause prohibits a State from constitutionally freezing the seats in its Senate, with the effect of maintaining numerical voting inequalities, even though that course reflects the expressed will of the people of the State. (Note 3, supra.)

In my view the matter should not be left in this equivocal posture. Both the orderly solution of this particular case, and the wider ramifications that are bound to follow in the wake of Baker v. Carr, demand that the Court come to grips now with the basic issue tendered by this case. This should be done either by dismissing the appeal for want of a substantial federal question or by noting probable jurisdiction and then deciding the issue one way or another. For reasons given in my separate dissent in the Baker case, I think dismissal is the right course.

Notes

[1] On appeals to the Supreme Court of Michigan the result of an equally divided court is that the judgment below is affirmed. Mich. Stat. Ann. § 27.46 (1938). Although no statute expressly controls, it appears that Michigan follows the general rule that no affirmative action may be taken on an original petition unless a majority of the justices considering the case vote to grant relief. Consequently the effect of an equal division on an original petition for a writ of mandamus would be a dismissal of the petition. Cf. In re Hartley, 317 Mich. 441, 27 N. W. 2d 48.

It appears, moreover, that in fact five members (a majority) of the Michigan Supreme Court concurred as to this issue. The separate concurring opinion of Justice Black of that court shows that he also concluded "that a State may—unfettered juridically by the Fourteenth Amendment—determine what as a matter of State policy shall be `a proper diffusion of political initiative' as between the thinly and heavily populated areas of the State." 360 Mich., at 119-120, 104 N. W. 2d, at 125.

[2] The appellant listed the following as the "Questions Presented":

"I. Does the Fourteenth Amendment to the U. S. Constitution prohibit the establishment by a state of permanent state legislative districts grossly unequal in population?

"II. Does the Fourteenth Amendment to the U. S. Constitution prohibit the establishment by a state of permanent legislative districts lacking any discernible, rational, uniform, non-arbitrary and non-discriminatory basis of representation whatever (save, only, the freezing by such enactment of legislative malapportionment theretofore invalid under prior constitutional provisions)?

"III. Does a suit duly brought in a state court of otherwise competent jurisdiction, challenging a state constitutional amendment respecting legislative apportionment and/or districting on grounds of asserted conflict with the Fourteenth Amendment to the United States Constitution, present a justiciable controversy of which such court has jurisdiction and the power to render relief?

"IV. Do the 1952 amendments to Art. V, § 2 and § 4 of the Michigan Constitution, and the implementing legislation thereto, offend the Fourteenth Amendment to the U. S. Constitution, including the due-process and equal protection clauses thereof?

"V. If so, may the Michigan Supreme Court, otherwise possessed of jurisdiction, entertain and render relief in an action to invalidate such enactments?"

The third of these questions does assert the issue of "justiciability." However, no reference to "justiciability" appears in the opinion written for four justices of the state court, and the appellees' motion to dismiss or affirm combined, entirely justifiably in face of the record, the appellant's five questions into the following single question:

"Does Article V, Section 2 of the Michigan Constitution, as amended by a majority vote in the general election of November 1952, of the people of the State of Michigan, which prescribes that the Michigan Senate shall consist of 34 members, each of whom is to be elected from a geographically described area, not subject to change because of fluctuations in population, violate the equal protection or due process clause of the Fourteenth Amendment to the United States Constitution?"

[3] The disputed provision of the Michigan Constitution, Art. V, § 2, which establishes permanent state senatorial districts not subject to change because of fluctuations in population, was adopted as initiative Proposition No. 3 in a referendum held throughout the State in November 1952.

Justice Harlan's dissent in Goldlawr, Inc. v. Heiman (April 30, 1962)

MR. JUSTICE HARLAN, whom MR. JUSTICE STEWART joins, dissenting.

The notion that a District Court may deal with an in personam action in such a way as possibly to affect a defendant's substantive rights without first acquiring jurisdiction over him is not a familiar one in federal jurisprudence. No one suggests that Congress was aware that 28 U. S. C. § 1406 (a) might be so used when it enacted that statute. The "interest of justice" of which the statute speaks and which the Court's opinion emphasizes in support of its construction of § 1406 (a) is assuredly not a one-way street. And it is incongruous to consider, as the Court's holding would seem to imply, that in the "interest of justice" Congress sought in § 1406 (a) to deal with the transfer of cases where both venue and jurisdiction are lacking in the district where the action is commenced, while neglecting to provide any comparable alleviative measures for the plaintiff who selects a district where venue is proper but where personal jurisdiction cannot be obtained.[*]

In these circumstances I think the matter is better left for further action by Congress, preferably after the Judicial Conference of the United States has expressed its views on the subject. Cf. Miner v. Atlass, 363 U. S. 641, 650-652. Meanwhile, substantially for the reasons elaborated in the opinion of Judge Moore, 288 F. 2d 579, I would affirm the judgment of the Court of Appeals.

[*] In an ordinary diversity suit, for example, a plaintiff may bring suit in the judicial district where he resides. 28 U. S. C. § 1391 (a). But if he is unable to get personal service on the defendant in the territory defined by Fed. Rule Civ. Proc. 4 (f), his suit will be dismissed. See Robertson v. Railroad Labor Board, 268 U. S. 619; cf. Mississippi Publishing Corp. v. Murphree, 326 U. S. 438, 442-443. Since this would not be "a case laying venue in the wrong division or district," § 1406 (a) would be inapplicable.

Justice Harlan's dissent in California v. FPC (April 30, 1962)

MR. JUSTICE HARLAN, whom MR. JUSTICE STEWART joins, dissenting.

In this case originating in the Federal Power Commission, the Court today announces a new and surprising antitrust procedural rule: If the Commission is asked to "proceed to a decision on the merits of a merger application when there is pending in the courts a suit challenging the validity of that [merger and its antecedent] transaction[s] under the antitrust laws," the Commission must abstain from a determination and "await decision in the antitrust suit before taking action." (Ante, pp. 487, 489.)

The holding does not turn on any facts or circumstances which may be said to be peculiar to this particular case. It is not limited to Federal Power Commission proceedings. Without adverting to any legal principle or statute to support its decision, the Court appears to lay down a pervasive rule, born solely of its own abstract notions of what "orderly procedure" requires, that seemingly will henceforth govern every agency action involving matters with respect to which the antitrust laws are applicable and antitrust litigation is then pending in the courts.

I cannot subscribe to a decision which broadly works such havoc with the proper relationship between the administrative and judicial functions in matters of this kind. The decision, on the one hand, in effect transfers to the Antitrust Division of the Department of Justice regulatory functions entrusted to administrative agencies, and on the other hand deprives the courts in government antitrust litigation of the authority given them by statute to determine whether or not interlocutory relief is necessary or appropriate. What this new rule entails is illustrated by this case: A business transaction of great magnitude and importance, which the Federal Power Commission has found to be in the public interest, is, at least for the time being, set for naught, without the slightest inquiry into whether the antitrust charges leveled against it are weighty or not. The Court's action is the more unusual because it is taken (1) despite the antitrust court's denial of interlocutory relief when such relief was belatedly sought by the Government; (2) in the face of the considered judgment of the Solicitor General, representing the public interests respectively involved in the administrative and antitrust proceedings, that determination of the ultimate effect of the Commission's order should be left to abide the event of the antitrust case, and that meanwhile such order should be allowed to stand; and (3) at the instance only of an intervenor in the Commission's proceeding which was not even a party to the Government's antitrust suit.

The undiscriminating nature and reach of this decision become apparent when attention is focused on the procedural events occurring prior to the order of the Commission which is here under attack. On July 22, 1957, the Department of Justice instituted a civil action in the United States District Court in Utah against the El Paso Natural Gas Company and the Pacific Northwest Pipeline Company, seeking to restrain an alleged violation of § 7 of the Clayton Act. This violation was said to have occurred when, beginning in January 1957, El Paso embarked on a program of acquiring nearly all of

Pacific's outstanding common stock. The complaint asked that the purchase be declared to be a violation of § 7 of the Clayton Act and that El Paso be directed to divest itself of Pacific's stock. No interlocutory relief appears to have been requested.

On August 7, 1957, El Paso filed with the Federal Power Commission its application for authorization to merge Pacific's assets with its own. Despite this announced intention further to intermingle the affairs of the two corporations, the Government did not seek temporary relief from the District Court in Utah. El Paso, on the other hand, contended that "primary jurisdiction" with regard to the merger resided with the Commission and sought to have the antitrust action stayed. Its motion was denied by the District Court, and on March 3, 1958, we denied leave to file a petition for common-law certiorari to that decision. 355 U. S. 950.

When the case was returned to the District Court the Government again made no effort to obtain from that court an order maintaining the status quo pending the outcome of the suit. Instead, the Assistant Attorney General in charge of the Antitrust Division suggested to the Commission that it stay its own proceedings until the antitrust suit had terminated. When this request was rejected by the Commission, the Antitrust Division withdrew from the Commission proceedings despite an express invitation from the Commission that it participate.

Hearings before the Commission's examiner were scheduled to begin on September 17, 1958, and the trial of the antitrust suit in the District Court was set for November 17, 1958. At a hearing on several pretrial matters held in the District Court on September 5 and 6, the Government, for the first time, moved for a temporary injunction to restrain the asset merger even if the Commission's approval were forthcoming.[1] That motion was denied and not renewed thereafter. The Commission's hearings began on September 17 and were recessed on September 26 until November 12.

El Paso again moved in the District Court for a continuance of the antitrust trial until after the Commission had passed on the merger application, and the Government once more asked the Commission to stay its proceedings pending the outcome of the antitrust case. While noting that the Government had refused the Commission's invitation to intervene in the merger proceedings, the Commission agreed to defer to the District Court. It notified the court that if El Paso's motion for a continuance of the trial were denied, the Commission would continue its merger proceeding to a later date. On October 13, 1958, the District Court issued an order granting El Paso's motion and continued the antitrust trial "until the final determination by the Federal Power Commission of the applications now pending before it." The Government has never sought to review this order by mandamus or by any other available means. The Commission subsequently held its hearings and authorized the merger of El Paso and Pacific in an order dated December 23, 1959. It is that order which the Court today in effect holds to have been entered without jurisdiction.

The Court relies on three "practical reasons" to support its perplexing conclusion that despite the Government's failure promptly to seek relief pendente lite in the antitrust suit, its failure to press for review of the denial of such relief when belatedly sought, and the Commission's expressed willingness to defer to the antitrust court, the Commission was nonetheless required to withhold approval of the merger application: (1) If the asset merger were approved and executed, and the stock purchase thereafter held to be illegal, an "unscrambling" involving "needless waste of time and money" would be necessary; (2) such an "unscrambling" would "raise complicated and perplexing problems on tax matters and otherwise"; (3) the Commission's approval of the asset merger "is bound to carry momentum into the antitrust suit." (Ante, pp. 488-489.) Whatever weight these considerations may be deemed to have, I think that "orderly procedure" required their determination, at least in the first instance, by the antitrust court, if indeed they were not rejected by the District Court on the Government's 1958 motion to enjoin consummation of the merger. Their consideration by this Court as an original matter is entirely inappropriate, and in no event do any of them affect the validity of the Commission's order approving the merger.[2]

 I.

 Section 15 of the Clayton Act, 15 U. S. C. § 25, grants jurisdiction to the United States District Courts "to prevent and restrain violations" of the Clayton Act, and empowers the United States Attorneys "to institute proceedings in equity to prevent and restrain such violations." The same statutory section provides that pending determination of the merits of a complaint filed by the United States "and before final decree, the court may at any time make such temporary restraining order or prohibition as shall be deemed just in the premises." Consequently, it is the duty of the District Court before which an antitrust suit is pending to pass on the desirability of temporary relief in order to avoid later problems of "unscrambling." In the case before us, it was not until more than a year after the Government knew of El Paso's intention to merge Pacific's assets with its own that it requested the District Court to enjoin the execution of this plan. The court's denial of the temporary injunction must be presumed to have been based on its evaluation of the likelihood of success of the antitrust suit and of the difficulties that might arise if interlocutory relief were denied. Not having renewed its motion, the Government may surely not revive it indirectly by attacking the Commission's order. Moreover, by what authority is petitioner, the State of California, an intervenor only in the Commission's proceedings, empowered to assert claims relating to the enforcement of the antitrust laws that are unavailable to the Government, the plaintiff in the antitrust action?

 II.

 Similarly, whatever is meant by the suggestion that the Commission's approval carries "momentum" into the antitrust suit, this factor is one that should be remedied, if necessary, by purging the antitrust proceedings of any improper influence deriving from the agency determination, not by invalidating the administrative action. The Court's holding—which is unnecessary to a decision of this case and, as the Government argues, also premature[3]—that the concluding proviso of § 7 of the Clayton Act gives the Commission's approval of this asset merger no immunizing effect against the antitrust claim, surely lends added support to the view that the agency is permitted to consider this application as it might consider any other which suggests no difficulties under the antitrust laws. If the Commission's approval is irrelevant to the merits of the Government's antitrust suit, it is the court considering the antitrust claim which should guard itself against giving weight to this irrelevancy, not the Commission passing on the merger application. And if the lower courts should ultimately go wrong in this regard, their error would be correctible in this Court.

Likewise there is little substance to the difficulty which this Court finds in a court "undoing what was done" (ante, p. 489) by the Commission. Had the antitrust trial court been fearful on that score it could have entered an appropriate interlocutory order ensuring that nothing would be done while the litigation was pending.

III.

Finally, I do not think that the record in this case justifies a conclusion that the Commission's refusal to postpone consideration of the merger application amounted to an abuse of discretion. On the Court's premise that the agency's approval did not immunize the transaction from antitrust liability, the Commission's action in granting the certificate of public convenience and necessity did no more than permit the merger to be consummated subject to all possible antitrust infirmities. And even proceeding on the Commission's premise that the proviso of § 7 of the Clayton Act gives it the power to immunize mergers from antitrust liability, its decision to go ahead after being notified by the District Court that the motion to continue the antitrust suit had been granted could hardly be regarded as an abuse of discretion.

In conclusion, the Court's decision in this case creates a wholly artificial imbalance between antitrust law enforcement and administrative regulation with respect to federally regulated industries. By displacing the continuing supervision of a court over such interlocutory terms as are "just in the premises" with an absolute rule prohibiting the regulating agency from considering applications relating to matters which are also involved in a pending antitrust suit, this decision seems to leave no room for sensible accommodation of the two sets of interests in a given instance. Neither the inflexible rule announced by the Court nor its decision on the facts of this case is supported by reason or authority.

I would affirm.

Notes

[1] The fact that such a motion was made and denied does not appear in the record before this Court. However, it is asserted in El Paso's brief and is not denied by any of the other parties.

[2] Because of the posture of this case, I would not reach the question as to what weight should be given to the pendency of administrative merger proceedings by an antitrust court which is asked to grant interlocutory relief. However, I think more can be said than the Court does in favor of staying the hand of an antitrust court pending

consideration by the appropriate agency of matters touching on "those areas . . . in which active regulation has been found necessary to compensate for the inability of competition to provide adequate regulation." Federal Communications Comm'n v. RCA Communications, Inc., 346 U. S. 86, 92.

[3] Whatever may be the impact on a § 7 action of the Commission's approval of this merger, it can be felt only in the antitrust suit. Consequently, I would, as the Solicitor General has suggested, leave this issue open for consideration in the District Court should the agency's order be asserted as a defense in that action.

Justice Harlan's dissent in In re McConnell (June 18, 1962)

MR. JUSTICE HARLAN, whom MR. JUSTICE STEWART joins, dissenting.

With respect to the contempt count that was sustained by the Court of Appeals, this case involves nothing more than an ordinary exercise of the District Court's contempt power in aid of maintaining discipline and decorum in the courtroom. The most, I think, that could appropriately be said of the conviction on this count is that petitioner's unlawyer-like conduct did not merit a jail sentence. The Court of Appeals has removed all basis for criticism on that score by reducing the sentence to a $100 fine. In other respects its opinion displays an alert regard for the undoubted fact that the contempt power should always be exercised circumspectly and dispassionately, particularly when called into play by the conduct of an attorney in the course of sharply contested litigation.

I can hardly believe that the Court intends its opinion to mean that only a physical obstruction of pending judicial proceedings is punishable under 18 U. S. C. § 401. For a court's power to punish summarily for contempt has always been available as a sanction against the use of abusive and insulting language in a courtroom. See, e. g., Offutt v. United States, 348 U. S. 11; Fisher v. Pace, 336 U. S. 155, 159-160; Ex parte Terry, 128 U. S. 289, 307-309. And it can scarcely be supposed that Congress' enactment of 18 U. S. C. § 401 was intended to abrogate this power, even as the forerunner to that section was construed in In re Michael, 326 U. S. 224, 228. Cf. Ex parte Hudgings, 249 U. S. 378, 383.

This routine intra-circuit affair presents nothing calling for the exercise of this Court's supervisory power, and the case would have been much better left with the Court of Appeals by a denial of certiorari.

I would affirm.

Justice Harlan's dissent in Rudolph v. US (June 18, 1962)

Separate opinion of MR. JUSTICE HARLAN.

Although the reasons given by the Court for dismissing the writ as improvidently granted should have been persuasive against granting certiorari, now that the case is here I think it better to decide it, two members of the Court having dissented on the merits.

The courts below concluded (1) that the value of this "all expense" trip to the company-sponsored insurance convention constituted "gross income" to the petitioners within the meaning of § 61 of the Internal Revenue Code of 1954, and (2) that the amount reflected was not deductible as an "ordinary and necessary" business expense under § 162 of the Code.[1] Both conclusions are, in my opinion, unassailable unless the findings of fact on which they rested are to be impeached by us as clearly erroneous. I do not think they can be on this record, especially in light of the "seasoned and wise rule of this Court" which "makes concurrent findings of two courts below final here in the absence of very exceptional showing of error." Comstock v. Group of Institutional Investors, 335 U. S. 211, 214.

The basic facts, found by the District Court, are as follows. Petitioners, husband and wife, reside in Dallas, Texas, where the home office of the husband's employer, the Southland Life Insurance Company, is located. By having sold a predetermined amount of insurance, the husband qualified to attend the company's convention in New York City in 1956 and, in line with company policy, to bring his wife with him. The petitioners, together with 150 other employees and officers of the insurance company and 141 wives, traveled to and from New York City on special trains, and were housed in a single hotel during their two-and-one-half-day visit. One morning was devoted to a "business meeting" and group luncheon, the rest of the time in New York City to "travel, sight-seeing, entertainment, fellowship or free time." The entire trip lasted one week.

The company paid all the expenses of the convention-trip which amounted to $80,000; petitioners' allocable share being $560. When petitioners did not include the latter amount in their joint income tax return, the Commissioner assessed a deficiency which was sustained by the District Court, 189 F. Supp. 2, and also by the Court of Appeals, one judge dissenting, in a per curiam opinion, 291 F. 2d 841, citing its recent decision in Patterson v. Thomas, 289 F. 2d 108, where the same result had been reached. The District Court held that the value of the trip being "in the nature of a bonus, reward, and compensation for a job well done," was income to Rudolph, but being "primarily a pleasure trip in the nature of a vacation," the costs were personal and nondeductible.

I.

Under § 61 of the 1954 Code was the value of the trip to the taxpayer-husband properly includible in gross income? That section defines gross income as "all income from whatever source derived," including, among other items, "compensation for services." Certain sections of the 1954 Code enumerate particular receipts which are included in the concept of "gross income,"[2] including prizes and awards (with certain exceptions);[3] while other sections, §§ 101-121, specifically exclude certain receipts from "gross income," including, for example, gifts and inheritances[4] (see Commissioner v. Duberstein, 363 U. S. 278), and meals or lodgings furnished for the convenience of the employer.[5] The Treasury Regulations emphasize the inclusiveness of the concept of "gross income."[6]

In light of the sweeping scope of § 61 taxing "all gains except those specifically exempted," Commissioner v. Glenshaw Glass Co., 348 U. S. 426, 430; see Commissioner v.

LoBue, 351 U. S. 243, 246; James v. United States, 366 U. S. 213, 219, and its purpose to include as taxable income "any economic or financial benefit conferred on the employee as compensation, whatever the form or mode by which it is effected," Commissioner v. Smith, 324 U. S. 177, 181, it seems clear that the District Court's findings, if sustainable, bring the value of the trip within the reach of the statute.

Petitioners do not claim that the value of the trip is within one of the statutory exclusions from "gross income" (see notes 4 and 5, supra) as did the taxpayer in Patterson v. Thomas, 289 F. 2d 108, 111-112; rather they characterize the amount as a "fringe benefit" not specifically excluded from § 61 by other sections of the statute, yet not intended to be encompassed by its reach. Conceding that the statutory exclusions from "gross income" are not exhaustive, as the Government seems to recognize is so under Glenshaw, it is not now necessary to explore the extent of any such nonstatutory exclusions.[7] For it was surely within the Commissioner's competence to consider as "gross income" a "reward, or a bonus given to . . . employees for excellence in service," which the District Court found was the employer's primary purpose in arranging this trip. I cannot say that this finding, confirmed as it has been by the Court of Appeals, is inadequately supported by this record.[8]

II.

There remains the question whether, though income, this outlay for transportation, meals, and lodging was deductible by petitioners as an "ordinary and necessary" business expense under § 162.[9] The relevant factors on this branch of the case are found in Treas. Reg. § 1.162-2.[10] In summary, the regulation in pertinent part provides:

Traveling expenses, including meals, lodgings and other incidentals, reasonable and necessary in the conduct of the taxpayer's business and directly attributable to it are deductible, but expenses of a trip "undertaken for other than business purposes" are "personal expenses" and the meals and lodgings are "living expenses." Treas. Reg. § 1.162-2 (a).

If a taxpayer who travels to a destination engages in both "business and personal activities," the traveling expenses are deductible only if the trip is "related primarily" to the taxpayer's business; if "primarily personal," the traveling expenses are not deductible even though the taxpayer engages in some business there; yet expenses allocable to the taxpayer's trade or business there are deductible even though the travel expenses to and fro are not.[11] Id., § 1.162-2 (b) (1).

Whether a trip is related primarily to the taxpayer's business or is primarily personal in nature "depends on the facts and circumstances in each case." Id., § 1.162-2 (b) (2); so too with expenses paid or incurred in attending a convention. Id., § 1.162-2 (d).

Finally, the deductibility of the expenses of a taxpayer's wife who accompanies her husband depends, first, on whether his trip is a "business trip." Id., § 1.162-2 (c); if so, it must further be shown that the wife's presence on the trip also had a bona fide business purpose. Ibid.

Where, as here, it may be arguable that the trip was both for business and personal reasons, the crucial question is whether, under all the facts and circumstances of the case, the purpose of the trip was "related primarily to business" or was, rather, "primarily personal in nature."

That other trips to other conventions or meetings by other taxpayers were held to be primarily related to business is of no relevance here; that certain doctors, lawyers, clergymen, insurance agents or others[12] have or have not been permitted similar deductions only shows that in the circumstances of those cases, the courts thought that the expenses were or were not deductible as "related primarily to business."

The husband places great emphasis on the fact that he is an entrapped "organization man," required to attend such conventions, and that his future promotions depend on his presence. Suffice it to say that the District Court did not find any element of compulsion; to the contrary, it found that the petitioners regarded the convention in New York City as a pleasure trip in the nature of a vacation. Again, I cannot say that these findings are without adequate evidentiary support. Supra, pp. 273-274.

The trip not having been primarily a business trip, the wife's expenses are not deductible. It is not necessary, therefore, to examine whether they would or would not be deductible if, to the contrary, the husband's trip was related primarily to business.

Where, as here, two courts below have resolved the determinative factual issues against the taxpayers, according to the rules of law set forth in the statute and regulations, it is not for this Court to re-examine the evidence, and disturb their findings, unless "clearly erroneous." That is not the situation here.

I would affirm.

Notes

[1] As I see this case, there is no need to explore whether the proper reporting procedure for a deductible expense is not to include it in income in the first place, cf. Treas. Reg. § 1.162-17 (b), or to "run it through" the taxpayer's income with an offsetting deduction in the same amount.

[2] E. g., § 71 (Alimony and separate maintenance payments), § 72 (Annuities; certain proceeds of endowment and life insurance contracts), § 73 (Services of child).

[3] § 74: "(a) GENERAL RULE.—Except as provided in subsection (b) and in section 117 (relating to scholarships and fellowship grants), gross income includes amounts received as prizes and awards.

"(b) EXCEPTION.—Gross income does not include amounts received as prizes and awards made primarily in recognition of religious, charitable, scientific, educational, artistic, literary, or civic achievement, but only if—

"(1) the recipient was selected without any action on his part to enter the contest or proceeding; and

"(2) the recipient is not required to render substantial future services as a condition to receiving the prize or award."

[4] § 102.

[5] § 119. Some of the other exclusions are § 101 (Certain death payments), § 103 (Interest on certain governmental obligations), § 104 (Compensation for injuries or sickness), § 105 (Amounts received under accident and health plans), § 113 (Mustering-out payments for members of the Armed Forces), § 117 (Scholarship and fellowship grants).

[6] Treas. Reg. § 1.61-1 (a) provides:

"Gross income means all income from whatever source derived, unless excluded by law. Gross income includes income realized in any form, whether in money, property, or services. Income may be realized, therefore, in the form of services, meals, accommodations, stock, or other property, as well as in cash." See also Treas. Reg. § 1.61-2 (a) (1), (d) and § 1.74-1 (a).

[7] Petitioners rely on § 3401 of the 1954 Code, relating to withholding taxes, and more especially on Treas. Reg. § 31.3401 (a)-1 (b) (10) providing that certain fringe benefits are not considered "wages" subject to withholding. The Government admits that not all "fringe benefits" have been taxed as income, but it is enough to point out here that the withholding tax analogy is not perfect, for payments to laid-off employees from company-financed supplemental unemployment benefit plans are "taxable income" to the employees although not "wages" subject to withholding. Rev. Rul. 56-249, 1956-1 Cum. Bull. 488, as amplified by Rev. Rul. 60-330, 1960-2 Cum. Bull. 46.

[8] The District Court said (189 F. Supp., at 4-5):

"All of the evidence considered, we think it irrefutably leads to this conclusion: That the insurance company was just doing a gracious magnanimous thing of awarding those leading agents a trip just as much as if it had awarded them an automobile, or suit of clothes . . . .

. . . . .

". . . [W]e conclude, that the trip was earned by . . . Rudolph, and was in the nature of a bonus, reward, and compensation for a job well done."

It is pertinent to note that in addition to the facts referred to on p. 271, supra, the record shows that company-sponsored conventions of the same kind have in recent years been held in Canada, Mexico City, Havana, Colorado and California, places well known for their appeal to tourists, and far removed from the home office in Dallas. While this factor alone does not render the expenses nondeductible, see I. R. S. News Rel. No. IR-394, August 3, 1961, it certainly was a relevant circumstance for the District Court to consider.

[9] "(a) IN GENERAL.—There shall be allowed as a deduction all the ordinary and necessary expenses paid or incurred during the taxable year in carrying on any trade or business, including—

. . . . .

"(2) traveling expenses (including the entire amount expended for meals and lodging) while away from home in the pursuit of a trade or business . . . ."

No question is raised in this case as to whether the $80,000 paid by the company for the total convention expense is deductible by the corporation.

There is no need to explore the lack of symmetry in certain "income" and "deductibility" areas in the 1954 Code permitting employers to provide certain "fringe benefits" to employees—such as parking facilities, swimming pools, medical services— which have not generally been considered income to the employee, but which, if paid for by the employee with his own funds, would not be a deductible expense. The practicalities of a tax system do not demand hypothetical or theoretical perfection, and these workaday problems are properly the concern of the Commissioner, not of the Courts.

[10] Although this Regulation is part of those promulgated on April 3, 1958, it is applicable to this 1956 transaction. The power to make the Regulations prospective only, Int. Rev. Code of 1954, § 7805 (b), was not exercised, and they were made applicable to taxable years beginning after December 31, 1953. T. D. 6291, 1958-1 Cum. Bull. 63. Moreover, the result here would not be different under the prior comparable Regulation. Treas. Reg. 118, § 39.23 (a)-2 (a).

[11] No claim has been made by the husband in this case that specific business expenses which may have been incurred at the convention in New York are deductible. The only issue is the deductibility of the entire trip expense. Compare Patterson v. Thomas, 289 F. 2d 108, 114 and n. 13.

[12] Deductions allowed: Coffey v. Commissioner, 21 B. T. A. 1242 (doctor); Coughlin v. Commissioner, 203 F. 2d 307 (lawyer); Shutter v. Commissioner, 2 B. T. A. 23 (clergyman); Callinan v. Commissioner, 12 T. C. M. 170 (legal secretary); see Rev. Rul. 59-316, 1959-2 Cum. Bull. 57; Rev. Rul. 60-16, 1960-1 Cum. Bull. 58.

Justice Harlan's concurrence and dissent in Brown Shoe v. US (June 25, 1962)

MR. JUSTICE HARLAN, dissenting in part and concurring in part.

I would dismiss this appeal for lack of jurisdiction, believing that the case in its present posture is prematurely here because the judgment sought to be reviewed is not yet final. Since the Court, however, holds that the case is properly before us, I consider it appropriate, after noting my dissent to this holding, to express my views on the merits because the issues are of great importance. On that aspect, I concur in the judgment of the Court but do not join its opinion, which I consider to go far beyond what is necessary to decide the case.

JURISDICTION.

The Court's authority to entertain this appeal depends on § 2 of the Expediting Act of 1903. That statute, in its present form, provides (15 U. S. C. § 29):

"In every civil action brought in any district court of the United States under any of said [antitrust] Acts, wherein the United States is complainant, an appeal from the final judgment of the district court will lie only to the Supreme Court." (Emphasis added.)

The Act was passed by a Congress which thereby "sought . . . to ensure speedy disposition of suits in equity brought by the United States under the Anti-Trust Act."

United States v. California Cooperative Canneries, 279 U. S. 553, 558. This major policy consideration emerges clearly from the otherwise meager legislative history of the Act. See H. R. Rep. No. 3020, 57th Cong., 2d Sess. (1903); 36 Cong. Rec. 1679, 1744, 1747. It was in keeping with this purpose that "Congress limited the right of review to an appeal from the decree which disposed of all matters . . . and . . . precluded the possibility of an appeal to either [the Supreme Court or the Court of Appeals] . . . from an interlocutory decree." United States v. California Cooperative Canneries, supra. For it was entirely consistent with its desire to expedite these cases for Congress to have eliminated the time-consuming delays occasioned by interlocutory appeals either to intermediate courts or to this Court.

By taking jurisdiction over this appeal at the present time, despite the fact that, even if affirmed, this case would doubtless reappear on the Court's docket if the terms of the District Court's divestiture decree are unsatisfactory to the appellant or to the Government, the Court is paving the way for dual appeals in all government antitrust cases where intricate divestiture judgments are involved. Whether or not such a procedure is advisable from the standpoint of judicial administration or practical business considerations—and I think such questions by no means free from doubt—I believe that it is contrary to the provisions and purposes of the Expediting Act, and that the construction now given the Act does violence to the accepted meaning of "final judgment" in the federal judicial system.

The judgment from which this appeal is taken directs the appellant to "relinquish and dispose of the stock, share capital and assets" of the G. R. Kinney Company and enjoins further interlocking interests between the two corporations. It does not specify how the divestiture is to be carried out, but directs appellant to file "a proposed plan to carry into effect the divestiture order" and grants the Government 30 days following such filing in which to submit "opposition or suggestions thereto." When considered in light of the District Court's opinion, this reservation emerges as much more than a mere retention of jurisdiction for the purpose of ministerially executing a definite and precise final judgment. See e. g., Ray v. Law, 3 Cranch 179; French v. Shoemaker, 12 Wall. 86, 98. In light of this Court's remarks in United States v. E. I. du Pont de Nemours & Co., 353 U. S. 586, 607-608, the District Court concluded that the particular form which the divestiture order was to take was a matter which "could have far-reaching effects and consequences," 179 F. Supp., at 741, and that it would be appropriate for the court to conduct hearings on the manner in which the Kinney stock ought to be disposed of by the appellant. Hence it is not farfetched to assume that particular terms of the remedy ordered by the District Court will be contested, and that this Court may well be asked to examine the details relating to the anticipated divestiture. E. g., United States v. E. I. du Pont de Nemours & Co., 366 U. S. 316.

The exacting obligation with respect to the terms of antitrust decrees cast upon this Court by the Expediting Act was commented upon only last Term. In United States v. E. I. du Pont de Nemours & Co., 366 U. S. 316, it was noted that it was the Court's practice, "particularly in cases of a direct appeal from the decree of a single judge, . . . to examine the District Court's action closely to satisfy ourselves that the relief is effective to redress the antitrust violation proved." 366 U. S., at 323; see International Boxing Club, Inc., v. United States, 358 U. S. 242, 253. In the present case the Court and the parties know nothing more of "this most significant phase of the case," United States v. United States Gypsum Co., 340 U. S. 76, 89, than that Brown will generally be required to divest itself of any interest in Kinney. Exactly how this separation is to be accomplished has not yet been determined, and there is no way of knowing now whether both parties to the suit will find the decree satisfactory or whether one or both will seek further review in this Court.

Despite the opportunity thus created for separate reviews of these kinds of cases at their "merits" and "relief" stages, the Court holds that the judgment now in effect has "sufficient indicia of finality" (ante, p. 308) to render it appealable now, notwithstanding that the terms of the ordered divestiture have not yet been fixed. This conclusion is based upon three discrete considerations, none of which, in my opinion, serves to overcome the "final judgment" requirement of the Expediting Act, as that term has hitherto been understood in federal law.[1]

First. The Court suggests that any further proceedings to be conducted in the District Court are "sufficiently independent of, and subordinate to, the issues presented by this appeal" to permit them to be considered and reviewed separately. But this judicially created exception to the embracing principle of finality has never heretofore been utilized by this Court to permit separate review of a District Court's decision on the underlying merits of a claim when the details of the relief that is to be awarded are yet uncertain. The present case does not present the possibility, as did Cohen v. Beneficial Industrial Loan Corp., 337 U. S. 541, and Forgay v. Conrad, 6 How. 201, that a delay in appellate review would result in irreparable harm, equivalent in effect to a denial of any review on the point at issue. See 337 U. S., at 546; 6 How., at 204. Nor is this a case in which the complaint's prayers for relief are so diversified that the resolution of one branch of the case "is independent of, and unaffected by, another litigation with which it happens to be entangled." Radio Station WOW, Inc., v. Johnson, 326 U. S. 120, 126; see Carondelet Canal Co. v. Louisiana, 233 U. S. 362, 372-373; Forgay v. Conrad, supra.

If the appellant were compelled to await the entry of a particularized divestiture order before being granted appellate review, it would suffer no irremediable loss; indeed, in this case the merger was allowed to proceed pendente lite, so any delay, to the extent that it could affect the parties, would benefit the appellant. Nor can it well be suggested that the particular conditions under which the divestiture is to be executed are matters that are only fortuitously "entangled" with the merits of the complaint. Despite the seemingly mandatory tone of the "divestiture" judgment now before us, the plain fact remains that it is by its own terms inoperative to a substantial extent until further proceedings are held in the District Court. Unlike the cases relied upon by the Court, therefore, this case comes up on appeal before the appellant knows exactly what it has been ordered to do or not to do. This is surely not the type of judgment "which ends the litigation on the merits and leaves nothing for the court to do but execute the judgment."

Catlin v. United States, 324 U. S. 229, 233; see Covington v. Covington First National Bank, 185 U. S. 270, 277.

Second. The Court finds significant the "character of the decree still to be entered in this suit." Ante, p. 309. Since the order of full divestiture requires "careful, and often extended, negotiation and formulation," ante, p. 309, it is suggested that a delay in carrying out its terms might render them impractical or unenforceable. Apart from the fact that this policy consideration is more appropriately addressed to the Congress than to this Court, it appears to me to call for a result directly contrary to that reached by the Court. For if the terms of the divestiture are indeed so difficult to formulate and so interrelated with market conditions, it is most unlikely that the decree to be issued by the District Court will turn out to be satisfactory to both parties. Consequently, on the Court's own reasoning, a second appearance of this case on our docket is not an imaginative possibility but a reasonable likelihood. In stating that the divestiture portion of this judgment "is disputed here on an `all or nothing' basis," and that "it is ripe for review now, and will, thereafter, be foreclosed," ante, p. 309, the Court can hardly mean that either the appellant or the Government will be precluded from seeking review of the divestiture terms if it deems them unsatisfactory. Indeed, neither side on this appeal has addressed itself to the propriety of the divestiture remedy, as such, that is independently of the question whether the merger itself runs afoul of the Clayton Act.

Moreover, if it is delay between formulation of the decree and its execution that is thought to be damaging, what reason is there to believe that this delay or its hazards will be any greater if the entire case is brought up here once than if review is separately sought from the divestiture decree once its terms have been settled? Nor can it be maintained that if the merits are now affirmed then an appeal on the question of relief is improbable. For insofar as complex "negotiation and formulation" is a factor, the probability of an appeal is equally likely in either instance.

Third. The Court's final reason for holding this judgment appealable is that similar judgments have often been reviewed here in the past with no issue ever having been raised regarding jurisdiction. But the cases are legion which have echoed the answer given by Chief Justice Marshall to a contention that the Court was bound on a jurisdictional point by its consideration on the merits of a case in which the jurisdictional question had gone unnoticed: "No question was made, in that case, as to the jurisdiction. It passed sub silentio, and the court does not consider itself as bound by that case." United States v. More, 3 Cranch 159, 172; see Snow v. United States, 118 U. S. 346, 354; Cross v. Burke, 146 U. S. 82, 87; Louisville Trust Co. v. Knott, 191 U. S. 225, 236; New v. Oklahoma, 195 U. S. 252, 256; United States ex rel. Arant v. Lane, 245 U. S. 166, 170; Stainback v. Mo Hock Ke Lok Po, 336 U. S. 368, 379; United States v. L. A. Tucker Truck Lines, 344 U. S. 33, 38. The fact that the Court may, in the past, have overlooked the lack of finality in some of the judgments that came here for review in similar posture to this one does not now free it from the requirements of the Expediting Act. Nor does the fact that none of the cases reviewed in what now appears to have been an interlocutory stage was ever appealed again justify disregard of the statute. This history might point to the desirability of an amendment to the Expediting Act, but it does not make into a "final judgment" a decree which reserves for future determination the terms of the precise relief to be afforded.

The Court suggests that a "pragmatic approach" to finality is called for in light of the policies of the Federal Rules of Civil Procedure, which direct the "just, speedy, and inexpensive determination of every action." Ante, p. 306. But this misconceives the nature of the issue that is presented. Whether this judgment is final and appealable is not a question turning on the Federal Rules of Civil Procedure or on any balance of policies by this Court. Congress has seen fit to make this Court, for reasons which are less than obvious, the sole appellate tribunal for civil antitrust suits instituted by the United States. In so doing, it has chosen to limit this Court's reviewing power to "final judgments." Whether the first of these legislative determinations, made in 1903, when appeal as of right to this Court was the rule rather than the exception, should survive the expansion in the Court's docket and the development, pursuant to the Judiciary Act of 1925, of this Court's discretionary certiorari jurisdiction, may never have been given adequate consideration by the Congress.[2]

At this period of mounting dockets there is certainly much to be said in favor of relieving this Court of the often arduous task of searching through voluminous trial testimony and exhibits to determine whether a single district judge's findings of fact are supportable. The legal issues in most civil antitrust cases are no longer so novel or unsettled as to make them especially appropriate for initial appellate consideration by this Court, as compared with those in a variety of other areas of federal law. And under modern conditions it may well be doubted whether direct review of such cases by this Court truly serves the purpose of expedition which underlay the original passage of the Expediting Act. I venture to predict that a critical reappraisal of the problem would lead to the conclusion that "expedition" and also, over-all, more satisfactory appellate review would be achieved in these cases were primary appellate jurisdiction returned to the Court of Appeals, leaving this Court free to exercise its certiorari power with respect to particular cases deemed deserving of further review. As things now stand this Court must deal with all government civil antitrust cases, often either at the unnecessary expenditure of its own time or at the risk of inadequate appellate review if a summary disposition of the appeal is made. Further, such a jurisdictional change would bid fair to satisfy the very "policy" arguments suggested by the Court in this case. For the Courts of Appeals, whose dockets are generally less crowded than those of this Court, would then be authorized to hear appeals from orders such as the one here in question. Since this order grants an injunction against interlocking interests between Brown and Kinney, it would come within 28 U. S. C. § 1292 (a) (1) were this not a case "where a direct review may be had in the Supreme Court."

So long, however, as the present Expediting Act continues to commend itself to Congress this Court is bound by its limitations, and since for the reasons already given the decree appealed cannot, in my opinion, be properly considered a "final judgment," I think the appeal, at this juncture, should have been dismissed.

THE MERITS.

Since the Court nonetheless holds that the judgment is appealable in its present form, and since the underlying questions are far-reaching, I consider it a duty to express my view on the merits. On this aspect of the case I join the disposition which affirms the judgment of the District Court, though I am not prepared to subscribe to all that is said or implied in the opinion of this Court.

The question presented by this case can be stated in narrow and concise terms: Are the District Court's conclusions that the effect of the Brown-Kinney merger may be, in the language of § 7 of the Clayton Act, "substantially to lessen competition, or to tend to create a monopoly" in "any line of commerce in any section of the country" sustainable? In other words, does the indefinite and general language in § 7 manifest a congressional purpose to proscribe a combination of this sort? Brown contends that in finding the merger illegal the District Court lumped together what are in fact discrete "lines of commerce," that it failed to define an appropriate "section of the country," and that when the case is properly viewed any lessening of competition that may be caused by the merger is not "substantial." For reasons stated below, I think that each of these contentions is untenable.

The dispositive considerations are, I think, found in the "vertical" effects of the merger, that is, the effects reasonably to be foreseen from combining Brown's manufacturing facilities with Kinney's retail outlets. In my opinion the District Court's conclusions as to such effects are supported by the record, and suffice to condemn the merger under § 7, without regard to what might be deemed to be the "horizontal" effects of the transaction.

1. "Line of Commerce."—In considering both the horizontal and vertical aspects of this merger, the District Court analyzed the probable impact on competition in terms of three relevant "lines of commerce"—men's shoes, women's shoes, and children's shoes. It rejected Brown's claim that shoes of different construction or of different price range constituted distinct lines of commerce. Whatever merit there might be to Brown's contention that the product market should be more narrowly defined when it is viewed from the vantage point of the ultimate consumer (whose pocketbook, for example, may limit his purchase to a definite price range), the same is surely not true of the shoe manufacturer. Although the record contains evidence tending to prove that a shoe manufacturing plant may be managed more economically if its production is limited to only one type and grade of shoe, the history of Brown's own factories reveals that a single plant may be used in successive years, or even at the same time, for the manufacture of varying grades of shoes and may, without undue difficulty, be shifted from the production of children's shoes to men's or women's shoes, or vice versa.

Because of this flexibility of manufacture, the product market with respect to the merger between Brown's manufacturing facilities and Kinney's retail outlets might more accurately be defined as the complete wearing-apparel shoe market, combining in one the three components which the District Court treated as separate lines of commerce. Such an analysis, taking into account the interchangeability of production, would seem a more realistic gauge of the possible anticompetitive effects in the shoe manufacturing industry of a merger between a shoe manufacturer and a retailer than the District Court's compartmentalization in terms of the buying public. For if a manufacturer of women's shoes is able, albeit at some expense, to convert his plant to the production of men's shoes, the possibility of such a shift should be considered in deciding whether the market for either men's shoes or women's shoes can be monopolized or whether a particular merger substantially lessens competition among manufacturers of either product. See Adelman, Economic Aspects of the Bethlehem Opinion, 45 Va. L. Rev. 684, 689-691; cf. United States v. Columbia Steel Co., 334 U. S. 495, 510-511; but see United States v. Bethlehem Steel Corp., 168 F. Supp. 576, 592.

The fact that § 7 speaks of the lessening of competition "in any line of commerce" (emphasis added) does not, of course, mean that the product market on which the effect of the merger is considered may be defined as narrowly or as broadly as the Government chooses to define it.[3] The duty rests with the District Court, and ultimately with this Court, to determine what is the appropriate market on an appraisal of the relevant economic considerations. Discovering the product market is "a necessary predicate to a finding of a violation of the Clayton Act," United States v. E. I. du Pont de Nemours & Co., 353 U. S. 586, 593, and the breadth of the statutory language provides no license for an abdication of this necessary function. In light of the production flexibility demonstrated by the undisputed facts in this case, I think the line of commerce by which the vertical aspects of the Brown-Kinney merger should be judged is the wearing-apparel shoe industry generally.

2. "Section of the Country."—This merger involves nationwide concerns which sell and purchase shoes in various localities throughout the country, so that it appears that the most suitable geographical market for appraising the alleged anticompetitive effects of the vertical combination is the Nation as a whole. This finding of the District Court (limited to the vertical aspect of the merger) is not contested by Brown and is properly accepted here. One caveat is in order, however. In judging the anticompetitive effect of the merger on the national market, it must be recognized that any decline in competition that might result need not have a uniform effect throughout the entire country. It is sufficient if the record proves that as a result of the merger competition will generally be lessened, though its most serious impact may be felt in certain localities.

3. "Substantially to Lessen Competition."—The remaining question is whether the merger of Brown's manufacturing facilities with Kinney's retail outlets "may . . . substantially lessen competition" or "tend to create a monopoly" in the nationwide market in which shoe manufacturers sell to shoe retailers. The findings of the District Court, supported by the evidence, when taken together with undisputed facts appearing in the record, justify the conclusion that a substantial lessening of competition in the relevant market is a "reasonable probability." S. Rep. No. 1775, 81st Cong., 2d Sess. 6 (1950).

On the date of the merger Kinney's retail stores numbered 352, and this figure had increased to more than 400 by the time of the trial. Nearly all these stores sell men's, women's, and children's shoes and are located in the downtown areas of cities of at least 10,000 population. In 116 of these cities, Kinney's combined pairage sale of shoes for 1955 exceeded 10% of all shoes sold in the city during the year. Its total retail shoe sales during the year constituted 1.2% of the national total in terms of dollar volume and 1.6% in terms of pairage. Of these shoes, only 20% were supplied by the Kinney manufacturing plants, the remainder coming from some 197 other sources.[4]

Prior to 1955 Kinney had bought none of its outside source shoes from Brown, and its records for 1955 reveal that the year's purchases were made from a diverse number of independent shoe manufacturers. There were 66 suppliers (including Brown) in that year each of whose total sales to Kinney exceeded $50,000, and only three of these (Brown, Endicott-Johnson Co., and Georgia Shoe Manufacturing Co.) were large companies whose output placed them among the 25 most productive nonrubber shoe manufacturers in the United States. Consequently, it appears that Kinney was a substantial purchaser of the shoes produced by many small independent shoe manufacturers throughout the country. In fact, the record affirmatively shows that at least five of Kinney's suppliers, three of which are located in the State of New York, one in Pennsylvania, and one in New Hampshire, each relied upon Kinney to purchase more than 40% of its total production in 1955.

That the merger between Brown's shoe production plants and Kinney's retail outlets will tend to foreclose some of the large market which smaller shoe manufacturers found in sales to Kinney hardly seems open to doubt. This conclusion is supported by the following facts which emerge indisputably from the record: (1) In the shoe industry, as in many others, the purchase of a retail chain by a manufacturer results in an increased flow of the purchasing manufacturer's shoes to the retail store. Hence independent shoe manufacturers find it more difficult to sell their shoes to an acquired retail chain than to an independent one. (2) The result of Brown's earlier acquisition of two retail chains was, in each instance, a substantial increase in the quantity of Brown shoe purchases by the previously independent chains.[5] (3) The history of many of Brown's plants proves that they may be readily adapted to the production of the grade and style of shoes customarily sold in Kinney stores.[6] (4) Although Brown supplied none of Kinney's requirements before the merger, it was supplying almost 8% of these requirements just two years thereafter.

The dollar volume of Kinney's outside shoe purchases in 1955 was between 16 and 17 million dollars, and this amount had increased to 19.4 million by 1957. While Kinney was making only about 1.2% of the total retail dollar sales in the United States in 1955, that percentage can hardly be deemed an accurate reflection of its proportion of nationwide shoe purchases by retailers since the retail-sales figure is based on a computation that includes all retail stores, whether or not they were vertically integrated or otherwise affiliated. In terms of available markets for independent shoe manufacturers, the percentage of Kinney's purchases must have been substantially larger—though the precise figure is unavailable on the record before us.[7]

If the controlling test were, as it may be under the similar language of § 3 of the Clayton Act, one of "quantitative substantiality," compare Standard Oil Co. v. United States, 337 U. S. 293, with Tampa Electric Co. v. Nashville Coal Co., 365 U. S. 320, the probable foreclosure of independent manufacturers from this substantial share of the available retail shoe market would be enough to render the vertical aspect of this merger unlawful under § 7. But since the merger can be shown to have an injurious effect on competition among manufacturers and among retailers, it is unnecessary to consider whether the Standard Stations formula is applicable.

The vertical affiliation between this shoe manufacturer and a primarily retail organization is surely not, as the dissenters thought the contractual tie in Standard Stations to be, "a device for waging competition" rather than "a device for suppressing competition." 337 U. S., at 323. Since Brown is able by reason of this merger to turn an independent purchaser into a captive market for its shoes it inevitably diminishes the available market for which shoe manufacturers compete. If Brown shoes replace those which had been previously produced by others, the displaced manufacturers have no choice but to enter some other market or go out of business. Since all manufacturers, including Brown, had competed for Kinney's patronage when it was unaffiliated, Brown's merger with Kinney potentially withdraws a share of the market previously available to the independent shoe manufacturers.

Not only may this merger, judged from a vertical standpoint, affect manufacturers who compete with Brown; it may also adversely affect competition on the retailing level. With a large manufacturer such as Brown behind it, the Kinney chain would have a great competitive advantage over the retail stores with which it vies for consumer patronage. As a manufacturer-owned outlet, the Kinney store would doubtless be able to sell its shoes at a lower profit margin and outlast an independent competitor. The merger would also effectively prevent the retail competitor from dealing in Brown shoes, since these might be offered at lower prices in Kinney stores than elsewhere.[8]

Brown contends that even if these anticompetitive effects are probable, they touch upon an insignificant share of the market and are not, therefore, "substantial" within the meaning of § 7. Our decision in Tampa Electric Co. v. Nashville Coal Co., 365 U. S. 320, is cited as authority for the proposition that a foreclosure of about 1% of the relevant market is necessarily insubstantial. But the opinion in Tampa Electric carefully noted that "substantiality in a given case" depends on a variety of factors. 365 U. S., at 329. Two of the considerations that were mentioned were "the relative strength of the parties" and "the probable immediate and future effects which pre-emption of that share of the market might have on effective competition therein." Ibid. When, as here, the foreclosure of what may be considered a small percentage of retailers' purchases may be caused by the combination of the country's third largest seller of shoes with the country's largest family-style shoe store chain, and when the volume of the latter's purchases from independent manufacturers in various parts of the country is large enough to render it probable that these suppliers, if displaced, will have to fall by the wayside, it cannot, in my opinion, be said that the effect on the shoe industry is "remote" or "insubstantial."

I reach this result without considering the findings of the District Court respecting the trend in the shoe industry towards "oligopoly" and vertical integration. The statistics in the record fall short of convincing me that any such trend exists.[9] I consider the District Court's judgment warranted apart from these findings.

Accordingly, bowing to the Court's decision that the case is properly before us, I join the judgment of affirmance.

Notes

[1] "A final judgment is one which disposes of the whole subject, gives all the relief that was contemplated, provides with reasonable completeness, for giving effect to the judgment and leaves nothing to be done in the cause save to superintend, ministerially, the execution of the decree." City of Louisa v. Levi, 140 F. 2d 512, 514. See, e. g., Grant v. Phoenix Ins. Co., 106 U. S. 429; Taylor v. Board of Education, 288 F. 2d 600.

[2] For example, the report which accompanied the 1925 Act to the floor of the Senate said of the cases in which direct appeal from a District Court to the Supreme Court was retained: "As is well known, there are certain cases which, under the present law, may be taken directly from the district court to the Supreme Court. Without entering into a description of these four classes of cases, it is sufficient to say that under the existing law these are cases which must be heard by three judges, one of whom is a circuit judge." S. Rep. No. 362, 68th Cong., 1st Sess. 3 (1924). (Emphasis added.) This generalization was obviously erroneous since the Expediting Act provided for direct review in this Court of government antitrust cases decided by a single district judge.

[3] As the Court noted in United States v. E. I. du Pont de Nemours & Co., 351 U. S. 377, 393, "one can theorize that we have monopolistic competition in every nonstandardized commodity with each manufacturer having power over the price and production of his own product." If the Government were permitted to choose its "line of commerce" it could presumably draw the market narrowly in a case that turns on the existence vel non of monopoly power and draw it broadly when the question is whether both parties to a merger are within the same competitive market.

[4] The schedule in the record of Kinney's outside shoe suppliers for the calendar year 1955 lists 319 vendors, but 122 of these supplied less than $1,000 worth of goods during the year.

[5] In 1951 Brown purchased the Wohl Shoe Company, which operated leased shoe departments in department stores throughout the country. Before its acquisition of Wohl, Brown had supplied 12.8% of Wohl's shoe requirements; by 1957, it was supplying 33.6% of Wohl's needs.

In 1953, Brown purchased a partial interest in a small chain of retail stores in Los Angeles known as Wetherby-Kayser. Before this purchase, Brown had supplied 10.4% of

Wetherby's shoes; within one year this percentage increased to almost 50%.

[6] In addition, it appears from the record that shortly after the merger was effected, Kinney abandoned its earlier policy of selling only Kinney-brand shoes (80% of which were "made up" for it by its manufacturers) and began selling a considerable number of Brown's branded and advertised shoes. Along with the indications in the record that Kinney was beginning also to sell higher-priced shoes in its suburban outlets, this suggests that Brown could supply much of Kinney's needs with only a minimal additional capital investment.

[7] The existence of such gaps in the record make a fair assessment of the effects of this merger more difficult than it would otherwise be. One of the reasons why I would not consider the horizontal aspect of this merger is my conviction that the data supplied by the Government is entirely inadequate for a proper evaluation of the impact of the horizontal merger on competition.

[8] The change in Kinney policy whereby it now carries shoes bearing the Brown brand (see note 6, supra) tends to make retailer competition still more difficult.

[9] In terms of bare numbers, the quantity of retail outlets owned or controlled by the major manufacturers has undoubtedly been increasing since 1947. But much of the data in the record is incomplete in this regard because it is based on varying standards. Thus, while the Government argues that the increase in percentage of national retail sales by shoe chains owning 101 or more outlets from 20.9% in 1948 to 25.5% in 1954 proves the trend toward "oligopoly," the appellant's statistics, founded upon retail sales by all outlets (including general merchandise and clothing stores), show that retail sales by chains of 11 or more stood at a constant 19.5% of national dollar volume in both 1948 and 1954. Moreover, the apparent decline in the proportional share of the country's shoe needs supplied by the largest manufacturers between 1947 and 1955 belies any claim that shoe production is becoming "oligopolistic." Whereas the largest four manufacturers supplied 25.9% of the Nation's needs in 1947, the largest eight supplied 31.4%, and the largest 15 supplied 36.2%, in 1955 the equivalent percentages were 22%, 27%, and 32.5%.

There is no suggestion in the record as to whether earlier purchases of retail chains by shoe manufacturers reduced the number of independent manufacturers or otherwise harmed competition. Consequently, while the record does establish that manufacturers have been increasing the number of their retail outlets, it is entirely silent on the effects of this vertical expansion.

Justice Harlan's concurrence and dissent in US v. Loew's (Nov 5, 1962)

MR. JUSTICE HARLAN, with whom MR. JUSTICE STEWART joins, concurring in part and dissenting in part.

I agree with and join in Parts I and II of the Court's opinion, relating to No. 43 and No. 44, respectively. As to Part III, relating to No. 42, I dissent. My disagreement goes not so much to the particular additional relief granted, but to the fact that the Court has deemed it appropriate to concern itself at all with such comparatively trivial remedial glosses upon the District Court's decree.

I think it distorts the proper relationship of this Court to the lower federal courts, whose assessment of a particular situation is bound to be more informed than ours, for us to exercise revisory power over the terms of antitrust relief, except in instances where things have manifestly gone awry. This is not such a case, as the meticulous handling of it by the District Court abundantly shows. In my view its decree should be left undisturbed.

Justice Harlan's dissent in Hewitt-Robins v. Eastern Freight-Ways (Nov 19, 1962)

MR. JUSTICE HARLAN, whom MR. JUSTICE STEWART and MR. JUSTICE WHITE join, dissenting.

With deference, I consider that the T. I. M. E. case, 359 U. S. 464, plainly controls this one. That it does control is not and could hardly be gainsaid to the extent that the complaint purports to allege a statutory cause of action, that is, one based on the terms of the Motor Carrier Act itself. T. I. M. E., at 468-472. However, construing the complaint as alleging also a common-law cause of action, the Court holds that such an action is "not inconsistent" with the Motor Carrier Act and is therefore preserved by § 216 (j) of the statute.

The Court's decision rests primarily on the significance it accords to the existence of certain administrative procedures available to shippers to challenge rates in advance of their application, see §§ 216 (g) and 217 (c) of the Act, and the lack of such protective remedies in the case of routing practices. In addition, three further considerations are asserted to support its conclusion: (1) a misrouting claim does not jeopardize the stability of tariffs or of certificated routes, whereas to permit actions attacking the reasonableness of rates would hamper the efficient administration of the Act; (2) the allowance of misrouting actions will deter misrouting practices and decrease the number of "cease and desist" proceedings before the I. C. C.; (3) the absence of any judicial remedy would put the shipper entirely at the mercy of the carrier, contrary to the purpose of the Motor Carrier Act. This reasoning, I submit, entirely misconceives the basis of the T. I. M. E. decision.

The result reached in T. I. M. E. basically rested on two interdependent considerations: (1) the courts may not adjudicate a matter over which the Commission has been given primary jurisdiction, 359 U. S., at 473-474; (2) since the Commission must decide whether a rate is reasonable and Congress has denied it the authority to award reparations for past unreasonable charges, to allow a judicial remedy for recovery of past rate charges would "permit the I. C. C. to accomplish indirectly what Congress has not chosen to give it the authority to accomplish directly," id., at 475.

Both of these factors are present here. There can be no doubt that under § 216 (b) and (e) of the Interstate Commerce Act the Commission has primary jurisdiction over the complained of misrouting practices,[1] as indeed the Commission's action taken with respect to these very practices, Hewitt-Robins, Inc., v. Eastern Freight-Ways, Inc., 302 I. C. C. 173, and the Court's opinion in this case show. Nor is it suggested that the Commission possesses any reparations authority with respect to such misrouting. The conjunction of these factors thus brings T. I. M. E., decided only four Terms ago, into full play.

1. It is true that in this instance the Act does not contain certain protective provisions as in the case of rate making. This cannot, however, serve to distinguish T. I. M. E., whose determination of the congressional purpose underlying the Motor Carrier Act was based on considerations that stand quite independently of the impact of particular provisions of the statute. It should also be noted that the absence of such provisions does not mean that carriers may follow misrouting practices with impunity. Section 212 (a) of the Act provides that the Commission may, on its own initiative or on complaint, suspend or revoke certificates, permits, or licenses for willful failure to comply with any provision of the Act or any order or regulation of the Commission. Under § 216 (e) the Commission may order the termination of an unjust practice and prescribe the lawful practice to be followed. Section 222 (a) imposes fines for violations of the Act, and § 222 (b) confers jurisdiction on the District Courts to enjoin violations of the Act when application is made by the Commission.

2. If the issue as to the reasonableness of a routing practice is referred to the Commission, a procedure the Court recognizes as essential, allowance of a judicial remedy for misrouting will not jeopardize the stability of tariffs or of certificated routes. But the suggestion that such a danger was presented by a court action challenging unreasonable rates and that this contributed to the decision in T. I. M. E. is manifestly untenable. It was conceded there, as of course it had to be under prior decisions of this Court,[2] that the primary jurisdiction doctrine compelled referral to the Commission of all issues as to the reasonableness of the rates. Since even if a judicial remedy were allowed the Commission would have been the tribunal deciding the basic question, the course of decision would have been uniform and there would not have been, any more than here, interference with the Commission's functioning in the area of its special competence or any threat to the stability of the rate structure. Moreover, the possibility that rate actions might constitute a threat to the rate structure through stimulating excessive litigation could hardly have been regarded as a significant factor in T. I. M. E., for it was there observed that only a handful of actions to recover for unreasonable charges had been brought in the previous 24 years. 359 U. S., at 479. And if the Court now believes that to have been a relevant consideration in T. I. M. E., it should certainly be of greater weight with respect to misrouting claims, which are likely to arise more frequently because, as the Court points out, "selection of the route is usually made on an ad hoc basis, precluding preshipment determination of its reasonableness."[3]

3. Finally, as to the suggestions that actions such as this should be allowed because of their incidental deterrent effect on misrouting practices and in the interest of

justice to shippers, it need only be said that these are matters for the Congress.[4] Our duty is to apply the statute as we find it.

I would affirm.

Notes

[1] Section 216 (b) of the Interstate Commerce Act, 49 U. S. C. § 316 (b), provides in pertinent part: "It shall be the duty of every common carrier of property by motor vehicle . . . to . . . observe . . . reasonable . . . practices . . . relating to or connected with the transportation of property in interstate . . . commerce." Section 216 (e) provides that whenever "the Commission shall be of the opinion that any . . . practice . . . is or will be unjust or unreasonable. . . it shall determine . . . the lawful . . . practice."

[2] See, e. g., Texas & Pacific R. Co. v. American Tie & Timber Co., 234 U. S. 138; Texas & Pacific R. Co. v. Abilene Cotton Oil Co., 204 U. S. 426.

[3] If the Court's reference to Commissioner Eastman's statement quoted in T. I. M. E., at 477-478, n. 18, is intended to imply that the present action may be characterized as one for rate "overcharges" and thus is permissible, it should be noted that the "overcharges" to which the Commissioner referred were, as his statement makes clear, charges "above published tariff rates," id., at 478, not those resulting, as alleged here, from the application of a wrong tariff. It is only the former that the Commissioner thought could be recovered "in court as the law now stands." Id., at 478.

[4] So far, Congress has refused to act. See H. R. 8031, 86th Cong., 1st Sess. (1959); 359 U. S., at 471-472 and notes 10, 11.

Justice Harlan's dissent in Mercantile Nat. Bank at Dallas v. Langdeau (Jan 21, 1963)

MR. JUSTICE HARLAN, dissenting.

The Court's opinion in these appeals, and some of the things said in Construction Laborers v. Curry, ante, p. 542, cut deeply into the statutory requirement of "finality" limiting our jurisdiction to review state court judgments.[1]

That requirement is more than a technical rule of procedure, yielding when need be to the exigencies of particular situations. Rather, it is a long-standing and healthy federal policy that protects litigants and courts from the disruptions of piecemeal review and forecloses this Court from passing on constitutional issues that may be dissipated by the final outcome of a case, thus helping to keep to a minimum undesirable federal-state conflicts. In this instance it precludes, in my opinion, the exercise of our appellate jurisdiction at this stage of the proceedings.

The state court judgments now sought to be reviewed are nothing more than a determination that venue was properly laid in the county where suit against these appellants was brought. Such a determination, being tantamount to a denial of a motion to dismiss, is a classic example of an interlocutory ruling that is only a step towards ultimate disposition and is not in itself reviewable as a final judgment. See Catlin v. United States, 324 U. S. 229; 6 Moore, Federal Practice ¶¶ 54.12 (1), 54.14; see also Clinton Foods v. United States, 188 F. 2d 289, 291-292, and cases cited therein.[2] It fits squarely within the general rule that a judgment is not final unless it terminates the litigation and leaves nothing to be done but to enforce by execution what has been demanded. See Parr v. United States, 351 U. S. 513.

It is true that several specific, and narrowly circumscribed, exceptions to this general rule have been developed in order to deal with extraordinary situations where a judgment is final in substance although not in form. But these appeals do not fall within any of these exceptions.

Thus this is not a situation in which what remains to be done in the state courts is a mere formality, or in which the appellants concede that their whole case must stand or fall on the federal claim. Compare Richfield Oil Corp. v. State Board of Equalization, 329 U. S. 69; Pope v. Atlantic Coast Line R. Co., 345 U. S. 379; Construction Laborers v. Curry, ante, p. 542. Quite the contrary, appellants vigorously deny their liability on the merits of the appellee's claim.

Nor are these appeals like Radio Station WOW v. Johnson, 326 U. S. 120, where the challenged order required an immediate transfer of property, and where the remaining matters left to be disposed of in the state court were wholly unrelated, would almost certainly have raised no federal question, and could not have mooted the question sought to be reviewed. Here, a victory for appellants on the merits would clearly moot the federal question before us today. "It is of course not our province to discourage appeals. But for the soundest of reasons we ought not to pass on constitutional issues before they have reached a definitive stop." Republic Natural Gas Co. v. Oklahoma, 334 U. S. 62, 71.

On the other hand, if appellants lost on the merits, the venue question raised in the present appeals would then be open for review by this Court. Hence the controversy is wholly different from Cohen v. Beneficial Industrial Loan Corp., 337 U. S. 541, 546, where the challenged order would not have been merged in the final judgment and where, unless immediate review had been granted, no appellate determination of the right claimed could ever have been obtained.

Failing to come within any of these limited exceptions, appellants fall back on the familiar assertion that they should not be subjected to a burdensome trial in the wrong forum, a claim which the Court finds compelling. But surely such a claim cannot be accepted, for there is a large variety of situations in which a ruling on a preliminary matter will determine whether or not the case is to continue; yet a decision that does not definitively terminate the case is plainly not final. To rely on the hardship of being subjected to trial is to do away with the distinction between interlocutory and final orders. It is for this reason that the Court has always held that the hazard of being subjected to trial does not invest a preliminary ruling with the finality requisite to appeal. E. g., Parr v. United States, 351 U. S. 513, 519-520.

This is not a case of first impression. In Cincinnati Street R. Co. v. Snell, 179 U. S.

395, the railway company sought to appeal from a determination by the highest court of the State directing a change of venue and remanding the case for further proceedings. The railway company contended that the state law under which the change of venue had been ordered was unconstitutional. The case is thus squarely in point, since the appellants here are also challenging the constitutionality of the application of local venue provisions. This Court unanimously dismissed the writ of error for lack of finality, stating:

"It is true that the order appealed from finally adjudges that a change of venue should have been allowed; but the same comment may be made upon dozens of interlocutory orders made in the progress of a cause. Indeed, scarcely an order is imaginable which does not finally dispose of some particular point arising in the case; but that does not justify a review of such order, until the action itself has been finally disposed of. If every order were final, which finally passes upon some motion made by one or the other of the parties to a cause, it might in some cases require a dozen writs of error to dispose finally of the case." 179 U. S., at 397.

The Cincinnati case also shows the invalidity of the argument of these appellants that they may be spared a trial if their venue claim is presently sustained. For the Court in Cincinnati was unmoved by the circumstance that the railway company there had already won a jury verdict which had been set aside by the state court because of faulty venue. A fortiori, in a proceeding where the action has not yet been tried, the Court should be deaf to the similar claims of these appellants.

The Court's decision in these appeals throws the law of finality into a state of great uncertainty and will, I am afraid, tend to increase future efforts at piecemeal review.[3]

Notes

[1] 28 U. S. C. § 1257 limits the appellate jurisdiction of this Court to review of "[f]inal judgments or decrees rendered by the highest court of a State in which a decision could be had."

[2] As the Court stated in the Catlin case, 324 U. S., at 236: "[D]enial of a motion to dismiss, even when the motion is based upon jurisdictional grounds, is not immediately reviewable. . . . Certainly this is true whenever the question may be saved for disposition upon review of final judgment disposing of all issues involved in the litigation . . . ."

[3] The Court appears to suggest that these appeals are unique because the decisions were appealable under state law and because national banks are making a substantial claim of a conflict between a federal and a state statute. But I fail to see how the appealability of interlocutory orders under state law, the identity of the appellants, or the substantiality of the federal claim asserted can have any bearing on whether the judgments appealed from are final.

Justice Harlan's dissent in Gallick v. Baltimore & Ohio R. (Feb 18, 1963)

MR. JUSTICE HARLAN, dissenting.

Heartrending as the petitioner's accident has turned out to be, I think this case should not have been brought here. It involves no unsettled questions of federal law calling for decision by this Court, nor, in any acceptable sense, a departure by the state courts from legal principles already decided requiring this Court's intervention. The case thus does not qualify for review under Rule 19.[*] See the dissenting opinion of Mr. Justice Frankfurter in Rogers v. Missouri Pacific R. Co., 352 U. S. 500, 524, and the separate opinion of this writer, p. 559. The case has necessarily required an inordinate amount of time, which the Court can ill afford in the present state of its docket.

Reaching the merits, however, id., pp. 559-562, I would affirm the judgment below. I agree with my Brothers STEWART and GOLDBERG as to the inconsistency of the jury's verdict. But in addition, I cannot say that the view of the record taken by the state courts, in holding that the evidence on the issue of causation was insufficient to make a case for the jury, was an arbitrary or unreasonable one. The opinion of the Ohio Court of Appeals evinces a conscientious effort to follow this Court's decisions under the Federal Employers' Liability Act, and more particularly the broad pronouncements made in the Rogers case, supra. On this score the Court's reversal seems to me no more than an exercise in second-guessing the state court's estimate of the record.

From another standpoint this case does have significance. It affords a particularly dramatic example of the inadequacy of ordinary negligence law to meet the social obligations of modern industrial society. The cure for that, however, lies with the legislature and not with the courts.

[*] In pertinent part, Rule 19 provides:

"1. A review on writ of certiorari is not a matter of right, but of sound judicial discretion, and will be granted only where there are special and important reasons therefor. The following, while neither controlling nor fully measuring the court's discretion, indicate the character of reasons which will be considered:

"(a) Where a state court has decided a federal question of substance not theretofore determined by this court, or has decided it in a way probably not in accord with applicable decisions of this court. . . ."

Justice Harlan's dissent in Fay v. Noia (March 18, 1963)

MR. JUSTICE HARLAN, whom MR. JUSTICE CLARK and MR. JUSTICE STEWART join, dissenting.

This decision, both in its abrupt break with the past and in its consequences for the future, is one of the most disquieting that the Court has rendered in a long time.

Section 2241 of the Judicial Code, 28 U. S. C. § 2241, entitled "Power to grant writ," which is part of the federal habeas corpus statute, provides among other things:

"(c) The writ of habeas corpus shall not extend to a prisoner unless—

.....

"(3) He is in custody in violation of the Constitution or laws or treaties of the

United States."

I dissent from the Court's opinion and judgment for the reason that the federal courts have no power, statutory or constitutional, to release the respondent Noia from state detention. This is because his custody by New York does not violate any federal right, since it is pursuant to a conviction whose validity rests upon an adequate and independent state ground which the federal courts are required to respect.

A full exposition of the matter is necessary, and I believe it will justify the statement that in what it does today the Court has turned its back on history and struck a heavy blow at the foundations of our federal system.

I.

DEPARTURE FROM HISTORY.

The history of federal habeas corpus jurisdiction, I believe, leaves no doubt that today's decision constitutes a square rejection of long-accepted principles governing the nature and scope of the Great Writ.[1]

Habeas corpus ad subjiciendum is today, as it has always been, a fundamental safeguard against unlawful custody. The importance of this prerogative writ, requiring the body of a person restrained of liberty to be brought before the court so that the lawfulness of the restraint may be determined, was recognized in the Constitution,[2] and the first Judiciary Act gave the federal courts authority to issue the writ "agreeable to the principles and usages of law."[3] Although the wording of earlier statutory provisions has been changed, the basic question before the court to which the writ is addressed has always been the same: in the language of the present statute, on the books since 1867, is the detention complained of "in violation of the Constitution or laws or treaties of the United States"? Supra, p. 448.

Detention can occur in many contexts, and in each the scope of judicial inquiry will differ. Thus a child may be detained by a parent, an alien excluded by an immigration official, or a citizen arrested by a policeman and held without being brought to a magistrate. But the custody with which we are here concerned is that resulting from a judgment of criminal conviction and sentence by a court of law. And the question before us is the circumstances under which that custody may be held to be inconsistent with the commands of the Federal Constitution. What does history show?

1. Pre-1915 period.—The formative stage of the development of habeas corpus jurisdiction may be said to have ended in 1915, the year in which Frank v. Mangum, 237 U. S. 309, was decided. During this period the federal courts, on applications for habeas corpus complaining of detention pursuant to a judgment of conviction and sentence, purported to examine only the jurisdiction of the sentencing tribunal. In the leading case of Ex parte Watkins, 3 Pet. 193, the Court stated:

"An imprisonment under a judgment cannot be unlawful, unless that judgment be an absolute nullity; and it is not a nullity if the court has general jurisdiction of the subject, although it should be erroneous." 3 Pet., at 203.

Many subsequent decisions, dealing with both state and federal prisoners, and involving both original applications to this Court for habeas corpus and review of lower court decisions, reaffirmed the limitation of the writ to consideration of the sentencing court's jurisdiction over the person of the defendant and the subject matter of the suit. E. g., Ex parte Parks, 93 U. S. 18; Andrews v. Swartz, 156 U. S. 272; In re Belt, 159 U. S. 95; In re Moran, 203 U. S. 96.

The concept of jurisdiction, however, was subjected to considerable strain during this period, and the strain was not lessened by the fact that until the latter part of the last century, federal criminal convictions were not generally reviewable by the Supreme Court.[4] The expansion of the definition of jurisdiction occurred primarily in two classes of cases: (1) those in which the conviction was for violation of an allegedly unconstitutional statute, and (2) those in which the Court viewed the detention as based on some claimed illegality in the sentence imposed, as distinguished from the judgment of conviction. An example of the former is Ex parte Siebold, 100 U. S. 371, in which the Court considered on its merits the claim that the acts under which the indictments were found were unconstitutional, reasoning that "[a]n unconstitutional law is void, and is as no law," and therefore "if the laws are unconstitutional and void, the Circuit Court acquired no jurisdiction of the causes." 100 U. S., at 376-377.[5] An example of the latter is Ex parte Lange, 18 Wall. 163, in which this Court held that if a valid sentence had been carried out, and if the governing statute permitted only one sentence, the sentencing judge lacked jurisdiction to impose further punishment:

"[W]hen the prisoner . . . by reason of a valid judgment, had fully suffered one of the alternative punishments to which alone the law subjected him, the power of the court to punish further was gone." 18 Wall., at 176.[6]

It was also during this period that Congress, in 1867, first made habeas corpus available by statute to prisoners held under state authority. Act of February 5, 1867, c. 28, § 1, 14 Stat. 385. In this 1867 Act the Court now seems to find justification for today's decision, relying on the statement of one of its proponents that the bill was "coextensive with all the powers that can be conferred" on the courts and judges of the United States. Cong. Globe, 39th Cong., 1st Sess. 4151. But neither the statute itself, its legislative history, nor its subsequent interpretation lends any support to the view that habeas corpus jurisdiction since 1867 has been exercisable whether or not the state detention complained of rested on decision of a federal question.

First, there is nothing in the language of the Act— which spoke of the availability of the writ to prisoners "restrained of . . . liberty in violation of the constitution. . ."—to suggest that there was any change in the nature of the writ as applied to one held pursuant to a judgment of conviction. The language was that typically employed in habeas corpus cases, and, as we have seen, it was not believed that a person so held was restrained in violation of law if the sentencing court had personal and subject matter jurisdiction. Rather, the change accomplished by the language of the Act related to the classes of prisoners (in particular, state as well as federal) for whom the writ would be available.

Second, what little legislative history there is does not suggest any change in the nature of the writ. The extremely brief debates indicated only a lack of understanding as to what the Act would accomplish, coupled with an effort by the proponents to make it clear that the purpose was to extend the availability of the writ to persons not then covered; there was no indication of any intent to alter its substantive scope.[7] Thus, less than 20 years after enactment, a congressional committee could say of the 1867 Act that it was not "contemplated by its framers or . . . properly . . . construed to authorize the overthrow of the final judgments of the State courts of general jurisdiction, by the inferior Federal judges . . . ."[8]

Third, cases decided under the Act during this period made it clear that the Court did not regard the Act as changing the character of the writ. In considering the lawfulness of the detention of state prisoners, the Court continued to confine itself to questions it regarded as "jurisdictional." See, e. g., In re Rahrer, 140 U. S. 545; Harkrader v. Wadley, 172 U. S. 148; Pettibone v. Nichols, 203 U. S. 192. And the Court repeatedly held that habeas corpus was not available to a state prisoner to consider errors, even constitutional errors, that did not go to the jurisdiction of the sentencing court. E. g., In re Wood, 140 U. S. 278; Andrews v. Swartz, 156 U. S. 272; Bergemann v. Backer, 157 U. S. 655.

At the same time, in dealing with applications by state prisoners the Court developed the doctrine of exhaustion of state remedies, a doctrine now embodied in 28 U. S. C. § 2254. In Ex parte Royall, 117 U. S. 241, the prisoner had brought federal habeas corpus seeking release from his detention pending a state prosecution, and alleging that the statute under which he was to be tried was void under the Contract Clause. The power of the federal court to act in this case, if the allegations could be established, was clear since under accepted principles the State would have lacked "jurisdiction" to detain the prisoner. But the Court observed that the question of constitutionality would be open to the prisoner at his state trial and, absent any showing of urgency, considerations of comity counseled the exercise of discretion to withhold the writ at this early stage. In subsequent decisions, the Court continued to insist that state remedies be exhausted, even when the applicant alleged a lack of jurisdiction in state authorities which, if true, would have enabled the federal court to act on the application immediately. E. g., Ex parte Fonda, 117 U. S. 516; Cook v. Hart, 146 U. S. 183; New York v. Eno, 155 U. S. 89. As stated in Cook v. Hart, 146 U. S., at 195, "The party charged waives no defect of jurisdiction by submitting to a trial of his case upon the merits . . . . Should . . . [his] rights be denied, his remedy in the Federal court will remain unimpaired." (Emphasis added.) The question whether the Constitution deprived the State of jurisdiction, in other words, would remain open under traditional doctrine, on collateral as well as direct attack.

There can be no doubt of the limited scope of habeas corpus during this formative period, and of the consistent efforts to confine the writ to questions of jurisdiction. But the cardinal point for present purposes is that in no case was it held, or even suggested, that habeas corpus would be available to consider any claims by a prisoner held pursuant to a state court judgment whose validity rested on an adequate nonfederal ground. Indeed, so long as the writ was confined to claims by state prisoners that the State was constitutionally precluded from exercising its jurisdiction in the particular case, it is difficult to conceive of a decision to detain in such cases resting on an adequate state ground. Even when the concept of jurisdiction was expanded, as in Ex parte Siebold, 100 U. S. 371, and other decisions, the matters open on habeas were still limited to those which were believed to have deprived the sentencing court of all competence to act, and which therefore could always be raised on collateral attack. It is for this reason that the Royall line of "exhaustion" cases, relied on so heavily by the Court, has no real bearing on the problem before us. For those cases dealt only with the discretion of the court to take action which, if the allegations of lack of state jurisdiction were upheld, it would have had power to take either before or after state consideration. The issue here, on the other hand, is one of power, and wholly different considerations are involved.

In those few instances during this early period when the Court discussed questions it did not regard as jurisdictional, it occasionally went so far as to suggest that a constitutional claim could not be raised on habeas even if the state decision to detain rested on an inadequate state ground—that the only avenue of relief was direct review. Thus in Andrews v. Swartz, 156 U. S. 272, where the claim made on federal habeas was the systematic exclusion of Negroes from a state jury, the Court held it "a sufficient answer to this contention that the state court had jurisdiction both of the offence charged and of the accused." Id., at 276. It continued:

"Even if it be assumed that the state court improperly denied to the accused . . . the right to show by proof that persons of his race were arbitrarily excluded. . . it would not follow that the court lost jurisdiction of the case within the meaning of the well-established rule that a prisoner under conviction and sentence of another court will not be discharged on habeas corpus unless the court that passed the sentence was so far without jurisdiction that its proceedings must be regarded as void." Ibid.

2. 1915-1953 period.—The next stage of development may be described as beginning in 1915 with Frank v. Mangum, 237 U. S. 309, and ending in 1953 with Brown v. Allen, 344 U. S. 443. In Frank, the prisoner had claimed before the state courts that the proceedings in which he had been convicted for murder had been dominated by a mob, and the State Supreme Court, after consideration not only of the record but of extensive affidavits, had concluded that mob domination had not been established.[9] Frank then sought federal habeas, and this Court affirmed the denial of relief. But in doing so the Court recognized that Frank's allegation of mob domination raised a constitutional question which he was entitled to have considered by a competent tribunal uncoerced by popular pressures. Such "corrective process" had been afforded by the State Supreme Court, however, and since Frank had received "notice, and a hearing, or an opportunity to be heard" on his constitutional claims (237 U. S., at 326), his detention was not in violation of federal law and habeas corpus would not lie.

It is clear that a new dimension was added to habeas corpus in this case, for in addition to questions previously thought of as "jurisdictional," the federal courts were now to consider whether the applicant had been given an adequate opportunity to raise his constitutional claims before the state courts. And if no such opportunity had been afforded in the state courts, the federal claim would be heard on its merits. The Court thus rejected the views expressed in Andrews v. Swartz, supra, p. 455, by holding, in effect, that a constitutional claim could be heard on habeas if the State's refusal to give it proper consideration rested on an inadequate state ground. But habeas would not lie to reconsider constitutional questions that had been fairly determined. And a fortiori it would not lie to consider a question when the state court's refusal to do so rested on an adequate and independent state ground.

In this connection, it is important to note the section of the opinion relating to Frank's separate constitutional claim that his involuntary absence from the courtroom at the time the verdict was rendered invalidated the conviction. Frank had failed to raise this point in his motion for a new trial; the state court held that it had been "waived"; and this Court decided that the state rule barring assertion of the point after failure to raise it in a motion for new trial was reasonable and did not violate due process.[10] Clearly, the significance of the Court's ruling was that as to this constitutional claim, whatever its merits if the point had been properly preserved, there was an adequate nonfederal ground for the detention.

In no case prior to Brown v. Allen, I submit, was there any substantial modification of the concepts articulated in the Frank decision. In Moore v. Dempsey, 261 U. S. 86, this Court did require a hearing on federal habeas of a claim similar to that in Frank, of mob domination of the trial, even though the state appellate court had purported to pass on the claim, but only by refusing to "assume that the trial was an empty ceremony."[11] The decision of this Court is sufficiently ambiguous that it seems to have meant all things to all men.[12] But I suggest that the decision cannot be taken to have overruled Frank; it did not purport to do so, and indeed it was joined by two Justices who had joined in the Frank opinion. Rather, what the Court appears to have held was that the state appellate court's perfunctory treatment of the question of mob domination, amounting to nothing more than reliance on the presumptive validity of the trial, was not in fact acceptable corrective process and federal habeas would therefore lie to consider the merits of the claim. Until today, the Court has consistently so interpreted the opinion, as in Ex parte Hawk, 321 U. S. 114, 118, where Moore was cited as an example of a case in which "the remedy afforded by state law proves in practice unavailable or seriously inadequate." See also Jennings v. Illinois, 342 U. S. 104, 111.

Certainly, there is no basis in the Moore opinion, whatever it may fairly be taken to mean, for concluding that the Court required consideration on federal habeas of a question which the state court had had an adequate state ground for refusing to consider. The claim of mob domination was considered, although apparently inadequately, by the state court, and it was only on this premise that the claim was required to be heard on habeas.

Subsequent decisions involving state prisoners continued to indicate that the controlling question on federal habeas—apart from matters going to lack of state jurisdiction in light of federal law—was whether or not the State had afforded adequate opportunity to raise the federal claim. If not, the federal claim could be considered on its merits. See, e. g., Mooney v. Holohan, 294 U. S. 103; White v. Ragen, 324 U. S. 760; Woods v. Nierstheimer, 328 U. S. 211; cf. Jennings v. Illinois, 342 U. S. 104.[13]

A development paralleling that in Frank v. Mangum took place during this period with regard to federal prisoners. The writ remained unavailable to consider questions that were or could have been raised in the original proceedings, or on direct appeal, see Sunal v. Large, 332 U. S. 174, but it was employed to permit consideration of constitutional questions that could not otherwise have been adequately presented to the courts. E. g., Johnson v. Zerbst, 304 U. S. 458; Walker v. Johnston, 312 U. S. 275; Waley v. Johnston, 316 U. S. 101. This limited scope of habeas corpus, and its statutory substitute 28 U. S. C. § 2255, in relation to federal prisoners may have survived Brown v. Allen and may still survive today. See, e. g., Franano v. United States, 303 F. 2d 470, cert. denied, 371 U. S. 865. Compare Jordan v. United States, 352 U. S. 904.

To recapitulate, then, prior to Brown v. Allen, habeas corpus would not lie for a prisoner who was in custody pursuant to a state judgment of conviction by a court of competent jurisdiction if he had been given an adequate opportunity to obtain full and fair consideration of his federal claim in the state courts. Clearly, under this approach, a detention was not in violation of federal law if the validity of the state conviction on which that detention was based rested on an adequate nonfederal ground.

3. Post-1953, Brown v. Allen, period.—In 1953, this Court rendered its landmark decisions in Brown v. Allen, 344 U. S. 443, and Daniels v. Allen, reported therewith, 344 U. S., at 482-487.[14] Both cases involved applications for federal habeas corpus by prisoners who were awaiting execution pursuant to state convictions. In both cases, the constitutional contentions made were that the trial court had erred in ruling confessions admissible and in overruling motions to quash the indictment on the basis of alleged discrimination in the selection of jurors.

In Brown, these contentions had been presented to the highest court of the State, on direct appeal from the conviction, and had been rejected by that court on the merits, State v. Brown, 233 N. C. 202, 63 S. E. 2d 99, after which this Court had denied certiorari, 341 U. S. 943. At this point, the Court held, Brown was entitled to full reconsideration of these constitutional claims, with a hearing if appropriate, in an application to a Federal District Court for habeas corpus.

It is manifest that this decision substantially expanded the scope of inquiry on an application for federal habeas corpus.[15] Frank v. Mangum and Moore v. Dempsey had denied that the federal courts in habeas corpus sat to determine whether errors of law, even constitutional law, had been made in the original trial and appellate proceedings. Under the decision in Brown, if a petitioner could show that the validity of a state decision to detain rested on a determination of a constitutional claim, and if he alleged that determination to be erroneous, the federal court had the right and the duty to satisfy itself of the correctness of the state decision.

But what if the validity of the state decision to detain rested not on the determination of a federal claim but rather on an adequate nonfederal ground which would have barred direct review by this Court? That was the question in Daniels. The attorney for the petitioners in that case had failed to mail the appeal papers on the last day for filing, and although he delivered them by hand the next day, the State Supreme Court refused to entertain the appeal, ruling that it had not been filed on time. This ruling, this Court held, barred federal habeas corpus consideration of the claims that the state appellate court had refused to consider. Language in Mr. Justice Reed's opinion for the Court appeared to support the result alternatively in terms of waiver,[16] failure to exhaust state remedies,[17] and the existence of an adequate state ground.[18] But while the explanation may have been ambiguous, the result was clear: habeas corpus would not lie for a prisoner who was detained pursuant to a state judgment which, in the view of the majority in Daniels, rested on a reasonable application of the State's own procedural requirements. Moreover, the issue was plainly viewed as one of authority, not of discretion. 344 U. S., at 485.

I do not pause to reconsider here the question whether the state ground in Daniels was an adequate one; persuasive arguments can be made that it was not. The important point for present purposes is that the approach in Daniels was wholly consistent with established principles in the field of habeas corpus jurisdiction. The problem, however, had been brought into sharper focus by the result in Brown. Once it is made clear that the questions open on federal habeas extend to such matters as the admissibility of confessions, or of other evidence, the possibility that inquiry may be precluded by the existence of a state ground adequate to support the judgment is substantially increased.

Issues similar to those in Daniels next came before the Court in Irvin v. Dowd, 359 U. S. 394. In that case, the state court's decision affirming Irvin's conviction for murder was ambiguous and it could have been interpreted to rest on a state ground even though Irvin's federal constitutional claims were considered. Irvin v. State, 236 Ind. 384, 139 N. E. 2d 898; see also the dissenting opinion of this writer in Irvin v. Dowd, supra, 412. This Court, in reversing a dismissal of an application for federal habeas corpus, concluded that the state court decision had rested on determination of Irvin's federal claims, and held that those claims could therefore be considered on federal habeas. The majority appeared to approach the problem as one of exhaustion,[19] but the basic determination was that the state court judgment, pursuant to which Irvin was detained, did not rest on an application of the State's procedural rules.

This brings us to the present case. There can, I think, be no doubt that today's holding—that federal habeas will lie despite the existence of an adequate and independent nonfederal ground for the judgment pursuant to which the applicant is detained—is wholly unprecedented. Indeed, it constitutes a direct rejection of authority that is squarely to the contrary. That the result now reached is a novel one does not, of course, mean that it is necessarily incorrect or unwise. But a decision which finds virtually no support in more than a century of this Court's experience should certainly be subject to the most careful scrutiny.

II.

CONSTITUTIONAL BARRIER.

The true significance of today's decision can perhaps best be laid bare in terms of a hypothetical case presenting questions of the powers of this Court on direct review, and of a Federal District Court on habeas corpus.

1. On direct review.—Assume that a man is indicted, and held for trial in a state court, by a grand jury from which members of his race have been systematically excluded. Assume further that the State requires any objection to the composition of the grand jury to be raised prior to the verdict, that no such objection is made, and that the defendant seeks to raise the point for the first time on appeal from his conviction. If the state appellate court refuses to consider the claim because it was raised too late, and if certiorari is sought and granted, the initial question before this Court will be whether there was an adequate state ground for the judgment below. If the petitioner was represented by counsel not shown to be incompetent, and if the necessary information to make the objection is not shown to have been unavailable at the time of trial, it is certain that the judgment of conviction will stand, despite the fact the indictment was obtained in violation of the petitioner's constitutional rights.[20]

What is the reason for the rule that an adequate and independent state ground of decision bars Supreme Court review of that decision—a rule which, of course, is as applicable to procedural as to substantive grounds? In Murdock v. Memphis, 20 Wall. 590, 632-636, it was concluded that under the governing statute (i) the Court did not have jurisdiction, on review of a state decision, to examine and decide "questions not of a Federal character," id., at 633, and (ii) an erroneous decision of a federal question by a state court could not warrant reversal if there were:

"any other matter or issue adjudged by the State court, which is sufficiently broad to maintain the judgment of that court, notwithstanding the error in deciding the issue raised by the Federal question." Id., at 636.

But as the Court in Murdock so strongly implied, and as emphasized in subsequent decisions, the adequate state ground rule has roots far deeper than the statutes governing our jurisdiction, and rests on fundamentals that touch this Court's habeas corpus jurisdiction equally with its direct reviewing power. An examination of the alternatives that might conceivably be followed will, I submit, confirm that the rule is one of constitutional dimensions going to the heart of the division of judicial powers in a federal system.

One alternative to the present rule would be for the Court to review and decide any federal questions in the case, even if the determination of nonfederal questions were adequate to sustain the judgment below, and then to send the case back to the state court for further consideration. But it needs no extended analysis to demonstrate that such action would exceed this Court's powers under Article III. As stated in Herb v. Pitcairn, 324 U. S. 117, 126:

"[O]ur power is to correct wrong judgments, not to revise opinions. We are not permitted to render an advisory opinion, and if the same judgment would be rendered by the state court after we corrected its views of federal laws, our review could amount to nothing more than an advisory opinion."

Another alternative, which would avoid the problem of advisory opinions, would be to take the entire case and to review on the merits the state court's decision of every question in it. For example, in our hypothetical case the Court might consider on its merits the question whether the state court correctly ruled that under state law objections to the composition of the grand jury must be made prior to the verdict.

To a limited extent, of course, this procedural ruling of the state court raises federal as well as state questions. It is clear that a State may not preclude Supreme Court review of federal claims by discriminating against or evading the assertion of a federal right, and indeed that state procedural grounds for refusal to consider a federal claim must rest on a "fair or substantial basis."[21] Occasionally this means that a state procedural rule which may properly preclude the raising of state claims in a state court cannot thwart review of federal claims in this Court.[22] These principles are inherent in the concept that a state ground, to be of sufficient breadth to support the judgment, must be both "adequate" and "independent."

But determination of the adequacy and independence of the state ground, I submit, marks the constitutional limit of our power in this sphere. The reason why this is so was perhaps most articulately expressed in a different but closely related context by Mr. Justice Field in his opinion in Baltimore & O. R. Co. v. Baugh, 149 U. S. 368, 401. He stated, in a passage quoted with approval by the Court in the historic decision in Erie R. Co. v. Tompkins, 304 U. S. 64, 78-79:

"[T]he Constitution of the United States . . . recognizes and preserves the autonomy and independence of the States—independence in their legislative and independence in their judicial departments. Supervision over either the legislative or the judicial action of the States is in no case permissible except as to matters by the Constitution specifically authorized or delegated to the United States. Any interference with either, except as thus permitted, is an invasion of the authority of the State and, to that extent, a denial of its independence."

For this Court to go beyond the adequacy of the state ground and to review and determine the correctness of that ground on its merits would, in our hypothetical case, be to assume full control over a State's procedures for the administration of its own criminal justice. This is and must be beyond our power if the federal system is to exist in substance as well as form. The right of the State to regulate its own procedures governing the conduct of litigants in its courts, and its interest in supervision of those procedures, stand on the same constitutional plane as its right and interest in framing "substantive" laws governing other aspects of the conduct of those within its borders.

There is still a third possible course this Court might follow if it were to reject the adequate state ground rule. The Act of 1867, which in § 1 extended the habeas corpus jurisdiction to state prisoners detained in violation of federal law, in § 2 gave the Supreme Court the authority, in cases coming from the state courts, to order execution directly without remanding the case. 14 Stat. 385, 386-387. That authority, which has been exercised at least once,[23] remained unimpaired through the modifications of appellate and certiorari jurisdiction,[24] and exists today.[25] Acting pursuant to that authority in our hypothetical case, this Court might grant certiorari, "ignore" the state ground of decision, decide the federal question and, instead of merely remanding the case, issue a writ requiring the petitioner's release from custody. By this simple device, the Court, it might be argued, would avoid problems of advisory opinions while at the same time refraining from consideration of questions of state law.

But apart from the unseemliness of such a disposition, it is apparent that what the Court would actually be doing would be to decide the state law question sub silentio and to reverse the state court judgment on that question. For if the petitioner is detained pursuant to the judgment, and his detention is to be terminated, that must mean that the state ground is not adequate to support the only purpose for which the judgment was rendered. The judgment, in other words, becomes a nullity.

Moreover, the future effect of such a disposition is precisely the same as a reversal on the merits of the question of state law. If noncompliance with a state rule requiring a particular constitutional claim to be raised before verdict does not preclude consideration of the claim by this Court, then the rule is invalid in every significant sense, since no judgment based on its application can ever be effective.

In short, the constitutional infirmities of such a disposition by this Court are the same as those inherent in review of the state question on its merits. The vice, however, is greater because the Court would, in actuality, be invalidating a state rule without even purporting to consider it.

2. On habeas corpus.—The adequate state ground doctrine thus finds its source in basic constitutional principles, and the question before us is whether this is as true in a collateral attack in habeas corpus as on direct review. Assume, then, that after dismissal of the writ of certiorari in our hypothetical case, the prisoner seeks habeas corpus in a Federal District Court, again complaining of the composition of the grand jury that indicted him. Is that federal court constitutionally more free than the Supreme Court on direct review to "ignore" the adequate state ground, proceed to the federal question, and order the prisoner's release?

The answer must be that it is not. Of course, as the majority states, a judgment is not a "jurisdictional prerequisite" to a habeas corpus application, ante, p. 430, but that is wholly irrelevant. The point is that if the applicant is detained pursuant to a judgment, termination of the detention necessarily nullifies the judgment. The fact that a District Court on habeas has fewer choices than the Supreme Court, since it can only act on the body of the prisoner, does not alter the significance of the exercise of its power. In habeas as on direct review, ordering the prisoner's release invalidates the judgment of conviction and renders ineffective the state rule relied upon to sustain that judgment. Try as the majority does to turn habeas corpus into a roving commission of inquiry into every possible invasion of the applicant's civil rights that may ever have occurred, it cannot divorce the writ from a judgment of conviction if that judgment is the basis of the detention.

Thus in the present case if this Court had granted certiorari to review the State's denial of coram nobis, had considered the coerced confession claim, and had ordered Noia's release, the necessary effects of that disposition would have been (1) to set aside the conviction and (2) to invalidate application of the New York rule requiring the claim to be raised on direct appeal in order to be preserved. It is, I think, beyond dispute that the Court does exactly the same thing by affirming the decision below in this case. In doing so, the Court exceeds its constitutional power if in fact the state ground relied upon to sustain the judgment of conviction is an adequate one. See pp. 472-476, infra. The effect of the approach adopted by the Court is, indeed, to do away with the adequate state ground rule entirely in every state case, involving a federal question, in which detention follows from a judgment.

The majority seems to recognize at least some of the consequences of its decision when it attempts to fill the void created by abolition of the adequate state ground rule in state criminal cases. But the substitute it has fashioned—that of "conscious waiver" or "deliberate by-passing" of state procedures—is, as I shall next try to show, wholly unsatisfactory.

III.

ATTEMPTED PALLIATIVES.

Apparently on the basis of a doctrine analogous to that of "unclean hands," the Court states that a federal judge, in his discretion, may deny relief on habeas corpus to one who has understandingly and knowingly refused to avail himself of state procedures. But such a test, if it is meant to constitute a limitation on interference with state administration of criminal justice, falls far short of the mark. In fact, as explained and applied in this case, it amounts to no limitation at all.

First, the Court explains that the test is one calling for the exercise of the district judge's discretion, that the judge may, in other words, grant relief even when a conscious waiver has been shown. Thus the Court does not merely tell the States that, if they wish to detain those whom they convict, they must revamp their entire systems of criminal procedures so that no forfeiture may be imposed in the absence of deliberate choice; the States are also warned that even a deliberate, explicit, intelligent choice not to assert a constitutional right may not preclude its assertion on federal habeas.

Second, the Court states (as it must if it is to adhere to its definition) that "[a] choice made by counsel not participated in by the petitioner does not automatically bar relief." Ante, p. 439. It is true that there are cases in which the adequacy of the state ground necessarily turns on the question whether the defendant himself expressly and intelligently waived a constitutional right. Foremost among these are the cases involving right to counsel, for the Court has made it clear that this right cannot be foregone without deliberate choice by the defendant. See Johnson v. Zerbst, 304 U. S. 458; Carnley v. Cochran, 369 U. S. 506. But to carry this principle over in full force to cases in which a defendant is represented by counsel not shown to be incompetent is to undermine the entire representational system. We have manifested an ever-increasing awareness of the fundamental importance of representation by counsel, see Gideon v. Wainwright, ante, p. 335, and yet today the Court suggests that the State may no more have a rule of forfeiture for one who is competently represented than for one who is not. The effect on state procedural rules may be disastrous.

Third, when it comes to apply the "waiver" test in this case, the Court then in effect reads its own creation out of existence. Recognizing that Noia himself decided not to appeal, and that he apparently made this choice after consultation with counsel, the Court states that his decision was nevertheless not a "waiver." Since a new trial might have resulted in a death sentence, Noia was, in the majority's view, confronted with a "grisly choice," and he quite properly declined to play "Russian roulette" by appealing his conviction. Ante, pp. 439-440.

Does the Court mean by these colorful phrases that it would be unconstitutional for the State to impose a heavier sentence in a second trial for the same offense? Apparently not, since the majority assures us that there may be some cases in which a risk of a heavier sentence must be run. What distinguishes this case, we are told, is that the risk of the death sentence on a new trial was substantial in view of the trial judge's statement that Noia's past record and his involvement in the crime almost led the judge to disregard the jury's recommendation against a death sentence.

What the Court seems to be saying in this exercise in fine distinctions is that no waiver of a right can be effective if some adverse consequence might reasonably be expected to follow from exercise of that right. Under this approach, of course, there could never be a binding waiver, since only an incompetent would give up a right without any good reason, and an incompetent cannot make an intelligent waiver. The Court wholly ignores the question whether the choice made by the defendant is one that the State could constitutionally require.

Looked at from any angle, the concept of waiver which the Court has created must be found wanting. Of gravest importance, it carries this Court into a sphere in which it has no proper place in the context of the federal system. The true limitations on our constitutional power are those inherent in the rule requiring that a judgment resting on an adequate state ground must be respected.

IV.

ADEQUACY OF THE STATE GROUND HERE INVOLVED.

It is the adequacy, or fairness, of the state ground that should be the controlling question in this case.[26] This controlling question the Court does not discuss.

New York asserts that a claim of the kind involved here must be raised on timely appeal if it is to be preserved, and contends that in permitting an appeal it has provided a reasonable opportunity for the claim to be made. The collateral post-conviction writ of

268

coram nobis, the State has said, remains a remedy only for the calling up of facts unknown at the time of the judgment. See People v. Noia, decided sub nom. People v. Caminito, 3 N. Y. 2d 596, 601, 148 N. E. 2d 139, 143. In other words, the State claims that it may constitutionally detain a man pursuant to a judgment of conviction, regardless of any error that may have led to that conviction, if the relevant facts were reasonably available and an appeal was not taken.

Under the circumstances here—particularly the fact that Noia was represented by counsel whose competence is not challenged—is this a reasonable ground for barring collateral assertion of the federal claim? Certainly the State has a vital interest in requiring that appeals be taken on the basis of facts known at the time, since the first assertion of a claim many years later might otherwise require release long after it was feasible to hold a new trial. And although in Daniels v. Allen it might have been argued that the State's refusal to entertain an appeal actually received on time amounted to an evasion of the federal claim, no such argument can be made here, since no appeal was ever sought.

Moreover, we should be slow to reject—as an invalid barrier to the raising of a federal right—a state determination that one forum rather than another must be resorted to for the assertion of that right. A far more rigid restriction of federal forums was upheld in Yakus v. United States, 321 U. S. 414. In that case, the Court sustained a federal statute permitting an attack on the validity of an administrative price regulation to be made only on timely review of the administrative order, and precluding the defense of invalidity in a later criminal prosecution for violation of the regulation. What the Court there said bears repetition here:

"No procedural principle is more familiar to this Court than that a constitutional right may be forfeited in criminal as well as civil cases by the failure to make timely assertion of the right before a tribunal having jurisdiction to determine it." 321 U. S., at 444.

But is there some special circumstance here that operates to invalidate the nonfederal ground? Certainly it cannot be that the claim of a coerced confession is of such a nature that a State is constitutionally compelled to permit its assertion at any time even if it could have been, but was not, raised on appeal. Many federal decisions have held that a federal prisoner held pursuant to a federal conviction may not assert such a claim in collateral proceedings when it was not, but could have been, asserted on appeal. E. g., Davis v. United States, 214 F. 2d 594, cert. denied, 353 U. S. 960; Smith v. United States, 88 U. S. App. D. C. 80, 187 F. 2d 192, cert. denied, 341 U. S. 927; see Hodges v. United States, 108 U. S. App. D. C. 375, 282 F. 2d 858, cert. dismissed, 368 U. S. 139.

Is it then a basis for invalidating the nonfederal ground that Noia's two codefendants are today free from custody on facts which Noia says are identical to those in his case? Does the nonfederal ground fall when the federal claim appears to have obvious merit? There may be some question whether the facts in Noia's case and those in Bonino's and Caminito's are identical,[27] but assuming that they are, I think it evident that the nonfederal ground must still stand.

Again, there is highly relevant precedent dealing with federal prisoners. In Sunal v. Large, 332 U. S. 174, Sunal and Kulick had been prosecuted for violation of the Selective Service Act, and both had sought to raise a defense the court had refused to consider. Both were convicted and sentenced to imprisonment but took no appeal, quite evidently because such an appeal would have been to no avail under the existing state of the law. Subsequently, in another case, this Court held on comparable facts that the defense in question must be permitted. Estep v. United States, 327 U. S. 114. Sunal and Kulick then sought relief on habeas corpus, and this relief was denied. The opinion of the Court observed that there had been no barrier to the perfection of appeals by these prisoners and no facts which were not then known. That an appeal may have appeared futile at the time (indeed, far more futile than was the case here) was held not a sufficient basis for collateral relief. The present case, I submit, would be less troublesome than Sunal even had it involved a federal prisoner.

Surely, the state ground is not rendered inadequate because on a new trial for the same offense, Noia might have received the death sentence. The State is well within constitutional limits in permitting such a sentence to be imposed. Of particular relevance here is the decision in Larson v. United States, 275 F. 2d 673. Two criminal defendants had been tried and sentenced to imprisonment by a federal court. One defendant, Juelich, had moved for a continuance or a change of venue, on the ground of community prejudice, and his motion had been denied. Both defendants were convicted; Juelich appealed from his conviction; and the Court of Appeals reversed, Juelich v. United States, 214 F. 2d 950, holding that the constitutional requirement of a fair trial had been violated by the refusal to grant a change of venue or a continuance. Larson, the other defendant, had chosen not to appeal, apparently because he feared that the death sentence might be imposed in a new trial, but after his codefendant's success, he sought collateral relief under § 2255. That relief was denied by the District Court, and the Court of Appeals affirmed, stating:

"We do not say . . . that in every instance, before resort can be had to Section 2255 there must be an appeal. We say only that, in the circumstances of this case, Larson, taking a calculated risk, made a free choice not to jeopardize his life, and he is bound by that decision. . . . Whatever errors there were in his trial were known to Larson and to his counsel —for the same errors formed the basis for Juelich's appeal. Manifest justice to an accused person requires only that he have an opportunity to correct errors that may have led to an unfair trial. The orderly administration of justice requires that even a criminal case some day come to an end." 275 F. 2d, at 679-680.

This Court denied certiorari. 363 U. S. 849.

Decisions such as Sunal and Larson are reasoned expressions by the federal judiciary of its views on the fair and proper administration of federal criminal justice. We cannot turn around and tell the State of New York that it is constitutionally prohibited from being governed by the same considerations.

I recognize that Noia's predicament may well be thought one that strongly calls for correction. But the proper course to that end lies with the New York Governor's powers of executive clemency, not with the federal courts.[28] Since Noia is detained pursuant to a state judgment whose validity rests on an adequate and independent state ground, the judgment below should be reversed.

Notes

[1] For a broad range of views, see the analytical discussions of the development of federal habeas corpus jurisdiction in Hart, Foreword, 73 Harv. L. Rev. 84; Reitz, Federal Habeas Corpus: Impact of an Abortive State Proceeding, 74 Harv. L. Rev. 1315; Brennan, Federal Habeas Corpus and State Prisoners: An Exercise in Federalism, 7 Utah L. Rev. 423; and Bator, Finality in Criminal Law and Federal Habeas Corpus for State Prisoners, 76 Harv. L. Rev. 441.

[2] U. S. Const., Art 1, § 9, cl. 2.

[3] Section 14 of the Judiciary Act of 1789, c. 20, 1 Stat. 73, 81-82.

[4] The statutory development relating to review of criminal cases by the Supreme Court is discussed in Bator, supra, note 1, at 473, n. 75.

[5] See also, e. g., Ex parte Jackson, 96 U. S. 727; Ex parte Yarbrough, 110 U. S. 651; Minnesota v. Brundage, 180 U. S. 499.

[6] See also, e. g., Ex parte Wilson, 114 U. S. 417; In re Snow, 120 U. S. 274; In re Bonner, 151 U. S. 242. Compare Ex parte Bigelow, 113 U. S. 328.

In addition, there were a few cases during the period in which the Court rejected claims made in habeas corpus, apparently on their merits, without clearly limiting itself to questions of "jurisdiction." See In re Converse, 137 U. S. 624; Felts v. Murphy, 201 U. S. 123. See also Bator, supra, note 1, at 484. These cases were infrequent, however, and must be considered as exceptions to the general rules held to be applicable in this formative period.

[7] The remarks of Congressman Lawrence quoted by the majority, ante, p. 417, were in response to a suggestion by Congressman LeBlond that the bill would not cover certain civilians in military custody. Cong. Globe, 39th Cong., 1st Sess. 4151. See also id., at 4229.

[8] H. R. Rep. No. 730, 48th Cong., 1st Sess. 5 (1884).

[9] Frank v. State, 141 Ga. 243, 280-281, 80 S. E. 1016, 1032-1033.

[10] See 237 U. S., at 343. The dissenting opinion, 237 U. S., at 345, 346, did not take issue with this holding, but rather focused on the allegations of mob domination.

[11] Hicks v. State, 143 Ark. 158, 162, 220 S. W. 308, 310.

[12] Compare Hart, supra, note 1, at 105; Reitz, supra, note 1, at 1328-1329; Bator, supra, note 1, at 488-491.

[13] It has been suggested that language in such cases as White v. Ragen, 324 U. S. 760, 765, and House v. Mayo, 324 U. S. 42, 48, supports the result reached today by indicating that federal habeas will lie when an adequate state ground bars direct review by this Court. See Brennan, supra, note 1, at 431-432, n. 51; Reitz, supra, note 1, at 1359-1360. But these cases do not stand for this proposition. In each of them the state court appeared

to have denied that the particular post-conviction remedy sought was available to redress a claim of federal right that could not have been adequately asserted in the original trial. In each of them, it remained possible that other state remedies might be open, in which event it seemed clear that the particular denial of relief rested on an adequate state ground. But if it was subsequently determined—either by further attempts to obtain state relief or by proof in a Federal District Court—that no state remedies of any kind were ever available in the state courts, then federal habeas would lie. For, "it is not simply a question of state procedure," and there is no truly adequate state ground, "when a state court of last resort closes the door to any consideration of a claim of denial of a federal right." Young v. Ragen, 337 U. S. 235, 238; cf. Ward v. Love County, 253 U. S. 17; General Oil Co. v. Crain, 209 U. S. 211. In other words, the proposition that cases such as White v. Ragen do stand for is that this Court will, as a matter of sound judicial administration, accept what appears on its face to be an adequate state ground because the Federal District Court remains open for more intensive consideration of the petitioner's claim of inadequacy. Cf. 28 U. S. C. § 2241 (b).

[14] A third case, Speller v. Allen, was also reported at the same time but was not significantly different, for present purposes, from Brown v. Allen.

[15] Brown v. Mississippi, 297 U. S. 278, cited by the Court, ante, p. 414, arose on direct review of a state conviction, and did not suggest that a claim of a coerced confession, once determined by the state courts, could be redetermined on federal habeas.

[16] See 344 U. S., at 486. See also Mr. Justice Frankfurter's separate opinion, 344 U. S., at 488, 503.

[17] "A failure to use a state's available remedy, in the absence of some interference or incapacity . . . bars federal habeas corpus. The statute requires that the applicant exhaust available state remedies. To show that the time has passed for appeal is not enough to empower the Federal District Court to issue the writ." 344 U. S., at 487.

[18] "[W]here the state action was based on an adequate state ground, no further examination is required, unless no state remedy for the deprivation of federal constitutional rights ever existed." 344 U. S., at 458.

[19] Analysis of the problem in terms of exhaustion of remedies no longer available has been severely criticized. Hart, supra, note 1, at 112-114. This "exhaustion" approach is today quite properly interred. Ante, pp. 434-435.

[20] See Michel v. Louisiana, 350 U. S. 91.

[21] Lawrence v. State Tax Comm'n, 286 U. S. 276, 282. See, e. g., Rogers v. Alabama, 192 U. S. 226; NAACP v. Alabama, 357 U. S. 449. See also Hart and Wechsler, The Federal Courts and the Federal System, 501.

[22] See Davis v. Wechsler, 263 U. S. 22. New York Central R. Co. v. New York & Pa. Co., 271 U. S. 124; NAACP v. Alabama, supra. See also the discussion in the dissenting opinion in Williams v. Georgia, 349 U. S. 375, 393, 399.

[23] In Tyler v. Magwire, 17 Wall. 253, 293, the Court issued a writ of possession and ordered its marshal to execute it against the state defendant in possession.

[24] The successive statutes are collected and set out in full in Robertson and Kirkham, Jurisdiction of the Supreme Court of the United States (Wolfson and Kurland ed. 1951), Appendix A.

[25] 28 U. S. C. § 2106 authorizes the Court to vacate, as well as reverse, affirm or modify, any judgment lawfully brought before it for review. 28 U. S. C. § 1651 (a) provides that the Court "may issue all writs necessary or appropriate" in aid of its jurisdiction. See also 28 U. S. C. § 2241 (a), giving this Court specific authority to issue writs of habeas corpus. Such writs are to be executed, under 28 U. S. C. § 672, by the marshal of this Court, who is authorized by 28 U. S. C. § 549, when acting within a State, to "exercise the same powers which a sheriff of such state may exercise in executing the laws thereof." The power to enter judgment and, when necessary, to enforce it by appropriate process, has been said to be inherent in the Court's appellate jurisdiction. Stanley v. Schwalby, 162 U. S. 255, 279-282. See also Hart and Wechsler, supra, note 21, at 420-421.

[26] In view of the concession by the State, I assume in this discussion that Noia's confession was coerced. A confession, of course, may be coerced and yet still be a wholly reliable admission of guilt. See Rogers v. Richmond, 365 U. S. 534. Whether or not Noia was guilty of the crime of felony murder, and whether the evidence of his guilt was accurate and substantial, are matters irrelevant to the question of coercion and also irrelevant here.

[27] See People v. Noia, 4 App. Div. 2d 698, 163 N. Y. S. 2d 796.

[28] At the oral argument the State District Attorney advised us that his office would support an application for clemency once the case had been disposed of in this Court.

Justice Harlan's concurrence in Lane v. Brown (March 18, 1963)

Separate opinion of MR. JUSTICE HARLAN, in which MR. JUSTICE CLARK concurs.

I think it falls short of the requirements of due process for a State to foreclose an indigent from appealing in a case such as this at the unreviewable discretion of a Public Defender by whom, or by whose office, the indigent has been represented at the trial. It ignores the human equation not to recognize the possibility that a Public Defender so circumstanced may decide not to appeal questions which a lawyer who has had no previous connection with the case might consider worthy of appellate review. (I do not of course remotely intimate that such is the situation here.)

Were it clear that the decision of this Public Defender not to appeal had been subject to judicial review at the instance of the prisoner, I should have voted to sustain this conviction. However, the State Attorney General has candidly informed us that the Indiana law is unclear on this score.

Accordingly, while agreeing with the Court's action in remanding this case, I would instruct the District Court to discharge the prisoner only if the Indiana Supreme

Court fails, within a reasonable time, to accord him a review of the Public Defender's decision not to appeal the denial of coram nobis.

Justice Harlan's dissent in Gibson v. Florida Legislative Investigation Comm. (March 25, 1963)

MR. JUSTICE HARLAN, whom MR. JUSTICE CLARK, MR. JUSTICE STEWART, and MR. JUSTICE WHITE join, dissenting.

The difficulties with this decision will become apparent once the case is deflated to its true size.

The essential facts are these. For several years before petitioner was convicted of this contempt, the respondent, a duly authorized Committee of the Florida Legislature, had been investigating alleged Communist "infiltration" into various organizations in Dade County, Florida, including the Miami Branch of the National Association for the Advancement of Colored People.[1] There was no suggestion that the branch itself had engaged in any subversive or other illegal activity, but the Committee had developed information indicating that 14 of some 52 present or past residents of Dade County, apparently at one time or another members of the Communist Party or connected organizations,[2] were or had been members or had "participated in the meetings and other affairs" of this local branch of the N. A. A. C. P.

Having failed to obtain from prior witnesses, other than its own investigator, any significant data as to the truth or falsity of this information, the Committee, in 1959, summoned the petitioner to testify, also requiring that he bring with him the membership records of the branch. Petitioner, a Negro clergyman, was then and for the past five years had been president of the local branch, and his custodianship of the records stands conceded.

On his appearance before the Committee petitioner was asked to consult these records himself and, after doing so, to inform the Committee which, if any, of the 52 individually identified persons were or had been members of the N. A. A. C. P. Miami Branch. He declined to do this on two grounds. First, he said that the N. A. A. C. P. itself had already undertaken action "excluding from our ranks any and all persons who may have subversive tendencies."

To substantiate this, petitioner furnished the Committee with copies of "Anti-Communism" resolutions which he stated had been adopted each year since 1950 at the Association's annual convention. Second, petitioner protested that production of the membership records would violate "a legal right of ours, the right of association." At the same time the petitioner expressed willingness to testify from recollection as to the membership or nonmembership in the local branch of any persons that the Committee might name to him.

The petitioner was then asked to state from recollection the N. A. A. C. P. membership vel non of the 14 persons mentioned above, photographs of each being exhibited to him. But he was unable to supply any information, disclaiming even knowledge of most of the names. He was then again asked to utilize the membership records as a testimonial aid, it having been earlier made clear to him that the Committee itself did not propose to look at the records:

"[By Committee counsel]. Now, are you aware of the fact, Reverend, that we're not actually asking you to turn over to this Committee those records, but that we're asking that you bring those records here for the purpose of consulting them yourself and telling us, under oath, after consulting them, whether or not certain people who we will name are members, or have been members of your organization? "[By the witness]. I'm aware of it."

Petitioner persisted in his refusal. This contempt charge and conviction, and its affirmance by the Supreme Court of Florida, 126 So. 2d 129, followed.

I.

This Court rests reversal on its finding that the Committee did not have sufficient justification for including the Miami Branch of the N. A. A. C. P. within the ambit of its investigation—that, in the language of our cases (Uphaus v. Wyman, 360 U. S. 72, 79), an adequate "nexus" was lacking between the N. A. A. C. P. and the subject matter of the Committee's inquiry.

The Court's reasoning is difficult to grasp. I read its opinion as basically proceeding on the premise that the governmental interest in investigating Communist infiltration into admittedly nonsubversive organizations, as distinguished from investigating organizations themselves suspected of subversive activities, is not sufficient to overcome the countervailing right to freedom of association. Ante, pp. 547-549. On this basis "nexus" is seemingly found lacking because it was never claimed that the N. A. A. C. P. Miami Branch had itself engaged in subversive activity, ante, pp. 554-555, and because none of the Committee's evidence relating to any of the 52 alleged Communist Party members was sufficient to attribute such activity to the local branch or to show that it was dominated, influenced, or used "by Communists." Ante, pp. 550-555.

But, until today, I had never supposed that any of our decisions relating to state or federal power to investigate in the field of Communist subversion could possibly be taken as suggesting any difference in the degree of governmental investigatory interest as between Communist infiltration of organizations and Communist activity by organizations. See, e. g., Barenblatt v. United States, 360 U. S. 109 (infiltration into education); Wilkinson v. United States, 365 U. S. 399, and Braden v. United States, 365 U. S. 431 (infiltration into basic industries); Russell v. United States, 369 U. S. 749, 773 (infiltration of newspaper business).

Considering the number of congressional inquiries that have been conducted in the field of "Communist infiltration" since the close of World War II, affecting such diverse interests as "labor, farmer, veteran, professional, youth, and motion picture groups" (Barenblatt, supra, at 119), it is indeed strange to find the strength of state interest in the same type of investigation now impugned. And it is not amiss to recall that government evidence in Smith Act prosecutions has shown that the sensitive area of race relations has long been a prime target of Communist efforts at infiltration. See Scales v. United States, 367 U. S. 203, 235, 245, 249 n. 26, 251, 255-256.

Given the unsoundness of the basic premise underlying the Court's holding as to the absence of "nexus," this decision surely falls of its own weight. For unless "nexus" requires an investigating agency to prove in advance the very things it is trying to find out, I do not understand how it can be said that the information preliminarily developed by the Committee's investigator was not sufficient to satisfy, under any reasonable test, the requirement of "nexus."

Apart from this, the issue of "nexus" is surely laid at rest by the N. A. A. C. P.'s own "Anti-Communism" resolution, first adopted in 1950, which petitioner had voluntarily furnished the Committee before the curtain came down on his examination:

"ANTI-COMMUNISM

"Whereas, certain branches of the National Association for the Advancement of Colored People are being rocked by internal conflicts between groups who follow the Communist line and those who do not, which threaten to destroy the confidence of the public in the Association and which will inevitably result in its eventual disruption; and

"Whereas, it is apparent from numerous attacks by Communists in their official organs `The Daily Worker' and `Political Affairs' upon officials of the Association that there is a well-organized, nationwide conspiracy by Communists either to capture or split and wreck the NAACP; therefore be it

"Resolved, that this Forty-First Convention of the National Association for the Advancement of Colored People go on record as unequivocally condemning attacks by Communists and their fellow-travelers upon the Association and its officials, and in order to safeguard the good-name of the Association, promote and develop unity, eliminate internal ideological friction, increase the membership and build the necessary power effectively to wage the fight for civil rights, herewith, call upon, direct and instruct the National Board of Directors to appoint a committee to investigate and study the ideological composition and trends of the membership and leadership of the local units with a view to determining causes of the aforementioned conflicts, confusion and loss of membership; be it further

"Resolved, that this Convention go on record as directing and instructing the Board of Directors to take the necessary action to eradicate such infiltration, and if necessary to suspend and reorganize, or lift the charter and expel any unit, which, in the judgment of the Board of Directors, upon a basis of the findings of the aforementioned investigation and study of local units comes under Communist or other political control and combination." (Emphasis added.)

It hardly meets the point at issue to suggest, as the Court does (ante, p. 554), that the resolution only serves to show that the Miami Branch was in fact free of any Communist influences—unless self-investigation is deemed constitutionally to block official inquiry.

II.

I also find it difficult to see how this case really presents any serious question as to interference with freedom of association. Given the willingness of the petitioner to testify from recollection as to individual memberships in the local branch of the N. A. A. C. P., the germaneness of the membership records to the subject matter of the Committee's investigation, and the limited purpose for which their use was sought—as an aid to refreshing the witness' recollection, involving their divulgence only to the petitioner himself (supra, pp. 577-578) —this case of course bears no resemblance whatever to NAACP v. Alabama, 357 U. S. 449, or Bates v. Little Rock, 361 U. S. 516. In both of those cases the State had sought general divulgence of local N. A. A. C. P. membership lists without any showing of a justifying state interest. In effect what we are asked to hold here is that the petitioner had a constitutional right to give only partial or inaccurate testimony, and that indeed seems to me the true effect of the Court's holding today.

I have scrutinized this record with care to ascertain whether any unfairness in the Committee's proceedings could be detected. I can find none. In the questioning and treatment of witnesses, explanations of pertinency, rulings on objections, and general conduct of the inquiry, I perceive nothing in this record which savors of other than a decorous attitude on the part of the Committee and a lawyerlike and considerate demeanor on the part of its counsel. Nor do I find in the opinion of the Florida Supreme Court the slightest indication of anything other than a conscientious application of the constitutional principles governing cases such as this.

There can be no doubt that the judging of challenges respecting legislative or executive investigations in this sensitive area demands the utmost circumspection on the part of the courts, as indeed the Florida Supreme Court has itself recognized. See Graham v. Florida Legislative Investigation Comm., 126 So. 2d 133, 135. But this also surely carries with it the reciprocal responsibility of respecting legitimate state and local authority in this field. With all respect, I think that in deciding this case as it has the Court has failed fully to keep in mind that responsibility.

I would affirm.

Notes

[1] We are told by counsel for the Committee, without contradiction by the petitioner, that the investigations of the predecessor committees have included the activities of such persons and organizations as John Casper, the Ku Klux Klan, and the Seaboard White Citizens Council.

[2] The Committee's information as to such membership has not been challenged in this case.

Justice Harlan's dissent in Basham v. Pennsylvania R. Co. (April 15, 1963)

MR. JUSTICE HARLAN, dissenting.
This is a run-of-the-mill negligence case, presenting no new question of law or

departure from established legal principles. The only question is whether there was enough evidence to take the case to the jury.

A total of 12 New York Judges—one at nisi prius, four on the Appellate Division (a fifth dissenting), and seven on the Court of Appeals—have held that the evidence was not sufficient to warrant submission of the case to the jury.

To bring such a case here for further review by nine more Justices seems to me a most futile expenditure of judicial time. Having reflected on the oral argument, briefs, and record, I conclude that the only premise on which this reversal can be justified is that anything a jury says goes.

I would affirm the judgment below.

Justice Harlan's dissent in Willner v. Committee on Character and Fitness, Appellate Div. of Supreme Court of NY (May 13, 1963)

MR. JUSTICE HARLAN, whom MR. JUSTICE CLARK joins, dissenting.

The majority and concurring opinions bear witness to the difficulty the Court has had divining from this messy and opaque record whether the case in truth presents a substantial federal question. Obviously much influenced by the amended remittitur of the Court of Appeals, the Court considers that the state courts have held that an applicant for membership in the New York Bar may be denied admission without having had the opportunity at any stage to confront persons whose unfavorable information may have led the Character Committee to refuse to certify the candidate's "character and fitness."

It would take a great deal to persuade me that either of these experienced and respected New York courts has been guilty of such a questionable constitutional holding. In light of the record, I do not believe that either the Court of Appeals' affirmance or its amended remittitur by any means points to the interpretation which this Court now places on the action of that court. In my view the more reasonable, and correct, interpretation is that the Court of Appeals simply held that, in light of what had gone before,[1] the Appellate Division's refusal to entertain petitioner's last de novo application for admission —the eighth proceeding before that court—involved no abuse of its discretion under Rule 1 of the New York Rules of Civil Practice. More particularly, in these prior proceedings no confrontation claim was raised until 1954—some 16 years after the original denial of admission —during which period the matter had already been before the Appellate Division five times (note 1, supra).[2]

So interpreting the Court of Appeals' action, I do not think this case presents a substantial federal question— no more so than did the petition for certiorari which was filed here in 1955, raising this same confrontation question in almost the same context of prior proceedings, and which this Court then denied. In re Willner, 348 U. S. 955.

Now that plenary consideration has shed more light on this case than in the nature of things was afforded at the time the petition for certiorari was acted upon, I think the proper course is to dismiss the writ as improvidently granted.

Notes

[1] The chronology of events was in substance this: The Appellate Division, upon the Character Committee's refusal to certify the applicant, originally denied admission in 1938. Refusal of certification had followed petitioner's appearance before the Committee at which, among other things, he had been informed and interrogated about complaints received from two lawyers, Wieder and Dempsey. (Wieder charged that petitioner had not completed his required "clerkship," having been discharged from Wieder's office for unsatisfactory performance before the end of the clerkship period. Dempsey's complaint related to certain litigation involving petitioner and one of Dempsey's clients, in which petitioner had been charged with fraud in connection with accountancy services performed for the client.) Apart from these ex parte charges, petitioner in his return to the Committee's written questionnaire had (1) stated that he had not been connected with any law offices, although in a later interview he had informed the Committee that he had in fact been employed in Wieder's office for a short time; (2) stated that he had served "no clerkship," although he had subsequently informed the Committee of the filing of a certificate of clerkship with the Court of Appeals in Albany; (3) failed to disclose the aforementioned suit brought against him by Dempsey's client; (4) failed to disclose an annulment suit that had been brought against him by his 16-year-old wife, later stating that he had omitted this information because "Some people consider it a heinous offense"; and (5) failed to include six other suits or judgments against him among those listed in the questionnaire. The Committee characterized petitioner's demeanor as one of "general evasiveness."

Although he made no contemporary effort to obtain review of the original denial of admission, petitioner thereafter sought to attack it before the Appellate Division on four successive occasions during the years 1943-1951—all to no avail. Again, he sought no review of any of these proceedings, one of which involved a de novo hearing before the Character Committee, and in none does he appear to have raised the confrontation claim now made here.

Lack of confrontation seems to have been asserted for the first time in 1954, when petitioner again unsuccessfully moved the Appellate Division for leave to file a de novo application for admission. Leave to appeal to the New York Court of Appeals, sought then for the first time, was denied, and this Court in turn denied certiorari. 348 U. S. 955.

Finally in 1960 and 1961 petitioner twice more unsuccessfully moved the Appellate Division for leave to file a de novo application for admission, the latter proceeding being the one presently before the Court.

[2] In his petition initiating the present proceeding petitioner alleged that during the interviews held in connection with his original application the Chairman of the Character Committee promised him "a confrontation." The record, however, discloses no such episode. Indeed at the third Committee hearing in 1938 petitioner was asked whether he had anything further to present and he responded simply by referring to one of the

affidavits submitted on his behalf purporting to refute the Wieder charge (note 1, supra). He made no request for confrontation.

Justice Harlan's concurrence and dissent in Railway Clerks v. Allen (May 13, 1963)

MR. JUSTICE HARLAN, concurring in part and dissenting in part.

I agree with the reversal of the interim and qualified permanent relief that was granted by the state courts respecting the obligation to pay union dues. But I disagree with what in effect amounts to an affirmance of the state judgment in other respects. I believe that dismissal of this action in its entirety is called for.

International Assn. of Machinists v. Street, 367 U. S. 740, decided only two years ago, stated in unmistakable terms that a plaintiff claiming relief in an action of this kind must show two things: (1) that he had made known to the union the particular political candidates or causes for whose support he did not wish his union dues used; (2) that membership dues had been used for such purposes.

The statement of these principles was reinforced on the very same day in Lathrop v. Donohue, 367 U. S. 820, the Wisconsin integrated bar case, where a plurality of the Court said (at 845-846):

"Even if the demurrer is taken as admitting all the factual allegations of the complaint, even if these allegations are construed most expansively, and even if, like the Wisconsin Supreme Court, we take judicial notice of the political activities of the State Bar, still we think that the issue of impingement upon rights of free speech through the use of exacted dues is no more concretely presented for adjudication than it was in Hanson [351 U. S. 225]. Compare International Association of Machinists v. Street, ante, p. 740, at pp. 747-749. Nowhere are we clearly apprised as to the views of the appellant on any particular legislative issues on which the State Bar has taken a position, or as to the way in which and the degree to which funds compulsorily exacted from its members are used to support the organization's political activities." See also what follows at pp. 846-848.

These requirements have not been met in this case. At best all that has been alleged or proved is that the union will expend a part of each respondent's still-unpaid membership dues for so-called political or other purposes not connected with collective bargaining, and that each respondent would object to the use of any part of his dues for matters other than those relating to collective bargaining. None of the respondents who testified could specify any particular expenditure, or even class of expenditure, to which he objected.

I do not understand how, consistently with Street, the Court can now hold that "it is enough that . . . [a union member] manifests his opposition to any political expenditures by the union" (ante, p. 118), or how it can say that in so holding "we are not inconsistent with" what the plurality was at such pains to point out in Lathrop (albeit in a constitutional context), id., note 5. The truth of the matter is that the Court has departed from the strict substantive limitations of Street and has given them (and, as I see it, also that case's remedial limitations, compare 367 U. S., at 772-775, 778-779, 779-780, 796-797, with ante, p. 122-123 and Appendix) an expansive thrust which can hardly fail to increase the volume of this sort of litigation in the future.

Believing that our decisions should have more lasting power than has been accorded Street, I must respectfully dissent. I would reverse the judgment and remand the case for dismissal of the complaint.

Justice Harlan's dissent in Gutierrez v. Waterman SS (May 13, 1963)

MR. JUSTICE HARLAN, dissenting.

The decision in this case has importance in admiralty law beyond what might appear on the surface. It marks another substantial stride toward the development by this Court of a doctrine that a shipowner is an insurer for those who perform any work on or around a ship subject to maritime jurisdiction. While my primary disagreement with the Court goes to its holding on unseaworthiness, I am also unable to agree with its views on the negligence issue.

I.

The shipowner's duty with respect to seaworthiness is a duty to furnish a vessel that is reasonably fit for its intended use—one that is staunch and strong, that is fitted out with all proper equipment and in good order, and that carries a sufficient and competent crew and complement of officers. Gilmore and Black, The Law of Admiralty, 158. As developed by this Court in cases involving injury to seamen and dock workers, the duty has become absolute and has been found to reach even transitory conditions arising after the outset of the voyage. See Mitchell v. Trawler Racer, Inc., 362 U. S. 539. But, except for the few unpersuasive instances noted in this opinion, the obligation has remained one relating essentially to the ship and its appurtenances. See id., at 550. Although the doctrine has been extended—in my view, quite questionably—to equipment brought on board by a stevedore, see Alaska S. S. Co. v. Petterson, 347 U. S. 396,[1] the shipowner has not been deemed an insurer of the condition of the cargo. His duty with respect to cargo has been to see that it is stowed in a manner that does not make the ship itself an unsafe place to work. See, e. g., Palazzolo v. Pan-Atlantic S. S. Corp., 211 F. 2d 277; Curtis v. A. Garcia y Cia., 241 F. 2d 30; Rich v. Ellerman & Bucknall S. S. Co., 278 F. 2d 704; Carabellese v. Naviera Aznar, S. A., 285 F. 2d 355.[2]

The Court, however, has concluded that it is bound by the determination last Term, in Atlantic & Gulf Stevedores, Inc., v. Ellerman Lines, Ltd., 369 U. S. 355, to hold that defective cargo may in and of itself render the shipowner liable for unseaworthiness. I must admit that some language in that case (369 U. S., at 364) does appear to stand for this proposition. But I think it fair to suggest that it was negligence, not unseaworthiness, on which attention was focused there—indeed unseaworthiness was neither briefed nor argued. At all events I am frank to say that in concurring in the result in that case, unseaworthiness as a distinct issue entirely eluded me, as it evidently did the dissenters, who interpreted the majority opinion as suggesting that the jury's finding was premised on a negligent failure to inspect the cargo containers. See 369 U. S., at 365. Moreover, the case cited by the Ellerman Court in support of its unseaworthiness conclusion, Weyerhaeuser S. S. Co. v. Nacirema Co., 355 U. S. 563, did not even touch upon such an issue. So casual a determination should not be blindly accepted as fastening on the law of admiralty such a far-reaching innovation. At least it should not preclude us from considering the question anew when it is now fully and squarely presented.[3]

The Court's decision after Ellerman, in Morales v. City of Galveston, 370 U. S. 165, is the strongest evidence that Ellerman was not regarded as establishing the fundamental change in the law of unseaworthiness for which it is now cited. In Morales, a longshoreman working in the hold of a ship had been injured by the fumes emanating from grain that had been improperly treated with an excessive amount of a chemical insecticide. The grain in question had been found to be "contaminated," although not due to the fault or with the knowledge of the city or the shipowner, and the question before this Court was whether the longshoreman could recover for unseaworthiness. The Court sustained the conclusion of the lower courts that he could not, because under the circumstances the absence of a forced ventilation system in the hold did not constitute unseaworthiness.

"What caused injury in the present case, however, was not the ship, its appurtenances, or its crew, but the isolated and completely unforeseeable introduction of a noxious agent from without. The trier of the facts ruled, under proper criteria, that the Grelmarion [the ship] was not in any manner unfit for the service to which she was to be put, and we cannot say that his determination was wrong." 370 U. S., at 171.

The crucial point for present purposes is that both the majority and the dissenting opinions in Morales viewed the issue in terms of the seaworthiness of the ship: whether or not it should have had a forced ventilation system in the hold. Nowhere was it even suggested that liability for unseaworthiness could arise solely by virtue of the defective state of the cargo itself, even though its contaminated and unsafe condition had clearly been established and was not in dispute. Thus the Court in Morales unanimously ignored the possibility of a doctrine which the Court today concludes was squarely established less than three months earlier, in Ellerman.[4]

II.

In order to conclude that the respondent shipowner was negligent in the circumstances presented here, it was necessary for the trier of fact to find that the respondent knew or should have known of the defective condition of the bags being unloaded. It is doubtful that such a finding was made by the trial judge in this case—the closest he came was the statement that the shipowner was negligent in permitting broken and weakened bags to be discharged "when it knew or should have known that injury was likely to result." This finding passes over the basic question: whether respondent had notice, or constructive notice, of the condition of the bags themselves.

Even assuming for present purposes that the necessary finding as to notice was made, I believe that the judgment on negligence cannot be sustained, for there is no evidence whatever to support such a finding. The evidence in the record, including the landing report, relates only to the stevedore company's knowledge of the condition of the bags. There is nothing to suggest that any agent or employee of the respondent was or should have been in the area, or knew or should have known of the condition of the cargo at the time of unloading.[5] And of course there is no basis in law for charging the shipowner with responsibility for any negligence on the part of the stevedore company.

Whether from the standpoint of negligence or unseaworthiness I see no basis for the holding in this case. Presumably the result reached by the Court would be the same—at least consistency demands that it should be the same—if this accident had occurred on the dock while the beans were being loaded rather than unloaded. Yet in neither case is there warrant for holding the shipowner to have breached any obligation, for in neither case does it own or control the place where the accident occurred and in neither case is the ship's equipment, property, or crew in any way responsible, with or without fault, for the injury.

Accordingly, I would affirm.

Notes

[1] A 6-3 unexplicated per curiam.

[2] The result in Reddick v. McAllister Lighterage Line, 258 F. 2d 297, the only other Court of Appeals case cited by the majority, is consistent with these decisions, for all three judges in Reddick agreed that the finding of unseaworthiness could be sustained on the basis of improper stowage. Two of the judges said, but only alternatively, that the finding could "also be predicated on the latent defect in the cargo-crate." 258 F. 2d, at 299. (Emphasis added.)

[3] I do not attach significance to the fact that in Ellerman the Court was asked in a petition for rehearing to reconsider whether cargo can itself be unseaworthy. Petitions for rehearing lie within the broad discretion of the Court and are almost never granted. Indeed, this petition for rehearing serves principally to underscore the fact that the point had not been briefed, argued, or apparently even considered by the parties as germane to the case prior to its decision.

[4] The Court in Morales cited Ellerman, along with several other cases, only for the proposition that a ship might be unseaworthy because "[t]he method of loading her cargo, or the manner of its stowage, might be improper." 370 U. S., at 170. Such a proposition, of course, is wholly different from the one for which Ellerman is cited today.

[5] The coopers sent aboard were employed by the stevedore company, not the steamship company.

Justice Harlan's concurrence and dissent in Peterson v. Greenville (May 20, 1963) [Excerpt]

[. . .] An individual's right to restrict the use of his property, however unregenerate a particular exercise of that right may be thought, lies beyond the reach of the Fourteenth Amendment. The dilution or virtual elimination of that right cannot well be justified either on the premise that it will hasten formal repeal of outworn segregation laws or on the ground that it will facilitate proof of state action in cases of this kind. Those laws have already found their just constitutional deserts in the decisions of this Court, and in many communities in which racial discrimination is no longer a universal or widespread practice such laws may have a purely formal existence and may indeed be totally unknown. Of course this is not to say that their existence on the books may never play a significant and even decisive role in private decision making. But the question in each case, if the right of the individual to make his own decisions is to remain viable, must be: was the discriminatory exclusion in fact influenced by the law? Cf. Truax v. Raich, 239 U. S. 33.[3] The inexorable rule which the Court lays down reflects insufficient reckoning with the course of history.

It is suggested that requiring proof of the effect of such laws in individual instances would involve "attempting to separate the mental urges of the discriminators" (ante, p. 248). But proof of state of mind is not a novel concept in the law of evidence, see 2 Wigmore, Evidence (3d ed. 1940), §§ 385-393, and such a requirement presents no special barriers in this situation. The mere showing of such an ordinance would, in my judgment, make out a prima facie case of invalid state action, casting on the State the burden of proving that the exclusion was in fact the product solely of private choice. In circumstances like these that burden is indeed a heavy one. This is the rule which, in my opinion, evenhanded constitutional doctrine and recognized evidentiary rules dictate. Its application here calls for reversal of these convictions. [. . .]

Justice Harlan's dissent in Reed v. The Yaka (May 27, 1963)

MR. JUSTICE HARLAN, whom MR. JUSTICE STEWART joins, dissenting.

This decision goes further than anything yet done by the Court in F. E. L. A. and admiralty cases (see, e. g., Rogers v. Missouri Pac. R. Co., 352 U. S. 500, and its offspring, and Gutierrez v. Waterman S. S. Corp., ante, p. 206) to do what it considers "justice" to those who have become the unfortunate victims of industrial accidents. For it is no exaggeration to say that in holding that a longshoreman may recover from his own employer for injuries suffered in the course of employment, the Court has effectively "repealed" a basic aspect of the Longshoremen's and Harbor Workers' Compensation Act.

The violence done to the statutory scheme is most simply shown merely by quoting the relevant portions of the two provisions that govern the question before us. The first is the definition of "employer" as:

"an employer any of whose employees are employed in maritime employment, in whole or in part, upon the navigable waters of the United States (including any dry dock)." § 2 (4), 44 Stat. 1425, 33 U. S. C. § 902 (4).

The second is § 5, a provision entitled "Exclusiveness of liability," which states:

"The liability of an employer [for the compensation] prescribed in section 4 shall be exclusive and in place of all other liability of such employer to the employee . . . at law or in admiralty on account of such injury or death . . . ." 44 Stat. 1426. 33 U. S. C. § 905.

There being no doubt that petitioner is an "employee" within the meaning of the Act,[1] there is thus no question that he is excluded from recovering from his employer, Pan-Atlantic, in this action. Under a statute which was specifically written to include shipowners who employed their own dockworkers, and which excluded liability at law or in admiralty, there is no room for concluding that an employer shipowner can be held liable to his own longshoreman employee for unseaworthiness. Indeed, the point is so clear that petitioner has had what I would have thought was the good sense not even to argue to the contrary. (He has instead based his argument wholly on the theory that the ship itself may be liable even in the absence of any underlying personal liability on the part of anyone.)

While conceding that the statute "on its face lends support" to the conclusion that neither party has challenged, the Court refuses to give what it describes as "blind adherence to the superficial meaning" of the Act. But if exclusiveness of liability is the "superficial" meaning, then what, may it be asked, is the "true" congressional purpose in enacting this legislation? The statutory design was nowhere more concisely or more accurately summarized than in the dissenting opinion in Ryan Stevedoring Co. v. Pan-Atlantic S. S. Corp., 350 U. S. 124, 140, where it was stated:

"Congress weighed the conflicting interests of employers and employees and struck what was considered to be a fair and constitutional balance. Injured employees thereby lost their chance to get large tort verdicts against their employers, but gained the right to get a sure though frequently a more modest recovery. However, § 33 did leave employees a chance to recover extra tort damages from third persons who negligently injured them. And while Congress imposed absolute liability on employers, they were also accorded counterbalancing advantages. They were no longer to be subjected to the hazards of large tort verdicts. Under no circumstances were they to be held liable to their own employees for more than the compensation clearly fixed in the Act. Thus employers were given every reason to believe they could buy their insurance and make other business arrangements on the basis of the limited Compensation Act liability." (Footnote omitted.)

Congress, then, deliberately gave employers certain "counterbalancing advantages" in exchange for imposing on them absolute liability. If these advantages are to be discarded as purely "superficial," then the true purpose of the statute was apparently to give an additional remedy to employees while not requiring them to relinquish any existing remedies as part of the bargain. This, of course, is precisely the opposite of what Congress explicitly aimed to do.

The Court is frank to admit that the real reason for its decision is that a contrary result would make little economic sense after the decision in Ryan, supra, holding that, on the basis of an implied contract of indemnity, a shipowner is entitled to reimbursement from an independent stevedore of a judgment obtained against the shipowner by the stevedore's employee. Admittedly, the liability imposed in Ryan is similar to the liability imposed on Pan-Atlantic in the present case. But what is overlooked is that the Ryan result can be squared with the statute, resting as it did on the stevedoring company's voluntarily assumed contractual obligation to indemnify the third-party shipowner, while the present result cannot. Granting that petitioner could have recovered in this case for faulty equipment brought aboard by longshoremen if the ship had been operated by an independent company, cf. Alaska S. S. Co. v. Petterson, 347 U. S. 396, I believe that any anomaly between that case and this one should be left to Congress to remedy, for it may be that it would choose means wholly different from those chosen by the Court. There is an outer limit beyond which judicial construction of the language of a statute ought not go, and I respectfully submit that that limit has been exceeded here.

Believing that there is no basis on which recovery by petitioner can be sustained,[2] I would affirm the judgment below.

Notes

[1] The Act in § 2 (3), 44 Stat. 1425, 33 U. S. C. § 902 (3), defines "employee," and excludes only masters and members of a crew and those engaged to load or unload any small vessel under 18 tons net.

[2] The basis of recovery urged by petitioner is that in rem liability of the ship can exist even without any underlying personal liability. But I fully agree with the court below (cf. Guzman v. Pichirilo, 369 U. S. 698, 704 (dissenting opinion)) that such a result would be a gross misapplication of a fiction whose principal modern function is as a procedural device to provide a convenient forum where none would otherwise be available. See Continental Grain Co. v. Barge FBL-585, 364 U. S. 19, 23-24. The reasons against its application to create substantive liability were eloquently stated by Mr. Justice Bradley, speaking for the Court in City of Norwich, 118 U. S. 468, 503: "To say that an owner is not liable, but that his vessel is liable, seems to us like talking in riddles. . . . In the matter of liability, a man and his property cannot be separated . . . ."

The Court also suggests that there may be another basis for recovery that is not reached apparently on the ground that it was not properly preserved: that Waterman, the demisor, was not absolved by the making of a bareboat charter from liability for unseaworthiness arising after the demise. I see no procedural barrier to consideration of this theory as possible support for petitioner's recovery against the ship, but I do not believe it can be sustained on its merits. I agree with the court below, and with the Court of Appeals for the Second Circuit, see Grillea v. United States, 229 F. 2d 687, 690, that a demisor should not be held liable for unseaworthiness resulting solely from the equipment brought on board by the demisee's employees. An analogy may concededly be drawn to this Court's holding in Alaska S. S. Co. v. Petterson, supra, relating to the shipowner's liability for equipment brought on board by a stevedore, but I would not extend that one-sentence 6-3 per curiam decision beyond its precise facts. Cf. Gutierrez v. Waterman S. S. Corp., supra, at 216 (dissenting opinion).

Justice Harlan's partial dissent in Arizona v. California (June 3, 1963)

MR. JUSTICE HARLAN, whom MR. JUSTICE DOUGLAS and MR. JUSTICE STEWART join, dissenting in part.

I dissent from so much of the Court's opinion as holds that the Secretary of the Interior has been given authority by Congress to apportion, among and within the States of California, Arizona, and Nevada, the waters of the mainstream of the Colorado River below Lee Ferry. I also dissent from the holding that in times of shortage the Secretary has discretion to select or devise any "reasonable method" he wishes for determining which users within these States are to bear the burden of that shortage. (In all other respects MR. JUSTICE STEWART and I—but not MR. JUSTICE DOUGLAS—agree with and join in the Court's opinion, though not without some misgivings regarding the amounts of water allocated to the Indian Reservations.)

In my view, it is the equitable principles established by the Court in interstate water-rights cases, as modified by the Colorado River Compact and the California limitation, that were intended by Congress to govern the apportionment of mainstream waters among the Lower Basin States, whether in surplus or in shortage. A fortiori, state law was intended to control apportionment among users within a single State.

I.

INTRODUCTION.

The Court's conclusions respecting the Secretary's apportionment powers, particularly those in times of shortage, result in a single appointed federal official being vested with absolute control, unrestrained by adequate standards, over the fate of a substantial segment of the life and economy of three States. Such restraint upon his actions as may follow from judicial review are, as will be shown, at best illusory. Today's result, I venture to say, would have dumbfounded those responsible for the legislation the Court construes, for nothing could have been farther from their minds or more inconsistent with their deeply felt convictions.

The Court professes to find this extraordinary delegation of power principally in § 5 of the Project Act, the provision authorizing the Secretary to enter into contracts for the storage and delivery of water. But § 5, as is more fully shown below, pp. 615-621, infra, had no design resembling that which the Court now extracts from it. Rather, it was intended principally as a revenue measure, and the clause requiring a contract as a condition of delivery was inserted at the insistence not of the Lower but of the Upper Basin States in an effort to insure that nothing would disturb that basin's rights under the Colorado River Compact. There was no thought that § 5 would give authority to apportion water among the Lower Basin States. Indeed, during the hearings on the third Swing-Johnson bill when

§ 5 took its present form, one of its principal proponents, Delph Carpenter of Colorado, specifically stated that the proposed condition of a contract was intended to require

"that the persons who receive the water shall respect and do so under the compact. It has nothing to do with the interstate relations between Arizona and California."[1] (Emphasis added.)

And Representative Swing, coauthor of the bill, made virtually the same point in explaining the provision before the House Rules Committee:

"The act says [in § 5] `The Secretary of the Interior is hereby authorized, under such general regulations as he may prescribe, to contract for the storage of water.' Whose water? It does not say. It might be a community like Imperial Valley that has already acquired a water right . . . or it may be someone who hereafter will acquire a water right, but that right will not be acquired under this bill; not from the United States Government. He will acquire his water right, if he acquires one, from the State and under the laws of the State, in which he puts the water to a beneficial use. There is nothing in this bill which puts the Government in conflict with the water laws of Arizona or Utah or any other State. As a matter of fact, the reclamation law is adopted by section 13 of this bill [now § 14], and section 8 of the reclamation act says that what the Government does must not be in conflict with the water laws of the States, so there can be no violence done State laws on this score."[2] (Emphasis added.)

The Court concedes, as indeed it must in the face of such unequivocal evidence, that this third Swing-Johnson bill, like its predecessors, established "no method whatever of apportioning the waters among the States of the Lower Basin." Ante, p. 560. This concession, one would think, would end this aspect of the controversy, since § 5 as ultimately adopted is virtually the same as that proposed in the third bill.[3] Yet a method of federal apportionment is discovered in the fourth Swing-Johnson bill as finally enacted, a method which ends by delegating to the Secretary of the Interior the awesome power over the "water" destiny of three States. To what provision does the Court attribute this startling metamorphosis? The fundamental change in approach is apparently found in § 4 (a), which as adopted contains provisions (1) conditioning the effectiveness of the Act on seven-state ratification of the Colorado River Compact or alternatively on California's agreement to limit its annual consumption of Colorado River water, together with six-state ratification of the Compact; and (2) giving permission to California. Arizona, and Nevada to enter a further compact apportioning certain waters to the latter two States pursuant to a stated formula.

It is manifest that § 4 (a), on which the Court so heavily relies, neither apportions the waters of the river nor vests power in any official to make such an apportionment. The first paragraph does not grant any water to anyone; it merely conditions the Act's effectiveness on seven-state ratification of the Compact or on six-state ratification, plus California's agreement to a limitation, i. e., a ceiling, on her appropriations. The source of authority to make such appropriations must be found elsewhere. And the second paragraph of § 4 (a), suggesting a particular interstate agreement, similarly makes no apportionment of water among the States and delegates no power to any official to make such an apportionment. Indeed, it was accepted by the Senator from California (Mr. Johnson) only after the following colloquy with its proponent, Senator Pittman of Nevada:

"Mr. JOHNSON. . . . [W]hat I want to make clear is that this amendment shall not be construed hereafter by any of the parties to it or any of the States as being the expression of the will or the demand or the request of the Congress of the United States.

"Mr. PITTMAN. Exactly, not.

"Mr. JOHNSON. Very well, then.

"Mr. PITTMAN. It is not the request of Congress.

"Mr. JOHNSON. I accept the amendment, then." 70 Cong. Rec. 472.

Senator Johnson would surely have been surprised to learn that the formula which was not even "the request of Congress" was in truth one which the Secretary was authorized to force down the throats of the States if they did not voluntarily agree to it.

Even this brief summary, I think, casts the gravest doubts upon the Court's construction of the Project Act as abolishing state law and accepted principles of equitable apportionment in effecting allocations of water among the States. A more detailed analysis will, I believe, demonstrate the incorrectness of the Court's conclusions on this score and will reveal the constitutional difficulties inherent in the uncontrolled delegation of power resulting from those conclusions.

II.

THE BACKGROUND OF THE BOULDER CANYON PROJECT ACT.

Judicial apportionment of interstate waters was established long before the Project Act as an effective means of resolving interstate water disputes. Kansas v. Colorado, 206 U. S. 46. Its acceptability had never been questioned. Priority of appropriation, the basic determinant of judicial apportionment as enunciated in Wyoming v. Colorado, 259 U. S. 419, was the law in six of the Colorado Basin States,[4] and senior appropriations were respected in the seventh.[5] The law of appropriation, which rests on the basic principle that a water right depends on beneficial use and which gives priority of right to the appropriator first in time, had been repeatedly declared to be indispensable to the development of the arid lands of the West.[6]

This backdrop of firm dedication to the principles of appropriation and of judicial apportionment is critical to an understanding of congressional purpose with respect to the Project Act. It is also critical to recognize that congressional compromise with these deeply respected principles was only partial; the problems facing Congress as a result of Wyoming v. Colorado were narrow. No Senator or Representative ever suggested that judicial apportionment was generally inappropriate; no Senator or Representative ever inveighed against the law of appropriation as such. The first problem was simply this: Interstate application of the doctrine of priority, unlimited by equitable considerations, threatened to deprive the four Upper Basin States of their fair share of the Colorado River because they were not so quick as California in development. The purpose of the Compact was simply to limit traditional doctrines to the extent necessary to avoid this extreme and harsh result, and to eliminate long and costly litigation.

It was perfectly plain that the Colorado River Compact merely guaranteed to the upper States a specified quantity of water immune from priorities below, subject to stated delivery requirements; it did nothing whatever to interfere with the law of priorities or the principles of equitable apportionment among the States of the Lower Basin.[7] It was precisely because it did not that Arizona refused to approve either the Project Act or the Compact until something was done to safeguard her share of Lower Basin water.[8] Similarly, the upper States feared that in the absence of ratification by Arizona, California would be free to appropriate all the Lower Basin's share under the Compact, and Arizona, not limited by that document, would be free to appropriate, as against the upper States, water the Compact sought to apportion to the Upper Basin.[9]

The remaining problem, therefore, was that California's acquisition of priorities as against Arizona and the upper States had to be further limited. A ceiling had to be put on her interstate appropriative priorities. Solution of this narrow problem likewise did not require complete abrogation of the principles of priority and interstate judicial apportionment.

Still another, and profoundly significant, factor in understanding the effect of the Project Act on the law of appropriation and judicial apportionment is the pervasive hostility that many westerners had to any form of federal control of water rights. Colorado's Delph Carpenter, who was as much responsible as any man for both the Compact and the contract requirement of § 5 of the Project Act, testified in 1925 to what he termed an insidious and calculated policy of the National Government, fostered particularly by the Departments of Interior and Justice, to encroach upon state prerogatives and supersede state authority with respect to the distribution of water. He made it clear, as did Wyoming's Senator Kendrick, that he deemed this policy oppressive, destructive, and deplorable.[10] Utah's Senator King made the same objection on the floor of the Senate. 69 Cong. Rec. 10262. When it was suggested that Congress might legislate to meet the problem of California's threatened preemption of the river, a storm of doubt arose as to its constitutional power to do so. Upper Basin and Arizona spokesmen—those who were to be benefited by limiting appropriations—repeatedly insisted that the only constitutional ways of apportioning the river were by suit in this Court or by interstate compact.[11] And Senator Bratton of New Mexico, hardly an opponent of the Project Act, objected that by merely suggesting in § 4 (a) the terms of a compact which the States were free to modify or to reject, Congress was infringing upon state sovereignty. 70 Cong. Rec. 470-471.

Congress' entire approach to the problems of prior appropriation was governed by this deep-seated hostility to federal dictation of water rights. When plans for development of the Lower Basin threatened the rights of the upper States, they did not seek the simple (and in my view constitutionally unobjectionable) solution of a legislative apportionment. They employed instead the cumbersome method of interstate compact, which required authorization by Congress and by seven state legislatures prior to negotiation and ratification by the same eight bodies thereafter. When it began to appear that Arizona would not ratify the Compact, Congress still did not legislate a general apportionment. It built the statute around the provisions of the Compact, insisting on ratification by as many States as possible, even at the cost of further delaying the already overdue Project Act. It simply conditioned the use of government property and of water stored behind the dam on compliance with the Compact. Attempts to divide the Lower Basin water by interstate agreement continued through the Denver Conference called by the Upper Basin Governors in the summer of 1927—nearly five years after negotiation of the Compact. Yet it was not until 1927 that an amendment was first offered to protect Arizona by a statutory limitation on California's consumption, and it was not until 1928 that the proposal was adopted into the bill.[12]

Finally, when Congress ultimately resigned itself to the necessity of legislating in some way with respect to the division of Lower Basin waters, it used narrow words suitable to its narrow purpose and to its regard both for the system of judicial apportionment and appropriation and for the rights of the States. Even then Congress did not attempt to legislate an apportionment of Lower Basin water; it simply prescribed a ceiling for California. In the words of Senator Johnson, "We write, then, that California shall use perpetually only a specific amount of water, naming the maximum amount which may be used." 69 Cong. Rec. 7250. Even this, Congress was unwilling to do directly. As reported from committee, the bill contained a provision directing the Secretary of the Interior to limit California's consumption in the exercise of his power of contract.[13] But this was replaced by the present provision, which reached the same result not via the Secretary's contract authority but by the awkward device of requiring California's legislature to consent to the limitation as a condition precedent to the effectiveness of the Project Act. And this was not all; to end the tale Congress added to § 4 (a) specific authorization to Arizona, California, and Nevada to enter into an agreement to complete the division of the Lower Basin water—the same cumbersome substitute for direct congressional apportionment that had been abortively mooted for six years.

This history bears recapitulation. First, the law of appropriation, basic to western water law, was greatly respected, and the solution of interstate water disputes by judicial apportionment in this Court was well established and accepted. Second, the problems created by these doctrines as applied in Wyoming v. Colorado were narrow ones, not requiring for their solution complete abrogation of well-tried principles; existing law was quite adequate to deal with all questions save those Congress expressly solved by imposing a ceiling on California. Third, Congress throughout the dispute exhibited great reluctance to interfere with the division of water by legislation, because of a deep and fundamental mistrust of federal intervention and a profound regard for state sovereignty, shared by many influential members. Finally, when Congress was forced to legislate with respect to this problem or face defeat of the entire Project Act, it chose narrow terms appropriate to the narrow problem before it, and even then acted only indirectly to require California's consent to limiting her consumption.

It is inconceivable that such a Congress intended that the sweeping federal power which it declined to exercise —a power even the most avid partisans of national authority might hesitate to grant to a single administrator —be exercised at the unbridled discretion of an administrative officer, especially in the light of complaints registered about "bureaucratic" and "oppressive" interference of the Department which that very officer headed.[14] It is utterly incredible that a Congress unwilling because of concern for States' rights even to limit California's maximum consumption to 4,400,000 acre-feet without the consent of her legislature intended to give the Secretary of the Interior authority without California's consent to reduce her share even below that quantity in a shortage.

III.

THE AUTHORITY OF THE SECRETARY UNDER SECTION 5 OF THE PROJECT ACT.

The Court holds that § 5 of the Project Act, which empowers the Secretary to contract for water delivery and forbids delivery of stored water without a contract, displaces the law of apportionment among the Lower Basin States, giving the Secretary power to divide the water by contract and to distribute the burden of shortages, without respecting appropriations.

But it does not follow that because no user is entitled to stored water without a contract the Secretary may award or withhold contracts independently of priorities. In fact, § 5 reflects no such intention. The Secretary's power to contract upon appropriate financial charges for water delivery, not included in the early bills, was added during the 1926 hearings in response to a request from Secretary of the Interior Work that users of water, as well as of power, be made to bear the cost of the project.[15] At the same time § 4 (b) for the first time provided that no work under the Act should begin until these revenues were assured by the Secretary's contracts. There was yet no provision prohibiting deliveries without contracts.[16]

Thus originally purely a financial tool, the contract power was later made to serve the additional purpose of enforcing the Compact's provisions against Arizona in the absence of her ratification. At the urging of the upper States § 8 had been amended to subject the United States in operating the dam to the Compact, to condition the enjoyment of the dam's benefits on compliance with the Compact, and to require that contracts from the United States should so provide.[17] The upper States then insisted on inserting the requirement in § 5 that no one was to receive stored water without a contract, expressly and solely for the purpose of tying the Compact's enforcement to the contract power.[18] There was no intent to confer absolute power to grant or withhold. Indeed, to give effect to priorities in time of shortage, up to the maximum quantities permitted California by § 4 (a), tends to promote the stability of water uses, a policy Congress sought to further in § 5 itself by requiring that contracts be for permanent service. In short, disregard of appropriations in one State in favor of those in another, except as required by the inter-basin apportionment of the Compact or by the California limitation, was no part of the purpose of this section; it was designed to insure revenue and to enforce the Compact and the California limitation.[19]

When the provision for water delivery contracts was first inserted in the Swing bill in 1926, it prescribed that "Contracts respecting water for domestic uses may be for permanent service but subject to rights of prior appropriators."[20] Proponents of the bill later altered this provision to apply to irrigation contracts as well as to require, rather than simply to permit, that contracts be for permanent service.[21] At the request of the upper States, the phrase "subject to rights of prior appropriators" was deleted.[22] The Court concludes from this bit of history that Congress considered but rejected the suggestion that the law of appropriation govern the distribution of water stored in Lake Mead. But deletion or rejection of a proposed amendment is not strong evidence of legislative intention; the reasons for deletion may be any of a great number, not the least frequent of which is that the suggestion is redundant. Here it seems clear that there was a further reason for the change. The phrase was dropped at the same time the provision requiring each user to have a contract was added. Under the bill as it stood prior to this no contract was required, and new contracts were made junior to all prior appropriators, even those initiating or perfecting rights only after the statute became effective. As amended the bill required a contract of every user of stored waters, and the deleted clause was no longer in accord with the contractual plan. It is surely stretching things to suggest that deletion of this no longer accurate language signifies that the Secretary may award contracts on his own authority, without regard for priorities that would obtain under state law.

In support of its construction of § 5 the Court relies in large part upon an exchange between Senator Johnson and Senator Walsh of Montana. 70 Cong. Rec. 168. The only thing this colloquy seems to make clear is that Senator Johnson had not comprehensively analyzed the relationship between § 5 and the law of appropriation. First he thought the Secretary would be required to deliver water to those who had appropriated it; then he said this would be required "[i]f they contract"; then he agreed the Secretary might withhold water "as he sees fit"; then he "doubt[ed] very much" whether the Secretary could disregard Los Angeles' appropriations; finally he said "possibly" the Secretary might utterly ignore appropriations. This shifting dialogue can scarcely be deemed an authoritative, or even useful, aid to construction of the statute.

Nor is there warrant for the Court's reliance on the statements of such opponents of the bill as Utah's Representative Colton and Arizona's Representative Douglas. Objections of opponents of a bill are seldom significant guides to its construction. See Schwegmann Bros. v. Calvert Distillers Corp., 341 U. S. 384, 394-395. And in any event in this instance the opponents themselves were far from consistent in their views.[23]

Of far greater significance are the statements of the bill's supporters, which confirm that no power to ignore appropriations was given to the Secretary.[24] Representative Swing, author of the bill, responded to Mr. Hayden's assertion that such a power was given with an emphatic denial: "the distribution will either be by agreement between the States or under their respective laws." House Hearings, supra, note 1, at 32. The following year he explained that the United States would not dispose of water rights under the bill; it would merely store water belonging to persons acquiring their rights under state law. See pp. 604-605, supra. In 1928, defending the House bill against an Arizona witness' charge that California might appropriate the entire Lower Basin supply, Mr. Swing did not dispute the statement as to California's rights but reinforced it by declaring that Arizona was free to make appropriations too. Hearings before House Committee on Irrigation and Reclamation on H. R. 5773, 70th Cong., 1st Sess. 57-58. He later assured the House that notwithstanding the bill Arizona "still has the benefit of the law of prior appropriation, and she still has the right to the beneficial use of any of the water she is able to put to use." 69 Cong. Rec. 9781. Delph Carpenter, proponent of the § 5 contract requirement, said that it was designed to burden storage water with the Compact, and thus to protect the Upper Basin, and that "[i]t has nothing to do with the interstate relations between Arizona and California."[25] Senator Johnson, sponsor of the Senate bill, told the Senate the bill was made a part of the reclamation law, which "specifically protects each State in its water rights and in the rights of the citizens of those States to water." 68 Cong. Rec. 4292. Senator Pittman insisted there was nothing in the bill (prior to the California limitation) to prevent either Arizona or California from appropriating all the water she could use.[26] Senator Phipps, whose amendment became the California limitation, declared that any dispute over the relative rights of Arizona and of Los Angeles would be resolved by the Secretary in accordance with priority of appropriation and the normal preference for domestic over agricultural use.[27]

Of further weight in supporting the view that Congress did not construe § 5 to destroy the law of appropriation and apportionment is the fact that the entire controversy over the California limitation took place after § 5 was added to the bill. Utah was so certain that Arizona remained free to appropriate water despite § 5 that she repealed her ratification of the six-state Compact thereafter.[28] While the original committee amendment to the Act would have required the Secretary to limit California's appropriations, the debates evidence no conviction that the Secretary had even a permissive authority to do so by virtue of the unamended § 5.

IV.

THE BEARING OF OTHER PROVISIONS OF THE PROJECT ACT.

Nothing in the Project Act expressly gives the Secretary power to ignore appropriations so long as financial conditions are met and the Compact and limitations are observed. Senators Hayden and Pittman, as the Court notes, did indicate that § 4 (a) provided for an apportionment of the water, although even they did not suggest that § 4 (a) gave any authority to the Secretary to make an apportionment by his contracts or to allocate the burdens in time of shortage. But in any event, as already noted, pp. 606-607, supra, § 4 does not by its terms make an apportionment; rather it simply requires six-state ratification of the Compact and an agreement by California to limit her share as conditions on the effectiveness of the Act, and authorizes an apportionment by the States themselves. In the words of Senator Johnson, the provision

". . . does not divide the water between Arizona and California. It fixes a maximum amount beyond which California can not go." 70 Cong. Rec. 385.

Nor does § 6, which requires that the dam be operated for the satisfaction of "present perfected rights" among other purposes, indicate by negative implication that the Secretary may ignore all other appropriations. This provision was drafted by the Upper Basin States in order to insure that the condition of the Compact had been met to relieve them from the claims of perfected users below.[29] That condition was the construction of an adequate storage reservoir against which those claims could be asserted; the Compact has nothing to do with whether rights perfected under state law since 1929 may be ignored by the Secretary in awarding contracts. Section 8 (b), which subjects the United States and all users of the Project to any compact allocating among the Lower Basin States "the benefits, including power, arising from the use of water accruing to said States," and which subjects such an agreement, if made after January 1, 1929, to any delivery contracts made prior to its approval, is similarly no authority for the Court's conclusion. Legislative history is virtually silent as to the reason for giving such contracts precedence, but the provision seems simply to have been intended to promote the entering of contracts by insuring their permanence in accordance with the requirement of § 5.[30] There is no indication in § 8 (b) whether or not the Secretary is free in awarding contracts to ignore existing appropriations; it merely evidences a policy that rights so perfected as to have been reduced to a contract for delivery at a consideration, whatever the basis on which they should be awarded, ought not to be destroyed by a subsequent interstate agreement.

If the statute were completely silent as to whether the Secretary may disregard appropriations, the normal inference would be that Congress did not mean to displace existing law. Enough has been said of the statute's history to buttress this inference beyond question. Moreover, the statute is by no means silent on this matter. The references in § 8 (a) and (b) to "appropriators" of water stored or delivered by the Project, and in § 4 (a) to the taking of steps "to initiate or perfect any claims to the use of water" made available by the dam, are only the least evidence.[31] Section 14 provides that the Reclamation Act shall govern the operation of Hoover Dam except as the Project Act otherwise provides. Section 8 of the Reclamation Act, 32 Stat. 390, 43 U. S. C. § 383, directs the Secretary of the Interior in carrying out his duties under the Act to proceed in accordance with state and territorial laws and declares that nothing in the federal act "shall in any way affect any right of any State or of the Federal Government or of any landowner, appropriator, or user of water in, to, or from any interstate stream or the waters thereof."

Both Representative Swing and Senator Johnson emphasized that this provision was deliberately incorporated into the Project Act to safeguard from federal destruction the rights of the States to their shares of the water.[32] This Court made clear in Wyoming v. Colorado, 259 U. S. 419, 463, that by thus protecting the rights of any State in an interstate stream Congress intended to leave untouched the law of interstate equitable apportionment. Ivanhoe Irrig. Dist. v. McCracken, 357 U. S. 275, 291, despite its dictum that § 8 applies only to the acquisition of rights by the United States and not to its operation of a dam, holds only that the clear command of § 5 of the Reclamation Act, 32 Stat. 389, 43 U. S. C. § 431—that water deliveries to each user not exceed the quantity required for 160 acres—prevails over state law, not that state law does not generally govern priorities in the use of water from federal reclamation projects under § 8.[33] The Court in Ivanhoe expressly stated that it was reaching its narrow conclusion:

"[w]ithout passing generally on the coverage of § 8 in the delicate area of federal-state relations in the irrigation field . . . ." 357 U. S., at 292.

This general question, with reference to what is undoubtedly the most important single water project in the United States, is precisely the question before us today. In view of the language of the Project Act, as well as its background and legislative history, there can, I think, be no doubt of the answer.

V.

THE LACK OF STANDARDS DEFINING THE LIMITS OF THE SECRETARY'S POWER.

The Secretary, the Court holds, has already apportioned the waters of the mainstream by his contracts with Arizona and Nevada and has done so in accordance with the formula suggested as a basis for an interstate agreement in § 4 (a). This holding may come as a surprise to those responsible for a statement such as that in the Arizona contract, which provides that its terms are

". . . without prejudice to, any of the respective contentions of said states and water users as to . . . (5) what limitations on use, rights of use, and relative priorities exist as to the waters of the Colorado River system . . . ."

But whether the quantum of the Secretary's apportionment was intentional or inadvertent, the Court holds that such an apportionment has been made, and the relevant question for the future is the one that is perhaps primarily responsible for this litigation: How is the burden of any shortage to be borne by the Lower Basin States? This question is not decided; the Court simply states that the initial determination is for the Secretary to make.

What yardsticks has Congress laid down for him to follow? There is, it is true, a duty imposed on the Secretary under § 6 to satisfy "present perfected rights," and if these rights are defined as those perfected on or before the effective date of the Act, it has been estimated that California's share amounts to approximately 3,000,000 acre-feet annually. This, then, would be the floor provided by the Act for California, assuming enough water is available to satisfy such present perfected rights. And the Act also has provided a ceiling for California: the 4,400,000 acre-feet of water (plus one-half of surplus) described in § 4 (a).

But what of that wide area between these two outer limits? Here, when we look for the standards defining the Secretary's authority, we find nothing.[34] Under the Court's construction of the Act, in other words, Congress has made a gift to the Secretary of almost 1,500,000 acre-feet of water a year, to allocate virtually as he pleases in the event of any shortage preventing the fulfillment of all of his delivery commitments.

The delegation of such unrestrained authority to an executive official raises, to say the least, the gravest constitutional doubts. See Schechter Poultry Corp. v. United States, 295 U. S. 495; Panama Refining Co. v. Ryan, 293 U. S. 388; cf. Youngstown Sheet & Tube Co. v. Sawyer, 343 U. S. 579, 587-589. The principle that authority granted by the legislature must be limited by adequate standards serves two primary functions vital to preserving the separation of powers required by the Constitution.[35] First, it insures that the fundamental policy decisions in our society will be made not by an appointed official but by the body immediately responsible to the people. Second, it prevents judicial review from becoming merely an exercise at large by providing the courts with some measure against which to judge the official action that has been challenged.

The absence of standards under the Court's construction is an instructive illustration of these points. The unrestrained power to determine the burden of shortages is the power to make a political decision of the highest order. Indeed, the political pressures that will doubtless be brought to bear on the Secretary as a result of this decision are disturbing to contemplate. Furthermore, whatever the Secretary decides to do, this Court will surely be unable effectively to review his actions, since it will not know what guides were intended by Congress to govern those actions.

These substantial constitutional doubts do not, of course, lead to the conclusion that the Project Act must be held invalid. Rather, they buttress the conviction, already firmly grounded in the Act and its history, that no such authority was vested in the Secretary by Congress. Its purpose instead was to leave these matters to state law, and developed principles of equitable apportionment, subject only to the explicit exceptions provided in the Act.

For these reasons I respectfully dissent from the construction which the Court puts upon this aspect of the Act.

Notes

[1] Hearings before House Committee on Irrigation and Reclamation on H. R. 6251 and H. R. 9826, 69th Cong., 1st Sess. 163.

[2] Hearings before House Committee on Rules on H. R. 9826, 69th Cong., 2d Sess. 116. The bill then under consideration, as recommended by the House Committee on Irrigation and Reclamation, appears in H. R. Rep. No. 1657, 69th Cong., 2d Sess. 29-34.

[3] The only change that need be noted for present purposes is the addition of a clause requiring contracts to conform to § 4 (a), discussed below, as well as to the Compact.

[4] Arizona: Clough v. Wing, 2 Ariz. 371, 17 P. 453; Colorado: Coffin v. Left Hand Ditch Co., 6 Colo. 443; Nevada: Jones v. Adams, 19 Nev. 78, 6 P. 442; New Mexico: Albuquerque Land & Irr. Co. v. Gutierrez, 10 N. Mex. 177, 61 P. 357; Utah: Stowell v. Johnson, 7 Utah 215, 26 P. 290; Wyoming: Moyer v. Preston, 6 Wyo. 308, 44 P. 845.

[5] California: Osgood v. El Dorado Water & Deep Gravel Mining Co., 56 Cal. 571.

[6] E. g., Coffin v. Left Hand Ditch Co., 6 Colo. 443, 446-447, 449-450; Stowell v.

Johnson, 7 Utah 215, 225, 26 P. 290, 291; Willey v. Decker, 11 Wyo. 496, 515-524, 73 P. 210, 215-218. "Irrigation," said the Nevada court, ". . . would be strangled by the enforcement of the riparian principle." Twaddle v. Winters, 29 Nev. 88, 106, 85 P. 280, 284.

[7] Ward Bannister, Denver attorney and spokesman for the Upper Basin States, said that "[t]he purpose of the compact is to provide the three lower States with a fund of water from which they may appropriate and the four upper States with a fund of water from which they may appropriate." Hearings before House Committee on Irrigation and Reclamation on H. R. 2903, 68th Cong., 1st Sess. 232.

[8] See the remarks of Senator Hayden, 70 Cong. Rec. 388.

[9] See, e. g., H. R. Rep. No. 1657, 69th Cong., 2d Sess., pt. 2, 3-4; Hearings, supra, note 2, at 34-37.

[10] Hearings before Senate Committee on Irrigation and Reclamation pursuant to S. Res. No. 320, 68th Cong., 2d Sess. 663-675. "It was the oppression of the National Government strangling development, preventing development in the States. . . . These two experiences and others taught Colorado, Wyoming, and New Mexico the extent to which a department of the United States would go in overriding State authority and oppressing whole communities. . . . Thus it came to the attention of the States, that the United States Government intended to supersede all State law and override State authority on that river. . . . [A]ny desire by a governmental bureau to ultimately, by insiduous [sic] or other methods, take over the control and dominion of the streams within the States and to override State authority at once becomes not only abhorrent but gives rise to a feeling of bitter resentment and sounds a call to arms for self-defense. . . ." Id., at 663, 665, 671, 673. See also his remarks at Hearings, supra, note 1, at 146-157.

[11] Senator KING: "If the Senator means by his statement that the Federal Government may go into a stream, whether it be the Colorado River, the Sacramento River, or a river in the State of Montana, and put its powerful hands down upon the stream and say, `This is mine; I can build a dam there and allocate water to whom I please, regardless of other rights, either suspended, inchoate, or perfected,' I deny the position which the Senator takes." 70 Cong. Rec. 169. The Senator in question was Carl Hayden; he denied that his statement, which concerned his authorization for a compact among the three lower States, meant any such thing.

Senator PHIPPS: "I am firmly convinced that there must be voluntary ratification on the part of each interested State in order to make the compact effective. This is the only method of settling possible controversies permanently and of putting the water of the stream to its highest beneficial use. It is the only satisfactory method; it is the only legal method to avoid proceedings in the courts which would prove costly and almost interminable." 68 Cong. Rec. 4515.

Senator HAYDEN: "There are only two ways in which this controversy can be settled. Either the States can agree upon an equitable apportionment of waters of the Colorado River or, in the absence of a compact, the Supreme Court of the United States can determine what the rights of the various States are in on [sic] that stream. . . . Arizona denies that it is within the power of Congress to apportion the waters of an interstate stream among the States." Hearings, supra, note 2, at 75, 76. (Emphasis added.)

Representative COLTON: "I have been informed that an attorney for the Reclamation Service of the United States claims that Congress has the power to allocate and apportion all of the Colorado River among the States regardless of their wishes in the matter. Such a theory is abhorrent to our whole plan of government and particularly to the theory on which our whole system of water rights has been built up." Hearings before House Committee on Irrigation and Reclamation on H. R. 5773, 70th Cong., 1st Sess. 414.

Representative LEATHERWOOD: "[T]here are only two agencies that can allocate the waters of this great river, the States themselves by treaty ratified by the Congress of the United States, or by the judicial branch of the Government; for the Congress has no power to allocate any of the waters of this river or any other river where the doctrine of prior appropriation is in force." Hearings, supra, note 2, at 31.

WARD BANNISTER: "[T]here is nothing in the Federal Constitution upon which to base the power of the Federal Government to divide this water among the States. . . . [T]he same thing that would invalidate a provision inserted by Congress direct would invalidate any rule promulgated by the Secretary of the Interior under Congressional permission, and the upper States would find themselves utterly helpless." Hearings, supra, n. 7, at 195.

[12] 68 Cong. Rec. 4763; S. Rep. No. 592, 70th Cong., 1st Sess. 2.

[13] S. Rep. No. 592, 70th Cong., 1st Sess. 2.

[14] See note 10, supra, and accompanying text.

[15] Hearings, supra, note 1, at 6, 46.

[16] H. R. 9826, 69th Cong., 1st Sess., § 5.

[17] S. 1868, 69th Cong., 1st Sess.; H. R. 6251, 69th Cong., 1st Sess.; H. R. 9826, 69th Cong., 1st Sess. This amendment, wrote Secretary Work in recommending the bill, "provides for the distribution and use of all water for irrigation, power and otherwise, in accordance with the Colorado River compact." Hearings, supra, note 1, at 8.

[18] See notes 1, 2, supra, and accompanying text. Contracts were later made subject also to the California limitation in § 4 (a).

[19] It is significant to contrast the language giving the Secretary authority to enter water delivery contracts with that in § 5 (c), relating to the distribution of electrical power. The latter provision explicitly gives the Secretary authority to resolve conflicts in applications, referring him for the governing standards to "the policy expressed in the Federal Water Power Act as to conflicting applications for permits and licenses."

[20] Hearings, supra, note 1, at 12.

[21] Id., at 115.

[22] Id., at 97, 115.

[23] Thus, almost in the same breath with which Representative Colton made his then seemingly dire prediction of national control, he declared that "Arizona is not a party

at all to this compact. She and her citizens may appropriate water at any time." 69 Cong. Rec. 9648. Arizona, as has already been pointed out, was busily opposing the bill on the specific ground that it left California free to appropriate from the river.

[24] The one apparent exception to the unanimity of view among the bill's supporters is the statement in Representative Smith's report of the third Swing bill to the House: "All rights respecting water or power under the project are, under the terms of the bill, to be disposed of by contract by the Government. It is not reasonable to assume that the Government will do anything of an unfair or prejudicial nature to Arizona." H. R. Rep. No. 1657, 69th Cong., 2d Sess. 11.

[25] See note 1, supra, and accompanying text. Mr. Carpenter's remarks also included the following: " `Except by contract made as herein stated' means this: If the flow of the Colorado River is controlled and regulated by the construction of the Black Canyon Dam, and any person in the State of Arizona attempt to take any water out of the stream which has been discharged from the reservoir and is being carried in the stream bed, as a natural conduit, for delivery to lower users, this law would be brought into effect and he would be prevented from using any of that water independent of the Colorado River compact but unincumbered by any other condition for the benefit of California and Nevada. In other words, the compact does not disturb the rights between Arizona, California, and Nevada, inter sese, as to their portion of the water." Hearings, supra, note 1, at 163.

[26] "If a dam shall be built at Boulder Canyon it will impound certain waters and equate the flow below. The water below will be subject to appropriation and use by both California and Arizona . . . . In other words, there is nothing in this proposed legislation that could prevent Arizona from appropriating from the Colorado River within her borders all of the water she could use for irrigation." 68 Cong. Rec. 4412.

[27] "It seems to me that in resolving such a difficulty, should it arise, there would be taken into consideration the fact that water for domestic use should take priority over water intended for purposes of irrigation. Aside from that, these filings are first in point as compared with those to which the Senator from Arizona referred. They are for a superior use, and, in addition thereto, the applicant who has made the filing has pursued the proper course in developing the manner of appropriation or the manner of diverting the water and putting it to the highest beneficial use. I do not anticipate any difficulty on that score in resolving the question of priority by the Secretary of the Interior." 70 Cong. Rec. 169.

[28] See 68 Cong. Rec. 3064-3065; Hearings before House Committee on Irrigation and Reclamation on H. R. 5773, 70th Cong., 1st Sess. 191, 193, 214-215.

[29] See Hearings, supra, note 1, at 98, 116, 117.

[30] Delph Carpenter said that the Secretary's contracts should be lagged for only a limited period of time in order to give the States complete freedom to agree. Id., at 204.

[31] It should also be noted that, as the Master held, § 18, quoted ante, p. 585, clearly leaves each State free to apply its own law in determining rights among users

within its borders. The Court's strained reading of this provision emasculates it entirely and sacrifices even matters of solely intrastate concern on the altar of federal supremacy.

[32] See pp. 604-605, 619-620, supra.

[33] Nor is anything said in City of Fresno v. California, 372 U. S. 627, relevant here, since the Court there stated only that if the Government exercises its power of eminent domain, "the effect of § 8 in such a case is to leave to state law the definition of the property interests, if any, for which compensation must be made." 372 U. S., at 630. Fresno did not consider the question now presented: the effect of § 8 in the absence of any exercise of the federal power of eminent domain.

[34] Nor, I submit, does the Court suggest any standards. Certainly, there is nothing in the enumeration of purposes in § 6 which will be of any assistance in helping the Secretary allocate the burden of shortages among competing irrigation and domestic uses within and among the Lower Basin States.

[35] See the discussion in Comment, 14 Stan. L. Rev. 372.

Justice Harlan's dissent in McNeese v. Board of Ed. for Community Unit School District (June 3, 1963) [Appendix omitted]

MR. JUSTICE HARLAN, dissenting.

In Burford v. Sun Oil Co., 319 U. S. 315, 317-318, this Court said:

"Although a federal equity court does have jurisdiction of a particular proceeding, it may, in its sound discretion, whether its jurisdiction is invoked on the ground of diversity of citizenship or otherwise, `refuse to enforce or protect legal rights, the exercise of which may be prejudicial to the public interest'; [citing United States v. Dern, 289 U. S. 352, 360] for it `is in the public interest that federal courts of equity should exercise their discretionary power with proper regard for the rightful independence of state governments in carrying out their domestic policy.'. . . [Citing Pennsylvania v. Williams, 294 U. S. 176, 185.] Assuming that the federal district court had jurisdiction, should it, as a matter of sound equitable discretion, have declined to exercise that jurisdiction here?"

This wise approach has been followed by the lower federal courts in "school segregation" cases (see, e.g., Carson v. Board of Education, 227 F. 2d 789; Carson v. Warlick, 238 F. 2d 724; Covington v. Edwards, 264 F. 2d 780; Holt v. Raleigh City Board of Education, 265 F. 2d 95; Parham v. Dove, 271 F. 2d 132; Shepard v. Board of Education, 207 F. Supp. 341), and more than once this Court has refused to interfere (see Carson v. Warlick, supra, cert. denied, 353 U. S. 910; Holt v. Raleigh City Board of Education, supra, cert. denied, 361 U. S. 818).[1] For several reasons I think the present case is peculiarly one where, as was said in Burford (at p. 334), "a sound respect for the independence of state action requires the federal equity court to stay its hand."

1. It is apparent on the face of the complaint that this case is quite atypical of others that have come before this Court, in that the Chenot School's student body includes

both white and Negro students—in almost equal numbers —and in that none of the petitioners (or others whom they purport to represent) has been refused enrollment in the school. The alleged discriminatory practices relate, rather, to the manner in which this particular school district was formed and to the way in which the internal affairs of the school are administered. These are matters in which the federal courts should not initially become embroiled. Their exploration and correction, if need be, are much better left to local authority in the first instance.

2. There is nothing that leaves room for serious doubt as to the efficacy of the administrative remedy which Illinois has provided. (The text of the statute is set forth in the Appendix to this opinion.) The fact that the Superintendent of Public Instruction himself possesses no corrective power and that he can only "request" the Attorney General to enforce his findings by appropriate court proceedings does not, in my opinion, leave the administrative proceeding sanctionless (compare United States Alkali Export Assn. v. United States, 325 U. S. 196), or, as in Lane v. Wilson, 307 U. S. 268, serve to remove this case from the "exhaustion" requirements of Burford. If the Superintendent refuses to activate the Attorney General, his decision (as with a contrary one) is subject to judicial review. It is not suggested that the Attorney General could not also be compelled to act if he improperly refused to do so. And it must of course be assumed that these two responsible public officials will fully perform their sworn duty. Moreover, the terms of the statute itself which, among other things, provides for the use of compulsory process, strongly attest to the fact that the administrative remedy was intended as serious business and not as an exercise that might abort before fulfillment.

Nor can this administrative remedy otherwise be regarded as deficient. The fact that it takes a minimal number of school district residents to initiate a complaint before the Superintendent can hardly be deemed an untoward or unduly burdensome requirement. And the proceeding surely finds a strong practical even though "indirect sanction" (ante, p. 676) in the power of the Superintendent at least to make it more difficult for a school, guilty of racial discrimination, to obtain state financial aid—either by revoking "recognition" of the school district (ante, p. 675) or, as suggested to us by respondents' attorneys, by refusing to certify such a school for state aid.[2]

3. Finally, we should be slow to hold unavailing an administrative remedy afforded by a State which long before Brown v. Board of Education, 347 U. S. 483, had outlawed both by its constitution and statutes racial discrimination in its public schools,[3] and which since Brown has passed the further implementing legislation drawn in question in this litigation (Appendix). For myself I am unwilling to assume that these solemn constitutional and legislative pronouncements of Illinois mean anything less than what they say or that the rights assured by them and by the Fourteenth Amendment will not be fully and promptly vindicated by the State if petitioners can make good their grievances.

I would affirm.

Notes

[1] Cases such as Mannings v. Board of Public Instruction, 277 F. 2d 370, and Borders v. Rippy, 247 F. 2d 268 (where the school boards had taken no affirmative steps whatever to desegregate the schools), and Orleans Parish School Board v. Bush, 242 F. 2d 156, and Gibson v. Board of Public Instruction, 246 F. 2d 913 (arising in States having school segregation statutes on their books), are wide of the mark in the circumstances of this case.

[2] Section 18-12 of the School Code of Illinois provides in part:

"No State aid claim may be filed for any district unless the clerk or secretary of the school board executes and files with the Superintendent of Public Instruction, on forms prescribed by him, a sworn statement that the district has complied with the requirements of Section 10-22.5 in regard to the non-segregation of pupils on account of color, creed, race or nationality."

[3] As early as 1901 the Supreme Court of Illinois in People v. Mayor of Alton, 193 Ill. 309, 312, 61 N. E. 1077, 1078, construing Art. VIII, § 1, of the Illinois Constitution, held:

"The complaint of the relator is that his children have been excluded, on account of their color, from the public school of said city located near his residence and been required to attend a school located a mile and a half distant from his residence, established exclusively for colored children. Such complaint is not met by showing that the schools established for colored children in said city equal or surpass in educational facilities the schools established in said city for white children. Under the law the common council of said city had no right to establish different schools for the white children and colored children of said city and to exclude the colored children from the schools established for white children, even though the schools established for colored children furnished educational facilities equal or superior to those of the schools established for white children."

Section 10-22.5 of the School Code of Illinois has provided since 1945 that:

". . . no pupil shall be excluded from or segregated in any such school on account of his color, race or nationality."

Sections 22-11 and 22-12 of the School Code, enacted in 1909, provide:

"Any school officer or other person who excludes or aids in excluding from the public schools, on account of color, any child who is entitled to the benefits of such school shall be fined not less than $5 nor more than $100."

"Whoever by threat, menace or intimidation prevents any colored child entitled to attend a public school in this State from attending such school shall be fined not exceeding $25."

Justice Harlan's dissent in US v. Philadelphia Nat. Bank (June 17, 1963)

MR. JUSTICE HARLAN, whom MR. JUSTICE STEWART joins, dissenting.

I suspect that no one will be more surprised than the Government to find that the Clayton Act has carried the day for its case in this Court.

In response to an apparently accelerating trend toward concentration in the commercial banking system in this country, a trend which existing laws were evidently ill-suited to control, numerous bills were introduced in Congress from 1955 to 1960.[1] During this period, the Department of Justice and the federal banking agencies[2] advocated divergent methods of dealing with the competitive aspects of bank mergers, the former urging the extension of § 7 of the Clayton Act to cover such mergers and the latter supporting a regulatory scheme under which the effect of a bank merger on competition would be only one of the factors to be considered in determining whether the merger would be in the public interest. The Justice Department's proposals were repeatedly rejected by Congress, and the regulatory approach of the banking agencies was adopted in the Bank Merger Act of 1960. See infra, pp. 379-383.

Sweeping aside the "design fashioned in the Bank Merger Act" as "predicated upon uncertainty as to the scope of § 7 of the Clayton Act (ante, p. 349), the Court today holds § 7 to be applicable to bank mergers and concludes that it has been violated in this case. I respectfully submit that this holding, which sanctions a remedy regarded by Congress as inimical to the best interests of the banking industry and the public, and which will in large measure serve to frustrate the objectives of the Bank Merger Act, finds no justification in either the terms of the 1950 amendment of the Clayton Act or the history of the statute.

I.

The key to this case is found in the special position occupied by commercial banking in the economy of this country. With respect to both the nature of the operations performed and the degree of governmental supervision involved, it is fundamentally different from ordinary manufacturing and mercantile businesses.

The unique powers of commercial banks to accept demand deposits, provide checking account services, and lend against fractional reserves permit the banking system as a whole to create a supply of "money," a function which is indispensable to the maintenance of the structure of our national economy. And the amount of the funds held by commercial banks is very large indeed; demand deposits alone represent approximately three-fourths of the money supply in the United States.[3] Since a bank's assets must be sufficiently liquid to accommodate demand withdrawals, short-term commercial and industrial loans are the major element in bank portfolios, thus making commercial banks the principal source of shortterm business credit. Many other services are also provided by banks, but in these more or less collateral areas they receive more active competition from other financial institutions.[4]

Deposit banking operations affect not only the volume of money and credit, but also the value of the dollar and the stability of the currency system. In this field, considerations other than simply the preservation of competition are relevant. Moreover, commercial banks are entrusted with the safekeeping of large amounts of funds belonging to individuals and corporations. Unlike the ordinary investor, these depositors do not regard their funds as subject to a risk of loss and, at least in the case of demand depositors, they do not receive a return for taking such a risk. A bank failure is a community disaster; its impact first strikes the bank's depositors most heavily, and then spreads throughout the economic life of the community.[5] Safety and soundness of banking practices are thus critical factors in any banking system.

The extensive blanket of state and federal regulation of commercial banking, much of which is aimed at limiting competition, reflects these factors. Since the Court's opinion describes, at some length, aspects of the supervision exercised by the federal banking agencies (ante, pp. 327-330), I do no more here than point out that, in my opinion, such regulation evidences a plain design grounded on solid economic considerations to deal with banking as a specialized field.

This view is confirmed by the Bank Merger Act of 1960 and its history.

Federal legislation dealing with bank mergers[6] dates from 1918, when Congress provided that, subject to the approval of the Comptroller of the Currency, two or more national banks could consolidate to form a new national bank;[7] similar provision was made in 1927 for the consolidation of a state and a national bank resulting in a national bank.[8] In 1952 mergers of national and state banks into national banks were authorized, also conditioned on approval by the Comptroller of the Currency.[9] In 1950 Congress authorized the theretofore prohibited[10] merger or consolidation of a national bank with a state bank when the assuming or resulting bank would be a state bank.[11] In addition, the Federal Deposit Insurance Act was amended to require the approval of the FDIC for all mergers and consolidations between insured and noninsured banks, and of specified federal banking agencies for conversions of insured banks into insured state banks if the conversion would result in the capital stock or surplus of the newly formed bank being less than that of the converting bank.[12] The Act further required insured banks merging with insured state banks to secure the approval of the Comptroller of the Currency if the assuming bank would be a national bank, and the approval of the Board of Governors of the Federal Reserve System and the FDIC, respectively, if the assuming or resulting bank would be a state member bank or nonmember insured bank.[13]

None of this legislation prescribed standards by which the appropriate federal banking agencies were to be guided in determining the significance to be attributed to the anticompetitive effects of a proposed merger. As previously noted (supra, p. 373), Congress became increasingly concerned with this problem in the 1950's. The antitrust laws apparently provided no solution; in only one case prior to 1960, United States v. Firstamerica Corp., Civil No. 38139, N. D. Cal., March 30, 1959, settled by consent decree, had either the Sherman or Clayton Act been invoked to attack a commercial bank merger.

Indeed the inapplicability to bank mergers of § 7 of the Clayton Act, even after it was amended in 1950, was, for a time, an explicit premise on which the Department of Justice performed its antitrust duties. In passing upon an application for informal clearance of a bank merger in 1955, the Department stated:

"After a complete consideration of this matter, we have concluded that this Department would not have jurisdiction to proceed under section 7 of the Clayton Act. For this reason this Department does not presently plan to take any action on this matter." Hearings before the Antitrust Subcommittee of the House Committee on the Judiciary, 84th Cong., 1st Sess., Ser. 3, pt. 3, p. 2141 (1955).

And in testifying before the Senate Committee on Banking and Currency in 1957 Attorney General Brownell, speaking of bank mergers, noted:

"On the basis of these provisions the Department of Justice has concluded, and all apparently agree, that asset acquisitions by banks are not covered by section 7 [of the Clayton Act] as amended in 1950." Hearings on the Financial Institutions Act of 1957 before a Subcommittee of the Senate Committee on Banking and Currency, 85th Cong., 1st Sess., pt. 2, p. 1030 (1957).

Similar statements were repeatedly made to Congress by Justice Department representatives in the years prior to the enactment of the Bank Merger Act.[14]

The inapplicability of § 7 to bank mergers was also an explicit basis on which Congress acted in passing the Bank Merger Act of 1960. The Senate Report on S. 1062, the bill that was finally enacted, stated:

"Since bank mergers are customarily, if not invariably, carried out by asset acquisitions, they are exempt from section 7 of the Clayton Act. (Stock acquisitions by bank holding companies, as distinguished from mergers and consolidations, are subject to both the Bank Holding Company Act of 1956 and sec. 7 of the Clayton Act.)" S. Rep. No. 196, 86th Cong., 1st Sess. 1-2 (1959).

"In 1950 (64 Stat. 1125) section 7 of the Clayton Act was amended to correct these deficiencies. Acquisitions of assets were included within the section, in addition to stock acquisitions, but only in the case of corporations subject to the jurisdiction of the Federal Trade Commission (banks, being subject to the jurisdiction of the Federal Reserve Board for purposes of the Clayton Act by virtue of section 11 of that act, were not affected)." Id., at 5.[15]

During the floor debates Representative Spence, the Chairman of the House Committee on Banking and Currency, recognized the same difficulty: "The Clayton Act is ineffective as to bank mergers because in the case of banks it covers only stock acquisitions and bank mergers are not accomplished that way." 106 Cong. Rec. 7257 (1960).[16]

But instead of extending the scope of § 7 to cover bank mergers, as numerous proposed amendments to that section were designed to accomplish,[17] Congress made the deliberate policy judgment that "it is impossible to subject bank mergers to the simple rule of section 7 of the Clayton Act. Under that act, a merger would be barred if it might tend substantially to lessen competition, regardless of the effects on the public interest." 105 Cong. Rec. 8076 (1959) (remarks of Senator Robertson, a sponsor of S. 1062). Because of the peculiar nature of the commercial banking industry, its crucial role in the economy, and its intimate connection with the fiscal and monetary operations of the Government, Congress rejected the notion that the general economic and business premises of the

Clayton Act should be the only considerations applicable to this field. Unrestricted bank competition was thought to have been a major cause of the panic of 1907 and of the bank failures of the 1930's,[18] and was regarded as a highly undesirable condition to impose on banks in the future:

"Banking is too important to depositors, to borrowers, to the Government, and the public generally, to permit unregulated and unrestricted competition in that field.

"The antitrust laws have reflected an awareness of the difference between banking and other regulated industries on the one hand, and ordinary unregulated industries and commercial enterprises on the other hand." 106 Cong. Rec. 9711 (1960) (remarks of Senator Fulbright, a sponsor of S. 1062).

"It is this distinction between banking and other businesses which justifies different treatment for bank mergers and other mergers. It was this distinction that led the Senate to reject the flat prohibition of the Clayton Act test which applies to other mergers." Id., at 9712.[19]

Thus the Committee on Banking and Currency recommended "continuance of the existing exemption from section 7 of the Clayton Act." 105 Cong. Rec. 8076 (1959). Congress accepted this recommendation; it decided to handle the problem of concentration in commercial banking "through banking laws, specially framed to fit the particular needs of the field . . . ." S. Rep. No. 196, 86th Cong., 1st Sess. 18 (1959). As finally enacted in 1960, the Bank Merger Act embodies the regulatory approach advocated by the banking agencies, vesting in them responsibility for its administration and placing the scheme within the framework of existing banking laws as an amendment to § 18 (c) of the Federal Deposit Insurance Act, 12 U. S. C. (Supp. IV, 1963), § 1828 (c).[20] It maintains the latter Act's requirement of advance approval by the appropriate federal agency for mergers between insured banks and between insured and noninsured banks (supra, pp. 375-377), but establishes that such approval is necessary in every merger of this type. To aid the respective agencies in determining whether to approve a merger, and in "the interests of uniform standards" (12 U. S. C. (Supp. IV, 1963) § 1828 (c)), the Act requires the two agencies not making the particular decision and the Attorney General to submit to the immediately responsible agency reports on the competitive factors involved. It further provides that in addition to considering the banking factors examined by the FDIC in connection with applications to become an insured bank, which focus primarily on matters of safety and soundness,[21] the approving agency "shall also take into consideration the effect of the transaction on competition (including any tendency toward monopoly), and shall not approve the transaction unless, after considering all of such factors, it finds the transaction to be in the public interest." 12 U. S. C. (Supp. IV, 1963) § 1828 (c).

The congressional purpose clearly emerges from the terms of the statute and from the committee reports, hearings, and floor debates on the bills. Time and again it was repeated that effect on competition was not to be the controlling factor in determining whether to approve a bank merger, that a merger could be approved as being in the public interest even though it would cause a substantial lessening of competition. The following statement is typical:

"The committee wants to make crystal clear its intention that the various banking factors in any particular case may be held to outweigh the competitive factors, and that the competitive factors, however favorable or unfavorable, are not, in and of themselves, controlling on the decision. And, of course, the banking agencies are not bound in their consideration of the competitive factors by the report of the Attorney General." S. Rep. No. 196, 86th Cong., 1st Sess. 24 (1959); id., at 19, 21.[22]

The foregoing statement also shows that it was the congressional intention to place the responsibility for approval squarely on the banking agencies; the report of the Attorney General on the competitive aspects of a merger was to be advisory only.[23] And there was deliberately omitted any attempt to specify or restrict the kinds of circumstances in which the agencies might properly determine that a proposed merger would be in the public interest notwithstanding its adverse effect on competition.[24]

What Congress has chosen to do about mergers and their effect on competition in the highly specialized field of commercial banking could not be more "crystal clear." (Supra, p. 382.) But in the face of overwhelming evidence to the contrary, the Court, with perfect equanimity, finds "uncertainty" in the foundations of the Bank Merger Act (ante, p. 349) and on this premise puts it aside as irrelevant to the task of construing the scope of § 7 of the Clayton Act.

I am unable to conceive of a more inappropriate case in which to overturn the considered opinion of all concerned as to the reach of prior legislation.[25] For 10 years everyone—the department responsible for antitrust law enforcement, the banking industry, the Congress, and the bar—proceeded on the assumption that the 1950 amendment of the Clayton Act did not affect bank mergers. This assumption provided a major impetus to the enactment of remedial legislation, and Congress, when it finally settled on what it thought was the solution to the problem at hand, emphatically rejected the remedy now brought to life by the Court.

The result is, of course, that the Bank Merger Act is almost completely nullified; its enactment turns out to have been an exorbitant waste of congressional time and energy. As the present case illustrates, the Attorney General's report to the designated banking agency is no longer truly advisory, for if the agency's decision is not satisfactory a § 7 suit may be commenced immediately.[26] The bank merger's legality will then be judged solely from its competitive aspects, unencumbered by any considerations peculiar to banking.[27] And if such a suit were deemed to lie after a bank merger has been consummated, there would then be introduced into this field, for the first time to any significant extent, the threat of divestiture of assets and all the complexities and disruption attendant upon the use of that sanction.[28] The only vestige of the Bank Merger Act which remains is that the banking agencies will have an initial veto.[29]

This frustration of a manifest congressional design is, in my view, a most unwarranted intrusion upon the legislative domain. I submit that whatever may have been the congressional purpose in 1950, Congress has now so plainly pronounced its current judgment that bank mergers are not within the reach of § 7 that this Court is duty bound to effectuate its choice.

But I need not rest on this proposition, for, as will now be shown, there is nothing in the 1950 amendment to § 7 or its legislative history to support the conclusion that Congress even then intended to subject bank mergers to this provision of the Clayton Act.

II.

Prior to 1950, § 7 of the Clayton Act read, in pertinent part, as follows:

"That no corporation engaged in commerce shall acquire, directly or indirectly, the whole or any part of the stock or other share capital of another corporation engaged also in commerce, where the effect of such acquisition may be to substantially lessen competition between the corporation whose stock is so acquired and the corporation making the acquisition, or to restrain such commerce in any section or community, or tend to create a monopoly of any line of commerce."

In 1950 this section was amended to read (the major amendments being indicated in italics):

"That no corporation engaged in commerce shall acquire, directly or indirectly, the whole or any part of the stock or other share capital *and no corporation subject to the jurisdiction of the Federal Trade Commission shall acquire the whole or any part of the assets* of another corporation engaged also in commerce, where *in any line of commerce in any section of the country,* the effect of such acquisition may be substantially to lessen competition, or to tend to create a monopoly."

If Congress did intend the 1950 amendment to reach bank mergers, it certainly went at the matter in a very peculiar way. While prohibiting asset acquisitions having the anticompetitive effects described in § 7, it limited the applicability of that provision to corporations subject to the jurisdiction of the Federal Trade Commission, which does not include banks. And it reenacted the stock-acquisition provision in the very same language which—as it was fully aware—had been interpreted not to reach the type of merger customarily used in the banking industry. See infra, pp. 389-393. In the past this Court has drawn the normal inference that such a reenactment indicates congressional adoption of the prior judicial statutory construction. E. g., United States v. Dixon, 347 U. S. 381; Overstreet v. North Shore Corp., 318 U. S. 125, 131-132.

In this instance, however, the Court holds that the stock-acquisition provision underwent an expansive metamorphosis, so that it now embraces all mergers or consolidations involving an exchange of stock. Since bank mergers usually, if not always, do involve exchanges of stock, the effect of this construction is to rob the Federal Trade Commission provision relating to asset acquisitions of all force as a substantive limitation upon the scope of § 7; according to the Court the purpose of that provision was merely to ensure the Commission's role in the enforcement of § 7. Ante, pp. 346-348. In short, under this reasoning bank mergers to all intents and purposes are fully within the reach of § 7.

A more circumspect look at the 1950 amendment of § 7 and its background will show that this construction is not tenable.

The language of the stock-acquisition provision itself is hardly congenial to the Court's interpretation. The PNB-Girard merger is technically a consolidation, governed by § 20 of the national banking laws, 12 U. S. C. (Supp. IV, 1963) § 215. Under that section, the corporate existence of both PNB and Girard, all of their rights, franchises, assets, and liabilities, would be automatically vested in the resulting bank, which would operate under the PNB charter. PNB itself would acquire nothing. Rather, the two banks would be creating a new entity by the amalgamation of their properties, and the subsequent conversion of Girard stock (which would then represent ownership in a nonfunctioning entity) into stock of the resulting bank would simply be part of the mechanics by which ownership in the new entity would be reflected. Clearly this is not a case of a corporation acquiring the stock of another functioning corporation, which is the only situation where "the effect of . . . [a stock] acquisition may be substantially to lessen competition." (Emphasis added.)

There are further crucial differences between a merger and a stock acquisition. A merger normally requires public notice and the approval of the holders of two-thirds of the outstanding shares of each corporation, and dissenting shareholders have the right to receive in cash the appraised value of their shares.[30] A purchase of stock may be done privately, and the only approval involved is that of the individual parties to the transaction. Unlike a merged company, a corporation whose stock is acquired usually remains in business as a subsidiary of the acquiring corporation.[31]

The Government, however, contends that a merger more closely resembles a stock acquisition than an asset acquisition because of one similarity of central importance: the acquisition by one corporation of an immediate voice in the management of the business of another corporation. But this is obviously true a fortiori of asset acquisitions of sufficient magnitude to fall within the prohibition of § 7; if a corporation buys the plants, equipment, inventory, etc., of another corporation, it acquires absolute control over, not merely a voice in the management of, another business.

The legislative history of the 1950 amendment also unquestionably negates any inference that Congress intended to reach bank mergers. It is true that the purpose was "to plug a loophole" in § 7 (95 Cong. Rec. 11485 (1949) (remarks of Representative Celler)). But simply to state this broad proposition does not answer the precise questions presented here: what was the nature of the loophole sought to be closed; what were the means chosen to close it?

The answer to the latter question is unmistakably indicated by the relationship between the 1950 amendment and previous judicial decisions. In Arrow-Hart & Hegeman Elec. Co. v. Federal Trade Comm'n, 291 U. S. 587, this Court, by a divided vote, ruled on the scope of the Federal Trade Commission's remedial powers under the original Clayton Act. After the Commission had issued a § 7 complaint against a holding company which had been formed by the stockholders of two manufacturing corporations, steps were taken to avoid the Commission's jurisdiction. Two new holding companies were formed, each acquired all the common stock of one of the manufacturing companies, and each issued its stock directly to the stockholders of the original holding company. This company then dissolved and the two new holding companies and their respective manufacturing subsidiaries merged into one corporation. This Court held that the Commission had no authority, after the merger, to order the resulting corporation to divest itself of assets. An essential part of this holding was that the merger in question, which was technically a consolidation similar to that here planned by PNB and Girard, was not a stock acquisition within the prohibitions of § 7: "If the merger of the two manufacturing corporations and the combination of their assets was in any respect a violation of any antitrust law, as to which we express no opinion, it was necessarily a violation of statutory prohibitions other than those found in the Clayton Act." 291 U. S., at 599; see id., at 595.[32]

This decision, along with two others earlier handed down by this Court (Thatcher Mfg. Co. v. Federal Trade Comm'n and Swift & Co. v. Federal Trade Comm'n, decided together with Federal Trade Comm'n v. Western Meat Co., 272 U. S. 554), perhaps provided more of a spur to enactment of the "assets" amendment to § 7 than any other single factor. These decisions were universally regarded as opening the unfortunate loophole whereby § 7 could be evaded through the use of an asset acquisition. Representative Celler expressed the view of Congress in this fashion:

"The result of these decisions has so weakened sections 7 and 11 . . . as to give to the Federal Trade Commission and the Department of Justice merely a paper sword to prevent improper mergers." 95 Cong. Rec. 11485 (1949).[33]

Since this Court's decisions were cast in terms of the scope of the Federal Trade Commission's jurisdiction, Congress, in amending § 7 so as to close that gap, emphasized its expectation—made plain in the committee reports, hearings, and debates—that the Commission would assume the principal role in enforcing the section.[34] Implicit here is that no change in the enforcement powers of the other agencies named in § 11 was contemplated.[35] Of more importance, the legislative history demonstrates that it was the asset-acquisition provision that was designed to plug the loophole created by Thatcher, Swift, and Arrow. Although Arrow, unlike Thatcher and Swift, involved a consolidation of the same type as the PNB-Girard merger, the members of Congress drew no distinction among these cases, invariably discussing all three of them in the same breath as examples of asset acquisitions.[36] Indeed, the House report stated that

"the Supreme Court . . . held [in Arrow] that if an acquiring corporation secured title to the physical assets of a corporation whose stock it had acquired before the Federal Trade Commission issues its final order, the Commission lacks power to direct divestiture of the physical assets . . . ." H. R. Rep. No. 1191, 81st Cong., 1st Sess. 5 (1949). (Emphasis added.)

And on the Senate floor it was pointed out that "the method by which . . . [the merger in Arrow] had been accomplished was an innocent one . . . ." 96 Cong. Rec. 16505 (1950). (Emphasis added.) Clearly the understanding of Congress was that a consolidation of two corporations was an acquisition of assets.[37]

Nor did Congress act inadvertently or without purpose in limiting the asset-acquisition provision to corporations subject to the jurisdiction of the Federal Trade Commission, thereby excluding bank mergers. The reports, hearings, and debates on the 1950 amendment reveal that Congress was then concerned with the rising tide of industrial concentration—i. e., "the external expansion. . . through mergers, acquisitions, and consolidations"[38] of corporations engaged in manufacturing, mining, merchandising, and of other kindred commercial endeavors. Specialized areas of the economy such as banking were not even considered. Thus the Federal Trade Commission's 1948 report on mergers recounted the statistics on concentration in a multitude of industries— e. g., steel, cement, electrical equipment, food and dairy products, tobacco, textiles, paper, chemicals, rubber—but included not one figure on banking concentration.[39] This report was repeatedly cited and heavily relied on by members of Congress and others to demonstrate the magnitude of the merger movement and the economic dangers it presented.[40] In the committee hearings the focus was exclusively upon amalgamation in the ordinary commercial fields,[41] and similarly the Senate and House reports spoke solely of industrial concentration as the evil to be remedied.[42] On the floor of the House, Representative Celler indicated the extent of concentration of industrial power:

"Four companies now have 64 percent of the steel business, four have 82 percent of the copper business, two have 90 percent of the aluminum business, three have 85 percent of the automobile business, two have 80 percent of the electric lamp business, four have 75 percent of the electric refrigerator business, two have 80 percent of the glass business, four have 90 percent of the cigarette business, and so forth.

"The antitrust laws are a complete bust unless we pass this bill." 95 Cong. Rec. 11485 (1949).

The legislatory history is thus singularly devoid of any evidence that Congress sought to deal with the special problem of banking concentration.

I do not mean to suggest, of course, that § 7 of the Clayton Act is thereby rendered applicable only to ordinary commercial and industrial corporations and not to firms in any "regulated" sector of the economy. The point is that when Congress included in § 7 asset acquisitions by corporations subject to the Federal Trade Commission's jurisdiction, and at the same time continued in § 11 the Federal Reserve Board's jurisdiction over banks, it was not acting irrationally. Rather, the absence of any mention of banks in the legislative history of the 1950 amendment, viewed in light of the prior congressional treatment of banking as a distinctive area with special characteristics and needs, compels the conclusion that bank mergers were simply not then regarded as part of the loophole to be plugged.[43]

This conclusion is confirmed by a number of additional considerations. It was not until after the passage of the 1950 amendment of § 7 that Representative Celler, its co-sponsor, requested the staff of the Antitrust Subcommittee of the House Committee on the Judiciary "to prepare a report indicating the concentration existing in our banking system." Staff of Subcommittee No. 5, House Committee on the Judiciary, 82d Cong., 2d Sess., Report on Bank Mergers and Concentration of Banking Facilities III (1952). The introduction to the report reveals that:

"On March 21, 1945, the Board of Governors of the Federal Reserve System wrote to the chairman of the Committee on the Judiciary requesting that the provisions of H. R. 2357, Seventy-ninth Congress, first session, one of the early predecessors of the Celler Antimerger Act, be extended so as to include corporations subject to the jurisdiction of the Federal Reserve Board under section 11 of the Clayton Act. Because of the revisions made in subsequent versions of antimerger bills, however, it became impracticable to include within the scope of the act corporations other than those subject to regulation by the Federal Trade Commission. Banks, which are placed squarely within the authority of the Federal Reserve Board by section 11 of the Clayton Act, are therefore circumscribed insofar as mergers are concerned only by the old provisions of section 7, and certain additional statutes which do not presently concern themselves substantively with the question of competition in the field of banking." Id., at VII.

It is also worth noting that in 1956 Representative Celler himself introduced another amendment to § 7, explaining that "all the bill [H. R. 5948] does is plug a loophole in the present law dealing with bank mergers . . . . This loophole exists because section 7 of the Clayton Act prohibits bank mergers . . . only if such mergers are accomplished by stock acquisition." 102 Cong. Rec. 2109 (1956). The bill read in pertinent part: "[N]o bank . . . shall acquire . . . the whole or any part of the assets of another corporation engaged also in commerce . . . ." Ibid. The amendment passed the House but was defeated in the Senate.

For all these reasons, I think the conclusion is inescapable that § 7 of the Clayton Act does not apply to the PNB-Girard merger. The Court's contrary conclusion seems to me little better than a tour de force.[44]

Notes

[1] See Wemple and Cutler, The Federal Bank Merger Law and the Antitrust Laws, 16 Bus. Law. 994, 995 (1961). Many of the bills are summarized in Funk, Antitrust Legislation Affecting Bank Mergers, 75 Banking L. J. 369 (1958).

[2] These agencies and the areas of their primary supervisory responsibility are: (1) the Comptroller of the Currency—national banks; (2) the Federal Reserve System—state Reserve-member banks; (3) the FDIC—insured nonmember banks.

[3] Samuelson, Economics (5th ed. 1961), p. 311.

[4] For example, savings and loan associations, credit unions, and other institutions compete with banks in installment lending to individuals, and banks are in competition with individuals in the personal trust field.

[5] Since bank insolvencies destroy sources of credit, not only borrowers but also others who rely on the borrowers' ability to secure loans may be adversely affected. See Berle, Banking Under the Anti-Trust Laws, 49 Col. L. Rev. 589, 592 (1949).

[6] The term "merger" is generally used throughout this opinion to designate any

form of corporate amalgamation. See note 7 in the Court's opinion, ante, p. 332. Occasionally, however, as in the above paragraph, the terms "merger" and "consolidation" are used in their technical sense.

[7] 40 Stat. 1043, as amended, 12 U. S. C. (Supp. IV, 1963) § 215.

[8] 44 Stat. 1225, as amended, 12 U. S. C. (Supp. IV, 1963) § 215.

[9] 66 Stat. 599, as amended, 12 U. S. C. (Supp. IV, 1963) § 215a.

[10] See Paton, Conversion, Merger and Consolidation Legislation— "Two-Way Street" For National and State Banks, 71 Banking L. J. 15 (1954).

[11] 64 Stat. 455, as amended, 12 U. S. C. § 214a.

[12] 64 Stat. 457; see 64 Stat. 892 (now 74 Stat. 129, 12 U. S. C. (Supp. IV, 1963) § 1828 (c)).

[13] Ibid. However, under the Act, insured banks merging with insured state banks did not have to obtain approval unless the capital stock or surplus of the resulting or assuming bank would be less than the aggregate capital stock or surplus of all the merging banks.

[14] See Hearings before the Antitrust Subcommittee of the House Committee on the Judiciary, 84th Cong., 1st Sess., Ser. 3, pt. 1, pp. 243-244 (1955); Hearings on S. 3911 before a Subcommittee of the Senate Committee on Banking and Currency, 84th Cong., 2d Sess. 60-61, 84 (1956); Hearings on S. 1062 before the Senate Committee on Banking and Currency, 86th Cong., 1st Sess. 9 (1959).

[15] See also H. R. Rep. No. 1416, 86th Cong., 2d Sess. 5 (1960) ("The Federal antitrust laws are also inadequate to the task of regulating bank mergers; while the Attorney General may move against bank mergers to a limited extent under the Sherman Act, the Clayton Act offers little help."); id., at 9 ("Because section 7 [of the Clayton Act] is limited, insofar as banks are concerned, to cases where a merger is accomplished through acquisition of stock, and because bank mergers are accomplished by asset acquisitions rather than stock acquisitions, the act offers `little help,' in the words of Hon Robert A. Bicks, acting head of the Antitrust Division, in controlling bank mergers.").

[16] In the Senate, a sponsor of S. 1062, Senator Fulbright, reported that the "1950 amendment to section 7 of the Clayton Act, which for the first time imposed controls over mergers by means other than stock acquisitions, did not apply to bank mergers which are practically invariably accomplished by means other than stock acquisition. Accordingly for all practical purposes bank mergers have been and still are exempt from section 7 of the Clayton Act." 106 Cong. Rec. 9711 (1960).

[17] E. g., H. R. 5948, 84th Cong. 1st Sess. (1955); S. 198, 85th Cong., 1st Sess. (1957); S. 722, 85th Cong., 1st Sess. (1957); see note 1, supra.

[18] S. Rep. No. 196, 86th Cong., 1st Sess. 17 (1959): "Time and again the Nation has suffered from the results of unregulated and uncontrolled competition in the field of banking, and from insufficiently regulated competition. . . . The rapid increase in the number of small weak banks, to such a large number that the Comptroller could not effectively supervise them or control any but the worst abuses, was one of the factors

which led to the panic of 1907.

"The banking collapse in the early 1930's again was in large part the result of insufficient regulation and control of banks, in effect the result of too much competition." See also 105 Cong. Rec. 8076 (1959): "But unlimited and unrestricted competition in banking is just not possible. We have had too many panics and banking crises and bank failures, largely as the result of excessive competition in banking, to consider for a moment going back to the days of free banking or unregulated banking."

[19] See also S. Rep. No. 196, 86th Cong., 1st Sess. 16 (1959): "But it is impossible to require unrestricted competition in the field of banking, and it would be impossible to subject banks to the rules applicable to ordinary industrial and commercial concerns, not subject to regulation and not vested with a public interest."

[20] For the pertinent text of the statute, see note 8 in the Court's opinion, ante, pp. 332-333.

[21] These factors are: "the financial history and condition of each of the banks involved, the adequacy of its capital structure, its future earnings prospects, the general character of its management, the convenience and needs of the community to be served, and whether or not its corporate powers are consistent with the purposes of this chapter." 12 U. S. C. (Supp. IV, 1963) § 1828 (c). Compare § 6 of the Federal Deposit Insurance Act, 12 U. S. C. § 1816.

[22] See also 106 Cong. Rec. 7259 (1960): "The language of S. 1062 as amended by the House Banking and Currency Committee and as it appears in the bill we are now about to pass in the House makes it clear that the competitive and monopolistic factors are to be considered along with the banking factors and that after considering all of the factors involved, if the resulting institution will be in the public interest, then the application should be approved and otherwise disapproved."

[23] 106 Cong. Rec. 7257 (1960): "This puts the responsibility for acting on a proposed merger where it belongs—in the agency charged with supervising and examining the bank which will result from the merger. Out of their years of experience in supervising banks, our Federal banking agencies have developed specialized knowledge of banking and the people who engage in it. They are experts at judging the condition of the banks involved, their prospects, their management, and the needs of the community for banking services. They should have primary responsibility in deciding whether a proposed merger would be in the public interest." (Emphasis added.)

[24] H. R. Rep. No. 1416, 86th Cong., 2d Sess. 11-12 (1960): "We are convinced, also, that approval of a merger should depend on a positive showing of some benefit to be derived from it. As previously indicated, your committee is not prepared to say that the cases enumerated in the hearings are the only instances in which a merger is in the public interest, nor are we prepared to devise a specific and exclusive list of situations in which a merger should be approved."

[25] Compare State Board of Ins. v. Todd Shipyards Corp., 370 U. S. 451, 457, in which this Court refused to reconsider certain prior decisions because Congress had

"posited a regime of state regulation" of the insurance business on their continuing validity. Cf. Toolson v. New York Yankees, Inc., 346 U. S. 356.

[26] If a bank merger such as this falls within the category of a "stock" acquisition, a § 7 suit to enjoin it may be brought not only by the Attorney General, but by the Federal Reserve Board as well. See § 11 of the Clayton Act, 15 U. S. C. § 21 (vesting authority in the Board to enforce § 7 "where applicable to banks"). In an attempt to retain some semblance of the structure erected by Congress in the Bank Merger Act, the Court states that it "supplanted . . . whatever authority the FRB may have acquired under § 11, by virtue of the amendment of § 7, to enforce § 7 against bank mergers." Ante, p. 344, note 22. Since both the Attorney General and the Federal Reserve Board have purely advisory roles where a bank merger will result in a national bank, the Court's reasoning with respect to the effect of the Bank Merger Act upon enforcement authority should apply with equal force to both.

[27] Indeed the Court has erected a simple yardstick in order to alleviate the agony of analyzing economic data—control of 30% of a commercial banking market is prohibited. Ante, pp. 363-364.

[28] Although § 7 of the Clayton Act is applicable to an outright purchase of bank stock, this form of amalgamation is infrequently used in the banking field and does not involve divestiture problems of the same magnitude as does an asset acquisition.

[29] It is true, as the Court points out (ante, p. 354), that Congress, in enacting the Bank Merger Act, agreed that the applicability of the Sherman Act to banking should not be disturbed. See, e. g., 105 Cong. Rec. 8076 (1959). But surely this alone provides no conceivable justification for applying the Clayton Act as well. Apart from the fact that the Sherman Act covers many kinds of restraints besides mergers, one of the sponsors of the Bank Merger Act (Senator Fulbright) expressed his expectation that in a Sherman Act case a bank merger would not be subjected to strict antitrust standards to the exclusion of all other considerations: "And even if the Sherman Act is held to apply to banking and to bank mergers, it seems clear that under the rule of reason spelled out in the Standard Oil case, different considerations will be found applicable, in a regulated field like banking, in determining whether activities would `unduly diminish competition,' in the words of the Supreme Court in that case." 106 Cong. Rec. 9711 (1960). Moreover, this Court has recognized in other areas that it may be necessary to accommodate the Sherman Act to regulatory policy. McLean Trucking Co. v. United States, 321 U. S. 67, 83; Federal Communications Comm'n v. RCA Communications, Inc., 346 U. S. 86, 91-92. See also United States v. Columbia Steel Co., 334 U. S. 495, 527. And of course the Sherman Act is concerned more with existing anticompetitive effects than with future probabilities, and thus would not reach incipient restraints to the same extent as would § 7 of the Clayton Act. See Brown Shoe Co. v. United States, 370 U. S. 294, 317-318 and notes 32, 33.

[30] In these respects a merger is precisely the contrary of what § 7 was originally designed to proscribe—the secret acquisition of corporate control. See the Court's opinion, ante, p. 338.

[31] That the stock-acquisition provision was not intended to cover mergers is

strongly suggested by the second paragraph of § 7: "No corporation shall acquire . . . any part of the stock . . . of one or more corporations . . . where . . . the effect . . . of the use of such stock by the voting or granting of proxies . . . may be substantially to lessen competition, or to tend to create a monopoly." 15 U. S. C. § 18. (Emphasis added.) After a merger has been consummated, the resulting corporation holds no stock in any party to the merger; thus there can be in this situation no such thing as a restraint of trade by "the use" of the voting power of acquired stock.

[32] On this point, the dissenters agreed: "It is true that the Clayton Act does not forbid corporate mergers . . . ." 291 U. S., at 600. See also United States v. Celanese Corp. of America, 91 F. Supp. 14.

[33] See also Hearings on H. R. 988, H. R. 1240, H. R. 2006, H. R. 2734 before Subcommittee No. 3 of the House Committee on the Judiciary, 81st Cong., 1st Sess. 38-39 (1949); Hearings on H. R. 2734 before a Subcommittee of the Senate Committee on the Judiciary, 81st Cong., 1st & 2d Sess. 109-110 (1950): "The loophole sought to be filled resulted from a series of Supreme Court decisions. (Swift & Co. v. FTC and Thatcher Mfg. Co. v. FTC (272 U. S. 554); Arrow-Hart & Hegeman Co. v. FTC (291 U. S. 587).) In these decisions the Supreme Court held that section 7 of the Clayton Act, while prohibiting the acquisition of stock of a competitor, gave the Federal Trade Commission no authority under section 11 to order divestiture of assets which had been acquired before a cease-and-desist order was issued, even though the acquisition resulted from the voting of illegally held stock."

[34] The Federal Trade Commission had assumed primary enforcement responsibility before the 1950 amendment. See Martin, Mergers and the Clayton Act (1959), p. 197.

[35] Compare note 26, supra.

[36] See note 33 supra; Hearings on H. R. 2734 before a Subcommittee of the Senate Committee on the Judiciary, 81st Cong., 1st & 2d Sess. 97 (1950). And this Court has, after the 1950 amendment, described Arrow as a case involving an asset acquisition. Brown Shoe Co. v. United States, 370 U. S. 294, 313 and note 20.

[37] The single excerpt quoted by the Court (ante, p. 345) casts no doubt on this proposition, for Senator Kilgore's remark occurred in the course of a discussion in which he was trying to make the point that there is no difference in practical effect, as opposed to the legal distinction, between a merger and a stock acquisition. Thus at the end of the paragraph quoted by the Court the Senator stated: ". . . I cannot see how on earth you can get the idea that the purchase of the stock of the corporation, all of it, does not carry with it the transfer of all of the physical assets in that corporation." Hearings on H. R. 2734 before a Subcommittee of the Senate Committee on the Judiciary, 81st Cong., 1st & 2d Sess. 176 (1950).

[38] H. R. Rep. No. 1191, 81st Cong., 1st Sess. 2 (1949).

[39] Federal Trade Commission, The Merger Movement: A Summary Report (1948), passim.

[40] E. g., Hearings on H. R. 988, H. R. 1240, H. R. 2006, H. R. 2734 before Subcommittee No. 3 of the House Committee on the Judiciary, 81st Cong., 1st Sess. 39-40 (1949); 95 Cong. Rec. 11503 (1949); 96 Cong. Rec. 16505 (1950).

[41] Hearings on H. R. 2734 before a Subcommittee of the Senate Committee on the Judiciary, 81st Cong., 1st & 2d Sess. 5-6, 17, 57-59 (1950); Hearings on H. R. 988, H. R. 1240, H. R. 2006, H. R. 2734 before Subcommittee No.3 of the House Committee on the Judiciary, 81st Cong., 1st Sess. 40, 113 (1949).

[42] S. Rep. No. 1775, 81st Cong., 2d Sess. 3 (1950): H. R. Rep. No. 1191, 81st Cong., 1st Sess. 2-3 (1949).

[43] It is interesting to note that in the same year in which § 7 was amended Congress passed an act facilitating certain kinds of bank mergers which had theretofore been prohibited. See note 11, supra, and accompanying text.

[44] Since the Court does not reach the Sherman Act aspect of this case, it wou

Justice Harlan's dissent in Sherbert v. Verner (June 17, 1963)

MR. JUSTICE HARLAN, whom MR. JUSTICE WHITE joins, dissenting.

Today's decision is disturbing both in its rejection of existing precedent and in its implications for the future. The significance of the decision can best be understood after an examination of the state law applied in this case.

South Carolina's Unemployment Compensation Law was enacted in 1936 in response to the grave social and economic problems that arose during the depression of that period. As stated in the statute itself:

"Economic insecurity due to unemployment is a serious menace to health, morals and welfare of the people of this State; involuntary unemployment is therefore a subject of general interest and concern . . . ; the achievement of social security requires protection against this greatest hazard of our economic life; this can be provided by encouraging the employers to provide more stable employment and by the systematic accumulation of funds during periods of employment to provide benefits for periods of unemployment, thus maintaining purchasing power and limiting the serious social consequences of poor relief assistance."

§ 68-38. (Emphasis added.)

Thus, the purpose of the legislature was to tide people over, and to avoid social and economic chaos, during periods when work was unavailable. But, at the same time, there was clearly no intent to provide relief for those who, for purely personal reasons, were or became unavailable for work. In accordance with this design, the legislature provided, in § 68-113, that

"[a]n unemployed insured worker shall be eligible to receive benefits with respect to any week only if the Commission finds that . . . [h]e is able to work and is available for work. . . ."

(Emphasis added.)

The South Carolina Supreme Court has uniformly applied this law in conformity with its clearly expressed purpose. It has consistently held that one is not "available for work" if his unemployment has resulted not from the inability of industry to provide a job, but rather from personal circumstances, no matter how compelling. The reference to "involuntary unemployment" in the legislative statement of policy, whatever a sociologist, philosopher, or theologian might say, has been interpreted not to embrace such personal circumstances. See, e.g., Judson Mills v. South Carolina Unemployment Compensation Comm'n, 204 S.C. 37, 28 S.E.2d 535 (claimant was "unavailable for work" when she became unable to work the third shift, and limited her availability to the other two, because of the need to care for her four children); Stone Mfg. Co. v. South Carolina Employment Security Comm'n, 219 S.C. 239, 64 S.E.2d 644; Hartsville Cotton Mill v. South Carolina Employment Security Comm'n, 224 S.C. 407, 79 S.E.2d 381.

In the present case, all that the state court has done is to apply these accepted principles. Since virtually all of the mills in the Spartanburg area were operating on a six-day week, the appellant was "unavailable for work," and thus ineligible for benefits, when personal considerations prevented her from accepting employment on a full-time basis in the industry and locality in which she had worked. The fact that these personal considerations sprang from her religious convictions was wholly without relevance to the state court's application of the law. Thus, in no proper sense can it be said that the State discriminated against the appellant on the basis of her religious beliefs or that she was denied benefits because she was a Seventh-day Adventist. She was denied benefits just as any other claimant would be denied benefits who was not "available for work" for personal reasons. [1]

With this background, this Court's decision comes into clearer focus. What the Court is holding is that, if the State chooses to condition unemployment compensation on the applicant's availability for work, it is constitutionally compelled to carve out an exception -- and to provide benefits -- for those whose unavailability is due to their religious convictions. [2] Such a holding has particular significance in two respects.

First, despite the Court's protestations to the contrary, the decision necessarily overrules Braunfeld v. Brown, 366 U. S. 599, which held that it did not offend the "Free Exercise" Clause of the Constitution for a State to forbid a Sabbatarian to do business on Sunday. The secular purpose of the statute before us today is even clearer than that involved in Braunfeld. And just as in Braunfeld -- where exceptions to the Sunday closing laws for Sabbatarians would have been inconsistent with the purpose to achieve a uniform day of rest and would have required case-by-case inquiry into religious beliefs -- so here, an exception to the rules of eligibility based on religious convictions would necessitate judicial examination of those convictions and would be at odds with the limited purpose of the statute to smooth out the economy during periods of industrial instability. Finally, the indirect financial burden of the present law is far less than that involved in Braunfeld. Forcing a store owner to close his business on Sunday may well have the effect of depriving him of a satisfactory livelihood if his religious convictions require him to close on Saturday as well. Here we are dealing only with temporary benefits, amounting to a fraction of regular weekly wages and running for not more than 22 weeks. See §§ 68-104, 68-105. Clearly, any differences between this case and Braunfeld cut against the present appellant. [3]

Second, the implications of the present decision are far more troublesome than its apparently narrow dimensions would indicate at first glance. The meaning of today's holding, as already noted, is that the State must furnish unemployment benefits to one who is unavailable for work if the unavailability stems from the exercise of religious convictions. The State, in other words, must single out for financial assistance those whose behavior is religiously motivated, even though it denies such assistance to others whose identical behavior (in this case, inability to work on Saturdays) is not religiously motivated. It has been suggested that such singling out of religious conduct for special treatment may violate the constitutional limitations on state action. See Kurland, Of Church and State and The Supreme Court, 29 U. of Chi.L.Rev. l; cf. Cammarano v. United States, 358 U. S. 498, 358 U. S. 515 (concurring opinion). My own view, however, is that, at least under the circumstances of this case, it would be a permissible accommodation of religion for the State, if it chose to do so, to create an exception to its eligibility requirements for persons like the appellant. The constitutional obligation of "neutrality," see School District of Abington Township v. Schempp, ante, p. 374 U. S. 222, is not so narrow a channel that the slightest deviation from an absolutely straight course leads to condemnation. There are too many instances in which no such course can be charted, too many areas in which the pervasive activities of the State justify some special provision for religion to prevent it from being submerged by an all-embracing secularism. The State violates its obligation of neutrality when, for example, it mandates a daily religious exercise in its public schools, with all the attendant pressures on the school children that such an exercise entails. See Engel v. Vitale, 370 U. S. 421; School District of Abington Township v. Schempp, supra. But there is, I believe, enough flexibility in the Constitution to permit a legislative judgment accommodating an unemployment compensation law to the exercise of religious beliefs such as appellant's.

For very much the same reasons, however, I cannot subscribe to the conclusion that the State is constitutionally compelled to carve out an exception to its general rule of eligibility in the present case. Those situations in which the Constitution may require special treatment on account of religion are, in my view, few and far between, and this view is amply supported by the course of constitutional litigation in this area. See, e.g., Braunfeld v. Brown, supra; Cleveland v. United States, 329 U. S. 14; Prince v. Massachusetts, 321 U. S. 158; Jacobson v. Massachusetts, 197 U. S. 11; Reynolds v. United States, 98 U. S. 145. Such compulsion in the present case is particularly inappropriate in light of the indirect, remote, and insubstantial effect of the decision below on the exercise of appellant's religion and in light of the direct financial assistance to religion that today's decision requires.

For these reasons I respectfully dissent from the opinion and judgment of the

Court. [4]

Notes

[1] I am completely at a loss to understand note 4 of the Court's opinion Certainly the Court is not basing today's decision on the unsupported supposition that, some day, the South Carolina Supreme Court may conclude that there is some personal reason for unemployment that may not disqualify a claimant for relief. In any event, I submit it is perfectly clear that South Carolina would not compensate persons who became unemployed for any personal reason, as distinguished from layoffs or lack of work, since the State Supreme Court's decisions make it plain that such persons would not be regarded as "available for work" within the manifest meaning of the eligibility requirements. Nor can I understand what this Court means when it says that,

"if the eligibility provisions were thus limited, it would have been unnecessary for the [South Carolina] court to have decided appellant's constitutional challenge. . . ."

[2] The Court does suggest, in a rather startling disclaimer, ante, pp. 374 U. S. 409-410, that its holding is limited in applicability to those whose religious convictions do not make them "nonproductive" members of society, noting that most of the Seventh-day Adventists in the Spartanburg area are employed. But surely this disclaimer cannot be taken seriously, for the Court cannot mean that the case would have come out differently if none of the Seventh-day Adventists in Spartanburg had been gainfully employed, or if the appellant's religion had prevented her from working on Tuesdays, instead of Saturdays. Nor can the Court be suggesting that it will make a value judgment in each case as to whether a particular individual's religious convictions prevent him from being "productive." I can think of no more inappropriate function for this Court to perform.

[3] The Court's reliance on South Carolina Code § 64, ante, p. 374 U. S. 406, to support its conclusion with respect to free exercise, is misplaced. Section 64-4, which is not a part of the Unemployment Compensation Law, is an extremely narrow provision that becomes operative only during periods of national emergency, and thus has no bearing in the circumstances of the present case. And plainly, under our decisions in the "Sunday law" cases, appellant can derive no support for her position from the State's general statutory provisions setting aside Sunday as a uniform day of rest.

[4] Since the Court states, ante, p. 374 U. S. 410, that it does not reach the appellant's "equal protection" argument, based upon South Carolina's emergency Sunday work provisions, §§ 64-4, 64-6, I do not consider it appropriate for me to do so.

Justice Harlan's dissent in Pickelsimer v. Wainwright (Oct 14, 1963)

MR. JUSTICE HARLAN, dissenting.

I am unable to agree with the Court's summary disposition of these 10 Florida cases, and believe that the federal question which they present in common is deserving of full-dress consideration. That question is whether the denial of an indigent defendant's right to court-appointed counsel in a state criminal trial as established last Term in Gideon v. Wainwright, 372 U. S. 335, overruling Betts v. Brady, 316 U. S. 455, invalidates his pre-Gideon conviction.

When this Court is constrained to change well-established constitutional rules governing state criminal proceedings, as has been done here and in other recent cases, see, e. g., Mapp v. Ohio, 367 U. S. 643; Ker v. California, 374 U. S. 23; Douglas v. California, 372 U. S. 353, it seems to me that the question whether the States are constitutionally required to apply the new rule retrospectively, which may well require the reopening of cases long since finally adjudicated in accordance with then applicable decisions of this Court, is one that should be decided only after informed and deliberate consideration. Surely no general answer is to be found in "the fiction that the law now announced has always been the law." Griffin v. Illinois, 351 U. S. 12, 26 (Frankfurter, J., concurring). Nor do I believe that the circumstance that Gideon was decided in the context of a state collateral proceeding rather than upon direct review, as were the new constitutional doctrines enunciated in Mapp and Ker, forecloses consideration of the retroactivity issue in this instance.[1]

In the current swift pace of constitutional change, the time has come for the Court to deal definitively with this important and far-reaching subject.[2] Without intimating any view as to how the question should be decided in these cases, I would set one or more of them for argument.[3]

Notes

[1] The Court's opinion in Gideon contains no discussion of this issue. Similarly, in cases decided last Term in which we summarily vacated the judgment and remanded for further consideration in light of Gideon, e. g., Bryant v. Wainwright, 374 U. S. 492, the question of retroactivity was not treated in the dispositions.

[2] Such cases as Eskridge v. Washington State Prison Board, 357 U. S. 214, and Norvell v. Illinois, 373 U. S. 420, hardly constitute precedents for a rule of general application.

[3] In all but two of these cases, the State suggests that the judgments can be supported on an adequate independent state ground, even though the Florida Supreme Court denied relief without hearing or explanatory opinion, and despite the apparent concession in Nos. 36 and 87 that the state court did face the federal question and rule adversely to the petitioners. It is abundantly clear that each of the state grounds suggested is either plainly unavailing or so tenuous that it would be disrespectful of the Florida Supreme Court to regard it as the basis of that court's judgment. Cf. Klinger v. Missouri, 13 Wall. 257; Adams v. Russell, 229 U. S. 353, 358-359; Williams v. Kaiser, 323 U. S. 471, 478-479. Accordingly, I am satisfied that the federal question is properly before this Court in all of the cases.

Justice Harlan's dissent in SEC v. Capital Gains Research Bureau (Dec 9,

1963)

MR. JUSTICE HARLAN, dissenting.

I would affirm the judgment below substantially for the reasons given by Judge Moore in his opinion for the majority of the Court of Appeals sitting en banc, 306 F. 2d 606, and in his earlier opinion for the panel. 300 F. 2d 745. A few additional observations are in order.

Contrary to the majority, I do not read the Court of Appeals' en banc opinion as holding that either § 206 (1) of the Investment Advisers Act of 1940, 54 Stat. 847 (prohibiting the employment of "any device, scheme, or artifice to defraud any client or prospective client"), or § 206 (2), 54 Stat. 847 (prohibiting the engaging "in any transaction, practice, or course of business which operates as a fraud or deceit upon any client or prospective client"), is confined by traditional common law concepts of fraud and deceit. That court recognized that "federal securities laws are to be construed broadly to effectuate their remedial purpose." 306 F. 2d, at 608. It did not hold or intimate that proof of "intent to injure and actual injury to clients" (ante, p. 186) was necessary to make out a case under these sections of the statute. Rather it explicitly observed: "Nor can there be any serious dispute that a relationship of trust and confidence should exist between the advisor and the advised," ibid., thus recognizing that no such proof was required. In effect the Court of Appeals simply held that the terms of the statute require, at least, some proof that an investment adviser's recommendations are not disinterested.

I think it clear that what was shown here would not make out a case of fraud or breach of fiduciary relationship under the most expansive concepts of common law or equitable principles. The nondisclosed facts indicate no more than that the respondents personally profited from the foreseeable reaction to sound and impartial investment advice.[1]

The cases cited by the Court (ante, p. 198) are wide of the mark as even a skeletonized statement of them will show. In Securities & Exchange Comm'n v. Torr, 15 F. Supp. 315, reversed on other grounds, 87 F. 2d 446, defendants were in effect bribed to recommend a certain stock. Although it was not apparent that they lied in making their recommendations, it was plain that they were motivated to make them by the promise of reward. In the case before us, there is no vestige of proof that the reason for the recommendations was anything other than a belief in the soundness of the investment advice given.

Charles Hughes & Co. v. Securities & Exchange Comm'n, 139 F. 2d 434, involved sales of stock by customers' men to those ignorant of the market value of the stocks at 16% to 41% above the over-the-counter price. Defendant's employees must have known that the customers would have refused to buy had they been aware of the actual market price.

The defendant in Norris & Hirshberg, Inc., v. Securities & Exchange Comm'n, 85 U. S. App. D. C. 268, 177 F. 2d 228, dealt in unlisted securities. Most of its customers believed that the firm was acting only on their behalf and that its income was derived from commissions; in fact the firm bought from and sold to its customers, and received its income from mark-ups and mark-downs. The nondisclosure of this basic relationship did not, the court stated, "necessarily establish that petitioner violated the antifraud provisions of the Securities and Securities Exchange Acts." Id., at 271, 177 F. 2d, at 231. Defendant's trading practices, however, were found to establish such a violation; an example of these was the buying of shares of stock from one customer and the selling to another at a substantially higher price on the same day. The opinion explicitly distinguishes between what is necessary to prove common law fraud and the grounds under securities legislation sufficient for revocation of a broker-dealer registration. Id., at 273, 177 F. 2d, at 233.

Arleen Hughes v. Securities & Exchange Comm'n, 85 U. S. App. D. C. 56, 174 F. 2d 969, concerned the revocation of the license of a broker-dealer who also gave investment advice but failed to disclose to customers both the best price at which the securities could be bought in the open market and the price which she had paid for them. Since the court expressly relied on language in statutes and regulations making unlawful "any omission to state a material fact," id., at 63, 174 F. 2d, at 976, this case hardly stands for the proposition that the result would have been the same had such provisions been absent.

In Speed v. Transamerica Corp., 235 F. 2d 369, the controlling stockholder of a corporation made a public offer to buy stock, concealing from the other shareholders information known to it as an insider which indicated the real value of the stock to be considerably greater than the price set by the public offer. Had shareholders been aware of the concealment, they would undoubtedly have refused to sell; as a consequence of selling they suffered ascertainable damages.

In Archer v. Securities & Exchange Comm'n 133 F. 2d 795, defendant copartners of a company dealing in unlisted securities concealed the name of Claude Westfall, who was found to be in control of the business. Westfall was thereby enabled to defraud the customers of the brokerage firm of Harris, Upham & Co., for which he worked as a trader. Securities of the customers of the latter firm were bought by defendants' company at under the market level, and defendants' company sold securities to the clients of Harris, Upham & Co. at prices above the market.

In all of these cases but Arleen Hughes, which turned on explicit provisions against nondisclosure, the concealment involved clearly reflected dishonest dealing that was vital to the consummation of the relevant transactions. No such factors are revealed by the record in the present case. It is apparent that the Court is able to achieve the result reached today only by construing these provisions of the Investment Advisers Act as it might a pure conflict of interest statute, cf. United States v. Mississippi Valley Co., 364 U. S. 520, something which this particular legislation does not purport to be.

I can find nothing in the terms of the statute or in its legislative history which lends support to the absolute rule of disclosure now established by the Court. Apart from the other factors dealt with in the two opinions of the Court of Appeals, it seems to me especially significant that Congress in enacting the Investment Advisers Act did not include the express disclosure provision found in § 17 (a) (2) of the Securities Act of 1933, 48 Stat. 84,[2] even though it did carry over to the Advisers Act the comparable fraud and deceit provisions of the Securities Act.[3]

To attribute the presence of a disclosure provision in the earlier statute to an "abundance of caution" (ante, p. 198) and its omission in the later statute to a congressional belief that its inclusion would be "surplusage" (ante, p. 199) is for me a singularly unconvincing explanation of this controlling difference between the two statutes.[4]

However salutary may be thought the disclosure rule now fashioned by the Court, I can find no authority for it either in the statute or in any regulation duly promulgated thereunder by the S. E. C. Only two Terms ago we refused to extend certain provisions of the Securities Exchange Act of 1934 to encompass "policy" considerations at least as cogent as those urged here by the S. E. C. Blau v. Lehman, 368 U. S. 403. The Court should have exercised the same wise judicial restraint in this case. This is particularly so at this interlocutory stage of the litigation. It is conceivable that at the trial the S. E. C. would have been able to make out a case under the statute construed according to its terms.

I respectfully dissent.

Notes

[1] According to respondents' brief (and the fact does not appear to be contested), the annual gross income of Capital Gains Research Bureau from publishing investment information and advice was some $570,000. Even accepting the S. E. C.'s figures, respondents' profit from the trading transactions in question was somewhat less than $20,000. Thus any basis for an inference that respondents' advice was tainted by self-interest, which might have been drawn had respondents' buying and selling activities been more significant, is lacking on this record.

[2] That section makes it unlawful "to obtain money or property by means of . . . any omission to state a material fact necessary in order to make the statements made, in the light of the circumstances under which they were made, not misleading . . . ."

[3] Section 17 (a) of the 1933 Act makes it unlawful "(1) to employ any device, scheme, or artifice to defraud . . . (3) to engage in any transaction, practice, or course of business which operates or would operate as a fraud or deceit upon the purchaser." Compare the language of these provisions with that of § 206 (1), (2) of the Investment Advisers Act, supra, p. 203.

[4] The argument is that by the time of enactment of the Investment Advisers Act in 1940 Congress had become aware that the courts "were merging the proscription against nondisclosure [contained in the 1933 Securities Act] into the general proscription against fraud" also found in the same act. Ante, p. 198. However, the only federal pre-1940 case cited is Securities & Exchange Comm'n v. Torr, ante, p. 198, and supra, p. 204. There the failure of a fiduciary to disclose that his advice was prompted by a "bribe" was equated by the trial judge with deceit. Such a decision can hardly be deemed to establish that any

nondisclosure of a fact material to the recipient of investment advice is fraud or deceit. Saying the least, it strains credulity that a provision expressly proscribing material omissions would be thought by Congress to be "surplusage" when it came to enacting the 1940 Act. This is particularly so when it is remembered that violation of the fraud and deceit section is punishable criminally (§ 217 of the Investment Advisers Act of 1940, 54 Stat. 857); Congress must have known that the courts do not favor expansive constructions of criminal statutes.

Justice Harlan's concurrence and dissent in Eichel v. New York Central R. (Dec 16, 1963)

MR. JUSTICE HARLAN, concurring in part and dissenting in part.

Once again, I am obliged to record my view that certiorari should not have been granted in a case of this kind, involving only a question of the admissibility of evidence in a suit under the Federal Employers' Liability Act, 35 Stat. 65, as amended, 45 U. S. C. § 51. See my dissenting opinion in Tipton v. Socony Mobil Oil Co., Inc., earlier this Term, ante, p. 37.

On the merits, I agree with the majority that the judgment below should be reversed, but for different reasons. Whether or not evidence that the petitioner was receiving disability pension payments under the Railroad Retirement Act of 1937, 50 Stat. 307, as amended, 45 U. S. C. § 228a, should have been admitted depends on a balance between its probative bearing on the issue as to which it was offered, in this case the respondent's claim that petitioner was a malingerer, and the possibility of prejudice to the petitioner resulting from the jury's consideration of the evidence on issues as to which it is irrelevant. When a balance of this sort has to be struck, it should, except in rare instances, be left to the discretion of the trial judge, subject to review for abuse. See Uniform Rules of Evidence, Rule 45; Model Code of Evidence, Rule 303. It is he who is in the best position to weigh the relevant factors, such as the value of the disputed evidence as compared with other proof adducible to the same end and the effectiveness of limiting instructions. Believing that this rule should have been followed here, I concur in reversing the judgment below, which not only held the evidence not inadmissible as a matter of law but also directed its admission on retrial.

For the same reasons, however, I dissent from the majority's holding that the evidence is required to be excluded. I see no reason why evidentiary questions should be given different treatment when they arise in an F. E. L. A. case than when they arise in other contexts.

Justice Harlan's dissent in Hardy v. US (Jan 6, 1964)

MR. JUSTICE HARLAN, dissenting.
I think the Court should not, in the name of exercising its supervisory powers,

engraft this further requirement on 28 U. S. C. § 1915.[1] The holding is that an indigent convict who—following the trial court's certification that his appeal was frivolous and not taken in good faith—has received at the direction of the Court of Appeals a free copy of that portion of the trial transcript germane to the errors asserted as grounds for appeal, is entitled as of right to a free copy of the balance of the transcript if his appellate counsel was not the lawyer who represented him at the trial. The theory is that this is necessary to enable the new lawyer to discover possible "plain error."

Four members of the Court would go further. They would furnish complete transcripts as a matter of course to all indigent appellants, whether or not represented at the appellate stage by the same lawyer who acted for them at the trial. Ante, p. 288. And recognizing that any indigent receiving such a transcript is thus advantaged over an appellant who has to pay for his transcript, they go on to suggest that fairness may require that appellants who are not indigent, but impoverished, should be furnished free transcripts to the extent that they cannot afford to pay for them. Ante, p. 289, n. 7. Although the majority opinion stops short of both of these propositions, given what is now done can it be said that these more expansive positions are without force? Be that as it may, the Court has taken a long step in derogation of the hitherto consistently maintained view, both in federal and state criminal cases, that an indigent defendant is not automatically entitled to a free transcript simply because those economically better situated can obtain their transcripts at will. See Johnson v. United States, 352 U. S. 565, 566; Griffin v. Illinois, 351 U. S. 12, 20; Eskridge v. Washington Prison Board, 357 U. S. 214, 216; Draper v. Washington, 372 U. S. 487, 495.

Granting that § 1915 has not caught up with this Court's recent pronouncements in this area (see concurring opinion of CLARK, J., ante, pp. 296-298) and that, as recommended in the recent report of the Attorney General's Committee,[2] the time has come for a comprehensive overhauling of the procedures governing in forma pauperis appeals in the federal system, I believe that such an undertaking is more appropriately to be accomplished by congressional action, taken in collaboration with the Judicial Conference of the United States, than by piecemeal adjudications of this Court. Especially meet for such a course is the innovation made today, a step which in countrywide application affects the public treasury to an unknown degree, and whose wisdom should not be judged in the abstract or upon the limited data presently before the Court.

A balanced solution of a problem having such unforeseeable ramifications requires consideration of the informed views of those on the firing line of the administration of criminal justice—District judges, Circuit judges, United States attorneys, defense lawyers and Legal Aid Societies—and exploration of differing conditions among the Circuits. It might be concluded that a nationwide requirement of this sort would be unsound, and that the matter is best left for discrete treatment by the Judicial Councils in the various Circuits, subject of course to constitutional limitations. Remotely situated as this Court is from the day-to-day workings of the criminal system, it should hesitate to promulgate blanket requirements on this subject based largely upon theoretical considerations. Cf. Sanders v. United States, 373 U. S. 1, 23 (dissenting opinion of this writer).

I would dispose of this case as the Government suggests by remanding it to the Court of Appeals for further consideration in light of that court's subsequent decision in Ingram v. United States, 315 F. 2d 29. I do not understand this Court's decision to rest on constitutional grounds, nor do I think it well could.

Notes

[1] "§ 1915. Proceedings in forma pauperis.

"(a) Any court of the United States may authorize the commencement, prosecution or defense of any suit, action or proceeding, civil or criminal, or appeal therein, without prepayment of fees and costs or security therefor, by a citizen who makes affidavit that he is unable to pay such costs or give security therefor. Such affidavit shall state the nature of the action, defense or appeal and affiant's belief that he is entitled to redress.

"An appeal may not be taken in forma pauperis if the trial court certifies in writing that it is not taken in good faith."

[2] Poverty and the Administration of Federal Criminal Justice, Report of the Attorney General's Committee on Poverty and the Administration of Federal Criminal Justice (1963).

Justice Harlan's concurrence and dissent in Humphrey v. Moore (Jan 6, 1964)

MR. JUSTICE HARLAN, concurring in part and dissenting in part.

I agree with the Court's opinion and judgment insofar as it relates to the claim that the Joint Conference Committee exceeded its authority under the collective bargaining agreement. Although it is undoubtedly true as a general proposition that bargaining representatives have power to alter the terms of a contract with an employer, the challenge here is not to a purported exercise of such power but to the validity of a grievance settlement reached under proceedings allegedly not authorized by the terms of the collective agreement. Moreover, a committee with authority to settle grievances whose composition is different from that in the multiunion-multiemployer bargaining unit cannot be deemed to possess power to effect changes in the bargaining agreement. When it is alleged that the union itself has engaged or acquiesced in such a departure from the collective bargaining agreement, I can see no reason why an individually affected employee may not step into the shoes of the union and maintain a § 301 suit himself.

But insofar as petitioners' claim rests upon alleged unfair union representation in the grievance proceeding, I agree with the views expressed in the concurring opinion of my Brother GOLDBERG (ante, 355-358) (except that I would expressly reserve the question of whether a suit of this nature would be maintainable under § 301 where it is alleged or proved that the employer was a party to the asserted unfair union representation). However, the conclusion that unilateral unfair union representation gives rise only to a cause of action for violation of a duty implicit in the National Labor Relations Act brings one face-to-face with a further question: Does such a federal cause of action come within the play of the preemption doctrine, San Diego Trades Council v. Garmon, 359 U. S. 236, contrary to what would be the case were such a suit to lie under § 301, Smith v. Evening News Assn., 371 U. S. 195? Short of deciding that question, I do not think it would be appropriate to dispose of this case simply by saying that no unfair union representation was shown in this instance. For if there be preemption in this situation, Garmon would not only preclude state court jurisdiction but would also require this Court initially to defer to the primary jurisdiction of the Labor Board.

The preemption issue is a difficult and important one, carrying ramifications extending far beyond this particular case. It should not be decided without our having the benefit of the views of those charged with the administration of the labor laws. To that end I would reverse the judgment of the state court to the extent that it rests upon a holding that the Joint Conference Committee acted beyond the scope of its authority, set the case for reargument on the unfair representation issue, and invite the National Labor Relations Board to present its views by brief and oral argument on the preemption question. Cf. Retail Clerks International Assn. v. Schermerhorn, 373 U. S. 746, 757; 375 U. S. 96.

Justice Harlan's dissent in Wesberry v. Sanders (Feb 17, 1964) [Notes omitted]

MR. JUSTICE HARLAN, dissenting.

I had not expected to witness the day when the Supreme Court of the United States would render a decision which casts grave doubt on the constitutionality of the composition of the House of Representatives. It is not an exaggeration to say that such is the effect of today's decision. The Court's holding that the Constitution requires States to select Representatives either by elections at large or by elections in districts composed "as nearly as is practicable" of equal population places in jeopardy the seats of almost all the members of the present House of Representatives.

In the last congressional election, in 1962, Representatives from 42 States were elected from congressional districts.[1] In all but five of those States, the difference between the populations of the largest and smallest districts exceeded 100,000 persons.[2] A difference of this magnitude in the size of districts the average population of which in each State is less than 500,000[3] is presumably not equality among districts "as nearly as is practicable," although the Court does not reveal its definition of that phrase.[4] Thus, today's decision impugns the validity of the election of 398 Representatives from 37 States, leaving a "constitutional" House of 37 members now sitting.[5]

Only a demonstration which could not be avoided would justify this Court in rendering a decision the effect of which, inescapably as I see it, is to declare constitutionally defective the very composition of a coordinate branch of the Federal Government. The Court's opinion not only fails to make such a demonstration, it is unsound logically on its face and demonstrably unsound historically.

I.

Before coming to grips with the reasoning that carries such extraordinary consequences, it is important to have firmly in mind the provisions of Article I of the Constitution which control this case:

"Section 2. The House of Representatives shall be composed of Members chosen every second Year by the People of the several States, and the Electors in each State shall have the Qualifications requisite for Electors of the most numerous Branch of the State Legislature.

.....

"Representatives and direct Taxes shall be apportioned among the several States which may be included within this Union, according to their respective Numbers, which shall be determined by adding to the whole Number of free Persons, including those bound to Service for a Term of Years, and excluding Indians not taxed, three fifths of all other Persons. The actual Enumeration shall be made within three Years after the first Meeting of the Congress of the United States, and within every subsequent Term of ten Years, in such Manner as they shall by Law direct. The Number of Representatives shall not exceed one for every thirty Thousand, but each State shall have at Least one Representative . . . .

"Section 4. The Times, Places and Manner of holding Elections for Senators and Representatives, shall be prescribed in each State by the Legislature thereof; but the Congress may at any time by Law make or alter such Regulations, except as to the Places of chusing Senators.

.....

"Section 5. Each House shall be the Judge of the Elections, Returns and Qualifications of its own Members . . . ."

As will be shown, these constitutional provisions and their "historical context," ante, p. 7, establish:

1. that congressional Representatives are to be apportioned among the several States largely, but not entirely, according to population;

2. that the States have plenary power to select their allotted Representatives in accordance with any method of popular election they please, subject only to the supervisory power of Congress; and

3. that the supervisory power of Congress is exclusive.

In short, in the absence of legislation providing for equal districts by the Georgia Legislature or by Congress, these appellants have no right to the judicial relief which they seek. It goes without saying that it is beyond the province of this Court to decide whether equally populated districts is the preferable method for electing Representatives, whether state legislatures would have acted more fairly or wisely had they adopted such a method, or whether Congress has been derelict in not requiring state legislatures to follow that course. Once it is clear that there is no constitutional right at stake, that ends the case.

II.

Disclaiming all reliance on other provisions of the Constitution, in particular those of the Fourteenth Amendment on which the appellants relied below and in this Court, the Court holds that the provision in Art. I, § 2, for election of Representatives "by the People" means that congressional districts are to be "as nearly as is practicable" equal in population, ante, pp. 7-8. Stripped of rhetoric and a "historical context," ante, p. 7, which bears little resemblance to the evidence found in the pages of history, see infra, pp. 30-41, the Court's opinion supports its holding only with the bland assertion that "the principle of a House of Representatives elected `by the People'" would be "cast aside" if "a vote is worth more in one district than in another," ante, p. 8, i. e., if congressional districts within a State, each electing a single Representative, are not equal in population. The fact is, however, that Georgia's 10 Representatives are elected "by the People" of Georgia, just as Representatives from other States are elected "by the People of the several States." This is all that the Constitution requires.[6]

Although the Court finds necessity for its artificial construction of Article I in the undoubted importance of the right to vote, that right is not involved in this case. All of the appellants do vote. The Court's talk about "debasement" and "dilution" of the vote is a model of circular reasoning, in which the premises of the argument feed on the conclusion. Moreover, by focusing exclusively on numbers in disregard of the area and shape of a congressional district as well as party affiliations within the district, the Court deals in abstractions which will be recognized even by the politically unsophisticated to have little relevance to the realities of political life.

In any event, the very sentence of Art. I, § 2, on which the Court exclusively relies confers the right to vote for Representatives only on those whom the State has found qualified to vote for members of "the most numerous Branch of the State Legislature." Supra, p. 22. So far as Article I is concerned, it is within the State's power to confer that right only on persons of wealth or of a particular sex or, if the State chose, living in specified areas of the State.[7] Were Georgia to find the residents of the Fifth District unqualified to vote for Representatives to the State House of Representatives, they could not vote for Representatives to Congress, according to the express words of Art. I, § 2. Other provisions of the Constitution would, of course, be relevant, but, so far as Art. I, § 2, is concerned, the disqualification would be within Georgia's power. How can it be, then, that this very same sentence prevents Georgia from apportioning its Representatives as it chooses? The truth is that it does not.

The Court purports to find support for its position in the third paragraph of Art. I, § 2, which provides for the apportionment of Representatives among the States. The appearance of support in that section derives from the Court's confusion of two issues: direct election of Representatives within the States and the apportionment of

Representatives among the States. Those issues are distinct, and were separately treated in the Constitution. The fallacy of the Court's reasoning in this regard is illustrated by its slide, obscured by intervening discussion (see ante, pp. 13-14), from the intention of the delegates at the Philadelphia Convention "that in allocating Congressmen the number assigned to each State should be determined solely by the number of the State's inhabitants," ante, p. 13, to a "principle solemnly embodied in the Great Compromise—equal representation in the House for equal numbers of people," ante, p. 14. The delegates did have the former intention and made clear provision for it.[8] Although many, perhaps most, of them also believed generally—but assuredly not in the precise, formalistic way of the majority of the Court[9]—that within the States representation should be based on population, they did not surreptitiously slip their belief into the Constitution in the phrase "by the People," to be discovered 175 years later like a Shakespearian anagram.

Far from supporting the Court, the apportionment of Representatives among the States shows how blindly the Court has marched to its decision. Representatives were to be apportioned among the States on the basis of free population plus three-fifths of the slave population. Since no slave voted, the inclusion of three-fifths of their number in the basis of apportionment gave the favored States representation far in excess of their voting population. If, then, slaves were intended to be without representation, Article I did exactly what the Court now says it prohibited: it "weighted" the vote of voters in the slave States. Alternatively, it might have been thought that Representatives elected by free men of a State would speak also for the slaves. But since the slaves added to the representation only of their own State, Representatives from the slave States could have been thought to speak only for the slaves of their own States, indicating both that the Convention believed it possible for a Representative elected by one group to speak for another nonvoting group and that Representatives were in large degree still thought of as speaking for the whole population of a State.[10]

There is a further basis for demonstrating the hollowness of the Court's assertion that Article I requires "one man's vote in a congressional election . . . to be worth as much as another's," ante, p. 8. Nothing that the Court does today will disturb the fact that although in 1960 the population of an average congressional district was 410, 481,[11] the States of Alaska, Nevada, and Wyoming each have a Representative in Congress, although their respective populations are 226, 167, 285, 278, and 330,066.[12] In entire disregard of population, Art. I, § 2, guarantees each of these States and every other State "at Least one Representative." It is whimsical to assert in the face of this guarantee that an absolute principle of "equal representation in the House for equal numbers of people" is "solemnly embodied" in Article I. All that there is is a provision which bases representation in the House, generally but not entirely, on the population of the States. The provision for representation of each State in the House of Representatives is not a mere exception to the principle framed by the majority; it shows that no such principle is to be found.

Finally in this array of hurdles to its decision which the Court surmounts only by knocking them down is § 4 of Art. I which states simply:

"The Times, Places and Manner of holding Elections for Senators and Representatives, shall be prescribed in each State by the Legislature thereof; but the Congress may at any time by Law make or alter such Regulations, except as to the Places of chusing Senators." (Emphasis added.)

The delegates were well aware of the problem of "rotten boroughs," as material cited by the Court, ante, pp. 14-15. and hereafter makes plain. It cannot be supposed that delegates to the Convention would have labored to establish a principle of equal representation only to bury it, one would have thought beyond discovery, in § 2, and omit all mention of it from § 4, which deals explicitly with the conduct of elections. Section 4 states without qualification that the state legislatures shall prescribe regulations for the conduct of elections for Representatives and, equally without qualification, that Congress may make or alter such regulations. There is nothing to indicate any limitation whatsoever on this grant of plenary imtial and supervisory power. The Court's holding is, of course, derogatory not only of the power of the state legislatures but also of the power of Congress, both theoretically and as they have actually exercised their power. See infra, pp. 42-45.[13] It freezes upon both, for no reason other than that it seems wise to the majority of the present Court, a particular political theory for the selection of Representatives.

III.

There is dubious propriety in turning to the "historical context" of constitutional provisions which speak so consistently and plainly. But, as one might expect when the Constitution itself is free from ambiguity, the surrounding history makes what is already clear even clearer.

As the Court repeatedly emphasizes, delegates to the Philadelphia Convention frequently expressed their view that representation should be based on population. There were also, however, many statements favoring limited monarchy and property qualifications for suffrage and expressions of disapproval for unrestricted democracy.[14] Such expressions prove as little on one side of this case as they do on the other. Whatever the dominant political philosophy at the Convention, one thing seems clear: it is in the last degree unlikely that most or even many of the delegates would have subscribed to the principle of "one person, one vote," ante, p. 18.[15] Moreover, the statements approving population-based representation were focused on the problem of how representation should be apportioned among the States in the House of Representatives. The Great Compromise concerned representation of the States in the Congress. In all of the discussion surrounding the basis of representation of the House and all of the discussion whether Representatives should be elected by the legislatures or the people of the States, there is nothing which suggests even remotely that the delegates had in mind the problem of districting within a State.[16]

The subject of districting within the States is discussed explicitly with reference to the provisions of Art. I, § 4, which the Court so pointedly neglects. The Court states: "The delegates referred to rotten borough apportionments in some of the state legislatures as the kind of objectionable governmental action that the Constitution should not tolerate in the election of congressional representatives." Ante, p. 15. The remarks of Madison cited by the Court are as follows:

"The necessity of a Genl. Govt. supposes that the State Legislatures will sometimes fail or refuse to consult the common interest at the expense of their local conveniency or prejudices. The policy of referring the appointment of the House of Representatives to the people and not to the Legislatures of the States, supposes that the result will be somewhat influenced by the mode, [sic] This view of the question seems to decide that the Legislatures of the States ought not to have the uncontrouled right of regulating the times places & manner of holding elections. These were words of great latitude. It was impossible to foresee all the abuses that might be made of the discretionary power. Whether the electors should vote by ballot or viva voce, should assemble at this place or that place; should be divided into districts or all meet at one place, shd all vote for all the representatives; or all in a district vote for a number allotted to the district; these & many other points would depend on the Legislatures. [sic] and might materially affect the appointments.

Whenever the State Legislatures had a favorite measure to carry, they would take care so to mould their regulations as to favor the candidates they wished to succeed. Besides, the inequality of the Representation in the Legislatures of particular States, would produce a like inequality in their representation in the Natl. Legislature, as it was presumable that the Counties having the power in the former case would secure it to themselves in the latter. What danger could there be in giving a controuling power to the Natl. Legislature?"[17] (Emphasis added.)

These remarks of Madison were in response to a proposal to strike out the provision for congressional supervisory power over the regulation of elections in Art. I, § 4. Supported by others at the Convention,[18] and not contradicted in any respect, they indicate as clearly as may be that the Convention understood the state legislatures to have plenary power over the conduct of elections for Representatives, including the power to district well or badly, subject only to the supervisory power of Congress. How, then, can the Court hold that Art. I, § 2, prevents the state legislatures from districting as they choose? If the Court were correct, Madison's remarks would have been pointless. One would expect, at the very least, some reference to Art. I, § 2, as a limiting factor on the States. This is the "historical context" which the Convention debates provide.

Materials supplementary to the debates are as unequivocal. In the ratifying conventions, there was no suggestion that the provisions of Art. I, § 2, restricted the power of the States to prescribe the conduct of elections conferred on them by Art. I, § 4. None of the Court's references to the ratification debates supports the view that the provision for election of Representatives "by the People" was intended to have any application to the apportionment of Representatives within the States; in each instance, the cited passage merely repeats what the Constitution itself provides: that Representatives were to be elected by the people of the States.[19]

In sharp contrast to this unanimous silence on the issue of this case when Art. I, §

2, was being discussed, there are repeated references to apportionment and related problems affecting the States' selection of Representatives in connection with Art. I, § 4. The debates in the ratifying conventions, as clearly as Madison's statement at the Philadelphia Convention, supra, pp. 32-33, indicate that under § 4, the state legislatures, subject only to the ultimate control of Congress, could district as they chose.

At the Massachusetts convention, Judge Dana approved § 4 because it gave Congress power to prevent a state legislature from copying Great Britain, where "a borough of but two or three cottages has a right to send two representatives to Parliament, while Birmingham, a large and populous manufacturing town, lately sprung up, cannot send one."[20] He noted that the Rhode Island Legislature was "about adopting" a plan which would deprive the towns of Newport and Providence of them weight."[21] Mr. King noted the situation in Connecticut, where "Hartford, one of their largest towns, sends no more delegates than one of their smallest corporations," and in South Carolina: "The back parts of Carolina have increased greatly since the adoption of their constitution, and have frequently attempted an alteration of this unequal mode of representation but the members from Charleston, having the balance so much in their favor, will not consent to an alteration, and we see that the delegates from Carolina in Congress have always been chosen by the delegates of that city."[22] King stated that the power of Congress under § 4 was necessary to "control in this case"; otherwise, he said, "The representatives . . . from that state [South Carolina], will not be chosen by the people, but will be the representatives of a faction of that state."[23]

Mr. Parsons was as explicit.

"Mr. PARSONS contended for vesting in Congress the powers contained in the 4th section [of Art. I]. not only as those powers were necessary for preserving the union, but also for securing to the people their equal rights of election. . . . [State legislatures] might make an unequal and partial division of the states into districts for the election of representatives. or they might even disqualify one third of the electors. Without these powers in Congress, the people can have no remedy; but the 4th section provides a remedy, a controlling power in a legislature, composed of senators and representatives of twelve states, without the influence of our commotions and factions, who will hear impartially, and preserve and restore to the people their equal and sacred rights of election. Perhaps it then will be objected, that from the supposed opposition of interests in the federal legislature, they may never agree upon any regulations; but regulations necessary for the interests of the people can never be opposed to the interests of either of the branches of the federal legislature; because that the interests of the people require that the mutual powers of that legislature should be preserved unimpaired, in order to balance the government. Indeed, if the Congress could never agree on any regulations, then certainly no objection to the 4th section can remain; for the regulations introduced by the state legislatures will be the governing rule of elections, until Congress can agree upon alterations."[24] (Emphasis added.)

In the New York convention, during the discussion of § 4, Mr. Jones objected to congressional power to regulate elections because such power "might be so construed as to deprive the states of an essential right, which, in the true design of the Constitution, was to be reserved to them."[25] He proposed a resolution explaining that Congress had such power only if a state legislature neglected or refused or was unable to regulate elections itself.[26] Mr. Smith proposed to add to the resolution ". . . that each state shall be divided into as many districts as the representatives it is entitled to, and that each representative shall be chosen by a majority of votes."[27] He stated that his proposal was designed to prevent elections at large, which might result in all the representatives being "taken from a small part of the state."[28]

He explained further that his proposal was not intended to impose a requirement on the other States but "to enable the states to act their discretion, without the control of Congress."[29] After further discussion of districting, the proposed resolution was modified to read as follows:

"[Resolved] . . . that nothing in this Constitution shall be construed to prevent the legislature of any state to pass laws, from time to time, to divide such state into as many convenient districts as the state shall be entitled to elect representatives for Congress, nor to prevent such legislature from making provision, that the electors in each district shall choose a citizen of the United States, who shall have been an inhabitant of the district, for the term of one year immediately preceding the time of his election, for one of the representatives of such state."[30]

Despite this careful, advertent attention to the problem of congressional districting, Art. I, § 2, was never mentioned. Equally significant is the fact that the proposed resolution expressly empowering the States to establish congressional districts contains no mention of a requirement that the districts be equal in population.

In the Virginia convention, during the discussion of § 4, Madison again stated unequivocally that he looked solely to that section to prevent unequal districting:

". . . [I]t was thought that the regulation of time, place, and manner, of electing the representatives, should be uniform throughout the continent. Some states might regulate the elections on the principles of equality, and others might regulate them otherwise. This diversity would be obviously unjust. Elections are regulated now unequally in some states, particularly South Carolina, with respect to Charleston, which is represented by thirty members. Should the people of any state by any means be deprived of the right of suffrage, it was judged proper that it should be remedied by the general government. It was found impossible to fix the time, place, and manner, of the election of representatives, in the Constitution. It was found necessary to leave the regulation of these, in the first place, to the state governments, as being best acquainted with the situation of the people, subject to the control of the general government, in order to enable it to produce uniformity, and prevent its own dissolution. And, considering the state governments and general government as distinct bodies, acting in different and independent capacities for the people, it was thought the particular regulations should be submitted to the former, and the general regulations to the latter. Were they exclusively under the control of the state governments, the general government might easily be dissolved. But if they be regulated properly by the state legislatures, the congressional control will very probably never be exercised. The power appears to me satisfactory, and as unlikely to be abused as any part of the Constitution."[31] (Emphasis added.)

Despite the apparent fear that § 4 would be abused, no one suggested that it could safely be deleted because § 2 made it unnecessary.

In the North Carolina convention, again during discussion of § 4, Mr. Steele pointed out that the state legislatures had the initial power to regulate elections, and that the North Carolina legislature would regulate the first election at least "as they think proper."[32] Responding to the suggestion that the Congress would favor the seacoast, he asserted that the courts would not uphold nor the people obey "laws inconsistent with the Constitution."[33] (The particular possibilities that Steele had in mind were apparently that Congress might attempt to prescribe the qualifications for electors or "to make the place of elections inconvenient."[34]) Steele was concerned with the danger of congressional usurpation, under the authority of § 4, of power belonging to the States. Section 2 was not mentioned.

In the Pennsylvania convention, James Wilson described Art. I, § 4, as placing "into the hands of the state legislatures" the power to regulate elections, but retaining for Congress "self-preserving power" to make regulations lest "the general government . . . lie prostrate at the mercy of the legislatures of the several states."[35] Without such power, Wilson stated, the state governments might "make improper regulations" or "make no regulations at all."[36] Section 2 was not mentioned.

Neither of the numbers of The Federalist from which the Court quotes, ante, pp. 15, 18, fairly supports its holding. In No. 57, Madison merely stated his assumption that Philadelphia's population would entitle it to two Representatives in answering the argument that congressional constituencies would be too large for good government.[37] In No. 54, he discussed the inclusion of slaves in the basis of apportionment. He said: "It is agreed on all sides, that numbers are the best scale of wealth and taxation, as they are the only proper scale of representation."[38] This statement was offered simply to show that the slave population could not reasonably be included in the basis of apportionment of direct taxes and excluded from the basis of apportionment of representation. Further on in the same number of The Federalist, Madison pointed out the fundamental cleavage which Article I made between apportionment of Representatives among the States and the selection of Representatives within each State:

"It is a fundamental principle of the proposed Constitution, that as the aggregate number of representatives allotted to the several States, is to be determined by a federal rule founded on the aggregate number of inhabitants, so the right of choosing this allotted number in each State is to be exercised by such part of the inhabitants, as the State itself may designate. The qualifications on which the right of suffrage depend, are not perhaps the same in any two States. In some of the States the difference is very material. In every State, a certain proportion of inhabitants are deprived of this right by the Constitution of the State, who will be included in the census by which the Foederal Constitution apportions the representatives. In this point of view, the southern States might retort the complaint, by insisting, that the principle laid down by the Convention required that no regard should be had to the policy of particular States towards their own inhabitants; and consequently, that the slaves as inhabitants should have been admitted into the census according to their full number, in like manner with other inhabitants, who by the policy of other States, are not admitted to all the rights of citizens."[39]

In The Federalist, No. 59, Hamilton discussed the provision of § 4 for regulation of elections. He justified Congress' power with the "plain proposition, that every government ought to contain in itself the means of its own preservation."[40] Further on, he said:

"It will not be alledged that an election law could have been framed and inserted into the Constitution, which would have been always applicable to every probable change in the situation of the country; and it will therefore not be denied that a discretionary power over elections ought to exist somewhere. It will, I presume, be as readily conceded, that there were only three ways, in which this power could have been reasonably modified and disposed, that it must either have been lodged wholly in the National Legislature, or wholly in the State Legislatures, or primarily in the latter, and ultimately in the former. The last mode has with reason been preferred by the Convention. They have submitted the regulation of elections for the Federal Government in the first instance to the local administrations; which in ordinary cases, and when no improper views prevail, may be both more convenient and more satisfactory; but they have reserved to the national authority a right to interpose, whenever extraordinary circumstances might render that interposition necessary to its safety."[41] (Emphasis added.)

Thus, in the number of The Federalist which does discuss the regulation of elections, the view is unequivocally stated that the state legislatures have plenary power over the conduct of congressional elections subject only to such regulations as Congress itself might provide.

The upshot of all this is that the language of Art. I, §§ 2 and 4, the surrounding text, and the relevant history are all in strong and consistent direct contradiction of the Court's holding. The constitutional scheme vests in the States plenary power to regulate the conduct of elections for Representatives, and, in order to protect the Federal Government, provides for congressional supervision of the States' exercise of their power. Within this scheme, the appellants do not have the right which they assert, in the absence of provision for equal districts by the Georgia Legislature or the Congress. The constitutional right which the Court creates is manufactured out of whole cloth.

IV.

The unstated premise of the Court's conclusion quite obviously is that the Congress has not dealt, and the Court believes it will not deal, with the problem of congressional apportionment in accordance with what the Court believes to be sound political principles. Laying aside for the moment the validity of such a consideration as a factor in constitutional interpretation, it becomes relevant to examine the history of congressional action under Art. I, § 4. This history reveals that the Court is not simply undertaking to exercise a power which the Constitution reserves to the Congress; it is also overruling congressional judgment.

Congress exercised its power to regulate elections for the House of Representatives for the first time in 1842, when it provided that Representatives from States "entitled to more than one Representative" should be elected by districts of contiguous territory, "no one district electing more than one Representative."[42] The requirement was later dropped,[43] and reinstated.[44] In 1872, Congress required that Representatives "be elected by districts composed of contiguous territory, and containing as nearly as practicable an equal number of inhabitants, . . . no one district electing more than one Representative."[45] This provision for equal districts which the Court exactly duplicates in effect, was carried forward in each subsequent apportionment statute through 1911.[46] There was no reapportionment following the 1920 census. The provision for equally populated districts was dropped in 1929,[47] and has not been revived, although the 1929 provisions for apportionment have twice been amended and, in 1941, were made generally applicable to subsequent censuses and apportionments.[48]

The legislative history of the 1929 Act is carefully reviewed in Wood v. Broom, 287 U. S. 1. As there stated:

"It was manifestly the intention of the Congress not to re-enact the provision as to compactness, contiguity, and equality in population with respect to the districts to be created pursuant to the reapportionment under the Act of 1929.

"This appears from the terms of the act, and its legislative history shows that the omission was deliberate. The question was up, and considered." 287 U. S., at 7.

Although there is little discussion of the reasons for omitting the requirement of equally populated districts, the fact that such a provision was included in the bill as it was presented to the House,[49] and was deleted by the House after debate and notice of intention to do so,[50] leaves no doubt that the omission was deliberate. The likely explanation for the omission is suggested by a remark on the floor of the House that "the States ought to have their own way of making up their apportionment when they know the number of Congressmen they are going to have."[51]

Debates over apportionment in subsequent Congresses are generally unhelpful to explain the continued rejection of such a requirement; there are some intimations that the feeling that districting was a matter exclusively for the States persisted.[52] Bills which would have imposed on the States a requirement of equally or nearly equally populated districts were regularly introduced in the House.[53] None of them became law.

For a period of about 50 years, therefore, Congress, by repeated legislative act, imposed on the States the requirement that congressional districts be equal in population. (This, of course, is the very requirement which the Court now declares to have been constitutionally required of the States all along without implementing legislation.) Subsequently, after giving express attention to the problem, Congress eliminated that requirement, with the intention of permitting the States to find their own solutions. Since then, despite repeated efforts to obtain congressional action again, Congress has continued to leave the problem and its solution to the States. It cannot be contended, therefore, that the Court's decision today fills a gap left by the Congress. On the contrary, the Court substitutes its own judgment for that of the Congress.

V.

The extent to which the Court departs from accepted principles of adjudication is further evidenced by the irrelevance to today's issue of the cases on which the Court relies.

Ex parte Yarbrough, 110 U. S. 651, was a habeas corpus proceeding, in which the Court sustained the validity of a conviction of a group of persons charged with violating federal statutes[54] which made it a crime to conspire to deprive a citizen of his federal rights, and in particular the right to vote. The issue before the Court was whether or not the Congress had power to pass laws protecting the right to vote for a member of Congress from fraud and violence; the Court relied expressly on Art. I, § 4, in sustaining this power. Id., at 660. Only in this context, in order to establish that the right to vote in a congressional election was a right protected by federal law, did the Court hold that the right was dependent on the Constitution and not on the law of the States. Indeed, the Court recognized that the Constitution "adopts the qualification" furnished by the States "as the qualification of its own electors for members of Congress." Id., at 663. Each of the other three cases cited by the Court, ante, p. 17, similarly involved acts which were prosecuted as violations of federal statutes. The acts in question were filing false election returns, United States v. Mosley, 238 U. S. 383, alteration of ballots and false certification of votes, United States v. Classic, 313 U. S. 299, and stuffing the ballot box, United States v. Saylor, 322 U. S. 385. None of those cases has the slightest bearing on the present situation.[55]

The Court gives scant attention, and that not on the merits, to Colegrove v. Green, 328 U. S. 549, which is directly in point; the Court there affirmed dismissal of a complaint alleging that "by reason of subsequent changes in population the Congressional districts for the election of Representatives in the Congress created by the Illinois Laws of 1901 . . . lacked compactness of territory and approximate equality of population." Id., at 550-551. Leaving to another day the question of what Baker v. Carr, 369 U. S. 186, did actually decide, it can hardly be maintained on the authority of Baker or anything else, that the Court does not today invalidate Mr. Justice Frankfurter's eminently correct statement in Colegrove that "the Constitution has conferred upon Congress exclusive authority to secure fair representation by the States in the popular House . . . . If Congress failed in exercising its powers, whereby standards of fairness are offended, the remedy ultimately lies with the people." 328 U. S., at 554. The problem was described by Mr. Justice Frankfurter as "an aspect of government from which the judiciary, in view of what is involved, has been excluded by the clear intention of the Constitution . . . ." Ibid. Mr. Justice Frankfurter did not, of course, speak for a majority of the Court in Colegrove; but refusal for that reason to give the opinion precedential effect does not justify refusal to give appropriate attention to the views there expressed.[56]

VI.

Today's decision has portents for our society and the Court itself which should be recognized. This is not a case in which the Court vindicates the kind of individual rights that are assured by the Due Process Clause of the Fourteenth Amendment, whose "vague contours," Rochin v. California, 342 U. S. 165, 170, of course leave much room for constitutional developments necessitated by changing conditions in a dynamic society. Nor is this a case in which an emergent set of facts requires the Court to frame new principles to protect recognized constitutional rights. The claim for judicial relief in this case strikes at one of the fundamental doctrines of our system of government, the separation of powers. In upholding that claim, the Court attempts to effect reforms in a field which the Constitution, as plainly as can be, has committed exclusively to the political process.

This Court, no less than all other branches of the Government, is bound by the Constitution. The Constitution does not confer on the Court blanket authority to step into every situation where the political branch may be thought to have fallen short. The stability of this institution ultimately depends not only upon its being alert to keep the other branches of government within constitutional bounds but equally upon recognition of the limitations on the Court's own functions in the constitutional system.

What is done today saps the political process. The promise of judicial intervention in matters of this sort cannot but encourage popular inertia in efforts for political reform through the political process, with the inevitable result that the process is itself weakened. By yielding to the demand for a judicial remedy in this instance, the Court in my view does a disservice both to itself and to the broader values of our system of government.

Believing that the complaint fails to disclose a constitutional claim, I would affirm the judgment below dismissing the complaint.

Justice Harlan's concurrence and dissent in US v. El Paso Natural Gas (April 6, 1964)

MR. JUSTICE HARLAN, concurring in part and dissenting in part.

I.

Contrary to what I had first thought, the Government is not asking in this case, as it did in United States v. Yellow Cab Co., 338 U. S. 338, that we "in effect . . . try the case de novo," id., at 340. Rather it contends that on the undisputed facts of record the ultimate determination below was clearly erroneous. See id., at 341-342. For reasons given in the Court's opinion, I agree that a violation of § 7 of the Clayton Act has been established, and that the District Court erred in deciding otherwise. On this score I shall comment only on two matters.

First. The Court's strictures concerning the District Court's findings seem to me to miss the mark. Findings of fact should, of course, be the product of the conscientious and independent judgment of the district judge. Nevertheless, if they are supported by evidence, they are not rendered suspect simply because the trial court, as here, has accepted in toto the findings proposed by one side or the other. The real lack in this case is that the District Court wrote no opinion setting forth the reasoning underlying any of the subsidiary findings on disputed issues of fact or connecting the subsidiary findings with its ultimate determination that the Clayton Act had not been violated by this merger.

Both as a practitioner and as a judge I have more than once felt that a closely contested government antitrust case, decided below in favor of the defendant, has foundered in this Court for lack of an illuminating opinion by the District Court. District Courts should not forget that such cases, the trials of which usually result in long and complex factual records, come here without the benefit of any sifting by the Courts of Appeals. The absence of an opinion by the District Court has been a handicap in this instance.

Second. This case affords another example of the unsatisfactoriness of the existing bifurcated system of antitrust and other regulation in various fields. In this case, the Federal Power Commission had indicated its approval of this merger as being in the public interest. The Department of Justice, however, considered the merger to be violative of the antitrust laws and, for that reason alone, against the public interest. This Court, under the present scheme of things has no choice on this record[*] but to sustain the position of the Department of Justice, as indeed it has felt constrained to do, albeit in my view with less justification, in other recent cases involving dual regulation. Cf. United States v. Philadelphia National Bank, 374 U. S. 321; United States v. First National Bank & Trust Co., decided today, post, p. 665, and my dissenting opinions in those cases. It would be unrealistic not to recognize that this state of affairs has the effect of placing the Department of Justice in the driver's seat even though Congress has lodged primary regulatory authority elsewhere.

It does seem to me that the time has come when this duplicative and, I venture to say, anachronistic system of dual regulation should be re-examined. Had the subtle and necessarily speculative questions involved in assessing the short-term and long-term effects of this merger been subject to appraisal by a single agency, under congressionally established standards marking the relationship between the different and often competing objectives of the antitrust laws and those governing the regulation of "interstate" natural gas, who can say that this case might not have called for a different outcome?

II.

While I agree with the Court's decision on the merits, I dissent from its peremptory ordering of divestiture. "The framing of" appropriate relief "should take place in the District rather than in Appellate Courts." International Salt Co., Inc., v. United States, 332 U. S. 392, 400 (footnote omitted). United States v. E. I. du Pont de Nemours & Co., 366 U. S. 316, is not to the contrary; that case had already been here before on the merits (353 U. S. 586), and when it came here again at the relief stage the Court observed that "the District Courts [have] the responsibility initially to fashion the remedy. . . ." 366 U. S., at 323. I know of no case where this Court has in the first instance itself directed divestiture or any other particular kind of relief. The fact that these appellees have been "on notice," ante, p. 662, of the charges against them affords no justification for this departure from normal practice. See the cases cited in the second du Pont case, 366 U. S., at 322.

I would remand the case to the District Court for the fashioning of appropriate relief.

Justice Harlan's dissent in US v. First Nat. Bank & Trust Co. of Lexington (April 6, 1964)

MR. JUSTICE HARLAN, whom MR. JUSTICE STEWART joins, dissenting.

But for the Court's return to a discarded theory of anti-trust law, this case would have little future importance. The decision last Term in United States v. Philadelphia National Bank, 374 U. S. 321, that § 7 of the Clayton Act, 15 U. S. C. § 18, is applicable to bank mergers surely marks the end of cases like this one, in which the Government relies solely on §§ 1 and 2 of the Sherman Act, 15 U. S. C. §§ 1, 2. Since, however, this case, doomed to be a novelty in the reports, has become the vehicle for turning the clock back to antitrust law of days long past, I am constrained to do more than merely register my dissent.

I.

Stripped of embellishments, the Court's opinion amounts to an invocation of formulas of antitrust numerology and a presumption that in the antitrust field good things come usually, if not always, in small packages.[1] The "facts relevant to the alleged restraint of trade under the Sherman Act," ante, p. 668, on which the Court relies, are: (1) the size relative to their competitors of First National and Security Trust before the consolidation and of First Security after the consolidation; (2) the competitive position before the consolidation of First National and Security Trust in the more limited area of trust business;[2] and (3) "testimony in the record from three of the four remaining banks that the consolidation will seriously affect their ability to compete effectively over the years . . . ," ante, p. 669.

The testimony to which the Court adverts was provided by competitors of First Security and was characterized by the district judge who heard it as seemingly "based merely upon surmise and . . . lacking in factual support." 208 F. Supp. 457, 460. Since the Court suggests no reason for regarding this evidentiary finding of the trial court as "clearly erroneous," it must be accepted here, e. g., United States v. Yellow Cab Co., 338 U. S. 338, 341-342, leaving as the factual basis for the Court's decision only the statistics unquestionably showing that First National and Security Trust were big and First Security is bigger. The embellishment which adorns these statistics is the proposition that "where merging companies are major competitive factors in a relevant market, the elimination of significant competition between them, by merger or consolidation, itself constitutes a violation of § 1 of the Sherman Act," ante, pp. 671-672.

The sole support for this proposition, which is defended by no independent reasoning whatever, is the four "railroad cases," a reiteration of which forms the bulk of the Court's opinion.[3] It is questionable whether those cases, three of which involved the combination of massive transportation systems[4] and the fourth a combination of "two great competing interstate carriers and . . . two great competing coal companies extensively engaged in interstate commerce"[5] have any relevance to the present factual situation. That question, however, need not be explored.

In United States v. Columbia Steel Co., 334 U. S. 495, these same cases were cited by the Government for the same proposition urged here: that "control by one competitor over another violates the Sherman Act . . . ," id., at 531. The Court relegated the cases to a footnote and stated that it would not "examine those cases to determine whether we would now approve either their language or their holdings." Ibid. The facts of the "railroad cases" were found to be "so dissimilar from that presented" that they could "furnish little guidance" in deciding the later case. Ibid. Beyond this explicit rejection of these cases as a basis for decision is their further rejection clearly implicit in the portion of the Columbia Steel opinion which the Court quotes, ante, p. 672.

"In determining what constitutes unreasonable restraint, we do not think the dollar volume is in itself of compelling significance; we look rather to the percentage of business controlled, the strength of the remaining competition, whether the action springs from business requirements or purpose to monopolize, the probable development of the industry, consumer demands, and other characteristics of the market." 334 U. S., at 527.

Quite obviously, if "bigness" alone provided a sufficient answer to the questions involved in a § 1 charge, it would be pointless to attend to the factors set out in Columbia Steel and reiterated here, in form approvingly but in fact without regard.

II.

If regard be had to the criteria enumerated in Columbia Steel, none of them except perhaps those which deal with "bigness" favor the Government here. Although for purposes of the Sherman Act, such statistics have little meaning in the absence of a context,[6] it may be admitted that the figures in this case of dollar volume[7] and the percentage of business controlled are large. So far as these figures have relevance under the Columbia Steel test, they perhaps speak against the appellee.

On the other hand, the strength of the remaining competition is attested by findings of fact in the District Court, not refused or even mentioned in the Court's opinion:

"As of December 31, 1960, there were in operation in Lexington, beside the First National Bank and Trust Company and Security Trust Company, four other commercial banks, namely:

"Citizens Union National Bank and Trust Company, with total assets of $27,876,000, total deposits of $24,569,000 and total net loans and discounts of $14,457,000;

"Bank of Commerce, with total assets of $21,230,000, total deposits of $19,500,000 and total net loans and discounts of $12,738,000;

"Central Bank and Trust Company, with total assets of $14,930,000, with total deposits of $14,144,000, and with total net loans and discounts of $7,799,000;

"Second National Bank and Trust Company, with total assets of $13,240,000, total deposits of $12,157,000 and total net loans and discounts of $5,362,000.

.....

"Before and since the consolidation herein referred to, all the banks in Fayette County have been operated successfully in the field of commercial banking and in competition with each other.

.....

"In the trial of the case, other than the officials and employees of the defendant, First Security National Bank and Trust Company, numerous witnesses, most of whom were men of long experience in the field of banking, testified to the effect that, in their opinion, the consolidation of the two Lexington banks herein referred to would not lessen competition in the banking field in Fayette County and did not tend to create a monopoly in that field.

"According to their testimony, the fact that the merged bank had a large percentage of the trust business of the community did not and would not substantially restrain or lessen competition in the field of commercial banking." 208 F. Supp., at 459-460.[8]

The motive behind the consolidation also is indicated by the findings below, similarly unchallenged, that ". . . the consolidation herein referred to clearly appears to have been the result of a lawful program of expansion on the part of the merging banks rather than an invidious scheme to restrain competition or to secure monopoly in the local field of banking." 208 F. Supp., at 460. Any doubts on this score are removed by the explicit concession of government counsel at oral argument before this Court that there is no evidence at all in the record of an anticompetitive motive behind the consolidation.

There is nothing whatever in the findings below or in the opinion of this Court pertinent to the other criteria laid down in Columbia Steel—the probable development of the industry, consumer demands, and other market characteristics—which supports the Court's conclusion.[9]

In sum, the Court's analysis of the facts of this case ends where it begins; the conclusion that the consolidation violates the Sherman Act collapses into the agreed premise that First Security is "big."

III.

The truth is, of course, that this is, if anything, a Clayton Act case masquerading in the garb of the Sherman Act. One can hardly doubt that it comes to us under these false colors only because the decision last Term that bank mergers could be reached under the Clayton Act was indeed a surprise to the Government. See my dissenting opinion in Philadelphia National Bank, supra, at 373. No one has more sympathy for the Government in this respect than I. Nevertheless, having "at the outset elected to proceed not under the Clayton but the Sherman Act," Times-Picayune Pub. Co. v. United States, 345 U. S. 594,

609, "the Government here must measure up to the criteria of the more stringent law," id., at 610.

The pernicious effect of allowing the Government to change horses in midstream in fact if not quite in form[10] goes beyond this case and, in the field of banking, beyond even the revitalization of a properly moribund rule of antitrust law. In combination with the Philadelphia National Bank case, today's decision effectively precludes any possibility that the will of the Congress with respect to bank mergers will be carried out. The Congress has plainly indicated that it does not intend that mergers in the banking field be measured solely by the antitrust considerations which are applied in other industries. Characteristic of such indications, set out in detail in my dissenting opinion in the Philadelphia National Bank case, supra, at 374-386, is the following excerpt from the Senate Report on the bill which became the Bank Merger Act of 1960, 12 U. S. C. (Supp. IV, 1963) § 1828 (c):

"The committee wants to make crystal clear its intention that the various banking factors in any particular case may be held to outweigh the competitive factors, and that the competitive factors, however favorable or unfavorable, are not, in and of themselves, controlling on the decision." S. Rep. No. 196, 86th Cong., 1st Sess., 24.

Adherence to the principles enunciated in Columbia Steel, supra, would leave room for an accommodation within the framework of the antitrust laws of the special features of banking recognized by Congress. It is difficult to see how features peculiar to banking or indeed any other features of a particular case which, in reason, should lead to a different result, can stand up against the bludgeon with which the Court now strikes at combinations which may well have no fault except "bigness."

I would affirm.

Notes

[1] Compare the dissenting opinion in United States v. Columbia Steel Co., 334 U. S. 495, 534.

[2] The reason for singling out this aspect of the banks' activities is unclear, since the Court does not determine even whether trust department services should be regarded as a relevant market. See ante, p. 667, note 3. In view of the majority's disposition of the case, I do not set out here my reasons for believing that the District Court's determination that the consolidation in question does not violate § 2 of the Sherman Act (monopoly) should be affirmed.

[3] United States v. Yellow Cab Co., 332 U. S. 218, cited by the Court, ante, p. 671, is wholly irrelevant.

[4] Northern Securities Co. v. United States, 193 U. S. 197; United States v. Union Pacific R. Co., 226 U. S. 61; United States v. Southern Pacific Co., 259 U. S. 214.

[5] United States v. Reading Co., 253 U. S. 26, 59.

[6] The presumption which the Court laid down in Philadelphia National Bank, supra, at 363, that "a merger which produces a firm controlling an undue percentage share

of the relevant market, and results in a significant increase in the concentration of firms in that market, is . . . inherently likely to lessen competition substantially. . ." was concerned with the application of § 7 of the Clayton Act. Compare Times-Picayune Pub. Co. v. United States, 345 U. S. 594, 612, a Sherman Act case in which the Court noted that "no magic inheres in numbers," and quoted with approval the statement in Columbia Steel, supra, at 528, that "the relative effect of percentage command of a market varies with the setting in which that factor is placed."

[7] As found by the District Court, in 1960, First National had "total assets of $65,069,000, total deposits of $58,673,000 and total net loans and discounts of $35,434,000." 208 F. Supp., at 459. Security Trust, in 1960, had "total assets of $21,033,000, total deposits of $17,402,000 and total net loans and discounts of $12,317,000." Ibid.

[8] The only contrary evidence, testimony of presidents of three of the four competing local banks who "expressed considerable fear that the consolidation would result in serious loss to the other banks and would be disastrous to some of them," 208 F. Supp., at 460, was discredited by the District Court. See supra, p. 674.

[9] With reference to the probable development of the industry, the Government turns to the past and notes that the number of local banks decreased from 10 to 7 between 1929 and 1938; but this statistic, more at home in a Clayton Act case, is of doubtful significance in the present context, particularly in view of the period during which the decrease occurred. The same may be said of the Government's reference to the testimony of the president of a competing bank that the consolidation from which his bank resulted was carried through (years before the First Security consolidation) principally to enable it "to better compete with the First National." In fact, in the three years since the First Security consolidation, there has been no further concentration.

[10] It is one thing to say, as the Court did in Times-Picayune, supra, at 609, that "the Clayton Act's more specific standards illuminate the public policy which the Sherman Act was designed to subserve . . . ." It is quite another thing to treat them as interchangeable. See id., at 609-610.

Justice Harlan's dissent in Reynolds v. Sims (June 15, 1964) [Notes and appendices omitted] [Asterisk note omitted]

MR. JUSTICE HARLAN, dissenting. *

In these cases the Court holds that seats in the legislatures of six States 1 are apportioned in ways that violate the Federal Constitution. Under the Court's ruling it is bound to follow that the legislatures in all but a few of the other 44 States will meet the same fate. 2 These decisions, with Wesberry v. Sanders, 376 U.S. 1, involving congressional districting by the States, and Gray v. Sanders, 372 U.S. 368, relating to elections for statewide office, have the effect of placing basic aspects of state political systems under the pervasive overlordship of the federal judiciary. Once again, 3 I must register my protest.

PRELIMINARY STATEMENT.

Today's holding is that the Equal Protection Clause of the Fourteenth Amendment requires every State to structure its legislature so that all the members of each house represent substantially the same number of people; other factors may be given play only to the extent that they do not significantly encroach on this basic "population" principle. Whatever may be thought of this holding as a piece of political ideology - and even on that score the political history and practices of this country from its earliest beginnings leave wide room for debate (see the dissenting opinion of Frankfurter, J., in Baker v. Carr, 369 U.S. 186, 266, 301-323) - I think it demonstrable that the Fourteenth Amendment does not impose this political tenet on the States or authorize this Court to do so.

The Court's constitutional discussion, found in its opinion in the Alabama cases (Nos. 23, 27, 41, ante, p. 533) and more particularly at pages 561-568 thereof, is remarkable (as, indeed, is that found in the separate opinions of my Brothers STEWART and CLARK, ante, pp. 588, 587) for its failure to address itself at all to the Fourteenth Amendment as a whole or to the legislative history of the Amendment pertinent to the matter at hand. Stripped of aphorisms, the Court's argument boils down to the assertion that appellees' right to vote has been invidiously "debased" or "diluted" by systems of apportionment which entitle them to vote for fewer legislators than other voters, an assertion which is tied to the Equal Protection Clause only by the constitutionally frail tautology that "equal" means "equal."

Had the Court paused to probe more deeply into the matter, it would have found that the Equal Protection Clause was never intended to inhibit the States in choosing any democratic method they pleased for the apportionment of their legislatures. This is shown by the language of the Fourteenth Amendment taken as a whole, by the understanding of those who proposed and ratified it, and by the political practices of the States at the time the Amendment was adopted. It is confirmed by numerous state and congressional actions since the adoption of the Fourteenth Amendment, and by the common understanding of the Amendment as evidenced by subsequent constitutional amendments and decisions of this Court before Baker v. Carr, supra, made an abrupt break with the past in 1962.

The failure of the Court to consider any of these matters cannot be excused or explained by any concept of "developing" constitutionalism. It is meaningless to speak of constitutional "development" when both the language and history of the controlling provisions of the Constitution are wholly ignored. Since it can, I think, be shown beyond doubt that state legislative apportionments, as such, are wholly free of constitutional limitations, save such as may be imposed by the Republican Form of Government Clause (Const., Art. IV, 4), 4 the Court's action now bringing them within the purview of the Fourteenth Amendment amounts to nothing less than an exercise of the amending power by this Court.

So far as the Federal Constitution is concerned, the complaints in these cases should all have been dismissed below for failure to state a cause of action, because what has been alleged or proved shows no violation of any constitutional right.

Before proceeding to my argument it should be observed that nothing done in Baker v. Carr, supra, or in the two cases that followed in its wake, Gray v. Sanders and Wesberry v. Sanders, supra, from which the Court quotes at some length, forecloses the conclusion which I reach.

Baker decided only that claims such as those made here are within the competence of the federal courts to adjudicate. Although the Court stated as its conclusion that the allegations of a denial of equal protection presented "a justiciable constitutional cause of action," 369 U.S., at 237, it is evident from the Court's opinion that it was concerned all but exclusively with justiciability and gave no serious attention to the question whether the Equal Protection Clause touches state legislative apportionments. 5 Neither the opinion of the Court nor any of the concurring opinions considered the relevant text of the Fourteenth Amendment or any of the historical materials bearing on that question. None of the materials was briefed or otherwise brought to the Court's attention. 6

In the Gray case the Court expressly laid aside the applicability to state legislative apportionments of the "one person, one vote" theory there found to require the striking down of the Georgia county unit system. See 372 U.S., at 376, and the concurring opinion of STEWART, J., joined by CLARK, J., id., at 381-382.

In Wesberry, involving congressional districting, the decision rested on Art. I, 2, of the Constitution. The Court expressly did not reach the arguments put forward concerning the Equal Protection Clause. See 376 U.S., at 8, note 10.

Thus it seems abundantly clear that the Court is entirely free to deal with the cases presently before it in light of materials now called to its attention for the first time. To these I now turn.

I.

A. The Language of the Fourteenth Amendment.

The Court relies exclusively on that portion of 1 of the Fourteenth Amendment which provides that no State shall "deny to any person within its jurisdiction the equal protection of the laws," and disregards entirely the significance of 2, which reads:

"Representatives shall be apportioned among the several States according to their respective numbers, counting the whole number of persons in each State, excluding Indians not taxed. But when the right to vote at any election for the choice of electors for President and Vice President of the United States, Representatives in Congress, the Executive and Judicial officers of a State, or the members of the Legislature thereof, is denied to any of the male inhabitants of such State, being twenty-one years of age, and citizens of the United States, or in any way abridged, except for participation in rebellion, or other crime, the basis of representation therein shall be reduced in the proportion which the number of such male citizens shall bear to the whole number of male citizens twenty-one years of age in such State." (Emphasis added.)

The Amendment is a single text. It was introduced and discussed as such in the

Reconstruction Committee, 7 which reported it to the Congress. It was discussed as a unit in Congress and proposed as a unit to the States, 8 which ratified it as a unit. A proposal to split up the Amendment and submit each section to the States as a separate amendment was rejected by the Senate. 9 Whatever one might take to be the application to these cases of the Equal Protection Clause if it stood alone, I am unable to understand the Court's utter disregard of the second section which expressly recognizes the States' power to deny "or in any way" abridge the right of their inhabitants to vote for "the members of the [State] Legislature," and its express provision of a remedy for such denial or abridgment. The comprehensive scope of the second section and its particular reference to the state legislatures preclude the suggestion that the first section was intended to have the result reached by the Court today. If indeed the words of the Fourteenth Amendment speak for themselves, as the majority's disregard of history seems to imply, they speak as clearly as may be against the construction which the majority puts on them. But we are not limited to the language of the Amendment itself.

B. Proposal and Ratification of the Amendment.

The history of the adoption of the Fourteenth Amendment provides conclusive evidence that neither those who proposed nor those who ratified the Amendment believed that the Equal Protection Clause limited the power of the States to apportion their legislatures as they saw fit. Moreover, the history demonstrates that the intention to leave this power undisturbed was deliberate and was widely believed to be essential to the adoption of the Amendment.

(i) Proposal of the amendment in Congress. - A resolution proposing what became the Fourteenth Amendment was reported to both houses of Congress by the Reconstruction Committee of Fifteen on April 30, 1866, 10 The first two sections of the proposed amendment read:

"SEC. 1. No State shall make or enforce any law which shall abridge the privileges or immunities of citizens of the United States; nor shall any State deprive any person of life, liberty, or property without due process of law; nor deny to any person within its jurisdiction the equal protection of the laws.

"SEC. 2. Representatives shall be apportioned among the several States which may be included within this Union, according to their respective numbers, counting the whole number of persons in each State, excluding Indians not taxed. But whenever, in any State, the elective franchise shall be denied to any portion of its male citizens not less than twenty-one years of age, or in any way abridged except for participation in rebellion or other crime, the basis of representation in such State shall be reduced in the proportion which the number of such male citizens shall bear to the whole number of male citizens not less than twenty-one years of age." 11

In the House, Thaddeus Stevens introduced debate on the resolution on May 8. In his opening remarks, Stevens explained why he supported the resolution although it fell "far short" of his wishes:

"I believe it is all that can be obtained in the present state of public opinion. Not only Congress but the several States are to be consulted. Upon a careful survey of the whole ground, we did not believe that nineteen of the loyal States could be induced to ratify any proposition more stringent than this." 12

In explanation of this belief, he asked the House to remember "that three months since, and more, the committee reported and the House adopted a proposed amendment fixing the basis of representation in such way as would surely have secured the enfranchisement of every citizen at no distant period," but that proposal had been rejected by the Senate. 13

He then explained the impact of the first section of the proposed Amendment, particularly the Equal Protection Clause.

"This amendment . . . allows Congress to correct the unjust legislation of the States, so far that the law which operates upon one man shall operate equally upon all. Whatever law punishes a white man for a crime shall punish the black man precisely in the same way and to the same degree. Whatever law protects the white man shall afford `equal' protection to the black man. Whatever means of redress is afforded to one shall be afforded to all. Whatever law allows the white man to testify in court shall allow the man of color to do the same. These are great advantages over their present codes. Now different degrees of punishment are inflicted, not on account of the magnitude of the crime, but according to the color of the skin. Now color disqualifies a man from testifying in courts, or being tried in the same way as white men. I need not enumerate these partial and oppressive laws. Unless the Constitution should restrain them those States will all, I fear, keep up this discrimination, and crush to death the hated freedmen." 14

He turned next to the second section, which he said he considered "the most important in the article." 15 Its effect, he said, was to fix "the basis of representation in Congress." 16 In unmistakable terms, he recognized the power of a State to withhold the right to vote:

"If any State shall exclude any of her adult male citizens from the elective franchise, or abridge that right, she shall forfeit her right to representation in the same proportion. The effect of this provision will be either to compel the States to grant universal suffrage or so to shear them of their power as to keep them forever in a hopeless minority in the national Government, both legislative and executive." 17

Closing his discussion of the second section, he noted his dislike for the fact that it allowed "the States to discriminate [with respect to the right to vote] among the same class, and receive proportionate credit in representation." 18

Toward the end of the debate three days later, Mr. Bingham, the author of the first section in the Reconstruction Committee and its leading proponent, 19 concluded his discussion of it with the following:

"Allow me, Mr. Speaker, in passing, to say that this amendment takes from no State any right that ever pertained to it. No State ever had the right, under the forms of law or otherwise, to deny to any freeman the equal protection of the laws or to abridge the privileges or immunities of any citizen of the Republic, although many of them have assumed and exercised the power, and that without remedy. The amendment does not give, as the second section shows, the power to Congress of regulating suffrage in the several States." 20 (Emphasis added.)

He immediately continued:

"The second section excludes the conclusion that by the first section suffrage is subjected to congressional law; save, indeed, with this exception, that as the right in the people of each State to a republican government and to choose their Representatives in Congress is of the guarantees of the Constitution, by this amendment a remedy might be given directly for a case supposed by Madison, where treason might change a State government from a republican to a despotic government, and thereby deny suffrage to the people." 21 (Emphasis added.)

He stated at another point in his remarks:

"To be sure we all agree, and the great body of the people of this country agree, and the committee thus far in reporting measures of reconstruction agree, that the exercise of the elective franchise, though it be one of the privileges of a citizen of the Republic, is exclusively under the control of the States." 22 (Emphasis added.)

In the three days of debate which separate the opening and closing remarks, both made by members of the Reconstruction Committee, every speaker on the resolution, with a single doubtful exception, 23 assumed without question that, as Mr. Bingham said, supra, "the second section excludes the conclusion that by the first section suffrage is subjected to congressional law." The assumption was neither inadvertent nor silent. Much of the debate concerned the change in the basis of representation effected by the second section, and the speakers stated repeatedly, in express terms or by unmistakable implication, that the States retained the power to regulate suffrage within their borders. Attached as Appendix A hereto are some of those statements. The resolution was adopted by the House without change on May 10. 24

Debate in the Senate began on May 23, and followed the same pattern. Speaking for the Senate Chairman of the Reconstruction Committee, who was ill, Senator Howard, also a member of the Committee, explained the meaning of the Equal Protection Clause as follows:

"The last two clauses of the first section of the amendment disable a State from depriving not merely a citizen of the United States, but any person, whoever he may be, of life, liberty, or property without due process of law, or from denying to him the equal protection of the laws of the State. This abolishes all class legislation in the States and does away with the injustice of subjecting one caste of persons to a code not applicable to another. It prohibits the hanging of a black man for a crime for which the white man is not to be hanged. It protects the black man in his fundamental rights as a citizen with the same shield which it throws over the white man. Is it not time, Mr. President, that we extend to the black man, I had almost called it the poor privilege of the equal protection of the law? . . .

"But, sir, the first section of the proposed amendment does not give to either of these classes the right of voting. The right of suffrage is not, in law, one of the privileges or immunities thus secured by the Constitution. It is merely the creature of law. It has always been regarded in this country as the result of positive local law, not regarded as one of those fundamental rights lying at the basis of all society and without which a people cannot exist except as slaves, subject to a depotism [sic]." 25 (Emphasis added.)

Discussing the second section, he expressed his regret that it did "not recognize the authority of the United States over the question of suffrage in the several States at all . . . ." 26 He justified the limited purpose of the Amendment in this regard as follows:

"But, sir, it is not the question here what will we do; it is not the question what you, or I, or half a dozen other members of the Senate may prefer in respect to colored suffrage; it is not entirely the question what measure we can pass through the two Houses; but the question really is, what will the Legislatures of the various States to whom these amendments are to be submitted do in the premises; what is it likely will meet the general approbation of the people who are to elect the Legislatures, three fourths of whom must ratify our propositions before they have the force of constitutional provisions?

. . . . .

"The committee were of opinion that the States are not yet prepared to sanction so fundamental a change as would be the concession of the right of suffrage to the colored race. We may as well state it plainly and fairly, so that there shall be no misunderstanding on the subject. It was our opinion that three fourths of the States of this Union could not be induced to vote to grant the right of suffrage, even in any degree or under any restriction, to the colored race. . . .

"The second section leaves the right to regulate the elective franchise still with the States, and does not meddle with that right." 27 (Emphasis added.)

There was not in the Senate, as there had been in the House, a closing speech in explanation of the Amendment. But because the Senate considered, and finally adopted, several changes in the first and second sections, even more attention was given to the problem of voting rights there than had been given in the House. In the Senate, it was fully understood by everyone that neither the first nor the second section interfered with the right of the States to regulate the elective franchise. Attached as Appendix B hereto are representative statements from the debates to that effect. After having changed the proposed amendment to the form in which it was adopted, the Senate passed the resolution on June 8, 1866. 28 As changed, it passed in the House on June 13. 29

(ii) Ratification by the "loyal" States. - Reports of the debates in the state legislatures on the ratification of the Fourteenth Amendment are not generally available. 30 There is, however, compelling indirect evidence. Of the 23 loyal States which ratified the Amendment before 1870, five had constitutional provisions for apportionment of at least one house of their respective legislatures which wholly disregarded the spread of population. 31 Ten more had constitutional provisions which gave primary emphasis to population, but which applied also other principles, such as partial ratios and recognition of political subdivisions, which were intended to favor sparsely settled areas. 32 Can it be seriously contended that the legislatures of these States, almost two-thirds of those concerned, would have ratified an amendment which might render their own States' constitutions unconstitutional?

Nor were these state constitutional provisions merely theoretical. In New Jersey, for example, Cape May County, with a population of 8, 349, and Ocean County, with a population of 13,628, each elected one State Senator, as did Essex and Hudson Counties, with populations of 143,839 and 129,067, respectively. 33 In the House, each county was entitled to one representative, which left 39 seats to be apportioned according to population. 34 Since there were 12 counties besides the two already mentioned which had populations over 30,000, 35 it is evident that there were serious disproportions in the House also. In New York, each of the 60 counties except Hamilton County was entitled to one of the 128 seats in the Assembly. 36 This left 69 seats to be distributed among counties the populations of which ranged from 15,420 to 942, 292. 37 With seven more counties having populations over 100,000 and 13 others having populations over 50,000, 38 the disproportion in the Assembly was necessarily large. In Vermont, after each county had been allocated one Senator, there were 16 seats remaining to be distributed among the larger counties. 39 The smallest county had a population of 4,082; the largest had a population of 40,651 and there were 10 other counties with populations over 20,000. 40

(iii) Ratification by the "reconstructed" States. - Each of the 10 "reconstructed" States was required to ratify the Fourteenth Amendment before it was readmitted to the Union. 41 The Constitution of each was scrutinized in Congress. 42 Debates over readmission were extensive. 43 In at least one instance, the problem of state legislative apportionment was expressly called to the attention of Congress. Objecting to the inclusion of Florida in the Act of June 25, 1868, Mr. Farnsworth stated on the floor of the House:

"I might refer to the apportionment of representatives. By this constitution representatives in the Legislature of Florida are apportioned in such a manner as to give to the sparsely-populated portions of the State the control of the Legislature. The sparsely-populated parts of the State are those where there are very few negroes, the parts inhabited by the white rebels, the men who, coming in from Georgia, Alabama, and other States, control the fortunes of their several counties. By this constitution every county in that State is entitled to a representative. There are in that State counties that have not thirty registered voters; yet, under this constitution, every one of those counties is entitled to a representative in the Legislature; while the populous counties are entitled to only one representative each, with an additional representative for every thousand inhabitants." 44

The response of Mr. Butler is particularly illuminating:

"All these arguments, all these statements, all the provisions of this constitution have been submitted to the Judiciary Committee of the Senate, and they have found the constitution republican and proper. This constitution has been submitted to the Senate, and they have found it republican and proper. It has been submitted to your own Committee on Reconstruction, and they have found it republican and proper, and have reported it to this House." 45

The Constitutions of six of the 10 States contained provisions departing substantially from the method of apportionment now held to be required by the Amendment. 46 And, as in the North, the departures were as real in fact as in theory. In North Carolina, 90 of the 120 representatives were apportioned among the counties without regard to population, leaving 30 seats to be distributed by numbers. 47 Since there were seven counties with populations under 5,000 and 26 counties with populations over 15,000, the disproportions must have been widespread and substantial. 48 In South Carolina, Charleston, with a population of 88,863, elected two Senators; each of the other counties, with populations ranging from 10, 269 to 42,486, elected one Senator. 49 In Florida, each of the 39 counties was entitled to elect one Representative; no county was entitled to more than four. 50 These principles applied to Dade County, with a population of 85, and to Alachua County and Leon County, with populations of 17, 328 and 15, 236, respectively. 51

It is incredible that Congress would have exacted ratification of the Fourteenth Amendment as the price of readmission, would have studied the State Constitutions for compliance with the Amendment, and would then have disregarded violations of it.

The facts recited above show beyond any possible doubt:

(1) that Congress, with full awareness of and attention to the possibility that the States would not afford full equality in voting rights to all their citizens, nevertheless deliberately chose not to interfere with the States' plenary power in this regard when it proposed the Fourteenth Amendment;

(2) that Congress did not include in the Fourteenth Amendment restrictions on the States' power to control voting rights because it believed that if such restrictions were included, the Amendment would not be adopted; and

(3) that at least a substantial majority, if not all, of the States which ratified the Fourteenth Amendment did not consider that in so doing, they were accepting limitations on their freedom, never before questioned, to regulate voting rights as they chose.

Even if one were to accept the majority's belief that it is proper entirely to disregard the unmistakable implications of the second section of the Amendment in construing the first section, one is confounded by its disregard of all this history. There is here none of the difficulty which may attend the application of basic principles to situations not contemplated or understood when the principles were framed. The problems which concern the Court now were problems when the Amendment was adopted. By the deliberate choice of those responsible for the Amendment, it left those problems untouched.

C. After 1868.

The years following 1868, far from indicating a developing awareness of the applicability of the Fourteenth Amendment to problems of apportionment, demonstrate precisely the reverse: that the States retained and exercised the power independently to apportion their legislatures. In its Constitutions of 1875 and 1901, Alabama carried forward earlier provisions guaranteeing each county at least one representative and fixing an upper limit to the number of seats in the House. 52 Florida's Constitution of 1885 continued the guarantee of one representative for each county and reduced the maximum number of representatives per county from four to three. 53 Georgia, in 1877, continued to favor the smaller counties. 54 Louisiana, in 1879, guaranteed each parish at least one representative in the House. 55 In 1890, Mississippi guaranteed each county one representative, established a maximum number of representatives, and provided that specified groups of counties should each have approximately one-third of the seats in the House, whatever the spread of population. 56 Missouri's Constitution of 1875 gave each county one representative and otherwise favored less populous areas. 57 Montana's original Constitution of 1889 apportioned the State Senate by counties. 58 In 1877, New Hampshire amended its Constitution's provisions for apportionment, but continued to favor sparsely settled areas in the House and to apportion seats in the Senate according to direct taxes paid; 59 the same was true of New Hampshire's Constitution of 1902. 60

In 1894, New York adopted a Constitution the peculiar apportionment provisions of which were obviously intended to prevent representation according to population: no county was allowed to have more than one-third of all the Senators, no two counties which were adjoining or "separated only by public waters" could have more than one-half of all the Senators, and whenever any county became entitled to more than three Senators, the total number of Senators was increased, thus preserving to the small counties their original number of seats. 61 In addition, each county except Hamilton was guaranteed a seat in the Assembly. 62 The North Carolina Constitution of 1876 gave each county at least one representative and fixed a maximum number of representatives for the whole House. 63 Oklahoma's Constitution at the time of its admission to the Union (1907) favored small counties by the use of partial ratios and a maximum number of seats in the House; in addition, no county was permitted to "take part" in the election of more than seven representatives. 64 Pennsylvania, in 1873, continued to guarantee each county one representative in the House. 65 The same was true of South Carolina's Constitution of 1895, which provided also that each county should elect one and only one Senator. 66 Utah's original Constitution of 1895 assured each county of one representative in the House. 67 Wyoming, when it entered the Union in 1889, guaranteed each county at least one Senator and one representative. 68

D. Today.

Since the Court now invalidates the legislative apportionments in six States, and has so far upheld the apportionment in none, it is scarcely necessary to comment on the situation in the States today, which is, of course, as fully contrary to the Court's decision as is the record of every prior period in this Nation's history. As of 1961, the Constitutions of all but 11 States, roughly 20% of the total, recognized bases of apportionment other than geographic spread of population, and to some extent favored sparsely populated areas by a variety of devices, ranging from straight area representation or guaranteed minimum area representation to complicated schemes of the kind exemplified by the provisions of New

York's Constitution of 1894, still in effect until struck down by the Court today in No. 20, post, p. 633. 69 Since Tennessee, which was the subject of Baker v. Carr, and Virginia, scrutinized and disapproved today in No. 69, post, p. 678, are among the 11 States whose own Constitutions are sound from the standpoint of the Federal Constitution as construed today, it is evident that the actual practice of the States is even more uniformly than their theory opposed to the Court's view of what is constitutionally permissible.

    E. Other Factors.

    In this summary of what the majority ignores, note should be taken of the Fifteenth and Nineteenth Amendments. The former prohibited the States from denying or abridging the right to vote "on account of race, color, or previous condition of servitude." The latter, certified as part of the Constitution in 1920, added sex to the prohibited classifications. In Minor v. Happersett, 21 Wall. 162, this Court considered the claim that the right of women to vote was protected by the Privileges and Immunities Clause of the Fourteenth Amendment. The Court's discussion there of the significance of the Fifteenth Amendment is fully applicable here with respect to the Nineteenth Amendment as well.

    "And still again, after the adoption of the fourteenth amendment, it was deemed necessary to adopt a fifteenth, as follows: `The right of citizens of the United States to vote shall not be denied or abridged by the United States, or by any State, on account of race, color, or previous condition of servitude.' The fourteenth amendment had already provided that no State should make or enforce any law which should abridge the privileges or immunities of citizens of the United States. If suffrage was one of these privileges or immunities, why amend the Constitution to prevent its being denied on account of race, &c.? Nothing is more evident than that the greater must include the less, and if all were already protected why go through with the form of amending the Constitution to protect a part?" Id., at 175.

    In the present case, we can go still further. If constitutional amendment was the only means by which all men and, later, women, could be guaranteed the right to vote at all, even for federal officers, how can it be that the far less obvious right to a particular kind of apportionment of state legislatures - a right to which is opposed a far more plausible conflicting interest of the State than the interest which opposes the general right to vote - can be conferred by judicial construction of the Fourteenth Amendment? 70 Yet, unless one takes the highly implausible view that the Fourteenth Amendment controls methods of apportionment but leaves the right to vote itself unprotected, the conclusion is inescapable that the Court has, for purposes of these cases, relegated the Fifteenth and Nineteenth Amendments to the same limbo of constitutional anachronisms to which the second section of the Fourteenth Amendment has been assigned.

    Mention should be made finally of the decisions of this Court which are disregarded or, more accurately, silently overruled today. Minor v. Happersett, supra, in which the Court held that the Fourteenth Amendment did not confer the right to vote on anyone, has already been noted. Other cases are more directly in point. In Colegrove v. Barrett, 330 U.S. 804, this Court dismissed "for want of a substantial federal question" an appeal from the dismissal of a complaint alleging that the Illinois legislative apportionment resulted in "gross inequality in voting power" and "gross and arbitrary and atrocious discrimination in voting" which denied the plaintiffs equal protection of the laws. 71 In Remmey v. Smith, 102 F. Supp. 708 (D.C. E. D. Pa.), a three-judge District Court dismissed a complaint alleging that the apportionment of the Pennsylvania Legislature deprived the plaintiffs of "constitutional rights guaranteed to them by the Fourteenth Amendment." Id., at 709. The District Court stated that it was aware that the plaintiffs' allegations were "notoriously true" and that "the practical disenfranchisement of qualified electors in certain of the election districts in Philadelphia County is a matter of common knowledge." Id., at 710. This Court dismissed the appeal " for the want of a substantial federal question." 342 U.S. 916 .

In Kidd v. McCanless, 200 Tenn. 273, 292 S. W. 2d 40, the supreme Court of Tennessee dismissed an action for a declaratory judgment that the Tennessee Apportionment Act of 1901 was unconstitutional. The complaint alleged that "a minority of approximately 37% of the voting population of the State now elects and controls 20 of the 33 members of the Senate; that a minority of 40% of the voting population of the State now controls 63 of the 99 members of the House of Representatives." Id., at 276, 292 S. W. 2d, at 42. Without dissent, this Court granted the motion to dismiss the appeal. 352 U.S. 920 . In Radford v. Gary, 145 F. Supp. 541 (D.C. W. D. Okla.), a three-judge District Court was convened to consider "the complaint of the plaintiff to the effect that the existing apportionment statutes of the State of Oklahoma violate the plain mandate of the Oklahoma Constitution and operate to deprive him of the equal protection of the laws guaranteed by the Fourteenth Amendment to the Constitution of the United States." Id., at 542. The plaintiff alleged that he was a resident and voter in the most populous county of the State, which had about 15% of the total population of the State but only about 2% of the seats in the State Senate and less than 4% of the seats in the House. The complaint recited the unwillingness or inability of the branches of the state government to provide relief and alleged that there was no state remedy available. The District Court granted a motion to dismiss. This Court affirmed without dissent. 352 U.S. 991 .

Each of these recent cases is distinguished on some ground or other in Baker v. Carr. See 369 U.S., at 235 -236. Their summary dispositions prevent consideration whether these after-the-fact distinctions are real or imaginary. The fact remains, however, that between 1947 and 1957, four cases raising issues precisely the same as those decided today were presented to the Court. Three were dismissed because the issues presented were thought insubstantial and in the fourth the lower court's dismissal was affirmed. 72

I have tried to make the catalogue complete, yet to keep it within the manageable limits of a judicial opinion. In my judgment, today's decisions are refuted by the language of the Amendment which they construe and by the inference fairly to be drawn from subsequently enacted Amendments. They are unequivocally refuted by history and by consistent theory and practice from the time of the adoption of the Fourteenth Amendment until today.

II.

The Court's elaboration of its new "constitutional" doctrine indicates how far - and how unwisely - it has strayed from the appropriate bounds of its authority. The consequence of today's decision is that in all but the handful of States which may already satisfy the new requirements the local District Court or, it may be, the state courts, are given blanket authority and the constitutional duty to supervise apportionment of the State Legislatures. It is difficult to imagine a more intolerable and inappropriate interference by the judiciary with the independent legislatures of the States.

In the Alabama cases (Nos. 23, 27, 41), the District Court held invalid not only existing provisions of the State Constitution - which this Court lightly dismisses with a wave of the Supremacy Clause and the remark that "it makes no difference whether a State's apportionment scheme is embodied in its constitution or in statutory provisions," ante, p. 584 - but also a proposed amendment to the Alabama Constitution which had never been submitted to the voters of Alabama for ratification, and "standby" legislation which was not to become effective unless the amendment was rejected (or declared unconstitutional) and in no event before 1966. Sims v. Frink, 208 F. Supp. 431. See ante, pp. 543-551. Both of these measures had been adopted only nine days before, 73 at an Extraordinary Session of the Alabama Legislature, convened pursuant to what was very nearly a directive of the District Court, see Sims v. Frink, 205 F. Supp. 245, 248. The District Court formulated its own plan for the apportionment of the Alabama Legislature, by picking and choosing among the provisions of the legislative measures. 208 F. Supp., at 441-442. See ante, p. 552. Beyond that, the court warned the legislature that there would be still further judicial reapportionment unless the legislature, like it or not, undertook the task for itself. 208 F. Supp., at 442. This Court now states that the District Court acted in "a most proper and commendable manner," ante, p. 586, and approves the District Court's avowed intention of taking "some further action" unless the State Legislature acts by 1966, ante, p. 587.

In the Maryland case (No. 29, post, p. 656), the State Legislature was called into Special Session and enacted a temporary reapportionment of the House of Delegates, under pressure from the state courts. 74 Thereafter, the Maryland Court of Appeals held that the Maryland Senate was constitutionally apportioned. Maryland Committee for Fair Representation v. Tawes, 229 Md. 406, 184 A. 2d 715. This Court now holds that neither branch of the State Legislature meets constitutional requirements. Post, p. 674. The Court presumes that since "the Maryland constitutional provisions relating to legislative apportionment [are] hereby held unconstitutional, the Maryland Legislature . . . has the inherent power to enact at least temporary reapportionment legislation pending adoption of state constitutional provisions" which satisfy the Federal Constitution, id., at 675. On this premise, the Court concludes that the Maryland courts need not "feel obliged to take further affirmative action" now, but that "under no circumstances should the 1966 election of members of the Maryland Legislature be permitted to be conducted pursuant to the existing or any other unconstitutional plan." Id., at 676.

In the Virginia case (No. 69, post, p. 678), the State Legislature in 1962 complied with the state constitutional requirement of regular reapportionment. 75 Two days later, a complaint was filed in the District Court. 76 Eight months later, the legislative reapportionment was declared unconstitutional. Mann v. Davis, 213 F. Supp. 577. The District Court gave the State Legislature two months within which to reapportion itself in special session, under penalty of being reapportioned by the court. 77 Only a stay granted by a member of this Court slowed the process; 78 it is plain that no stay will be forthcoming in the future. The Virginia Legislature is to be given "an adequate opportunity to enact a valid plan"; but if it fails "to act promptly in remedying the constitutional defects in the State's legislative apportionment plan," the District Court is to "take further action." Post, p. 693.

In Delaware (No. 307, post, p. 695), the District Court entered an order on July 25, 1962, which stayed proceedings until August 7, 1962, "in the hope and expectation" that the General Assembly would take "some appropriate action" in the intervening 13 days. Sincock v. Terry, 207 F. Supp. 205, 207. By way of prodding, presumably, the court noted that if no legislative action were taken and the court sustained the plaintiffs' claim, "the present General Assembly and any subsequent General Assembly, the members of which were elected pursuant to Section 2 of Article 2 [the challenged provisions of the Delaware Constitution], might be held not to be a de jure legislature and its legislative acts might be held invalid and unconstitutional." Id., at 205-206. Five days later, on July 30, 1962, the General Assembly approved a proposed amendment to the State Constitution. On August 7, 1962, the District Court entered an order denying the defendants' motion to dismiss. The court said that it did not wish to substitute its judgment "for the collective wisdom of the General Assembly of Delaware," but that "in the light of all the circumstances," it had to proceed promptly. 210 F. Supp. 395, 396. On October 16, 1962, the court declined to enjoin the conduct of elections in November. 210 F. Supp. 396. The court went on to express its regret that the General Assembly had not adopted the court's suggestion, see 207 F. Supp., at 206-207, that the Delaware Constitution be amended to make apportionment a statutory rather than a constitutional matter, so as to facilitate further changes in apportionment which might be required. 210 F. Supp., at 401. In January 1963, the General Assembly again approved the proposed amendment of the apportionment provisions of the Delaware Constitution, which thereby became effective on January 17, 1963. 79 Three months later, on April 17, 1963, the District Court reached "the reluctant conclusion" that Art. II, 2, of the Delaware Constitution was unconstitutional, with or without the 1963 amendment. Sincock v. Duffy, 215 F. Supp. 169, 189. Observing that "the State of Delaware, the General Assembly, and this court all seem to be trapped in a kind of box of time," id., at 191, the court gave the General Assembly until October 1, 1963, to adopt acceptable provisions for apportionment. On May 20, 1963, the District Court enjoined the defendants from conducting any elections, including the general election scheduled for November 1964, pursuant to the old or the new constitutional provisions. 80 This Court now approves all these proceedings, noting particularly that in allowing the 1962 elections to go forward, "the District Court acted in a wise and temperate manner." Post, p. 710. 81

Records such as these in the cases decided today are sure to be duplicated in most of the other States if they have not been already. They present a jarring picture of courts threatening to take action in an area which they have no business entering, inevitably on the basis of political judgments which they are incompetent to make. They show legislatures of the States meeting in haste and deliberating and deciding in haste to avoid the threat of judicial interference. So far as I can tell, the Court's only response to this unseemly state of affairs is ponderous insistence that "a denial of constitutionally protected rights demands judicial protection," ante, p. 566. By thus refusing to recognize the bearing which a potential for conflict of this kind may have on the question whether the claimed rights are in fact constitutionally entitled to judicial protection, the Court assumes, rather than supports, its conclusion.

It should by now be obvious that these cases do not mark the end of reapportionment problems in the courts. Predictions once made that the courts would never have to face the problem of actually working out an apportionment have proved false. This Court, however, continues to avoid the consequences of its decisions, simply assuring us that the lower courts "can and . . . will work out more concrete and specific standards," ante, p. 578. Deeming it "expedient" not to spell out "precise constitutional tests," the Court contents itself with stating "only a few rather general considerations." Ibid.

Generalities cannot obscure the cold truth that cases of this type are not amenable to the development of judicial standards. No set of standards can guide a court which has to decide how many legislative districts a State shall have, or what the shape of the districts shall be, or where to draw a particular district line. No judicially manageable standard can determine whether a State should have single-member districts or multimember districts or some combination of both. No such standard can control the balance between keeping up with population shifts and having stable districts. In all these respects, the courts will be called upon to make particular decisions with respect to which a principle of equally populated districts will be of no assistance whatsoever. Quite obviously, there are limitless possibilities for districting consistent with such a principle. Nor can these problems be avoided by judicial reliance on legislative judgments so far as possible. Reshaping or combining one or two districts, or modifying just a few district lines, is no less a matter of choosing among many possible solutions, with varying political consequences, than reapportionment broadside. 82

The Court ignores all this, saying only that "what is marginally permissible in one State may be unsatisfactory in another, depending on the particular circumstances of the case," ante, p. 578. It is well to remember that the product of today's decisions will not be readjustment of a few districts in a few States which most glaringly depart from the principle of equally populated districts. It will be a redetermination, extensive in many cases, of legislative districts in all but a few States.

Although the Court - necessarily, as I believe - provides only generalities in elaboration of its main thesis, its opinion nevertheless fully demonstrates how far removed these problems are from fields of judicial competence. Recognizing that "indiscriminate districting" is an invitation to "partisan gerrymandering," ante, pp. 578-579, the Court nevertheless excludes virtually every basis for the formation of electoral districts other than "indiscriminate districting." In one or another of today's opinions, the Court declares it unconstitutional for a State to give effective consideration to any of the following in establishing legislative districts:

(1) history; 83

(2) "economic or other sorts of group interests"; 84

(3) area; 85

(4) geographical considerations; 86

(5) a desire "to insure effective representation for sparsely settled areas"; 87

(6) "availability of access of citizens to their representatives"; 88

(7) theories of bicameralism (except those approved by the Court); 89

(8) occupation; 90

(9) "an attempt to balance urban and rural power." 91

(10) the preference of a majority of voters in the State. 92

So far as presently appears, the only factor which a State may consider, apart from numbers, is political subdivisions. But even "a clearly rational state policy" recognizing this factor is unconstitutional if "population is submerged as the controlling consideration . . . ." 93

I know of no principle of logic or practical or theoretical politics, still less any constitutional principle, which establishes all or any of these exclusions. Certain it is that the Court's opinion does not establish them. So far as the Court says anything at all on this score, it says only that "legislators represent people, not trees or acres," ante, p. 562; that "citizens, not history or economic interests, cast votes," ante, p. 580; that "people, not land or trees or pastures, vote," ibid. 94 All this may be conceded. But it is surely equally obvious, and, in the context of elections, more meaningful to note that people are not ciphers and that legislators can represent their electors only by speaking for their interests - economic, social, political - many of which do reflect the place where the electors live. The Court does not establish, or indeed even attempt to make a case for the proposition that conflicting interests within a State can only be adjusted by disregarding them when voters are grouped for purposes of representation.

CONCLUSION.

With these cases the Court approaches the end of the third round set in motion by the complaint filed in Baker v. Carr. What is done today deepens my conviction that judicial entry into this realm is profoundly ill-advised and constitutionally impermissible. As I have said before, Wesberry v. Sanders, supra, at 48, I believe that the vitality of our political system, on which in the last analysis all else depends, is weakened by reliance on the judiciary for political reform; in time a complacent body politic may result.

These decisions also cut deeply into the fabric of our federalism. What must follow from them may eventually appear to be the product of state legislatures. Nevertheless, no thinking person can fail to recognize that the aftermath of these cases, however desirable it may be thought in itself, will have been achieved at the cost of a radical alteration in the relationship between the States and the Federal Government, more particularly the Federal Judiciary. Only one who has an overbearing impatience with the federal system and its political processes will believe that that cost was not too high or was inevitable.

Finally, these decisions give support to a current mistaken view of the Constitution and the constitutional function of this Court. This view, in a nutshell, is that every major social ill in this country can find its cure in some constitutional "principle," and that this Court should "take the lead" in promoting reform when other branches of government fail to act. The Constitution is not a panacea for every blot upon the public welfare, nor should this Court, ordained as a judicial body, be thought of as a general haven for reform movements. The Constitution is an instrument of government, fundamental to which is the premise that in a diffusion of governmental authority lies the greatest promise that this Nation will realize liberty for all its citizens. This Court, limited in function in accordance with that premise, does not serve its high purpose when it exceeds its authority, even to satisfy justified impatience with the slow workings of the political process. For when, in the name of constitutional interpretation, the Court adds something to the Constitution that was deliberately excluded from it, the Court in reality substitutes its view of what should be so for the amending process.

I dissent in each of these cases, believing that in none of them have the plaintiffs stated a cause of action. To the extent that Baker v. Carr, expressly or by implication, went beyond a discussion of jurisdictional doctrines independent of the substantive issues involved here, it should be limited to what it in fact was: an experiment in venturesome constitutionalism. I would reverse the judgments of the District Courts in Nos. 23, 27, and 41 (Alabama), No. 69 (Virginia), and No. 307 (Delaware), and remand with directions to dismiss the complaints. I would affirm the judgments of the District Courts in No. 20 (New York), and No. 508 (Colorado), and of the Court of Appeals of Maryland in No. 29.

Justice Harlan's dissent in US v. Continental Can Co. (June 22, 1964)

MR. JUSTICE HARLAN, whom MR. JUSTICE STEWART joins, dissenting.

Measured by any antitrust yardsticks with which I am familiar, the Court's conclusions are, to say the least, remarkable. Before the merger which is the subject of this case, Continental Can manufactured metal containers and Hazel-Atlas manufactured glass containers.[1] The District Court found, with ample support in the record, that the Government had wholly failed to prove that the merger of these two companies would adversely affect competition in the metal container industry, in the glass container industry, or between the metal container industry and the glass container industry. Yet this Court manages to strike down the merger under § 7 of the Clayton Act, because, in the

Court's view, it is anticompetitive.[2] With all respect, the Court's conclusion is based on erroneous analysis, which makes an abrupt and unwise departure from established antitrust law.

I agree fully with the Court that "we must recognize meaningful competition where it is found," ante, p. 449, and that "inter-industry" competition, such as that involved in this case, no less than "intra-industry" competition is protected by § 7 from anticompetitive mergers. As this Court has, in effect, recognized in past cases, the concept of an "industry," or "line of commerce," is not susceptible of reduction to a precise formula. See Brown Shoe Co., Inc., v. United States, 370 U. S. 294, 325; United States v. E. I. du Pont de Nemours & Co., 351 U. S. 377, 394-396; Times-Picayune Publishing Co. v. United States, 345 U. S. 594, 611. It would, therefore, be artificial and inconsistent with the broad protective purpose of § 7, see Brown Shoe, supra, at 311-323, to attempt to differentiate between permitted and prohibited mergers merely by asking whether a probable reduction in competition, if it is found, will be within a single "industry" or between two or more "industries."

Recognition that the purpose of § 7 is not to be thwarted by limiting its protection to intramural competition within strictly defined "industries," does not mean, however, that the concept of a "line of commerce" is no longer serviceable. More precisely, it does not, as the majority seems to think, entail the conclusion that wherever "meaningful competition" exists, a "line of commerce" is to be found. The Court declares the initial question of this case to be "whether the admitted competition between metal and glass containers for uses other than packaging beer was of the type and quality deserving of § 7 protection and therefore the basis for defining a relevant product market." Ante, p. 449. (Emphasis added.) And the Court's answer is similarly phrased: ". . . [W]e hold that the interindustry competition between glass and metal containers is sufficient to warrant treating as a relevant product market the combined glass and metal container industries and all end uses for which they compete." Ante, p. 457. (Emphasis added.) Quite obviously, such a conclusion simply reads the "line of commerce" element out of § 7, and destroys its usefulness as an aid to analysis.

The distortions to which this approach leads are evidenced by the Court's application of it in this case.

Having found that there is "interindustry competition between glass and metal containers" the Court concludes that "the combined glass and metal container industries" is the relevant line of commerce or "product market" in which anticompetitive effects must be measured. Ante, p. 457. Applying that premise, the Court then notes Continental's "dominant position" in the metal can industry, ante, p. 458, and finds that Continental has a "major position" in the "relevant product market—the combined metal and glass container industries," ante, p. 459. (Emphasis added.) Hazel-Atlas, being the third largest producer of glass containers, is found to rank sixth in the relevant product market—again, the combined metal and glass container industries. Ante, p. 460. This "evidence," coupled with the market shares of Continental and Hazel-Atlas in the combined product market,[3] leads the Court to conclude that the merger violates § 7.

"The resulting percentage of the combined firms," the Court says, "approaches that held presumptively bad in United States v. Philadelphia National Bank, 374 U. S. 321." Ante, p. 461. The Philadelphia Bank case, which involved the merger of two banks plainly engaged in the same line of commerce,[4] is, however, entirely distinct from the present situation, which involves two separate industries. The bizarre result of the Court's approach is that market percentages of a nonexistent market enable the Court to dispense with "elaborate proof of market structure, market behavior and probable anticompetitive effects," ante, p. 458. As I shall show, the Court has "dispensed with" proof which, given heed, shows how completely fanciful its market-share analysis is.

In fairness to the District Court it should be said that it did not err in failing to consider the "line of commerce" on which this Court now relies. For the Government did not even suggest that such a line of commerce existed until it got to this Court.[5] And it does not seriously suggest even now that such a line of commerce exists.[6] The truth is that "glass and metal containers" form a distinct line of commerce only in the mind of this Court.

The District Court found, and this Court accepts the finding, that this case "deals with three separate and distinct industries manufacturing separate and distinct types of products": metal, glass, and plastic containers. 217 F. Supp., at 780.

"Concededly there was substantial and vigorous inter-industry competition between these three industries and between various of the products which they manufactured. Metal can, glass container and plastic container manufacturers were each seeking to enlarge their sales to the thousands of packers of hundreds of varieties of food, chemical, toiletry and industrial products, ranging from ripe olives to fruit juices to tuna fish to smoked tongue; from maple syrup to pet food to coffee; from embalming fluid to floor wax to nail polish to aspirin to veterinary supplies, to take examples at random.

"Each industry and each of the manufacturers within it was seeking to improve their products so that they would appeal to new customers or hold old ones. Hazel-Atlas and Continental were part of this overall industrial pattern, each in a recognized separate industry producing distinct products but engaged in inter-industry competition for the favor of various end users of their products." 217 F. Supp., at 780-781.

Only this Court will not be "concerned," ante, p. 457, that without support in reason or fact, it dips into this network of competition and establishes metal and glass containers as a separate "line of commerce," leaving entirely out of account all other kinds of containers: "plastic, paper, foil and any other materials competing for the same business," ibid.[7] Brown Shoe, supra, on which the Court relies for this travesty of economics, ante, p. 458, spoke of "well-defined submarkets" within a broader market, and said that "the boundaries of such a submarket" were to be determined by "practical indicia," 370 U. S., at 325.[8] (Emphasis added.) Since the Court here provides its own definition of a market, unrelated to any market reality whatsoever, Brown Shoe must in this case be regarded as a bootstrap.

The Court is quite wrong when it says that the District Court "employed an unduly narrow construction of the `competition' protected by § 7" and that it held that "the competition protected by § 7 [is limited] to competition between identical products," ante, p. 452. Quite to the contrary, the District Court expressly stated that "Section 7 is applicable to conglomerate mergers where the facts warrant," 217 F. Supp., at 783 (footnote omitted).[9] The difference between the District Court and this Court lies rather in the District Court's next sentence: "But there must be evidence that the facts warrant such application." Ibid.

If attention is paid to the conclusions of the court below, it is obvious that this Court's analysis has led it to substitute a meaningless figure—the merged companies' share of a nonexistent "market"—for the sound, careful factual findings of the District Court.

The District Court found:[10]

(1) With respect to the merger's effect on competition within the metal container industry, that "prior to its acquisition Hazel-Atlas did not manufacture or sell metal cans . . . ." 217 F. Supp., at 770.

(2) With respect to the merger's effect on competition within the glass container industry, that "Continental did not, directly or through subsidiaries, manufacture or sell glass containers . . . ." Ibid.

(3) With respect to the merger's effect on the metal container industry's efforts to compete with the glass container industry,

"The Government fared no better on its claim that as a result of the merger Continental was likely to lose the incentive to push can sales at the expense of glass. The Government introduced no evidence showing either that there had been or was likely to be any slackening of effort to push can sales. On the contrary, as has been pointed out, the object of the merger was diversification, and Continental was actively promoting intra-company competition between its various product lines. Since by far the largest proportion of Continental's business was in metal cans, it scarcely seemed likely that cans would suffer at the expense of glass.

"Moreover, subsequent to the merger Continental actively engaged in a vigorous research and promotion program in both its metal and glass container lines. In the light of the record and of the competitive realities, the notion that it was likely to cease being an innovator in either line is patently absurd." 217 F. Supp., at 790 (footnote omitted). (Emphasis added.)

(4) With respect to the merger's effect on the glass container industry's efforts to compete with the metal container industry,

"In addition the Government advanced the converse of the proposition which it urged with respect to the metal can line—that as a result of the merger Continental was likely to lose the incentive to push glass container sales at the expense of cans. In view of what has been said concerning the purpose of Continental's diversification program and the course it pursued after the merger, it is no more likely that Continental would slacken its efforts to promote glass than that it would slacken its efforts to promote cans. Indeed, if it had planned to do so there would have been little, if any, point to acquiring Hazel-Atlas, a major glass container producer." 217 F. Supp., at 793.

It is clear from the foregoing that the District Court fully considered the possibility that a merger of leading producers in two industries between which there was competition would dampen the inter-industry rivalry. The basis of the decision below was not, therefore, an erroneous belief that § 7 did not reach such competition but a careful study of the Government's proof, which led to the conclusion that "in the light of the record and of the competitive realities, the notion that . . . [the merged company] was likely to cease being an innovator in either line is patently absurd."

Surely this failure of the Court's mock-statistical analysis to reflect the facts as found on the record demonstrates what the Government concedes,[11] and what one would in any event have thought to be obvious: When a merger is attacked on the ground that competition between two distinct industries, or lines of commerce, will be affected, the shortcut "market share" approach developed in the Philadelphia Bank case, see 374 U. S., at 362-365; ante, p. 458, has no place. In such a case, the legality of the merger must surely depend, as it did below, on an inquiry into competitive effects in the actual lines of commerce which are involved. In this case, the result depends—or should depend—on the impact of the merger in the two lines of commerce here involved: the metal container industry and the glass container industry.[12] As the findings of the District Court which are quoted above make plain, reference to these two actual lines of commerce does not preclude protection of inter-industry competition. Indeed, by placing the merged company in the setting of other companies in each of the respective lines of commerce which are also engaged in inter-industry competition, this approach is far more likely than the Court's to give § 7 full, but not artificial, scope.

The Court's spurious market-share analysis should not obscure the fact that the Court is, in effect, laying down a "per se" rule that mergers between two large companies in related industries are presumptively unlawful under § 7. Had the Court based this new rule on a conclusion that such mergers are inherently likely to dampen inter-industry competition or that so few mergers of this kind would fail to have that effect that a "per se" rule is justified, I could at least understand the thought process which lay behind its decision. It would, of course, be inappropriate to prescribe per se rules in the first case to present a problem, cf. White Motor Co. v. United States, 372 U. S. 253, let alone a case in which the facts suggest that a per se rule is unsound. And to lay down a rule on either of the bases suggested would require a much more careful look at the nature of competition between industries than the Court's casual glance in that direction.

In any event, the Court does not take this tack. It chooses instead to invent a line of commerce the existence of which no one, not even the Government, has imagined; for which businessmen and economists will look in vain; a line of commerce which sprang into existence only when the merger took place and will cease to exist when the merger is undone. I have no idea where § 7 goes from here, nor will businessmen or the antitrust bar. Hitherto, it has been thought that the validity of a merger was to be tested by examining its effect in identifiable, "well-defined" (Brown Shoe, supra, at 325) markets. Here-after, however slight (or even nonexistent) the competitive impact of a merger on any actual market, businessmen must rest uneasy lest the Court create some "market," in which the merger presumptively dampens competition, out of bits and pieces of real ones. No one could say that such a fear is unfounded, since the Court's creative powers in this respect are declared to be as extensive as the competitive relationships between industries. This is said to be recognizing "meaningful competition where it is found to exist." It is in fact imagining effects on competition where none has been shown.

I would affirm the judgment of the District Court.

Notes

[1] Both companies manufactured other related products which for present purposes may be disregarded. See the description of the two companies in the opinion of the District Court, 217 F. Supp. 761, 769-770.

[2] Section 7 of the Clayton Act, as amended by the Act of December 29, 1950, 64 Stat. 1125, 15 U. S. C. § 18, provides in pertinent part:

"No corporation engaged in commerce shall acquire, directly or indirectly, the whole or any part of the stock or other share capital and no corporation subject to the jurisdiction of the Federal Trade Commission shall acquire the whole or any part of the assets of another corporation engaged also in commerce, where in any line of commerce in any section of the country, the effect of such acquisition may be substantially to lessen competition, or to tend to create a monopoly."

[3] The Court confesses to some difficulty in determining market shares. See ante, pp. 459-460, n. 10.

[4] "We have no difficulty in determining the `line of commerce' (relevant product or services market) . . . in which to appraise the probable competitive effects of appellees' proposed merger. We agree with the District Court that the cluster of products (various kinds of credit) and services (such as checking accounts and trust administration) denoted by the term `commercial banking'. . . composes a distinct line of commerce. . . . In sum, it is clear that commercial banking is a market `sufficiently inclusive to be meaningful in terms of trade realities.' Crown Zellerbach Corp. v. Federal Trade Comm'n, 296 F. 2d 800, 811 (C.A. 9th Cir. 1961)." 374 U. S., at 356-357.

[5] In the District Court, the Government relied on 10 "lines of commerce." In addition to "the packaging industry," "the can industry," "the glass container industry," and "metal closures" (not relevant here), the Government argued that there were six "lines of commerce" which were defined by the end product for which the containers were used, e. g., "containers for the beer industry." See 217 F. Supp., at 778-779.

[6] Although the Government makes the suggestion, which the Court now accepts, that wherever there is competition there is a "line of commerce," so that "the `line of commerce' within which the merger's effect on competition should be appraised is the production and sale of containers used for all purposes for which metal or glass containers

may be used . . ." (Brief, p. 18), it concedes the artificiality of this approach and, in so doing, itself rejects the market-share analysis adopted by the Court. The Government states that its suggested test of illegality of a merger involving inter-industry competition "omits analysis of statistics regarding market shares simply because those traditional yardsticks are generally unavailable to measure the full consequences which an interindustry merger would have on competition." (Brief, p. 22.)

The test which the Government advocates is that it "can satisfy its burden of showing that the merger may have the effect of substantially lessening competition by proving (a) the existence of substantial competition between two industries; (b) a high degree of concentration in either or both of the competing industries; and (c) the dominant positions of each of the merging companies in its respective industry." (Brief, p. 22.) This approach, which has at least the virtue of facing up to its own logic, frankly disavows attention to a "line of commerce." The effect of the Court's approach is not markedly different from that of the Government's test, see infra, p. 476, and there is some suggestion in the last few pages of the Court's opinion that the Court appreciates this. As discussed hereafter, however, there is nothing in the Court's opinion to support adoption of the Government's "per se" approach, and the facts developed in the District Court demonstrate that, so far as one can tell from this case at least, a per se approach to the problem of inter-industry competition is wholly inappropriate.

[7] If the competition between metal and glass containers is sufficient to constitute them collectively a "line of commerce," why does their competition with plastic containers and "other materials competing for the same business" not require that all such containers be included in the same line of commerce? The Court apparently concedes that the competition is multilateral.

[8] The "practical indicia" specified by the Court were: "industry or public recognition of the submarket as a separate economic entity, the product's peculiar characteristics and uses, unique production facilities, distinct customers, distinct prices, sensitivity to price changes, and specialized vendors." 370 U. S., at 325 (footnote omitted). While many of these factors weigh against the Court's conclusion that metal and glass containers should be combined in a single line of commerce, not one of them speaks for the Court's conclusion that they should be segregated from all other kinds of containers and together form a separate line of commerce.

[9] The District Court observed also that "relevant markets are neither economic abstractions nor artificial conceptions." 217 F. Supp., at 768. In this respect, in view of the majority's present opinion, the district judge must, I suppose, be deemed to have erred.

[10] This summary of the District Court's findings includes only so much as is relevant to the majority's opinion. The District Court gave detailed attention to each of the Government's contentions, in an opinion of 48 pages. Its conclusions were summarized in the following statement:

"Viewing the evidence as a whole, quite apart from theory, there was a total failure by the Government to establish the essential elements of a violation of Section 7. As will be apparent from a discussion of the proof relating to each specific line of commerce, the Government did not lay either the statistical or testimonial foundations required to establish its case. It was this failure of proof which required the dismissal of the complaint and entry of judgment for the defendants." 217 F. Supp., at 787.

[11] See note 6, supra.

[12] The Government urged other lines of commerce below, see note 5, supra, but has abandoned all of them here except "containers for the canning industry," a line of commerce defined by end use and including "all metal cans and glass containers for the end uses of `canning' food." 217 F. Supp., at 799. The District Court gave detailed reasons, which the record fully supports, for rejecting the Government's contention that this was a distinct line of commerce. See 217 F. Supp., at 799-802.

Justice Harlan's concurrence and dissent in NLRB v. Burnup & Sims, Inc. (Nov 9, 1964)

MR. JUSTICE HARLAN, concurring in part and dissenting in part.

Both the rule adopted by the lower court and that now announced by this Court seem to me unacceptable. On the one hand, it impinges on the rights assured by §§ 7 and 8 (a) (1) to hold, as the Court of Appeals did, that the employee must bear the entire brunt of his honest, but mistaken, discharge. On the other hand, it is hardly fair that the employer should be faced with the choice of risking damage to his business or incurring a penalty for taking honest action to thwart it.

Between these two one-way streets lies a middle two-way course: a rule which would require reinstatement of the mistakenly discharged employee and back pay only as of the time that the employer learned, or should have learned, of his mistake, subject, however, to a valid business reason for refusing reinstatement.[1] Such a rule gives offense neither to any policy of the statute nor to the dictates of fairness to the employer, and in my opinion represents a reasonable accommodation between the two inflexible points of view evinced by the opinions below and here.

Since I do not believe that this case presents the rare situation in which the Board can ignore motive,[2] I would vacate the judgment of the Court of Appeals and remand the case to the Board for further appropriate proceedings in light of what I believe to be the proper rule.

Notes

[1] As for example, if a replacement had been hired and the discharged employee unduly delayed in apprising the employer of the mistake.

[2] See Teamsters Local v. Labor Board, 365 U. S. 667, 677 (1961) (concurring opinion). Respondent here had a significant business justification—to avoid dynamiting of a silo—for discharging the employees, unlike the situations presented in Allis-Chalmers Mfg. Co. v. Labor Board, 162 F. 2d 435; Cusano v. Labor Board, 190 F. 2d 898, and Labor

Board v. Industrial Cotton Mills, 208 F. 2d 87. See Teamsters Local, supra, at 680.

In Allis-Chalmers the employer downgraded the status of plant inspectors after they had voted to join a union, and it was apparent that the employer acted only because of the inspectors' membership in the union. There was no business justification for the employer's action except for his feeling that union members should not exercise supervisory powers and the Board was therefore justified in treating this as an unfair labor practice without a specific finding of discriminatory motive.

Cusano involved a mistaken belief by the employer that an employee had made a misstatement about company profits, which might well have been protected campaign "oratory" even if the employee had made the misstatement. Since the employer could simply have denied the truth of the profit figures, there was no business justification for discharging the employee.

Industrial Cotton Mills presents the closest analogy to the case before us. There an employee was refused reinstatement following a strike for alleged strike misconduct—throwing tacks on the street during a strike—which he did not commit. The Court of Appeals recognized the special congressional concern for the right to strike embodied in §§ 2 (3) and 13 of the Act, and held that the employer's lack of antiunion motive was irrelevant. There was also little business justification for punishing the employee after the strike had ended, unlike the fear in this case of future sabotage by the employees.

Justice Harlan's dissent in Brulotte v. Thys Co. (Nov 16, 1964)

MR. JUSTICE HARLAN, dissenting.

The Court holds that the Thys Company unlawfully misused its patent monopoly by contracting with purchasers of its patented machines for royalty payments based on use beyond the patent term. I think that more discriminating analysis than the Court has seen fit to give this case produces a different result.

The patent laws prohibit post-expiration restrictions on the use of patented ideas; they have no bearing on use restrictions upon nonpatented, tangible machines. We have before us a mixed case involving the sale of a tangible machine which incorporates an intangible, patented idea. My effort in what follows is to separate out these two notions, to show that there is no substantial restriction on the use of the Thys idea, and to demonstrate that what slight restriction there may be is less objectionable than other post-expiration use restrictions which are clearly acceptable.

I.

It surely cannot be questioned that Thys could have lawfully set a fixed price for its machine and extended credit terms beyond the patent period. It is equally unquestionable, I take it, that if Thys had had no patent or if its patent had expired, it could have sold its machines at a flexible, undetermined price based on use; for example, a phonograph record manufacturer could sell a recording of a song in the public domain to a juke-box owner for an undetermined consideration based on the number of times the record was played.

Conversely it should be equally clear that if Thys licensed another manufacturer to produce hop-picking machines incorporating any of the Thys patents, royalties could not be exacted beyond the patent term. Such royalties would restrict the manufacturer's exploitation of the idea after it falls into the public domain, and no such restriction should be valid. To give another example unconnected with a tangible machine, a song writer could charge a royalty every time his song—his idea—was sung for profit during the period of copyright. But once the song falls into the public domain each and every member of the public should be free to sing it.

In fact Thys sells both a machine and the use of an idea. The company should be free to restrict the use of its machine, as in the first two examples given above. It may not restrict the use of its patented idea once it has fallen into the public domain. Whether it has done so must be the point of inquiry.

Consider the situation as of the day the patent monopoly ends. Any manufacturer is completely free to produce Thys-type hop-pickers. The farmer who has previously purchased a Thys machine is free to buy and use any other kind of machine whether or not it incorporates the Thys idea, or make one himself if he is able. Of course, he is not entitled as against Thys to the free use of any Thys machine. The Court's opinion must therefore ultimately rest on the proposition that the purchasing farmer is restricted in using his particular machine, embodying as it does an application of the patented idea, by the fact that royalties are tied directly to use.

To test this proposition I again put a hypothetical. Assume that a Thys contract called for neither an initial flat-sum payment nor any annual minimum royalties; Thys' sole recompense for giving up ownership of its machine was a royalty payment extending beyond the patent term based on use, without any requirement either to use the machine or not to use a competitor's. A moment's thought reveals that, despite the clear restriction on use both before and after the expiration of the patent term, the arrangement would involve no misuse of patent leverage.[1] Unless the Court's opinion rests on technicalities of contract draftsmanship and not on the economic substance of the transaction, the distinction between the hypothetical and the actual case lies only in the cumulative investment consisting of the initial and minimum payments independent of use, which the purchaser obligated himself to make to Thys. I fail to see why this distinguishing feature should be critical. If anything the investment will encourage the purchaser to use his machine in order to amortize the machine's fixed cost over as large a production base as possible. Yet the gravamen of the majority opinion is restriction. not encouragement, of use.

II.

The essence of the majority opinion may lie in some notion that "patent leverage" being used by Thys to exact use payments extending beyond the patent term somehow allows Thys to extract more onerous payments from the farmers than would otherwise be obtainable. If this be the case, the Court must in some way distinguish longterm use payments from long-term installment payments of a flat-sum purchase price. For the danger which it seems to fear would appear to inhere equally in both, and as I read the Court's opinion, the latter type of arrangement is lawful despite the fact that failure to pay an installment under a conditional sales contract would permit the seller to recapture the machine, thus terminating —not merely restricting—the farmer's use of it. Furthermore, since the judgments against petitioners were based almost entirely on defaults in paying the $500 minimums and not on failures to pay for above-minimum use,[2] any such distinction of extended use payments and extended installments, even if accepted, would not justify eradicating all petitioners' obligations beyond the patent term, but only those based on use above the stated minimums; for the minimums by themselves, being payable whether or not a machine has been used, are precisely identical in substantive economic effect to flat installments.

In fact a distinction should not be accepted based on the assumption that Thys, which exploits its patents by selling its patented machines rather than licensing others to manufacture them, can use its patent leverage to exact more onerous payments from farmers by gearing price to use instead of charging a flat sum. Four possible situations must be considered. The purchasing farmer could overestimate, exactly estimate, underestimate, or have no firm estimate of his use requirements for a Thys machine. If he overestimates or exactly estimates, the farmer will be fully aware of what the machine will cost him in the long run, and it is unrealistic to suppose that in such circumstances he would be willing to pay more to have the machine on use than on straight terms. If the farmer underestimates, the thought may be that Thys will take advantage of him; but surely the farmer is in a better position than Thys or anyone else to estimate his own requirements and is hardly in need of the Court's protection in this respect. If the farmer has no fixed estimate of his use requirements he may have good business reasons entirely unconnected with "patent leverage" for wanting payments tied to use, and may indeed be willing to pay more in the long run to obtain such an arrangement. One final example should illustrate my point:

At the time when the Thys patent term still has a few years to run, a farmer who has been picking his hops by hand comes into the Thys retail outlet to inquire about the mechanical pickers. The salesman concludes his description of the advantages of the Thys machine with the price tag—$20,000. Value to the farmer depends completely on the use he will derive from the machine; he is willing to obligate himself on long credit terms to pay $10,000, but unless the machine can substantially outpick his old hand-picking methods, it is worth no more to him. He therefore offers to pay $2,000 down, $400 annually for 20 years, and an additional payment during the contract term for any production he can derive from the machine over and above the minimum amount he could pick by hand. Thys accepts, and by doing so, according to the majority, commits a per se misuse of its patent. I cannot believe that this is good law.[3]

III.

The possibility remains that the Court is basing its decision on the technical framing of the contract and would have treated the case differently if title had been declared to pass at the termination instead of the outset of the contract term, or if the use payments had been verbally disassociated from the patent licenses and described as a convenient means of spreading out payments for the machine. If indeed the impact of the opinion is that Thys must redraft its contracts to achieve the same economic results, the decision is not only wrong, but conspicuously ineffectual.

I would affirm.

Notes

[1] Installment of a patented, coin-operated washing machine in the basement of an apartment building without charge except that the landlord and his tenants must deposit 25 cents for every use, should not constitute patent misuse.

[2] Petitioner Charvet was indebted to Thys only to the extent of the minimums; petitioner Brulotte was in default approximately $4,500 of which $3,120 was attributable to minimums.

[3] The Court also adverts to the provisions in the license agreements prohibiting "assignment of the machines or their removal from Yakima County" (ante, p. 32) during the terms of the agreements. Such provisions, however, are surely appropriate to secure performance of what are in effect conditional sales agreements and they do not advance the argument for patent misuse.

Furthermore, it should not be overlooked that we are dealing here with a patent, not an antitrust, case, there being no basis in the record for concluding that Thys' arrangements with its licensees were such as to run afoul of the antitrust laws.

Justice Harlan's dissent in Schlagenhauf v. Holder (Nov 23, 1964)

MR. JUSTICE HARLAN, dissenting.

In my view the Court's holding that mandamus lies in this case cannot be squared with the course of decisions to which the majority at the threshold pays lip service. Ante, pp. 109-110. As the Court recognizes, mandamus, like the other extraordinary writs, is available to correct only those decisions of inferior courts which involve a "usurpation of judicial power" or, what is tantamount thereto, "a clear abuse of discretion"; such a writ "is not to be used as a substitute for appeal." Ibid.

Mandamus is found to be an appropriate remedy in this instance, however, because (1) petitioner's challenge was based on an asserted lack of power in the District Court to issue the examination order, and (2) that being so, the Court of Appeals had the right also to inquire into the application of the "in controversy" and "good cause" requirements of Rule 35 (a), particularly since those issues, like the question of "power," were matters of "first impression" which in "these special circumstances" should be determined by the Court of Appeals "so as to avoid piecemeal litigation and to settle new and important problems." Ante, p. 111.

For me this reasoning is unacceptable. Of course a court of appeals when confronted with a substantial challenge to the power of a district court to act in the premises may proceed to examine that question without awaiting its embodiment in a final judgment, as the Court of Appeals did here by issuing an order to show cause why a writ of mandamus should not issue. But once it is determined that the challenged power did exist, and that the district court acted within the limit of that power, an extraordinary writ should be denied. I know of no case which suggests that a court of appeals' right to consider such a question at an interlocutory stage of the litigation also draws to the court the right to consider other questions—here the "in controversy" and "good cause" issues— which otherwise would not be examinable upon a petition for an extraordinary writ. Indeed, were an extraordinary writ to issue following a determination that the district court lacked power, that would put an end to the litigation and these questions would never be reached. And, as the Court correctly states, the fact that "hardship may result from delay and perhaps unnecessary trial," ante, p. 110, is not a factor that makes for the issuance of such a writ.

Manifestly, today's procedural holding, when stripped of its sugar-coating, is born of the Court's belief that the petitioner should not be exposed to the rigors of these examinations before the proper "guidelines" have been established by this tribunal. Understandable as that point of view may be, it can only be indulged at the expense of making a deep inroad into the firmly established federal policy which, with narrow exceptions,[1] permits appellate review only of the final judgments of district courts. To be sure the Court is at pains to warn that what is done today puts an end to future "interlocutory" review of Rule 35 questions. Ante, p. 112. Nevertheless, I find it hard to escape the conclusion that this decision may open the door to the extraordinary writs being used to test any question of "first impression," if it can be geared to an alleged lack of "power" in the district court. As such, it seems to me out of keeping with the rule of "finality," with respect to which Congress, wisely I think, has been willing to make only cautious exceptions.[2]

The Court of Appeals having correctly concluded, as this Court now holds and as I agree, that the District Court had power to order the physical and mental examinations of this petitioner, and since I believe that there was no clear abuse of discretion in its so acting, I think the lower court was quite right in denying mandamus, and I would affirm its judgment on that basis.

Notes

[1] See, e. g., 28 U. S. C. §§ 1292 (a) (1), (b) (1958 ed.).

[2] See note 1, supra.

Justice Harlan's dissent in Beck v. State of Ohio (Nov 23, 1964)

MR. JUSTICE HARLAN, dissenting.

Judge Zimmerman of the Supreme Court of Ohio stated as a fact,[1] "Information was given to the police by an informer that defendant would be in a certain locality at a certain time pursuing his unlawful activities. He was found in that locality, as predicted, driving an automobile." I regard this as the crucial point in the case, for if the informant did give the police that information, the fact of its occurrence would sufficiently indicate the informant's reliability to provide a basis for petitioner's arrest, Draper v. United States, 358 U. S. 307, 3 L. Ed. 2d 327, 79 S. Ct. 329. It is this court's function, therefore, to determine whether the state's finding is adequately supportable. In doing so it is essential to consider what are the appropriate standards of appellate review.

Generally "our inquiry clearly is limited to a study of the undisputed portions of the record." Thomas v. Arizona, 356 U. S. 390, 402, 2 L. Ed.2d 863, 78 S. Ct. 885."[T]here has been complete agreement that any conflict in testimony as to what actually led to a contested confession [or to a contested arrest] is not this court's concern. Such conflict comes here authoritatively resolved by the state's adjudication." Watts v. Indiana, 338 U. S. 49, 51-52, 93 L. Ed. 1801, 69 S. Ct. 1347. See also, Gallegos v. Nebraska, 342 U. S. 55, 60-61, 96 L. Ed. 86, 72 S. Ct. 141; Haley v. Ohio, 332 U. S. 596, 597-598, 92 L. Ed. 224, 68 S. Ct. 302. It is equally clear that in cases involving asserted violations of constitutional rights the Court is free to draw its own inferences from established facts, giving due weight to the conclusions of the state court, but not being conclusively bound by them, Ker v. California, 374 U. S. 23, 10 L. Ed.2d 726, 83 S. Ct. 1683; Spano v. New York, 360 U. S. 315, 3 L. Ed.2d 1265, 79 S. Ct. 1202.

A distinction between facts and inferences may often be difficult to draw, but the guiding principle for this Court should be that when a question is in doubt and demeanor and credibility of witnesses, or contemporaneous understandings of the parties, have a part to play in its resolution, this Court should be extremely slow to upset a state court's inferential findings. The impetus for our exercising de novo review of the facts comes from the attitude that unless this Court can fully redetermine the facts of each case for itself, it will be unable to afford complete protection for constitutional rights. But when the "feel" of the trial may have been a proper element in resolving an issue which is unclear on the record, our independent judgment should give way to the greater capability of the state trial court[2] in determining whether a constitutional right has been infringed.[3] Proper regard for the duality of the American judicial system demands no less.

Federal habeas corpus, which allows a federal court in appropriate circumstances to develop a fresh record, Townsend v. Sain, 372 U. S. 293, 9 L. Ed.2d 770, 83 S. Ct. 745, provides a far more satisfactory vehicle for resolving such unclear issues, for the judge can evaluate for himself the on-the-spot considerations which no appellate court can estimate with assurance on a cold record. Those considerations are important to the case at bar.

While I agree that the record is not free from all doubt, I believe that the following selected portions of the arresting officer's testimony are sufficient to carry the day for the State's judgment:

"Q. Did you have reasonable and probable cause to stop this man?

"A. Yes, I did.

* * *

"Q. Based on his previous record? A. Information and previous record and observation. (Emphasis added.)

* * *

"Q. When you left the station, did you have in mind stopping Mr. Beck? A. I had in mind looking for him in the area of East 115th Street and Beulah, stopping him if I did see him make a stop in that area.

* * *

"Q. You indicated that you were operating on information? A. Yes.

"Q. From whom did you get this information? A. I couldn't divulge that information.

"Q. But someone specifically did relate that information to you? A. Yes.

"Q. And you knew who that person was? A. Yes."

It is true that the officer never specifically said "The informant told me that Beck was operating in the area of East 115th Street and Beulah," but he did testify that he went looking for Beck in that specific area, that he was acting in part on information, and that his information had been related to him by some specific person whose name he felt privileged not to divulge. I find the state court inference reasonable, even on the basis of the admittedly sparse record before us, that the informant told the officer that Beck was operating in the mentioned area.

Furthermore, in reaching this inference, on-the-spot considerations might well have come into play. There appears to have been no lack of common understanding at trial that the informant had given the officer the crucial information. Petitioner argued in the Ohio Supreme Court, "the pattern is obvious, an officer testifies he had information from a confidential source that a particular person is `picking up' numbers in a given area and based on that information they arrest such person `on sight' without a warrant."[4] Judge Zimmerman of the Supreme Court of Ohio found it to be the fact without seeing any need for elaboration. Respondent, in its brief in this court, assumed it to be the fact.[5] And petitioner raised no question as to this inference in either his petition or brief. Indeed the question is raised for the first time, sua sponte, by the court's opinion.

On this basis I vote to affirm.

Notes

[1] Although it was Judge Zimmerman's opinion for the Supreme Court of Ohio which articulated the specific finding in question here, that finding must be attributed to the trial court, for we must presume that its conclusion that the arrest was constitutionally permissible was based on the factual findings necessary to support it. If the Court is unwilling to accept this presumption, it should, at least, remand the case to the Ohio courts in order that any question on this score may be set at rest.

[2] See note 1, supra.

[3] NORRIS v. ALABAMA, 294 U. S. 587, 55 S. Ct. 579, 79 L. Ed. 1074, in which the Court concluded, contrary to a state court finding, that Negroes' names had been unlawfully added to a jury book, would at first glance appear to be an exception, but in fact it proves the rule. The evidence on which the conclusion was based was documentary and no "on-the-spot" considerations were involved.

[4] Reply brief for appellant in the Supreme Court of Ohio, p. 5.

[5] Brief for respondent, p. 8.

Justice Harlan's dissent in Farmer v. Arabian American Oil (Dec 14, 1964)

MR. JUSTICE HARLAN, with whom MR. JUSTICE STEWART joins, dissenting.

The only possible justification for bringing this case here was to settle the question of whether the 100-mile subpoena rule deprives a district court of power to tax as costs the traveling expenses of witnesses reasonably brought by the prevailing litigant from places beyond that distance. The Court, however, declines to make any precise holding on this question. The scope of the discretion of a district judge acting within his powers, which is the foundation of today's decision, is in my opinion a matter which should be left with the courts of appeals. I would affirm the judgment below for the reasons stated in the opinion of Chief Judge Lumbard for the majority of the Court of Appeals, 324 F. 2d 359.

Justice Harlan's dissent in Hamm v. Rock Hill (Dec 14, 1964)

MR. JUSTICE HARLAN, dissenting.

The Court holds that these state trespass convictions, occurring before the passage of the Civil Rights Act of 1964, must be set aside by virtue of the federal doctrine of criminal abatement. This remarkable conclusion finds no support in reason or authority.

The common-law rule of abatement is basically a canon of construction conceived by the courts as a yardstick for determining whether a legislature, which has enacted a statute making conduct noncriminal which was proscribed by an earlier criminal statute, also intended to put an end to nonfinal convictions under the former legislation. In effect, the doctrine of abatement establishes a presumption that such was the purpose of the legislature in the absence of a demonstrated contrary intent, as evidenced, for example, in the case of congressional enactments by the federal saving statute,[1] see United States v. Reisinger, 128 U. S. 398. As was said in United States v. Tynen, 11 Wall. 88, 95:

"By the repeal of the 13th section of the act of 1813 all criminal proceedings taken under it fell. There can be no legal conviction, nor any valid judgment pronounced upon conviction, unless the law creating the offence be at the time in existence. By the repeal the legislative will is expressed that no further proceedings be had under the act repealed."

The doctrine has its origins in the English common law, see, e. g., Rex v. Cator, 4 Burr. 2026, 98 Eng. Rep. 56; King v. Davis, 1 Leach Crown Cases 306 (3d ed.), 168 Eng.

Rep. 238, and has been embraced in American state and federal jurisprudence.

The abatement doctrine serves a useful and appropriate purpose in a framework of the legislation of a single political sovereignty. The doctrine strikes a jarring note, however, when it is applied so as to affect the legislation of a different sovereignty, as the federal doctrine is now used to abate these state convictions. Our federal system tolerates wide differences between state and federal legislative policies,[2] and the presumption of retroactive exculpation that readily attaches to a federal criminal statute which unreservedly repeals earlier federal legislation cannot, in my opinion, be automatically thought to embrace exoneration from earlier wrongdoing under a state statute.[3]

I know of no case which suggests that the doctrine of abatement can be applied to affect the existing legislation of another jurisdiction. Until today the doctrine has always been applied only with respect to legislation of the same sovereignty, e. g., Rex v. Cator, supra; King v. Davis, supra; United States v. Tynen, supra; Yeaton v. United States, 5 Cranch 281. And all of the cases relied on by the Court are of that character.

The Supremacy Clause cannot serve as a vehicle for extending the federal doctrine of abatement beyond proper bounds. That provision of the Constitution would come into play only if it appeared from the Civil Rights Act itself or from its legislative history and setting that Congress' purpose was to displace past as well as prospective applications of state laws touching upon the matters with which the federal statute is concerned. For me, this would have to be made to appear in unmistakable terms, for such a purpose would represent an exercise of federal legislative power wholly unprecedented in our history.

I entirely agree with my Brother BLACK'S poignant observations on this score; there is not a scintilla of evidence which remotely suggests that Congress had any such revolutionary course in mind. Section 1104 of the Civil Rights Act indeed provides that nothing in the statute is to be "construed as invalidating any provision of State law unless . . . inconsistent with any of the purposes of this Act, or any provision thereof." Whether or not state trespass laws as applied to "racial trespasses" occurring after the effective date of the Civil Rights Act are to be deemed inconsistent with the provisions of § 203 (c) of the Act,[4] a question which I find unnecessary to decide at this juncture, there is certainly no such plain inconsistency between § 203 (c) and state trespass laws as applied in those situations arising before the passage of the Civil Rights Act as would justify this Court's attributing to Congress a purpose to pre-empt state law in such instances.

Moreover, the contrary conclusion would confront us with constitutional questions of the gravest import, for the legislative record is barren of any evidence showing that giving effect to past state trespass convictions would result in placing any burden on present interstate commerce.[5] Such evidence, at the very least, would be a prerequisite to the validity of any purported exercise of the Commerce power in this regard. See Heart of Atlanta Motel, Inc. v. United States, ante, p. 241; Katzenbach v. McClung, ante, p. 294. There is, indeed, nothing to indicate that Congress even adverted to such a question.

Finally, the Court's decision cannot be justified under the rule of avoidance of constitutional questions, see Court's opinion. ante, p. 316. That rule does not reach to the extent of enabling this Court to fabricate nonconstitutional grounds of decision out of whole cloth.

" ` A statute must be construed, if fairly possible, so as to avoid not only the conclusion that it is unconstitutional, but also grave doubts upon that score.' United States v. Jin Fuey Moy, supra [241 U. S. 394, 401]. But avoidance of a difficulty will not be pressed to the point of disingenuous evasion." Moore Ice Cream Co. v. Rose, 289 U. S. 373, 379 (Cardozo, J.).[6]

Concluding that these trespass convictions are not abated, I would affirm the judgments in both of these cases for the reasons given by MR. JUSTICE BLACK in his dissenting opinion in Bell v. Maryland, 378 U. S. 226, 318, in which I joined.

Notes

[1] 1 U. S. C. § 109 (1958 ed.):

"The repeal of any statute shall not have the effect to release or extinguish any penalty, forfeiture, or liability incurred under such statute, unless the repealing Act shall so expressly provide, and such statute shall be treated as still remaining in force for the purpose of sustaining any proper action or prosecution for the enforcement of such penalty, forfeiture, or liability. The expiration of a temporary statute shall not have the effect to release or extinguish any penalty, forfeiture, or liability incurred under such statute, unless the temporary statute shall so expressly provide, and such statute shall be treated as still remaining in force for the purpose of sustaining any proper action or prosecution for the enforcement of such penalty, forfeiture, or liability."

I accept the Court's conclusion that this section has no application here, but only because there has been no repeal or amendment of an existing federal statute.

[2] Arkansas, for example, has a saving clause, Ark. Stat. Ann. §§ 1-103, 1-104, similar to 1 U. S. C. § 109, which expresses a state policy to save the conviction of Lupper. See Mack v. Connor, 220 Ga. 450, 139 S. E. 2d 286 (1964). Cf. Bell v. Maryland, 378 U. S. 226, conviction affirmed on remand, 236 Md. 356, 204 A. 2d 54; rehearing granted and argument deferred "awaiting the outcome of similar issues now pending before the United States Supreme Court," quite obviously referring to these cases.

[3] See Cohens v. Virginia, 6 Wheat. 264, 443, quoted in my Brother BLACK'S opinion, ante, p. 321.

[4] Quoted in the Court's opinion, ante, pp. 310-311.

[5] No attempt is made by the Court to justify the retroactive application of the Civil Rights Act under the Fourteenth Amendment.

[6] See also International Association of Machinists v. Street, 367 U. S. 740, 797 (Frankfurter, J., dissenting).

Justice Harlan's dissent in California v. Lo-Vaca Gathering (Jan 18, 1965)

MR. JUSTICE HARLAN, dissenting.

Today's decision furnishes a too-ready answer to an intricate problem of administrative regulation. It reflects the sort of decision that is to be expected when the Court is willing to make a bare choice between two unrefined points of view as to regulatory method, without first being informed by the regulating agency concerned as to its evaluation of the competing factors—something that is indispensable to achieving a well-balanced solution of a problem such as this. The respective positions of the parties here each possesses the capacity to frustrate the scope of natural gas regulation ordained by the Congress. The Commission's molecular theory, accepted by the Court with undefined reservations, results in expanding the regulatory scheme by sweeping within the Commission's authority gas that has not been supplied or used for interstate resale ("nonjurisdictional" gas). The respondents' contract-allocation position, on the other hand, might serve to contract the legitimate scope of regulation by interfering with the ability of the Commission to deal with gas restricted under a supply contract to "not-for-sale," but which has been actually used by the pipeline-purchaser for interstate resale ("jurisdictional" gas).

Whether or not there is a middle ground that would more closely fulfill the purposes of the Natural Gas Act than either of the proposals now before us is something that this Court is not competent to assess without expert guidance from the Commission, and we have been given none. Lacking this, I am unwilling to accept at this juncture the position of either party to this litigation. I think the Court should decline to pass upon these cases until the Commission has first illumined the regulatory problems involved through an appropriate exercise of its rule-making powers.[1]

The complexity and elusiveness of the matters with which we are asked to deal are best exposed from the vantage point of this Court by considering some of the questions to which allocation contracts in varying contexts give rise.

The Commission has, at least until this case, accepted the proposition that a single supplier to a pipeline may allocate by contract between the amount of gas used for jurisdictional purposes and the amount used nonjurisdictionally. For example, in City of Hastings v. Federal Power Comm'n, 221 F. 2d 31, a pipeline company sold gas to the city through one pipeline under two contracts, one covering the gas to be resold by the city, and the other gas to be used by the city in its own plants. Although the gas was mingled in the common pipeline, the allocation was approved, and the latter gas was, without more, considered not subject to Commission regulation. A similar situation was presented in United States v. Public Utilities Comm'n of California, 345 U. S. 295, where a power company sold electricity to the Navy for use in its power plants and also for resale to dependent families. The absence of any allocation was fatal in that case, but the Court recognized that a different question would be presented if there had been two separate transactions. 345 U. S., at 316-318.

The result does not change when two or more suppliers are involved, provided that the allocation of nonjurisdictional gas is prorated among all of the suppliers. For example, if a pipeline company consumed 30% of its total volume of gas in its own plants, and sold 10% of the total volume in the State of production, each supplier could allocate 40% of its gas supply to nonjurisdictional use. Such was essentially the case in North Dakota v. Federal Power Comm'n, 247 F. 2d 173, where the allocation was upheld with Commission approval. If these cases are accepted by the Court, two corollaries follow: since gas is a fungible commodity, the mingling of gas does not alone render ineffective for purposes of Commission jurisdiction the allocation contracts, although the molecular identification of the nonjurisdictional gas is destroyed; and the fact that the prices paid for nonjurisdictional gas[2] may affect the rate base for the jurisdictional gas, is also not a critical factor at this stage.[3]

The issue now before the Court arises only when some suppliers are allocating part or all of their gas to nonjurisdictional use, but others are not. This issue could arise commonly in two contexts: if existing suppliers were allocating pro rata, and new suppliers were added which did not allocate, the addition of the new suppliers might be thought not to destroy the validity of the existing allocation contracts since the new suppliers might be satisfying an increase in the demand for jurisdictional gas.[4] The converse situation is presented in this case, where the new suppliers are attempting to allocate, and existing suppliers are not. One possible test in such cases might be to determine the source of the demand for the gas supplied to El Paso by Houston and Lo-Vaca. To modify the argument used by respondents, if a separate pipeline were constructed from the Coquat station (at which the gas enters the El Paso system) to the point along El Paso's system where the outflow will increase, would the sale be jurisdictional or not? If in fact El Paso has formerly been using the same amount of gas in its compressors that it intends to use in the future, then the purpose of the Lo-Vaca allocation will be merely to release for interstate sale—to satisfy the interstate demand—gas from other suppliers which formerly was used for nonjurisdictional purposes.

The record before us does not answer the question put. There is some indication that El Paso intends to construct new compressor plants, and may have to use more nonjurisdictional gas at its existing plants to handle the added gas received from Lo-Vaca under the unrestricted contract. Such a use would satisfy a nonjurisdictional demand.

However, there is also evidence that in fact El Paso's consumption for nonjurisdictional purposes will remain constant, and that Lo-Vaca's supplies will be used to satisfy an increased demand from interstate consumers. The fact that Lo-Vaca gas purportedly replaces the compressor gas supplies formerly furnished by other suppliers, thus releasing that gas for interstate resale, should not defeat Commission jurisdiction under this analysis.

Another possible standard which suggests itself would be to determine the probable percentages of gas from each supplier which will be used for nonjurisdictional purposes, and only permit each supplier to allocate by contract to nonjurisdictional use his pro rata share of the total estimated nonjurisdictional gas. For example, if we suppose a pipeline running from the Gulf coast of Texas through New Mexico into California, as does the El Paso system, then each supplier should determine what percentage of the total volume of gas flowing west from the point of its input will be ultimately used for a nonjurisdictional purpose. It would then be mathematically probable that his gas would be used for nonjurisdictional purposes in the same percentage, and he could allocate that amount by contract, subject to change should new supplies be added to the system.[5]

I recognize, of course, that there may be pitfalls in both of these possible methods, and that there may be other formulae that are preferable to either. I have ventured them only as support for my belief that the Commission's molecular theory, which in the name of protecting the Commission's jurisdiction in reality involves a judicial expansion of its authority, should not be accepted until the Commission, after due exploration in a rule-making proceeding, is able to satisfy this Court that no other feasible method—more particularly no modification of the respondents' contract-allocation theory—exists that would better fit the boundaries of the Commission's jurisdiction as fixed by Congress.

It is undoubtedly true that normally an administrative agency may decide for itself whether to proceed in a given field of its regulatory functions through the promulgation of general rules[6] or by the process of case-by-case adjudication.[7] This Commission from the outset has usually proceeded, with the Court's approval,[8] in developing its procedures by the adjudicatory process. Nevertheless, there are good reasons why the rule-making power appears to be the more promising avenue of approach in this instance. First, the adjudicatory process has not yielded any satisfactory basic principle to serve as a point of departure for judicial assessment of cases of this kind, or indeed for a consistent administrative approach;[9] even in this litigation the Commission's position is far from clear as to what room, if any, there may be for restrictive allocation contracts. Second, the gas industry is entitled to know the fundamental ground rules by which it should conduct itself in this regard with some degree of predictability, as witness the situation of these respondents whose good faith in the transactions giving rise to this litigation has not been impugned in any way. Third, that unlike the line of cases in which agency jurisdiction is conceded,[10] here the Commission should not be permitted to adopt a theory which expands its jurisdiction beyond statutory limits[11] without full hearings and the formulation of a rule interpreting its jurisdiction in this area which conforms to the jurisdictional limits of § 1 (b) of the Natural Gas Act. Fourth, because these matters are fraught with technical "perplexities, both geological and economic," Railroad Comm'n of Texas v. Rowan & Nichols Oil Co., 311 U. S. 570, 574, the informed expertise of the Commission is a necessary adjunct to satisfactory judicial resolution of particular cases. "Had the Commission, acting upon its experience and peculiar competence, promulgated a general rule of which its order here was a particular application, the problem for our consideration would be very different." Securities & Exchange Comm'n v. Chenery Corp., 318 U. S. 80, 92. The courts have a right to the informed judgment of the Commission before acting further in this presently opaque area.

I would vacate the judgment of the Court of Appeals and remand the case to the Commission for further proceedings after the promulgation of interpretive rules to cover this, and like cases.[12]

Notes

[1] See Elman, Comment, Rulemaking Procedures in the FTC's Enforcement of the Merger Law, 78 Harv. L. Rev. 385 (1964).

[2] See Court's opinion, ante, p. 370. In fact, the price charged by Lo-Vaca for its nonjurisdictional gas is exactly the same as the price established for its concededly jurisdictional sale, and the Houston sale is for a price lower than either of the Lo-Vaca sales.

[3] Both Lo-Vaca and El Paso are constructing pipelines to connect with the El Paso system at its Coquat station, and both must obtain Commission certification under § 7 of the Natural Gas Act in order to construct such pipelines. The Commission could take many of the factors presented in this case into account when ruling on the applications, see Federal Power Comm'n v. Transcontinental Gas Pipe Line Corp., 365 U. S. 1. The Commission could also take into account the reasonableness of the prices charged for nonjurisdictional gas should El Paso apply for a rate increase on its jurisdictional sales.

[4] See Amerada Petroleum Corp. v. Federal Power Comm'n, 334 F. 2d 404 (C. A. 8th Cir. 1964), cert. pending, No. 585, this Term, where the suppliers in the North Dakota case, supra, had been allocating, and the pipeline then added new suppliers which did not allocate. The Court of Appeals upheld the allocation contracts.

[5] Corrections would have to be made, of course, where gas is withdrawn for intrastate consumption from a trunk line before the gas is mingled with the interstate system. Such gas would all be attributed to the suppliers feeding the trunk line, and this gas would not be used in computing the total percentages. Cf. Peoples Natural Gas Co. v. Public Service Comm'n of Pennsylvania, 270 U. S. 550. This method of allocation would only operate with natural gas, which flows in one direction only; different considerations would be applicable were we dealing with electric power, which can flow in both directions along a system.

[6] See United States v. Storer Broadcasting Co., 351 U. S. 192. See generally 1 Davis, Administrative Law Treatise, § 5.01 (1958).

[7] See Securities & Exchange Comm'n v. Chenery Corp., 332 U. S. 194.

[8] See, e. g., United States v. Public Utilities Comm'n of California, supra, at 318, n. 28.

[9] See Lo-Vaca Gathering Co., 26 F. P. C. 606, 615:

"To the extent that North Dakota may be inconsistent with the action we take here, we believe it was erroneously decided." Compare, supra, p. 373.

[10] As for example, in rate-making proceedings.

[11] Natural Gas Act, § 1 (b), quoted in the Court's opinion, ante, p. 368, n. 1.

[12] See Addison v. Holly Hill Fruit Prods., Inc., 322 U. S. 607, 619.

Justice Harlan's dissent in Henry v. Mississippi (Jan 18, 1965)

MR. JUSTICE HARLAN, with whom MR. JUSTICE CLARK and MR. JUSTICE STEWART join, dissenting.

Flying banners of federalism, the Court's opinion actually raises storm signals of a most disquieting nature. While purporting to recognize the traditional principle that an adequate procedural, as well as substantive, state ground of decision bars direct review here of any federal claim asserted in the state litigation, the Court, unless I wholly misconceive what is lurking in today's opinion, portends a severe dilution, if not complete abolition, of the concept of "adequacy" as pertaining to state procedural grounds.

In making these preliminary observations I do not believe I am seeing ghosts. For I cannot account for the remand of this case in the face of what is a demonstrably adequate state procedural ground of decision by the Mississippi Supreme Court except as an early step toward extending in one way or another the doctrine of Fay v. Noia, 372 U. S. 391, to direct review. In that case, decided only two Terms ago, the Court turned its back on history (see dissenting opinion of this writer, at 448 et seq.), and did away with the adequate state ground doctrine in federal habeas corpus proceedings.

Believing that any step toward extending Noia to direct review should be flushed out and challenged at its earliest appearance in an opinion of this Court, I respectfully dissent.

I.

The Mississippi Supreme Court did not base its ultimate decision upon petitioner's federal claim that his wife's consent could not validate an otherwise improper police search of the family car, but on the procedural ground that petitioner (who was represented by three experienced lawyers) had not objected at the time the fruits of this search were received in evidence. This Court now strongly implies, but does not decide (in view of its remand on the "waiver" issue) that enforcement of the State's "contemporaneous-objection" rule was inadequate as a state ground of decision because the petitioner's motion for a directed verdict of acquittal afforded the trial judge a satisfactory opportunity to take "appropriate corrective action" with reference to the allegedly inadmissible evidence. Thus, it is suggested, this may be a situation where "giving effect to the contemporaneous-objection rule for its own sake `would be to force resort to an arid ritual of meaningless form.' " (Ante, p. 449.)

From the standpoint of the realities of the courtroom, I can only regard the Court's analysis as little short of fanciful. The petitioner's motion for a verdict could have provoked one of three courses of action by the trial judge, none of which can reasonably be considered as depriving the State's contemporaneous-objection rule of its capacity to serve as an adequate state ground.

1. The trial judge might have granted the directed verdict. But had this action been appropriate, the Supreme Court of Mississippi, in its first opinion, would have ordered the prosecution dismissed. Since it did not, and the matter is entirely one of state law, further speculation by this Court should be foreclosed.[1]

2. The trial judge might have directed a mistrial. The State's interest in preventing mistrials through the contemporaneous-objection requirement is obvious.

3. The remaining course of action is the example given by the Court; the trial judge could have denied the motion for a directed verdict, but, sua sponte, called for elaboration of the argument, determined that the search of the automobile was unconstitutional, and given cautionary instructions to the jury to disregard the inadmissible evidence when the case was submitted to it.

The practical difficulties with this approach are manifestly sufficient to show a substantial state interest in their avoidance, and thus to show an "adequate" basis for the State's adherence to the contemporaneous-objection rule. To make my point I must quote the motion for directed verdict in full.

"Atty Carter: We're going to make a motion, your Honor, for a directed verdict in this case. We are going to base our motion on several grounds. First, we think that this whole process by which this defendant was brought or attempted to be brought into the jurisdiction of this Court is illegal and void. There is nothing in the record in this case to show that the warrant that was issued against this defendant was based upon—it must be based in this State and any other State on an affidavit, on a proper affidavit or a proper complaint by any party. True, there is some testimony that some affidavit was made, and the complaining witness said so, but in the record in this case which is before the Court, no such affidavit is present and there is a verification from the Justice of the Peace that no such affidavit is present in this case; therefore, we contend that the warrant under which this defendant was subjected to arrest was illegal and without force and effect. Secondly, we contend that the warrant having been issued and the testimony of this Mr. Collins on the stand to the effect that after he had placed this man under arrest, he then proceeded to go and search his car, and clearly, this is a violation of his rights under the Fourth Amendment, and it is unlawful search and seizure so the evidence that they have secured against this defendant is illegal and unlawful. Finally, we contend that on the basis of these facts that the affidavit under which the defendant was tried before the Justice of the Peace Court, as we contended yesterday, based upon the statement that was sworn to by the County Attorney, not on information and belief, but directly that this is void and defective and could give the Justice of the Peace no jurisdiction in this case. We contend under these circumstances that the State—that this is an illegal process; that this man's rights have been violated under the Fourteenth Amendment, and finally, we contend that the State has failed to prove beyond a reasonable doubt to any extent to implicate this man in this case. Now, on these basis [sic] we contend that this whole process is illegal and void, and that it has permeated and contended [sic] the whole process insofar as the jurisdiction of this Court is concerned or jurisdiction over this individual is concerned; therefore, he should be released, and we move for a directed verdict."

"Court: Motion overruled. Bring the jury back."

The motion was renewed at the completion of the defense in the following language:

"Atty Carter: Your Honor, at this time at the close of the case we want to make a motion for a directed verdict. We base it on the grounds and the reasons which we set forth in our motion for a directed verdict at the close of the State's case. We make it now at the close of the entire case on those grounds and on the grounds that the evidence has not shown beyond any reasonable doubt under the law that the defendant is guilty of the charge. We therefore make a motion for a directed verdict at this time.

"Court: Motion is overruled."

The single sentence in the first motion (supra, p. 460) is the only direct reference to the search and seizure question from beginning to end of the trial.

As every trial lawyer of any experience knows, motions for directed verdicts are generally made as a matter of course at the close of the prosecution's case, and are generally denied without close consideration unless the case is clearly borderline. It is simply unrealistic in this context to have expected the trial judge to pick out the single vague sentence from the directed verdict motion and to have acted upon it with the refined imagination the Court would require of him. Henry's three lawyers apparently regarded the search and seizure claim as makeweight. They had not mentioned it earlier in the trial and gave no explanation for their laxity in raising it. And when they did mention it, they did so in a cursory and conclusional sentence placed in a secondary position in a directed verdict motion. The theory underlying the search and seizure argument—that a wife's freely given permission to search the family car is invalid —is subtle to say the very least, and as the matter was presented to the trial judge it would have been extraordinary had he caught it, or even realized that there was a serious problem to catch. But this is not all the Court would require of him. He must, in addition, realize that despite the inappropriateness of granting the directed verdict requested of him, he could partially serve the cause of the defense by taking it upon himself to frame and give cautionary instructions to the jury to disregard the evidence obtained as fruits of the search.[2]

Contrast with this the situation presented by a contemporaneous objection. The objection must necessarily be directed to the single question of admissibility; the judge must inevitably focus on it; there would be no doubt as to the appropriate form of relief, and the effect of the trial judge's decision would be immediate rather than remote. Usually the proper timing of an objection will force an elaboration of it. Had objection been made in this case during the officer's testimony about the search, it would have called forth of its own force the specific answer that the wife had given her permission and, in turn, the assertion that the permission was ineffective. The issue, in short, would have been advertently faced by the trial judge and the likelihood of achieving a correct result maximized.

Thus the state interest which so powerfully supports the contemporaneous-objection rule is that of maximizing correct decisions and concomitantly minimizing errors requiring mistrials and retrials. The alternative for the State is to reverse a trial judge who, from a long motion, fails to pick out and act with remarkable imagination upon a single vague sentence relating to admissibility of evidence long since admitted. A trial judge is a decision-maker, not an advocate. To force him out of his proper role by requiring him to coax out the arguments and imaginatively reframe the requested remedies for the counsel before him is to place upon him more responsibility than a trial judge can be expected to discharge.

There was no "appropriate corrective action" that could have realistically satisfied the purposes of the contemporaneous-objection rule. Without question the State had an interest in maintaining the integrity of its procedure, and thus without doubt reliance on the rule in question is "adequate" to bar direct review of petitioner's federal claim by this Court.[3]

II.

The real reason for remanding this case emerges only in the closing pages of the Court's opinion. It is pointed out that even were the contemporaneous-objection rule considered to be an adequate state ground, this would not, under Fay v. Noia, preclude consideration of Henry's federal claim in federal habeas corpus unless it were made to appear that Henry had deliberately waived his federal claim in the state proceedings. It is then said that in the interest of "efficient administration of criminal justice" and "harmonious" relations between the federal and state judiciaries the Mississippi courts should be given the opportunity to pass, in the first instance, on the waiver issue; the prospect is entertained that such action on the part of this Court will encourage the States to grasp the "opportunity" afforded by Fay v. Noia and Townsend v. Sain by providing "state procedures, direct or collateral, for a full airing of federal claims." It is "suggested" that were this to be done "irritation" and "friction" respecting the exercise of federal habeas corpus power vis-a-vis state convictions "might be ameliorated."

What does all this signify? The States are being invited to voluntarily obliterate all state procedures, however conducive they may be to the orderly conduct of litigation, which might thwart state-court consideration of federal claims. But what if the States do not accept the invitation? Despite the Court's soft-spoken assertion that "settled principles" will be applied in the future, I do not think the intimation will be missed by any discerning reader of the Court's opinion that at the least a substantial dilution of the adequate state-ground doctrine may be expected. A contrary prediction is belied by the implication of the opinion that under "settled principles," the contemporaneous-objection rule relied upon in this case could be declared inadequate.

To me this would not be a move toward "harmonious" federalism; any further disrespect for state procedures, no longer cognizable at all in federal habeas corpus, would be the very antithesis of it. While some may say that, given Fay v. Noia, what the Court is attempting to do is justifiable as a means of promoting "efficiency" in the administration of criminal justice, it is the sort of efficiency which, though perhaps appropriate in some watered-down form of federalism, is not congenial to the kind of federalism I had supposed was ours. I venture to say that to all who believe the federal system as we have known it to be a priceless aspect of our Constitutionalism, the spectre implicit in today's decision will be no less disturbing than what the Court has already done in Fay v. Noia.

Believing that the judgment below rests on an adequate independent state ground, I would dismiss the writ issued in this case as improvidently granted.

Notes

[1] The court, as a matter of state law, could have found (a) that there was sufficient corroborative evidence, (b) that none was necessary, or (c) that retrial was necessary to prevent defendants in criminal cases from hanging back until the completion of the State's case and then for the first time moving to strike a piece of evidence crucial to getting the case to the jury.

The Court's suggestion (ante, p. 449, n. 4) that we may proceed on the speculation that the Mississippi Supreme Court "overlooked" the renewal of the motion for directed verdict made at the completion of the case hardly requires comment.

[2] Furthermore, even if counsel had fully elaborated the argument and had made it in the context of a motion to strike rather than a motion for directed verdict, the trial judge could properly have exercised his discretion (as the Mississippi Supreme Court did) and denied any relief. This power is recognized in trial judges in the federal system in order to prevent the "ambushing" of a trial through the withholding of an objection that should have been made when questionable evidence was first introduced. Federalism is turned upside down if it is denied to judges in the state systems. See Fed. Rules Crim. Proc. 41 (e) and 26; United States v. Milanovich, 303 F. 2d 626, cert. denied, 371 U. S. 876; Hollingsworth v. United States, 321 F. 2d 342, 350; Isaacs v. United States, 301 F. 2d 706, 734-735, cert. denied, 371 U. S. 818; United States v. Murray, 297 F. 2d 812, 818, cert. denied, 369 U. S. 828; Metcalf v. United States, 195 F. 2d 213, 216-217.

[3] As the first opinion by the Mississippi Supreme Court shows, there is discretion in certain circumstances to lower the procedural bar. It does not follow that this Court is completely free to exercise that discretion. Even in cases from lower federal courts we do so only if there has been an abuse. If, in order to insulate its decisions from reversal by this Court, a state court must strip itself of the discretionary power to differentiate between different sets of circumstances, the rule operates in a most perverse way.

Justice Harlan's concurrence and dissent in Fortson v. Toombs (Jan 18, 1965)

MR. JUSTICE HARLAN, with whom MR. JUSTICE STEWART joins, concurring in part and dissenting in part.

This is the first time that the Court, after plenary briefing and argument, has been called on to consider the propriety of interim arrangements prescribed by a district court pending the effectuation of its decision requiring reapportionment of a branch of a state legislature.

After holding that the House of Representatives of the General Assembly of Georgia was unconstitutionally composed, a decision which is not called into question on this appeal, the three-judge District Court ordered: (1) that the election in 1964 of the legislature to serve in 1965 (the 1965 legislature) might proceed under the State's existing methods of apportionment; (2) that until a properly apportioned legislature took office no other legislature could propose to the electorate, except through the calling of a convention of popularly elected delegates, the adoption of a new state constitution; and (3) that (except for reapportionment legislation) the 1965 House should be "limited," notwithstanding any provision of state law, "to the enactment of such legislation as shall properly come before the said Legislature during the regular 1965 45-day session" provided by Georgia law. After the State's appeal was filed in this Court this last provision was in effect abrogated by the District Court with the approval of the parties.[1]

This appeal draws in question the validity of items (2) and (3) above, similarly numbered in the District Court's order. It is contended by the appellees, however, that both these issues have now become moot.

I.

The Court's disposition of this case, of course, involves a holding that at least as to item (2) the case is not moot. For, contrary to what my Brother GOLDBERG says in his dissenting opinion (post, pp. 636-638) and as my Brother CLARK seems to recognize (ante), the Court does not remand the case to the District Court for a determination on the issue of mootness, but only to decide whether any injunctive relief is now appropriate in light of what has transpired since such relief was first granted.

While it may be that the Court's implicit holding on mootness does not reach beyond the portion of the District Court's decree that goes to the submission of a proposed new state constitution (par. (2) of the decree), I would also hold not moot the pronouncement of that decree placing limitations on the functioning of the 1965 State Legislature (original par. (3) of the decree).

As to paragraph (2), it is sufficient to say that the injunction has continuing effect, not only with respect to the 1965 legislature, but also as to any successor legislature if it is found to be "malapportioned." Any alleged "speculativeness" as to whether a new state constitution may be proposed to the electorate before a "constitutional" legislature comes into being, goes not to mootness but only to the question whether the District Court (assuming its power in the premises, see below) should have granted any relief on this score.[2] So far as original paragraph (3) of the decree is concerned (limiting the activities of the 1965 legislature) it was not rendered moot by the District Court's modification after the case had been taken for review by this Court. Analytically, the situation is tantamount to a confession of error at this level, at most relieving this Court of the necessity of making a definitive exposition of its views on this subject (compare the suggestion of my Brother GOLDBERG, post, pp. 638-639), but not depriving the question of the attribute of justiciability. Cf. Young v. United States, 315 U. S. 257, 258-259.

The position adopted by the Court is that although the case is not moot, at least as to the "constitution-submission" issue, decision of that question could be avoided if the District Court chose to vacate that part of its injunction in light of the change in circumstance which has made the need for such relief speculative; the Court therefore remands the case to afford the District Court that opportunity. I do not think that such avoidance as to either question is called for in this case. The Court's reapportionment decisions have pressed district courts onto an uncharted and highly sensitive field of federalstate relations with little more to guide them than the elusive "one-person-one-vote" aphorism. District courts, as courts of first instance, must necessarily fashion remedies for themselves, and the passage of time and the variety of remedies chosen by them may ultimately help this Court to wend its way through this treacherous constitutional terrain. But it is essential that the lower courts at least be launched in the right general direction and not allowed to range so far afield as to hamstring state legislatures and deprive States of effective legislative government. Paragraphs (2) and (3) of the injunction involved in this case do range that far afield. Absent disapproval by this Court, the decision below, rendered by a distinguished panel, cannot fail to furnish a strong practical, if not legal, precedent for other district courts. I do not think this should be allowed to happen.

II.

I would hold the decree below improvident in both the aspects before us.

As to the provision forbidding submission to the electorate of a legislatively proposed new state constitution, I can find nothing in the Fourteenth Amendment, elsewhere in the Constitution, or in any decision of this Court which requires a State to initiate complete or partial constitutional change only by some method in which every voice in the voting population is given an opportunity to express itself. Can there be the slightest constitutional doubt that a State may lodge the power to initiate constitutional changes in any select body it pleases, such as a committee of the legislature, a group of constitutional lawyers, or even a "malapportioned" legislature—particularly one whose composition was considered, prior to this Court's reapportionment pronouncements of June 15, 1964, to be entirely and solely a matter of state concern?[3]

Similarly as to the provision of the lower court's original decree limiting the functions of the 1965 legislature, it seems scarcely open to serious doubt that so long as the federal courts allow this Georgia Legislature to sit, it must be regarded as the de facto legislature of the State, possessing the full panoply of legislative powers accorded by Georgia law.

I think that the State of Georgia is entitled to a clearcut pronouncement from this Court that nothing in its reapportionment decisions contemplated such unheard-of federal court intrusion into state political affairs as the decree before us evinces. Beyond that, for this Court to temporize with important interstitial matters of this kind, deeply affecting the even course of federal-state relations, can only serve to aggravate the confusion which last June's reapportionment cases have left in their wake.[4]

I would modify the decree below by striking therefrom paragraph (2) and approving the substitute for original paragraph (3) as framed by the District Court.

Notes

[1] The full text of the District Court's order and the amendment of item 3 are printed in the dissenting opinion of MR. JUSTICE GOLDBERG as Appendices A and B, respectively. Post, pp. 639, 641.

[2] See Labor Board v. Pennsylvania Greyhound Lines. Inc., 303 U. S. 261, 271; Southern Pac. Terminal Co. v. Interstate Commerce Comm'n, 219 U. S. 498, 514-515.

[3] If, as I believe, a State is not federally restricted in its choice of means for initiating constitutional change, the question of whether, under Georgia law, the proposed new Georgia Constitution should have been initiated by a popularly elected convention instead of by the legislature is not a matter for federal cognizance.

[4] To hold as I think the Court should on these issues would not in any way impair the federal courts' ability to prevent frustration of their reapportionment decrees.

Justice Harlan's dissent in Carrington v. Rash (March 1, 1965)

MR. JUSTICE HARLAN, dissenting.

I.

Anyone not familiar with the provisions of the Fourteenth Amendment, the history of that Amendment, and the decisions of the Court in this constitutional area, would gather from today's opinion that it is an established constitutional tenet that state laws governing the qualifications of voters are subject to the limitations of the Equal Protection Clause. Yet any dispassionate survey of the past will reveal that the present decision is the first to so hold.

In making this holding the Court totally ignores, as it did in last Term's reapportionment cases, Reynolds v. Sims, 377 U. S. 533 (and companion cases), all the history of the Fourteenth Amendment and the course of judicial decisions which together plainly show that the Equal Protection Clause was not intended to touch state electoral matters. See my dissenting opinion in Reynolds v. Sims, at 589. If that history does not prove what I think it does, we are at least entitled to be told why. While I cannot express surprise over today's decision after the reapportionment cases, which though bound to follow I continue to believe are constitutionally indefensible, I can and do respectfully, but earnestly, record my protest against this further extension of federal judicial power into the political affairs of the States. The reapportionment cases do not require this extension. They were concerned with methods of constituting state legislatures; this case involves state voter qualifications. The Court is quite right in not even citing them.[1]

I deplore the added impetus which this decision gives to the current tendency of judging constitutional questions on the basis of abstract "justice" unleashed from the limiting principles that go with our constitutional system. Constitutionally principled adjudication, high in the process of which is due recognition of the just demands of federalism, leaves ample room for the protection of individual rights. A constitutional democracy which in order to cope with seeming needs of the moment is willing to temporize with its basic distribution and limitation of governmental powers will sooner or later find itself in trouble.

For reasons set forth at length in my dissent in Reynolds, I would dismiss the complaint in this case for failure to state a claim of federal right.

II.

I also think this decision wrong even on the Court's premise that it is free to extend the Equal Protection Clause so as to reach state-established voter qualifications. The question here is simply whether the differentiation in voting eligibility requirements which Texas has made is founded on a rational classification. In judging this question I think that the dictates of history, even though the Court has seen fit to disregard them for the purpose of determining whether it should get into the matter at all, should cause the Court to take a hard look before striking down a traditional state policy in this area as rationally indefensible.

Essentially the Texas statute establishes a rule that servicemen from other States stationed at Texas bases are to be treated as transients for voting purposes. No one disputes that in the vast majority of cases Texas' view of things accords with fact. Although it is doubtless true that this rule may operate in some instances contrary to the actual facts, I do not think that the Federal Constitution prevents the State from ignoring that possibility in the overall picture. In my opinion Texas could rationally conclude that such instances would likely be too minimal to justify the administrative expenditure involved in coping with the "special problems" (ante, p. 96) entailed in winnowing out the bona fide permanent residents from among the transient servicemen living off base and sending their children to local schools.

Beyond this, I think a legitimate distinction may be drawn between those who come voluntarily into Texas in connection with private occupations and those ordered into Texas by military authority. Residences established by the latter are subject to the doubt, not present to the same degree with the former, that when the military compulsion ends, so also may the desire to remain in Texas.

And finally, I think that Texas, given the traditional American notion that control of the military should always be kept in civilian hands, emphasized in the case of Texas by its own special historical experience,[2] could rationally decide to protect state and local politics against the influences of military voting strength by, in effect, postponing the privilege of voting otherwise attaching to a service-acquired domicile until the serviceman becomes a civilian and by limiting Texan servicemen to voting in the counties of their original domicile.[3] Such a policy on Texas' part may seem to many unduly provincial in light of modern conditions, but it cannot, in my view, be said to be unconstitutional.

Thus, whether or not this Court has subject matter jurisdiction in this case, the judgment of the Supreme Court of Texas should not be disturbed.

Notes

[1] None of the cases on which the Court does rely lends any support to its decision.

In Pope v. Williams, 193 U. S. 621, the Court upheld a Maryland statute which required voters to have been registered in the State for at least a year. The Court said of the right to vote:

"It is not a privilege springing from citizenship of the United States. . . . It may not be refused on account of race, color or previous condition of servitude, but it does not follow from mere citizenship of the United States. In other words, the privilege to vote in a State is within the jurisdiction of the State itself, to be exercised as the State may direct, and upon such terms as to it may seem proper, provided, of course, no discrimination is made between individuals in violation of the Federal Constitution [obviously referring to the Fifteenth and not the Fourteenth Amendment]. . . . The question whether the conditions prescribed by the State might be regarded by others as reasonable or unreasonable is not a Federal one." 193 U. S., at 632-633.

Lassiter v. Northampton Election Bd., 360 U. S. 45, upheld the literacy test applied in North Carolina against an attack made on its face. The Court noted that:

"Of course a literacy test, fair on its face, may be employed to perpetuate that discrimination which the Fifteenth Amendment was designed to uproot." 360 U. S., at 53. (Emphasis added.)

Gray v. Sanders, 372 U. S. 368, struck down Georgia's county-unit system for counting votes in a party primary election for the nomination of a United States Senator. It did not deal with voter qualifications.

United States v. Classic, 313 U. S. 299, dealt with stuffing ballot boxes, and Ex parte Yarbrough, 110 U. S. 651, with intimidation of Negroes attempting to vote. Neither dealt with voter qualifications.

None of the other federal cases cited by the Court was concerned in any way with voting.

[2] The 1837 election law of the Republic of Texas, § 9, provided "That regular enlisted soldiers, and volunteers for during the war, shall not be eligible to vote for civil officers." 2 Laws of Republic of Texas, p. 8, in 1 Gammel, Laws of Texas, p. 1350. "This provision was no doubt inspired by the mutinous conduct of the nonresident volunteers who had been recruited in the United States after the Battle of San Jacinto. They had defied the provisional government and on one occasion in July, 1836, had sent an officer to arrest President David G. Burnett and his cabinet to bring them to trial before the army. They had continued their rebellious conduct after Sam Houston became the first president under the Constitution of 1836. It was not until May, 1837, that Houston was able to dissolve the army and eliminate this threat to civil authority. This provision disfranchising soldiers in the regular army was placed in the 1845 Constitution of the State of Texas and has remained in each succeeding constitution. It was modified in 1932 to exempt the National Guard and reserve and retired officers and men." McCall, History of Texas Election Laws, 9 Vernon's Ann. Tex. Civ. Stat., pp. XVII-XVIII (1952).

Other States which had similar provisions in their early constitutions included Alabama, Const. of 1819, Art. III, § 5; Arkansas, Const. of 1836, Art. IV, § 2; Indiana,

Const. of 1816, Art. VI, § 1: Louisiana, Const. of 1845, Art. 12; Missouri, Const. of 1820, Art. III, § 10; South Carolina, Const. of 1790 (as amended in 1810), Art. I, § 4; Virginia, Const. of 1830, Art. III, § 14.

The 1932 amendment to the Texas Constitution was replaced in 1954 by the present provision.

[3] Tex. Const., Art. VI, § 2, quoted in Court's opinion, ante, n. 1.

Justice Harlan's dissent in O'Keeffe v. Smith, Hinchman & Grylls Associates, Inc. (March 29, 1965)

MR. JUSTICE HARLAN, whom MR. JUSTICE CLARK and MR. JUSTICE WHITE join, dissenting.

Ecker was employed in Seoul, Korea, as an assistant administrative officer for Smith, Hinchman & Grylls Associates, Inc., an engineering management concern working under contracts with the United States and Korean Governments. His duties were restricted to Seoul where he was responsible for personnel in the stenographic and clerical departments. He was subject to call at the job site at any time, but the usual work week was 44 hours, and employees were accustomed to travel far from the job site on weekends and holidays for recreational purposes. Ecker did not live at the job site; he was given an allowance to live on the economy in Seoul. On his Memorial Day weekend he went to a lake 30 miles east of Seoul where a friend of his (not a co-employee) had a house. Ecker intended to spend the holiday there with his friend and another visitor. Their Saturday afternoon project was to fill in the beach in front of the house with sand, but none was readily available. In order to obtain it the three crossed the lake in a small aluminum boat to a sandy part of the shore. There they filled the boat with a load of sand, intending to transport it back to the house. The return trip, however, put Archimedes' Principle to the test; in the middle of the lake the boat capsized and sank. Two of the three men drowned, including Ecker.

The Longshoremen's and Harbor Workers' Compensation Act,[1] as extended by the Defense Bases Act,[2] provides workmen's compensation for any

"accidental injury or death arising out of and in the course of employment, and such occupational disease or infection as arises naturally out of such employment or as naturally or unavoidably results from such accidental injury, and includes an injury caused by the willful act of a third person directed against an employee because of his employment." 33 U. S. C. § 902 (2).

The Court holds, per curiam, that Ecker died in the course of his employment. I see no meaningful interpretation of the statute which will support this result except a rule that any decision made by a Deputy Commissioner must be upheld (compare Rogers v. Missouri Pac. R. Co., 352 U. S. 500). That interpretation, although meaningful, is unsupportable.

O'Leary v. Brown-Pacific-Maxon, Inc., 340 U. S. 504, relied upon by the Court, did not establish such a rule. The Court there upheld a compensation award arising from the accidental death of an employee of a government contractor on the island of Guam. The employer maintained for its employees a recreation center near the shoreline along which ran a very dangerous channel. After spending the afternoon at the employer's recreation center, and while waiting for the employer's bus, the employee heard cries for help from two men in trouble in the channel. He drowned in his attempt to rescue them. Mr. Justice Frankfurter, writing for the Court, stated the standard of coverage as:

"All that is required is that the `obligations or conditions' of employment create the `zone of special danger' out of which the injury arose." 340 U. S., at 507.

That language was intended to mean only that where the employer had placed a facility for employees in an especially dangerous location and thus had created a danger of accidents, a "reasonable rescue attempt" could be "one of the risks of the employment." This was made crystal clear by the caveat: "We hold only that rescue attempts such as that before us are not necessarily excluded from the coverage of the Act as the kind of conduct that employees engage in as frolics of their own." Ibid.

He went on to state that the standard of review to be applied to the Deputy Commissioner's finding that the employee died in the course of his employment was the same as that set out in Universal Camera Corp. v. Labor Board, 340 U. S. 474, for review of Labor Board decisions. Mr. Justice Frankfurter wrote both Universal Camera and Brown-Pacific-Maxon, and delivered the opinions on the same day. Reliance upon Universal Camera in Brown-Pacific-Maxon shows beyond doubt that the Court was not establishing a rule that any compensation award by a Deputy Commissioner would be automatically upheld, for it was the whole purpose of Universal Camera to effectuate congressional intent that the courts expand their scope of review over administrative decisions. That opinion defined judicial responsibility for examining the whole record in Labor Board cases, and not just those parts of the record which tended to support the Board. It remains today as the leading judicial guide for administrative review, and the most prominent directive to lower courts not to underestimate their responsibilities in this regard. I think it untenable to read a case which purports to apply the Universal Camera standard of review as embodying a philosophy of judicial abdication.

I read Brown-Pacific-Maxon to mean that some questions of application of "arising out of and in the course of employment" to the facts of a case will be left to the discretion of the administrator, and review of his decision treated as review of a finding of fact. The cases in which this limited review of the administrator's decision is appropriate are those in which one application of the statute to the external facts of the case effectuates the judicially recognizable purpose of the statute as well as another. Dominion over the broad or clear purposes of the statute thus remains firmly in the courts' hands, while within the confines of such statutory purposes, administrators are left discretion to provide the intimate particularizations of statutory application.[3] Brown-Pacific-Maxon is illustrative. The employee drowned in a particularly treacherous channel with which his job brought him into proximity. The danger was not great that circumstance would force him to swim in the channel, but the danger existed and was peculiar to the locality to which his job brought him; and it was out of this special danger that the employee's injury arose. This, taken together with the other elements of job connection which the administrator thought relevant, rendered an award in the case consistent with the broad purposes of the compensation statute. Yet had the Deputy Commissioner come out the other way, I think that his decision would have been equally supportable. Although it was true that the injury was related to an especially dangerous channel with which the employee's job brought him into proximity, the administrator could have ruled that the danger, although special, was so remote that the connection between the job and the injury was not sufficient to justify compensation. Either result would have been consistent with the statutory purpose of compensating all job-connected injuries on the actual job site and, additionally, those injuries off the job site which result from the "special" dangers of the employment. In the sense that both results would have been supportable, the review of the choice actually made by the Deputy Commissioner was treated as review of a finding of fact.

In the case before us, the Deputy Commissioner's ruling is not consistent with the statutory purpose. The injury did not take place on the actual job site, and it did not arise out of any special danger created by the job. In no sense can it be said that Ecker's job created any "special" danger of his drowning in a lake, or more particularly of his loading a small boat with sand and capsizing it. Nothing indicates that the lake was rougher, the boat tippier, or the sand heavier than their counterparts in the United States. If there were "exacting and unconventional conditions" in Korea it does not appear that the lake, boat, or sand was one of them. There is nothing more than a "but for" relationship between the accident and the employment. To permit the award of compensation to stand reads the "job-connected" emphasis right out of the statute, an emphasis which is clearly there. Only injuries "arising out of" the employment are compensated. A disease or infection is covered if it arises "naturally out of such employment." Injuries willfully inflicted by third persons upon an employee are covered only if inflicted "because of his employment." A "but for" relationship between the injury and the employment should not in itself be sufficient to bring about coverage.

Whether the injury is compensable should depend to some degree on the cause of the injury as well as the time of day, location, and momentary activity of the employee at the time of the accident. I would distinguish between a case in which Ecker smashed his hand in a filing cabinet while at the office and one in which he tripped over a pebble while off on a weekend hike. In the first case Ecker's injury would have arisen out of and in the course of his employment, whereas the statute would not apply to the second case unless the injury were traceable to some special danger peculiar to the employment, which was clearly not the case. Thus, if while off on that same weekend hike Ecker stepped on a mine left over from the Korean conflict, a different result could follow.

This view of the statute makes far more sense to me than the view adopted by the Court as indicated by the result in this case and its approving citation of such cases as Self

v. Hanson, 305 F. 2d 699, and Pan American World Airways, Inc. v. O'Hearne, 335 F. 2d 70, cert. denied today. It is difficult to determine just what such cases stand for. In Self v. Hanson, for instance, Miss Williams was in the company of a gentleman in a pick-up truck parked at the end of a breakwater on Guam Island at 11 o'clock in the evening. The gentleman said that he wanted to show her a ship in the harbor. Apparently they had been looking at it for over half an hour when the driver of another vehicle on the breakwater lost control and ran into the pick-up truck, causing Miss Williams spinal injuries. The Ninth Circuit upheld the Deputy Commissioner's ruling that she was injured in the course of her employment as a secretary on a Guam defense project.

To permit compensation for such injuries is to impose absolute liability upon the employer for any and all injuries, whatever their nature, whatever their cause, just so long as the Deputy Commissioner makes an award and the job location is one to which the reviewing judge would not choose to go if he had his choice of vacation spots. Before setting its stamp of approval on such an interpretation of the statute, the Court at the very least should hear argument and receive briefs on the merits. The Solicitor General has pointed out that "there are several thousands of injury cases reported annually" under this Act.[4] He urged that this question be definitively resolved by this Court. Because of the importance placed by all parties upon resolution of the proper application of the Act to these cases, and because I do not believe Brown-Pacific-Maxon, supra, dictates the Court's result, I respectfully dissent from its decision to treat O'Keeffe v. Smith, Hinchman & Grylls Associates, Inc., summarily, from its decision on the merits in that case, and from its denial of certiorari in Pan-American World Airways, Inc. v. O'Hearne, No. 474, and Pan American World Airways, Inc. v. O'Keeffe, No. 852.

Notes

[1] 44 Stat. 1424, as amended, 33 U. S. C. § 901 et seq. (1958 ed.).

[2] 55 Stat. 622, as amended, 42 U. S. C. § 1651 et seq. (1958 ed.)

[3] See generally, Jaffe, Judicial Review: Question of Law, 69 Harv. L. Rev. 239 (1955).

[4] Petition for certiorari in No. 307, p. 11.

Justice Harlan's concurrence in Hanna v. Plumer (April 26, 1965)

MR. JUSTICE HARLAN, concurring.

It is unquestionably true that up to now Erie and the cases following it have not succeeded in articulating a workable doctrine governing choice of law in diversity actions. I respect the Court's effort to clarify the situation in today's opinion. However, in doing so I think it has misconceived the constitutional premises of Erie and has failed to deal adequately with those past decisions upon which the courts below relied.

Erie was something more than an opinion which worried about "forum-shopping and avoidance of inequitable administration of the laws," ante, p. 468, although to be sure these were important elements of the decision. I have always regarded that decision as one of the modern cornerstones of our federalism, expressing policies that profoundly touch the allocation of judicial power between the state and federal systems. Erie recognized that there should not be two conflicting systems of law controlling the primary activity of citizens, for such alternative governing authority must necessarily give rise to a debilitating uncertainty in the planning of everyday affairs.[1] And it recognized that the scheme of our Constitution envisions an allocation of law-making functions between state and federal legislative processes which is undercut if the federal judiciary can make substantive law affecting state affairs beyond the bounds of congressional legislative powers in this regard. Thus, in diversity cases Erie commands that it be the state law governing primary private activity which prevails.

The shorthand formulations which have appeared in some past decisions are prone to carry untoward results that frequently arise from oversimplification. The Court is quite right in stating that the "outcome-determinative" test of Guaranty Trust Co. v. York, 326 U. S. 99, if taken literally, proves too much, for any rule, no matter how clearly "procedural," can affect the outcome of litigation if it is not obeyed. In turning from the "outcome" test of York back to the unadorned forum-shopping rationale of Erie, however, the Court falls prey to like over-simplification, for a simple forum-shopping rule also proves too much; litigants often choose a federal forum merely to obtain what they consider the advantages of the Federal Rules of Civil Procedure or to try their cases before a supposedly more favorable judge. To my mind the proper line of approach in determining whether to apply a state or a federal rule, whether "substantive" or "procedural," is to stay close to basic principles by inquiring if the choice of rule would substantially affect those primary decisions respecting human conduct which our constitutional system leaves to state regulation.[2] If so, Erie and the Constitution require that the state rule prevail, even in the face of a conflicting federal rule.

The Court weakens, if indeed it does not submerge, this basic principle by finding, in effect, a grant of substantive legislative power in the constitutional provision for a federal court system (compare Swift v. Tyson, 16 Pet. 1), and through it, setting up the Federal Rules as a body of law inviolate.

"[T]he constitutional provision for a federal court system . . . carries with it congressional power . . . to regulate matters which, though falling within the uncertain area between substance and procedure, are rationally capable of classification as either." Ante, p. 472. (Emphasis supplied.)

So long as a reasonable man could characterize any duly adopted federal rule as "procedural," the Court, unless I misapprehend what is said, would have it apply no matter how seriously it frustrated a State's substantive regulation of the primary conduct and affairs of its citizens. Since the members of the Advisory Committee, the Judicial Conference, and this Court who formulated the Federal Rules are presumably reasonable men, it follows that the integrity of the Federal Rules is absolute. Whereas the unadulterated outcome and forum-shopping tests may err too far toward honoring state rules, I submit that the Court's "arguably procedural, ergo constitutional" test moves too fast and far in the other direction.

The courts below relied upon this Court's decisions in Ragan v. Merchants Transfer Co., 337 U. S. 530, and Cohen v. Beneficial Loan Corp., 337 U. S. 541. Those cases deserve more attention than this Court has given them, particularly Ragan which, if still good law, would in my opinion call for affirmance of the result reached by the Court of Appeals. Further, a discussion of these two cases will serve to illuminate the "diversity" thesis I am advocating.

In Ragan a Kansas statute of limitations provided that an action was deemed commenced when service was made on the defendant. Despite Federal Rule 3 which provides that an action commences with the filing of the complaint, the Court held that for purposes of the Kansas statute of limitations a diversity tort action commenced only when service was made upon the defendant. The effect of this holding was that although the plaintiff had filed his federal complaint within the state period of limitations, his action was barred because the federal marshal did not serve a summons on the defendant until after the limitations period had run. I think that the decision was wrong. At most, application of the Federal Rule would have meant that potential Kansas tort defendants would have to defer for a few days the satisfaction of knowing that they had not been sued within the limitations period. The choice of the Federal Rule would have had no effect on the primary stages of private activity from which torts arise, and only the most minimal effect on behavior following the commission of the tort. In such circumstances the interest of the federal system in proceeding under its own rules should have prevailed.

Cohen v. Beneficial Loan Corp. held that a federal diversity court must apply a state statute requiring a small stockholder in a stockholder derivative suit to post a bond securing payment of defense costs as a condition to prosecuting an action. Such a statute is not "outcome determinative"; the plaintiff can win with or without it. The Court now rationalizes the case on the ground that the statute might affect the plaintiff's choice of forum (ante, p. 469, n. 10), but as has been pointed out, a simple forum-shopping test proves too much. The proper view of Cohen is, in my opinion, that the statute was meant to inhibit small stockholders from instituting "strike suits," and thus it was designed and could be expected to have a substantial impact on private primary activity. Anyone who was at the trial bar during the period when Cohen arose can appreciate the strong state policy reflected in the statute. I think it wholly legitimate to view Federal Rule 23 as not purporting to deal with the problem. But even had the Federal Rules purported to do so, and in so doing provided a substantially less effective deterrent to strike suits, I think the state rule should still have prevailed. That is where I believe the Court's view differs from mine; for the Court attributes such overriding force to the Federal Rules that it is hard to think of a case where a conflicting state rule would be allowed to operate, even though the state rule reflected policy considerations which, under Erie, would lie within the realm of state legislative authority.

It remains to apply what has been said to the present case. The Massachusetts rule provides that an executor need not answer suits unless in-hand service was made upon him or notice of the action was filed in the proper registry of probate within one year of his giving bond. The evident intent of this statute is to permit an executor to distribute the estate which he is administering without fear that further liabilities may be outstanding for which he could be held personally liable. If the Federal District Court in Massachusetts applies Rule 4 (d) (1) of the Federal Rules of Civil Procedure instead of the Massachusetts service rule, what effect would that have on the speed and assurance with which estates are distributed? As I see it, the effect would not be substantial. It would mean simply that an executor would have to check at his own house or the federal courthouse as well as the registry of probate before he could distribute the estate with impunity. As this does not seem enough to give rise to any real impingement on the vitality of the state policy which the Massachusetts rule is intended to serve, I concur in the judgment of the Court.

Notes

[1] Since the rules involved in the present case are parallel rather than conflicting, this first rationale does not come into play here.

[2] See Hart and Wechsler, The Federal Courts and the Federal System 678.

Byrd v. Blue Ridge Coop., Inc., 356 U. S. 525, 536-540, indicated that state procedures would apply if the State had manifested a particularly strong interest in their employment. Compare Dice v. Akron, C. & Y. R. Co., 342 U. S. 359. However, this approach may not be of constitutional proportions.

Justice Harlan's dissent in Travia v. Lomenzo (June 1, 1965)

MR. JUSTICE HARLAN, dissenting.

An application has been made to me, as Circuit Justice, for a stay pending appeal from an order of a three-judge District Court, dated May 24, 1965, ordering New York to hold a special legislative election on November 2, 1965, under the electoral scheme embodied in reapportionment "Plan A"[1] passed by the New York Legislature, signed by the Governor, and held unconstitutional under the State Constitution by the New York Court of Appeals. The stay application was accompanied by a motion, addressed to the Court, asking for an acceleration and immediate hearing of the appeal, to which the relief sought from me is incident. Because the stay and acceleration questions were in my opinion inextricably related and involved issues of far-reaching importance, I referred the stay application to the full Court for determination (see Sup. Ct. Rule 50 (6)) in conjunction with the motion to accelerate the appeal. The Court now denies both the stay and motion to accelerate, and I respectfully dissent.

"Plan A" was one of four alternative reapportionment plans passed by the New York Legislature under the impact of an order of the District Court, dated July 27, 1964, entered pursuant to this Court's decision in WMCA, Inc. v. Lomenzo, 377 U. S. 633, which held New York's then-existing method of legislative apportionment violative of the

Fourteenth Amendment. The District Court order provided by way of interim relief that (1) the November 1964 legislative elections could proceed under the invalidated apportionment system, but the legislators would be permitted to serve for only a one-year period, instead of the two-year term provided in the State Constitution; (2) a special November 1965 election must be held under a constitutionally valid apportionment plan to be enacted by the New York Legislature and submitted to the District Court for approval not later than April 1, 1965 (later extended to May 5, 1965), the legislators so elected again to serve for only one year; and (3) the regularly scheduled November 1966 election, for a normal two-year term, would be held under the same or some other court-approved reapportionment plan. This Court summarily affirmed the District Court's order. Hughes v. WMCA, Inc., 379 U. S. 694. Two dissenting Justices would have set the case for plenary consideration, and two concurring Justices expressly noted that the Court's action did not foreclose the District Court from modifying its interim order in light of subsequent developments.

In December 1964 the 1964 Legislature, meeting in special session, passed and the Governor signed four alternative reapportionment plans, one of which, "Plan A," is involved in the matter now before us. On January 26, 1965, the three-judge District Court found that "Plan A" satisfied federal constitutional requirements, but that each of the other plans did not. 238 F. Supp. 916. On April 14, 1965, the New York Court of Appeals held all four plans invalid under the State Constitution, in that each provided for an Assembly of more than 150 members, thus exceeding the membership limit prescribed by the New York Constitution, Art. 3, § 2. In re Orans, 15 N. Y. 2d 339, 206 N. E. 2d 854.

Ignoring the New York Court of Appeals' holding that Plan A violated the State Constitution, a majority of the District Court, on May 18, 1965, ordered the November 1965 state legislative election to proceed under that plan. One judge dissented, considering that a more appropriate, though admittedly not wholly satisfactory, "interim" solution would be to permit the November 1965 election to go forward under the old reapportionment formula, with the legislators thus elected being accorded "weighted votes" in the legislature based on population.

On May 24, 1965, the State Legislature passed three bills, the substantial effects of which were (1) to adopt the dissenting district judge's weighted voting formula for the 1966 legislative session, without holding an election this fall;[2] (2) to create a bi-partisan commission to devise a new reapportionment formula for the 1966 election, meeting both federal and state constitutional requirements;[3] and (3) to issue a call for a constitutional convention to promulgate a permanent reapportionment plan to govern the 1968 and subsequent elections.[4] The Speaker of the Assembly and the President pro tem of the State Senate (the intervenors-appellants here) thereupon sought leave to intervene in the district court proceedings and to persuade the court to modify the interim relief in accordance with these legislative proposals. Their application for leave to intervene was granted, but the District Court refused to modify its earlier order. These applications for a stay and accelerated appeal followed immediately.

These matters bristle with difficult and important questions that touch the nerve centers of the sound operation of our federal and state judicial and political systems. They involve, among other things, the right of a federal court to order that one house of a state legislature shall temporarily be of greater size than is permitted by the State Constitution. Surely such questions are deserving of plenary consideration and reasoned explication. By denying a stay and refusing to accelerate this appeal, the Court, instead, has in effect decided them not only summarily but also sub silentio. For while the denial of a stay does not technically moot the appeal, it is manifest that such is the practical effect of the Court's action, since in normal course the appeal will not even be heard until after the presently ordered November election has taken place.

Without prejudging the question, the propriety of a federal court's ordering a state election to proceed under a plan which the highest court of the State has found to violate the State Constitution in respects not claimed to be violative of the Federal Constitution, when a number of alternatives are available, raises what I consider to be very serious federal questions which this Court should at least hear. All parties have shown themselves willing to argue the case promptly. I would set the case for immediate argument, and would have the Court render its decision on the stay promptly thereafter, with opinions on the merits of the controversy to follow in due course. Compare Cooper v. Aaron, 358 U. S. 1.[5]

I am wholly at a loss to understand the Court's casual way of disposing of this matter and I can find no considerations of any kind which justify it. The Court should be willing to face up articulately to these difficult problems which have followed as a not unnatural aftermath of its reapportionment decisions of last Term.

Notes

[1] New York Laws 1964, c. 976. At the same time the Legislature passed three successive amendments to c. 976: New York Laws 1964, cc. 977-978 (Plan "B"), c. 979 (Plan "C"), and c. 981 (Plan "D"). These four acts have been referred to throughout the proceedings as Plans A, B, C, and D.

[2] New York Assembly Intro. 6051, Print: 7067, vetoed by the Governor on May 27, 1965.

[3] New York Assembly Intro. 6050, Print. 7066, vetoed by the Governor on May 27, 1965.

[4] New York Assembly Intro. 5695, Print. 5988.

[5] The necessity for a prompt disposition is evidenced by the fact that the State's primary machinery must be set in motion today if an election next November is to take place.

Justice Harlan's concurrence in Estes v. Texas (June 7, 1965)

MR. JUSTICE HARLAN, concurring.

I concur in the opinion of the Court, subject, however, to the reservations and only to the extent indicated in this opinion.

The constitutional issue presented by this case is farreaching in its implications for the administration of justice in this country. The precise question is whether the Fourteenth Amendment prohibits a State, over the objection of a defendant, from employing television in the courtroom to televise contemporaneously, or subsequently by means of videotape, the courtroom proceedings of a criminal trial of widespread public interest. The issue is no narrower than this because petitioner has not asserted any isolatable prejudice resulting from the presence of television apparatus within the courtroom or from the contemporaneous or subsequent broadcasting of the trial proceedings. On the other hand, the issue is no broader, for we are concerned here only with a criminal trial of great notoriety, and not with criminal proceedings of a more or less routine nature.

The question is fraught with unusual difficulties. Permitting television in the courtroom undeniably has mischievous potentialities for intruding upon the detached atmosphere which should always surround the judicial process. Forbidding this innovation, however, would doubtless impinge upon one of the valued attributes of our federalism by preventing the States from pursuing a novel course of procedural experimentation. My conclusion is that there is no constitutional requirement that television be allowed in the courtroom, and, at least as to a notorious criminal trial such as this one, the considerations against allowing television in the courtroom so far outweigh the countervailing factors advanced in its support as to require a holding that what was done in this case infringed the fundamental right to a fair trial assured by the Due Process Clause of the Fourteenth Amendment.

Some preliminary observations are in order: All would agree, I am sure, that at its worst, television is capable of distorting the trial process so as to deprive it of fundamental fairness. Cables, kleig lights, interviews with the principal participants, commentary on their performances, "commercials" at frequent intervals, special wearing apparel and makeup for the trial participants—certainly such things would not conduce to the sound administration of justice by any acceptable standard. But that is not the case before us. We must judge television as we find it in this trial—relatively unobtrusive, with the cameras contained in a booth at the back of the courtroom.

I.

No constitutional provision guarantees a right to televise trials. The "public trial" guarantee of the Sixth Amendment, which reflects a concept fundamental to the administration of justice in this Country, In re Oliver, 333 U. S. 257, certainly does not require that television be admitted to the courtroom. See United Press Assns. v. Valente, 308 N. Y. 71, 123 N. E. 2d 777. Essentially, the public-trial guarantee embodies a view of human nature, true as a general rule, that judges, lawyers, witnesses, and jurors will perform their respective functions more responsibly in an open court than in secret proceedings. In re Oliver, supra, at 266-273. A fair trial is the objective, and "public trial" is an institutional safeguard for attaining it.

Thus the right of "public trial" is not one belonging to the public, but one belonging to the accused, and inhering in the institutional process by which justice is administered. Obviously, the public-trial guarantee is not violated if an individual member of the public cannot gain admittance to a courtroom because there are no available seats. The guarantee will already have been met, for the "public" will be present in the form of those persons who did gain admission. Even the actual presence of the public is not guaranteed. A public trial implies only that the court must be open to those who wish to come, sit in the available seats, conduct themselves with decorum, and observe the trial process. It does not give anyone a concomitant right to photograph, record, broadcast, or otherwise transmit the trial proceedings to those members of the public not present, although to be sure, the guarantee of public trial does not of itself prohibit such activity.

The free speech and press guarantees of the First and Fourteenth Amendments are also asserted as embodying a positive right to televise trials, but the argument is greatly overdrawn. Unquestionably, television has become a very effective medium for transmitting news. Many trials are newsworthy, and televising them might well provide the most accurate and comprehensive means of conveying their content to the public. Furthermore, television is capable of performing an educational function by acquainting the public with the judicial process in action. Albeit these are credible policy arguments in favor of television, they are not arguments of constitutional proportions. The rights to print and speak, over television as elsewhere, do not embody an independent right to bring the mechanical facilities of the broadcasting and printing industries into the courtroom. Once beyond the confines of the courthouse, a news-gathering agency may publicize, within wide limits, what its representatives have heard and seen in the courtroom. But the line is drawn at the courthouse door; and within, a reporter's constitutional rights are no greater than those of any other member of the public. Within the courthouse the only relevant constitutional consideration is that the accused be accorded a fair trial. If the presence of television substantially detracts from that goal, due process requires that its use be forbidden.

I see no force in the argument that to exclude television apparatus from the courtroom, while at the same time permitting newspaper reporters to bring in their pencils and notebooks, would discriminate in favor of the press as against the broadcasting services. The distinctions to be drawn between the accouterments of the press and the television media turn not on differences of size and shape but of function and effect. The presence of the press at trials may have a distorting effect, but it is not caused by their pencils and notebooks. If it were, I would not hesitate to say that such physical paraphernalia should be barred.

II.

The probable impact of courtroom television on the fairness of a trial may vary according to the particular kind of case involved. The impact of television on a trial exciting wide popular interest may be one thing; the impact on a run-of-the-mill case may be quite another. Furthermore, the propriety of closed circuit television for the purpose of making a court recording or for limited use in educational institutions obviously presents markedly different considerations. The Estes trial was a heavily publicized and highly sensational affair. I therefore put aside all other types of cases; in so doing, however, I wish to make it perfectly clear that I am by no means prepared to say that the constitutional issue should ultimately turn upon the nature of the particular case involved. When the issue of television in a non-notorious trial is presented it may appear that no workable distinction can be drawn based on the type of case involved, or that the possibilities for prejudice, though less severe, are nonetheless of constitutional proportions. Compare Powell v. Alabama, 287 U. S. 45; Betts v. Brady, 316 U. S. 455; Gideon v. Wainwright, 372 U. S. 335. The resolution of those further questions should await an appropriate case; the Court should proceed only step by step in this unplowed field. The opinion of the Court necessarily goes no farther, for only the four members of the majority who unreservedly join the Court's opinion would resolve those questions now.

I do not deem the constitutional inquiry in this case ended by the finding, in effect conceded by petitioner's counsel, that no isolatable prejudice was occasioned by the manner in which television was employed in this case.[1] Courtroom television introduces into the conduct of a criminal trial the element of professional "showmanship," an extraneous influence whose subtle capacities for serious mischief in a case of this sort will not be underestimated by any lawyer experienced in the elusive imponderables of the trial arena. In the context of a trial of intense public interest, there is certainly a strong possibility that the timid or reluctant witness, for whom a court appearance even at its traditional best is a harrowing affair, will become more timid or reluctant when he finds that he will also be appearing before a "hidden audience" of unknown but large dimensions. There is certainly a strong possibility that the "cocky" witness having a thirst for the limelight will become more "cocky" under the influence of television. And who can say that the juror who is gratified by having been chosen for a front-line case, an ambitious prosecutor, a publicity-minded defense counsel, and even a conscientious judge will not stray, albeit unconsciously, from doing what "comes naturally" into pluming themselves for a satisfactory television "performance"?

Surely possibilities of this kind carry grave potentialities for distorting the integrity of the judicial process bearing on the determination of the guilt or innocence of the accused, and, more particularly, for casting doubt on the reliability of the fact-finding process carried on under such conditions. See Douglas. The Public Trial and the Free Press, 46 A. B. A. J. 840 (1960). To be sure, such distortions may produce no telltale signs, but in a highly publicized trial the danger of their presence is substantial, and their effects may be far more pervasive and deleterious than the physical disruptions which all concede would vitiate a conviction. A lively public interest could increase the size of the viewing audience immensely, and the masses of spectators to whom the trial is telecast would have become emotionally involved with the case through the dissemination of pretrial publicity, the usual concomitant of such a case. The presence of television would certainly emphasize to the trial participants that the case is something "special." Particularly treacherous situations are presented in cases where pretrial publicity has been massive[2] even when jurors positively state they will not be influenced by it; see Rideau v. Louisiana, 373 U. S. 723; Irvin v. Dowd, 366 U. S. 717. To increase the possibility of influence and the danger of a "popular verdict" by subjecting the jurors to the view of a mass audience whose approach to the case has been conditioned by pretrial publicity can only make a bad situation worse. The entire thrust of rules of evidence and the other protections attendant upon the modern trial is to keep extraneous influences out of the courtroom. Turner v. Louisiana, 379 U. S. 466, 472-473. As we recently observed in Turner, "Mr. Justice Holmes stated no more than a truism when he observed that `Any judge who has sat with juries knows that in spite of forms they are extremely likely to be impregnated by the environing atmosphere.' Frank v. Mangum, 237 U. S. 309, at 349 (dissenting opinion)." Id., at 472.[3] The knowledge on the part of the jury and other trial participants that they are being televised to an emotionally involved audience can only aggravate the atmosphere created by pretrial publicity.

The State argues that specific prejudice must be shown for the Due Process Clause to apply. I do not believe that the Fourteenth Amendment is so impotent when the trial practices in question are instinct with dangers to constitutional guarantees. I am at a loss to understand how the Fourteenth Amendment can be thought not to encompass protection of a state criminal trial from the dangers created by the intrusion of collateral and wholly irrelevant influences into the courtroom. The Court has not hesitated in the past to condemn such practices, even without any positive showing of isolatable prejudice. In Turner v. Louisiana, supra, decided just this Term, we held that the "potentialities" for distortion of the trial created by a key witness serving as bailiff to a sequestered jury were sufficient to violate the Due Process Clause of the Fourteenth Amendment. In Jackson v. Denno, 378 U. S. 368, the Court made the judgment that a trial judge's determination of a coerced-confession issue is more likely to avoid prejudice than a jury determination, a judgment which indeed overrode a long-standing contrary state practice. And in Irvin v. Dowd, 366 U. S. 717, we held that flamboyant pretrial publicity cast sufficient doubt on the impartiality of the jury to vitiate a conviction, even in the face of statements by all the jurors that they were not subject to its influence. See 366 U. S., at 729 (Frankfurter. J., concurring). Other examples of instances in which the Court has exercised its judgment as to the effects of one thing or another on human behavior are plentiful. See, e. g., Griffin v. California, 380 U. S. 609; Tancil v. Woolls, 379 U. S. 19; Mapp v. Ohio, 367 U. S. 643 (compare People v. Defore, 242 N. Y. 13, 150 N. E. 585); Avery v. Georgia, 345 U. S. 559; Brown v. Board of Education, 347 U. S. 483; Tumey v. Ohio, 273 U. S. 510.

The judgment that the presence of television in the courtroom represents a serious danger to the trial process is supported by a vast segment of the Bar of this country, as evidenced by Canon 35 of the Canons of Judicial Ethics of the American Bar Association, counselling against such practices,[4] the views of the Judicial Conference of the United States (infra, p. 601), Rule 53 of the Federal Rules of Criminal Procedure, and even the "personal views" (post, pp. 601-602) of the Justices on the dissenting side of the present case.

The arguments advanced against the constitutional banning of televised trials seem to me peculiarly unpersuasive. It is said that the pictorial broadcasting of trials will serve to educate the public as to the nature of the judicial process. Whatever force such arguments might have in run-of-the-mill cases, they carry little weight in cases of the sort before us, where the public's interest in viewing the trial is likely to be engendered more by curiosity about the personality of the well-known figure who is the defendant (as here), or about famous witnesses or lawyers who will appear on the television screen, or about the details of the particular crime involved, than by innate curiosity to learn about the workings of the judicial process itself. Indeed it would be naive not to suppose that it would be largely such factors that would qualify a trial for commercial television "billing," and it is precisely that kind of case where the risks of permitting television coverage of the proceedings are at their greatest.

It is also asserted that televised trials will cause witnesses to be more truthful, and jurors, judges, and lawyers more diligent. To say the least this argument is sophistic, for it is impossible to believe that the reliability of a trial as a method of finding facts and determining guilt or innocence increases in relation to the size of the crowd which is watching it. Attendance by interested spectators in the courtroom will fully satisfy the safeguards of "public trial." Once openness is thus assured, the addition of masses of spectators would, I venture to say, detract rather than add to the reliability of the process. See Cox v. Louisiana, 379 U. S. 559, 562. A trial in Yankee Stadium, even if the crowd sat in stony silence, would be a substantially different affair from a trial in a traditional courtroom under traditional conditions, and the difference would not. I think, be that the witnesses, lawyers, judges, and jurors in the stadium would be more truthful, diligent, and capable of reliably finding facts and determining guilt or innocence.[5] There will be no disagreement, I am sure, among those competent to judge that precisely the opposite would likely be the case.

Finally, we should not be deterred from making the constitutional judgment which this case demands by the prospect that the day may come when television will have become so commonplace an affair in the daily life of the average person as to dissipate all reasonable likelihood that its use in courtrooms may disparage the judicial process. If and when that day arrives the constitutional judgment called for now would of course be subject to re-examination in accordance with the traditional workings of the Due Process Clause. At the present juncture I can only conclude that televised trials, at least in cases like this one, possess such capabilities for interfering with the even course of the judicial process that they are constitutionally banned. On these premises I concur in the opinion of the Court.

Notes

[1] The trial judge ordered that there was to be no audio transmission of the

witnesses' testimony. The witnesses, however, were present at the September hearing when everything was broadcast, and the record does not show affirmatively that they were aware that the microphone which confronted them during the actual trial was not being used for the same purpose.

[2] Petitioner in this case amassed 11 volumes of pretrial press clippings.

[3] The Court had occasion to recognize in Cox v. Louisiana, 379 U. S. 559, 565, that even "judges are human" and not immune from outside environmental influences.

[4] The consistent position of the American Bar Association is set out in the Appendix.

[5] There may, of course, be a difference in impact upon the atmosphere and trial participants between the physical presence of masses of people and the presence of a camera lens which permits masses of people to observe the process remotely. However, the critical element is the knowledge of the trial participants that they are subject to such visual observation, an element which is, of course, present in this case.

Justice Harlan's dissent in Gondeck v. Pan Am. World Airways (Oct 18, 1965)

MR. JUSTICE HARLAN, dissenting.

The result reached in this case has been achieved at the expense of the sound legal principle that litigation must at some point come to an end.

I can find nothing in the train of events on which the Court relies in overturning this more than three-year-old final judgment that justifies bringing into play the dubious doctrine of United States v. Ohio Power Co., 353 U. S. 98, a case which was decided by a closely divided vote of less than a full bench,[1] which deviated from long-established practices of this Court,[2] and which, so far as I can find, has had no sequel in subsequent decisions of the Court.[3]

The judgment against this petitioner became final as long ago as June 11, 1962. 370 U. S. 918. The Court refused to reconsider it four months later when it denied rehearing on October 8, 1962. 371 U. S. 856. When some two years later, July 13, 1964, the Court of Appeals for the Fourth Circuit upheld a compensation award with respect to a co-employee of Gondeck killed in the same accident, Pan American World Airways, Inc. v. O'Hearne, 335 F. 2d 70, petitioner did not even seek to file another petition for rehearing here. A few months later the Fifth Circuit might be thought to have indicated some doubt about its earlier decision in the Gondeck case, O'Keeffe v. Pan American World Airways, Inc., 338 F. 2d 319, 325, but again no attempt was made to file a further petition for rehearing here in Gondeck.

It was this Court's decision of last Term in O'Keeffe v. Smith, Hinchman & Grylls Associates, Inc., 380 U. S. 359, which itself was a debatable innovation in this area of the law,[4] that triggered the undoing of this judgment of four Terms ago. It should be noted that the subject matter in O'Keeffe v. Pan American World Airways, Inc., was an entirely different accident from the one in which petitioner's decedent was involved.

This, then, is hardly one of those rare cases in which " `the interest in finality of litigation must yield' " because " `the interests of justice would make unfair the strict application of our rules,' " ante, pp. 26-27. On the contrary, the situation is one in which the prevailing party in this litigation had every reason to count on the judgment in its favor remaining firm. Believing that this decision holds seeds of mischief for the future orderly administration of justice, I respectfully dissent.

Notes

[1] The vote was 4 to 3, MR. JUSTICE BRENNAN and Mr. Justice Whittaker, since retired, not participating. 353 U. S., at 99.

[2] See dissenting opinion of HARLAN, J., 353 U. S., at 99.

[3] My Brother CLARK'S citation of Cahill v. New York, N. H. & H. R. Co., 351 U. S. 183, ante, p. 28, for the proposition that this petition for rehearing must be granted is inapposite. Cahill was an FELA case in which this Court reversed summarily a judgment of the Court of Appeals overturning a district court judgment for the plaintiff, 350 U. S. 898. Later that same Term, after a petition for rehearing had been denied, 350 U. S. 943, the Court was persuaded on "a motion to recall and amend the judgment" that its mandate, which simply reinstated the District Court's judgment, was incorrect and that the case should properly have been remanded to the Court of Appeals for further proceedings. It is difficult for me to see how the correction during the same Term of our own error in Cahill can be thought to compel or justify a general "rule of `no finality' " (as my Brother CLARK puts it, ante, p. 29) which requires the granting of a second petition for rehearing three years after the first one was denied in a case which this Court never heard.

[4] The case was decided without argument by a substantially divided Court, 380 U. S. 359. See dissenting opinion of HARLAN, J., joined by CLARK and WHITE, JJ., 380 U. S., at 365. See also separate opinion of DOUGLAS, J., 380 U. S., at 371.

Justice Harlan's dissent in FTC v. Mary Carter Paint Co. (Nov 8, 1965)

MR. JUSTICE HARLAN, dissenting.

In my opinion the basis for the Commission's action is too opaque to justify an upholding of its order in this case. A summary discussion of the facts and Commission proceedings will suffice to show why I cannot subscribe to the majority's disposition.

Since 1951 the enterprise now known as Mary Carter Paint Company has been manufacturing paint products for direct distribution through its own outlets and franchised dealers. For most or all of this period, its practice has been to establish its prices on a per-can basis but to give each customer a second can without further charge for each can purchased. Mary Carter's advertisements, while disclosing that the first can of each pair must be bought at the listed price, have always described the second can as "free"; typical slogans are: "Buy one get one free" and "Every second can free." It is this advertising which the Commission now condemns as unfair and deceptive under § 5 of the

Federal Trade Commission Act, as amended, 52 Stat. 111, 15 U. S. C. § 45 (1964 ed.).

To the extent that the Commission's order may rest on the proposition that the second can is not "free" because its receipt is "tied" to the purchase of the first can, it is manifestly inconsistent with the rules governing use of the word "free" maintained by the Commission for over a decade. No one suggests that the additional can of Mary Carter paint is free in the sense that no conditions are attached to its receipt, but the FTC forsook this commercially unrealistic definition in 1953. In that year, first by its decision in Walter J. Black, Inc., 50 F. T. C. 225, and then a general policy statement, 4 CCH Trade Reg. Rep. ¶ 40,210, it sanctioned use of the word "free" to describe an item given without extra charge on condition of another purchase so long as the condition was plainly stated and the "tying" product was not increased in price for the occasion or decreased in quantity or quality. The FTC prefaced these rules in Black by saying that "[t]he businessmen of the United States are entitled to a clear and unequivocal answer" and it represented that its new position would be maintained until either Congress or the courts decided otherwise. 50 F. T. C., at 232, 235.

There is presently no charge by the Commission that Mary Carter failed to comply with this general statement which continued in force through the proceedings and decision affecting Mary Carter. Rather, for the greater period of its advertising operations Mary Carter could properly claim to have relied on the FTC's official pronouncement while it was establishing its "every second can free" slogan in the public mind, an investment now seemingly lost. Without inflexibly holding the Commission to its promise and avowed position, certainly solid justification should be demanded before the courts agree that this departure is not "arbitrary, capricious, [or] an abuse of discretion." Administrative Procedure Act § 10 (e), 60 Stat. 243, 5 U. S. C. § 1009 (e) (1964 ed.).

At the very least the Commission should be required to demonstrate real deception and public injury in a decision that allows the courts to evaluate its reasoning and businessmen to comply with assurance with its latest views; these standards are not met by the FTC's opinion in this case. The Department of Justice suggests that the FTC regards the advertisements as implying that Mary Carter regularly sells its paint for the present percan price without giving an extra can free;[1] from this premise, it might be argued, the buyer may then conclude that each can of Mary Carter is the equal of similarly priced rivals with whom it has regularly competed on equal terms in the past, making the present "free" can offer appear an excellent bargain. But the advertising in the present case does not really suggest that the "free" can is a departure from Mary Carter's usual pricing policy. Certainly nothing in any of the publicity states that the extra can is a "new" bargain or asserts that the opportunity may lapse in the near future. To the contrary, a number of Mary Carter advertisements, not separately treated by the Commission, affirmatively suggest that the extra-can offer has been and will continue to be the sales policy. Far from trying to imply that its extra-can offer represents a temporary saving for the customer, Mary Carter has striven over a number of years to associate itself irrevocably in the public mind with the notion that every second can is free; the catchphrase appears in one form or another in nearly all the ads before us and is even imprinted on the top of Mary Carter paint cans. Finally, it is not without irony that the Commission, presumably seeking to protect the consumer from any unfounded ultimate conclusions that a can of Mary Carter is as good as its high-priced rivals, rejected an offer of proof from the company that a single can of Mary Carter is scientifically equal or superior to the leading paints that sell at the same per-can price level without giving bonus cans. Actually, there is no suggestion that any volume of consumer complaints has been received, which further deepens the mystery why this frail proceeding was ever initiated.[2]

The temptation to gloss over the analytical failings of the rationale now asserted for the FTC by relying on agency expertise must be short-lived in this case. Any findings by the FTC as to what the public may conclude from particular phrasings are most inexplicit, no distinction is taken between the various ads in question, and the conduct prescribed is never sharply identified. Surely there can be no resort to uninvoked expertise to buttress an unarticulated theory.

The opaqueness of the Commission's opinion and order makes their approval difficult for yet other reasons. The bite of the FTC decision is in its order, which even the Commission recognizes to be unclear; how the Commission order can be upheld before this Court is told what exactly it means is indeed a puzzling question. Additionally, by failing to spell out its rationale the FTC decision breeds the suspicion that it is not merely ad hoc[3] but quite possibly irreconcilable with the Black case seemingly reaffirmed by the Commission in this very proceeding. If the Commission is able to write an opinion and order that can cure these defects and draw the plain distinctions necessary to assure fair warning and equal treatment for other advertisers, it has not done so yet.

In administering § 5 in the context of the many elusive questions raised by modern advertising, it is the duty of the Commission to speak and rule clearly so that lawabiding businessmen may know where they stand. In proscribing a practice uncomplained of by the public. effectively harmless to the consumer, allowed by the Commission's long-established policy statement, and only a hairbreadth away from advertising practices that the Commission will continue to permit, I think that the Commission in this instance has fallen far short of what is necessary to entitle its order to enforcement.

For these reasons I would not disturb the judgment of the Court of Appeals setting aside the Commission's order.

Notes

[1] Such an implication might be thought to run counter to the spirit of the now-superseded Guide V, Guides Against Deceptive Pricing, 23 Fed. Reg. 7965 (1958), requiring that the sales price for two articles in a two-for-the-price-of-one sale must be the usual and customary price for one. Mary Carter can, of course, reasonably claim to have complied with the letter of Guide V; assuming that it is making a two-for-the-price-of-one offer in substance, the advertised sum is the usual and customary price which a purchaser

has to pay in order to acquire a single can. There is evidence that on at least a few occasions customers took only one can, paying the advertised per-can price. There is no evidence that Mary Carter permitted or tolerated sales of single cans at less than the advertised per-can price.

[2] I put aside the argument that might arise from Mary Carter's practice of selling its paint in both gallon and quart cans. Conceivably, one might order a gallon and receive an unneeded extra gallon, never realizing that two quarts purchased plus two quarts free could be had for a smaller sum. The FTC ignored and the Government expressly disclaims reliance on any such argument. Moreover, many ads seem to give both quart and gallon prices.

[3] Of the post-1952 cases cited in the majority's note 2 (ante, p. 47), none is authority for condemning Mary Carter's advertising. Puro Co., 50 F. T. C. 454 (1953), and Ray S. Kalwajtys, 52 F. T. C. 721, enforced, 237 F. 2d 654 (1956), both involved plain deceptions as to the usual prices of the items in question. Book-of-the-Month Club, Inc., 50 F. T. C. 778 (1954), and the Black case both exculpate sellers under the rule finally appearing in the 1953 policy statement, with whose terms Mary Carter has complied.

Justice Harlan's concurrence and dissent in United Gas Improvement Co. v. Callery Properties (Dec 7, 1965)

MR. JUSTICE HARLAN, concurring in part and dissenting in part.

While the Commission's expansive view of its powers seems to me largely defensible in the abstract, I believe its actual decision reveals error and unfairness in important respects.

I.

The price condition, alone of the three key prongs of the Commission's order, can in my view be wholly sustained. The chief challenge to it stems from the exclusion in the § 7 hearing of a mass of cost and supply-demand evidence tendered by producers.[1] Although the encompassing § 7 standard of public convenience and necessity encourages a broad inquiry, the Commission has given valid reasons for limiting itself to the in-line price for the time being. Area pricing ultimately aims to simplify proceedings under the statute, but the transition to it is said to strain the Commission's present resources for investigation. See Wisconsin v. FPC, 373 U. S. 294, 298-300, 313-314. The in-line price, comparatively easy to fix, provides a firm basis for producers, helps avoid unrefundable initial overcharges, and exerts a downward pressure on price; at the same time, producers can file increases under § 4 with a six-month delay at most. The Commission has given a fair trial to cost evidence,[2] and nothing in the offer of proof suggests a supply-demand crisis warranting court intervention with this administrative approach.

In locating the in-line price, the Commission has ignored a number of contemporaneous high-price contracts labeled "suspect" because then under review, disapproved, or deemed influenced by those under review or disapproved. Although the danger of using a crooked measuring rod demands some precaution, this blanket exclusion also chances some distortion in favor of an unduly low in-line price. In the main the producers have chosen not to brief this question, apparently under the misapprehension that the Government has not here sought to sustain the exclusion of these contracts or that the lower court's failure to reach the question precluded this Court from doing so.[3] But while the suspect order rule may by default be abided in this instance, I would not close the door to future arguments for a different solution of the dilemma.

A last troubling aspect of the in-line price derives from a critical and unusual circumstance: it, like the other conditions in this case, was imposed for the first time on remand, several years after an unconditioned permanent certificate had issued. Presumably for six months hence, producers will be compelled to sell at a price they might not have accepted when free to refuse; for all that appears, the price may even be below cost, let alone a fair profit. However, in general the producers apparently did not seek an option to cancel future sales if dissatisfied by the newly conditioned certificates, the six-month delay is both brief and familiar, and I cannot say the Commission did not have a legitimate interest in imposing the in-line price at the time it did.

II.

The price-increase moratorium also seems to me a measure not generally beyond the Commission's grasp, but it should not be sustained on the record before us. Recognizing force in the contrary view of the Court of Appeals, I do not believe that § 4 must be read to bestow on producers an invincible right to raise prices subject only to a six-month delay and refund liability. Cf. FPC v. Texaco Inc., 377 U. S. 33; FPC v. Hunt, 376 U. S. 515. A freeze until 1967 is not permanent price-fixing, and in this interregnum between individual and area pricing, the hazard of irreversible price increases warrants imposing some brake. A lengthy moratorium—coupled with a refusal to consider cost or supply-demand figures in setting prices for the duration—might present a real risk of choking off supply, but such a case is not before us.

Nevertheless, a moratorium instituted on remand is a hazardous device at best, and the present one is simply not supported by evidence. Because the producers have no chance to refuse the certificates after commencing delivery, the ceiling may coerce sales at unfairly low prices. Yet while the present moratorium must be endured longer than the in-line price, at least it permits the producers to charge a markedly higher amount; and as the safety valve for a price explosion, the moratorium could be upheld. At this point, however, the Government's argument fails for lack of proof that a price explosion is likely if increases rise above the moratorium figure. The Commission's figure was not considered by its hearing examiner, who made no recommendation for a moratorium. The Commission report itself devotes no more than one conclusory sentence, qualified by a footnote, to the question of what specific price rise will trigger increases at large, 30 F. P. C., at 298; rather than amplifying, the Government brief merely contends that the point has not been adequately preserved under § 19—a contention I do not accept.[4] Several producers state that the Commission's fear of triggering has not been realized although sales are currently being made by them at levels above the intended moratorium price.

III.

While agreeing that the Commission has power to order refunds in the case before us, I believe the measure of repayment it selected is illogical and harsh. On the initial question of power, it must be conceded that nothing in the statute provides for refunds when a sale has been approved without qualification; but approval in the present instances had not become final for want of judicial review, and an equitable power to order refunds may fairly be implied.

The measure of refunds is another matter. The Commission has now directed that the producers repay the difference between the amounts collected over four to six years and the figure it has now established as the original in-line price.[5] Since the in-line price has been fixed without reference to cost evidence and falls below the opening levels set in the negotiated contracts, the producers may well be receiving less than cost, as some of them expressly claim; and this imposed revision downward of prices covers not six months but a period of years.

The obvious refund formula, implicated by the statute itself and adopted by the Court of Appeals, would call for repayment of all amounts collected in excess of the "just and reasonable" price; that price, measured under §§ 4 and 5, naturally takes due account of costs. The Government retorts that producers have no "right" to sell their gas for a "just and reasonable" price under the statute, a proposition perhaps true in the limited sense that the public convenience and necessity might yet exclude fair-profit sales by a uniquely high cost producer or in the face of a glutted market. No attempt is made, however, to class the present facts with such imaginable situations. Nor is advance exclusion from the interstate market so fearsome as an unexpected repricing of a completed sale depriving the seller of profit or costs.

On the present facts the Government has failed to point to any public interest overriding the potent claims of the producers to a fair return on their past four to six years of sales. Any triggering caused by the amounts previously charged has already spent its force and cannot be undone. Unconvincingly, the Government implies the producers may be comparatively well off with the present formula because it provides a final figure now and the "just and reasonable" price might prove to be below the in-line price; however, instant certainty as to past prices is no great gain since taxes and royalties have already been paid, and the chance that producers may get more than they deserve by following the in-line price is not a substitute for assuring them a fair return. About the only concrete advantage cited by the Government for the in-line price is that it speeds refunds to consumers. Assuming that a compromise cannot be reached as in other cases,[6] elaborate cost data should become available in the next year or two with the completion of the southern Louisiana area rate proceeding. Consumers, who assuredly expected no refunds when they paid their gas bills as long ago as six years, certainly do not suffer seriously in waiting a bit longer for refunds that individually must be minute in most cases.

The incongruity of the Commission's refund formula is well portrayed by considering what would have happened if the Commission had originally granted the certificates now thought proper by this Court. By accepting certificates conditioning sales at the in-line price, the producers could immediately have filed for increases, suffering at most a six-month delay. Even if the Commission's moratorium survived, the ceiling during this four-to-six-year period would have been 23.55 cents rather than the 18.5-cent figure now imposed. Thus, even had the Commission not erred in the first instance in favor of the producers, they still could have collected payments well in excess of 18.5 cents subject only to the ultimate finding of a "just and reasonable" price now denied them by the Commission.

In line with the foregoing discussion, I would uphold the Commission's decision fixing an in-line price, remand the case for further findings on the triggering price for a moratorium if the Commission wishes to pursue the point, and set aside the refund with leave to order repayments based on the "just and reasonable" price.

Notes

[1] Section citations herein are all to the Natural Gas Act, 52 Stat. 821, as amended, 15 U. S. C. §§ 717-717w (1964 ed.).

[2] See the majority's note 3, ante, p. 228.

[3] See Petition of the FPC for Certiorari, p. 15, n. 14.

[4] This precise ground of attack upon the moratorium was set forth by at least one producer. See ODECO Application for Rehearing Before the FPC. R. 603. Applications of other producers argued instead that any moratorium was plainly illegal under the Fifth Circuit's decision in Hunt v. FPC, 306 F. 2d 334, which had not then been reversed by this Court. 376 U. S. 515. See Petition of Placid Oil et al. for Rehearing Before the FPC, p. 35. Under these circumstances, § 19 does not seem to me to preclude allowing all producers the benefit of the error pinpointed by ODECO.

[5] Deliveries commenced under all or nearly all the contracts in 1959 at prices exceeding 18.5 cents. The Commission's order directing the in-line price, refunds, and the moratorium issued four years later in 1963, and it has been under judicial review for the past two years. The record does not clearly indicate what rate increases the producers may already have filed with the Commission.

[6] On several occasions, the Commission has approved agreements by producers to refund a fixed fraction of the difference between the amounts collected and the settlement price. See Texaco Inc., 28 F. P. C. 247 (other producers severed from the instant case); Continental Oil Co., 28 F. P. C. 1090 (on remand from CATCO).

Justice Harlan's concurrence and dissent in Rosenblatt v. Baer (Feb 21, 1966)

MR. JUSTICE HARLAN, concurring in part and dissenting in part.

I agree with the Court's opinion except for Part II, in which a section of the trial court's charge is characterized as depending upon a "theory" of "impersonal" libel, which we held constitutionally impermissible in New York Times Co. v. Sullivan, 376 U. S. 254.

In New York Times, in addition to establishing a constitutional standard governing actions for defamation of public officials, we went on to examine the evidence in that particular case. We found that "it was incapable of supporting the jury's finding that the allegedly libelous statements were made `of and concerning' respondent." 376 U. S., at 288. The statements in question, in general terms, attributed misconduct to the police of Montgomery, Alabama, during civil rights activities. The plaintiff in the libel suit, the Commissioner of Public Affairs, pressed his action not on the theory that the statements referred to him, but instead "solely on the unsupported assumption that, because of his official position," the statements must be taken as indicating that he had been involved in the misconduct. 376 U. S., at 289. The Supreme Court of Alabama held that "[i]n measuring the performance or deficiencies of . . . groups [such as the police], praise or criticism is usually attached to the official in complete control of the body," 273 Ala. 656, at 674-675, 144 So. 2d 25, at 39, and allowed the action by the Commissioner.

In setting aside the state judgment we noted that this proposition had "disquieting implications for criticism of governmental conduct," 376 U. S., at 291, for it permitted any general statement criticizing some governmental activity to be transmuted into a cause of action for personal libel by the official in charge of that activity. We stated that the liberty of expression embodied in the Fourteenth Amendment forbade a State from permitting "an otherwise impersonal attack on governmental operations" to be used as the basis of "a libel of an official responsible for those operations." 376 U. S., at 292.

This salutary principle has been applied, I believe incorrectly, to the facts of this case. It is true that, on its face, the alleged libel here seems to discuss only the conduct of governmental operations, viz., the comparative improvement in the management of the ski area. However, the theory on which respondent based his claim is that the rhetorical question, "What happened to all the money last year? and every other year?" was read as accusing him of peculation or culpable mismanagement. The trial court and the Supreme Court of New Hampshire, as well as this Court, have found this a permissible reading of the newspaper article.

The charge of the trial court did not leave the jury free to convert an "impersonal" into a "personal" libel. The court merely instructed the jury that if it interpreted the article as an accusation of misconduct the jury could find for the plaintiff if either he alone was found to be libeled, or he was one of a small group of persons so libeled.[*] This is conventional tort law. "[I]f the group is small enough numerically or sufficiently restricted geographically so that people reasonably think the defamatory utterance was directed to or intended to include the plaintiff, there may be a recovery." 1 Harper & James, Torts § 5.7, at 367 (1956). See also Prosser, Torts § 106, at 767-768 (1964); Riesman, Democracy and Defamation: Control of Group Libel, 42 Col. L. Rev. 727, 759-760 (1942). The Restatement of Torts § 564, Comment c (1938), includes this aspect of defamation in language very similar to that of the charge in this case:

"The size of the class may be so small as to indicate that the plaintiff is the person intended or at least to cast such grave suspicion upon him as to be defamatory of him. Thus, a statement that all members of a school board or a city council are corrupt is sufficiently definite to constitute a defamatory publication of each member thereof. If, however, the group or class disparaged is a large one, some particular circumstances must point to the plaintiff as the person defamed. Thus, a statement that all lawyers are dishonest or that all ministers are liars is not defamatory of any particular lawyer or minister unless the surrounding circumstances indicate that he was the person intended."

This and the trial court's formulation can scarcely be thought too indefinite, for they reflect standards successfully applied over the years in numerous state cases. See, e. g., Gross v. Cantor, 270 N. Y. 93, 200 N. E. 592; cases cited in Harper & James, supra, § 5.7, at 367; and Prosser, supra, § 106, at 767-768. The rule is an eminently sound one.

As to the facts at hand, it seems to be agreed— apart of course from the public-official "malice" rule which would apply in any event—that if the article in question is read by the jury as an accusation of wrong-doing by Baer, he has a good cause of action in libel. I see no reason why that cause of action should fail if the jury finds that the article was read as accusing the three Commissioners along with Baer. This is a very different case from New York Times, where the alleged libel concerned not an identified small group responsible for the running of a particular public enterprise, but a criticism of "the police" generally in the discharge of their duties. It seems manifest that in instructing the jury as to a "small group," the trial judge was not allowing the plaintiff to transform impersonal governmental criticism into an individual cause of action, but was simply referring to this traditional tort doctrine that more than one person can be libeled by the same statement. I cannot understand why a statement which a jury is permitted to read as meaning "A is a thief" should become absolutely privileged if it is read as meaning "A, B, C, and D are thieves."

Without receding in any way from our ruling in New York Times that impersonal criticism of government cannot be made a basis for a libel action by an official who heads the branch or agency involved, I dissent from the Court's conclusion that this is such a case. In all other respects I join the Court's opinion.

[*] The trial judge charged the jury as follows:
"An insinuation of a crime is actionable as a positive assertion if the meaning is reasonably plain and clear, and the putting of the words in the form of a question does not change the liability of the defendant if the form and sense of the question is defamatory or derogatory. Now, an imputation of impropriety or a crime to one or some of a small group that casts suspicion upon all is actionable. It is sufficient if Mr. Baer, the plaintiff here, proves on the balance of probabilities by his evidence that he was one of a group upon whom suspicion was cast, and the fact that others in this group might also have been libeled is not a defense; but Mr. Baer has the burden of showing that the defamation, if you find that there was one, either was directed to him or could have been as one of a

small group." R. Vol. V, pp. 148-149.

.....

"Now, as to any part of the article which you, if you do, find defamatory, and that Mr. Baer was intended, or he with a few others was intended, he and a small group, if you find that it was derogatory of him and charged him with a crime, held him up to scorn and ridicule, that he was the fellow, either singly or in a small group, then you can go on to consider—and you should—whether the publication was privileged or justified . . . ." R. Vol. V, pp. 151-152.

Justice Harlan's dissent in Pate v. Robinson (March 7, 1966)

MR. JUSTICE HARLAN, whom MR. JUSTICE BLACK joins, dissenting.

The facts now canvassed by this Court to support its constitutional holding were fully sifted by the Illinois Supreme Court. I cannot agree that the state court's unanimous appraisal was erroneous and still less that it was error of constitutional proportions.

The Court appears to hold that a defendant's present incompetence may become sufficiently manifest during a trial that it denies him due process for the trial court to fail to conduct a hearing on that question on its own initiative. I do not dissent from this very general proposition, and I agree also that such an error is not "waived" by failure to raise it and that it may entitle the defendant to a new trial without further proof. Waiver is not an apposite concept where we premise a defendant so deranged that he cannot oversee his lawyers. Since our further premise is that the trial judge should and could have avoided the error, a new trial seems not too drastic an exaction in view of the proof problems arising after a significant lapse of time.[1] However, I do not believe the facts known to the trial judge in this case suggested Robinson's incompetence at time of trial with anything like the force necessary to make out a violation of due process in the failure to pursue the question.

Before turning to the facts, it is pertinent to consider the quality of the incompetence they are supposed to indicate. In federal courts—and I assume no more is asked of state courts—the test of incompetence that warrants postponing the trial is reasonably well settled. In language this Court adopted on the one occasion it faced the issue, "the `test must be whether . . . [the defendant] has sufficient present ability to consult with his lawyer with a reasonable degree of rational understanding—and whether he has a rational as well as factual understanding of the proceedings against him.' " Dusky v. United States, 362 U. S. 402. In short, emphasis is on capacity to consult with counsel and to comprehend the proceedings, and lower courts have recognized that this is by no means the same test as those which determine criminal responsibility at the time of the crime.[2] The question, then, is not whether the facts before the trial judge suggested that Robinson's crime was an insane act but whether they suggested he was incompetent to stand trial.

The Court's affirmative answer seemingly rests on two kinds of evidence, principally adduced by Robinson to prove an insanity defense after the State rested its main case. First, there was evidence of a number of episodes of severe irrationality in Robinson's past. Among them were the slaying of his infant son, his attempted suicide, his efforts to burn his wife's clothing, his fits of temper and of abstraction, and his seven-week incarceration in a state hospital eight years before the trial. This evidence may be tempered by the State's counterarguments, for example, that Robinson was found guilty of his son's killing and that alcoholism may explain his hospitalization, but it cannot be written off entirely. The difficulty remains that while this testimony may suggest that Flossie May Ward's killing was just one more irrational act, I cannot say as a matter of common knowledge that it evidences incapacity during the trial. Indeed, the pattern revealed may best indicate that Robinson did function adequately during most of his life interrupted by periods of severe derangement that would have been quite apparent had they occurred at trial. The second class of data pertinent to the Court's theory, remarks by witnesses and counsel that Robinson was "presently insane," deserves little comment. I think it apparent that these statements were addressed to Robinson's responsibility for the killing, that is, his ability to do insane acts, and not to his general competency to stand trial.[3]

Whatever mild doubts this evidence may stir are surely allayed by positive indications of Robinson's competence at the trial. Foremost is his own behavior in the courtroom. The record reveals colloquies between Robinson and the trial judge which undoubtedly permitted a reasonable inference that Robinson was quite cognizant of the proceedings and able to assist counsel in his defense.[4] Turning from lay impressions to those of an expert, it was stipulated at trial that a Dr. Haines, Director of the Behavior Clinic of the Criminal Court of Cook County, had examined Robinson several months earlier and, if called, would testify that Robinson "knows the nature of the charge and is able to cooperate with his counsel." The conclusive factor is that Robinson's own lawyers, the two men who apparently had the closest contact with the defendant during the proceedings, never suggested he was incompetent to stand trial and never moved to have him examined on incompetency grounds during trial;[5] indeed, counsel's remarks to the jury seem best read as an affirmation of Robinson's present "lucidity" which would be highly peculiar if Robinson had been unable to assist properly in his defense. See p. 386, n. 8, ante, of the Court's opinion.

Thus, I cannot agree with the Court that the requirements of due process were violated by the failure of the trial judge, who had opportunities for personal observation of the defendant that we do not possess, to halt the trial and hold a competency hearing on his own motion.

Several other grounds have been urged as a basis for habeas corpus relief for Robinson. These other grounds are understandably not discussed in the Court's opinion, and I think it is sufficient for me to say I do not believe that they warrant further proceedings. In my view, the Court of Appeals should be reversed and the District Court's dismissal of the petition reinstated.

Notes

[1] The constitutional violation alleged is the failure to make an inquiry. In the more usual case, the simple claim that a defendant was convicted while incompetent during the trial, there is of course no proof of a constitutional violation until that incompetence is established in appropriate proceedings.

[2] See James v. Boles, 339 F. 2d 431; United States v. Kendrick, 331 F. 2d 110; Lyles v. United States, 103 U. S. App. D. C. 22, 254 F. 2d 725.

[3] At the time Robinson's mother and Mrs. Calhoun made the statements noted in the Court's opinion, p. 383, n. 5, ante, they also stated Robinson did not know the difference between right and wrong. Counsel's statement, too, quoted by the Court at p. 386, n. 8, ante, was directed to acquittal, not postponement. See, n. 5, infra, Mrs. Moore, a family friend, responded to the question on Robinson's sanity by saying: "When he is in those moods, I think he is insane; when he is in those moods, because he is terrible."

[4] The Illinois Supreme Court stated in its opinion: "[T]he record reflects several instances where defendant displayed his ability to assist in the conduct of his defense in a reasonable and rational manner. Typical instances of when defendant displayed mental alertness, as well as understanding and knowledge of the proceeding, appear in his remarks to the court as follows: `Your honor, they were on the State's witness list and the State said they have several witnesses. They produced two. For what reason, I don't know, but I am on trial here and I would like to be given every consideration, and I would like that the court be adjourned until tomorrow morning—to give me time to confer with counsel for the calling of witnesses.' Again, when discussing witnesses with the court, defendant said: `Well, the police are contending that the clothes they have found in Moore's apartment was mine. That is the reason at the beginning of trial, I asked the attorney to have a pre-trial preliminary to determine the admissibility and validity of the evidence that the State was intending to use against me.' " 22 Ill. 2d, at 168, 174 N. E. 2d, at 823.

[5] The record in my view does not bear out any suggestion that Robinson's counsel apprised the trial judge that he believed Robinson incompetent to stand trial, even granting that "insane" was a synonym for "incompetent" under then-existing state law (pp. 384-385, n. 6, ante). Under Illinois law, as one would naturally expect, incompetence at the time of trial has been a ground not for acquitting the defendant but for postponing his trial; and nowhere in the record does Robinson's counsel even hint to the judge that he believes the trial should be deferred or abated because his client is not fit to continue. The ready explanation for counsel's references to "present insanity," apart from emphasizing Robinson's general lack of criminal responsibility, is that Illinois law provided that one acquitted on grounds of insanity at the time of the crime shall by the same verdict be found cured of or still afflicted with "such insanity" and committed in the latter instance. Ill. Rev. Stat., c. 38, § 592 (1959).

Justice Harlan's dissent in Perry v. Commerce Loan Co. (March 7, 1966)

MR. JUSTICE HARLAN, dissenting.

The result reached by the Court may well be desirable, but in my opinion it is one that cannot be attained under the present statute within the proper limits of the judicial function.

Chapter XIII of the Bankruptcy Act establishes procedures for the relief of wage earners who are unable to meet their debts as they mature. Two types of procedures are made available: extension plans under which the wage earner's debts are intended to be paid off in full over a period of time, and composition plans under which only a percentage of debts are recoverable. Referring to both types of plans, § 656 of the Bankruptcy Act, 11 U. S. C. § 1056 (1964 ed.), provides that "a plan" shall not be confirmed if the debtor has "been guilty of any of the acts or failed to perform any of the duties which would be a bar to the discharge of the bankrupt . . . ." To ascertain what would be a bar to the discharge of a bankrupt one must turn to § 14 (c), 11 U. S. C. § 32 (c) (1964 ed.), which provides, among other things, that no discharge may be granted if the bankrupt has been granted a previous discharge within six years. § 14 (c) (5). It is undisputed that petitioner here was so discharged, and there is no question but that he would have been refused another discharge in bankruptcy at the time he applied for this extension plan. The statutory scheme thus plainly seems to bar him from obtaining Chapter XIII relief as well.

The process by which the Court has undertaken to release the debtor from the impact of these straightforward statutory provisions seems to me wholly unavailing. The Court's major argument is built upon its reading of the word "guilty" in § 656 (a) (3). As already noted that section denies confirmation to an extension plan if the debtor has been "guilty" of any act that would bar a discharge in bankruptcy. The argument is that since receiving a prior discharge is neither unlawful nor morally reprehensible one cannot be "guilty" of it, and hence that the six-year "discharge" provision cannot be a bar to a Chapter XIII extension plan.

This argument presupposes that the word "guilty" was intentionally used in § 656 in a discriminating sense, that is, to distinguish among those acts catalogued in § 14 (c) which under § 656 would bar confirmation of an extension plan. The fact of the matter is, however, that when Congress in 1938 enacted Chapter XIII, 52 Stat. 930-938, it took as its model the form and language of the prior bankruptcy act, more specifically § 12d, 30 Stat. 550, dealing with compositions.[1] The "guilty" phrase was appropriate in that 1898 statute because at that time the only bars to a discharge in the predecessor of § 14 (c) were offenses punishable by imprisonment or fraudulent concealment. Section 14b, 30 Stat. 550. In 1903, Congress amended § 14b to include the six-year bar, 32 Stat. 797, and over the years other grounds for refusing confirmation have been added to that section. But the word "guilty" was never changed, and has obviously remained in several chapters of the Act merely as a shorthand way of referring back to those items that preclude the granting of a discharge. Thus, Chapter XI of the Bankruptcy Act, which deals with arrangements, has almost an exact duplicate of § 656 (a) (3) containing the same "guilty" phraseology. § 366 (3), 11 U. S. C. § 766 (3) (1964 ed.). Chapter XII, which deals with real property arrangements, contains a similar provision. § 472 (3), 11 U. S. C. § 872 (3) (1964 ed.). And of course Chapter XIII, dealing with both compositions and extensions for wage earners, uses this language. These parallel provisions all derive from the same section framed in 1898.

This history and this parallelism indubitably demonstrate two things: first, that the Congress did not devise the "guilty" terminology in 1938 as a means of making a subtle distinction between the morally reprehensible bars to bankruptcy contained in § 14 (c) and the other bars there enumerated; and second, that the word "guilty" means the same thing when applied to general arrangements in § 366, to real property arrangements in § 472, and to compositions and extensions in § 656. If the word "guilty" excludes the six-year bar for extension plans, it is impossible to see what sort of statutory interpretative sleight of hand would save it for general arrangements, real property arrangements, and wage-earner composition plans. Moreover, it seems already accepted that as applied to Chapter XI arrangements, the "guilty" provision does refer back to the six-year bar. See In re Jensen, 200 F. 2d 58; 9 Collier, Bankruptcy ¶ 9.19, at 310-311 (14th ed. 1964); Kennedy, Hospitality for Repeaters Under the Bankruptcy Act, 68 Com. L. J. 117, 119-120 (1963). The same would appear to be true of the meaning of "guilty" in Chapter XII. See 9 Collier, supra, ¶ 9.07, at 1146. And the Court in its present opinion appears to concede that when applied to compositions, § 656 is somehow transformed to include the six-year bar.

In short, construing "guilty" to refer only to "reprehensible" aspects of § 14 (c) has no basis in legislative history, and requires a strained attempt to distinguish other applications of the identical section and of parallel sections which concededly are applied more generally. Because of its ramifications, this construction may do serious harm to the administration of Chapter XIII compositions, Chapter XII real property arrangements, and Chapter XI arrangements.

The Court also advances another argument in support of its conclusion that confirmation of this extension plan was not barred by virtue of §§ 656 and 14 (c). This argument rests essentially on § 602 of the Bankruptcy Act, 11 U. S. C. § 1002 (1964 ed.). Section 602 provides that the provisions of Chapters I through VII shall apply to Chapter XIII "insofar as they are not inconsistent or in conflict with the provisions of this chapter . . . ." It seems to be said that the six-year bar is inconsistent with the provisions of Chapter XIII because the extension plan is designed to give wage earners relief, and the six-year bar would preclude some such people from receiving that relief without good reason.

This argument likewise does not withstand analysis. To be sure the six-year bar makes it impossible for certain wage earners to get relief by way of extension plans, but so do all the other restrictions on this form of relief. Nobody would suggest that it is "inconsistent" with Chapter XIII to withhold extension-plan relief from those who engage in fraud on the ground that such a restriction cuts down the number of people who can take advantage of Chapter XIII. Section 656 clearly does establish restrictions on the class of people to whom relief is available; the question before us is whether the six-year bar is such a limitation; citation of § 602 is conclusory only, and makes no positive contribution to a meaningful analysis.

My conclusion that the statute should be read literally to preclude the confirmation of an extension plan if the applicant has been granted a discharge within the previous six years is reinforced by § 686 (5) of Chapter XIII, 11 U. S. C. § 1086 (5) (1964 ed.). Section 686 (5) in its entirety declares that "confirmation of a plan under this chapter shall not be refused because of a discharge granted or a composition confirmed prior to the effective date of this amendatory Act." The inclusion of this provision indicates quite clearly that Congress did believe that a prior discharge would be a bar to a Chapter XIII plan, and that it decided to remove that restriction only for discharges granted before September 22, 1938, the effective date of the statute in question. See 10 Collier, supra, ¶ 33.05, at 477. Such a provision is perfectly understandable. Before the enactment of the extension-plan amendment, wage earners who sought a bankruptcy remedy could obtain only a discharge through straight bankruptcy or composition. There would be no reason to preclude wage earners who availed themselves of such relief prior to September 1938 from obtaining a more favorable extension plan subsequently. On the other hand, after enactment of Chapter XIII, wage earners would have the opportunity to apply for an extension plan. It is not difficult to understand why Congress should have refused to permit wage earners who chose a discharge in bankruptcy rather than an extension plan a second opportunity, within six years, to receive statutory relief. I am frank to say that I am unable to perceive the basis for the Court's contrary explanation of this provision.

The short of the matter is that the Court's arguments do not support the conclusion it reaches. The conclusion is of course supportable as a legislative judgment, even though arguments can be made for both sides. Thus, it might be argued for the six-year bar in a Chapter XIII context somewhat as follows: the wage-earner extension plan is a new and very advantageous procedure for the debtor, but it is a burden on the courts. It is also a constraint on creditors who will be delayed in collecting, will be precluded from garnishing, and may not receive full repayment if the debtor obtains a discharge under § 661 of the Act, 11 U. S. C. § 1061 (1964 ed.). It is therefore reasonable to limit the availability of this kind of relief to those wage earners who have not had the advantage of a discharge in bankruptcy in the previous six years. Furthermore, it is certainly arguable that the six-year bar encourages wage earners to make use of the Chapter XIII procedure. With the prior-discharge bar eliminated, a debtor might eschew an extension plan and decide instead to go through straight bankruptcy first, waiting a few months until the going once again "gets tough" to take advantage of the extension plan.

I venture considerations such as these not as overcoming the countervailing ones relied on by the Court, and heretofore espoused by others,[2] but simply to point up the fact that this is not one of those cases where seemingly straightforward statutory language must yield its literal meaning to a contrary congressional intent. What we have here are but two contrasting legislative policies, wherein the Court's duty is to take the statute as it is presently plainly written.

I would affirm the judgment of the Court of Appeals.

Notes

[1] "The judge shall confirm a composition if satisfied that (1) it is for the best interests of the creditors; (2) the bankrupt has not been guilty of any of the acts or failed to perform any of the duties which would be a bar to his discharge . . . ." § 12d, 30 Stat. 550.

[2] See the proposed amendments of the Bankruptcy Act by the National Bankruptcy Conference, note 8, ante, p. 404; Kennedy, Hospitality for Repeaters Under the Bankruptcy Act, 68 Com. L. J. 117 (1963).

Justice Harlan's concurrence and dissent in Brenner v. Manson (March 21, 1966)

MR. JUSTICE HARLAN, concurring in part and dissenting in part.

While I join the Court's opinion on the issue of certiorari jurisdiction, I cannot agree with its resolution of the important question of patentability.

Respondent has contended that a workable chemical process, which is both new and sufficiently nonobvious to satisfy the patent statute, is by its existence alone a contribution to chemistry and "useful" as the statute employs that term.[1] Certainly this reading of "useful" in the statute is within the scope of the constitutional grant, which states only that "[t]o promote the Progress of Science and useful Arts," the exclusive right to "Writings and Discoveries" may be secured for limited times to those who produce them. Art. I, § 8. Yet the patent statute is somewhat differently worded and is on its face open both to respondent's construction and to the contrary reading given it by the Court. In the absence of legislative history on this issue, we are thrown back on policy and practice. Because I believe that the Court's policy arguments are not convincing and that past practice favors the respondent, I would reject the narrow definition of "useful" and uphold the judgment of the Court of Customs and Patent Appeals (hereafter CCPA).

The Court's opinion sets out about half a dozen reasons in support of its interpretation. Several of these arguments seem to me to have almost no force. For instance, it is suggested that "[u]ntil the process claim has been reduced to production of a product shown to be useful, the metes and bounds of that monopoly are not capable of precise delineation" (p. 534, ante) and "[i]t may engross a vast, unknown, and perhaps unknowable area" (p. 534, ante). I fail to see the relevance of these assertions; process claims are not disallowed because the products they produce may be of "vast" importance nor, in any event, does advance knowledge of a specific product use provide much safeguard on this score or fix "metes and bounds" precisely since a hundred more uses may be found after a patent is granted and greatly enhance its value.

The further argument that an established product use is part of "[t]he basic quid pro quo" (p. 534, ante) for the patent or is the requisite "successful conclusion" (p. 536, ante) of the inventor's search appears to beg the very question whether the process is "useful" simply because it facilitates further research into possible product uses. The same infirmity seems to inhere in the Court's argument that chemical products lacking immediate utility cannot be distinguished for present purposes from the processes which create them, that respondent appears to concede and the CCPA holds that the products are nonpatentable, and that therefore the processes are nonpatentable. Assuming that the two classes cannot be distinguished, a point not adequately considered in the briefs, and assuming further that the CCPA has firmly held such products nonpatentable,[2] this permits us to conclude only that the CCPA is wrong either as to the products or as to the processes and affords no basis for deciding whether both or neither should be patentable absent a specific product use.

More to the point, I think, are the Court's remaining, prudential arguments against patentability: namely, that disclosure induced by allowing a patent is partly undercut by patent-application drafting techniques, that disclosure may occur without granting a patent, and that a patent will discourage others from inventing uses for the product. How far opaque drafting may lessen the public benefits resulting from the issuance of a patent is not shown by any evidence in this case but, more important, the argument operates against all patents and gives no reason for singling out the class involved here. The thought that these inventions may be more likely than most to be disclosed even if patents are not allowed may have more force; but while empirical study of the industry might reveal that chemical researchers would behave in this fashion, the abstractly logical choice for them seems to me to maintain secrecy until a product use can be discovered. As to discouraging the search by others for product uses, there is no doubt this risk exists but the price paid for any patent is that research on other uses or improvements may be hampered because the original patentee will reap much of the reward. From the standpoint of the public interest the Constitution seems to have resolved that choice in favor of patentability.

What I find most troubling about the result reached by the Court is the impact it may have on chemical research. Chemistry is a highly interrelated field and a tangible benefit for society may be the outcome of a number of different discoveries, one discovery building upon the next. To encourage one chemist or research facility to invent and disseminate new processes and products may be vital to progress, although the product or process be without "utility" as the Court defines the term, because that discovery permits someone else to take a further but perhaps less difficult step leading to a commercially useful item. In my view, our awareness in this age of the importance of achieving and publicizing basic research should lead this Court to resolve uncertainties in its favor and uphold the respondent's position in this case.

This position is strengthened, I think, by what appears to have been the practice of the Patent Office during most of this century. While available proof is not conclusive, the commentators seem to be in agreement that until Application of Bremner, 37 C. C. P. A. (Pat.) 1032, 182 F. 2d 216, in 1950, chemical patent applications were commonly granted although no resulting end use was stated or the statement was in extremely broad terms.[3] Taking this to be true, Bremner represented a deviation from established practice which the CCPA has now sought to remedy in part only to find that the Patent Office does not want to return to the beaten track. If usefulness was typically regarded as inherent during a long and prolific period of chemical research and development in this country, surely this is added reason why the Court's result should not be adopted until Congress expressly mandates it, presumably on the basis of empirical data which this Court does not possess.

Fully recognizing that there is ample room for disagreement on this problem when, as here, it is reviewed in the abstract, I believe the decision below should be affirmed.

Notes

[1] The statute in pertinent part is set out in the Court's opinion, p. 529, ante.

[2] Any concession by respondent would hardly be controlling on an issue of this general importance, but I am less clear than the Court that such a concession exists. See, e. g., Brief for Respondent, p. 53. As to the CCPA, it is quite true that that court purports in the very case under review and in others to distinguish product patents, although its actual practice may be somewhat less firm. See Application of Adams, 50 C. C. P. A. (Pat.) 1185, 316 F. 2d 476, Application of Nelson, 47 C. C. P. A. (Pat.) 1031, 280 F. 2d 172.

[3] See, e. g., the statement of a Patent Office Examiner-in-Chief: "Until recently it was also rather common to get patents on chemical compounds in cases where no use was indicated for the claimed compounds or in which a very broad indication or suggestion as to use was included in the application. [Bremner and another later ruling] . . . have put an end to this practice." Wolffe, Adequacy of Disclosure as Regards Specific Embodiment and Use of Invention, 41 J. Pat. Off. Soc. 61, 66 (1959). The Government's brief in this case is in accord: "[I]t was apparently assumed by the Patent Office [prior to 1950] . . . that chemical compounds were necessarily useful . . . and that specific inquiry beyond the success of the process was therefore unnecessary . . . ." Brief for the Commissioner, p. 25. See also Cohen & Schwartz, Do Chemical Intermediates Have Patentable Utility? 29 Geo. Wash. L. Rev. 87, 91 (1960); Note, 53 Geo. L. J. 154, 183 (1964); 14 Am. U. L. Rev. 78 (1964).

Justice Harlan's concurrence and dissent in US v. Guest (March 28, 1966)

MR. JUSTICE HARLAN, concurring in part and dissenting in part.

I join Parts I and II[1] of the Court's opinion, but I cannot subscribe to Part III in its full sweep. To the extent that it is there held that 18 U. S. C. § 241 (1964 ed.) reaches conspiracies, embracing only the action of private persons, to obstruct or otherwise interfere with the right of citizens freely to engage in interstate travel, I am constrained to dissent. On the other hand, I agree that § 241 does embrace state interference with such interstate travel, and I therefore consider that this aspect of the indictment is sustainable on the reasoning of Part II of the Court's opinion.

This right to travel must be found in the Constitution itself. This is so because § 241 covers only conspiracies to interfere with any citizen in the "free exercise or enjoyment" of a right or privilege "secured to him by the Constitution or laws of the United States," and no "right to travel" can be found in § 241 or in any other law of the United States. My disagreement with this phase of the Court's opinion lies in this: While past cases do indeed establish that there is a constitutional "right to travel" between States free from unreasonable governmental interference, today's decision is the first to hold that such movement is also protected against private interference, and, depending on the constitutional source of the right, I think it either unwise or impermissible so to read the Constitution.

Preliminary, nothing in the Constitution expressly secures the right to travel. In contrast the Articles of Confederation provided in Art. IV:

"The better to secure and perpetuate mutual friendship and intercourse among the people of the different States in this Union, the free inhabitants of each of these States . . . shall be entitled to all privileges and immunities of free citizens in the several States; and the people of each State shall have free ingress and regress to and from any other State, and shall enjoy therein all the privileges of trade and commerce, subject to the same duties, impositions and restrictions as the inhabitants thereof respectively . . . ."

This right to "free ingress and regress" was eliminated from the draft of the Constitution without discussion even though the main objective of the Convention was to create a stronger union. It has been assumed that the clause was dropped because it was so obviously an essential part of our federal structure that it was necessarily subsumed under more general clauses of the Constitution. See United States v. Wheeler, 254 U. S. 281, 294. I propose to examine the several asserted constitutional bases for the right to travel, and the scope of its protection in relation to each source.

I.

Because of the close proximity of the right of ingress and regress to the Privileges and Immunities Clause of the Articles of Confederation it has long been declared that the right is a privilege and immunity of national citizenship under the Constitution. In the influential opinion of Mr. Justice Washington on circuit, Corfield v. Coryell, 4 Wash. C. C. 371 (1825), the court addressed itself to the question—"what are the privileges and immunities of citizens in the several states?" Id., at 380. Corfield was concerned with a New Jersey statute restricting to state citizens the right to rake for oysters, a statute which the court upheld. In analyzing the Privileges and Immunities Clause of the Constitution, Art. IV, § 2, the court stated that it confined "these expressions to those privileges and immunities which are, in their nature, fundamental," and listed among them "The right of a citizen of one state to pass through, or to reside in any other state, for purposes of trade, agriculture, professional pursuits, or otherwise . . . ." Id., at 380-381.

The dictum in Corfield was given general approval in the first opinion of this Court to deal directly with the right of free movement, Crandall v. Nevada, 6 Wall. 35, which struck down a Nevada statute taxing persons leaving the State. It is first noteworthy that in his concurring opinion Mr. Justice Clifford asserted that he would hold the statute void exclusively on commerce grounds for he was clear "that the State legislature cannot impose any such burden upon commerce among the several States." 6 Wall., at 49. The majority opinion of Mr. Justice Miller, however, eschewed reliance on the Commerce Clause and the Import-Export Clause and looked rather to the nature of the federal union:

"The people of these United States constitute one nation. . . . This government has necessarily a capital established by law . . . . That government has a right to call to this point any or all of its citizens to aid in its service . . . . The government, also, has its offices of secondary importance in all other parts of the country. On the sea-coasts and on the rivers it has its ports of entry. In the interior it has its land offices, its revenue offices, and its sub-treasuries. In all these it demands the services of its citizens, and is entitled to bring them to those points from all quarters of the nation, and no power can exist in a State to obstruct this right that would not enable it to defeat the purposes for which the government was established." 6 Wall., at 43-44.

Accompanying this need of the Federal Government, the Court found a correlative right of the citizen to move unimpeded throughout the land:

"He has the right to come to the seat of government to assert any claim he may have upon that government, or to transact any business he may have with it. To seek its protection, to share its offices, to engage in administering its functions. He has a right to free access to its sea-ports, through which all the operations of foreign trade and commerce are conducted, to the sub-treasuries, the land offices, the revenue offices, and the courts of justice in the several States, and this right is in its nature independent of the will of any State over whose soil he must pass in the exercise of it." 6 Wall., at 44.

The focus of that opinion, very clearly, was thus on impediments by the States on free movement by citizens. This is emphasized subsequently when Mr. Justice Miller asserts that this approach is "neither novel nor unsupported by authority," because it is, fundamentally, a question of the exercise of a State's taxing power to obstruct the functions of the Federal Government: "[T]he right of the States in this mode to impede or embarrass the constitutional operations of that government, or the rights which its citizens hold under it, has been uniformly denied." 6 Wall., at 44-45.

Later cases, alluding to privileges and immunities, have in dicta included the right to free movement. See Paul v. Virginia, 8 Wall. 168, 180; Williams v. Fears, 179 U. S. 270, 274; Twining v. New Jersey, 211 U. S. 78.

Although the right to travel thus has respectable precedent to support its status as a privilege and immunity of national citizenship, it is important to note that those cases all dealt with the right of travel simply as affected by oppressive state action. Only one prior case in this Court, United States v. Wheeler, 254 U. S. 281, was argued precisely in terms of a right to free movement as against interference by private individuals. There the Government alleged a conspiracy under the predecessor of § 241 against the perpetrators of the notorious Bisbee Deportations.[2] The case was argued straightfowardly in terms of whether the right to free ingress and egress, admitted by both parties to be a right of national citizenship, was constitutionally guaranteed against private conspiracies. The Brief for the Defendants in Error, whose counsel was Charles Evans Hughes, later Chief Justice of the United States, gives as one of its main points: "So far as there is a right pertaining to Federal citizenship to have free ingress or egress with respect to the several States, the right is essentially one of protection against the action of the States themselves and of those acting under their authority." Brief, at p. i. The Court, with one dissent, accepted this interpretation of the right of unrestricted interstate movement, observing that Crandall v. Nevada, supra, was inapplicable because, inter alia, it dealt with state action. 254 U. S., at 299. More recent cases discussing or applying the right to interstate travel have always been in the context of oppressive state action. See, e. g., Edwards v. California, 314 U. S. 160, and other cases discussed, infra.[3]

It is accordingly apparent that the right to unimpeded interstate travel, regarded as a privilege and immunity of national citizenship, was historically seen as a method of breaking down state provincialism, and facilitating the creation of a true federal union. In the one case in which a private conspiracy to obstruct such movement was heretofore presented to this Court, the predecessor of the very statute we apply today was held not to encompass such a right.

II.

A second possible constitutional basis for the right to move among the States without interference is the Commerce Clause. When Mr. Justice Washington articulated the right in Corfield, it was in the context of a state statute impeding economic activity by outsiders, and he cast his statement in economic terms. 4 Wash. C. C., at 380-381. The two concurring Justices in Crandall v. Nevada, supra, rested solely on the commerce argument, indicating again the close connection between freedom of commerce and travel as principles of our federal union. In Edwards v. California, 314 U. S. 160, the Court held squarely that the right to unimpeded movement of persons is guaranteed against oppressive state legislation by the Commerce Clause, and declared unconstitutional a California statute restricting the entry of indigents into that State.

Application of the Commerce Clause to this area has the advantage of supplying a longer tradition of case law and more refined principles of adjudication. States do have rights of taxation and quarantine, see Edwards v. California, 314 U. S., at 184 (concurring opinion), which must be weighed against the general right of free movement, and Commerce Clause adjudication has traditionally been the means of reconciling these interests. Yet this approach to the right to travel, like that found in the privileges and immunities cases, is concerned with the interrelation of state and federal power, not—with an exception to be dealt with in a moment—with private interference.

The case of In re Debs, 158 U. S. 564, may be thought to raise some doubts as to this proposition. There the United States sought to enjoin Debs and members of his union from continuing to obstruct—by means of a strike—interstate commerce and the passage of the mails. The Court held that Congress and the Executive could certainly act to keep the channels of interstate commerce open, and that a court of equity had no less power to enjoin what amounted to a public nuisance. It might be argued that to the extent Debs permits the Federal Government to obtain an injunction against the private conspiracy alleged in the present indictment,[4] the criminal statute should be applicable as well on the ground that the governmental interest in both cases is the same, namely to vindicate the underlying policy of the Commerce Clause. However, § 241 is not directed toward the vindication of governmental interests; it requires a private right under federal law. No such right can be found in Debs, which stands simply for the proposition that the Commerce Clause gives the Federal Government standing to sue on a basis similar to that of private individuals under nuisance law. The substantive rights of private persons to enjoin such impediments, of course, devolve from state not federal law; any seemingly inconsistent discussion in Debs would appear substantially vitiated by Erie R. Co. v. Tompkins, 304 U. S. 64.

I cannot find in any of this past case law any solid support for a conclusion that the Commerce Clause embraces a right to be free from private interference. And the Court's opinion here makes no such suggestion.

III.

One other possible source for the right to travel should be mentioned. Professor Chafee, in his thoughtful study, "Freedom of Movement,"[5] finds both the privileges and immunities approach and the Commerce Clause approach unsatisfactory. After a thorough review of the history and cases dealing with the question he concludes that this "valuable human right," id., at 209, is best seen in due process terms:

"Already in several decisions the Court has used the Due Process Clause to safeguard the right of the members of any race to reside where they please inside a state, regardless of ordinances and injunctions. Why is not this clause equally available to assure the right to live in any state one desires? And unreasonable restraints by the national government on mobility can be upset by the Due Process Clause in the Fifth Amendment . . . . Thus the `liberty' of all human beings which cannot be taken away without due process of law includes liberty of speech, press, assembly, religion, and also liberty of movement." Id., at 192-193.

This due process approach to the right to unimpeded movement has been endorsed by this Court. In Kent v. Dulles, 357 U. S. 116, the Court asserted that "The right to travel is a part of the `liberty' of which the citizen cannot be deprived without due process of law under the Fifth Amendment," id., at 125, citing Crandall v. Nevada, supra, and Edwards v. California, supra. It is true that the holding in that case turned essentially on statutory grounds. However, in Aptheker v. Secretary of State, 378 U. S. 500, the Court, applying this constitutional doctrine, struck down a federal statute forbidding members of Communist organizations to obtain passports. Both the majority and dissenting opinions affirmed the principle that the right to travel is an aspect of the liberty guaranteed by the Due Process Clause.

Viewing the right to travel in due process terms, of course, would clearly make it inapplicable to the present case, for due process speaks only to governmental action.

IV.

This survey of the various bases for grounding the "right to travel" is conclusive only to the extent of showing that there has never been an acknowledged constitutional right to be free from private interference, and that the right in question has traditionally been seen and applied, whatever the constitutional underpinning asserted, only against governmental impediments. The right involved being as nebulous as it is, however, it is necessary to consider it in terms of policy as well as precedent.

As a general proposition it seems to me very dubious that the Constitution was intended to create certain rights of private individuals as against other private individuals. The Constitutional Convention was called to establish a nation, not to reform the common law. Even the Bill of Rights, designed to protect personal liberties, was directed at rights against governmental authority, not other individuals. It is true that there is a very narrow range of rights against individuals which have been read into the Constitution. In Ex parte Yarbrough, 110 U. S. 651, the Court held that implicit in the Constitution is the right of citizens to be free of private interference in federal elections. United States v. Classic, 313 U. S. 299, extended this coverage to primaries. Logan v. United States, 144 U. S. 263, applied the predecessor of § 241 to a conspiracy to injure someone in the custody of a United States marshal; the case has been read as dealing with a privilege and immunity of citizenship, but it would seem to have depended as well on extrapolations from statutory provisions providing for supervision of prisoners. The Court in In re Quarles, 158 U. S. 532, extending Logan, supra, declared that there was a right of federal citizenship to inform federal officials of violations of federal law. See also United States v. Cruikshank, 92 U. S. 542, 552, which announced in dicta a federal right to assemble to petition the Congress for a redress of grievances.

Whatever the validity of these cases on their own terms, they are hardly persuasive authorities for adding to the collection of privileges and immunities the right to be free of private impediments to travel. The cases just discussed are narrow, and are essentially concerned with the vindication of important relationships with the Federal Government—voting in federal elections, involvement in federal law enforcement, communicating with the Federal Government. The present case stands on a considerably different footing.

It is arguable that the same considerations which led the Court on numerous occasions to find a right of free movement against oppressive state action now justify a similar result with respect to private impediments. Crandall v. Nevada, supra, spoke of the need to travel to the capital, to serve and consult with the offices of government. A basic reason for the formation of this Nation was to facilitate commercial intercourse; intellectual, cultural, scientific, social, and political interests are likewise served by free movement. Surely these interests can be impeded by private vigilantes as well as by state action. Although this argument is not without force, I do not think it is particularly persuasive. There is a difference in power between States and private groups so great that analogies between the two tend to be misleading. If the State obstructs free intercourse of goods, people, or ideas, the bonds of the union are threatened; if a private group effectively stops such communication, there is at most a temporary breakdown of law and order, to be remedied by the exercise of state authority or by appropriate federal legislation.

To decline to find a constitutional right of the nature asserted here does not render the Federal Government helpless. As to interstate commerce by railroads, federal law already provides remedies for "undue or unreasonable prejudice," 24 Stat. 380, as amended, 49 U. S. C. § 3 (1) (1964 ed.), which has been held to apply to racial discrimination. Henderson v. United States, 339 U. S. 816. A similar statute applies to motor carriers, 49 Stat. 558, as amended, 49 U. S. C. § 316 (d) (1964 ed.), and to air carriers, 72 Stat. 760, 49 U. S. C. § 1374 (b) (1964 ed.). See Boynton v. Virginia, 364 U. S. 454; Fitzgerald v. Pan American World Airways, 229 F. 2d 499. The Civil Rights Act of 1964, 78 Stat. 243, deals with other types of obstructions to interstate commerce. Indeed, under the Court's present holding, it is arguable that any conspiracy to discriminate in public accommodations having the effect of impeding interstate commerce could be reached under § 241, unaided by Title II of the Civil Rights Act of 1964. Because Congress has wide authority to legislate in this area, it seems unnecessary— if prudential grounds are of any relevance, see Baker v. Carr, 369 U. S. 186, 258-259 (CLARK, J., concurring)— to strain to find a dubious constitutional right.

V.

If I have succeeded in showing anything in this constitutional exercise, it is that until today there was no federal right to be free from private interference with interstate transit, and very little reason for creating one. Although the Court has ostensibly only "discovered" this private right in the Constitution and then applied § 241 mechanically to punish those who conspire to threaten it, it should be recognized that what the Court has in effect done is to use this all-encompassing criminal statute to fashion federal common-law crimes, forbidden to the federal judiciary since the 1812 decision in United States v. Hudson, 7 Cranch 32. My Brother DOUGLAS, dissenting in United States v. Classic, supra, noted well the dangers of the indiscriminate application of the predecessor of § 241: "It is not enough for us to find in the vague penumbra of a statute some offense about which Congress could have legislated, and then to particularize it as a crime because it is highly offensive." 313 U. S., at 331-332.

I do not gainsay that the immunities and commerce provisions of the Constitution leave the way open for the finding of this "private" constitutional right, since they do not speak solely in terms of governmental action Nevertheless, I think it wrong to sustain a criminal indictment on such an uncertain ground. To do so subjects § 241 to serious challenge on the score of vagueness and serves in effect to place this Court in the position of making criminal law under the name of constitutional interpretation. It is difficult to subdue misgivings about the potentialities of this decision.

I would sustain this aspect of the indictment only on the premise that it sufficiently alleges state interference with interstate travel, and on no other ground.

Notes

[1] The action of three of the Justices who join the Court's opinion in nonetheless cursorily pronouncing themselves on the far-reaching constitutional questions deliberately not reached in Part II seems to me, to say the very least, extraordinary.

[2] For a discussion of the deportations, see The President's Mediation Comm'n, Report on the Bisbee Deportations (November 6, 1917).

[3] The Court's reliance on United States v. Moore, 129 F. 630, is misplaced. That case held only that it was not a privilege or immunity to organize labor unions. The reference to "the right to pass from one state to any other" was purely incidental dictum.

[4] It is not even clear that an equity court would enjoin a conspiracy of the kind alleged here, for traditionally equity will not enjoin a crime. See Developments in the Law—Injunctions, 78 Harv. L. Rev. 994, 1013-1018 (1965).

[5] In Three Human Rights in the Constitution of 1787, at 162 (1956).

Justice Harlan's separate opinion in Brookhart v. Janis (April 18, 1966)

Separate opinion of MR. JUSTICE HARLAN.

I do not find the issue in this case as straightforward as does the Court. If the record were susceptible only of the reading given it by the Court, I would concur in the judgment. However, for me this case presents problems of two sorts.

First, the precise nature of the "rights" that were allegedly "waived" is not wholly clear. One view, adopted by the Court, is that petitioner's lawyer in effect entered a conditional plea of guilty for the defendant. Another interpretation, which is certainly arguable, would find the agreement between petitioner's counsel and the trial court to involve no more than a matter of trial procedure. I believe a lawyer may properly make a tactical determination of how to run a trial even in the face of his client's incomprehension or even explicit disapproval. The decision, for example, whether or not to cross-examine a specific witness is, I think, very clearly one for counsel alone. Although it can be contended that the waiver here was nothing more than a tactical choice of this nature, I believe for federal constitutional purposes the procedure agreed to in this instance involved so significant a surrender of the rights normally incident to a trial that it amounted almost to a plea of guilty or nolo contendere. And I do not believe that under the Due Process Clause of the Fourteenth Amendment such a plea may be entered by counsel over his client's protest.

Second, given the need for petitioner's approval of the entry of such a plea, the further question arises whether petitioner did in fact agree to be tried in a "prima facie" trial without the opportunity to cross-examine witnesses. The Supreme Court of Ohio, on the basis of an examination of the record, found that petitioner "agreed that all the state had to prove was a prima facie case, that he would not contest it, and that there would be no cross-examination of witnesses." Brookhart v. Haskins, 2 Ohio St. 2d 36, 38, 205 N. E. 2d 911, 913. This Court, after an independent examination of the relevant portion of the same record, reprinted, ante, pp. 5-6, finds that petitioner "did not intelligently and knowingly agree to be tried in a proceeding which was the equivalent of a guilty plea . . . ." Ante, p. 7.

The decisive fact is of course the state of petitioner's mind—his understanding and his intention—when his counsel stated to the trial court: "Prima facie, Your Honor, is all we are interested in." My reading of the record leaves me in substantial doubt as to what petitioner's actual understanding was at the end of the pertinent courtroom colloquy, a doubt that is enhanced by the general unfamiliarity that seems to exist with this Ohio "prima facie" practice.[*] I cannot see how the question can be satisfactorily resolved solely on the existing record. I would therefore vacate this judgment and remand the case for a hearing under appropriate state procedures to determine whether petitioner did in fact knowingly and freely choose to have his guilt determined in this type of trial. Failing the availability of such proceedings in the state courts, the avenue of federal habeas corpus would then be open to petitioner for determination of that issue.

[*] The Supreme Court of Ohio characterized the procedure as "unusual," 2 Ohio St. 2d, at 39, 205 N. E. 2d, at 914. At oral argument, the Assistant Attorney General of Ohio noted that he had been unaware of such a procedure, and that the practice could not be found in any statute or rules of court. The State explains the procedure as follows: "There is no statutory plea of nolo contendere in Ohio in felony cases, therefore, when one is charged with a crime which he knows that he cannot successfully defend, but a plea of guilty will subject him to a penalty in a civil suit arising out of the same factual situation, he is without recourse to a plea of nolo contendere as is permitted in federal courts and certain other state courts. To circumvent this difficulty some Ohio courts have allowed, as was done here, the accused to enter a plea of not guilty and by arrangement require the prosecution to prove only a prima facie case." Brief, at 44-45, note 41.

Justice Harlan's concurrence in Burns v. Richardson (April 25, 1966)

MR. JUSTICE HARLAN, concurring in the result.

Because judicial responsibility requires me, as I see things, to bow to the authority of Reynolds v. Sims, 377 U. S. 533, despite my original and continuing belief that the decision was constitutionally wrong (see my dissenting opinion, 377 U. S., at 589 et seq.), I feel compelled to concur in the Court's disposition of this case. Even under Reynolds, however, I cannot agree with the rationale, elaborated in Part III of the Court's opinion, by which Hawaii's registered voter base is sustained. As I read today's opinion, registered voter figures are an acceptable basis for apportionment only so long as they substantially approximate the results that would be reached under some other type of population-based scheme of apportionment.

Many difficult questions of judgment, relating both to policy and to administrative convenience, must be resolved by a State in determining what statistics to use in establishing its apportionment plan. I would not read Reynolds as precluding a State from apportioning its legislature on any rational basis consistent with Reynolds' philosophy that "people," not other interests, must be the basis of state legislative apportionment. I think apportionment on the basis of registered voters is a rational system of this type, and that it is therefore permissible under Reynolds regardless of whether in the particular case it approximates some other kind of a population apportionment.

Justice Harlan's dissent in Amell v. US (May 16, 1966)

MR. JUSTICE HARLAN, whom MR. JUSTICE STEWART joins, dissenting.

In my opinion a course of legal history, reflecting both decisions of this Court and congressional enactments, precludes the interpretation that is now placed on the Suits in Admiralty Act, 41 Stat. 525, as amended, 46 U. S. C. § 741 et seq. (1964 ed.).

I.

The Suits in Admiralty Act was enacted in 1920 to deal with problems created by the formation of a large government-owned merchant fleet during World War I. The Act established a method to sue the United States in admiralty that would protect the interests of libellants while at the same time prevent in rem attachments of government vessels during a possible emergency. See S. Rep. No. 223, 66th Cong., 1st Sess. (1919); H. R. Rep. No. 497, 66th Cong., 2d Sess. (1919); 58 Cong. Rec. 7317 (1919); 59 Cong. Rec. 1684-1688 (1920). Although the creation of this statutory procedure for suits in admiralty was occasioned by particular needs, the early cases, discussed below, held unmistakably, first, that the Act provided the exclusive admiralty remedy against the United States, and, second, that it was exclusive of all other remedies affording relief for an underlying claim cognizable in admiralty.

The Suits in Admiralty Act provides the procedure for suits against the United States or a government-owned corporation "[i]n cases where if such vessel were privately owned or operated, or if such cargo were privately owned or possessed, or if a private person or property were involved, a proceeding in admiralty could be maintained. . . ." 46 U. S. C. § 742. A narrow construction of the statute was unanimously rejected in Eastern Transp. Co. v. United States, 272 U. S. 675, where the Court held that the Act made the Government amenable to any cause of action in admiralty, in rem or in personam, to which a private owner would be liable. 272 U. S., at 690. This view was reiterated and reinforced in Fleet Corp. v. Rosenberg Bros., 276 U. S. 202. There the libellants sued the government-owned Fleet Corporation in admiralty. The cause was time-barred under the Suits in Admiralty Act, but the respondents argued that the remedy provided by the Act did not preclude a nonstatutory suit in admiralty against the public corporation. The Court held that the Act provided the exclusive admiralty remedy against the United States or its agencies. It left open, however, the question whether "the Act also prevents a resort to any concurrent remedies against the United States . . . on like causes of action in the Court of Claims or in courts of law . . . ." 276 U. S., at 214.

This reservation was laid at rest in Johnson v. Fleet Corp., 280 U. S. 320. There four cases were consolidated: two involved seamen's allegations of negligence; the third alleged breach of contract affecting cargo; the fourth alleged loss of cargo due to negligence. The suits were barred by the Suits in Admiralty statute of limitations, but it was argued that Tucker Act and common-law remedies were still available. The Court held squarely for the Government in spite of well-briefed arguments and some support from legislative history that the admiralty jurisdiction was not meant to be exclusive in such cases.[1] Reviewing the structure of the Act and basic congressional intent, the Court stated that the Act's purposes would not be served "if suits under the Tucker Act and in the Court of Claims be allowed against the United States and actions at law in state and federal courts be permitted against the Fleet Corporation or other agents for enforcement of the maritime causes of action covered by the Act." 280 U. S., at 327. The Court concluded "that the remedies given by the Act are exclusive in all cases where a libel might be filed under it." Ibid.

This interpretation of the Suits in Admiralty Act was subsequently recognized and ultimately adopted by the Congress, which on various occasions has amended the Act or passed supporting legislation premised on the exclusivity of the Act over all claims that might be heard in admiralty. Soon after the Johnson case, supra, was decided, the Congress acted to mitigate its effects on those who were barred by its two-year limitation. In an Act of June 30, 1932, 47 Stat. 420, § 5 of the Suits in Admiralty Act was amended to waive the two-year period for suitors who had filed timely actions elsewhere before the Johnson decision.[2] In 1950, in order to eliminate any remaining confusion, § 5 was again amended to codify the Johnson rule as applied to government agents, namely, "[t]hat where a remedy is provided by . . . [the Suits in Admiralty Act] it shall hereafter be exclusive of any other action by reason of the same subject matter against the agent or employee of the United States . . . ." 64 Stat. 1112, 46 U. S. C. § 745 (1964 ed.).

See S. Rep. No. 2535, 81st Cong., 2d Sess. (1950), quoted in note 2, supra; H. R. Rep. No. 1292. 81st Cong., 1st Sess. (1949).

The statutes affecting the Court of Claims directly were also altered by Congress to conform with the basic structure of the exclusive admiralty jurisdiction. In 1948 the Tucker Act was amended to strike the word "admiralty" from the scope of that court's jurisdiction. Act of June 25, 1948, c. 646, 62 Stat. 940, 28 U. S. C. § 1491 (1964 ed.).[3] In 1960, an Act was passed to facilitate transfers of admiralty actions from the Court of Claims to the federal district courts and to toll the running of the statute of limitations in such cases so that litigants who sued, incorrectly, in the Court of Claims would not be required to file a new suit in the district court which might by then be time-barred. Act of September 13, 1960, 74 Stat. 912, 28 U. S. C. § 1506 (1964 ed.). Recognition of the exclusive admiralty jurisdiction of the district courts prompted enactment of this statute. See H. R. Rep. No. 523, 86th Cong., 1st Sess. (1959); S. Rep. No. 1894, 86th Cong., 2d

Sess. (1960).

II.

This survey of case law and statutory development indicates quite clearly that the jurisdiction of the district courts is exclusive in actions falling within the purview of the Suits in Admiralty Act, and that the test for determining whether an action falls within that class is whether "a libel might be filed under [the Act]," Johnson v. Fleet Corp., supra, at 327, or in the words of the statute directly, whether "if such vessel were privately owned or operated . . . a proceeding in admiralty could be maintained." 46 U. S. C. § 742.

Until today the basic test for the Act's applicability has been a familiar historical one, for the statutory term "proceeding in admiralty" is quite obviously coextensive with its meaning in ordinary legal usage. In the case now before us, the question for the Court is whether the claim for back wages by these seamen would be heard by an admiralty court if their employer were a private person. The answer is clearly in the affirmative, see Sheppard v. Taylor, 5 Pet. 675; Kossick v. United Fruit Co., 365 U. S. 731, 735. It is stated in 1 Benedict, The Law of American Admiralty 124 (6th ed. Knauth 1940): "The mariners of a ship are commonly said to be wards of the admiralty. Their wages, their rights, their wrongs and injuries have always been a special subject of the admiralty jurisdiction." It is true that the claim against a private employer might also be litigated in a common-law court, see Leon v. Galceran, 11 Wall. 185; 1 Benedict, supra, at 35. But the fact that there is concurrent jurisdiction over such a claim in private litigation is irrelevant for purposes of a suit against the sovereign, for as shown above, the Suits in Admiralty Act is exclusive over any action which "could be maintained" in admiralty. This is indubitably such a claim.

III.

The Court, while recognizing "that the Suits in Admiralty Act specifically repealed the Tucker Act so far as the two conflicted," ante, p. 163, avoids the result compelled by prior interpretation of the Suits in Admiralty Act and conventional admiralty law, by formulating a new test for the statute's applicability. Instead of asking whether this suit is one traditionally within the scope of admiralty jurisdiction, it sees the interrelation of the Tucker Act and the Suits in Admiralty Act as requiring an inquiry into the question whether the petitioners are more like federal employees than like mariners, and after weighing the factors involved concludes that they are more civil servants than seafarers. I believe this test presents a false basis for determining whether or not exclusive jurisdiction lies in admiralty and puts a mischievous gloss on the relevant statutes.

Obviously these petitioners are both federal employees and seamen. One label refers to their employer; the other to the type of work they perform. This dual classification might well be made of the status of employees in many private industries. A large corporation might have thousands of employees, some of whom are employed in maritime activities. Because of the evolution of our legal system these maritime employees can sue their employer in an admiralty court as well as at law; their land-based co-workers do not have that option. The fact that the contracts, pension rights, and other benefits and obligations may be similar for both types of employees is irrelevant for purposes of defining the admiralty court's jurisdiction over the claims of these maritime employees. Cf. The Steam-Boat Thomas Jefferson, 10 Wheat. 428; International Stevedoring Co. v. Haverty, 272 U. S. 50. The position of federal maritime employees should be no different. The argument of the Court showing that in many respects the rights of federal employees who are seamen are similar to the rights of federal employees who are not seamen, whatever its merits on its own terms, see Part IV, infra, does not negate the fact that the claims of these seamen are within the traditional scope of the admiralty jurisdiction. See McCrea v. United States, 294 U. S. 23, a claim for wages, inter alia, under the Suits in Admiralty Act.

Not only is the Court's approach based upon a false yardstick, but it contrives an impracticable test for applying a jurisdictional statute. The rule heretofore used for the application of the Suits in Admiralty Act has been that, absent any clear statutory exception,[4] it encompasses any claim that could have been brought before an admiralty court were the defendant a private shipper. Since the scope of the admiralty jurisdiction is long established and generally well understood, suitors would normally know in what forum their cases should be brought. The Court's new test for determining the proper forum is whether the underlying cause of action is primarily of "a maritime nature." As the Court's opinion indicates, this inquiry can be resolved only after what in many instances will be a complicated and elusive process. Indeed, in this case, only after several pages of analysis is the Court able to determine that "with respect to these wage claims, Congress thought of these petitioners more as government employees who happened to be seamen than as seamen who by chance worked for the Government," ante, p. 163. Putting aside the fact that there is nothing to show that Congress ever contemplated such a "jurisdictional" standard, replacing the straightforward "admiralty jurisdiction" test by the unpredictable "primarily of a maritime nature" rule is bound to introduce confusion and uncertainty into determinations of the appropriateness of a particular forum, the very type of question that should have a reasonably definitive answer.

IV.

The Court quite obviously construes the Act as it does because it is reluctant to deprive federally employed seamen of the longer statute of limitations available under the Tucker Act. Apart from anything else, this can be accomplished, however, only at the expense of forfeiting other substantial advantages available under the Suits in Admiralty Act.

First, an admiralty court is likely to be better acquainted with many underlying questions involved in suits such as these, and to be more sensitive to the tradition that seamen are the "wards of the admiralty." For example, the Classification Act of 1949, 63 Stat. 954, as amended, 5 U. S. C. § 1082 (8) (1964 ed.), provides that federally employed crew members shall be compensated "as nearly as is consistent with the public interest in accordance with prevailing rates and practices in the maritime industry . . . ." One of the suits consolidated in this action raises the question of overtime payment for "port watch tours of duty," and the petitioner, citing the Classification Act, alleges that "prevailing rates" in the trade require "16 hours at overtime rates per 24 hour port watch tour of duty." Another complaint involves, inter alia, a naval rule regarding lunch periods where, due to the nature of the work, "it may not be administratively desirable to allow a specified period of time off for lunch." Navy Civilian Personnel Instruction 610.2-1k. Questions involving such subject matter are best heard in admiralty.[5]

Second, venue under the Tucker Act, for suits over $10,000 and all suits involving pension rights, is limited to the Court of Claims. 28 U. S. C. § 1346 (a), (d) (1964 ed.). Three of the four suits consolidated here are above the $10,000 limit, and thus can only be brought in the District of Columbia. Of these three cases, two involve naval facilities at Fort Lauderdale, Florida. The interests of most maritime employees of the United States would probably be better served by allowing the more favorable venue provisions in admiralty.[6]

Third, interest provisions under the Suits in Admiralty Act are more favorable than under the Tucker Act. Under the latter statute interest runs at most from the date of judgment, 28 U. S. C. §§ 2411 (b), 2516 (1964 ed.), while in admiralty the court may award interest from the date the libel is filed. 46 U. S. C. §§ 743, 745 (1964 ed.). Greater court costs may also be awarded in admiralty. Compare 46 U. S. C. § 743 with 28 U. S. C. § 2412 (b) (1964 ed.).

Because of the Court's ruling today, all of these benefits are lost to all federally employed seamen, not merely to those involved in this case. The untoward results to which this decision leads in themselves engender the most serious misgivings as to the soundness of the Court's ruling, albeit it may be thought to produce a beneficent result in this particular instance.

I would affirm the judgment of the Court of Claims.

Notes

[1] Legislative history bearing on this aspect of the question is meager, although one colloquy during the House Committee on the Judiciary hearings on this bill suggests that concurrent jurisdiction with the Court of Claims might have been contemplated in certain situations. Hearing before the House Committee on the Judiciary on the Attorney General's Substitute for S. 3076 and H. R. 7124, 66th Cong., 1st Sess., ser. 8, at 48 (1919).

[2] Again in 1950 Congress extended the limitations period to accommodate those employees who, in reliance upon a prior decision, Hust v. Moore-McCormack Lines, 328 U. S. 707, overruled in Cosmopolitan Co. v. McAllister, 337 U. S. 783, had not filed suit against the United States under the Suits in Admiralty Act for a tort committed when a government-owned ship was being operated by a private company as general agent for the Government. 64 Stat. 1112, 46 U. S. C. § 745 (1964 ed.). The Senate report noted that "[t]o prevent future repetition of such mistakes the bill expressly restates the existing law that the remedy by suit against the United States is exclusive of every other type of action by reason of the same subject matter against the United States or against its employees or agents." S. Rep. No. 2535, 81st Cong., 2d Sess., 1 (1950).

[3] The House report noted: "the Court of Claims has no admiralty jurisdiction, but the Suits in Admiralty Act . . . vests exclusive jurisdiction over suits in admiralty against the United States in the district courts." H. R. Rep. No. 308, 80th Cong., 1st Sess., App. p. 138 (1947).

[4] Compare Johansen v. United States, 343 U. S. 427, and Patterson v. United States, 359 U. S. 495, in which it was held that the Federal Employees' Compensation Act of 1916, 39 Stat. 742, 5 U. S. C. § 751 et seq. (1964 ed.), provided the sole remedy for seamen injured on board government-owned vessels, thus barring suits under the Suits in Admiralty Act.

[5] The Court's argument that this factor is offset by the peculiar expertise of the Court of Claims with respect to the nonmaritime components of government seamen wage claims is not persuasive. District courts, too, possess such expertise, born of their concurrent jurisdiction with the Court of Claims in government contract actions involving less than $10,000. 28 U. S. C. § 1346 (a) (1964 ed.).

[6] 46 U. S. C. § 742 provides that suits under the Suits in Admiralty Act "shall be brought in the district court of the United States for the district in which the parties so suing, or any of them, reside or have their principal place of business in the United States, or in which the vessel or cargo charged with liability is found."

Justice Harlan's dissent in US v. Standard Oil Co. (May 23, 1966)

MR. JUSTICE HARLAN, whom MR. JUSTICE BLACK and MR. JUSTICE STEWART join, dissenting.

Had the majority in judging this case been content to confine itself to applying relevant rules of law and to leave policies affecting the proper conservation of the Nation's rivers to be dealt with by the Congress, I think that today's decision in this criminal case would have eventuated differently. The best that can be said for the Government's case is that the reach of the provision of § 13 of the Rivers and Harbors Act of 1899, 30 Stat. 1152, 33 U. S. C. § 407 (1964 ed.), under which this indictment is laid, is uncertain. This calls into play the traditional rule that penal statutes are to be strictly construed. In my opinion application of that rule requires a dismissal of the indictment.

I.

Section 13 forbids the deposit of all kinds of "refuse matter" into navigable rivers "other than that flowing from streets and sewers and passing therefrom in a liquid state." As the Court notes, this 1899 Act was part of a codification of prior statutes. This revamping was not discussed at any length on the floor of either House of Congress; the Senate was informed only that the provisions were merely a codification of existing law, without changes in substance. 32 Cong. Rec. 2296-2297 (1899). Section 13 was in fact based on two very similar prior statutes. The rivers and harbors appropriation act of 1890 provided the first national anti-obstruction provision, 26 Stat. 453:

"Sec. 6. That it shall not be lawful to cast, throw, empty, or unlade, or cause, suffer, or procure to be cast, thrown, emptied, or unladen, either from or out of any ship, vessel, lighter, barge, boat, or other craft, or from the shore, pier, wharf, furnace, manufacturing establishments, or mills of any kind whatever, any ballast, stone, slate, gravel, earth, rubbish, wreck, filth, slabs, edgings, sawdust, slag, cinders, ashes, refuse, or other waste of any kind, into any port, road, roadstead, harbor, haven, navigable river, or navigable waters of the United States which shall tend to impede or obstruct navigation . . . ."

A later statute, § 6 of the Rivers and Harbors Act of 1894, 28 Stat. 363, provided somewhat similarly:

"That it shall not be lawful to place, discharge, or deposit, by any process or in any manner, ballast, refuse, dirt, ashes, cinders, mud, sand, dredgings, sludge, acid, or any other matter of any kind other than that flowing from streets, sewers, and passing therefrom in a liquid state, in the waters of any harbor or river of the United States, for the improvement of which money has been appropriated by Congress . . . ."

The Court relies primarily on the latter Act, contending that its applicability to "any other matter of any kind" would surely encompass oil, even though commercially valuable. Further, the Court notes (ante, p. 228) that the 1894 statute was modeled after a federal statute of 1888 dealing with New York Harbor, 25 Stat. 209. Under this New York Harbor Act, which still remains on the books, 33 U. S. C. § 441 et seq. (1964 ed.), prosecutions for accidental deposits of commercially useful oil have been sustained. The Colombo, 42 F. 2d 211. This background is thought to reinforce the view that oil of any type would fall within the 1894 statute's purview. Since the present enactment was intended to be merely a codification, the majority concludes that the construction of the broader 1894 predecessor should govern.

Whatever might be said about how properly to interpret the 1890 and, more especially, the 1894 statutes, it is the 1899 Act that has been on the books for the last 67 years, and its purposes and language must guide the determination of this case. To the extent that there were some differences in scope between the 1890 and 1894 Acts, these were necessarily resolved in the 1899 codification, which, while embodying the essential thrust of both prior statutes, appears from its plain language to have favored the more restrictive coverage of the 1890 Act. Moreover, it is questionable to what extent the Court's speculation as to the meaning of a phrase in one of the prior statutes is relevant at all when the language of the present statute, which is penal in nature, is in itself explicit and unambiguous.

The purpose of § 13 was essentially to eliminate obstructions to navigation and interference with public works projects. This 1899 enactment, like the two pre-existing statutes which it was intended to codify, was a minor section attached to a major appropriation act together with other measures dealing with sunken wrecks,[1] trespassing at public works sites,[2] and obstructions caused by improperly constructed bridges, piers, and other structures.[3] These statutes were rendered necessary primarily because navigable rivers, which the Congress was appropriating funds to improve, were being obstructed by depositing of waste materials by factories and ships.[4] It is of course true, as the Court observes, that "oil is oil." ante, p. 226, and that the accidental spillage of valuable oil may have substantially the same "deleterious effect on waterways" as the wholesale depositing of waste oil. But the relevant inquiry is not the admittedly important concerns of pollution control, but Congress' purpose in enacting this anti-obstruction Act, and that appears quite plainly to be a desire to halt through the imposition of criminal penalties the depositing of obstructing refuse matter in rivers and harbors.

The Court's construction eschews the everyday meaning of "refuse matter"—waste, rubbish, trash, debris, garbage, see Webster's New International Dictionary, 3d ed.—and adopts instead an approach that either reads "refuse" out of the Act altogether, or gives to it a tortured meaning. The Court declares, at one point, that "The word `refuse' includes all foreign substances and pollutants apart from those `flowing from streets and sewers and passing therefrom in a liquid state' into the watercourse." Ante, p. 230. Thus, dropping anything but pure water into a river would appear to be a federal misdemeanor. At the same time, the Court also appears to endorse the Second Circuit's somewhat narrower view that "refuse matter" refers to any material, however valuable, which becomes unsalvageable when introduced into the water. Ante, pp. 229-230. On this latter approach, the imposition of criminal penalties would in effect depend in each instance on a prospective estimate of salvage costs. Such strained definitions of a phrase that is clear as a matter of ordinary English hardly commend themselves, and at the very least raise serious doubts as to the intended reach of § 13.

II.

Given these doubts as to the proper construction of "refuse matter" in § 13, we must reckon with a traditional canon that a penal statute will be narrowly construed. See II Hale, Historia Placitorum Coronae 335 (1736); United States v. Wiltberger, 5 Wheat. 76, 95. The reasons underlying this maxim are various. It appears likely that the rule was originally adopted in order to spare people from the effects of exceedingly harsh penalties. See Hall, Strict or Liberal Construction of Penal Statutes, 48 Harv. L. Rev. 748, 750 (1935). Even though this rationale might be thought to have force were the defendant a natural person,[5] I cannot say that it is particularly compelling in this instance where the maximum penalty to which Standard Oil might be subject is a fine of $2,500. 33 U. S. C. § 411 (1964 ed.).

A more important contemporary purpose of the notion of strict construction is to give notice of what the law is, in order to guide people in their everyday activities. Again, however, it is difficult to justify a narrow reading of § 13 on this basis. The spilling of oil of any type into rivers is not something one would be likely to do whether or not it is legally proscribed by a federal statute. A broad construction would hardly raise dangers of penalizing people who have been innocently pouring valuable oil into navigable waters, for such conduct in Florida is unlawful whatever the effect of § 13. A Florida statute penalizing as a misdemeanor the depositing into waters within the State of "any rubbish, filth, or poisonous or deleterious substance or substances, liable to affect the health of persons, fish, or live stock . . . ," Fla. Stat. Ann., § 387.08 (1960 ed.), quite evidently reaches the dumping of commercial oil. And Florida's nuisance law would likewise seem to make this conduct actionable in equity. See, e. g., The Ferry Pass Inspectors' & Shippers' Assn. v. The Whites River Inspectors' & Shippers' Assn., 57 Fla. 399, 48 So. 643. Finally, as noted earlier, ante, p. 229, n. 5, prior decisions by some lower courts have held § 13 applicable to spillage of oil. For these reasons this justification for the canon of strict construction is not persuasive in this instance.

There is, however, a further reason for applying a seemingly straightforward statute in a straightforward way. In McBoyle v. United States, 283 U. S. 25, this Court held that a statute making it a federal crime to move a stolen "motor vehicle" in interstate commerce did not apply to a stolen airplane. That too was a case in which precise clarity was not required in order to give due warning of the line between permissible and wrongful conduct, for there could not have been any question but that stealing aircraft was unlawful. Nevertheless, Mr. Justice Holmes declared that "Although it is not likely that a criminal will carefully consider the text of the law before he murders or steals, it is reasonable that a fair warning should be given to the world in language that the common world will understand, of what the law intends to do if a certain line is passed." 283 U. S., at 27. The policy thus expressed is based primarily on a notion of fair play: in a civilized state the least that can be expected of government is that it express its rules in language all can reasonably be expected to understand. Moreover, this requirement of clear expression is essential in a practical sense to confine the discretion of prosecuting authorities, particularly important under a statute such as § 13 which imposes criminal penalties with a minimal, if any, scienter requirement.[6]

In an area in which state or local law has traditionally regulated primary activity,[7] there is good reason to restrict federal penal legislation within the confines of its language. If the Federal Government finds that there is sufficient obstruction or pollution of navigable waters caused by the introduction of commercial oil or other nonrefuse material, it is an easy matter to enact appropriate regulatory or penal legislation.[8] Such legislation can be directed at specific types of pollution, and the remedies devised carefully to ensure compliance. Indeed, such a statute was enacted in 1924 to deal with oil pollution in coastal waters caused by vessels, 43 Stat. 605, 33 U. S. C. §§ 433, 434 (1964 ed.).

To conclude that this attempted prosecution cannot stand is not to be oblivious to the importance of preserving the beauties and utility of the country's rivers. It is simply to take the statute as we find it. I would affirm the judgment of the District Court.

Notes

[1] Rivers and Harbors Act of 1899, § 15, 30 Stat. 1152, 33 U. S. C. § 409 (1964 ed.).

[2] Rivers and Harbors Act of 1899, § 14, 30 Stat. 1152, 33 U. S. C. § 408 (1964 ed.).

[3] Rivers and Harbors Act of 1899, § 12, 30 Stat. 1151, 33 U. S. C. § 406 (1964 ed.).

[4] Congress was presented, when considering one of the predecessors of the 1899 Act, with the representations of the Office of the Chief of Army Engineers that there had been "serious injury to navigable waters by the discharge of sawmill waste into streams . . . . In fair-ways of harbors, channels are injured from deposits of ballast, steam-boat ashes, oysters, and rubbish from passing vessels." S. Rep. No. 224, 50th Cong., 1st Sess., 2 (1888). See also H. R. Rep. No. 1826, 55th Cong., 3rd Sess., 3-4 (1899). There is no support for the proposition that these statutes were directed at "pollution" independently of "obstruction."

[5] The minimum sentence for an individual convicted of violating § 13 is a $500 fine or 30 days' imprisonment, not an insignificant penalty for accidentally dropping foreign matter into a river. 33 U. S. C. § 411 (1964 ed.).

[6] The parties were not in agreement as to what scienter requirement the statute imposes. This question is not before us under the restricted jurisdiction granted to this Court under 18 U. S. C. § 3731 (1964 ed.), see United States v. Petrillo, 332 U. S. 1; United States v. Borden Co., 308 U. S. 188, and the Court today intimates no views on the question.

[7] Besides the Florida pollution statute adverted to earlier, Fla. Stat. Ann., § 387.08 (1960 ed.), the city of Jacksonville has enacted ordinances dealing generally with fire prevention, Jacksonville Ordinance Code §§ 19-4.1 to 19-4.24 (1958 Supp.), disposal of waste material, § 21-12 (1958 Supp.), and pollution of the city water supply, § 27-52 (1953 Code).

[8] See, e. g., special message of the President dealing with new antipollution legislation, Preservation of Our Natural Heritage—Message from the President of the United States, H. Doc. No. 387, 89th Cong., 2d Sess., Cong. Rec., Feb. 23, 1966, pp. 3519-3522.

Justice Harlan's dissent in Rinaldi v. Yeager (May 31, 1966)

MR. JUSTICE HARLAN, dissenting.

New Jersey recoups the cost of trial transcripts furnished to indigents out of prison allowances made to incarcerated prisoners, but does not seek reimbursement from parolees or convicted defendants not imprisoned. The Court holds this differentiation to violate the Equal Protection Clause. I am unable to agree. Under conventional equal-protection standards which disapprove only irrational and arbitrary classifications, the statute is plainly valid. See McLaughlin v. Florida, 379 U. S. 184, 190-191; McGowan v. Maryland, 366 U. S. 420, 426; Lindsley v. Natural Carbonic Gas Co., 220 U. S. 61, 78-79. Surely the State might reasonably choose to reimburse itself for such transcript costs out of prison allowances, but deem it not worth the added time and trouble, or even advisable, to attempt to extract such charges from a convict not in prison who must support himself on his own resources. Adhering to the traditional test of rationality, I would affirm the decision of the District Court.[*]

[*] I find no substance to appellant's main argument, which the Court lays aside, that to permit any such recoupment from an indigent is an unconstitutional deterrent to appeal. Nor do I think there is any force to the argument in n. 4 (ante, p. 308), not even suggested by appellant, which at best goes to the validity of the statutes governing compensation and not to the reimbursement statute being reviewed.

Justice Harlan's concurrence and dissent in Cheff v. Schnackenberg (June 6, 1966)

MR. JUSTICE HARLAN, concurring in the result in No. 67 and dissenting in Nos. 412 and 442.

By the opinions in these cases, two new limitations on the use of the federal contempt power are inaugurated. In Cheff, it is announced that prison sentences for criminal contempt in a federal court must be limited to six months unless the defendant is afforded a trial by jury. In Shillitani and Pappadio, an automatic "purge" clause and related indicia are found to convert a criminal sentence into a civil sanction which cannot survive the grand jury's expiration. I believe these limitations are erroneous in reasoning and result alike.

I.

The decision to extend the right to jury trial to criminal contempts ending in sentences greater than six months is the product of the views of four Justices who rest that conclusion on the Court's supervisory power and those of two others who believe that jury trials are constitutionally required in all but "petty" criminal contempts. The four Justices who rely on the supervisory power also find the constitutional question a "difficult" one. Ante, at 365. However, as recently as 1958, this Court in Green v. United States, 356 U. S. 165, unequivocally declared that the prosecution of criminal contempts was not subject to the grand and petit jury requirements of Art. III, § 2, of the Constitution and the Fifth and Sixth Amendments. This doctrine, which was accepted by federal judges in the early days of the Republic[1] and has been steadfastly adhered to in case after case in this Court,[2] should be recognized now as a definitive answer to petitioners' constitutional claims in each of the cases before us.

The prevailing opinion's new supervisory-power rule seems to me equally infirm. The few sentences devoted to this dictum give no reason why a six-month limitation is desirable. Nor is there anything about the sentences actually imposed in these instances that warrants reappraisal of the present practice in contempt sentencing. In Cheff itself the sentence was for six months. Shillitani and Pappadio involved two-year sentences but each was moderated by a purge clause and seemingly in neither case were there disputed facts suitable for a jury. Among the prominent shortcomings of the new rule, which are simply disregarded, is the difficulty it may generate for federal courts seeking to implement locally unpopular decrees. Another problem is in administration: to decide whether to proffer a jury trial, the judge must now look ahead to the sentence, which itself depends on the precise facts the trial is to reveal.

In my view, before this Court improvises a rule necessarily based on pure policy that largely shrugs off history, a far more persuasive showing can properly be expected.

II.

No less remarkable is the Court's upsetting of the sentences in Shillitani and Pappadio on the ground that the jailings were really for civil contempt which cannot endure beyond the grand jury's term.[3] It can hardly be suggested that the lower courts did not intend to invoke the criminal contempt power to keep the petitioners in jail after the grand jury expired; the contrary is demonstrated by the entire record.[4] Instead, the Court attempts to characterize the proceedings by a supposed primary or essential "purpose" and then lops off so much of the sentences as do not conform to that purpose. What the Court fails to do is to give any reason in policy, precedent, statute law, or the Constitution for its unspoken premise that a sentencing judge cannot combine two purposes into a single sentence of the type here imposed.

Without arguing about which purpose was primary, obviously a fixed sentence with a purge clause can be said to embody elements of both criminal and civil contempt. However, so far as the safeguards of criminal contempt proceedings may be superior to civil, the petitioners have not been disadvantaged in this regard, nor do they claim otherwise. Adding a purge clause to a fixed sentence is a benefit for the petitioners, not a reason for complaint. Similarly the public interest is served by exerting strong pressure to obtain answers while tailoring the length of imprisonment so that it may punish the defendant only for his period of recalcitrance and no more. I see no reason why a fixed sentence with an automatic purge clause should be deemed impermissible.

For the foregoing reasons, I would affirm the judgments in all three cases on the basis of Green and leave the authority of that case unimpaired.[5]

Notes

[1] E. g., Ex parte Burr, 4 Fed. Cas. 791, 797 (No. 2,186) (C. C. D. C. 1823) (Cranch, C. J.):

"[C]ases of contempt of court have never been considered as crimes within the meaning and intention of the second section of the third article of the constitution of the United States; nor have attachments for contempt ever been considered as criminal prosecutions within the sixth amendment. . . . Many members of the [constitutional] convention were members of the first congress, and it cannot be believed that they would have silently acquiesced in so palpable a violation of the then recent constitution, as would have been contained in the seventeenth section of the judiciary act of 1789 (1 Stat. 73),— which authorizes all the courts of the United States `to punish by fine and imprisonment, at the discretion of the said courts, all contempts of authority in any cause or hearing before the same,'—if their construction of the constitution had been that which has, in this case, been contended for at the bar."

[2] See Ex parte Terry, 128 U. S. 289, 313 (1888) (Harlan, J.); Savin, Petitioner, 131 U. S. 267, 278 (1889) (Harlan, J.); Eilenbecker v. Plymouth County, 134 U. S. 31, 36 (1890) (Miller, J.); Interstate Commerce Comm'n v. Brimson, 154 U. S. 447, 489 (1894) (Harlan, J.); Bessette v. W. B. Conkey Co., 194 U. S. 324, 336-337 (1904) (Brewer, J.); Gompers v. Bucks Stove & Range Co., 221 U. S. 418, 450 (1911) (Lamar, J.); Gompers v. United States, 233 U. S. 604, 610-611 (1914) (Holmes, J.); Ex parte Hudgings, 249 U. S. 378, 383 (1919) (White, C. J.); Myers v. United States, 264 U. S. 95, 104-105 (1924) (McReynolds, J.); Michaelson v. United States, 266 U. S. 42, 67 (1924) (Sutherland, J.); Ex parte Grossman, 267 U. S. 87, 117-118 (1925) (Taft, C. J.); Fisher v. Pace, 336 U. S. 155, 159-160 (1949) (Reed, J.); Offutt v. United States, 348 U. S. 11, 14 (1954) (Frankfurter, J.).

[3] This question was never raised in Pappadio nor encompassed by the limited grant of certiorari in that case, see 382 U. S. 916; in Shillitani, where the issue is properly before the Court, petitioner filed a certiorari petition discussing the point but tendered no brief on the merits on any phase of the case.

[4] For example, in each case the Judgment and Commitment states that "the defendant is guilty of criminal contempt" and orders him committed "for a period of Two (2) Years, or until further order of this Court," should the questions be answered within that period before the grand jury expires.

[5] The two-year sentences imposed on Shillitani and Pappadio do not call for the exercise of this Court's corrective power over contempt sentences, see Green, 356 U. S., at 187-189; as has been noted, both sentences carried purge clauses.

Justice Harlan's dissent in US v. Grinnell Corp. (June 13, 1966)

MR. JUSTICE HARLAN, dissenting.

I cannot agree with the Court that the relevant market has been adequately proved. I do not dispute that a national market may be found even though immediate competition takes place only within individual communities, some of which are themselves natural monopolies. For a national monopoly of such local enterprises may still have serious long-term impact on competition and be vulnerable on its own plane to the antitrust laws. In the product market also the Court seems to me to make out a good enough case for lumping together the different kinds of central station protective service (CSPS). But I cannot agree that the facts so far developed warrant restricting the product market to accredited CSPS.

Because the ultimate issue is the effective power to control price and competition, this Court has always recognized that the market must include products or services "reasonably interchangeable" with those of the alleged monopolist. United States v. du Pont & Co., 351 U. S. 377, 395. In this instance, there is no doubt that the accredited CSPS business does compete in some measure with many other forms of hazard protection:

watchmen, local alarms, proprietary systems, telephone-connected services, unaccredited CSPS, direct-connected (to police and fire stations) systems, and so forth. The critical question, then, is the extent of competition from these rivals.

The Government and the majority have stressed that differences in cost, reliability and insurance discounts may disqualify a competing form of protection for a particular customer. For example, it is said that proprietary systems are too expensive for any but large companies and local alarms may go unanswered in some neighborhoods. But if in general a CSPS customer has a feasible alternative to CSPS, it does not much matter that other ones are foreclosed to him, nor that other CSPS customers have different second choices. From this record, it may well be that other forms of protection are each competitive enough with segments of the CSPS market so that in sum CSPS rarely has a monopoly position.

From the defense standpoint, there is substantial evidence showing that the defendants do feel themselves under pressure from other forms of protection, that they do compete for customers, and that they do lower prices even in areas where no CSPS competition is present. This concrete evidence of market behavior seems to me to rank higher than the kind of inference proof heavily relied on by the Government—physical differences between competing forms of protection, self-advertising claims of CSPS companies that they represent a superior service, and varying insurance discounts. Given that the burden of proof rests upon the Government, the record leaves me with such misgivings as to the validity of the District Court's findings on this score that I am not prepared to agree that the Government has made the showing of market domination that the law demands before a business is sundered.

At the same time the case must be recognized as a close one, and I am not ready to say at this stage that the findings and conclusions of the District Court might not be supportable. All things considered, I join with my Brothers FORTAS and STEWART to the extent of voting to remand the case for further proceedings so that new findings can be made as to the relevant product market. This course seems to me the more appropriate in light of the fact that because of the Expediting Act, 15 U. S. C. § 29 (1964 ed.), we have not had the benefit of any intermediate appellate sifting of this record. In view of the disposition I propose, I do not consider any of the other questions in the case.

Justice Harlan's concurrence and dissent in Nicholas v. US (June 13, 1966)

MR. JUSTICE HARLAN, concurring in part and dissenting in part.

Recognizing the case to be difficult, I would affirm the Court of Appeals' decision to allow both the interest and the penalty as administration expenses. On both points, I think there are fair policy arguments which can be mustered to support either result. On balance, it seems to me that the entire period starting with the Chapter XI operation and carrying through the bankruptcy proceeding should be regarded as a continuum of court administration. See especially § 378 (2) of the Bankruptcy Act, 11 U. S. C. § 778 (2) (1964 ed.). From this I think it follows that interest should not be stopped when bankruptcy succeeds the Chapter XI period, and that the court-appointed trustee does fall heir to the responsibilities of the court-supervised debtor in possession to file returns.

Justice Harlan's dissent in Bank of Marin v. England (Nov 21, 1966)

MR. JUSTICE HARLAN, dissenting.

The Court, in its haste to alleviate an indisputable inequity to the bank, disregards, in my opinion, both the proper principles of statutory construction and the most permanent interests of bankruptcy administration. I must dissent.[1]

The Act itself is unambiguous. Section 70a vests title to the bankrupt's property in the trustee "as of the date of the filing of the petition." 52 Stat. 879, 11 U. S. C. § 110 (a). Section 70d nonetheless sustains bona fide transfers of the property made after filing and "before adjudication or before a receiver takes possession. . . whichever first occurs. . . ." 52 Stat. 881, 11 U. S. C. § 110 (d). Transactions excluded from the shelter of § 70d are, so far as pertinent, within § 70d (5), which provides that "no [such] transfer by or in behalf of the bankrupt . . . shall be valid against the trustee . . . ." 52 Stat. 882, 11 U. S. C. § 110 (d) (5). The adjudication of voluntary petitions results by operation of law from filing. § 18f, 73 Stat. 109, 11 U. S. C. § 41 (f).

In the situation before us, the remaining issue is accordingly whether this transfer occurred before or after September 26, the day on which Seafoods filed its petition in bankruptcy and was perforce adjudicated bankrupt. I do not understand petitioner to contend, or the Court to suggest that this occurred at a time other than presentment of the checks, October 2. Given the law of California, by which a check is not a pro tanto transfer of the drawer's rights until presentment, I cannot see that another moment is possible. California Civil Code § 3265e; California Commercial Code § 3409. In sum, I find it unavoidable that the Act's plain words hold the bank liable to the trustee for the value of its payment on Seafoods' behalf.[2]

I do not suggest that this Court should confine its attention to the unadorned terms of the Bankruptcy Act. Nonetheless, where Congress has pointed so unmistakably in one direction, prudence and simple propriety surely require that we examine carefully the impulses which beckon us to another. The Court explains its resolution of this case by two apparently alternative contentions. I am unpersuaded that either permits us to circumvent the Act's demands.

The Court first intimates, without expressly deciding, that the bank is shielded by its contractual right to a seasonable revocation of its duty to honor checks drawn upon it. The Court vouches for this the doctrine that a trustee in bankruptcy takes rights no wider or more complete than his bankrupt had. It is doubtless true that a trustee is not a bona fide purchaser or encumbrancer, and that he ordinarily assumes the bankrupt's property subject to existing claims, liens, and equities. Hewit v. Berlin Machine Works, 194 U. S. 296. Unfortunately, these maxims scarcely suffice to decide this case. They are interstitial rules, valid no further than the Act's positive requirements permit. First National Bank v. Staake, 202 U. S. 141. 4 Collier, Bankruptcy ¶ 70.04, at 954.2. The Act in several respects clothes the trustee in powers denied to his bankrupt: A trustee may thus avoid, although his bankrupt may not, transactions deemed fraudulent under the Act, liens obtained and preferential transfers completed within four months of bankruptcy, and statutory liens within the prohibition of § 67c (2). 4 Collier, Bankruptcy ¶ 70.04, at 957.

The Court does not assert that this transfer is protected by § 70d. I understand it instead to concede that, equitable considerations aside, the bank's payment is invalid against the trustee. I must conclude that the Court has reasoned that a contractual defense retained against the bankrupt suffices to preclude use of a power expressly conferred upon the trustee. If this is the Court's meaning, it has traversed both logic and authority, and has emasculated the powers given to trustees under the Act.

The Court's principal contention seems to be that equitable considerations oblige it to release the bank from liability. Its premise plainly is that equity is here a solvent to which we may appropriately resort; I am unable to accept that premise. This is not a case in which the statute is imprecise. Nor is it a case in which the legislature's intentions have been misshapen by the statute's words; even a cursory examination of the history of § 70 will evidence that its terms faithfully reflect Congress' purposes.

The Act of 1898 vested title to the bankrupt's property in the trustee at adjudication, but contained nothing to prevent its dissipation in the interval after filing.[3] The courts were therefore left free to devise protective rules to reconcile the competing interests of the estate and of those who dealt with the bankrupt in this period. The fulcrum of those rules was the proposition that a "petition [in bankruptcy] is a caveat to all the world, and in effect an attachment and injunction." Mueller v. Nugent, 184 U. S. 1, 14. The courts softened its severity by a series of exceptions, either employing or distinguishing it as equity or convenience suggested. The result, as a principal draftsman of the Chandler Act reforms described it, was that "no consistent theory of protected transactions has been developed," and the situation was "conducive to confusion and uncertainty, with potentialities for argument, `bluffing,' litigation, expense and delay."[4]

The law consisted essentially of "nebulous vagaries."[5]

The Chandler Act stemmed chiefly from a sustained investigation of these and other problems by the National Bankruptcy Conference.[6] Its members were the Act's principal draftsmen. The revisions they made to § 70 entirely restructured the basis both of the trustee's title and of the protection given to transactions which occur after filing. Their purpose, as one of them explained to the Chandler subcommittee, was to provide "a clear statutory basis" to the issues of title and protected transactions, in "lieu of a crazy quilt of contradictory judicial statements."[7] The effect of their revisions was to define "the full extent to which bona fide transactions with the bankrupt, after bankruptcy, will be protected."[8]

Adjudication and receivership were plainly expected to mark the perimeters of this protection. Various factors determined this choice. First, none of the several exceptions to Mueller v. Nugent reached transactions which occurred after adjudication.[9] More important, once the draftsmen had elected to vest title in the trustee from filing, they were chiefly anxious to shield debtors from the consequences of unwarranted involuntary petitions.[10] They feared that such a petition might ruin a debtor by inducing others to avoid dealings with him. Section 70d was expected to immunize bona fide transactions after filing, and thus to encourage dealings with the solvent debtor. There is no need for such protection after adjudication. Finally, adjudication and receivership signal the beginning of bankruptcy administration, and they are therefore both appropriate moments at which to forbid all further meddling with the estate.[11]

It is equally plain that the protection offered by § 70d must have been intended principally for involuntary proceedings. There are several indications of this. Most important, the hazard to which the section was chiefly directed, the consequences of an unwarranted petition upon a debtor's credit, is entirely absent from voluntary proceedings. Thus, the discussion of this problem before the Chandler subcommittee was explicitly confined to involuntary petitions.[12] Further, the protection offered by § 63b, which closely supplements § 70d, extends only to involuntary proceedings.[13] Finally, the draftsmen must surely have known that the adjudication of voluntary petitions ordinarily followed quickly and routinely after filing.[14] It was certainly not unknown for adjudication to occur on the day of filing.[15] The draftsmen could only have intended that any protection given in voluntary proceedings by § 70d be fleeting and minimal.[16]

In short, § 70 was tailored to provide carefully measured protection to bona fide transfers. It was intended to preclude further confusion and uncertainty. There is every indication that its terms faithfully reflect its purposes.

I fully sympathize with the discomfort of the bank's position, but I cannot escape the impact of what Congress has done.[17] The Court has not found § 70 constitutionally impermissible.[18] It has simply measured the statute by the standard of its own conscience, and concluded that equity requires a result which the statute forbids. I had thought it well settled that equity may supplement, but may never supersede, the Act. 1 Collier, Bankruptcy ¶ 2.09, at 171-172. The Act's language is neither imprecise nor infelicitous; I can therefore see no room for the interposition of equity.

More important, the Court today permits the dilution of the Chandler amendments to § 70. The Court's disposition of this case may be taken to suggest that whenever equity is thought strongly to demand relief from the strictures of the Act, further exceptions may be appropriately created to the statutory scheme. I fear that the Court may have set in motion once more the protracted process which before 1938 resulted in "confusion and uncertainty," "litigation, expense and delay."

If so, the Chandler amendments will have had no more permanent result than to wipe the judicial slate momentarily clean.

I would affirm the judgment of the Court of Appeals.

Notes

[1] Like the Court, I believe that this case is not moot. In addition to what has been said by the majority, compare Fishgold v. Sullivan Drydock & Repair Corp., 328 U. S. 275, and Aeronautical Industrial Dist. Lodge v. Campbell, 337 U. S. 521.

[2] It is true that the negotiability proviso to § 70d (5) has once been held to protect a bank in analogous circumstances. Rosenthal v. Guaranty Bank & Trust Co., 139 F. Supp. 730. The proviso's legislative history throws little light on its intended scope. It appears inapplicable here. First, presentment is not strictly a negotiation. Second and more important, other constructions are more consonant with the balance of § 70d. Cf. 70 Harv. L. Rev. 548, 550. 4 Collier, Bankruptcy ¶ 70.68, at 1502, n. 3 (14th ed. 1964). I do not understand the Court to rely upon the proviso.

[3] This Court had held that despite the cleavage at adjudication, the trustee took the title as it was at filing. Everett v. Judson, 228 U. S. 474. The situation is summarized in McLaughlin, Aspects of the Chandler Bill to Amend the Bankruptcy Act, 4 U. Chi. L. Rev. 369, 383.

[4] McLaughlin, Amendment of the Bankruptcy Act (pts. 1 & 2), 40 Harv. L. Rev. 341, 583, at 615. The same conclusions are reached by Weinstein, The Bankruptcy Law of 1938, at 161.

[5] 4 Collier, Bankruptcy ¶ 70.66, at 1495.

[6] A brief history of the Conference's work may be found in McLaughlin, 4 U. Chi. L. Rev., at 375.

[7] Hearing before the House Committee on the Judiciary on H. R. 6439, 75th Cong., 1st Sess., 212. Professor McLaughlin quoted from his article in 40 Harv. L. Rev. 341. He subsequently acknowledged that § 70 would permit an area in which the courts could continue to balance the competing interests of the parties. Ibid. In light of the importance attached to adjudication as a line of cleavage, and the comparative insignificance intended for § 70d in voluntary proceedings, see infra, I do not believe that this acknowledgment can be taken to reach this case.

[8] 4 Collier, Bankruptcy ¶ 70.67, at 1500.

[9] 4 Collier, Bankruptcy ¶ 70.66, at 1498. In the one apparent exception, Jones v. Springer, 226 U. S. 148, a dredge had been placed in the hands of a receiver under an attachment levied before filing. The Court concluded that this sufficed to avoid the ordinary limitations imposed by adjudication.

[10] Hearing before the House Committee on the Judiciary on H. R. 6439, 75th Cong., 1st Sess., 211. Professor McLaughlin described this to the subcommittee as "the next most pressing problem." He concluded that "[w]e have put in a provision [70d] to cover that [the problem of unwarranted petitions]." His explanation to the subcommittee of § 70d was based entirely on this problem. There is of course evidence that the draftsmen also expected to alleviate unfairness which § 70a might otherwise produce. See Analysis of H. R. 12889, House Committee on the Judiciary, 74th Cong., 2d Sess., 230 (Comm. Print 1936).

[11] MacLachlan, Handbook of the Law of Bankruptcy 346.

[12] Hearing before the House Committee on the Judiciary on H. R. 6439, 75th Cong., 1st Sess., 211.

[13] 52 Stat. 873, 11 U. S. C. § 103 (b). Section 63b provides that "In the interval after the filing of an involuntary petition and before the appointment of a receiver or the adjudication, whichever first occurs, a claim arising in favor of a creditor by reason of property transferred or services rendered by the creditor to the bankrupt for the benefit of the estate shall be provable to the extent of the value of such property or services."

[14] MacLachlan, Handbook of the Law of Bankruptcy 40.

[15] See, e. g., New York County National Bank v. Massey, 192 U. S. 138.

[16] Further, the 1959 amendments to § 18, by which adjudication results by operation of law from filing, were adopted upon the recommendation of the Judicial Conference and its Committee on Bankruptcy Administration. Annual Report of the Proceedings of the Judicial Conference, 1958, p. 28. The bill received the endorsement of the National Bankruptcy Conference. H. R. Rep. No. 241, 86th Cong., 1st Sess., 2. It therefore seems quite improbable that the 1959 amendments could have inadvertently excluded voluntary proceedings from the scope of § 70d.

[17] Judge Soper's reasoning in Lake v. New York Life Insurance Co., 218 F. 2d 394, 399, seems entirely persuasive: "Whether the line which has been drawn is the best possible solution of the problem is not for the courts to say. The line has in fact been drawn by competent authority and it is no longer necessary for the courts to make the attempt, which has not been conspicuously successful in the past, to decide cases on the facts as they arise . . . ." See also Kohn v. Myers, 266 F. 2d 353.

[18] I cannot in any event accept petitioner's contention that these provisions have denied it due process. In exercise of its express constitutional authority over bankruptcy, Art. I, § 8, Congress has attached great importance to swift and efficient administration; to this purpose it devised a statutory scheme by which it balanced the competing rights of the interested parties. Congress' purposes are permissible, and the scheme it has adopted is reasonably calculated to achieve those purposes. In this context I cannot say that the Constitution requires that all whose rights may be reached by bankruptcy proceedings must first have actual notice of them. Cf. Hanover National Bank v. Moyses, 186 U. S. 181.

Justice Harlan's dissent in Parker v. Gladden (Dec 12, 1966)

MR. JUSTICE HARLAN, dissenting.

By not setting forth the background of this proceeding the Court has put seriously out of focus the constitutional issue involved in this case.

Parker was convicted of second degree murder on May 19, 1961, and sentenced to life imprisonment. On September 7, 1961, he addressed a letter to several jurors protesting his innocence, condemning his attorneys for incompetence, intimating that witnesses were coerced into lying, and chiding the jurors for being duped into finding him guilty. After affirmance of his conviction by the Supreme Court of Oregon on September 15, 1963—some two years after the jury verdict—Parker again set out to take his case to the jury. He furnished his wife with a tape recording in which he propounded a series of questions designed to uncover possible improprieties in the jury's deliberations. The jury had deliberated a long time and Parker had been told that their discussion was heated. Although unaware of any irregularities he commenced "shooting in the dark." (Tr., p. 16.) Mrs. Parker then acquired a jury list and discovered those jurors who had been most sympathetic to her husband.[1] She invited two regular jurors and an alternate to her home to listen to the recording and discuss the case. An attorney was then retained to prepare affidavits detailing the allegations before us and to institute this post-conviction proceeding. The statements before this Court were found to have been made by this apparently Elizabethan-tongued bailiff, but, contrary to this Court's assertion, the trial court found that these statements were only prejudicial in nature and not that they had a prejudicial effect.[2] The Oregon Supreme Court did not find the trial proceedings fundamentally unfair.

This Court finds the bailiff's remarks to be in violation of the Sixth Amendment's confrontation requirement. Although I believe that "a right of confrontation is `implicit in the concept of ordered liberty,' " Pointer v. Texas, 380 U. S. 400, 408 (concurring opinion of HARLAN, J.), I cannot accede to the view that the Sixth Amendment is directly applicable to the States through the Fourteenth. As to the confrontation problem here asserted, I know of no case in which this Court has held that jurors must have been absolutely insulated from all expressions of opinion on the merits of the case or the judicial process at the risk of declaration of a new trial. Irvin v. Dowd, 366 U. S. 717. Even where this Court has acted in its supervisory capacity it has refused to hold that jury contact with outside information is always a cause for overthrowing a verdict, wisely preferring to allow "each case . . . [to] turn on its special facts." Marshall v. United States, 360 U. S. 310, 312. The Court notes that these remarks were made by a state officer, but does not explain why the bailiff's official capacity would in this instance make him any more a "witness" than any other person able to communicate with the jury. Thus, though I believe unintentionally, the Court's opinion leaves open the possibility of automatically requiring a mistrial on constitutional grounds whenever any juror is exposed to any potentially prejudicial expression of opinion.

Considering this case, as I would, under the doctrine of fundamental fairness implicit in the Due Process Clause of the Fourteenth Amendment, I think a different result follows. Much reliance has been placed upon Turner v. Louisiana, 379 U. S. 466. But in Turner we faced a situation in which the trial court allowed two deputy sheriffs who were key witnesses to be placed in "continuous and intimate association" with the jury, and it would have been "blinking reality not to recognize the extreme prejudice inherent in this" situation. 379 U. S., at 473. There too we faced "a procedure employed by the State" involving "such a probability that prejudice will result" that we deemed it "inherently lacking in due process." Estes v. Texas, 381 U. S. 532, 542-543. Here no procedure adopted by the State is to be faulted and it seems clear to me that the rule of Stroble v. California, 343 U. S. 181, and Irvin v. Dowd, supra, should apply and a substantial showing of prejudice in fact must be made before a due process violation can be found.

On this basis the occurrences before us seem inconsequential to me in light of the eight-day trial and twenty-six-hour jury deliberation. And my feeling is confirmed by the extremely trivial evidence of prejudice amounting to no more than an assertion by one obviously highly emotional and "guilt-ridden" juror that she might have been influenced without realizing it.[3] "[I]t is an impossible standard to require that tribunal [the jury] to be a laboratory, completely sterilized and freed from any external factors." Rideau v. Louisiana, 373 U. S. 723, 733 (CLARK, J., dissenting).

The potentialities of today's decision may go far beyond what, I am sure, the Court intends. Certainly the Court does not wish to encourage convicted felons to "intimidate, beset and harass," Stein v. New York, 346 U. S. 156, 178, a discharged jury in an effort to establish possible grounds for a new trial. Our courts have always been alert to protect the sanctity of the jury process. McDonald v. Pless, 238 U. S. 264; see Castaldi v. United States, 251 F. Supp. 681. But in allowing Parker to overturn his conviction on the basis of what are no more than inconsequential incidents in an otherwise constitutionally flawless proceeding, the Court encourages others to follow his example in pursuing the jury and may be thought by some to commit federal courts in habeas corpus proceedings to interrogate the jury upon the mere allegation that a prejudicial remark has reached the ears of one of its members. Remmer v. United States, 347 U. S. 227. To any such result I cannot subscribe.

I think the Oregon Supreme Court correctly assessed the constitutional issue before us, and I would affirm its judgment.

Notes

[1] The record shows that Mrs. Parker first called juror number one, Mrs. Inwards, and upon finding her sympathetic obtained from her the names of those who had held out longest. Mrs. Inwards also informed Mrs. Parker that an alternate juror, Mrs. Gattman, was sympathetic to Parker's cause.

[2] The trial court purported to follow the State Supreme Court's decision in State v. Kristich, 226 Ore. 240, 359 P. 2d 1106, which held that where a bailiff had communicated with a jury on a point of law prejudice would be presumed. Thus the trial court said that "if the matters alleged in plaintiff's petition had been called to the Court's attention, the Court, on its own motion, would have granted the defendant a new trial," and held that Parker deserved a new trial because the communication was of a prejudicial nature. The Oregon Supreme Court reversed because it held that the trial court erroneously applied the new-trial standard to a post-conviction proceeding where only error of constitutional magnitude would serve to overthrow the verdict. The Supreme Court made no specific finding on prejudice but in distinguishing Turner v. Louisiana, 379 U. S. 466, noted a "difference in degree of the out-of-courtroom influence . . . so great as to

lead us to the conclusion that the bailiff's misconduct did not deprive defendant of a constitutionally correct trial." 245 Ore. ___, ___, 407 P. 2d 246, 249.

[3] Mrs. Inwards, who on recall testified that she must have been unconsciously influenced, denied any influence when first examined. In her further testimony she admitted that she was extremely upset by the verdict and would do anything short of committing perjury to overturn it. She stated, however, that although she had gone to the trial judge to discuss the verdict she had never mentioned the bailiff's remarks to him. In specifying that the bailiff's remarks "must" have influenced her she limited herself to declaring that they did so in connection with the pressure put on her by other jurors during the deliberations thus stating that "all in all" she "must" have been influenced.

Justice Harlan's dissent in Swann v. Adams (Jan 9, 1967)

MR. JUSTICE HARLAN, whom MR. JUSTICE STEWART joins, dissenting.

Reynolds v. Sims, 377 U. S. 533, laid down a "one man, one vote" mandate for the structuring of all state legislatures, but the Court there recognized, as it does again today, that "mathematical exactness . . . is not required," ante, at 443, and that variations are acceptable if they "are based on legitimate considerations incident to the effectuation of a rational state policy . . . ." 377 U. S., at 579, cited, ante, at 444. The Court refuses, however, to accept Florida's present legislative apportionment plan, at least on the record before us, because neither the State nor the District Court justified the relatively minor variations in population among some of the districts.

This holding seems to me to stand on its head the usual rule governing this Court's approach to the validity of legislative enactments, state as well as federal, which is, of course, that they come to us with a strong presumption of regularity and constitutionality. See, e. g., Butler v. Pennsylvania, 10 How. 402; Davis v. Department of Labor, 317 U. S. 249; Flemming v. Nestor, 363 U. S. 603. Accordingly, I do not believe the burden is on the State to justify every aspect of a complex plan completely restructuring its legislature, on pain of its being declared constitutionally invalid by the judiciary. I can think of no other area of law in which there is an analogous presumption of invalidity attaching to a legislative enactment of a State in an area of its admitted competence and superior experience. The burden of showing unconstitutionality should be left here, as in other cases, on the attacking party.

I would affirm the judgment of the District Court on the grounds (1) that the plan enacted by the Florida Legislature is in substantial compliance with the rule of Reynolds v. Sims, supra, and (2) that the appellants have not shown any invidious purpose for, or effect flowing from, the mathematical variations among certain districts.

Justice Harlan's concurrence and dissent in Time v. Hill (Jan 9, 1967)

MR. JUSTICE HARLAN, concurring in part and dissenting in part.

While I find much with which I agree in the opinion of the Court, I am constrained to express my disagreement with its view of the proper standard of liability to be applied on remand. Were the jury on retrial to find negligent rather than, as the Court requires, reckless or knowing "fictionalization," I think that federal constitutional requirements would be met.

I.

The Court's opinion demonstrates that the fictionalization doctrine upon which New York premises liability is one which would strip newsworthy material, otherwise protected, of its constitutional shield upon a mere showing of substantial falsity. I agree that the compensatory damage instruction given by the trial court required only such a determination and a finding of "commercial purpose" to sustain liability. And reading the opinion of the Appellate Division in the light of other New York decisions I believe that this was the theory upon which the jury finding was sustained.[1] True, the trial court told the jury that it must find that the appellant "altered or changed the true facts." But it did not specify whether this alteration or change would have to be reckless or negligent, or whether innocent variation from the facts as found by the jury would suffice for the award of damages. Clearly knowing falsification was not required, for the court refused appellant's request to charge that the jury must find in its favor unless it found knowing falsification.

The instructions on punitive damages required the jury to find at least "failure to make a reasonable investigation," in my view a crucial determination. However, the entire damage award was set aside as excessive by the Appellate Division which found it unduly influenced by inflammatory evidence. On remand for reconsideration of damages, only a compensatory award was made. This was the award affirmed by the Court of Appeals in the decision we are reviewing. With the case in this posture, I do not think it can fairly be said that there has been a binding jury interpretation of the degree of fault involved in the fictionalization and I agree with the Court that the conduct involved would bear a variety of interpretations.

Like the Court, I consider that only a narrow problem is presented by these facts. To me this is not "privacy" litigation in its truest sense. See Prosser, Law of Torts § 112; Silver, Privacy and the First Amendment, 34 Ford. L. Rev. 553; but see Bloustein, Privacy as an Aspect of Human Dignity: An Answer to Dean Prosser, 39 N. Y. U. L. Rev. 962. No claim is made that there was any intrusion upon the Hills' solitude or private affairs in order to obtain information for publication. The power of a State to control and remedy such intrusion for newsgathering purposes cannot be denied, cf. Mapp v. Ohio, 367 U. S. 643, but is not here asserted. Similarly it may be strongly contended that certain facts are of such limited public interest and so intimate and potentially embarrassing to an individual that the State may exercise its power to deter publication. Feeney v. Young, 191 App. Div. 501, 181 N. Y. Supp. 481; see Sidis v. F-R Pub. Corp., 113 F. 2d 806, 808. But the instructions to the jury, the opinions in the New York appellate courts, and indeed the arguments advanced by both sides before this Court all recognize that the theme of the article in question was a perfectly proper one and that an article of this type could have been prepared without liability. Winters v. New York, 333 U. S. 507, 510. The record is replete with articles commenting on the genesis of The Desperate Hours, one of which was prepared by the author himself and used by appellee to demonstrate the supposed falsity of the Life piece. Finally no claim is made that appellant published the article to advance a commercial interest in the play. There is no evidence to show that Time, Inc., had any financial interest in the production or even that the article was published as an advertisement. Thus the question whether a State may apply more stringent limitations to the use of the personality in "purely commercial advertising" is not before the Court. See Valentine v. Chrestensen, 316 U. S. 52.

II.

Having come this far in step with the Court's opinion, I must part company with its sweeping extension of the principles of New York Times Co. v. Sullivan, 376 U. S. 254. It was established in New York Times that mere falsity will not suffice to remove constitutional protection from published matter relating to the conduct of a public official that is of public concern. But that decision and those in which the Court has developed its doctrine, Rosenblatt v. Baer, 383 U. S. 75, Garrison v. Louisiana, 379 U. S. 64, have never found independent value in false publications[2] nor any reason for their protection except to add to the protection of truthful communication. And the Court has been quick to note that where private actions are involved the social interest in individual protection from falsity may be substantial. Rosenblatt v. Baer, supra, at 86-87, n. 13. Thus I believe that rigorous scrutiny of the principles underlying the rejection of the mere falsity criterion and the imposition of ancillary safeguards, as well as the interest which the State seeks to protect, is necessary to reach a proper resolution of this case.

Two essential principles seem to underlie the Court's rejection of the mere falsity criterion in New York Times. The first is the inevitability of some error in the situation presented in free debate especially when abstract matters are under consideration. Certainly that is illustrated here in the difficulty to be encountered in making a precise description of the relationship between the Hill incident and The Desperate Hours. The second is the Court's recognition that in many areas which are at the center of public debate "truth" is not a readily identifiable concept, and putting to the pre-existing prejudices of a jury the determination of what is "true" may effectively institute a system of censorship. Any nation which counts the Scopes trial as part of its heritage cannot so readily expose ideas to sanctions on a jury finding of falsity. See Cantwell v. Connecticut, 310 U. S. 296, 310. "The marketplace of ideas" where it functions still remains the best testing ground for truth.

But these arguments against suppressing what is found to be "false" on that ground alone do not negative a State's interest in encouraging the publication of well researched materials more likely to be true. Certainly it is within the power of the State to use positive means— the provision of facilities[3] and training of students[4]— to further this end. The issue presented in this case is the constitutionality of a State's employment of sanctions to accomplish that same goal. The Court acknowledges that sanctions may be employed against knowing or reckless falsehoods but would seem to grant a "talismanic immunity" to all unintentional errors. However, the distinction between the facts presented to us here and the situation at issue in the New York Times case and its progeny casts serious doubt on that grant of immunity and calls for a more limited "breathing space" than that granted in criticism of public officials.

First, we cannot avoid recognizing that we have entered an area where the "marketplace of ideas" does not function and where conclusions premised on the existence of that exchange are apt to be suspect. In Rosenblatt v. Baer, supra, the Court made the New York Times rationale operative where "the public has an independent interest in the qualifications and performance of the person who holds it [government position], beyond the general public interest in the qualifications and performance of all government employees . . . ." Id., at 86. In elaboration the Court said: "The employee's position must be one which would invite public scrutiny and discussion of the person holding it, entirely apart from the scrutiny and discussion occasioned by the particular charges in controversy." Id., at 87, n. 13. To me this seems a clear recognition of the fact that falsehood is more easily tolerated where public attention creates the strong likelihood of a competition among ideas. Here such competition is extremely unlikely for the scrutiny and discussion of the relationship of the Hill incident and the play is "occasioned by the particular charges in controversy" and the matter is not one in which the public has an "independent interest." It would be unreasonable to assume that Mr. Hill could find a forum for making a successful refutation of the Life material or that the public's interest in it would be sufficient for the truth to win out by comparison as it might in that area of discussion central to a free society. Thus the state interest in encouraging careful checking and preparation of published material is far stronger than in New York Times. The dangers of unchallengeable untruth are far too well documented to be summarily dismissed.[5]

Second, there is a vast difference in the state interest in protecting individuals like Mr. Hill from irresponsibly prepared publicity and the state interest in similar protection for a public official. In New York Times we acknowledged public officials to be a breed from whom hardiness to exposure to charges, innuendoes, and criticisms might be demanded and who voluntarily assumed the risk of such things by entry into the public arena. 376 U. S., at 273. But Mr. Hill came to public attention through an unfortunate circumstance not of his making rather than his voluntary actions and he can in no sense be considered to have "waived" any protection the State might justifiably afford him from irresponsible publicity. Not being inured to the vicissitudes of journalistic scrutiny such an individual is more easily injured and his means of self-defense are more limited. The public is less likely to view with normal skepticism what is written about him because it is not accustomed to seeing his name in the press and expects only a disinterested report.

The coincidence of these factors in this situation leads me to the view that a State should be free to hold the press to a duty of making a reasonable investigation of the underlying facts and limiting itself to "fair comment"[6] on the materials so gathered. Theoretically, of course, such a rule might slightly limit press discussion of matters touching individuals like Mr. Hill. But, from a pragmatic standpoint, until now the press, at least in New York, labored under the more exacting handicap of the existing New York privacy law and has certainly remained robust. Other professional activity of great social value is carried on under a duty of reasonable care[7] and there is no reason to suspect the press would be less hardy than medical practitioners or attorneys for example. The "freedom of the press" guaranteed by the First Amendment, and as reflected in the Fourteenth, cannot be thought to insulate all press conduct from review and responsibility for harm inflicted.[8] The majority would allow sanctions against such conduct only when it is morally culpable. I insist that it can also be reached when it creates a severe risk of irremediable harm to individuals involuntarily exposed to it and powerless to protect themselves against it. I would remand the case to the New York courts for possible retrial under that principle.

A constitutional doctrine which relieves the press of even this minimal responsibility in cases of this sort seems to me unnecessary and ultimately harmful to the permanent good health of the press itself. If the New York Times case has ushered in such a trend it will prove in its long-range impact to have done a disservice to the true values encompassed in the freedoms of speech and press.

Notes

[1] The majority in the New York Appellate Division denied that the article could "be characterized as a mere dissemination of news, nor even an effort to supply legitimate newsworthy information. . . ." They added that "points of similarity in the book and the occurrence . . . justified neither the identification nor the commercial exploitation of plaintiffs' name and family with the play." Justice Rabin, concurring, agreed that the subject could have been presented without liability "albeit the presentation of such newsworthy material increases the publisher's circulation." The New York Court of Appeals affirmed "on the majority and concurring opinions at the Appellate Division." The decision below seems to have ample support in New York law. See, e. g., Spahn v. Julian Messner, Inc., 18 N. Y. 2d 324, 221 N. E. 2d 543; Binns v. Vitagraph Co., 147 App. Div. 783, 132 N. Y. Supp. 237, aff'd 210 N. Y. 51, 103 N. E. 1108; Youssoupoff v. CBS, Inc., 41 Misc. 2d 42, 244 N. Y. S. 2d 701, aff'd, 19 App. Div. 2d 865, 244 N. Y. S. 2d 1; Koussevitzky v. Allen, Towne & Heath, Inc., 188 Misc. 479, 68 N. Y. S. 2d 779, aff'd, 272 App. Div. 759, 69 N. Y. S. 2d 432.

[2] The passage from Garrison v. Louisiana, supra, quoted in the opinion of the Court makes clear that the only interest in protecting falsehood is to give added "breathing space" to truth. It is undeniable that falsity may be published, especially in the political arena, with what may be considered "good" motives—for example a good-faith belief in the absolute necessity of defeating an "evil" candidate. But the Court does not remove state power to control such conduct, thus underlining the strong social interest in discouraging

false publication.

[3] Thus the State may take land for the construction of library facilities. E. g., Hayford v. Bangor, 102 Me. 340, 66 A. 731; Laird v. Pittsburg, 205 Pa. 1, 54 A. 324.

[4] Thus many state universities have professional schools of journalism. See 3 Department of Health, Educ. & Welfare, Education Directory—Higher Education.

[5] See Riesman, Democracy and Defamation: Fair Game and Fair Comment I, 42 Col. L. Rev. 1085; Beauharnais v. Illinois, 343 U. S. 250; State v. Klapprott, 127 N. J. L. 395, 22 A. 2d 877. And despite the Court's denial that the opportunity for rebuttal is germane, it must be the circulation of falsity and the harm stemming from it which lead the Court to allow the imposition of liability at all. For the Court finds the subject of the Life article "a matter of public interest." And it states that "[e]xposure of the self to others in varying degrees is a concomitant of life in a civilized community." Thus it could not permit New York to allow compensation for mere exposure unless it is holding, as I am sure it is not, that the presence of some reckless falsehood in written material strips it of all constitutional protection. The Court's suggestion that Mr. Hill might not be anxious to rebut the falsehood because it might increase his harm from exposure is equally applicable to libel actions where the opportunity to rebut may be limited by fear of reiterating the libel. And this factor emphasizes, rather than lessens, the state interest in discouraging falsehood for it increases the likelihood that falsity will continue to circulate to the detriment of some when truth should be encouraged "for the benefit of all of us."

[6] A negligence standard has been applied in libel actions both where the underlying facts are alleged to be libelous, Layne v. Tribune Co., 108 Fla. 177, 146 So. 234, and where comment is the subject of the action, Clancy v. Daily News Corp., 202 Minn. 1, 277 N. W. 264. Similarly the press should not be constitutionally insulated from privacy actions brought by parties in the position of Mr. Hill when reasonable care has not been taken in ascertaining or communicating the underlying facts or where the publisher has not kept within the traditional boundaries of "fair comment" with relation to underlying facts and honest opinion. See Prosser, Law of Torts § 110, at 815-816. Similar standards of reasonable investigation and presentation have long been applied in misrepresentation cases. See, e. g., International Products Co. v. Erie R. Co., 244 N. Y. 331, 155 N. E. 662; Nash v. Minnesota Title Ins. & Trust Co., 163 Mass. 574, 40 N. E. 1039. Under such a standard the fact that the publication involved in this case was not defamatory would enter into a determination of the amount of care which would have been reasonable in the preparation of the article.

[7] See, e. g., McCoid, The Care Required of Medical Practitioners, 12 Vand. L. Rev. 549; Wade, The Attorney's Liability for Negligence, 12 Vand. L. Rev. 755. It may be argued that other professions are distinguishable because practitioners may insure against liability. But this course is also open to the press. Developments in the Law, Defamation, 69 Harv. L. Rev. 875, 906.

[8] This Court has never held that the press has an absolute privilege to publish falsity. There is nothing in the history of the First Amendment, or the Fourteenth, to

indicate that the authors contemplated restrictions on the ability of private persons to seek legal redress for press-inflicted injury. See generally Levy, Legacy of Suppression; Duniway, The Development of Freedom of the Press in Massachusetts. The Founders rejected an attempt by Madison to add to Art. I, § 10, a guarantee of freedom of the press against state action. The main argument advanced against it was that it would unduly interfere with the proper powers of the States. See 5 Madison's Writings 378 (Hunt ed.); 1 Annals of Cong. 756.

Justice Harlan's dissent in Garrity v. New Jersey (Jan 16, 1967)

MR. JUSTICE HARLAN, whom MR. JUSTICE CLARK and MR. JUSTICE STEWART join, dissenting.

The majority opinion here and the plurality opinion in Spevack v. Klein, post, p. 511, stem from fundamental misconceptions about the logic and necessities of the constitutional privilege against self-incrimination. I fear that these opinions will seriously and quite needlessly hinder the protection of other important public values. I must dissent here, as I do in Spevack.

The majority employs a curious mixture of doctrines to invalidate these convictions, and I confess to difficulty in perceiving the intended relationships among the various segments of its opinion. I gather that the majority believes that the possibility that these policemen might have been discharged had they refused to provide information pertinent to their public responsibilities is an impermissible "condition" imposed by New Jersey upon petitioners' privilege against self-incrimination. From this premise the majority draws the conclusion that the statements obtained from petitioners after a warning that discharge was possible were inadmissible. Evidently recognizing the weakness of its conclusion, the majority attempts to bring to its support illustrations from the lengthy series of cases in which this Court, in light of all the relevant circumstances, has adjudged the voluntariness in fact of statements obtained from accused persons.

The majority is apparently engaged in the delicate task of riding two unruly horses at once: it is presumably arguing simultaneously that the statements were involuntary as a matter of fact, in the same fashion that the statements in Chambers v. Florida, 309 U. S. 227, and Haynes v. Washington, 373 U. S. 503, were thought to be involuntary, and that the statements were inadmissible as a matter of law, on the premise that they were products of an impermissible condition imposed on the constitutional privilege. These are very different contentions and require separate replies, but in my opinion both contentions are plainly mistaken, for reasons that follow.

I.

I turn first to the suggestion that these statements were involuntary in fact. An assessment of the voluntariness of the various statements in issue here requires a more comprehensive examination of the pertinent circumstances than the majority has undertaken.

The petitioners were at all material times policemen in the boroughs of Bellmawr and Barrington, New Jersey. Garrity was Bellmawr's chief of police and Virtue one of its police officers; Holroyd, Elwell, and Murray were police officers in Barrington. Another defendant below, Mrs. Naglee, the clerk of Bellmawr's municipal court, has since died. In June 1961 the New Jersey Supreme Court sua sponte directed the State's Attorney General to investigate reports of traffic ticket fixing in Bellmawr and Barrington. Subsequent investigations produced evidence that the petitioners, in separate conspiracies, had falsified municipal court records, altered traffic tickets, and diverted moneys produced from bail and fines to unauthorized purposes. In the course of these investigations the State obtained two sworn statements from each of the petitioners; portions of those statements were admitted at trial. The petitioners were convicted in two separate trials of conspiracy to obstruct the proper administration of the state motor traffic laws, the cases being now consolidated for purposes of our review. The Supreme Court of New Jersey affirmed all the convictions.

The first statements were taken from the petitioners by the State's Deputy Attorney General in August and November 1961. All of the usual indicia of duress are wholly absent. As the state court noted, there was "no physical coercion, no overbearing tactics of psychological persuasion, no lengthy incommunicado detention, or efforts to humiliate or ridicule the defendants." 44 N. J. 209, 220, 207 A. 2d 689, 695. The state court found no evidence that any of the petitioners were reluctant to offer statements, and concluded that the interrogations were conducted with a "high degree of civility and restraint." Ibid.

These conclusions are fully substantiated by the record. The statements of the Bellmawr petitioners were taken in a room in the local firehouse, for which Chief Garrity himself had made arrangements. None of the petitioners were in custody before or after the depositions were taken; each apparently continued to pursue his ordinary duties as a public official of the community. The statements were recorded by a court stenographer, who testified that he witnessed no indications of unwillingness or even significant hesitation on the part of any of the petitioners. The Bellmawr petitioners did not have counsel present, but the Deputy Attorney General testified without contradiction that Garrity had informed him as they strolled between Garrity's office and the firehouse that he had arranged for counsel, but thought that none would be required at that stage. The interrogations were not excessively lengthy, and reasonable efforts were made to assure the physical comfort of the witnesses. Mrs. Naglee, the clerk of the Bellmawr municipal court, who was known to suffer from a heart ailment, was assured that questioning would cease if she felt any discomfort.

The circumstances in which the depositions of the Barrington petitioners were taken are less certain, for the New Jersey Supreme Court found that there was an informal agreement at the Barrington trial that the defendants would argue simply that the possibility of dismissal made the statements "involuntary as a matter of law." The defense did not contend that the statements were the result of physical or mental coercion, or that the wills of the Barrington petitioners were overborne. Accordingly, the State was never obliged to offer evidence of the voluntariness in fact of the statements. We are, however, informed that the three Barrington petitioners had counsel present as their depositions were taken. Insofar as the majority suggests that the Barrington statements are involuntary in fact, in the fashion of Chambers or Haynes, it has introduced a factual contention never urged by the Barrington petitioners and never considered by the courts of New Jersey.

As interrogation commenced, each of the petitioners was sworn, carefully informed that he need not give any information, reminded that any information given might be used in a subsequent criminal prosecution, and warned that as a police officer he was subject to a proceeding to discharge him if he failed to provide information relevant to his public responsibilities. The cautionary statements varied slightly, but all, except that given to Mrs. Naglee, included each of the three warnings.[1] Mrs. Naglee was not told that she could be removed from her position at the court if she failed to give information pertinent to the discharge of her duties. All of the petitioners consented to give statements, none displayed any significant hesitation, and none suggested that the decision to offer information was motivated by the possibility of discharge.

A second statement was obtained from each of the petitioners in September and December 1962. These statements were not materially different in content or circumstances from the first. The only significant distinction was that the interrogator did not advert even obliquely to any possibility of dismissal. All the petitioners were cautioned that they were entitled to remain silent, and there was no evidence whatever of physical or mental coercion.

All of the petitioners testified at trial, and gave evidence essentially consistent with the statements taken from them. At a preliminary hearing conducted at the Bellmawr trial to determine the voluntariness of the statements, the Bellmawr petitioners offered no evidence beyond proof of the warning given them.

The standards employed by the Court to assess the voluntariness of an accused's statements have reflected a number of values, and thus have emphasized a variety of factual criteria. The criteria employed have included threats of imminent danger, Payne v. Arkansas, 356 U. S. 560, physical deprivations, Reck v. Pate, 367 U. S. 433, repeated or extended interrogation, Chambers v. Florida, 309 U. S. 227, limits on access to counsel or friends, Crooker v. California, 357 U. S. 433, length and illegality of detention under state law, Haynes v. Washington, 373 U. S. 503, individual weakness or incapacity, Lynumn v. Illinois, 372 U. S. 528, and the adequacy of warnings of constitutional rights, Davis v. North Carolina, 384 U. S. 737. Whatever the criteria employed, the duty of the Court has been "to examine the entire record," and thereby to determine whether the accused's will "was overborne by the sustained pressures upon him." Davis v. North Carolina, 384 U. S. 737, 741, 739.

It would be difficult to imagine interrogations to which these criteria of duress were more completely inapplicable, or in which the requirements which have subsequently been imposed by this Court on police questioning were more thoroughly satisfied. Each of the petitioners received a complete and explicit reminder of his constitutional privilege. Three of the petitioners had counsel present; at least a fourth had consulted counsel but freely determined that his presence was unnecessary. These petitioners were not in any fashion "swept from familiar surroundings into police custody, surrounded by antagonistic forces, and subjected to the techniques of persuasion . . . ." Miranda v. Arizona, 384 U. S. 436, 461. I think it manifest that, under the standards developed by this Court to assess voluntariness, there is no basis for saying that any of these statements were made involuntarily.

II.

The issue remaining is whether the statements were inadmissible because they were "involuntary as a matter of law," in that they were given after a warning that New Jersey policemen may be discharged for failure to provide information pertinent to their public responsibilities. What is really involved on this score, however, is not in truth a question of "voluntariness" at all, but rather whether the condition imposed by the State on the exercise of the privilege against self-incrimination, namely dismissal from office, in this instance serves in itself to render the statements inadmissible. Absent evidence of involuntariness in fact, the admissibility of these statements thus hinges on the validity of the consequence which the State acknowledged might have resulted if the statements had not been given. If the consequence is constitutionally permissible, there can surely be no objection if the State cautions the witness that it may follow if he remains silent. If both the consequence and the warning are constitutionally permissible, a witness is obliged, in order to prevent the use of his statements against him in a criminal prosecution, to prove under the standards established since Brown v. Mississippi, 297 U. S. 278, that as a matter of fact the statements were involuntarily made. The central issues here are therefore identical to those presented in Spevack v. Klein, supra: whether consequences may properly be permitted to result to a claimant after his invocation of the constitutional privilege, and if so, whether the consequence in question is permissible. For reasons which I have stated in Spevack v. Klein, in my view nothing in the logic or purposes of the privilege demands that all consequences which may result from a witness' silence be forbidden merely because that silence is privileged. The validity of a consequence depends both upon the hazards, if any, it presents to the integrity of the privilege and upon the urgency of the public interests it is designed to protect.

It can hardly be denied that New Jersey is permitted by the Constitution to establish reasonable qualifications and standards of conduct for its public employees. Nor can it be said that it is arbitrary or unreasonable for New Jersey to insist that its employees furnish the appropriate authorities with information pertinent to their employment. Cf. Beilan v. Board of Education, 357 U. S. 399; Slochower v. Board of Education, 350 U. S. 551. Finally, it is surely plain that New Jersey may in particular require its employees to assist in the prevention and detection of unlawful activities by officers of the state government. The urgency of these requirements is the more obvious here, where the conduct in question is that of officials directly entrusted with the administration of justice. The importance for our systems of justice of the integrity of local police forces can scarcely be exaggerated. Thus, it need only be recalled that this Court itself has often intervened in state criminal prosecutions precisely on the ground that this might encourage high standards of police behavior. See, e. g., Ashcraft v. Tennessee, 322 U. S. 143; Miranda v. Arizona, supra. It must be concluded, therefore, that the sanction at issue here is reasonably calculated to serve the most basic interests of the citizens of New Jersey.

The final question is the hazard, if any, which this sanction presents to the constitutional privilege. The purposes for which, and the circumstances in which, an officer's discharge might be ordered under New Jersey law plainly may vary. It is of course possible that discharge might in a given case be predicated on an imputation of guilt drawn from the use of the privilege, as was thought by this Court to have occurred in Slochower v. Board of Education, supra. But from our vantage point, it would be quite improper to assume that New Jersey will employ these procedures for purposes other than to assess in good faith an employee's continued fitness for public employment. This Court, when a state procedure for investigating the loyalty and fitness of public employees might result either in the Slochower situation or in an assessment in good faith of an employee, has until today consistently paused to examine the actual circumstances of each case. Beilan v. Board of Education, supra; Nelson v. Los Angeles County, 362 U. S. 1. I am unable to see any justification for the majority's abandonment of that process; it is well calculated both to protect the essential purposes of the privilege and to guarantee the most generous opportunities for the pursuit of other public values. The majority's broad prohibition, on the other hand, extends the scope of the privilege beyond its essential purposes, and seriously hampers the protection of other important values. Despite the majority's disclaimer, it is quite plain that the logic of its prohibitory rule would in this situation prevent the discharge of these policemen. It would therefore entirely forbid a sanction which presents, at least on its face, no hazard to the purposes of the constitutional privilege, and which may reasonably be expected to serve important public interests. We are not entitled to assume that discharges will be used either to vindicate impermissible inferences of guilt or to penalize privileged silence, but must instead presume that this procedure is only intended and will only be used to establish and enforce standards of conduct for public employees.[2] As such, it does not minimize or endanger the petitioners' constitutional privilege against self-incrimination.[3]

I would therefore conclude that the sanction provided by the State is constitutionally permissible. From this, it surely follows that the warning given of the possibility of discharge is constitutionally unobjectionable. Given the constitutionality both of the sanction and of the warning of its application, the petitioners would be constitutionally entitled to exclude the use of their statements as evidence in a criminal prosecution against them only if it is found that the statements were, when given, involuntary in fact. For the reasons stated above, I cannot agree that these statements were involuntary in fact.

I would affirm the judgments of the Supreme Court of New Jersey.

Notes

[1] The warning given to Chief Garrity is typical. "I want to advise you that anything you say must be said of your own free will and accord without any threats or promises or coercion, and anything you say may be, of course, used against you or any other person in any subsequent criminal proceedings in the courts of our state.

"You do have, under our law, as you probably know, a privilege to refuse to make any disclosure which may tend to incriminate you. If you make a disclosure with knowledge of this right or privilege, voluntarily, you thereby waive that right or privilege in relation to any other questions which I might put to you relevant to such disclosure in this investigation.

"This right or privilege which you have is somewhat limited to the extent that you as a police officer under the laws of our state, may be subjected to a proceeding to have you removed from office if you refuse to answer a question put to you under oath pertaining to your office or your function within that office. It doesn't mean, however, you can't exercise the right. You do have the right."

A. "No, I will cooperate."

Q. "Understanding this, are you willing to proceed at this time and answer any questions?"

A. "Yes."

[2] The legislative history of N. J. Rev. Stat. 2A:81-17.1 provides nothing which clearly indicates the purposes of the statute, beyond what is to be inferred from its face. In any event, the New Jersey Supreme Court noted below that the State would be entitled, even without the statutory authorization, to discharge state employees who declined to provide information relevant to their official responsibilities. There is therefore nothing to which this Court could properly now look to forecast the purposes for which or circumstances in which New Jersey might discharge those who have invoked the constitutional privilege.

[3] The late Judge Jerome Frank thus once noted, in the course of a spirited defense of the privilege, that it would be entirely permissible to discharge police officers who decline, on grounds of the privilege, to disclose information pertinent to their public responsibilities. Judge Frank quoted the following with approval:

" `Duty required them to answer. Privilege permitted them to refuse to answer. They chose to exercise the privilege, but the exercise of such privilege was wholly inconsistent with their duty as police officers. They claim that they had a constitutional right to refuse to answer under the circumstances, but . . . they had no constitutional right to remain police officers in the face of their clear violation of the duty imposed upon them.' Christal v. Police Commission of San Francisco." Citing 33 Cal. App. 2d 564, 92 P. 2d 416. (Emphasis added by Judge Frank.) United States v. Field, 193 F. 2d 92, 106 (separate opinion).

Justice Harlan's dissent in Spevack v. Klein (Jan 16, 1967)

MR. JUSTICE HARLAN, whom MR. JUSTICE CLARK and MR. JUSTICE STEWART join, dissenting.

This decision, made in the name of the Constitution, permits a lawyer suspected of professional misconduct to thwart direct official inquiry of him without fear of disciplinary action. What is done today will be disheartening and frustrating to courts and bar associations throughout the country in their efforts to maintain high standards at the bar.

It exposes this Court itself to the possible indignity that it may one day have to admit to its own bar such a lawyer unless it can somehow get at the truth of suspicions, the investigation of which the applicant has previously succeeded in blocking. For I can perceive no distinction between "admission" and "disbarment" in the rationale of what is now held. The decision might even lend some color of support for justifying the appointment to the bench of a lawyer who, like petitioner, prevents full inquiry into his professional behavior. And, still more pervasively, this decision can hardly fail to encourage oncoming generations of lawyers to think of their calling as imposing on them no higher standards of behavior than might be acceptable in the general market-place. The soundness of a constitutional doctrine carrying such denigrating import for our profession is surely suspect on its face.

Six years ago a majority of this Court, in Cohen v. Hurley, 366 U. S. 117, set its face against the doctrine that now prevails, bringing to bear in support of the Court's holding, among other things, the then-established constitutional proposition that the Fourteenth Amendment did not make applicable to the States the Fifth Amendment as such. Three years later another majority of the Court, in Malloy v. Hogan, 378 U. S. 1, decided to make the Fifth Amendment applicable to the States and in doing so cast doubt on the continuing vitality of Cohen v. Hurley. The question now is whether Malloy requires the overruling of Cohen in its entirety. For reasons that follow I think it clear that it does not.

It should first be emphasized that the issue here is plainly not whether lawyers may "enjoy first-class citizenship."

Nor is the issue whether lawyers may be deprived of their federal privilege against self-incrimination, whether or not criminal prosecution is undertaken against them. These diversionary questions have of course not been presented or even remotely suggested by this case either here or in the courts of New York. The plurality opinion's vivid rhetoric thus serves only to obscure the issues with which we are actually confronted, and to hinder their serious consideration. The true question here is instead the proper scope and effect of the privilege against self-incrimination under the Fourteenth Amendment in state disciplinary proceedings against attorneys.[1] In particular, we are required to determine whether petitioner's disbarment for his failure to provide information relevant to charges of misconduct in carrying on his law practice impermissibly vitiated the protection afforded by the privilege. This important question warrants more complete and discriminating analysis than that given to it by the plurality opinion.

This Court reiterated only last Term that the constitutional privilege against self-incrimination "has never been given the full scope which the values it helps to protect suggest." Schmerber v. California, 384 U. S. 757, 762. The Constitution contains no formulae with which we can calculate the areas within this "full scope" to which the privilege should extend, and the Court has therefore been obliged to fashion for itself standards for the application of the privilege. In federal cases stemming from Fifth Amendment claims, the Court has chiefly derived its standards from consideration of two factors: the history and purposes of the privilege, and the character and urgency of the other public interests involved. See, e. g., Orloff v. Willoughby, 345 U. S. 83; Davis v. United States, 328 U. S. 582; Shapiro v. United States, 335 U. S. 1. If, as Malloy v. Hogan, supra, suggests, the federal standards imposed by the Fifth Amendment are now to be extended to the States through the Fourteenth Amendment, see also Griffin v. California, 380 U. S. 609, it would follow that these same factors must be no less relevant in cases centering on Fourteenth Amendment claims. In any event, the construction consistently given to the Fourteenth Amendment by this Court would require their consideration. Bates v. City of Little Rock, 361 U. S. 516. I therefore first turn to these factors to assess the validity under the Fourteenth Amendment of petitioner's disbarment.

It cannot be claimed that the purposes served by the New York rules at issue here, compendiously aimed at "ambulance chasing" and its attendant evils, are unimportant or unrelated to the protection of legitimate state interests. This Court has often held that the States have broad authority to devise both requirements for admission and standards of practice for those who wish to enter the professions. E. g., Hawker v. New York, 170 U. S. 189; Dent v. West Virginia, 129 U. S. 114; Barsky v. Board of Regents, 347 U. S. 442. The States may demand any qualifications which have "a rational connection with the applicant's fitness or capacity," Schware v. Board of Bar Examiners, 353 U. S. 232, 239, and may exclude any applicant who fails to satisfy them. In particular, a State may require evidence of good character, and may place the onus of its production upon the applicant. Konigsberg v. State Bar of California, 366 U. S. 36. Finally, a State may without constitutional objection require in the same fashion continuing evidence of professional and moral fitness as a condition of the retention of the right to practice. Cohen v. Hurley, 366 U. S. 117. All this is in no way questioned by today's decision.

As one prerequisite of continued practice in New York, the Appellate Division, Second Department, of the Supreme Court of New York has determined that attorneys must actively assist the courts and the appropriate professional groups in the prevention and detection of unethical legal activities. The Second Department demands that attorneys maintain various records, file statements of retainer in certain kinds of cases, and upon request provide information, all relevant to the use by the attorneys of contingent fee arrangements in such cases. These rules are intended to protect the public from the abuses revealed by a lengthy series of investigations of malpractices in the geographical area represented by the Second Department. It cannot be said that these conditions are arbitrary or unreasonable, or that they are unrelated to an attorney's continued fitness to practice. English courts since Edward I have endeavored to regulate the qualification and practice of lawyers, always in hope that this might better assure the integrity and evenhandedness of the administration of justice.[2] Very similar efforts have been made in the United States since the 17th century.[3] These efforts have protected the systems of justice in both countries from abuse, and have directly contributed to public confidence in those systems. Such efforts give appropriate recognition to the principle accepted both here and in England that lawyers are officers of the court who perform a fundamental role in the administration of justice.[4] The rules at issue here are in form and spirit a continuation of these efforts, and accordingly are reasonably calculated to serve the most enduring interests of the citizens of New York.

Without denying the urgency or significance of the public purposes served by these rules, the plurality opinion has seemingly concluded that they may not be enforced because any consequence of a claim of the privilege against self-incrimination which renders that claim "costly" is an "instrument of compulsion" which impermissibly infringes on the protection offered by the privilege. Apart from brief obiter dicta in recent opinions of this Court, this broad proposition is entirely without support in the construction hitherto given to the privilege, and is directly inconsistent with a series of cases in which this Court has indicated the principles which are properly applicable here. The Court has not before held that the Federal Government and the States are forbidden to permit any consequences to result from a claim of the privilege; it has instead recognized that such consequences may vary widely in kind and intensity, and that these differences warrant individual examination both of the hazard, if any, offered to the essential purposes of the privilege, and of the public interests protected by the consequence. This process is far better calculated than the broad prohibition embraced by the plurality to serve both the purposes of the privilege and the other important public values which are often at stake in such cases. It would assure the integrity of the privilege, and yet guarantee the most generous opportunities for the pursuit of other public values, by selecting the rule or standard most appropriate for the hazards and characteristics of each consequence.

One such rule has already been plainly approved by this Court. It seems clear to me that this rule is applicable to the situation now before us. The Court has repeatedly recognized that it is permissible to deny a status or authority to a claimant of the privilege against self-incrimination if his claim has prevented full assessment of his qualifications for the status or authority. Under this rule, the applicant may not both decline to disclose information necessary to demonstrate his fitness, and yet demand that he receive the benefits of the status. He may not by his interjection of the privilege either diminish his obligation to establish his qualifications, or escape the consequences exacted by the State for a failure to satisfy that obligation.

This rule was established by this Court in Orloff v. Willoughby, 345 U. S. 83. The Court there held that a doctor who refused, under a claim of the privilege against self-incrimination, to divulge whether he was a Communist was not entitled by right to receive a commission as an Army officer, although he had apparently satisfied every other prerequisite for a commission. The Court expressly noted that "[n]o one believes he can be punished" for asserting the privilege, but said that it had "no hesitation" in holding that the petitioner nonetheless could not both rely on the privilege to deny relevant information to the commissioning authorities and demand that he be appointed to a position of "honor and trust." 345 U. S., at 91. The Court concluded that "we cannot doubt that the President of the United States, before certifying his confidence in an officer and appointing him to a commissioned rank, has the right to learn whatever facts the President thinks may affect his fitness." Ibid.

Analogous problems were involved in Kimm v. Rosenberg, 363 U. S. 405, in which the Court held that an alien whose deportation had been ordered was ineligible for a discretionary order permitting his voluntary departure. The alien was held to be ineligible because he had failed to establish that he was not affiliated with the Communist Party, in that he refused to answer questions about membership in the Party on grounds that the answers might incriminate him. The petitioner could not prevent the application of a sanction imposed as a result of his silence by interposing the privilege against self-incrimination as a basis for that silence.

These principles have also been employed by this Court to hold that failure to incriminate one's self can result in denial of the removal of one's case from a state to a federal court, Maryland v. Soper (No. 1), 270 U. S. 9, and by the Fourth Circuit to hold that a bankrupt's failure to disclose the disposition of his property, although disclosure might incriminate him, requires the denial of a discharge in bankruptcy. Kaufman v. Hurwitz, 176 F. 2d 210.

This Court has applied similar principles in a series of cases involving claims under the Fourteenth Amendment. These cases all antedate Malloy v. Hogan, and thus are presumably now subject to the "federal standards," but until today those standards included the principles of Orloff v. Willoughby, and Malloy v. Hogan therefore could not alone require a different result. The fulcrum of these cases has been Slochower v. Board of Education, 350 U. S. 551. The appellant there was an associate professor at Brooklyn College who invoked the Fifth Amendment privilege before an investigating committee of the United States Senate, and was subsequently discharged from his position at the college by reason of that occurrence. The Court held that his removal was a denial of the due process demanded by the Fourteenth Amendment. Its reasons were apparently two: first, the Board had attached a "sinister meaning," in the form of an imputation of guilt, to Slochower's invocation of the privilege; and second, the Board was not engaged in a bona fide effort to elicit information relevant to assess the "qualifications of its employees." The state authorities "had possessed the pertinent information for 12 years," and in any event the questions put to Slochower by the committee were "wholly unrelated" to his university functions. 350 U. S., at 558.

The elements of the holding in Slochower have subsequently been carefully considered on several occasions by this Court. See, e. g., Beilan v. Board of Education, 357 U. S. 399; Lerner v. Casey, 357 U. S. 468; Nelson v. Los Angeles County, 362 U. S. 1. These cases, when read with Slochower, make plain that so long as state authorities do not derive any imputation of guilt from a claim of the privilege, they may in the course of a bona fide assessment of an employee's fitness for public employment require that the employee disclose information reasonably related to his fitness, and may order his discharge if he declines. Identical principles have been applied by this Court to applicants for admission to the bar who have refused to produce information pertinent to their professional and moral qualifications. Konigsberg v. State Bar of California, 366 U. S. 36; In re Anastaplo, 366 U. S. 82. In sum, all these cases adopted principles under the Fourteenth Amendment which are plainly congruent with those applied in Orloff v. Willoughby, supra, and other federal cases to Fifth Amendment claims.

The petitioner here does not contend, and the plurality opinion does not suggest, that the state courts have derived any inference of guilt from petitioner's claim of the privilege. The state courts have expressly disclaimed all such inferences. 24 App. Div. 2d 653, 654. Nor is it suggested that the proceedings against petitioner were not an effort in good faith to assess his qualifications for continued practice in New York, or that the information sought from petitioner was not reasonably relevant to those qualifications. It would therefore follow that under the construction consistently given by this Court both to the privilege under the Fifth Amendment and to the Due Process Clause of the Fourteenth Amendment, petitioner's disbarment is constitutionally permissible.

The plurality opinion does not pause either to acknowledge the previous handling of these issues or to explain why the privilege must now be supposed to forbid all consequences which may result from privileged silence. This is scarcely surprising, for the plurality opinion would create a novel and entirely unnecessary extension of the privilege which would exceed the needs of the privilege's purpose and seriously inhibit the protection of other public interests. The petitioner was not denied his privilege against self-incrimination, nor was he penalized for its use; he was denied his authority to practice law within the State of New York by reason of his failure to satisfy valid obligations imposed by the State as a condition of that authority. The only hazard in this process to the integrity of the privilege is the possibility that it might induce involuntary disclosures of incriminating materials; the sanction precisely calculated to eliminate that hazard is to exclude the use by prosecuting authorities of such materials and of their fruits. This Court has, upon proof of involuntariness, consistently forbidden their use since Brown v. Mississippi, 297 U. S. 278, and now, as my Brother WHITE has emphasized, the plurality has intensified this protection still further with the broad prohibitory rule it has announced today in Garrity v. New Jersey, ante, p. 493. It is true that this Court has on occasion gone a step further, and forbidden the practices likely to produce involuntary disclosures, but those cases are readily distinguishable. They have uniformly involved either situations in which the entire process was thought both to present excessive risks of coercion and to be foreign to our accusatorial system, as in Miranda v. Arizona, 384 U. S.

436, or situations in which the only possible purpose of the practice was thought to be to penalize the accused for his use of the constitutional privilege, as in Griffin v. California, 380 U. S. 609. Both situations are plainly remote from that in issue here. None of the reasons thought to require the prohibitions established in those cases have any relevance in the situation now before us; nothing in New York's efforts in good faith to assure the integrity of its judicial system destroys, inhibits, or even minimizes the petitioner's constitutional privilege. There is therefore no need to speculate whether lawyers, or those in any other profession or occupation, have waived in some unspecified fashion a measure of the protection afforded by the constitutional privilege; it suffices that the State is earnestly concerned with an urgent public interest, and that it has selected methods for the pursuit of that interest which do not prevent attainment of the privilege's purposes.

I think it manifest that this Court is required neither by the logic of the privilege against self-incrimination nor by previous authority to invalidate these state rules, and thus to overturn the disbarment of the petitioner. Today's application of the privilege serves only to hamper appropriate protection of other fundamental public values.[5]

In view of these conclusions, I find it unnecessary to reach the alternative basis of the Court of Appeals' decision, the "required records doctrine." See Shapiro v. United States, 335 U. S. 1.

I would affirm the judgment of disbarment.

Notes

[1] No claim has been made either here or in the state courts that the underlying facts representing petitioner's alleged conduct were not such as to entitle him to claim the privilege against self-incrimination. We therefore deal with the case on the premise that his claim of privilege was properly asserted.

[2] The history of these efforts is outlined in Cohen, A History of the English Bar and Attornatus to 1450, 277 et seq., 2 Holdsworth, A History of English Law 317, 504 et seq.; 6 id., 431 et seq.

[3] These efforts are traced in Warren, History of the American Bar, passim.

[4] Evidences of this principle may be found in the opinions of this Court. See, e. g., Ex parte Bradley, 7 Wall. 364; Powell v. Alabama, 287 U. S. 45; Gideon v. Wainwright, 372 U. S. 335.

[5] It should be noted that the principle that a license or status may be denied to one who refuses, under the shelter of the constitutional privilege, to disclose information pertinent to that status or privilege, has been adopted in a variety of situations by statute. See, e. g., 12 U. S. C. § 481; 47 U. S. C. §§ 308 (b), 312 (a) (4): 5 U. S. C. § 2283.

Justice Harlan's dissent in Chapman v. California (Feb 20, 1967)

MR. JUSTICE HARLAN, dissenting.
The Court today holds that the harmlessness of a trial error in a state criminal

prosecution, such error resulting from the allowance of prosecutorial comment barred by the Fourteenth Amendment, must be determined under a "necessary rule" of federal law. The Court imposes a revised version of the standard utilized in Fahy v. Connecticut, 375 U. S. 85, on state appellate courts, not because the Constitution requires that particular standard, but because the Court prefers it.

My understanding of our federal system, and my view of the rationale and function of harmless-error rules and their status under the Fourteenth Amendment, lead me to a very different conclusion. I would hold that a state appellate court's reasonable application of a constitutionally proper state harmless-error rule to sustain a state conviction constitutes an independent and adequate state ground of judgment. Believing this to be the situation here, I would dismiss the writ. Viator v. Stone, 336 U. S. 948.

I.

The key to the Court's opinion can, I think, be found in its statement that it cannot "leave to the States the formulation of the authoritative laws, rules, and remedies designed to protect people from infractions by the States of federally guaranteed rights," and that "in the absence of appropriate congressional action" the Court must fashion protective rules. The harmless-error rule now established flows from what is seemingly regarded as a power inherent in the Court's constitutional responsibilities rather than from the Constitution itself. The Court appears to acknowledge that other harmless-error formulations would be constitutionally permissible. It certainly indicates that Congress, for example, could impose a different formulation.[1]

I regard the Court's assumption of what amounts to a general supervisory power over the trial of federal constitutional issues in state courts as a startling constitutional development that is wholly out of keeping with our federal system and completely unsupported by the Fourteenth Amendment where the source of such a power must be found. The Fourteenth Amendment guarantees individuals against invasions by the States of fundamental rights, Palko v. Connecticut, 302 U. S. 319, and under more recent decisions of this Court some of the specifics of the Bill of Rights as well. See, e. g., in the context of this case, Malloy v. Hogan, 378 U. S. 1; Griffin v. California, 380 U. S. 609. It thus serves as a limitation on the actions of the States, and lodges in this Court the same power over state "laws, rules, and remedies" as the Court has always had over the "laws, rules, and remedies" created by Congress. This power was classically described by Chief Justice Marshall in Marbury v. Madison, 1 Cranch 137, 178:

"So if a law be in opposition to the constitution; if both the law and the constitution apply to a particular case, so that the court must either decide that case conformably to the law, disregarding the constitution; or conformably to the constitution, disregarding the law; the court must determine which of these conflicting rules governs the case. . . ."

Nothing in the Fourteenth Amendment purports to give federal courts supervisory powers, in the affirmative sense of McNabb v. United States, 318 U. S. 332, over state courts. See id., at 340-341. Moreover, where the constitutional power described by

Marshall has been invoked, the Court has always been especially reluctant to interfere with state procedural practices. See Spencer v. Texas, 385 U. S. 554. From the beginning of the federal Union, state courts have had power to decide issues of federal law and to formulate "authoritative laws, rules, and remedies" for the trial of those issues. The primary responsibility for the trial of state criminal cases still rests upon the States, and the only constitutional limitation upon these trials is that the laws, rules, and remedies applied must meet constitutional requirements. If they do not, this Court may hold them invalid. The Court has no power, however, to declare which of many admittedly constitutional alternatives a State may choose.[2] To impose uniform national requirements when alternatives are constitutionally permissible would destroy that opportunity for broad experimentation which is the genius of our federal system.

Even assuming that the Court has the power to fashion remedies and procedures binding on state courts for the protection of particular constitutional rights, I could not agree that a general harmless-error rule falls into that category. The harmless-error rules now utilized by all the States and in the federal judicial system are the product of judicial reform early in this century. Previously most American appellate courts, concerned about the harshness of criminal penalties, followed the rule imposed on English courts through the efforts of Baron Parke, and held that any error of substance required a reversal of conviction. See Orfield, Criminal Appeals in America 190. The reform movement, led by authorities like Roscoe Pound and Learned Hand, resulted in allowing courts to discontinue using reversal as a "necessary" remedy for particular errors and "to substitute judgment for the automatic application of rules . . . ." 4 Barron, Federal Practice and Procedure § 2571, at 438. This Court summarized the need for that development in the leading case of Kotteakos v. United States, 328 U. S. 750, 759:

"§ 269 [a federal harmless error provision] and similar state legislation grew out of widespread and deep conviction over the general course of appellate review in American criminal causes. This was shortly, as one trial judge put it after § 269 had become law, that courts of review `tower above the trials of criminal cases as impregnable citadels of technicality.' . . . [C]riminal trial became a game for sowing reversible error in the record."

Holding, as is done today, that a special harmless-error rule is a necessary remedy for a particular kind of error revives the unfortunate idea that appellate courts must act on particular errors rather than decide on reversal by an evaluation of the entire proceeding to determine whether the cause as a whole has been determined according to properly applicable law. In this case, California has recognized the impropriety of the trial comment here involved, and has given clear direction to state trial courts for the future. Certainly this is the appropriate remedy for the constitutional error committed. The challenged decision has no direct relation to federal constitutional provisions, rather it is an analysis of the question whether this admittedly improper comment had any significant impact on the outcome of the trial. In Kotteakos, supra, this Court described the "material factors" in harmless-error determinations as "the character of the proceeding, what is at stake upon its outcome, and the relation of the error asserted to casting the balance for decision on the case as a whole . . . ." Id., at 762. None of these factors has any relation to substantive constitutional provisions, and I think the Court errs in conceiving of an application of harmless-error rules as a remedy designed to safeguard particular constitutional rights.[3] It seems clear to me that harmless-error rules concern, instead, the fundamental integrity of the judicial proceedings as a whole.

As indicated above, I am of the opinion that the validity of a challenged state harmless-error rule itself is a federal constitutional question. Harmless-error rules may, as the Court says, "work very unfair and mischievous results." And just concern can be expressed over the possibility that state harmless-error decisions may result in the dilution of new constitutional doctrines because of state hostility to them. However, the record is barren of any showing that the California courts, which have been in the vanguard in the development of individual safeguards in criminal trials,[4] are using their harmless-error rule to destroy or dilute constitutional guarantees. If the contrary were the case and the harmless-error rule itself were shown to have resulted in a course of convictions significantly influenced by constitutionally impermissible factors, I think it clear that constitutional due process could not countenance the continued application of the rule.[5] And individual applications of a permissible rule would still be subject to scrutiny as to the tenability of the independent and adequate state ground. See Thompson v. Louisville, 362 U. S. 199; Terre Haute & Indianapolis Railroad Co. v. Indiana ex rel. Ketcham, 194 U. S. 579; Note, The Untenable Nonfederal Ground in the Supreme Court, 74 Harv. L. Rev. 1375.

I thus see no need for this new constitutional doctrine.[6] Decision of this case should turn instead on the answers to two questions: Is the California harmless-error provision consistent with the guarantee of fundamental fairness embodied in the Due Process Clause of the Fourteenth Amendment? See Palko v. Connecticut, supra. Was its application in this instance by the California Supreme Court a reasonable one or was the rule applied arbitrarily to evade the underlying constitutional mandate of fundamental fairness? These issues will now be considered.

II.

The California harmless-error rule is incorporated in that State's constitution. It was first adopted by a vote of the people in 1911 and readopted as part of the revised constitution in 1966. While its language allows reversal only where there has been a "miscarriage of justice," a long course of judicial decisions has shaped the rule in a manner which cannot be ignored. California courts will not allow a conviction based upon an improperly obtained confession to stand. See, e. g., People v. Dorado, 62 Cal. 2d 338, 398 P. 2d 361; People v. Sears, 62 Cal. 2d 737, 401 P. 2d 938. Nor will the fact that sufficient evidence to support the conviction is present absent the tainted evidence preclude a reversal. See, e. g., People v. Patubo, 9 Cal. 2d 537, 71 P. 2d 270; People v. Mahoney, 201 Cal. 618, 258 P. 607. And reversal will be required when the tainted evidence is introduced in intentional violation of constitutional standards. See People v. Sarazzawski, 27 Cal. 2d 7, 161 P. 2d 934. Thus the California rule and the "federal rule" today declared applicable to state adjudication are parallel in these special instances[7] and their divergence, if any, arises from the general formulation found in the opinions of the California Supreme Court.

In People v. Watson, 46 Cal. 2d 818, 299 P. 2d 243, the California Supreme Court undertook a general discussion of the application of the state harmless-error rule. It declared that the "final test" was "the `opinion' of the reviewing court, in the sense of its belief or conviction, as to the effect of the error; and that ordinarily where the result appears just, and it further appears that such result would have been reached if the error had not been committed, a reversal will not be ordered." Reversal would be required only when "it is reasonably probable that a result more favorable to the appealing party would have been reached," and this judgment "must necessarily be based upon reasonable probabilities rather than upon mere possibilities; otherwise the entire purpose of the constitutional provision would be defeated." 46. Cal. 2d, at 835-837, 299 P. 2d, at 254-255. This formulation may sound somewhat different from that announced today, but on closer analysis the distinction between probability and possibility becomes essentially esoteric. In fact, California courts have at times equated the California standard with the standard utilized by this Court in Fahy v. Connecticut, supra. See, e. g., People v. Jacobson, 63 Cal. 2d 319, 331, 405 P. 2d 555, 563.

Similarly, members of this Court have used a variety of verbal formulae in deciding questions of harmless error in federal cases, ranging from today's "reasonable doubt" standard to the ability to "say with fair assurance. . . that the jury was not substantially swayed . . . ." Fiswick v. United States, 329 U. S. 211, 218. And the circuit courts have been equally varied in their expressions.

See United States v. Brown, 79 F. 2d 321; United States v. Feinberg, 140 F. 2d 592; United States v. McMaster, 343 F. 2d 176.

Against this background the California rule can hardly be said to be out of keeping with fundamental fairness, and I see no reason for striking it down on its face as a violation of the guarantee of "due process."[8]

III.

A summary of the evidence introduced against the petitioners and the events of the trial will make it apparent that the application of the California rule in this case was not an unreasonable one. California courts have not hesitated to declare that comment has caused a miscarriage of justice when that conclusion has been warranted by the circumstances, see, e. g., People v. Keller, 234 Cal. App. 2d 395, 44 Cal. Rptr. 432; People v. Sigal, 235 Cal. App. 2d 449, 45 Cal. Rptr. 481, but the posture of this case minimized the possible impact of the comment.

Petitioners were tried for the murder of a night club bartender in the course of a robbery of the club. The State established that petitioners were the last customers remaining in the club on the night of the murder. Three people with descriptions matching those of Chapman, Teale, and the victim were seen leaving the club together. The club had been ransacked and its condition indicated that the victim had been forced out of it. He was later shot from close range with a .22-caliber weapon and left beside a country road. It was shown that Chapman had purchased a similar weapon five days before the murder and this weapon was in Teale's possession when he was arrested. Blood matching the type of the victim was found on the floormat of the vehicle in which Chapman and Teale had been traveling. Other scientific testimony established that the victim had been in petitioners' car. Blood (untypable) was found on Chapman's clothes, and blood matching the victim's was found on her shoes. Similar evidence connected Teale with the murder.

After his arrest Teale made admissions, amounting almost to a full confession, to a fellow prisoner and these were introduced against him. The jury was cautioned to disregard them as against Chapman. Petitioners pleaded not guilty, but offered no defense on the merits. The only defense witness was a Dr. Sheuerman who was called by Chapman in an effort to establish a defense of lack of capacity to form the requisite intent because of "disassociative reaction."

The prosecutor's comment on petitioners' failure to explain away or challenge the evidence presented against them was admittedly extensive.[9] The California Supreme Court found it harmless error for a number of reasons. First the court noted the convincing and unchallenged evidence presented by the State. It next observed that the jurors were certain to take notice of petitioners' silence whether or not there was comment since the evidence itself cried for an explanation. I think this point crucial, since it seems to me that this Court has confused the impact of petitioners' silence on the jury with the impact of the prosecution's comment upon that silence. The added impact of that comment would seem marginal in a case of this type where the jury must inevitably look to petitioners for an explanation of the innuendo of the real evidence and in Teale's case of his damaging admissions. Finally the California Supreme Court noted that Chapman, against whom the evidence was less strong, had keyed her defense to evidence of her mental defect, a subject upon which the comment had not touched. From this discriminating analysis it was concluded that another result was not "reasonably probable" absent the erroneous comments.

I cannot see how this resolution can be thought other than a reasonable, and therefore constitutional, application of the California harmless-error rule.

IV.

When we consider how little is empirically known about the workings of a jury, see Kalven & Zeisel, The American Jury, passim, it seems to me highly inappropriate for this Court to presume to take upon itself the power to pass directly on the correctness of impact evaluations coming from 50 different jurisdictions. Juries must invariably react differently to particular items of evidence because of local predispositions and experience factors. The state courts, manned by local judges aware of and in touch with the special factors affecting local criminal trials, seem the best, and the constitutionally required, final authority for ruling on the effect of the admission of inadmissible evidence in state criminal proceedings, absent the application of a fundamentally unfair rule, or any unreasonable application of a proper rule manifesting a purpose to defeat federal constitutional rights. Once it appears that neither of these factors is present in a state harmless-constitutional-error decision, federal judicial responsibility should be at an end. This decision, however, encompasses much more. It imposes on this Court, in cases coming here directly from state courts, and on the lower federal courts, in cases arising on habeas corpus, the duty of determining for themselves whether a constitutional error was harmless. In all but insubstantial instances, this will entail a de novo assessment of the entire state trial record.

For one who believes that among the constitutional values which contribute to the preservation of our free society none ranks higher than the principles of federalism, and that this Court's responsibility for keeping such principles intact is no less than its responsibility for maintaining particular constitutional rights, the doctrine announced today is a most disturbing one. It cuts sharply into the finality of state criminal processes; it bids fair to place an unnecessary substantial burden of work on the federal courts; and it opens the door to further excursions by the federal judiciary into state judicial domains. I venture to hope that as time goes on this new doctrine, even in its present manifestation, will be found to have been strictly contained, still more that it will not be pushed to its logical extremes.

I respectfully dissent.

Notes

[1] For myself, I intimate no view on congressional power with respect to state courts in this regard.

[2] Cases in which lower federal courts, acting under the authority of the Fourteenth Amendment, as expanded by this Court's decision in Reynolds v. Sims, 377 U. S. 533, have promulgated their own reapportionment plans may superficially be thought to support such a power. E. g., Reynolds v. State Election Board, 233 F. Supp. 323. But such cases are quite apart from the present one because they arise from a situation where some positive constitutional action is a necessity and thus require the exercise of special equity powers. Here the ordinary remedy of striking down unconstitutional harmless-error rules and applications is sufficient to deal with any problem that may arise. There is no necessity for a State to have a harmless-error rule at all.

[3] The Court indeed recognizes, as does my Brother STEWART in his concurring opinion, that errors of constitutional dimension can be harmless, a proposition supported by ample precedent. See Snyder v. Massachusetts, 291 U. S. 97; Motes v. United States, 178 U. S. 458; Haines v. United States, 188 F. 2d 546; United States v. Donnelly, 179 F. 2d 227. Presumably all errors in the federal courts will continue to be evaluated under the single standard of 28 U. S. C. § 2111 as interpreted today. Certainly there is nothing in the substantive provisions of the Bill of Rights which suggests any standard for assessing the impact of their violation.

[4] See, e. g., People v. Cahan, 44 Cal. 2d 434, 282 P. 2d 905; People v. Dorado, 62 Cal. 2d 338, 398 P. 2d 361.

[5] It is clear enough that this is not the rationale that the Court is employing. The Court would leave California free to apply its harmless-error rule to errors of state law and must thus consider the rule itself consistent with constitutional due process. This leaves the anomalous situation where the impact of a particular piece of evidence is to be assessed by a different "constitutional" standard depending only on whether state law or federal constitutional law barred its admittance.

[6] Fahy v. Connecticut, 375 U. S. 85, should not be deemed dispositive on such a far-reaching matter, which was entirely passed over in the Court's opinion in that case.

[7] Some special limitations on harmless error have always been respected by this Court and seem to me essential to the fundamental fairness guaranteed by the Due Process Clauses of the Fifth and Fourteenth Amendments. These limitations stem from what I perceive as two distinct considerations. The first is a recognition that particular types of error have an effect which is so devastating or inherently indeterminate that as a matter of law they cannot reasonably be found harmless. E. g., Payne v. Arkansas, 356 U. S. 560 (confessions); see Fahy v. Connecticut, supra, at 95 (dissenting opinion of HARLAN, J.); cf. Bollenbach v. United States, 326 U. S. 607 (independently sufficient evidence). The second is a recognition that certain types of official misbehavior require reversal simply because society cannot tolerate giving final effect to a judgment tainted with such intentional misconduct. E. g., Berger v. United States, 295 U. S. 78 (prosecutorial misconduct). Although they have never been viewed in this light, I would see violations of Gideon v. Wainwright, 372 U. S. 335, as falling in the first category, and violations of Tumey v. Ohio, 273 U. S. 510, as falling in the second. However, as I understand my Brother STEWART'S opinion concurring in the result, he would read all such limitations into the content of the Due Process Clause and limit the application of harmless-error rules with respect to constitutional errors to an undefined category of instances. I think it preferable to resolve these special problems from an analysis of the nature of the error involved rather than by an attempt to discover limitations in the policy underlying the substantive constitutional provisions. The latter course seems to me to blur analysis and lead to distinction by fiat among equally specific constitutional guarantees.

[8] The rule was upheld by the Ninth Circuit in Sampsell v. California, 191 F. 2d 721, against an attack on its constitutionality.

[9] The decision in Griffin v. California, 380 U. S. 609, was not announced until after the trial of the case. Hence the trial was conducted according to what was, at the time, constitutional California law. No implication of prosecutorial misconduct can be drawn from these circumstances.

Justice Harlan's dissent in Iacurci v. Lummus Co. (May 15, 1967)

MR. JUSTICE HARLAN, dissenting.

In Neely v. Eby Construction Co., 386 U. S. 317, we held that a court of appeals might, despite denial by the trial judge of motions for a new trial and for judgment notwithstanding the verdict, appropriately instruct the district court to enter judgment against the jury-verdict winner. We also recognized in Neely, however, that there might be situations in which the necessity for a new trial would be better determined by the trial court, and that in such situations the court of appeals should return the case to the district court for such an assessment.

In joining Neely, I did not understand the opinion to require this Court to interpose in each case its own judgment of the relative competence of the court of appeals and of the district court to pass on the new trial motion. Rather, I understood Neely to place upon the court of appeals the responsibility for determining "in its informed discretion," supra, at 329, which, if any, of the issues urged in support of a new trial "should be reserved for the trial court." Ibid. I think that sound judicial administration demands that this Court should overturn a considered judgment of a court of appeals on such issues only in situations of manifest abuse of discretion.

The Court in this instance states that it does "not share the Court of Appeals' confidence as to the meaning, in light of the trial court's instructions, of the jury's failure to answer" subquestions included in the interrogatories. The ambiguities upon which the Court now relies were earnestly urged by petitioner in her petition for rehearing to the Court of Appeals. Petition for Rehearing 5-6, 7-8. They were, as the Court in Neely intended, before the Court of Appeals for its judgment whether the case should be returned to the District Court for determination of the necessity for a new trial. Had I been sitting on the Court of Appeals I might not have agreed with the view taken of this case by the majority there, but I cannot agree that their conclusion was a manifest abuse of their "informed discretion." I hope that this decision does not indicate that the Court is about to embark on a course comparable to that it set for itself in FELA cases.

I would affirm the judgment of the Court of Appeals.

Justice Harlan's dissent in Afroyim v. Rusk (May 29, 1967)

MR. JUSTICE HARLAN, whom MR. JUSTICE CLARK, MR. JUSTICE STEWART, and MR. JUSTICE WHITE join, dissenting.

Almost 10 years ago, in Perez v. Brownell, 356 U. S. 44, the Court upheld the constitutionality of § 401 (e) of the Nationality Act of 1940, 54 Stat. 1169. The section deprives of his nationality any citizen who has voted in a foreign political election. The Court reasoned that Congress derived from its power to regulate foreign affairs authority to expatriate any citizen who intentionally commits acts which may be prejudicial to the foreign relations of the United States, and which reasonably may be deemed to indicate a dilution of his allegiance to this country. Congress, it was held, could appropriately consider purposeful voting in a foreign political election to be such an act.

The Court today overrules Perez, and declares § 401 (e) unconstitutional, by a remarkable process of circumlocution. First, the Court fails almost entirely to dispute the reasoning in Perez; it is essentially content with the conclusory and quite unsubstantiated assertion that Congress is without "any general power, express or implied," to expatriate a citizen "without his assent."[1] Next, the Court embarks upon a lengthy, albeit incomplete, survey of the historical background of the congressional power at stake here, and yet, at the end, concedes that the history is susceptible of "conflicting inferences." The Court acknowledges that its conclusions might not be warranted by that history alone, and disclaims that the decision today relies, even "principally," upon it. Finally, the Court declares that its result is bottomed upon the "language and the purpose" of the Citizenship Clause of the Fourteenth Amendment; in explanation, the Court offers only the terms of the clause itself, the contention that any other result would be "completely incongruous," and the essentially arcane observation that the "citizenry is the country and the country is its citizenry."

I can find nothing in this extraordinary series of circumventions which permits, still less compels, the imposition of this constitutional constraint upon the authority of Congress. I must respectfully dissent.

There is no need here to rehearse Mr. Justice Frankfurter's opinion for the Court in Perez; it then proved and still proves to my satisfaction that § 401 (e) is within the power of Congress.[2] It suffices simply to supplement Perez with an examination of the historical evidence which the Court in part recites, and which provides the only apparent basis for many of the Court's conclusions. As will be seen, the available historical evidence is not only inadequate to support the Court's abandonment of Perez, but, with due regard for the restraints that should surround the judicial invalidation of an Act of Congress, even seems to confirm Perez' soundness.

I.

Not much evidence is available from the period prior to the adoption of the Fourteenth Amendment through which the then-prevailing attitudes on these constitutional questions can now be determined. The questions pertinent here were only tangentially debated; controversy centered instead upon the wider issues of whether a citizen might under any circumstances renounce his citizenship, and, if he might, whether that right should be conditioned upon any formal prerequisites.[3] Even the discussion of these issues was seriously clouded by the widely accepted view that authority to regulate the incidents of citizenship had been retained, at least in part, by the several States.[4] It should therefore be remembered that the evidence which is now available may not necessarily represent any carefully considered, still less prevailing, viewpoint upon the present issues.

Measured even within these limitations, the Court's evidence for this period is remarkably inconclusive; the Court relies simply upon the rejection by Congress of legislation proposed in 1794, 1797, and 1818, and upon an isolated dictum from the opinion of Chief Justice Marshall in Osborn v. Bank of the United States, 9 Wheat. 738. This, as will appear, is entirely inadequate to support the Court's conclusion, particularly in light of other and more pertinent evidence which the Court does not notice.

The expatriation of unwilling citizens was apparently first discussed in the lengthy congressional debates of 1794 and 1795, which culminated eventually in the Uniform Naturalization Act of 1795.[5] 1 Stat. 414. Little contained in those debates is pertinent here. The present question was considered only in connection with an amendment, offered by Congressman Hillhouse of Connecticut, which provided that any American who acquired a foreign citizenship should not subsequently be permitted to repatriate in the United States. Although this obscure proposal scarcely seems relevant to the present issues, it was apparently understood at least by some members to require the automatic expatriation of an American who acquired a second citizenship. Its discussion in the House consumed substantially less than one day, and of this debate only the views of two Congressmen, other than Hillhouse, were recorded by the Annals.[6] Murray of Maryland, for reasons immaterial here, supported the proposal. In response, Baldwin of Georgia urged that foreign citizenship was often conferred only as a mark of esteem, and that it would be unfair to deprive of his domestic citizenship an American honored in this fashion. There is no indication that any member believed the proposal to be forbidden by the Constitution. The measure was rejected by the House without a reported vote and no analogous proposal was offered in the Senate. Insofar as this brief exchange is pertinent here, it establishes at most that two or more members believed the proposal both constitutional and desirable, and that some larger number determined, for reasons that are utterly obscure, that it should not be adopted.

The Court next relies upon the rejection of proposed legislation in 1797. The bill there at issue would have forbidden the entry of American citizens into the service of any foreign state in time of war; its sixth section included machinery by which a citizen might voluntarily expatriate himself.[7] The bill contained nothing which would have expatriated unwilling citizens, and the debates do not include any pronouncements relevant to that issue. It is difficult to see how the failure of that bill might be probative here.

The debates in 1817 and 1818, upon which the Court so heavily relies, are scarcely more revealing. Debate centered upon a brief bill[8] which provided merely that any citizen who wished to renounce his citizenship must first declare his intention in open court, and thereafter depart the United States. His citizenship would have terminated at the moment of his renunciation. The bill was debated only in the House; no proposal permitting the involuntary expatriation of any citizen was made or considered there or in the Senate. Nonetheless, the Court selects portions of statements made by three individual Congressmen, who apparently denied that Congress had authority to enact legislation to deprive unwilling citizens of their citizenship. These brief dicta are, by the most generous standard, inadequate to warrant the Court's broad constitutional conclusion. Moreover, it must be observed that they were in great part deductions from constitutional premises which have subsequently been entirely abandoned. They stemmed principally from the Jeffersonian contention that allegiance is owed by a citizen first to his State, and only through the State to the Federal Government. The spokesmen upon whom the Court now relies supposed that Congress was without authority to dissolve citizenship, since "we have no control" over "allegiance to the State . . . ."[9] The bill's opponents urged that "The relation to the State government was the basis of the relation to the General Government, and therefore, as long as a man continues a citizen of a State, he must be considered a citizen of the United States."[10] Any statute, it was thought, which dissolved federal citizenship while a man remained a citizen of a State "would be inoperative."[11] Surely the Court does not revive this entirely discredited doctrine; and yet so long as it does not, it is difficult to see that any significant support for the ruling made today may be derived from the statements on which the Court relies. To sever the statements from their constitutional premises, as the Court has apparently done, is to transform the meaning these expressions were intended to convey.

Finally, it must be remembered that these were merely the views of three Congressmen; nothing in the debates indicates that their constitutional doubts were shared by any substantial number of the other 67 members who eventually opposed the bill. They were plainly not accepted by the 58 members who voted in the bill's favor. The bill's opponents repeatedly urged that, whatever its constitutional validity, the bill was imprudent and undesirable. Pindall of Virginia, for example, asserted that a citizen who employed its provisions would have "motives of idleness or criminality,"[12] and that the bill would thus cause "much evil."[13] McLane of Delaware feared that citizens would use the bill to escape service in the armed forces in time of war; he warned that the bill would, moreover, weaken "the love of country, so necessary to individual happiness and national prosperity."[14] He even urged that "The commission of treason, and the objects of plunder and spoil, are equally legalized by this bill."[15] Lowndes of South Carolina cautioned the House that difficulties might again arise with foreign governments over the rights of seamen if the bill were passed.[16] Given these vigorous and repeated arguments, it is quite impossible to assume, as the Court apparently has, that any substantial portion of the House was motivated wholly, or even in part, by any particular set of constitutional assumptions. These three statements must instead be taken as representative only of the beliefs of three members, premised chiefly upon constitutional doctrines which have subsequently been rejected, and expressed in a debate in which the present issues were not directly involved.

The last piece of evidence upon which the Court relies for this period is a brief obiter dictum from the lengthy opinion for the Court in Osborn v. Bank of the United States, 9 Wheat. 738, 827, written by Mr. Chief Justice Marshall. This use of the dictum is entirely unpersuasive, for its terms and context make quite plain that it cannot have been intended to reach the questions presented here. The central issue before the Court in Osborn was the right of the bank to bring its suit for equitable relief in the courts of the United States. In argument, counsel for Osborn had asserted that although the bank had been created by the laws of the United States, it did not necessarily follow that any cause involving the bank had arisen under those laws. Counsel urged by analogy that the naturalization of an alien might as readily be said to confer upon the new citizen a right to bring all his actions in the federal courts. Id., at 813-814. Not surprisingly, the Court rejected the analogy, and remarked that an act of naturalization "does not proceed to give, to regulate, or to prescribe his capacities," since the Constitution demands that a naturalized citizen must in all respects stand "on the footing of a native." Id., at 827. The Court plainly meant no more than that counsel's analogy is broken by Congress' inability to offer a naturalized citizen rights or capacities which differ in any particular from those given to a native-born citizen by birth. Mr. Justice Johnson's discussion of the analogy in dissent confirms the Court's purpose. Id., at 875-876.

Any wider meaning, so as to reach the questions here, wrenches the dictum from its context, and attributes to the Court an observation extraneous even to the analogy before it. Moreover, the construction given to the dictum by the Court today requires the assumption that the Court in Osborn meant to decide an issue which had to that moment scarcely been debated, to which counsel in Osborn had never referred, and upon which no case had ever reached the Court. All this, it must be recalled, is in an area of the law in which the Court had steadfastly avoided unnecessary comment. See, e. g., M`Ilvaine v. Coxe's Lessee, 4 Cranch 209, 212-213; The Santissima Trinidad, 7 Wheat. 283, 347-348. By any standard, the dictum cannot provide material assistance to the Court's position in the present case.[17]

Before turning to the evidence from this period which has been overlooked by the Court, attention must be given an incident to which the Court refers, but upon which it apparently places relatively little reliance. In 1810, a proposed thirteenth amendment to the Constitution was introduced into the Senate by Senator Reed of Maryland; the amendment, as subsequently modified, provided that any citizen who accepted a title of nobility, pension, or emolument from a foreign state, or who married a person of royal blood, should "cease to be a citizen of the United States."[18] The proposed amendment was, in a modified form, accepted by both Houses, and subsequently obtained the approval of all but one of the requisite number of States.[19] I have found nothing which indicates with any certainty why such a provision should then have been thought necessary,[20] but two reasons suggest themselves for the use of a constitutional amendment. First, the provisions may have been intended in part as a sanction for Art. I, § 9, cl. 8;[21] it may therefore have been thought more appropriate that it be placed within the Constitution itself. Second, a student of expatriation issues in this period has dismissed the preference for an amendment with the explanation that "the dominant Jeffersonian view held that citizenship was within the jurisdiction of the states; a statute would thus have been a federal usurpation of state power."[22] This second explanation is fully substantiated by the debate in 1818; the statements from that debate set out in the opinion for the Court were, as I have noted, bottomed on the reasoning that since allegiance given by an individual to a State could not be dissolved by Congress, a federal statute could not regulate expatriation. It surely follows that this "obscure enterprise"[23] in 1810, motivated by now discredited constitutional premises, cannot offer any significant guidance for solution of the important issues now before us.

The most pertinent evidence from this period upon these questions has been virtually overlooked by the Court. Twice in the two years immediately prior to its passage of the Fourteenth Amendment, Congress exercised the very authority which the Court now suggests that it should have recognized was entirely lacking. In each case, a bill was debated and adopted by both Houses which included provisions to expatriate unwilling citizens.

In the spring and summer of 1864, both Houses debated intensively the Wade-Davis bill to provide reconstruction governments for the States which had seceded to form the Confederacy. Among the bill's provisions was § 14, by which "every person who shall hereafter hold or exercise any office . . . in the rebel service . . . is hereby declared not to be a citizen of the United States."[24] Much of the debate upon the bill did not, of course, center on the expatriation provision, although it certainly did not escape critical attention.[25] Nonetheless, I have not found any indication in the debates in either House that it was supposed that Congress was without authority to deprive an unwilling citizen of his citizenship. The bill was not signed by President Lincoln before the adjournment of Congress, and thus failed to become law, but a subsequent statement issued by Lincoln makes quite plain that he was not troubled by any doubts of the constitutionality of § 14.[26] Passage of the Wade-Davis bill of itself "suffices to destroy the notion that the men who drafted the Fourteenth Amendment felt that citizenship was an `absolute.' "[27]

Twelve months later, and less than a year before its passage of the Fourteenth Amendment, Congress adopted a second measure which included provisions that permitted the expatriation of unwilling citizens. Section 21 of the Enrollment Act of 1865 provided that deserters from the military service of the United States "shall be deemed and taken to have voluntarily relinquished and forfeited their rights of citizenship and their rights to become citizens . . . ."[28] The same section extended these disabilities to persons who departed the United States with intent to avoid "draft into the military or naval service . . . ."[29] The bitterness of war did not cause Congress here to neglect the requirements of the Constitution; for it was urged in both Houses that § 21 as written was ex post facto, and thus was constitutionally impermissible.[30] Significantly, however, it was never suggested in either debate that expatriation without a citizen's consent lay beyond Congress' authority. Members of both Houses had apparently examined intensively the section's constitutional validity, and yet had been undisturbed by the matters upon which the Court now relies.

Some doubt, based on the phrase "rights of citizenship," has since been expressed[31] that § 21 was intended to require any more than disfranchisement, but this is, for several reasons, unconvincing. First, § 21 also explicitly provided that persons subject to its provisions should not thereafter exercise various "rights of citizens";[32] if the section had not been intended to cause expatriation, it is difficult to see why these additional provisions would have been thought necessary. Second, the executive authorities of the United States afterwards consistently construed the section as causing expatriation.[33] Third, the section was apparently understood by various courts to result in expatriation; in particular, Mr. Justice Strong, while a member of the Supreme Court of Pennsylvania, construed the section to cause a "forfeiture of citizenship," Huber v. Reily,

53 Pa. 112, 118, and although this point was not expressly reached, his general understanding of the statute was approved by this Court in Kurtz v. Moffitt, 115 U. S. 487, 501. Finally, Congress in 1867 approved an exemption from the section's provisions for those who had deserted after the termination of general hostilities, and the statute as adopted specifically described the disability from which exemption was given as a "loss of his citizenship." 15 Stat. 14. The same choice of phrase occurs in the pertinent debates.[34]

It thus appears that Congress had twice, immediately before its passage of the Fourteenth Amendment, unequivocally affirmed its belief that it had authority to expatriate an unwilling citizen.

The pertinent evidence for the period prior to the adoption of the Fourteenth Amendment can therefore be summarized as follows. The Court's conclusion today is supported only by the statements, associated at least in part with a now abandoned view of citizenship, of three individual Congressmen, and by the ambiguous and inapposite dictum from Osborn. Inconsistent with the Court's position are statements from individual Congressmen in 1794, and Congress' passage in 1864 and 1865 of legislation which expressly authorized the expatriation of unwilling citizens. It may be that legislation adopted in the heat of war should be discounted in part by its origins, but, even if this is done, it is surely plain that the Court's conclusion is entirely unwarranted by the available historical evidence for the period prior to the passage of the Fourteenth Amendment. The evidence suggests, to the contrary, that Congress in 1865 understood that it had authority, at least in some circumstances, to deprive a citizen of his nationality.

II.

The evidence with which the Court supports its thesis that the Citizenship Clause of the Fourteenth Amendment was intended to lay at rest any doubts of Congress' inability to expatriate without the citizen's consent is no more persuasive. The evidence consists almost exclusively of two brief and general quotations from Howard of Michigan, the sponsor of the Citizenship Clause in the Senate, and of a statement made in a debate in the House of Representatives in 1868 by Van Trump of Ohio. Measured most generously, this evidence would be inadequate to support the important constitutional conclusion presumably drawn in large part from it by the Court; but, as will be shown, other relevant evidence indicates that the Court plainly has mistaken the purposes of the clause's draftsmen.

The Amendment as initially approved by the House contained nothing which described or defined citizenship.[35] The issue did not as such even arise in the House debates; it was apparently assumed that Negroes were citizens, and that it was necessary only to guarantee to them the rights which sprang from citizenship. It is quite impossible to derive from these debates any indication that the House wished to deny itself the authority it had exercised in 1864 and 1865; so far as the House is concerned, it seems that no issues of citizenship were "at all involved."[36]

In the Senate, however, it was evidently feared that unless citizenship were defined, or some more general classification substituted, freedmen might, on the premise that they were not citizens, be excluded from the Amendment's protection. Senator Stewart thus offered an amendment which would have inserted into § 1 a definition of citizenship,[37] and Senator Wade urged as an alternative the elimination of the term "citizen" from the Amendment's first section.[38] After a caucus of the chief supporters of the Amendment, Senator Howard announced on their behalf that they favored the addition of the present Citizenship Clause.[39]

The debate upon the clause was essentially cursory in both Houses, but there are several clear indications of its intended effect. Its sponsors evidently shared the fears of Senators Stewart and Wade that unless citizenship were defined, freedmen might, under the reasoning of the Dred Scott decision,[40] be excluded by the courts from the scope of the Amendment. It was agreed that, since the "courts have stumbled on the subject," it would be prudent to remove the "doubt thrown over" it.[41] The clause would essentially overrule Dred Scott, and place beyond question the freedmen's right of citizenship because of birth. It was suggested, moreover, that it would, by creating a basis for federal citizenship which was indisputably independent of state citizenship, preclude any effort by state legislatures to circumvent the Amendment by denying freedmen state citizenship.[42] Nothing in the debates, however, supports the Court's assertion that the clause was intended to deny Congress its authority to expatriate unwilling citizens. The evidence indicates that its draftsmen instead expected the clause only to declare unreservedly to whom citizenship initially adhered, thus overturning the restrictions both of Dred Scott and of the doctrine of primary state citizenship, while preserving Congress' authority to prescribe the methods and terms of expatriation.

The narrow, essentially definitional purpose of the Citizenship Clause is reflected in the clear declarations in the debates that the clause would not revise the prevailing incidents of citizenship. Senator Henderson of Missouri thus stated specifically his understanding that the "section will leave citizenship where it now is."[43] Senator Howard, in the first of the statements relied upon, in part, by the Court, said quite unreservedly that "This amendment [the Citizenship Clause] which I have offered is simply declaratory of what I regard as the law of the land already, that every person born within the limits of the United States, and subject to their jurisdiction, is . . . a citizen of the United States."[44] Henderson had been present at the Senate's consideration both of the Wade-Davis bill and of the Enrollment Act, and had voted at least for the Wade-Davis bill.[45]

Howard was a member of the Senate when both bills were passed, and had actively participated in the debates upon the Enrollment Act.[46] Although his views of the two expatriation measures were not specifically recorded, Howard certainly never expressed to the Senate any doubt either of their wisdom or of their constitutionality. It would be extraordinary if these prominent supporters of the Citizenship Clause could have imagined, as the Court's construction of the clause now demands, that the clause was only "declaratory" of the law "where it now is," and yet that it would entirely withdraw a power twice recently exercised by Congress in their presence.

There is, however, even more positive evidence that the Court's construction of the clause is not that intended by its draftsmen. Between the two brief statements from Senator Howard relied upon by the Court, Howard, in response to a question, said the following:

"I take it for granted that after a man becomes a citizen of the United States under the Constitution he cannot cease to be citizen, except by expatriation or the commission of some crime by which his citizenship shall be forfeited."[47] (Emphasis added.)

It would be difficult to imagine a more unqualified rejection of the Court's position; Senator Howard, the clause's sponsor, very plainly believed that it would leave unimpaired Congress' power to deprive unwilling citizens of their citizenship.[48]

Additional confirmation of the expectations of the clause's draftsmen may be found in the legislative history, wholly overlooked by the Court, of the Act for the Relief of certain Soldiers and Sailors, adopted in 1867. 15 Stat. 14. The Act, debated by Congress within 12 months of its passage of the Fourteenth Amendment, provided an exception from the provisions of § 21 of the Enrollment Act of 1865 for those who had deserted from the Union forces after the termination of general hostilities. Had the Citizenship Clause been understood to have the effect now given it by the Court, surely this would have been clearly reflected in the debates; members would at least have noted that, upon final approval of the Amendment, which had already obtained the approval of 21 States, § 21 would necessarily be invalid. Nothing of the sort occurred; it was argued by some members that § 21 was imprudent and even unfair,[49] but Congress evidently did not suppose that it was, or would be, unconstitutional. Congress simply failed to attribute to the Citizenship Clause the constitutional consequences now discovered by the Court.[50]

Nonetheless, the Court urges that the debates which culminated in the Expatriation Act of 1868 materially support its understanding of the purposes of the Citizenship Clause. This is, for several reasons, wholly unconvincing. Initially, it should be remembered that discussion of the Act began in committee some six months after the passage of the Relief Act of 1867, by the Second Session of the Congress which had approved the Relief Act; the Court's interpretation of the history of the Expatriation Act thus demands, at the outset, the supposition that a view of the Citizenship Clause entirely absent in July had appeared vividly by the following January. Further, the purposes and background of the Act should not be forgotten. The debates were stimulated by repeated requests both from President Andrew Johnson and from the public that Congress assert the rights of naturalized Americans against the demands of their former countries.[51] The Act as finally adopted was thus intended "primarily to assail the conduct of the British Government [chiefly for its acts toward naturalized Americans resident in Ireland] and to declare the right of naturalized Americans to renounce their native allegiance";[52] accordingly, very little of the lengthy debate was in the least pertinent to the present issues. Several members did make plain, through their proposed amendments to the bill or their interstitial comments, that they understood Congress to have authority to expatriate unwilling citizens,[53] but in general both the issues now before the Court and questions of the implications of the Citizenship Clause were virtually untouched in the debates.

Nevertheless, the Court, in order to establish that Congress understood that the Citizenship Clause denied it such authority, fastens principally upon the speeches of Congressman Van Trump of Ohio. Van Trump sponsored, as one of many similar amendments offered to the bill by various members, a proposal to create formal machinery by which a citizen might voluntarily renounce his citizenship.[54] Van Trump himself spoke at length in support of his proposal; his principal speech consisted chiefly of a detailed examination of the debates and judicial decisions pertinent to the issues of voluntary renunciation of citizenship.[55] Never in his catalog of relevant materials did Van Trump even mention the Citizenship Clause of the Fourteenth Amendment;[56] so far as may be seen from his comments on the House floor, Van Trump evidently supposed the clause to be entirely immaterial to the issues of expatriation. This is completely characteristic of the debate in both Houses; even its draftsmen and principal supporters, such as Senator Howard, permitted the Citizenship Clause to pass unnoticed. The conclusion seems inescapable that the discussions surrounding the Act of 1868 cast only the most minimal light, if indeed any, upon the purposes of the clause, and that the Court's evidence from the debates is, by any standard, exceedingly slight.[57]

There is, moreover, still further evidence, overlooked by the Court, which confirms yet again that the Court's view of the intended purposes of the Citizenship Clause is mistaken. While the debate on the Act of 1868 was still in progress, negotiations were completed on the first of a series of bilateral expatriation treaties, which "initiated this country's policy of automatic divestment of citizenship for specified conduct affecting our foreign relations." Perez v. Brownell, supra, at 48. Seven such treaties were negotiated in 1868 and 1869 alone;[58] each was ratified by the Senate. If, as the Court now suggests, it was "abundantly clear" to Congress in 1868 that the Citizenship Clause had taken from its hands the power of expatriation, it is quite difficult to understand why these conventions were negotiated, or why, once negotiated, they were not immediately repudiated by the Senate.[59]

Further, the executive authorities of the United States repeatedly acted, in the 40 years following 1868, upon the premise that a citizen might automatically be deemed to have expatriated himself by conduct short of a voluntary renunciation of citizenship; individual citizens were, as the Court indicated in Perez, regularly held on this basis to have lost their citizenship. Interested Members of Congress, and others, could scarcely have been unaware of the practice; as early as 1874, President Grant urged Congress in his Sixth Annual Message to supplement the Act of 1868 with a statutory declaration of the acts by which a citizen might "be deemed to have renounced or to have lost his citizenship."[60] It was the necessity to provide a more satisfactory basis for this practice that led first to the appointment of the Citizenship Board of 1906, and subsequently to the Nationality Acts of 1907 and 1940. The administrative practice in this period was described by the Court in Perez; it suffices here merely to emphasize that the Court today has not ventured to explain why the Citizenship Clause should, so shortly after its adoption, have been, under the Court's construction, so seriously misunderstood.

It seems to me apparent that the historical evidence which the Court in part recites is wholly inconclusive, as indeed the Court recognizes; the evidence, to the contrary, irresistibly suggests that the draftsmen of the Fourteenth Amendment did not intend, and could not have expected, that the Citizenship Clause would deprive Congress of authority which it had, to their knowledge, only recently twice exercised. The construction demanded by the pertinent historical evidence, and entirely consistent with the clause's terms and purposes, is instead that it declares to whom citizenship, as a consequence either of birth or of naturalization, initially attaches. The clause thus served at the time of its passage both to overturn Dred Scott and to provide a foundation for federal citizenship entirely independent of state citizenship; in this fashion it effectively guaranteed that the Amendment's protection would not subsequently be withheld from those for whom it was principally intended. But nothing in the history, purposes, or language of the clause suggests that it forbids Congress in all circumstances to withdraw the citizenship of an unwilling citizen. To the contrary, it was expected, and should now be understood, to leave Congress at liberty to expatriate a citizen if the expatriation is an appropriate exercise of a power otherwise given to Congress by the Constitution, and if the methods and terms of expatriation adopted by Congress are consistent with the Constitution's other relevant commands.

The Citizenship Clause thus neither denies nor provides to Congress any power of expatriation; its consequences are, for present purposes, exhausted by its declaration of the classes of individuals to whom citizenship initially attaches. Once obtained, citizenship is of course protected from arbitrary withdrawal by the constraints placed around Congress' powers by the Constitution; it is not proper to create from the Citizenship Clause an additional, and entirely unwarranted, restriction upon legislative authority. The construction now placed on the Citizenship Clause rests, in the last analysis, simply on the Court's ipse dixit, evincing little more, it is quite apparent, than the present majority's own distaste for the expatriation power.

I believe that Perez was rightly decided, and on its authority would affirm the judgment of the Court of Appeals.

Notes

[1] It is appropriate to note at the outset what appears to be a fundamental ambiguity in the opinion for the Court. The Court at one point intimates, but does not expressly declare, that it adopts the reasoning of the dissent of THE CHIEF JUSTICE in Perez. THE CHIEF JUSTICE there acknowledged that "actions in derogation of undivided allegiance to this country" had "long been recognized" to result in expatriation, id., at 68; he argued, however, that the connection between voting in a foreign political election and abandonment of citizenship was logically insufficient to support a presumption that a

citizen had renounced his nationality. Id., at 76. It is difficult to find any semblance of this reasoning, beyond the momentary reference to the opinion of THE CHIEF JUSTICE, in the approach taken by the Court today; it seems instead to adopt a substantially wider view of the restrictions upon Congress' authority in this area. Whatever the Court's position, it has assumed that voluntariness is here a term of fixed meaning; in fact, of course, it has been employed to describe both a specific intent to renounce citizenship, and the uncoerced commission of an act conclusively deemed by law to be a relinquishment of citizenship. Until the Court indicates with greater precision what it means by "assent," today's opinion will surely cause still greater confusion in this area of the law.

[2] It is useful, however, to reiterate the essential facts of this case, for the Court's very summary statement might unfortunately cause confusion about the situation to which § 401 (e) was here applied. Petitioner emigrated from the United States to Israel in 1950, and, although the issue was not argued at any stage of these proceedings, it was assumed by the District Court that he "has acquired Israeli citizenship." 250 F. Supp. 686, 687. He voted in the election for the Israeli Knesset in 1951, and, as his Israeli Identification Booklet indicates, in various political elections which followed. Transcript of Record 1-2. In 1960, after 10 years in Israel, petitioner determined to return to the United States, and applied to the United States Consulate in Haifa for a passport. The application was rejected, and a Certificate of Loss of Nationality, based entirely on his participation in the 1951 election, was issued. Petitioner's action for declaratory judgment followed. There is, as the District Court noted, "no claim by the [petitioner] that the deprivation of his American citizenship will render him a stateless person." Ibid.

[3] See generally Tsiang, The Question of Expatriation in America Prior to 1907, 25-70; Roche, The Expatriation Cases, 1963 Sup. Ct. Rev. 325, 327-330; Roche, Loss of American Nationality, 4 West. Pol. Q. 268.

[4] Roche, The Expatriation Cases, 1963 Sup. Ct. Rev. 325, 329. Although the evidence, which consists principally of a letter to Albert Gallatin, is rather ambiguous, Jefferson apparently believed even that a state expatriation statute could deprive a citizen of his federal citizenship. 1 Writings of Albert Gallatin 301-302 (Adams ed. 1879). His premise was presumably that state citizenship was primary, and that federal citizenship attached only through it. See Tsiang, supra, at 25. Gallatin's own views have been described as essentially "states' rights"; see Roche, Loss of American Nationality, 4 West. Pol. Q. 268, 271.

[5] See 4 Annals of Cong. 1004 et seq.

[6] The discussion and rejection of the amendment are cursorily reported at 4 Annals of Cong. 1028-1030.

[7] The sixth section is set out at 7 Annals of Cong. 349.

[8] The bill is summarized at 31 Annals of Cong. 495.

[9] 31 Annals of Cong. 1046.

[10] 31 Annals of Cong. 1057.

[11] Ibid. Roche describes the Congressmen upon whom the Court chiefly relies as

"the states' rights opposition." Loss of American Nationality, 4 West. Pol. Q. 268, 276.

[12] 31 Annals of Cong. 1047.

[13] 31 Annals of Cong. 1050.

[14] 31 Annals of Cong. 1059.

[15] Ibid.

[16] 31 Annals of Cong. 1051.

[17] Similarly, the Court can obtain little support from its invocation of the dictum from the opinion for the Court in United States v. Wong Kim Ark, 169 U. S. 649, 703. The central issue there was whether a child born of Chinese nationals domiciled in the United States is an American citizen if its birth occurs in this country. The dictum upon which the Court relies, which consists essentially of a reiteration of the dictum from Osborn, can therefore scarcely be considered a reasoned consideration of the issues now before the Court. Moreover, the dictum could conceivably be read to hold only that no power to expatriate an unwilling citizen was conferred either by the Naturalization Clause or by the Fourteenth Amendment; if the dictum means no more, it would of course not even reach the holding in Perez. Finally, the dictum must be read in light of the subsequent opinion for the Court, written by Mr. Justice McKenna, in Mackenzie v. Hare, 239 U. S. 299. Despite counsel's invocation of Wong Kim Ark, id., at 302 and 303, the Court held in Mackenzie that marriage between an American citizen and an alien, unaccompanied by any intention of the citizen to renounce her citizenship, nonetheless permitted Congress to withdraw her nationality. It is immaterial for these purposes that Mrs. Mackenzie's citizenship might, under the statute there, have been restored upon termination of the marital relationship; she did not consent to the loss, even temporarily, of her citizenship, and, under the proposition apparently urged by the Court today, it can therefore scarcely matter that her expatriation was subject to some condition subsequent. It seems that neither Mr. Justice McKenna, who became a member of the Court after the argument but before the decision of Wong Kim Ark, supra, at 732, nor Mr. Chief Justice White, who joined the Court's opinions in both Wong Kim Ark and Mackenzie, thought that Wong Kim Ark required the result reached by the Court today. Nor, it must be supposed, did the other six members of the Court who joined Mackenzie, despite Wong Kim Ark.

[18] The various revisions of the proposed amendment may be traced through 20 Annals of Cong. 530, 549, 572-573, 635, 671.

[19] Ames, The Proposed Amendments to the Constitution of the United States during the First Century of Its History, 2 Ann. Rep. Am. Hist. Assn. for the Year 1896, 188.

[20] Ames, supra, at 187, speculates that the presence of Jerome Bonaparte in this country some few years earlier might have caused apprehension, and concludes that the amendment was merely an expression of "animosity against foreigners." Id., at 188.

[21] The clause provides that "No Title of Nobility shall be granted by the United States: And no Person holding any Office of Profit or Trust under them, shall, without the Consent of the Congress, accept of any present, Emolument, Office, or Title, of any kind whatever, from any King, Prince, or foreign State."

[22] Roche, The Expatriation Cases, 1963 Sup. Ct. Rev. 325, 335.

[23] Ibid.

[24] 6 Richardson, Messages and Papers of the Presidents 226.

[25] See, e. g., the comments of Senator Brown of Missouri, Cong. Globe, 38th Cong., 1st Sess., 3460.

[26] Lincoln indicated that although he was "unprepared" to be "inflexibly committed" to "any single plan of restoration," he was "fully satisfied" with the bill's provisions. 6 Richardson, Messages and Papers of the Presidents 222-223.

[27] Roche, The Expatriation Cases, 1963 Sup. Ct. Rev. 325, 343.

[28] 13 Stat. 490. It was this provision that, after various recodifications, was held unconstitutional by this Court in Trop v. Dulles, 356 U. S. 86. A majority of the Court did not there hold that the provision was invalid because Congress lacked all power to expatriate an unwilling citizen. In any event, a judgment by this Court 90 years after the Act's passage can scarcely reduce the Act's evidentiary value for determining whether Congress understood in 1865, as the Court now intimates that it did, that it lacked such power.

[29] 13 Stat. 491.

[30] Cong. Globe, 38th Cong., 2d Sess., 642-643, 1155-1156.

[31] Roche, The Expatriation Cases, 1963 Sup. Ct. Rev. 325, 336.

[32] 13 Stat. 490.

[33] Hearings before House Committee on Immigration and Naturalization on H. R. 6127, 76th Cong., 1st Sess., 38.

[34] See, e. g., the remarks of Senator Hendricks, Cong. Globe, 40th Cong., 1st Sess., 661.

[35] The pertinent events are described in Flack, Adoption of the Fourteenth Amendment 83-94.

[36] Id., at 84.

[37] Cong. Globe, 39th Cong., 1st Sess., 2560.

[38] Wade would have employed the formula "persons born in the United States or naturalized under the laws thereof" to measure the section's protection. Cong. Globe, 39th Cong., 1st Sess., 2768-2769.

[39] Cong. Globe, 39th Cong., 1st Sess., 2869. The precise terms of the discussion in the caucus were, and have remained, unknown. For contemporary comment, see Cong. Globe, 39th Cong., 1st Sess., 2939.

[40] Scott v. Sandford, 19 How. 393.

[41] Cong. Globe, 39th Cong., 1st Sess., 2768.

[42] See, e. g., the comments of Senator Johnson of Maryland, Cong. Globe, 39th Cong., 1st Sess., 2893. It was subsequently acknowledged by several members of this Court that a central purpose of the Citizenship Clause was to create an independent basis of federal citizenship, and thus to overturn the doctrine of primary state citizenship. The Slaughter-House Cases, 16 Wall. 36, 74, 95, 112. The background of this issue is traced in

tenBroek, The Antislavery Origins of the Fourteenth Amendment 71-93.

[43] Cong. Globe, 39th Cong., 1st Sess., 3031. See also Flack, The Adoption of the Fourteenth Amendment 93. In the same fashion, tenBroek, supra, at 215-217, concludes that the whole of § 1 was "declaratory and confirmatory." Id., at 217.

[44] Cong. Globe, 39th Cong., 1st Sess., 2890. See also the statement of Congressman Baker, Cong. Globe, 39th Cong., 1st Sess., App. 255, 256. Similarly, two months after the Amendment's passage through Congress, Senator Lane of Indiana remarked that the clause was "simply a re-affirmation" of the declaratory citizenship section of the Civil Rights Bill. Fairman, Does the Fourteenth Amendment Incorporate the Bill of Rights? 2 Stan. L. Rev. 5, 74.

[45] Senator Henderson participated in the debates upon the Enrollment Act and expressed no doubts about the constitutionality of § 21, Cong. Globe, 38th Cong., 2d Sess., 641, but the final vote upon the measure in the Senate was not recorded. Cong. Globe, 38th Cong., 2d Sess., 643.

[46] See, e. g., Cong. Globe, 38th Cong., 2d Sess., 632.

[47] Cong. Globe, 39th Cong., 1st Sess., 2895.

[48] The issues pertinent here were not, of course, matters of great consequence in the ratification debates in the several state legislatures, but some additional evidence is nonetheless available from them. The Committee on Federal Relations of the Texas House of Representatives thus reported to the House that the Amendment's first section "proposes to deprive the States of the right . . . to determine what shall constitute citizenship of a State, and to transfer that right to the Federal Government." Its "object" was, they thought, "to declare negroes to be citizens of the United States." Tex. House J. 578 (1866). The Governor of Georgia reported to the legislature that the "prominent feature of the first [section] is, that it settles definitely the right of citizenship in the several States, . . . thereby depriving them in the future of all discretionary power over the subject within their respective limits, and with reference to their State Governments proper." Ga. Sen. J. 6 (1866). See also the message of Governor Cox to the Ohio Legislature, Fairman, supra, 2 Stan. L. Rev., at 96, and the message of Governor Fletcher to the Missouri Legislature, Mo. Sen. J. 14 (1867). In combination, this evidence again suggests that the Citizenship Clause was expected merely to declare to whom citizenship initially attaches, and to overturn the doctrine of primary state citizenship.

[49] Senator Hendricks, for example, lamented its unfairness, declared that its presence was an "embarrassment" to the country, and asserted that it "is not required any longer." Cong. Globe, 40th Cong., 1st Sess., 660-661.

[50] Similarly, in 1885, this Court construed § 21 without any apparent indication that the section was, or had ever been thought to be, beyond Congress' authority. Kurtz v. Moffitt, 115 U. S. 487, 501-502.

[51] Tsiang, supra, n. 3, at 95. President Johnson emphasized in his Third Annual Message the difficulties which were then prevalent. 6 Richardson, Messages and Papers of the Presidents 558, 580-581.

[52] Tsiang, supra, at 95. See also 3 Moore, Digest of International Law 579-580.

[53] See, e. g., Cong. Globe, 40th Cong., 2d Sess., 968, 1129-1131.

[54] Van Trump's proposal contained nothing which would have expatriated any unwilling citizen, see Cong. Globe, 40th Cong., 2d Sess., 1801; its ultimate failure therefore cannot, despite the Court's apparent suggestion, help to establish that the House supposed that legislation similar to that at issue here was impermissible under the Constitution.

[55] Cong. Globe, 40th Cong., 2d Sess., 1800-1805.

[56] It should be noted that Van Trump, far from a "framer" of the Amendment, had not even been a member of the Congress which adopted it. Biographical Directory of the American Congress 1774-1961, H. R. Doc. No. 442, 85th Cong., 2d Sess., 1750.

[57] As General Banks, the Chairman of the House Committee on Foreign Affairs, carefully emphasized, the debates were intended simply to produce a declaration of the obligation of the United States to compel other countries "to consider the rights of our citizens and to bring the matter to negotiation and settlement"; the bill's proponents stood "for that and nothing more." Cong. Globe, 40th Cong., 2d Sess., 2315.

[58] The first such treaty was that with the North German Union, concluded February 22, 1868, and ratified by the Senate on March 26, 1868. 2 Malloy, Treaties, Conventions, International Acts, Protocols and Agreements between the United States and other Powers 1298. Similar treaties were reached in 1868 with Bavaria, Baden, Belgium, Hesse, and Württemberg; a treaty was reached in 1869 with Norway and Sweden. An analogous treaty was made with Mexico in 1868, but, significantly, it permitted rebuttal of the presumption of renunciation of citizenship. See generally Tsiang, supra, at 88.

[59] The relevance of these treaties was certainly not overlooked in the debates in the Senate upon the Act of 1868. See, e. g., Cong. Globe, 40th Cong., 2d Sess., 4205, 4211, 4329, 4331. Senator Howard attacked the treaties, but employed none of the reasons which might be suggested by the opinion for the Court today. Id., at 4211.

[60] 7 Richardson, Messages and Papers of the Presidents 284, 291. See further Borchard, Diplomatic Protection of Citizens Abroad §§ 319, 324, 325.

Justice Harlan's dissent in Reitman v. Mulkey (May 29, 1967)

MR. JUSTICE HARLAN, whom MR. JUSTICE BLACK, MR. JUSTICE CLARK, and MR. JUSTICE STEWART join, dissenting.

I consider that this decision, which cuts deeply into state political processes, is supported neither by anything "found" by the Supreme Court of California nor by any of our past cases decided under the Fourteenth Amendment. In my view today's holding, salutary as its result may appear at first blush, may in the long run actually serve to handicap progress in the extremely difficult field of racial concerns. I must respectfully dissent.

The facts of this case are simple and undisputed. The legislature of the State of California has in the last decade enacted a number of statutes restricting the right of private landowners to discriminate on the basis of such factors as race in the sale or rental of property. These laws aroused considerable opposition, causing certain groups to organize themselves and to take advantage of procedures embodied in the California Constitution permitting a "proposition" to be presented to the voters for a constitutional amendment. "Proposition 14" was thus put before the electorate in the 1964 election and was adopted by a vote of 4,526,460 to 2,395,747. The Amendment, Art. I, § 26, of the State Constitution, reads in relevant part as follows:

"Neither the State nor any subdivision or agency thereof shall deny, limit or abridge, directly or indirectly, the right of any person, who is willing or desires to sell, lease or rent any part or all of his real property, to decline to sell, lease or rent such property to such person or persons as he, in his absolute discretion, chooses."[1]

I am wholly at a loss to understand how this straightforward effectuation of a change in the California Constitution can be deemed a violation of the Fourteenth Amendment, thus rendering § 26 void and petitioners' refusal to rent their properties to respondents, because of their race, illegal under prior state law. The Equal Protection Clause of the Fourteenth Amendment, which forbids a State to use its authority to foster discrimination based on such factors as race, Takahashi v. Fish & Game Comm'n, 334 U. S. 410; Brown v. Board of Education, 347 U. S. 483; Goss v. Board of Education, 373 U. S. 683, does not undertake to control purely personal prejudices and predilections, and individuals acting on their own are left free to discriminate on racial grounds if they are so minded, Civil Rights Cases, 109 U. S. 3. By the same token, the Fourteenth Amendment does not require of States the passage of laws preventing such private discrimination, although it does not of course disable them from enacting such legislation if they wish.

In the case at hand California, acting through the initiative and referendum, has decided to remain "neutral" in the realm of private discrimination affecting the sale or rental of private residential property; in such transactions private owners are now free to act in a discriminatory manner previously forbidden to them. In short, all that has happened is that California has effected a pro tanto repeal of its prior statutes forbidding private discrimination. This runs no more afoul of the Fourteenth Amendment than would have California's failure to pass any such antidiscrimination statutes in the first instance. The fact that such repeal was also accompanied by a constitutional prohibition against future enactment of such laws by the California Legislature cannot well be thought to affect, from a federal constitutional standpoint, the validity of what California has done. The Fourteenth Amendment does not reach such state constitutional action any more than it does a simple legislative repeal of legislation forbidding private discrimination.

I do not think the Court's opinion really denies any of these fundamental constitutional propositions. Rather it attempts to escape them by resorting to arguments which appear to me to be entirely ill-founded.

I.

The Court attempts to fit § 26 within the coverage of the Equal Protection Clause by characterizing it as in effect an affirmative call to residents of California to discriminate.

The main difficulty with this viewpoint is that it depends upon a characterization of § 26 that cannot fairly be made. The provision is neutral on its face, and it is only by in effect asserting that this requirement of passive official neutrality is camouflage that the Court is able to reach its conclusion. In depicting the provision as tantamount to active state encouragement of discrimination the Court essentially relies on the fact that the California Supreme Court so concluded. It is said that the findings of the highest court of California as to the meaning and impact of the enactment are entitled to great weight. I agree of course, that findings of fact by a state court should be given great weight, but this familiar proposition hardly aids the Court's holding in this case.

There is no disagreement whatever but that § 26 was meant to nullify California's fair-housing legislation and thus to remove from private residential property transactions the state-created impediment upon freedom of choice. There were no disputed issues of fact at all, and indeed the California Supreme Court noted at the outset of its opinion that "[i]n the trial court proceedings allegations of the complaint were not factually challenged, no evidence was introduced, and the only matter placed in issue was the legal sufficiency of the allegations." 64 Cal. 2d 529, 531-532, 413 P. 2d 825, 827. There was no finding, for example, that the defendants' actions were anything but the product of their own private choice. Indeed, since the alleged racial discrimination that forms the basis for the Reitman refusal to rent on racial grounds occurred in 1963, it is not possible to contend that § 26 in any way influenced this particular act. There was no findings as to the general effect of § 26. The Court declares that the California court "held the intent of § 26 was to authorize private racial discriminations in the housing market . . . ," ante, p. 376, but there is no supporting fact in the record for this characterization. Moreover, the grounds which prompt legislators or state voters to repeal a law do not determine its constitutional validity. That question is decided by what the law does, not by what those who voted for it wanted it to do, and it must not be forgotten that the Fourteenth Amendment does not compel a State to put or keep any particular law about race on its books. The Amendment only forbids a State to pass or keep in effect laws discriminating on account of race. California has not done this.

A state enactment, particularly one that is simply permissive of private decision-making rather than coercive and one that has been adopted in this most democratic of processes, should not be struck down by the judiciary under the Equal Protection Clause without persuasive evidence of an invidious purpose or effect. The only "factual" matter relied on by the majority of the California Supreme Court was the context in which Proposition 14 was adopted, namely, that several strong antidiscrimination acts had been passed by the legislature and opposed by many of those who successfully led the movement for adoption of Proposition 14 by popular referendum. These circumstances, and these alone, the California court held, made § 26 unlawful under this Court's cases interpreting the Equal Protection Clause. This, of course, is nothing but a legal conclusion as to federal constitutional law, the California Supreme Court not having relied in any way upon the State Constitution. Accepting all the suppositions under which the state court acted, I cannot see that its conclusion is entitled to any special weight in the discharge of our own responsibilities. Put in another way, I cannot transform the California court's conclusion of law into a finding of fact that the State through the adoption of § 26 is actively promoting racial discrimination. It seems to me manifest that the state court decision rested entirely on what that court conceived to be the compulsion of the Fourteenth Amendment, not on any factfinding by the state courts.

II.

There is no question that the adoption of § 26, repealing the former state antidiscrimination laws and prohibiting the enactment of such state laws in the future, constituted "state action" within the meaning of the Fourteenth Amendment. The only issue is whether this provision impermissibly deprives any person of equal protection of the laws. As a starting point, it is clear that any statute requiring unjustified discriminatory treatment is unconstitutional. E. g., Nixon v. Herndon, 273 U. S. 536; Brown v. Board of Education, supra; Peterson v. City of Greenville, 373 U. S. 244. And it is no less clear that the Equal Protection Clause bars as well discriminatory governmental administration of a statute fair on its face. E. g., Yick Wo v. Hopkins, 118 U. S. 356. This case fits within neither of these two categories: Section 26 is by its terms inoffensive, and its provisions require no affirmative governmental enforcement of any sort. A third category of equal-protection cases, concededly more difficult to characterize, stands for the proposition that when governmental involvement in private discrimination reaches a level at which the State can be held responsible for the specific act of private discrimination, the strictures of the Fourteenth Amendment come into play. In dealing with this class of cases, the inquiry has been framed as whether the State has become "a joint participant in the challenged activity, which, on that account, cannot be considered to have been so `purely private' as to fall without the scope of the Fourteenth Amendment." Burton v. Wilmington Parking Authority, 365 U. S. 715, 725.

Given these latter contours of the equal-protection doctrine, the assessment of particular cases is often troublesome, as the Court itself acknowledges. Ante, pp. 378-379.

However, the present case does not seem to me even to approach those peripheral situations in which the question of state involvement gives rise to difficulties. See, e. g., Evans v. Newton, 382 U. S. 296; Lombard v. Louisiana, 373 U. S. 267. The core of the Court's opinion is that § 26 is offensive to the Fourteenth Amendment because it effectively encourages private discrimination. By focusing on "encouragement" the Court, I fear, is forging a slippery and unfortunate criterion by which to measure the constitutionality of a statute simply permissive in purpose and effect, and inoffensive on its face.

It is true that standards in this area have not been definitely formulated, and that acts of discrimination have been included within the compass of the Equal Protection Clause not merely when they were compelled by a state statute or other governmental pressures, but also when they were said to be "induced" or "authorized" by the State. Most of these cases, however, can be approached in terms of the impact and extent of affirmative state governmental activities, e. g., the action of a sheriff, Lombard v. Louisiana, supra; the official supervision over a park, Evans v. Newton, supra; a joint venture with a lessee in a municipally owned building, Burton v. Wilmington Parking Authority, supra.[2] In situations such as these the focus has been on positive state cooperation or partnership in affirmatively promoted activities, an involvement that could have been avoided. Here, in contrast, we have only the straightforward adoption of a neutral provision restoring to the sphere of free choice, left untouched by the Fourteenth Amendment, private behavior within a limited area of the racial problem. The denial of equal protection emerges only from the conclusion reached by the Court that the implementation of a new policy of governmental neutrality, embodied in a constitutional provision and replacing a former policy of antidiscrimination, has the effect of lending encouragement to those who wish to discriminate. In the context of the actual facts of the case, this conclusion appears to me to state only a truism: people who want to discriminate but were previously forbidden to do so by state law are now left free because the State has chosen to have no law on the subject at all. Obviously whenever there is a change in the law it will have resulted from the concerted activity of those who desire the change, and its enactment will allow those supporting the legislation to pursue their private goals.

A moment of thought will reveal the far-reaching possibilities of the Court's new doctrine, which I am sure the Court does not intend. Every act of private discrimination is either forbidden by state law or permitted by it. There can be little doubt that such permissiveness —whether by express constitutional or statutory provision, or implicit in the common law—to some extent "encourages" those who wish to discriminate to do so. Under this theory "state action" in the form of laws that do nothing more than passively permit private discrimination could be said to tinge all private discrimination with the taint of unconstitutional state encouragement.

This type of alleged state involvement, simply evincing a refusal to involve itself at all, is of course very different from that illustrated in such cases as Lombard, Peterson, Evans, and Burton, supra, where the Court found active involvement of state agencies and officials in specific acts of discrimination. It is also quite different from cases in which a state enactment could be said to have the obvious purpose of fostering discrimination. Anderson v. Martin, 375 U. S. 399. I believe the state action required to bring the Fourteenth Amendment into operation must be affirmative and purposeful, actively fostering discrimination. Only in such a case is ostensibly "private" action more properly labeled "official." I do not believe that the mere enactment of § 26, on the showing made here, falls within this class of cases.

III.

I think that this decision is not only constitutionally unsound, but in its practical potentialities short-sighted. Opponents of state antidiscrimination statutes are now in a position to argue that such legislation should be defeated because, if enacted, it may be unrepealable. More fundamentally, the doctrine underlying this decision may hamper, if not preclude, attempts to deal with the delicate and troublesome problems of race relations through the legislative process. The lines that have been and must be drawn in this area, fraught as it is with human sensibilities and frailties of whatever race or creed, are difficult ones. The drawing of them requires understanding, patience, and compromise, and is best done by legislatures rather than by courts. When legislation in this field is unsuccessful there should be wide opportunities for legislative amendment, as well as for change through such processes as the popular initiative and referendum. This decision, I fear, may inhibit such flexibility. Here the electorate itself overwhelmingly wished to overrule and check its own legislature on a matter left open by the Federal Constitution. By refusing to accept the decision of the people of California, and by contriving a new and ill-defined constitutional concept to allow federal judicial interference, I think the Court has taken to itself powers and responsibilities left elsewhere by the Constitution.

I believe the Supreme Court of California misapplied the Fourteenth Amendment, and would reverse its judgments, and remand the case for further appropriate proceedings.

Notes

[1] "Real Property" is defined by § 26 as "any interest in real property of any kind or quality, present or future, irrespective of how obtained or financed, which is used, designed, constructed, zoned or otherwise devoted to or limited for residential purposes whether as a single family dwelling or as a dwelling for two or more persons or families living together or independently of each other."

[2] In McCabe v. Atchison, Topeka & Santa Fe R. Co., 235 U. S. 151, cited by the Court, the complaint of the Negro appellants was held to have been properly dismissed on the ground that its allegations were "altogether too vague and indefinite," id., at 163. In dictum the Court stated that where a State regulated the facilities of a common carrier it could not constitutionally enact a statute that did not comply with the "separate but equal" doctrine. Whatever the implications of the Fourteenth Amendment may be as to common carriers, compare the opinions of Goldberg, J., concurring, and BLACK, J., dissenting, in Bell v. Maryland, 378 U. S. 226, 286, 318, nothing in McCabe would appear to have much relevance to the problem before us today.

Neither is there force in the Court's reliance on Nixon v. Condon, 286 U. S. 73, a voting case decided under the Fifteenth as well as the Fourteenth Amendment.

Justice Harlan's dissent in Udall v. FPC (June 5, 1967)

MR. JUSTICE HARLAN, whom MR. JUSTICE STEWART joins, dissenting.

I had thought it indisputable, first, that a court may not overturn a determination made by an administrative agency upon a question committed to the agency's judgment unless the determination is "unsupported by substantial evidence,"[1] and, second, that the substantiality of the evidence must be measured through, and only after, an examination of the "whole record."[2]

The Commission has determined, on the basis of 14,327 pages of testimony and exhibits, of "extensive material"[3] submitted after the close of the record by the Secretary of the Interior,[4] and of the Commission's own "general knowledge of the Columbia River System," 31 F. P. C. 247, 277, that the application of Pacific Northwest was "best adapted to a comprehensive plan," 49 Stat. 842, 16 U. S. C. § 803 (a), of development for this portion of the Columbia River Basin, and that, as a consequence, this site should not now be reserved for later development by the United States.[5]

The Court of Appeals unanimously concluded that this evidentiary record establishes that "the Commission was amply justified in refusing to recommend federal development and in issuing a license for private construction." 123 U. S. App. D. C. 209, 217, 358 F. 2d 840, 848. I agree. Doubtless much of the evidence was not, as it was submitted, labeled as pertinent to a determination of the Commission's responsibilities under § 7 (b), but I had not before understood that evidence marshaled in support of an agency's finding must, if it is to be credited, have been tidily categorized at the hearing according to the purposes for which it might subsequently be employed.

I can only conclude that the Court, despite its self-serving disclaimer, ante, pp. 450-451, has, in its haste to give force to its own findings of fact on the breeding requirements of anadromous fish[6] and on the likelihood that solar and nuclear power will shortly be alternative sources of supply, substituted its own preferences for the discretion given by Congress to the Federal Power Commission. In particular, it must be emphasized that the Court, alone among the Secretary of the Interior, the Commission, Pacific Northwest, the Washington Public Power Supply System, and the various other intervenors, apparently supposes that no dam at all may now be needed at High Mountain Sheep.[7] Wherever the right lies on that issue, it need only be said that Congress has entrusted its resolution to the Commission's informed discretion, and that, on the basis of an ample evidentiary record, the Commission has determined that Pacific Northwest should now be licensed to construct the project.

I would affirm the judgments in both cases substantially for the reasons given in Judge Miller's opinion below, as amplified by the considerations contained in this opinion.

Notes

[1] Administrative Procedure Act § 10 (e), 5 U. S. C. § 706 (2) (E) (1964 ed., Supp. II). See also Universal Camera Corp. v. Labor Board, 340 U. S. 474, 488; Jaffe, Judicial Control of Administrative Action 600 et seq. (1965).

[2] 5 U. S. C. § 706 (1964 ed., Supp. II).

[3] 31 F. P. C. 247, 275.

[4] The history of the Secretary's extraordinary series of belated and apparently indecisive interventions in these proceedings warrants a more complete chronicle than the Court has given. On March 31, 1958, Pacific Northwest applied for a license for the High Mountain Sheep site, and on October 21, 1959, the Commission solicited the views of the

Secretary of the Interior. On November 21, 1960, the Secretary replied substantively, and urged that the entire project be postponed, since the available power supply in the region was, in his view, then sufficient. The hearings nonetheless continued. On March 15, 1961, the Secretary wrote once more, first to indicate that he was withdrawing permission for Interior Department employees to testify at the hearings on questions of the alternative power sources and of the protection of the anadromous fish, and second to suggest that the hearings should be recessed or suspended until the end of 1964, more than three years later. There was, in these various communications, no intimation that federal development of the site was desirable or even appropriate. The hearings concluded on September 12, 1961.

On June 28, 1962, the Secretary suggested, for the first time, that federal development might be suitable; he did not, however, urge that either he or the Commission should immediately seek congressional approval of such a federal project, a precondition to its commencement. Nor did the Secretary intimate that the evidentiary record that had been compiled by the Commission might be incomplete, or request that it be reopened so that he might supplement it. Nonetheless, the Commission sua sponte ordered the parties to respond to the Secretary's suggestion.

On October 8, 1962, the Examiner completed his recommendations, concluding that Pacific Northwest's proposal was "best adapted" to the river's development, in part because federal development could not reasonably be immediately anticipated. The Secretary thereupon sought to intervene out of time, and to file exceptions. He did not request that the record be reopened. His motions were granted, and very extensive exceptions were filed. Oral argument of the exceptions was subsequently heard. Neither in the exceptions nor, apparently, in the oral argument did the Secretary seek to reopen the record to supplement the evidence before the Commission.

The Commission's decision, rejecting the Secretary's suggestions, was announced on February 5, 1964. The Secretary sought a rehearing on March 26, 1964, and only then did he ask that the record be reopened. He offered only the most general indications of the evidence he would introduce if his motion were granted. Not surprisingly, the Commission denied the motion, and, after consideration of various "pleadings," affirmed, with certain minor modifications, its first order. 31 F. P. C. 1051. These actions for review followed. The Secretary, apparently for the first time, announced in his petition to this Court for a writ of certiorari that he was now prepared to seek immediate congressional approval for federal construction of a dam at High Mountain Sheep.

[5] Section 7 (b) of the Federal Power Act, 49 Stat. 842, 16 U. S. C. § 800 (b), requires the Commission to refuse any application when it concludes that the project should be undertaken by the United States.

[6] It must be noted that nothing in the terms, purposes, or legislative history of the Anadromous Fish Act of 1965, 79 Stat. 1125, suggests in any way that it was expected to provide the Secretary or this Court with any retroactive "mandate" to overturn the Commission's judgment. The only pertinent portions of the legislative history are plain

and uncontradicted acknowledgments from the Federal Power Commission that the Act would not "have any effect" on its authority. Anadromous Fish, Hearings before the Subcommittee on Fisheries and Wildlife Conservation of the House Committee on Merchant Marine and Fisheries, 88th Cong., 2d Sess., 45; H. R. Rep. No. 1007, 89th Cong., 1st Sess., 21. Ironically, the Commission twice during the course of those hearings called attention, without any rejoinder from the Secretary, to the High Mountain Sheep project as an illustration of its continuing and earnest concern for the protection of anadromous fish. Hearings, supra, at 45; Report, supra, at 22.

[7] Contrary to his earlier position, supra, p. 452, the Secretary, as has been noted, now apparently entertains no doubt that the project should be immediately commenced.

Justice Harlan's dissent in Commissioner v. Estate of Bosch (June 5, 1967)

MR. JUSTICE HARLAN, whom MR. JUSTICE FORTAS joins, dissenting.

The central issue presented by these two cases is whether and in what circumstances a judgment of a lower state court is entitled to conclusiveness in a subsequent federal proceeding, if the state judgment establishes property rights from which stem federal tax consequences. The issue is doubly important: it is a difficult and intensely practical problem, and it involves basic questions of the proper relationship in this context between the state and federal judicial systems. For reasons which follow, I am constrained to dissent from the resolution reached by the Court in both cases.

I.

It is useful first to summarize the legal and factual circumstances out of which these cases arose.

In No. 240, Second National Bank, the decedent's will and codicil provided that one-third of the residuary estate should be held in trust for the decedent's widow, who was given a general testamentary power of appointment over the corpus, and that the balance should be held in separate trusts for his nine grandchildren. The widow's trust was plainly within the terms of the marital deduction provided by § 2056 (b) (5) of the Internal Revenue Code of 1954; the issue in this instance thus simply involves determination of the amount of this trust, and hence the amount of the marital deduction. Under Connecticut's tax-proration statute, Conn. Gen. Stat. Rev. § 12-401, a bequest exempt from estate tax, as here by reason of the federal marital deduction, is not reduced by any portion of such tax. Accordingly, if the proration statute is applicable to this decedent's will, the widow's trust would bear no part of the federal estate tax, and its entire burden would instead fall upon the grandchildren's trusts. The amount of the marital deduction would be correspondingly increased.

By its terms, the state proration statute is to be applied unless the "testator otherwise directs." Article I of the decedent's will provided, without apparent ambiguity, that the "provisions of any statute requiring the apportionment or proration of [estate] taxes . . . shall be without effect in the settlement of my estate." Nonetheless, the executor, petitioner here, contended to the Commissioner that the statute was applicable, and, upon receipt of the 30-day deficiency letter,[1] applied to the Probate Court for the District of Hamden, Connecticut, for a determination that the estate taxes should be apportioned under the terms of the state statute. Notice of the application was given to the District Director of Internal Revenue, but, in accord with the Service's consistent position with reference to such state proceedings, Mim. 6134, Apr. 3, 1947, 1947 CCH Fed. Tax Rep. ¶ 6137, no appearance was entered in his behalf.

Apart from the executor's application, the probate court had the benefit only of argument from the guardian ad litem of the grandchildren; the guardian acknowledged that proration under the statute would place the burden of the estate tax entirely upon his wards' trusts, but nevertheless concluded that he had "no objection" to the executor's application. The court, filing a written opinion, determined that the decedent's disclaimer of the statute was ambiguous, and therefore concluded that the statute was applicable. Petitioner thereupon paid the assessed deficiency, and brought this suit for a refund. The District Court and the Court of Appeals both concluded that, because of the character of Connecticut's probate court system,[2] the state judgment was not conclusive of the applicability of the proration statute. 222 F. Supp. 446; 351 F. 2d 489.

In No. 673, Estate of Bosch, the decedent created in 1930 a revocable inter vivos trust in favor of his wife, which also granted to her a general testamentary power of appointment over the corpus. In 1951, the decedent's wife, in order to take advantage of the Powers of Appointment Act of 1951, 65 Stat. 91, executed an instrument which purportedly converted the general power into a special power of appointment. Upon the decedent's death in 1957, his executor sought a marital deduction for the amount of the inter vivos trust; under § 2056 (b) (5), the trust would qualify for the deduction only if the decedent's wife held at his death a general power of appointment over the corpus.

The Commissioner, on the basis of the release signed in 1951 by the widow, disallowed the deduction, but the executor sought from the Tax Court a redetermination of the resulting deficiency. While the Tax Court proceeding was still pending, the executor petitioned in the New York Supreme Court for a determination under state law of the validity of the 1951 release. The Tax Court, with the Commissioner's assent, temporarily suspended its proceeding. In the state court, each of the three parties—the trustee, the widow, and the guardian ad litem of an infant who was a possible beneficiary—contended that the release was a nullity. The state court adopted their unanimous view. The Tax Court thereupon accepted the state trial court decision as an "authoritative exposition" of the requirements of state law. 43 T. C. 120. A divided Court of Appeals affirmed. 363 F. 2d 1009.

II.

The issue here, despite its importance in general, is essentially quite a narrow one. The questions of law upon which taxation turns in these cases are not among those for which federal definitions or standards have been provided; compare Burnet v. Harmel, 287 U. S. 103, 110; Heiner v. Mellon, 304 U. S. 271, 279; Lyeth v. Hoey, 305 U. S. 188, 194;

it is, on the contrary, accepted that federal tax consequences have here been imposed by Congress on property rights as those rights have been defined and delimited by the pertinent state laws. The federal revenue interest thus consists entirely of the expectation that the absence or presence of the rights will be determined accurately in accordance with the prevailing state rules. The question here is, however, not how state law must in the context of federal taxation ordinarily be determined; it is instead the more narrow one of whether and under what conditions a lower state court adjudication of a taxpayer's property rights is conclusive when subsequently the federal tax consequences of those rights are at issue in a federal court.

The problem may not, as the Court properly observes, be resolved by reference to the principles of res judicata or collateral estoppel, see generally Cromwell v. County of Sac, 94 U. S. 351, 352-353; the Revenue Service has not, and properly need not have, entered an appearance in either of the state court proceedings in question here. Nor do the pertinent provisions of the revenue laws, or their legislative history, provide an adequate guide to the solution of the problem; the only direct reference in that lengthy history relevant to these questions is imprecise and equivocal.[3] The cases in this Court are scarcely more revealing; they are, as Judge Friendly remarked below, "cryptic" and "rather dated." 363 F. 2d 1009, 1015.

It is, of course, plain that the Rules of Decision Act, 28 U. S. C. § 1652, is applicable here, as it is, by its terms, to any situation in which a federal court must ascertain and apply the law of any of the several States. Nor may it be doubted that the judgments of state courts must be accepted as a part of the state law to which the Act gives force in federal courts, Erie R. Co. v. Tompkins, 304 U. S. 64; it is not, for that purpose, material whether the jurisdiction of the federal court in a particular case is founded upon diversity of citizenship or involves a question arising under the laws of the United States.[4] This need not mean, however, that every state judgment must be accepted by federal courts as conclusive of state law. The Court has, for example, never held, even in diversity cases, where the federal interest consists at most in affording a "neutral" forum, that the judgments of state trial courts must in all cases be taken as conclusive statements of state law;[5] apart from a series of cases decided at the 1940 Term,[6] the Court has consistently acknowledged that the character both of the state proceeding and of the state court itself may be relevant in determining a judgment's conclusiveness as a statement of state law.[7] This same result must surely follow a fortiori in cases in which the application of a federal statute is at issue.

Similarly, it is difficult to see why the formula now ordinarily employed to determine state law in diversity cases—essentially that, absent a recent judgment of the State's highest court, state cases are only data from which the law must be derived—is necessarily applicable without modification in all situations in which federal courts must ascertain state law. The relationship between the state and federal judicial systems is simply too delicate and important to be reduced to any single standard. See Hill, The Erie Doctrine in Bankruptcy, 66 Harv. L. Rev. 1013; Note, The Competence of Federal Courts to

Formulate Rules of Decision, 77 Harv. L. Rev. 1084. Compare, e. g., Morgan v. Commissioner, 309 U. S. 78, 80-81; Cardozo, Federal Taxes and the Radiating Potencies of State Court Decisions, 51 Yale L. J. 783. The inadequacy of this formula is particularly patent here, where, unlike the cases in which it was derived, the federal court is confronted by precisely the legal and factual circumstances upon which the state court has already passed.

Accordingly, although the Rules of Decision Act and the Erie doctrine plainly offer relevant guidance to the appropriate result here, they can scarcely be said to demand any single conclusion.

III.

Given the inconclusiveness of these sources, it is essential to approach these questions in terms of the various state and federal interests fundamentally at stake. It suffices for present purposes simply to indicate the pertinent factors. On one side are certain of the principles which ultimately are the wellsprings both of the Rules of Decision Act and of the Erie doctrine. First among those is the expectation that scrupulous adherence by federal courts to the provisions of state law, as reflected both in local statutes and in state court decisions, will promote an appropriate uniformity in the administration of law within each of the States. Uniformity will, in turn, assure proper regard in the federal courts for the areas of law left by the Constitution to state discretion and administration, and, in addition, will prevent the incongruity that stems from dissimilar treatment by state and federal courts of the same or similar factual situations. Finally, it must be acknowledged that state courts are unquestionably better positioned to measure the requirements of their own laws; even the lowest state court possesses the tangible advantage of a close familiarity with the meaning and purposes of its local rules of law.

On the other side are important obligations which spring from the practical exigencies of the administration of federal revenue statutes. It can scarcely be doubted that if conclusiveness for federal tax purposes were attributed to any lower state court decree, whether the product of genuinely adversary litigation or not, there would be many occasions on which taxpayers might readily obtain favorable, but entirely inaccurate, determinations of state law from unsuspecting state courts. One need not, to envision this hazard, assume either fraud by the parties or any lack of competence or dis-interestedness among state judges; no more would be needed than a complex issue of law, a crowded calendar, and the presentation to a busy judge of but essentially a single viewpoint. The consequence of any such occurrence would be an explication of state law that would not necessarily be either a reasoned adjudication of the issues or a consistent application of the rules adopted by the State's appellate courts.

It is difficult to suppose that adherence by federal courts to such judgments would contribute materially to the uniformity of the administration of state law, or that the taxpayer would be unfairly treated if he were obliged to act, for purposes of federal taxation, as if he were governed by a more accurate statement of the requirements of state law. Certainly it would contribute nothing to the uniformity or accuracy of the administration of the federal revenue statutes if federal courts were compelled to adhere in all cases to such judgments.[8]

IV.

The foregoing factors might, of course, be thought consistent with a variety of disparate resolutions of the questions these two cases present. If emphasis is placed principally upon the importance of uniformity in the application of law within each of the several States, and thereby upon the apparent unfairness to an individual taxpayer if an issue of state law were differently decided by state and federal courts, it might seem appropriate to accept, in all but the most exceptional of circumstances, the judgment of any state court that has addressed the question at issue. This is the viewpoint identified with the opinion of the Court of Appeals for the Third Circuit in Gallagher v. Smith, 223 F. 2d 218; it is, in addition, apparently the rule adopted today by my Brother DOUGLAS. Conversely, if emphasis is placed principally upon the hazards to the federal fisc from dubious decisions of lower state courts, it might be thought necessary to require federal courts to examine for themselves, absent a judgment by the State's highest court, the content in each case of the pertinent state law. This, as I understand it, is the rule adopted by a majority of the Court today.

In my opinion, neither of these positions satisfactorily reconciles the relevant factors involved. The former would create excessive risks that federal taxation will be evaded through the acquisition of inadequately considered judgments from lower state courts, resulting from proceedings brought, in reality, not to resolve truly conflicting interests among the parties but rather as a predicate for gaining foreseeable tax advantages, and in which the point of view of the United States had never been presented or considered. The judgment resulting from such a proceeding might well differ only in form from a consent decree. The United States would be compelled either to accept as binding upon its interests such a judgment, or to participate in every state court proceeding, brought at the taxpayer's pleasure, which might establish state property rights with federal tax consequences.

The second position, on the other hand, would require federal intervention into the administration of state law far more frequently than the federal interests here demand; absent a judgment of the State's highest court, federal courts must under this rule re-examine and, if they deem it appropriate, disregard the previous judgment of a state court on precisely the identical question of state law. The result might be widely destructive both of the proper relationship between state and federal law and of the uniformity of the administration of law within a State.

The interests of the federal treasury are essentially narrow here; they are entirely satisfied if a considered judgment is obtained from either a state or a federal court, after consideration of the pertinent materials, of the requirements of state law. For this purpose, the Commissioner need not have, and does not now ask, an opportunity to relitigate in federal courts every issue of state law that may involve federal tax consequences; the federal interest requires only that the Commissioner be permitted to obtain from the federal courts a considered adjudication of the relevant state law issues in cases in which, for whatever reason, the state courts have not already provided such an adjudication. In turn, it may properly be assumed that the state court has had an opportunity to make, and has made, such an adjudication if, in a proceeding untainted by fraud, it has had the benefit of reasoned argument from parties holding genuinely inconsistent interests.

I would therefore hold that in cases in which state-adjudicated property rights are contended to have federal tax consequences, federal courts must attribute conclusiveness to the judgment of a state court, of whatever level in the state procedural system, unless the litigation from which the judgment resulted does not bear the indicia of a genuinely adversary proceeding. I need not undertake to define with any particularity the weight I should give to the various possible factors involved in such an assessment; it suffices to illustrate the more important of the questions which I believe to be pertinent. The principal distinguishing characteristic of a state proceeding to which, in my view, conclusiveness should be attributed is less the number of parties represented before the state court than it is the actual adversity of their financial and other interests. It would certainly be pertinent if it appeared that all the parties had instituted the state proceeding solely for the purpose of defeating the federal revenue. The taking of an appeal would be significant, although scarcely determinative. The burden would be upon the taxpayer, in any case brought either for a redetermination of a deficiency or for a refund, to overturn the presumption, Welch v. Helvering, 290 U. S. 111, 115, that the Commissioner had correctly assessed the necessary tax by establishing that the state court had had an opportunity to make, and had made, a reasoned resolution of the state law issues, after a proceeding in which the pertinent viewpoints had been presented. Proceedings in which one or more of the parties had been guilty of fraud in the presentation of the issues to the state court would, of course, ordinarily be entitled to little or no weight in the federal court's determination of state law.

I recognize, of course, that this approach lacks the precision of both the contrasting yardsticks suggested by the Court and by my Brother DOUGLAS. Yet I believe that it reflects more faithfully than either of those resolutions the demands of our federal system and of the competing interests involved.[9]

V.

I would apply these general principles to the present cases in the following manner. In No. 240, the Court of Appeals agreed with the District Court that "it was unnecessary" to make a finding on whether the proceedings in the Connecticut probate court were collusive or "nonadversary," since the decrees of the probate court could " `under no circumstances' " be considered binding. 351 F. 2d 489, 494. I would therefore vacate the judgment of the Court of Appeals and remand the cause for further proceedings in accordance with the views expressed herein.

In No. 673, the Court of Appeals apparently concluded that, absent fraud or collusion, any state court proceeding which terminates in a judgment binding on the parties as to their rights under state law is also conclusive for purposes of federal taxation. 363 F. 2d 1009, 1014. I would therefore reverse the judgment of the Court of Appeals, and again would remand the cause for further proceedings consistent with the views expressed in this opinion.

Notes

[1] The deficiency was assessed at $1,333,194.35, plus interest. If the proration statute is applicable, as the executor has contended, the marital deduction attributable to the widow's trust would be approximately $3,600,000. If the statute is not applicable, as the Commissioner has held, the marital deduction would be approximately $1,700,000.

[2] The District Court concluded that Connecticut probate courts are not courts of records (but see Shelton v. Hadlock, 62 Conn. 143, 25 A. 483, and 1 Locke & Kohn, Connecticut Probate Practice 30 (1951)), that its decrees are without legal effect in the State's higher courts, and that their decrees are also subject to collateral attack even in another probate district. 222 F. Supp., at 457; see also 351 F. 2d, at 494.

[3] A supplementary report of the Senate Finance Committee, concerned with the legislation which eventually became the Revenue Act of 1948, said simply that "proper regard should be given to interpretations of the will rendered by a court in a bona fide adversary proceeding." S. Rep. No. 1013, Pt. 2, 80th Cong., 2d Sess., 4. This language is doubtless broadly consistent with virtually any resolution of these issues, but it is difficult to see the pertinence of the sentence's last four words if, as the Court suggests, conclusiveness was intended to be given to the State's highest court, but to none other.

[4] See, e. g., Maternally Yours, Inc. v. Your Maternity Shop, Inc., 234 F. 2d 538; Friendly, In Praise of Erie—and of the New Federal Common Law, 39 N. Y. U. L. Rev. 383, 408, n. 122; Note, The Competence of Federal Courts to Formulate Rules of Decision, 77 Harv. L. Rev. 1084, 1087.

[5] See King v. Order of Travelers, 333 U. S. 153. Compare Bernhardt v. Polygraphic Co., 350 U. S. 198, 204, 209-211.

[6] Fidelity Union Trust Co. v. Field, 311 U. S. 169; Six Companies of California v. Joint Highway District, 311 U. S. 180; West v. A. T. & T. Co., 311 U. S. 223; and Stoner v. New York Life Ins. Co., 311 U. S. 464. See also Vandenbark v. Owens-Illinois Glass Co., 311 U. S. 538. All these cases, with the possible exception of Field, and apart from the rather different issue in Vandenbark, concerned intermediate state courts. They have been strongly and repeatedly criticized by commentators. Judge Friendly, for example, described them as "outrages," supra, at 401. See also Corbin, The Laws of the Several States, 50 Yale L. J. 762, 766-768; Clark, State Law in the Federal Courts, 55 Yale L. J. 267, 290-292; and 2 Crosskey, Politics and the Constitution 922-927 (1953). It may also be wondered whether these cases have any vitality left after King and Bernhardt, supra.

[7] Freuler v. Helvering, 291 U. S. 35; King v. Order of Travelers, supra; Bernhardt v. Polygraphic Co., supra.

[8] See, on the importance of uniformity in federal taxation, Hylton v. United

States, 3 Dall. 171, 180; Cahn, Local Law in Federal Taxation, 52 Yale L. J. 799.

[9] It may be doubted, however, whether this approach would actually produce serious practical disadvantages. It is essentially the standard which has been embodied in the Treasury Regulations since 1919, see now Treas. Reg. §§ 20.2053-1 (b) (2), 20.2056(e)-2(d) (2), and which was urged before this Court in these cases by counsel for the United States. It is, moreover, similar to the standards employed in various opinions by a number of the courts of appeals. See, e. g., Saulsbury v. United States, 199 F. 2d 578; Brodrick v. Gore, 224 F. 2d 892; In re Sweet's Estate, 234 F. 2d 401; Old Kent Bank & Trust Co. v. United States, 362 F. 2d 444. See also Cahn, supra, at 818-819; Braverman & Gerson, The Conclusiveness of State Court Decrees in Federal Tax Litigation, 17 Tax L. Rev. 545. If any practical difficulties actually attend this standard, they have apparently not, despite its wide use, yet appeared.

Justice Harlan's dissent in NLRB v. Great Dane Trailers, Inc. (June 12, 1967)

MR. JUSTICE HARLAN, whom MR. JUSTICE STEWART joins, dissenting.

Because I think that the Court puts forth a premise which misinterprets the recent decision in NLRB v. C & C Plywood Corp., 385 U. S. 421, and has proposed a determining rule based on a distillation of prior opinions which is, in my view, substantially inaccurate, I am constrained to express my dissent from its opinion. I believe that the Fifth Circuit correctly analyzed the problem, and that its decision should be affirmed.

The Court begins by stating that vacation benefits had "accrued" under the contract, and implies that striking employees had a contractual right to such benefits which was arbitrarily disregarded by Great Dane in order to punish those employees for engaging in protected activity. Were these the properly established facts of the case, I would have little difficulty in concurring in the result reached by the majority. Employer action which undercuts rights protected by § 7 of the National Labor Relations Act, as amended, 61 Stat. 140, and has no inferable, legitimate business purpose has been held a violation of §§ 8 (a) (3) and (1). Republic Aviation Corp. v. Labor Board, 324 U. S. 793. But the contract dispute is not so frivolous as to be determined without examination,[1] and the issue framed by the Court is not properly before us. Moreover, contrary to the Court's assertion, neither the Board nor the lower court limited itself to considering this issue, and both recognized a limitation on the Board's contract interpretation powers in light of § 301 (a) of the Labor Management Relations Act, 1947.[2]

The Board disclaimed "interpreting the contract for the parties" and held only that "strikers must be treated uniformly with nonstrikers with respect to whatever benefits accrue to the latter from the existence of the employment relationship." It explained that its order would merely force the employer to use the same vacation pay criteria for all employees and only prevent Great Dane from using the requirement that a recipient be at work as of July 1, 1963. The Court of Appeals considered the "term or condition of employment" at issue to be the employer's unilaterally declared vacation "policy." It explicitly disregarded "the question of whether the Board would have acted improperly . . . to decide whether it was an unfair labor practice to withhold benefits due under the contract . . . ." 363 F. 2d 130, 133. (Emphasis in original.)

I think the Board and the Court of Appeals were correct in disregarding the contract issue. In NLRB v. C & C Plywood Corp., supra, which the Court says upholds jurisdiction to consider the contract, we faced a situation in which an employer had taken a unilateral action with respect to wages which was a prima facie violation of § 8 (a) (3) and was attempting to justify that action by contractual privilege. The Court held that the interposition of a contractual defense could not deprive the Board of jurisdiction to "enforce a statutory right" where the Board had "not construed a labor agreement to determine the extent of the contractual rights which were given the union by the employer." Id., at 428. Also the agreement involved in that case did not contain an arbitration clause and thus the strong policy favoring arbitration was not infringed by the Board's action. Id., at 426. Here the Court's statement of the issue would imply that the Board may consider an unfair labor practice founded solely on breach of a contractual duty, and the labor agreement seems to invoke the remedy of arbitration.[3] In these circumstances, I think the only issue properly before the Court is whether the employer's unilaterally declared vacation policy, considered on its own bottom, constitutes a violation of § 8 (a) (3) absent a showing of improper motivation by evidence independent of the policy itself.

The Court attempts to resolve this issue as well as the contractual one. In the Court's view an employer must "come forward with evidence of legitimate and substantial business justifications" whenever any of his actions are challenged in a § 8 (a) (3) proceeding. Prior to today's decision, § 8 (a) (3) violations could be grouped into two general categories: those based on actions serving no legitimate business purposes or actions inherently severely destructive of employee rights where improper motive could be inferred from the actions themselves, and, in the latter instance, even a legitimate business purpose could be held by the Board not to justify the employer's conduct, Labor Board v. Erie Resistor Corp., 373 U. S. 221; and those not based on actions "demonstrably so destructive of employee rights and so devoid of significant service to any legitimate business end," where independent evidence evincing the employer's antiunion animus would be required to find a violation. Labor Board v. Brown, 380 U. S. 278, 286. The Court is unable to conclude that the employer's conduct in this case falls into the first category, and has proposed its rule as an added gloss on the second whose contours were fixed only two years ago in Brown.

Under today's formulation, the Board is required to find independent evidence of the employer's antiunion motive only when the employer has overcome the presumption of unlawful motive which the Court raises. This alteration of the burden in § 8 (a) (3) cases may either be a rule of convenience important to the resolution of this case alone or may, more unfortunately, portend an important shift in the manner of deciding employer unfair labor practice cases under § 8 (a) (3). In either event, I believe it is unwise.

The "legitimate and substantial business justifications" test may be interpreted as requiring only that the employer come forward with a nonfrivolous business purpose in order to make operative the usual requirement of proof of antiunion motive. If this is the result of today's decision, then the Court has merely penalized Great Dane for not anticipating this requirement when arguing before the Board. Such a penalty seems particularly unfair in view of the clarity of our recent pronouncements that "the Board must find from evidence independent of the mere conduct involved that the conduct was primarily motivated by an antiunion animus," Labor Board v. Brown, 380 U. S., at 288, and that "the Board must find that the employer acted for a proscribed purpose." American Ship Building Co. v. Labor Board, 380 U. S. 300, 313.

On the other hand, the use of the word "substantial" in the burden of proof formulation may give the Board a power which it formerly had only in § 8 (a) (3) cases like Erie Resistor, supra. The Board may seize upon that term to evaluate the merits of the employer's business purposes and weigh them against the harm that befalls the union's interests as a result of the employer's action. If this is the Court's meaning, it may well impinge upon the accepted principle that "the right to bargain collectively does not entail any `right' to insist on one's position free from economic disadvantage." American Ship Building Co. v. Labor Board, supra, at 309. Employers have always been free to take reasonable measures which discourage a strike by pressuring the economic interests of employees, including the extreme measure of hiring permanent replacements, without having the Board inquire into the "substantiality" of their business justifications. Labor Board v. Mackay Radio & Telegraph Co., 304 U. S. 333. If the Court means to change this rule, though I assume it does not, it surely should not do so without argument of the point by the parties and without careful discussion.

In my opinion, the Court of Appeals correctly held that this case fell into the category in which independent evidence of antiunion motive is required to sustain a violation. As was pointed out in the Court of Appeals opinion, a number of legitimate motives for the terms of the vacation policy could be inferred, 363 F. 2d, at 134, and an unlawful motive is not the sole inference to be drawn from the conduct. Nor is the employer's conduct here, like the super-seniority plan in Erie Resistor, supra, such that an unlawful motive can be found by "an application of the common-law rule that a man is held to intend the foreseeable consequences of his conduct." Radio Officers v. Labor Board, 347 U. S. 17, 45. The differences between the facts of this case and those of Erie Resistor, supra, are, as the parties recognize, so significant as to preclude analogy. Unlike the granting of super-seniority, the vacation pay policy here had no potential long-term impact on the bargaining situation. The vacation policy was not employed as a weapon against the strike as was the super-seniority plan. Notice of the date of required presence for vacation pay eligibility was not given until after the date had passed. The record shows clearly that Great Dane had no need to employ any such policy to combat the strike, since it had successfully replaced almost all of the striking employees.[4] The Trial Examiner rejected all union claims that particular actions by Great Dane demonstrated antiunion animus. In these circumstances, the Court of Appeals correctly found no substantial evidence of a violation of § 8 (a) (3).

Plainly the Court is concerned lest the strikers in this case be denied their "rights" under the collective bargaining agreement that expired at the commencement of the strike. Equally plainly, a suit under § 301 is the proper manner by which to secure these "rights," if they indeed exist. I think it inappropriate to becloud sound prior interpretations of § 8 (a) (3) simply to reach what seems a sympathetic result.

Notes

[1] The union elected to terminate the contract raising the question whether any right to vacation pay survived the termination. Also the contract provided for vacation pay when the employee was not actually granted a vacation, and the initial choice lay with the employer. Thus under the contract the employer was not obligated to grant two weeks' additional pay, but could choose to grant vacation instead and lower the total cash outlay. Termination precluded exercise of that choice.

[2] 61 Stat. 156, 29 U. S. C. § 185 (a). This position is supported by the legislative history discussed in NLRB v. C & C Plywood Corp., 385 U. S. 421, at 427.

[3] Article XIV of the contract provided that arbitration would not be required after one party had given notice of intent to terminate or modify the contract. This disclaimer clearly implies that arbitration would be required in the resolution of disputes arising under the contract.

[4] By July 1, 1963, almost 75% of the striking employees had been replaced. By August 1, 1963, when the dispute over vacation pay was coming to a head almost 90% had been replaced. All strikers had been replaced by October 8, 1963.

Justice Harlan's dissent in Berger v. New York (June 12, 1967)

MR. JUSTICE HARLAN, dissenting.

The Court in recent years has more and more taken to itself sole responsibility for setting the pattern of criminal law enforcement throughout the country. Time-honored distinctions between the constitutional protections afforded against federal authority by the Bill of Rights and those provided against state action by the Fourteenth Amendment have been obliterated, thus increasingly subjecting state criminal law enforcement policies to oversight by this Court. See, e. g., Mapp v. Ohio, 367 U. S. 643; Ker v. California, 374 U. S. 23; Malloy v. Hogan, 378 U. S. 1; Murphy v. Waterfront Commission, 378 U. S. 52. Newly contrived constitutional rights have been established without any apparent concern for the empirical process that goes with legislative reform. See, e. g., Miranda v. Arizona, 384 U. S. 436. And overlying the particular decisions to which this course has given rise is the fact that, short of future action by this Court, their impact can only be undone or modified by the slow and uncertain process of constitutional amendment.

Today's decision is in this mold. Despite the fact that the use of electronic eavesdropping devices as instruments of criminal law enforcement is currently being comprehensively addressed by the Congress and various other bodies in the country, the Court has chosen, quite unnecessarily, to decide this case in a manner which will seriously restrict, if not entirely thwart, such efforts, and will freeze further progress in this field, except as the Court may itself act or a constitutional amendment may set things right.

In my opinion what the Court is doing is very wrong, and I must respectfully dissent.

I.

I am, at the outset, divided from the majority by the way in which it has determined to approach the case. Without pausing to explain or to justify its reasoning, it has undertaken both to circumvent rules which have hitherto governed the presentation of constitutional issues to this Court, and to disregard the construction consistently attributed to a state statute by the State's own courts. Each of these omissions is, in my opinion, most unfortunate.

The Court declares, without further explanation, that since petitioner was "affected" by § 813-a, he may challenge its validity on its face. Nothing in the cases of this Court supports this wholly ambiguous standard; the Court until now has, in recognition of the intense difficulties so wide a rule might create for the orderly adjudication of constitutional issues, limited the situations in which state statutes may be challenged on their face. There is no reason here, apart from the momentary conveniences of this case, to abandon those limitations: none of the circumstances which have before properly been thought to warrant challenges of statutes on their face is present, cf. Thornhill v. Alabama, 310 U. S. 88, 98, and no justification for additional exceptions has been offered. See generally United States v. National Dairy Products Corp., 372 U. S. 29, 36; Aptheker v. Secretary of State, 378 U. S. 500, 521 (dissenting opinion). Petitioner's rights, and those of others similarly situated, can be fully vindicated through the adjudication of the consistency with the Fourteenth Amendment of each eavesdropping order.

If the statute is to be assessed on its face, the Court should at least adhere to the principle that, for purposes of assessing the validity under the Constitution of a state statute, the construction given the statute by the State's courts is conclusive of its scope and meaning. Fox v. Washington, 236 U. S. 273; Winters v. New York, 333 U. S. 507; Poulos v. New Hampshire, 345 U. S. 395. This principle is ultimately a consequence of the differences in function of the state and federal judicial systems. The strength with which it has hitherto been held may be estimated in part by the frequency with which the Court has in the past declined to adjudicate issues, often of great practical and constitutional importance, until the state courts "have been afforded a reasonable opportunity to pass upon them." Harrison v. NAACP, 360 U. S. 167, 176. See, e. g., Railroad Comm'n v. Pullman Co., 312 U. S. 496; Spector Motor Service, Inc. v. McLaughlin, 323 U. S. 101; Shipman v. DuPre, 339 U. S. 321; Albertson v. Millard, 345 U. S. 242; Government Employees v. Windsor, 353 U. S. 364.

The Court today entirely disregards this principle. In its haste to give force to its distaste for eavesdropping, it has apparently resolved that no attention need be given to the construction of § 813-a adopted by the state courts. Apart from a brief and partial acknowledgment, spurred by petitioner's concession, that the state cases might warrant exploration, the Court has been content simply to compare the terms of the statute with the provisions of the Fourth Amendment; upon discovery that their words differ, it has concluded that the statute is constitutionally impermissible. In sharp contrast, when confronted by Fourth Amendment issues under a federal statute which did not, and does not now, reproduce ipsissimis verbis the Fourth Amendment, 26 U. S. C. § 7607 (2), the Court readily concluded, upon the authority of cases in the courts of appeals, that the statute effectively embodied the Amendment's requirements. Draper v. United States, 358 U. S. 307, 310 n. And the Court, without the assistance even of state authorities, reached an identical conclusion as to a similar state statute in Ker v. California, 374 U. S. 23, 36 n. The circumstances of the present case do not come even within the narrow exceptions to the rule that the Court ordinarily awaits a state court's construction before adjudicating the validity of a state statute. Cf. Dombrowski v. Pfister, 380 U. S. 479; Baggett v. Bullitt, 377 U. S. 360. The Court has shown no justification for its disregard of existing and pertinent state authorities.

II.

The Court's precipitate neglect of the New York cases is the more obviously regrettable when their terms are examined, for they make quite plain that the state courts have fully recognized the applicability of the relevant federal constitutional requirements, and that they have construed § 813-a in conformity with those requirements. Opinions of the state courts repeatedly suggest that the "reasonable grounds" prescribed by the section are understood to be synonymous with the "probable cause" demanded by the Fourth and Fourteenth Amendments. People v. Cohen, 42 Misc. 2d 403, 404, 248 N. Y. S. 2d 339, 341; People v. Grossman, 45 Misc. 2d 557, 568, 257 N. Y. S. 2d 266, 277; People v. Beshany, 43 Misc. 2d 521, 525, 252 N. Y. S. 2d 110, 115. The terms are frequently employed interchangeably, without the least suggestion of any shadings of meaning. See, e. g., People v. Rogers, 46 Misc. 2d 860, 863, 261 N. Y. S. 2d 152, 155; People v. McDonough, 51 Misc. 2d 1065, 1069, 275 N. Y. S. 2d 8, 12. Further, a lower state court has stated quite specifically that "the same standards, at the least, must be applied" to orders under § 813-a as to warrants for the search and seizure of tangible objects. People v. Cohen, supra, at 407-408, 248 N. Y. S. 2d, at 344. Indeed, the court went on to say that the standards "should be much more stringent than those applied to search warrants." Id., at 408, 248 N. Y. S. 2d, at 344. Compare Siegel v. People, 16 N. Y. 2d 330, 332, 213 N. E. 2d 682, 683. The court in Cohen was concerned with a wiretap order, but the order had been issued under § 813-a, and there was no suggestion there or elsewhere that eavesdropping orders should be differently treated. New York's statutory requirements for search warrants, it must be emphasized, are virtually a literal reiteration of the terms of the Fourth Amendment. N. Y. Code Crim. Proc. § 793. If the Court wished a precise invocation of the terms of the Fourth Amendment, it had only to examine the pertinent state authorities.

There is still additional evidence that the State fully recognizes the applicability to eavesdropping orders of the Fourth Amendment's constraints. The Legislature of New York adopted in 1962 comprehensive restrictions upon the use of eavesdropped information obtained without a prior § 813-a order. N. Y. Civ. Prac. § 4506. The restrictions were expected and intended to give full force to the mandate of the opinion for this Court in Mapp v. Ohio, 367 U. S. 643. See 2 McKinney's Session Laws of New York 3677 (1962); New York State Legislative Annual 16 (1962). If it was then supposed that information obtained without a prior § 813-a order must, as a consequence of Mapp, be excluded from evidence, but that evidence obtained with a § 813-a order need not be excluded, it can only have been assumed that the requirements applicable to the issuance of § 813-a orders were entirely consistent with the demands of the Fourth and Fourteenth Amendments. The legislature recognized the "hiatus" in its law created by Mapp, and wished to set its own "house . . . in order." New York State Legislative Annual, supra, at 18. It plainly understood that the Amendments were applicable, and intended to adhere fully to their requirements.

New York's permissive eavesdropping statute must, for purposes of assessing its constitutional validity on its face, be read "as though" this judicial gloss had been "written into" it. Poulos v. New Hampshire, supra, at 402. I can only conclude that, so read, the statute incorporates as limitations upon its employment the requirements of the Fourth Amendment.

III.

The Court has frequently observed that the Fourth Amendment's two clauses impose separate, although related, limitations upon searches and seizures; the first "is general and forbids every search that is unreasonable," Go-Bart Co. v. United States, 282 U. S. 344, 357; the second places a number of specific constraints upon the issuance and character of warrants. It would be inappropriate and fruitless to undertake now to set the perimeters of "reasonableness" with respect to eavesdropping orders in general; any limitations, for example, necessary upon the period over which eavesdropping may be conducted, or upon the use of intercepted information unconnected with the offenses for which the eavesdropping order was first issued, should properly be developed only through a case-by-case examination of the pertinent questions. It suffices here to emphasize that, in my view, electronic eavesdropping, as such or as it is permitted by this statute, is not an unreasonable search and seizure.

At the least, reasonableness surely implies that this Court must not constrain in any grudging fashion the development of procedures, consistent with the Amendment's essential purposes, by which methods of search and seizure unknown in 1789 may be appropriately controlled.

It is instead obliged to permit, and indeed even to encourage, serious efforts to approach constructively the difficult problems created by electronic eavesdropping. In this situation, the Court should recognize and give weight to the State's careful efforts to restrict the excessive or unauthorized employment of these devices. New York has provided that no use may be made of eavesdropping devices without a prior court order, and that such an order is obtainable only upon the application of state prosecutorial authorities or of policemen of suitable seniority. N. Y. Code Crim. Proc. § 813-a. Eavesdropping conducted without an order is punishable by imprisonment for as much as two years. N. Y. Pen. Law §§ 738, 740. Information obtained through impermissible eavesdropping may not be employed for any purpose in any civil or criminal action, proceeding, or hearing, except in the criminal prosecution of the unauthorized eavesdropper himself. N. Y. Civ. Prac. § 4506. These restrictions are calculated to prevent the "unbridled,"[1] "unauthorized,"[2] and "indiscriminate"[3] electronic searches and seizures which members of this Court have frequently condemned. Surely the State's efforts warrant at least a careful, and even sympathetic, examination of the fashion in which the state courts have construed these provisions, and in which they have applied them to the situation before us. I cannot, in any event, agree that the Fourth Amendment can properly be taken as a roadblock to the use, within appropriate limits, of law enforcement techniques necessary to keep abreast of modern-day criminal activity. The importance of these devices as a tool of effective law enforcement is impressively attested by the data marshalled in my Brother WHITE'S dissenting opinion. Post, p. 107.

IV.

I turn to what properly is the central issue in this case: the validity under the Warrants Clause of the Fourth Amendment of the eavesdropping order under which the recordings employed at petitioner's trial were obtained. It is essential first to set out certain of the pertinent facts.

The disputed recordings were made under the authority of a § 813-a order, dated June 12, 1962, permitting the installation of an eavesdropping device in the business office of one Harry Steinman; the order, in turn, was, so far as this record shows, issued solely upon the basis of information contained in affidavits submitted to the issuing judge by two assistant district attorneys. The first affidavit, signed by Assistant District Attorney Goldstein, indicated that the Rackets Bureau of the District Attorney's Office of New York County was then conducting an investigation of alleged corruption in the State Liquor Authority, and that the Bureau had received information that persons desiring to obtain or retain liquor licenses were obliged to pay large sums to officials of the Authority. It described the methods by which the bribe money was transmitted through certain attorneys to the officials. The affidavit asserted that one Harry Neyer, a former employee of the Authority, served as a "conduit." It indicated that evidence had been obtained "over a duly authorized eavesdropping device installed in the office of the aforesaid Harry Neyer," that conferences "relative to the payment of unlawful fees" occurred in Steinman's office. The number and street address of the office were provided. The affidavit specified that the "evidence indicates that the said Harry Steinman has agreed to pay, through the aforesaid Harry Neyer, $30,000" in order to secure a license for the Palladium Ballroom, an establishment within New York City. The Palladium, it was noted, had been the subject of hearings before the Authority "because of narcotic arrests therein." On the basis of this information, the affidavit sought an order to install a recording device in Steinman's business office.

The second affidavit, signed by Assistant District Attorney Scotti, averred that Scotti, as the Chief of the Bureau to which Goldstein was assigned, had read Goldstein's affidavit, and had concluded that the order might properly issue under § 813-a.

The order as issued permitted the recording of "any and all conversations, communications and discussions" in Steinman's business office for a period of 60 days.

The central objections mounted to this order by petitioner, and repeated as to the statute itself by the Court, are three: first, that it fails to specify with adequate particularity the conversations to be seized; second, that it permits a general and indiscriminate search and seizure; and third, that the order was issued without a showing of probable cause.[4]

Each of the first two objections depends principally upon a problem of definition: the meaning in this context of the constitutional distinction between "search" and "seizure." If listening alone completes a "seizure," it would be virtually impossible for state authorities at a probable cause hearing to describe with particularity the seizures which would later be made during extended eavesdropping; correspondingly, seizures would unavoidably be made which lacked any sufficient nexus with the offenses for which the order was first issued. Cf. Kremen v. United States, 353 U. S. 346; Warden v. Hayden, 387 U. S. 294. There is no need for present purposes to explore at length the question's subtleties; it suffices to indicate that, in my view, conversations are not "seized" either by eavesdropping alone, or by their recording so that they may later be heard at the eavesdropper's convenience. Just as some exercise of dominion, beyond mere perception, is necessary for the seizure of tangibles, so some use of the conversation beyond the initial listening process is required for the seizure of the spoken word. Cf. Lopez v. United States, 373 U. S. 427, 459 (dissenting opinion); United States v. On Lee, 193 F. 2d 306, 313-314 (dissenting opinion); District of Columbia v. Little, 85 U. S. App. D. C. 242, 247, 178 F. 2d 13, 18, affirmed on other grounds, 339 U. S. 1. With this premise, I turn to these three objections.

The "particularity" demanded by the Fourth Amendment has never been thought by this Court to be reducible "to formula"; Oklahoma Press Pub. Co. v. Walling, 327 U. S. 186, 209; it has instead been made plain that its measurement must take fully into account the character both of the materials to be seized and of the purposes of the seizures. Accordingly, where the materials "are books, and the basis for their seizure is the ideas which they contain," the most "scrupulous exactitude" is demanded in the warrant's description; Stanford v. Texas, 379 U. S. 476, 485; see also Marcus v. Search Warrant, 367 U. S. 717; but where the special problems associated with the First Amendment are not involved, as they are not here, a more "reasonable particularity," Brown v. United States, 276 U. S. 134, 143; Consolidated Rendering Co. v. Vermont, 207 U. S. 541, 554, is permissible. The degree of particularity necessary is best measured by that requirement's purposes. The central purpose of the particularity requirement is to leave "nothing . . . to the discretion of the officer executing the warrant," Marron v. United States, 275 U. S. 192,

196, by describing the materials to be seized with precision sufficient to prevent "the seizure of one thing under a warrant describing another." Ibid. The state authorities are not compelled at the probable cause hearing to wager, upon penalty of a subsequent reversal, that they can successfully predict each of the characteristics of the materials which they will later seize, cf. Consolidated Rendering Co. v. Vermont, supra, at 554; such a demand would, by discouraging the use of the judicial process, defeat the Amendment's central purpose. United States v. Ventresca, 380 U. S. 102, 108.

The materials to be seized are instead described with sufficient particularity if the warrant readily permits their identification both by those entrusted with the warrant's execution and by the court in any subsequent judicial proceeding. "It is," the Court has said with reference to the particularity of the place to be searched, "enough if the description is such that the officer . . . can with reasonable effort ascertain and identify" the warrant's objects. Steele v. United States No. 1, 267 U. S. 498, 503.

These standards must be equally applicable to the seizure of words, and, under them, this order did not lack the requisite particularity. The order here permitted the interception, or search, of any and all conversations occurring within the order's time limitations at the specified location; but this direction must be read in light of the terms of the affidavits, which, under § 813, form part of the authority for the eavesdropping. The affidavits make plain that, among the intercepted conversations, the police were authorized to seize only those "relative to the payment of unlawful fees necessary to obtain liquor licenses." These directions sufficed to provide a standard which left nothing in the choice of materials to be seized to the "whim," Stanford v. Texas, supra, at 485, of the state authorities. There could be no difficulty, either in the course of the search or in any subsequent judicial proceeding, in determining whether specific conversations were among those authorized for seizure by the order. The Fourth and Fourteenth Amendments do not demand more. Compare Kamisar, The Wiretapping-Eavesdropping Problem: A Professor's View, 44 Minn. L. Rev. 891, 913.

Nor was the order invalid because it permitted the search of any and all conversations occurring at the specified location; if the requisite papers have identified the materials to be seized with sufficient particularity, as they did here, and if the search was confined to an appropriate area, the order is not invalidated by the examination of all within that area reasonably necessary for discovery of the materials to be seized. I do not doubt that searches by eavesdrop must be confined in time precisely as the search for tangibles is confined in space, but the actual duration of the intrusion here, or for that matter the total period authorized by the order, was not, given the character of the offenses involved, excessive. All the disputed evidence was obtained within 13 days, scarcely unreasonable in light of an alleged conspiracy involving many individuals and a lengthy series of transactions.

The question therefore remains only whether, as petitioner suggests, the order was issued without an adequate showing of probable cause. The standards for the measurement of probable cause have often been explicated in the opinions of this Court;

see, e. g., United States v. Ventresca, 380 U. S. 102; its suffices now simply to emphasize that the information presented to the magistrate or commissioner must permit him to "judge for himself the persuasiveness of the facts relied on by a complaining officer." Giordenello v. United States, 357 U. S. 480, 486. The magistrate must "assess independently the probability" that the facts are as the complainant has alleged; id., at 487; he may not "accept without question the complainant's mere conclusion." Id., at 486.

As measured by the terms of the affidavits here, the issuing judge could properly have concluded that probable cause existed for the order. Unlike the situations in Nathanson v. United States, 290 U. S. 41, and Giordenello v. United States, supra, the judge was provided the evidence which supported the affiants' conclusions; he was not compelled to rely merely on their "affirmation of suspicion and belief," Nathanson v. United States, supra, at 46. Compare Rugendorf v. United States, 376 U. S. 528; Aguilar v. Texas, 378 U. S. 108. In my opinion, taking the Steinman affidavits on their face, the constitutional requirements of probable cause were fully satisfied.

V.

It is, however, plain that the Steinman order was issued principally upon the basis of evidence obtained under the authority of the Neyer order; absent the Neyer eavesdropped evidence, the Steinman affidavits consist entirely of conclusory assertions, and they would, in my judgment, be insufficient. It is, therefore, also necessary to examine the Neyer order.

The threshold issue is whether petitioner has standing to challenge the validity under the Constitution of the Neyer order. Standing to challenge the constitutional validity of a search and seizure has been an issue of some difficulty and uncertainty;[5] it has, nevertheless, hitherto been thought to hinge, not upon the use against the challenging party of evidence seized during the search, but instead upon whether the privacy of the challenging party's premises or person has been invaded. Jones v. United States, 362 U. S. 257; Wong Sun v. United States, 371 U. S. 471. These cases centered upon searches conducted by federal authorities and challenged under Fed. Rule Crim. Proc. 41 (e), but there is no reason now to suppose that any different standard is required by the Fourteenth Amendment for searches conducted by state officials. See generally Maguire, Evidence of Guilt 215-216 (1959).

The record before us does not indicate with precision what information was obtained under the Neyer order, but it appears, and petitioner does not otherwise assert, that petitioner was never present in Neyer's office during the period in which eavesdropping was conducted. There is, moreover, no suggestion that petitioner had any property interest in the premises in which the eavesdropping device was installed. Apart from the use of evidence obtained under the Neyer order to justify issuance of the Steinman order, under which petitioner's privacy was assuredly invaded, petitioner is linked with activities under the Neyer order only by one fleeting and ambiguous reference in the record.

In a pretrial hearing conducted on a motion to suppress the Steinman recordings, counsel for the State briefly described the materials obtained under the Neyer order. Counsel indicated that

"Mr. Neyer then has conversations with Mr. Steinman and other persons. In the course of some of these conversations, we have one-half of a telephone call, of several telephone calls between Mr. Neyer and a person he refers to on the telephone as Mr. Berger; and in the conversation with Mr. Berger Mr. Neyer discusses also the obtaining of a liquor License for the Palladium and mentions the fact that this is going to be a big one."

Counsel for petitioner responded, shortly after, that "I take it . . . that none of the subject matter to which [counsel for the State] has just adverted is any part of this case . . . ." Counsel for the State responded:

"That's right, your Honor. I am not—I think evidence can be brought out during the trial that Berger, who Mr. Steinman, Mr. Neyer speaks to concerning the Palladium, is, in fact, the defendant Ralph Berger."

However oblique this invasion of petitioner's personal privacy might at first seem, it would entirely suffice, in my view, to afford petitioner standing to challenge the validity of the Neyer order. It is surely without significance in these circumstances that petitioner did not conduct the conversation from a position physically within the room in which the device was placed; the fortuitousness of his location can matter no more than if he had been present for a conference in Neyer's office, but had not spoken, or had been seated beyond the limits of the device's hearing. The central question should properly be whether his privacy has been violated by the search; it is enough for this purpose that he participated in a discussion into which the recording intruded. Standing should not, in any event, be made an insuperable barrier which unnecessarily deprives of an adequate remedy those whose rights have been abridged; to impose distinctions of excessive refinement upon the doctrine "would not comport with our justly proud claim of the procedural protections accorded to those charged with crime." Jones v. United States, supra, at 267. It would instead "permit a quibbling distinction to overturn a principle which was designed to protect a fundamental right." United States v. Jeffers, 342 U. S. 48, 52. I would conclude that, under the circumstances here, the recording of a portion of a telephone conversation to which petitioner was party would suffice to give him standing to challenge the validity under the Constitution of the Neyer order.[6]

Given petitioner's standing under federal law to challenge the validity of the Neyer order, I would conclude that such order was issued without an adequate showing of probable cause. It seems quite plain, from the facts described by the State, that at the moment the Neyer order was sought the Rackets Bureau indeed had ample information to justify the issuance of an eavesdropping order. Nonetheless, the affidavits presented at the Neyer hearing unaccountably contained only the most conclusory allegations of suspicion. The record before us is silent on whether additional information might have been orally presented to the issuing judge.[7] Under these circumstances, I am impelled to the view that the judge lacked sufficient information to permit him to assess the circumstances as a "neutral and detached magistrate," Johnson v. United States, 333 U. S. 10, 14, and accordingly that the Neyer order was impermissible.

VI.

It does not follow, however, that evidence obtained under the Neyer order could not properly have been employed to support issuance of the Steinman order. The basic question here is the scope of the exclusionary rule fashioned in Weeks v. United States, 232 U. S. 383, and made applicable to state proceedings in Mapp v. Ohio, 367 U. S. 643. The Court determined in Weeks that the purposes of the Fourth Amendment could be fully vindicated only if materials seized in violation of its requirements were excluded from subsequent use against parties aggrieved by the seizure. Despite broader statements in certain of the cases, see, e. g., Silverthorne Lumber Co. v. United States, 251 U. S. 385, 392, the situations for which the Weeks rule was devised, and to which it has since been applied, have uniformly involved misconduct by police or prosecutorial authorities. The rule's purposes have thus been said to be both to discourage "disobedience to the Federal Constitution," Mapp v. Ohio, supra, at 657, and to avoid any possibility that the courts themselves might be "accomplices in the willful disobedience of a Constitution they are sworn to uphold." Elkins v. United States, 364 U. S. 206, 223. The Court has cautioned that the exclusionary rule was not intended to establish supervisory jurisdiction over the administration of state criminal justice, and that the States might still fashion "workable rules governing arrests, searches and seizures." Ker v. California, 374 U. S. 23, 34.

I find nothing in the terms or purposes of the rule which demands the invalidation, under the circumstances at issue here, of the Steinman order. The state authorities appeared, as the statute requires, before a judicial official, and held themselves ready to provide information to justify the issuance of an eavesdropping order. The necessary evidence was at hand, and there was apparently no reason for the State to have preferred that it not be given to the issuing judge. The Neyer order is thus invalid simply as a consequence of the judge's willingness to act upon substantially less information than the Fourteenth Amendment obliged him to demand; correspondingly, the only "misconduct" that could be charged against the prosecution consists entirely of its failure to press additional evidence upon him. If the exclusionary rule were to be applied in this and similar situations, praiseworthy efforts of law enforcement authorities would be seriously, and quite unnecessarily, hampered; the evidence lawfully obtained under a lengthy series of valid warrants might, for example, be lost by the haste of a single magistrate. The rule applied in that manner would not encourage police officers to adhere to the requirements of the Constitution; it would simply deprive the State of evidence it has sought in accordance with those requirements.

I would hold that where, as here, authorities have obtained a warrant in a judicial proceeding untainted by fraud, a second warrant issued on the authority of evidence gathered under the first is not invalidated by a subsequent finding that the first was issued without a showing of probable cause.

VII.

It follows that the Steinman order was, as a matter of constitutional requirement, validly issued, that the recordings obtained under it were properly admitted at petitioner's trial, and, accordingly, that his conviction must be affirmed.[8]

Notes

[1] Hoffa v. United States, 385 U. S. 293, 317 (dissenting opinion).

[2] Silverman v. United States, 365 U. S. 505, 510.

[3] Lopez v. United States, 373 U. S. 427, 441 (opinion concurring in result).

[4] Two of petitioner's other contentions are plainly foreclosed by recent opinions of this Court. His contention that eavesdropping unavoidably infringes the rule forbidding the seizure of "mere evidence" is precluded by Warden v. Hayden, 387 U. S. 294. His contention that eavesdropping violates his constitutional privilege against self-incrimination is answered by Osborn v. United States, 385 U. S. 323, and Hoffa v. United States, 385 U. S. 293.

[5] See, e. g., Edwards, Standing to Suppress Unreasonably Seized Evidence, 47 Nw. U. L. Rev. 471; Comment, Standing to Object to an Unreasonable Search and Seizure, 34 U. Chi. L. Rev. 342; Recent Development, Search and Seizure: Admissibility of Illegally Acquired Evidence Against Third Parties, 66 Col. L. Rev. 400.

[6] While on this record it cannot be said with entire assurance that the "Berger" mentioned in the Neyer eavesdropped conversation was this petitioner, I think it proper to proceed at this juncture on the basis that such is the case, leaving whatever questions of identity there may be to such state proceedings as, on the premises of this opinion, might subsequently eventuate in the state courts. See n. 8, infra.

[7] The only additional reference in the record possibly pertinent to the content of the Neyer hearing is a conclusory assertion by counsel for the State in argument on the motion to suppress that the State had shown its evidence to the issuing judge. The reference is obscure, but its context suggests strongly that counsel meant only that the Steinman affidavits were adequate for purposes of probable cause.

[8] Whether N. Y. Civ. Prac. § 4506, as amended to take effect July 1, 1962, some 18 days after the issuance of the Steinman order, would be deemed, under the premises of this opinion, to render inadmissible at Berger's trial the evidence procured under it, is a matter for the state courts to decide. See People v. Cohen, 42 Misc. 2d 403, 408, 409, 248 N. Y. S. 2d 339, 344, 345; People v. Beshany, 43 Misc. 2d 521, 532, 252 N. Y. S. 2d 110, 121. Further state proceedings on that score would of course not be foreclosed under a disposition in accordance with this opinion.

Justice Harlan's dissent in US v. Sealy, Inc. (June 12, 1967)

MR. JUSTICE HARLAN, dissenting.

I cannot agree that on this record the restrictive territorial arrangements here challenged are properly to be classified as "horizontal," and hence illegal per se under established antitrust doctrine. I believe that they should be regarded as "vertical" and thus, as the Court recognizes, subject to different antitrust evaluation.

Sealy, Inc., is the owner of trademarks for Sealy branded bedding. Sealy licenses manufacturers in various parts of the country to produce and sell its products. In addition, Sealy provides technical and managerial services for them, conducts advertising and other promotional programs, and engages in technical research and quality control activities. The Government's theory of this case in the District Court was essentially that the allocation of territories by Sealy to its various licensees was unlawful per se because in spite of these other legitimate activities Sealy was actually a "front" created and used by the various manufacturers of Sealy products "to camouflage their own collusive activities . . . ." Plaintiff's Brief in Opposition to Defendants' Briefs, October 12, 1961, pp. 12, 15.

If such a characterization of Sealy had been proved at trial I would agree that the division of territories is illegal per se. Horizontal agreements among manufacturers to divide territories have long been held to violate the antitrust laws without regard to any asserted justification for them. See Addyston Pipe & Steel Co. v. United States, 175 U. S. 211; United States v. National Lead Co., 332 U. S. 319; Timken Roller Bearing Co. v. United States, 341 U. S. 593. The reason is that territorial divisions prevent open competition, and where they are effected horizontally by manufacturers or by sellers who in the normal course of things would be competing among themselves, such restraints are immediately suspect. As the Court noted in White Motor Co. v. United States, 372 U. S. 253, 263, they are "naked restraints of trade with no purpose except stifling of competition." On the other hand, vertical restraints—that is, limitations imposed by a manufacturer on his own dealers, as in White Motor Co., supra, or by a licensor on his licensees—may have independent and valid business justifications. The person imposing the restraint cannot necessarily be said to be acting for anticompetitive purposes. Quite to the contrary, he can be expected to be acting to enhance the competitive position of his product vis-à-vis other brands.

With respect to vertical restrictions, it has long been recognized that in order to engage in effective interbrand competition, some limitations on intrabrand competition may be necessary. Restraints of this type "may be allowable protections against aggressive competitors or the only practicable means a small company has for breaking into or staying in business (cf. Brown Shoe [v. United States, 370 U. S. 294], at 330; United States v. Jerrold Electronics Corp., 187 F. Supp. 545, 560-561, aff'd, 365 U. S. 567) and within the `rule of reason,' " White Motor Co., supra, at 263; see also id., at 267-272 (concurring opinion of BRENNAN, J.). For these reasons territorial limitations imposed vertically should be tested by the rule of reason, namely, whether in the context of the particular industry, "the restraint imposed is such as merely regulates and perhaps thereby promotes competition or whether it is such as may suppress or even destroy competition." Chicago Board of Trade v. United States, 246 U. S. 231, 238. Indeed the Court reaffirms these principles in the opinion which it announces today in United States v. Arnold, Schwinn & Co., post, p. 365.

The question in this case is whether Sealy is properly to be regarded as an independent licensor which, as a prima facie matter, can be deemed to have imposed these restraints on its licensees for its own business purposes, or as equivalent to a horizontal combination of licensees, that is as simply a vehicle for effectuating horizontal arrangements between its licensees. On the basis of the findings made by the District Court, I am unable to accept the Court's classification of these restraints as horizontally contrived. The District Court made the following findings:

"84. The preceding [detailed factual] findings indicate the type of evidence in this record that demonstrates that there has never been a central conspiratorial purpose on the part of Sealy and its licensees to divide the United States into territories in which competitors would not compete. Their main purpose has been the proper exploitation of the Sealy name and trademarks by licensing bedding manufacturers to manufacture and sell Sealy products in exchange for royalties to Sealy. The fact remains that each licensee was restricted in the territory in which he could manufacture and sell Sealy products. However, the record shows that this restriction was imposed by Sealy and was also secondary, or ancillary, to the main purpose of Sealy's license contracts.

.....

"119. Plaintiff's evidence, read as a whole, conclusively proves that the Sealy licensing arrangements were developed in the early 1920's for entirely legitimate business purposes, including royalty income to Sugar Land Industries, which owned the Sealy name, trademarks and patents, and the benefits to licensees of joint purchasing, research, engineering, advertising and merchandising. These objectives were carried out by successor companies, including defendant, whose activities have been directed not toward market division among licensees but toward obtaining additional licensees and more intensive sales coverage."

The Solicitor General in presenting the appeal to this Court stated explicitly that he did not contend "that Sealy, Inc. was no more than a facade for a conspiracy to suppress competition," Brief, p. 12, since it admittedly did have genuine and lawful purposes. For me these District Court findings, which the Government accepts for purposes of this appeal, take this case out of the category of horizontal agreements, and thus out of the per se category as well.[1] Sealy has wholly legitimate interests and purposes of its own: it is engaged in vigorous interbrand competition with large integrated bedding manufacturers and with retail chains selling their own products.[2] Sealy's goal is to maximize sales of its products nationwide, and thus to maximize its royalties. The test under such circumstances should be the same as that governing other vertical relationships, namely, whether in the context of the market structure of this industry, these territorial restraints are reasonable business practices, given the true purposes of the antitrust laws. See White Motor Co., supra; Sandura Co. v. FTC, 339 F. 2d 847. It is true that in this case the shareholders of Sealy are the licensees. Such a relationship no doubt requires special scrutiny.[3] But I cannot agree that this fact by itself automatically requires striking down Sealy's policy of territorialization. The correct approach, in my view, is to consider Sealy's corporate structure and decision-making process as one (but only one) relevant factor in determining whether the restraint is an unreasonable one. Compare United States v. Penn-Olin Chem. Co., 378 U. S. 158, 170.

The Court in reaching its result relies heavily on the fact that these territorial limitations were part of "an `aggregation of trade restraints,' " ante, p. 354, because the District Court has held that appellee did violate the Sherman Act by engaging in unlawful price fixing. "The territorial restraints," the Court says, "were a part of the unlawful price-fixing and policing," ante, p. 356. Nothing, however, in the findings of the District Court supports this conclusion. Indeed, the opposite conclusion is the more tenable one since the District Court that found Sealy guilty of price fixing found at the same time that it had not unlawfully conspired to allocate territories. The Government has not contended here that it is entitled to an injunction against territorial restrictions as a part of its relief in the price-fixing aspect of the case. The price-fixing issue was not appealed to this Court, and we can assume that the Government will obtain adequate and effective injunctive relief from the District Court. For these reasons the Court's "aggregation of trade restraints" theory seems to me ill-conceived.

I find nothing in the Court's opinion that persuades me to abandon the traditional "rule of reason" approach to this type of business practice in the context of the facts found by the trial court. The District Court, however, made no findings in respect to this theory for judging liability since the Government insisted on trying the case in per se terms, attempting to prove only a horizontal conspiracy. Although Sealy did introduce some evidence concerning the bedding industry, the territorialization issue was not tried in the terms of the reasonableness of the territorial restrictions. A motion to suppress Sealy's subpoena seeking discovery with respect to one of its leading competitors was successfully supported by the Government,[4] and no evidence directly aimed at justifying territorial limitations as a reasonable method of competition in the bedding industry was taken. Accordingly, the District Court made no findings as to such justification.

Although in the normal course of things I would have voted to remand the case for further proceedings and findings under the correct rules of law, I believe that since the Government deliberately chose to stand on its per se approach, and did not prevail, it should not be able to relitigate the case on an alternative theory, especially when it opposed appellee's efforts to present the case that way.

I would affirm the dismissal of this aspect of the case by the District Court.

Notes

[1] Compare United States v. General Motors, 384 U. S. 127, where the undisputed facts as found by the District Court, id., at 140-141, proved a horizontal conspiracy among Chevrolet dealers to initiate and police a boycott of sales by dealers to discount houses. It is precisely because no such horizontal impetus was shown to exist here that I view this case differently. See my opinion concurring in the result in General Motors, 384 U. S., at 148.

[2] The District Court made no findings as to the position of Sealy in the bedding

industry, but on the basis of testimony introduced and not seriously contravened it appears that Sealy products are by no means the largest selling bedding products, that Sealy manufacturers have many competitors both nationwide and local, and that advertising—particularly nationwide advertising—is an important competitive factor in the industry.

[3] The Sealy trademark was originally owned by Sugar Land Industries, and its products were manufactured by a subsidiary, Sealy Mattress Co. In the 1920's independent manufacturers were licensed to produce Sealy products, and in 1925 Sugar Land sold the trademarks to a new corporation, Sealy Corp., owned by one E. E. Edwards and the various Sealy licensees. In 1933, when the economic depression eliminated a number of Sealy producers, the corporation was reorganized into the present Sealy, Inc. At present there are about 30 licensees owning approximately 90% of the stock. This joint-venture approach was created and maintained, the District Court found, "for entirely legitimate business purposes," such as obtaining the benefits "of joint purchasing, research, engineering, advertising and merchandising." Finding 119.

[4] See United States v. Serta Associates, Inc., 29 F. R. D. 136, where in a companion action against another licensor of bedding products a similar subpoena was quashed after it was opposed by the Government. The District Court there noted: "The complaint alleges price fixing and market allocations by Serta, which it has denied. Defendant alleges the agreements made were reasonable ancillary restraints, valid under the Sherman Act, and the evidence sought by this subpoena would completely corroborate the reasonableness. The plaintiff, the Government, has also filed a brief supportive of the motion to quash the subpoena. It asserts that the complaint raises per se violations of the Sherman Act which fact renders completely irrelevant the subpoenaed material, tending to confirm the reasonableness of defendant's conduct."

Justice Harlan's dissent in Roberts v. LaVallee (Oct 23, 1967)

MR. JUSTICE HARLAN, dissenting.

As the Court states, petitioner was told that if he wished a transcript of his preliminary hearing he would have to pay for it. The Court fails to add, however, that petitioner and his counsel were both present at the preliminary hearing, that they were furnished a free transcript of the grand jury testimony of the state witness in question but made no use of this transcript at trial, and that at no time has petitioner suggested any use to which the preliminary hearing transcript could have been put, although he is in a position to know what it contains.

The decisions cited in the majority opinion fall far short of declaring that any document related to the criminal process, no matter how demonstrably trivial its significance, must be supplied free to indigents simply because the State is willing to make it available to others able to pay for it. Rather than formulate such an undiscriminating rule, a rule that predictably may lead to a narrowing of the availability of documents that a

State is not constitutionally required to furnish to any criminal defendant, I would at least undertake to examine the importance of the particular document in question.

This examination is not necessary in the present case, however, for, as the Court's opinion recognizes, there exists an adequate basis under state law for affording petitioner the relief that he seeks here. Believing, as did the Court of Appeals, that federal courts should not unnecessarily interfere with the administration of justice in state courts, particularly when this involves reaching federal constitutional questions unnecessarily, see Harrison v. NAACP, 360 U. S. 167, I would affirm the decision below.

In addition, in the circumstances depicted by this record, I consider the Court's disposition of this case improvident even under the postulates of its opinion. I understand the Court to require the issuance of a writ of habeas corpus, and hence the setting aside of the state conviction, without any further investigation of whether the constitutional error now found to have been committed by the state courts actually prejudiced this defendant. Since there appears every likelihood that further examination would reveal that the denial of a preliminary hearing transcript to this petitioner was "harmless beyond a reasonable doubt," Chapman v. California, 386 U. S. 18, at 24, the case should have been sent back to the Court of Appeals with instruction to remand to the District Court for a hearing to determine the possibility of prejudice. Cf. Roberts v. United States, ate, p. 18. Due respect for state criminal processes requires at least this much.

Justice Harlan's concurrence in Wyandotte Transp. v. US (Dec 4, 1967)

MR. JUSTICE HARLAN, concurring.

I concur in the Court's holding that under § 15 of the Rivers and Harbors Act of 1899, 33 U. S. C. § 409, the United States may recover the costs of removing a vessel negligently sunk in navigable waters from those responsible for the sinking. I further agree with the holding that the United States is entitled to the declaratory relief sought in the Cargill action. In affording this latter relief it is my understanding that the Court does not purport to decide whether the United States may also obtain an injunction compelling removal, but has left that question to be answered in light of a full development of the facts, and in accordance with normal standards of equity.

In reaching these conclusions, I have not been unmindful of the view stated by me in dictum in my dissenting opinion in United States v. Republic Steel Corp., 362 U. S. 482, 493, to the effect that the courts are precluded from supplying relief not expressly found in the Rivers and Harbors Act. Insofar as that dictum might be taken to encompass the present case, where, contrary to my view in Republic Steel, I do believe that the relief afforded by this Court is fairly to be implied from the statute, candor would compel me to say that the dictum was ill-founded.

On these premises I join the opinion of the Court.

Justice Harlan's dissent in Mine Workers v. Illinois Bar Assn. (Dec 5, 1967)

MR. JUSTICE HARLAN, dissenting.

This decision cuts deeply into one of the most traditional of state concerns, the maintenance of high standards within the state legal profession. I find myself unable to subscribe to it.

The Canons of Professional Ethics of the Illinois State Bar Association forbid the unauthorized practice of law by any lay agency.[1] The Illinois Supreme Court, acting in light of these canons and in exercise of its common-law power of supervision over the Bar,[2] prohibited the United Mine Workers of America, District 12, from employing a salaried lawyer to represent its members in workmen's compensation actions before the Illinois Industrial Commission. I do not believe that this regulation of the legal profession infringes upon the rights of speech, petition, or assembly of the Union's members, assured by the Fourteenth Amendment.

I.

As I stated at greater length in my dissenting opinion in NAACP v. Button, 371 U. S. 415, 448, 452-455, the freedom of expression guaranteed against state interference by the Fourteenth Amendment includes the liberty of individuals not only to speak but also to unite to make their speech effective. The latter right encompasses the right to join together to obtain judicial redress. However, litigation is more than speech; it is conduct. And the States may reasonably regulate conduct even though it is related to expression. The pivotal point is how these competing interests should be resolved in this instance.

My brethren are apparently in accord. The majority begins by noting that this activity of the Union is related to expression and therefore is of a type which may be sheltered from state regulation by the Constitution. But the majority's inquiry does not stop there; it goes on to examine the state concerns and concludes that the decree "is not needed to protect the State's interest in high standards of legal ethics." See ante, at 225.[3] I agree, of course, with this "balancing" approach. See, e. g., NAACP v. Button, supra, at 452-455 (dissenting opinion); Konigsberg v. California Bar, 366 U. S. 36, 49-51; Talley v. California, 362 U. S. 60, 66 (concurring opinion). Indeed, I cannot conceive of any other sound method of attacking this type of problem. For if an "absolute" approach were adopted, as some members of this Court have from time to time insisted should be so with "First Amendment" cases,[4] and the state interest in regulation given no weight, there would be no apparent reason why, for example, a group might not employ a layman to represent its members in court or before an agency because it felt that his low fee made up for his deficiencies in legal knowledge. Cf. Hackin v. Arizona, ante, p. 143 (DOUGLAS, J., dissenting).

II.

Although I agree with the balancing approach employed by the majority, I find the scales tip differently. I believe that the majority has weighed the competing interests badly, according too much force to the claims of the Union and too little to those of the public interest at stake. As indicated previously, the interest of the Union stems from its members' constitutionally protected right to seek redress in the courts or, as here, before an agency. By the plan at issue, the Union has sought to make it easier for members to obtain benefits under the Illinois Workmen's Compensation Act.[5] The plan is evidently designed to help injured union members in three ways: (1) by assuring that they will have knowledge of and access to an attorney capable of handling their claims; (2) by guaranteeing that they will not be charged excessive legal fees; and (3) by protecting them from crippling, even though reasonable, fees by making legal costs payable collectively through union dues. These are legitimate and laudable goals. However, the union plan is by no means necessary for their achievement. They all may be realized by methods which are proper under the laws of Illinois.

The Illinois Supreme Court in this case repeated its statement in a prior case that a union may properly make known to its members the names of attorneys it deems capable of handling particular types of claims.[6]

Such union notification would serve to assure union members of access to competent lawyers.

As regards the protection of union members against the charging of unreasonable fees, a fully efficient safeguard would seem to be found in the Illinois Workmen's Compensation Act itself. An amendment to the Act in 1915, shortly after its initial passage,[7] provided that the Industrial Commission

"shall have the power to determine the reasonableness and fix the amount of any fee or compensation charged by any person for any service performed in connection with this Act, or for which payment is to be made under this Act or rendered in securing any right under this Act."[8]

In 1927, the words "including attorneys, physicians, surgeons and hospitals" were added following the phrase "or compensation charged by any person."[9] Thus, there would now appear to be no reasonable grounds for fearing that union members will be subjected to excessive legal fees.

The final interest sought to be promoted by the present plan is in the collective payment of legal fees. That objective could presumably be realized by imposing assessments on union members for the establishment of a fund out of which injured members would be reimbursed for their legal expenses.[10] There is no reason to believe that this arrangement would be improper under Illinois law, since the union's obligation would run only to the member and there would be no financial connection between union and attorney.

The regulatory interest of the State in this instance is found in the potential for abuse inherent in the union plan. The plan operates as follows. The Union employs a licensed lawyer on a salary basis[11] to represent members and their dependents in connection with their claims under the Workmen's Compensation Act. Members are told that they may employ other attorneys if they wish. The attorney is selected by the Executive Board of District 12, and the terms of employment specify that the attorney's sole obligation is to the person represented and that there will be no interference by the

Union. Injured union members are furnished by the Union with a form which advises them to send the form to the Union's legal department. Upon receipt of the form, the attorney assumes it to constitute a request that he file on behalf of the injured member a claim with the Industrial Commission, though no such explicit request is contained in the form. The application for compensation is prepared by secretaries in the union offices, and when complete it is sent directly to the Industrial Commission. In most instances, the attorney has neither seen nor talked with the union member at this stage, though the attorney is available for consultation at specified times. After the filing of the claim and prior to the hearing before the Commission, the attorney prepares for its presentation by resorting to his file and to the application, usually without conferring with the injured member. Ordinarily the member and this attorney first meet at the time of the hearing before the Commission.

The attorney determines what he thinks the claim to be worth and attempts to settle with the employer's attorney during prehearing negotiations. If agreement is reached, the attorney recommends to the injured member that he accept the result. If no settlement occurs, a hearing on the merits is held before the Industrial Commission. The full amount of the settlement or award is paid to the injured member. The attorney retains for himself no part of the amount received, his sole compensation being his annual salary paid by the Union.

This union plan contains features which, in my opinion, Illinois may reasonably consider to present the danger of lowering the quality of representation furnished by the attorney to union members in the handling of their claims. The union lawyer has little contact with his client. He processes the applications of injured members on a mass basis. Evidently, he negotiates with the employer's counsel about many claims at the same time. The State was entitled to conclude that, removed from ready contact with his client, insulated from interference by his actual employer, paid a salary independent of the results achieved, faced with a heavy caseload,[12] and very possibly with other activities competing for his time,[13] the attorney will be tempted to place undue emphasis upon quick disposition of each case. Conceivably, the desire to process forms rapidly might influence the lawyer not to check with his client regarding ambiguities or omissions in the form, or to miss facts and circumstances which face-to-face consultation with his client would have brought to light. He might be led, so the State might consider, to compromise cases for reasons unrelated to their own intrinsic merits, such as the need to "get on" with negotiations or a promise by the employer's attorney of concessions relating to other cases. The desire for quick disposition also might cause the attorney to forgo appeals in some cases in which the amount awarded seemed unusually low.[14]

III.

Thus, there is solid support for the Illinois Supreme Court's conclusion that the union plan presents a danger of harm to the public interest in a regulated bar. The reasonableness of this result is further buttressed by the numerous prior decisions, both in Illinois and elsewhere, in which courts have prohibited the employment of salaried attorneys by groups for the benefit of their members.[15]

The majority dismisses the State's interest in regulation by pointing out that there have been no proven instances of abuse or actual disadvantage to union members resulting from the operation of the union plan. See ante, at 225. But the proper question is not whether this particular plan has in fact caused any harm.[16] It is, instead, settled that in the absence of any dominant opposing interest a State may enforce prophylactic measures reasonably calculated to ward off foreseeable abuses, and that the fact that a specific activity has not yet produced any undesirable consequences will not exempt it from regulation. See, e. g., Hoopeston Canning Co. v. Cullen, 318 U. S. 313, 321-322; Daniel v. Family Sec. Life Ins. Co., 336 U. S. 220, 222-225.

It is also irrelevant whether we would proscribe the union plan were we sitting as state judges or state legislators. The sole issue before us is whether the Illinois Supreme Court is forbidden to do so because the plan unduly impinges upon rights guaranteed to the Union's members by the Fourteenth Amendment. Since the finding that the union plan presents dangers to the public and legal profession is not an arbitrary one, and since the limitation upon union members is so slight, in view of the permissible alternatives still open to them, I would hold that there has been no denial of constitutional rights occasioned by Illinois' prohibition of the plan.

IV.

This decision, which again manifests the peculiar insensitivity to the need for seeking an appropriate constitutional balance between federal and state authority that in recent years has characterized so many of the Court's decisions under the Fourteenth Amendment, puts this Court more deeply than ever in the business of supervising the practice of law in the various States. From my standpoint, what is done today is unnecessary, undesirable, and constitutionally all wrong. In the absence of demonstrated arbitrary or discriminatory regulation, state courts and legislatures should be left to govern their own Bars, free from interference by this Court.[17] Nothing different accords with longstanding and unquestioned tradition and with the most elementary demands of our federal system.

I would affirm.

Notes

[1] Canons 35, 47, Canons of Ethics of the Illinois State Bar Association. These canons are identical to the corresponding canons of the American Bar Association.

[2] Even in the absence of applicable statutes, state courts have held themselves empowered to promulgate and enforce standards of professional conduct drawn from the common law and the closely related prohibitions of the Canons of Ethics. See, e. g., In re Maclub of America, Inc., 295 Mass. 45, 3 N. E. 2d 272, and cases therein cited. See generally Drinker, Legal Ethics 26-30, 35-48.

[3] This weighing of the competing interests involved is the same approach as that used in NAACP v. Button, 371 U. S. 415, and in Railroad Trainmen v. Virginia Bar, 377 U.

S. 1. However, since a new balance must be struck whenever the competing interests are significantly different, this decision is not controlled by those cases. The union members in this case are not asserting legal rights which stem either from the Constitution or from a federal statute, sources of origin stressed respectively in Button, see 371 U. S., at 429-431, 441-444, and in Railroad Trainmen, see 377 U. S., at 3-6. Furthermore, the union plan at issue here differs from the referral practice involved in Railroad Trainmen because it involves the services of a union-salaried lawyer.

Similarly, the interests in this case are very different from those in cases involving legal aid to the indigent. The situation of a salaried lawyer representing indigent clients was expressly distinguished by the court below. See 35 Ill. 2d 112, 121, 219 N. E. 2d 503, 508.

[4] See, e. g., Lathrop v. Donohue, 367 U. S. 820, 865, 871-874 (dissenting opinion); Konigsberg v. California Bar, 366 U. S. 36, 56, 60-71 (dissenting opinion).

[5] Ill. Rev. Stat., c. 48, § 138.1 et seq. (1963).

[6] See 35 Ill. 2d, at 118-119, 219 N. E. 2d, at 506-507. The earlier Illinois decision referred to was In re Brotherhood of R. R. Trainmen, 13 Ill. 2d 391, 150 N. E. 2d 163.

[7] It may be significant that the union plan was instituted in 1913, prior to this amendment of the Act. See ante, at 219.

[8] Ill. Laws, 1915, p. 408.

[9] Ill. Laws, 1927, p. 511.

[10] Cf. American Bar Association, Committee on Professional Ethics, Informal Opinion No. 469 (December 26, 1961) (union may reimburse member client for legal expenses).

[11] The salary paid at the time of this action was $12,400 per annum.

[12] The attorney employed by the Union in this case handled more than 400 workmen's compensation claims a year.

[13] The attorney employed by the Mine Workers was also an Illinois state senator and had a private practice other than the Mine Workers' representation.

[14] Of 351 workmen's compensation cases, from all sources, which were appealed to the Illinois courts during the period 1936-1967, only one was appealed by a miner affiliated with District 12. No such miner has appealed since 1942. See Respondents' Brief, at 17-18.

[15] See, e. g., People ex rel. Courtney v. Association of Real Estate Tax-payers, 354 Ill. 102, 187 N. E. 823; In re Maclub of America, Inc., 295 Mass. 45, 3 N. E. 2d 272, and cases therein cited; Richmond Assn. of Credit Men, Inc. v. Bar Assn. of Richmond, 167 Va. 327, 189 S. E. 153. The Canons of Ethics of the American Bar Association have also been interpreted as forbidding arrangements of the kind at issue here. See American Bar Association, Committee on Unauthorized Practice of the Law, Informative Opinion No. A of 1950, 36 A. B. A. J. 677.

[16] It is possible that the operation of the plan did result in union members receiving a lower quality of legal representation than they otherwise would have had. For

example, the Mine Workers' present attorney recovered an average of $1,160 per case, while his predecessor secured an average of $1,350, even though the permissible rates of recovery were lower during the predecessor's tenure. See Record, at 53-54, 58-60; Brief for Respondents 18. See also n. 14, supra.

[17] It has been suggested both in this case and elsewhere, cf. Hackin v. Arizona, ante, p. 143 (DOUGLAS, J., dissenting), that prevailing Canons of Ethics and traditional customs in the legal profession will have to be modified to keep pace with the needs of new social developments, such as the Federal Poverty Program. That may well be true, but such considerations furnish no justification for today's heavy-handed action by the Court. The American Bar Association and other bodies throughout the country already have such matters under consideration. See, e. g., 1964 ABA Reports 381-383 (establishment of Special Committee on Ethical Standards); 1966 ABA Reports 589-594 (Report of Special Committee on Availability of Legal Services); 39 Calif. State Bar Journal 639-742 (Report of Committee on Group Legal Services). Moreover, the complexity of these matters makes them especially suitable for experimentation at the local level. And, all else failing, the Congress undoubtedly has the power to implement federal programs by establishing overriding rules governing legal representation in connection therewith.

Justice Harlan's concurrence and dissent in Case-Swayne Co. v. Sunkist Growers (Dec 18, 1967)

MR. JUSTICE HARLAN, concurring in part and dissenting in part.

I agree with the Court's holding that Congress did not intend that nonstock organizations with nonproducer members should qualify for the antitrust exemption conferred by § 1 of the Capper-Volstead Act, 7 U. S. C. § 291, and that the Sunkist system therefore is technically not a properly constituted Capper-Volstead cooperative. However, like my Brother WHITE, I am unable to ignore the possible effect of the Court's holding insofar as it subjects this large agricultural organization to antitrust liability extending far beyond the confines of this suit.

There is nothing in the record to indicate that Sunkist intended to evade the mandate of the Capper-Volstead Act when it allowed privately owned "agency association" packing houses to become members of the Sunkist system. Sunkist's only apparent motive in including the agency associations as members was to provide a greater range of packing facilities for citrus growers who desired to market through Sunkist. The agency associations have been an integral part of the Sunkist system for many years.[1] Until the bringing of the present action, this aspect of Sunkist's organization had apparently gone without challenge from private persons who dealt with Sunkist. Its legality never seems to have been questioned by any agency of government. Sunkist argued before us, without challenge to its sincerity, that the membership of the agency associations did not deprive it of antitrust immunity so long as all of its actions were taken for the benefit of the growers. There is no reason to doubt that this has been Sunkist's belief through the years.

In these circumstances, it seems inequitable that the membership of the agency associations should cause Sunkist to lose all of its previously assumed immunity from liability under § 1 of the Sherman Act. This would evidently be the consequence of the Court's holding, and if not mitigated in any way it would appear to expose Sunkist to very large liabilities. Many of the activities of a marketing organization the size of Sunkist presumably amount to restraints of trade, and under the Court's rationale Sunkist would be subject to treble damage suits in respect of all of them. The chief result would be to allow windfall treble damage recoveries to persons with whom Sunkist dealt at arm's length and in good faith. The main burden would ultimately fall on the growers at the base of the Sunkist organization.

I would hold that Sunkist is not liable under § 1 of the Sherman Act for past acts merely because the agency associations participated in its government by virtue of their membership. It seems to me that this result is not only more equitable but accords better with the basic purpose of Congress, which was to aid producers, than does the Court's holding, which burdens the growers with heavy potential liabilities. This belief is supported by the frequent reference in the congressional debates to the forerunner of this very organization as one which Congress intended by the Act to protect.[2]

Sufficient precedent for this type of equitable mitigation is found in Sunkist Growers, Inc. v. Winckler & Smith Citrus Products Co., 370 U. S. 19, in which this Court held that Sunkist's former "tripartite" structure did not deprive it of its § 1 immunity. The Court there stated that

"To hold otherwise would be to impose grave legal consequences upon organizational distinctions that are of de minimis meaning and effect to these growers who have banded together for processing and marketing purposes within the purview of the Clayton and Capper-Volstead Acts." Id., at 29.

The very words of Capper-Volstead § 1, however, make it clear that Congress granted antitrust immunity to agricultural cooperatives only on condition that all of the benefits of cooperative organization were received by agricultural producers. Therefore, I would also hold that Sunkist may not assert antitrust immunity if the damage complained of resulted from attempts by the agency associations to use their power within Sunkist for their own benefit as distinguished from that of the growers.

The Court holds, and, for the future, I agree, that even those organizations in which all gains are channeled to the producers may not qualify under Capper-Volstead § 1 if they have nonproducer members. Congress may have excluded nonproducers simply because it felt that the benefits to producers from nonproducer membership were outweighed by the dangers of admitting nonproducer foxes into the cooperative hen roost. However, as the Court recognizes, see ante, at 394-395, the evident congressional concern about the possibility of monopoly by organizations immunized from antitrust prosecution by Capper-Volstead[3] indicates that in restricting membership to producers Congress also intended to limit in a rough way the amount of market power which could be controlled by such organizations. The resources of nonproducers were to be available to the cooperatives, not through the broad avenue of membership, but by the narrower path of contract: the Act provides that qualifying organizations and their members "may make the necessary contracts and agreements" to effect the Act's purposes. To give effect to this legislative intent, I would hold that the marketing agreements of the agency associations with Sunkist and with individual growers must be tested by the standard applicable to contracts with nonmembers.

The Court of Appeals held that, treated as contracts with nonmembers, the agreements in question were proper under the Act. 369 F. 2d 449, 461-462. I agree. Regarded as contracts, these agreements provide essentially that a grower who desires to market through the Sunkist system and have his fruit packed by an agency association shall deliver to such association his entire crop for the year, that the agency association shall pack it in return for cost plus a fixed fee, and that the entire crop shall then be marketed by Sunkist. The contract may be canceled by the grower in August of any year. Since the main effect of these agreements is simply to give the growers who want to market through Sunkist a wider choice of packing facilities than they would enjoy if limited to cooperative packing houses, I would hold that the agreements are permissible when looked upon as contracts with nonmembers.

In accord with this opinion, I would remand the case to the District Court so that Case-Swayne may show what, if any, of the damage allegedly suffered by it resulted from actions taken by the agency associations for their own benefit as distinguished from that of the growers. I need hardly say that for the future Sunkist would forfeit its entire Capper-Volstead antitrust exemption were it to elect to continue the membership of the agency associations.

Notes

[1] It appears that the agency associations have been members of the system at least since 1924. See McKay & Stevens, Organization and Development of a Cooperative Citrus-Fruit Marketing Agency 22-23 (U. S. Dept. of Agriculture, Bull. No. 1237, 1924).

[2] See n. 12, ante, at 394.

[3] See, e. g., 62 Cong. Rec. 2217-2226, 2257-2280.

Justice Harlan's dissent in Damico v. California (Dec 18, 1967)

MR. JUSTICE HARLAN, dissenting.

California's Aid to Families with Dependent Children program provides welfare assistance to mothers and children rendered destitute through desertion by or separation from the fathers of the children. The law requires that, unless a suit for divorce has been filed, the desertion or separation be of at least three months' duration before AFDC aid will be granted.

Appellants were informed by a social worker that, no suit for divorce having been filed, they could not receive AFDC aid before the end of the three-month period; they then brought this suit for a declaration that the three-month requirement violated the Federal Constitution. The District Court, without reaching the question whether it should "abstain" pending appropriate state proceedings for relief, and without reaching the merits, dismissed on the ground that the plaintiffs had failed to exhaust "adequate administrative remedies."

This Court, without plenary consideration and without stating its reasons, now reverses the District Court's dismissal, citing McNeese v. Board of Education, 373 U. S. 668. In McNeese, the Court held that Negro students, seeking relief from alleged school racial segregation, did not have to pursue and exhaust certain administrative remedies available under state law before bringing their federal action. Although I did not at the time and do not now fully understand the Court's opinion in McNeese,[*] the net result of the case as I see it was that the right to assert, in a federal court, that state officials had acted in a manner depriving the plaintiff of clear constitutional rights could not be delayed by the interposition of intentionally or unintentionally inadequate state remedies for the alleged discrimination.

If that is a correct description of the exhaustion problem in McNeese, it bears little relation to the exhaustion question here. State AFDC relief was created pursuant to the provisions of the federal Social Security Act, 49 Stat. 627, 42 U. S. C. § 601 et seq. The Federal Government pays the major share of the cost of state aid, see 42 U. S. C. § 603, and in return closely supervises both how it shall be administered and what remedies shall be available to those who have complaints about its operation. Each State receiving federal assistance (which includes California) must formulate and submit to the Secretary of Health, Education, and Welfare, for his approval, a plan of operation of its AFDC program. 42 U. S. C. § 602. In particular, the plan must provide that "aid to families with dependent children . . . shall be furnished with reasonable promptness to all eligible individuals," 42 U. S. C. § 602 (a) (9), and must "provide for granting . . . a fair hearing before the State agency [whose creation is required by a separate provision, 42 U. S. C. § 602 (a) (3)] to any individual whose claim for aid to families with dependent children is denied or is not acted upon with reasonable promptness." 42 U. S. C. § 602 (a) (4). The California plan approved by the Secretary apparently includes both California's three-month requirement and California's hearing procedure.

The Court simply ignores the highly successful federal-state working relationship created by Congress in this area. The right of these appellants to receive AFDC funds involves not only questions of state law, but also the propriety of that law under federal statutory law. For the determination of these questions Congress has specified a state forum in the first instance. Today's holding, made without benefit of briefs and oral argument and on a skimpy record, that 42 U. S. C. § 1983 may be used to bypass 42 U. S. C. § 602 is a disservice to both of these important statutes.

I would affirm the judgment below.

[*] The source of my difficulty is a compound of the occasional use of language

broader than was necessary or warranted by the facts as the majority viewed them, and of my own disagreement with the majority's view of the facts. In Monroe v. Pape, 365 U. S. 167, in an opinion which I joined, the Court declared that one complaining of unlawful search and seizure by state officials could sue them in a federal court under 42 U. S. C. § 1983, notwithstanding the availability of similar remedies under state law. That case did not say that one who is engaged in a course of dealing with an administrative agency may bypass the orderly procedures established by that agency and the procedures for review of agency action and sue its members individually at any stage. In McNeese it was the prevailing view, with which I disagreed under the circumstances, that the administrative procedures established by the State were inadequate for the vindication of federal rights. Reading Monroe to have interpreted 42 U. S. C. § 1983 "to provide a remedy where state law was inadequate, [and] `to provide a federal remedy where the state remedy, though adequate in theory, was not available in practice,' " 373 U. S., at 672, the Court concluded that "[w]hen federal rights are subject to such tenuous protection, prior resort to a state proceeding is not necessary." Id., at 676.

The majority opinion in McNeese also, however, attributed to Monroe the establishment of the principle that 42 U. S. C. § 1983 provides a "supplementary" remedy to any a State might have. This language is now interpreted by the Court to mean that there can be no requirement that a person dealing with an administrative agency continue to deal with it in an orderly fashion, no matter how adequate his remedy there. If this is what the majority opinion in McNeese meant to say, its dictum was gratuitous both in the sense that it was not compelled by the facts as the Court viewed them and in the sense that it was an incorrect interpretation of Monroe.

Justice Harlan's dissent in Rockefeller v. Wells (Dec 18, 1967)

MR. JUSTICE HARLAN, dissenting.

This action was brought by appellees under the Civil Rights Act. 42 U. S. C. §§ 1983, 1988, for declaratory and other relief. Their complaint alleged that New York's congressional districting statute does not conform to the requirements of Art. I, § 2, of the United States Constitution, as those requirements are defined in Wesberry v. Sanders, 376 U. S. 1. A three-judge court was convened.

The court found, on the basis of 1960 census statistics, that the population of one of New York's 41 congressional districts varied from the average population of the districts by 15.1%, and that 12 other districts varied from the population average by as much as 10%. It concluded that such a variation from average, without a suitable explanation, "violates constitutional requirements." 273 F. Supp. 984, at 989. The court noted that there have been "substantial" population changes in these districts since 1960, and that complete accuracy in redistricting must await the results of the 1970 census, but reasoned that a suitable compromise would be to require redistricting immediately, premised on the best population figures now available. Revisions could then be made when the 1970 census statistics were released. This Court simply affirms, without elaboration or opinion.

There are, in my opinion, two principal issues here worthy of plenary consideration. First, the District Court thought it "too clear for debate" that this districting statute "violates constitutional requirements as enunciated by the Supreme Court." 273 F. Supp., at 989. There are few issues in reapportionment cases that are clear beyond debate, and, with respect, the invalidity of this statute is certainly not among them. It is true that variations of as much as 18.28% were disapproved in Swann v. Adams, 385 U. S. 440, but the Court there also re-emphasized that the approval or disapproval of the variations in one State "has little bearing on the validity of a similar variation in another State." Id., at 445. And see Reynolds v. Sims, 377 U. S. 533, 578. The impossibility of calculating the proper result in these cases from numerical variations is illustrated by Toombs v. Fortson, 241 F. Supp. 65. The District Court there said specifically that "we will base any test as to the reasonableness of variances on the departure figure of 15 percent." Id., at 70. This Court simply affirmed without opinion. 384 U. S. 210. See also Moore v. Moore, 246 F. Supp. 578, 582. Yet in this case, in which variations no greater than 15.1% are in issue, the Court again summarily affirms.

Presumably the size of the numerical variation is not alone decisive,[1] but if the "particular circumstances of the case," Reynolds v. Sims, supra, at 578, Swann v. Adams, supra, at 445, may be crucial to the validity of districting statutes, then surely the Court should endeavor to define what such circumstances are, and to indicate how they are relevant. Instead, the Court more and more often disposes of reapportionment cases summarily, see, e. g., Toombs v. Fortson, supra; Duddleston v. Grills, 385 U. S. 455; Kirkpatrick v. Preisler, 385 U. S. 450; Lucas v. Rhodes, ante, p. 212; and when the Court does issue an opinion, it is content simply to recite that such circumstances may be relevant, without undertaking any elucidation. See, e. g., Swann v. Adams, supra. All this has the effect of leaving the state legislatures,[2] the lower courts, and even Congress[3] without meaningful guidance.

Second, the confusion created by the Court's reticence is compounded, in cases in which it is held that a districting statute does not satisfy constitutional requirements, by uncertainty as to the appropriate next step. See, e. g., Lucas v. Rhodes, supra. The District Court here noted that the Court's cases provided "[l]ittle guidance or help," but concluded, nonetheless, that immediate redistricting should be ordered, based on the best available population figures. It thought that this expedient was in the pattern set by Swann v. Adams, 383 U. S. 210. Swann, however, was merely a brief per curiam opinion, which did not purport to establish any general rule on appropriate remedies. As the elections of 1968 approach, it seems to me that the time has come for this Court to provide clearer guidance to the lower courts on the proper remedy in reapportionment cases. More particularly, some indication should be given as to what part, if any, 1960 census figures are to play, alone or in combination with later, albeit incomplete or unverified, population figures. See Lucas v. Rhodes, supra.

I would note probable jurisdiction, and set the case for argument.

Notes

[1] I note, however, that the District Court in Preisler v. Secretary of State of Missouri, 257 F. Supp. 953, said specifically that "population and population alone is the sole standard for congressional representation." Id., at 973. This Court affirmed without opinion. 385 U. S. 450. See also Bush v. Martin, 224 F. Supp. 499, 511, aff'd, 376 U. S. 222.

[2] The New York Legislature, for example, made careful efforts to comply with the constitutional requirements, as they had been enunciated by this Court. The Joint Legislative Committee on Reapportionment thus expressly recognized "the absence of Federal and State constitutional and statutory standards," but concluded that "the most important standard is substantial equality of population." Interim Report of the Joint Legislative Committee on Reapportionment, 1961 N. Y. Leg. Doc. No. 45, p. 4. It added that "[w]hile exact equality of population is the ideal, it is an ideal that, for practical reasons, can never be attained. Some variation from it will always be necessary. The question arises as to what is a permissible fair variation." Ibid.

[3] The House Committee on the Judiciary, for example, reported favorably in 1965 on a bill which was intended to implement the requirements of Wesberry v. Sanders, supra, by creating a series of standards for the apportionment of congressional districts. The Committee noted that "[t]he courts . . . have been reluctant to prescribe standards . . . ." H. R. Rep. No. 140, 89th Cong., 1st Sess., 2. One standard included in the bill was a maximum permissible variation of 15% above or below the average population of the congressional districts within a State. Id., at 2-3. Given the present state of the law in this area, it is difficult to imagine how a legislator could sensibly decide whether such a maximum variation satisfied applicable constitutional requirements. Indeed, Representative Kastenmeier dissented from the Committee's report, noting that "there is serious doubt whether H. R. 5505 can, in light of the Wesberry case, withstand constitutional attack." Id., at 5.

Justice Harlan's concurrence in Zschernig v. Miller (Jan 15, 1968)

MR. JUSTICE HARLAN, concurring in the result.

Although I agree with the result reached in this case, I am unable to subscribe to the Court's opinion, for three reasons. First, by resting its decision on the constitutional ground that this Oregon inheritance statute infringes the federal foreign relations power, without pausing to consider whether the 1923 Treaty of Friendship, Commerce and Consular Rights with Germany[1] itself vitiates this application of the state statute, the Court has deliberately turned its back on a cardinal principle of judicial review. Second, correctly construed the 1923 treaty, in my opinion, renders Oregon's application of its statute in this instance impermissible, thus requiring reversal of the state judgment. Third, the Court's constitutional holding, which I reach only because the majority has done so, is in my view untenable. The impact of today's holding on state power in this field, and perhaps in other areas of the law as well, justifies a full statement of my views upon the case.

I.

Even in this age of rapid constitutional change, the Court has continued to proclaim adherence to the principle that decision of constitutional issues should be avoided wherever possible.[2] In his celebrated concurring opinion in Ashwander v. Valley Authority, 297 U. S. 288, 341, Mr. Justice Brandeis listed the self-imposed rules by which the Court has avoided the unnecessary decision of constitutional questions. In his fourth rule he dealt with the situation presented by this case, declaring that:

"The Court will not pass upon a constitutional question although properly presented by the record, if there is also present some other ground upon which the case may be disposed of. . . . Thus, if a case can be decided on either of two grounds, one involving a constitutional question, the other a question of statutory construction or general law, the Court will decide only the latter. Siler v. Louisville & Nashville R. Co., 213 U. S. 175, 191; Light v. United States, 220 U. S. 523, 538." Id., at 347.[3]

The above rule should control the disposition of this case, for there is what I think must be regarded, within the meaning of Ashwander, as a nonconstitutional ground on which the decision could be founded. Although the appellants chose to argue only the constitutional question, the United States, as amicus curiae, forcefully, and I believe correctly, contended that the full relief sought by the appellants should be afforded by overruling the construction of the 1923 treaty, rather than the constitutional holding, in Clark v. Allen, 331 U. S. 503. The Court simply states that "[w]e do not accept the invitation to re-examine our ruling in Clark v. Allen." See ante, at 432. I believe that the principle of avoiding unnecessary constitutional adjudication obliges us to accept that invitation and to inquire whether the treaty might provide an adequate alternative ground for affording the appellants their due.[4]

II.

Article IV of the 1923 treaty with Germany provides:

"Where, on the death of any person holding real or other immovable property or interests therein within the territories of one High Contracting Party, such property or interests therein would, by the laws of the country or by a testamentary disposition, descend or pass to a national of the other High Contracting Party, whether resident or non-resident, were he not disqualified by the laws of the country where such property or interests therein is or are situated, such national shall be allowed a term of three years in which to sell the same, this term to be reasonably prolonged if circumstances render it necessary, and withdraw the proceeds thereof, without restraint or interference, and exempt from any succession, probate or administrative duties or charges other than those which may be imposed in like cases upon the nationals of the country from which such proceeds may be drawn.

"Nationals of either High Contracting Party may have full power to dispose of their personal property of every kind within the territories of the other, by testament, donation, or otherwise, and their heirs, legatees and donees, of whatsoever nationality, whether resident or non-resident, shall succeed to such personal property, and may take possession thereof, either by themselves or by others acting for them, and retain or dispose of the same at their pleasure subject to the payment of such duties or charges only as the nationals of the High Contracting Party within whose territories such property may be or belong shall be liable to pay in like cases."

In Clark v. Allen, supra, this Court considered the application of this treaty provision to a case much like the present one. In Clark one who was apparently an American citizen died in California and left her real and personal property to German nationals. The California Probate Code provided that

"The rights of aliens not residing within the United States . . . to take either real or personal property or the proceeds thereof in this State by succession or testamentary disposition, upon the same terms and conditions as residents and citizens of the United States is dependent in each case upon the existence of a reciprocal right upon the part of citizens of the United States to take real and personal property and the proceeds thereof upon the same terms and conditions as residents and citizens of the respective countries of which such aliens are inhabitants and citizens and upon the rights of citizens of the United States to receive by payment to them within the United States or its territories money originating from the estates of persons dying within such foreign countries." Cal. Prob. Code § 259, added by Stats. 1941, c. 895, § 1.

The Clark Court first considered whether the 1923 treaty with Germany had survived the events of the years 1923-1947. It concluded that the treaty was still in effect and that it clearly entitled the German citizens to take the real estate left them by the decedent.

The Court then went on to discuss the application of the treaty to personalty. It noted that a practically identical provision of a treaty with Wurttemburg had been held in the 1860 case of Frederickson v. Louisiana, 23 How. 445, not to govern "[t]he case of a citizen or subject of the respective countries residing at home, and disposing of [personal] property there in favor of a citizen or subject of the other . . . ," id., at 447, and that the Frederickson decision had been followed in 1917 cases involving three other treaties.[5] The Court then said:

"The construction adopted by those cases is, to say the least, permissible when the syntax of the sentences dealing with realty and personalty is considered. So far as realty is concerned, the testator includes `any person'; and the property covered is that within the territory of either of the high contracting parties. In case of personalty, the provision governs the right of `nationals' of either contracting party to dispose of their property within the territory of the `other' contracting party; and it is `such personal property' that the `heirs, legatees and donees' are entitled to take.

"Petitioner, however, presents a detailed account of the history of the clause which was not before the Court in Frederickson v. Louisiana, supra, and which bears out the construction that it grants the foreign heir the right to succeed to his inheritance or the proceeds thereof. But we do not stop to review that history. For the consistent judicial construction of the language since 1860 has given it a character which the treaty-making agencies have not seen fit to alter. And that construction is entirely consistent with the plain language of the treaty. We therefore do not deem it appropriate to change that construction at this late date, even though as an original matter the other view might have much to commend it." 331 U. S., at 515-516.

In the case now before us, an American citizen died in Oregon, leaving property to relatives in East Germany. An Oregon statute conditioned a nonresident alien's right to inherit property in Oregon upon the existence of a reciprocal right of American citizens to inherit in the alien's country upon the same terms as citizens of that country; upon the right of American citizens to receive payment within the United States from the estates of decedents dying in that country; and upon proof that the alien heirs of the American decedent would receive the benefit, use, and control of their inheritance without confiscation.[6] The Oregon Supreme Court affirmed the finding of the trial court that the evidence did not establish that American citizens were accorded reciprocal rights to take property from or to receive the proceeds of East German estates. However, it found that the 1923 treaty was still effective with respect to East Germany, and consequently held that under Clark v. Allen the East German heirs must be permitted to take the real, though not the personal, property despite the Oregon statute.

I, too, believe that the 1923 treaty is still applicable to East Germany.[7] However, I am satisfied that Clark v. Allen should not be followed insofar as the Court there held that the words of the 1923 treaty must be taken to bear the meaning ascribed to them in Frederickson v. Louisiana because of the "consistent judicial construction of the language since 1860." This reasoning assumes both that the drafters of the 1923 treaty knew of the Frederickson decision and that they thought Frederickson would control the interpretation of that treaty. The first assumption seems open to substantial doubt, and the second is not beyond question.

There is evidence that in 1899, almost 40 years after the Frederickson decision, the State Department's treaty draftsmen were not aware of the meaning given to the crucial treaty language in that opinion. For in 1895 the British Ambassador initiated correspondence with the State Department in which he proposed a treaty which would assure that "no greater charges [would] be imposed. . . on real or personal property in the United States inherited by British subjects, whether domiciled within the union or not, than are imposed upon property inherited by American citizens," in return for provisions assuring to American citizens reciprocal rights in Great Britain.[8] The ensuing treaty of 1899[9] contained language substantially identical to that in the subsequent 1923 treaty with Germany. Since it is highly unlikely that the British Ambassador intended that British subjects should be able to inherit personal property from American decedents only if those decedents happened also to be British subjects, or that the State Department so understood him, it is clear enough that the draftsmen in 1899 must have been unaware of Frederickson.

It is also conceivable that the drafters of the 1923 treaty thought that Frederickson was inapplicable to that treaty. Because the article of the Wurttemburg treaty dealing with realty was not brought to the attention of the Frederickson Court, the Frederickson decision was based largely upon the Court's understanding that

"The case of a citizen or subject of the respective countries residing at home, and disposing of property there in favor of a citizen or subject of the other, was not in the contemplation of the contracting Powers, and is not embraced in this article of the treaty." 23 How., at 447-448.

Hence, the drafters of the 1923 treaty might have assumed that Frederickson was not applicable to that treaty, in which the inclusion of the realty provision made it clear that the parties did consider the case of a citizen dying in his own country. In view of these indications that the draftsmen of the 1923 treaty very likely did not intend that the words of the treaty should bear the meaning given them in Frederickson, it seems to me that the Court in Clark v. Allen erred in holding the question foreclosed. Accordingly, a de novo inquiry into the meaning of the treaty seems entirely appropriate.

III.

The language of Article IV of the 1923 treaty with Germany, which was quoted earlier, is based upon Article X of the treaty of 1785 with Prussia.[10] Article X provided:

"The citizens or subjects of each party shall have power to dispose of their personal goods within the jurisdiction of the other, by testament, donation or otherwise; and their representatives, being subjects or citizens of the other party, shall succeed to their said personal goods . . . and dispose of the same at their will, paying such dues only as the inhabitants of the country wherein the said goods are, shall be subject to pay in like cases. . . . And where, on the death of any person holding real estate within the territories of the one party, such real estate would by the laws of the land descend on a citizen or subject of the other, were he not disqualified by alienage, such subject shall be allowed a reasonable time to sell the same, and to withdraw the proceeds without molestation, and exempt from all rights of detraction on the part of the government of the respective states."

This part of the treaty with Prussia was in turn founded upon earlier treaties with France, the Netherlands, and Sweden.[11] The treaty of 1778 with France specifically freed American citizens from the burdens of two restrictions on the right of aliens to dispose of or inherit property which were then common in the civil law countries: the droit d'aubaine and the droit de détraction. The droit d'aubaine was the feudal right of the sovereign to appropriate the property of an alien who died within the realm; an aspect of this doctrine was "the complementary incapacity of an alien to inherit, even from a citizen." Nielsen v. Johnson, 279 U. S. 47, 55, n. 2.[12] The droit d'aubaine was replaced during the 18th century by the droit de détraction, a tax "imposed on the right of an alien to [inherit] . . . the property of persons dying within the realm," Nielsen v. Johnson, supra, at 56, n. 2, and levied upon the removal of the inherited property by the alien from the decedent's country.[13]

The 1782 treaty with the Netherlands and the 1783 treaty with Sweden were framed more generally. They provided that:

"The subjects of the contracting parties in the respective states, may freely dispose of their goods and effects either by testament, donation or otherwise, in favour of such persons as they think proper; and their heirs in whatever place they shall reside, shall receive the succession . . . ."[14]

The 1785 treaty with Prussia, which is substantially identical to the 1923 treaty, differed from the earlier treaties in two important respects. For one thing, it dealt separately with realty and with personalty.[15] This separate treatment stemmed from the fact that at common law aliens could freely inherit personalty but could not succeed to realty.[16] The Continental Congress, apparently fearing that under the Articles of Confederation it lacked power thus to alter the laws of the States, instructed the Commissioners who negotiated the treaty "[t]hat no rights be stipulated for aliens to hold real property within the States, this being utterly inadmissible by their several laws and policy," but that a person who would inherit realty but for his alienage should be permitted to sell the property and withdraw the proceeds within a reasonable time.[17]

The other important difference was that the provision of the Prussian treaty dealing with the disposal and inheritance of personalty, though generally based upon the corresponding language in the Dutch and Swedish treaties, was altered by the addition of the phrase "within the jurisdiction of the other," so as to read:

"The citizens or subjects of each party shall have power to dispose of their personal goods within the jurisdiction of the other, by testament, donation or otherwise, and their representatives, being subjects or citizens of the other party, shall succeed to their said personal goods . . . and dispose of the same at their will, paying such dues only as the inhabitants of the country wherein the said goods are, shall be subject to pay in like cases. . . ." (Emphasis added.)

There is no precise indication why this phrase was added. Its function seems to have been to define more clearly than the earlier treaties the cases in which disposition of property required protection from the droit d'aubaine, namely those instances when property was disposed of in a country other than that of the citizenship of the owner. Under this construction, the phrase would modify the word "dispose" rather than the words "personal goods" (or "personal property" in the 1923 treaty). The right of succession would be unaffected, since the words "said personal goods" (or "such personal property" in the 1923 treaty) would refer to all "personal goods" (or to "personal property of every kind" in the 1923 treaty) and not merely to those personal goods within the territory of the other party to the treaty.

Several factors point to the conclusion that this construction is correct, and that the phrase "within the jurisdiction of the other" was not intended to modify the words "personal goods" and thereby to limit the right of succession. The addition of the phrase "within the jurisdiction of the other" was unrelated to the problem of freeing rights of succession from the droit de détraction, since that exaction was imposed upon succession by an alien to the property of any person dying within the realm, regardless of the citizenship of the decedent. The phrase therefore cannot have been intended to modify the right of succession in order to enlarge or contract this freedom.

Moreover, the terms of the newly added real property clause affirmatively indicate that the "personal goods" clause of the 1785 treaty (and therefore the "personal property" clause of the 1923 treaty) was intended to confer the right to inherit personal property from both alien and citizen decedents. The first draft of the 1785 treaty was substantially similar to the earlier Dutch and Swedish treaties, and quite clearly would have permitted aliens to succeed to real or personal property regardless of whether the decedent died in his own country.[18] However, as noted earlier, the Continental Congress out of caution instructed the Commissioners that aliens should not be allowed by the treaty to succeed to and hold real estate but should be limited to sale of the land and removal of the proceeds. This indicates that the real estate clause was intended purely as a limitation on the rights accorded with respect to personal property and was not supposed to confer any greater rights. The real property clause certainly permitted inheritance from both alien and citizen, for it allowed succession "on the death of any person holding real estate." This was acknowledged by the Court in Clark v. Allen, supra, at 517, with respect to the 1923 treaty. It would seem to follow that the more liberal personal property clause was also intended to allow inheritance regardless of the decedent's nationality.

The conclusion that the personal property clause of the 1785 (and hence of the 1923) treaty was intended to grant a right of inheritance no matter what the decedent's citizenship finds additional support in the State Department's interpretations of similar treaty provisions during the 19th century. When negotiating substantially identical provisions in treaties with German states in the 1840's, the then Minister to Prussia, Mr. Wheaton, indicated his belief that the proposed treaties would protect "naturalized Germans, resident in the U[nited] States, who are entitled to inherit the property of their relations deceased in Germany."[19] There was no suggestion that the treaties would apply only to real property or, with respect to personal property, only to the small class of naturalized Germans whose "relations" in Germany happened also to be American citizens. In responding to Mr. Wheaton, the State Department instructed him to take as his "general guide" the treaty with Prussia and others similarly worded, and instructed him that the object should be "the removal of all obstructions. . . to the withdrawal from the one country, by the citizens or subjects of the other, of any property which may have been transferred to them by . . . will,— or which they may have inherited ab intestato."[20]

Later in the century, after the Frederickson decision, the State Department several times indicated that it regarded similarly worded treaties as assuring citizens of one country the right to inherit personal property of citizens of the other dying in their own country. In 1868 and 1880 the Department asserted, under a similarly worded treaty,[21] the right of American citizens to inherit personal property of Swiss decedents who dies in Switzerland.[22] In 1877, it took the same position with respect to the rights of Russian heirs to inherit the personal property of American decedents under a like treaty with

Russia.[23] The negotiations leading to the British treaty of 1899, which have previously been described, reveal the same attitude.

This course of history, coupled with the general principle that "where a provision of a treaty fairly admits of two constructions, one restricting, the other enlarging, rights which may be claimed under it, the more liberal interpretation is to be preferred,"[24] leads in my opinion to the conclusion that Article IV of the 1923 treaty should be construed as guaranteeing to citizens of the contracting parties the right to inherit personal property from a decedent who dies in his own country. I would overrule Frederickson v. Louisiana, supra, and Clark v. Allen, supra, insofar as they hold the contrary. Considerations of stare decisis should not stand in the way of rectifying two decisions that rest on such infirm foundations. Compare Swift & Co., Inc. v. Wickham, 382 U. S. 111, with Kesler v. Department of Public Safety, 369 U. S. 153. Properly construed, the 1923 treaty, which of course takes precedence over the Oregon statute under the Supremacy Clause, entitles the appellants in this case to succeed to the personal as well as the real property of the decedent despite the state statute.

IV.

Upon my view of this case, it would be unnecessary to reach the issue whether Oregon's statute governing inheritance by aliens amounts to an unconstitutional infringement upon the foreign relations power of the Federal Government. However, since this is the basis upon which the Court has chosen to rest its decision, I feel that I should indicate briefly why I believe the decision to be wrong on that score, too.

As noted earlier, the Oregon statute conditions an alien's right to inherit Oregon property upon the satisfaction of three conditions: (1) a reciprocal right of Americans to inherit property in the alien's country; (2) the right of Americans to receive payment in the United States from the estates of decedents dying in the alien's country; and (3) proof that the alien heirs of the Oregon decedent would receive the benefit, use, and control of their inheritance without confiscation. In Clark v. Allen, supra, the Court upheld the constitutionality of a California statute which similarly conditioned the right of aliens to inherit upon reciprocity but did not contain the other two restrictions. The Court in Clark dismissed as "farfetched" the contention that the statute unconstitutionally infringed upon the federal foreign relations power. See 331 U. S., at 517. The Court noted that California had not violated any express command of the Constitution by entering into a treaty, agreement or compact with foreign countries. It said that "[w]hat California has done will have some incidental or indirect effect in foreign countries. But that is true of many state laws which none would claim cross the forbidden line." Ibid.

It seems to me impossible to distinguish the present case from Clark v. Allen in this respect in any convincing way. To say that the additional conditions imposed by the Oregon statute amount to such distinctions would be to suggest that while a State may legitimately place inheritance by aliens on a reciprocity basis, it may not take measures to assure that reciprocity exists in practice and that the inheritance will actually be enjoyed by the person whom the testator intended to benefit. The years since the Clark decision have revealed some instances in which state court judges have delivered intemperate or ill-advised remarks about foreign governments in the course of applying such statutes, but nothing has occurred which could not readily have been foreseen at the time Clark v. Allen was decided.

Nor do I believe that this aspect of the Clark v. Allen decision should be overruled, as my Brother STEWART would have it. Prior decisions have established that in the absence of a conflicting federal policy or violation of the express mandates of the Constitution the States may legislate in areas of their traditional competence even though their statutes may have an incidental effect on foreign relations.[25] Application of this rule to the case before us compels the conclusion that the Oregon statute is constitutional. Oregon has so legislated in the course of regulating the descent and distribution of estates of Oregon decedents, a matter traditionally within the power of a State. See ante, at 440. Apart from the 1923 treaty, which the Court finds it unnecessary to consider, there is no specific interest of the Federal Government which might be interfered with by this statute. The appellants concede that Oregon might deny inheritance rights to all nonresident aliens.[26] Assuming that this is so, the statutory exception permitting inheritance by aliens whose countries permit Americans to inherit would seem to be a measure wisely designed to avoid any offense to foreign governments and thus any conflict with general federal interests: a foreign government can hardly object to the denial of rights which it does not itself accord to the citizens of other countries.

The foregoing would seem to establish that the Oregon statute is not unconstitutional on its face. And in fact the Court seems to have found the statute unconstitutional only as applied. Its notion appears to be that application of the parts of the statute which require that reciprocity actually exist and that the alien heir actually be able to enjoy his inheritance will inevitably involve the state courts in evaluations of foreign laws and governmental policies, and that this is likely to result in offense to foreign governments. There are several defects in this rationale. The most glaring is that it is based almost entirely on speculation. My Brother DOUGLAS does cite a few unfortunate remarks made by state court judges in applying statutes resembling the one before us. However, the Court does not mention, nor does the record reveal, any instance in which such an occurrence has been the occasion for a diplomatic protest, or, indeed, has had any foreign relations consequence whatsoever.[27] The United States says in its brief as amicus curiae that it

"does not . . . contend that the application of the Oregon escheat statute in the circumstances of this case unduly interferes with the United States' conduct of foreign relations."[28]

At an earlier stage in this case, the Solicitor General told this Court:

"The Department of State has advised us . . . that State reciprocity laws, including that of Oregon, have had little effect on the foreign relations and policy of this country. . . . Appellants' apprehension of a deterioration in international relations, unsubstantiated by experience, does not constitute the kind of `changed conditions' which might call for re-examination of Clark v. Allen."[29]

Essentially, the Court's basis for decision appears to be that alien inheritance laws afford state court judges an opportunity to criticize in dictum the policies of foreign governments, and that these dicta may adversely affect our foreign relations. In addition to finding no evidence of adverse effect in the record, I believe this rationale to be untenable because logically it would apply to many other types of litigation which come before the state courts. It is true that, in addition to the many state court judges who have applied alien inheritance statutes with proper judicial decorum,[30] some judges have seized the opportunity to make derogatory remarks about foreign governments. However, judges have been known to utter dicta critical of foreign governmental policies even in purely domestic cases, so that the mere possibility of offensive utterances can hardly be the test.

If the flaw in the statute is said to be that it requires state courts to inquire into the administration of foreign law, I would suggest that that characteristic is shared by other legal rules which I cannot believe the Court wishes to invalidate. For example, the Uniform Foreign Money-Judgments Recognition Act provides that a foreign-country money judgment shall not be recognized if it "was rendered under a system which does not provide impartial tribunals or procedures compatible with the requirements of due process of law."[31] When there is a dispute as to the content of foreign law, the court is required under the common law to treat the question as one of fact and to consider any evidence presented as to the actual administration of the foreign legal system.[32] And in the field of choice of law there is a nonstatutory rule that the tort law of a foreign country will not be applied if that country is shown to be "uncivilized."[33] Surely, all of these rules possess the same "defect" as the statute now before us. Yet I assume that the Court would not find them unconstitutional.

I therefore concur in the judgment of the Court upon the sole ground that the application of the Oregon statute in this case conflicts with the 1923 Treaty of Friendship, Commerce and Consular Rights with Germany.

Notes

[1] Dec. 8, 1923, 44 Stat. 2132, T. S. No. 725.

[2] See, e. g., Giles v. Maryland, 386 U. S. 66, 80-81; Hamm v. City of Rock Hill, 379 U. S. 306, 316; Bell v. Maryland, 378 U. S. 226, 237; Communist Party v. Catherwood, 367 U. S. 389, 392; Poe v. Ullman, 367 U. S. 497, 503; Machinists v. Street, 367 U. S. 740, 749.

[3] See also Alma Motor Co. v. Timken Co., 329 U. S. 129, 136-137.

[4] It is true, of course, that the treaty would displace the Oregon statute only by virtue of the Supremacy Clause of the Constitution. Yet I think it plain that this fact does not render inapplicable the teachings of Ashwander. Disposition of the case pursuant to the treaty would involve no interpretation of the Constitution, and this is what the Ashwander rules seek to bring about. Cf. Swift & Co., Inc. v. Wickham, 382 U. S. 111, 126-

127.

[5] Petersen v. Iowa, 245 U. S. 170; Duus v. Brown, 245 U. S. 176; Skarderud v. Tax Commission, 245 U. S. 633.

[6] The statute appears in the majority opinion in n. 1, ante, at 430.

[7] The appellees argue that a substantial part of the 1923 treaty has been terminated or abrogated by the 1954 Treaty of Friendship, Commerce and Navigation with the Federal Republic of Germany, 7 U. S. T. 1839, T. I. A. S. No. 3593. However, Article XXVI of the 1954 treaty specifies that it extends only to "all areas of land and water under the sovereignty or authority of" the Federal Republic of Germany, and to West Berlin. The United States does not challenge the holding of the Oregon Supreme Court that the 1923 treaty still applies to East Germany. See Brief for the United States as amicus curiae 6, n. 5.

[8] 125 Notes from Great Britain, Sept. 24, 1895, MSS., Nat. Archives.

[9] Treaty of March 2, 1899, with Great Britain, 31 Stat. 1939.

[10] July, Aug., Sept., 1785, 8 Stat. 88.

[11] See Art. XI, Treaty of Feb. 6, 1778, with France, 8 Stat. 18; Art. VI, Treaty of Oct. 8, 1782, with the Netherlands, 8 Stat. 36; Art. VI, Treaty of April 3, 1783, with Sweden, 8 Stat. 64.

[12] See also 3 Vattel, The Law of Nations or the Principles of Natural Law § 112, at 147-148 (1916 ed.); Wheaton, Elements of International Law § 82, at 115-116 (1866 ed.).

[13] See Borchard, Diplomatic Protection of Citizens Abroad § 39, at 88 (1916 ed.); 4 Miller, Treaties and other International Acts of the United States of America 547 (1934).

[14] The quotation is from the Swedish treaty. The wording of the Dutch treaty differs only slightly.

[15] The earlier treaties used the words "effects" and "goods," which have been held to include realty. Todok v. Union State Bank, 281 U. S. 449, 454.

[16] See 1 Blackstone, Commentaries 372; 2 Kent, Commentaries 61-63.

[17] See XXVI Journals of the Continental Congress 357, 360-361.

[18] See 2 Diplomatic Correspondence of the United States 1783-1789, at 111, 116-117.

[19] Despatch, Wheaton to Legare, June 14, 1843, 3 Despatches, Prussia, No. 226, MSS., Nat. Archives; see 4 Miller, Treaties and other International Acts of the United States of America 547-548 (1934).

[20] 4 Miller, supra, at 546, 548.

[21] Treaty of Nov. 25, 1850, with Switzerland, 11 Stat. 587, 590.

[22] See Diplomatic Correspondence of the United States, 1868, Pt. II, 194, 196-197; Foreign Relations of the United States, 1880, 952-953.

[23] See 4 Moore, Digest of International Law 6 (1906). The treaty was the Treaty of Dec. 18, 1832, with Russia, 8 Stat. 444.

[24] Bacardi Corp. v. Domenech, 311 U. S. 150, 163, citing Jordan v. Tashiro, 278 U. S. 123, 127; Nielsen v. Johnson, 279 U. S. 47, 52.

[25] See, e. g., Clarke v. Deckebach, 274 U. S. 392; Frick v. Webb, 263 U. S. 326; Webb v. O'Brien, 263 U. S. 313; Terrace v. Thompson, 263 U. S. 197; Heim v. McCall, 239 U. S. 175.

[26] Brief for Appellants 13. Thus, this case does not present the question whether a uniform denial of rights to nonresident aliens might be a denial of equal protection forbidden by the Fourteenth Amendment. Cf. Blake v. McClung, 172 U. S. 239, 260-261.

[27] The communication from the Bulgarian Government mentioned in the majority opinion in n. 7, ante, at 437, apparently refers not to intemperate comments by state-court judges but to the very existence of state statutes which result in the denial of inheritance rights to Bulgarians.

[28] Brief for the United States as amicus curiae 6, n. 5.

[29] Memorandum for the United States 5.

[30] See, e. g., Estate of Larkin, 65 Cal. 2d 60, 416 P. 2d 473.

[31] Uniform Foreign Money-Judgments Recognition Act § 4 (a) (1), 9B Unif. Laws Ann. 67.

[32] See generally Schlesinger, Comparative Law 31-143 (2d ed. 1959).

[33] See Slater v. Mexican National R. Co., 194 U. S. 120, 129 (Holmes, J.); American Banana Co. v. United Fruit Co., 213 U. S. 347, 355-356 (Holmes, J.); Cuba R. Co. v. Crosby, 222 U. S. 473, 478 (Holmes, J.); Walton v. Arabian American Oil Co., 233 F. 2d 541, 545.

Justice Harlan's dissent in Hardin v. Kentucky Util. (Jan 16, 1968)

MR. JUSTICE HARLAN, dissenting.

These cases present a narrow question of statutory construction, upon which differing views might reasonably be entertained. I cannot, however, agree that the position now adopted by the Court will satisfactorily achieve the purposes evidently sought by Congress in 1959. I therefore respectfully dissent.

The scope of judicial review of administrative action is, of course, governed principally by the terms and purposes of the underlying statutory system. Compare generally 4 Davis, Administrative Law Treatise § 30.03 (1958); Jaffe, Judicial Review: Question of Law, 69 Harv. L. Rev. 239; Jaffe, Judicial Control of Administrative Action 546 et seq. (1965). The purposes of these statutory provisions are uncommonly plain. The Court acknowledges, as it must, that "it is clear and undisputed that protection of private utilities from TVA competition was almost universally regarded as the primary objective of the [service area] limitation." Ante, at 7.

The provisions in question were expected to protect private utilities by "defin[ing]" and "limit[ing]" the "working arrangement that now exists with respect to" the Authority's service area. S. Rep. No. 470, 86th Cong., 1st Sess., 8. They were thus intended to constrict the Authority's discretion as to the expansion of its area of service. It is no disparagement of the Authority to recognize that an orderly system of law does not place the enforcement of a restraint upon discretion into the un-fettered hands of the party sought to be restrained; surely, therefore, the scope of judicial review of proceedings involving such limitations should be measured generously.

The role of the courts should, in particular, be viewed hospitably where, as here, the question sought to be reviewed does not significantly engage the agency's expertise. This is an instance "where the only or principal dispute relates to the meaning of the statutory term," NLRB v. Marcus Trucking Co., 286 F. 2d 583, 591; it may, as Judge Friendly has noted, therefore appropriately be denominated a "question of law." Ibid. It presents issues on which courts, and not the Authority, are relatively more expert. See 4 Davis, supra, at § 30.04. No doubt "economic and engineering aspects," ante, at 9, including topography, may influence the Authority's wish to expand its area of service, but such factors can hardly prescribe the terms or stringency of Congress' prohibitions against expansion.

In light of these considerations, I am unable to accept this decision, the effect of which is to restrict severely the scope of judicial review of the Authority's determinations under § 15d (a). The Court forbids reviewing courts to set aside such determinations unless they lack "reasonable support," and then discovers such support here in the most minimal evidence.[1] At bottom, the support adduced for this determination by the Court consists of two facts: first, the Authority's distributor served on July 1, 1957, eight customers in New Tazewell and 20 customers in Tazewell;[2] and second, at least some of the other residents of the two municipalities quite understandably would prefer to pay the lower rates for electrical power charged by the Authority.[3] If these facts illustrate the "reasonable support" demanded by the Court, Congress' stringent limitation upon the Authority has proved extraordinarily fragile.[4]

Neither the statute nor the pertinent legislative history provides any formula for the precise measurement of the Authority's service area. However, given Congress' clear purpose to restrict stringently the expansion of the area served by the Authority on July 1, 1957, I think that the emphasis placed by the Court of Appeals on the number of customers served on that date by respondent and the Authority offers the basis of a sensible and practical standard. Certainly Congress did not wish or expect that, as this Court now holds, the question should be left largely, if not entirely, in the hands of the Authority. I would therefore affirm the judgment below for the reasons given in Judge O'Sullivan's opinion for the Court of Appeals, 375 F. 2d 403, supplemented by the considerations discussed in this opinion.

Notes

[1] It should be noted that the agency determination upon which the Court places so much weight was reached at a "special meeting" of the Board of Directors on August 26, 1964, more than eight months after respondent filed its complaint, and only three weeks before trial. One of the staff memoranda upon which the determination was based refers specifically to this litigation. One might have supposed that a determination which was

made post litem motam warranted at least cautious treatment.

[2] The Court's choice of descriptive phrase is noteworthy. The Court suggests that the Authority's distributor served "a substantial minority" of the customers in the two Tazewells. The District Court found, in fact, that on July 1, 1957, respondent served 95.3% of those customers. 237 F. Supp. 502, 513.

[3] The Court intimates darkly that "economic dislocations" have occurred. The pertinent evidence appears to consist at bottom of allegations that housing and other forms of economic development tend to locate in areas in which the Authority's less expensive electrical power is available. Surely the Court does not suppose that Congress in 1959 was unaware that the Authority's electrical power is relatively inexpensive, or that it did not recognize that those who reside outside the Authority's service area would find it economically desirable to have that area extended so as to include themselves.

[4] It is pertinent to note that neither of the two staff memoranda upon which the Authority's belated determination was explicitly based included among the "facts which appear to be relevant" (Memorandum from the Manager of Power to the General Manager, Tennessee Valley Authority, August 25, 1964, 2 Transcript of Record 801) any references to "economic and engineering aspects" (ante, at 9), or even to any "economic dislocations" (ante, at 13). Whatever the relevance of these factors in the eyes of the Court, the Authority's staff appears to have thought them immaterial. The determination itself does not, of course, refer to these factors.

Justice Harlan's dissent in Smith v. Illinois (Jan 29, 1968)

MR. JUSTICE HARLAN, dissenting.

We granted certiorari in this case believing that it presented with requisite clarity the issue whether a defendant in a state criminal trial may constitutionally be denied on cross-examination of a principal state witness the right to question such witness as to his actual name and address. Were I still of the view, after examination of the record, that this case clearly presents that question, I would concur in the Court's judgment on due process, but not on Sixth Amendment "incorporation," grounds.[*] The record, however, raises serious doubt that this petitioner was denied any information that he did not already have, thus either rendering the error harmless or at least making the issue inappropriate for constitutional adjudication.

The State's witness identified himself as "James Jordan." Apparently knowing that this was not his real or his only name, defense counsel asked Jordan whether that was his correct name, and received a negative reply. Further inquiry was disallowed by the trial judge as to both the witness' name and address. Later, however, defense counsel said of the witness "I represented him before, I know him." Still later, when asked by defense counsel on direct examination how long he had known James Jordan, the defendant replied, "I'd say a few years or so, casually." The defendant also indicated that he knew Jordan to be a narcotics addict, and that he knew that Jordan was acquainted with a person whose legal name he knew to be Herbert Simpson.

In the face of these developments, the Court's suggestion that perhaps the defense nevertheless did not know Jordan's name or address is, to say the least, exceedingly dubious. At no point did defense counsel, or defendant, state that he lacked the requested information, nor did counsel pursue the point with any vigor after the State's objections to the questions; he simply turned to another series of questions without suggesting any way in which his attempt to present a defense had been prejudiced. The inference seems to me patent that counsel was asking routine questions, to which he already knew the answers, and that his failure to get answers in court was of no consequence.

I would not reverse a state conviction on a record so opaque, indeed one savoring of a disingenuous constitutional contention. Cf. Rescue Army v. Municipal Court, 331 U. S. 549; Poe v. Ullman, 367 U. S. 497. I would therefore dismiss the writ as improvidently granted.

[*] See my opinion concurring in the result in Pointer v. Texas, 380 U. S. 400, 408.

Justice Harlan's dissent in Albrecht v. Herald Co. (March 4, 1968)

MR. JUSTICE HARLAN, dissenting.

While I entirely agree with the views expressed by my Brother STEWART and have joined his dissenting opinion, the Court's disregard of certain economic considerations underlying the Sherman Act warrants additional comment.

I.

The practice of setting genuine price "ceilings," that is maximum prices, differs from the practice of fixing minimum prices, and no accumulation of pronouncements from the opinions of this Court can render the two economically equivalent.

The allegation of a combination of persons to fix maximum prices undoubtedly states a Sherman Act cause of action. In order for a plaintiff to win such a § 1 case, however, he must be able to prove the existence of the alleged combination, and the defendant must be unable, either by virtue of a per se rule or by failure of proof at trial, to show an adequate justification. It is on these two points that price ceilings differ from price floors: to hold that a combination may be inferred from the vertical dictation of a maximum price simply because it may be permissible to infer a combination from the vertical dictation of a minimum price ignores economic reality; to conclude that no acceptable justification for fixing maximum prices can be found simply because there is no acceptable justification for fixing minimum prices is to substitute blindness for analysis.

Resale price maintenance, a practice not involved here, lessens horizontal intrabrand competition. The effects, higher prices, less efficient use of resources, and an easier life for the resellers, are the same whether the price maintenance policy takes the form of a horizontal conspiracy among resellers or of vertical dictation by a manufacturer plus reseller acquiescence. This means two things. First, it is frequently possible to infer a combination of resellers behind what is presented to the world as a vertical and unilateral price policy, because it is the resellers and not the manufacturer who reap the direct benefits of the policy. Second, price floors are properly considered per se restraints, in the sense that once a combination to create them has been demonstrated, no proffered justification is an acceptable defense. Following the rule of reason, combinations to fix price floors are invariably unreasonable: to the extent that they achieve their objective, they act to the direct detriment of the public interest as viewed in the Sherman Act. In the absence of countervailing fair trade laws, all asserted justifications are, upon examination, found wanting, either because they are too trivial or elusive to warrant the expense of a trial (as is the case, for example, with a defense that price floors maintain the prestige of a product) or because they run counter to Sherman Act premises (as is the case with the defense that price maintenance enables inefficient sellers to stay in business).

Vertically imposed price ceilings are, as a matter of economic fact that this Court's words cannot change, an altogether different matter. Other things being equal, a manufacturer would like to restrict those distributing his product to the lowest feasible profit margin, for in this way he achieves the lowest overall price to the public and the largest volume. When a manufacturer dictates a minimum resale price he is responding to the interest of his customers, who may treat his product better if they have a secure high margin of profits. When the same manufacturer dictates a price ceiling, however, he is acting directly in his own interest, and there is no room for the inference that he is merely a mechanism for accomplishing anticompetitive purposes of his customers.[1]

Furthermore, the restraint imposed by price ceilings is of a different order from that imposed by price floors. In the present case the Court uses again the fallacious argument that price ceilings and price floors must be equally unreasonable because both "cripple the freedom of traders and thereby restrain their ability to sell in accordance with their own judgment."[2] The fact of the matter is that this statement does not in itself justify a per se rule in either the maximum or minimum price case, and that the real justification for a per se rule in the case of minimums has not been shown to exist in the case of maximums.

It has long been recognized that one of the objectives of the Sherman Act was to preserve, for social rather than economic reasons, a high degree of independence, multiplicity, and variety in the economic system. Recognition of this objective does not, however, require this Court to hold that every commercial act that fetters the freedom of some trader is a proper subject for a per se rule in the sense that it has no adequate provable justification. See, e. g., White Motor Co. v. United States, 372 U. S. 253. The per se treatment of price maintenance is justified because analysis alone, without the burden of a trial in each individual case, demonstrates that price floors are invariably harmful on balance.[3] Price ceilings are a different matter: they do not lessen horizontal competition; they drive prices toward the level that would be set by intense competition, and they cannot go below this level unless the manufacturer who dictates them and the customer who accepts them have both miscalculated. Since price ceilings reflect the manufacturer's view that there is insufficient competition to drive prices down to a competitive level, they have the arguable justification that they prevent retailers or wholesalers from reaping monopoly or supercompetitive profits.

When price floors and price ceilings are placed side by side, then, and the question is asked of each, "Does analysis justify a no-trial rule?" the answers must be quite different. Both practices share the negative attribute that they restrict individual discretion in the pricing area, but only the former imposes upon the public the much more significant evil of lessened competition, and, as just seen, the latter has an important arguable justification that the former does not possess. As the Court's opinion partially but inexplicitly recognizes, in a maximum price case the asserted justification must be met on its merits, and not by incantation of a per se rule developed for an altogether different situation.[4]

II.

The Court's discovery in this case of (a) a combination and (b) a restraint that is per se unreasonable is beset with pitfalls. The Court relies directly on combinations with Milne and Kroner, two third parties who were simply hired and paid to do telephoning and distributing jobs that respondent could as effectively have done itself. Neither had any special interest in respondent's objective of setting a price ceiling. If the critical question is whether a company pays one of its own employees to perform a routine task, or hires an outsider to do the same thing, the requirement of a "combination" in restraint of trade has lost all significant meaning. The point is more than that the words in a statute ought to be taken to mean something of substance. The premise of § 1 adjudication has always been that it is quite proper for a firm to set its own prices and determine its own territories, but that it may not do so in conjunction with another firm with which, in combination, it can generate market power that neither would otherwise have. A firm is not "combining" to fix its own prices or territory simply because it hires outside accountants, market analysts, advertisers by telephone or otherwise, or delivery boys. Once it is recognized that Kroner had no interest whatever in forcing his competitor to lower his price, and was merely being paid to perform a delivery job that respondent could have done itself, it is clear respondent's activity was in its essence unilateral.

The Court, quite evidently dissatisfied with the Milne and Kroner theories of combination, goes on to suggest two others not claimed. First, it is said, petitioner might have alleged a combination with other carriers who accepted respondent's maximum price. The difficulty with this thesis is that such a "combination" would have been wholly irrelevant to what was done to petitioner. In a price maintenance situation, each distributor does have an interest in preventing others from breaking the price line and driving everyone's prices down, and there is thus a real symphony of interests behind the pressure exerted on any individual retailer. However, in contrast, the effectiveness of a price ceiling imposed on one distributor does not depend upon the imposition of ceilings on other distributors, be they competitive or not. Each distributor's maximum price agreement is, for reasons already discussed, a vertical matter only, independent of agreements by other dealers. Hence the result of the Court's theory here would be to make what was done to this petitioner illegal because of the coincidental existence of unrelated similar agreements, and to base petitioner's right to recover upon activities that are altogether irrelevant to whatever harm he has suffered.

The Court also suggests that, under Parke, Davis, "petitioner could have claimed a combination between respondent and himself, at least as of the day he unwillingly complied with respondent's advertised price." This theory is intriguing, because although it is unsound on its face, it has within it the ring of something familiar. Obviously it makes no sense to deny recovery to a pressured retailer who resists temptation to the last and grant it to one who momentarily yields but is restored to virtue by the vision of treble damages. It is not the momentary acquiescence but the punishment for refusing to acquiesce that does the damage on which recovery is based.

The Court's difficulties on all of its theories stem from its unwillingness to face the ultimate conclusion at which it has actually arrived: it is unlawful for one person to dictate price floors or price ceilings to another; any pressure brought to bear in support of such dictation renders the dictator liable to any dictatee who is damaged. The reason for the Court's reluctance to state this conclusion bluntly is transparent: this statement of the matter takes no account of the absence of a combination or conspiracy.

This does not mean, however, that no combination or conspiracy could ever be inferred in such an ostensibly unilateral situation. It would often be proper to infer, in situations in which a manufacturer dictates a minimum price to a retailer, that the manufacturer is the mechanism for enforcing a very real combinatorial restraint among retailers who should be competing horizontally.[5] Instead of undertaking to analyze when this inference would be proper, the Court has in the past followed the rough approximation adopted in Parke, Davis:[6] there is no "combination" when a manufacturer simply states a resale price and announces that he will not deal with those who depart from it; there is a combination when the manufacturer goes one inch further. The magical quality in this transformation is more apparent than real, for the underlying horizontal combination may frequently be there and the Court has simply failed to state what it is.[7]

When a manufacturer dictates a maximum price, however, the Parke, Davis approach does not yield even a satisfactory rough answer to the question "[I]s there a combination?" For the manufacturer who purports to act unilaterally in dictating a maximum price really is acting unilaterally. No one is economically interested in the price squeeze but himself. Had the Court been in the habit of analyzing the economics on which the inference of a combination may be based, it would have seen that even if combinations to fix maximum prices are as illegal as combinations to fix minimum prices the circumstances under which a combination to fix maximum prices may be inferred are different from those which imply a combination to keep prices up.

It was for this reason that in Kiefer-Stewart Co. v. Seagram & Sons, 340 U. S. 211, the only case in this Court in which maximum resale prices have actually been held unlawful, the key question was whether there was an actual horizontal combination of manufacturers to impose on retailers a maximum resale price. The Court refused to hold that dictation of price ceilings to a single retailer by a single manufacturer was unlawful, but instead insisted upon, and found, a situation in which two manufacturers, in their common interest, combined to impose upon retailers a condition of doing business which they might not have been able to demand individually.

Kiefer-Stewart's treatment of the combination requirement is instructive. Any manufacturer is at perfect liberty to set the prices at which he will sell to retailers, and in that way maximize his profits while lessening theirs. Competition, that is the threat that the purchasing seller will simply turn to another manufacturer, prevents the manufacturer from raising his prices beyond a certain point. It is per se unlawful, however, for two manufacturers to combine to raise their prices together, rendering each of them secure because the retailer or wholesaler has nowhere else to turn. From the manufacturer's viewpoint, putting a ceiling on the resale price may be simply an alternative means to the end of maximizing his own profits by lessening distribution costs: instead of squeezing the reseller from the bottom he squeezes from the top. The holding of Kiefer-Stewart was that the squeeze from the top, like the squeeze from the bottom, was lawful unless by a combination of persons between whom competition would otherwise have limited the power to squeeze from either direction. No combination of the kind required in Kiefer-Stewart exists here, and the Court has found no sensible substitute theory of combination.

The Court's second difficulty in this case is to state why imposition of price ceilings is a per se unlawful restraint. The respondent offered as a defense the contention that since there was no competition between distributors to keep resale prices down, a fixed maximum price was in the interest of both the respondent itself and the public. The Court, recognizing that despite scattered dicta about maximum and minimum prices both being per se illegal there was here an alleged justification that would have to be faced on its merits, attempts to show that the defense may be disposed of without hearing evidence on it.

The Court has not been persuasive. The question in this case is not whether dictation of maximum prices is ever illegal, but whether it is always illegal. Petitioner is seeking, and now receives, a judgment notwithstanding the verdict of a jury that he had failed to show that the practice was unreasonable in this case. The best the Court can do is to list certain unfortunate consequences that maximum price dictation might have in other cases but was not shown to have here. Then, in rejecting the significant affirmative justification offered for respondent's practice, the Court merely says, "The assertion that illegal price fixing is justified because it blunts the pernicious consequences of another distribution practice is unpersuasive." Ante, at 154. I shall ignore the insertion of the word "illegal," which merely assumes the conclusion. I cannot understand why, in deciding whether a practice is an unreasonable restraint of trade, the Court finds it "unpersuasive" that the practice blunts pernicious attributes of an existing distribution system.

The Court's only answer is that the courts below did not consider whether the existing distribution system might itself be illegal. But even assuming that respondent can conceivably be penalized for failure to raise the question whether the distribution system, unchallenged by petitioner, was lawful, the Court's argument falls short. The Court has decided that exclusive territories and consequent market power can never be a justification for dictation of maximum prices because exclusive territories are sometimes unlawful. But they are neither always unlawful nor have they been demonstrated to be unlawful in this case.

It may well be that the mechanics of newspaper distribution are such that a city quite naturally divides itself into one or more relatively exclusive territories (sometimes called "paper routes"), giving each distributor a large degree of monopoly power. It is hardly farfetched to assume that a newspaper might be able to prove (if given the opportunity it is today denied) that rough territorial exclusivity is simply a fact of economic life in the newspaper distributing business, both because the nature of the enterprise dictates compactness of routes and because the number of distributors that a particular area can sustain is necessarily so small that they naturally fall into oligopolistic respect for each other's territories, and into a pattern of price leadership.

There is no question that the ideal situation, from the point of view of both the publisher and the public, is to have a very large number of distributors intensely vying with each other in both price and service. This situation, however, may be one that it is impossible to achieve in some, perhaps in all, cities. It seems quite possible that a publisher who does not want to do his own distributing must live with the fact that there will always be a relatively small number of competing distributors, who consequently will be likely to fall into lawful but undesirable oligopolistic behavior—price leadership and territorial exclusivity.

Confronted by this situation, the publisher, who is competing with other publishers in, among other things, price and service to the public, will seek to provide efficient distribution service at the lowest possible price. These objectives would be realized by intense competition without the publisher's interference, but in the absence of such competition the publisher must take steps of his own.

The present respondent took two steps. First, it insisted on the right to approve each distributor. Naturally, since newspapermen are notoriously realistic, it referred to the acquisition of a distributorship as the purchase of a "route." Second, it set a maximum home delivery price and enforced it; the price could not be below the level that perfect competition would dictate without driving the distributors out of business and defeating the publisher's whole objective. Hence the price set cannot be supposed to have been unreasonable.[8] Respondent had no need to go to the extreme of cutting off distributors preferring to do a high-profit, low-volume business, and did not do so. It simply advertised the maximum home delivery price and created competition with any distributor not observing it. Today's decision leaves respondent with no alternative but to use its own trucks.

For the reasons stated in my Brother STEWART'S opinion and those stated here, I would affirm the judgment below.

Notes

[1] See the opinion of Judge Coffin in Quinn v. Mobil Oil Co., 375 F. 2d 273, 276.

[2] Kiefer-Stewart Co. v. Seagram & Sons, 340 U. S. 211, 213.

[3] See the analysis in the leading case, United States v. Trenton Potteries Co., 273 U. S. 392, at 395-402. Price floors, or other agreements to prevent price cutting, are there held to be per se unreasonable because they inevitably lessen competition. There is no reference to the purely collateral effect of limiting individual trader discretion, still less to a program such as the one involved in this case that does not inhibit competitive price cutting.

[4] The same points may be made from the perspective of the retailers or wholesalers subject to the price dictation. When the issue is minimum resale prices, those sellers who are more efficient and ambitious are likely to object to price restrictions, while the lazier and less efficient sellers will welcome their protection. When the issue is price ceilings, the matter is different. Assuming the ceilings are high enough to permit a return that will enable the seller to stay in business, a seller will object to price ceilings only because they deny him the supercompetitive return that the imperfections of competition would otherwise permit. At the same time, in stark contrast to the situation involved in resale price maintenance, no seller has any interest in insisting that price ceilings be imposed on his competitors; he is not worried that they may sell at a higher price than his own. Thus while resale price maintenance establishes what is the equivalent of a single horizontal restraint on otherwise competitive sellers, price ceilings establish merely a series of distinct vertical relationships between manufacturer and seller, with no one seller economically interested in the maintenance of the vertical relationship with any other seller.

[5] See Turner, The Definition of Agreement Under the Sherman Act: Conscious Parallelism and Refusals to Deal, 75 Harv. L. Rev. 655. Professor Turner (as he then was) suggested the overruling of United States v. Colgate & Co., 250 U. S. 300, arguing, inter alia, that Colgate behavior by a manufacturer tends to produce tacit or implied minimum price agreements among otherwise competitive retailers. He suggested that "it should be perfectly clear to any manufacturer that a policy of refusing to deal with price cutters is no more nor less than an invitation [to retailers] to agree [with each other as well as with the manufacturer] on . . . a minimum price . . . ." Id., at 689. (Emphasis added.)

[6] United States v. Parke, Davis & Co., 362 U. S. 29.

[7] I thought at the time Parke, Davis was decided (see my dissenting opinion in that case, 362 U. S., at 49) and continue to believe, that the result reached could not be supported on the majority's reasoning. I am frank to say, however, that I now consider that the Parke, Davis result can be supported on Professor Turner's rationale. See Turner, supra, n. 5, at 684-691. Further reflection on the matter also leads me to say that my

statement in dissent to the effect that Parke, Davis had overruled the Colgate case was overdrawn, and further that I am not yet prepared to say that Professor Turner's rationale necessarily carries the total discard of Colgate.

[8] Reasonableness is also evidenced by the abundance of persons willing to distribute newspapers at or below the fixed ceilings. The point is not affected by the fact that the distributors willing to accept respondent's conditions were buying monopolies. The principal virtue of a monopoly is the power of the monopolist to charge supercompetitive prices. Hence it cannot be argued that the ceilings might have proved too low to attract buyers but for the fact that they were accompanied by monopoly power.

Justice Harlan's concurrence and dissent in US v. Third Nat. Bank in Nashville (March 4, 1968)

MR. JUSTICE HARLAN, whom MR. JUSTICE STEWART joins, concurring in part and dissenting in part.

My understanding of the procedural structure of the Bank Merger Act of 1966,[1] based on our decision last Term in United States v. First City National Bank of Houston, 386 U. S. 361, 364, is that the Act requires the District Court to engage in a two-step process. First, the District Court must decide whether the merger, considered solely from an antitrust viewpoint, would violate the Clayton Act standard embodied in the Bank Merger Act. If it would not, the inquiry is over. If there would be a violation, then the District Court must go on to decide whether "the anticompetitive effects of the proposed transaction are clearly outweighed in the public interest by the probable effect of the transaction in meeting the convenience and needs of the community to be served."[2] In making the latter decision, the District Court must again evaluate the antitrust factor, this time in a less polar way. For a comparatively minor violation of the Clayton Act, like that in this case, obviously may be more readily outweighed by factors relating to "convenience and needs" than may a relatively serious infraction.

Turning to the application of the Act to this case, the first question is whether the merger, as an antitrust matter, would violate the Clayton Act. I continue to disagree, particularly in the banking field, with the "numbers game" test for determining Clayton Act violations which was adopted by this Court in United States v. Philadelphia National Bank, 374 U. S. 321. However, I consider myself bound by that decision, and under its dictates I concur in the Court's finding that this merger would violate the Act.

I also concur in the Court's decision that this case must be remanded so that there may be a new application of the second-step balancing process. In this case, which was decided before our decision in Houston Bank, supra, the District Court either omitted the first of the two indicated procedural steps or concluded, incorrectly, that the merger would not violate the Clayton Act.[3] In either event, the error may have caused the District Court to misconceive the antitrust "threshold" at which the second-step balancing process was intended to come into play. This, in turn, may have led the court to give the "anticompetitive effect" of the merger a different weight in the balance than was intended by the framers of the Bank Merger Act. Hence, the case must be remanded to the District Court so that it may reweigh the competing factors in light of the correct antitrust threshold.

With regard to the "convenience and needs" side of the balance, I am in accord with the Court's ruling that a merger should not be approved under the 1966 Act unless the District Court finds that the benefits conferred upon the community by the merger could not reasonably have been achieved in other ways. Unlike the Court, however, I conclude from the record that the District Court did make adequate findings on this issue. The record reveals that many witnesses testified that Nashville Bank had problems of real magnitude, the greatest being to find replacements for key executives. Mr. Weaver, the leader of the group which purchased control of the bank not long before the merger, testified that initially his group had intended to operate the bank themselves, but that talks with many bankers had convinced him that his group could not solve the bank's problems. The head of an executive-placement firm testified that he did not believe that he could have found new executives for Nashville Bank, in light of its overall situation.[4] Although there was testimony in rebuttal, including that of another recruiter of executives, to the effect that the problems were not unsolvable, I cannot conclude that the District Court committed error when it held that

"While there is some conflict, the preponderance of the evidence is that it would have been practically impossible within any reasonable period of time to obtain adequate managerial replacements either from within the bank or from the outside, a product of the bank's failure . . . to provide itself with the facilities, procedures and equipment required to maintain a competitive posture." 260 F. Supp. 869, 881.

In sum, what I would consider to be the scope of the proceedings on remand is this. In light of our holding that a Clayton Act violation has been made out, further consideration of the first-step antitrust issue by the District Court is foreclosed. Believing, as I do but contrary to the Court, that the findings already made by the District Court as to the alternatives to merger are adequate, in my view the only question for the District Court to consider respecting the second step is whether, because of its character in light of the antitrust standard now set forth, the antitrust violation should yield to other factors bearing on public "convenience and needs."

Notes

[1] 80 Stat. 7, 12 U. S. C. § 1828 (c) (1964 ed., Supp. II).

[2] Bank Merger Act of 1966, amending § 18 (c) (5) (B) of the Federal Deposit Insurance Act, 12 U. S. C. § 1828 (c) (5) (B) (1964 ed., Supp. II).

[3] The District Court's opinion is unclear as to whether the court considered it necessary to make a discrete finding under the Clayton Act.

[4] An account of Nashville Bank's overall situation appears in the Court's opinion, ante, at 175-176.

Justice Harlan's concurrence and dissent in Interstate Circuit v. Dallas (April 22, 1968)

MR. JUSTICE HARLAN, concurring in No. 47, ante, p. 629, and dissenting in Nos. 56 and 64.

These cases usher the Court into a new phase of the intractable obscenity problem: may a State prevent the dissemination of obscene or other obnoxious material to juveniles upon standards less stringent than those which would govern its distribution to adults?

In No. 47, the Ginsberg case, the Court upholds a New York statute applicable only to juveniles which, as construed by the state courts, in effect embodies in diluted form the "adult" obscenity standards established by Roth v. United States, 354 U. S. 476, and the prevailing opinion in Memoirs v. Massachusetts, 383 U. S. 413. In Nos. 56 and 64, the Interstate Circuit and United Artists cases, the Court strikes down on the ground of vagueness a similar Dallas ordinance, not couched, however, entirely in obscenity terms. In none of these cases does the Court pass judgment on the particular material condemned by the state courts.

As the Court enters this new area of obscenity law it is well to take stock of where we are at present in this constitutional field. The subject of obscenity has produced a variety of views among the members of the Court unmatched in any other course of constitutional adjudication.[1] Two members of the Court steadfastly maintain that the First and Fourteenth Amendments render society powerless to protect itself against the dissemination of even the filthiest materials.[2] No other member of the Court, past or present, has ever stated his acceptance of that point of view. But there is among present members of the Court a sharp divergence as to the proper application of the standards in Roth, supra,[3] Memoirs, supra,[4] and Ginzburg v. United States, 383 U. S. 463,[5] for judging whether given material is constitutionally protected or unprotected. Most of the present Justices who believe that "obscenity" is not beyond the pale of governmental control seemingly consider that the Roth-Memoirs-Ginzburg tests permit suppression of material that falls short of so-called "hard core pornography," on equal terms as between federal and state authority.[6] Another view is that only "hard core pornography" may be suppressed, whether by federal or state authority.[7] And still another view, that of this writer, is that only "hard core pornography" may be suppressed by the Federal Government, whereas under the Fourteenth Amendment States are permitted wider authority to deal with obnoxious matter than might be justifiable under a strict application of the Roth-Memoirs-Ginzburg rules.[8]

There are also differences among us as to how our appellate process should work in reviewing obscenity determinations. One view is that we should simply examine the proceedings below to ascertain whether the lower federal or state courts have made a genuine effort to apply the Roth-Memoirs-Ginzburg tests, and that if such is the case, their determinations that the questioned material is obscene should be accepted, much as would any findings of fact.[9] Another view is that the question of whether particular material is obscene inherently entails a constitutional judgment for which the Court has ultimate responsibility, and hence that it is incumbent upon us to judge for ourselves, de novo as it were, the obscenity vel non of the challenged matter.[10]

The upshot of all this divergence in viewpoint is that anyone who undertakes to examine the Court's decisions since Roth which have held particular material obscene or not obscene would find himself in utter bewilderment.[11] From the standpoint of the Court itself the current approach has required us to spend an inordinate amount of time in the absurd business of perusing and viewing the miserable stuff that pours into the Court, mostly in state cases, all to no better end than second-guessing state judges. In all except rare instances, I venture to say, no substantial free-speech interest is at stake, given the right of the States to control obscenity.

I believe that no improvement in this chaotic state of affairs is likely to come until it is recognized that this whole problem is primarily one of state concern, and that the Constitution tolerates much wider authority and discretion in the States to control the dissemination of obscene materials than it does in the Federal Government. Reiterating the viewpoint that I have expressed in earlier opinions, I would limit federal control of obscene materials to those which all would recognize as what has been called "hard core pornography," and would withhold the federal judicial hand from interfering with state determinations except in instances where the state action clearly appears to be but the product of prudish overzealousness. See Roth v. United States, supra, at 496; Manual Enterprises v. Day, 370 U. S. 478; Jacobellis v. Ohio, 378 U. S. 184, 203; Memoirs v. Massachusetts, supra, at 455. And in the juvenile field I think that the Constitution is still more tolerant of state policy and its applications. If current doctrinaire views as to the reach of the First Amendment into state affairs are thought to stand in the way of such a functional approach, I would revert to basic constitutional concepts that until recent times have been recognized and respected as the fundamental genius of our federal system, namely the acceptance of wide state autonomy in local affairs.

I come now to the cases at hand. In No. 47, Ginsberg, I concur in the judgment and join the opinion of the Court, fully preserving, however, the views repeatedly expressed in my earlier opinions in this field.

In Nos. 56 and 64, the Interstate Circuit and United Artists cases, I respectfully dissent. I do not agree that the Dallas ordinance can be struck down, as the Court now holds, on the score of vagueness. The ambiguities about which the Court expresses concern are essentially two.[12] First, the ordinance does not include a definition of "sexual promiscuity."[13] Second, the ordinance provides that a film "shall be considered `likely to incite or encourage' crime delinquency or sexual promiscuity . . . if, in the judgment of the Board, there is a substantial probability that it will create the impression on young persons that such conduct is profitable, desirable, acceptable, respectable, praiseworthy or commonly accepted." The Court is concerned that many may disagree as to whether any specific materials create such impressions on young persons.

These seem to me entirely inadequate grounds on which to strike down the ordinance. It must be granted, of course, that people may differ as to the application of these standards; but the central lesson of this Court's efforts in this area is that under all verbal formulae, including even this Court's own definition of obscenity, reasonable men can, and ordinarily do, differ as to the proper assessment of challenged materials. The truth is that the Court has demanded greater precision of language from the City of Dallas than the Court can itself give, or even than can sensibly be expected in this area of the law.

The Court has not always asked so much.[14] In Roth, the federal statute under which the petitioner had been sentenced to five years' imprisonment forbade the mailing of material that was "obscene. lewd, lascivious, or filthy . . . or other publication of an indecent character."[15] 354 U. S., at 491. In Alberts v. California, the companion case to Roth, the California statute provided that the materials must have a "tendency to deprave or corrupt its readers." Id., at 498. No definitions were included in either statute, yet the Court there explicitly rejected the argument that they did not "provide reasonably ascertainable standards of guilt . . . ." Id., at 491. The Court recognized that the terms of obscenity statutes are necessarily imprecise, but emphasized, quoting United States v. Petrillo, 332 U. S. 1, 7-8, that the " `Constitution does not require impossible standards'; all that is required is that the language `conveys sufficiently definite warning as to the proscribed conduct when measured by common understanding and practices. . . .' "[16] Ibid. Yet it should be repeated that the Interstate Circuit cases, unlike Roth and Alberts, involve merely the classification, not the proscription by criminal prosecution, of objectionable materials. In my opinion, the ordinance does not fail either to give adequate notice of the films that are to be restricted, or to provide sufficiently definite standards for its administration.[17]

Although the Court finds it unnecessary to pass judgment upon the materials involved in these cases, I consider it preferable to face that question. Upon the premises set forth in my Roth and Memoirs opinions, and reiterated here, I would hold that in condemning these materials New York and the City of Dallas have acted within constitutional limits.

I would affirm the judgments in all three cases.

Notes

[1] In the following 13 obscenity cases from the date Roth was decided, in which signed opinions were written for a decision or judgment of the Court, there has been a total of 55 separate opinions among the Justices. Kingsley Books, Inc. v. Brown, 354 U. S. 436 (four opinions); Roth v. United States, supra (four opinions); Kingsley Int'l Pictures Corp. v. Regents, 360 U. S. 684 (six opinions); Smith v. California, 361 U. S. 147 (five opinions); Times Film Corp. v. Chicago, 365 U. S. 43 (three opinions); Marcus v. Search Warrant, 367 U. S. 717 (two opinions); Manual Enterprises v. Day, 370 U. S. 478 (three opinions); Bantam Books, Inc. v. Sullivan, 372 U. S. 58 (four opinions); Jacobellis v. Ohio,

378 U. S. 184 (six opinions); A Quantity of Books v. Kansas, 378 U. S. 205 (four opinions); Memoirs v. Massachusetts, supra (five opinions); Ginzburg v. United States, 383 U. S. 463 (five opinions); Mishkin v. New York, 383 U. S. 502 (four opinions).

[2] See Roth v. United States, supra, at 508 (dissenting opinion); Jacobellis v. Ohio, supra, at 196 (separate opinion); Ginzburg v. United States, supra, at 476, 482 (dissenting opinions).

[3] Roth stated the test to be "whether to the average person, applying contemporary community standards, the dominant theme of the material taken as a whole appeals to prurient interest." 354 U. S., at 489 (note omitted).

[4] Memoirs elaborated the Roth test as follows: "it must be established that (a) the dominant theme of the material taken as a whole appeals to a prurient interest in sex; (b) the material is patently offensive because it affronts contemporary community standards relating to the description or representation of sexual matters; and (c) the material is utterly without redeeming social value." 383 U. S., at 418.

[5] The Ginzburg "test" is difficult to state with any precision. The Court held that "in close cases evidence of pandering may be probative with respect to the nature of the material in question and thus satisfy the Roth test." 383 U. S., at 474. But this "simply elaborates the test by which the obscenity vel non of the material must be judged." Id., at 475. Yet evidence of pandering may "support the determination that the material is obscene even though in other contexts the material would escape such condemnation." Id., at 476. Pandering itself evidently encompasses every form of the " `business of purveying textual or graphic matter openly advertised to appeal to the erotic interest of their customers.' " Id., at 467 (note omitted).

[6] See, e. g., Jacobellis v. Ohio, supra, at 193-195 (opinion of BRENNAN, J.).

[7] See id., at 197 (concurring opinion of STEWART, J.).

[8] See Roth v. United States, supra, at 496 (concurring and dissenting opinion); Memoirs v. Massachusetts, supra, at 455 (dissenting opinion).

[9] See Jacobellis v. Ohio, supra, at 202 (dissenting opinion).

[10] See Jacobellis, at 190 (opinion of BRENNAN, J.); Roth v. United States, supra, at 497-498 (concurring and dissenting opinion); Kingsley Int'l Pictures Corp. v. Regents, supra, at 708 (concurring in result).

[11] See, e. g., Keney v. New York, 388 U. S. 440; Friedman v. New York, 388 U. S. 441; Ratner v. California, 388 U. S. 442; Cobert v. New York, 388 U. S. 443; Sheperd v. New York, 388 U. S. 444; Avansino v. New York, 388 U. S. 446; Aday v. United States, 388 U. S. 447; Corinth Publications, Inc. v. Wesberry, 388 U. S. 448; Books, Inc. v. United States, 388 U. S. 449; Rosenbloom v. Virginia, 388 U. S. 450; A Quantity of Copies of Books v. Kansas, 388 U. S. 452; Mazes v. Ohio, 388 U. S. 453; Schackman v. California, 388 U. S. 454; Landau v. Fording, 388 U. S. 456; Potomac News Co. v. United States, 389 U. S. 47; Conner v. City of Hammond, 389 U. S. 48; Central Magazine Sales, Ltd. v. United States, 389 U. S. 50; Chance v. California, 389 U. S. 89.

[12] The Court emphasizes at greater length the failure of the Board and the Texas

courts to proffer any clarification of the ordinance. This compels examination of the ordinance's terms, but it does not, of course, offer any independent basis for a conclusion that the ordinance is ambiguous.

[13] The Court acknowledges that the city has since adopted a definition of sexual promiscuity, but it expresses no views as to the definition's adequacy.

[14] It is pertinent to note that a majority of the Court did not hold that the New York statute at issue in Kingsley Int'l Pictures Corp. v. Regents, supra, was impermissibly vague. The statute forbade the exhibition of a film "which portrays acts of sexual immorality. . . or . . . presents such acts as desirable, acceptable or proper patterns of behavior." Id., at 685. It appears that only the opinion of Mr. Justice Clark, concurring in the result, upon which the Court now relies so heavily, described this standard as vague. Indeed, Mr. Justice Frankfurter said in his separate opinion that the "Court does not strike the law down because of vagueness . . . ." Id., at 695. See also id., at 704. Mr. Justice Frankfurter went on to say that " `[s]exual immorality' is not a new phrase in this branch of law and its implications dominate the context. I hardly conceive it possible that the Court would strike down as unconstitutional the federal statute against mailing lewd, obscene and lascivious matter, which has been the law of the land for nearly a hundred years, see the Act of March 3, 1865, 13 Stat. 507, and March 3, 1873, 17 Stat. 599, whatever specific instances may be found not within its allowable prohibition. In sustaining this legislation this Court gave the words `lewd, obscene and lascivious' concreteness by saying that they concern `sexual immorality.' " Id., at 695-696.

[15] The statute involved in Roth now provides in part that it is a criminal offense to import or transport in interstate commerce any "obscene, lewd, lascivious, or filthy book, pamphlet, picture, motion-picture film, paper, letter, writing, print, or other matter of indecent character . . . ." 18 U. S. C. § 1462. Similarly, § 1461 provides that it is a criminal offense to mail any "obscene, lewd, lascivious, indecent, filthy or vile" article. See also §§ 1463, 1464, 1465. Although each of these sections makes profuse use of the disjunctive, no definitions of any of these descriptive terms are provided.

[16] The Court went on to say that it "is argued that because juries may reach different conclusions as to the same material, the statutes must be held to be insufficiently precise to satisfy due process requirements. But, it is common experience that different juries may reach different results under any criminal statute. That is one of the consequences we accept under our jury system." 354 U. S., at 492, n. 30. Precisely similar reasoning should be applicable to boards like that created by the Dallas ordinance, although the cost of differences in result is here measured (at least initially) by film classifications, and not by lengthy terms of imprisonment.

[17] It is difficult to see how the Court could suppose that its Memoirs formula offers more precise warnings to film makers than does the Dallas ordinance. Surely the Court cannot now believe that "redeeming social value," "patent offensiveness," and "prurient interest" are, particularly as modified so as to apply to children, terms of common understanding and clarity. Moreover, one wonders whether the pandering

rationale adopted in Ginzburg v. United States, supra, is thought to give more "guidance to those who seek to adjust their conduct" than does the Dallas ordinance. It is difficult to imagine any standard more vague, or more overbroad, than the "new subjectivity" created by the Court's search for the "leer of the sensualist." See Magrath, The Obscenity Cases: Grapes of Roth, 1966 Sup. Ct. Rev. 7, 61.

Justice Harlan's dissent in Glona v. American Guarantee & Liability Ins. (May 20, 1968)

MR. JUSTICE HARLAN, whom MR. JUSTICE BLACK and MR. JUSTICE STEWART join, dissenting.[*]

These decisions can only be classed as constitutional curiosities.

At common law, no person had a legally cognizable interest in the wrongful death of another person, and no person could inherit the personal right of another to recover for tortious injuries to his body.[1] By statute, Louisiana has created both rights in favor of certain classes of persons. The question in these cases is whether the way in which Louisiana has defined the classes of persons who may recover is constitutionally permissible. The Court has reached a negative answer to this question by a process that can only be described as brute force.

One important reason why recovery for wrongful death had everywhere to await statutory delineation is that the interest one person has in the life of another is inherently intractable. Rather than hear offers of proof of love and affection and economic dependence from every person who might think or claim that the bell had tolled for him, the courts stayed their hands pending legislative action. Legislatures, responding to the same diffuseness of interests, generally defined classes of proper plaintiffs by highly arbitrary lines based on family relationships, excluding issues concerning the actual effect of the death on the plaintiff.[2]

Louisiana has followed the traditional pattern. There the actions lie in favor of the surviving spouse and children of the deceased, if any; if none, then in favor of the surviving parents of the deceased, if any; if none, then in favor of the deceased's brothers and sisters, if any; if none, then no action lies. According to this scheme, a grown man may sue for the wrongful death of parents he did not love,[3] even if the death relieves him of a great economic burden or entitles him to a large inheritance. But an employee who loses a job because of the death of his employer has no cause of action, and a minor child cared for by neighbors or relatives "as if he were their own son" does not therefore have a right to sue for their death.[4] Perhaps most dramatic, a surviving parent, for example, of a Louisiana deceased may sue if and only if there is no surviving spouse or child: it does not matter who loved or depended on whom, or what the economic situation of any survivor may be, or even whether the spouse or child elects to sue.[5] In short, the whole scheme of the Louisiana wrongful death statute, which is similar in this respect to that of most other States, makes everything the Court says about affection and nurture and dependence altogether irrelevant. The only question in any case is whether the plaintiff falls within the classes of persons to whom the State has accorded a right of action for the death of another.

Louisiana has chosen, as have most other States in one respect or another, to define these classes of proper plaintiffs in terms of their legal rather than their biological relation to the deceased. A man may recover for the death of his wife, whether he loved her or not, but may not recover for the death of his paramour.[6] A child may recover for the death of his adopted parents. An illegitimate may recover for the wrongful death of a parent who has taken a few hours to acknowledge him formally, but not for the death of a person who he claims is his parent but who has not acknowledged him.[7] A parent may recover for the death of an illegitimate child he has acknowledged, but not for the death of an illegitimate child whom he did not bother to acknowledge until the possibility of tort recovery arose.

The Court today, for some reason which I am at a loss to understand, rules that the State must base its arbitrary definition of the plaintiff class on biological rather than legal relationships. Exactly how this makes the Louisiana scheme even marginally more "rational" is not clear, for neither a biological relationship nor legal acknowledgment is indicative of the love or economic dependence that may exist between two persons. It is, frankly, preposterous to suggest that the State has made illegitimates into "nonpersons," or that, by analogy with what Louisiana has done here it might deny illegitimates constitutional rights or the benefits of doing business in corporate form.[8] The rights at issue here stem from the existence of a family relationship, and the State has decided only that it will not recognize the family relationship unless the formalities of marriage, or of the acknowledgment of children by the parent in question, have been complied with.

There is obvious justification for this decision. If it be conceded, as I assume it is, that the State has power to provide that people who choose to live together should go through the formalities of marriage and, in default, that people who bear children should acknowledge them, it is logical to enforce these requirements by declaring that the general class of rights that are dependent upon family relationships shall be accorded only when the formalities as well as the biology of those relationships are present. Moreover, and for many of the same reasons why a State is empowered to require formalities in the first place, a State may choose to simplify a particular proceeding by reliance on formal papers rather than a contest of proof.[9] That suits for wrongful death, actions to determine the heirs of intestates, and the like, must as a constitutional matter deal with every claim of biological paternity or maternity on its merits is an exceedingly odd proposition.

The Equal Protection Clause states a complex and difficult principle. Certain classifications are "inherently suspect," which I take to mean that any reliance upon them in differentiating legal rights requires very strong affirmative justification. The difference between a child who has been formally acknowledged and one who has not is hardly one of these. Other classifications are impermissible because they bear no intelligible proper relation to the consequences that are made to flow from them. This does not mean that any classification this Court thinks could be better drawn is unconstitutional. But even if the power of this Court to improve on the lines that Congress and the States have drawn were very much broader than I consider it to be, I could not understand why a State which bases the right to recover for wrongful death strictly on family relationships could not demand that those relationships be formalized.

I would affirm the decisions of the state court and the Court of Appeals for the Fifth Circuit.

[*] This opinion applies also to No. 508, Levy v. Louisiana, ante, p. 68.

Notes

[1] See Van Beeck v. Sabine Towing Co., 300 U. S. 342, 344-345, and cases there cited.

[2] An English statute, Lord Campbell's Act, 9 & 10 Vict., c. 93 (1846), "has served as the model for similar acts in most of the states in this country." F. Tiffany, Death By Wrongful Act 5 (2d ed., 1913). The statute provided that the action "shall be for the Benefit of the Wife, Husband, Parent, and Child . . . ." It is note-worthy that English and Canadian courts held the words "child" and "parent" to exclude illegitimate relationships. Dickinson v. North Eastern R. Co., 2 Hurl. & Colt. 735, 9 L. T. R. (N. S.) 299; Gibson v. Midland R. Co., 2 Ont. 658. A recent comprehensive survey of American law in the field comments that "[i]f there is a general rule today, it is probably that the word `child' or `children' when used in a statute pertaining to wrongful death beneficiaries, refers to a legitimate child or legitimate children, and thus only legitimates can recover for the wrongful death of their parents. This is merely an application of the principle that statutes patterned after Lord Campbell's Act which use the word `kin' mean legitimate kin, and that where such statutes say `father' or `mother,' `children,' `brothers' or `sister,' they mean only legitimate father, mother, children, brothers or sisters." S. Speiser, Recovery for Wrongful Death 587 (1966).

[3] He may even, like Shakespeare's Edmund, have spent his life contriving treachery against his family. Supposing that the Bard had any views on the law of legitimacy, they might more easily be discerned from Edmund's character than from the words he utters in defense of the only thing he cares for, himself.

[4] Numerous Louisiana cases, reflecting the difficulty of attempting to determine the "real" interest of one person in the death of another, have insisted upon strict conformity to the required statutory relationship, and stated that the statute may not be extended by interpretation to analogous cases. E. g., Bradley v. Swift & Co., 167 La. 249, 119 So. 37 (1928). As it happens, this Court has had occasion to recognize Louisiana's interest in strict construction. See Mobile Life Ins. Co. v. Brame, 95 U. S. 754, holding that an insurance company, having paid the insurance after the wrongful death of its insured, had no cause of action against the tortfeasor under Louisiana law.

[5] See, e. g., Burthlong v. Huber, 4 So. 2d 480; Doucet v. Travelers Ins. Co., 91 F. Supp. 864. The Court speaks in Levy of tortfeasors going free. However, the deceased in

that case left a legitimate parent. Under the Court's opinion, the right of legitimate and perhaps dependent parents to sue will henceforth be cut off by the mere existence of an illegitimate child, though the child be a self-supporting adult, and though the child elect not to sue. Incidentally, the burden of proving the nonexistence of such a child will be on the plaintiff parent. Trahan v. Southern Pacific Co., 209 F. Supp. 334.

[6] Vaughan v. Dalton-Lard Lumber Co., 119 La. 61, 43 So. 926 (1907). At the same time, a wife may recover for the death of a man to whom she is lawfully married, although she is not dependent on him for support and, indeed, is living adulterously with someone else. Jones v. Massachusetts Bonding & Ins. Co., 55 So. 2d 88.

[7] In Thompson v. Vestal Lumber & Mfg. Co., 16 So. 2d 594, 596, aff'd, 208 La. 83, 22 So. 2d 842 (1944), the court stated: "Children referred to in this law [the wrongful death statute] include only those who are the issue of lawful wedlock or who, being illegitimate, have been acknowledged or legitimated pursuant to methods expressly established by law." Article 203 of the Louisiana Civil Code provides that children may be acknowledged by a declaration, by either or both parents, executed in the presence of a notary public and two witnesses.

[8] A more obvious analogy from the law of corporations than the rather farfetched example the Court has suggested is the elementary rule that the benefits of doing business in corporate form may be denied, to the willful, the negligent, and the innocent alike, if the formalities of incorporation have not been properly complied with.

[9] Even where liability arises under a federal statute defining rights in terms of a family relationship to the deceased, federal courts have generally looked to the law and the formalities of the appropriate State. In Seaboard Air Line v. Kenney, 240 U. S. 489, arising under the Federal Employers' Liability Act, 35 Stat. 65, as amended, 36 Stat. 291, this Court relied upon the North Carolina determination that the "next of kin" of an illegitimate deceased were his half siblings rather than his father. In De Sylva v. Ballentine, 351 U. S. 570, arising under the Copyright Act, 61 Stat. 652, 17 U. S. C. § 1 et seq., we held that the word "children" in § 24 of that federal statute should be defined by reference to California law; California law provided that an illegitimate who had been acknowledged in writing by his father could inherit from him; since the illegitimate involved in De Sylva had been acknowledged, we held he was included within the statutory term. Two Justices, concurring in the unanimous result, argued that it was not proper to look to state law for a definition of the federal statutory term "children." Nowhere, however, was it suggested that we look to the Constitution. In Bell v. Tug Shrike, 332 F. 2d 330, the Fourth Circuit looked to Virginia law to determine whether the plaintiff was a "widow" entitled to bring suit under the Jones Act, 41 Stat. 1007, 46 U. S. C. § 688. Plaintiff had "married" her "husband" at a time when he was already married. Although the pre-existing marriage was later dissolved by divorce, after which plaintiff continued to live with the "husband," Virginia does not recognize common-law marriages. Consequently, plaintiff was held not to be a "widow." There was no suggestion that equal protection was in any way involved.

Justice Harlan's dissent in Duncan v. Louisiana (May 20, 1968)

MR. JUSTICE HARLAN, whom MR. JUSTICE STEWART joins, dissenting.

Every American jurisdiction provides for trial by jury in criminal cases. The question before us is not whether jury trial is an ancient institution, which it is; nor whether it plays a significant role in the administration of criminal justice, which it does; nor whether it will endure, which it shall. The question in this case is whether the State of Louisiana, which provides trial by jury for all felonies, is prohibited by the Constitution from trying charges of simple battery to the court alone. In my view, the answer to that question, mandated alike by our constitutional history and by the longer history of trial by jury, is clearly "no."

The States have always borne primary responsibility for operating the machinery of criminal justice within their borders, and adapting it to their particular circumstances. In exercising this responsibility, each State is compelled to conform its procedures to the requirements of the Federal Constitution. The Due Process Clause of the Fourteenth Amendment requires that those procedures be fundamentally fair in all respects. It does not, in my view, impose or encourage nationwide uniformity for its own sake; it does not command adherence to forms that happen to be old; and it does not impose on the States the rules that may be in force in the federal courts except where such rules are also found to be essential to basic fairness.

The Court's approach to this case is an uneasy and illogical compromise among the views of various Justices on how the Due Process Clause should be interpreted. The Court does not say that those who framed the Fourteenth Amendment intended to make the Sixth Amendment applicable to the States. And the Court concedes that it finds nothing unfair about the procedure by which the present appellant was tried. Nevertheless, the Court reverses his conviction: it holds, for some reason not apparent to me, that the Due Process Clause incorporates the particular clause of the Sixth Amendment that requires trial by jury in federal criminal cases—including, as I read its opinion, the sometimes trivial accompanying baggage of judicial interpretation in federal contexts.

I have raised my voice many times before against the Court's continuing undiscriminating insistence upon fastening on the States federal notions of criminal justice,[1] and I must do so again in this instance. With all respect, the Court's approach and its reading of history are altogether topsy-turvy.

I.

I believe I am correct in saying that every member of the Court for at least the last 135 years has agreed that our Founders did not consider the requirements of the Bill of Rights so fundamental that they should operate directly against the States.[2] They were wont to believe rather that the security of liberty in America rested primarily upon the dispersion of governmental power across a federal system.[3] The Bill of Rights was considered unnecessary by some[4] but insisted upon by others in order to curb the possibility of abuse of power by the strong central government they were creating.[5]

The Civil War Amendments dramatically altered the relation of the Federal Government to the States. The first section of the Fourteenth Amendment imposes highly significant restrictions on state action. But the restrictions are couched in very broad and general terms: citizenship; privileges and immunities; due process of law; equal protection of the laws. Consequently, for 100 years this Court has been engaged in the difficult process Professor Jaffe has well called "the search for intermediate premises."[6] The question has been, Where does the Court properly look to find the specific rules that define and give content to such terms as "life, liberty, or property" and "due process of law"?

A few members of the Court have taken the position that the intention of those who drafted the first section of the Fourteenth Amendment was simply, and exclusively, to make the provisions of the first eight Amendments applicable to state action.[7] This view has never been accepted by this Court. In my view, often expressed elsewhere,[8] the first section of the Fourteenth Amendment was meant neither to incorporate, nor to be limited to, the specific guarantees of the first eight Amendments. The overwhelming historical evidence marshalled by Professor Fairman demonstrates, to me conclusively, that the Congressmen and state legislators who wrote, debated, and ratified the Fourteenth Amendment did not think they were "incorporating" the Bill of Rights[9] and the very breadth and generality of the Amendment's provisions suggest that its authors did not suppose that the Nation would always be limited to mid-19th century conceptions of "liberty" and "due process of law" but that the increasing experience and evolving conscience of the American people would add new "intermediate premises." In short, neither history, nor sense, supports using the Fourteenth Amendment to put the States in a constitutional straitjacket with respect to their own development in the administration of criminal or civil law.

Although I therefore fundamentally disagree with the total incorporation view of the Fourteenth Amendment, it seems to me that such a position does at least have the virtue, lacking in the Court's selective incorporation approach, of internal consistency: we look to the Bill of Rights, word for word, clause for clause, precedent for precedent because, it is said, the men who wrote the Amendment wanted it that way. For those who do not accept this "history," a different source of "intermediate premises" must be found. The Bill of Rights is not necessarily irrelevant to the search for guidance in interpreting the Fourteenth Amendment, but the reason for and the nature of its relevance must be articulated.

Apart from the approach taken by the absolute incorporationists, I can see only one method of analysis that has any internal logic. That is to start with the words "liberty" and "due process of law" and attempt to define them in a way that accords with American traditions and our system of government. This approach, involving a much more discriminating process of adjudication than does "incorporation," is, albeit difficult, the one that was followed throughout the 19th and most of the present century. It entails a "gradual process of judicial inclusion and exclusion,"[10] seeking, with due recognition of constitutional tolerance for state experimentation and disparity, to ascertain those "immutable principles . . . of free government which no member of the Union may disregard."[11] Due process was not restricted to rules fixed in the past, for that "would be to deny every quality of the law but its age, and to render it incapable of progress or improvement."[12] Nor did it impose nationwide uniformity in details, for

"[t]he Fourteenth Amendment does not profess to secure to all persons in the United States the benefit of the same laws and the same remedies. Great diversities in these respects may exist in two States separated only by an imaginary line. On one side of this line there may be a right of trial by jury, and on the other side no such right. Each State prescribes its own modes of judicial proceeding."[13]

Through this gradual process, this Court sought to define "liberty" by isolating freedoms that Americans of the past and of the present considered more important than any suggested countervailing public objective. The Court also, by interpretation of the phrase "due process of law," enforced the Constitution's guarantee that no State may imprison an individual except by fair and impartial procedures.

The relationship of the Bill of Rights to this "gradual process" seems to me to be twofold. In the first place it has long been clear that the Due Process Clause imposes some restrictions on state action that parallel Bill of Rights restrictions on federal action. Second, and more important than this accidental overlap, is the fact that the Bill of Rights is evidence, at various points, of the content Americans find in the term "liberty" and of American standards of fundamental fairness.

An example, both of the phenomenon of parallelism and the use of the first eight Amendments as evidence of a historic commitment, is found in the partial definition of "liberty" offered by Mr. Justice Holmes, dissenting in Gitlow v. New York, 268 U. S. 652:

"The general principle of free speech . . . must be taken to be included in the Fourteenth Amendment, in view of the scope that has been given to the word `liberty' as there used, although perhaps it may be accepted with a somewhat larger latitude of interpretation than is allowed to Congress by the sweeping language that governs or ought to govern the laws of the United States." Id., at 672.

As another example, Mr. Justice Frankfurter, speaking for the Court in Wolf v. Colorado, 338 U. S. 25, 27-28, recognized that

"[t]he security of one's privacy against arbitrary intrusion by the police—which is at the core of the Fourth Amendment—is basic to a free society. It is therefore implicit in `the concept of ordered liberty' and as such enforceable against the States through the Due Process Clause."

The Court has also found among the procedural requirements of "due process of law" certain rules paralleling requirements of the first eight Amendments. For example, in Powell v. Alabama, 287 U. S. 45, the Court ruled that a State could not deny counsel to an accused in a capital case:

"The fact that the right involved is of such a character that it cannot be denied without violating those `fundamental principles of liberty and justice which lie at the base of all our civil and political institutions' . . . is obviously one of those compelling considerations which must prevail in determining whether it is embraced within the due process clause of the Fourteenth Amendment, although it be specifically dealt with in another part of the federal Constitution." Id., at 67. (Emphasis added.)

Later, the right to counsel was extended to all felony cases.[14] The Court has also ruled, for example, that "due process" means a speedy process, so that liberty will not be long restricted prior to an adjudication, and evidence of fact will not become stale;[15] that in a system committed to the resolution of issues of fact by adversary proceedings the right to confront opposing witnesses must be guaranteed;[16] and that if issues of fact are tried to a jury, fairness demands a jury impartially selected.[17] That these requirements are fundamental to procedural fairness hardly needs redemonstration.

In all of these instances, the right guaranteed against the States by the Fourteenth Amendment was one that had also been guaranteed against the Federal Government by one of the first eight Amendments. The logically critical thing, however, was not that the rights had been found in the Bill of Rights, but that they were deemed, in the context of American legal history, to be fundamental. This was perhaps best explained by Mr. Justice Cardozo, speaking for a Court that included Chief Justice Hughes and Justices Brandeis and Stone, in Palko v. Connecticut, 302 U. S. 319:

"If the Fourteenth Amendment has absorbed them, the process of absorption has had its source in the belief that neither liberty nor justice would exist if they were sacrificed." Id., at 326.

Referring to Powell v. Alabama, supra, Mr. Justice Cardozo continued:

"The decision did not turn upon the fact that the benefit of counsel would have been guaranteed to the defendants by the provisions of the Sixth Amendment if they had been prosecuted in a federal court. The decision turned upon the fact that in the particular situation laid before us in the evidence the benefit of counsel was essential to the substance of a hearing." Id., at 327.

Mr. Justice Cardozo then went on to explain that the Fourteenth Amendment did not impose on each State every rule of procedure that some other State, or the federal courts, thought desirable, but only those rules critical to liberty:

"The line of division may seem to be wavering and broken if there is a hasty catalogue of the cases on the one side and the other. Reflection and analysis will induce a different view. There emerges the perception of a rationalizing principle which gives to discrete instances a proper order and coherence. The right to trial by jury and the immunity from prosecution except as the result of an indictment may have value and importance. Even so, they are not of the very essence of a scheme of ordered liberty. To abolish them is not to violate a `principle of justice so rooted in the traditions and conscience of our people as to be ranked as fundamental.'. . . Few would be so narrow or provincial as to maintain that a fair and enlightened system of justice would be impossible without them." Id., at 325. (Emphasis added.)

Today's Court still remains unwilling to accept the total incorporationists' view of the history of the Fourteenth Amendment. This, if accepted, would afford a cogent reason for applying the Sixth Amendment to the States. The Court is also, apparently, unwilling to face the task of determining whether denial of trial by jury in the situation before us, or in other situations, is fundamentally unfair. Consequently, the Court has compromised on the ease of the incorporationist position, without its internal logic. It has simply assumed that the question before us is whether the Jury Trial Clause of the Sixth Amendment should be incorporated into the Fourteenth, jot-for-jot and case-for-case, or ignored. Then the Court merely declares that the clause in question is "in" rather than "out."[18]

The Court has justified neither its starting place nor its conclusion. If the problem is to discover and articulate the rules of fundamental fairness in criminal proceedings, there is no reason to no reason to assume that the whole body of rules developed in this Court constituting Sixth Amendment jury trial must be regarded as a unit. The requirement of trial by jury in federal criminal cases has given rise to numerous subsidiary questions respecting the exact scope and content of the right. It surely cannot be that every answer the Court has given, or will give, to such a question is attributable to the Founders; or even that every rule announced carries equal conviction of this Court; still less can it be that every such subprinciple is equally fundamental to ordered liberty.

Examples abound. I should suppose it obviously fundamental to fairness that a "jury" means an "impartial jury."[19] I should think it equally obvious that the rule, imposed long ago in the federal courts, that "jury" means "jury of exactly twelve,"[20] is not fundamental to anything: there is no significance except to mystics in the number 12. Again, trial by jury has been held to require a unanimous verdict of jurors in the federal courts,[21] although unanimity has not been found essential to liberty in Britain, where the requirement has been abandoned.[22]

One further example is directly relevant here. The co-existence of a requirement of jury trial in federal criminal cases and a historic and universally recognized exception for "petty crimes" has compelled this Court, on occasion, to decide whether a particular crime is petty, or is included within the guarantee.[23] Individual cases have been decided without great conviction and without reference to a guiding principle. The Court today holds, for no discernible reason, that if and when the line is drawn its exact location will be a matter of such fundamental importance that it will be uniformly imposed on the States. This Court is compelled to decide such obscure borderline questions in the course of administering federal law. This does not mean that its decisions are demonstrably sounder than those that would be reached by state courts and legislatures, let alone that they are of such importance that fairness demands their imposition throughout the Nation.

Even if I could agree that the question before us is whether Sixth Amendment jury trial is totally "in" or totally "out," I can find in the Court's opinion no real reasons for concluding that it should be "in." The basis for differentiating among clauses in the Bill of Rights cannot be that only some clauses are in the Bill of Rights, or that only some are old and much praised, or that only some have played an important role in the development of federal law. These things are true of all. The Court says that some clauses are more "fundamental" than others, but it turns out to be using this word in a sense that would have astonished Mr. Justice Cardozo and which, in addition, is of no help. The word does not mean "analytically critical to procedural fairness" for no real analysis of the role of the jury in making procedures fair is even attempted. Instead, the word turns out to mean "old," "much praised," and "found in the Bill of Rights." The definition of "fundamental" thus turns out to be circular.

II.

Since, as I see it, the Court has not even come to grips with the issues in this case, it is necessary to start from the beginning. When a criminal defendant contends that his state conviction lacked "due process of law," the question before this Court, in my view, is whether he was denied any element of fundamental procedural fairness. Believing, as I do, that due process is an evolving concept and that old principles are subject to re-evaluation in light of later experience, I think it appropriate to deal on its merits with the question whether Louisiana denied appellant due process of law when it tried him for simple assault without a jury.

The obvious starting place is the fact that this Court has, in the past, held that trial by jury is not a requisite of criminal due process. In the leading case, Maxwell v. Dow, 176 U. S. 581, Mr. Justice Peckham wrote as follows for the Court:[24]

"Trial by jury has never been affirmed to be a necessary requisite of due process of law. . . .

. . . . .

". . . The right to be proceeded against only by indictment, and the right to a trial by twelve jurors, are of the same nature, and are subject to the same judgment, and the people in the several States have the same right to provide by their organic law for the change of both or either. . . . [T]he State has full control over the procedure in its courts, both in civil and criminal cases, subject only to the qualification that such procedure must not work a denial of fundamental rights or conflict with specific and applicable provisions of the Federal Constitution. The legislation in question is not, in our opinion, open to either of these objections." Id., at 603-605.

In Hawaii v. Mankichi, 190 U. S. 197, the question was whether the Territory of Hawaii could continue its pre-annexation procedure of permitting conviction by non-unanimous juries. The Congressional Resolution of Annexation had provided that municipal legislation of Hawaii that was not contrary to the United States Constitution could remain in force. The Court interpreted the resolution to mean only that those requirements of the Constitution that were "fundamental" would be binding in the Territory. After concluding that a municipal statute allowing a conviction of treason on circumstantial evidence would violate a "fundamental" guarantee of the Constitution, the Court continued:

"We would even go farther, and say that most, if not all, the privileges and immunities contained in the bill of rights of the Constitution were intended to apply from the moment of annexation; but we place our decision of this case upon the ground that the two rights alleged to be violated in this case [Sixth Amendment jury trial and grand jury indictment] are not fundamental in their nature, but concern merely a method of procedure which sixty years of practice had shown to be suited to the conditions of the islands, and well calculated to conserve the rights of their citizens to their lives, their property and their well-being." Id., at 217-218.

Numerous other cases in this Court have assumed that jury trial is not fundamental to ordered liberty.[25]

Although it is of course open to this Court to reexamine these decisions, I can see no reason why they should now be overturned. It can hardly be said that time has altered the question, or brought significant new evidence to bear upon it. The virtues and defects of the jury system have been hotly debated for a long time,[26] and are hotly debated today, without significant change in the lines of argument.[27]

The argument that jury trial is not a requisite of due process is quite simple. The central proposition of Palko, supra, a proposition to which I would adhere, is that "due process of law" requires only that criminal trials be fundamentally fair. As stated above, apart from the theory that it was historically intended as a mere shorthand for the Bill of Rights, I do not see what else "due process of law" can intelligibly be thought to mean. If due process of law requires only fundamental fairness,[28] then the inquiry in each case must be whether a state trial process was a fair one. The Court has held, properly I think, that in an adversary process it is a requisite of fairness, for which there is no adequate substitute, that a criminal defendant be afforded a right to counsel and to cross-examine opposing witnesses. But it simply has not been demonstrated, nor, I think, can it be demonstrated, that trial by jury is the only fair means of resolving issues of fact.

The jury is of course not without virtues. It affords ordinary citizens a valuable opportunity to participate in a process of government, an experience fostering, one hopes, a respect for law.[29] It eases the burden on judges by enabling them to share a part of their sometimes awesome responsibility.[30] A jury may, at times, afford a higher justice by refusing to enforce harsh laws (although it necessarily does so haphazardly, raising the questions whether arbitrary enforcement of harsh laws is better than total enforcement, and whether the jury system is to be defended on the ground that jurors sometimes disobey their oaths).[31] And the jury may, or may not, contribute desirably to the willingness of the general public to accept criminal judgments as just.[32]

It can hardly be gainsaid, however, that the principal original virtue of the jury trial—the limitations a jury imposes on a tyrannous judiciary—has largely disappeared. We no longer live in a medieval or colonial society. Judges enforce laws enacted by democratic decision, not by regal fiat. They are elected by the people or appointed by the people's elected officials, and are responsible not to a distant monarch alone but to reviewing courts, including this one.[33]

The jury system can also be said to have some inherent defects, which are multiplied by the emergence of the criminal law from the relative simplicity that existed when the jury system was devised.[34] It is a cumbersome process, not only imposing great cost in time and money on both the State and the jurors themselves,[35] but also contributing to delay in the machinery of justice.[36] Untrained jurors are presumably less adept at reaching accurate conclusions of fact than judges, particularly if the issues are many or complex.[37] And it is argued by some that trial by jury, far from increasing public respect for law, impairs it: the average man, it is said, reacts favorably neither to the notion that matters he knows to be complex are being decided by other average men,[38] nor to the way the jury system distorts the process of adjudication.[39]

That trial by jury is not the only fair way of adjudicating criminal guilt is well attested by the fact that it is not the prevailing way, either in England or in this country. For England, one expert makes the following estimates. Parliament generally provides that new statutory offenses, unless they are of "considerable gravity" shall be tried to judges; consequently, summary offenses now outnumber offenses for which jury trial is afforded by more than six to one. Then, within the latter category, 84% of all cases are in fact tried to the court. Over all, "the ratio of defendants actually tried by jury becomes in some years little more than 1 per cent."[40]

In the United States, where it has not been as generally assumed that jury waiver is permissible,[41] the statistics are only slightly less revealing. Two experts have estimated that, of all prosecutions for crimes triable to a jury, 75% are settled by guilty plea and 40% of the remainder are tried to the court.[42] In one State, Maryland, which has always provided for waiver, the rate of court trial appears in some years to have reached 90%.[43] The Court recognizes the force of these statistics in stating,

"We would not assert, however, that every criminal trial—or any particular trial—held before a judge alone is unfair or that a defendant may never be as fairly treated by a judge as he would be by a jury." Ante, at 158.

I agree. I therefore see no reason why this Court should reverse the conviction of appellant, absent any suggestion that his particular trial was in fact unfair, or compel the State of Louisiana to afford jury trial in an as yet unbounded category of cases that can, without unfairness, be tried to a court.

Indeed, even if I were persuaded that trial by jury is a fundamental right in some criminal cases, I could see nothing fundamental in the rule, not yet formulated by the Court, that places the prosecution of appellant for simple battery within the category of "jury crimes" rather than "petty crimes." Trial by jury is ancient, it is true. Almost equally ancient, however, is the discovery that, because of it,

"the King's most loving Subjects are much travailed and otherwise encumbered in coming and keeping of the said six Weeks Sessions, to their Costs, Charges, Unquietness."[44]

As a result, through the long course of British and American history, summary procedures have been used in a varying category of lesser crimes as a flexible response to the burden jury trial would otherwise impose.

The use of summary procedures has long been widespread. British procedure in 1776 exempted from the requirement of jury trial

"[v]iolations of the laws relating to liquor, trade and manufacture, labor, smuggling, traffic on the highway, the Sabbath, `cheats,' gambling, swearing, small thefts, assaults, offenses to property, servants and seamen, vagabondage . . . [and] at least a hundred more . . . ."[45] (Emphasis added.)

Penalties for such offenses included heavy fines (with imprisonment until they were paid), whippings, and imprisonment at hard labor.[46]

Nor had the Colonies a cleaner slate, although practices varied greatly from place to place with conditions. In Massachusetts, crimes punishable by whipping (up to 10 strokes), the stocks (up to three hours), the ducking stool, and fines and imprisonment were triable to magistrates.[47] The decision of a magistrate could, in theory, be appealed to a jury, but a stiff recognizance made exercise of this right quite rare.[48] New York was somewhat harsher. For example, "anyone adjudged by two magistrates to be an idle, disorderly or vagrant person might be transported whence he came, and on reappearance be whipped from constable to constable with thirty-one lashes by each."[49] Anyone committing a criminal offense "under the degree of Grand Larceny" and unable to furnish bail within 48 hours could be summarily tried by three justices.[50] With local variations, examples could be multiplied.

The point is not that many offenses that English-speaking communities have, at one time or another, regarded as triable without a jury are more serious, and carry more serious penalties, than the one involved here. The point is rather that until today few people would have thought the exact location of the line mattered very much. There is no obvious reason why a jury trial is a requisite of fundamental fairness when the charge is robbery, and not a requisite of fairness when the same defendant, for the same actions, is charged with assault and petty theft.[51] The reason for the historic exception for relatively minor crimes is the obvious one: the burden of jury trial was thought to outweigh its marginal advantages. Exactly why the States should not be allowed to make continuing adjustments, based on the state of their criminal dockets and the difficulty of summoning jurors, simply escapes me.

In sum, there is a wide range of views on the desirability of trial by jury, and on the ways to make it most effective when it is used; there is also considerable variation from State to State in local conditions such as the size of the criminal caseload, the ease or difficulty of summoning jurors, and other trial conditions bearing on fairness. We have before us, therefore, an almost perfect example of a situation in which the celebrated dictum of Mr. Justice Brandeis should be invoked. It is, he said,

"one of the happy incidents of the federal system that a single courageous State may, if its citizens choose, serve as a laboratory . . . ." New State Ice Co. v. Liebmann, 285 U. S. 262, 280, 311 (dissenting opinion).

This Court, other courts, and the political process are available to correct any experiments in criminal procedure that prove fundamentally unfair to defendants. That is not what is being done today: instead, and quite without reason, the Court has chosen to impose upon every State one means of trying criminal cases; it is a good means, but it is not the only fair means, and it is not demonstrably better than the alternatives States might devise.

I would affirm the judgment of the Supreme Court of Louisiana.

Notes

[1] See, e. g., my opinions in Mapp v. Ohio, 367 U. S. 643, 672 (dissenting); Ker v. California, 374 U. S. 23, 44 (concurring); Malloy v. Hogan, 378 U. S. 1, 14 (dissenting); Pointer v. Texas, 380 U. S. 400, 408 (concurring); Griffin v. California, 380 U. S. 609, 615 (concurring); Klopfer v. North Carolina, 386 U. S. 213, 226 (concurring).

[2] Barron v. Baltimore, 7 Pet. 243 (1833), held that the first eight Amendments restricted only federal action.

[3] The locus classicus for this viewpoint is The Federalist No. 51 (Madison).

[4] The Bill of Rights was opposed by Hamilton and other proponents of a strong central government. See The Federalist No. 84; see generally C. Rossiter, 1787: The Grand Convention 284, 302-303.

[5] In Barron v. Baltimore, supra, at 250, Chief Justice Marshall said, "These amendments demanded security against the apprehended encroachments of the general government—not against those of the local governments."

[6] Jaffe, Was Brandeis an Activist? The Search for Intermediate Premises, 80 Harv. L. Rev. 986 (1967).

[7] See Adamson v. California, 332 U. S. 46, 71 (dissenting opinion of BLACK, J.); O'Neil v. Vermont, 144 U. S. 323, 366, 370 (dissenting opinion of Harlan, J.) (1892); H. Black, "Due Process of Law," in A Constitutional Faith 23 (1968).

[8] In addition to the opinions cited in n. 1, supra, see, e. g., my opinions in Poe v. Ullman, 367 U. S. 497, 522, at 539-545 (dissenting), and Griswold v. Connecticut, 381 U. S. 479, 499 (concurring).

[9] Fairman, Does the Fourteenth Amendment Incorporate the Bill of Rights? The Original Understanding, 2 Stan. L. Rev. 5 (1949). Professor Fairman was not content to rest upon the overwhelming fact that the great words of the four clauses of the first section of the Fourteenth Amendment would have been an exceedingly peculiar way to say that "The rights heretofore guaranteed against federal intrusion by the first eight Amendments are henceforth guaranteed against state intrusion as well." He therefore sifted the mountain of material comprising the debates and committee reports relating to the Amendment in both Houses of Congress and in the state legislatures that passed upon it. He found that in the immense corpus of comments on the purpose and effects of the proposed amendment, and on its virtues and defects, there is almost no evidence whatever for "incorporation." The first eight Amendments are so much as mentioned by only two members of Congress, one of whom effectively demonstrated (a) that he did not understand Barron v. Baltimore, 7 Pet. 243, and therefore did not understand the question

of incorporation, and (b) that he was not himself understood by his colleagues. One state legislative committee report, rejected by the legislature as a whole, found § 1 of the Fourteenth Amendment superfluous because it duplicated the Bill of Rights: the committee obviously did not understand Barron v. Baltimore either. That is all Professor Fairman could find, in hundreds of pages of legislative discussion prior to passage of the Amendment, that even suggests incorporation.

To this negative evidence the judicial history of the Amendment could be added. For example, it proved possible for a Court whose members had lived through Reconstruction to reiterate the doctrine of Barron v. Baltimore, that the Bill of Rights did not apply to the States, without so much as questioning whether the Fourteenth Amendment had any effect on the continued validity of that principle. E. g., Walker v. Sauvinet, 92 U. S. 90; see generally Morrison, Does the Fourteenth Amendment Incorporate the Bill of Rights? The Judicial Interpretation, 2 Stan. L. Rev. 140 (1949).

[10] Davidson v. New Orleans, 96 U. S. 97, 104.

[11] Holden v. Hardy, 169 U. S. 366, 389.

[12] Hurtado v. California, 110 U. S. 516, 529.

[13] Missouri v. Lewis, 101 U. S. 22, 31.

[14] Gideon v. Wainwright, 372 U. S. 335. The right to counsel was found in the Fourteenth Amendment because, the Court held, it was essential to a fair trial. See 372 U. S., at 342-345.

[15] Klopfer v. North Carolina, 386 U. S. 213.

[16] Pointer v. Texas, 380 U. S. 400.

[17] Irvin v. Dowd, 366 U. S. 717.

[18] The same illogical way of dealing with a Fourteenth Amendment problem was employed in Malloy v. Hogan, 378 U. S. 1, which held that the Due Process Clause guaranteed the protection of the Self-Incrimination Clause of the Fifth Amendment against state action. I disagreed at that time both with the way the question was framed and with the result the Court reached. See my dissenting opinion, id., at 14. I consider myself bound by the Court's holding in Malloy with respect to self-incrimination. See my concurring opinion in Griffin v. California, 380 U. S. 609, 615. I do not think that Malloy held, nor would I consider myself bound by a holding, that every question arising under the Due Process Clause shall be settled by an arbitrary decision whether a clause in the Bill of Rights is "in" or "out."

[19] The Court has so held in, e. g., Irvin v. Dowd, 366 U. S. 717. Compare Dennis v. United States, 339 U. S. 162.

[20] E. g., Rassmussen v. United States, 197 U. S. 516.

[21] E. g., Andres v. United States, 333 U. S. 740. With respect to the common-law number and unanimity requirements, the Court suggests that these present no problem because "our decisions interpreting the Sixth Amendment are always subject to reconsideration. . . ." Ante, at 158, n. 30. These examples illustrate a major danger of the "incorporation" approach—that provisions of the Bill of Rights may be watered down in

the needless pursuit of uniformity. Cf. my concurring opinion in Ker v. California, 374 U. S. 23, 44. MR. JUSTICE WHITE alluded to this problem in his dissenting opinion in Malloy v. Hogan, supra, at 38.

[22] Criminal Justice Act of 1967, § 13.

[23] E. g., Callan v. Wilson, 127 U. S. 540; District of Columbia v. Clawans, 300 U. S. 617; District of Columbia v. Colts, 282 U. S. 63.

[24] The precise issue in Maxwell was whether a jury of eight rather than 12 jurors could be employed in criminal prosecutions in Utah. The Court held that this was permissible because the Fourteenth Amendment did not require the States to provide trial by jury at all. The Court seems to think this was dictum. As a technical matter, however, a statement that is critical to the chain of reasoning by which a result is in fact reached does not become dictum simply because a later court can imagine a totally different way of deciding the case. See Jordan v. Massachusetts, 225 U. S. 167, 176, citing Maxwell for the proposition that "the requirement of due process does not deprive a State of the power to dispense with jury trial altogether."

[25] E. g., Irvin v. Dowd, supra, at 721; Fay v. New York, 332 U. S. 261, 288; Palko v. Connecticut, supra, at 325; Snyder v. Massachusetts, 291 U. S. 97, 105; Brown v. New Jersey, 175 U. S. 172, 175; Missouri v. Lewis, supra, at 31.

[26] E. g., Deady, Trial by Jury, 17 Am. L. Rev. 398, 399-400 (1883):

"Still in these days of progress and experiment, when everything is on trial at the bar of human reason or conceit, it is quite the fashion to speak of jury trial as something that has outlived its usefulness. Intelligent and well-meaning people often sneer at it as an awkward and useless impediment to the speedy and correct administration of justice, and a convenient loop-hole for the escape of powerful and popular rogues. Considering the kind of jury trials we sometimes have in the United States, it must be admitted that this criticism is not without foundation."

[27] See generally Kalven, Memorandum Regarding Jury System, printed in Hearings on Recording of Jury Deliberations before the Subcommittee to Investigate the Administration of the Internal Security Act of the Senate Committee on the Judiciary, 84th Cong., 1st Sess., 63-81. In particular,

"the debate has been going on for a long time (at least since 1780) and the arguments which were advanced pro and con haven't changed much in the interim. Nor, contrary to my first impression, does there seem to be any particular period in which the debate grows hotter or colder. It has always been a hot debate." Id., at 63.

[28] See, e. g., Snyder v. Massachusetts, supra, at 107-108 (Cardozo, J.):

"So far as the Fourteenth Amendment is concerned, the presence of a defendant [at trial] is a condition of due process to the extent that a fair and just hearing would be thwarted by his absence, and to that extent only."

[29] The point is made by, among others, A. Tocqueville. 1 Democracy in America 285 (Reeve tr.).

[30] The argument is developed by Curtis, The Trial Judge and the Jury, 5 Vand.

L. Rev. 150 (1952). For example,

"Juries relieve the judge of the embarrassment of making the necessary exceptions. They do this, it is true, by violating their oaths, but this, I think, is better than tempting the judge to violate his oath of office." Id., at 157.

[31] See generally G. Williams, The Proof of Guilt 257-263; W. Forsyth, History of Trial by Jury 261.

[32] See J. Stephen, A General View of the Criminal Law of England 208-209.

[33] See, e. g., Sunderland, The Inefficiency of the American Jury, 13 Mich. L. Rev. 302, 305:

"But times have changed, and the government itself is now under the absolute control of the people. The judges, if appointed, are selected by the agents of the people, and if elected are selected by the people directly. The need for the jury as a political weapon of defense has been steadily diminishing for a hundred years, until now the jury must find some other justification for its continuance."

[34] See, e. g., Sunderland, supra, at 303:

"Life was simple when the jury system was young, but with the steadily growing complexity of society and social practices, the facts which enter into legal controversies have become much more complex."

[35] Compare Green, Jury Injustice, 20 Jurid. Rev. 132, 133.

[36] Cf. Lummus, Civil Juries and the Law's Delay, 12 B. U. L. Rev. 487.

[37] See, e. g., McWhorter, Abolish the Jury, 57 Am. L. Rev. 42. Statistics on this point are difficult to accumulate for the reason that the only way to measure jury performance is to compare the result reached by a jury with the result the judge would have reached in the same case. While judge-jury comparisons have many values, it is impossible to obtain a statistical comparison of accuracy in this manner. See generally H. Kalven & H. Zeisel, The American Jury, passim.

[38] E. g., Boston, Some Practical Remedies for Existing Defects in the Administration of Justice, 61 U. Pa. L. Rev. 1, 16:

"There is not one important personal or property interest, outside of a Court of justice, which any of us would willingly commit to the first twelve men that come along the street . . . ."

[39] E. g., McWhorter, supra, at 46:

"It is the jury system that consumes time at the public expense in gallery playing and sensational and theatrical exhibitions before the jury, whereby the public interest and the dignity of the law are swallowed up in a morbid, partisan or emotional personal interest in the parties immediately concerned."

[40] Williams, supra, at 302.

[41] For example, in the federal courts the right of the defendant to waive a jury was in doubt as recently as 1930, when it was established in Patton v. United States, 281 U. S. 276. It was settled in New York only in 1957, People v. Carroll, 7 Misc. 2d 581, 161 N. Y. S. 2d 339, aff'd, 3 N. Y. 2d 686, 148 N. E. 2d 875.

[42] Kalven & Zeisel, supra, at 12-32.

[43] See Oppenheim, Waiver of Trial by Jury in Criminal Cases, 25 Mich. L. Rev. 695, 728.

[44] 37 Hen. 8, c. 7.

[45] Frankfurter & Corcoran, Petty Federal Offenses and the Constitutional Guaranty of Trial by Jury, 39 Harv. L. Rev. 917, 928. The source of the authors' information is R. Burn, Justice of the Peace (1776).

[46] Frankfurter & Corcoran, supra, at 930-934.

[47] See, id., at 938-942.

[48] Ibid.

[49] Frankfurter & Corcoran, supra, at 945. They refer to the Vagrancy Act of 1721, 2 Col. L. (N. Y.) 56.

[50] Frankfurter & Corcoran, supra, at 945.

[51] The example is taken from Day, Petty Magistrates' Courts in Connecticut, 17 J. Crim. L. C. & P. S., 343, 346-347, cited in Kalven & Zeisel, supra, at 17. The point is that the "huge proportion" of criminal charges for which jury trial has not been available in America, E. Puttkammer, Administration of Criminal Law 87-88, is increased by the judicious action of weary prosecutors.

Justice Harlan's dissent in Bloom v. Illinois (May 20, 1968)

MR. JUSTICE HARLAN, whom MR. JUSTICE STEWART joins, dissenting.

I dissent for the reasons expressed in my dissenting opinion in Duncan v. Louisiana, ante, p. 171, and in my separate opinion in Cheff v. Schnackenberg, 384 U. S. 373, 380. See also United States v. Barnett, 376 U. S. 681; Green v. United States, 356 U. S. 165.

This case completes a remarkable circle. In Duncan, supra, the Court imposed on the States a rule of procedure that was neither shown to be fundamental to procedural fairness nor held to be part of the originally understood content of the Fourteenth Amendment. The sole justification was that the rule was found in the Bill of Rights. The Court now, without stating any additional reasons, imposes on the States a related rule that, as recently as Cheff v. Schnackenberg, supra, the Court declined to find in the Bill of Rights. That the words of Mr. Justice Holmes,[*] inveighing against a century of "unconstitutional assumption of [state] powers by the Courts of the United States" in derogation of the central premise of our Constitution, should be invoked to support the Court's action here can only be put down to the vagaries of the times.

Justice Harlan's dissent in Food Employees v. Logan Valley Plaza (May 20, 1968)

MR. JUSTICE HARLAN, dissenting.

The petitioners argue for reversal of the decision below on two separate grounds: first, that petitioners' picketing was protected by the First Amendment from state injunctive interference of this kind; second, that the Pennsylvania courts have strayed into a sphere where the power of initial decision is reserved by federal labor laws to the National Labor Relations Board. I think that, if available, the second or "pre-emption" ground would plainly be a preferable basis for decision. Because reliance on pre-emption would invoke the authority of a federal statute through the Constitution's Supremacy Clause, it would avoid interpretation of the Constitution itself, which would be necessary if the case were treated under the First Amendment. See, e. g., Zschernig v. Miller, 389 U. S. 429, 443, 444-445 (opinion of the writer concurring in the result). Dependence on pre-emption would also assure that the Court does not itself disrupt the statutory scheme of labor law established by the Congress, a point to which I shall return.

On the merits, it seems clear from the facts stated by the Court, see ante, at 310-312 and from our past decisions[1] that the petitioners have a substantial pre-emption claim. However, upon examination of the record I have come reluctantly to the conclusion that this Court is precluded from reaching the merits of that question because of the petitioners' failure to raise any such issue in the Pennsylvania Supreme Court. The rule that in cases coming from state courts this Court may review only those issues which were presented to the state court is not discretionary but jurisdictional. Section 1257 of Title 28, which defines this Court's certiorari jurisdiction, states:

"Final judgments or decrees rendered by the highest court of a State in which a decision could be had, may be reviewed by the Supreme Court . . . [b]y writ of certiorari, . . . where any title, right, privilege or immunity is specially set up or claimed under the Constitution, treaties or statutes of . . . the United States."

Since the Pennsylvania Supreme Court did not advert in its majority opinion to the pre-emption issue,[2] it is necessary to determine whether that question was "specially set up or claimed" within the meaning of § 1257. In deciding that question, it is relevant and usually sufficient to ask whether the petitioners satisfied the state rules governing presentation of issues. See, e. g., Beck v. Washington, 369 U. S. 541, 549-554; Wolfe v. North Carolina, 364 U. S. 177, 195; John v. Paullin, 231 U. S. 583, 585.[3] Rule 59 of the Pennsylvania Supreme Court provides:

"The [appellant's] statement of the questions involved must set forth each question separately, in the briefest and most general terms . . . . This rule is to be considered in the highest degree mandatory, admitting no exception; ordinarily no point will be considered which is not thus set forth in or necessarily suggested by the statement of questions involved."

The Pennsylvania Supreme Court has consistently held that it will not consider points not presented in the manner prescribed by this rule, and that such points are regarded as abandoned or waived.[4] In this case, the petitioners' statement of questions involved did not refer to the possibility of federal pre-emption,[5] and of course the Pennsylvania Supreme Court's majority opinion did not mention it either. A similar rule of the Washington Supreme Court was involved in Beck v. Washington, supra, and we held that when a defendant has failed to comply with such a rule "the argument cannot be entertained here under an unbroken line of precedent. E. g., Ferguson v. Georgia, 365 U. S. 570, 572 (1961); Capital City Dairy Co. v. Ohio, 183 U. S. 238, 248 (1902)." 369 U. S., at 553-554.[6] I am therefore led to conclude that we have no jurisdiction to consider the question of pre-emption.[7]

Turning to the First Amendment question, I believe that in the circumstances it is not an appropriate one for this Court to decide. This controversy arose in the course of a labor union's efforts to achieve labor goals by informational picketing. Although no pre-emption question is properly before us, I do think that we can take notice that this is an area in which Congress has enacted detailed legislation, see, e. g., 29 U. S. C. § 158 (b) (7) (C), and has set up an administrative agency to resolve such disputes in the first instance. The reason why it was deemed necessary to fashion the doctrine of pre-emption under the federal labor laws was that it would be intolerably disruptive if this statutory scheme were interpreted differently by state and federal courts. See, e. g., Garner v. Teamsters Union, 346 U. S. 485, 490-491; San Diego Unions v. Garmon, 359 U. S. 236, 242-245. It seems to me that a similar objection applies to this Court's resolution of such disputes by resort to the Constitution. For the establishment by this Court of a rigid constitutional rule in a field where Congress has attempted to strike a delicate balance between competing economic forces, and in circumstances where we cannot know how the controversy would be settled by Congress' chosen instrument, may also have a considerable disruptive effect. I therefore believe that we should exercise our discretion not to reach the First Amendment issue, and that we should dismiss the writ as improvidently granted. Such a disposition would not be unfair to the petitioners, since the failure to bring the preemption question properly before us was their own.

Notes

[1] See, e. g., Construction Laborers v. Curry, 371 U. S. 542, 546-548; Hotel Employees Local 255 v. Sax Enterprises, Inc., 358 U. S. 270; Youngdahl v. Rainfair, Inc., 355 U. S. 131, 139; NLRB v. Babcock & Wilcox Co., 351 U. S. 105, 112-114; NLRB v. Stowe Spinning Co., 336 U. S. 226, 229-232; cf. Amalgamated Meat Cutters v. Fairlawn Meats, Inc., 353 U. S. 20, 24-25. See also Marshall Field & Co., 98 N. L. R. B. 88, 93, enforced as modified sub nom. Marshall Field & Co. v. NLRB, 200 F. 2d 375, 380.

[2] Where the highest state court has actually ruled on a federal question, this Court's concern with the proper raising of the question in the state court disappears. See, e. g., Raley v. Ohio, 360 U. S. 423, 436; Whitney v. California, 274 U. S. 357, 360-361; Manhattan Life Ins. Co. v. Cohen, 234 U. S. 123, 134.

[3] The only circumstances in which a federal claim will be entertained despite the petitioners' failure to raise it below in the prescribed manner are when the State's rules do not afford a reasonable opportunity for a hearing on the federal issue, see, e. g., Central Union Tel. Co. v. Edwardsville, 269 U. S. 190, 194-195, or are applied in a discriminatory

fashion to evade the federal claim, see, e. g., Hartford Life Ins. Co. v. Johnson, 249 U. S. 490, 493. No. such allegation is made in this case.

[4] See, e. g., Dunmore v. McMillan, 396 Pa. 472, 152 A. 2d 708; Kuhns v. Brugger, 390 Pa. 331, 135 A. 2d 395; Kerr v. O'Donovan, 389 Pa. 614, 134 A. 2d 213.

[5] The petitioners stated that the question involved was:

"Did the lower court err in granting a Preliminary Injunction . . . where in a suit in equity by the owner of a shopping center and one of its tenants it is established that the appellant-union peacefully picketed near tenant's building within the confines of said shopping center; that no picketing efforts were directed toward the shopping center or other tenants; that picketing efforts were merely to inform the public of the labor dispute?"

[6] See also Wolfe v. North Carolina, 364 U. S. 177, 195; Parker v. Illinois, 333 U. S. 571; CIO v. McAdory, 325 U. S. 472, 477.

[7] The petitioners contend that this Court has jurisdiction to consider the pre-emption issue despite the petitioners' failure to raise it below, because the question is one of "subject matter jurisdiction." Although some implied support for this proposition may be found in Seaboard Air Line R. Co. v. Daniel, 333 U. S. 118, 122-123, I am unable to perceive how the nature of the federal question involved can affect the specific limitation on our jurisdiction contained in 28 U. S. C. § 1257.

Justice Harlan's dissent in Flast v. Cohen (June 10, 1968)

MR. JUSTICE HARLAN, dissenting.

The problems presented by this case are narrow and relatively abstract, but the principles by which they must be resolved involve nothing less than the proper functioning of the federal courts, and so run to the roots of our constitutional system. The nub of my view is that the end result of Frothingham v. Mellon, 262 U. S. 447, was correct, even though, like others,[1] I do not subscribe to all of its reasoning and premises. Although I therefore agree with certain of the conclusions reached today by the Court,[2] I cannot accept the standing doctrine that it substitutes for Frothingham, for it seems to me that this new doctrine rests on premises that do not withstand analysis. Accordingly, I respectfully dissent.

I.

It is desirable first to restate the basic issues in this case. The question here is not, as it was not in Frothingham, whether "a federal taxpayer is without standing to challenge the constitutionality of a federal statute." Ante, at 85. It could hardly be disputed that federal taxpayers may, as taxpayers, contest the constitutionality of tax obligations imposed severally upon them by federal statute. Such a challenge may be made by way of defense to an action by the United States to recover the amount of a challenged tax debt, see, e. g., Hylton v. United States, 3 Dall. 171; McCray v. United States, 195 U. S. 27; United States v. Butler, 297 U. S. 1; or to a prosecution for willful failure to pay or to report the tax. See, e. g., Marchetti v. United States, 390 U. S. 39. Moreover, such a challenge may provide the basis of an action by a taxpayer to obtain the refund of a previous tax payment. See, e. g., Bailey v. Drexel Furniture Co., 259 U. S. 20.

The lawsuits here and in Frothingham are fundamentally different. They present the question whether federal taxpayers qua taxpayers may, in suits in which they do not contest the validity of their previous or existing tax obligations, challenge the constitutionality of the uses for which Congress has authorized the expenditure of public funds. These differences in the purposes of the cases are reflected in differences in the litigants' interests. An action brought to contest the validity of tax liabilities assessed to the plaintiff is designed to vindicate interests that are personal and proprietary. The wrongs alleged and the relief sought by such a plaintiff are unmistakably private; only secondarily are his interests representative of those of the general population. I take it that the Court, although it does not pause to examine the question, believes that the interests of those who as taxpayers challenge the constitutionality of public expenditures may, at least in certain circumstances, be similar. Yet this assumption is surely mistaken.[3]

The complaint in this case, unlike that in Frothingham, contains no allegation that the contested expenditures will in any fashion affect the amount of these taxpayers' own existing or foreseeable tax obligations. Even in cases in which such an allegation is made, the suit cannot result in an adjudication either of the plaintiff's tax liabilities or of the propriety of any particular level of taxation. The relief available to such a plaintiff consists entirely of the vindication of rights held in common by all citizens. It is thus scarcely surprising that few of the state courts that permit such suits require proof either that the challenged expenditure is consequential in amount or that it is likely to affect significantly the plaintiff's own tax bill; these courts have at least impliedly recognized that such allegations are surplusage, useful only to preserve the form of an obvious fiction.[4]

Nor are taxpayers' interests in the expenditure of public funds differentiated from those of the general public by any special rights retained by them in their tax payments. The simple fact is that no such rights can sensibly be said to exist. Taxes are ordinarily levied by the United States without limitations of purpose; absent such a limitation, payments received by the Treasury in satisfaction of tax obligations lawfully created become part of the Government's general funds. The national legislature is required by the Constitution to exercise its spending powers to "provide for the common Defence and general Welfare." Art. I, § 8, cl. 1. Whatever other implications there may be to that sweeping phrase, it surely means that the United States holds its general funds, not as stakeholder or trustee for those who have paid its imposts, but as surrogate for the population at large. Any rights of a taxpayer with respect to the purposes for which those funds are expended are thus subsumed in, and extinguished by, the common rights of all citizens. To characterize taxpayers' interests in such expenditures as proprietary or even personal either deprives those terms of all meaning or postulates for taxpayers a scintilla juris in funds that no longer are theirs.

Surely it is plain that the rights and interests of taxpayers who contest the constitutionality of public expenditures are markedly different from those of "Hohfeldian" plaintiffs,[5] including those taxpayer-plaintiffs who challenge the validity of their own tax liabilities. We must recognize that these non-Hohfeldian plaintiffs complain, just as the petitioner in Frothingham sought to complain, not as taxpayers, but as "private attorneys-general."[6] The interests they represent, and the rights they espouse, are bereft of any personal or proprietary coloration. They are, as litigants, indistinguishable from any group selected at random from among the general population, taxpayers and nontaxpayers alike. These are and must be, to adopt Professor Jaffe's useful phrase, "public actions" brought to vindicate public rights.[7]

It does not, however, follow that suits brought by non-Hohfeldian plaintiffs are excluded by the "case or controversy" clause of Article III of the Constitution from the jurisdiction of the federal courts. This and other federal courts have repeatedly held that individual litigants, acting as private attorneys-general, may have standing as "representatives of the public interest." Scripps-Howard Radio v. Comm'n, 316 U. S. 4, 14. See also Commission v. Sanders Radio Station, 309 U. S. 470, 477; Associated Industries v. Ickes, 134 F. 2d 694; Reade v. Ewing, 205 F. 2d 630; Scenic Hudson Preservation Conf. v. FPC, 354 F. 2d 608; Office of Communication of United Church of Christ v. FCC, 123 U. S. App. D. C. 328, 359 F. 2d 994. Compare Oklahoma v. Civil Service Comm'n, 330 U. S. 127, 137-139. And see, on actions qui tam, Marvin v. Trout, 199 U. S. 212, 225; United States ex rel. Marcus v. Hess, 317 U. S. 537, 546. The various lines of authority are by no means free of difficulty, and certain of the cases may be explicable as involving a personal, if remote, economic interest, but I think that it is, nonetheless, clear that non-Hohfeldian plaintiffs as such are not constitutionally excluded from the federal courts. The problem ultimately presented by this case is, in my view, therefore to determine in what circumstances, consonant with the character and proper functioning of the federal courts, such suits should be permitted.[8] With this preface, I shall examine the position adopted by the Court.

II.

As I understand it, the Court's position is that it is unnecessary to decide in what circumstances public actions should be permitted, for it is possible to identify situations in which taxpayers who contest the constitutionality of federal expenditures assert "personal" rights and interests, identical in principle to those asserted by Hohfeldian plaintiffs. This position, if supportable, would of course avoid many of the difficulties of this case; indeed, if the Court is correct, its extended exploration of the subtleties of Article III is entirely unnecessary. But, for reasons that follow, I believe that the Court's position is untenable.

The Court's analysis consists principally of the observation that the requirements of standing are met if a taxpayer has the "requisite personal stake in the outcome" of his suit. Ante, at 101. This does not, of course, resolve the standing problem; it merely restates it. The Court implements this standard with the declaration that taxpayers will be "deemed" to have the necessary personal interest if their suits satisfy two criteria: first, the challenged expenditure must form part of a federal spending program, and not merely be "incidental" to a regulatory program; and second, the constitutional provision under which the plaintiff claims must be a "specific limitation" upon Congress' spending powers. The difficulties with these criteria are many and severe, but it is enough for the moment to emphasize that they are not in any sense a measurement of any plaintiff's interest in the outcome of any suit. As even a cursory examination of the criteria will show, the Court's standard for the determination of standing and its criteria for the satisfaction of that standard are entirely unrelated.

It is surely clear that a plaintiff's interest in the outcome of a suit in which he challenges the constitutionality of a federal expenditure is not made greater or smaller by the unconnected fact that the expenditure is, or is not, "incidental" to an "essentially regulatory" program.[9] An example will illustrate the point. Assume that two independent federal programs are authorized by Congress, that the first is designed to encourage a specified religious group by the provision to it of direct grants-in-aid, and that the second is designed to discourage all other religious groups by the imposition of various forms of discriminatory regulation. Equal amounts are appropriated by Congress for the two programs. If a taxpayer challenges their constitutionality in separate suits,[10] are we to suppose, as evidently does the Court, that his "personal stake" in the suit involving the second is necessarily smaller than it is in the suit involving the first, and that he should therefore have standing in one but not the other?

Presumably the Court does not believe that regulatory programs are necessarily less destructive of First Amendment rights, or that regulatory programs are necessarily less prodigal of public funds than are grants-in-aid, for both these general propositions are demonstrably false. The Court's disregard of regulatory expenditures is not even a logical consequence of its apparent assumption that taxpayer-plaintiffs assert essentially monetary interests, for it surely cannot matter to a taxpayer qua taxpayer whether an unconstitutional expenditure is used to hire the services of regulatory personnel or is distributed among private and local governmental agencies as grants-in-aid. His interest as taxpayer arises, if at all, from the fact of an unlawful expenditure, and not as a consequence of the expenditure's form. Apparently the Court has repudiated the emphasis in Frothingham upon the amount of the plaintiff's tax bill, only to substitute an equally irrelevant emphasis upon the form of the challenged expenditure.

The Court's second criterion is similarly unrelated to its standard for the determination of standing. The intensity of a plaintiff's interest in a suit is not measured, even obliquely, by the fact that the constitutional provision under which he claims is, or is not, a "specific limitation" upon Congress' spending powers. Thus, among the claims in Frothingham was the assertion that the Maternity Act, 42 Stat. 224, deprived the petitioner of property without due process of law. The Court has evidently concluded that this claim did not confer standing because the Due Process Clause of the Fifth Amendment is not a specific limitation upon the spending powers.[11] Disregarding for the moment the formidable obscurity of the Court's categories, how can it be said that Mrs. Frothingham's interests in her suit were, as a consequence of her choice of a constitutional claim, necessarily less intense than those, for example, of the present appellants? I am quite unable to understand how, if a taxpayer believes that a given public expenditure is unconstitutional, and if he seeks to vindicate that belief in a federal court, his interest in the suit can be said necessarily to vary according to the constitutional provision under which he states his claim.

The absence of any connection between the Court's standard for the determination of standing and its criteria for the satisfaction of that standard is not merely a logical ellipsis. Instead, it follows quite relentlessly from the fact that, despite the Court's apparent belief, the plaintiffs in this and similar suits are non-Hohfeldian, and it is very nearly impossible to measure sensibly any differences in the intensity of their personal interests in their suits. The Court has thus been compelled simply to postulate situations in which such taxpayer-plaintiffs will be "deemed" to have the requisite "personal stake and interest." Ante, at 101. The logical inadequacies of the Court's criteria are thus a reflection of the deficiencies of its entire position. These deficiencies will, however, appear more plainly from an examination of the Court's treatment of the Establishment Clause.

Although the Court does not altogether explain its position, the essence of its reasoning is evidently that a taxpayer's claim under the Establishment Clause is "not merely one of ultra vires," but one which instead asserts "an abridgment of individual religious liberty" and a "governmental infringement of individual rights protected by the Constitution." Choper, The Establishment Clause and Aid to Parochial Schools, 56 Calif. L. Rev. 260, 276. It must first be emphasized that this is apparently not founded upon any "preferred" position for the First Amendment, or upon any asserted unavailability of other plaintiffs.[12] The Court's position is instead that, because of the Establishment Clause's historical purposes, taxpayers retain rights under it quite different from those held by them under other constitutional provisions.

The difficulties with this position are several. First, we have recently been reminded that the historical purposes of the religious clauses of the First Amendment are significantly more obscure and complex than this Court has heretofore acknowledged.[13] Careful students of the history of the Establishment Clause have found that "it is impossible to give a dogmatic interpretation of the First Amendment, and to state with any accuracy the intention of the men who framed it . . . ."[14] Above all, the evidence seems clear that the First Amendment was not intended simply to enact the terms of Madison's Memorial and Remonstrance against Religious Assessments.[15] I do not suggest that history is without relevance to these questions, or that the use of federal funds for religious purposes was not a form of establishment that many in the 18th century would have found objectionable. I say simply that, given the ultimate obscurity of the Establishment Clause's historical purposes, it is inappropriate for this Court to draw fundamental distinctions among the several constitutional commands upon the supposed authority of isolated dicta extracted from the clause's complex history. In particular, I have not found, and the opinion of the Court has not adduced, historical evidence that properly permits the Court to distinguish, as it has here, among the Establishment Clause, the Tenth Amendment, and the Due Process Clause of the Fifth Amendment as limitations upon Congress' taxing and spending powers.[16]

The Court's position is equally precarious if it is assumed that its premise is that the Establishment Clause is in some uncertain fashion a more "specific" limitation upon Congress' powers than are the various other constitutional commands. It is obvious, first, that only in some Pickwickian sense are any of the provisions with which the Court is concerned "specific[ally]" limitations upon spending, for they contain nothing that is expressly directed at the expenditure of public funds. The specificity to which the Court repeatedly refers must therefore arise, not from the provisions' language, but from something implicit in their purposes. But this Court has often emphasized that Congress' powers to spend are coterminous with the purposes for which, and methods by which, it may act, and that the various constitutional commands applicable to the central government, including those implicit both in the Tenth Amendment and in the General Welfare Clause, thus operate as limitations upon spending. See United States v. Butler, 297 U. S. 1. And see, e. g., Veazie Bank v. Fenno, 8 Wall. 533, 541; Loan Association v. Topeka, 20 Wall. 655, 664; Thompson v. Consolidated Gas Co., 300 U. S. 55, 80; Carmichael v. Southern Coal Co., 301 U. S. 495; Everson v. Board of Education, 330 U. S. 1, 6. Compare Steward Machine Co. v. Davis, 301 U. S. 548; Helvering v. Davis, 301 U. S. 619. I can attach no constitutional significance to the various degrees of specificity with which these limitations appear in the terms or history of the Constitution. If the Court accepts the proposition, as I do, that the number and scope of public actions should be restricted, there are, as I shall show, methods more appropriate, and more nearly permanent, than the creation of an amorphous category of constitutional provisions that the Court has deemed, without adequate foundation, "specific limitations" upon Congress' spending powers.

Even if it is assumed that such distinctions may properly be drawn, it does not follow that federal taxpayers hold any "personal constitutional right" such that they may each contest the validity under the Establishment Clause of all federal expenditures. The difficulty, with which the Court never comes to grips, is that taxpayers' suits under the Establishment Clause are not in these circumstances meaningfully different from other public actions. If this case involved a tax specifically designed for the support of religion, as was the Virginia tax opposed by Madison in his Memorial and Remonstrance,[17] I would agree that taxpayers have rights under the religious clauses of the First Amendment that would permit them standing to challenge the tax's validity in the federal courts. But this is not such a case, and appellants challenge an expenditure, not a tax. Where no such tax is involved, a taxpayer's complaint can consist only of an allegation that public funds have been, or shortly will be, expended for purposes inconsistent with the Constitution. The taxpayer cannot ask the return of any portion of his previous tax payments, cannot prevent the collection of any existing tax debt, and cannot demand an adjudication of the propriety of any particular level of taxation. His tax payments are received for the general purposes of the United States, and are, upon proper receipt, lost in the general revenues.

Compare Steward Machine Co. v. Davis, supra, at 585. The interests he represents, and the rights he espouses, are, as they are in all public actions, those held in common by all citizens. To describe those rights and interests as personal, and to intimate that they are in some unspecified fashion to be differentiated from those of the general public, reduces constitutional standing to a word game played by secret rules.[18]

Apparently the Court, having successfully circumnavigated the issue, has merely returned to the proposition from which it began. A litigant, it seems, will have standing if he is "deemed" to have the requisite interest, and "if you . . . have standing, then you can be confident you are" suitably interested. Brown, Quis Custodiet Ipsos Custodes?—The School-Prayer Cases, 1963 Sup. Ct. Rev. 1, 22.

III.

It seems to me clear that public actions, whatever the constitutional provisions on which they are premised, may involve important hazards for the continued effectiveness of the federal judiciary. Although I believe such actions to be within the jurisdiction conferred upon the federal courts by Article III of the Constitution, there surely can be little doubt that they strain the judicial function and press to the limit judicial authority. There is every reason to fear that unrestricted public actions might well alter the allocation of authority among the three branches of the Federal Government. It is not, I submit, enough to say that the present members of the Court would not seize these opportunities for abuse, for such actions would, even without conscious abuse, go far toward the final transformation of this Court into the Council of Revision which, despite Madison's support, was rejected by the Constitutional Convention.[19] I do not doubt that there must be "some effectual power in the government to restrain or correct the infractions"[20] of the Constitution's several commands, but neither can I suppose that such power resides only in the federal courts. We must as judges recall that, as Mr. Justice Holmes wisely observed, the other branches of the Government "are ultimate guardians of the liberties and welfare of the people in quite as great a degree as the courts." Missouri, Kansas & Texas R. Co. v. May, 194 U. S. 267, 270. The powers of the federal judiciary will be adequate for the great burdens placed upon them only if they are employed prudently, with recognition of the strengths as well as the hazards that go with our kind of representative government.

Presumably the Court recognizes at least certain of these hazards, else it would not have troubled to impose limitations upon the situations in which, and purposes for which, such suits may be brought. Nonetheless, the limitations adopted by the Court are, as I have endeavored to indicate, wholly untenable. This is the more unfortunate because there is available a resolution of this problem that entirely satisfies the demands of the principle of separation of powers. This Court has previously held that individual litigants have standing to represent the public interest, despite their lack of economic or other personal interests, if Congress has appropriately authorized such suits. See especially Oklahoma v. Civil Service Comm'n, 330 U. S. 127, 137-139. Compare Perkins v. Lukens Steel Co., 310 U. S. 113, 125-127. I would adhere to that principle.[21] Any hazards to the proper allocation of authority among the three branches of the Government would be substantially diminished if public actions had been pertinently authorized by Congress and the President. I appreciate that this Court does not ordinarily await the mandate of other branches of the Government, but it seems to me that the extraordinary character of public actions, and of the mischievous, if not dangerous, consequences they involve for the proper functioning of our constitutional system, and in particular of the federal courts, makes such judicial forbearance the part of wisdom.[22] It must be emphasized that the implications of these questions of judicial policy are of fundamental significance for the other branches of the Federal Government.

Such a rule could readily be applied to this case. Although various efforts have been made in Congress to authorize public actions to contest the validity of federal expenditures in aid of religiously affiliated schools and other institutions, no such authorization has yet been given.[23]

This does not mean that we would, under such a rule, be enabled to avoid our constitutional responsibilities, or that we would confine to limbo the First Amendment or any other constitutional command. The question here is not, despite the Court's unarticulated premise, whether the religious clauses of the First Amendment are hereafter to be enforced by the federal courts; the issue is simply whether plaintiffs of an additional category, heretofore excluded from those courts, are to be permitted to maintain suits. The recent history of this Court is replete with illustrations, including even one announced today (supra, at n. 12), that questions involving the religious clauses will not, if federal taxpayers are prevented from contesting federal expenditures, be left "unacknowledged, unresolved, and undecided."

Accordingly, for the reasons contained in this opinion, I would affirm the judgment of the District Court.

Notes

[1] See, e. g., Davis, Standing to Challenge Governmental Action, 39 Minn. L. Rev. 353; L. Jaffe, Judicial Control of Administrative Action 483-495 (1965).

[2] In particular, I agree, essentially for the reasons stated by the Court, that we do not lack jurisdiction under 28 U. S. C. § 1253 to consider the judgment of the three-judge District Court.

[3] I put aside, for the moment, the suggestion that a taxpayer's rights under the Establishment Clause are more "personal" than they are under any other constitutional provision.

[4] See generally Comment, Taxpayers' Suits: A Survey and Summary, 69 Yale L. J. 895, 905-906.

[5] The phrase is Professor Jaffe's, adopted, of course, from W. Hohfeld, Fundamental Legal Conceptions (1923). I have here employed the phrases "Hohfeldian" and "non-Hohfeldian" plaintiffs to mark the distinction between the personal and proprietary interests of the traditional plaintiff, and the representative and public interests

of the plaintiff in a public action. I am aware that we are confronted here by a spectrum of interests of varying intensities, but the distinction is sufficiently accurate, and convenient, to warrant its use at least for purposes of discussion.

[6] Cf. Associated Industries v. Ickes, 134 F. 2d 694, 704; Reade v. Ewing, 205 F. 2d 630, 632.

[7] L. Jaffe, Judicial Control of Administrative Action 483 (1965).

[8] I agree that implicit in this question is the belief that the federal courts may decline to accept for adjudication cases or questions that, although otherwise within the perimeter of their constitutional jurisdiction, are appropriately thought to be unsuitable at least for immediate judicial resolution. Compare Ashwander v. Tennessee Valley Authority, 297 U. S. 288, 345-348 (concurring opinion); H. Wechsler, Principles, Politics, and Fundamental Law 9-15 (1961); and Bickel, Foreword: The Passive Virtues, The Supreme Court, 1960 Term, 75 Harv. L. Rev. 40, 45-47 (1961).

[9] I must note at the outset that I cannot determine with any certainty the Court's intentions with regard to this first criterion. Its use of Doremus v. Board of Education, 342 U. S. 429, as an analogue perhaps suggests that it intends to exclude only those cases in which there are virtually no public expenditures. See, e. g., Howard v. City of Boulder, 132 Colo. 401, 290 P. 2d 237. On the other hand, the Court also emphasizes that the contested programs may not be "essentially regulatory" programs, and that the statute challenged here "involves a substantial expenditure of federal tax funds." Ante, at 102, 103 (emphasis added). Presumably this means that the Court's standing doctrine also excludes any program in which the expenditures are "insubstantial" or which cannot be characterized as a "spending" program.

[10] I am aware that the attack upon the second program would presumably be premised, at least in large part, upon the Free Exercise Clause, and that the Court does not today hold that that clause is within its standing doctrine. I cannot, however, see any meaningful distinction for these purposes, even under the Court's reasoning, between the two religious clauses.

[11] It should be emphasized that the Court finds it unnecessary to examine the history of the Due Process Clause to determine whether it was intended as a "specific limitation" upon Congress' spending and taxing powers. Nor does the Court pause to examine the purposes of the Tenth Amendment, another of the premises of the constitutional claims in Frothingham. But see Gibbons v. Ogden, 9 Wheat. 1, 199; Veazie Bank v. Fenno, 8 Wall. 533, 541; United States v. Butler, 297 U. S. 1. And compare Everson v. Board of Education, 330 U. S. 1, 6.

[12] The Court does make one reference to the availability vel non of other plaintiffs. It indicates that where a federal statute is directed at a specified class, "the proper party emphasis in the federal standing doctrine would require that standing be limited to the taxpayers within the affected class." Ante, at 104, n. 25. Assuming arguendo the existence of such a federal "best-plaintiff" rule, it is difficult to see why this rule would not altogether exclude taxpayers as plaintiffs under the Establishment Clause, since there

plainly may be litigants under the Clause with the personal rights and interests of Hohfeldian plaintiffs. See, e. g., Board of Education v. Allen, decided today, post, p. 236.

[13] See, in particular, M. Howe, The Garden and the Wilderness 1-31 (1965); C. Antieau, A. Downey & E. Roberts, Freedom from Federal Establishment (1964). Not all members of the Court have of course ignored the complexities of the clause's history. See especially McCollum v. Board of Education, 333 U. S. 203, 238 (dissenting opinion of Reed, J.).

[14] Antieau, Downey & Roberts, supra, at 142. See also Howe, supra, at 10-12.

[15] See, in particular, Antieau, Downey & Roberts, supra, at 126-128, 144-146, 207-208. And see 1 Annals of Cong. 730-731. It has elsewhere been observed, I think properly, that "to treat [Madison's Remonstrance] as authoritatively incorporated in the First Amendment is to take grotesque liberties with the simple legislative process, and even more with the complex and diffuse process of ratification of an Amendment by three-fourths of the states." Brown, Quis Custodiet Ipsos Custodes?—The School-Prayer Cases, 1963 Sup. Ct. Rev. 1, 8.

[16] I will of course grant that claims under, for example, the Tenth Amendment may present "generalized grievances about the conduct of government or the allocation of power in the Federal System." Ante, at 106. I will also grant that it would be well if such questions could be avoided by the federal courts. Unfortunately, I cannot see how these considerations are relevant under the Court's principal criterion, which I understand to be merely whether any given constitutional provision is, or is not, a limitation upon Congress' spending powers. It is difficult to see what there is in the fact that a constitutional provision is held to be such a limitation that could sensibly give the Court "confidence" about the fashion in which a given plaintiff will present a given issue.

[17] The bill was intended to establish "a provision for teachers of the Christian religion." It and the Memorial and Remonstrance are reprinted in Everson v. Board of Education, supra, at 63-74.

[18] I have equal difficulty with the argument that the religious clauses of the First Amendment create a "personal constitutional right," held by all citizens, such that any citizen may, under those clauses, contest the constitutionality of federal expenditures. The essence of the argument would presumably be that freedom from establishment is a right that inheres in every citizen, thus any citizen should be permitted to challenge any measure that conceivably involves establishment. Certain provisions of the Constitution, so the argument would run, create the basic structure of our society and of its government, and accordingly should be enforceable at the demand of every individual. Unlike the position taken today by the Court, such a doctrine of standing would at least be internally consistent, but it would also threaten the proper functioning both of the federal courts and of the principle of separation of powers. The Establishment Clause is, after all, only one of many provisions of the Constitution that might be characterized in this fashion. Certain of these provisions, e. g., the Ninth and Tenth Amendments, would provide the basis for cases that, absent a standing question, could not readily be excluded from the federal

courts as involving political questions, or as otherwise unsuitable for adjudication under the principles formulated for these purposes by the Court. Compare United Public Workers v. Mitchell, 330 U. S. 75, 94-96; Griswold v. Connecticut, 381 U. S. 479. Indeed, it might even be urged that the Ninth and Tenth Amendments, since they are largely confirmatory of rights created elsewhere in the Constitution, were intended to declare the standing of individual citizens to contest the validity of governmental activities. It may, of course, also be argued that these amendments are merely "tub[s] for the whale," 1 W. Crosskey, Politics and the Constitution 688 (1953); but lacking such an argument, any doctrine of standing premised upon the generality or relative importance of a constitutional command would, I think, very substantially increase the number of situations in which individual citizens could present for adjudication "generalized grievances about the conduct of government." I take it that the Court, apart from my Brother DOUGLAS, and I are agreed that any such consequence would be exceedingly undesirable.

[19] See 1 M. Farrand, The Records of the Federal Convention of 1787, at 21, 97-98, 108-110, 138-140 (1911); 2 Farrand, id., at 73-80.

[20] The Federalist No. 80 (Hamilton).

[21] My premise is, as I have suggested, that non-Hohfeldian plaintiffs as such are not excluded by Article III from the jurisdiction of the federal courts. The problem is therefore to determine in what situations their suits should be permitted, and not whether a "statute constitutionally could authorize a person who shows no case or controversy to call on the courts . . . ." Scripps-Howard Radio v. Comm'n, 316 U. S. 4, 21 (dissenting opinion). I do not, of course, suggest that Congress' power to authorize suits by specified classes of litigants is without constitutional limitation. This Court has recognized a panoply of restrictions upon the actions that may properly be brought in federal courts, or reviewed by this Court after decision in state courts. It is enough now to emphasize that I would not abrogate these restrictions in situations in which Congress has authorized a suit. The difficult case of Muskrat v. United States, 219 U. S. 346, does not require more. Whatever the other implications of that case, it is enough to note that there the United States, as statutory defendant, evidently had "no interest adverse to the claimants." Id., at 361.

[22] I am aware that there is a second category of cases in which the Court has entertained claims by non-Hohfeldian plaintiffs: suits brought by state or local taxpayers in state courts to vindicate federal constitutional claims. A certain anomaly may be thought to have resulted from the Court's consideration of such cases while it has refused similar suits brought by federal taxpayers in the federal courts. This anomaly, if such it is, will presumably continue even under the standing doctrine announced today, since we are not told that the standing rules will hereafter be identical for the two classes of taxpayers. Although these questions are not now before the Court, I think it appropriate to note that one possible solution would be to hold that standing to raise federal questions is itself a federal question. See Freund, in E. Cahn, Supreme Court and Supreme Law 35 (1954).

This would demand partial reconsideration of, for example, Doremus v. Board of Education, 342 U. S. 429. Cf. United States v. Raines, 362 U. S. 17, 23, n. 3; Cramp v. Board of Public Instruction, 368 U. S. 278, 282; Baker v. Carr, 369 U. S. 186, 204.

[23] This question was, however, extensively discussed in the course of the debates upon the Elementary and Secondary Education Act of 1965, 79 Stat. 27. See, e. g., 111 Cong. Rec. 5973, 6132, 7316-7318.

Justice Harlan's dissent in Harrison v. US (June 10, 1968)

MR. JUSTICE HARLAN, dissenting.

Like my Brother BLACK and my Brother WHITE, I am unable to understand why the Court reverses this petitioner's conviction. There is no suggestion that the testimony in question, given on the stand with the advice of counsel, was somehow unreliable. Nor, as the opinion of MR. JUSTICE WHITE amply demonstrates, is there any plausible argument that a rule excluding such evidence from use at a later trial adds an ounce of deterrence against police violation of the Mallory rule.

I do not doubt that "voluntariness" is not always a purely subjective question as to the defendant's state of mind; it may involve an objective analysis of the fairness of the situation in which government agents placed him. Nor would I rule out the possibility that a direct product of unlawful official activity might properly be excludable as a fruit of that activity—even where the product is so unforeseeable that a deterrent rationale for exclusion will not suffice—on the ground that the Government should not play an ignoble part.

But these concepts do not reach this case. Here, apparently in all good faith, the Government offered at one trial an out-of-court confession by petitioner. It was objected to on the ground that it had been obtained in violation of the Mallory rule. That objection was overruled, and the defense had to decide how to proceed. While defense counsel may have believed he had good grounds for reversal on appeal (as the Court of Appeals later held he did) he also had to present a defense in an effort to persuade the jury to acquit. That defense had of course to be structured to meet the Government's case as it stood—including but not limited to the admitted confession—and counsel decided to put his client on the stand.[*]

The situation was one that criminal and civil defendants face all the time: believing that error has been committed that will result in reversal on appeal, they must nevertheless present a defense, and in doing so may help the other side on retrial. The situation here is no different in principle from the sacrifice of surprise, or the conveyance of important leads to the other side, that may occur because a trial continues even after error has been committed. It is a price that is paid for having a system of justice that insists, generally, upon full trials before appellate review of points of law. It is a problem that can be avoided, within our system, only by doing what is done here, namely, reaching the wrong result as between the litigants. For me this is not acceptable doctrine.

[*] This case is altogether different from Darwin v. Connecticut, 391 U. S. 346, 350, in which I took the position that when a first confession is involuntary a later confession produced by the erroneous impression that the cat was already out of the bag should also be considered involuntary. Here (1) petitioner's out-of-court confession was not involuntary; (2) petitioner's in-court statements were given upon the advice of counsel, and there is no indication whatever that petitioner misunderstood the position he was in; (3) the in-court testimony could not possibly have been thought merely cumulative of the confession, for it (a) was given in order to rebut the confession and (b) damaged petitioner's position in a manner quite independent of the use of the confession.

Justice Harlan's dissent in Jones v. Alfred H. Mayer Co. (June 17, 1968)

MR. JUSTICE HARLAN, whom MR. JUSTICE WHITE joins, dissenting.

The decision in this case appears to me to be most ill-considered and ill-advised.

The petitioners argue that the respondents' racially motivated refusal to sell them a house entitles them to judicial relief on two separate grounds. First, they claim that the respondents acted in violation of 42 U. S. C. § 1982; second, they assert that the respondents' conduct amounted in the circumstances to "state action"[1] and was therefore forbidden by the Fourteenth Amendment even in the absence of any statute. The Court, without reaching the second ground alleged, holds that the petitioners are entitled to relief under 42 U. S. C. § 1982, and that § 1982 is constitutional as legislation appropriate to enforce the Thirteenth Amendment.

For reasons which follow, I believe that the Court's construction of § 1982 as applying to purely private action is almost surely wrong, and at the least is open to serious doubt. The issues of the constitutionality of § 1982, as construed by the Court, and of liability under the Fourteenth Amendment alone, also present formidable difficulties. Moreover, the political processes of our own era have, since the date of oral argument in this case, given birth to a civil rights statute[2] embodying "fair housing" provisions[3] which would at the end of this year make available to others, though apparently not to the petitioners themselves,[4] the type of relief which the petitioners now seek. It seems to me that this latter factor so diminishes the public importance of this case that by far the wisest course would be for this Court to refrain from decision and to dismiss the writ as improvidently granted.

I.

I shall deal first with the Court's construction of § 1982, which lies at the heart of its opinion. That construction is that the statute applies to purely private as well as to state-authorized discrimination.

A.

The Court's opinion focuses upon the statute's legislative history, but it is worthy of note that the precedents in this Court are distinctly opposed to the Court's view of the statute.

In the Civil Rights Cases, 109 U. S. 3, decided less than two decades after the enactment of the Civil Rights Act of 1866, from which § 1982 is derived, the Court said in dictum of the 1866 Act:

"This law is clearly corrective in its character, intended to counteract and furnish redress against State laws and proceedings, and customs having the force of law, which sanction the wrongful acts specified.. . . The Civil Rights Bill here referred to is analogous in its character to what a law would have been under the original Constitution, declaring that the validity of contracts should not be impaired, and that if any person bound by a contract should refuse to comply with it, under color or pretence that it had been rendered void or invalid by a State law, he should be liable to an action upon it in the courts of the United States, with the addition of a penalty for setting up such an unjust and unconstitutional defence." Id., at 16-17.[5]

In Corrigan v. Buckley, 271 U. S. 323, the question was whether the courts of the District of Columbia might enjoin prospective breaches of racially restrictive covenants. The Court held that it was without jurisdiction to consider the petitioners' argument that the covenant was void because it contravened the Fifth, Thirteenth, and Fourteenth Amendments and their implementing statutes. The Court reasoned, inter alia, that the statutes, including the immediate predecessor of § 1982,[6] were inapplicable because

"they, like the Constitutional Amendment under whose sanction they were enacted, do not in any manner prohibit or invalidate contracts entered into by private individuals in respect to the control and disposition of their own property." Id., at 331.[7]

In Hurd v. Hodge, 334 U. S. 24, the issue was again whether the courts of the District might enforce racially restrictive covenants. At the outset of the process of reasoning by which it held that judicial enforcement of such a covenant would violate the predecessor of § 1982, the Court said:

"We may start with the proposition that the statute does not invalidate private restrictive agreements so long as the purposes of those agreements are achieved by the parties through voluntary adherence to the terms. The action toward which the provisions of the statute under consideration is [sic] directed is governmental action. Such was the holding of Corrigan v. Buckley . . . ." Id., at 31.[8]

B.

Like the Court, I begin analysis of § 1982 by examining its language. In its present form, the section provides:

"All citizens of the United States shall have the same right, in every State and Territory, as is enjoyed by white citizens thereof to inherit, purchase, lease, sell, hold, and convey real and personal property."

The Court finds it "plain and unambiguous," ante, at 420, that this language forbids purely private as well as state-authorized discrimination. With all respect, I do not find it so. For me, there is an inherent ambiguity in the term "right," as used in § 1982. The "right" referred to may either be a right to equal status under the law, in which case the statute operates only against state-sanctioned discrimination, or it may be an "absolute" right enforceable against private individuals. To me, the words of the statute, taken alone, suggest the former interpretation, not the latter.[9]

Further, since intervening revisions have not been meant to alter substance, the intended meaning of § 1982 must be drawn from the words in which it was originally enacted. Section 1982 originally was a part of § 1 of the Civil Rights Act of 1866, 14 Stat. 27. Sections 1 and 2 of that Act provided in relevant part:

"That all persons born in the United States and not subject to any foreign power . . . are hereby declared to be citizens of the United States; and such citizens, of every race and color . . . , shall have the same right, in every State and Territory in the United States, . . . to inherit, purchase, lease, sell, hold, and convey real and personal property . . . as is enjoyed by white citizens, and shall be subject to like punishment, pains, and penalties, and to none other, any law, statute, ordinance, regulation, or custom, to the contrary notwithstanding.

"Sec. 2. That any person who, under color of any law, statute, ordinance, regulation, or custom, shall subject, or cause to be subjected, any inhabitant of any State or Territory to the deprivation of any right secured or protected by this act . . . shall be deemed guilty of a misdemeanor . . . ."

It seems to me that this original wording indicates even more strongly than the present language that § 1 of the Act (as well as § 2, which is explicitly so limited) was intended to apply only to action taken pursuant to state or community authority, in the form of a "law, statute, ordinance, regulation, or custom."[10] And with deference I suggest that the language of § 2, taken alone, no more implies that § 2 "was carefully drafted to exempt private violations of § 1 from the criminal sanctions it imposed," see ante, at 425, than it does that § 2 was carefully drafted to enforce all of the rights secured by § 1.

C.

The Court rests its opinion chiefly upon the legislative history of the Civil Rights Act of 1866. I shall endeavor to show that those debates do not, as the Court would have it, overwhelmingly support the result reached by the Court, and in fact that a contrary conclusion may equally well be drawn. I shall consider the legislative history largely in chronological sequence, dealing separately with the Senate and House debates.

The First Session of the Thirty-ninth Congress met on December 4, 1865, some six months after the preceding Congress had sent to the States the Thirteenth Amendment, and a few days before word was received of that Amendment's ratification. On December 13, Senator Wilson introduced a bill which would have invalidated all laws in the former rebel States which discriminated among persons as to civil rights on the basis of color, and which would have made it a misdemeanor to enact or enforce such a statute.[11] On the same day, Senator Trumbull said with regard to Senator Wilson's proposal:

"The bill does not go far enough, if what we have been told to-day in regard to the treatment of freedmen in the southern States is true. . . . [U]ntil [the Thirteenth

Amendment] is adopted there may be some question . . . as to the authority of Congress to pass such a bill as this, but after the adoption of the constitutional amendment there can be none.

"The second clause of that amendment was inserted for some purpose, and I would like to know . . . for what purpose? Sir, for the purpose, and none other, of preventing State Legislatures from enslaving, under any pretense, those whom the first clause declared should be free."[12]

Senator Trumbull then indicated that he would introduce separate bills to enlarge the powers of the recently founded Freedmen's Bureau and to secure the freedmen in their civil rights, both bills in his view being authorized by the second clause of the Thirteenth Amendment.[13]

Since he had just stated that the purpose of that clause was to enable Congress to nullify acts of the state legislatures, it seems inferable that this was also to be the aim of the promised bills.

On January 5, Senator Trumbull introduced both the Freedmen's bill and the civil rights bill.[14] The Freedmen's bill would have strengthened greatly the existing system by which agents of the Freedmen's Bureau exercised protective supervision over freedmen wherever they were present in large numbers. Inter alia, the Freedmen's bill would have permitted the President, acting through the Bureau, to extend "military protection and jurisdiction" over all cases in which persons in the former rebel States were

"in consequence of any State or local law, ordinance, police or other regulation, custom, or prejudice, [denied or refused] any of the civil rights or immunities belonging to white persons, including the right . . . to inherit, purchase, lease, sell, hold and convey real and personal property, . . . on account of race . . . ."[15]

The next section of the Freedmen's bill provided that the agents of the Freedmen's Bureau might try and convict of a misdemeanor any person who deprived another of such rights on account of race and "under color of any State or local law, ordinance, police, or other regulation or custom . . . ." Thus, the Freedmen's bill, which was generally limited in its application to the Southern States and which was correspondingly more sweeping in its protection of the freedmen than the civil rights bill,[16] defined both the rights secured and the denials of those rights which were criminally punishable in terms of acts done under the aegis of a State or locality. The only significant distinction was that denials which occurred "in consequence of a State or local . . . prejudice" would have entitled the victim to military protection but would not have been criminal. In the corresponding section of the companion and generally parallel civil rights bill, which was to be effective throughout the Nation, the reference to "prejudice" was omitted from the rights-defining section. This would seem to imply that the more widely applicable civil rights bill was meant to provide protection only against those discriminations which were legitimated by a state or community sanction sufficiently powerful to deserve the name "custom."

The form of the Freedmen's bill also undercuts the Court's argument, ante, at 424, that if § 1 of the Civil Rights Act were construed as extending only to "state action," then "much of § 2 [which clearly was so limited] would have made no sense at all." For the similar structure of the companion Freedmen's bill, drafted by the same hand and largely parallel in structure, would seem to confirm that the limitation to "state action" was deliberate.

The civil rights bill was debated intermittently in the Senate from January 12, 1866, until its eventual passage over the President's veto on April 6. In the course of the debates, Senator Trumbull, who was by far the leading spokesman for the bill, made a number of statements which can only be taken to mean that the bill was aimed at "state action" alone. For example, on January 29, 1866, Senator Trumbull began by citing a number of recently enacted Southern laws depriving men of rights named in the bill. He stated that "[t]he purpose of the bill under consideration is to destroy all these discriminations, and carry into effect the constitutional amendment."[17] Later the same day, Senator Trumbull quoted § 2 of the bill in full, and said:

"This is the valuable section of the bill so far as protecting the rights of freedmen is concerned. . . . When it comes to be understood in all parts of the United States that any person who shall deprive another of any right . . . in consequence of his color or race will expose himself to fine and imprisonment, I think such acts will soon cease."[18]

These words contain no hint that the "rights" protected by § 2 were intended to be any less broad than those secured by § 1. Of course, § 2 plainly extended only to "state action." That Senator Trumbull viewed §§ 1 and 2 as co-extensive appears even more clearly from his answer the following day when asked by Senator Cowan whether there was "not a provision [in the bill] by which State officers are to be punished?" Senator Trumbull replied: "Not State officers especially, but everybody who violates the law. It is the intention to punish everybody who violates the law."[19]

On January 29, Senator Trumbull also uttered the first of several remarkably similar and wholly unambiguous statements which indicated that the bill was aimed only at "state action." He said:

"[This bill] may be assailed as drawing to the Federal Government powers that properly belong to `States'; but I apprehend, rightly considered, it is not obnoxious to that objection. It will have no operation in any State where the laws are equal, where all persons have the same civil rights without regard to color or race. It will have no operation in the State of Kentucky when her slave code and all her laws discriminating between persons on account of race or color shall be abolished."[20]

Senator Trumbull several times reiterated this view. On February 2, replying to Senator Davis of Kentucky, he said:

"Why, sir, if the State of Kentucky makes no discrimination in civil rights between its citizens, this bill has no operation whatever in the State of Kentucky. Are all the rights of the people of Kentucky gone because they cannot discriminate and punish one man for doing a thing that they do not punish another for doing? The bill draws to the Federal Government no power whatever if the States will perform their constitutional obligations."[21]

On April 4, after the President's veto of the bill, Senator Trumbull stated that "If an offense is committed against a colored person simply because he is colored, in a State where the law affords him the same protection as if he were white, this act neither has nor was intended to have anything to do with his case, because he has adequate remedies in the State courts . . . ."[22] Later the same day, he said:

"This bill in no manner interferes with the municipal regulations of any State which protects all alike in their rights of person and property. It could have no operation in Massachusetts, New York, Illinois, or most of the States of the Union."[23]

The remarks just quoted constitute the plainest possible statement that the civil rights bill was intended to apply only to state-sanctioned conduct and not to purely private action. The Court has attempted to negate the force of these statements by citing other declarations by Senator Trumbull and others that the bill would operate everywhere in the country. See ante, at 426, n. 35. However, the obvious and natural way to reconcile these two sets of statements is to read the ones about the bill's nationwide application as declarations that the enactment of a racially discriminatory law in any State would bring the bill into effect there.[24] It seems to me that very great weight must be given these statements of Senator Trumbull, for they were clearly made to reassure Northern and Border State Senators about the extent of the bill's operation in their States.

On April 4, Senator Trumbull gave two additional indications that the bill was intended to reach only state-sanctioned action. The first occurred during Senator Trumbull's defense of the part of § 3 of the bill which gave federal courts jurisdiction "of all causes, civil and criminal, affecting persons who are denied or cannot enforce in the courts . . . of the State or locality where they may be any of the rights secured to them by the first section of this act . . . ." Senator Trumbull said:

"If it be necessary in order to protect the freedman in his rights that he should have authority to go into the Federal courts in all cases where a custom prevails in a State, or where there is a statute-law of the State discriminating against him, I think we have the authority to confer that jurisdiction under the second clause of the [Thirteenth Amendment]."[25]

If the bill had been intended to reach purely private discrimination it seems very strange that Senator Trumbull did not think it necessary to defend the surely more dubious federal jurisdiction over cases involving no state action whatsoever. A few minutes later, Senator Trumbull reiterated that his reason for introducing the civil rights bill was to bring about "the passage of a law by Congress, securing equality in civil rights when denied by State authorities to freedmen and all other inhabitants of the United States . . . ."[26]

Thus, the Senate debates contain many explicit statements by the bill's own author, to whom the Senate naturally looked for an explanation of its terms, indicating that the bill would prohibit only state-sanctioned discrimination.

The Court puts forward in support of its construction an impressive number of quotations from and citations to the Senate debates. However, upon more circumspect analysis than the Court has chosen to give, virtually all of these appear to be either irrelevant or equally consistent with a "state action" interpretation. The Court's mention, ante, at 427, of a reference in the Senate debates to "white employers who refused to pay their Negro workers" surely does not militate against a "state action" construction, since "state action" would include conduct pursuant to "custom," and there was a very strong "custom" of refusing to pay slaves for work done. The Court's citation, ante, at 427-428, of Senate references to "white citizens who assaulted Negroes" is not in point, for the debate cited by the Court concerned the Freedmen's bill, not the civil rights bill.[27] The former by its terms forbade discrimination pursuant to "prejudice," as well as "custom," and in any event neither bill provided a remedy for the victim of a racially motivated assault.[28]

The Court's quotation, ante, at 429-430, of Senator Trumbull's December 13 reference to the then-embryonic civil rights bill is also compatible with a "state action" interpretation, at least when it is recalled that the unedited quotation, see supra, at 455, includes a statement that the second clause of the Thirteenth Amendment, the authority for the proposed bill, was intended solely as a check on state legislatures. Senator Trumbull's declaration the following day that the forthcoming bill would be aimed at discrimination pursuant to "a prevailing public sentiment" as well as to legislation, see ante, at 431, is also consistent with a "state action" reading of the bill, for the bill explicitly prohibited actions done under color of "custom" as well as of formal laws.

The three additional statements of Senator Trumbull and the remarks of senatorial opponents of the bill, quoted by the Court, ante, at 431-433, to show the bill's sweeping scope, are entirely ambiguous as to whether the speakers thought the bill prohibited only state-sanctioned conduct or reached wholly private action as well. Indeed, if the bill's opponents thought that it would have the latter effect, it seems a little surprising that they did not object more strenuously and explicitly.[29] The remark of Senator Lane which is quoted by the Court, ante, at 433, to prove that he viewed the bill as reaching " `the white man . . . [who] would invoke the power of local prejudice' against the Negro," seems to have been quoted out of context. The quotation is taken from a part of Senator Lane's speech in which he defended the section of the bill permitting the President to invoke military authority when necessary to enforce the bill. After noting that there might be occasions "[w]here organized resistance to the legal authority assumes that shape that the officers cannot execute a writ,"[30] Senator Lane concluded that "if [the white man] would invoke the power of local prejudice to override the laws of the country, this is no Government unless the military may be called in to enforce the order of the civil courts and obedience to the laws of the country."[31] It seems to me manifest that, taken in context, this remark is beside the point in this case.

The post-veto remarks of opponents of the bill, cited by the Court, ante, at 435, also are inconclusive. Once it is recognized that the word "right" as used in the bill is ambiguous, then Senator Cowan's statement, ante, at 435, that the bill would confer "the right . . . to purchase . . . real estate . . . without any qualification"[32] must inevitably share that ambiguity. The remarks of Senator Davis, ibid., with respect to rental of hotel rooms and sale of church pews are, when viewed in context, even less helpful to the Court's thesis. For these comments were made immediately following Senator Davis' plaintive acknowledgment that "this measure proscribes all discriminations . . . that may be made . . . by any `ordinance, regulation, or custom,' as well as by `law or statute.' "[33] Senator Davis then observed that ordinances, regulations, and customs presently conferred upon white persons the most comfortable accommodations in ships and steamboats, hotels, churches, and railroad cars, and stated that "[t]his bill . . . declares all persons who enforce those distinctions to be criminals against the United States . . . ."[34] Thus, Senator Davis not only tied these obnoxious effects of the bill to its "customs" provision but alleged that they were brought about by § 2 as well as § 1. There is little wonder that his remarks "elicited no reply," see ibid., from the bill's supporters.

The House debates are even fuller of statements indicating that the civil rights bill was intended to reach only state-endorsed discrimination. Representative Wilson was the bill's sponsor in the House. On the very first day of House debate, March 1, Representative Wilson said in explaining the bill:

"[I]f the States, seeing that we have citizens of different races and colors, would but shut their eyes to these differences and legislate, so far at least as regards civil rights and immunities, as though all citizens were of one race or color, our troubles as a nation would be well-nigh over. . . . It will be observed that the entire structure of this bill rests on the discrimination relative to civil rights and immunities made by the States on `account of race, color, or previous condition of slavery.' "[35]

A few minutes later, Representative Wilson said:

"Before our Constitution was formed, the great fundamental rights [which are embodied in this bill] belonged to every person who became a member of our great national family. . . . The entire machinery of government . . . was designed, among other things, to secure a more perfect enjoyment of these rights. . . . I assert that we possess the power to do those things which Governments are organized to do; that we may protect a citizen of the United States against a violation of his rights by the law of a single State; . . . that this power permeates our whole system, is a part of it, without which the States can run riot over every fundamental right belonging to citizens of the United States . . . ."[36]

These statements surely imply that Representative Wilson believed the bill to be aimed at state-sanctioned discrimination and not at purely private discrimination, which of course existed unhindered "[b]efore our Constitution was formed."

Other congressmen expressed similar views. On March 2, Representative Thayer, one of the bill's supporters, said:

"The events of the last four years . . . have changed [the freedmen] from a condition of slavery to that of freedom. The practical question now to be decided is whether they shall be in fact freemen. It is whether they shall have the benefit of this great charter of liberty given to them by the American people.

"Sir, if it is competent for the new-formed Legislatures of the rebel States to enact laws . . . which declare, for example, that they shall not have the privilege of purchasing a home for themselves and their families; . . . then I demand to know, of what practical value is the amendment abolishing slavery . . .?"[37]

A few minutes later, he said:

"Do you give freedom to a man when you allow him to be deprived of those great natural rights to which every man is entitled by nature? . . . [W]hat kind of freedom is that by which the man placed in a state of freedom is subject to the tyranny of laws which deprive him of [those] rights . . .?"[38]

A little later, Representative Thayer added:

"[The freedmen] are entitled to the benefit of that guarantee of the Constitution which secures to every citizen the enjoyment of life, liberty, and property, and no just reason exists why they should not enjoy the protection of that guarantee . . . .

"What is the necessity which gives occasion for that protection? Sir, in at least six of the lately rebellious States the reconstructed Legislatures of those States have enacted laws which, if permitted to be enforced, would strike a fatal blow at the liberty of the freedmen . . . ."[39]

An opponent of the bill, Representative Bingham, said on March 9:

"[W]hat, then, is proposed by the provision of the first section? Simply to strike down by congressional enactment every State constitution which makes a discrimination on account of race or color in any of the civil rights of the citizen."[40]

Representative Shellabarger, a supporter of the bill, discussed it on the same day. He began by stating that he had no doubt of the constitutionality of § 2 of the bill, provided Congress might enact § 1. With respect to § 1, he said:

"Its whole effect is not to confer or regulate rights, but to require that whatever of these enumerated rights and obligations are imposed by State laws shall be for and upon all citizens alike . . . . Self-evidently this is the whole effect of this first section. It secures . . . equality of protection in those enumerated civil rights which the States may deem proper to confer upon any races. . . . It must . . . be noted that the violations of citizens' rights, which are reached and punished by this bill, are those which are inflicted under `color of law,' &c. The bill does not reach mere private wrongs, but only those done under color of state authority . . . . [I]ts whole force is expended in defeating an attempt, under State laws, to deprive races and the members thereof as such of the rights enumerated in this act. This is the whole of it."[41]

Thus, Representative Shellabarger said in so many words that the bill had no impact on "mere private wrongs."

After the President's veto of the bill, Representative Lawrence, a supporter, stated his views. He said:

"The bill does not declare who shall or shall not have the right to sue, give evidence, inherit, purchase, and sell property. These questions are left to the States to determine, subject only to the limitation that there are some inherent and inalienable rights pertaining to every citizen, which cannot be abolished or abridged by State constitutions or laws. . . .

"Now, there are two ways in which a State may undertake to deprive citizens of these . . . rights: either by prohibitory laws, or by a failure to protect any one of them.

"If the people of a State should become hostile to a large class of naturalized citizens and should enact laws to prohibit them and no other citizens . . . from inheriting, buying, holding, or selling property, . . . that would be prohibitory legislation. If the State should simply enact laws for native-born citizens and provide no law under which naturalized citizens could enjoy any one of these rights, and should deny them all protection by civil process or penal enactments, that would be a denial of justice."[42]

From this passage it would appear that Representative Lawrence conceived of the word "right" in § 1 of the bill as referring to a right to equal legal status, and that he believed that the sole effect of the bill was to prohibit state-imposed discrimination.

The Court quotes and cites a number of passages from the House debates in aid of its construction of the bill. As in the case of the Senate debates, most of these appear upon close examination to provide little support. The first significant citation, ante, at 425, n. 33, is a dialogue between Representative Wilson and Representative Loan, another of the bill's supporters.

The full exchange went as follows:

"Mr. LOAN. Mr. Speaker, I . . . ask the chairman. . . why the committee limit the provisions of the second section to those who act under the color of law. Why not let them apply to the whole community where the acts are committed?

"Mr. WILSON, of Iowa. That grows out of the fact that there is discrimination in reference to civil rights under the local laws of the States. Therefore we provide that the persons who under the color of these local laws should do these things shall be liable to this punishment.

"Mr. LOAN. What penalty is imposed upon others than officers who inflict these wrongs on the citizen?

"Mr. WILSON, of Iowa. We are not making a general criminal code for the States.

"Mr. LOAN. Why not abrogate those laws instead of inflicting penalties upon officers who execute writs under them?

"Mr. WILSON, of Iowa. A law without a sanction is of very little force.

"Mr. LOAN. Then why not put it in the bill directly?

"Mr. WILSON, of Iowa. That is what we are trying to do."[43]

The interpretation which the Court places on Representative Wilson's remarks, see ante, at 425, n. 33, is a conceivable one.[44] However, it is equally likely that, since both participants in the dialogue professed concern solely with § 2 of the bill, their remarks carried no implication about the scope of § 1. Moreover, it is possible to read the entire exchange as concerned with discrimination in communities having discriminatory laws, with Representative Loan urging that the laws should be abrogated directly or that all persons, not merely officers, who discriminated pursuant to them should be criminally punishable.

The next significant reliance upon the House debates is the Court's mention of references in the debates "to white employers who refused to pay their Negro workers, white planters who agreed among themselves not to hire freed slaves without the permission of their former masters, white citizens who assaulted Negroes or who combined to drive them out of their communities." Ante, at 427-428.[45] (Footnotes omitted.) As was pointed out in the discussion of the Senate debates, supra, at 462, the references to white men's refusals to pay freedmen and their agreements not to hire freedmen without their "masters' " consent are by no means contrary to a "state action" view of the civil rights bill, since the bill expressly forbade action pursuant to "custom" and both of these practices reflected "customs" from the time of slavery. The Court cites two different House references to assaults on Negroes by whites. The first was by Congressman Windom,[46] and close examination reveals that his only mention of assaults was with regard to a Texas "pass system," under which freedmen were whipped if found abroad without passes, and a South Carolina law permitting freedmen to be whipped for insolence.[47] Since these assaults were sanctioned by law, or at least by "custom," they would be reached by the bill even under a "state action" interpretation. The other allusion to assaults, as well as the mention of combinations of whites to drive freedmen from communities, occurred in a speech by Representative Lawrence.[48] These references were shortly preceded by the remarks of Congressman Lawrence quoted, supra, at 468, and were immediately followed by his comment that "If States should undertake to authorize such offenses, or deny to a class of citizens all protection against them, we may then inquire whether the nation itself may be destroyed . . . ."[49] These fore and aft remarks imply that Congressman Lawrence's concern was that the activities referred to would receive state sanction.

The Court, ante, at 428, n. 40, quotes a statement of Representative Eldridge, an opponent of the bill, in which he mentioned references by the bill's supporters to "individual cases of wrong perpetrated upon the freedmen of the South . . . ."[50] However, up to that time there had been no mention whatever in the House debates of any purely private discrimination,[51] so one can only conclude that by "individual cases" Representative Eldridge meant "isolated cases," not "cases of purely private discrimination."

The last significant reference[52] by the Court to the House debates is its statement, ante, at 434, that "Representative Cook of Illinois thought that, without appropriate federal legislation, any `combination of men in [a] neighborhood [could] prevent [a Negro] from having any chance' to enjoy" the benefits of the Thirteenth Amendment. This quotation seems to be taken out of context. What Representative Cook said was:

"[W]hen those rights which are enumerated in this bill are denied to any class of men on account of race or color, when they are subject to a system of vagrant laws which sells them into slavery or involuntary servitude, which operates upon them as upon no other part of the community, they are not secured in the rights of freedom. If a man can be sold, the man is a slave. If he is nominally freed by the amendment to the Constitution, . . . he has simply the labor of his hands on which he can depend. Any combination of men in his neighborhood can prevent him from having any chance to support himself by his labor. They can pass a law that a man not supporting himself by labor shall be deemed a vagrant, and that a vagrant shall be sold."[53]

These remarks clearly were addressed to discriminations effectuated by law, or sanctioned by "custom." As such, they would have been reached by the bill even under a "state action" interpretation.

D.

The foregoing analysis of the language, structure, and legislative history of the 1866 Civil Rights Act shows, I believe, that the Court's thesis that the Act was meant to extend to purely private action is open to the most serious doubt, if indeed it does not render that thesis wholly untenable. Another, albeit less tangible, consideration points in the same direction. Many of the legislators who took part in the congressional debates inevitably must have shared the individualistic ethic of their time, which emphasized personal freedom[54] and embodied a distaste for governmental interference which was soon to culminate in the era of laissez-faire.[55] It seems to me that most of these men would have regarded it as a great intrusion on individual liberty for the Government to take from a man the power to refuse for personal reasons to enter into a purely private transaction involving the disposition of property, albeit those personal reasons might reflect racial bias. It should be remembered that racial prejudice was not uncommon in 1866, even outside the South.[56] Although Massachusetts had recently enacted the Nation's first law prohibiting racial discrimination in public accommodations,[57] Negroes could not ride within Philadelphia streetcars[58] or attend public schools with white children in New York City.[59] Only five States accorded equal voting rights to Negroes,[60] and it appears that Negroes were allowed to serve on juries only in Massachusetts.[61] Residential segregation was the prevailing pattern almost everywhere in the North.[62] There were no state "fair housing" laws in 1866, and it appears that none had ever been proposed.[63] In this historical context, I cannot conceive that a bill thought to prohibit purely private discrimination not only in the sale or rental of housing but in all property transactions would not have received a great deal of criticism explicitly directed to this feature. The fact that the 1866 Act received no criticism of this kind[64] is for me strong additional evidence that it was not regarded as extending so far.

In sum, the most which can be said with assurance about the intended impact of the 1866 Civil Rights Act upon purely private discrimination is that the Act probably was envisioned by most members of Congress as prohibiting official, community-sanctioned discrimination in the South, engaged in pursuant to local "customs" which in the recent time of slavery probably were embodied in laws or regulations.[65] Acts done under the color of such "customs" were, of course, said by the Court in the Civil Rights Cases, 109 U. S. 3, to constitute "state action" prohibited by the Fourteenth Amendment. See id., at 16, 17, 21. Adoption of a "state action" construction of the Civil Rights Act would therefore have the additional merit of bringing its interpretation into line with that of the Fourteenth Amendment, which this Court has consistently held to reach only "state action." This seems especially desirable in light of the wide agreement that a major purpose of the Fourteenth Amendment, at least in the minds of its congressional proponents, was to assure that the rights conferred by the then recently enacted Civil Rights Act could not be taken away by a subsequent Congress.[66]

II.

The foregoing, I think, amply demonstrates that the Court has chosen to resolve this case by according to a loosely worded statute a meaning which is open to the strongest challenge in light of the statute's legislative history. In holding that the Thirteenth Amendment is sufficient constitutional authority for § 1982 as interpreted, the Court also decides a question of great importance. Even contemporary supporters of the aims of the 1866 Civil Rights Act doubted that those goals could constitutionally be achieved under the Thirteenth Amendment,[67] and this Court has twice expressed similar doubts. See Hodges v. United States, 203 U. S. 1, 16-18; Corrigan v. Buckley, 271 U. S. 323, 330. But cf. Civil Rights Cases, 109 U. S. 3, 22. Thus, it is plain that the course of decision followed by the Court today entails the resolution of important and difficult issues.

The only apparent way of deciding this case without reaching those issues would be to hold that the petitioners are entitled to relief on the alternative ground advanced by them: that the respondents' conduct amounted to "state action" forbidden by the Fourteenth Amendment. However, that route is not without formidable obstacles of its own, for the opinion of the Court of Appeals makes it clear that this case differs substantially from any "state action" case previously decided by this Court. See 379 F. 2d, at 40-45.

The fact that a case is "hard" does not, of course, relieve a judge of his duty to decide it. Since, the Court did vote to hear this case, I normally would consider myself obligated to decide whether the petitioners are entitled to relief on either of the grounds on which they rely. After mature reflection, however, I have concluded that this is one of those rare instances in which an event which occurs after the hearing of argument so diminishes a case's public significance, when viewed in light of the difficulty of the questions presented, as to justify this Court in dismissing the writ as improvidently granted.

The occurrence to which I refer is the recent enactment of the Civil Rights Act of 1968, Pub. L. 90-284, 82 Stat. 73. Title VIII of that Act contains comprehensive "fair housing" provisions, which by the terms of § 803 will become applicable on January 1, 1969, to persons who, like the petitioners, attempt to buy houses from developers. Under those provisions, such persons will be entitled to injunctive relief and damages from developers who refuse to sell to them on account of race or color, unless the parties are able to resolve their dispute by other means. Thus, the type of relief which the petitioners seek will be available within seven months' time under the terms of a presumptively constitutional Act of Congress.[68] In these circumstances, it seems obvious that the case has lost most of its public importance, and I believe that it would be much the wiser course for this Court to refrain from deciding it. I think it particularly unfortunate for the Court to persist in deciding this case on the basis of a highly questionable interpretation of a sweeping, century-old statute which, as the Court acknowledges, see ante, at 415, contains none of the exemptions which the Congress of our own time found it necessary to include in a statute regulating relationships so personal in nature. In effect, this Court, by its construction of § 1982, has extended the coverage of federal "fair housing" laws far beyond that which Congress in its wisdom chose to provide in the Civil Rights Act of 1968. The political process now having taken hold again in this very field, I am at a loss to understand why the Court should have deemed it appropriate or, in the circumstances of this case, necessary to proceed with such precipitate and insecure strides.

I am not dissuaded from my view by the circumstance that the 1968 Act was enacted after oral argument in this case, at a time when the parties and amici curiae had invested time and money in anticipation of a decision on the merits, or by the fact that the 1968 Act apparently will not entitle these petitioners to the relief which they seek.[69] For the certiorari jurisdiction was not conferred upon this Court "merely to give the defeated party in the . . . Court of Appeals another hearing," Magnum Co. v. Coty, 262 U. S. 159, 163, or "for the benefit of the particular litigants," Rice v. Sioux City Cemetery, 349 U. S. 70, 74, but to decide issues, "the settlement of which is of importance to the public as distinguished from . . . the parties," Layne & Bowler Corp. v. Western Well Works, Inc., 261 U. S. 387, 393. I deem it far more important that this Court should avoid, if possible, the decision of constitutional and unusually difficult statutory questions than that we fulfill the expectations of every litigant who appears before us.

One prior decision of this Court especially suggests dismissal of the writ as the proper course in these unusual circumstances. In Rice v. Sioux City Cemetery, supra, the issue was whether a privately owned cemetery might defend a suit for breach of a contract to bury on the ground that the decedent was a Winnebago Indian and the contract restricted burial privileges to Caucasians. In considering a petition for rehearing following an initial affirmance by an equally divided Court, there came to the Court's attention for the first time an Iowa statute which prohibited cemeteries from discriminating on account of race, but which would not have benefited the Rice petitioner because of an exception for "pending litigation." Mr. Justice Frankfurter, speaking for a majority of the Court, held that the writ should be dismissed. He pointed out that the case presented "evident difficulties," 349 U. S., at 77, and noted that "[h]ad the statute been properly brought to our attention . . . , the case would have assumed such an isolated significance that it would hardly have been brought here in the first instance." Id., at 76-77. This case certainly presents difficulties as substantial as those in Rice. Compare what has been said in this opinion with 349 U. S., at 72-73; see also Bell v. Maryland, 378 U. S. 226. And if the petition for a writ of certiorari in this case had been filed a few months after, rather than a few months before, the passage of the 1968 Civil Rights Act, I venture to say that the case would have been deemed to possess such "isolated significance," in comparison with its difficulties, that the petition would not have been granted.

For these reasons, I would dismiss the writ of certiorari as improvidently granted.

Notes

[1] This "state action" argument emphasizes the respondents' role as housing developers exercising continuing authority over a suburban housing complex with about 1,000 inhabitants.

[2] The Civil Rights Act of 1968, Pub. L. 90-284, 82 Stat. 73.

[3] Id., §§ 801-819.

[4] See ante, at 417, n. 21.

[5] See also Virginia v. Rives, 100 U. S. 313, 317-318.

[6] Section 1978 of the Revised Statutes.

[7] See also Buchanan v. Warley, 245 U. S. 60, 78-79.

[8] It seems to me that this passage is not dictum, as the Court terms it, ante, at 419 and n. 25, but a holding. For if the Court had held the covenants in question invalid as between the parties, then it would not have had to rely upon a finding of "state action."

[9] Despite the Court's view that this reading flies in the face of the "plain and unambiguous terms" of the statute, see ante, at 420, it is not without precedent. In the Civil Rights Cases, 109 U. S. 3, the Court said of identical language in the predecessor statute to § 1982:

"[C]ivil rights, such as are guaranteed by the Constitution against State aggression, cannot be impaired by the wrongful acts of individuals, unsupported by State authority . . . . The wrongful act of an individual, unsupported by any such authority, is simply a private wrong, or a crime of that individual; an invasion of the rights of the injured party, it is true . . . ; but if not sanctioned in some way by the State, or not done under State authority, his rights remain in full force, and may presumably be vindicated by resort to the laws of the State for redress. An individual cannot deprive a man of his right . . . to hold property, to buy and sell . . . ; he may, by force or fraud, interfere with the enjoyment of the right in a particular case; . . . but, unless protected in these wrongful acts by some shield of State law or State authority, he cannot destroy or injure the right . . . ." 109 U. S., at 17.

[10] The Court does not claim that the deletion from § 1 of the statute, in 1874, of the words "any law, statute, ordinance, regulation, or custom, to the contrary notwithstanding" was intended to have any substantive effect. See ante, at 422, n. 29.

[11] See Cong. Globe, 39th Cong., 1st Sess., 39-42.

[12] Id., at 43.

[13] See ibid.

[14] See Cong. Globe, 39th Cong., 1st Sess., 129.

[15] Freedmen's bill, § 7. The text of the bill may be found in E. McPherson, The Political History of the United States of America During the Period of Reconstruction 72 (1871). The Freedmen's bill was passed by both the Senate and the House, but the Senate

failed to override the President's veto. See Cong. Globe, 39th Cong., 1st Sess., 421, 688, 742, 748, 775, 915-916, 943.

[16] Section 7 of the Freedmen's bill would have permitted the President to extend "military protection and jurisdiction" over all cases in which the specified rights were denied, while § 3 of the Civil Rights Act merely gave the federal courts concurrent jurisdiction over such actions. Section 8 of the Freedmen's bill would have allowed agents of the Freedmen's Bureau to try and convict those who violated the bill's criminal provisions, while § 3 of the Civil Rights Act only gave the federal courts exclusive jurisdiction over such actions.

[17] Cong. Globe, 39th Cong., 1st Sess., 474. (Emphasis added.)

[18] Id., at 475. (Emphasis added.)

[19] Id., at 500. (Emphasis added.) The Civil Rights Cases, 109 U. S. 3, suggest how Senator Trumbull might have expected § 2 to affect persons other than "officers" in spite of its "under color" language, for it was there said in dictum that:

"The Civil Rights Bill . . . is analogous . . . to [a law] under the original Constitution, declaring that the validity of contracts should not be impaired, and that if any person bound by a contract should refuse to comply with it, under color or pretence that it had been rendered void or invalid by a State law, he should be liable to an action upon it in the courts of the United States, with the addition of a penalty for setting up such an unjust and unconstitutional defence." 109 U. S., at 17. (Emphasis added.)

[20] Cong. Globe, 39th Cong., 1st Sess., 476. (Emphasis added.)

[21] Id., at 600. (Emphasis added.)

[22] Id., at 1758.

[23] Id., at 1761. (Emphasis added.)

[24] Moreover, a few Northern States apparently did have laws which denied to Negroes rights enumerated in the Act. See G. Stephenson, Race Distinctions in American Law 36-39 (1910); L. Litwack, North of Slavery: The Negro in the Free States, 1790-1860, at 93-94 (1961).

[25] Cong. Globe, 39th Cong., 1st Sess., 1759.

[26] Id., at 1760. (Emphasis added.)

[27] See Cong. Globe, 39th Cong., 1st Sess., 339-340.

[28] The Court also gives prominence, see ante, at 428-429, to a report by General Carl Schurz which described private as well as official discrimination against freedmen in the South. However, it is apparent that the Senate regarded the report merely as background, and it figured relatively little in the debates. Moreover, to the extent that the described discrimination was the product of "custom," it would have been prohibited by the bill.

[29] See infra, at 473-475.

[30] Cong. Globe, 39th Cong., 1st Sess., 603.

[31] Ibid.

[32] See Cong. Globe, 39th Cong., 1st Sess., 1781.

[33] Cong. Globe, 39th Cong., 1st Sess., Appendix, 183.

[34] Ibid.

[35] Cong. Globe, 39th Cong., 1st Sess., 1118. (Emphasis added.)

[36] Id., at 1119. (Emphasis added.)

[37] Id., at 1151. (Emphasis added.)

[38] Id., at 1152. (Emphasis added.)

[39] Id., at 1153. (Emphasis added.)

[40] Id., at 1291. (Emphasis added.)

[41] Id., at 1293-1294. It is quite clear that Representative Shellabarger was speaking of the bill's first section, for he did not mention the second section until later in his speech, and then only briefly and in terms which indicated that he thought it co-extensive with the first ("I cannot remark on the second section further than to say that it is the ordinary case of providing punishment for violating a law of Congress."). See id., at 1294.

[42] Cong. Globe, 39th Cong., 1st Sess., 1832-1833. (Emphasis added.)

[43] Id., at 1120.

[44] It is worthy of note, however, that if Representative Wilson believed that § 2 of the bill would apply only to state officers, and not to other members of the community, he apparently differed from the bill's author. See the remarks of Senator Trumbull quoted, supra, at 458.

[45] The Court's reliance, see ante, at 425, n. 33, on the statement of Representative Shellabarger that "the violations of citizens' rights, which are reached and punished by this bill, are those which are . . . done under color of state authority . . . ," Cong. Globe, 39th Cong., 1st Sess., 1294, seems very misplaced when the statement is taken in context. A fuller version of Representative Shellabarger's remarks will be found, supra, at 467-468.

[46] See Cong. Globe, 39th Cong., 1st Sess., 1160.

[47] See ibid.

[48] See Cong. Globe, 39th Cong., 1st Sess., 1835.

[49] Ibid. (Emphasis added.)

[50] Cong. Globe, 39th Cong., 1st Sess., 1156.

[51] See id., at 1115-1124, 1151-1155.

[52] The emphasis given by the Court to the statement of Representative Thayer which is quoted, ante, at 433-434, surely evaporates when the statement is viewed in conjunction with Representative Thayer's immediately following remarks, quoted, supra, at 466-467.

[53] Id., at 1124. (Emphasis added.) Earlier in the same speech, Representative Cook had described actual vagrancy laws which had recently been passed by reconstructed Southern legislatures. See id., at 1123-1124.

[54] An eminent American historian has said that the events of the last third of the 19th century took place "in a framework of pioneer individualistic mores . . . ." S. Morison,

The Oxford History of the American People 788 (1965). See also 3 V. Parrington, Main Currents in American Thought 7-22 (1930).

[55] It has been suggested that the effort of the congressional radicals to enact a program of land reform in favor of the freedmen during Reconstruction failed in part because it smacked too much of "paternalism" and interference with property rights. See K. Stampp, The Era of Reconstruction 126-131 (1965).

[56] See generally M. Konvitz & T. Leskes, A Century of Civil Rights (1961); L. Litwack, North of Slavery: The Negro in the Free States, 1790-1860 (1961); K. Stampp, supra, at 12-17; G. Stephenson, Race Distinctions in American Law (1910); Maslow & Robison, Civil Rights Legislation and the Fight for Equality, 1862-1952, 20 U. Chi. L. Rev. 363 (1953).

[57] See M. Konvitz & T. Leskes, supra, at 155-156; 1864-1865 Mass. Acts and Resolves 650.

[58] Negroes were permitted to ride only on the front platforms of the cars. See L. Litwack, supra, at 112.

[59] Negro students in New York City were compelled to attend separate schools, called African schools, under authority of an 1864 New York State statute which empowered school officials to establish separate, equal schools for Negro children. See L. Litwack, supra, at 121, 133-134, 136, 151; G. Stephenson, supra, at 185; 1864 N. Y. Laws 1281. In 1883, the New York Court of Appeals held that students in Brooklyn might constitutionally be segregated pursuant to the statute. See People ex rel. King v. Gallagher, 93 N. Y. 438. In 1900, the statute was finally repealed and segregation legally forbidden. See 1900 N. Y. Laws, Vol. II, at 1173.

[60] See L. Litwack, supra, at 91-92. The States were Massachusetts, Rhode Island, Maine, New Hampshire, and Vermont. See id., at 91.

[61] See L. Litwack, supra, at 94.

[62] See id., at 168-170.

[63] It has been noted that:

"Residential housing, despite its importance . . . , appears to be the last of the major areas of discrimination that the states have been willing to attack." M. Konvitz & T. Leskes, supra, at 236.

And as recently as 1953, it could be said:

"Bills have been introduced in state legislatures to forbid racial or religious discrimination in `multiple dwellings' (those housing three or more families), . . . but these proposals have not been considered seriously by any legislative body." Maslow & Robison, supra, at 408. (Footnotes omitted.)

[64] In contrast, the bill was repeatedly and vehemently attacked, in the face of emphatic denials by its sponsors, on the ground that it allegedly would invalidate two types of state laws: those denying Negroes equal voting rights and those prohibiting intermarriage. See, e. g., Cong. Globe, 39th Cong., 1st Sess., 598, 600, 604, 606, 1121, 1157, 1263.

[65] The petitioners do not argue, and the Court does not suggest, that the discrimination complained of in this case was the product of such a "custom."

[66] See, e. g., H. Flack, The Adoption of the Fourteenth Amendment 94 (1908); J. James, The Framing of the Fourteenth Amendment 126-128, 179 (1956); 2 S. Morison & H. Commager, The Growth of the American Republic 39 (4th ed. 1950); K. Stampp, supra, at 136; J. tenBroek, Equal Under Law 224 (1965); L. Warsoff, Equality and the Law 126 (1938).

[67] See, e. g., Cong. Globe, 39th Cong., 1st Sess., 504-505 (Senator Johnson); id., at 1291-1293 (Representative Bingham).

[68] Of course, the question of the constitutionality of the "fair housing" provisions of the 1968 Civil Rights Act is not before us, and I intend no implication about how I would decide that issue.

[69] See ante, at 417, n. 21.

Justice Harlan's dissent in Grunenthal v. Long Island R. (Nov 18, 1968)

MR. JUSTICE HARLAN, dissenting.

I think it clear that the only issue which might conceivably justify the presence of this case in this Court is whether a United States Court of Appeals may constitutionally review the refusal of a district court to set aside a verdict for excessiveness. The Court purports not to decide that question, preferring to rest its decision upon the alleged correctness of the District Court's action in the circumstances of this case. Like my Brother STEWART, I am at an utter loss to understand how the Court manages to review the District Court's decision and find it proper while at the same time proclaiming that it has avoided decision of the issue whether appellate courts ever may review such actions.

Even assuming that this feat of legal gymnastics has been successfully performed, I believe that the correctness of this particular District Court decision, a matter whose proper resolution depends upon a detailed examination of the trial record and which possesses little if any general significance, is not a suitable issue for this Court. Accordingly, I think it appropriate to vote to dismiss the writ as improvidently granted, even though the case formally is here on an unlimited writ. See my dissenting opinion in Protective Committee v. Anderson, 390 U. S. 414, 454 (1968). To the extent that this position is inconsistent with my having joined the per curiam opinion in Neese v. Southern R. Co., 350 U. S. 77 (1955), in which the Court adopted a course similar to that followed today, I feel bound frankly to say that the incongruity of today's decision brings me face-to-face with the question whether that earlier disposition was correct, and that I now believe it to have been wrong.[*]

Since the Court professes not to reach the constitutional issue in this case, I consider it inappropriate for me, as an individual Justice, to express my opinion on it.

[*] See ante, at 157, n. 3.

Justice Harlan's concurrence in Oestereich v. Selective Serv. System Local Bd. No. 11 (Dec 16, 1968)

MR. JUSTICE HARLAN, concurring in the result.

I concur in the holding that pre-induction review is available in this case, but I reach this conclusion by means of a somewhat different analysis from that contained in the opinion of my Brother DOUGLAS.

At the outset, I think it is important to state what this case does and does not involve. Petitioner does not contend that the Selective Service System has improperly resolved factual questions, or wrongfully exercised its discretion, or even that it has acted without any "basis in fact," as that phrase is commonly used in this area of law. See Estep v. United States, 327 U. S. 114, 122-123 (1946); ante, at 238, n. 7. He asserts, rather, that the procedure pursuant to which he was reclassified and ordered to report for induction—a procedure plainly mandated by the System's self-promulgated published regulations, 32 CFR, pt. 1642—is unlawful. Specifically, he asserts that the delinquency reclassification scheme is not authorized by any statute, that it is inconsistent with his statutory exemption as a ministerial student, 50 U. S. C. App. § 456 (g), and that, whether or not approved by Congress, the regulations are facially unconstitutional.[1]

The pivotal language of § 10 (b) (3), for present purposes, is the statute's proscription of pre-induction judicial review "of the classification or processing of any registrant . . . ." I take the phrase "classification or processing" to encompass the numerous discretionary, factual, and mixed law-fact determinations which a Selective Service Board must make prior to issuing an order to report for induction. I do not understand that phrase to prohibit review of a claim, such as that made here by petitioner, that the very statutes or regulations which the Board administers are facially invalid.

"Classification is the key to selection," 32 CFR § 1622.1 (b), and among a local Board's most important functions is "to decide, subject to appeal, the class in which each registrant shall be placed." 32 CFR § 1622.1 (c). Classification is a highly individualized process, in which a Board must consider all pertinent information presented to it. Ibid. Thus, a Board may be required to determine, on a conflicting record, whether a registrant is conscientiously opposed to participation in war in any form, 32 CFR § 1622.14, or whether the registrant's deferment "is in the national interest and of paramount importance to our national security . . . ." 32 CFR § 1622.20. A Board also exercises considerable discretion in the processing of registrants—for example, in securing information relevant to classification, 32 CFR §§ 1621.9-1621.15, scheduling of physical examinations, 32 CFR, pt. 1628, and scheduling and postponement of induction itself, 32 CFR, pt. 1632.

Congress' decision to defer judicial review of such decisions by the Selective Service Boards until after induction was, I believe, responsive to two major considerations. First, because these determinations are of an individualized and discretionary nature, a reviewing court must often examine Board records and other documentary evidence, hear testimony, and resolve controversies on a sizable record. Even though the scope of judicial review is narrow, see Estep v. United States, supra, at 122-123, this cannot be done quickly. To stay induction pending such review would work havoc with the orderly processing of registrants into the Nation's armed forces. See 113 Cong. Rec. 15426 (Senator Russell); cf. Estep v. United States, supra, at 137 (Mr. Justice Frankfurter, concurring in the result).

Second, the registrant has been afforded, prior to his induction, the opportunity for a hearing and administrative appeals within the Selective Service System. 32 CFR, pts. 1624-1627. It is properly presumed that a registrant's Board has fully considered all relevant information presented to it, and that it has classified and processed him regularly, and in accordance with the applicable statutes and regulations. Greer v. United States, 378 F. 2d 931 (1967); Storey v. United States, 370 F. 2d 255 (1966); cf. United States v. Chemical Foundation, 272 U. S. 1, 14-15 (1926); Chin Yow v. United States, 208 U. S. 8, 12 (1908); Martin v. Mott, 12 Wheat. 19 (1827).

These factors are significantly altered where the registrant contends that the procedure employed by the Board is invalid on its face.

First, such a claim does not invite the court to review the factual and discretionary decisions inherent in the "classification or processing" of registrants, and does not, therefore, present opportunity for protracted delay. To be sure, collateral factual determinations—for example, whether the registrant was subjected to the statute or regulation drawn in question (in this case, the delinquency reclassification procedure)—may sometimes be necessary. But, in general, a court may dispose of a challenge to the validity of the procedure on the pleadings.

Insubstantial claims can usually be weeded out with dispatch.[2]

Second, a challenge to the validity of the administrative procedure itself not only renders irrelevant the presumption of regularity,[3] but also presents an issue beyond the competence of the Selective Service Boards to hear and determine. Adjudication of the constitutionality of congressional enactments[4] has generally been thought beyond the jurisdiction of administrative agencies. See Public Utilities Comm'n v. United States, 355 U. S. 534, 539 (1958); Engineers Public Service Co. v. SEC, 78 U. S. App. D. C. 199, 215-216, 138 F. 2d 936, 952-953 (1943), dismissed as moot, 332 U. S. 788. The Boards have no power to promulgate regulations, and are not expressly delegated any authority to pass on the validity of regulations or statutes. Such authority cannot readily be inferred, for the composition of the Boards, and their administrative procedures, render them wholly unsuitable forums for the adjudication of these matters: local and appeal Boards consist of part-time, uncompensated members, chosen ideally to be representative of the registrants' communities;[5] the fact that a registrant may not be represented by counsel in Selective Service proceedings, 32 CFR § 1624.1 (b), seems incompatible with the Boards' serious consideration of such purely legal claims. Indeed, the denial of counsel has been justified on the ground that the proceedings are nonjudicial. United States v. Sturgis, 342 F. 2d 328, 332 (1965), cert. denied, 382 U. S. 879; cf. United States v. Capehart, 141 F. Supp.

708, 719 (1956), aff'd, 237 F. 2d 388 (1956), cert. denied, 352 U. S. 971.

To withhold pre-induction review in this case would thus deprive petitioner of his liberty without the prior opportunity to present to any competent forum—agency or court—his substantial claim that he was ordered inducted pursuant to an unlawful procedure. Such an interpretation of § 10 (b) (3) would raise serious constitutional problems,[6] and is not indicated by the statute's history,[7] language, or purpose. On the foregoing basis I agree that § 10 (b) (3) does not forbid pre-induction review in this instance.

Because both the District Court and the Court of Appeals passed on the merits of petitioner's challenge to the delinquency reclassification regulations, this issue is ripe for our consideration. Whatever validity the procedure may have under other circumstances, I agree that the delinquency reclassification of petitioner for failure to possess his registration certificate is inconsistent with petitioner's conceded statutory exemption as a student of the ministry.

Notes

[1] Petitioner makes several other arguments which I do not find necessary to discuss.

[2] Moreover, a court should be hesitant to grant a preliminary injunction staying induction except upon a strong showing that the registrant is likely to succeed on the merits.

[3] A suggestive analogy may be found in the Court's construction of the civil rights removal statute, 28 U. S. C. § 1443. Where state statutory procedure is valid on its face, it is presumed that the state courts will treat a defendant fairly, and removal is not permitted. Georgia v. Rachel, 384 U. S. 780, 803-804 (1966); Virginia v. Rives, 100 U. S. 313, 321-323 (1880). But, subject to qualifications not here pertinent, a defendant may remove the cause when the state statutory procedure is facially invalid: "When a statute of the State denies his right, or interposes a bar to his enforcing it, in the judicial tribunals, the presumption is fair that they will be controlled by it in their decisions . . . ." Id., at 321. See also Greenwood v. Peacock, 384 U. S. 808 (1966).

[4] It may be noted that the Selective Service System urges that the delinquency reclassification provisions have been approved by Congress. Brief for the Respondents 71.

[5] See 32 CFR §§ 1603.3, 1604.22; Memorandum from General Hershey, S. Doc. No. 82, 89th Cong., 2d Sess., 4; Weekly Compilation of Presidential Documents, March 13, 1967, p. 395; Report of the National Advisory Commission on Selective Service 74-79 (1967).

Although each local Board has assigned to it a part-time, uncompensated appeal agent—"whenever possible, a person with legal training and experience," 32 CFR § 1604.71 (c)—his pertinent responsibilities to the Board are limited to assisting its members by "interpreting for them laws, regulations, and other directives," 32 CFR § 1604.71 (d) (4), and he must be "equally diligent in protecting the interests of the Government and the rights of the registrant in all matters." 32 CFR § 1604.71 (d) (5).

[6] It is doubtful whether a person may be deprived of his personal liberty without the prior opportunity to be heard by some tribunal competent fully to adjudicate his claims. Cf. Kwong Hai Chew v. Colding, 344 U. S. 590, 596-598 (1953); Opp Cotton Mills, Inc. v. Administrator, 312 U. S. 126, 152-153 (1941); United States v. Illinois Central R. Co., 291 U. S. 457, 463 (1934); Londoner v. City and County of Denver, 210 U. S. 373, 385 (1908); Dixon v. Alabama State Board of Education, 294 F. 2d 150 (1961). But cf. Ewing v. Mytinger & Casselberry, Inc., 339 U. S. 594 (1950); Bowles v. Willingham, 321 U. S. 503, 520 (1944); North American Cold Storage Co. v. Chicago, 211 U. S. 306 (1908). The validity of summary administrative deprivation of liberty without a full hearing may turn on the availability of a prompt subsequent hearing, cf. U. S. Const., Amdt. VI; United States v. Ewell, 383 U. S. 116, 120 (1966); Freedman v. Maryland, 380 U. S. 51 (1965)—something not made meaningfully available to petitioner here, either by the option of defending a criminal prosecution for refusing to report for induction, see Ex parte Young, 209 U. S. 123 (1908); Oklahoma Operating Co. v. Love, 252 U. S. 331 (1920); cf. Reisman v. Caplin, 375 U. S. 440 (1964), or by filing a petition for a writ of habeas corpus after induction. See ante, at 235-236; Estep v. United States, supra, at 129-130 (concurring opinion of Mr. Justice Murphy).

The problem is exacerbated by petitioner's nonfrivolous argument that induction pursuant to the delinquency reclassification procedure constitutes "punishment" for violation of collateral regulations, without jury trial, right to counsel, and other constitutional requisites. See Kennedy v. Mendoza-Martinez, 372 U. S. 144, 168-169 (1963). It is not necessary to decide this issue. If petitioner's claim is valid, however, then postponement of a hearing until after induction is tantamount to permitting the imposition of summary punishment, followed by loss of liberty, without possibility of bail, until such time as the petitioner is able to secure his release by a writ of habeas corpus. This would, at the very least, cut against the grain of much that is fundamental to our constitutional tradition. Cf. Hart, The Power of Congress to Limit the Jurisdiction of Federal Courts: An Exercise in Dialectic, 66 Harv. L. Rev. 1362, 1380-1383 (1953).

[7] The salient parts of the statute's sparse legislative history are set out in my Brother STEWART'S dissenting opinion, post, at 247-248. Both the House and Senate committees were "disturbed by the apparent inclination of some courts to review the classification action of local or appeal Boards before the registrant had exhausted his administrative remedies." H. R. Rep. No. 267, 90th Cong., 1st Sess., 30 (1967); S. Rep. No. 209, 90th Cong., 1st Sess., 10 (1967). As I have discussed in the preceding text, the Boards can provide no remedy for a registrant's claim that the regulations or statutes are themselves invalid. (This is not to say that a registrant making such a claim may come into court before he has exhausted his administrative appeals, for the System may decide in his favor on other grounds, obviating the need for further review. Cf. my dissent in Public Utilities Comm'n v. United States, supra, at 549-550; Aircraft & Diesel Equipment Corp. v. Hirsch, 331 U. S. 752, 772 (1947). Petitioner here has exhausted available remedies.

Appendix 4.)

Section 10 (b) (3) was likely precipitated by the Second Circuit's well-publicized decision in Wolff v. Selective Service Bd., 372 F. 2d 817 (1967). See dissenting opinion of MR. JUSTICE STEWART, post, at 247; Brief for Respondent 18, n. 4, 69, n. 32. Wolff, as well as the other "recent cases" to which the committee reports probably referred, and this Court's decisions construing the antecedent to § 10 (b) (3), all involved claims that the Selective Service Boards had maladministered or misapplied the applicable statutes or regulations, and not challenges to the validity of the laws themselves. Wolff v. Selective Service Bd., supra (loss of deferment for participating in demonstration); Townsend v. Zimmerman, 237 F. 2d 376 (1956) (failure to follow proper appeal procedure); Schwartz v. Strauss, 206 F. 2d 767 (1953) (concurring opinion) (misclassification); Ex parte Fabiani, 105 F. Supp. 139 (1952) (refusal to recognize foreign medical school for deferment); Tomlinson v. Hershey, 95 F. Supp. 72 (1949) (refusal to hear request for deferment); Estep v. United States, supra (entitlement to ministerial exemption); Falbo v. United States, 320 U. S. 549 (1944) (entitlement to conscientious objector status).

Justice Harlan's concurrence in Smith v. Hooey (Jan 20, 1969)

Separate opinion of MR. JUSTICE HARLAN.

I agree that a State may not ignore a criminal accused's request to be brought to trial, merely because he is incarcerated in another jurisdiction, but that it must make a reasonable effort to secure his presence for trial. This much is required by the Due Process Clause of the Fourteenth Amendment, and I would rest decision of this case on that ground, and not on "incorporation" of the Sixth Amendment's speedy-trial provision into the Fourteenth.

See my opinion concurring in the result in Klopfer v. North Carolina, 386 U. S. 213, 226 (1967).

I believe, however, that the State is entitled to more explicitness from us as to what is to be expected of it on remand than what is conveyed merely by the requirement that further proceedings not be "inconsistent with this opinion." Must the charges against petitioner be dismissed? Or may Texas now secure his presence and proceed to try him? If petitioner contends that he has been prejudiced by the nine-year delay, how is this claim to be adjudicated?

This case is one of first impression for us, and decides a question on which the state and lower federal courts have been divided. Under these particular circumstances, I do not believe that Texas should automatically forfeit the right to try petitioner. If the State still desires to bring him to trial, it should do so forthwith. At trial, if petitioner makes a prima facie showing that he has in fact been prejudiced by the State's delay, I would then shift to the State the burden of proving the contrary.

Justice Harlan's concurrence in dissent in Hunter v. Erickson (Jan 20, 1969)

MR. JUSTICE HARLAN, whom MR. JUSTICE STEWART joins, concurring.

At the outset, I think it well to sketch my constitutional approach to state statutes which structure the internal governmental process and which are challenged under the Equal Protection Clause of the Fourteenth Amendment. For equal protection purposes, I believe that laws which define the powers of political institutions fall into two classes. First, a statute may have the clear purpose of making it more difficult for racial and religious minorities to further their political aims. Like any other statute which is discriminatory on its face, such a law cannot be permitted to stand unless it can be supported by state interests of the most weighty and substantial kind. McLaughlin v. Florida, 379 U. S. 184, 192 (1964).

Most laws which define the structure of political institutions, however, fall into a second class. They are designed with the aim of providing a just framework within which the diverse political groups in our society may fairly compete and are not enacted with the purpose of assisting one particular group in its struggle with its political opponents. Consider, for example, Akron's procedure which requires that almost any ordinance be submitted to a general referendum if 10% of the electorate signs an appropriate petition.[*] This rule obviously does not have the purpose of protecting one particular group to the detriment of all others. It will sometimes operate in favor of one faction; sometimes in favor of another. Akron has adopted the referendum system because its citizens believe that whenever an action of the City Council raises the emotional opposition of any significant group in the community, the people should have a right to decide the matter directly. Statutes of this type, which are grounded upon general democratic principle, do not violate the Equal Protection Clause simply because they occasionally operate to disadvantage Negro political interests. If a governmental institution is to be fair, one group cannot always be expected to win. If the Council's fair housing legislation were defeated at a referendum, Negroes would undoubtedly lose an important political battle, but they would not thereby be denied equal protection.

This same analysis applies to other institutions of government which are even more solidly rooted in our history than is the referendum. The existence of a bicameral legislature or an executive veto may on occasion make it more difficult for minorities to achieve favorable legislation; nevertheless, they may not be attacked on equal protection grounds since they are founded on neutral principles. Similarly, the rule which makes it relatively difficult to amend a state constitution is commonly justified on the theory that constitutional provisions should be more thoroughly scrutinized and more soberly considered than are simple statutory enactments. Here, too, Negroes may stand to gain by the rule if a fair housing law is made part of the constitution, or they may lose if the constitution adopts a position of strict neutrality on the question. See Reitman v. Mulkey, 387 U. S. 369, 389 (1967) (dissenting opinion of HARLAN, J.). But even if Negroes are obliged to undertake the arduous task of amending the state constitution, they are not thereby denied equal protection. For the rule making constitutional amendment difficult is grounded in neutral principle.

In the case before us, however, the city of Akron has not attempted to allocate governmental power on the basis of any general principle. Here, we have a provision that has the clear purpose of making it more difficult for certain racial and religious minorities to achieve legislation that is in their interest. Since the charter amendment is discriminatory on its face, Akron must "bear a far heavier burden of justification" than is required in the normal case. McLaughlin v. Florida, 379 U. S. 184, 194 (1964). And Akron has failed to sustain this burden. The city's principal argument in support of the charter amendment relies on the undisputed fact that fair housing legislation may often be expected to raise the passions of the community to their highest pitch. It was not necessary, however, to pass this amendment in order to assure that particularly sensitive issues will ultimately be decided by the general electorate. Akron has already provided a procedure, which is grounded in neutral principle, that requires a general referendum on this issue if 10% of the voters insist. If the prospect of fair housing legislation really arouses passionate opposition, the voters will have the final say. Consequently, the charter amendment will have its real impact only when fair housing does not arouse extraordinary controversy. This being the case, I can perceive no legitimate state interest which in any degree vindicates the action taken by the City here.

As I read the Court's opinion to be entirely consistent with the basic principles which I believe control this case, I join in it.

[*] Section 25 of Akron's city charter exempts the following ordinances from the referendum procedure:

"(a) Annual appropriation ordinances. (b) Ordinances or resolutions providing for the approval or disapproval of appointments or removals and appointments or removals made by Council. (c) Actions by Council on the approval of official bonds. (d) Ordinances or resolutions providing for the submission of any proposition to the vote of the electors. (e) Ordinances providing for street improvements petitioned for by owners of a majority of the feet front of the property benefited and to be specially assessed for the cost thereof."

It is not suggested that any of these exceptions were made with the purpose of disadvantaging Negro political interests.

Justice Harlan's dissent in Alabama Teachers Assn. v. Alabama Public School and College Authority (Jan 20, 1969)

MR. JUSTICE HARLAN, dissenting.

Only two years ago, Moody v. Flowers, 387 U. S. 97, 101 (1967), made it clear that a three-judge court need not be convoked whenever "a state statute is involved but only when a state statute of general and statewide application is sought to be enjoined." Although this holding was solidly grounded in precedent and in policy, the Court today abandons Moody without explanation by taking jurisdiction to affirm this judgment summarily.

The case before us does not involve a statute of "general and statewide application." Appellants are simply trying to prevent the construction of a single public college to be located in the City of Montgomery. Appellants merely attack a statute which "authorize[s] the Alabama public school and college authority . . . to issue . . . additional bonds in the . . . amount of $5,000,000 for the purpose of constructing . . . a four-year college at Montgomery under the supervision and control of the board of trustees of Auburn University." Ala. Acts, No. 403 (1967).[1] The fate of this one school, like the fate of a county-wide reapportionment plan, Moody v. Flowers, supra, or the affairs of a regional drainage district, Rorick v. Commissioners, 307 U. S. 208 (1939), is not to be decided by a special three-judge court. As Moody and Rorick teach, the bare fact that a state statute is involved is not enough to trigger 28 U. S. C. § 2281.[2]

We do not deal here with a state statute which "embodies a policy of statewide concern," Spielman Motor Sales Co. v. Dodge, 295 U. S. 89, 94 (1935), but one which expresses a judgment that more educational facilities are needed in a particular locality. Indeed, appellants' constitutional attack on the statute is entirely based on the peculiar local situation existing in Montgomery. At present, there are two state-supported institutions of higher learning in the city. Alabama State is a four-year college which has traditionally been attended by Negroes. Alabama Extension Center, on the other hand, has a predominantly white enrollment, but does not at present grant degrees, offering its students a set of "extension" courses. The Extension Center, however, will be enlarged to create Montgomery's new four-year college, while Negro Alabama State has been entirely ignored in the planning. Appellants contend that, at a minimum, the State's College Authority was constitutionally obliged to consider the possibility of coordinating the new college's operations with those of Alabama State before the Authority could properly embark on its present course.

This brief outline of the facts demonstrates that we are dealing with an essentially local dispute which could properly be heard first by a single District Judge and then by the Court of Appeals before it came to us on certiorari.[3]

I would dismiss this appeal for want of jurisdiction.

Notes

[1] Although the appellants' original complaint also contained a challenge to the constitutionality of the Alabama statute creating the State's Public School and College Authority, Ala. Acts, No. 243 (1965), this challenge was abandoned at the hearing on the merits. See 289 F. Supp. 784, 785, n. 1 (1968).

[2] While my Brother DOUGLAS is quite right in noting that Brown v. Board of Education and two of its companion cases, 347 U. S. 483 (1954), were heard on appeal from three-judge District Courts, he fails to recognize that in each of those cases, appellants had sought to enjoin the operation of a state statute or constitutional provision of general application that either required or authorized racial segregation in public and

secondary schools. Id., at 486, n. 1. See also, McLaurin v. Oklahoma State Regents, 339 U. S. 637 (1950). In contrast, our "freedom-of-choice" decisions of last Term, Green v. County School Board, 391 U. S. 430 (1968); Raney v. Board of Education, 391 U. S. 443 (1968); Monroe v. Board of Commissioners, 391 U. S. 450 (1968), came to us on certiorari from the Fourth, Eighth, and Sixth Circuits respectively, precisely because the plans promulgated by the school boards in those cases were not of state-wide scope. See also Cooper v. Aaron, 358 U. S. 1 (1958) (on certiorari to the Eighth Circuit); Griffin v. School Board, 377 U. S. 218 (1964) (on certiorari to the Fourth Circuit); Bradley v. School Board, 382 U. S. 103 (1965) (on certiorari to the Fourth Circuit); Rogers v. Paul, 382 U. S. 198 (1965) (on certiorari to the Eighth Circuit); cf. Watson v. Memphis, 373 U. S. 526 (1963) (on certiorari to the Sixth Circuit).

Indeed, even when there is an attack on a state-wide statute which requires racial discrimination on its face, a three-judge court need not be convoked if the statute is clearly invalid under pre-existing case law. Bailey v. Patterson, 369 U. S. 31 (1962).

[3] Appellants themselves seem to have recognized that this Court's jurisdiction is questionable. They filed a protective appeal with the Court of Appeals for the Fifth Circuit on August 23, 1968. That court is holding the appeal in abeyance pending our decision in this case. See Jurisdictional Statement 2, n. 1.

Justice Harlan's concurrence in Presbyterian Church in US v. Mary Elizabeth Blue Hull Memorial Presbyterian Church (Jan 27, 1969)

MR. JUSTICE HARLAN, concurring.

I am in entire agreement with the Court's rejection of the "departure-from-doctrine" approach taken by the Georgia courts, as that approach necessarily requires the civilian courts to weigh the significance and the meaning of disputed religious doctrine. I do not, however, read the Court's opinion to go further to hold that the Fourteenth Amendment forbids civilian courts from enforcing a deed or will which expressly and clearly lays down conditions limiting a religious organization's use of the property which is granted. If, for example, the donor expressly gives his church some money on the condition that the church never ordain a woman as a minister or elder, see ante, at 442, n. 1, or never amend certain specified articles of the Confession of Faith, he is entitled to his money back if the condition is not fulfilled. In such a case, the church should not be permitted to keep the property simply because church authorities have determined that the doctrinal innovation is justified by the faith's basic principles. Cf. Watson v. Jones, 13 Wall. 679, 722-724 (1872).

On this understanding, I join the Court's opinion.

Justice Harlan's concurrence and dissent in SEC v. National Securities, Inc. (Jan 27, 1969)

MR. JUSTICE HARLAN, whom MR. JUSTICE STEWART joins, concurring in part and dissenting in part.

I concur entirely in Parts I and II of the Court's opinion construing the McCarran-Ferguson Act. But I am at a loss to understand why the Court finds it necessary to go further and construe Rule 10b-5 promulgated under § 10 (b) of the Securities Exchange Act of 1934. The Court of Appeals did not reach this question since it believed that the McCarran-Ferguson Act entirely exempted the transaction involved here from the commands of the federal securities laws. The Government's petition for certiorari is similarly limited. The only issue it raises is "[w]hether the McCarran-Ferguson Act . . . precludes the application of the anti-fraud provisions of the Securities Exchange Act of 1934. . . ." See Petition for Certiorari 2. When the respondents' brief on the merits argued that Rule 10b-5 did not apply to the present case, the Solicitor General did not even attempt to present the Government's position on that score because he quite properly believed that "the question is not appropriately before this Court for decision." Government's Reply Brief 2.

Despite the fact that we have not heard the views of the Securities and Exchange Commission, the Court chooses this case as a vehicle to construe for the first time one of the most important and elusive provisions of the securities laws. Moreover, the decision has far-reaching radiations, despite the fact that the precise issue presented is a narrow one. Courts and commentators have long debated whether Rule 10b-5 should be read as a sweeping prohibition against fraud in the securities industry when this results in rendering nullities of the other antifraud provisions of more limited scope which can be found in the statute books. See, e. g., §§ 11 (a), 12 (2), and 13 of the Securities Act of 1933; § 18 of the Securities and Exchange Act of 1934. The late Judge Jerome Frank,[1] Professor Louis Loss,[2] and Milton Cohen,[3]—to mention only three of those particularly eminent in this field—have warned that Rule 10b-5 should not be construed to supersede the special statutory schemes which Congress has devised to assure fair dealing in various aspects of the securities business. But see A. Bromberg, Securities Law § 2.5 (1967); Ellis v. Carter, 291 F. 2d 270 (1961). Even those who take an extremely broad view of the scope of the Rule have recognized that it could well be argued that the courts should not rush in to apply § 10 (b) to regulate proxy solicitations where Congress has refused to permit the Commission to intervene under § 14. See Bromberg, supra, § 6.5 (2), n. 93.1. Indeed, at one time the SEC itself was of the opinion that the Rule did not apply in cases of this sort. National Supply Co. v. Leland Stanford University, 134 F. 2d 689, 694 (1943). Nevertheless, the majority believes it can answer this question "rather quickly," ante, at 468, without any real recognition of the basic principles which hang in the balance.

In addition, the Court has chosen to adopt a very loose construction of the requirement, first enunciated by Judge Augustus Hand in Birnbaum v. Newport Steel Corp., 193 F. 2d 461 (1951), cert. denied 343 U. S. 956 (1952), that a transaction must involve a "purchase" or "sale" of securities before it may be found to violate Rule 10b-5. While some commentators have welcomed the erosion of this doctrine, see Lowenfels, The

Demise of the Birnbaum Doctrine: A New Era for Rule 10b-5, 54 Va. L. Rev. 268 (1968), especially in injunction actions initiated by the SEC, Note, The Purchaser-Seller Limitation to SEC Rule 10b-5, 53 Cornell L. Rev. 684, 694-697 (1968), others believe that "Birnbaum seems basically correct." 3 L. Loss, Securities Regulation 1469. As recently as 1964, the Second Circuit rendered a decision which has been commonly understood to have reaffirmed the vitality of the Birnbaum doctrine, with my Brother MARSHALL casting the deciding vote. O'Neill v. Maytag, 339 F. 2d 764, 768 (1964);[4] see Lowenfels, supra, at 270.

I am unwilling to decide these fundamental matters without full-dress argument. Indeed, if the courts of appeals are not to be permitted to develop the law in this area on a case-by-case basis, I think it much wiser for us to consider the basic issues in a case which squarely raises them rather than in one which is of marginal importance.

Notes

[1] Fischman v. Raytheon Manufacturing Co., 188 F. 2d 783 (1951).

[2] 3 Securities Regulation 1787-1791 (1961).

[3] "Truth in Securities" Revisited, 79 Harv. L. Rev. 1340, 1370 n. 89 (1966).

[4] Both O'Neill and Birnbaum were of course private actions, and I do not mean to suggest that my Brother MARSHALL is flatly inconsistent in now ruling that the "purchase" and "sale" requirement has been met in this case involving the SEC's request for an injunction. Nevertheless, both private and public actions arise under the same Rule, and the legal problems involved in the two situations, while not identical, are closely related.

Justice Harlan's dissent in Tinker v. Des Moines Indept. Comm. Sch. Dist. (Feb 24, 1969)

MR. JUSTICE HARLAN, dissenting.

I certainly agree that state public school authorities in the discharge of their responsibilities are not wholly exempt from the requirements of the Fourteenth Amendment respecting the freedoms of expression and association. At the same time I am reluctant to believe that there is any disagreement between the majority and myself on the proposition that school officials should be accorded the widest authority in maintaining discipline and good order in their institutions. To translate that proposition into a workable constitutional rule, I would, in cases like this, cast upon those complaining the burden of showing that a particular school measure was motivated by other than legitimate school concerns—for example, a desire to prohibit the expression of an unpopular point of view, while permitting expression of the dominant opinion.

Finding nothing in this record which impugns the good faith of respondents in promulgating the armband regulation, I would affirm the judgment below.

Justice Harlan's concurrence and dissent in Allen v. State Bd. of Elections (March 3, 1969)

MR. JUSTICE HARLAN, concurring in part and dissenting in part.

The Court's opinion seeks to do justice by granting each side half of what it requests. The majority first grants appellants all they could hope for, by adopting an overly broad construction of § 5 of the Voting Rights Act. As if to compensate for its generosity, the Court then denies some of the same appellants the relief that they deserve. Section 5 is thereby reduced to a dead letter in a very substantial number of situations in which it was intended to have its full effect.[1]

I.

I shall first consider the Court's extremely broad construction of § 5. It is best to begin by delineating the precise area of difference between the position the majority adopts and the one which I consider represents the better view of the statute. We are in agreement that in requiring federal review of changes in any "standard, practice, or procedure with respect to voting," Congress intended to include all state laws that changed the process by which voters were registered and had their ballots counted. The Court, however, goes further to hold that a State covered by the Act must submit for federal approval all those laws that could arguably have an impact on Negro voting power, even though the manner in which the election is conducted remains unchanged. I believe that this reading of the statute should be rejected on several grounds. It ignores the place of § 5 in the larger structure of the Act; it is untrue to the statute's language; and it is unsupported by the legislative history.

A.

First, and most important, the Court's construction ignores the structure of the complex regulatory scheme created by the Voting Rights Act. The Court's opinion assumes that § 5 may be considered apart from the rest of the Act. In fact, however, the provision is clearly designed to march in lock-step with § 4—the two sections cannot be understood apart from one another. Section 4 is one of the Act's central provisions, suspending the operation of all literacy tests and similar "devices"[2] for at least five years in States whose low voter turnout indicated that these "tests" and "devices" had been used to exclude Negroes from the suffrage in the past. Section 5, moreover, reveals that it was not designed to implement new substantive policies but that it was structured to assure the effectiveness of the dramatic step that Congress had taken in § 4. The federal approval procedure found in § 5 only applies to those States whose literacy tests or similar "devices" have been suspended by § 4. As soon as a State regains the right to apply a literacy test or similar "device" under § 4, it also escapes the commands of § 5.

The statutory scheme contains even more striking characteristics which indicate that § 5's federal review procedure is ancillary to § 4's substantive commands. A State may escape § 5, even though it has consistently violated this provision, so long as it has complied with § 4, and has suspended the operation of literacy tests and other "devices" for five years. On the other hand, no matter how faithfully a State complies with § 5, it remains subject to its commands so long as it has not consistently obeyed § 4.[3]

As soon as it is recognized that § 5 was designed solely to implement the policies of § 4, it becomes apparent that the Court's decision today permits the tail to wag the dog. For the Court has now construed § 5 to require a revolutionary innovation in American government that goes far beyond that which was accomplished by § 4. The fourth section of the Act had the profoundly important purpose of permitting the Negro people to gain access to the voting booths of the South once and for all. But the action taken by Congress in § 4 proceeded on the premise that once Negroes had gained free access to the ballot box, state governments would then be suitably responsive to their voice, and federal intervention would not be justified. In moving against "tests and devices" in § 4, Congress moved only against those techniques that prevented Negroes from voting at all. Congress did not attempt to restructure state governments. The Court now reads § 5, however, as vastly increasing the sphere of federal intervention beyond that contemplated by § 4, despite the fact that the two provisions were designed simply to interlock. The District Court for the District of Columbia is no longer limited to examining any new state statute that may tend to deny Negroes their right to vote, as the "tests and devices" suspended by § 4 had done. The decision today also requires the special District Court to determine whether various systems of representation favor or disfavor the Negro voter—an area well beyond the scope of § 4. Section 4, for example, does not apply to States and localities which have in the past permitted Negroes to vote freely, but which arguably have limited minority voting power by adopting a system in which various legislative bodies are elected on an at-large basis. And yet, in Fairley v. Patterson, No. 25, the Court holds that a statute permitting the at-large election of county boards of supervisors must be reviewed by federal authorities under § 5. Moreover, it is not clear to me how a court would go about deciding whether an at-large system is to be preferred over a district system. Under one system, Negroes have some influence in the election of all officers; under the other, minority groups have more influence in the selection of fewer officers. If courts cannot intelligently compare such alternatives, it should not be readily inferred that Congress has required them to undertake the task.

The Court's construction of § 5 is even more surprising in light of the Act's regional application. For the statute, as the Court now construes it, deals with a problem that is national in scope. I find it especially difficult to believe that Congress would single out a handful of States as requiring stricter federal supervision concerning their treatment of a problem that may well be just as serious in parts of the North as it is in the South.[4]

The difficulties with the Court's construction increase even further when the language of the statute is considered closely. When standing alone, the statutory formula requiring federal approval for changes in any "standard, practice, or procedure with respect to voting" can be read to support either the broad construction adopted by the majority or the one which I have advanced. But the critical formula does not stand alone. Immediately following the statute's description of the federal approval procedure, § 5 proceeds to describe the type of relief an aggrieved voter may obtain if a State enforces a new statute without obtaining the consent of the appropriate federal authorities: "no person shall be denied the right to vote for failure to comply with such qualification, prerequisite, standard, practice, or procedure." (Emphasis supplied.) This remedy serves to delimit the meaning of the formula in question. Congress was clearly concerned with changes in procedure with which voters could comply. But a law, like that in Fairley v. Patterson, No. 25, which permits all members of the County Board of Supervisors to run in the entire county and not in smaller districts, does not require a voter to comply with anything at all, and so does not come within the scope of the language used by Congress. While the Court's opinion entirely ignores the obvious implications of this portion of the statute, the Solicitor General's amicus brief candidly admits that this provision is flatly inconsistent with the broad reading the Government has advanced and this Court has adopted. The Government's brief simply suggests that Congress' choice of the verb "comply" was merely the result of an oversight. I cannot accept such a suggestion, however, when Congress' choice of language seems to me to be consistent with the general statutory framework as I understand it.

    B.

    While the Court's opinion does not confront the factors I have just canvassed, it does attempt to justify its holding on the basis of its understanding "of the legislative history and an analysis of the basic purposes of the Act." Ante, at 569. Turning first to consider the Act's basic purposes, the Court suggests that Congress intended to adopt the concept of voting articulated in Reynolds v. Sims, 377 U. S. 533 (1964), and protect Negroes against a dilution of their voting power. See ante, at 565-566, 569. It is clear, of course, that the Court's reapportionment decisions do not apply of their own force to the problem before us. This is a statute we are interpreting, not a broad constitutional provision whose contours must be defined by this Court. The States are required to submit certain kinds of legislation for federal approval only if Congress, acting within its powers, so provided. And the fact is that Congress consciously refused to base § 5 of the Voting Rights Act on its powers under the Fourteenth Amendment, upon which the reapportionment cases are grounded. The Act's preamble states that it is intended "[t]o enforce the fifteenth amendment to the Constitution of the United States, and for other purposes." When Senator Fong of Hawaii suggested that the preamble include a citation to the Fourteenth Amendment as well, the Attorney General explained that he "would have quite a strong preference not to," because "I believe that S. 1564 as drafted can be squarely based on the 15th amendment." Hearings on S. 1564 before the Senate Committee on the Judiciary, 89th Cong., 1st Sess., pt. 1, p. 193. Attorney General Katzenbach's position was restated repeatedly,[5] and any mention of the Fourteenth Amendment is absent from this portion of the statute.[6]

    As the reapportionment cases rest upon the Equal Protection Clause, they cannot be cited to support the claim that Congress, in passing this Act, intended to proceed against state statutes regulating the nature of the constituencies legislators could properly represent. If Congress intended, as it clearly did, to ground § 5 on the Fifteenth Amendment, the leading voting case is not Reynolds v. Sims, but Gomillion v. Lightfoot, 364 U. S. 339 (1960). While that case establishes the proposition that redistricting done with the purpose of excluding Negroes from a municipality violates the Fifteenth Amendment, it also maintains the distinction between an attempt to exclude Negroes totally from the relevant constituency, and a statute that permits Negroes to vote but which uses the gerrymander to contain the impact of Negro suffrage.

It is unnecessary, of course, to decide whether Gomillion v. Lightfoot marks the limit of the Fifteenth Amendment. It is enough to recognize that Congress did not in any way adopt the reapportionment cases' expansive concept of voting when it enacted the Voting Rights Act of 1965. Once it is determined that Reynolds v. Sims holds no magic key to the "basic purposes" of this statute, one is obliged to determine the Act's purposes in more traditional ways. And it is here where the Court's opinion fails to convince. As I have already suggested, the Act's structure assigns to § 5 a role that is a good deal more modest than the one which the majority gives it.[7]

The majority is left, then, relying on its understanding of the legislative history. With all deference, I find that the history the Court has garnered undermines its case, insofar as it is entitled to any weight at all. I refer not only to the unequivocal statement of Assistant Attorney General Burke Marshall, ante, at 564, which the Court concedes to be diametrically opposed to the construction it adopts. For the lengthy testimony of Attorney General Katzenbach, upon which the Court seems to rely, actually provides little more support for its position. Mr. Katzenbach, unlike his principal assistant, was never directly confronted with the question raised here, and we are left to guess as to his views. If guesses are to be made, however, surely it is important to note that though the Attorney General used many examples to illustrate the operation of § 5, each of them concerned statutes that had an immediate impact on voter qualifications or which altered the manner in which the election was conducted.[8] One would imagine that if the Attorney General believed that § 5 had the remarkable sweep the majority has now given it, one of his hypotheticals would have betrayed that fact.[9]

C.

Section 5, then, should properly be read to require federal approval only of those state laws that change either voter qualifications or the manner in which elections are conducted. This does not mean, however, that the District Courts in the four cases before us were right in unanimously concluding that the Voting Rights Act did not apply. Rather, it seems to me that only the judgment in Fairley v. Patterson, No. 25, should be affirmed, as that case involves a state statute which simply gives each county the right to elect its Board of Supervisors on an at-large basis.

In Whitley v. Williams, No. 36, however, Mississippi's new statute both imposes new qualifications on independent voters who wish to nominate a candidate by petition and alters the manner in which such nominations are made.[10] Since the Voting Rights Act explicitly covers "primary" elections, see § 14 (c) (1), the only significant question presented is whether a petitioning procedure should be considered a "primary" within the meaning of the Act. As the nominating petition is the functional equivalent of the political primary, I can perceive no good reason why it should not be included within the ambit of the Act.

The statute involved in Bunton v. Patterson, No. 26, raises a somewhat more difficult problem of statutory interpretation. If one looks to its impact on the voters, the State's law making the office of school superintendent appointive enacts a "voting qualification" of the most drastic kind. While under the old regime all registered voters could cast a ballot, now none are qualified. On the other hand, one can argue that the concept of a "voting qualification" presupposes that there will be a vote. On balance, I would hold that the statute comes within § 5. Cf. Gomillion v. Lightfoot, supra. Such a holding would not, of course, disable the State from adopting an appointive system after the force of § 5 has spent itself.

Finally, Virginia has quite obviously altered the manner in which an election is conducted when for the first time it has been obliged to issue regulations concerning the way in which illiterate voters shall be processed at the polls. Consequently, I would reverse the lower court's decision in the Allen case, No. 3.

II.

After straining to expand the scope of § 5 beyond its proper limits, the majority surprisingly refuses to grant appellants in the Mississippi cases[11] the only relief that will effectively implement the Act's purposes. As the Court recognizes, ante, at 572, the Voting Rights Act only applies to the States for a limited period of time— Mississippi may free itself from § 5's requirements in 1970.[12] And yet the Court affords appellants in the Mississippi cases only declaratory relief, permitting state officials selected in violation of § 5 to hold office until their four-year terms expire in 1971.[13] An election for these offices may never be held in compliance with Congress' commands. And of course, the Court's decision respecting relief does not only control these particular cases. There may have been hundreds of officials throughout the South who began serving long terms in office this November under procedures that have not been federally approved. As a result of this part of the Court's decision, the Voting Rights Act may never play the full role that Congress intended for it.

It seems clear to me that we should issue a conditional injunction in the Mississippi cases along the lines suggested by the Solicitor General, except of course in the Fairley case which I think should be affirmed. Unless Mississippi promptly submits its laws to either the Attorney General or the District Court for the District of Columbia, new elections under the pre-existing law should be ordered. Of course, if the laws are promptly submitted for approval, a new election should be required only if the District Court determines that the statute in question is discriminatory either in its purpose or in its effect.

Notes

[1] I concur in the Court's disposition of the complex jurisdictional issues these cases present. While I consider the question whether § 5 authorizes a three-judge court a close one, it is clear to me that we would not avoid very many three-judge courts whatever we decide. I would suspect that generally a plaintiff attacking a state statute because it has not been federally approved under § 5 could also make at least a substantial constitutional claim that the state statute is discriminatory in its purpose or effect. Consequently, in the usual case a three-judge court would always be convened under 28 U. S. C. § 2281. Once convened, the Court would, of course, first consider the plaintiff's § 5 argument in the name of avoiding a constitutional question. Therefore, it appears to me that there is no good reason to invoke the normal rule that three-judge court statutes should be construed as narrowly as possible. As the Court suggests, the more natural reading of the statute confers jurisdiction on three-judge courts even in an action brought by private parties.

[2] Section 4 (c) reads:

"The phrase `test or device' shall mean any requirement that a person as a prerequisite for voting or registration for voting (1) demonstrate the ability to read, write, understand, or interpret any matter, (2) demonstrate any educational achievement or his knowledge of any particular subject, (3) possess good moral character, or (4) prove his qualifications by the voucher of registered voters or members of any other class."

[3] The Solicitor General expressly adopts this construction of the statute in his supplemental amicus brief. In any event, the Act is clear: § 4 (a) permits a State to free itself from § 4 by proving to a District Court in the District of Columbia that no "test or device has been used during the five years preceding the filing of the action for the purpose or with the effect of denying or abridging the right to vote on account of race or color." (Emphasis supplied.) As already noted, see n. 2, supra, the phrase "test or device" is a term of art including a class of statutes much narrower than those included under § 5. However, since § 5 applies by its own terms only to "a State or political subdivision with respect to which the prohibitions set forth in section 4 (a) are in effect," a State that escapes from § 4, escapes from § 5 as well, even though it has not complied with that section.

[4] Indeed, I would have very substantial constitutional difficulties with the statute if I were to accept such a construction.

[5] See, e. g., Senate Hearings, supra, at 35, 141; Hearings on H. R. 6400 before Subcommittee No. 5 of the House Committee on the Judiciary, 89th Cong., 1st Sess., ser. 2, p. 102.

[6] When, in § 10 of the Act, Congress moved against the imposition of poll taxes, it expressly invoked the Fourteenth Amendment as providing an additional basis for its action in this specific area. See § 10 (b).

[7] The Court seeks to strengthen its case by looking to the language of one of the definitional sections of the Act. Ante, at 565-566. Section 14 (c) (1) defines the term "vote" or "voting" to "include all action necessary to make a vote effective in any primary, special, or general election, including, but not limited to, registration, listing pursuant to this Act,

or other action required by law prerequisite to voting, casting a ballot, and having such ballot counted properly and included in the appropriate totals of votes cast with respect to candidates for public or party office and propositions for which votes are received in an election." (Emphasis supplied.) All of the aspects of voting that are enumerated in this definition concern the procedures by which voters are processed. When the statute cautions that its enumeration of stages in the election process is not exclusive, it merely indicates that the change of any other procedure that prevents the voter from having his ballot finally counted is also included within the range of the Act's concern. Surely the Court is entirely ignoring the textual context when it seeks to read the italicized phrases as embracing all electoral laws that affect the amount of political power Negroes will derive from the exercise of the franchise, even when the way in which voters are processed remains unchanged.

[8] The examples given by the Attorney General concerned changes in a State's voting age, residence, or property requirements; changes in the frequency that registrars' offices are open; and changes from paper ballots to machines or vice versa. See House Hearings, supra, n. 5, at 60-62, 95; Senate Hearings, supra, at 191-192, 237.

[9] The Court emphasizes three specific colloquies in which Mr. Katzenbach participated to support its understanding of the legislative history. In the most important one, see ante, at 566-567, n. 31, Senator Fong expressed concern that § 5, which at that time merely required federal review of changes in state "procedures," would not encompass a state regulation which would radically limit the hours during which new voters could register. The Attorney General agreed that the statute should be elaborated to more clearly include such a change. Since such a law alters the manner in which voters are processed, I fail to see how this colloquy undermines my construction of the section—which clearly requires federal review in cases of the sort Mr. Katzenbach and Senator Fong were discussing. Similarly, a second extract highlighted by the Court, ante, at 567-568, is one in which the Attorney General emphasizes that § 5 is intended to prevent the States from evading the requirements of § 4—a point I believe to count strongly in favor of the interpretation I deem the correct one. Finally, it is quite true that the Attorney General opposed carving out exceptions from § 5 that would permit the State to switch from paper ballots to voting machines without federal approval. See ante, at 568. But this fact hardly indicates that he or anyone else was of the opinion that the section required review of statutes that did not concern themselves with voting procedures. In fact, on the one occasion that Mr. Katzenbach discussed the reapportionment cases in connection with § 5, he indicated no awareness whatever that § 5 could be construed to apply to cases involving laws that change the voting power of various groups. See House Hearings, supra, at 93-94.

[10] The statute requires supporters of a candidate to write their own names on the nominating petition, together with their polling district. Moreover, petitions must be filed by an earlier date and must contain many more signatures. The Act also imposes a "voting qualification" on those who wish to vote in a party primary, by providing that they may not subsequently compete with the primary victor by running as an independent

candidate.

[11] In the Allen case, coming from Virginia, the term of the Congressman who gained his seat under procedures that have not been approved under § 5 has already expired. Consequently, only a grant of declaratory relief is appropriate in this case, as the appellants themselves recognize.

[12] Since the Voting Rights Act became effective in Mississippi in August 1965, the State will be able to escape the requirements of § 5 in 1970 by proving that it has not imposed a "test or device" in violation of § 4 for a five-year period. See text, at n. 3, supra. Section 5 will only continue to apply after 1970 if Mississippi is found to have continued imposing "tests or devices" after 1965. The Court's decision today, however, does not consider whether any of the statutes involved in these cases impose a "test" or "device" within the meaning of § 4, see n. 2, supra. It simply holds that the statutes fall into the much broader class of laws that modify a "standard, practice, or procedure with respect to voting" under § 5.

[13] The state senator, state representative, county supervisor, justice of the peace, and constable involved in Whitley v. Williams, No. 36, were all elected for four-year terms ending in 1971. See Mississippi Code § 3238 (1942). Similarly, the affected county superintendents of education in Bunton v. Patterson, No. 26, were appointed to four-year terms, expiring in 1971.

While I would affirm in Fairley v. Patterson, No. 25, the incumbents in that case also will serve until 1971.

Justice Harlan's dissent in Desist v. US (March 24, 1969)

MR. JUSTICE HARLAN, dissenting.

In the four short years since we embraced the notion that our constitutional decisions in criminal cases need not be retroactively applied, Linkletter v. Walker, 381 U. S. 618 (1965),[1] we have created an extraordinary collection of rules to govern the application of that principle. We have held that certain "new" rules are to be applied to all cases then subject to direct review, Linkletter v. Walker, supra; Tehan v. Shott, 382 U. S. 406 (1966); certain others are to be applied to all those cases in which trials have not yet commenced, Johnson v. New Jersey, 384 U. S. 719 (1966); certain others are to be applied to all those cases in which the tainted evidence has not yet been introduced at trial, Fuller v. Alaska, 393 U. S. 80 (1968); and still others are to be applied only to the party involved in the case in which the new rule is announced and to all future cases in which the proscribed official conduct has not yet occurred. Stovall v. Denno, 388 U. S. 293 (1967); DeStefano v. Woods, 392 U. S. 631 (1968).

Although it has more than once been said that "new" rules affecting "the very integrity of the fact-finding process," are to be retroactively applied, Linkletter v. Walker, supra, at 639; see also Tehan v. Shott, supra, at 416; Fuller v. Alaska, supra, at 81, this requirement was eroded to some extent in Johnson v. New Jersey, supra, at 728-729, and yet further in Stovall v. Denno, supra, at 299; see also DeStefano v. Woods, supra. Again, although it has been said that a decision will be retroactively applied when it has been "clearly foreshadowed" in our prior case law, Johnson v. New Jersey, supra, at 731; Berger v. California, 393 U. S. 314 (1969), the Court today rejects such a contention. Ante, at 248. Indeed, the Court now also departs from pre-existing doctrine in refusing retroactive application within the federal system of the "new" rule ultimately laid down in Katz v. United States, 389 U. S. 347 (1967), despite its concession that "relatively few" federal cases would have to be reconsidered. Compare ante, at 251-252, with Linkletter v. Walker, supra, at 637; Tehan v. Shott, supra, at 418-419; Johnson v. New Jersey, supra, at 731-732; Stovall v. Denno, supra, at 300.

I have in the past joined in some of those opinions which have, in so short a time, generated so many incompatible rules and inconsistent principles. I did so because I thought it important to limit the impact of constitutional decisions which seemed to me profoundly unsound in principle. I can no longer, however, remain content with the doctrinal confusion that has characterized our efforts to apply the basic Linkletter principle. "Retroactivity" must be rethought.

I.

RETROACTIVITY ON DIRECT REVIEW.

Upon reflection, I can no longer accept the rule first announced two years ago in Stovall v. Denno, supra, and reaffirmed today, which permits this Court to apply a "new" constitutional rule entirely prospectively, while making an exception only for the particular litigant whose case was chosen as the vehicle for establishing that rule. Indeed, I have concluded that Linkletter was right in insisting that all "new" rules of constitutional law must, at a minimum, be applied to all those cases which are still subject to direct review by this Court at the time the "new" decision is handed down.

Matters of basic principle are at stake. In the classical view of constitutional adjudication, which I share, criminal defendants cannot come before this Court simply to request largesse. This Court is entitled to decide constitutional issues only when the facts of a particular case require their resolution for a just adjudication on the merits. See Marbury v. Madison, 1 Cranch 137 (1803). We do not release a criminal from jail because we like to do so, or because we think it wise to do so, but only because the government has offended constitutional principle in the conduct of his case. And when another similarly situated defendant comes before us, we must grant the same relief or give a principled reason for acting differently. We depart from this basic judicial tradition when we simply pick and choose from among similarly situated defendants those who alone will receive the benefit of a "new" rule of constitutional law.

The unsound character of the rule reaffirmed today is perhaps best exposed by considering the following hypothetical. Imagine that the Second Circuit in the present case had anticipated the line of reasoning this Court subsequently pursued in Katz v. United States, supra, at 352-353, concluding—as this Court there did— that "the underpinnings of Olmstead and Goldman have been so eroded by our subsequent decisions that the `trespass' doctrine there enunciated can no longer be regarded as controlling." Id., at 353. Would we have reversed the case on the ground that the principles the Second Circuit had announced—though identical with those in Katz—should not control because Katz is not retroactive? To the contrary, I venture to say that we would have taken satisfaction that the lower court had reached the same conclusion we subsequently did in Katz. If a "new" constitutional doctrine is truly right, we should not reverse lower courts which have accepted it; nor should we affirm those which have rejected the very arguments we have embraced. Anything else would belie the truism that it is the task of this Court, like that of any other, to do justice to each litigant on the merits of his own case. It is only if our decisions can be justified in terms of this fundamental premise that they may properly be considered the legitimate products of a court of law, rather than the commands of a super-legislature.

Re-examination of prior developments in the field of retroactivity leads me irresistibly to the conclusion that the only solid disposition of this case lies in vacating the judgment of the Court of Appeals and in remanding this case to that court for further consideration in light of Katz.

II.

RETROACTIVITY ON HABEAS CORPUS.

What has already been said is, from my standpoint, enough to dispose of the case before us. Ordinarily I would not go further. But in this instance I consider it desirable and appropriate to venture some observations on the application of the retroactivity doctrine in habeas corpus cases, under the prevailing scope of the "Great Writ" as set forth in this Court's 1963 decision in Fay v. Noia, 372 U. S. 391, and in today's decision in Kaufman v. United States, ante, p. 217. I believe this course is fitting because none of the Court's prior retroactivity decisions has faced up to the quite different factors which should govern the application of retroactivity in habeas corpus cases; because the retroactive application of Katz in habeas corpus cases would seem to be foreclosed by the present decision; because principled habeas retroactivity now seems to me to demand much more than the "purpose," "reliance," and judicial "administration" standards, ante, at 249, which have so far been regarded as the tests governing retroactivity in direct review and habeas corpus cases alike; and because the retroactivity doctrine is still in a developing stage. In what ensues I shall simply try to suggest some of the considerations which appear to me to lay bare the complexities of the retroactivity problem on habeas which I feel have not been sufficiently explored in past decisions, leaving expression of definitive views upon any of such considerations for future habeas cases to which they are germane.

A.

While, as I have argued, a reviewing court has the obligation to rule upon every decisive issue properly raised by the parties on direct review, the federal courts have never had a similar obligation on habeas corpus.

Indeed, until Brown v. Allen, 344 U. S. 443 (1953), federal courts would never consider the merits of a constitutional claim if the habeas petitioner had a fair opportunity to raise his arguments in the original proceeding.[2] See my dissent in Fay v. Noia, supra, at 449-463; see also Bator, Finality in Criminal Law and Federal Habeas Corpus for State Prisoners, 76 Harv. L. Rev. 441, 463 (1963). With habeas restricted in this way, the question of applying a "new" constitutional rule to convictions which had become final arose so infrequently that the retroactivity issue could not be considered a significant one in those days. Even under Brown, the retroactive application of "new" rules in habeas cases did not serve to erode the finality of criminal judgments to any substantial degree. It was the rare case in which the habeas petitioner had raised a "new" constitutional argument both at his original trial and on appeal. Yet it was only in such a case that Brown would permit a habeas court to apply the "new" rule. Cf. Sunal v. Large, 332 U. S. 174 (1947).

The conflict between retroactivity and finality only became of major importance with the Court's decision in Fay v. Noia, supra. For the first time, it was there held that, at least in some instances, a habeas petitioner could successfully attack his conviction collaterally despite the fact that the "new" rule had not even been suggested in the original proceedings. Thus, Noia opened the door for large numbers of prisoners to relitigate their convictions each time a "new" constitutional rule was announced by this Court.

I continue to believe that Noia, which has been given even broader scope in Kaufman v. United States, supra, constitutes an indefensible departure both from the historical principles which defined the scope of the "Great Writ" and from the principles of federalism which have formed the bedrock of our constitutional development. Nevertheless, my views on this score have not prevailed, and pending re-examination of the scope of habeas corpus, I believe myself obliged to consider on its own bottom the retroactivity problem which Noia has spawned, since it is a matter of the greatest importance if the integrity of the federal judicial process is to be maintained in this era of increasingly rapid constitutional change.

B.

The greatly expanded writ of habeas corpus seems at the present time to serve two principal functions. See Kaufman v. United States, supra, at 229; Mishkin, The Supreme Court, 1964 Term—Foreword: The High Court, The Great Writ, and the Due Process of Time and Law, 79 Harv. L. Rev. 56, 77-101 (1965). First, it seeks to assure that no man has been incarcerated under a procedure which creates an impermissibly large risk that the innocent will be convicted. It follows from this that all "new" constitutional rules which significantly improve the pre-existing fact-finding procedures are to be retroactively applied on habeas. See my Brother BLACK'S dissent in Kaufman v. United States, supra, at 235-236. The new habeas, however, is not only concerned with those rules which substantially affect the fact-finding apparatus of the original trial. Under the prevailing notions, Kaufman v. United States, supra, at 224-226, the threat of habeas serves as a necessary additional incentive for trial and appellate courts throughout the land to conduct their proceedings in a manner consistent with established constitutional standards. In order to perform this deterrence function, the habeas court need not, as prior cases make clear, necessarily apply all "new" constitutional rules retroactively. In these cases, the habeas court need only apply the constitutional standards that prevailed at the time the original proceedings took place.

The theory that the habeas petitioner is entitled to the law prevailing at the time of his conviction is, however, one which is more complex than the Court has seemingly recognized. First, it is necessary to determine whether a particular decision has really announced a "new" rule at all or whether it has simply applied a well-established constitutional principle to govern a case which is closely analogous to those which have been previously considered in the prior case law. Only a short time ago, for example, we attempted to define with more precision the conditions governing the issuance of a search warrant under the Fourth Amendment. Spinelli v. United States, 393 U. S. 410 (1969). While we had never previously encountered the precise situation raised in Spinelli, our decision in that case rested upon the established doctrine that a magistrate may issue a warrant only when he can judge for himself the validity of the affiant's conclusion that criminal activity is involved. Johnson v. United States, 333 U. S. 10, 14 (1948); Aguilar v. Texas, 378 U. S. 108 (1964). Surely, it could not be thought that Spinelli should not be retroactively applied under the expanded habeas process because it was not announced until 1969. One need not be a rigid partisan of Blackstone to recognize that many, though not all, of this Court's constitutional decisions are grounded upon fundamental principles whose content does not change dramatically from year to year, but whose meanings are altered slowly and subtly as generation succeeds generation. In such a context it appears very difficult to argue against the application of the "new" rule in all habeas cases since one could never say with any assurance that this Court would have ruled differently at the time the petitioner's conviction became final.

In the Katz case, however, one can say with assurance that there was a time at which this Court would have ruled differently. For in Olmstead, Goldman, and On Lee,[3] the Court did just that. Even under the prevailing view of habeas, this fact should be of significance. Although the threat of collateral attack may be necessary to assure that the lower federal and state courts toe the constitutional line, the lower courts cannot be faulted when, following the doctrine of stare decisis, they apply the rules which have been authoritatively announced by this Court. If anyone is responsible for changing these rules, it is this Court.

Even in this situation, however, the doctrine of stare decisis cannot always be a complete answer to the retroactivity problem if a habeas petitioner is really entitled to the constitutional law which prevailed at the time of his conviction. Consider, for example, the state of Fourth Amendment law as it existed after our decision in Silverman v. United States, 365 U. S. 505 (1961). As my Brother STEWART notes today, ante, at 248, Silverman went a long way toward rejecting the principles supporting the Goldman and Olmstead rules. The Court in Silverman cautioned that the scope of the Fourth Amendment's protection is "not inevitably measurable in terms of ancient niceties of tort or real property law." 365 U. S., at 511. The majority's opinion concluded with the warning:

"We find no occasion to re-examine Goldman here, but we decline to go beyond it, by even a fraction of an inch." Id., at 512. It is hard to believe that any lawyer worthy of the name could, after reading Silverman, rely with confidence on the continuing vitality of the Goldman rule. Nor is it by any means clear to me that it would have been improper for a lower court to have declined to follow Goldman in the light of Silverman.[4] Given the deterrence purpose of the expanded habeas corpus, it thus could be persuasively argued that the Katz rule should be applied to all cases which had not become final at the time Silverman was decided.[5]

C.

Katz, of course, has been one of the lesser innovations of a decade that has witnessed revolutionary changes in the most fundamental premises of hitherto accepted constitutional law. And similar difficulties arise as to the retroactive application of the Court's other landmark decisions if one is to insist that a habeas petitioner is entitled to the law as it stood at the time of his conviction. It is possible to argue, for example, that the Court's decision in Mapp v. Ohio, 367 U. S. 643 (1961), imposing the exclusionary rule on the States, was a sufficient indication to the lower courts that they should no longer rely on the doctrine of stare decisis when confronted with the claim that other Bill of Rights guarantees should be incorporated into the Due Process Clause of the Fourteenth Amendment. It would follow from this position that all subsequent decisions incorporating various other provisions of the Bill of Rights into Due Process should be applied to all cases arising on habeas which were pending on appeal at the time Mapp was decided.

On the other hand, one could argue that stare decisis was still the appropriate rule for the lower courts until this Court made it clear that a particular guarantee was applicable to the States. It would follow from this position that the Court's decision in Griffin v. California, 380 U. S. 609 (1965), should be retroactively applied only to Malloy v. Hogan, 378 U. S. 1 (1964), which was the first case beginning the process of incorporating the Fifth Amendment's privilege against self-incrimination, and that Duncan v. Louisiana, 391 U. S. 145 (1968), should not be applied to any of those cases which had become final before that decision required the States to provide criminal jury trials on the same basis as the Federal Government.

Neither of these positions would be squarely inconsistent with the Court's new view of habeas corpus. Indeed, if the Court in Mapp had given any indication whatever that it accepted my Brother BLACK'S "incorporationist" philosophy in its pristine purity, see Adamson v. California, 332 U. S. 46, 68-123 (1947), it would appear that it would have been improper for the lower courts to rely on the old precedents to respond to the new claims advanced by criminal defendants. However, the Court has never accepted MR. JUSTICE BLACK'S constitutional premises in full-blown form. Instead, it has embarked on a course of "selective incorporation" in which the nature of each particular Bill of Rights guarantee has been examined before it was imposed upon the States. Given the ad hoc character of this approach, and given the fundamental place of federalism in the traditional conception of constitutional adjudication, it could certainly be strongly argued that the lower courts could properly follow the traditional due process approach until the time this Court made it clear that a particular Bill of Rights guarantee had been incorporated.

The relationship for retroactivity purposes among the Escobedo, Miranda, Wade, and Gilbert decisions[6] presents another difficult problem under the new habeas corpus concept. It can be argued that the "line-up" cases, Wade and Gilbert, should be retroactively applied to all those cases pending when Miranda was decided. Since Miranda placed affirmative requirements upon police officers to assure that the accused would have an opportunity to obtain counsel at one "critical stage" of the criminal process, neither police officials nor the lower courts, it might be argued, could properly assume that other critical stages would not be comparably treated. Similarly, it may be suggested that the rules announced in both Miranda and the "line-up" cases should be applied to all cases still pending on appeal when Escobedo v. Illinois announced that the Sixth Amendment applied in the police station. For Gideon v. Wainwright, 372 U. S. 335 (1963), had already established the proposition that the State must provide free counsel to indigents at the criminal trial.

It is doubtless true that a habeas court encounters difficult and complex problems if it is required to chart out the proper implications of the governing precedents at the time of a petitioner's conviction. One may well argue that it is of paramount importance to make the "choice of law" problem on habeas as simple as possible, applying each "new" rule only to those cases pending at the time it is announced. While this would obviously be simpler, simplicity would be purchased at the cost of compromising the principle that a habeas petitioner is to have his case judged by the constitutional standards dominant at the time of his conviction.

I do not pretend to have exhausted in the foregoing discussion all the complexities of the retroactivity problem on habeas. But the considerations I have canvassed suggest that we should take a hard look at where we are going in the retroactivity field so that this new doctrine may be administered in accordance with the basics of the judicial tradition. Unfortunately, the Court does not even attempt this task.

For the reasons stated in Part I of this opinion I cannot subscribe to the affirmance of the judgment of the Court of Appeals. I would remand the case to that court for reconsideration in light of Katz v. United States.

Notes

[1] In one instance this doctrine has been applied to a nonconstitutional decision. See Lee v. Florida, 392 U. S. 378 (1968), and its aftermath in Fuller v. Alaska, 393 U. S. 80 (1968).

[2] An exception to this general rule was made, however, when the habeas petitioner attacked the constitutionality of the state statute under which he had been convicted. See, e. g., Ex parte Siebold, 100 U. S. 371 (1880). Since, in this situation, the

State had no power to proscribe the conduct for which the petitioner was imprisoned, it could not constitutionally insist that he remain in jail.

[3] Olmstead v. United States, 277 U. S. 438 (1928); Goldman v. United States, 316 U. S. 129 (1942); On Lee v. United States, 343 U. S. 747 (1952).

[4] After Silverman was decided, we were careful to frame our decisions in such a way that a direct consideration of the "trespass" doctrine could be avoided. In Lopez v. United States, 373 U. S. 427, 439 (1963), we noted that: "The validity of [Olmstead and Goldman] is not in question here. Indeed this case involves no `eavesdropping' whatever in any proper sense of that term. The Government did not use an electronic device to listen in on conversations it could not otherwise have heard. Instead, the device was used only to obtain the most reliable evidence possible of a conversation in which the Government's own agent was a participant. . . ." In Berger v. New York, 388 U. S. 41, the Court found that New York's eavesdropping statute contained impermissibly vague standards even with regard to the authorization of electronic surveillance requiring a trespass. It concluded that "[t]his disposition obviates the necessity for any discussion of the other points raised." Id., at 44. Moreover, Berger made it clear that we had rejected Olmstead's declaration that the Fourth Amendment did not protect the integrity of private conversations. Such an action would hardly strengthen a lawyer's or lower court's confidence in the continuing vitality of the "trespass" doctrine, which is also rooted in Olmstead.

Finally, the Court's suggestion that our unexplicated per curiam reversal in Clinton v. Virginia, 377 U. S. 158 (1964), was premised upon the "trespass" doctrine, see ante, at 248, n. 11, is not supported by the opinion in that case. Only Mr. Justice Clark expressly predicated his decision upon the doctrine. The other seven members of the majority did not state the ground upon which the reversal was based.

[5] While I do not question much that my Brother FORTAS says in his dissenting opinion, I am unable to adopt the extreme position on retroactivity he proposes. Before Silverman was decided in 1961, no decision of this Court had undermined the conceptual basis of the Olmstead rule. Before 1961, even the most conscientious police department or judge had no reason to doubt the validity of the "trespass" rule. Nevertheless, MR. JUSTICE FORTAS would grant habeas corpus to prisoners whose convictions became final before Silverman. This result cannot be justified even if one assumes that it is proper for a habeas court to require "conceptual faithfulness" to our opinions and "not merely decisional obedience" to the rules they announce. See post, at 277.

[6] Escobedo v. Illinois, 378 U. S. 478 (1964); Miranda v. Arizona, 384 U. S. 436 (1966); United States v. Wade, 388 U. S. 218 (1967); Gilbert v. California, 388 U. S. 263 (1967).

Justice Harlan's dissent in Kaiser v. New York (March 24, 1969)

MR. JUSTICE HARLAN, dissenting.

It is conceded that petitioner's conviction rested largely upon evidence acquired by nontrespassory wiretapping conducted pursuant to a warrant issued under N. Y. Code Crim. Proc. § 813-a. The Court affirms the conviction on the ground that today's decision in Desist v. United States, ante, p. 244, necessarily dictates that evidence obtained by an illegal, nontrespassory wiretap will be inadmissible only if the tapping occurred after the date of the decision in Katz v. United States, 389 U. S. 347 (1967). The wiretapping in this case took place prior to Katz. However, the case is here on direct review, and for the reasons stated in Part I of my dissenting opinion in Desist, supra, at 258-259, I would hold that petitioner is entitled to benefit from the Katz rule.

It is therefore necessary for me to consider whether petitioner's federal constitutional rights were violated by the wiretapping. Were I free to do so, I would decide this issue by inquiring whether, on the facts of this particular case and in light of New York decisions construing § 813-a, the wiretapping was valid under the Warrants Clause of the Fourth Amendment. See Ker v. California, 374 U. S. 23, 30-34 (1963); see also Mapp v. Ohio, 367 U. S. 643 (1961). However, I believe that this approach is foreclosed by this Court's decision in Berger v. New York, 388 U. S. 41 (1967). In Berger, the Court held that a "bugging" pursuant to a § 813-a warrant violated the petitioner's Fourth Amendment rights because on its face the statute did not contain constitutionally required safeguards. It is true that the "bugging" in Berger involved a trespass and that the Court did not reach the question whether Olmstead should be overruled. But the holding that § 813-a was to be considered on its face rather than as applied depended in no way upon the fact of physical intrusion. The warrant procedure prescribed in § 813-a applies equally to "bugging" and to wiretapping. Hence, the Court's "on its face" approach would seem necessarily to embrace § 813-a wiretapping.

I dissented from the "on its face" approach adopted in Berger. See 388 U. S., at 89 et seq. I continue to disagree with that approach. Yet I think that Berger must be taken as having decided that a warrant issued pursuant to the version of § 813-a then in effect could not possibly satisfy the requirements of the Fourth Amendment.[*] Since I regard myself as bound by Berger, I am reluctantly compelled to conclude that the wiretap evidence introduced against petitioner was seized in violation of the Constitution, and that his conviction consequently cannot stand.

[*] There were no amendments to § 813-a between June 1962, the date of the "bugging" in Berger, and July 1964, the date of the wiretapping in this case. Nor in my view is it necessary to decide whether Berger should be "retroactive." The present case was on direct appeal in the New York courts at the time Berger was decided, and petitioner is therefore entitled to invoke Berger under the rule advanced in Part I of my dissenting opinion in Desist.

Justice Harlan's dissent in Wells v. Rockefeller (April 7, 1969)

MR. JUSTICE HARLAN, with whom MR. JUSTICE STEWART joins,

dissenting.[*]

Whatever room remained under this Court's prior decisions for the free play of the political process in matters of reapportionment is now all but eliminated by today's Draconian judgments. Marching to the nonexistent "command of Art. I, § 2" of the Constitution,[1] the Court now transforms a political slogan into a constitutional absolute. Strait indeed is the path of the righteous legislator. Slide rule in hand, he must avoid all thought of county lines, local traditions, politics, history, and economics, so as to achieve the magic formula: one man, one vote.

As my Brothers WHITE and FORTAS demonstrate, insistence on mathematical perfection does not make sense even on its own terms. Census figures themselves are inexact; our mobile population rapidly renders them obsolete; large groups of ineligible voters are unevenly distributed throughout the State. Nevertheless, the Court refuses to permit any room for legislative common sense to compensate for Census Bureau inadequacies. If no "scientific" data are available to justify a divergence from census figures, the Court holds that nothing can be done—"we mean to open no avenue for subterfuge." Kirkpatrick v. Preisler, ante, at 535.

This all-pervasive distrust of the legislative process is completely alien to established notions of judicial review. See Butler v. Pennsylvania, 10 How. 402 (1851); Davis v. Department of Labor, 317 U. S. 249 (1942); Flemming v. Nestor, 363 U. S. 603 (1960). Nor does it have precedent in the prior reapportionment decisions themselves. "Reynolds v. Sims . . . recognized that mathematical exactness is not required in state apportionment plans. De minimis deviations are unavoidable . . . ." Swann v. Adams, 385 U. S. 440, 444 (1967); see also Wesberry v. Sanders, 376 U. S. 1, 18 (1964).[2]

Even more important, the Court's exclusive concentration upon arithmetic blinds it to the realities of the political process, as the Rockefeller case makes so clear. The fact of the matter is that the rule of absolute equality is perfectly compatible with "gerrymandering" of the worst sort. A computer may grind out district lines which can totally frustrate the popular will on an overwhelming number of critical issues. The legislature must do more than satisfy one man, one vote; it must create a structure which will in fact as well as theory be responsive to the sentiments of the community. On the record before us, however, there is absolutely no indication that the New York Legislature can satisfy this Court's demand for absolute equality and yet create a structure which will permit New York's multitude of political groups to have a fair chance at having their voices heard in Congress.

Even the appellant himself does not suggest that it is possible to create a proper apportionment plan which is at the same time consistent with the demands of perfect mathematical equality. The plan he advances contemplates a maximum deviation of 4.7% from the state average, which represents an improvement of only 1.9 percentage points on the State's 6.6% deviation. Moreover, under the State's plan, a majority of the congressional delegation can represent no less than 49.3% of the population. The appellant's scheme "improves" this figure by 0.5%, increasing the number to 49.8%. See

Appellant's Appendix D. Perfection, however, is still 0.2% away.

Although the appellant's plan offers such marginal benefits of voting egalitarianism, and although the record contains no suggestion of any other plan which even arguably permits the coherent expression of the popular will, the Court rejects the legislature's considered proposal simply because it seeks to remain true to traditional county and regional lines. In doing so, the majority ignores the salutary warning to be found in Reynolds v. Sims, 377 U. S. 533, 578-579 (1964): "Indiscriminate districting, without any regard for political subdivision or natural or historical boundary lines, may be little more than an open invitation to partisan gerrymandering." Yet, today the Court condemns the legislature's approach because it "permit[s] groups of districts with defined interest orientations to be overrepresented at the expense of districts with different interest orientations." Ante, at 546. Of course, all districting decisions inevitably involve choices between different interest groups. But as Reynolds recognized, legislatures prefer to follow traditional county and regional lines so that the demands of blatant partisanship will be tempered by the constraints of history and tradition. If the Court believes it has struck a blow today for fully responsive representative democracy, it is sorely mistaken. Even more than in the past, district lines are likely to be drawn to maximize the political advantage of the party temporarily dominant in public affairs.

We do not deal here with the hopelessly malapportioned legislature unwilling to set its own house in order. Rather, the question before us is whether the Constitution requires that mathematics be a substitute for common sense in the art of statecraft. As I do not think that the apportionment plans submitted by the States of New York and Missouri can properly be regarded as offensive to the requirement of equality imposed in Wesberry—a case whose constitutional reasoning I still find it impossible to swallow, but by whose dictate I consider myself bound—I dissent.

I would reverse the judgments of the District Court in the Missouri cases and affirm the decision of the District Court in the New York case.

[*] [This opinion applies also to No. 30, Kirkpatrick v. Preisler, ante, p. 526.]

Notes

[1] See ante, at 546; Kirkpatrick v. Preisler, ante, at 531. I have discussed in my dissenting opinion in Wesberry v. Sanders, 376 U. S. 1, 20 (1964), the extraordinary historical leap involved in reading the straightforward constitutional provision that "The House of Representatives shall be composed of Members chosen every second Year by the People of the several States . . ." as a command for equal districts.

[2] While Wesberry cautions that "it may not be possible to draw congressional districts with mathematical precision," 376 U. S., at 18, it did not attempt to delineate the extent to which the States may properly deviate from the "ideal."

Justice Harlan's dissent in Shapiro v. Thompson (April 21, 1969) [Notes omitted]

MR. JUSTICE HARLAN, dissenting.

The Court today holds unconstitutional Connecticut, Pennsylvania, and District of Columbia statutes which restrict certain kinds of welfare benefits to persons who have lived within the jurisdiction for at least one year immediately preceding their applications. The Court has accomplished this result by an expansion of the comparatively new constitutional doctrine that some state statutes will be deemed to deny equal protection of the laws unless justified by a "compelling" governmental interest, and by holding that the Fifth Amendment's Due Process Clause imposes a similar limitation on federal enactments. Having decided that the "compelling interest" principle is applicable, the Court then finds that the governmental interests here asserted are either wholly impermissible or are not "compelling." For reasons which follow, I disagree both with the Court's result and with its reasoning.

I.

These three cases present two separate but related questions for decision. The first, arising from the District of Columbia appeal, is whether Congress may condition the right to receive Aid to Families with Dependent Children (AFDC) and Aid to the Permanently and Totally Disabled in the District of Columbia upon the recipient's having resided in the District for the preceding year.[1] The second, presented in the Pennsylvania and Connecticut appeals, is whether a State may, with the approval of Congress, impose the same conditions with respect to eligibility for AFDC assistance.[2] In each instance, the welfare residence requirements are alleged to be unconstitutional on two grounds: first, because they impose an undue burden upon the constitutional right of welfare applicants to travel interstate; second, because they deny to persons who have recently moved interstate and would otherwise be eligible for welfare assistance the equal protection of the laws assured by the Fourteenth Amendment (in the state cases) or the analogous protection afforded by the Fifth Amendment (in the District of Columbia case). Since the Court basically relies upon the equal protection ground, I shall discuss it first.

II.

In upholding the equal protection argument,[3] the Court has applied an equal protection doctrine of relatively recent vintage: the rule that statutory classifications which either are based upon certain "suspect" criteria or affect "fundamental rights" will be held to deny equal protection unless justified by a "compelling" governmental interest. See ante, at 627, 634, 638.

The "compelling interest" doctrine, which today is articulated more explicitly than ever before, constitutes an increasingly significant exception to the long-established rule that a statute does not deny equal protection if it is rationally related to a legitimate governmental objective.[4] The "compelling interest" doctrine has two branches. The branch which requires that classifications based upon "suspect" criteria be supported by a compelling interest apparently had its genesis in cases involving racial classifications, which have, at least since Korematsu v. United States, 323 U. S. 214, 216 (1944), been regarded as inherently "suspect."[5] The criterion of "wealth" apparently was added to the list of "suspects" as an alternative justification for the rationale in Harper v. Virginia Bd. of Elections, 383 U. S. 663, 668 (1966), in which Virginia's poll tax was struck down. The criterion of political allegiance may have been added in Williams v. Rhodes, 393 U. S. 23 (1968).[6] Today the list apparently has been further enlarged to include classifications based upon recent interstate movement, and perhaps those based upon the exercise of any constitutional right, for the Court states, ante, at 634:

"The waiting-period provision denies welfare benefits to otherwise eligible applicants solely because they have recently moved into the jurisdiction. But in moving . . . appellees were exercising a constitutional right, and any classification which serves to penalize the exercise of that right, unless shown to be necessary to promote a compelling governmental interest, is unconstitutional."[7]

I think that this branch of the "compelling interest" doctrine is sound when applied to racial classifications, for historically the Equal Protection Clause was largely a product of the desire to eradicate legal distinctions founded upon race. However, I believe that the more recent extensions have been unwise. For the reasons stated in my dissenting opinion in Harper v. Virginia Bd. of Elections, supra, at 680, 683-686, I do not consider wealth a "suspect" statutory criterion. And when, as in Williams v. Rhodes, supra, and the present case, a classification is based upon the exercise of rights guaranteed against state infringement by the Federal Constitution, then there is no need for any resort to the Equal Protection Clause; in such instances, this Court may properly and straightforwardly invalidate any undue burden upon those rights under the Fourteenth Amendment's Due Process Clause. See, e. g., my separate opinion in Williams v. Rhodes, supra, at 41.

The second branch of the "compelling interest" principle is even more troublesome. For it has been held that a statutory classification is subject to the "compelling interest" test if the result of the classification may be to affect a "fundamental right," regardless of the basis of the classification. This rule was foreshadowed in Skinner v. Oklahoma, 316 U. S. 535, 541 (1942), in which an Oklahoma statute providing for compulsory sterilization of "habitual criminals" was held subject to "strict scrutiny" mainly because it affected "one of the basic civil rights." After a long hiatus, the principle reemerged in Reynolds v. Sims, 377 U. S. 533, 561-562 (1964), in which state apportionment statutes were subjected to an unusually stringent test because "any alleged infringement of the right of citizens to vote must be carefully and meticulously scrutinized." Id., at 562. The rule appeared again in Carrington v. Rash, 380 U. S. 89, 96 (1965), in which, as I now see that case,[8] the Court applied an abnormally severe equal protection standard to a Texas statute denying certain servicemen the right to vote, without indicating that the statutory distinction between servicemen and civilians was generally "suspect." This branch of the doctrine was also an alternate ground in Harper v. Virginia Bd. of Elections, supra, see 383 U. S., at 670, and apparently was a basis of the holding in Williams v. Rhodes, supra.[9] It has reappeared today in the Court's cryptic suggestion, ante, at 627, that the "compelling interest" test is applicable merely because the result of the classification may be to deny the appellees "food, shelter, and other necessities of life," as well as in the Court's statement, ante, at 638, that "[s]ince the classification here touches on the fundamental right of interstate movement, its constitutionality must be judged by the stricter standard of whether it promotes a compelling state interest."[10]

I think this branch of the "compelling interest" doctrine particularly unfortunate and unnecessary. It is unfortunate because it creates an exception which threatens to swallow the standard equal protection rule. Virtually every state statute affects important rights. This Court has repeatedly held, for example, that the traditional equal protection standard is applicable to statutory classifications affecting such fundamental matters as the right to pursue a particular occupation,[11] the right to receive greater or smaller wages[12] or to work more or less hours,[13] and the right to inherit property.[14] Rights such as these are in principle indistinguishable from those involved here, and to extend the "compelling interest" rule to all cases in which such rights are affected would go far toward making this Court a "super-legislature." This branch of the doctrine is also unnecessary. When the right affected is one assured by the Federal Constitution, any infringement can be dealt with under the Due Process Clause. But when a statute affects only matters not mentioned in the Federal Constitution and is not arbitrary or irrational, I must reiterate that I know of nothing which entitles this Court to pick out particular human activities, characterize them as "fundamental," and give them added protection under an unusually stringent equal protection test.

I shall consider in the next section whether welfare residence requirements deny due process by unduly burdening the right of interstate travel. If the issue is regarded purely as one of equal protection, then, for the reasons just set forth, this nonracial classification should be judged by ordinary equal protection standards. The applicable criteria are familiar and well established. A legislative measure will be found to deny equal protection only if "it is without any reasonable basis and therefore is purely arbitrary." Lindsley v. Natural Carbonic Gas Co., 220 U. S. 61, 78 (1911). It is not enough that the measure results incidentally "in some inequality," or that it is not drawn "with mathematical nicety," ibid.; the statutory classification must instead cause "different treatments . . . so disparate, relative to the difference in classification, as to be wholly arbitrary." Walters v. City of St. Louis, 347 U. S. 231, 237 (1954). Similarly, this Court has stated that where, as here, the issue concerns the authority of Congress to withhold "a noncontractual benefit under a social welfare program. . . , the Due Process Clause [of the Fifth Amendment] can be thought to interpose a bar only if the statute manifests a patently arbitrary classification, utterly lacking in rational justification." Flemming v. Nestor, 363 U. S. 603, 611 (1960).

For reasons hereafter set forth, see infra, at 672-677, a legislature might rationally find that the imposition of a welfare residence requirement would aid in the accomplishment of at least four valid governmental objectives.

It might also find that residence requirements have advantages not shared by other methods of achieving the same goals. In light of this undeniable relation of residence requirements to valid legislative aims, it cannot be said that the requirements are "arbitrary" or "lacking in rational justification." Hence, I can find no objection to these residence requirements under the Equal Protection Clause of the Fourteenth Amendment or under the analogous standard embodied in the Due Process Clause of the Fifth Amendment.

    III.

    The next issue, which I think requires fuller analysis than that deemed necessary by the Court under its equal protection rationale, is whether a one-year welfare residence requirement amounts to an undue burden upon the right of interstate travel. Four considerations are relevant: First, what is the constitutional source and nature of the right to travel which is relied upon? Second, what is the extent of the interference with that right? Third, what governmental interests are served by welfare residence requirements? Fourth, how should the balance of the competing considerations be struck?

    The initial problem is to identify the source of the right to travel asserted by the appellees. Congress enacted the welfare residence requirement in the District of Columbia, so the right to travel which is invoked in that case must be enforceable against congressional action. The residence requirements challenged in the Pennsylvania and Connecticut appeals were authorized by Congress in 42 U. S. C. § 602 (b), so the right to travel relied upon in those cases must be enforceable against the States even though they have acted with congressional approval.

    In my view, it is playing ducks and drakes with the statute to argue, as the Court does, ante, at 639-641, that Congress did not mean to approve these state residence requirements. In 42 U. S. C. § 602 (b), quoted more fully, ante, at 638-639, Congress directed that:

      "[t]he Secretary shall approve any [state assistance] plan which fulfills the conditions specified in subsection (a) of this section, except that he shall not approve any plan which imposes as a condition of eligibility for [AFDC aid] a residence requirement [equal to or greater than one year]."

    I think that by any fair reading this section must be regarded as conferring congressional approval upon any plan containing a residence requirement of up to one year.

    If any reinforcement is needed for taking this statutory language at face value, the overall scheme of the AFDC program and the context in which it was enacted suggest strong reasons why Congress would have wished to approve limited state residence requirements. Congress determined to enlist state assistance in financing the AFDC program, and to administer the program primarily through the States. A previous Congress had already enacted a one-year residence requirement with respect to aid for dependent children in the District of Columbia.[15] In these circumstances, I think it only sensible to conclude that in allowing the States to impose limited residence conditions despite their possible impact on persons who wished to move interstate,[16] Congress was motivated by a desire to encourage state participation in the AFDC program,[17] as well as by a feeling that the States should at least be permitted to impose residence requirements as strict as that already authorized for the District of Columbia. Congress therefore had a genuine federal purpose in allowing the States to use residence tests. And I fully agree with THE CHIEF JUSTICE that this purpose would render § 602 (b) a permissible exercise of Congress' power under the Commerce Clause, unless Congress were prohibited from acting by another provision of the Constitution.

Nor do I find it credible that Congress intended to refrain from expressing approval of state residence requirements because of doubts about their constitutionality or their compatibility with the Act's beneficent purposes. With respect to constitutionality, a similar residence requirement was already in effect for the District of Columbia, and the burdens upon travel which might be caused by such requirements must, even in 1935, have been regarded as within the competence of Congress under its commerce power. If Congress had thought residence requirements entirely incompatible with the aims of the Act, it could simply have provided that state assistance plans containing such requirements should not be approved at all, rather than having limited approval to plans containing residence requirements of less than one year. Moreover, when Congress in 1944 revised the AFDC program in the District of Columbia to conform with the standards of the Act, it chose to condition eligibility upon one year's residence,[18] thus strongly indicating that it doubted neither the constitutionality of such a provision nor its consistency with the Act's purposes.[19]

Opinions of this Court and of individual Justices have suggested four provisions of the Constitution as possible sources of a right to travel enforceable against the federal or state governments: the Commerce Clause;[20] the Privileges and Immunities Clause of Art. IV, § 2;[21] the Privileges and Immunities Clause of the Fourteenth Amendment;[22] and the Due Process Clause of the Fifth Amendment.[23] The Commerce Clause can be of no assistance to these appellees, since that clause grants plenary power to Congress,[24] and Congress either enacted or approved all of the residence requirements here challenged. The Privileges and Immunities Clause of Art. IV, § 2,[25] is irrelevant, for it appears settled that this clause neither limits federal power nor prevents a State from distinguishing among its own citizens, but simply "prevents a State from discriminating against citizens of other States in favor of its own." Hague v. CIO, 307 U. S. 496, 511 (1939) (opinion of Roberts, J.); see Slaughter-House Cases, 16 Wall. 36, 77 (1873). Since Congress enacted the District of Columbia residence statute, and since the Pennsylvania and Connecticut appellees were residents and therefore citizens of those States when they sought welfare, the clause can have no application in any of these cases.

The Privileges and Immunities Clause of the Fourteenth Amendment provides that: "No State shall make or enforce any law which shall abridge the privileges or immunities of citizens of the United States." It is evident that this clause cannot be applicable in the District of Columbia appeal, since it is limited in terms to instances of state action. In the Pennsylvania and Connecticut cases, the respective States did impose and enforce the residence requirements. However, Congress approved these requirements in 42 U. S. C. § 602 (b). The fact of congressional approval, together with this Court's past statements about the nature of the Fourteenth Amendment Privileges and Immunities Clause, leads me to believe that the clause affords no additional help to these appellees, and that the decisive issue is whether Congress itself may impose such requirements. The view of the Privileges and Immunities Clause which has most often been adopted by the Court and by individual Justices is that it extends only to those "privileges and immunities" which "arise or grow out of the relationship of United States citizens to the national government." Hague v. CIO, 307 U. S. 496, 520 (1939) (opinion of Stone, J.).[26] On the authority of Crandall v. Nevada, 6 Wall. 35 (1968), those privileges and immunities have repeatedly been said to include the right to travel from State to State,[27] presumably for the reason assigned in Crandall: that state restrictions on travel might interfere with intercourse between the Federal Government and its citizens.[28] This kind of objection to state welfare residence requirements would seem necessarily to vanish in the face of congressional authorization, for except in those instances when its authority is limited by a constitutional provision binding upon it (as the Fourteenth Amendment is not), Congress has full power to define the relationship between citizens and the Federal Government.

Some Justices, notably the dissenters in the Slaughter-House Cases, 16 Wall. 36, 83, 111, 124 (1873) (Field, Bradley, and Swayne, JJ., dissenting), and the concurring Justices in Edwards v. California, 314 U. S. 160, 177, 181 (1941) (DOUGLAS and Jackson, JJ., concurring), have gone further and intimated that the Fourteenth Amendment right to travel interstate is a concomitant of federal citizenship which stems from sources even more basic than the need to protect citizens in their relations with the Federal Government. The Slaughter-House dissenters suggested that the privileges and immunities of national citizenship, including freedom to travel, were those natural rights "which of right belong to the citizens of all free governments," 16 Wall., at 98 (Field, J.). However, since such rights are "the rights of citizens of any free government," id., at 114 (Bradley, J.), it would appear that they must be immune from national as well as state abridgment. To the extent that they may be validly limited by Congress, there would seem to be no reason why they may not be similarly abridged by States acting with congressional approval.

The concurring Justices in Edwards laid emphasis not upon natural rights but upon a generalized concern for the functioning of the federal system, stressing that to allow a State to curtail "the rights of national citizenship would be to contravene every conception of national unity," 314 U. S., at 181 (DOUGLAS, J.), and that "[i]f national citizenship means less than [the right to move interstate] it means nothing." Id., at 183 (Jackson, J.). However, even under this rationale the clause would appear to oppose no obstacle to congressional delineation of the rights of national citizenship, insofar as Congress may do so without infringing other provisions of the Constitution. Mr. Justice Jackson explicitly recognized in Edwards that: "The right of the citizen to migrate from state to state . . . [is] subject to all constitutional limitations imposed by the federal government," id., at 184. And nothing in the nature of federalism would seem to prevent Congress from authorizing the States to do what Congress might validly do itself. Indeed, this Court has held, for example, that Congress may empower the States to undertake regulations of commerce which would otherwise be prohibited by the negative implications of the Commerce Clause. See Prudential Ins. Co. v. Benjamin, 328 U. S. 408 (1946). Hence, as has already been suggested, the decisive question is whether Congress may legitimately enact welfare residence requirements, and the Fourteenth Amendment Privileges and Immunities Clause adds no extra force to the appellees' attack on the requirements.

The last possible source of a right to travel is one which does operate against the Federal Government: the Due Process Clause of the Fifth Amendment.[29] It is now settled that freedom to travel is an element of the "liberty" secured by that clause. In Kent v. Dulles, 357 U. S. 116, 125-126 (1958), the Court said:

"The right to travel is a part of the `liberty' of which the citizen cannot be deprived without due process of law under the Fifth Amendment. . . . Freedom of movement across frontiers . . . , and inside frontiers as well, was a part of our heritage. . . ."

The Court echoed these remarks in Aptheker v. Secretary of State, 378 U. S. 500, 505-506 (1964), and added:

"Since this case involves a personal liberty protected by the Bill of Rights, we believe that the proper approach to legislation curtailing that liberty must be that adopted by this Court in NAACP v. Button, 371 U. S. 415, and Thornhill v. Alabama, 310 U. S. 88. . . . [S]ince freedom of travel is a constitutional liberty closely related to rights of free speech and association, we believe that appellants. . . should not be required to assume the burden of demonstrating that Congress could not have written a statute constitutionally prohibiting their travel." Id., at 516-517.

However, in Zemel v. Rusk, 381 U. S. 1 (1965), the First Amendment cast of the Aptheker opinion was explained as having stemmed from the fact that Aptheker was forbidden to travel because of "expression or association on his part," id., at 16. The Court noted that Zemel was "not being forced to choose between membership in an organization and freedom to travel," ibid., and held that the mere circumstance that Zemel's proposed journey to Cuba might be used to collect information of political and social significance was not enough to bring the case within the First Amendment category.

Finally, in United States v. Guest, 383 U. S. 745 (1966), the Court again had occasion to consider the right of interstate travel. Without specifying the source of that right, the Court said:

"The constitutional right to travel from one State to another . . . occupies a position fundamental to the concept of our Federal Union. It is a right that has been firmly established and repeatedly recognized.. . . [The] right finds no explicit mention in the Constitution. The reason, it has been suggested, is that a right so elementary was conceived from the beginning to be a necessary concomitant of the stronger Union the Constitution created. In any event, freedom to travel throughout the United States has long been recognized as a basic right under the Constitution." Id., at 757-758. (Footnotes omitted.)

I therefore conclude that the right to travel interstate is a "fundamental" right which, for present purposes, should be regarded as having its source in the Due Process Clause of the Fifth Amendment.

The next questions are: (1) To what extent does a one-year residence condition upon welfare eligibility interfere with this right to travel?; and (2) What are the governmental interests supporting such a condition? The consequence of the residence requirements is that persons who contemplate interstate changes of residence, and who believe that they otherwise would qualify for welfare payments, must take into account the fact that such assistance will not be available for a year after arrival. The number or proportion of persons who are actually deterred from changing residence by the existence of these provisions is unknown. If one accepts evidence put forward by the appellees,[30] to the effect that there would be only a minuscule increase in the number of welfare applicants were existing residence requirements to be done away with, it follows that the requirements do not deter an appreciable number of persons from moving interstate.

Against this indirect impact on the right to travel must be set the interests of the States, and of Congress with respect to the District of Columbia, in imposing residence conditions. There appear to be four such interests. First, it is evident that a primary concern of Congress and the Pennsylvania and Connecticut Legislatures was to deny welfare benefits to persons who moved into the jurisdiction primarily in order to collect those benefits.[31] This seems to me an entirely legitimate objective. A legislature is certainly not obliged to furnish welfare assistance to every inhabitant of the jurisdiction, and it is entirely rational to deny benefits to those who enter primarily in order to receive them, since this will make more funds available for those whom the legislature deems more worthy of subsidy.[32]

A second possible purpose of residence requirements is the prevention of fraud. A residence requirement provides an objective and workable means of determining that an applicant intends to remain indefinitely within the jurisdiction. It therefore may aid in eliminating fraudulent collection of benefits by nonresidents and persons already receiving assistance in other States. There can be no doubt that prevention of fraud is a valid legislative goal. Third, the requirement of a fixed period of residence may help in predicting the budgetary amount which will be needed for public assistance in the future. While none of the appellant jurisdictions appears to keep data sufficient to permit the making of detailed budgetary predictions in consequence of the requirement,[33] it is probable that in the event of a very large increase or decrease in the number of indigent newcomers the waiting period would give the legislature time to make needed adjustments in the welfare laws. Obviously, this is a proper objective. Fourth, the residence requirements conceivably may have been predicated upon a legislative desire to restrict welfare payments financed in part by state tax funds to persons who have recently made some contribution to the State's economy, through having been employed, having paid taxes, or having spent money in the State. This too would appear to be a legitimate purpose.[34]

The next question is the decisive one: whether the governmental interests served by residence requirements outweigh the burden imposed upon the right to travel. In my view, a number of considerations militate in favor of constitutionality. First, as just shown, four separate, legitimate governmental interests are furthered by residence requirements. Second, the impact of the requirements upon the freedom of individuals to travel interstate is indirect and, according to evidence put forward by the appellees themselves, insubstantial. Third, these are not cases in which a State or States, acting alone, have attempted to interfere with the right of citizens to travel, but one in which the States have acted within the terms of a limited authorization by the National Government, and in which Congress itself has laid down a like rule for the District of Columbia. Fourth, the legislatures which enacted these statutes have been fully exposed to the arguments of the appellees as to why these residence requirements are unwise, and have rejected them. This is not, therefore, an instance in which legislatures have acted without mature deliberation.

Fifth, and of longer-range importance, the field of welfare assistance is one in which there is a widely recognized need for fresh solutions and consequently for experimentation. Invalidation of welfare residence requirements might have the unfortunate consequence of discouraging the Federal and State Governments from establishing unusually generous welfare programs in particular areas on an experimental basis, because of fears that the program would cause an influx of persons seeking higher welfare payments. Sixth and finally, a strong presumption of constitutionality attaches to statutes of the types now before us. Congressional enactments come to this Court with an extremely heavy presumption of validity. See, e. g., Brown v. Maryland, 12 Wheat. 419, 436 (1827); Insurance Co. v. Glidden Co., 284 U. S. 151, 158 (1931); United States v. Butler, 297 U. S. 1, 67 (1936); United States v. National Dairy Corp., 372 U. S. 29, 32 (1963). A similar presumption of constitutionality attaches to state statutes, particularly when, as here, a State has acted upon a specific authorization from Congress. See, e. g., Powell v. Pennsylvania, 127 U. S. 678, 684-685 (1888); United States v. Des Moines N. & R. Co., 142 U. S. 510, 544-545 (1892).

I do not consider that the factors which have been urged to outweigh these considerations are sufficient to render unconstitutional these state and federal enactments. It is said, first, that this Court, in the opinions discussed, supra, at 669-671, has acknowledged that the right to travel interstate is a "fundamental" freedom. Second, it is contended that the governmental objectives mentioned above either are ephemeral or could be accomplished by means which do not impinge as heavily on the right to travel, and hence that the requirements are unconstitutional because they "sweep unnecessarily broadly and thereby invade the area of protected freedoms." NAACP v. Alabama, 377 U. S. 288, 307 (1964). The appellees claim that welfare payments could be denied those who come primarily to collect welfare by means of less restrictive provisions, such as New York's Welfare Abuses Law;[35] that fraud could be prevented by investigation of individual applicants or by a much shorter residence period; that budgetary predictability is a remote and speculative goal; and that assurance of investment in the community could be obtained by a shorter residence period or by taking into account prior intervals of residence in the jurisdiction.

Taking all of these competing considerations into account, I believe that the balance definitely favors constitutionality. In reaching that conclusion, I do not minimize the importance of the right to travel interstate. However, the impact of residence conditions upon that right is indirect and apparently quite insubstantial. On the other hand, the governmental purposes served by the requirements are legitimate and real, and the residence requirements are clearly suited to their accomplishment. To abolish residence requirements might well discourage highly worthwhile experimentation in the welfare field. The statutes come to us clothed with the authority of Congress and attended by a correspondingly heavy presumption of constitutionality. Moreover, although the appellees assert that the same objectives could have been achieved by less restrictive means, this is an area in which the judiciary should be especially slow to fetter the judgment of Congress and of some 46 state legislatures[36] in the choice of methods. Residence requirements have advantages, such as administrative simplicity and relative certainty, which are not shared by the alternative solutions proposed by the appellees. In these circumstances, I cannot find that the burden imposed by residence requirements upon ability to travel outweighs the governmental interests in their continued employment. Nor do I believe that the period of residence required in these cases—one year—is so excessively long as to justify a finding of unconstitutionality on that score.

I conclude with the following observations. Today's decision, it seems to me, reflects to an unusual degree the current notion that this Court possesses a peculiar wisdom all its own whose capacity to lead this Nation out of its present troubles is contained only by the limits of judicial ingenuity in contriving new constitutional principles to meet each problem as it arises. For anyone who, like myself, believes that it is an essential function of this Court to maintain the constitutional divisions between state and federal authority and among the three branches of the Federal Government, today's decision is a step in the wrong direction. This resurgence of the expansive view of "equal protection" carries the seeds of more judicial interference with the state and federal legislative process, much more indeed than does the judicial application of "due process" according to traditional concepts (see my dissenting opinion in Duncan v. Louisiana, 391 U. S. 145, 171 (1968)), about which some members of this Court have expressed fears as to its potentialities for setting us judges "at large."[37] I consider it particularly unfortunate that this judicial roadblock to the powers of Congress in this field should occur at the very threshold of the current discussions regarding the "federalizing" of these aspects of welfare relief.

Justice Harlan's dissent in NLRB v. Wyman-Gordon Co. (April 23, 1969)

MR. JUSTICE HARLAN, dissenting.

The language of the Administrative Procedure Act does not support the Government's claim that an agency is "adjudicating" when it announces a rule which it refuses to apply in the dispute before it. The Act makes it clear that an agency "adjudicates" only when its procedures result in the "formulation of an order." 5 U. S. C. § 551 (7). (Emphasis supplied.) An "order" is defined to include "the whole or a part of a final disposition. . . of an agency in a matter other than rule making . . . ." 5 U. S. C. § 551 (6). (Emphasis supplied.) This definition makes it apparent that an agency is not adjudicating when it is making a rule, which the Act defines as "an agency statement of general or particular applicability and future effect . . . ." 5 U. S. C. § 551 (4). (Emphasis supplied.) Since the Labor Board's Excelsior rule was to be effective only 30 days after its promulgation, it clearly falls within the rule-making requirements of the Act.[1]

Nor can I agree that the natural interpretation of the statute should be rejected because it requires the agency to choose between giving its rules immediate effect or initiating a separate rule-making proceeding. An agency chooses to apply a rule prospectively only because it represents such a departure from pre-existing understandings that it would be unfair to impose the rule upon the parties in pending matters. But it is precisely in these situations, in which established patterns of conduct are revolutionized, that rule-making procedures perform the vital functions that my Brother DOUGLAS describes so well in a dissenting opinion with which I basically agree.

Given the fact that the Labor Board has promulgated a rule in violation of the governing statute, I believe that there is no alternative but to affirm the judgment of the Court of Appeals in this case. If, as the plurality opinion suggests, the NLRB may properly enforce an invalid rule in subsequent adjudications, the rule-making provisions of the Administrative Procedure Act are completely trivialized. Under today's prevailing approach, the agency may evade the commands of the Act whenever it desires and yet coerce the regulated industry into compliance. It is no answer to say that "respondent was under no compulsion to furnish the list because no statute and no validly adopted rule required it to do so," ante, at 766, when the Labor Board was threatening to issue a subpoena which the courts would enforce. In what other way would the administrative agency compel obedience to its invalid rule?

One cannot always have the best of both worlds. Either the rule-making provisions are to be enforced or they are not. Before the Board may be permitted to adopt a rule that so significantly alters pre-existing labor-management understandings, it must be required to conduct a satisfactory rule-making proceeding, so that it will have the benefit of wide-ranging argument before it enacts its proposed solution to an important problem.

In refusing to adopt this position, the prevailing opinion not only undermines the Administrative Procedure Act, but also compromises the most basic principles governing judicial review of agency action established in our past decisions. This Court's landmark opinion in SEC v. Chenery Corp., 318 U. S. 80, 94 (1943), makes it clear that we are obliged to remand a case if the agency has relied upon an improper reason to justify its action:

"If the action rests upon an administrative determination —an exercise of judgment in an area which Congress has entrusted to the agency—of course it must not be set aside because the reviewing court might have made a different determination were it empowered to do so. But if the action is based upon a determination of law as to which the reviewing authority of the courts does come into play, an order may not stand if the agency has misconceived the law. In either event the orderly functioning of the process of review requires that the grounds upon which the administrative agency acted be clearly disclosed and adequately sustained."

Chenery's teachings are applicable here. The Regional Office that issued the order under review refused to consider the merits of the arguments against the Excelsior rule which were raised by Wyman-Gordon on the ground that they had been rejected by the Board in the Excelsior case itself:

"[I]t is well known that Excelsior issued only after oral argument and briefs, including amicus curiae briefs by interested parties. The Board has considered arguments such as those made here and nevertheless established the requirement embodied in Excelsior and the undersigned [Acting Regional Director] is bound by it." Appendix 33.

The Board denied review of this decision on the ground that "it raises no substantial issues warranting review." Appendix 35.

Since the major reason the Board has given in support of its order is invalid, Chenery requires remand. See also Bell v. United States, 366 U. S. 393, 412-413 (1961); Burlington Truck Lines v. United States, 371 U. S. 156, 167-168 (1962); cf. Phelps Dodge Corp. v. NLRB, 313 U. S. 177, 196-197 (1941). The prevailing opinion explains its departure from our leading decisions in this area on the ground that: "There is not the slightest uncertainty as to the outcome of [this] proceeding" on remand. Ante, n. 6, at 767. I can perceive no justification whatever for this assertion. Since the Excelsior rule was invalidly promulgated, it is clear that, at a minimum, the Board is obliged on remand to recanvass all of the competing considerations before it may properly announce its decision in this case.[2] We cannot know what the outcome of such a reappraisal will be. Surely, it cannot be stated with any degree of certainty that the Board will adopt precisely the same solution as the one which was embraced in Excelsior. The plurality simply usurps the function of the National Labor Relations Board when it says otherwise.

I would affirm the judgment of the Court of Appeals.

Notes

[1] For the reasons advanced by Chief Judge Aldrich in his opinion below, 397 F. 2d 394, I think it clear that the Excelsior rule involves matters of substance and not procedure, and so does not fall within the exception created by 5 U. S. C. § 553 (b) (A) of the Act.

[2] As I have indicated, supra, at 781, I would go further and require the Board to initiate a new rule-making proceeding where, as here, it has previously recognized that the

proposed new rule so departs from prior practices that it cannot fairly be applied retroactively. In the absence of such a proceeding, the administrative agency must be obliged to follow its earlier decisions which did not require employers to furnish Excelsior lists to unions during organizing campaigns.

Justice Harlan's concurrence in National Bd. of YMCA v. U.S. (May 19, 1969)

MR. JUSTICE HARLAN, concurring in the result.

At the time the military retreated into the YMCA and the Masonic Temple, three alternative courses of action were open to the army commander. First, the troops could have continued their prior strategy and stood their ground in front of the buildings without returning the rioters' hostile sniper fire; second, the troops could have stood their ground and attempted to repel the mob by the use of deadly force; third, the troops could have retreated from the entire area, leaving the mob temporarily in control. The petitioners argue that if the troops had adopted either of the first two of these alternative strategies, their buildings would not have suffered the damage which resulted from the military's occupation.

But what if the military had adopted the third strategy open to it? If the army had completely abandoned the area to the rioters, and regrouped for a later counter-attack, there can be little doubt on this record that the rioters would have subjected the buildings to greater damage than that which was in fact suffered. I believe this fact to be decisive. For it appears to me that, in riot control situations, the Just Compensation Clause may only be properly invoked when the military had reason to believe that its action placed the property in question in greater peril than if no form of protection had been provided at all.

I.

I start from the premise that, generally speaking, the Government's complete failure to provide police protection to a particular property owner on a single occasion does not amount to a "taking" within the meaning of the Fifth Amendment. Every man who is robbed on the street cannot demand compensation from the Government on the ground that the Fifth Amendment requires fully effective police protection at all times. The petitioners do not, of course, argue otherwise. Yet surely the Government may not be required to guarantee fully effective protection during serious civil disturbances when it is apparent that the police and the military are unable to defend all the property which is threatened by the mob. If the owners of unprotected property remain uncompensated, however, there seems little justice in compensating petitioners, who merely contend that the military occupation of their buildings provided them with inadequate protection.

Petitioners' claim that they may recover on a bare showing that they were afforded "inadequate" protection has an additional defect which should be noted. If courts were required to consider whether the military or police protection afforded a particular property owner was "adequate," they would be required to make judgments which are best left to officials directly responsible to the electorate. In the present case, for example, petitioners could argue that it was possible for the troops to maintain their position in front of the buildings if they had been willing to kill a large number of rioters. In rebuttal, the Government could persuasively argue that the indiscriminate use of deadly force would have enraged the mob still further and would have increased the likelihood of future disturbances. Which strategy is a court to accept? Clearly, it is far sounder to defer to the other duly constituted branches of government in this regard.

It is, then, both unfair and unwise to favor those who have obtained some form of police protection over those who have received none at all. It is only if the military or other protective action foreseeably increased the risk of damage that compensation should be required. Since, in the present case, the military reasonably believed that petitioners' property was better protected if the troops retreated into the buildings, rather than from the entire area, the property owners have no claim to compensation on the ground that the protection afforded to them was "inadequate."

I must emphasize, however, that the test I have advanced should be applied only to government actions taken in an effort to control a riot. The Army could not, for example, appropriate the YMCA today and claim that no payment was due because the building would have been completely demolished if the military had not intervened during the riot. Once tranquility has been restored, property owners may legitimately expect that the Government will not deprive them of the property saved from the mob. But while the rioters are surging through the streets out of control, everyone must recognize that the Government cannot protect all property all of the time. I think it appropriate to say, however, that our decision today does not in any way suggest that the victims of civil disturbances are undeserving of relief. But it is for the Congress, not this Court, to decide the extent to which those injured in the riot should be compensated, regardless of the extent to which the police or military attempted to protect the particular property which each individual owns.

II.

While I agree with the Court that no compensation is constitutionally available under the facts of this case, I have thought it appropriate to state my own views on this matter since the precise meaning of the rules the majority announces remains obscure at certain critical points. Moreover, in deciding this particular case we should spare no effort to search for principles that seem best calculated to fit others that may arise before American democracy once again regains its equilibrium.

The Court sets out two tests to govern the application of the Just Compensation Clause in riot situations. It first denies petitioners recovery on the ground that each was the "particular intended beneficiary" of the Government's military operations. Ante, at 92. I do not disagree with this formula if it means that the Fifth Amendment does not apply whenever the policing power reasonably believes that its actions will not increase the risk of riot damage beyond that borne by the owners of unprotected buildings. But the language the Court has chosen leaves a good deal of ambiguity as to its scope. If, for example, the military deliberately destroyed a building so as to prevent rioters from looting its contents and burning it to the ground, it would be difficult indeed to call the building's owner the "particular intended beneficiary" of the Government's action. Nevertheless, if the military reasonably believed that the rioters would have burned the building anyway, recovery should be denied for the same reasons it is properly denied in the case before us. Cf. United States v. Caltex, Inc., 344 U. S. 149 (1952).

Moreover, the Court's formula might be taken to indicate that if the military's subjective intention was to protect the building, the courts need not consider whether this subjective belief was a reasonable one.

While the widest leeway must, of course, be given to good-faith military judgment, I am not prepared to subscribe to judicial abnegation to this extent. If a court concludes, upon convincing evidence, that the military had good reason to know that its actions would significantly increase the risk of riot damage to a particular property, compensation should be awarded regardless of governmental good faith.

While I accept the Court's "intended beneficiary" test with these caveats, I cannot subscribe to the second ground the majority advances to deny recovery in the present case. The majority analogizes this case to one in which the military simply posted a guard in front of petitioners' properties. It is said that if the rioters had damaged the buildings as a part of their attack on the troops standing in front of them, the property damage caused would be too "indirect" a consequence of the military's action to warrant awarding Fifth Amendment compensation. It follows, says the Court, that even if the military's occupation of the buildings increased the risk of harm far beyond any alternative military strategy, the Army's action is nevertheless too "indirect" a cause of the resulting damage.

This argument, however, ignores a salient difference between the case the Court hypothesizes and the one which we confront. If the troops had remained on the street, they would not have obtained any special benefit from the use of petitioners' buildings. In contrast, the military did in this instance receive a benefit not enjoyed by members of the general public when the troops were ordered to occupy the YMCA and the Masonic Temple. As the Court's statement of the facts makes clear, the troops retreated into the buildings to protect themselves from sniper fire. Ordinarily, the Government pays for private property used to shelter its officials, and I would see no reason to make an exception here if the military had reason to know that the buildings would have been exposed to a lesser risk of harm if they had been left entirely unprotected.

On the premises set forth in this opinion, I concur in the judgment of the Court.

Justice Harlan's dissent in Jenkins v. Delaware (June 2, 1969)

MR. JUSTICE HARLAN, dissenting.

As one who has never agreed with the Miranda case but nonetheless felt bound by it,[*] I now find myself in the uncomfortable position of having to dissent from a holding which actually serves to curtail the impact of that decision.

I feel compelled to dissent because I consider that the new "retroactivity" ruling which the Court makes today is indefensible. Were I free to do so, I would hold that this petitioner is entitled to the benefits of Miranda, this case being before us on direct review and being one which had not become final prior to the decision of Miranda. See my dissenting opinion in Desist v. United States, 394 U. S. 244, 256 (1969); Linkletter v. Walker, 381 U. S. 618 (1965). But since as to the retroactivity issue I am also bound by Johnson v. New Jersey, 384 U. S. 719 (1966), I must judge that issue within the confines of Johnson, which does not appear to have been overruled by what was done in Desist v. United States, supra.

In the Johnson case we held that the "guidelines" of Miranda should apply to all "persons whose trials had not begun as of June 13, 1966," 384 U. S., at 734, the date on which Miranda was handed down. Today, however, the Court holds that Miranda does not apply to persons whose retrials have commenced after that date, if the original trial had begun before Miranda was decided. I find it quite impossible to discern in the rationale of Johnson any solid basis for the distinction now drawn.

The Court states that the retroactivity rule adopted in Johnson was "an effort to extend the protection of Miranda to as many defendants as was consistent with society's legitimate concern that convictions already validly obtained not be needlessly aborted." Ante, at 219. I too believe that a desire not to interfere with trials which were concluded or already under way at the time of Miranda lay at the core of what was done in Johnson. See 384 U. S., at 732-735. But that rationale would seem to require application of Miranda to subsequent retrials, rather than the contrary result mandated by the Court. When a defendant has had his pre-Miranda conviction set aside on other than Miranda grounds and is being retried, there is by hypothesis no "conviction . . . validly obtained" which might be "needlessly aborted" by application of the Miranda standards. There is no ongoing trial in which the prosecution's strategy might have been premised on pre-Miranda confession rules.

I am also left wholly unpersuaded by the Court's statement that application of Miranda to retrials would impose an intolerable "evidentiary burden" on prosecutors, for the Court ignores the fact that Miranda will impose a very similar burden whenever a defendant's first trial has for one reason or another been substantially delayed and its commencement carried beyond the Johnson cut-off date.

Apart from the two propositions just discussed, the Court offers nothing in justification of its trial-retrial distinction beyond the general observation that the retroactivity "technique" necessarily entails "incongruities" which must be tolerated because of "the impetus the technique provides for the implementation of long overdue reforms, which otherwise could not be practicably effected." Ante, at 218. But surely it is incumbent upon this Court to endeavor to keep such incongruities to a minimum. This in my opinion can only be done by turning our backs on the ad hoc approach that has so far characterized our decisions in the retroactivity field and proceeding to administer the doctrine on principle. See my dissenting opinion in Desist, supra. What is done today leads me again, see ibid., to urge that the time has come for us to take a fresh look at the whole problem of retroactivity.

I would reverse the judgment of the Supreme Court of Delaware. It would be less than frank were I not to say that I cast this vote with reluctance, feeling as I do about the unsoundness of Miranda.

[*] See my dissenting opinion in Miranda v. Arizona, 384 U. S. 436, 504 (1966), and my concurring opinion in Orozco v. Texas, 394 U. S. 324, 327 (1969).

Justice Harlan's dissent in Boykin v. Alabama (June 2, 1969)

MR. JUSTICE HARLAN, whom MR. JUSTICE BLACK joins, dissenting.

The Court today holds that petitioner Boykin was denied due process of law, and that his robbery convictions must be reversed outright, solely because "the record [is] inadequate to show that petitioner . . . intelligently and knowingly pleaded guilty." Ante, at 241. The Court thus in effect fastens upon the States, as a matter of federal constitutional law, the rigid prophylactic requirements of Rule 11 of the Federal Rules of Criminal Procedure. It does so in circumstances where the Court itself has only very recently held application of Rule 11 to be unnecessary in the federal courts. See Halliday v. United States, 394 U. S. 831 (1969). Moreover, the Court does all this at the behest of a petitioner who has never at any time alleged that his guilty plea was involuntary or made without knowledge of the consequences. I cannot possibly subscribe to so bizarre a result.

I.

In June 1966, an Alabama grand jury returned five indictments against petitioner Boykin, on five separate charges of common-law robbery. He was determined to be indigent, and on July 11 an attorney was appointed to represent him. Petitioner was arraigned three days later. At that time, in open court and in the presence of his attorney, petitioner pleaded guilty to all five indictments. The record does not show what inquiries were made by the arraigning judge to confirm that the plea was made voluntarily and knowingly.[1]

Petitioner was not sentenced immediately after the acceptance of his plea. Instead, pursuant to an Alabama statute, the court ordered that "witnesses . . . be examined, to ascertain the character of the offense," in the presence of a jury which would then fix petitioner's sentence. See Ala. Code, Tit. 14, § 415 (1958); Tit. 15, § 277. That proceeding occurred some two months after petitioner pleaded guilty. During that period, petitioner made no attempt to withdraw his plea. Petitioner was present in court with his attorney when the witnesses were examined. Petitioner heard the judge state the elements of common-law robbery and heard him announce that petitioner had pleaded guilty to that offense and might be sentenced to death. Again, petitioner made no effort to withdraw his plea.

On his appeal to the Alabama Supreme Court, petitioner did not claim that his guilty plea was made involuntarily or without full knowledge of the consequences. In fact, petitioner raised no questions at all concerning the plea.[2] In his petition and brief in this Court, and in oral argument by counsel, petitioner has never asserted that the plea was coerced or made in ignorance of the consequences.

II.

Against this background, the Court holds that the Due Process Clause of the Fourteenth Amendment requires the outright reversal of petitioner's conviction. This result is wholly unprecedented. There are past holdings of this Court to the effect that a federal habeas corpus petitioner who makes sufficiently credible allegations that his state guilty plea was involuntary is entitled to a hearing as to the truth of those allegations. See, e. g., Waley v. Johnston, 316 U. S. 101 (1942); cf. Machibroda v. United States, 368 U. S. 487 (1962). These holdings suggest that if equally convincing allegations were made in a petition for certiorari on direct review, the petitioner might in some circumstances be entitled to have a judgment of affirmance vacated and the case remanded for a state hearing on voluntariness. Cf. Jackson v. Denno, 378 U. S. 368, 393-394 (1964). However, as has been noted, this petitioner makes no allegations of actual involuntariness.

The Court's reversal is therefore predicated entirely upon the failure of the arraigning state judge to make an "adequate" record. In holding that this is a ground for reversal, the Court quotes copiously from McCarthy v. United States, 394 U. S. 459 (1969), in which we held earlier this Term that when a federal district judge fails to comply in every respect with the procedure for accepting a guilty plea which is prescribed in Rule 11 of the Federal Rules of Criminal Procedure, the plea must be set aside and the defendant permitted to replead, regardless of lower-court findings that the plea was in fact voluntary. What the Court omits to mention is that in McCarthy we stated that our decision was based "solely upon our construction of Rule 11," and explicitly disavowed any reliance upon the Constitution. Id., at 464. Thus McCarthy can provide no support whatever for today's constitutional edict.

III.

So far as one can make out from the Court's opinion, what is now in effect being held is that the prophylactic procedures of Criminal Rule 11 are substantially applicable to the States as a matter of federal constitutional due process. If this is the basis upon which Boykin's conviction is being reversed, then the Court's disposition is plainly out of keeping with a sequel case to McCarthy, decided only last month. For the Court held in Halliday v. United States, 394 U. S. 831 (1969), that "in view of the large number of constitutionally valid convictions that may have been obtained without full compliance with Rule 11, we decline to apply McCarthy retroactively." Id., at 833. The Court quite evidently found Halliday's conviction to be "constitutionally valid," for it affirmed the conviction even though Halliday's guilty plea was accepted in 1954 without any explicit inquiry into whether it was knowingly and understandingly made, as now required by present Rule 11. In justification, the Court noted that two lower courts had found in collateral proceedings that the plea was voluntary. The Court declared that:

"[A] defendant whose plea has been accepted without full compliance with Rule

11 may still resort to appropriate post-conviction remedies to attack his plea's voluntariness. Thus, if his plea was accepted prior to our decision in McCarthy, he is not without a remedy to correct constitutional defects in his conviction." Id., at 833.

It seems elementary that the Fifth Amendment due process to which petitioner Halliday was entitled must be at least as demanding as the Fourteenth Amendment process due petitioner Boykin. Yet petitioner Halliday's federal conviction has been affirmed as "constitutionally valid," despite the omission of any judicial inquiry of record at the time of his plea, because he initiated collateral proceedings which revealed that the plea was actually voluntary. Petitioner Boykin, on the other hand, today has his Alabama conviction reversed because of exactly the same omission, even though he too "may . . . resort to appropriate post-conviction remedies to attack his plea's voluntariness" and thus "is not without a remedy to correct constitutional defects in his conviction." In short, I find it utterly impossible to square today's holding with what the Court has so recently done.

I would hold that petitioner Boykin is not entitled to outright reversal of his conviction simply because of the "inadequacy" of the record pertaining to his guilty plea. Further, I would not vacate the judgment below and remand for a state-court hearing on voluntariness. For even if it is assumed for the sake of argument that petitioner would be entitled to such a hearing if he had alleged that the plea was involuntary, a matter which I find it unnecessary to decide, the fact is that he has never made any such claim. Hence, I consider that petitioner's present arguments relating to his guilty plea entitle him to no federal relief.[3]

Notes

[1] The record states only that:

"This day in open court came the State of Alabama by its District Attorney and the defendant in his own proper person and with his attorney, Evan Austill, and the defendant in open court on this day being arraigned on the indictment in these cases charging him with the offense of Robbery and plead guilty." Appendix 4.

[2] However, I am willing to accept the majority's view that we do have jurisdiction to consider the question.

[3] Petitioner advances two additional constitutional arguments: that imposition of the death penalty for common-law robbery is "cruel and unusual punishment" in violation of the Fourteenth Amendment; and thus to permit a jury to inflict the death penalty without any "standards" to guide its discretion amounts to a denial of due process. I do not reach these issues because the Court has not done so.

Justice Harlan's dissent in O'Callahan v. Parker (June 2, 1969)

MR. JUSTICE HARLAN, whom MR. JUSTICE STEWART and MR. JUSTICE WHITE join, dissenting.

I consider that the terms of the Constitution and the precedents in this Court point clearly to sustaining court-martial jurisdiction in this instance. The Court's largely one-sided discussion of the competing individual and governmental interests at stake, and its reliance upon what are at best wholly inconclusive historical data, fall far short of supporting the contrary conclusion which the majority has reached. In sum, I think that the Court has grasped for itself the making of a determination which the Constitution has placed in the hands of the Congress, and that in so doing the Court has thrown the law in this realm into a demoralizing state of uncertainty. I must dissent.

    I.

    My starting point is the language of Art. I, § 8, cl. 14, of the Constitution, which empowers the Congress "[t]o make Rules for the Government and Regulation of the land and naval Forces," and the Fifth Amendment's correlative exception for "cases arising in the land or naval forces."

    Writing for a plurality of the Court in Reid v. Covert, 354 U. S. 1 (1957), MR. JUSTICE BLACK explained that if the "language of Clause 14 is given its natural meaning. . . [t]he term `land and naval Forces' refers to persons who are members of the armed services . . . ," id., at 19-20, and that accordingly the Fifth Amendment's exception encompasses persons " `in' the armed services." Id., at 22-23. In Kinsella v. Singleton, 361 U. S. 234 (1960), again looking to the constitutional language, the Court noted that "military jurisdiction has always been based on the `status' of the accused, rather than on the nature of the offense," id., at 243; that is, whether the accused "is a person who can be regarded as falling within the term `land and naval Forces.' " Id., at 241.

    In these cases and many others, Ex parte Milligan, 4 Wall. 2, 123 (1866); Coleman v. Tennessee, 97 U. S. 509 (1879); Smith v. Whitney, 116 U. S. 167, 184-185 (1886); Johnson v. Sayre, 158 U. S. 109, 114 (1895); Grafton v. United States, 206 U. S. 333, 348 (1907), this Court has consistently asserted that military "status" is a necessary and sufficient condition for the exercise of court-martial jurisdiction. The Court has never previously questioned what the language of Clause 14 would seem to make plain—that, given the requisite military status, it is for Congress and not the Judiciary to determine the appropriate subject-matter jurisdiction of courts-martial. See Coleman v. Tennessee, supra, at 514.

    II.

    English constitutional history provides scant support for the Court's novel interpretation of Clause 14, and the pertinent American history proves, if anything, quite the contrary.

    The English history on which the majority relies reveals a long-standing and multifaceted struggle for power between the military and the Crown, on the one hand, and Parliament on the other, which focused, inter alia, on the King's asserted independent prerogative to try soldiers by court-martial in time of peace. See generally J. Tanner, English Constitutional Conflicts of the Seventeenth Century (1961). The martial law of the time was, moreover, arbitrary, and alien to established legal principles. See 1 W. Blackstone's Commentaries 413; M. Hale, History and Analysis of the Common Law in

England 42 (6th ed. 1820). Thus, when, with the Glorious Revolution of 1688, Parliament gained exclusive authority to create peacetime court-martial jurisdiction, it exercised that authority sparingly: the early Mutiny Acts permitted trial by court-martial only for the crimes of mutiny, sedition, and desertion. E. g., Mutiny Act of 1689, 1 W. & M., Sess. 2, c. 4.

Parliament subsequently expanded the military's peacetime jurisdiction both abroad and at home. See Mutiny Act of 1712, 12 Anne, c. 13; Mutiny Act of 1803, 43 Geo. 3, c. 20. And, significantly, § 46 of the Mutiny Act of 1720, 7 Geo. 1, c. 6, authorized trial by court-martial for offenses of a nonmilitary nature, if the injured civilian made no request that the accused be tried in the civil courts. See F. Wiener, Civilians Under Military Justice 13-14, 245-246 (1967).[1]

The burden of English history was not lost on the Framers of our Constitution, who doubtless feared the Executive's assertion of an independent military authority unchecked by the people acting through the Legislature. Article 9, § 4, of the Articles of Confederation— from which Art. I, § 8, cl. 14, of the Constitution was taken[2]—was responsive to this apprehension:

"The United States in Congress assembled shall. . . have the sole and exclusive right and power of . . . making rules for the government and regulation of the . . . land and naval forces, and directing their operations." (Emphasis added.)

But nothing in the debates over our Constitution indicates that the Congress was forever to be limited to the precise scope of court-martial jurisdiction existing in 17th century England. To the contrary, Alexander Hamilton stated that Congress' power to prescribe rules for the government of the armed forces "ought to exist without limitation: Because it is impossible to foresee or define the extent and variety of national exigencies, or the corresponding extent & variety of the means which may be necessary to satisfy them." The Federalist, No. 23. (Emphasis omitted.)

American exercise of court-martial jurisdiction prior to, and contemporaneous with, adoption of the Constitution lends no support to the Court's position. Military records between the end of the War of Independence and the beginning of the War of 1812 show frequent instances of trials by court-martial, east of the frontier, for offenses against civilians and the civil laws, such as theft, assault, and killing livestock.[3] Military authority to try soldiers for such offenses derived initially from the "general article" of war, first enacted by the Continental Congress in 1775,[4] and incorporated today in Art. 134, 10 U. S. C. § 934. W. Winthrop's Military Law and Precedents (2d ed. 1896), the leading 19th century treatise on military law, recognized that the general article encompassed crimes "committed upon or against civilians . . . at or near a military camp or post," id., at 724 (1920 reprint) (second emphasis added), and noted that even this limiting principle was not strictly observed. Id., at 725, 730-732. And in Grafton v. United States, 206 U. S. 333, 348 (1907), the Court held, with respect to the general article, that:

"The crimes referred to in that article manifestly embrace those not capital, committed by officers or soldiers of the Army in violation of public law as enforced by the civil power. No crimes committed by officers or soldiers of the Army are excepted by the . . . article from the jurisdiction thus conferred upon courts-martial, except those that are capital in their nature. . . . [T]he jurisdiction of general courts-martial [is] . . . concurrent with that of the civil courts."[5]

Even if the practice of early American courts-martial had been otherwise, this would hardly lead to the conclusion that Congress lacked power to authorize military trials under the present circumstances. It cannot be seriously argued as a general matter that the constitutional limits of congressional power are coterminous with the extent of its exercise in the late 18th and early 19th centuries.[6] And however restrictively the power to define court-martial jurisdiction may be construed, it would be patently wrong so to limit that power. The disciplinary requirements of today's armed force of over 3,000,000 men[7] are manifestly different from those of the 718-man army[8] in existence in 1789. Cf. The Federalist, No. 23, quoted, supra, at 277. By the same token, given an otherwise valid exercise of the Article I power, I can perceive no basis for judicial curtailment of court-martial jurisdiction as Congress has enacted it.

III.

In the light of the language and history of Art. 1, § 8, cl. 14, of the Constitution, and this Court's hitherto consistent interpretation of this provision, I do not believe that the resolution of the controversy before us calls for any balancing of interests. But if one does engage in a balancing process, one cannot fairly hope to come up with a meaningful answer unless the interests on both sides are fully explored. The Court does not do this. Rather, it chooses to ignore strong and legitimate governmental interests which support the exercise of court-martial jurisdiction even over "nonmilitary" crimes.

The United States has a vital interest in creating and maintaining an armed force of honest, upright, and well-disciplined persons, and in preserving the reputation, morale, and integrity of the military services. Furthermore, because its personnel must, perforce, live and work in close proximity to one another, the military has an obligation to protect each of its members from the misconduct of fellow servicemen.[9] The commission of offenses against the civil order manifests qualities of attitude and character equally destructive of military order and safety. The soldier who acts the part of Mr. Hyde while on leave is, at best, a precarious Dr. Jekyll when back on duty. Thus, as General George Washington recognized:

"All improper treatment of an inhabitant by an officer or soldier being destructive of good order and discipline as well as subversive of the rights of society is as much a breach of military, as civil law and as punishable by the one as the other." 14 Writings of George Washington 140-141 (Bicent. ed.).

A soldier's misconduct directed against civilians, moreover, brings discredit upon the service of which he is a member:

"Under every system of military law for the government of either land or naval forces, the jurisdiction of courts martial extends to the trial and punishment of acts of military or naval officers which tend to bring disgrace and reproach upon the service of which they are members, whether those acts are done in the performance of military duties, or in a civil position . . . ." Smith v. Whitney, 116 U. S. 167, 183-184 (1886).

The Government, thus, has a proper concern in keeping its own house in order, by deterring members of the armed forces from engaging in criminal misconduct on or off the base, and by rehabilitating offenders to return them to useful military service.[10]

The exercise of military jurisdiction is also responsive to other practical needs of the armed forces. A soldier detained by the civil authorities pending trial, or subsequently imprisoned, is to that extent rendered useless to the service. Even if he is released on bail or recognizance, or ultimately placed on probation, the civil authorities may require him to remain within the jurisdiction, thus making him unavailable for transfer with the rest of his unit or as the service otherwise requires.

In contrast, a person awaiting trial by court-martial may simply be restricted to limits, and may "participate in all military duties and activities of his organization while under such restriction." Manual for Courts-Martial, United States (1969), ¶ 20 b. The trial need not be held in the jurisdiction where the offense was committed. Id., ¶ 8. See, e. g., United States v. Voorhees, 4 U. S. C. M. A. 509, 515, 16 C. M. R. 83, 89 (1954); cf. United States v. Gravitt, 5 U. S. C. M. A. 249, 256, 17 C. M. R. 249, 256 (1954). And punishments—such as forfeiture of pay, restriction to limits, and hard labor without confinement—may be imposed that do not keep the convicted serviceman from performing his military duties. See Manual for Courts-Martial, supra, ¶¶ 126 g, h, k.

IV.

The Court does not explain the scope of the "service-connected" crimes as to which court-martial jurisdiction is appropriate, but it appears that jurisdiction may extend to "nonmilitary" offenses in appropriate circumstances. Thus, the Court intimates that it is relevant to the jurisdictional issue in this case that petitioner was wearing civilian clothes rather than a uniform when he committed the crimes. Ante, at 259. And it also implies that plundering, abusing, and stealing from, civilians may sometimes constitute a punishable abuse of military position, ante, at 270, n. 14, and that officers may be court-martialed for purely civilian crimes, because "[i]n the 18th century . . . the `honor' of an officer was thought to give a specific military connection to a crime otherwise without military significance."[11] Ibid. But if these are illustrative cases, the Court suggests no general standard for determining when the exercise of court-martial jurisdiction is permissible.

Whatever role an ad hoc judicial approach may have in some areas of the law, the Congress and the military are at least entitled to know with some certainty the allowable scope of court-martial jurisdiction. Otherwise, the infinite permutations of possibly relevant factors are bound to create confusion and proliferate litigation over the jurisdictional issue in each instance. Absolutely nothing in the language, history, or logic of the Constitution justifies this uneasy state of affairs which the Court has today created.

I would affirm the judgment of the Court of Appeals.

Notes

[1] This proviso was dropped in the Mutiny Act of 1721, 8 Geo. 1, c. 3, and court-martial jurisdiction over such offenses was thereafter limited by the articles of war to, inter alia, "Place[s] beyond the Seas . . . where there is no form of Our Civil Judicature in Force." F. Wiener, Civilians Under Military Justice 14 (1967).

[2] See 2 M. Farrand, The Records of the Federal Convention of 1787, p. 330 (1911); 5 J. Elliot, Debates in the Several State Conventions on the Adoption of the Federal Constitution as Recommended by the General Convention at Philadelphia in 1787, p. 443 (1836).

[3] For example: The general orders of George Washington report the trial of soldiers for "killing a Cow . . . , stealing Fowls . . . , and stealing eleven Geese . . . ." 26 Writings of George Washington 73 (Bicent. ed.) (H. Q., Newburgh, January 28, 1783), and "for stealing a number of Shirts and blanketts out of the public store at Newburgh . . . ." Id., at 322 (H. Q., Newburgh, April 15, 1783). The Orderly Books of the Corps of Artillerists and Engineers report the court-martial of Sergeant Harris for "beating a Mr. Williams an inhabitant living near this garrison," Book 1, pp. 157-158 (West Point, October 5, 1795), and of Private Kelly for "abusing and using violence on Mrs. Cronkhyte, a citizen of the United States." Book 3, pp. 45-46 (West Point, July 5, 1796). Numerous other instances of military punishment for nonmilitary crimes during the period 1775-1815 are summarized in the appendix to the Brief for the United States 35-52.

[4] "All crimes, not capital, and all disorders and neglects, which officers and soldiers may be guilty of, to the prejudice of good order and military discipline, though not mentioned in the articles of war, are to be taken cognizance of by a general or regimental court-martial, according to the nature and degree of the offence, and be punished at their discretion." W. Winthrop, Military Law and Precedents 957 (2d ed. 1896, 1920 reprint).

[5] In 1916, Congress for the first time explicitly authorized peacetime court-martial jurisdiction for specific noncapital offenses. Article 93, Articles of War, 39 Stat. 664. It also revised the general article, renumbered Article 96, to read:

"Though not mentioned in these articles, all disorders and neglects to the prejudice of good order and military discipline, all conduct of a nature to bring discredit upon the military service, and all crimes or offenses not capital, of which persons subject to military law may be guilty, shall be taken cognizance of by a general or special or summary court-martial, according to the nature and degree of the offense, and punished at the discretion of such court."

Testifying before the Senate Subcommittee on Military Affairs, Brigadier General Crowder, the Judge Advocate General of the Army, explained the revision (cf. n. 4, supra):

"You will notice some transposition of language. The phrase `to the prejudice of good order and military discipline' is put in in such a way that it qualifies only `all disorders and neglects.' As the law stands to-day it was often contended that this phrase qualified also `all crimes not capital.' There was some argument about whether it would reach back through that clause, `all disorders and neglects,' to the clause `all crimes not capital' and qualify the latter clause. . . . [B]ut Justice Harlan, in the decision in the Grafton case, seems to have set the matter at rest, and I am proposing legislation along the lines of Justice Harlan's decision." Hearings before the Senate Subcommittee on Military Affairs, an Appendix to S. Rep. No. 130, 64th Cong., 1st Sess., 25, 91.

The Act of March 3, 1863, § 30, 12 Stat. 736, authorized punishment for specific nonmilitary crimes, including capital ones, in time of war, insurrection, or rebellion. Article 92 of the 1916 Articles of War, 39 Stat. 664, made murder and rape punishable by death, but provided that "no person shall be tried by court-martial for murder or rape committed within the geographical limits of the States of the Union and the District of Columbia in time of peace." This proviso was deleted in the Uniform Code of Military Justice, Articles 118, 120, 10 U. S. C. §§ 918, 920, so that today there is no jurisdictional distinction between capital and noncapital offenses.

[6] On such a theory, for example, Congress could not have permissibly waited, as it did, until 1875, see Act of March 3, 1875, § 1, 18 Stat. 470, to confer general federal-question jurisdiction on the district courts; the present-day exercise of this jurisdiction, see 28 U. S. C. § 1331, would be unconstitutional.

[7] Statistical Abstract of The United States 257 (1968).

[8] R. Weigley, History of the United States Army 566 (1967).

[9] Congress may also assume the responsibility of protecting civilians from harms perpetrated by members of the armed forces. For the military is often responsible for bringing to a locality thousands of its personnel—whose numbers may be as great as, and sometimes exceed, the neighboring population—thereby imposing on the local law-enforcement agencies a burden which they may be unable to carry.

[10] Thus, at petitioner's presentence hearing, Captain Powell testified that "through proper rehabilitation, O'Callahan can make a good soldier," Record Transcript 61, and Major Turner testified:

"He has given superior performance, as far as I know. . . . He has gone through school and the Army does have a lot of money wrapped up in this man. . . . I think at this time, here that a rehabilitation program is in order." Id., at 64.

[11] It is, to say the least, strange that as a constitutional matter the military is without authority to discipline an enlisted man for an offense that is punishable if committed by an officer.

Justice Harlan's dissent in Jenkins v. McKeithen (June 9, 1969)

MR. JUSTICE HARLAN, whom MR. JUSTICE STEWART and MR. JUSTICE WHITE join, dissenting.

Swept up in a constitutional revolution of its own making, the Court has a tendency to lose sight of the principles that have traditionally defined and limited its role in our political system. Constitutional adjudication is a responsibility we cannot shirk. But it is a grave and extraordinary process, one of last resort. And when it cannot legitimately be avoided, it is a function that must be performed with the utmost circumspection and precision, lest the Court's opinions emanate radiations which unintentionally, and spuriously, indicate views on matters we have not fully considered.

Over the years, the Court has evolved a number of principles designed to assure that we act within our proper confines. Perhaps the most fundamental of these is that we adjudicate only when, and to the extent that, we are presented with an actual and concrete controversy. Today, in its haste to make new constitutional doctrine, the Court turns this principle on its head, as it attempts to create a controversy out of a complaint which alleges none. With respect, I must dissent.

I.

Only last Term, in Flast v. Cohen, 392 U. S. 83 (1968), the Court reaffirmed the proposition that "when standing [to sue] is placed in issue in a case, the question is whether the person whose standing is challenged is a proper party to request an adjudication of a particular issue . . . ," id., at 99-100, that is, "whether there is a logical nexus between the status asserted and the claim sought to be adjudicated." Id., at 102. In the present context, this means, simply, that for a plaintiff to challenge a particular course of conduct pursued or threatened to be pursued by a defendant, it is not enough for the plaintiff to allege that he has been or will be injured by the defendant; the plaintiff must further claim that the injury to him (or to those whom he has status to represent[1]) results from the particular course of conduct he challenges.

Appellant in the case at bar attacks the constitutional validity of certain specific statutory procedures of the Louisiana Labor-Management Commission of Inquiry. Applying the principle stated above, it is not sufficient that he may be injured by the Commission or its members in some way. The injury must be alleged to arise out of, or relate to, the application of the procedures in question. The most generous reading of appellant's complaint cannot mask the simple truth that it falls short of this minimal requirement.

At the risk of wearying the reader, I must deal with appellant's pleadings in some detail. The relevant portion of the complaint, and that relied upon by the Court, is part IV ("Facts"), which contains 17 operative paragraphs.

Paragraphs 1-3 identify the plaintiff and defendants.

Paragraphs 4-6 characterize the Commission as an "executive trial agency," and outline its investigative functions. Paragraph 7 avers that the Commission's procedures for performing these functions are constitutionally defective with respect to matters of counsel, confrontation, compulsory process, rules of evidence, standards of guilt, right of appeal, and self-incrimination. Nowhere, either directly or indirectly, do these paragraphs intimate that appellant (or for that matter, anyone else) has been affected by the procedures themselves and their asserted effects.

Paragraph 8 should be quoted in full:

"Furthermore complainant alleges that said defendants, their agents, representatives and employees, and those acting in concert with them, in connection with the administration of the provisions of said Act, have singled out complainant and members of Teamsters Local No. 5 as a special class of persons for repressive and willfully punitive action, solely because they are members of said Teamsters Local No. 5, in furtherance of which a deliberate effort has been made and continues to be made by said officials, spearheaded by defendant McKeithen, while acting under color of state law, to destroy the current power structure of the labor union aforesaid and said union to which complainant belongs as a member and through which he experiences economic survival, and to install a new power structure oriented and subservient to the James R. Hoffa group or clique of the International Brotherhood of Teamsters, Chauffeurs, Warehousemen and Helpers of America; this effort has included and continues to include (a) the deliberate circulation for public consumption of willful falsehoods about members of said labor union, such as characterizing said members as `hoodlums' and `gangsters,' comparable in depravity to the sinister Mafia gangsters of underworld criminals, while masking such lawless conduct behind a verbal facade of law and order, (b) the indiscriminate filing of criminal charges against members of said labor union, where there exists no justifiable basis therefor and the concomitant exaction of excessive bail bonds, (c) the intimidating of public officials into carrying out the tyrannical aims of such indiscriminate criminal prosecution, and (d) the dictatorial use of the powers of the office of Governor of Louisiana in furtherance thereof."

In paragraph 9, appellant avers, "as more specifically applies to him," that appellees conspired to file false criminal charges against him. Paragraphs 10-14 describe in detail the chronology and conduct of the resulting criminal proceedings.

Paragraph 15 alleges that appellees intimidated certain persons (not including appellant) in order to elicit false statements to bring about the prosecution of other persons (not including appellant).

Finally, paragraph 16 contains the usual averments requisite to equitable and declaratory relief, and paragraph 17 requests a temporary restraining order.

Reading and re-reading these many paragraphs of legal and factual averments, one cannot help but be struck by the conspicuous absence of any claim that appellant has been or will be investigated by the Commission, or called as a witness before it, or identified in its findings, or, indeed, subjected to any of its processes.[2] Can this lacuna be filled by implication? I believe not.

Only paragraphs 9-14 relate specifically to appellant, and they contain no hint that the filing of the criminal informations against him was the result of the Commission's use of any of the procedures which the Court today indicates are constitutionally suspect. And assuming, contrary to fact, see n. 1, supra, that appellant represents others besides himself in this action, the only other arguably germane paragraph is ¶ 8 (a), which alleges the "deliberate circulation for public consumption of willful falsehoods about members of said labor union." This paragraph conspicuously omits any suggestion that such "falsehoods" were the result of testimony before the Commission or that they were contained in the Commission's "findings"—a term that is repeatedly emphasized in the earlier description of the Commission's functions.

The complaint's utter failure to allege any connection between the injuries asserted to have been suffered by appellant and the procedures complained of is not, on any objective reading of the complaint, an accidental omission or the result of counsel's "inartfulness"—as my Brother MARSHALL would put it. In my view, the only plausible inference—especially when it is remembered that appellant was represented by counsel throughout this litigation—is that such allegations were omitted because appellant had no facts to support them.[3]

The prevailing opinion's strained construction of the complaint goes well beyond the principle, with which I have no quarrel, that federal pleadings should be most liberally construed. It entirely undermines an important function of the federal system of procedure—that of disposing of unmeritorious and unjusticiable claims at the outset, before the parties and courts must undergo the expense and time consumed by evidentiary hearings.

Accordingly, I would sustain the dismissal of the complaint on the ground that appellant has not shown himself to have standing to challenge the Commission's procedures.

II.

Because the complaint is barren of any indication of the manner in which appellant is affected by the Commission's formal procedures, the prevailing opinion is required to make its own assumptions. It places appellant in the vague position of "a person being investigated" by the Commission, ante, at 428, 429, and thence proceeds to discuss the rights of such a person to confront witnesses and to offer evidence in his own behalf. The prevailing opinion appears understandably reluctant to commit itself to very much. As I read the opinion, it does not state that any of the Commission's procedures are actually unconstitutional, but holds only that there is enough latent in the complaint that the case should proceed to trial.

Of necessity, however, my Brother MARSHALL has to examine some of the constitutional issues sought to be raised by appellant in order to justify a remand, and his discussion leaves radiations which are, at least, unclear. Reluctant as I am, under the circumstances of this case, to discuss the merits, I therefore feel compelled to outline my own views. I am not certain to what extent they comport with those of the majority.

The prevailing opinion fails to articulate what I deem to be a constitutionally significant distinction between two kinds of governmental bodies. The first is an agency whose sole or predominant function, without serving any other public interest, is to expose and publicize the names of persons it finds guilty of wrongdoing. To the extent that such a determination—whether called a "finding" or an "adjudication"—finally and directly affects the substantial personal interests, I do not doubt that the Due Process Clause may require that it be accompanied by many of the traditional adjudicatory procedural safeguards. Cf. Joint Anti-Fascist Refugee Committee v. McGrath, 341 U. S. 123 (1951).

By the terms of the Louisiana legislation, the appellee Commission is not of this sort. Its authority is "investigatory and fact finding only." La. Rev. Stat. Ann. § 23:880.6 A (Supp. 1969). Its stated purpose is "to supplement and assist the efforts and activities of the several district attorneys, grand juries and other law enforcement officials and agencies of the State of Louisiana." Preamble to Act No. 2. Its duty, when it finds probable cause to believe that the criminal laws have been violated, is to "report its findings and recommendations to the proper federal and state authorities . . . charged with the responsibility for prosecution of criminal offenses," or to file charges itself. La. Rev. Stat. Ann. § 23:880.7 B (Supp. 1969). The Commission has no authority to adjudicate a person's guilt or innocence, and its recommendations and findings have no legal consequences whatsoever. Id., § 23:880.7 A (Supp. 1969).

The Commission thus bears close resemblance to certain federal administrative agencies, infra, this page and 440, and to the offices of prosecuting attorneys. These agencies have one salient feature in common, which distinguishes them from those designed simply to "expose." None of them is the final arbiter of anyone's guilt or innocence. Each, rather, plays only a preliminary role, designed, in the usual course of events, to initiate a subsequent formal proceeding in which the accused will enjoy the full panoply of procedural safeguards. For this reason, and because such agencies could not otherwise practicably pursue their investigative functions, they have not been required to follow "adjudicatory" procedures.

I see no constitutionally relevant distinction between this State Commission and the federal administrative agencies that perform investigative functions designed to discover violations which may result in the initiation of criminal proceedings. In Hannah v. Larche, 363 U. S. 420, 445-448, 454-485 (1960), the Court expressly condoned the denial of "rights such as apprisal, confrontation, and cross-examination" in such "nonadjudicative, fact-finding investigations." Id., at 446. The Court recognized, for example, that the Federal Trade Commission

"could not conduct an efficient investigation if persons being investigated were permitted to convert the investigation into a trial. We have found no authorities suggesting that the rules governing Federal Trade Commission investigations violate the Constitution, and this is understandable since any person investigated by the Federal Trade Commission will be accorded all the traditional judicial safeguards at a subsequent adjudicative proceeding. . . ." Id., at 446.

And the Court said of the Securities and Exchange Commission:

"Although the Commission's Rules provide that parties to adjudicative proceedings shall be given detailed notice of the matters to be determined, . . . and a right to cross-examine witnesses appearing at the hearing, . . . those provisions of the Rules are made specifically inapplicable to investigations, . . . even though the Commission is required to initiate civil or criminal proceedings if an investigation discloses violations of law. Undoubtedly, the reason for this distinction is to prevent the sterilization of investigations by burdening them with trial-like procedures." Id., at 446-448. (Emphasis added.)

The statutory safeguards afforded persons being investigated by the Louisiana Commission are at least equal to those provided by most of these federal agencies. See id., at 454-485.

The Commission's functions also find close analogies in the investigations and determinations that take place daily in the offices of state and federal prosecuting attorneys. In both instances, the responsible officials proceed by interrogating persons with knowledge of possible violations of the criminal law. If the prosecutor believes that an individual has committed a crime, he files an information or seeks a grand jury indictment. When the Commission reaches a similar conclusion, it turns its intelligence over to a prosecutor so that he may initiate the formal criminal process.

For obvious reasons, it has not been seriously suggested that a "person under investigation" by a district attorney has any of the "adjudicative" constitutional rights at the investigative stage.[4] These rights attach only after formal proceedings have been initiated. Nor, of course, does one under investigations have a constitutional right that the investigations be conducted in secrecy, or that the official keep his plans to prosecute confidential. The decision whether or not to disclose these matters rests in the sound discretion of the responsible public official. Various factors, such as the fear that a suspect will flee or the concern for obtaining an unbiased jury when the matter comes to trial, may militate in favor of secrecy. On the other hand, an appropriate disclosure of a pending investigation may bring forth witnesses and evidence, and serves a proper ancillary function in keeping the public informed.[5]

The Commission's operations differ from those of a prosecuting attorney in one important respect, however. The very formality of the Commission's investigatory process may lend greater credibility and a greater aura of official sanction to the testimony given before it and to its findings. Although in this respect the Commission is not different from the federal agencies discussed above, I am not ready to say that the collateral consequences of government-sanctioned opprobrium may not under some circumstances entitle a person to some right, consistent with the Commission's efficient performance of its investigatory duties, to have his public say in rebuttal. However, the Commission's procedures are far from being niggardly in this respect. They include not only the right to make a personal appearance, but also the right to submit the statements of others, and, under some circumstances, to present questions to adverse witnesses. This is far more than is given persons under investigation by the federal agencies, and certainly serves adequately to neutralize any adverse collateral effects of the Commission's investigative proceedings.

As I noted above, the very insubstantiality of appellant's complaint leaves it unclear what the Court holds today. It may be that some of my Brethren understand the complaint to allege that in fact the Commission acts primarily as an agency of "exposure," rather than one which serves the ends required by the state statutes. If so—although I do not believe that the complaint can be reasonably thus construed—the area of disagreement between us may be small or nonexistent.

Before the Court holds that a purely investigatory agency must adopt the full roster of adjudicative safeguards however, it would do well to heed carefully its own warning in Hannah, that such a requirement "would make a shambles of the investigation and stifle the agency in its gathering of facts." 363 U. S., at 444. Such a requirement would not only incapacitate state criminal investigatory bodies at a time when their need cannot be gainsaid, but would cast a broad shadow of doubt over the propriety of long-standing procedures employed by many federal agencies—procedures which less than a decade ago the Court believed to be proper and necessary.

Notes

[1] As the prevailing opinion notes, ante, at 420, and n. 3, appellant does not assign as error the District Court's holding that this was not a proper class action.

[2] And, of course, there is no suggestion that appellant ever requested that the Commission accord him any of the rights of whose absence he complains.

[3] This inference is supported by the Report of the Labor-Management Commission of Inquiry, filed in this Court, which, other than mentioning the litigation challenging the Commission, nowhere refers to this appellant.

[4] Of course, a person called upon to participate in the investigation, e. g., by answering questions, may have relevant rights at this stage. Cf., e. g., Mancusi v. DeForte, 392 U. S. 364 (1968). But appellant does not intimate, and the majority does not assume, that he has been or will be subpoenaed to testify or produce documents.

[5] It is ironic that appellant should complain of the open nature of the Commission's proceedings. The statutory requirement that the Commission "shall base its findings and reports only upon evidence and testimony given at public hearings," La. Rev. Stat. Ann. § 23:880.12 A (Supp. 1969), is plainly designed to protect witnesses and persons under investigation from what some members of the Court have criticized as secret inquisitions or Star Chamber proceedings. See In re Groban, 352 U. S. 330, 337 (1957) (BLACK, J., dissenting); Anonymous v. Baker, 360 U. S. 287, 298 (1959) (BLACK, J., dissenting).

Justice Harlan's dissent in Utah Public Service Comm'n v. El Paso Gas Co. (June 16, 1969)

MR. JUSTICE HARLAN, whom MR. JUSTICE STEWART joins, dissenting.

The action taken by the Court today will be dismaying to all who are accustomed to regard this institution as a court of law.

All semblance of judicial procedure has been discarded in the headstrong effort to reach a result that four members of this Court believe desirable. In violation of the Court's rules, the majority asserts the power to dispose of this case according to its own notions, despite the fact that all the parties participating in the lower court proceedings are satisfied that the District Court's decree is in the public interest. The majority seeks to justify this extraordinary step on the ground that District Judge Chilson's painstaking opinion of over 30 pages is in violation of the mandate issued in Cascade Natural Gas Corp. v. El Paso Natural Gas Co., 386 U. S. 129 (1967), although (1) we have heard no oral argument directed to this question[1] and (2) we have not ordered the interested parties to file full briefs on this issue. Actually, as will appear, what the Court has done is to substitute, sua sponte, a new mandate for its old one. I cannot possibly subscribe to such an abuse of the judicial process.

Moreover, even if the impropriety of the Court's precipitate course is swallowed, it seems to me clear that the District Court's decision in the present case did not violate any prior mandate this Court has entered in this long and complicated litigation.[2] Rather than frustrating Cascade's command that "a new company be at once restored to a position where it could compete with El Paso in the California market," 386 U. S., at 136, Judge Chilson's decree adopted the solution which, so far as one can now tell, most effectively realized the goals of § 7 of the Clayton Act. Indeed, it is unlikely that as a result of the Court's order today, California's natural gas consumers will ever obtain the benefits of competition that this lawsuit was intended to achieve when it was initiated by the Department of Justice in 1957.

I.

In addition to 17 private parties, the States of California, Arizona, Nevada, Utah, and Washington intervened in the proceedings below. The Department of Justice of course represented the interests of the United States as plaintiff, and the Federal Power Commission participated as amicus curiae. Only the State of Utah, however, chose to file a Jurisdictional Statement in this Court challenging Judge Chilson's decree. All other parties have signified their belief that the District Court's judgment is satisfactory. The State of Utah now wishes to dismiss its appeal, reasonably suggesting that its interests in the present dispute are peripheral, and that if the State of California and the United States do not believe that the decree will prejudice the interests of California's consumers, Utah considers it inappropriate to contest the matter further.

The majority, however, refuses to permit Utah to dismiss its appeal, despite the command of Rule 60 of the rules of this Court:

"Whenever the parties thereto shall, by their attorneys of record, file with the clerk an agreement in writing that an appeal, petition for or writ of certiorari, or motion for leave to file or petition for [an] extraordinary writ be dismissed, specifying the terms as respects costs, and shall pay to the clerk any fees that may be due him, the clerk shall, without further reference to the court, enter an order of dismissal." (Emphasis supplied.)

The language of the rule could not be clearer—the parties to a lawsuit are given the absolute right to dismiss their appeal without judicial scrutiny. Since 1858, the rules of this Court have expressly recognized the existence of this right, see Revised Rules of the Sup. Ct. of the United States, Rule No. 29 (1858),[3] and I have found no decision in which this right has ever been questioned or limited. Nevertheless, the Court today, without any discussion whatever, ignores the heretofore unquestioned interpretation of the rule and declares that "there is an exception where the dismissal implicates a mandate we have entered in a cause." Ante, at 466.

In handing down this ipse dixit, the Court not only overlooks the teachings of more than a century of judicial practice, but also undermines the basic policies which support Rule 60. The rule is not a mere technicality but is predicated upon the classical view that it is the function of this Court to decide controversies between parties only when they cannot be settled by the litigants in any other way. See Marbury v. Madison, 1 Cranch 137 (1803). On this view of the judicial process, it is difficult to perceive why the Court should feel constrained to enforce its mandate when the parties have subsequently agreed, in a completely voluntary and bona fide way, that a different solution will better accommodate their interests. We have labor enough in deciding those pressing disputes which the parties are unable to resolve; there is no need to "do justice" when no litigant is complaining that a wrong has been committed. Nor will it do to say, as the Court seems to suggest, that antitrust decrees, being affected with a public interest, as they surely are, are always subject to sua sponte enforcement by the Court. "Enforcement" of the laws of the United States is the province of the Executive Branch. It is no more a proper function of this Court to thwart the Department of Justice when it decides to terminate an antitrust litigation than it is to order this department of the Executive Branch to commence an antitrust case which some members of this Court may feel should be brought.[4]

Although the Court's decision to police its own mandates sua sponte thus offends fundamental conceptions of the judicial process, I do not mean to suggest that this Court lacks the constitutional power to act in the way it has done. Cf. Continental Co. v. United States, 259 U. S. 156, 165-166 (1922). The Court does have a legitimate interest in maintaining the integrity of its mandates within the entire judicial system and it may be argued that the lower courts will not conscientiously effectuate our decisions unless all know that the Court will act when it learns of abuses. Yet, although this argument may be enough to establish the constitutionality of a practice in which this Court sits as an investigatory body with a roving commission to travel the length and breadth of this land policing its mandates, Rule 60 indicates that such an extraordinary departure from traditional judicial norms has never been thought necessary to insure the integrity of our mandates. Even during periods of history in which there was a greater risk that lower courts would seek to frustrate our decisions, it has been considered sufficient to rely upon the parties to bring violations of a mandate to our attention either by prosecuting a second appeal or by petitioning for a writ of mandamus.[5]

I see no reason why we should turn our back on such basic traditions at this late date. Moreover, if we are to take such drastic action, surely we should not do so in an ad hoc manner, under the pressures of the closing days of the Term. Rather, if we are to change Rule 60, we should do so in an appropriate rule-making proceeding, in which the arguments on both sides of the question may be canvassed with the dispassionate neutrality that is appropriate.

For all of these reasons, I would grant Utah's motion to dismiss its appeal and put an end to this 12-year-old lawsuit.[6]

II.

It is with great hesitation that I turn to consider the Court's decision finding Judge Chilson's decree in violation of Cascade's mandate. The case before us is one of enormous complexity. In addition to the plaintiff and defendant, 22 intervenors and nine applicants for the acquisition of the New Company participated in the proceedings below. Judge Chilson heard testimony for more than three months; the record in this case covers more than 14,000 pages, not to mention voluminous exhibits. And yet, we have not received any briefs which even attempt a complete discussion either of the merits of this case or of the question whether our mandate has been followed in a satisfactory way. The Jurisdictional Statement submitted by the State of Utah properly does not suggest that this case is suitable for summary disposition and simply attempts to persuade the Court that the questions presented are substantial. The documents filed in support of Judge Chilson's decision are no more satisfactory. While many of the parties who participated below have tendered motions in support of Utah's request to dismiss its appeal, these papers principally discuss the reasons why each party was satisfied with the result reached below and do not attempt a full-scale analysis of the merits of this extended and complicated controversy. Only the Memorandum submitted by the Solicitor General deals with the substance of the case in any significant way, since it contains the Government's Motion to Affirm which had been prepared as an answer to Utah's Jurisdictional Statement. Yet the Government's 18-page document does not pretend to deal thoroughly with this case's factual intricacies.

Despite the inadequate briefing, however, enough emerges from the record to suggest that, far from disobeying Cascade's mandate, Judge Chilson made a decision which may well be the only one which realistically promises to fulfill the purposes of the Clayton Act.

The District Court found that "time is of the essence" if the New Company is to compete successfully in the California market. 291 F. Supp. 3, 28. Judge Chilson's analysis of the competitive situation existing today powerfully supports his conclusion that the chances of successful entry are becoming more remote with every passing year. The District Court noted that when this lawsuit began in 1957, El Paso was the only out-of-state supplier in the California market; in contrast, two additional strong companies have entered the State in the past decade. Moreover:

"Although the expanding California market appears to offer opportunities for New Company to enter the market, the recommendation of the Federal Power Commission staff that a 42-inch pipeline should be constructed to California is a matter of grave concern, for according to the evidence before the Court, a 42-inch line would serve all increments to the southern California market for the foreseeable future. The Supreme Court recognized that competition in the California market is limited to future increments, which have not yet been certified for service. Once an increment has been certified, it is withdrawn from competition. The recommendations of the Commission's staff for the construction of a 42-inch line have been commended by the FPC examiner in a current proceeding as `bold and constructive.'. . .

    .....

    "The Government . . . [in] its Brief . . . states:

    `It is too early to predict the ultimate direction or final outcome of this current FPC proceeding. The opportunity it presents to the new company which is to emerge from this law suit is evident. If a full scale 42-inch proceeding gets underway . . . the new company should be equipped to enter as a contender with at least the minimum qualifications for serious consideration.' " 291 F. Supp., at 27-28.

The District Court found that the Colorado Interstate Gas Company (CIG) was the only potential purchaser which had a real opportunity to convince the FPC that it should operate the new Texas pipeline that holds the key to successful competition in California. Surely this finding has a substantial basis in fact, since no other prospective purchaser of the New Company has ever operated a pipeline and only one has ever had any connection at all with the oil and gas industry. Nevertheless, the Court today substantially decreases the chances of successful competition by the New Company by requiring years more litigation before the day will come when operations finally commence. During this lengthy period, existing gas companies will become even more solidly entrenched in the market and the Texas pipeline proceeding may well have progressed to the point where the New Company could not obtain serious consideration from the FPC.

Despite the fact that the Clayton Act may well be the loser, the majority prolongs this lawsuit for two reasons. First, it is said that the District Court violated Cascade's requirement that "[t]he gas reserves granted the New Company must be no less in relation to present existing reserves than Pacific Northwest had when it was independent; and the new gas reserves developed since the merger must be equitably divided between El Paso and the New Company." 386 U. S., at 136-137. But the Court's own discussion of this question unmistakably demonstrates that Judge Chilson fully complied with this branch of Cascade's mandate. The Court cannot and does not deny that Judge Chilson granted reserves to the New Company which are "`no less in relation to present existing reserves' than Northwest had when it was independent." See ante, at 469. The only question that remains is whether the District Court decreed an "equitable" division of gas resources discovered since the merger. The answer to this question also seems quite easy, since the Court does not deny that Judge Chilson granted New Company about 50% of these reserves, which is much more than its proportionate share of the assets.

Although this equal division seems more than equitable to the New Company, the majority fastens on the fact that even with this distribution of resources, the New Company will not be assured of sufficient gas both to meet the anticipated demand of New Company's present customers in the Pacific Northwest and to satisfy the requirements of its potential customers in the California market. This indeed would be a source of concern if it were found that New Company could not practically obtain additional gas resources if it decides to compete in California. But Judge Chilson concluded that just the opposite situation obtains; the District Court found that the New Company "can obtain the reserves necessary to compete in the California market." 291 F. Supp., at 20. The Court, however, ignores this finding completely and does not even attempt to show how, given this fact, New Company's equal share of reserves can in any sense be called "inequitable." Indeed, it is perfectly clear that the Court, under the guise of enforcing its mandate, is really creating a new, and more stringent, standard by which to test this divestiture. But surely this is completely illegitimate in a case where no party has challenged the legality of the District Court's decision, and where, at the most, the issue is the lower court's compliance with our previous mandate.

The Court's second ground for claiming disobedience with Cascade's command is equally untenable. It is said that Cascade ordered "complete divestiture" without delay and we are told that no divestiture can be complete unless there is a cash sale. Since the trial court did not order a cash sale, the majority finds that Cascade's mandate has not been obeyed.

There are several things wrong with this line of argument. First, Cascade expressly states that a cash sale is not required under the standards it sets down:

"Disposition of all of the stock with all convenient speed is necessary and conditions must be imposed to make sure that El Paso interests do not acquire a controlling interest." 386 U. S., at 141. (Emphasis supplied.)

Since Cascade did not require a cash sale it is difficult to see how the present divestiture plan, in which all the common stock of the New Company is transferred to CIG is a per se violation of this Court's earlier mandate. Once again, the Court has created a new standard for judging the validity of the District Court's decision instead of limiting itself to a consideration of whether the decree fulfilled Cascade's demand "that El Paso interests do not acquire a controlling interest" in the New Company.

I pass, then, to consider whether the divestiture plan before us violates our mandate in permitting El Paso domination of its competitor. While this standard is a rather vague one, MR. JUSTICE DOUGLAS, speaking for the Court in Cascade, gave it specific content by explaining why the proposed terms of divestiture then under review were unsatisfactory. This explanation is of the highest importance in determining whether Judge Chilson's decree contravened Cascade's command and it must be considered with care. MR. JUSTICE DOUGLAS began his analysis by noting that the decree had taken some steps to insulate the New Company from El Paso control since it did bar El Paso officers, directors, and owners of more than one-half of one percent of El Paso stock from buying into New Company at the public offering. The Court, however, found this limitation insufficient because:

"the decree does not prohibit members of the families of such prohibited purchasers from obtaining New Company stock. Further, under the terms of the decree, it would be possible for a group of El Paso stockholders, each with less than one-half of one percent of El Paso stock, to acquire at the initial public offering enough New Company stock substantially to influence or even to dominate the New Company. Or, such a group could combine with the families of prohibited purchasers in order to control the New Company. After the exchange or public offering, there is no restriction on the number of New Company shares El Paso shareholders may acquire. Thus, there is a danger that major El Paso stockholders may, subsequent to the exchange or public offering, purchase large blocks of New Company stock and obtain effective control." 386 U. S., at 140-141.

Judge Chilson's decree took steps to remedy each and every defect MR. JUSTICE DOUGLAS noted in Cascade. No members of the immediate family of any officer, director, or owner of one-half of one percent of El Paso shares may convert their nonvoting preference shares into voting common shares at any time. Moreover, any person who acts in concert with any director, officer, or substantial owner of El Paso is included within the ban. In addition, these same individuals are not permitted to obtain control of significant proportions of CIG stock, thereby achieving control over the New Company indirectly. Officers, directors, and their associates are barred from owning more than one-tenth of one percent of CIG stock during the next 10 years and substantial owners of El Paso may not own more than 5% of the outstanding common stock of CIG.[7]

It may be that, on appeal, even these stringent conditions may not be found to have fully satisfied the purposes of the Clayton Act. A decision of this question would of course require an analysis of the financial structure of El Paso in order to determine whether it was possible for the Company or its owners to evade the conditions imposed upon them. But it is surely impossible to hold on this record that Judge Chilson's decree is a violation of the mandate issued in Cascade when the present divestiture plan manifests a conscientious effort to comply with all of the suggestions advanced by the Court in that opinion.[8] Indeed, the majority today does not even attempt to make such a claim. Instead, it ignores the fact that the District Court carefully framed conditions to assure the New Company's independence. At no point in its brief opinion does the Court analyze this aspect of Judge Chilson's decree, contenting itself with the cryptic comment that "it is said . . . [that] there will be provisions to restrict El Paso control over the New Company." Ante, at 468.

III.

The Court's conclusion that its mandate has been disobeyed is, in short, based upon completely erroneous factual premises born of a superficial acquaintance with this 14,000-page record. This is not surprising since the majority has seen fit to decide this important case without the benefit of significant oral or written argument. And yet it is upon this tenuous basis that the Court has chosen to shatter centuries of judicial tradition in order to reach a decision which does not even promise to further the interests of California's gas consumers.

What eventuates today evidences a course of unjudicial action that transcends even that which marked the last appearance of the case in this Court. See the dissenting opinion of STEWART, J., in Cascade, 386 U. S. 129, 143.

I respectfully dissent.

Notes

[1] The Court's opinion incorrectly states that we "ordered oral argument at which all parties concerned were afforded an opportunity to be heard on the question whether there had been compliance with the mandate." Ante, at 466. The complete text of the Court's order directing a hearing unequivocally shows that the parties were requested to address themselves only to the motion filed by the State of Utah requesting permission to dismiss its appeal and that the parties were not asked to argue the merits of the appeal:

"The motion of appellant to dismiss the appeal under Rule 60 and the motion of William M. Bennett for a hearing are set for oral argument on April 29, 1969. The Solicitor General is invited to file a brief and present oral argument if he so desires. MR. JUSTICE HARLAN and MR. JUSTICE STEWART dissent, believing that the action taken by the Court abuses its own processes. See Rule 60. MR. JUSTICE WHITE, MR. JUSTICE FORTAS, and MR. JUSTICE MARSHALL took no part in the consideration or decision of this matter." 394 U. S. 970 (1969).

Pursuant to the Court's order, the parties used their limited time for oral argument in an effort to satisfy the Court that they had acted properly in refusing to take an appeal from the District Court's decision. No party presented any substantial arguments on the merits of this case.

[2] See Cascade Natural Gas Corp. v. El Paso Natural Gas Co., supra; United States v. El Paso Natural Gas Co., 376 U. S. 651 (1964); cf. California v. Federal Power Commission, 369 U. S. 482 (1962).

[3] Rule 29 provided:

"Whenever the plaintiff and defendant in a writ of error pending in this court, or the appellant and appellee in any appeal, shall at any time hereafter, in vacation and out of term time, by their respective attorneys, who are entered as such on the record, sign and file with the clerk an agreement in writing, directing the case to be dismissed, and specifying the terms upon which it is to be dismissed as to costs, and also paying to the clerk any fees that may be due to him, it shall be the duty of the clerk to enter the case dismissed, and to give to either party which may request it a copy of the agreement filed; but no mandate or other process is to issue without an order by the court."

While this rule by its terms provided for dismissal of cases only during vacation, there is no indication that a different procedure was followed during the Term. Surely there would be little reason to permit automatic dismissal during vacation but forbid it at other times.

Rule 29, with minor amendments, was a part of the Court's rules until July 1, 1954, when it was replaced by the present Rule 60.

[4] It is of course perfectly appropriate for a court to make an independent judgment as to the merits of an antitrust consent decree which the parties submit for approval. See, e. g., United States v. Pan American World Airways, Inc., 1959 Trade Cas. ¶ 69,300, at 75,138 (D. C. S. D. N. Y.). For in the consent decree context, the parties are requesting affirmative action from the judiciary in order to resolve their dispute, while in

the situation we confront, none of the parties are requesting further judicial relief.

[5] See In re Potts, 166 U. S. 263 (1897); cf. In re Sanford Fork & Tool Co., 160 U. S. 247 (1895); Ex parte The Union Steamboat Co., 178 U. S. 317 (1900).

[6] The Court does not decide whether the papers opposing Utah's motion to dismiss which were presented by John J. Flynn and I. Daniel Stewart, as amicus curiae, and those tendered by William M. Bennett, as "consumer spokesman," may be properly considered at this late stage in the proceedings. Since the Court does not reach this question, I do not believe it appropriate to state my views on the matter; nor have I believed it proper to consider in any way the arguments made by Messrs. Flynn, Stewart, and Bennett.

[7] These conditions were approved by the District Court on November 7, 1968, in an order approving the Implementing Documents filed by the appropriate parties pursuant to Judge Chilson's decision naming CIG as the successful applicant. The Implementing Documents are a part of the record in this case.

In addition to the restrictions mentioned in the text, the District Court also forbade El Paso's officers and directors as well as their associates, from owning more than one-tenth of one percent of New Company stock for the next 10 years; moreover, El Paso and its affiliates are forbidden to acquire any New Company or CIG stock at any time in the future. Steps have also been taken to assure that El Paso will have no officers or directors in common with New Company or CIG.

[8] The Court relies heavily on United States v. du Pont & Co., 366 U. S. 316 (1961), to support its claim that Cascade's mandate has been breached. But du Pont only holds that the District Court must assure itself that "the intercorporate community of interest which we found to violate the law" must be dissolved by divestiture. 366 U. S., at 331. Nothing in du Pont suggests, let alone holds, that a cash sale is the only way to accomplish this objective. Like Cascade, du Pont established no per se rule in this area.

Justice Harlan's concurrence and dissent in NC v. Pearce (June 23, 1969)

MR. JUSTICE HARLAN, concurring in part and dissenting in part.

Were these cases to be judged entirely within the traditional confines of the Due Process Clause of the Fourteenth Amendment, I should, but not without some difficulty, find myself in substantial agreement with the result reached by the Court. However, the Court today, in Benton v. Maryland, post, p. 784, has held, over my dissent, that the Double Jeopardy Clause of the Fifth Amendment is made applicable to the States by the Fourteenth Amendment Due Process Clause. While my usual practice is to adhere until the end of Term to views I have expressed in dissent during the Term, I believe I should not proceed in these important cases as if Benton had turned out otherwise.

Given Benton, it is my view that the decision of this Court in Green v. United States, 355 U. S. 184 (1957), from which I dissented at the time, points strongly to the conclusion, also reached by my Brother DOUGLAS, ante, p. 726, that the Double Jeopardy

Clause of the Fifth Amendment governs both issues presently decided by the Court. Accordingly, I join in Part I of the Court's opinion, and concur in the result reached in Part II, except in one minor respect.[1]

Green v. United States, supra, held in effect that a defendant who is convicted of a lesser offense included in that charged in the original indictment, and who thereafter secures reversal, may be retried only for the lesser included offense. Mr. Justice Frankfurter observed, in a dissent which I joined, that:

"As a practical matter, and on any basis of human values, it is scarcely possible to distinguish a case in which the defendant is convicted of a greater offense from one in which he is convicted of an offense that has the same name as that of which he was previously convicted but carries a significantly [increased] . . . punishment . . . ." Id., at 213.

Further reflection a decade later has not changed my view that the two situations cannot be meaningfully distinguished.

Every consideration enunciated by the Court in support of the decision in Green applies with equal force to the situation at bar. In each instance, the defendant was once subjected to the risk of receiving a maximum punishment, but it was determined by legal process that he should receive only a specified punishment less than the maximum. See id., at 190. And the concept or fiction of an "implicit acquittal" of the greater offense, ibid., applies equally to the greater sentence: in each case it was determined at the former trial that the defendant or his offense was of a certain limited degree of "badness" or gravity only, and therefore merited only a certain limited punishment. Most significantly, perhaps, in each case a contrary rule would place the defendant considering whether to appeal his conviction in the same "incredible dilemma" and confront him with the same "desperate" choice. Id., at 193. His decision whether or not to appeal would be burdened by the consideration that success,[2] followed by retrial and conviction, might place him in a far worse position than if he remained silent and suffered what seemed to him an unjust punishment.[3] In terms of Green, that the imposition of a more severe sentence on retrial is a matter of pure chance, rather than the result of purposeful retaliation for having taken an appeal, renders the choice no less "desperate."

If, as a matter of policy and practicality, the imposition of an increased sentence on retrial has the same consequences whether effected in the guise of an increase in the degree of offense or an augmentation of punishment, what other factors render one route forbidden and the other permissible under the Double Jeopardy Clause? It cannot be that the provision does not comprehend "sentences"—as distinguished from "offenses" —for it has long been established that once a prisoner commences service of sentence, the Clause prevents a court from vacating the sentence and then imposing a greater one. See United States v. Benz, 282 U. S. 304, 306-307 (1931); Ex parte Lange, 18 Wall. 163, 168, 173 (1874).

The Court does not suggest otherwise,[4] but in its view, apparently, when the conviction itself and not merely the consequent sentence has been set aside, or when either has been set aside at the defendant's behest,[5] the "slate has been wiped clean," ante, at 721, and the Double Jeopardy Clause presents no bar to the imposition of a sentence greater than that originally imposed. In support of this proposition, the Court relies chiefly on two cases, Stroud v. United States, 251 U. S. 15 (1919), and United States v. Ball, 163 U. S. 662 (1896). I do not believe that either of these cases provides an adequate basis for the Court's seemingly incongruous conclusion.

Stroud v. United States, supra, held that a defendant who received a life sentence for first-degree murder could, upon securing a reversal of the conviction, be retried for first-degree murder and sentenced to death. However, the opinion does not explicitly advert to the question whether the Double Jeopardy Clause bars the imposition of an increased punishment, and an examination of the briefs in that case confirms the doubt expressed by the Court of Appeals in Patton v. North Carolina, 381 F. 2d 636, 644 (1967), whether this question was squarely presented to the Court.[6] Assuming that Stroud stood for the proposition which the majority attributes to it, that decision simply cannot be squared with the subsequent decision in Green v. United States, 355 U. S. 184 (1957). See id., at 213 (dissenting opinion); People v. Henderson, 60 Cal. 2d 482, 386 P. 2d 677 (1963).

The Court does not rest solely on this ambiguous and doubtful precedent, however. Its main point seems to be that to limit the punishment on retrial to that imposed at the former trial "would be to cast doubt upon the whole validity of the basic principle enunciated in United States v. Ball," 163 U. S. 662 (1896), and its progeny. Ante, at 721.

Ball held, simply, that a defendant who succeeds in getting his first conviction set aside may thereafter be retried for the same offense of which he was formerly convicted. This is, indeed, a fundamental doctrine in our criminal jurisprudence, and I would be the last to undermine it. But Ball does not speak to the question of what punishment may be imposed on retrial. I entirely fail to understand the Court's suggestion, unless it assumes that Ball must stand or fall on the question-begging notion that, to quote the majority today, "the original conviction has, at the defendant's behest, been wholly nullified and the slate wiped clean."[7] Ante, at 721.

In relying on this conceptual fiction, the majority forgets that Green v. United States, supra, prohibits the imposition of an increased punishment on retrial precisely because convictions are usually set aside only at the defendant's behest, and not in spite of that fact. 355 U. S., at 193-194; supra, at 746: the defendant's choice to appeal an erroneous conviction is protected by the rule that he may not again be placed in jeopardy of suffering the greater punishment not imposed at the first trial. Moreover, in its exaltation of form over substance and policy, the Court misconceives, I think, the essential principle of Ball itself:

"While different theories have been advanced to support the permissibility of retrial, of greater importance than the conceptual abstractions employed to explain the Ball principle are the implications of that principle for the sound administration of justice.

Corresponding to the right of an accused to be given a fair trial is the societal interest in punishing one whose guilt is clear after he has obtained such a trial. It would be a high price indeed for society to pay were every accused granted immunity from punishment because of any defect sufficient to constitute reversible error in the proceedings leading to conviction." United States v. Tateo, 377 U. S. 463, 466 (1964).

To be sure, this societal interest is compromised to a degree if the second judge is forbidden to impose a greater punishment on retrial than was meted out at the first trial. For example, new facts may develop between the first and second trial which would, as an initial matter, be considered in aggravation of sentence. By the same token, however, the prosecutor who was able to prove only second-degree murder at the former trial might improve his case in the interim and acquire sufficient evidence to prove murder in the first degree. In either instance, if one views the second trial in a vacuum, the defendant has received less punishment than is his due. But in both cases, the compromise is designed to protect other societal interests, and it is, after Green, a compromise compelled by the Double Jeopardy Clause.[8]

I therefore conclude that, consistent with the Fifth Amendment, a defendant who has once been convicted and sentenced to a particular punishment may not on retrial be placed again in jeopardy of receiving a greater punishment than was first imposed. Because the Double Jeopardy Clause has now been held applicable to the States, Benton v. Maryland, supra, I would affirm the judgment of the Court of Appeals in No. 418, and vacate and remand in No. 413, so that respondent Pearce may finish serving his first, valid sentence. See n. 1, supra.

Notes

[1] An outright affirmance in No. 413 would carry the consequence of relieving the respondent Pearce from serving the remaining few months of his original state sentence. See the Court's opinion, ante, at 713-714 and n. 1. There is no basis, whether the result in this case is governed by due process or double jeopardy, for such an interference with the State's legitimate criminal processes. I would therefore vacate the judgment of the Court of Appeals for the Fourth Circuit in No. 413 and remand the case so that an order may be entered releasing Pearce at, but not before, the expiration of his first sentence. Cf. Peyton v. Rowe, 391 U. S. 54 (1968).

[2] A prohibition against enhanced punishment on retrial does not, of course, tend in any manner to encourage frivolous appeals. A contrary rule does not discourage frivolous appeals, except insofar as it discourages all appeals.

[3] The would-be appellant's quandary is most clearly seen when the first trial and conviction for a capital offense result in a sentence of life imprisonment. Cf., e. g., Green v. United States, supra.

[4] Indeed, the Court relies on these cases in Part I of its opinion to hold that a prisoner must be afforded credit for time served pursuant to a subsequently vacated sentence.

[5] Neither Lange nor Benz indicates that the principle prohibiting the imposition of an enhanced sentence on the same judgment of conviction depends on whether the original sentence is vacated on the prisoner's application, or is set aside sua sponte by the court. (It appears, though not clearly, that Lange's sentence was set aside at his behest.)

In Murphy v. Massachusetts, 177 U. S. 155 (1900), however, the Court indicated that one who successfully moves to vacate his sentence occupies "the same posture as if he had sued out his writ of error on the day he was first sentenced, and the mere fact that by reason of his delay in doing so he had served a portion of the erroneous sentence could not entitle him to assert that he was being twice punished." Id., at 161-162. Thus, the Court concluded in Murphy not only that the sentence could be augmented, but also that the petitioner was not constitutionally entitled to any credit for time served under the first sentence.

This proves too much, as the Court today holds in Part I of its opinion. In my view, neither conclusion survives Green.

[6] Stroud pitched his double jeopardy claim on the theory that, although "the constitutional prohibition does not prevent a second trial after reversal in non-capital cases," it does—without reference to the sentence imposed—preclude "a second trial upon reversal of a conviction in a capital case." Brief for Plaintiff in Error in No. 276, O. T. 1919, p. 32. Stroud's argument as to the enhanced sentence appears based solely on nonconstitutional grounds. See id., at 89 et seq.

[7] This fiction would seem to lead to a result which even the majority might have difficulty reconciling with the Double Jeopardy Clause's prohibition of multiple punishment. Consider the situation of a defendant who successfully vacates a conviction and is then retried and convicted after he has fully served the sentence first imposed. See Street v. New York, 394 U. S. 576 (1969); Sibron v. New York, 392 U. S. 40 (1968); Ginsberg v. New York, 390 U. S. 629 (1968). Although the sentence was fully served, the defendant himself has caused the judgment to be vacated, and the majority's "nullification" principle would seem to allow the judge to impose a new sentence of imprisonment on him—so long as the new sentence was an "increased" sentence rather than the result of the court's failure to "credit" the defendant with the sentence he had completed.

[8] That the new facts may consist of misdeeds committed by the defendant since the first trial, rather than prior misconduct only subsequently discovered, should not, in my view, alter the outcome under Green and the other double jeopardy cases. If subsequent misdeeds amount to criminal violations, the defendant may properly be tried and punished for them. If they amount to something less, the very uncertainty as to what kinds of noncriminal conduct may be considered in aggravation of the sentence on retrial would, analytically, seem to thwart the concerns protected by Green. In either event, I do not understand what rational policy distinguishes a defendant whose appeal is successful from one who takes no appeal and whose sentence may not, consistent with the Double Jeopardy Clause, be augmented. See supra, at 747.

Of course, nothing in the Double Jeopardy Clause forbids a prosecutor from introducing new and harmful evidence at the second trial in order to improve his chances of obtaining a conviction for the lesser offense of which the defendant was previously convicted or to assure that the defendant receives the full punishment imposed at the first trial.

Justice Harlan's concurrence and dissent in Detroit & Toledo Shore Line R. Co. v. Transportation Union (Dec 9, 1969)

MR. JUSTICE HARLAN, with whom THE CHIEF JUSTICE joins, concurring in part and dissenting in part.

I fully agree that the application of § 6 should not be restricted to only those terms of employment that the parties have seen fit to embody in a written agreement. Section 6 may properly, in some circumstances, be extended to "freeze" de facto conditions of employment. I cannot, however, accept what appears to be the majority's test for determining when a § 6 freeze is appropriate.[1] Any work practice is, in the words of the majority, an "actual, objective working condition." However, the practice of today may not be the accepted condition of yesterday, but rather a temporary expedient in which neither party acquiesces. I find it difficult to think that Congress intended that either party, by serving a § 6 notice, should be able to shackle his adversary and tie him to a condition that has been historically and consistently controverted.

Rather, what persuades me to countenance the extension of § 6 beyond the terms of a written collective-bargaining agreement is the fact, observed by the Court, that "[w]here a condition is satisfactorily tolerable to both sides, it is often omitted from the agreement . . . ," ante, at 155. Taking this observation as a point of departure, I favor a more subjective approach than the objective and mechanical one implicit in the majority's language. The question that should be asked is whether in the context of the relationship between the principals, taken as a whole, there is a basis for implying an understanding on the particular practice involved. To this end it is necessary to consider not only the duration of the practice but also all the dealings between the parties, as for example, whether the particular condition has been the subject of prior negotiations.

While I recognize, of course, that any subjective test is not easily applied, I cannot subscribe to a rule that may have the incongruous effect of perpetuating what both parties in fact view as a disputed practice, simply because neither party, for reasons of convenience, has exercised a recognized option of resorting to self-help.

Under this standard I consider that the proper disposition of the case before us is to remand to the District Court for additional findings.[2] While the District Court found that "[f]or many years prior to 1961" Lang Yard was the established terminal point for reporting to duty, that finding alone would not satisfy a subjective test in light of subsequent events that may have negatived any understanding that might have existed prior to 1961.[3] In 1961 the Shore Line advised the union of a contemplated shifting of reporting to its Trenton terminal some 30 miles north. The proposal apparently met with employee resistance and the union served a § 6 notice seeking to modify the agreement with the railroad. By 1963 the parties had exhausted the statutory mediation route without reconciling their differences and the Mediation Board recommended arbitration to break the impasse. This proposal was rejected by the company which declared the dispute moot since, by that time, it had abandoned its Trenton project. Meanwhile, the company embarked on a practice of transporting employees at its own expense and on company time from its Dearoad terminal, 11 miles north of Trenton, a practice which is the subject of a separate § 6 notice.

In my opinion a remand is called for to determine whether the company's voluntary abandonment of its Trenton project, coupled with its undertaking to transport employees from Dearoad at its own cost and the long-established practice prior to 1961, amounted to acceptance in principle of Lang Yard as the reporting location.

For that reason I respectfully dissent from the Court's affirmance of the Court of Appeals.

Notes

[1] The majority first announces a test looking to "actual, objective working conditions," ante, at 153. This is later qualified by a durational requirement, but no general principle of decision is set forth.

[2] While the District Court and the Court of Appeals both properly rejected petitioner's theory, restricting § 6 to terms embodied in a written agreement, it is by no means clear to me precisely what standard they followed in concluding that the Act was applicable.

[3] The District Court, as I read its findings, does not appear to have considered the possible impact of the train of events revealed by the record in connection with 1961-1963 proceedings before the Board.

Justice Harlan's dissent in Hellenic Lines Ltd. v. Rhoditis (June 8, 1970)

MR. JUSTICE HARLAN, with whom THE CHIEF JUSTICE and MR. JUSTICE STEWART join, dissenting.

I dissent from today's decision holding that a Greek seaman who signs articles in Greece for employment on a Greek-owned, Greek-flag vessel may recover under the Jones Act for shipboard injuries sustained while the vessel was in American territorial waters. This result is supported neither by precedent, nor realistic policy, and in my opinion is far removed from any intention that can reasonably be ascribed to Congress.

A

Section 688 of Title 46, U. S. C., 41 Stat. 1007, the Jones Act, provides:

"Any seaman who shall suffer personal injury in the course of his employment may, at his election, maintain an action for damages at law, with the right of trial by jury, and in such action all statutes of the United States modifying or extending the common-law right or remedy in cases of personal injury to railway employees shall apply; and in case of the death of any seaman as a result of any such personal injury the personal representative of such seaman may maintain an action for damages at law with the right of trial by jury, and in such action all statutes of the United States conferring or regulating the right of action for death in the case of railway employees shall be applicable. Jurisdiction in such actions shall be under the court of the district in which the defendant employer resides or in which his principal office is located."

The language of § 688 is, as Mr. Justice Jackson noted in Lauritzen v. Larsen, 345 U. S. 571 (1953), all-embracing. By its terms it is not limited to American seamen nor to vessels bearing the American flag. Yet despite the sweeping language it can hardly be doubted that congressional concern stopped short of the lengths to which the literal terms of the statute carry the Jones Act. This was emphasized in Lauritzen which pointed out that Congress wrote against a backdrop of "usage as old as the Nation," that "such statutes have been construed to apply only to areas and transactions in which American law would be considered operative under prevalent doctrines of international law." 345 U. S., at 577. This principle the Court reiterated in Romero v. International Terminal Co., 358 U. S. 354 (1959), where we reaffirmed the presumption that domestic legislation has been enacted with "respect for the relevant interests of foreign nations in the regulation of maritime commerce as part of the legitimate concern of the international community." 358 U. S., at 383.

This Court only recently applied this principle in McCulloch v. Sociedad Nacional, 372 U. S. 10 (1963), where we were called upon to determine whether labor relations dealing with an alien crew on a foreign-flag vessel, beneficially owned by an American corporation, affected "commerce" within the meaning of the National Labor Relations Act. In holding that the Act was not "intended to have any application to foreign registered vessels employing alien seamen," the Court declined to rely on the beneficial ownership of the vessel and other "substantial United States contacts," including regular visits to the United States and the "integrated maritime operation" of the United Fruit Company, the beneficial owner of the vessel, to override the well-settled principle that the law of the country whose flag a ship flies governs shipboard transactions, absent some "clear expression" from Congress to the contrary. See Wildenhus's Case, 120 U. S. 1 (1887); United States v. Flores, 289 U. S. 137, 155-159 (1933); Cunard Steamship Co. v. Mellon, 262 U. S. 100, 124 (1923); cf. Murray v. The Charming Betsy, 2 Cranch 64, 118 (1804).[1]

The McCulloch case followed a course marked early in our jurisprudence, and , in fact, built upon Lauritzen which had announced that the law of the flag, "the most venerable and universal rule of maritime law," would in Jones Act cases "overbear most other connecting events in determining applicable law . . . unless some heavy counterweight appears." 345 U. S., at 584, 585-586.

Such a counterweight would exist only in circumstances where the application of the American rule of law would further the purpose of Congress. While some legislation in its purpose obviously requires extension beyond our borders to achieve national policy, this is not so, in my opinion, with an Act concerned with prescribing particular remedies, rather than one regulating commerce or creating a standard for conduct.

The only justification that I can see for extending extraterritorially a remedial-type provision like § 688 is that the injured seaman is an individual whose well-being is a concern of this country. It was for this reason that Lauritzen recognized the residence of the plaintiff as a factor that should properly be considered in deciding who is a "seaman" as Congress employed that term in § 688. See D. Cavers, The Choice-of-Law Process 96-97 (1965). In so doing it reflected earlier decisions where recovery was had by resident alien seamen who were serving aboard foreign-flag vessels. See, e. g., Gambera v. Bergoty, 132 F. 2d 414 (C. A. 2d Cir. 1942); cf. Uravic v. F. Jarka Co., 282 U. S. 234 (1931).

In the early decisions involving citizen and resident alien seamen serving on foreign vessels, some additional factor, such as the vessel's presence in American waters or beneficial American ownership, was considered to be an element justifying recovery. See Uravic v. F. Jarka Co., supra; Gerradin v. United Fruit Co., 60 F. 2d 927 (C. A. 2d Cir. 1932); compare Gambera v. Bergoty, supra, with O'Neill v. Cunard White Star, 160 F. 2d 446 (C. A. 2d Cir. 1947). Lauritzen in enumerating these factors ("contacts") as independent considerations, was attempting to focus analysis on those factors that are the necessary ingredients for a statutory cause of action: first, as a matter of statutory construction, is plaintiff within that class of seamen that Congress intended to cover by the statute? and, second, is there a sufficient nexus between the defendant and this country so as to justify the assertion of legislative jurisdiction?[2] In other words the Court must define "seaman" and "employer" as those words are used in § 688. In this regard the situs of the accident or the vessel's contacts with this country by virtue of its beneficial ownership or the frequency of calls at our ports simply serves as an adequate nexus between this country and defendant to assert jurisdiction in a case where congressional policy is otherwise furthered. But no matter how qualitatively substantial or numerous these kinds of contacts may be, they have no bearing in themselves on whether Jones Act recovery is appropriate in a given instance. For transactions occurring aboard foreign-flag vessels that question should be answered by reference to the plaintiff's relationship to this country. See Note, Admiralty and the Choice of Law: Lauritzen v. Larsen Applied, 47 Va. L. Rev. 1400 (1961).

Viewed in this perspective, today's decision and decisions of several lower courts that have taken the phenomenon of "convenient" foreign registry as a wedge for displacing the law of the flag, see, e. g., Southern Cross Steamship Co. v. Firipis, 285 F. 2d 651 (C. A. 4th Cir. 1960); Pavlou v. Ocean Traders Marine Corp., 211 F. Supp. 320 (D. C. S. D. N. Y. 1962); Voyiatzis v. National Shipping & Trading Corp., 199 F. Supp. 920 (D. C. S. D. N. Y. 1961), have, I believe, misconstrued these basic premises on which Lauritzen was founded. This is underscored by the fact that the Lauritzen allusion to the practice of American owners of finding a "convenient" flag "to avoid stringent shipping laws by seeking foreign registration eagerly offered by some countries," 345 U. S., at 587, was prefaced by citation and discussion of Skiriotes v. Florida, 313 U. S. 69 (1941), and Steele v. Bulova Watch Co., 344 U. S. 280 (1952), both of which dealt with the question of when legislative jurisdiction existed to apply domestic law to American nationals abroad. In both cases the application of domestic law presupposed or construed legislative purpose to be furthered by reaching across the border.[3]

The Lauritzen statement, lifted out of context, has acquired a dynamism and become the justification for recovery by foreign seamen simply on the ground that convenient "registry" somehow circumvents an obligation that Congress desired to impose on all owners within its jurisdiction.[4]

This underlies today's decision which relies on the fact that Hellenic Lines is an American-based operation and its vessels would be accorded a competitive advantage over American-flag vessels were we to permit petitioners to avoid responsibility under the Jones Act. Liability is only one factor that contributes to the higher cost of operating an American-flag vessel. Indeed, recognizing the insurance factor, it is doubtful that this factor is a significant contribution to the competitive advantage of foreign-flag ships, especially given the higher crew wages (see 46 U. S. C. § 1132 requiring American crews) and construction costs for American-flag ships, which must be built in American yards if they are to participate in the congressional programs specifically designed to offset the higher costs that the Court today takes as justification for displacing settled international principles of choice of law. See, e. g., 46 U. S. C. § 883 (coastwise trade); 46 U. S. C. § 1180 (subsidy). See generally S. Lawrence, United States Merchant Shipping Policies and Politics 61-67 (1966).

Even were Jones Act liability a significant uncompensated cost in the operation of an American ship, I could not regard this as a reason for extending Jones Act recovery to foreign seamen when the underlying concern of the legislation before us is the adjustment of the risk of loss between individuals and not the regulation of commerce or competition.

B

Today's decision suggests that courts have become mesmerized by contacts, and notwithstanding the purported eschewal of a mechanical application of the Lauritzen test, they have lost sight of the primary purpose of Lauritzen which, as I conceive it, was to reconcile the all-embracing language of the Jones Act with those principles of comity embodied in international and maritime law that are designed to "foster amicable and workable commercial relations." 345 U. S., at 582. Lauritzen, properly understood, should, I submit, be taken to focus the judicial inquiry on the purpose of Congress and the presence or absence of an adequate basis for the assertion of American jurisdiction, when that purpose may be furthered by application of the statute in the circumstances presented.

Where, as in the case before us, the injured plaintiff has no American ties, the inquiry should be directed toward determining what jurisdiction is primarily concerned with plaintiff's welfare and whether that jurisdiction's rule may, consistent with those notions of due process that determine the presence of legislative jurisdiction, govern recovery. In the case before us, there is no reason to disregard either the law of the flag or plaintiff's contractual undertaking to accept Greek law as controlling, thereby in effect assuming that he signed articles under conditions that would justify disregarding the contractual choice of law. Rhoditis is a Greek national who resides in Greece. Under these circumstances Greek law provides the appropriate rule.

I would reverse the judgment of the Court of Appeals, and hold that the Jones Act affords no redress to this seaman.

Notes

[1] The principle of deference to the law of the flag had its origins in the fiction that the vessel was an extension of the sovereign territory of the country whose ensign it flew. As Mr. Justice Jackson noted in Lauritzen, the principle draws strength from the practical necessity of providing predictable rules for shipboard conduct, rules that would, under conventional territorial principles, be changing as the vessel traveled over the high seas and through different territorial waters. "It is true that the criminal jurisdiction of the United States is in general based on the territorial principle, and criminal statutes of the United States are not by implication given an extra-territorial effect. [Citations omitted.] But that principle has never been thought to be applicable to a merchant vessel which, for purposes of the jurisdiction of the courts of the sovereignty whose flag it flies to punish crimes committed upon it, is deemed to be a part of the territory of that sovereignty, and not to lose that character when in navigable waters within the territorial limits of another sovereignty. . . ." United States v. Flores, 289 U. S., at 155-156. See Restatement, Conflict of Laws §§ 405, 406 (1934).

[2] There must be at least some minimal contact between a State and the regulated subject before it can, consistently with the requirements of due process, exercise legislative jurisdiction. See, e. g., Home Ins. Co. v. Dick, 281 U. S. 397 (1930); Watson v. Employers Liability Assurance Corp., 348 U. S. 66 (1954).

[3] In Skiriotes the precise question was whether a State could prohibit by statute the use of diving equipment for the purpose of gathering deep sea sponges in waters within its territorial limits. This Court sustained the State's legislative jurisdiction to regulate the conduct of its own citizens. Thus the Court said: "Even if it were assumed that the locus of the offense was outside the territorial waters of Florida, it would not follow that the State could not prohibit its own citizens from the use of the . . . drivers' equipment at that place. No question as to the authority of the United States over these waters, or over the sponge fishery, is here involved. No right of a citizen of another State is here asserted. The question is solely between appellant and his own State. . . . If the United States may control the conduct of its citizens upon the high seas, we see no reason why the State of Florida may not likewise govern the conduct of its citizens upon the high seas with respect to matters in which the State has a legitimate interest . . . ." 313 U. S., at 76-77.

Steele involved the question of whether a district court "has jurisdiction to award relief to an American corporation against acts of trade-mark infringement and unfair competition consummated in a foreign country by a citizen and resident of the United States." 344 U. S., at 281. There was no question that plaintiff had suffered the injury and American commerce had been adversely affected in the way that the Lanham Act sought to prevent. The court concluded that in such circumstances liability could not be avoided simply by performing the forbidden acts in a foreign territory. Cf. Continental Ore Co. v. Union Carbide, 370 U. S. 690, 704 (1962); United States v. Sisal Sales Corp., 274 U. S. 268 (1927)

[4] The Second Circuit quite properly relied on the beneficial ownership of the ship to permit recovery in Bartholomew v. Universe Tankships. Inc., 263 F. 2d 437 (C. A. 2d Cir. 1959), where the injured plaintiff was an American domiciliary. Bartholomew, unfortunately, apprehended what I conceive to be unintended reverberations in Justice Jackson's Lauritzen language which it all but echoed: "looking through the facade of foreign registration and incorporation to the American ownership . . . is essential unless the purposes of the Jones Act are to be frustrated by American shipowners intent upon evading their obligations under the law by the simple expedient of incorporating in a foreign country and registering their vessels under a foreign flag." 263 F. 2d 437, 442.

Justice Harlan's concurrence in Welsh v. US (June 15, 1970) [Notes omitted]

MR. JUSTICE HARLAN, concurring in the result.

Candor requires me to say that I joined the Court's opinion in United States v. Seeger, 380 U. S. 163 (1965), only with the gravest misgivings as to whether it was a legitimate exercise in statutory construction, and today's decision convinces me that in doing so I made a mistake which I should now acknowledge.[1]

In Seeger the Court construed § 6 (j) of the Universal Military Training and Service Act so as to sustain a conscientious objector claim not founded on a theistic belief. The Court, in treating with the provision of the statute that limited conscientious objector claims to those stemming from belief in "a Supreme Being," there said: "Congress, in using the expression `Supreme Being' rather than the designation `God,' was merely clarifying the meaning of religious training and belief so as to embrace all religions and to exclude essentially political, sociological, or philosophical views," and held that the test of belief " `in a relation to a Supreme Being' is whether a given belief that is sincere and meaningful occupies a place in the life of its possessor parallel to that filled by the orthodox belief in God of one who clearly qualifies for the exemption." 380 U. S., at 165-166. Today the prevailing opinion makes explicit its total elimination of the statutorily required religious content for a conscientious objector exemption. The prevailing opinion now says: "If an individual deeply and sincerely holds beliefs that are purely ethical or moral in source and content but that nevertheless impose upon him a duty of conscience to refrain from participating in any war at any time" (emphasis added), he qualifies for a § 6 (j) exemption.

In my opinion, the liberties taken with the statute both in Seeger and today's decision cannot be justified in the name of the familiar doctrine of construing federal statutes in a manner that will avoid possible constitutional infirmities in them. There are limits to the permissible application of that doctrine, and, as I will undertake to show in this opinion, those limits were crossed in Seeger, and even more apparently have been exceeded in the present case. I therefore find myself unable to escape facing the constitutional issue that this case squarely presents: whether § 6 (j) in limiting this draft exemption to those opposed to war in general because of theistic beliefs runs afoul of the religious clauses of the First Amendment. For reasons later appearing I believe it does, and on that basis I concur in the judgment reversing this conviction, and adopt the test announced by MR. JUSTICE BLACK, not as a matter of statutory construction, but as the touchstone for salvaging a congressional policy of long standing that would otherwise have to be nullified.

I

Section 6 (j) provided during the period relevant to this case:

"Nothing contained in this title shall be construed to require any person to be subject to combatant training and service in the armed forces of the United States who, by reason of religious training and belief, is conscientiously opposed to participation in war in any form. Religious training and belief in this connection means an individual's belief in a relation to a Supreme Being involving duties superior to those arising from any human relation, but does not include essentially political, sociological, or philosophical views or a merely personal moral code." Universal Military Training and Service Act of 1948, § 6 (j), 62 Stat. 612, 50 U. S. C. App. § 456 (j).

The issue is then whether Welsh's opposition to war is founded on "religious training and belief" and hence "belief in a relation to a Supreme Being" as Congress used those words. It is of course true that certain words are more plastic in meaning than others. "Supreme Being" is a concept of theology and philosophy, not a technical term, and consequently may be, in some circumstances, capable of bearing a contemporary construction as notions of theology and philosophy evolve. Cf. United States v. Storrs, 272 U. S. 652 (1926). This language appears, however, in a congressional enactment; it is not a phrase of the Constitution, like "religion" or "speech," which this Court is freer to construe in light of evolving needs and circumstances. Cf. Joseph Burstyn, Inc. v. Wilson, 343 U. S. 495 (1952), and my concurring opinion in Estes v. Texas, 381 U. S. 532, 595-596 (1965), and my opinion concurring in the judgment in Garner v. Louisiana, 368 U. S. 157, 185 (1961). Nor is it so broad a statutory directive, like that of the Sherman Act, that we may assume that we are free to adopt and shape policies limited only by the most general statement of purpose. Cf. e. g., Standard Oil Co. v. United States, 221 U. S. 1 (1911). It is Congress' will that must here be divined. In that endeavor it is one thing to give words a meaning not necessarily envisioned by Congress so as to adapt them to circumstances also uncontemplated by the legislature in order to achieve the legislative policy, Holy Trinity Church v. United States, 143 U. S. 457 (1892); it is a wholly different matter to define words so as to change policy. The limits of this Court's mandate to stretch concededly elastic congressional language are fixed in all cases by the context of its usage and legislative history, if available, that are the best guides to congressional purpose and the lengths to which Congress enacted a policy. Rosado v. Wyman, 397 U. S. 397 (1970).[2] The prevailing opinion today snubs both guidelines for it is apparent from a textual analysis of § 6 (j) and the legislative history that the words of this section, as used and understood by Congress, fall short of enacting the broad policy of exempting from military service all individuals who in good faith oppose all war.

A

The natural reading of § 6 (j), which quite evidently draws a distinction between theistic and nontheistic religions, is the only one that is consistent with the legislative history. Section 5 (g) of the 1940 Draft Act exempted individuals whose opposition to war could be traced to "religious training and belief," 54 Stat. 889, without any allusion to a Supreme Being. In United States v. Kauten, 133 F. 2d 703 (C. A. 2d Cir. 1943), the Second Circuit, speaking through Judge Augustus Hand, broadly construed "religious training and belief" to include a "belief finding expression in a conscience which categorically requires the believer to disregard elementary self-interest and to accept martyrdom in preference to transgressing its tenets." 133 F. 2d, at 708. The view was further elaborated in subsequent decisions of the Second Circuit, see United States ex rel. Phillips v. Downer, 135 F. 2d 521 (C. A. 2d Cir. 1943); United States ex rel. Reel v. Badt, 141 F. 2d 845 (C. A. 2d Cir. 1944). This expansive interpretation of § 5 (g) was rejected by a divided Ninth Circuit in Berman v. United States, 156 F. 2d 377, 380-381 (1946):

"It is our opinion that the expression `by reason of religious training and belief' . . . was written into the statute for the specific purpose of distinguishing between a conscientious social belief, or a sincere devotion to a high moralistic philosophy, and one based upon an individual's belief in his responsibility to an authority higher and beyond any worldly one.

. . . . .

"[I]n United States v. Macintosh, 283 U. S. 605 . . . Mr. [Chief] Justice Hughes in his dissent . . . said: `The essence of religion is belief in a relation to God involving duties superior to those arising from any human relation.' "

The unmistakable and inescapable thrust of the Berman opinion, that religion is to be conceived in theistic terms, is rendered no less straightforward by the court's elaboration on the difference between beliefs held as a matter of moral or philosophical conviction and those inspired by religious upbringing and adherence to faith.

"There are those who have a philosophy of life, and who live up to it. There is evidence that this is so in regard to appellant. However, no matter how pure and admirable his standard may be, and no matter how devotedly he adheres to it, his philosophy and morals and social policy without the concept of deity cannot be said to be religion in the sense of that term as it is used in the statute. It is said in State v. Amana Society, 132 Iowa 304, 109 N. W. 894, 898 . . . : `Surely a scheme of life designed to obviate such results (man's inhumanity to man), and by removing temptations, and all the inducements of ambition and avarice, to nurture the virtues of unselfishness, patience, love, and service, ought not to be denounced as not pertaining to religion when its devotee regards it as an essential tenet of their [sic] religious faith.' " (Emphasis of Court of Appeals.) Ibid.

In the wake of this intercircuit dialogue, crystallized by the dissent in Berman which espoused the Second Circuit interpretation in Kauten, supra, Congress enacted § 6 (j) in 1948. That Congress intended to anoint the Ninth Circuit's interpretation of § 5 (g) would seem beyond question in view of the similarity of the statutory language to that used by Chief Justice Hughes in his dissenting opinion in Macintosh and quoted in Berman and the Senate report. The first half of the new language was almost word for word that of Chief Justice Hughes in Macintosh, and quoted by the Berman majority;[3] and the Senate Committee report adverted to Berman, thus foreclosing any possible speculation as to whether Congress was aware of the possible alternatives. The report stated:

"This section reenacts substantially the same provisions as were found in subsection 5 (g) of the 1940 act. Exemption extends to anyone who, because of religious training and belief in his relationship to a Supreme Being, is conscientiously opposed to combatant military service or to both combatant and noncombatant military service. (See United States v. Berman [sic], 156 F. (2d) 377, certiorari denied, 329 U. S. 795.)" S. Rep. No. 1268, 80th Cong., 2d Sess., 14.[4]

B

Against this legislative history it is a remarkable feat of judicial surgery to remove, as did Seeger, the theistic requirement of § 6 (j). The prevailing opinion today, however, in the name of interpreting the will of Congress, has performed a lobotomy and completely transformed the statute by reading out of it any distinction between religiously acquired beliefs and those deriving from "essentially political, sociological, or philosophical views or a merely personal moral code."

In the realm of statutory construction it is appropriate to search for meaning in the congressional vocabulary in a lexicon most probably consulted by Congress. Resort to Webster's[5] reveals that the meanings of "religion" are: "1. The service and adoration of God or a god as expressed in forms of worship, in obedience to divine commands . . . ; 2. The state of life of a religious . . . ; 3. One of the systems of faith and worship; a form of theism; a religious faith . . . ; 4. The profession or practice of religious beliefs; religious observances collectively; pl. rites; 5. Devotion or fidelity; . . . conscientiousness; 6. An apprehension, awareness, or conviction of the existence of a supreme being, or more widely, of supernatural powers or influences controlling one's own, humanity's, or nature's destiny; also, such an apprehension, etc., accompanied by or arousing reverence, love, gratitude, the will to obey and serve, and the like . . . ." (Emphasis added.)

Of the five pertinent definitions four include the notion of either a Supreme Being or a cohesive, organized group pursuing a common spiritual purpose together. While, as the Court's opinion in Seeger points out, these definitions do not exhaust the almost infinite and sophisticated possibilities for defining "religion," there is strong evidence that Congress restricted, in this instance, the word to its conventional sense. That it is difficult to plot the semantic penumbra of the word "religion" does not render this term so plastic in meaning that the Court is entitled, as matter of statutory construction, to conclude that any asserted and strongly held belief satisfies its requirements. It must be recognized that the permissible shadow of connotation is limited by the context in which words are used. In § 6 (j) Congress has included not only a reference to a Supreme Being but has also explicitly contrasted "religious" beliefs with those that are "essentially political, sociological, or philosophical" and a "personal moral code." This exception certainly is, at the very least, the statutory boundary, the "asymptote," of the word "religion."[6]

For me this dichotomy reveals that Congress was not embracing that definition of religion that alone speaks in terms of "devotion or fidelity" to individual principles acquired on an individualized basis but was adopting, at least, those meanings that associate religion with formal, organized worship or shared beliefs by a recognizable and cohesive group. Indeed, this requirement was explicit in the predecessor to the 1940 statute. The Draft Act of 1917 conditioned conscientious objector status on membership in or affiliation with a "well-recognized religious sect or organization [then] organized and existing and whose existing creed or principles for[ade] its members to participate in war in any form . . . ." § 4, 40 Stat 78. That § 5 (g) of the 1940 Act eliminated the affiliation and membership requirement does not, in my view, mean as the Court, in effect, concluded in Seeger that Congress was embracing a secular definition of religion.[7]

Unless we are to assume an Alice-in-Wonderland world where words have no meaning, I think it fair to say that Congress' choice of language cannot fail to convey to the discerning reader the very policy choice that the prevailing opinion today completely obliterates: that between conventional religions that usually have an organized and formal structure and dogma and a cohesive group identity, even when nontheistic, and cults that represent schools of thought and in the usual case are without formal structure or are, at most, loose and informal associations of individuals who share common ethical, moral, or intellectual views.

II

When the plain thrust of a legislative enactment can only be circumvented by distortion to avert an inevitable constitutional collision, it is only by exalting form over substance that one can justify this veering off the path that has been plainly marked by the statute. Such a course betrays extreme skepticism as to constitutionality, and, in this instance, reflects a groping to preserve the conscientious objector exemption at all cost.

I cannot subscribe to a wholly emasculated construction of a statute to avoid facing a latent constitutional question, in purported fidelity to the salutary doctrine of avoiding unnecessary resolution of constitutional issues, a principle to which I fully adhere. See Ashwander v. Tennessee Valley Authority, 297 U. S. 288, 348 (1936) (Brandeis, J., concurring). It is, of course, desirable to salvage by construction legislative enactments whenever there is good reason to believe that Congress did not intend to legislate consequences that are unconstitutional, but it is not permissible, in my judgment, to take a lateral step that robs legislation of all meaning in order to avert the collision between its plainly intended purpose and the commands of the Constitution. Cf. Yates v. United States, 354 U. S. 298 (1957). As the Court stated in Aptheker v. Secretary of State, 378 U. S. 500, 515 (1964):

"It must be remembered that `[a]lthough this Court will often strain to construe legislation so as to save it against constitutional attack, it must not and will not carry this to the point of perverting the purpose of a statute . . .' or judicially rewriting it. Scales v. United States [367 U. S. 203, 211]. To put the matter another way, this Court will not consider the abstract question of whether Congress might have enacted a valid statute but instead must ask whether the statute that Congress did enact will permissibly bear a construction rendering it free from constitutional defects."

The issue comes sharply into focus in Mr. Justice Cardozo's statement for the Court in Moore Ice Cream Co. v. Rose, 289 U. S. 373, 379 (1933):

"`A statute must be construed, if fairly possible, so as to avoid not only the conclusion that it is unconstitutional, but also grave doubts upon that score.' . . . But avoidance of a difficulty will not be pressed to the point of disingenuous evasion. Here the intention of the Congress is revealed too distinctly to permit us to ignore it because of mere misgivings as to power. The problem must be faced and answered."

If an important congressional policy is to be perpetuated by recasting unconstitutional legislation, as the prevailing opinion has done here, the analytically sound approach is to accept responsibility for this decision. Its justification cannot be by resort to legislative intent, as that term is usually employed, but by a different kind of legislative intent, namely the presumed grant of power to the courts to decide whether it more nearly accords with Congress' wishes to eliminate its policy altogether or extend it in order to render what Congress plainly did intend, constitutional. Compare, e. g., Yu Cong Eng v. Trinidad, 271 U. S. 500 (1926); United States v. Reese, 92 U. S. 214 (1876), with Skinner v. Oklahoma, 316 U. S. 535 (1942); Nat. Life Ins. Co. v. United States, 277 U. S. 508 (1928). I therefore turn to the constitutional question.

III

The constitutional question that must be faced in this case is whether a statute that defers to the individual's conscience only when his views emanate from adherence to theistic religious beliefs is within the power of Congress. Congress, of course, could, entirely consistently with the requirements of the Constitution, eliminate all exemptions for conscientious objectors. Such a course would be wholly "neutral" and, in my view, would not offend the Free Exercise Clause, for reasons set forth in my dissenting opinion in Sherbert v. Verner, 374 U. S. 398, 418 (1963). See Jacobson v. Massachusetts, 197 U. S. 11, 29 (1905) (dictum); cf. McGowan v. Maryland, 366 U. S. 420 (1961); Davis v. Beason, 133 U. S. 333 (1890); Hamilton v. Board of Regents, 293 U. S. 245, 264-265 (1934); Reynolds v. United States, 98 U. S. 145 (1879); Kurland, of Church and State and the Supreme Court, 29 U. Chi. L. Rev. 1 (1961). However, having chosen to exempt, it cannot draw the line between theistic or nontheistic religious beliefs on the one hand and secular beliefs on the other. Any such distinctions are not, in my view, compatible with the Establishment Clause of the First Amendment. See my separate opinion in Walz v. Tax Comm'n, 397 U. S. 664, 694 (1970); Epperson v. Arkansas, 393 U. S. 97 (1968); School District of Abington Township v. Schempp, 374 U. S. 203, 305 (1963) (Goldberg, J., concurring); Engel v. Vitale, 370 U. S. 421 (1962); Torcaso v. Watkins, 367 U. S. 488, 495 (1961); Fowler v. Rhode Island, 345 U. S. 67 (1953). The implementation of the neutrality principle of these cases requires, in my view, as I stated in Walz v. Tax Comm'n, supra, "an equal protection mode of analysis. The Court must survey meticulously the circumstances of governmental categories to eliminate, as it were, religious gerrymanders. In any particular case the critical question is whether the scope of legislation encircles a class so broad that it can be fairly concluded that [all groups that] could be thought to fall within the natural perimeter [are included]." 397 U. S., at 696.

The "radius" of this legislation is the conscientiousness with which an individual opposes war in general, yet the statute, as I think it must be construed, excludes from its "scope" individuals motivated by teachings of nontheistic religions,[8] and individuals guided by an inner ethical voice that bespeaks secular and not "religious" reflection. It not only accords a preference to the "religious" but also disadvantages adherents of religions that do not worship a Supreme Being. The constitutional infirmity cannot be cured, moreover, even by an impermissible construction that eliminates the theistic requirement and simply draws the line between religious and nonreligious. This in my view offends the Establishment Clause and is that kind of classification that this Court has condemned. See my separate opinion in Walz v. Tax Comm'n, supra; School District of Abington Township v. Schempp (Goldberg, J., concurring), supra; Engel v. Vitale, supra; Torcaso v. Watkins, supra.

If the exemption is to be given application, it must encompass the class of individuals it purports to exclude, those whose beliefs emanate from a purely moral, ethical, or philosophical source.[9] The common denominator must be the intensity of moral conviction with which a belief is held.[10] Common experience teaches that among "religious" individuals some are weak and others strong adherents to tenets and this is no less true of individuals whose lives are guided by personal ethical considerations.

The Government enlists the Selective Draft Law Cases, 245 U. S. 366 (1918), as precedent for upholding the constitutionality of the religious conscientious objector provision. That case involved the power of Congress to raise armies by conscription and only incidentally the conscientious objector exemption. The language emphasized by the Government to the effect that the exemption for religious objectors and ministers constituted neither an establishment nor interference with free exercise of religion can only be considered an after-thought since the case did not involve any individuals who claimed to be nonreligious conscientious objectors.[11] This conclusory assertion, unreasoned and unaccompanied by citation, surely cannot foreclose consideration of the question in a case that squarely presents the issue.

Other authorities assembled by the Government, far from advancing its case, demonstrate the unconstitutionality of the distinction drawn in § 6 (j) between religious and nonreligious beliefs. Everson v. Board of Education, 330 U. S. 1 (1947), the Sunday Closing Law Cases, 366 U. S. 420, 582, 599, and 617 (1961), and Board of Education v. Allen, 392 U. S. 236 (1968), all sustained legislation on the premise that it was neutral in its application and thus did not constitute an establishment, notwithstanding the fact that it may have assisted religious groups by giving them the same benefits accorded to nonreligious groups.[12] To the extent that Zorach v. Clauson, 343 U. S. 306 (1952), and Sherbert v. Verner, supra, stand for the proposition that the Government may (Zorach), or must (Sherbert), shape its secular programs to accommodate the beliefs and tenets of religious groups, I think these cases unsound.[13] See generally Kurland, supra. To conform with the requirements of the First Amendment's religious clauses as reflected in the mainstream of American history, legislation must, at the very least, be neutral. See my separate opinion in Walz v. Tax Comm'n, supra.

IV

Where a statute is defective because of underinclusion there exist two remedial alternatives: a court may either declare it a nullity and order that its benefits not extend to the class that the legislature intended to benefit, or it may extend the coverage of the statute to include those who are aggrieved by exclusion. Cf. Skinner v. Oklahoma, 316 U. S. 535 (1942); Iowa-Des Moines National Bank v. Bennett, 284 U. S. 239 (1931).[14]

The appropriate disposition of this case, which is a prosecution for refusing to submit to induction and not an action for a declaratory judgment on the constitutionality of § 6 (j), is determined by the fact that at the time of Welsh's induction notice and prosecution the Selective Service was, as required by statute, exempting individuals whose beliefs were identical in all respects to those held by petitioner except that they derived from a religious source. Since this created a religious benefit not accorded to petitioner, it is clear to me that this conviction must be reversed under the Establishment Clause of the First Amendment unless Welsh is to go remediless. Cf. Iowa-Des Moines National Bank v. Bennett, supra; Smith v. Cahoon, 283 U. S. 553 (1931).[15]

This result, while tantamount to extending the statute, is not only the one mandated by the Constitution in this case but also the approach I would take had this question been presented in an action for a declaratory judgment or "an action in equity where the enforcement of a statute awaits the final determination of the court as to validity and scope." Smith v. Cahoon, 283 U. S., at 565.[16] While the necessary remedial operation, extension, is more analogous to a graft than amputation, I think the boundaries of permissible choice may properly be considered fixed by the legislative pronouncement on severability.

Indicative of the breadth of the judicial mandate in this regard is the broad severability clause, 65 Stat. 88, which provides that "[i]f any provision of this Act or the application thereof to any person or circumstances is held invalid, the validity of the remainder of the Act and of the application of such provision to other persons and circumstances shall not be affected thereby." While the absence of such a provision would not foreclose the exercise of discretion in determining whether a legislative policy should be repaired or abandoned, cf. United States v. Jackson, 390 U. S. 570, 585 n. 27 (1968), its existence "discloses an intention to make the Act divisible and creates a presumption that, eliminating invalid parts, the legislature would have been satisfied with what remained . . . ." Champlin Rfg. Co. v. Commission, 286 U. S. 210, 235 (1932). See also Skinner v. Oklahoma, supra; Nat. Life Ins. Co. v. United States, 277 U. S. 508 (1928).[17]

In exercising the broad discretion conferred by a severability clause it is, of course, necessary to measure the intensity of commitment to the residual policy and consider the degree of potential disruption of the statutory scheme that would occur by extension as opposed to abrogation. Cf. Nat. Life Ins. Co. v. United States, supra (Brandeis, J., dissenting); Dorchy v. Kansas, 264 U. S. 286 (1924).

The policy of exempting religious conscientious objectors is one of longstanding tradition in this country and accords recognition to what is, in a diverse and "open" society, the important value of reconciling individuality of belief with practical exigencies whenever possible. See Girouard v. United States, 328 U. S. 61 (1946). It dates back to colonial times and has been perpetuated in state and federal conscription statutes. See Mr. Justice Cardozo's separate opinion in Hamilton v. Board of Regents, 293 U. S., at 267; Macintosh v. United States, 42 F. 2d 845, 847 (1930). That it has been phrased in religious terms reflects, I assume, the fact that ethics and morals, while the concern of secular philosophy, have traditionally been matters taught by organized religion and that for most individuals spiritual and ethical nourishment is derived from that source. It further reflects, I would suppose, the assumption that beliefs emanating from a religious source are probably held with great intensity.

When a policy has roots so deeply embedded in history, there is a compelling reason for a court to hazard the necessary statutory repairs if they can be made within the administrative framework of the statute and without impairing other legislative goals, even though they entail, not simply eliminating an offending section, but rather building upon it.[18] Thus I am prepared to accept the prevailing opinion's conscientious objector test, not as a reflection of congressional statutory intent but as patchwork of judicial making that cures the defect of under-inclusion in § 6 (j) and can be administered by local boards in the usual course of business.[19] Like the prevailing opinion, I also conclude that petitioner's beliefs are held with the required intensity and consequently vote to reverse the judgment of conviction.

Justice Harlan's concurrence and dissent in Coleman v. Alabama (June 22, 1970)

MR. JUSTICE HARLAN, concurring in part and dissenting in part.

If I felt free to consider this case upon a clean slate I would have voted to affirm these convictions.[*] But—in light of the lengths to which the right to appointed counsel has been carried in recent decisions of this Court, see Miranda v. Arizona, 384 U. S. 436 (1966); United States v. Wade, 388 U. S. 218 (1967); Gilbert v. California, 388 U. S. 263 (1967); Mathis v. United States, 391 U. S. 1 (1968); and Orozco v. Texas, 394 U. S. 324 (1969)—I consider that course is not open to me with due regard for the way in which the adjudicatory process of this Court, as I conceive it, should work. The continuing viability of the cases just cited is not directly before us for decision, and if and when such an occasion arises I would face it in terms of considerations that I have recently expressed elsewhere. See my dissenting opinion in Baldwin v. New York, decided today, post, p. 117, and my opinion concurring in the result in Welsh v. United States, 398 U. S. 333, 344 (1970).

Accordingly I am constrained to agree with the Court's conclusion that petitioners' constitutional rights were violated when Alabama refused to appoint counsel to represent them at the preliminary hearing. I dissent, however, from the terms of the Court's remand on this issue, as well as from the refusal to accord petitioners the benefit of the Wade case in connection with their police "lineup" contentions.

I

It would indeed be strange were this Court, having held a suspect or an accused entitled to counsel at such pretrial stages as "in-custody" police investigation, whether at the station house (Miranda) or even in the home (Orozco), now to hold that he is left to fend for himself at the first formal confrontation in the courtroom.

While, given the cases referred to, I cannot escape the conclusion that petitioners' constitutional rights must be held to have been violated by denying them appointed counsel at the preliminary hearing, I consider the scope of the Court's remand too broad and amorphous. I do not think that reversal of these convictions, for lack of counsel at the preliminary hearing, should follow unless petitioners are able to show on remand that they have been prejudiced in their defense at trial, in that favorable testimony that might otherwise have been preserved was irretrievably lost by virtue of not having counsel to help present an affirmative case at the preliminary hearing. In this regard, of course, as with any other erroneously excluded testimony, petitioners would have to show that its weight at trial would have been such as to constitute its "exclusion" reversible error, as well as demonstrate the actual likelihood that such testimony could have been presented and preserved at the preliminary hearing. In my opinion mere speculation that defense counsel might have been able to do better at trial had he been present at the preliminary hearing should not suffice to vitiate a conviction. The Court's remand under the Chapman harmless-error rule seems to me to leave the way open for that sort of speculation.

II

Despite my continuing disagreement with United States v. Wade, supra, I must dissent from the refusal to accord petitioners the benefit of the Wade holding, neither petitioner having been afforded counsel at the police "lineup" identification. The majority's action results from the holding in Stovall v. Denno, 388 U. S. 293 (1967), making Wade applicable only to lineups occurring after the date of that decision, the present lineup having taken place well before. For reasons explained in my dissent in

Desist v. United States, 394 U. S. 244, 256 (1969), I can no longer follow the "retroactivity" doctrine announced in Stovall in cases before us on direct review. That being the situation here, I would judge the case in light of Wade.

The Wade rule requires the exclusion of any in-court identification preceded by a pretrial lineup where the accused was not represented by counsel, unless the in-court identification is found to be derived from a source "independent" of the tainted pretrial viewing. Such a determination must, in the first instance, be made by the trial court. I would therefore send the case back on this score too.

[*] From the standpoint of Fourteenth Amendment due process, which is the way in which I think state cases of this kind should be judged (see, e. g., my concurring opinion in Gideon v. Wainwright, 372 U. S. 335, 349 (1963)), I could not have said that the denial of appointed counsel at a preliminary hearing, carrying no consequences beyond those involved in the Alabama procedure, is offensive to the concept of "fundamental fairness" embodied in the Due Process Clause. The case would, of course, be different if the State were permitted to introduce at trial evidence collected and presented at the preliminary hearing. A fortiori, I would not have thought that the lack of counsel at a police "line-up" is, as held in United States v. Wade, 388 U. S. 218 (1967), a denial of due process such as to require reversal. Even from the standpoint of the Sixth Amendment, I would have found it difficult to say that the language, "In all criminal prosecutions, the accused shall enjoy the right . . . to have the Assistance of Counsel for his defence" (emphasis supplied), was intended to reach such pre-indictment events. Cf. Sanders v. United States, 373 U. S. 1, 23 (1963).

Justice Harlan's concurrence and dissent in Chambers v. Maroney (June 22, 1970)

MR. JUSTICE HARLAN, concurring in part and dissenting in part.

I find myself in disagreement with the Court's disposition of this case in two respects.

I

I cannot join the Court's casual treatment of the issue that has been presented by both parties as the major issue in this case: petitioner's claim that he received ineffective assistance of counsel at his trial. As the Court acknowledges, petitioner met Mr. Tamburo, his trial counsel, for the first time en route to the court-room on the morning of trial. Although a different Legal Aid Society attorney had represented petitioner at his first trial, apparently neither he nor anyone else from the society had conferred with petitioner in the interval between trials. Because the District Court did not hold an evidentiary hearing on the habeas petition, there is no indication in the record of the extent to which Mr. Tamburo may have consulted petitioner's previous attorney, the attorneys for the other defendants, or the files of the Legal Aid Society. What the record does disclose on this claim is essentially a combination of two factors: the entry of counsel into the case immediately before trial, and his handling of the issues that arose during the trial.[1]

As respondent must concede, counsel's last-minute entry into the case precluded his compliance with the state rule requiring that motions to suppress evidence be made before trial, even assuming that he had sufficient acquaintance with the case to know what arguments were worth making. Furthermore, the record suggests that he may have had virtually no such acquaintance.

In the first place, he made no objection to the admission in evidence of the objects found during the search of the car at the station house after the arrest of its occupants, although that search was of questionable validity under Fourth Amendment standards, see infra.

Second, when the prosecution offered in evidence the bullets found in the search of petitioner's home, which had been excluded on defense objection at the first trial, Mr. Tamburo objected to their admission, but in a manner that suggested that he was a stranger to the facts of the case. While he indicated that he did know of the earlier exclusion, he apparently did not know on what ground the bullets had been excluded, and based his objection only on their asserted irrelevance.[2] Later in the trial he renewed his objection on the basis of the inadequacy of the warrant, stating, "I didn't know a thing about the search Warrant until this morning." App. 130.[3]

Third, when prosecution witness Havicon made an in-court identification of petitioner as the man who had threatened him with a gun during one of the robberies, Mr. Tamburo asked questions in cross-examination that suggested that he had not had time to settle upon a trial strategy or even to consider whether petitioner would take the stand. Mr. Tamburo asked whether, at a pretrial lineup, a detective had not told Havicon that petitioner "was the man with the gun." After Havicon's negative answer, this colloquy ensued:

"THE COURT: I take it you will be able to disprove that, will you?

"MR. TAMBURO: What?

"THE COURT: You shouldn't ask that question unless you are prepared to disprove that, contradict him.

"MR. TAMBURO: I have the defendant's testimony.

"THE COURT: Disprove it in any way at all.

"MR. MEANS [the prosecutor]: I don't understand how the defendant would know what the detectives told him.

"THE COURT: He said he is going to disprove it by the defendant, that's all right, go ahead." App. 34.

The next witness was a police officer who had been present at the lineup, and who testified that no one had told Havicon whom to pick out. Petitioner's counsel did not cross-examine, and petitioner never took the stand.

On this state of the record the Court of Appeals ruled that, although the late appointment of counsel necessitated close scrutiny into the effectiveness of his representation, petitioner "was not prejudiced by the late appointment of counsel" because neither of the Fourth Amendment claims belatedly raised justified reversal of the conviction. 408 F. 2d 1186, 1196. I agree that the strength of the search and seizure claims is an element to be considered in the assessment of whether counsel was adequately prepared to make an effective defense, but I cannot agree that the relevance of those claims in this regard disappears upon a conclusion by an appellate court that they do not invalidate the conviction.

This Court recognized long ago that the duty to provide counsel "is not discharged by an assignment at such a time or under such circumstances as to preclude the giving of effective aid in the preparation and trial of the case." Powell v. Alabama, 287 U. S. 45, 71 (1932); Hawk v. Olson, 326 U. S. 271, 278 (1945). While "the Constitution nowhere specifies any period which must intervene between the required appointment of counsel and trial," the Court has recognized that

"the denial of opportunity for appointed counsel to confer, to consult with the accused and to prepare his defense, could convert the appointment of counsel into a sham and nothing more than a formal compliance with the Constitution's requirement that an accused be given the assistance of counsel." Avery v. Alabama, 308 U. S. 444, 446 (1940).

Where counsel has no acquaintance with the facts of the case and no opportunity to plan a defense, the result is that the defendant is effectively denied his constitutional right to assistance of counsel.

It seems to me that what this record reveals about counsel's handling of the search and seizure claims and about the tenor of his cross-examination of the government witness Havicon, when coupled with his late entry into the case, called for more exploration by the District Court before petitioner's ineffective assistance of counsel claim could be dismissed. Such an exploration should have been directed to ascertaining whether the circumstances under which Mr. Tamburo was required to undertake petitioner's defense at the second trial were such as to send him into the courtroom with so little knowledge of the case as to render him incapable of affording his client adequate representation. The event of that exploration would turn, not on a mere assessment of particular missteps or omissions of counsel, whether or not caused by negligence, cf. McMann v. Richardson, 397 U. S. 759 (1970), but on the District Court's evaluation of the total picture, with the objective of determining whether petitioner was deprived of rudimentary legal assistance. See Williams v. Beto, 354 F. 2d 698 (C. A. 5th Cir. 1965). And, of course, such an exploration would not be confined to the three episodes that, in my opinion, triggered the necessity for a hearing.

It is not an answer to petitioner's claim for a reviewing court simply to conclude that he has failed after the fact to show that, with adequate assistance, he would have prevailed at trial. Glasser v. United States, 315 U. S. 60, 75-76 (1942); cf. White v. Maryland, 373 U. S. 59 (1963); Reynolds v. Cochran, 365 U. S. 525, 530-533 (1961). Further inquiry might show, of course, that counsel's opportunity for preparation was adequate to protect petitioner's interests,[4] but petitioner did, in my view, raise a sufficient doubt on that score to be entitled to an evidentiary hearing.[5]

    II

    In sustaining the search of the automobile I believe the Court ignores the framework of our past decisions circumscribing the scope of permissible search without a warrant. The Court has long read the Fourth Amendment's proscription of "unreasonable" searches as imposing a general principle that a search without a warrant is not justified by the mere knowledge by the searching officers of facts showing probable cause. The "general requirement that a search warrant be obtained" is basic to the Amendment's protection of privacy, and " `the burden is on those seeking [an] exemption . . . to show the need for it.' " E. g., Chimel v. California, 395 U. S. 752, 762 (1969); Katz v. United States, 389 U. S. 347, 356-358 (1967); Warden v. Hayden, 387 U. S. 294, 299 (1967); Preston v. United States, 376 U. S. 364, 367 (1964); United States v. Jeffers, 342 U. S. 48, 51 (1951); McDonald v. United States, 335 U. S. 451, 455-456 (1948); Agnello v. United States, 269 U. S. 20, 33 (1925).

    Fidelity to this established principle requires that, where exceptions are made to accommodate the exigencies of particular situations, those exceptions be no broader than necessitated by the circumstances presented. For example, the Court has recognized that an arrest creates an emergency situation justifying a warrantless search of the arrestee's person and of "the area from within which he might gain possession of a weapon or destructible evidence"; however, because the exigency giving rise to this exception extends only that far, the search may go no further. Chimel v. California, 395 U. S., at 763; Trupiano v. United States, 334 U. S. 699, 705, 708 (1948). Similarly we held in Terry v. Ohio, 392 U. S. 1 (1968), that a warrantless search in a "stop and frisk" situation must "be strictly circumscribed by the exigencies which justify its initiation." Id., at 26. Any intrusion beyond what is necessary for the personal safety of the officer or others nearby is forbidden.

    Where officers have probable cause to search a vehicle on a public way, a further limited exception to the warrant requirement is reasonable because "the vehicle can be quickly moved out of the locality or jurisdiction in which the warrant must be sought." Carroll v. United States, 267 U. S. 132, 153 (1925). Because the officers might be deprived of valuable evidence if required to obtain a warrant before effecting any search or seizure, I agree with the Court that they should be permitted to take the steps necessary to preserve evidence and to make a search possible.[6] Cf. ALI, Model Code of Pre-Arraignment Procedure § 6.03 (Tent. Draft No. 3, 1970). The Court holds that those steps include making a warrantless search of the entire vehicle on the highway—a conclusion reached by the Court in Carroll without discussion—and indeed appears to go further and to condone the removal of the car to the police station for a warrantless search there at the convenience of the police.[7] I cannot agree that this result is consistent with our insistence in other areas that departures from the warrant requirement strictly conform to the exigency presented.

    The Court concedes that the police could prevent removal of the evidence by temporarily seizing the car for the time necessary to obtain a warrant. It does not dispute that such a course would fully protect the interests of effective law enforcement; rather it states that whether temporary seizure is a "lesser" intrusion than warrantless search "is itself a debatable question and the answer may depend on a variety of circumstances." Ante, at 51-52.[8] I believe it clear that a warrantless search involves the greater sacrifice of Fourth Amendment values.

The Fourth Amendment proscribes, to be sure, unreasonable "seizures" as well as "searches." However, in the circumstances in which this problem is likely to occur, the lesser intrusion will almost always be the simple seizure of the car for the period—perhaps a day— necessary to enable the officers to obtain a search warrant. In the first place, as this case shows, the very facts establishing probable cause to search will often also justify arrest of the occupants of the vehicle. Since the occupants themselves are to be taken into custody, they will suffer minimal further inconvenience from the temporary immobilization of their vehicle. Even where no arrests are made, persons who wish to avoid a search— either to protect their privacy or to conceal incriminating evidence—will almost certainly prefer a brief loss of the use of the vehicle in exchange for the opportunity to have a magistrate pass upon the justification for the search. To be sure, one can conceive of instances in which the occupant, having nothing to hide and lacking concern for the privacy of the automobile, would be more deeply offended by a temporary immobilization of his vehicle than by a prompt search of it. However, such a person always remains free to consent to an immediate search, thus avoiding any delay. Where consent is not forthcoming, the occupants of the car have an interest in privacy that is protected by the Fourth Amendment even where the circumstances justify a temporary seizure. Terry v. Ohio, supra. The Court's endorsement of a warrantless invasion of that privacy where another course would suffice is simply inconsistent with our repeated stress on the Fourth Amendment's mandate of " `adherence to judicial processes.' " E. g., Katz v. United States, 389 U. S., at 357.[9]

Indeed, I believe this conclusion is implicit in the opinion of the unanimous Court in Preston v. United States, 376 U. S. 364 (1964). The Court there purported to decide whether a factual situation virtually identical to the one now before us was "such as to fall within any of the exceptions to the constitutional rule that a search warrant must be had before a search may be made." Id., at 367 (emphasis added). The Court concluded that no exception was available, stating that "since the men were under arrest at the police station and the car was in police custody at a garage, [there was no] danger that the car would be moved out of the locality or jurisdiction." Id., at 368. The Court's reliance on the police custody of the car as its reason for holding "that the search of the car without a warrant failed to meet the test of reasonableness under the Fourth Amendment," ibid., can only have been based on the premise that the more reasonable course was for the police to retain custody of the car for the short time necessary to obtain a warrant. The Court expressly did not rely, as suggested today, on the fact that an arrest for vagrancy provided "no cause to believe that evidence of crime was concealed in the auto." Ante, at 47; see 376

U. S., at 368; Wood v. Crouse, 417 F. 2d 394, 397-398 (C. A. 10th Cir. 1969). The Court now discards the approach taken in Preston, and creates a special rule for automobile searches that is seriously at odds with generally applied Fourth Amendment principles.

III

The Court accepts the conclusion of the two courts below that the introduction of the bullets found in petitioner's home, if error, was harmless. Although, as explained above, I do not agree that this destroys the relevance of the issue to the ineffectiveness of counsel claim, I agree that the record supports the lower courts' conclusion that this item of evidence, taken alone, was harmless beyond a reasonable doubt.

Notes

[1] Respondent concedes in this Court that "no other facts are available to determine the amount and the quality of the preparation for trial pursued by Mr. Tamburo or the amount of evidentiary material known by and available to him in determining what, if any, evidentiary objections were mandated or what, if any, defenses were available to petitioner." Brief for Respondent 13. The Court of Appeals stated: "We do not know what preparation, if any, counsel was able to accomplish prior to the date of the trial as he did not testify in the state habeas corpus proceeding and there was no evidentiary hearing in the district court. From the lower court opinion, as will appear later, we are led to believe that counsel was not wholly familiar with all aspects of the case before trial." 408 F. 2d 1186, 1191.

[2] Mr. Tamburo stated to the trial court:

"Your Honor, at the first trial, the District Attorney attempted to introduce into evidence some .38 calibre bullets that were found at the Chambers' home after his arrest. . . . At that trial, it was objected to and the objection was sustained, and I would also like to object to it now, I don't think it is good for the Jury to hear it. I don't feel there is any relevancy or connection between the fact there were .38 calibre bullets at his home and the fact that a .38 calibre gun was found, not on the person of Chambers, but in the group." App. 82.

This was the only instance in which Mr. Tamburo expressed any knowledge of what had transpired at the first trial, and it does not appear whether he learned of the exclusion from his brief talk with petitioner en route to the courtroom or from sources within the Legal Aid Society. The record does not disclose the reason for the exclusion of the bullets at the first trial.

[3] This colloquy followed the renewed objection:

"THE COURT: Well, of course, you have known about this from the other trial three weeks ago.

"MR. TAMBURO: I wasn't the attorney at the other trial.

"THE COURT: But, you knew about it?

"MR. TAMBURO: I didn't know a thing about the search Warrant until this morning.

"THE COURT: You knew about the evidence about to be introduced, you told me about it.

"MR. TAMBURO: It wasn't admitted.

"THE COURT: That doesn't mean I have to exclude it now." Id., at 130.

The court proceeded to overrule the objection on the ground that it had not been made in a pretrial motion, adding that "I think there is reasonable ground for making a search here, even without a Warrant." Id., at 130-131.

[4] In Avery, this Court concluded on the basis of a hearing: "That the examination and preparation of the case, in the time permitted by the trial judge, had been adequate for counsel to exhaust its every angle is illuminated by the absence of any indication, on the motion and hearing for new trial, that they could have done more had additional time been granted." 308 U. S., at 452.

[5] The absence of any request by counsel for a continuance of the trial should not, in my opinion, serve to vitiate petitioner's claim at this juncture.

[6] Where a suspect is lawfully arrested in the automobile, the officers may, of course, perform a search within the limits prescribed by Chimel as an incident to the lawful arrest. However, as the Court recognizes, the search here exceeded those limits. Nor was the search here within the limits imposed by pre-Chimel law for searches incident to arrest; therefore, the retroactivity of Chimel is not drawn into question in this case. See Preston v. United States, 376 U. S. 364 (1964).

[7] The Court disregards the fact that Carroll, and each of this Court's decisions upholding a warrantless vehicle search on its authority, involved a search for contraband. Brinegar v. United States, 338 U. S. 160 (1949); Scher v. United States, 305 U. S. 251 (1938); Husty v. United States, 282 U. S. 694 (1931); see United States v. Di Re, 332 U. S. 581, 584-586 (1948). Although subsequent dicta have omitted this limitation, see Dyke v. Taylor Implement Mfg. Co., 391 U. S. 216, 221 (1968); United States v. Ventresca, 380 U. S. 102, 107 n. 2 (1965); United States v. Rabinowitz, 339 U. S. 56, 61 (1950), id., at 73 (Frankfurter, J., dissenting), the Carroll decision has not until today been held to authorize a general search of a vehicle for evidence of crime, without a warrant, in every case where probable cause exists.

[8] The Court, unable to decide whether search or temporary seizure is the "lesser" intrusion, in this case authorizes both. The Court concludes that it was reasonable for the police to take the car to the station, where they searched it once to no avail. The searching officers then entered the station, interrogated petitioner and the car's owner, and returned later for another search of the car—this one successful. At all times the car and its contents were secure against removal or destruction. Nevertheless, the Court approves the searches without even an inquiry into the officers' ability promptly to take their case before a magistrate.

[9] Circumstances might arise in which it would be impracticable to immobilize the car for the time required to obtain a warrant—for example, where a single police officer must take arrested suspects to the station, and has no way of protecting the suspects' car

during his absence. In such situations it might be wholly reasonable to perform an on-the-spot search based on probable cause. However, where nothing in the situation makes impracticable the obtaining of a warrant, I cannot join the Court in shunting aside that vital Fourth Amendment safeguard.

Justice Harlan's concurrence and dissent in Williams v. Florida (June 22, 1970) [Notes omitted]

MR. JUSTICE HARLAN, dissenting in No. 188, ante, p. 66, and concurring in the result in No. 927.

In Duncan v. Louisiana, 391 U. S. 145 (1968), the Court held, over my dissent, joined by MR. JUSTICE STEWART, that a state criminal defendant is entitled to a jury trial in any case which, if brought in a federal court, would require a jury under the Sixth Amendment. Today the Court concludes, in No. 188, Baldwin v. New York, that New York cannot constitutionally provide that misdemeanors carrying sentences up to one year shall be tried in New York City without a jury.[1] At the same time the Court holds in No. 927, Williams v. Florida, that Florida's six-member-jury statute satisfies the Sixth Amendment as carried to the States by the Duncan holding.[2] The necessary consequence of this decision is that 12-member juries are not constitutionally required in federal criminal trials either.

The historical argument by which the Court undertakes to justify its view that the Sixth Amendment does not require 12-member juries is, in my opinion, much too thin to mask the true thrust of this decision. The decision evinces, I think, a recognition that the "incorporationist" view of the Due Process Clause of the Fourteenth Amendment, which underlay Duncan and is now carried forward into Baldwin, must be tempered to allow the States more elbow room in ordering their own criminal systems. With that much I agree. But to accomplish this by diluting constitutional protections within the federal system itself is something to which I cannot possibly subscribe. Tempering the rigor of Duncan should be done forthrightly, by facing up to the fact that at least in this area the "incorporation" doctrine does not fit well with our federal structure, and by the same token that Duncan was wrongly decided.

I would sustain both the Florida and New York statutes on the constitutional premises discussed in my dissenting opinion in Duncan, 391 U. S., at 161 et seq. In taking that course in Baldwin, I cannot, in a matter that goes to the very pulse of sound constitutional adjudication, consider myself constricted by stare decisis.[3]

Accordingly, I dissent in No. 188 and, as to the jury issue, concur in the result in No. 927. Given Malloy v. Hogan, 378 U. S. 1 (1964), I join that part of the Court's opinion in No. 927 relating to the Florida "alibi" procedure.

I

As a predicate for my conclusions, it is useful to map the circuitous route that has been taken in order to reach the results. In both cases, more patently in Williams than in

Baldwin, the history of jury trial practice in both the state and federal systems has been indiscriminately jumbled together as opposed to the point of departure having been taken from the language in which the federal guarantee is expressed and the historical precedent that brings it to life. The consequence of this inverted approach to interpreting the Sixth Amendment results, fortuitously,[4] in Baldwin in a Sixth Amendment rule that would be reached under the correct approach, given the "incorporationist" philosophy of Duncan, but, unhappily, imposes it on the one jurisdiction in the country that has seen fit to do otherwise; and in Williams results in a Sixth Amendment rule that could only be reached by standing the constitutional dialectic on its head.

A

To the extent that the prevailing opinion premises its conclusions in the Baldwin case on federal precedent and the common-law practice, I agree that the federal right to jury trial attaches where an offense is punishable by as much as six months' imprisonment. I think this follows both from the breadth of the language of the Sixth Amendment, which provides for a jury in "all criminal prosecutions," and the evidence of historical practice. In this regard I believe that contemporary usage in the States is of little, if any, significance.[5] For if exceptions are to be created out of the all-embracing language of the Sixth Amendment they should only be those that are anchored in history.

It is to the distinction between "petty" and "serious" offenses, rooted in the common law, that this Court has looked to ascertain the metes and bounds of the federal right guaranteed by the Sixth Amendment. See District of Columbia v. Clawans, 300 U. S. 617 (1937); Schick v. United States, 195 U. S. 65 (1904); Callan v. Wilson, 127 U. S. 540, 552 (1888). Since the conventional, if not immutable practice at common law appears to have been to provide juries for offenses punishable by fines of more than £100 or sentences to hard labor of more than six months in prison, see Frankfurter & Corcoran, Petty Federal Offenses and the Constitutional Guaranty of Trial by Jury, 39 Harv. L. Rev. 917 (1926),[6] I think it appropriate to draw the line at six months in federal cases,[7] although, for reasons to follow, I would not encumber the States by this requirement.[8]

B

In Williams the Court strangely does an about-face. Rather than bind the States by the hitherto undeviating and unquestioned federal practice of 12-member juries, the Court holds, based on a poll of state practice, that a six-man jury satisfies the guarantee of a trial by jury in a federal criminal system and consequently carries over to the States. This is a constitutional renvoi. With all respect, I consider that before today it would have been unthinkable to suggest that the Sixth Amendment's right to a trial by jury is satisfied by a jury of six, or less, as is left open by the Court's opinion in Williams, or by less than a unanimous verdict, a question also reserved in today's decision.

1. The Court, in stripping off the livery of history from the jury trial, relies on a two-step analysis. With arduous effort the Court first liberates itself from the "intent of the Framers" and "the easy assumption in our past decisions that if a given feature existed in a jury at common law in 1789, then it was necessarily preserved in the Constitution." Ante,

at 92-93. Unburdened by the yoke of history the Court then concludes that the policy protected by the jury guarantee does not require its perpetuation in common-law form.

Neither argument is, in my view, an acceptable reason for disregarding history and numerous pronouncements of this Court that have made "the easy assumption" that the Sixth Amendment's jury was one composed of 12 individuals. Even assuming ambiguity as to the intent of the Framers,[9] it is common sense and not merely the blessing of the Framers that explains this Court's frequent reminders that: "The interpretation of the Constitution of the United States is necessarily influenced by the fact that its provisions are framed in the language of the English common law, and are to be read in the light of its history." Smith v. Alabama, 124 U. S. 465, 478 (1888). This proposition was again put forward by Mr. Justice Gray speaking for the Court in United States v. Wong Kim Ark, 169 U. S. 649 (1898), where the Court was called upon to define the term "citizen" as used in the Constitution. "The Constitution nowhere defines the meaning of these words [the Citizenship Clause]. . . . In this, as in other respects, it must be interpreted in the light of the common law, the principles and history of which were familiarly known to the framers of the Constitution." 169 U. S., at 654. History continues to be a wellspring of constitutional interpretation. Indeed, history was even invoked by the Court in such decisions as Townsend v. Sain, 372 U. S. 293 (1963), and Fay v. Noia, 372 U. S. 391 (1963), where it purported to interpret the constitutional provision for habeas corpus according to the "historic conception of the writ" and took note that the guarantee was one rooted in common law and should be so interpreted.[10] Cf. United States v. Brown, 381 U. S. 437, 458 (1965). In accordance with these precepts, sound constitutional interpretation requires, in my view, fixing the federal jury as it was known to the common law.

It is, of course, true that history should not imprison those broad guarantees of the Constitution whose proper scope is to be determined in a given instance by a blend of historical understanding and the adaptation of purpose to contemporary circumstances. Cf. Katz v. United States, 389 U. S. 347 (1967); Estes v. Texas, 381 U. S. 532, 595-596 (1965) (concurring opinion); Olmstead v. United States, 277 U. S. 438, 471 (1928) (Brandeis, J., dissenting); United States v. Lovett, 328 U. S. 303, 318 (1946) (Frankfurter, J., concurring).[11] B. Cardozo, The Nature of the Judicial Process (1921). This is not, however, a circumstance of giving a term "a meaning not necessarily envisioned . . . so as to adapt [it] to circumstances . . . uncontemplated." See my opinion concurring in the result in Welsh v. United States, 398 U. S. 333, 344 (1970). The right to a trial by jury, however, has no enduring meaning apart from historical form.

The second aspect of the Court's argument is that the number "12" is a historical accident—even though one that has recurred without interruption since the 14th century (see ante, at 89)—and is in no way essential to the "purpose of the jury trial" which is to "safeguard against the corrupt or overzealous prosecutor and against the complaint, biased, or eccentric judge." Ante, at 100. Thus history, the Court suggests, is no guide to the meaning of those rights whose form bears no relation to the policy they reflect. In this context the 12-member feature of the classical common-law jury is apparently regarded by the Court as mere adornment.

This second justification for cutting the umbilical cord that ties the form of the jury to the past is itself, as I see it, the most compelling reason for maintaining that guarantee in its common-law form. For if 12 jurors are not essential, why are six? What if New York, now compelled by virtue of Baldwin to provide juries for the trial of misdemeanors, concludes that three jurors are adequate "interposition between the accused and his accuser of the common-sense judgment of a group of laymen," and constitute adequate "community participation and [provide] shared responsibility which results from that group's determination of guilt or innocence"? The Court's elaboration of what is required provides no standard and vexes the meaning of the right to a jury trial in federal courts, as well as state courts, by uncertainty. Can it be doubted that a unanimous jury of 12 provides a greater safeguard than a majority vote of six? The uncertainty that will henceforth plague the meaning of trial by jury is itself a further sufficient reason for not hoisting the anchor to history.

2. The circumvention of history is compounded by the cavalier disregard of numerous pronouncements of this Court that reflect the understanding of the jury as one of 12 members and have fixed expectations accordingly. Thus in Thompson v. Utah a unanimous Court answered in the affirmative the question whether the Sixth Amendment jury "is a jury constituted, as it was at common law, of twelve persons, neither more nor less." 170 U. S. 343, 349 (1898),[12] and it appears that before Duncan no Justice of this Court has seen fit to question this holding, one that has often been reiterated. See Patton v. United States, 281 U. S. 276, 288 (1930), where the Court reaffirmed earlier pronouncements and stated that the Sixth Amendment jury is characterized by three essential features: "(1) that the jury should consist of twelve men, neither more nor less; (2) that the trial should be in the presence and under the superintendence of a judge having power to instruct them as to the law and advise them in respect of the facts; and (3) that the verdict should be unanimous." See also Maxwell v. Dow, 176 U. S. 581, 586 (1900); Rassmussen v. United States, 197 U. S. 516, 527 (1905); Andres v. United States, 333 U. S. 740, 748 (1948) (unanimity).[13] As Mr. Justice Frankfurter stated in Gore v. United States, 357 U. S. 386, 392 (1958), in applying a constitutional provision "rooted in history . . . a long course of adjudication in this Court carries impressive authority."

The principle of stare decisis is multifaceted. It is a solid foundation for our legal system; yet care must be taken not to use it to create an unmovable structure. It provides the stability and predictability required for the ordering of human affairs over the course of time and a basis of "public faith in the judiciary as a source of impersonal and reasoned judgments." Moragne v. States Marine Lines, 398 U. S. 375, 403 (1970). See also Helvering v. Hallock, 309 U. S. 106 (1940); Boys Markets v. Retail Clerks, 398 U. S. 235 (1970); Hertz v. Woodman, 218 U. S. 205, 212 (1910); Burnet v. Coronado Oil & Gas Co., 285 U. S. 393, 405-406 (1932) (Brandeis, J., dissenting). Woodenly applied, however, it builds a stockade of precedent that confines the law by rules, ill-conceived when promulgated, or if sound in origin, unadaptable to present circumstances. No precedent is sacrosanct and one should not hesitate to vote to overturn this Court's previous holdings— old or recent—or reconsider settled dicta where the principles announced prove either practically (e. g., Moragne v. States Marine Lines, supra; Boys Markets v. Retail Clerks, supra), or jurisprudentially (e. g., Desist v. United States, 394 U. S. 244, 256 (1969) (dissenting opinion)) unworkable, or no longer suited to contemporary life (e. g., Katz v. United States, 389 U. S. 347, 360 (1967) (concurring opinion)). See also Welsh v. United States, 398 U. S. 333 (1970); Chimel v. California, 395 U. S. 752 (1969); Marchetti v. United States, 390 U. S. 39 (1968); Estes v. Texas, 381 U. S., at 595-596 (concurring opinion); Warden v. Hayden, 387 U. S. 294 (1967); Swift & Co. v. Wickham, 382 U. S. 111 (1965); James v. United States, 366 U. S. 213, 241 (1961) (separate opinion of HARLAN, J.). Indeed, it is these considerations that move me to depart today from the framework of Duncan. It is, in part, the disregard of stare decisis in circumstances where it should apply, to which the Court is, of necessity, driven in Williams by the "incorporation" doctrine, that leads me to decline to follow Duncan. Surely if the principle of stare decisis means anything in the law, it means that precedent should not be jettisoned when the rule of yesterday remains viable, creates no injustice, and can reasonably be said to be no less sound than the rule sponsored by those who seek change, let alone incapable of being demonstrated wrong. The decision in Williams, however, casts aside workability and relevance and substitutes uncertainty. The only reason I can discern for today's decision that discards numerous judicial pronouncements and historical precedent that sound constitutional interpretation would look to as controlling, is the Court's disquietude with the tension between the jurisprudential consequences wrought by "incorporation" in Duncan and Baldwin and the counter-pulls of the situation in Williams which presents the prospect of invalidating the common practice in the States of providing less than a 12-member jury for the trial of misdemeanor cases.

II

These decisions demonstrate that the difference between a "due process" approach, that considers each particular case on its own bottom to see whether the right alleged is one "implicit in the concept of ordered liberty," see Palko v. Connecticut, 302 U. S. 319, 325 (1937), and "selective incorporation" is not an abstract one whereby different verbal formulae achieve the same results. The internal logic of the selective incorporation doctrine cannot be respected if the Court is both committed to interpreting faithfully the meaning of the federal Bill of Rights and recognizing the governmental diversity that exists in this country. The "backlash" in Williams exposes the malaise, for there the Court dilutes a federal guarantee in order to reconcile the logic of "incorporation," the "jot-for-jot and case-for-case" application of the federal right to the States, with the reality of federalism. Can one doubt that had Congress tried to undermine the common-law right to trial by jury before Duncan came on the books the history today recited would have barred such action? Can we expect repeat performances when this Court is called upon to give definition and meaning to other federal guarantees that have been "incorporated"?

In Ker v. California, 374 U. S. 23 (1963), I noted in an opinion concurring in the result that: "The rule [of `incorporation'] is unwise because the States, with their differing law enforcement problems, should not be put in a constitutional strait jacket . . . . And if the Court is prepared to relax [federal] standards in order to avoid unduly fettering the States, this would be in derogation of law enforcement standards in the federal system . . . ." Id., at 45-46. Only last Term in Chimel v. California, supra, I again expressed my misgivings that "incorporation" would neutralize the potency of guarantees in federal courts in order to accommodate the diversity of our federal system. I reiterate what I said in dissent in Duncan, 391 U. S., at 175-176: "[N]either history, nor sense, supports using the Fourteenth Amendment to put the States in a constitutional straitjacket with respect to their own development in the administration of criminal or civil law." Since we now witness the first major attempt to wriggle free of that "straitjacket," it is appropriate, I think, to step back and view in perspective how far the incorporation doctrine has taken us, and to put the spotlight on a constitutional revolution that has inevitably become obscured by the process of case-by-case adjudication.

A

The recent history of constitutional adjudication in state criminal cases is the ascendancy of the doctrine of ad hoc ("selective") incorporation, an approach that absorbs one-by-one individual guarantees of the federal Bill of Rights into the Due Process Clause of the Fourteenth Amendment, and holds them applicable to the States with all the subtleties and refinements born of history and embodied in case experience developed in the context of federal adjudication. Thus, with few exceptions the Court has "incorporated," each time over my protest,[14] almost all the criminal protections found within the first eight Amendments to the Constitution, and made them "jot-for-jot and case-for-case" applicable to the States.

The process began with Mapp v. Ohio, 367 U. S. 643 (1961), where the Court applied to the States the so-called exclusionary rule, rendering inadmissible at trial evidence seized in violation of the Fourth Amendment, and thereby overruling pro tanto Wolf v. Colorado, 338 U. S. 25 (1949). See my dissenting opinion, 367 U. S., at 672. The particular course embarked upon in Mapp was blindly followed to its end in Ker v. California, 374 U. S. 23 (1963), where the Court made federal standards of probable cause for search and seizure applicable to the States, thereby overruling the remainder of Wolf. See my opinion concurring in the result, 374 U. S., at 44. Thereafter followed Malloy v. Hogan, 378 U. S. 1 (1964), and Griffin v. California, 380 U. S. 609 (1965), overruling Twining v. New Jersey, 211 U. S. 78 (1908), and Adamson v. California, 332 U. S. 46 (1947), and incorporating the Fifth Amendment privilege against self-incrimination by holding that "the same standards must determine whether an accused's silence in either a federal or state proceeding is justified." 378 U. S., at 11. See my dissenting opinion in Malloy, 378 U. S., at 14, and my concurring opinion in Griffin, 380 U. S., at 615. The year of Griffin also brought forth Pointer v. Texas, 380 U. S. 400 (1965), overruling Snyder v. Massachusetts, 291 U. S. 97 (1934), and Stein v. New York, 346 U. S. 156, 194 (1953), by holding that the Sixth Amendment's Confrontation Clause applied equally to the States and Federal Government. See my opinion concurring in the result, 380 U. S., at 408. In 1967 incorporation swept in the "speedy trial" guarantee of the Sixth Amendment. Klopfer v. North Carolina, 386 U. S. 213 (1967), and in 1968 Duncan v. Louisiana, supra, rendered the Sixth Amendment jury trial a right secured by the Fourteenth Amendment Due Process Clause. Only last Term the Court overruled Palko v. Connecticut, supra, and held that the "double jeopardy" protection of the Fifth Amendment was incorporated into the Fourteenth, and hence also carried to the States. Benton v. Maryland, 395 U. S. 784 (1969); see my opinion concurring in the result in Klopfer, 386 U. S., at 226; my dissenting opinion in Duncan, 391 U. S., at 171; my dissenting opinion in Benton, 395 U. S., at 801, and my separate opinion in North Carolina v. Pearce, 395 U. S. 711, 744 (1969).[15] In combination these cases have in effect restructured the Constitution in the field of state criminal law enforcement.

There is no need to travel again over terrain trod in earlier opinions in which I have endeavored to lay bare the historical and logical infirmities of this "incorporationist" approach. On that score I am content to rest on what I said in dissent in Duncan, 391 U. S., at 171. I continue to consider the principles therein expressed as the sound basis for approaching the adjudication of state cases of the kind now before us. It is my firm conviction that "incorporation" distorts the "essentially federal nature of our national government," Atlantic Coast Line R. Co. v. Brotherhood of Locomotive Engineers, 398 U. S. 281, 285 (1970), one of whose basic virtues is to leave ample room for governmental and social experimentation in a society as diverse as ours, and which also reflects the view of the Framers that "the security of liberty in America rested primarily upon the dispersion of governmental power across a federal system," 391 U. S., at 173. The Fourteenth Amendment tempered this basic philosophy but did not unstitch the basic federalist pattern woven into our constitutional fabric. The structure of our Government still embodies a philosophy that presupposes the diversity that engendered the federalist system.

That these doctrines are not only alive in rhetoric but vital in the world of practical affairs is evidenced by contemporary debate concerning the desirability of returning to "local" government the administration of many programs and functions that have in late years increasingly been centralized in the hands of the National Government.

B

But the best evidence of the vitality of federalism is today's decision in Williams. The merits or demerits of the jury system can, of course, be debated and those States that have diluted the common-law requirements evince a conclusion that the protection as known at common law is not necessary for a fair trial, or is only such marginal assurance of a fair trial that the inconvenience of assembling 12 individuals outweighs other gains in the administration of justice achieved by using only six individuals (or none at all as was the case in New York City).

The prevailing opinion rejects in Baldwin what would be the consistent approach, requiring affirmance, simply because New York City is the single jurisdiction in the Nation that sees fit to try misdemeanants without a jury. In doing so it, in effect, holds that "due process" is more offended by a trial without a jury for an offense punishable by no more than a year in prison than it is by a trial with a jury of six or less for offenses punishable by life imprisonment. This ignores both the basic fairness of the New York procedure and the peculiar local considerations that have led the New York Legislature to conclude that trial by jury is more apt to retard than further justice for criminal defendants in New York City.

I, for one, find nothing unfair in the New York system which provides the city defendant with an option, in lieu of a jury, of a bench trial before three judges, N. Y. C. Crim. Ct. Act § 40. Moreover, I think it counterproductive of fairness in criminal trials to hold by way of incorporation that juries are required of States in these days when congested calendars and attendant delays make what many students of criminal justice feel is one of the most significant contributions to injustice and hardship to criminal defendants.

The statistics cited by the New York Court of Appeals and amplified in the briefs are revealing and trenchant evidence of the crisis that presently bedevils the administration of criminal justice in New York City. New York's population density, a factor which is, as noted by the President's Commission on Law Enforcement and Administration of Justice, The Challenge of Crime in a Free Society 5, 28 (1967), directly associated with crime, is twice that of Buffalo, the second largest city in the State. Statistics supplied by the Office of the State Administrator of the Judicial Conference of the State of New York show that: "From July, 1966 through December, 1968 the New York City Criminal Court disposed of 321, 368 nontraffic misdemeanor cases; whereas in the next largest city, Buffalo, the City Court disposed of 8,189 nontraffic misdemeanor cases." 24 N. Y. 2d 207, 218, 247 N. E. 2d 260, 266 (1969). Thus, New York City's misdemeanor caseload is 39 times that of Buffalo's although its population is only 17 times greater. After today each of such defendants in New York is entitled to a trial by some kind of a jury. It can hardly be gainsaid that a jury requirement with the attendant time for selection of jurors and deliberation, even if not invoked by all defendants, will increase delays in calendars, depriving all defendants of a prompt trial. Impressive evidence suggests that this requirement could conceivably increase delays in New York City courts by as much as a factor of eight. A study done of the administration of the Municipal Court in Minneapolis shows that the requirement of a trial by jury in cases of intoxicated driving increased court delays there from three to 24 months. Note, Right to a Jury Trial for Persons Accused of an Ordinance Violation, 47 Minn. L. Rev. 93 (1962).

Notwithstanding this critical situation the Court concludes that the Constitution requires a procedure fraught with delay even though the American Bar Association Project on Standards for Criminal Justice, Trial By Jury, has recognized the New York City three-judge procedure as a possible compromise measure where jury trials are not permitted or waived, and the further fact that one-half the defendants tried for misdemeanors in New York City are acquitted.[16]

III

Today's decisions demonstrate a constitutional schizophrenia born of the need to cope with national diversity under the constraints of the incorporation doctrine. In Baldwin the prevailing opinion overrides the consideration of local needs, but in Williams the Court seeks out a minimum standard to avoid causing disruption in numerous instances even though, a priori, incorporation would surely require a jury of 12. The six-man, six-month rule of today's decisions simply reflects the lowest common denominator in the scope and function of the right to trial by jury in this country, but the circumstance that every jurisdiction except New York City has a trial by a jury for offenses punishable by six months in prison obscures the variety of opinion that actually exists as to the proper place for the jury in the administration of justice. More discriminating analysis indicates that four States besides Florida authorize a jury of less than 12 to try felony offenses[17] and three States authorize a nonunanimous verdict[18] in felony cases, and at least two other States provide a trial without jury in the first instance for certain offenses punishable by more than one year with a right to de novo trial on appeal.[19] Eight States provide for juries ranging from five to 12 to try crimes punishable by one year in prison, and one State has provided for a verdict by nine in a jury of 12.[20] Five States first provide a bench trial for misdemeanors from which the defendant can seek a trial de novo by jury,[21] a procedure that this Court, in a federal trial, has deemed incompatible with the Sixth Amendment for putting the accused to the burden of two trials if he wishes a jury verdict. See Callan v. Wilson, 127 U. S. 540 (1888).[22]

These varying provisions, reflecting as they do differing estimates of the importance of the jury in securing a fair trial and the feasibility of administering such a procedure given the local circumstances, and the extensive study and debate about the merits and demerits of the jury system, demonstrate that the relevance and proper role of trial by jury in the administration of criminal justice is yet far from sure.

"Incorporation" in Duncan closed the door on debate,[23] irrespective of local circumstances, such as the backlogs in urban courts like those of New York City, and has, without justification, clouded with uncertainty the constitutionality of these differing state modes of proceeding, see Appendix, pending approval by this Court; it now promises to dilute in other ways the settled meaning of the federal right to a trial by jury. Flexibility for experimentation in the administration of justice should be returned to the States here and in other areas that now have been swept into the rigid mold of "incorporation." I agree with THE CHIEF JUSTICE: "That the `near-uniform judgment of the Nation' is otherwise than the judgment in some of its parts affords no basis . . . to read into the Constitution something not found there." Opinion of THE CHIEF JUSTICE in Baldwin, ante, at 77.

It is time, I submit, for this Court to face up to the reality implicit in today's holdings and reconsider the "incorporation" doctrine before its leveling tendencies further retard development in the field of criminal procedure by stifling flexibility in the States and by discarding the possibility of federal leadership by example.

Justice Harlan's concurrence and dissent in US v. Phillipsburg Nat. Bank & Trust Co. (June 29, 1970)

MR. JUSTICE HARLAN, with whom THE CHIEF JUSTICE joins, concurring in part and dissenting in part.

My first reaction to this case, from the vantage point of what is depicted in the record and briefs, was wonderment that the Department of Justice had bothered to sue. How could that agency of government, I asked myself, be efficiently allocating its own scarce resources if it chose to attack a merger between two banks as small as those involved in this case? When compared with any of the 10 prior cases in which a bank merger was contested, the total assets of the bank that would result from this merger are minuscule.[1] Moreover, measured by trust assets, the Phillipsburg National Bank in 1968 ranked 1346th and the Second National Bank of Phillipsburg 2429th out of the approximately 3100 banks with trust powers in the United States. If the two banks were merged, the resulting bank would have ranked 1323d— only 23 places ahead of the Phillipsburg National alone.[2] With tigers still at large in our competitive jungle, why should the Department be taking aim at such small game?

The Court's disposition of this case provides justification enough from the Department's point of view. After today's opinion the legality of every merger of two directly competing banks—no matter how small—is placed in doubt if a court, through what has become an exercise in "antitrust numerology," United States v. First National Bank & Trust Co. of Lexington, 376 U. S. 665, 673 (1964) (HARLAN, J., dissenting), concludes that the merger "produces a firm controlling an undue percentage share of the relevant market," ante, at 366.

I

Under the Bank Merger Act it is now settled that a court must engage in a two-step process in order to decide whether a proposed merger passes muster. First, the effect of the merger upon competition must be evaluated, applying the standards under § 7 of the Clayton Act, United States v. Third National Bank in Nashville, 390 U. S. 171, 181-183 (1968). If there would be a violation, the court must then proceed to decide whether "the anticompetitive effects of the proposed transaction are clearly outweighed in the public interest by the probable effect of the transaction in meeting the convenience and needs of the community to be served."[3]

For the first stage of the analysis, the Court appears to decide whether the effect of this proposed merger "may be substantially to lessen competition" by the following process: First, the Court defines the relevant product market as commercial banking. Second, it defines the geographic market as Phillipsburg-Easton.[4] The Court next calculates the percentage share of this market that would be held by the proposed merged bank,[5] and the resulting changes in "concentration," as measured by the percent of market held by the two largest[6] and three largest banks.[7] It appears that from the magnitude of these figures alone, the Court concludes that the proposed merger would "significantly increase commercial banking concentration" in an "already concentrated" market.[8] On the basis of the magnitude of these figures alone the Court concludes that this merger would violate § 7 of the Clayton Act.

I have voiced my disagreement before, particularly in the banking field, with the " `numbers game' test for determining Clayton Act violations," United States v. Third National Bank, supra, at 193 (HARLAN, J., concurring in part and dissenting in part); see United States v. First National Bank, supra, at 673 (HARLAN, J., dissenting). Although I consider myself bound by the Court's decision in Philadelphia Bank, see United States v. Third National Bank, supra, at 193, I cannot concur in the simplistic way in which the Court applies the numbers test here.

Philadelphia Bank did not hold that all bank mergers resulting in an "undue percentage share of the relevant market" and "in a significant increase in the concentration of firms in that market," 374 U. S., at 363, necessarily violated § 7 of the Clayton Act. Instead that case established a rule by which the percentage figures alone do no more than "raise an inference," id., at 365, that the merger will significantly lessen competition. Philadelphia Bank left room, however, for the merging companies to show that the "merger is not likely to have such anticompetitive effects," id., at 363. In short, under the Philadelphia Bank test, the percentage figures create a rebuttable presumption of illegality.

In this case there are two aspects of market structure, each largely ignored by the Court, that I think might well rebut the presumption raised by the percentage figures that the merger will have a significant effect on competition. Consequently, I think the appellees should on remand be given an opportunity to show by "clear evidence" that despite the percentage figures, the anticompetitive effects of this merger are not significant.

II

The first of these aspects of the market structure concerns "entry." The percentage figures alone tell nothing about the conditions of entry in a particular market. New entry can, of course, quickly alleviate "undue" concentration. And the possibility of entry can act as a substantial check on the market power of existing competitors.

Entry into banking is not simply governed by free market conditions, of course, for it is also limited by regulatory laws. When the complaint in this case was filed, entry into the Phillipsburg-Easton market was very much restricted by both the Pennsylvania and New Jersey banking statutes.[9] However, a recent change in the New Jersey statute[10] together with a new opinion of the Court of Appeals for the Third Circuit rendered since the trial in this case,[11] appears to increase considerably the possibility of new entry into Phillipsburg. For the first time it may be possible for any national bank already operating anywhere in the northern region of New Jersey to open, under certain circumstances, a new office in Phillipsburg.[12]

If one assumes the regulatory barriers to entry have been permanently lowered, it would seem that the competitive significance of this merger may well be considerably overstated by the percentage figures alone. Certainly new entry into the market involved in this case would be both easier and of much greater competitive significance than in the Philadelphia Bank market. In a market dominated by banks of enormous absolute size, with assets of hundreds of millions and even billions of dollars, it is of course unlikely that a new entrant will quickly become a substantial competitive force. The same is not true, however, of a market in which the largest competitor is, in absolute terms, rather small.

In short, I think the significance of the percentage figures recited in the Court's opinion can only be fully evaluated after consideration of the present entry conditions in the Phillipsburg-Easton area. Because of the new developments in the New Jersey regulation of banking that have occurred since the trial of this case, I think it inexcusable of the majority not to give the appellee banks an opportunity on remand to demonstrate whether there is now a substantial possibility of new entry, and if so, what effect that possibility would have on the market power of the combined bank.[13]

III

Quite apart from entry, there is another aspect of the market structure relevant here that affects the significance of the percentage figures cited by the Court. Relying on Philadelphia Bank, the Court concludes that the "cluster of products . . . and services . . . denoted by the term `commercial banking'. . . composes a distinct line of commerce" for purposes of this case. The Court eschews all analysis of the composition of the products and services offered by appellee banks, however. The Court thus manages to ignore completely the extent to which competition from savings and loan companies, mutual savings banks, and other financial institutions that are not commercial banks affects the market power of the appellee banks.

A closer analysis of what the merging banks here do, plainly shows that they have more in common with savings and loan institutions and mutual savings banks than with the big city commercial banks considered in Philadelphia Bank. In particular, a much higher percentage of the total deposits of the banks here comes from savings accounts as opposed to demand deposits than is true of big city commercial banks.[14] Moreover, a much larger proportion of the total loans of these small banks is in the form of real estate or personal loans as opposed to commercial loans.[15] Savings and loan companies, savings banks, credit unions, etc., are of much greater competitive significance in this market than in the market analyzed in Philadelphia Bank. For in this market, these nonbank financial institutions offer close substitutes for the products and services that are most important to the appellee banks.

In choosing its product market, the Court largely ignores these subtleties and instead emphasizes the cluster of services and products which in the Court's words "makes commercial banking a distinct line of commerce." Because the Court does not explain why that combination has any substantial synergistic effect, cf. Anderson's-Black Rock, Inc. v. Pavement Salvage Co., Inc., 396 U. S. 57, 61 (1969), the Court's choice of a product market here can be seriously questioned. Certainly a more discriminating conclusion concerning the antitrust implication of this merger could be made if separate concentration percentages were calculated for each of the important products and services provided by appellee banks, and then an overall appraisal made of the effect of this merger on competition.

In any event, even assuming that for purposes of a preliminary analysis one were to use commercial banking as the line of commerce for the antitrust analysis—if only for the sake of convenience—that does not excuse the majority's failure to consider the competitive realities of the case in appraising the significance of the concentration percentages thus calculated, see United States v. First National Bank of Maryland, 310 F. Supp. 157, 175 (D. C. Md. 1970). The bare percentages themselves are not affected by the presence or absence of significant competition for important bank products or services from firms outside commercial banking. By treating these percentages as no different from those found in Philadelphia Bank, the Court blithely assumes that percentages of the same order of magnitude represent the same degree of market power, irrespective of the amount of competition from neighboring markets.

Seen another way, the Court's mode of analysis makes too much turn on the all-or-nothing determination that the relevant product market either includes or does not include products and services of savings and loan companies, and other competition. A far better approach would be to recognize the fact that a product or geographic market is at best an approximation—necessary to calculate some percentage figures. In evaluating such figures, however, the Court should not decide the case simply by the magnitude of the numbers alone— it should give the appellees on remand an opportunity to demonstrate that the numbers here significantly "overstate" the competitive effects of this merger because of the approximate nature of the assumptions underlying the Court's definition of the relevant market.

In short, I think that this case should be remanded to the District Court so that it might re-evaluate whether, in light of the entry conditions and existing competition from savings and loan and similar financial institutions, the merger can fairly be said to threaten a substantial loss of competition in the Phillipsburg-Easton area. Cf. White Motor Co. v. United States, 372 U. S. 253 (1963). If the District Court concludes that the merger would so threaten competition, it should then, in the manner the Court's opinion suggests, proceed to decide whether there are countervailing public interest advantages.

Notes

[1] The Appendix (at 831) contains the following table (somewhat modified herein) showing, inter alia, the total assets of the resulting banks in the contested bank merger cases initiated up to the time of suit in this case.

CONTESTED SECTION 7 BANK MERGER CASES: ASSETS

Case	Assets (in millions)
1. Manufacturers Hanover	$6,001.8
2. Continental Illinois	3,248.3

3. Crocker-Citizens 3,217.4

4. California Bank—First Western 2,421.2

5. Philadelphia National Bank 1,805.3

6. Provident—Central Penn 1,069.1

7. First City—Southern National (Houston) 1,042.9

8. Mercantile Trust—Security Trust 1,040.4

9. Third National—Nashville Bank & Trust 428.2

10. First National—Cooke Trust Company 389.7

11. Phillipsburg National—Second National 41.1

[2] App. 840.

[3] Bank Merger Act of 1966, amending § 18 (c) (5) (B) of the Federal Deposit Insurance Act, 12 U. S. C. § 1828 (c) (5) (B) (1964 ed., Supp. V). I do not quarrel with the Court's conclusion that the District Court improperly analyzed "convenience and needs," in the second stage, because of its erroneous choice of Phillipsburg alone as the relevant "community."

[4] I accept the Court's conclusion that the appropriate geographic market here is the Phillipsburg-Easton area, and agree that the geographic market designated by the District Court was too broad, given the small size of the banks involved in this case.

[5] PERCENTAGE OF PHILLIPSBURG-EASTON MARKET HELD BY MERGED BANKS Bank Assets 19.3 Total Deposits 23.4 Total Loans 27.3

[6] PERCENTAGE OF PHILLIPSBURG-EASTON MARKET HELD BY TWO LARGEST BANKS Before After Change Bank Assets 49 55 6 Total Deposits 56 65 9 Total Loans 49 63 14

[7] PERCENTAGE OF PHILLIPSBURG-EASTON MARKET HELD BY THREE LARGEST BANKS Before After Change Bank Assets 60 68 8 Total Deposits 70 80 10 Total Loans 64 76 12

[8] It is significant to note that the percentage figures in this case are themselves smaller, on the whole, than those found either in the Philadelphia Bank case supra, or Third National Bank case, supra.

PERCENTAGE OF TOTAL ASSETS IN RELEVANT MARKET
HELD BY MERGED BANKS

This case	19.3
Third Nat. Bank	38.4
Philadelphia Bank (at least 30%)	36*

PERCENTAGE OF TOTAL ASSETS IN RELEVANT MARKET
HELD BY TWO LARGEST BANKS

	Before	After
This case	49	55
Third Nat. Bank	72	77
Philadelphia Bank	44	59

PERCENTAGE OF TOTAL ASSETS IN RELEVANT MARKET

HELD BY THREE LARGEST BANKS**

	Before	After
This case	60	68
Third Nat. Bank	93	98

* For purposes of its holding in Philadelphia Bank, the Court "shade[d]" the 36% figure downward to "at least 30%" to compensate for the approximate nature of certain assumptions implicit in the manner in which it calculated the market shares, see Philadelphia Bank, supra, at 364 and n. 40.

** Because Philadelphia Bank involved a merger between the second and third largest banks, the percentage held by the three largest was not used in that case.

[9] New Jersey, at the time suit was filed here, (1) prohibited the merger of banks located in different countries; (2) restricted branch banking to the county in which the parent bank was located; (3) precluded branching altogether into cities in which another bank had a "principal office" (i. e., home office), or into communities in which a bank or branch was already located. See N. J. Stat. Ann. § 17:9A-19 (B) (1963).

[10] On July 17, 1969, a new banking statute came into effect that regulates, not on the basis of counties, but instead on the basis of three banking districts, of which Phillipsburg is in the first. District-wide de novo branching and mergers are authorized, subject to a "principal office" protection provision, N. J. Stat. Ann. § 17:9A-19 (B) (3) (Supp. 1970).

[11] Ramapo Bank v. Camp, 425 F. 2d 333 (C. A. 3d Cir. 1970). I intimate, of course, no views concerning the correctness of this decision.

[12] Because Phillipsburg is the location of a home office, the home-office protection proviso might be thought to preclude de novo branching there. However, the Ramapo Bank decision of the Third Circuit, supra, held that a national bank, by moving its main office into a protected community while simultaneously reopening its former main office as a branch, could avoid the operation of the "home-office protection" proviso of the New Jersey law. Under Ramapo, therefore, it is possible for any national bank willing to shift its "home office" to Phillipsburg to enter that market.

[13] It is simply untenable for the majority to ignore the bearing of this issue on the "anticompetitive effect" of this merger on the ground that "[n]othing in the present record suggests that any national bank now located outside Phillipsburg will apply to move its main office to that city," ante, at 369. At the time the present record was developed, existing law rendered that inquiry irrelevant. Moreover, the District Court found, quite apart from entry, that the proposed merger had no significant anticompetitive effect. It is therefore quite inappropriate for the majority to suggest that the failure of the District Court to reopen the record in light of its Ramapo decision is of any significance.

[14] TIME AND SAVINGS DEPOSITS AND DEMAND DEPOSITS AS PERCENTAGE OF TOTAL DEPOSITS Time & Savings Demand PNB 71 29 SNB 72 28

Large Bank Average* 45 55 * The average for 341 banks with assets over $100 million which submit weekly reports to the Federal Reserve Board.

Calculated from App. 788.

[15] REAL ESTATE LOANS AND PERSONAL LOANS AS PERCENTAGE OF TOTAL LOANS Real Estate Personal Combined PNB 54 28 82 SNB 72 14 86 Large Bank Average** 14 8 22 ** See n. 14, supra.

Calculated from App. 788.

Justice Harlan's concurrence in Williams v. Illinois (June 29, 1970)

MR. JUSTICE HARLAN, concurring in the result.

I concur in today's judgment, but in doing so wish to dissociate myself from the "equal protection" rationale employed by the Court to justify its conclusions.

The "equal protection" analysis of the Court is, I submit, a "wolf in sheep's clothing," for that rationale is no more than a masquerade of a supposedly objective standard for subjective judicial judgment as to what state legislation offends notions of "fundamental fairness." Under the rubric of "equal protection" this Court has in recent times effectively substituted its own "enlightened" social philosophy for that of the legislature no less than did in the older days the judicial adherents of the now discredited doctrine of "substantive" due process. I, for one, would prefer to judge the legislation before us in this case in terms of due process, that is to determine whether it arbitrarily infringes a constitutionally protected interest of this appellant. Due process, as I noted in my dissenting opinion in Poe v. Ullman, 367 U. S. 497, 541 (1961), is more than merely a procedural safeguard; it is also a " `bulwark . . . against arbitrary legislation.' Hurtado v. California, 110 U. S. 516, at 532." See Flemming v. Nestor, 363 U. S. 603 (1960), and my dissenting opinion in Shapiro v. Thompson, 394 U. S. 618, 655 (1969).

The matrix of recent "equal protection" analysis is that the "rule that statutory classifications which either are based upon certain `suspect' criteria or affect `fundamental rights' will be held to deny equal protection unless justified by a `compelling' governmental interest," Shapiro v. Thompson, supra, at 658 (HARLAN, J., dissenting). In Shapiro, Harper v. Virginia Board of Elections, 383 U. S. 663, 680 (1966), and Williams v. Rhodes, 393 U. S. 23, 41 (1968), I attempted to expose the weakness in the precedential and jurisprudential foundation upon which the current doctrine of "equal protection" sits. See also Griffin v. Illinois, 351 U. S. 12, 34-36 (1956) (dissenting opinion); Douglas v. California, 372 U. S. 353, 360 (1963) (dissenting opinion). I need not retrace the views expressed in these cases, except to object once again to this rhetorical preoccupation with "equalizing" rather than analyzing the rationality of the legislative distinction in relation to legislative purpose.

An analysis under due process standards, correctly understood, is, in my view, more conducive to judicial restraint than an approach couched in slogans and ringing phrases, such as "suspect" classification or "invidious" distinctions, or "compelling" state interest, that blur analysis by shifting the focus away from the nature of the individual interest affected, the extent to which it is affected, the rationality of the connection between legislative means and purpose, the existence of alternative means for effectuating the purpose, and the degree of confidence we may have that the statute reflects the legislative concern for the purpose that would legitimately support the means chosen. Accordingly, I turn to the case at hand.

I

The State of Illinois has made the unquestionably legitimate determination that the crime of petty larceny should be punished by a jail term of days, up to one year, in combination with a fine of a dollar amount. Anyone who, in the judgment of the trial judge, should receive the stiffest penalty known to Illinois law for this crime may, if he possesses funds, satisfy the demands of the criminal law by paying the fine superimposed on the jail term. If he cannot pay his debt to society, it is surely not unequal, but, to the contrary, most equal, that some substitute sanction be imposed lest the individual of means be subjected to a harsher penalty than one who is impoverished. If equal protection implications of the Court's opinion were to be fully realized, it would require that the consequence of punishment be comparable for all individuals; the State would be forced to embark on the impossible task of developing a system of individualized fines, so that the total disutility of the entire fine, or the marginal disutility of the last dollar taken, would be the same for all individuals. Cf. Michelman, Foreword: On Protecting the Poor Through the Fourteenth Amendment, 83 Harv. L. Rev. 7 (1969). Today's holding, and those in the other so-called "equal protection" decisions, e. g., Douglas v. California, supra; Anders v. California, 386 U. S. 738 (1967), offer no pretense to actually providing such equal treatment. It cannot be argued that the requirement of counsel on appeal is the right to the most skilled advocate who is theoretically at the call of the defendant of means. However desirable and enlightened a theory of social and economic equality may be, it is not a theory that has the blessing of the Fourteenth Amendment. Not "every major social ill in this country can find its cure in some constitutional `principle,' and . . . this Court [is not equipped to] `take the lead' in promoting reform when other branches of government fail to act. The Constitution is not a panacea for every blot upon the public welfare, nor should this Court, ordained as a judicial body, be thought of as a general haven for reform movements." Reynolds v. Sims, 377 U. S. 533, 624-625 (1964) (dissenting opinion).

II

The reluctance of the Court to carry its "equal protection" approach to its most logical consequences accents what I deem to be the true considerations involved in this case, namely, whether the legislature has impermissibly affected an individual right or has done so in an arbitrary fashion. Cf. Michelman, supra. While legislation usually will not be deemed arbitrary if its means can arguably be supposed to be related to a legitimate purpose (see my dissenting opinion in Shapiro v. Thompson, supra) and generally the burden of demonstrating the existence of a rational connection between means and ends is not borne by the State) see Flemming v. Nestor, supra, and my dissenting opinion in

Swann v. Adams, 385 U. S. 440, 447 (1967)), the presumption of regularity that comes with legislative judgment is one that is not equally acceptable in all instances, nor is it blind to the nature of the interests affected.

Thus, as a due process matter I have subscribed to the admonition of Skinner v. Oklahoma, 316 U. S. 535, 541 (1942), where the Court cautioned that there are limits to the extent to which the presumption of constitutionality can be pressed where a "basic liberty" is concerned. See my dissenting opinion in Poe v. Ullman, supra, at 543. The same viewpoint was implicit in Flemming v. Nestor, supra, where the Court noted the breadth of latitude to be accorded to a legislative judgment when the interest was that of a "noncontractual benefit under a social welfare program." 363 U. S., at 611. Thus while that "interest . . . is of sufficient substance to fall within the protection from arbitrary governmental action afforded by the Due Process Clause," when that interest is the "withholding of a noncontractual benefit under a social welfare program . . . , we must recognize that the Due Process Clause can be thought to interpose a bar only if the statute manifests a patently arbitrary classification, utterly lacking in rational justification." Ibid.

The implication of Flemming is, however, that the deference owed to legislative judgment is not the same in all cases. Thus legislation that regulates conduct but incidentally affects freedom of expression may, although it is a rational choice to effectuate a legitimate legislative purpose, be invalid because it imposes a burden on that right, or because other means, entailing less imposition, may exist. See NAACP v. Alabama, 357 U. S. 449 (1958); Lovell v. City of Griffin, 303 U. S. 444 (1938); Garner v. Louisiana, 368 U. S. 157, 185 (1961) (concurring in the judgment); United States v. O'Brien, 391 U. S. 367, 388 (1968) (concurring opinion).

These decisions, by no means dispositive of the case before us, unquestionably show that this Court will squint hard at any legislation that deprives an individual of his liberty—his right to remain free. Cf. my dissenting opinion in Poe v. Ullman, supra. While the interest of the State, that of punishing one convicted of crime is no less substantial, cf. concurring opinion of MR. JUSTICE BRENNAN in Illinois v. Allen, 397 U. S. 337, 347 (1970), the "balance which our Nation, built upon postulates of respect for the liberty of the individual, has struck between that liberty and the demands of organized society." Poe v. Ullman, supra, at 542, "having regard to what history teaches" is not such that the State's interest here outweighs that of the individual so as to bring into full play the application of the usual salutary presumption of rationality.

III

The State by this statute, or any other statute fixing a penalty of a fine, has declared its penological interest— deterrence, retribution, and rehabilitation—satisfied by a monetary payment, and disclaimed, as serving any penological purpose in such cases, a term in jail. While there can be no question that the State has a legitimate concern with punishing an individual who cannot pay the fine, there is serious question in my mind whether, having declared itself indifferent as between fine and jail, it can consistently with due process refrain from offering some alternative such as payment on the installment plan.

There are two conceivable justifications for not doing so. The most obvious and likely justification for the present statute is administrative convenience. Given the interest of the individual affected, I do not think a State may, after declaring itself indifferent between a fine and jail, rely on the convenience of the latter as a constitutionally acceptable means for enforcing its interest, given the existence of less restrictive alternatives. Cf. Mullane v. Central Hanover Trust Co., 339 U. S. 306 (1950).

The second conceivable justification is that the jail alternative serves a penological purpose that cannot be served by collection of a fine over time. It is clear that having declared itself satisfied by a fine, the alternative of jail to a fine serves neither a rehabilitative nor a retributive interest. The question is, then, whether the requirement of a lump-sum payment can be sustained as a rational legislative determination that deterrence is effective only when a fine is exacted at once after sentence and by lump sum, rather than over a term. This is a highly doubtful proposition, since, apart from the mere fact of conviction and the humiliation associated with it and the token of punishment evidenced by the forfeiture, the deterrent effect of a fine is apt to derive more from its pinch on the purse than the time of payment.

That the Illinois statute represents a considered judgment, evincing the belief that jail is a rational and necessary trade-off to punish the individual who possesses no accumulated assets seems most unlikely, since the substitute sentence provision, phrased in terms of a judgment collection statute, does not impose a discretionary jail term as an alternative sentence, but rather equates days in jail with a fixed sum. Thus, given that the only conceivable justification for this statute that would satisfy due process—that a lump-sum fine is a better deterrent than one payable over a period of time—is the one that is least likely to represent a considered legislative judgment, I would hold this statute invalid.

The conclusion I reach is only that when a State declares its penal interest may be satisfied by a fine or a forfeiture in combination with a jail term the administrative inconvenience in a judgment collection procedure does not, as a matter of due process, justify sending to jail, or extending the jail term of, individuals who possess no accumulated assets.[*] I would reserve the question as to whether a considered legislative judgment that a lump-sum fine is the only effective kind of forfeiture for deterrence and that the alternative must be jail, would be constitutional. It follows, a fortiori, that no conclusion reached herein casts any doubt on the conventional "$30 or 30 days" if the legislature decides that should be the penalty for the crime. Note, Discriminations Against the Poor and the Fourteenth Amendment, 81 Harv. L. Rev. 435 (1967). Such a statute evinces the perfectly rational determination that some individuals will be adequately punished by a money fine, and others, indifferent to money—whether by virtue of indigency or other reasons—can be punished only by a jail term. Still more patently nothing said herein precludes the State from punishing ultimately by jail individuals who fail to pay fines or imprisoning immediately individuals who, in the judgment of a court, will not undertake to pay their fines.

On these premises I join the Court's judgment vacating appellant's sentence and remanding to the Supreme Court of Illinois to afford it an opportunity to instruct the sentencing judge as to any permissible alternatives under Illinois law. It may be that Illinois courts have the power to fashion a procedure pending further consideration of this problem by the state legislature. Cf. Rosado v. Wyman, 397 U. S. 397, 421-422 (1970), and my opinion concurring in the result in Welsh v. United States, 398 U. S. 333, 344 (1970).

[*] In this regard, unlike the Court, I see no distinction between circumstances where the State through its judicial agent determines that effective punishment requires less than the maximum prison term plus a fine, or a fine alone, and the circumstances of this case.

Justice Harlan's dissent in US v. City of Chicago (Oct 19, 1970)

MR. JUSTICE HARLAN, with whom MR. JUSTICE BLACK joins, dissenting.
I think these cases do not lend themselves to summary disposition.
The Chicago & Eastern Illinois Railroad Co. and the Louisville & Nashville Railroad Co. jointly operated a train known as the "Georgian" which provided passenger service between Chicago, Illinois, and Atlanta, Georgia. At Evansville, Indiana, between the two terminal points on the "Georgian" run, the railroad companies switched engines and train crews; passengers, however, could remain in the railroad cars and continue through to the end of the run. The Chicago & Eastern Illinois sought ICC approval of its discontinuance of the Chicago-Evansville portion of the run; notice of the proposed discontinuance proceedings was not served on the Governors and residents of the States served by the Evansville-Atlanta portion of the "Georgian" run. After our remand in City of Chicago v. United States, 396 U. S. 162 (1969), the District Court held that notice of the ICC discontinuance proceedings should have been given to the Governors and residents of all the States served by the "Georgian" run. The Court, in Nos. 386 and 410, now summarily reverses that decision, holding that § 13a (1) of the Interstate Commerce Act, 49 U. S. C. § 13a (1), requires that a carrier seeking to discontinue passenger service give notice only in those States having regulatory authority over the carrier.[1]

The issue, in my opinion, is not one justifying summary resolution, as an examination of the Court's opinion indicates. The Court relies in the first instance on the absence of an explicit provision in § 13a (1) of the Act for notice to States served by "connecting railroads." However, the statutory provision in question is manifestly highly ambiguous with regard to the scope of the notice obligation in situations where two carriers, though subject to different state regulatory authorities, offer their services to the public in a manner which, from the consumer standpoint, is indistinguishable from passenger service offered by a single carrier. Section 13a (1) provides in relevant part:

"A carrier or carriers . . . if their rights with respect to the discontinuance or change, in whole or in part, of the operation or service of any train . . . operating from a point in one State to a point in any other State . . . are subject to any provision of the constitution or statutes of any State or any regulation or order of (or are the subject of any proceeding pending before) any court or an administrative or regulatory agency of any State, may, but shall not be required to, file with the Commission, and upon such filing shall mail to the Governor of each State in which such train . . . is operated, and post in every station, depot or other facility served thereby, notice at least thirty days in advance of any such proposed discontinuance or change. . . ."

Appellants in Nos. 386 and 410 argue that since § 13a (1) accords carriers a right to commence discontinuance proceedings before the ICC if their rights with respect to the operation of train service are subject to any state regulatory authority, the scope of the notice requirement should be limited by the reach of the state regulatory power giving rise, in the first instance, to the carrier's right to go before the ICC. Appellees in Nos. 386 and 410, for their part, contend that the notice requirement is geared to the areas through which "such train" is operated, not merely the areas reached by a State's regulatory power over the carrier. For my part, I find the language and structure of the statutory provision singularly opaque; and I am not aided in my choice between these competing constructions by the Court's observation that § 13a (1) makes no provision for notice in States served by "connecting railroads."

In view of the structural and linguistic ambiguity of the statutory provision, the Court's reliance on the absence of an explicit reference to carrier arrangements of this sort would carry weight only if the legislative policy underlying § 13a (1) of the Act solidly supported the result reached today. Lacking that, the description of congressional policy in n. 3 of the Court's opinion, ante, at 11, hardly warrants the Court's inference in the text of its opinion that the statutory purpose underpinning § 13a (1) is served by a limitation of the notice requirements according to the reach of the State's regulatory power over the carrier filing with the ICC.[2] Indeed, the concern with state regulatory parochialism, and the resulting burden on interstate commerce caused by economically wasteful passenger service arrangements, argue with at least equal force for an interpretation of the notice requirements of § 13a (1) as reaching beyond the relatively narrow parochial interests likely to be called forth by only a particular State's participation in a hearing on the discontinuance of multicarrier service.

Apparently, the Court recognizes the inherent ambiguity of the statute. Thus, its opinion finally comes to rest on the principle of deference to the administrative agency's construction of the statute. Suffice it to say that I am not persuaded by the deference argument as applied to the agency's pro forma finding of adequate notice in this very litigation where the notice issue evidently was not before the agency at the time of its ruling. See 331 I. C. C. 447, 448.

The above considerations are not meant to reflect any conclusions concerning the merits of the statutory construction issue presented in these cases. To the contrary, my point is simply that, without briefs and oral argument by the parties on the merits of the question, I would refrain from choosing between the conflicting constructions of § 13a (1) pressed upon the Court by the parties. Therefore, I would note probable jurisdiction in Nos. 386 and 410. I would withhold action in No. 387 pending dispositions in Nos. 386 and 410. In No. 396, I would note probable jurisdiction, limited to the questions concerning the District Court's action in reinstating the restraining order of September 6, 1968.

Notes

[1] Nos. 387 and 396 are appeals by the Government, the ICC, and the Louisville & Nashville Railroad Co. challenging the District Court's holding that the issues involving the discontinuance of the Louisville & Nashville Railroad Co.'s "Hummingbird" train are so factually related to the discontinuance of the "Georgian" run that the "Hummingbird" discontinuance should be remanded in light of the projected reconsideration of the "Georgian" discontinuance. In addition, the Louisville & Nashville Railroad Co., in No. 396, challenges the District Court's action in reinstating the September 6, 1968, restraining order entered by Judge Robson; that restraining order prohibited discontinuance of the "Hummingbird" trains pending resolution of the case in the District Court. On April 3, 1970, this Court stayed the District Court's action in reinstating the earlier restraining order. 397 U. S. 1019. The effect of today's opinion on the status of that restraining order is unclear.

[2] The disconnected nature of the Court's reasoning is nicely illustrated in n. 3 of its opinion, ante, at 11. We are offered two quotations—one from the Senate Report and the other from the Association of American Railroads—as legislative history supporting the Court's construction of § 13a (1). The substance of both clearly supports the view of § 13a (1) as seeking to remedy state regulatory parochialism. Unfortunately, neither quotation speaks to the question put in issue by the Court's rationale for summarily disposing of these cases; i. e., whether the congressional decision to proffer an alternative national forum as a remedy for state parochialism is to be construed solely in light of the carrier interest in escaping state regulatory agencies. Yet the Court, after reciting these quotations, chooses to draw the inference that the statute cannot be easily construed to do more than serve that interest of the carriers. I must respectfully submit that this is a rather obvious non sequitur.

Justice Harlan's dissent in Lines v. Frederick (Nov 9, 1970)

MR. JUSTICE HARLAN, dissenting.

In my view this case is another instance in which the pressure of an overcrowded docket has led the Court to deal summarily with an issue which, if deserving of our attention at all, is deserving of full-dress treatment. Cf. United States v. Maryland Savings-Share Insurance Corp., ante, p. 4; United States v. Chicago, ante, p. 8. Moreover, the Court disposes of the case despite the opaqueness of the record and the uncertainty with regard to relevant California law.

Under the terms of respondent Frederick's employment, his employer credited him with one day's vacation pay for each month's work.[1] From September 15, the date of bankruptcy, to December 23, the beginning of the shutdown and the enforced "vacation," Mr. Frederick presumably became entitled to a little over three days' pay. The same amount would have accrued to a person starting work on the date of bankruptcy with no debts or assets, the paradigm of "an unencumbered fresh start." Indeed, the order not only permitted Mr. Frederick a fresh start; it gave him a head start, to the extent of half a day's pay.[2] Segal v. Rochelle, 382 U. S. 375 (1966), and Local Loan Co. v. Hunt, 292 U. S. 234 (1934), therefore tend to support the position of the trustee rather than "compel a decision for the bankrupt." Ante, p. 20. However, respondents can muster forceful arguments in their support, even on the assumption that the accrued vacation pay was subject to the claims of creditors —a point of California law which the court below found it unnecessary to decide.

Since the question tendered for review is close and has split the courts of appeals, I would set the case for argument.

Notes

[1] While neither the stipulated facts nor the opinions below reveal the rate of accrual of vacation pay, I take as true the uncontested representation in Mr. Frederick's petition for review of the referee's order.

[2] The case of respondent Harris is similar, but it is complicated by the fact that he could have chosen to forgo his vacation. As he observed in his petition to review the turnover order, the record is silent on whether such a choice would have wiped out his accrued vacation time and left nothing for him to turn over.

Justice Harlan's concurrence and dissent in Oregon v. Mitchell (Dec 21, 1970) [Notes and appendix omitted]

MR. JUSTICE HARLAN, concurring in part and dissenting in part.

From the standpoint of this Court's decisions during an era of judicial constitutional revision in the field of the suffrage, ushered in eight years ago by Baker v. Carr, 369 U. S. 186 (1962), I would find it difficult not to sustain all three aspects of the Voting Rights Act Amendments of 1970, Pub. L. 91-285, 84 Stat. 314, here challenged. From the standpoint of the bedrock of the constitutional structure of this Nation, these cases bring us to a crossroad that is marked with a formidable "Stop" sign. That sign compels us to pause before we allow those decisions to carry us to the point of sanctioning Congress' decision to alter state-determined voter qualifications by simple legislation, and to consider whether sound doctrine does not in truth require us to hold that one or more of the changes which Congress has thus sought to make can be accomplished only by constitutional amendment.

The four cases require determination of the validity of the Voting Rights Act Amendments in three respects. In Nos. 43, Orig., and 44, Orig., Oregon and Texas have sought to enjoin the enforcement of § 302 of the Act as applied to lower the voting age in those States from 21 to 18.[1]

In Nos. 46, Orig., and 47, Orig., the United States seeks a declaration of the validity of the Act and an injunction requiring Arizona and Idaho to conform their laws to it. The Act would lower the voting age in each State from 21 to 18. It would suspend until August 6, 1975, the Arizona literacy test, which requires that applicants for registration be able to read the United States Constitution in English and write their names. It would require Idaho to make several changes in its laws governing residency, registration, and absentee voting in presidential elections. Among the more substantial changes, Idaho's present 60-day state residency requirement will in effect be lowered to 30-days; its 30-day county residency requirement for intrastate migrants will be abolished; Idaho will have to permit voting by citizens of other States formerly domiciled in Idaho who emigrated too recently to register in their new homes; and it must permit absentee registration and voting by persons who have lived in Idaho for less than six months. The relevant provisions of the Act and of the constitutions and laws of the four States are set out in an Appendix to this opinion.

Each of the States contests the power of Congress to enact the provisions of the Act involved in its suit.[2] The Government places primary reliance on the power of Congress under § 5 of the Fourteenth Amendment to enforce the provisions of that Amendment by appropriate legislation. For reasons to follow, I am of the opinion that the Fourteenth Amendment was never intended to restrict the authority of the States to allocate their political power as they see fit and therefore that it does not authorize Congress to set voter qualifications, in either state or federal elections. I find no other source of congressional power to lower the voting age as fixed by state laws, or to alter state laws on residency, registration, and absentee voting, with respect to either state or federal elections. The suspension of Arizona's literacy requirement, however, can be deemed an appropriate means of enforcing the Fifteenth Amendment, and I would sustain it on that basis.

I

It is fitting to begin with a quotation from one of the leading members of the 39th Congress, which proposed the Fourteenth Amendment to the States in 1866:

"Every Constitution embodies the principles of its framers. It is a transcript of their minds. If its meaning in any place is open to doubt, or if words are used which seem to have no fixed signification, we cannot err if we turn to the framers; and their authority increases in proportion to the evidence which they have left on the question." Cong. Globe, 39th Cong., 1st Sess., 677 (1866) (Sen. Sumner).

Believing this view to be undoubtedly sound, I turn to the circumstances in which the Fourteenth Amendment was adopted for enlightenment on the intended reach of its provisions. This, for me, necessary undertaking has unavoidably led to an opinion of more than ordinary length. Except for those who are willing to close their eyes to constitutional history in making constitutional interpretations or who read such history with a preconceived determination to attain a particular constitutional goal, I think that the history of the Fourteenth Amendment makes it clear beyond any reasonable doubt that no part of the legislation now under review can be upheld as a legitimate exercise of congressional power under that Amendment.

A. Historical Setting[3]

The point of departure for considering the purpose and effect of the Fourteenth Amendment with respect to the suffrage should be, I thin, the pre-existing provisions of the Constitution. Article I, § 2, provided that in determining the number of Representatives to which a State was entitled, only three-fifths of the slave population should be counted.[4] The section also provided that the qualifications of voters for such Representatives should be the same as those established by the States for electors of the most numerous branch of their respective legislatures. Article I, § 4, provided that, subject to congressional veto, the States might prescribe the times, places, and manner of holding elections for Representatives. Article II, § 1, provided that the States might direct the manner of choosing electors for President and Vice President, except that Congress might fix a uniform time for the choice.[5] Nothing in the original Constitution controlled the way States might allocate their political power except for the guarantee of a Republican Form of Government, which appears in Art. IV, § 4.[6] No relevant changes in the constitutional structure were made until after the Civil War.

At the close of that war, there were some four million freed slaves in the South, none of whom were permitted to vote. The white population of the Confederacy had been overwhelmingly sympathetic with the rebellion. Since there was only a comparative handful of persons in these States who were neither former slaves nor Confederate sympathizers, the place where the political power should be lodged was a most vexing question. In a series of proclamations in the summer of 1865, President Andrew Johnson had laid the groundwork for the States to be controlled by the white populations which had held power before the war, eliminating only the leading rebels and those unwilling to sign a loyalty oath.[7] The Radicals, on the other hand, were ardently in favor of Negro suffrage as essential to prevent resurgent rebellion, requisite to protect the freedmen, and necessary to ensure continued Radical control of the government. This ardor cooled as it ran into northern racial prejudice. At that time, only six States—Maine, New Hampshire, Vermont, Massachusetts, Rhode Island, and New York— permitted Negroes to vote, and New York imposed special property and residency requirements on Negro voters.[8] In referenda late that year, enfranchising proposals were roundly beaten in Connecticut, Wisconsin, Minnesota, the Territory of Colorado, and the District of Columbia. Gillette, supra, n. 3, at 25-26. Such popular rebuffs led the Radicals to pull in their horns and hope for a protracted process of reconstruction during which the North could be educated to the advisability of Negro suffrage, at least for the South. In the meantime, of course, it would be essential to bar southern representation in Congress lest a combination of southerners and Democrats obtain control of the government and frustrate Radical goals.

The problem of congressional representation was acute. With the freeing of the slaves, the Three-Fifths Compromise ceased to have any effect. While predictions of the precise effect of the change varied with the person doing the calculating, the consensus was that the South would be entitled to at least 15 new members of Congress, and, of course, a like number of new presidential electors. The Radicals had other rallying cries which they kept before the public in the summer of 1865, but one author gives this description of the mood as Congress convened:[9]

"Of all the movements influencing the Fourteenth Amendment which developed prior to the first session of the Thirty-ninth Congress, that for Negro suffrage was the most outstanding. The volume of private and public comment indicates that it was viewed as an issue of prime importance. The cry for a changed basis of representation was, in reality, subsidiary to this, and was meant by Radicals to secure in another way what Negro suffrage might accomplish for them: removal of the danger of Democratic dominance as a consequence of Southern restoration. The danger of possible repudiation of the national obligations, and assumption of the rebel debt, was invariably presented to show the need for Negro suffrage or a new basis of representation. Sentiment for disqualification of ex-Confederates, though a natural growth, well suited such purposes. The movement to guarantee civil rights, sponsored originally by the more conservative Republicans, received emphasis from Radicals only when state elections indicated that suffrage would not serve as a party platform."

When Congress met, the Radicals, led by Thaddeus Stevens, were successful in obtaining agreement for a Joint Committee on Reconstruction, composed of 15 members, to "inquire into the condition of the States which formed the so-called confederate States of America, and report whether they, or any of them, are entitled to be represented in either House of Congress . . . ." Cong. Globe, 39th Cong., 1st Sess., 30, 46 (1865) (hereafter Globe).

All papers relating to representation of the Southern States were to be referred to the Committee of Fifteen without debate. The result, which many had not foreseen, was to assert congressional control over Reconstruction and at the same time to put the congressional power in the hands of a largely Radical secret committee.

The Joint Committee began work with the beginning of 1866, and in due course reported a joint resolution, H. R. 51, to amend the Constitution. The proposal would have based representation and direct taxes on population, with a proviso that

"whenever the elective franchise shall be denied or abridged in any State on account of race or color, all persons of such race or color shall be excluded from the basis of representation." Globe 351.

The result, if the Southern States did not provide for Negro suffrage, would be a decrease in southern representation in Congress and the electoral college by some 24 seats from their pre-war position instead of an increase of 15. The House, although somewhat balky, approved the measure after lengthy debate. Globe 538. The Senate proved more intractable. An odd combination of Democrats, moderate Republicans, and extreme Radicals combined to defeat the measure, with the Radicals basing their opposition largely on the fear that the proviso would be read to authorize racial voter qualifications and thus prevent Congress from enfranchising the freedmen under powers assertedly granted by other clauses of the Constitution. See, e. g., Globe 673-687 (Sen. Sumner).

At about this same time the Civil Rights Bill and the Second Freedmen's Bureau Bill were being debated. Both bills provided a list of rights secured, not including voting.[10] Senator Trumbull, who reported the Civil Rights Bill on behalf of the Senate Judiciary Committee, stated: "I do not want to bring up the question of negro suffrage in the bill." Globe 606. His House counterpart exhibited the same reluctance. Globe 1162 (Cong. Wilson of Iowa). Despite considerable uncertainty as to the constitutionality of the measures, both ultimately passed. In the midst of the Senate debates on the basis of representation, President Johnson vetoed the Freedmen's Bureau Bill, primarily on constitutional grounds. This veto, which was narrowly sustained, was followed shortly by the President's bitter attack on Radical Reconstruction in his Washington's Birthday speech. These two actions, which were followed a month later by the veto of the Civil Rights Bill, removed any lingering hopes among the Radicals that Johnson would support them in a thoroughgoing plan of reconstruction. By the same token they increased the Radicals' need for an articulated plan of their own to be put before the country in the upcoming elections as an alternative to the course the President was taking.

The second major product of the Reconstruction Committee, before the resolution which became the Fourteenth Amendment, was a proposal to add an equal rights provision to the Constitution. This measure, H. R. 63, which foreshadowed § 1 of the Fourteenth Amendment, read as follows:

"The Congress shall have power to make all laws which shall be necessary and proper to secure to the citizens of each State all privileges and immunities of citizens in the several States, and to all persons in the several States equal protection in the rights of life, liberty, and property." Globe 1034.

It was reported by Congressman Bingham of Ohio, who later opposed the Civil Rights Bill because he believed it unconstitutional. Globe 1292-1293. The amendment immediately ran into serious opposition in the House and the subject was dropped.[11]

Such was the background of the Fourteenth Amendment. Congress, at loggerheads with the President over Reconstruction, had not come up with a plan of its own after six months of deliberations; both friends and foes prodded it to develop an alternative. The Reconstruction Committee had been unable to produce anything which could even get through Congress, much less obtain the adherence of three-fourths of the States. The Radicals, committed to Negro suffrage, were confronted with widespread public opposition to that goal and the necessity for a reconstruction plan that could do service as a party platform in the elections that fall. The language of the Fourteenth Amendment must be read with awareness that it was designed in response to this situation.

B. The Language of the Amendment and Reconstruction
Measures

Sections 1 and 2 of the Fourteenth Amendment as originally reported read as
follows:[12]

"SEC. 1. No State shall make or enforce any law which shall abridge the
privileges or immunities of citizens of the United States; nor shall any State deprive any
person of life, liberty, or property without due process of law; nor deny to any person
within its jurisdiction the equal protection of the laws.

"SEC. 2. Representatives shall be apportioned among the several States which
may be included within this Union, according to their respective numbers, counting the
whole number of persons in each State, excluding Indians not taxed. But whenever, in any
State, the elective franchise shall be denied to any portion of its male citizens not less than
twenty-one years of age, or in any way abridged except for participation in rebellion or
other crime, the basis of representation in such State shall be reduced in the proportion
which the number of such male citizens shall bear to the whole number of male citizens
not less than twenty-one years of age." Globe 2286.

In the historical context, no one could have understood this language as anything
other than an abandonment of the principle of Negro suffrage, for which the Radicals had
been so eager. By the same token, the language could hardly have been understood as
affecting the provisions of the Constitution placing voting qualifications in the hands of
the States. Section 1 must have been seen as little more than a constitutionalization of the
1866 Civil Rights Act, concededly one of the primary goals of that portion of the
Amendment.[13]

While these conclusions may, I think, be confidently asserted, it is not so easy to
explain just how contemporary observers would have construed the three clauses of § 1 to
reach this result.[14] No doubt in the case of many congressmen it simply never occurred
to them that the States' longstanding plenary control over voter qualifications would be
affected without explicit language to that effect. And since no speaker during the debates
on the Fourteenth Amendment pursued the contention that § 1 would be construed to
include the franchise, those who took the opposite view rarely explained how they arrived
at their conclusions.

In attempting to unravel what was seldom articulated, the appropriate starting
point is the fact that the framers of the Amendment expected the most significant portion
of § 1 to be the clause prohibiting state laws "which shall abridge the privileges or
immunities of citizens of the United States." These privileges were no doubt understood to
include the ones set out in the first section of the Civil Rights Act. To be prohibited by law
from enjoying these rights would hardly be consistent with full membership in a civil
society.

The same is not necessarily true with respect to prohibitions on participation in
the political process. Many members of Congress accepted the jurisprudence of the day, in
which the rights of man fell into three categories: natural, civil, and political. The

privileges of citizens, being "civil" rights, were distinct from the rights arising from governmental organization, which were political in character.[15] Others no doubt relied on the experience under the similar language of Art. IV, § 2, which had never been held to guarantee the right to vote. The remarks of Senator Howard of Michigan, who as spokesman for the Joint Committee explained in greater detail than most why the Amendment did not reach the suffrage, contain something of each view. See Globe 2766, quoted infra, at 187; nn. 56 and 57, infra; cf. Blake v. McClung, 172 U. S. 239, 256 (1898) (dictum).

Since the Privileges and Immunities Clause was expected to be the primary source of substantive protection, the Equal Protection and Due Process Clauses were relegated to a secondary role, as the debates and other contemporary materials make clear.[16] Those clauses, which appear on their face to correspond with the latter portion of § 1 of the Civil Rights Act, see n. 13, supra, and to be primarily concerned with person and property, would not have been expected to enfranchise the freedmen if the Privileges and Immunities Clause did not.

Other members of Congress no doubt saw § 2 of the proposed Amendment as the Committee's resolution of the related problems of suffrage and representation. Since that section did not provide for enfranchisement, but simply reduced representation for disfranchisement, any doubts about the effect of the broad language of § 1 were removed. Congressman Bingham, who was primarily responsible for the language of § 1, stated this view. Globe 2542, quoted infra, at 185. Finally, characterization of the Amendment by such figures as Stevens and Bingham in the House and Howard in the Senate, not contested by the Democrats except in passing remarks, was no doubt simply accepted by many members of Congress; they, repeating it, gave further force to the interpretation, with the result that, as will appear below, not one speaker in the debates on the Fourteenth Amendment unambiguously stated that it would affect state voter qualifications, and only three, all opponents of the measure, can fairly be characterized as raising the possibility.[17] Further evidence of this original understanding can be found in later events.

The 39th Congress, which proposed the Fourteenth Amendment, also enacted the first Reconstruction Act, c. 153, 14 Stat. 428 (1867). This Act required, as a condition precedent to readmission of the Southern States, that they adopt constitutions providing that the elective franchise should be enjoyed by all male citizens over the age of 21 who had been residents for more than one year and were not disfranchised for treason or common-law felony; even so, no State would be readmitted until a legislature elected under the new Constitution had ratified the proposed Fourteenth Amendment and that Amendment had become part of the Constitution.

The next development came when the ratification drive in the North stalled. After a year had passed during which only one Northern State had ratified the proposed Fourteenth Amendment, Arkansas was readmitted to the Union by the Act of June 22, 1868, 15 Stat. 72. This readmission was based on the "fundamental condition" that the state constitution should not be amended to restrict the franchise, except with reference to residency requirements. Three days later the Act of June 25, 1868, 15 Stat. 73, held out a promise of similar treatment to North Carolina, South Carolina, Louisiana, Georgia, Alabama, and Florida if they would ratify the Fourteenth Amendment. By happy coincidence, the assent of those six States was just sufficient to complete the ratification process. It can hardly be suggested, therefore, that the "fundamental condition" was exacted from them as a measure of caution lest the Fourteenth Amendment fail of ratification.

The 40th Congress, not content with enfranchisement in the South, proposed the Fifteenth Amendment to extend the suffrage to northern Negroes. See Gillette, supra, n. 3, at 46. This fact alone is evidence that they did not understand the Fourteenth Amendment to have accomplished such a result. Less well known is the fact that the 40th Congress considered and very nearly adopted a proposed amendment which would have expressly prohibited not only discriminatory voter qualifications but discriminatory qualifications for office as well. Each House passed such a measure by the required two-thirds margin. Cong. Globe, 40th Cong., 3d Sess., 1318, 1428 (1869). A conference committee, composed of Senators Stewart and Conkling and Representatives Boutwell, Bingham, and Logan, struck out the officeholding provision, id., at 1563, 1593, and with Inauguration Day only a week away, both Houses accepted the conference report. Id., at 1564, 1641. See generally Gillette 58-77. While the reasons for these actions are unclear, it is unlikely that they were provoked by the idea that the Fourteenth Amendment covered the field; such a rationale seemingly would have made the enfranchising provision itself unnecessary.

The 41st Congress readmitted the remaining three States of the Confederacy. The admitting act in each case recited good-faith ratification of the Fourteenth and Fifteenth Amendments, and imposed the fundamental conditions that the States should not restrict the elective franchise[18] and "[t]hat it shall never be lawful for the said State to deprive any citizen of the United States, on account of his race, color, or previous condition of servitude, of the right to hold office under the constitution and laws of said State." Act of Jan. 26, 1870, c. 10, 16 Stat. 62, 63 (Virginia); Act of Feb. 23, 1870, c. 19, 16 Stat. 67, 68 (Mississippi); Act of Mar. 30, 1870, c. 39, 16 Stat. 80, 81 (Texas).

These materials demonstrate not only that § 1 of the Fourteenth Amendment is susceptible of an interpretation that it does not reach suffrage qualifications, but that this is the interpretation given by the immediately succeeding Congresses. Such an interpretation is the most reasonable reading of the section in view of the background against which it was proposed and adopted, particularly the doubts about the constitutionality of the Civil Rights Act, the prejudice in the North against any recognition of the principle of Negro suffrage, and the basic constitutional structure of leaving suffrage qualifications with the States.[19] If any further clarification were needed, one would have thought it provided by the second section of the same Amendment, which specifically contemplated that the right to vote would be denied or abridged by the States on racial or other grounds. As a unanimous Court once asked, "Why this, if it was not in the power of the [state] legislature to deny the right of suffrage to some male inhabitants?" Minor v. Happersett, 21 Wall. 162, 174 (1875).

The Government suggests that the list of protected qualifications in § 2 is "no more than descriptive of voting laws as they then stood." Brief for the United States, Nos. 46, Orig., and 47, Orig., 75. This is wholly inaccurate. Aside from racial restrictions, all States had residency requirements and many had literacy, property, or taxation qualifications. On the other hand, several of the Western States permitted aliens to vote if they had satisfied certain residency requirements and had declared their intention to become citizens.[20] It hardly seems necessary to observe that the politicians who framed the Fourteenth Amendment were familiar with the makeup of the electorate. In any event, the congressional debates contain such proof in ample measure.[21]

Assuming, then, that § 2 represents a deliberate selection of the voting qualifications to be penalized, what is the point of it? The Government notes that "it was intended—although it has never been used—to provide a remedy against exclusion of the newly freed slaves from the vote." Brief for the Defendant, Nos. 43, Orig., and 44, Orig., 20. Undoubtedly this was the primary purpose. But the framers of the Amendment, with their attention thus focused on racial voting qualifications, could hardly have been unaware of § 1. If they understood that section to forbid such qualifications, the simple means of penalizing this conduct would have been to impose a reduction of representation for voting discrimination in violation of § 1. Their adoption instead of the awkward phrasing of § 2 is therefore significant.

To be sure, one might argue that § 2 is simply a rhetorical flourish, and that the qualifications listed there are merely the ones which the framers deemed to be consistent with the alleged prohibition of § 1. This argument is not only unreasonable on its face and untenable in light of the historical record; it is fatal to the validity of the reduction of the voting age in § 302 of the Act before us.

The only sensible explanation of § 2, therefore, is that the racial voter qualifications it was designed to penalize were understood to be permitted by § 1 of the Fourteenth Amendment. The Amendment was a halfway measure, adopted to deprive the South of representation until it should enfranchise the freedmen, but to have no practical effect in the North. It was politically acceptable precisely because of its regional consequences and its avoidance of an explicit recognition of the principle of Negro suffrage. As my Brother BLACK states: "[I]t cannot be successfully argued that the Fourteenth Amendment was intended to strip the States of their power, carefully preserved in the original Constitution, to govern themselves." Ante, at 127. The detailed historical materials make this unmistakably clear.

C. The Joint Committee

The first place to look for the understanding of the framers of the Fourteenth Amendment is the Journal of the Joint Committee on Reconstruction.[22] The exact sequence of the actions of this Committee presumably had little or no effect on the members of Congress who were not on the Committee, for the Committee attempted to keep its deliberations secret,[23] and the Journal itself was lost for nearly 20 years.[24] Nevertheless the Journal, although only a record of proposals and votes, illustrates the thoughts of those leading figures of Congress who were members and participated in the drafting of the Amendment.

Two features emerge from such a review with startling clarity. First, the Committee regularly rejected explicitly enfranchising proposals in favor of plans which would postpone enfranchisement, leave it to congressional discretion, or abandon it altogether. Second, the abandonment of Negro suffrage as a goal exactly corresponded with the adoption of provisions to reduce representation for discriminatory restrictions on the ballot.

This correspondence was present from the start. Five plans were proposed to deal with representation. One would have prohibited racial qualifications for voters and based representation on the whole number of citizens in the State; the other four proposals contained no enfranchising provision but in various ways would have reduced representation for States where the vote was racially restricted. Kendrick 41-44. A subcommittee reduced the five proposals to two, one prohibiting discrimination and the other reducing representation where it was present. On Stevens' motion the latter alternative was accepted by a vote of 11 to 3, Kendrick 51; with minor changes it was subsequently reported as H. R. 51.

The subcommittee also proposed that whichever provision on the basis of representation was adopted, the Congress should be empowered to legislate to secure all citizens "the same political rights and privileges" and also "equal protection in the enjoyment of life, liberty and property." Kendrick 51. After the Committee reported H. R. 51, it turned to consideration of this proposal. At a meeting attended by only 10 members, a motion to strike out the clause authorizing Congress to legislate for equal political rights and privileges lost by a vote of six to four. Kendrick 57. At a subsequent meeting, however, Bingham had the subcommittee proposal replaced with another which did not mention political rights and privileges, but was otherwise quite similar. Kendrick 61; see the opinion of MR. JUSTICE BRENNAN, MR. JUSTICE WHITE, and MR. JUSTICE MARSHALL, post, at 258-259, for the text of the two provisions. The Committee reported the substitute as H. R. 63. In the House so much concern was expressed over the centralization of power the amendment would work—a few said it would even authorize Congress to regulate the suffrage—that the matter was dropped. Post, at 260.

The Fourteenth Amendment had as its most direct antecedent a proposal drafted by Robert Dale Owen, who was not a member of Congress, and presented to the Joint Committee by Stevens.[25] Originally the plan provided for mandatory enfranchisement in 1876 and for reduction of representation until that date. Kendrick 82-84. However, Stevens was pressured by various congressional delegations who wanted nothing to do with Negro suffrage, even at a remove of 10 years.[26] He therefore successfully moved to strike out the enfranchising provision and correspondingly to abolish the 10-year limitation on reduction of representation for racial discrimination. The motion carried by a vote of 12 to 2. Kendrick 101.

Bingham was then successful in replacing § 1 of Owen's proposal, which read:

"No discrimination shall be made by any State, or by the United States, as to the civil rights of persons, because of race, color, or previous condition of servitude"

with the following now-familiar language:

"No State shall make or enforce any law which shall abridge the privileges or immunities of citizens of the United States; nor shall any State deprive any person of life, liberty, or property, without due process of law, nor deny to any person within its jurisdiction the equal protection of the laws." Kendrick 106.

The summary style of the Journal leaves unclear the reasons for the change. However, Bingham himself had rather consistently voted against proposals for direct and immediate enfranchisement,[27] and on the face of things it seems unlikely that the other members of the Joint Committee understood his provision to be an enfranchising proposal.[28] That they did not so understand is demonstrated by the speeches in the debates on the floor.[29]

Before I examine those debates, a word of explanation is in order. For obvious reasons, the discussions of voter qualifications in the 39th Congress and among the public were cast primarily in terms of racial disqualifications. This does not detract from their utility as guides to interpretation. When an individual speaker said that the Amendment would not result in the enfranchisement of Negroes, he must have taken one of two views: either the Amendment did not reach voter qualifications at all; or it set standards limiting state restrictions on the ballot, but those standards did not prohibit racial discrimination. I have already set out some of the reasons which lead me to conclude that the former interpretation is correct, and that it is the understanding shared by the framers of the Amendment, as well as by almost all of the opponents. The mere statement of the latter position appears to me to be a complete refutation of it. Even on its wholly unsupportable assumptions (1) that certain framers of the Amendment contemplated that the privileges and immunities of citizens included the vote, (2) that they intended to permit state laws to abridge the privileges and immunities of citizens whenever it was rational to do so, and (3) that they agreed on the rationality of prohibiting the freed slaves from voting, this remarkable theory still fails to explain why they understood the Amendment to permit racial voting qualifications in the free States of the North.

D. In Congress

On May 8, 1866, Thaddeus Stevens led off debate on H. R. 127, the Joint Resolution proposing the Fourteenth Amendment. After explaining the delay of the Joint Committee in coming up with a plan of reconstruction, he apologized for his proposal in advance:

"This proposition is not all that the committee desired. It falls far short of my wishes, but it fulfills my hopes. I believe it is all that can be obtained in the present state of public opinion. Not only Congress but the several States are to be consulted. Upon a careful survey of the whole ground, we did not believe that nineteen of the loyal States could be induced to ratify any proposition more stringent than this." Globe 2459.

In the climate of the times, Stevens could hardly have been understood as referring to anything other than the failure of the measure to make some provision for the enfranchisement of the freedmen. However, lest any mistake be made, he recounted the history of the Committee's prior effort in the field of representation and suffrage, H. R. 51, which "would surely have secured the enfranchisement of every citizen at no distant period." That measure was dead, "slaughtered by a puerile and pedantic criticism," and "unless this (less efficient, I admit) shall pass, its death has postponed the protection of the colored race perhaps for ages." Ibid.

With this explanation made, Stevens turned to a section-by-section study of the proposed resolution. The results to be achieved by § 1, as he saw it, would be equal punishment for crime, equal entitlement to the benefits of "[w]hatever law protects the white man," equal means of redress, and equal competence to testify. Ibid. If he thought the section provided equal access to the polls, despite his immediately preceding apology for the fact that it did not, his failure to mention that application is remarkable.[30]

Turning then to § 2, Stevens again discussed racial qualification for voting. He explained the section as follows:

"If any State shall exclude any of her adult male citizens from the elective franchise, or abridge that right, she shall forfeit her right to representation in the same proportion. The effect of this provision will be either to compel the States to grant universal suffrage or so to shear them of their power as to keep them forever in a hopeless minority in the national Government, both legislative and executive." Ibid.

Stevens recognized that it might take several years for the coercive effect of the Amendment to result in Negro suffrage, but since this would give time for education and enlightenment of the freedmen, "That short delay would not be injurious." Ibid. He did not indicate that he believed it would be unconstitutional. He admitted that § 2 was not so good as the proposal which had been defeated in the Senate, for that, by reducing representation by all the members of a race if any one was discriminated against, would have hastened full enfranchisement. Section 2 allowed proportional credit. "But it is a short step forward. The large stride which we in vain proposed is dead . . . ." Globe 2460.

I have dealt at length with Stevens' remarks because of his prominent position in the House and in the Joint Committee. The remaining remarks, except for Bingham's summation, can be treated in more summary fashion. Of the supporters of the Amendment, Garfield of Ohio,[31] Kelley of Pennsylvania,[32] Boutwell of Massachusetts (a member of the Joint Committee),[33] Eliot of Massachusetts,[34] Beaman of Michigan,[35] and Farnsworth of Illinois,[36] expressed their regret that the Amendment did not prohibit restrictions on the franchise. As the quotations set out in the margin indicate, the absence of such a prohibition was generally attributed to prejudice in the Congress, in the States, or both, to such an extent that an enfranchising amendment could not pass. This corresponds with the first part of Stevens' introductory speech.

Other supporters of the Amendment obviously based their remarks on their understanding that it did not affect state laws imposing discriminatory voting qualifications, but did not indicate that the omission was a drawback in their view. In this group were Thayer of Pennsylvania,[37] Broomall of Pennsylvania,[38] Raymond of New York,[39] McKee of Kentucky,[40] Miller of Pennsylvania,[41] Banks of Massachusetts,[42] and Eckley of Ohio.[43]

The remaining members of the House who supported the Fourteenth Amendment either did not speak at all or did not address themselves to the suffrage issue in any very clear terms. Those in the latter group who gave speeches on the proposed Amendment included Spalding of Ohio,[44] Longyear of Michigan,[45] and Shellabarger of Ohio.[46] The remaining Republican members of the Joint Committee—Washburne of Illinois, Morrill of Vermont, Conkling of New York, and Blow of Missouri —did not participate in the debates over the Amendment.

In the opposition to the Amendment were only the handful of Democrats. Even they, with one seeming exception, did not assert that the Amendment was applicable to suffrage, although they would have been expected to do so if they thought such a reading plausible. Finck of Ohio and Shanklin of Kentucky did not even mention Negro suffrage in their attacks on the Amendment, although Finck discussed the reasons why the Southern States could not be expected to ratify it, Globe 2460-2462, and Shanklin characterized the Amendment as "tyrannical and oppressive." Globe 2501. Eldridge of Wisconsin[47] and Randall of Pennsylvania[48] affirmatively indicated their understanding that with the Amendment the Radicals had at least temporarily abandoned their crusade for Negro suffrage, as did Finck when the measure returned from the Senate with amendments.[49]

The other two Democrats to participate in the three days of debate on H. R. 127, Boyer of Pennsylvania and Rogers of New Jersey, have been a source of great comfort to those who set out to prove that the history of the Fourteenth Amendment is inconclusive on this issue. Each, in the course of a lengthy speech, included a sentence which, taken out of context, can be read to indicate a fear that § 1 might prohibit racial restrictions on the ballot. Boyer said, "The first section embodies the principles of the civil rights bill, and is intended to secure ultimately, and to some extent indirectly, the political equality of the negro race." Globe 2467. Rogers, commenting on the uncertain scope of the Privileges and Immunities Clause, observed: "The right to vote is a privilege." Globe 2538.

While these two statements are perhaps innocuous enough to be left alone, it is noteworthy that each speaker had earlier in the session delivered a tirade against the principle of Negro suffrage;[50] if either seriously believed that the Fourteenth Amendment might enfranchise the freedmen, he was unusually calm about the fact. That they did not seriously interpret the Amendment in this way is indicated as well by other portions of their speeches.[51]

Two other opponents of the Fourteenth Amendment, Phelps of Maryland and Niblack of Indiana, made statements which have been adduced to show that there was no consensus on the applicability of the Fourteenth Amendment to suffrage laws. Phelps voiced his sentiments on May 5, three days before the beginning of debate.[52] In the course of a speech urging a soft policy on reconstruction, he expressed the fear that the Amendment would authorize Congress to define the privileges of citizens to include the suffrage—or indeed that it might have that effect proprio vigore. Globe 2398. Phelps did not repeat this sentiment after he was contradicted by speaker after speaker during the debates proper; indeed, he did not take part in the debates at all, but simply voted against the Amendment, along with most of his Democratic colleagues. Globe 2545.[53]

As for Niblack, on the first day of debate he made the following remarks:

"I give notice that I will offer the following amendment if I shall have the opportunity:

"`Add to the fifth section as follows:

"`Provided, That nothing contained in this article shall be so construed as to authorize Congress to regulate or control the elective franchise within any State, or to abridge or restrict the power of any State to regulate or control the same within its own jurisdiction, except as in the third section hereof prescribed.' " Globe 2465.

Like Phelps, Niblack found it unnecessary to participate in the debates. He was not heard from again until the vote on the call for the previous question. As Garfield ascertained at the time, the only opportunity to amend H. R. 127 would arise if the demand was voted down. Niblack voted to sustain it. Globe 2545.

Debate in the House was substantially concluded by Bingham, the man primarily responsible for the language of § 1. Without equivocation, he stated:

"The amendment does not give, as the second section shows, the power to Congress of regulating suffrage in the several States.

"The second section excludes the conclusion that by the first section suffrage is subjected to congressional law; save, indeed, with this exception, that as the right in the people of each State to a republican government and to choose their Representatives in Congress is of the guarantees of the Constitution, by this amendment a remedy might be given directly for a case supposed by Madison, where treason might change a State government from a republican to a despotic government, and thereby deny suffrage to the people." Globe 2542.

Stevens then arose briefly in rebuttal. He attacked Bingham for saying in another portion of his speech that the disqualification provisions of § 3 were unenforceable. He did not contradict—or even refer to—Bingham's interpretation of §§ 1 and 2. Globe 2544. The vote was taken and the resolution passed immediately thereafter. Globe 2545.

To say that Stevens did not contradict Bingham is to minimize the force of the record. Not once, during the three days of debate, did any supporter of the Amendment criticize or correct any of the Republicans or Democrats who observed that the Amendment left the ballot "exclusively under the control of the States." Globe 2542 (Bingham). This fact is tacitly admitted even by those who find the debates "inconclusive." The only contrary authority they can find in the debates is the pale remarks of the four Democrats already discussed.[54]

In the Senate, which did not have a gag rule, matters proceeded at a more leisurely pace. The introductory speech would normally have been given by Senator Fessenden of Maine, the Chairman of the Joint Committee on behalf of the Senate, but he was still weak with illness and unable to deliver a lengthy speech. The duty of presenting the views of the Joint Committee therefore devolved on Senator Howard of Michigan.[55]

Howard minced no words. He stated that

"the first section of the proposed amendment does not give to either of these classes the right of voting. The right of suffrage is not, in law, one of the privileges or immunities thus secured by the Constitution. It is merely the creature of law. It has always been regarded in this country as the result of positive local law, not regarded as one of those fundamental rights lying at the basis of all society and without which a people cannot exist except as slaves, subject to a depotism [sic]. Globe 2766.

"The second section leaves the right to regulate the elective franchise still with the States, and does not meddle with that right." Ibid. Howard stated that while he personally would have preferred to see the freedmen enfranchised, the Committee was confronted with the necessity of proposing an amendment which could be ratified.

"The committee were of opinion that the States are not yet prepared to sanction so fundamental a change as would be the concession of the right of suffrage to the colored race. We may as well state it plainly and fairly, so that there shall be no misunderstanding on the subject. It was our opinion that three fourths of the States of this Union could not be induced to vote to grant the right of suffrage, even in any degree or under any restriction, to the colored race." Ibid.

Howard's forthright attempt to prevent misunderstanding was completely successful insofar as the Senate was concerned; at least, no one has yet discovered a remark during the Senate debates on the proposed Fourteenth Amendment which indicates any contrary impression.[56]

For some, however, time has muddied the clarity with which he spoke.[57]

The Senate, like the House, made frequent reference to the fact that the proposed amendment would not result in the enfranchisement of the freedmen. The supporters who expressed their regret at the fact were Wade of Ohio,[58] Poland of Vermont,[59] Stewart of Nevada,[60] Howe of Wisconsin,[61] Henderson of Missouri,[62] and Yates of Illinois.[63] The remarks of Senator Sherman of Ohio, whose support for the amendment was lukewarm, see Globe 2986, seem to have been based on the common interpretation.[64]

Doolittle of Wisconsin, whose support for the President resulted in his virtually being read out of the Republican Party, proposed to base representation on adult male voters. Globe 2942. In a discussion with Senator Grimes of Iowa, a member of the Joint Committee, about the desirability of this change, Doolittle defended himself by pointing out that: "Your amendment proposes to allow the States to say who shall vote." Globe 2943. Grimes did not respond. Among the Democrats, no different view was expressed. Those whose remarks are informative are Hendricks of Indiana,[65] Cowan of Pennsylvania,[66] Davis of Kentucky,[67] and Johnson of Maryland.[68]

Senator Howard, who had opened debate, made the last remarks in favor of the Amendment. He said:

"We know very well that the States retain the power, which they have always possessed, of regulating the right of suffrage in the States. It is the theory of the Constitution itself. That right has never been taken from them; no endeavor has ever been made to take it from them; and the theory of this whole amendment is, to leave the power of regulating the suffrage with the people or Legislatures of the States, and not to assume to regulate it by any clause of the Constitution of the United States." Globe 3039.

Shortly thereafter the Amendment was approved. Globe 3041-3042.

In the House, there was a brief discussion of the Senate amendments and the measure generally, chiefly by the Democrats. Stevens then concluded the debate as he had begun it, expressing his regret that the Amendment would not enfranchise the freedmen.[69] The House accepted the Senate changes and sent the measure to the States. Globe 3149.

E. Collateral Evidence of Congressional Intent

It has been suggested that despite this evidence of congressional understanding, which seems to me overwhelming, the history is nonetheless inconclusive. Primary reliance is placed on debates over H. R. 51, the Joint Committee's first effort in the field of the basis of representation. In these debates, some of the more extreme Radicals, typified by Senator Sumner of Massachusetts, suggested that Congress had power to interfere with state voter qualifications at least to the extent of enfranchising the freedmen. This power was said to exist in a variety of constitutional provisions, including Art. I, § 2, Art. I, § 4, the war power, the power over territories, the guarantee of a republican form of government, and § 2 of the Thirteenth Amendment. Those who held this view expressed concern lest the Committee's proposal be read to authorize the States to discriminate on racial grounds and stated that they could not vote for the measure if such was the correct construction. They were sometimes comforted by supporters of the committee proposal, who assured them that there would be no such effect. From these statements, and the fact that some of those who took the extreme view ultimately did vote for the proposed Fourteenth Amendment, it is sought to construct a counter-argument: if H. R. 51, properly interpreted, would not have precluded congressional exercise of power otherwise existing under the constitutional provisions referred to, then § 2 of the Fourteenth Amendment, properly interpreted, does not preclude the exercise of congressional power under §§ 1 and 5 of that Amendment.

This argument, however, is even logically fallacious, and quite understandably none of the opinions filed today place much reliance on it. I do not maintain that the framers of the Fourteenth Amendment took away with one hand what they had given with the other, but simply that the Amendment must be construed as a whole, and that for the reasons already given, supra, at 167-170, the inclusion of § 2 demonstrates that the framers never intended to confer the power which my Brethren seek to find in §§ 1 and 5. Bingham, for one, distinguished between these two positions. When it was suggested in the debates over H. R. 51 that the proviso would remove pre-existing congressional power over voting qualifications, Bingham made the response quoted by my colleagues. Globe 431-432; see post, at 276-277. When it was observed during the debates over the proposed Fourteenth Amendment that § 2 demonstrated that the Amendment did not reach state control over voting qualifications, Bingham was the one making the observation. Globe 2542, quoted supra, at 185. As Bingham seems to have recognized, the sort of argument he made in connection with H. R. 51 is beside the point with respect to the Fourteenth Amendment.

In any event, even disregarding its analytical difficulties, the argument is based on blatant factual shortcomings. All but one of the speakers on whose statements primary reliance is placed stated, either during the debates on the Fourteenth Amendment or subsequently, that the Amendment did not enfranchise the freedmen.[70]

Finally, some of those determined to sustain the legislation now before us rely on speeches made between two and three years after Congress had sent the proposed Amendment to the States. Boutwell and Stevens in the House, and Sumner in the Senate, argued that the Fifteenth Amendment or enfranchising legislation was unnecessary because the Fourteenth Amendment prohibited racial discrimination in voter qualifications. Each had earlier expressed the opposite position.[71] Their subsequent attempts to achieve by assertion what they had not had the votes to achieve by constitutional processes can hardly be entitled to weight.

F. Ratification

State materials relating to the ratification process are not very revealing. For the most part only gubernatorial messages and committee reports have survived.[72] So far as my examination of these materials reveals, while the opponents of the Amendment were divided and sometimes equivocal on whether it might be construed to require enfranchisement,[73] the supporters of the Amendment in the States approached the congressional proponents in the unanimity of their interpretation. I have discovered only one brief passage in support of the Amendment which appears to be based on the assumption that it would result in enfranchisement.[74] These remarks, in the message of the Governor of Illinois, had to compete in the minds of the legislators with the viewpoint of the Chicago Tribune. This Radical journal repeatedly criticized the Amendment's lack of an enfranchising provision, and at one time it even expressed the hope that the South would refuse to ratify the Amendment so that the North would turn to enfranchisement of the freedmen as the only means of reconstruction. June 25, 1866, quoted in James 177. In all the other States I have examined, where the materials are sufficiently full for the understanding of a supporter of the Amendment to appear, his understanding has been that enfranchisement would not result.[75]

The scanty official materials can be supplemented by other sources. There was a congressional election in the fall of the year the Fourteenth Amendment went to the States. The Radicals ran on the Amendment as their reconstruction program, attempting to force voters to choose between their plan and that of President Johnson. From the campaign speeches and from newspaper reactions, we can get some further idea of the understanding of the States.

The tone of the campaign was set by the formal report of the Joint Committee, which Fessenden openly stated he had composed as a partisan document. James 147. Indeed, it was not even submitted to Congress until the day the Senate approved the measure, and then only in manuscript form. Globe 3038. On the delicate issue of Negro suffrage, the report read as follows:[76]

"Doubts were entertained whether Congress had power, even under the amended Constitution, to prescribe the qualifications of voters in a State, or could act directly on the subject. It was doubtful, in the opinion of your committee, whether the States would consent to surrender a power they had always exercised, and to which they were attached. As the best if not the only method of surmounting the difficulty, and as eminently just and proper in itself, your committee came to the conclusion that political power should be possessed in all the States exactly in proportion as the right of suffrage should be granted, without distinction of color or race.

This it was thought would leave the whole question with the people of each State, holding out to all the advantage of increased political power as an inducement to allow all to participate in its exercise. Such a provision would be in its nature gentle and persuasive, and would lead, it was hoped, at no distant day, to an equal participation of all, without distinction, in all the rights and privileges of citizenship, thus affording a full and adequate protection to all classes of citizens, since all would have, through the ballot-box, the power of self-protection.

"Holding these views, your committee prepared an amendment to the Constitution to carry out this idea, and submitted the same to Congress. Unfortunately, as we think, it did not receive the necessary constitutional support in the Senate, and therefore could not be proposed for adoption by the States. The principle involved in that amendment is, however, believed to be sound, and your committee have again proposed it in another form, hoping that it may receive the approbation of Congress."

Newspapers expressed the same view of the reach of the Amendment. Even while deliberations were underway, predictions that Congress would come up with a plan involving enfranchisement of the freedmen had gradually ceased. James 91. When the Amendment was released to the press, Andrew Johnson was reported as seeing in it a "practical abandonment of the negro suffrage issue." Cincinnati Daily Commercial, April 30, 1866, quoted in James 117. The New York Herald had reported editorially that the Amendment reflected an abandonment of the Radical push for Negro suffrage and acceptance of Johnson's position that control over suffrage rested exclusively with the States. May 1, 1866, reported in James 119. The Nation, a Radical organ, attributed the absence of any provision on Negro suffrage to "sheer want of confidence in the public." 2 Nation 545 (May 1, 1866), quoted in James 120. The Chicago Tribune, another Radical organ, complained that § 1 was objectionable as "surplusage," May 5, 1866, quoted in James 123, and later in the same month criticized the measure for "postponing, and not settling" the matter of equal political rights for Negroes. May 31, 1866, quoted in James 146. As deliberations continued, the reporting went on in the same vein. The New York Times reported that with elections approaching, "No one now talks or dreams of forcing Negro suffrage upon the Southern States." June 6, 1866. The Cincinnati Daily Commercial and the Boston Daily Journal for June 7, 1866, commented on the Radicals' abandonment of Negro suffrage. James 145.

Much the same picture emerges from the campaign speeches. Although an occasional Democrat expressed the fear that the Amendment would or might result in political equality,[77] the supporters of the Amendment denied such effects without exception that I have discovered. Among the leading congressional figures who stated in campaign speeches that the Amendment did not prohibit racial voting qualifications were Senators Howe, Lane, Sherman, Sumner, and Trumbull, and Congressmen Bingham, Delano, Schenck, and Stevens. See James 159-168, 173, 178; Fairman, Does the Fourteenth Amendment Incorporate the Bill of Rights?, 2 Stan. L. Rev. 5, 70-78 (1949).

As was pointed out above, all but a handful of Northern States prohibited blacks from voting at all, and opposition to a change was intense. Between 1865 and 1869 referenda on the issue rejected impartial Negro suffrage in Colorado Territory, Connecticut, Wisconsin, Minnesota (twice), the District of Columbia, Nebraska Territory, Kansas, Ohio, Michigan, Missouri, and New York. Only Iowa and Minnesota accepted it, and that on the day Grant was elected to the Presidency.[78] It is inconceivable that those States, in that climate, could have ratified the Amendment with the expectation that it would require them to permit their black citizens to vote.

Small wonder, then, that in early 1869 substantially the same group of men who three years earlier had proposed the Fourteenth Amendment felt it necessary to make further modifications in the Constitution if state suffrage laws were to be controlled even to the minimal degree of prohibiting qualifications which on their face discriminated on the basis of race. If the consequences for our federal system were not so serious, the contention that the history is "inconclusive" would be undeserving of attention. And, with all respect, the transparent failure of attempts to cast doubt on the original understanding is simply further evidence of the force of the historical record.

II

The history of the Fourteenth Amendment with respect to suffrage qualifications is remarkably free of the problems which bedevil most attempts to find a reliable guide to present decision in the pages of the past. Instead, there is virtually unanimous agreement, clearly and repeatedly expressed, that § 1 of the Amendment did not reach discriminatory voter qualifications. In this rather remarkable situation, the issue of the bearing of the historical understanding on constitutional interpretation squarely arises.

I must confess to complete astonishment at the position of some of my Brethren that the history of the Fourteenth Amendment has become irrelevant. Ante, at 139-140. In the six years since I first set out much of this history,[79] I have seen no justification for such a result which appears to me at all adequate. With matters in this posture, I need do no more by way of justifying my reliance on these materials than sketch the familiar outlines of our constitutional system.

When the Constitution with its original Amendments came into being, the States delegated some of their sovereign powers to the Federal Government, surrendered other powers, and expressly retained all powers not delegated or surrendered. Amdt. X. The power to set state voting qualifications was neither surrendered nor delegated, except to the extent that the guarantee of a republican form of government[80] may be thought to require a certain minimum distribution of political power. The power to set qualifications for voters for national office, created by the Constitution, was expressly committed to the States by Art. I, § 2, and Art. II, § 1.[81] By Art. V, States may be deprived of their retained powers only with the concurrence of two-thirds of each House of Congress and three-fourths of the States. No one asserts that the power to set voting qualifications was taken from the States or subjected to federal control by any Amendment before the Fourteenth. The historical evidence makes it plain that the Congress and the States proposing and ratifying that Amendment affirmatively understood that they were not limiting state power over voting qualifications. The existence of the power therefore survived the amending process, and, except as it has been limited by the Fifteenth, Nineteenth, and Twenty-fourth Amendments, it still exists today.[82] Indeed, the very fact that constitutional amendments were deemed necessary to bring about federal abolition of state restrictions on voting by reason of race (Amdt. XV), sex (Amdt. XIX), and, even with respect to federal elections, the failure to pay state poll taxes (Amdt. XXIV), is itself forceful evidence of the common understanding in 1869, 1919, and 1962, respectively, that the Fourteenth Amendment did not empower Congress to legislate in these respects.

It must be recognized, of course, that the amending process is not the only way in which constitutional understanding alters with time. The judiciary has long been entrusted with the task of applying the Constitution in changing circumstances, and as conditions change the Constitution in a sense changes as well. But when the Court gives the language of the Constitution an unforeseen application, it does so, whether explicitly or implicitly, in the name of some underlying purpose of the Framers.[83] This is necessarily so; the federal judiciary, which by express constitutional provision is appointed for life, and therefore cannot be held responsible by the electorate, has no inherent general authority to establish the norms for the rest of society. It is limited to elaboration and application of the precepts ordained in the Constitution by the political representatives of the people. When the Court disregards the express intent and understanding of the Framers, it has invaded the realm of the political process to which the amending power was committed, and it has violated the constitutional structure which it is its highest duty to protect.[84]

As the Court is not justified in substituting its own views of wise policy for the commands of the Constitution, still less is it justified in allowing Congress to disregard those commands as the Court understands them. Although Congress' expression of the view that it does have power to alter state suffrage qualifications is entitled to the most respectful consideration by the judiciary, coming as it does from a coordinate branch of government,[85] this cannot displace the duty of this Court to make an independent determination whether Congress has exceeded its powers. The reason for this goes beyond Marshall's assertion that: "It is emphatically the province and duty of the judicial department to say what the law is." Marbury v. Madison, 1 Cranch 137, 177 (1803).[86] It inheres in the structure of the constitutional system itself. Congress is subject to none of the institutional restraints imposed on judicial decisionmaking; it is controlled only by the political process. In Article V, the Framers expressed the view that the political restraints on Congress alone were an insufficient control over the process of constitution making. The concurrence of two-thirds of each House and of three-fourths of the States was needed for the political check to be adequate. To allow a simple majority of Congress to have final say on matters of constitutional interpretation is therefore fundamentally out of keeping with the constitutional structure. Nor is that structure adequately protected by a requirement that the judiciary be able to perceive a basis for the congressional interpretation, the only restriction laid down in Katzenbach v. Morgan, 384 U. S. 641 (1966).

It is suggested that the proper basis for the doctrine enunciated in Morgan lies in the relative factfinding competence of Court, Congress, and state legislatures. Post, at 246-249. In this view, as I understand it, since Congress is at least as well qualified as a state legislature to determine factual issues, and far better qualified than this Court, where a dispute is basically factual in nature the congressional finding of fact should control, subject only to review by this Court for reasonableness.

In the first place, this argument has little or no force as applied to the issue whether the Fourteenth Amendment covers voter qualifications. Indeed, I do not understand the adherents of Morgan to maintain the contrary.

But even on the assumption that the Fourteenth Amendment does place a limit on the sorts of voter qualifications which a State may adopt, I still do not see any real force in the reasoning.

When my Brothers refer to "complex factual questions," post, at 248, they call to mind disputes about primary, objective facts dealing with such issues as the number of persons between the ages of 18 and 21, the extent of their education, and so forth. The briefs of the four States in these cases take no issue with respect to any of the facts of this nature presented to Congress and relied on by my Brothers DOUGLAS, ante, at 141-143, and BRENNAN, WHITE, and MARSHALL, post, at 243-246, 279-280. Except for one or two matters of dubious relevance, these facts are not subject to rational dispute. The disagreement in these cases revolves around the evaluation of this largely uncontested factual material.[87] On the assumption that maturity and experience are relevant to intelligent and responsible exercise of the elective franchise, are the immaturity and inexperience of the average 18-, 19-, or 20-year-old sufficiently serious to justify denying such a person a direct voice in decisions affecting his or her life? Whether or not this judgment is characterized as "factual," it calls for striking a balance between incommensurate interests. Where the balance is to be struck depends ultimately on the values and the perspective of the decisionmaker. It is a matter as to which men of good will can and do reasonably differ.

I fully agree that judgments of the sort involved here are beyond the institutional competence and constitutional authority of the judiciary. See, e. g., Baker v. Carr, 369 U. S. 186, 266-330 (1962) (Frankfurter, J., dissenting); Kramer v. Union School District, 395 U. S. 621, 634-641 (1969) (STEWART, J., dissenting). They are pre-eminently matters for legislative discretion, with judicial review, if it exists at all, narrowly limited. But the same reasons which in my view would require the judiciary to sustain a reasonable state resolution of the issue also require Congress to abstain from entering the picture.

Judicial deference is based, not on relative factfinding competence, but on due regard for the decision of the body constitutionally appointed to decide. Establishment of voting qualifications is a matter for state legislatures. Assuming any authority at all, only when the Court can say with some confidence that the legislature has demonstrably erred in adjusting the competing interests is it justified in striking down the legislative judgment. This order of things is more efficient and more congenial to our system and, in my judgment, much more likely to achieve satisfactory results than one in which the Court has a free hand to replace state legislative judgments with its own. See Ferguson v. Skrupa, 372 U. S. 726 (1963).

The same considerations apply, and with almost equal force, to Congress' displacement of state decisions with its own ideas of wise policy. The sole distinction between Congress and the Court in this regard is that Congress, being an elective body, presumptively has popular authority for the value judgment it makes. But since the state legislature has a like authority, this distinction between Congress and the judiciary falls short of justifying a congressional veto on the state judgment. The perspectives and values of national legislators on the issue of voting qualifications are likely to differ from those of state legislators, but I see no reason a priori to prefer those of the national figures, whose collective decision, applying nationwide, is necessarily less able to take account of peculiar local conditions. Whether one agrees with this judgment or not, it is the one expressed by the Framers in leaving voter qualifications to the States. The Supremacy Clause does not, as my colleagues seem to argue, represent a judgment that federal decisions are superior to those of the States whenever the two may differ.

To be sure, my colleagues do not expressly say that Congress or this Court is empowered by the Constitution to substitute its own judgment for those of the States. However, before sustaining a state judgment they require a "clear showing that the burden imposed is necessary to protect a compelling and substantial governmental interest."[88] Post, at 238; see post, at 247 n. 30. I should think that if the state interest were truly "compelling" and "substantial," and a clear showing could be made that the voter qualification was "necessary" to its preservation, no reasonable person would think the qualification undesirable. Equivalently, if my colleagues or a majority of Congress deem a given voting qualification undesirable as a matter of policy, they must consider that the state interests involved are not "compelling" or "substantial" or that they can be adequately protected in other ways. It follows that my colleagues must be prepared to hold invalid as a matter of federal constitutional law all state voting qualifications which they deem unwise, as well as all such qualifications which Congress reasonably deems unwise. For this reason, I find their argument subject to the same objection as if it explicitly acknowledged such a conclusion.

It seems to me that the notion of deference to congressional interpretation of the Constitution, which the Court promulgated in Morgan, is directly related to this higher standard of constitutionality which the Court intimated in Harper v. Virginia Board of Elections, 383 U. S. 663 (1966), and brought to fruition in Kramer. When the scope of federal review of state determinations became so broad as to be judicially unmanageable, it was natural for the Court to seek assistance from the national legislature. If the federal role were restricted to its traditional and appropriate scope, review for the sort of "plain error" which is variously described as "arbitrary and capricious," "irrational," or "invidious," there would be no call for the Court to defer to a congressional judgment on this score that it did not find convincing. Whether a state judgment has so exceeded the bounds of reason as to authorize federal intervention is not a matter as to which the political process is intrinsically likely to produce a sounder or more acceptable result. It is a matter of the delicate adjustment of the federal system. In this area, to rely on Congress would make that body a judge in its own cause. The role of final arbiter belongs to this Court.

III

Since I cannot agree that the Fourteenth Amendment empowered Congress, or the federal judiciary, to control voter qualifications. I turn to other asserted sources of congressional power. My Brother BLACK would find that such power exists with respect to federal elections by virtue of Art. I, § 4, and seemingly other considerations that he finds implicit in federal authority.

The constitutional provisions controlling the regulation of congressional elections are the following:

Art. I, § 2: "the Electors [for Representatives] in each State shall have the Qualifications requisite for Electors of the most numerous Branch of the State Legislature."

Art. I, § 4: "The Times, Places and Manner of holding Elections for Senators and Representatives, shall be prescribed in each State by the Legislature thereof; but the Congress may at any time by Law make or alter such Regulations, except as to the Places of chusing Senators."

Amdt. XVII: "The electors [for Senators] in each State shall have the qualifications requisite for electors of the most numerous branch of the State legislatures."

It is difficult to see how words could be clearer in stating what Congress can control and what it cannot control. Surely nothing in these provisions lends itself to the view that voting qualifications in federal elections are to be set by Congress. The reason for the scheme is not hard to find. In the Constitutional Convention, Madison expressed the view that: "The qualifications of electors and elected were fundamental articles in a Republican Govt. and ought to be fixed by the Constitution. If the Legislature could regulate those of either, it can by degrees subvert the Constitution." 2 M. Farrand, Records of the Federal Convention of 1787, pp. 249-250 (1911). He explained further in The Federalist No. 52, p. 326 (C. Rossiter ed. 1961):

"To have reduced the different qualifications in the different States to one uniform rule would probably have been as dissatisfactory to some of the States as it would have been difficult to the convention. The provision made by the convention appears, therefore, to be the best that lay within their option. It must be satisfactory to every State, because it is conformable to the standard already established, or which may be established, by the State itself. It will be safe to the United States because, being fixed by the State constitutions, it is not alterable by the State governments, and it cannot be feared that the people of the States will alter this part of their constitutions in such a manner as to abridge the rights secured to them by the federal Constitution."

See also Federalist No. 60, p. 371 (C. Rossiter ed. 1961) (Hamilton), quoted in the opinion of MR. JUSTICE STEWART, post, at 290, which is to the same effect.

As to presidential elections, the Constitution provides:

"Each State shall appoint, in such Manner as the Legislature thereof may direct, a Number of Electors. . . ." Art. II, § 1, cl. 2.

"The Congress may determine the Time of chusing the Electors, and the Day on which they shall give their Votes; which Day shall be the same throughout the United States." Art. II, § 1, cl. 4.

Even the power to control the "Manner" of holding elections, given with respect to congressional elections by Art. I, § 4, is absent with respect to the selection of presidential electors.[89] And, of course, the fact that it was deemed necessary to provide separately for congressional power to regulate the time of choosing presidential electors and the President himself demonstrates that the power over "Times, Places and Manner" given by Art. I, § 4, does not refer to presidential elections, but only to the elections for Congressmen. Any shadow of a justification for congressional power with respect to congressional elections therefore disappears utterly in presidential elections.

IV

With these major contentions resolved, it is convenient to consider the three sections of the Act individually to determine whether they can be supported by any other basis of congressional power.

A. Voting Age

The only constitutional basis advanced in support of the lowering of the voting age is the power to enforce the Equal Protection Clause, a power found in § 5 of the Fourteenth Amendment. For the reasons already given, it cannot be said that the statutory provision is valid as declaratory of the meaning of that clause. Its validity therefore must rest on congressional power to lower the voting age as a means of preventing invidious discrimination that is within the purview of that clause.

The history of the Fourteenth Amendment may well foreclose the possibility that § 5 empowers Congress to enfranchise a class of citizens so that they may protect themselves against discrimination forbidden by the first section, but it is unnecessary for me to explore that question. For I think it fair to say that the suggestion that members of the age group between 18 and 21 are threatened with unconstitutional discrimination, or that any hypothetical discrimination is likely to be affected by lowering the voting age, is little short of fanciful. I see no justification for stretching to find any such possibility when all the evidence indicates that Congress—led on by recent decisions of this Court—thought simply that 18-year-olds were fairly entitled to the vote and that Congress could give it to them by legislation.[90]

I therefore conclude, for these and other reasons given in this opinion, that in § 302 of the Voting Rights Act Amendments of 1970 Congress exceeded its delegated powers.

B. Residency

For reasons already stated, neither the power to regulate voting qualifications in presidential elections, asserted by my Brother BLACK, nor the power to declare the meaning of § 1 of the Fourteenth Amendment, relied on by my Brother DOUGLAS, can support § 202 of the Act. It would also be frivolous to contend that requiring States to allow new arrivals to vote in presidential elections is an appropriate means of preventing local discrimination against them in other respects, or of forestalling violations of the Fifteenth Amendment. The remaining grounds relied on are the Privileges and Immunities Clause of Art. IV, § 2,[91] and the right to travel across state lines.

While the right of qualified electors to cast their ballots and to have their votes counted was held to be a privilege of citizenship in Ex parte Yarbrough, 110 U. S. 651 (1884), and United States v. Classic, 313 U. S. 299 (1941), these decisions were careful to observe that it remained with the States to determine the class of qualified voters. It was federal law, acting on this state-defined class, which turned the right to vote into a privilege of national citizenship. As the Court has consistently held, the Privileges and Immunities Clauses do not react on the mere status of citizenship to enfranchise any citizen whom an otherwise valid state law does not allow to vote. Minor v. Happersett, 21 Wall. 162, 170-175 (1875); Pope v. Williams, 193 U. S. 621, 632 (1904); Breedlove v. Suttles, 302 U. S. 277, 283 (1937); cf. Snowden v. Hughes, 321 U. S. 1, 6-7 (1944). Minors, felons, insane persons, and persons who have not satisfied residency requirements are among those citizens who are not allowed to vote in most States.[92] The Privileges and Immunities Clause of Art. IV of the Constitution is a direct descendent of Art. IV of the Articles of Confederation:

"The better to secure and perpetuate mutual friendship and intercourse among the people of the different States in this Union, the free inhabitants of each of these States, paupers, vagabonds and fugitives from justice excepted, shall be entitled to all privileges and immunities of free citizens in the several States . . . ."

It is inconceivable that these words when used in the Articles could have been understood to abolish state durational residency requirements.[93] There is not a vestige of evidence that any further extent was envisioned for them when they were carried over into the Constitution. And, as I have shown, when they were substantially repeated in § 1 of the Fourteenth Amendment it was affirmatively understood that they did not include the right to vote. The Privileges and Immunities Clause is therefore unavailing to sustain any portion of § 202.

The right to travel across state lines, see United States v. Guest, 383 U. S. 745, 757-758 (1966), and Shapiro v. Thompson, 394 U. S. 618, 630 (1969), is likewise insufficient to require Idaho to conform its laws to the requirements of § 202. MR. JUSTICE STEWART justifies § 202 solely on the power under § 5 of the Fourteenth Amendment to enforce the Privileges and Immunities Clause of § 1 which he deems the basis for the right to travel. Post, at 285-287. I find it impossible to square the position that § 5 authorizes Congress to abolish state voting qualifications based on residency with the position that it does not authorize Congress to abolish such qualifications based on race. Since the historical record compels me to accept the latter position, I must reject the former.

MR. JUSTICE BRENNAN, MR. JUSTICE WHITE, and MR. JUSTICE MARSHALL do not anchor the right of interstate travel to any specific constitutional provision. Post, at 237-238. Past decisions to which they refer have relied on the two Privileges and Immunities Clauses, just discussed, the Due Process Clause of the Fifth Amendment, and the Commerce Clause. See Shapiro v. Thompson, 394 U. S., at 630 n. 8; id., at 663-671 (dissenting opinion). The Fifth Amendment is wholly inapplicable to state laws; and surely the Commerce Clause cannot be seriously relied on to sustain the Act here challenged. With no specific clause of the Constitution empowering Congress to enact § 202, I fail to see how that nebulous judicial construct, the right to travel, can do so.

C. Literacy

The remaining provision of the Voting Rights Act Amendments involved in these cases is the five-year suspension of Arizona's requirement that registrants be able to read the Constitution in English and to write their names. Although the issue is not free from difficulty, I am of the opinion that this provision can be sustained as a valid means of enforcing the Fifteenth Amendment.

Despite the lack of evidence of specific instances of discriminatory application or effect, Congress could have determined that racial prejudice is prevalent throughout the Nation, and that literacy tests unduly lend themselves to discriminatory application, either conscious or unconscious.[94] This danger of violation of § 1 of the Fifteenth Amendment was sufficient to authorize the exercise of congressional power under § 2.

Whether to engage in a more particularized inquiry into the extent and effects of discrimination, either as a condition precedent or as a condition subsequent to suspension of literacy tests, was a choice for Congress to make.[95] The fact that the suspension is only for five years will require Congress to re-evaluate at the close of that period. While a less sweeping approach in this delicate area might well have been appropriate, the choice which Congress made was within the range of the reasonable.[96] I therefore agree that § 201 of the Act is a valid exercise of congressional power to the extent it is involved in this case. I express no view about its validity as applied to suspend tests such as educational qualifications, which do not lend themselves so readily to discriminatory application or effect.

For the reasons expressed in this opinion, I would grant the relief requested in Nos. 43, Orig., and 44, Orig. I would dismiss the complaint in No. 47, Orig., for failure to state a claim on which relief can be granted. In No. 46, Orig., I would grant declaratory relief with respect to the validity of § 201 of the Voting Rights Act Amendments as applied to Arizona's current literacy test; I would deny relief in all other respects, with leave to reapply to the United States District Court for the District of Arizona for injunctive relief in the event it proves necessary, which I am confident it will not.

V

In conclusion I add the following. The consideration that has troubled me most in deciding that the 18-year-old and residency provisions of this legislation should be held unconstitutional is whether I ought to regard the doctrine of stare decisis as preventing me from arriving at that result. For as I indicated at the outset of this opinion, were I to continue to consider myself constricted by recent past decisions holding that the Equal Protection Clause of the Fourteenth Amendment reaches state electoral processes, I would, particularly perforce of the decisions cited in n. 84, supra, be led to cast my vote with those of my Brethren who are of the opinion that the lowering of the voting age and the abolition of state residency requirements in presidential elections are within the ordinary legislative power of Congress.

After much reflection I have reached the conclusion that I ought not to allow stare decisis to stand in the way of casting my vote in accordance with what I am deeply convinced the Constitution demands. In the annals of this Court few developments in the march of events have so imperatively called upon us to take a fresh hard look at past decisions, which could well be mustered in support of such developments, as do the legislative lowering of the voting age and, albeit to a lesser extent, the elimination of state residential requirements in presidential elections. Concluding, as I have, that such decisions cannot withstand constitutional scrutiny, I think it my duty to depart from them, rather than to lend my support to perpetuating their constitutional error in the name of stare decisis.

In taking this position, I feel fortified by the evident malaise among the members of the Court with those decisions. Despite them, a majority of the Court holds that this congressional attempt to lower the voting age by simple legislation is unconstitutional, insofar as it relates to state elections. Despite them, four members of the Court take the same view of this legislation with respect to federal elections as well; and the fifth member of the Court who considers the legislation constitutionally infirm as regards state elections relies not at all on any of those decisions in reaching the opposite conclusion in federal elections. And of the eight members of the Court who vote to uphold the residential provision of the statute, only four appear to rely upon any of those decisions in reaching that result.

In these circumstances I am satisfied that I am free to decide these cases unshackled by a line of decisions which I have felt from the start entailed a basic departure from sound constitutional principle.

Justice Harlan's concurrence in US Bulk Carriers v. Arguelles (Jan 13, 1971)

MR. JUSTICE HARLAN, concurring.

I join in the opinion and judgment of the Court, but deem it advisable to add some thoughts of my own.

I

I do not think that the mere provision by federal statute of a judicial forum for enforcement of the wage claims of a subclass of workers forecloses application of the arbitration principles of Textile Workers v. Lincoln Mills, 353 U. S. 448 (1957), and Republic Steel Corp. v. Maddox, 379 U. S. 650 (1965); nor do I understand the Court's opinion today to so hold. In Smith v. Evening News Assn., 371 U. S. 195 (1962), we held that a suit in the state courts by an individual employee charging employer discrimination in violation of the collective-bargaining agreement was not foreclosed by the availability of an unfair labor practice proceeding before the National Labor Relations Board based on the same conduct. There we explicitly noted the absence of a grievance arbitration provision in the contract which had to be exhausted before recourse could be had to the courts. Id., at 196 n. 1. Later, in Republic Steel Corp. v. Maddox, supra, at 652, we cited this portion of Smith as support for the broadly stated proposition that "[a]s a general rule in cases to which federal law applies, federal labor policy requires that individual employees wishing to assert contract grievances must attempt use of the contract grievance procedure agreed upon by employer and union as the mode of redress." (Emphasis omitted.) Maddox held that an employee was compelled to exhaust contractual grievance machinery as a prelude to commencing a § 301 suit on the contract in the state court. Finally, in Carey v. Westinghouse Corp., 375 U. S. 261 (1964), we held that a union could compel an employer to arbitrate a contractual grievance arising out of events which also might support proceedings before the NLRB for either an unfair labor practice under § 8 (a) (5) of the National Labor Relations Act, as amended, or a petition clarifying the union's representation certificate under § 9 (c) (1). See also Old Dutch Farms v. Local 584, I. B. T., 243 F. Supp. 246 (EDNY 1965); United States Steel Corp. v. Seafarers, 237 F. Supp. 529 (ED Pa. 1965). See generally Vaca v. Sipes, 386 U. S. 171, 183-184 (1967).

Smith, Carey, and Maddox together evince the fundamental role arbitration plays in implementing national labor relations policy. They also evince the crucial role of the federal judiciary in forging the proper relationships among available arbitral, administrative, and judicial forums for vindicating contractual and statutory rights of employers, unions, and employees. In light of these cases, I cannot infer, from the mere provision by Congress of a federal judicial forum for enforcement of the wage claims of a subclass of workers' wages, that this Court is foreclosed from requiring arbitration under the collective-bargaining contract.

But in forging this relationship among potentially competing forums for the effectuation of contractual and statutory rights of individuals and organizations, we have always proceeded with close attention to the policies underpinning both the duty to arbitrate and the provision by Congress of rights and remedies in alternative forums. This Court has always recognized that the choice of forums inevitably affects the scope of the substantive right to be vindicated before the chosen forum. In particular, where arbitration is concerned, the Court has been acutely sensitive to these differences. Thus, in Wilko v. Swan, 346 U. S. 427 (1953), the Court faced a conflict between congressional policy favoring arbitration, as manifested in § 3 of the United States Arbitration Act, 9 U. S. C. § 3, and congressional policy favoring protection of securities purchasers from fraud, as manifested in § 12 (2) of the Securities Act of 1933, 48 Stat. 84, 15 U. S. C. § 77l (2). The Court carefully analyzed the impact which remission to arbitration would have on the scope of the substantive federal right involved in that case and concluded that conflicting congressional goals would best be served by construing the nonwaiver provisions of the Securities Act[1] as applying to the choice of a judicial forum as well as the substance of the Act's protection. See Wilko v. Swan, supra, at 434-439. Central to the process of reconciliation in that case was the recognition that the effectiveness of any pro-arbitration policy is dependent, in the first instance, on a limited scope of judicial review of the arbitrator's determination.

And in Bernhardt v. Polygraphic Co., 350 U. S. 198 (1956), in holding that state law controlled on the question of reference to arbitration in a diversity suit brought in a federal court, the Court offered the following considerations on the impact which reference to arbitration has on the scope of the substantive right:

"The nature of the tribunal where suits are tried is an important part of the parcel of rights behind a cause of action. The change from a court of law to an arbitration panel may make a radical difference in ultimate result. . . . Arbitrators do not have the benefit of judicial instruction on the law; they need not give their reasons for their results; the record of their proceedings is not as complete as it is in a court trial; and judicial review of an award is more limited than judicial review of a trial—all as discussed in Wilko v. Swan . . . ." 350 U. S., at 203.

Normally, the impact on the substantive right resulting from the decision to remit the individual to the arbitral forum is acceptable because the parties themselves have consented to that forum. Compare Atkinson v. Sinclair Refining Co., 370 U. S. 238 (1962), with Drake Bakeries v. Local 50, American Bakery Workers, 370 U. S. 254 (1962). And, with respect to the individual employee seeking to bypass the arbitral forum in a suit brought "simply on the contract," see Maddox, supra, at 657, the fact that his substantive rights derive solely from the contract, and that he owes those rights to the actions of his union representative in the collective-bargaining process, warrants the extension of the boundaries of collective consent to his individual remedial preferences. A suit simply on the contract to enforce contractual grievances is the normal labor arbitration situation, and "it cannot be said, in the normal situation, that contract grievance procedures are inadequate to protect the interests of an aggrieved employee until the employee has attempted to implement the procedures and found them so." Maddox, supra, at 653. In Maddox, we laid out in full the strong policy concerns which support exclusivity in the arbitral forum, supra, at 653-656, and then expressly noted the absence of countervailing positive reasons where the suit was simply on the contract. Supra, at 657. It is this state of affairs that supports the presumption of comprehensiveness underpinning this Court's § 301 labor arbitration doctrines. Maddox, supra, at 657.

II

Arguelles' suit, unlike Maddox's suit, is not "simply on the contract"; he invokes the court's jurisdiction seeking, in addition to the overtime wages allegedly due him under the collective-bargaining agreement, a statutory claim for refusal or neglect to pay his wages according to the timetable prescribed in 46 U. S. C. § 596 "without sufficient cause." In this circumstance, the presumption of comprehensiveness of the arbitral remedy is, in my view, rebutted.

But, of course, the policies underpinning Maddox are still relevant to the process of forging relationships among potentially competing forums in this case. Here, as in Maddox, the union's status as exclusive bargaining representative will most certainly be bolstered by requiring the employee to vindicate both his contractual and statutory rights in the arbitral forum. Supra, at 653. And, even more importantly, here as in Maddox, the availability of an alternative forum for vindicating both statutory and contractual rights allegedly abridged in the same transaction cuts significantly into the desirability of the arbitral forum from the employer's negotiating viewpoint. Maddox, supra, at 656-657. But, in the present context, it is crucial to recognize that these policy considerations underpinning arbitration argue, not merely for reference to the arbitrator as a matter of prior exhaustion of internal organizational remedies, but also for extremely limited judicial review of the arbitrator's decision. Indeed, this Court's decisions in the Steelworkers Trilogy make very clear that the scope of judicial review of the arbitrator's judgment where matters of contract rights are concerned is limited to a threshold determination of the arbitrability of the dispute. United Steelworkers v. American Mfg. Co., 363 U. S. 564 (1960); United Steelworkers v. Warrior & Gulf Navigation Co., 363 U. S. 574 (1960); United Steelworkers v. Enterprise Wheel & Car Corp., 363 U. S. 593 (1960). The extreme limitation of judicial review, and the expansive reading of consent, are both important to the task of effectuating national labor policy; both are legitimized, in my view, by the derivation of the individual's substantive legal right from the collective-bargaining agreement.

Where, however, the § 301 dispute implicates federal statutory rights, it is incumbent upon this Court to fashion the relationship among forums according to an analysis of the policies underpinning both § 301 and the federal statute the employee invokes, rather than simply transposing ipso facto the Court's labor arbitration jurisprudence. Thus, in the analogous situation where the disputed transaction implicates both contractual rights and rights enforceable in NLRB proceedings, we do not simply assume that because the dispute involves a contract grievance, and the contract contains a typically broad arbitration provision, remission to arbitration on the presumption of consent—combined with virtually no judicial review—follows automatically. Rather, the Court takes account of the views of the NLRB, as the agency charged with enforcement of the substantive statutory right in question, on the difficult issue whether the interests of national labor policy, as manifested both in § 301 and the unfair labor practice provision, will best be served by remission to arbitration. See, e. g., Carey v. Westinghouse Corp., 375 U. S., at 271-272; Smith v. Evening News Assn., 371 U. S., at 197-198.

III

Here Seaman Arguelles seeks to vindicate a federal statutory right to prompt payment of wages due him. His original complaint stated a cause of action under 46 U. S. C. § 596, which provides as follows:

"The master or owner of any vessel making coasting voyages shall pay to every seaman his wages within two days after the termination of the agreement under which he was shipped, or at the time such seaman is discharged, whichever first happens; and in case of vessels making foreign voyages, or from a port on the Atlantic to a port on the Pacific, or vice versa, within twenty-four hours after the cargo has been discharged, or within four days after the seaman has been discharged, whichever first happens; and in all cases the seaman shall be entitled to be paid at the time of his discharge on account of wages a sum equal to one-third part of the balance due him. Every master or owner who refuses or neglects to make payment in the manner hereinbefore mentioned without sufficient cause shall pay to the seaman a sum equal to two days' pay for each and every day during which payment is delayed beyond the respective periods, which sum shall be recoverable as wages in any claim made before the court . . . ."

These provisions of Title 46 derive from § 6 of the Act of July 20, 1790; see 1 Stat. 133. Also derived from § 6 of the original Act is 46 U. S. C. § 597, providing for part payment of wages earned during interim stops in port for the discharge of cargo.[2] Sections 596 and 597 go beyond the mere provision of a federal judicial forum for vindication of a worker's wage claims; they represent a congressional policy to secure to the individual seaman the prompt payment of his wages[3] as part of a broader protective and remedial scheme intended for the benefit of seamen. See Isbrandtsen Co. v. Johnson, 343 U. S. 779, 784-786 (1952). This legislation, though antedating the emergence of modern collective-bargaining institutions, must be taken to represent a continuing congressional policy to protect seamen as individual laborers.

In the instant case, remission to arbitration under the usual assumption concerning the scope of judicial review would mean that a denial of the grievance without any explanation on the arbitrator's part would have to stand. Given the assumption concerning scope of judicial review, the seaman's statutory right to double wages in the event of failure, "without sufficient cause" to pay promptly within the meaning of § 596 is, as a practical matter, subject to the unreviewable discretion of the arbitrator.

But the usual assumption concerning judicial review need not necessarily obtain in situations of this sort, any more than the usual assumptions concerning the boundaries of the individual's consent to the actions of his bargaining representative in agreeing to the broad arbitration provision need necessarily obtain. Two possibilities suggest themselves: the arbitrator's award might be reviewable to some unspecified extent, to ascertain whether the rights under §§ 596 and 597 have been adequately protected, or the claim may, in some fashion, be split, either by declining jurisdiction at the outset over the contract portion of the litigation, or by utilizing the various devices of abstention. Cf., e. g., United States Steel Corp. v. Seafarers, 273 F. Supp. 529 (ED Pa. 1965). As an abstract proposition, both options have the undesirable consequence of cutting substantially into the very exclusivity of the contractual forum which we said in Maddox is important to effectuation of the national labor policy favoring arbitration. See Maddox, supra, at 653. And the difficulties of analyzing the respective boundaries of the contractual right and the statutory right forbode ill for the efficient resolution of disputes implicating both the contract right and the federal statutory right. But the matter is not one to be decided abstractly; it may well be that certain types of federal statutory benefits will lend themselves to arbitration or splitting without an unacceptable sacrifice in competing policy interests.

However, this is not such a statute, because the very essence of the legislative policy at stake here is ensuring promptness in the payment of wages. I think it obvious that the least desirable of all solutions would be to create a necessity for suits in both forums. In this circumstance, I think conflicting congressional policies are best reconciled by construing 46 U. S. C. § 596 and § 301 of the Labor Management Relations Act as securing to the seaman an option to choose between arbitral and judicial forums where he states a claim under both the contract and 46 U. S. C. § 596.

Notes

[1] Section 14 of the Securities Act of 1933, 15 U. S. C. § 77n, provides:

"Any condition, stipulation, or provision binding any person acquiring any security to waive compliance with any provision of this subchapter or of the rules and regulations of the Commission shall be void."

[2] Arguelles attempted to amend his complaint prior to the summary judgment hearing to state a complaint under 46 U. S. C. § 597 as well as § 596. The court refused the proffered amendment pending its ruling on the summary judgment motion. Brief for Respondent 7 n. 4.

[3] In Collie v. Fergusson, 281 U. S. 52, 55 (1930), in discussing what constitutes sufficient cause for delay in payment under § 596, the Court noted that "the evident purpose of the section [is] to secure prompt payment of seamen's wages . . . and thus to

protect them from the harsh consequences of arbitrary and unscrupulous action of their employers, to which, as a class, they are peculiarly exposed."

Justice Harlan's concurrence and dissent in Perkins v. Matthews (Jan 14, 1971)

MR. JUSTICE HARLAN, concurring in part and dissenting in part.

Our role in this case, as the Court correctly recognizes, is limited to determination whether § 5 of the Voting Rights Act of 1965, 42 U. S. C. § 1973c (1964 ed., Supp. V), required the city of Canton to obtain federal approval of the way it proposed to run its 1969 elections. For this reason, I am unable to join the dissenting opinion of MR. JUSTICE BLACK, post, p. 401, although, like him, I see little likelihood that the changes here involved had a discriminatory purpose or effect.

I agree with the Court, and for substantially the reasons it gives, that the city should have submitted the relocation of polling places for federal approval. But I cannot agree that it was obliged to follow that course with respect to the other two matters here at issue.

I

Whether or not Congress could constitutionally require a State to submit all changes in its laws for federal approval, cf. South Carolina v. Katzenbach, 383 U. S. 301, 358-362 (1966) (separate opinion of BLACK, J.), the Voting Rights Act does not purport to do so. Section 5 requires submission of changes "with respect to voting" only. The Court seems to interpret this restriction as including any change in state law which has an effect on voting, if changes of that type have "a potential for racial discrimination in voting." Ante, p. 389. The limitation implied by the latter clause will prove meaningless as a practical matter. Given a change with an effect on voting, a set of circumstances may be conceived with respect to almost any situation in which the change will bear more heavily on one race than on another. In effect, therefore, the Court requires submission of any change which has an effect on voting. I think it plain that the statutory phrase—"with respect to voting"—was intended to have more limited compass.

The legislative history of the Voting Rights Act was examined in the majority opinion and a separate opinion in Allen v. State Board of Elections, 393 U. S. 544, 564-571, 588-591 (1969). No useful purpose would be served by retraversing ground covered there. The Court concluded from its review of the history that § 5 was "intended to reach any state enactment which altered the election law of a covered State in even a minor way." Id., at 566. The Court's opinions in both Allen and this case are devoid of evidence of a legislative intent to go beyond the State's election law and to reach matters such as annexations, which affect voting only incidentally and peripherally. Fairley v. Patterson, decided with Allen, and the remarks of the Solicitor General in his amicus brief in that case are plainly distinguishable on this basis. At least in the absence of a contrary administrative interpretation, I would not go beyond Allen to hold that annexations are within the scope of § 5. The Court's assertion that the Attorney General does in fact interpret the Act differently seems to me to give too much weight to the passing remark of an Assistant Attorney General. Cf. Allen v. State Board of Elections, 393 U. S., at 568-569.[1]

II

Fairley v. Patterson held that a change from election by districts to election at large was within the scope of § 5. The question for determination here is which of the two procedures was "in force or effect on November 1, 1964." The Court interprets the quoted phrase to mean the procedure which probably would have been followed if an election had been held on the crucial date, regardless of the provisions of controlling state law. While this interpretation is not wholly unreasonable, I find it unlikely that it is the one Congress would have preferred if it had thought about the problem. Resolution of the hypothetical factual question required by the Court's test would be quite inconvenient, if not unmanageable, for the Attorney General or the District Court for the District of Columbia, far from the scene.[2] Moreover, under the Court's test, results may turn on the seeming fortuity that in the first election after November 1, 1964, local officials forgot about a controlling statute of statewide application and no private citizen brought suit to have the election set aside. Barring state attempts to resurrect long-ignored statutes, I would interpret "procedure . . . in force or effect on November 1, 1964," to mean the procedure required by state law. Under this interpretation I would hold that the change from election by wards to election at large occurred on the effective date of the 1962 state statute, and therefore that it did not require approval under § 5.

III

I must confess that I am somewhat mystified by the Court's discussion of the appropriate remedy in this case. For the reasons set out in my partial dissent in Allen, 393 U. S., at 593-594, I would direct the holding of new elections if, and only if, the city fails to obtain approval from the appropriate federal officials within a reasonable time. If such approval is forthcoming, I see no justification for requiring a rerun of the 1969 elections. See the opinion of MR. JUSTICE BLACK, post, this page. If the approval is not forthcoming, the fact of violation of the federal statute, as interpreted by this Court, and the possibility that the changes had a discriminatory purpose or effect seem to me to require new elections in the absence of exceptional circumstances which I cannot now foresee. In any event, the District Court is entitled to more guidance on this score than the Court provides.

Notes

[1] The fact that the Attorney General has expressed his opinion on the merits of the handful of border changes which have been presented to him, rather than dismissing them as not within the scope of § 5, seems to me to be entitled to little weight in the face of the enormous number of annexations which have not been submitted to him and which he has done nothing about. In the fiscal year beginning July 1, 1967, there were over 40

municipal annexations in South Carolina. 1967-1968 Report of the Secretary of State of South Carolina 165-166. None of these were submitted for the approval of the Attorney General. Hearings on Voting Rights Act Extension before Subcommittee No. 5 of the House Committee on the Judiciary, 91st Cong., 1st Sess., ser. 3, pp. 310-312 (1969). The Georgia Session Laws for the years 1965 to 1969 reveal over 100 boundary changes in Georgia cities. Only one was submitted to the Attorney General, and that one also involved redrawing of ward lines. So far as the face of the statute, Act of March 2, 1966, No. 235, Ga. Laws 1966, p. 2729, reveals, the redrawing of ward lines may have completely altered the political map of the city. In the case at hand, the old ward lines were simply extended to the new city limits.

[2] Assuming that the statute requires determination of this hypothetical factual question, I would have thought that it should be passed on by the District Court in the first instance. The record is simply too sparse to reveal why the 1962 statute was not followed in 1965, or whether the same cause would have been operative a year earlier. If the defendants are not entitled to prevail on the theory that the plaintiffs failed to come forward with adequate proof of the procedure in force or effect in 1964, they are at least entitled to a hearing at which they may address themselves to the issue.

Justice Harlan's dissent in Usner v. Luckenbach Overseas (Jan 25, 1971)

MR. JUSTICE HARLAN, dissenting.

Past decisions of this Court have expanded the doctrine of unseaworthiness almost to the point of absolute liability. I have often protested against this development. See, e. g., the cases cited by the Court, ante, at 497 n. 6. But I must in good conscience regard the particular issue in this case as having been decided by Crumady v. The J. H. Fisser, 358 U. S. 423 (1959), even if prior decisions did not inexorably point to that result. As my Brother DOUGLAS states, Crumady cannot justly be distinguished from the case before us. Much as I would welcome a thoroughgoing re-examination of the past course of developments in the unseaworthiness doctrine, I fear that the Court's action today can only result in compounding the current difficulties of the lower courts with this area of the law.

Justice Harlan's dissent in Time, Inc. v. Pape (Feb 24, 1971)

MR. JUSTICE HARLAN, dissenting.

I would affirm the judgment of the Court of Appeals, essentially for the reasons stated in Judge Duffy's opinion for that court. The treatment of this case by our Court, however, prompts me to venture these additional comments.

I fully agree with the rule first enunciated in New York Times Co. v. Sullivan, 376 U. S. 254 (1964), that restricts the liability of those who utter defamatory falsehoods regarding public officials. We there recognized that because "erroneous statement is inevitable in free debate," id., at 271, "neither factual error nor defamatory content suffices to remove the constitutional shield from criticism of official conduct." Id., at 273. But these considerations did not persuade us to rule that the Constitution grants absolute immunity to everyone, be it the news media or anyone else, who libels a public official, or to conclude that the usual processes of law are inadequate for dealing with this kind of litigation. Rather, we decided that the substantial First Amendment interests implicated in any libel suit of this sort would be adequately served by a constitutional rule that subjects such a statement to the sanctions of the common law of libel only where it was uttered "with `actual malice'— that is, with knowledge that it was false or with reckless disregard of whether it was false or not." Id., at 280.

The step taken today, whereby this Court undertakes to judge, "on the specific facts of this case," ante, at 292, whether a jury could reasonably find that Time magazine's characterization of the Commission's report was sufficiently inaccurate to permit the concomitant finding that it was published with "malice," is, in my judgment, not warranted.

I can perceive no rational basis for distinguishing this case from one in which a newspaper or an individual seeks to have this Court review the record upon which a properly instructed jury found liability, where evidence sufficient to support its verdict exists, and where these matters have been reviewed by a court of appeals applying correct legal standards. As I see things, the Court identifies no such distinguishing feature about this case.

While it is true, of course, that this Court is free to re-examine for itself the evidentiary bases upon which rest decisions that allegedly impair or punish the exercise of Fourteenth Amendment freedoms, this does not mean that we are of necessity always, or even usually, compelled to do so. Indeed, it is almost impossible to conceive how this Court might continue to function effectively were we to resolve afresh the underlying factual disputes in all cases containing constitutional issues. Nor can I discern in those First Amendment considerations that led us to restrict the States' powers to regulate defamation of public officials any additional interest that is not served by the actual-malice rule of New York Times, supra, but is substantially promoted by utilizing this Court as the ultimate arbiter of factual disputes in those libel cases where no unusual factors, such as allegations of harassment or the existence of a jury verdict resting on erroneous instructions, cf. New York Times, supra, are present. While I am confident that the Court does not intend its decision to have any such broad reach, I fear that what is done today may open a door that will prove difficult to close.

Having determined that the court below properly defined the quality of proof required of Pape by New York Times and that it applied the correct standard of review in passing upon the trial judge's decision to grant a directed verdict—determinations that I do not think my Brethren dispute—I would stop the inquiry at this point and affirm the judgment of the Court of Appeals.

Justice Harlan's dissent in Investment Co. Institute v. Camp (April 5, 1971)

MR. JUSTICE HARLAN, dissenting.

The Court holds that the Investment Company Institute has standing as a competitor to challenge the action of the Comptroller of the Currency because Congress "arguably legislated against the competition that the petitioners sought to challenge, and from which flowed their injury." The ICI, says the Court, is entitled to prevail because "Congress did legislate against the competition that the petitioners challenge." Ante, at 620, 621 (emphasis added.) I understand the Court to mean by "legislated against the competition" not only that Congress prohibited banks from entering this field of endeavor, but that it did so in part for reasons stemming from the fact of the resulting competition. See ante, at 631-634, 636-638. However, the Court cannot mean by this phrase that it was Congress' purpose to protect petitioners' class against competitive injury for, as all three judges on the court below agreed, neither the language of the pertinent provisions of the Glass-Steagall Act nor the legislative history evinces any congressional concern for the interests of petitioners and others like them in freedom from competition.[1] Indeed, it appears reasonably plain that, if anything, the Act was adopted despite its anticompetitive effects rather than because of them. Cf. ante, at 630, 636.

This being the case, the discussion of standing in Hardin v. Kentucky Utilities Co., 390 U. S. 1, 5-6 (1968), is directly in point:

"This Court has, it is true, repeatedly held that the economic injury which results from lawful competition cannot, in and of itself, confer standing on the injured business to question the legality of any aspect of its competitor's operations. Railroad Co. v. Ellerman, 105 U. S. 166 (1882); Alabama Power Co. v. Ickes, 302 U. S. 464 (1938); Tennessee Power Co. v. TVA, 306 U. S. 118 (1939); Perkins v. Lukens Steel Co., 310 U. S. 113 (1940). But competitive injury provided no basis for standing in the above cases simply because the statutory and constitutional requirements that the plaintiff sought to enforce were in no way concerned with protecting against competitive injury. In contrast, it has been the rule, at least since the Chicago Junction Case, 264 U. S. 258 (1924), that when the particular statutory provision invoked does reflect a legislative purpose to protect a competitive interest, the injured competitor has standing to require compliance with that provision."

I do not believe that Data Processing Service v. Camp, 397 U. S. 150 (1970), and Arnold Tours v. Camp, 400 U. S. 45 (1970), require the opposite result from the one suggested by this passage from Hardin. Data Processing held that, aside from "case-or-controversy" problems not present here, the crucial question in ruling on a challenge to standing is "whether the interest sought to be protected by the complainant is arguably within the zone of interest to be protected or regulated by the statute or constitutional guarantee in question." 397 U. S., at 153. That question was resolved in favor of the data processors because "§ 4 [of the Bank Service Corporation Act] arguably brings a competitor within the zone of interests protected by it." Id., at 156.[2] In Arnold Tours the

Court observed that it was again dealing with § 4 of the Bank Service Corporation Act, and that "[n]othing in the [Data Processing] opinion limited § 4 to protecting only competitors in the data-processing field." 400 U. S., at 46. Plainly these cases provide little support for the Court's conclusion here that competitors, as such, have standing under the Glass-Steagall Act as well.

The Court's holding—that if Congress prohibited entry into a field of business for reasons relating to competition, then a competitor has standing to seek observance of the prohibition—has a surface appeal, but, so far as I can see, no sound analytical basis. Certainly none is offered. In any event, it appears to me that our prior decisions, particularly Hardin, require the conclusion that the petitioners in No. 61 lack standing to challenge the Comptroller's action. While I would not foreclose the possibility that those cases should be further modified in some respect,[3] the Court has not undertaken to re-examine them, and I deem it inappropriate for me to do so as a single Justice.

The view that I take with regard to petitioners' standing in No. 61 makes it unnecessary for me to reach the merits in that case, but it does require me to rule on the contentions made in No. 59. Like MR. JUSTICE BLACKMUN, see post, at 645, I find lengthy discussion of this topic superfluous. At issue is the propriety of the action of the Securities and Exchange Commission in increasing from two to three the number of seats open to bank officers on the five-man committee which serves as a board of directors of the account.[4] Substantially for the reasons given by the judges of the court below, 136 U. S. App. D. C. 241, 249-253, 266, 420 F. 2d 83, 91-95, 108, I am of the opinion that the Commission did not abuse its discretion in determining that the facts of this case made appropriate an exercise of the dispensing power explicitly vested in the Commission by 15 U. S. C. § 80a-6 (c).

For the reasons given herein, I would affirm the two judgments under review.

Notes

[1] "It is equally clear that giving even the broadest reading of the legislative history embellishing the Act will not support the conclusion that Congress meant to bestow upon Appellees any protection from competitive injury." 136 U. S. App. D. C. 241, 263, 420 F. 2d 83, 105 (Burger, J., joined by Miller, J.) (footnote omitted); see also id., at 254, 256-258, 420 F. 2d, at 96, 98-100 (Bazelon, C. J.).

[2] See also Barlow v. Collins, 397 U. S. 159, 164 (1970).

[3] For one suggestion to this effect, see Jaffe, Standing Again, 84 Harv. L. Rev. 633 (1971).

[4] By virtue of the "person or party aggrieved" provision of the Investment Company Act, 15 U. S. C. § 80a-42 (a), there is no difficulty supporting petitioner's standing in No. 59.

Justice Harlan's dissent in US v. White (April 5, 1971) [Notes omitted]

MR. JUSTICE HARLAN, dissenting.

The uncontested facts of this case squarely challenge the continuing viability of On Lee v. United States, 343 U. S. 747 (1952). As the plurality opinion of MR. JUSTICE WHITE itself makes clear, important constitutional developments since On Lee mandate that we reassess that case, which has continued to govern official behavior of this sort in spite of the subsequent erosion of its doctrinal foundations. With all respect, my agreement with the plurality opinion ends at that point.

I think that a perception of the scope and role of the Fourth Amendment, as elucidated by this Court since On Lee was decided, and full comprehension of the precise issue at stake lead to the conclusion that On Lee can no longer be regarded as sound law. Nor do I think the date we decided Katz v. United States, 389 U. S. 347 (1967), can be deemed controlling both for the reasons discussed in my dissent in Desist v. United States, 394 U. S. 244, 256 (1969), and my separate opinion in Mackey v. United States (and companion cases), ante, p. 675 (the case before us being here on direct review), and because, in my view, it requires no discussion of the holding in Katz, as distinguished from its underlying rationale as to the reach of the Fourth Amendment, to comprehend the constitutional infirmity of On Lee.

I

Before turning to matters of precedent and policy, several preliminary observations should be made. We deal here with the constitutional validity of instantaneous third-party electronic eavesdropping, conducted by federal law enforcement officers, without any prior judicial approval of the technique utilized, but with the consent and cooperation of a participant in the conversation,[1] and where the substance of the matter electronically overheard[2] is related in a federal criminal trial by those who eavesdropped as direct, not merely corroborative, evidence of the guilt of the nonconsenting party. The magnitude of the issue at hand is evidenced not simply by the obvious doctrinal difficulty of weighing such activity in the Fourth Amendment balance, but also, and more importantly, by the prevalence of police utilization of this technique. Professor Westin has documented in careful detail the numerous devices that make technologically feasible the Orwellian Big Brother. Of immediate relevance is his observation that " `participant recording,' in which one participant in a conversation or meeting, either a police officer or a co-operating party, wears a concealed device that records the conversation or broadcasts it to others nearby . . . is used tens of thousands of times each year throughout the country, particularly in cases involving extortion, conspiracy, narcotics, gambling, prostitution, corruption by police officials . . . and similar crimes."[3]

Moreover, as I shall undertake to show later in this opinion, the factors that must be reckoned with in reaching constitutional conclusions respecting the use of electronic eavesdropping as a tool of law enforcement are exceedingly subtle and complex. They have provoked sharp differences of opinion both within and without the judiciary, and the entire problem has been the subject of continuing study by various governmental and nongovernmental bodies.[4]

Finally, given the importance of electronic eavesdropping as a technique for coping with the more deep-seated kinds of criminal activity, and the complexities that are encountered in striking a workable constitutional balance between the public and private interests at stake, I believe that the courts should proceed with specially measured steps in this field. More particularly, I think this Court should not foreclose itself from reconsidering doctrines that would prevent the States from seeking, independently of the niceties of federal restrictions as they may develop, solutions to such vexing problems, see Mapp v. Ohio, 367 U. S. 643 (1961), and Ker v. California, 374 U. S. 23 (1963), and see also Berger v. New York, 388 U. S. 41 (1967); Baldwin v. New York, 399 U. S. 66, 117 (1970) (dissenting opinion); California v. Green, 399 U. S. 149, 172 (1970) (concurring opinion). I also think that in the adjudication of federal cases, the Court should leave ample room for congressional developments.

II

On these premises I move to the problem of third-party "bugging." To begin by tracing carefully the evolution of Fourth Amendment doctrine in post-On Lee decisions has proved useful in several respects. It serves to cast in perspective both the issue involved here and the imperative necessity for reconsidering On Lee afresh. Additionally, a full exposition of the dynamics of the decline of the trespass rationale underlying On Lee strikingly illuminates the deficiencies of the plurality opinion's retroactivity analysis.

A

On Lee involved circumstances virtually identical to those now before us. There, Government agents enlisted the services of Chin Poy, a former friend of Lee, who was suspected of engaging in illegal narcotics traffic. Poy was equipped with a "minifon" transmitting device which enabled outside Government agents to monitor Poy's conversations with Lee. In the privacy of his laundry, Lee made damaging admissions to Poy which were overheard by the agents and later related at trial. Poy did not testify. Mr. Justice Jackson, writing for five Justices, held the testimony admissible. Without reaching the question of whether a conversation could be the subject of a "seizure" for Fourth Amendment purposes, as yet an unanswered if not completely open question,[5] the Court concluded that in the absence of a trespass,[6] no constitutional violation had occurred.[7]

The validity of the trespass rationale was questionable even at the time the decision was rendered. In this respect On Lee rested on common-law notions and looked to a waning era of Fourth Amendment jurisprudence. Three members of the Court refused to join with Justice Jackson, and within 10 years the Court expressly disavowed an approach to Fourth Amendment questions that looked to common-law distinctions. See, e. g., Jones v. United States, 362 U. S. 257 (1960); Silverman v. United States, 365 U. S. 505 (1961); Lanza v. New York, 370 U. S. 139 (1962).

It is, of course, true that the opinion in On Lee drew some support from a brief additional assertion that "eavesdropping on a conversation, with the connivance of one of the parties" raises no Fourth Amendment problem. 343 U. S., at 754. But surely it is a misreading of that opinion to view this unelaborated assertion as a wholly independent ground for decision. At the very least, this rationale needs substantial buttressing if it is to persist in our constitutional jurisprudence after the decisions I discuss below. Indeed, the plurality opinion in the present case, in greatly elaborating the point, tacitly recognizes the analytic inability of this bare hypothesis to support a rule of law so profoundly important to the proper administration of justice. Moreover, if this was the true rationale of On Lee from the outset, it is difficult to see the relevance of Desist to the resolution of the instant case, for Katz surely does not speak directly to the continued viability of that ground for decision. See Katz v. United States, 389 U. S., at 363 n. (WHITE, J., concurring).

By 1963, when we decided Lopez v. United States, 373 U. S. 427, four members of the Court were prepared to pronounce On Lee and Olmstead v. United States, 277 U. S. 438 (1928), dead.[8] The pyre, they reasoned, had been stoked by decisions like Wong Sun v. United States, 371 U. S. 471 (1963), which, on the one hand, expressly brought verbal communication within the sweep of the Fourth Amendment,[9] and, on the other, reinforced our Silverman and Jones decisions which "refused to crowd the Fourth Amendment into the mold of local property law," 373 U. S., at 460 (BRENNAN, J., dissenting).

Although the Court's decision in Lopez is cited by the Government as a reaffirmation of On Lee, it can hardly be thought to have nurtured the questionable rationale of that decision or its much-criticized ancestor, Olmstead. To the discerning lawyer Lopez could only give pause, not comfort. While the majority opinion, of which I was the author, declined to follow the course favored by the dissenting and concurring Justices by sounding the death knell for Olmstead and On Lee, our holding, despite an allusion to the absence of "an unlawful . . . invasion of a constitutionally protected area," 373 U. S., at 438-439, was bottomed on two premises: the corroborative use that was made of the tape recordings, which increased reliability in the factfinding process, and the absence of a "risk" not fairly assumed by petitioner. The tape recording was made by a participant in the conversation and the opinion emphasized this absence of a third-party intrusion, expressly noting that there was no "electronic eavesdropping on a private conversation which government agents could not otherwise have overheard." 373 U. S., at 440.[10] As I point out in Part III of this opinion, it is one thing to subject the average citizen to the risk that participants in a conversation with him will subsequently divulge its contents to another, but quite a different matter to foist upon him the risk that unknown third parties may be simultaneously listening in.

While Lopez cited On Lee without disavowal of its holding, 373 U. S., at 438, it is entirely accurate to say that we did not there reaffirm it.[11] No decision since Lopez gives a breath of life to the reasoning that led to the On Lee and Olmstead results, and it required little clairvoyance to predict the demise of the basic rationale of On Lee and Olmstead foreshadowed by our subsequent opinions in Osborn v. United States, 385 U. S. 323 (1966), and Berger v. New York, 388 U. S. 41 (1967).

Only three years after Lopez, MR. JUSTICE STEWART writing for the Court in

Osborn v. United States, supra, expressly abjured reliance on Lopez and, instead, approved identical conduct based on the "circumstances under which the tape recording was obtained in [that] case," facts that involved "using [a recorder] under the most precise and discriminate circumstances, circumstances which fully met the `requirement of particularity' which the dissenting opinion in Lopez found necessary." Osborn v. United States, 385 U. S., at 327, 329.[12]

Since Osborn our decisions have shown no tolerance for the old dividing lines resting, as they did, on fiction and common-law distinctions without sound policy justification in the realm of values protected by the Fourth Amendment. Thus, in abolishing the "mere evidence rule" we announced that "the principal object of the Fourth Amendment is the protection of privacy rather than property," and once again noted the trend to discard "fictional and procedural barriers rested on property concepts." Warden v. Hayden, 387 U. S. 294, 304 (1967). That same Term the Court demonstrated the new flexibility in Fourth Amendment doctrine when it held that the warrant protections would be applied to administrative searches. Camara v. Municipal Court, 387 U. S. 523 (1967).

Certainly if Osborn, Warden, and Camara did not plainly draw into question the vigor of earlier precedents, Berger v. New York, 388 U. S. 41, did, and expunged any remnants of former doctrine which might have been thought to have survived Osborn and Warden.[13] There, the Court, following a path opened by Mr. Justice Brandeis' dissent in Olmstead, and smoothed in Osborn and Camara, expressed concern about scientific developments that have put within the reach of the Government the private communications of "anyone in almost any given situation," 388 U. S., at 47; it left no doubt that, as a general principle, electronic eavesdropping was an invasion of privacy and that the Fourth Amendment prohibited unsupervised "bugging." Disturbed by the extent of intrusion which "[b]y its very nature . . . is broad in scope," and nothing that "[f]ew threats to liberty exist which are greater than that posed by the use of eavesdropping devices," id., at 63, the Court brought to life the principle of reasonableness adumbrated in Osborn. Mr. Justice Clark, writing for the majority, reiterated the new approach:

"[T]he `indiscriminate use of such [bugging] devices in law enforcement raises grave constitutional questions under the Fourth and Fifth Amendments,' and imposes `a heavier responsibility on this Court in its supervision of the fairness of procedures . . . .' " 388 U. S., at 56, quoting from Osborn v. United States, 385 U. S. 323, 329 n. 7.

Nor did the Court waver in resolve in the face of respondent's dire prediction that "neither a warrant nor a statute authorizing eavesdropping can be drawn so as to meet the Fourth Amendment's requirements."[14] It was said that "[i]f that be true then the `fruits' of eavesdropping devices are barred under the Amendment." 388 U. S., at 63.[15]

If Berger did not flatly sound a dirge for Olmstead, it articulated principles that led MR. JUSTICE DOUGLAS, by way of concurrence, to comment on its quiet burial. 388 U. S., at 64. While it was left to Katz to perform the last rites, that decision inevitably followed from Osborn and Berger. The Berger majority's affirmative citation of On Lee for the principle that "under specific conditions and circumstances" eavesdropping may be lawful, 388 U. S., at 63, serves only to underscore the emerging operative assumptions: that the particular circumstances of each case will be scrutinized to the end of ascertaining the reasonableness of the search, and that will depend in large measure on whether prior judicial authorization, based on a particularized showing, has been obtained. Katz v. United States, supra.

Viewed in perspective, then, Katz added no new dimension to the law. At most it was a formal dispatch of Olmstead and the notion that such problems may usefully be resolved in the light of trespass doctrine, and, of course, it freed from speculation what was already evident, that On Lee was completely open to question.

B

But the decisions of this Court since On Lee do more than demonstrate that the doctrine of that case is wholly open for reconsideration, and has been since well before Katz was decided. They also establish sound general principles for application of the Fourth Amendment that were either dimly perceived or not fully worked out at the time of On Lee. I have already traced some of these principles in Part II-A, supra: that verbal communication is protected by the Fourth Amendment, that the reasonableness of a search does not depend on the presence or absence of a trespass, and that the Fourth Amendment is principally concerned with protecting interests of privacy, rather than property rights.

Especially when other recent Fourth Amendment decisions, not otherwise so immediately relevant, are read with those already discussed, the primacy of an additional general principle becomes equally evident: official investigatory action that impinges on privacy must typically, in order to be constitutionally permissible, be subjected to the warrant requirement. Particularly significant in this regard are Camara v. Municipal Court, 387 U. S. 523 (1967); Terry v. Ohio, 392 U. S. 1 (1968), and Chimel v. California, 395 U. S. 752 (1969).

In Camara the Court brought under the Fourth Amendment administrative searches that had once been thought to be without its sweep. In doing so the opinion emphasized the desirability of establishing in advance those circumstances that justified the intrusion into a home and submitting them for review to an independent assessor,[16] principles that this Court has always deemed to be at the core of Fourth Amendment protections.[17]

In bringing such searches within the ambit of the warrant requirement, Camara rejected the notion that the "less hostile" nature of the search relegated this invasion of privacy to the "periphery" of Fourth Amendment concerns. 387 U. S., at 530. The central consideration was, the Court concluded, that these administrative actions, no less than the typical search, involved government officials in an invasion of privacy, and that it was against the possible arbitrariness of invasion that the Fourth Amendment with its warrant machinery was meant to guard. Berger and Katz built, as noted earlier, on Osborn v. United States, supra, and Camara, and gave further expression to the principle.[18] It was not enough that government agents acted with restraint, for reasonableness must in the first instance be judged in a detached realm.[19]

The scope and meaning of the rule have emerged with even greater clarity by virtue of our holdings setting the boundaries for the exceptions. Recently, in Chimel v. California, 395 U. S. 752 (1969), we reiterated the importance of the prior independent determination of a neutral magistrate and underscored its centrality to the reasonableness requirement of the Fourth Amendment, and abandoned the holdings of Harris v. United States, 331 U. S. 145 (1947), and United States v. Rabinowitz, 339 U. S. 56 (1950). We were concerned by the breadth of searches occasioned by the Rabinowitz rule which frequently proved to be an invitation to a hunting expedition. Searches incident to arrest, we held, must be confined to a locus no greater than necessary to prevent injury to the arresting officer or destruction of evidence. 395 U. S., at 763, 767; cf. Terry v. Ohio, 392 U. S. 1 (1968).

To complete the tapestry, the strands of doctrine reflected in the search cases must be interwoven with the Court's other contemporary holdings. Most significant are Terry v. Ohio, supra, and Davis v. Mississippi, 394 U. S. 721 (1969), which were also harbingers of the new thrust in Fourth Amendment doctrine. There the Court rejected the contention that only an arrest triggered the "incident-to-arrest" exception to the warrant requirement of the Fourth Amendment, and held that any restraint of the person, however brief and however labeled, was subject to a reasonableness examination. 392 U. S., at 19. The controlling principle is "to recognize that the Fourth Amendment governs all intrusions by agents of the public upon personal security, and to make the scope of the particular intrusion, in light of all the exigencies of the case, a central element in the analysis of reasonableness." 392 U. S., at 18 n. 15. See also Davis v. Mississippi, 394 U. S., at 727.[20]

III

A

That the foundations of On Lee have been destroyed does not, of course, mean that its result can no longer stand. Indeed, the plurality opinion today fastens upon our decisions in Lopez, Lewis v. United States, 385 U. S. 206 (1966), and Hoffa v. United States, 385 U. S. 293 (1966), to resist the undercurrents of more recent cases emphasizing the warrant procedure as a safeguard to privacy. But this category provides insufficient support. In each of these cases the risk the general populace faced was different from that surfaced by the instant case. No surreptitious third ear was present, and in each opinion that fact was carefully noted.

In Lewis, a federal agent posing as a potential purchaser of narcotics gained access to petitioner's home and there consummated an illegal sale, the fruits of which were admitted at trial along with the testimony of the agent. Chief Justice Warren, writing for the majority, expressly distinguished the third-party overhearing involved, by way of example, in a case like Silverman v. United States, supra, noting that "there, the conduct proscribed was that of eavesdroppers, unknown and unwanted intruders who furtively listened to conversations occurring in the privacy of a house." 385 U. S., at 212. Similarly in Hoffa, MR. JUSTICE STEWART took care to mention that "surreptitious" monitoring was not there before the Court, and so too in Lopez, supra.

The plurality opinion seeks to erase the crucial distinction between the facts before us and these holdings by the following reasoning: if A can relay verbally what is revealed to him by B (as in Lewis and Hoffa), or record and later divulge it (as in Lopez), what difference does it make if A conspires with another to betray B by contemporaneously transmitting to the other all that is said? The contention is, in essence, an argument that the distinction between third-party monitoring and other undercover techniques is one of form and not substance. The force of the contention depends on the evaluation of two separable but intertwined assumptions: first, that there is no greater invasion of privacy in the third-party situation, and, second, that uncontrolled consensual surveillance in an electronic age is a tolerable technique of law enforcement, given the values and goals of our political system.[21]

The first of these assumptions takes as a point of departure the so-called "risk analysis" approach of Lewis, and Lopez, and to a lesser extent On Lee, or the expectations approach of Katz. See discussion in Part II, supra. While these formulations represent an advance over the unsophisticated trespass analysis of the common law, they too have their limitations and can, ultimately, lead to the substitution of words for analysis.[22] The analysis must, in my view, transcend the search for subjective expectations or legal attribution of assumptions of risk. Our expectations, and the risks we assume, are in large part reflections of laws that translate into rules the customs and values of the past and present.

Since it is the task of the law to form and project, as well as mirror and reflect, we should not, as judges, merely recite the expectations and risks without examining the desirability of saddling them upon society. The critical question, therefore, is whether under our system of government, as reflected in the Constitution, we should impose on our citizens the risks of the electronic listener or observer without at least the protection of a warrant requirement.

This question must, in my view, be answered by assessing the nature of a particular practice and the likely extent of its impact on the individual's sense of security balanced against the utility of the conduct as a technique of law enforcement. For those more extensive intrusions that significantly jeopardize the sense of security which is the paramount concern of Fourth Amendment liberties, I am of the view that more than self-restraint by law enforcement officials is required and at the least warrants should be necessary. Cf. Terry v. Ohio, supra; Davis v. Mississippi, supra.

B

The impact of the practice of third-party bugging, must, I think, be considered such as to undermine that confidence and sense of security in dealing with one another that is characteristic of individual relationships between citizens in a free society. It goes beyond the impact on privacy occasioned by the ordinary type of "informer" investigation upheld in Lewis and Hoffa. The argument of the plurality opinion, to the effect that it is irrelevant whether secrets are revealed by the mere tattletale or the transistor, ignores the differences occasioned by third-party monitoring and recording which insures full and accurate disclosure of all that is said, free of the possibility of error and oversight that inheres in human reporting.

Authority is hardly required to support the proposition that words would be measured a good deal more carefully and communication inhibited if one suspected his conversations were being transmitted and transcribed. Were third-party bugging a prevalent practice, it might well smother that spontaneity—reflected in frivolous, impetuous, sacrilegious, and defiant discourse—that liberates daily life.[23] Much off-hand exchange is easily forgotten and one may count on the obscurity of his remarks, protected by the very fact of a limited audience, and the likelihood that the listener will either overlook or forget what is said, as well as the listener's inability to reformulate a conversation without having to contend with a documented record.[24] All these values are sacrificed by a rule of law that permits official monitoring of private discourse limited only by the need to locate a willing assistant.

It matters little that consensual transmittals are less obnoxious than wholly clandestine eavesdrops. This was put forward as justification for the conduct in Boyd v. United States, 116 U. S. 616 (1886), where the Government relied on mitigating aspects of the conduct in question. The Court, speaking through Mr. Justice Bradley, declined to countenance literalism:

"Though the proceeding in question is divested of many of the aggravating incidents of actual search and seizure, yet, as before said, it contains their substance and essence, and effects their substantial purpose. It may be that it is the obnoxious thing in its mildest and least repulsive form; but illegitimate and unconstitutional practices get their first footing in that way, namely, by silent approaches and slight deviations from legal modes of procedure." 116 U. S., at 635.

Finally, it is too easy to forget—and, hence, too often forgotten—that the issue here is whether to interpose a search warrant procedure between law enforcement agencies engaging in electronic eavesdropping and the public generally. By casting its "risk analysis" solely in terms of the expectations and risks that "wrongdoers" or "one contemplating illegal activities" ought to bear, the plurality opinion, I think, misses the mark entirely. On Lee does not simply mandate that criminals must daily run the risk of unknown eavesdroppers prying into their private affairs; it subjects each and every law-abiding member of society to that risk. The very purpose of interposing the Fourth Amendment warrant requirement is to redistribute the privacy risks throughout society in a way that produces the results the plurality opinion ascribes to the On Lee rule. Abolition of On Lee would not end electronic eavesdropping. It would prevent public officials from engaging in that practice unless they first had probable cause to suspect an individual of involvement in illegal activities and had tested their version of the facts before a detached judicial officer. The interest On Lee fails to protect is the expectation of the ordinary citizen, who has never engaged in illegal conduct in his life, that he may carry on his private discourse freely, openly, and spontaneously without measuring his every word against the connotations it might carry when instantaneously heard by others unknown to him and unfamiliar with his situation or analyzed in a cold, formal record played days, months, or years after the conversation. Interposition of a warrant requirement is designed not to shield "wrongdoers," but to secure a measure of privacy and a sense of personal security throughout our society.

The Fourth Amendment does, of course, leave room for the employment of modern technology in criminal law enforcement, but in the stream of current developments in Fourth Amendment law I think it must be held that third-party electronic monitoring, subject only to the self-restraint of law enforcement officials, has no place in our society.

IV

I reach these conclusions notwithstanding seemingly contrary views espoused by both Congress and an American Bar Association study group.[25] Both the ABA study and Title III of the Omnibus Crime Control and Safe Streets Act of 1968, 82 Stat. 212, 18 U. S. C. § 2510 et seq. (1964 ed., Supp. V), appear to reflect little more than this Court's prior decisions. Indeed, the comprehensive provisions of Title III are evidence of the extent of congressional concern with the impact of electronic surveillance on the right to privacy. This concern is further manifested in the introductory section of the Senate Committee Report.[26] Although § 2511 (2) (c) exempts consensual and participant monitoring by law enforcement agents from the general prohibitions against surveillance without prior judicial authorization and makes the fruits admissible in court, see § 2515, congressional malaise with such conduct is evidenced by the contrastingly limited endorsement of consensual surveillance carried out by private individuals.[27] While individual Congressmen expressed concern about and criticized the provisions for unsupervised consensual electronic surveillance contained in § 2511,[28] the Senate Committee Report comment, to the effect that "[i]t [§ 2511 (2) (c)] largely reflects existing law," S. Rep. No. 1097, 90th Cong., 2d Sess., 93-94 (1968), followed by citations to On Lee and Lopez,[29] strongly suggests that the provisions represent not intractable approval of these practices, but rather an intention to adopt these holdings and to leave to the courts the task of determining their viability in light of later holdings such as Berger, Osborn, and Katz.[30]

I find in neither the ABA study nor Title III any justification for ignoring the identifiable difference— albeit an elusive one in the present state of knowledge— between the impact on privacy of single-party informer bugging and third-party bugging, which in my opinion justifies drawing the constitutional line at this juncture between the two as regards the necessity for obtaining a warrant. Recognition of this difference is, at the very least, necessary to preserve the openness which is at the core of our traditions and is secure only in a society that tolerates official invasion of privacy simply in circumscribed situations.

The Fourth Amendment protects these traditions, and places limitations on the means and circumstances by which the Government may collect information about its citizens by intruding into their personal lives. The spirit of the principle is captured by the oft-quoted language of Boyd v. United States, 116 U. S., at 630:

"The principles laid down in this opinion [speaking of Entick v. Carrington, 19 How. St. Tr. 1029 (1765)] affect the very essence of constitutional liberty and security. They reach farther than the concrete form of the case then before the court, with its adventitious circumstances; they apply to all invasions on the part of the government and its employes of the sanctity of a man's home and the privacies of life. It is not the breaking of his doors, and the rummaging of his drawers, that constitutes the essence of the offence; but it is the invasion of his indefeasible right of personal security . . . ."

What this means is that the burden of guarding privacy in a free society should not be on its citizens; it is the Government that must justify its need to electronically eavesdrop.

V

Not content to rest upon the proposition that On Lee remains sound law, the plurality opinion would also hold that the Court of Appeals erred further in disposing "of this case based on its understanding of the principles announced in the Katz case," ante, at 754, because Desist v. United States, 394 U. S. 244 (1969), held that Katz governed only governmental conduct occurring after the decision in Katz. It is difficult to know where to begin to analyze such a truly extraordinary assertion respecting the operation of the judicial process.

Because this case is here on direct review, even were the issues squarely controlled by Katz, I would unhesitatingly apply here the rule there adopted, for the reasons first expressed in my dissent in Desist, 394 U. S., at 256, and elaborated in my separate opinion in Mackey v. United States (and companion cases), ante, p. 675. I see no purpose in repeating at this point the analysis I set forth in those opinions. Suffice it to say that, in Desist, I went to some length to point out, by discussing a hypothetical proposition, that the failure to apply any new decision by this Court to cases which had not yet run their course on direct review was inconsistent with the case-by-case approach to constitutional decision and with the proper relationship of this Court to the lower federal courts. In particular, I noted that the logic of Desist suggested that it would constitute error for a lower federal court to adopt a new constitutional rule which this Court subsequently approved. 394 U. S., at 259. Today's opinion stands as eloquent evidence of that defect.

Indeed, I find this decision even more troubling than Desist. For the errors of Desist are not merely repeated here; they are plainly compounded. Upon the plurality opinion's own analysis of the instant case, it is clear that Katz has no direct relevance to the present viability of On Lee. "Katz involved no revelation to the Government by a party to conversations with the defendant nor did the Court indicate in any way that a defendant has a justifiable and constitutionally protected expectation that a person with whom he is conversing will not then or later reveal the conversation to the police." Ante, at 749. As I have already shown, one need not cite Katz to demonstrate the inability of On Lee to survive recent developments without at least substantial reformulation. To hold, then, that a mere citation of Katz, or drawing upon the philosophical underpinnings of that case in order to employ a general constitutional approach in tune with that of the decisions of this Court, conflicts with the holding of Desist is to let this obsession with prospectivity run riot.

Apparently Desist is now to be understood as holding that all lower federal courts are disabled from adjudicating on their merits all allegations of Fourth Amendment error not squarely supported by a prior decision of this Court. If so, one wonders what purpose is served by providing intermediate appellate review of constitutional issues in the federal criminal process. We must not forget that this Court is not the only tribunal in the entire federal system charged with a responsibility for the nurture and development of the Fourth Amendment. It is one thing to disable all federal courts, including this Court, from applying the settled law of the land to cases and controversies before them—as Desist does with Katz—and at least another giant step backward to preclude lower courts from resolving wholly disparate controversies in the light of constitutional principles. Can it be seriously contended, as the plurality opinion necessarily implies, that the Court of Appeals should not be reversed today on these alternative grounds had it simply omitted to discuss Katz? To force lower federal courts to adjudicate controversies either mechanistically or disingenuously is for me indefensible. Yet this is precisely what the plurality opinion does with its assertion that it is error for lower courts to "dispose" of a case based on their "understanding of the principles announced" in Katz for the next year or so.

I would hold that On Lee is no longer good law and affirm the judgment below.

Justice Harlan's dissenting as to jurisdiction in US v. Vuitch (April 21, 1971)

MR. JUSTICE HARLAN, with whom MR. JUSTICE BRENNAN, MR. JUSTICE MARSHALL, and MR. JUSTICE BLACKMUN join, dissenting as to jurisdiction.

Appellee Vuitch was indicted in the United States District Court for the District of Columbia for violations of D. C. Code Ann. § 22-201 (1967), the District of Columbia abortion statute. This statute is applicable only within the District of Columbia. On pretrial motion by Vuitch, the indictments were dismissed on the ground that the abortion statute was unconstitutionally vague. The United States appealed directly to this Court under the terms of the Criminal Appeals Act of 1907, 18 U. S. C. § 3731, relying on the provision allowing direct appeal "[f]rom a decision or judgment setting aside, or dismissing any indictment or information, or any count thereof, where such decision or judgment is based upon the invalidity or construction of the statute upon which the indictment or information is founded."[1] It is not contested that, but for this provision of the Criminal Appeals Act, the Government would have a right of appeal to the Court of Appeals for the District of Columbia Circuit under D. C. Code Ann. § 23-105 (Supp. 1970), which provides:

"In all criminal prosecutions the United States or the District of Columbia, as the case may be, shall have the same right of appeal that is given to the defendant, including the right to a bill of exceptions: Provided, That if on such appeal it shall be found that there was error in the rulings of the court during a trial, a verdict in favor of the defendant shall not be set aside."

The Court today—relying on the generic reference to "statutes" and "all criminal cases" in the text of 18 U. S. C. § 3731 and the absence of an express exclusion of statutes applicable only within the District of Columbia —concludes that 18 U. S. C. § 3731 rather than D. C. Code Ann. § 23-105 provides the proper appellate route for this case. I must disagree.

I

The historical development of the Government's right to appeal in criminal cases both in the District of Columbia and throughout the Nation is surveyed in Carroll v. United States, 354 U. S. 394 (1957). Section 23-105 of the D. C. Code was passed in 1901 as § 935 of the Code of 1901. 31 Stat. 1341. Prior to the Criminal Appeals Act of 1907, the Government had no right of appeal in criminal cases outside of the District of Columbia. To remedy this situation, a bill was introduced in the House of Representatives. That bill practically tracked the language of the D. C. statute, and made no provision for direct appeal to this Court. 40 Cong. Rec. 5408. The accompanying House Report described the bill as follows: "The accompanying bill will extend [§ 935] of the code of the District of Columbia to all districts in the United States." H. R. Rep. No. 2119, 59th Cong., 1st Sess., 2 (1906). That bill passed the House, but the Senate Committee on the Judiciary rejected the House approach of simply extending the provisions of the D. C. appeals statute to the rest of the Nation; the Senate Committee instead substituted a more narrowly drawn measure which enumerated specific substantive categories of criminal cases to be appealable by the Government and allocated jurisdiction over these appeals between the Supreme Court and the then Circuit Courts of Appeals according to the allocation of appellate jurisdiction for civil cases established in the Circuit Court of Appeals Act of 1891. S. Rep. No. 3922, 59th Cong., 1st Sess. (1906). See Carroll v. United States, supra, at 402 n. 11. Even that bill as narrowed could not pass the Senate; it provoked extended debate in which the opponents of the measure focused on the potential for abuse of individual rights arising from repeated court proceedings, delays in appeals, and restraints on personal freedom while the Government prosecuted its appeal. See generally United States v. Sisson, 399 U. S. 267 (1970). The upshot of these debates was that Senator Nelson, the bill's floor manager in the Senate, agreed to accept a variety of amendments which further narrowed the categories of cases appealable by the Government and made special provision for the defendant's release on his own recognizance. See 41 Cong. Rec. 2818-2825.[2]

It is at this point that Senator Clarke of Arkansas offered an amendment limiting the Government's right to appeal decisions dismissing indictments or arresting judgments for insufficiency of the indictment to instances where the decision was based upon "the invalidity or construction of the statute." The purpose of that amendment was described by Senator Clarke as follows:

"Mr. President, the object of the amendment is to limit the right of appeal upon the part of the General Government to the validity or constitutionality of the statute in which the prosecution is proceeding. It has been enlarged by the addition of another clause, which gives the right of appeal where the construction by the trial court is such as to decide that there is no offense committed, notwithstanding the validity of the statute, and in other respects the proceeding may remain intact. I think that is a broad enough right to concede to the General Government in the prosecution of persons in the court.

.....

"In view of the defects that recent years have disclosed, I do not believe it to be sound policy to go beyond the necessities as they have developed defects in our procedure. A case recently occurring has drawn attention to the fact that if a circuit judge or a district judge holding the circuit should determine that a statute of Congress was invalid, the United States is without means of having that matter submitted to a tribunal that under the Constitution has power to settle that question. I do not believe the remedy ought to be any wider than the mischief that has been disclosed. I do not believe that any additional advantages ought to be given to the General Government in the prosecution of persons arraigned in court, but I do believe the paragraph ought to be perfected in that behalf, so as to provide that there shall be an appeal to the court having authority to give uniformity to the practice which shall prevail in all the courts of the United States, and that they shall be ready to say, and say promptly, what the statute means and whether or not it is a valid statute.

.....

"So I think this amendment gives expression to the proposition that the remedy we provide here now should be no wider than the defect that has been disclosed in the preceding criminal procedure; and that is that whenever the validity of a statute has been adversely decided by a trial court, wherever its unconstitutionality has been pronounced by a trial court, the Government ought to have the right to promptly submit that to the tribunal having authority to dispose of such questions in order that there may be a uniform enforcement of the law throughout the entire limits of the United States.

"This is the purpose I have, Mr. President, and having discussed it with the distinguished Senator from Wisconsin . . . and the distinguished Senator from Minnesota [Mr. NELSON], we agreed that that would probably meet the defect." 41 Cong. Rec. 2819-2820.

See generally 41 Cong. Rec. 2819-2822.

The bill as thus amended passed the Senate; the House disagreed to the Senate amendment, but yielded in conference. The bill in conference was amended to provide for direct appeals to the Supreme Court. See H. R. Conf. Rep. No. 8113, 59th Cong., 2d Sess. (1907). No explanation was given in the conference report for the exclusive direct appeal route.

I draw from these legislative materials the following relevant propositions: (1) The Congress was definitely advertent to the existence of a Governmental appeal right in criminal cases within the District; (2) the Congress explicitly rejected the simple approach of extending the D. C. provision to the Nation; (3) the particular provision of the Act relied on by the Government as supporting its direct appeal in this case was amended with a view to limiting its reach to a relatively precise defect, i. e., the debilitating effect on the enforcement of criminal laws arising from conflicting judicial interpretations; and (4) the substitution of an exclusive direct appeal to this Court, while not expressly explained, is perfectly compatible with the goal of promptly achieving uniformity in construction of statutes applicable nationwide, while at the same time being wholly unnecessary to the resolution of conflicting district court constructions of local D. C. statutes, given the existence of a right of appeal to the Court of Appeals for the District of Columbia Circuit.

II

The question of overlap between the appellate routes available to the Government in criminal cases under the D. C. Code and 18 U. S. C. § 3731 was first dealt with by this Court in United States v. Burroughs, 289 U. S. 159 (1933). In Burroughs the defendants were indicted in the then Supreme Court of the District of Columbia for violation of the Federal Corrupt Practices Act, a statute of nationwide applicability. They successfully demurred on two grounds: one involving the construction of the statute, and the other involving the sufficiency of the indictment as a pleading. The Government took an appeal to the Court of Appeals for the District of Columbia under the D. C. appeals statute. The appellate court certified to this Court the question whether it had jurisdiction over an appeal where a § 3731-type challenge was joined with a challenge to the sufficiency of the indictment as a pleading. The Court disposed of the question by holding that the Criminal Appeals Act is inapplicable to any criminal case appealable under the provisions of the D. C. Code:

"The Criminal Appeals Act, in naming the courts from which appeals may be taken to this court, employs the phrase `district courts'; not `courts of the United States,' or `courts exercising the same jurisdiction as district courts.' We need not, however, determine whether the statute should be construed to embrace criminal cases tried in the Supreme Court of the District if § 935 of the District Code were not in effect. That section deals comprehensively with appeals in criminal cases from all of the courts of first instance of the District and confers on the Court of Appeals jurisdiction of appeals by the Government seeking review of the judgments of those courts. The Criminal Appeals Act, on the other hand, affects only certain specified classes of decisions in district courts, contains no repealing clause, and no reference to the courts of the District of Columbia or the territorial courts, upon many of which jurisdiction is conferred by language quite similar to that of the Code of Law of the District. We cannot construe it as impliedly repealing the complete appellate system created for the District of Columbia by § 935 of the Code, in the absence of expression on the part of Congress indicating that purpose. Implied repeals are not favored; and if effect can reasonably be given to both statutes, the presumption is that the earlier is intended to remain in force. . . ." 289 U. S., at 163-164.[3] (Emphasis added.)

The holding in Burroughs established a complete separation of the two statutory schemes for Government appeals in criminal cases; the essence of the Court's rationale was a presumption against implied repeals.

In 1942, Congress amended the Criminal Appeals Act to provide for Government appeals to the Courts of Appeals from all decisions dismissing indictments or arresting judgments of convictions except where a right of direct appeal to this Court exists. 56 Stat. 271. The new amendment expressly included the United States Court of Appeals for the District of Columbia Circuit as one of the intermediate appellate tribunals to which the Government could appeal;[4] in addition, the Act added a new provision to the Judicial Code establishing appellate jurisdiction in the then circuit courts of appeals "in criminal cases on appeals taken by the United States in cases where such appeals are permitted by law." 56 Stat. 272. The latter provision also expressly incorporated the United States Court of Appeals for the District of Columbia Circuit.[5] Ibid.

The legislative history of the 1942 amendment offers no explication of congressional intent in including the D. C. courts within the Act.[6] It is certain that this amendment generates some form of overlap between the two statutory schemes for Governmental appeals in criminal cases. In Carroll v. United States, 354 U. S. 394, 411 (1957), the Court recognized the new situation created by the 1942 amendment:

"It may be concluded, then, that even today criminal appeals by the Government in the District of Columbia are not limited to the categories set forth in 18 U. S. C. § 3731, although as to cases of the type covered by that special jurisdictional statute, its explicit directions will prevail over the general terms of [the D. C. statute] . . . ."

That, however, leaves open the question which cases come within the categories set forth in 18 U. S. C. § 3731.

III

After this Court's holding in Burroughs, it was clear that if Congress wished to effectuate any displacement of the pre-1907 route for Government appeals of criminal cases within the District of Columbia, some express manifestation of its intent was required. The 1942 amendment followed the Burroughs decision. Since Congress then acted to create some overlap between the two statutes without further limiting the categories of directly appealable criminal cases, it may be argued that we should presume Congress intended, as of 1942, to embrace within the very special appeals procedures of 18 U. S. C. § 3731 criminal cases based upon statutes applicable only within the District.

But that presumption from a completely silent legislative record flies in the face of the principle that statutes creating a right of direct appeal to this Court should be narrowly construed. Cf. Swift & Co. v. Wickham, 382 U. S. 111, 128-129 (1965); Florida Lime Growers v. Jacobsen, 362 U. S. 73, 92-93 (1960) (Frankfurter, J., dissenting). And, in light of the legislative history of the 1907 Act and this Court's explicit holding in Burroughs that the 1907 Act had no impact on cases appealable under the D. C. provision, it is especially inappropriate to rely on the absence of any further limiting language in the 1942 amendment as a justification for reading the term "statute" as encompassing criminal prosecutions in the District based on local as well as nationwide statutes.

The legislative history of the 1907 Act suggests a perfectly plausible reason for interpreting the language "based upon the invalidity or construction of the statute" as excluding D. C. statutes: that language was put in the Act by Senator Clarke with the express intention of limiting the Act's goal to remedying the precise defect of inconsistent enforcement of criminal statutes arising from the lack of a Government appeal. The Court of Appeals for the District of Columbia Circuit constitutes a perfectly adequate appellate tribunal for resolving conflicting interpretations given local statutes by judges within the District of Columbia.[7] Where, however, the Government brings a prosecution in the District of Columbia based on a statute of nationwide applicability, the Court of Appeals for the District of Columbia Circuit cannot achieve uniformity in the enforcement of the statute.

As an original proposition, then, a construction of the relevant provisions of the 1907 Act as excluding criminal cases in the District brought under local statutes but including cases brought under nationwide statutes would have been consistent both with the express purpose of Senator Clarke's amendment and the canon of strict construction as applied to direct appeals statutes.[8] But the Court in Burroughs took the position that Congress could not displace the pre-existing appellate route to any extent without indicating an express intent to do so; Burroughs, significantly, involved a prosecution under a statute of nationwide applicability. Subsequently, Congress did expressly indicate an intent to displace the alternative appellate route available within the District. The extent of that displacement, I think, should now be measured by the express goal of the relevant provision of the 1907 Act, as limited by Senator Clarke: avoidance of inconsistent enforcement of criminal laws. That theory of legislative purpose—combined with the Burroughs holding that Congress should be required to affirmatively indicate an intent to displace the prior appellate route— yields an interpretation of the 1907 Act as amended in 1942 which is consistent with the canon of strict construction generally applied to direct appeals statutes.[9]

IV

I have little doubt that, had the Criminal Appeals Act not been recently amended to dispense with direct appeals to this Court, see n. 1, supra, the interpretation of the Act I have suggested would be adopted by the Court. This Court has never taken jurisdiction over a direct appeal from a dismissal of a prosecution brought in the District of Columbia for violation of a statute applicable within the District. It is worth noting that, given the Court's adherence to the principles of Carroll v. United States, supra, the rather absurd waste of our judicial resources on cases such as United States v. Waters, 175 F. 2d 340, appeal dismissed on motion of the United States, 335 U. S. 869 (1948), and United States v. Sweet, 399 U. S. 517 (1970), see n. 8, supra, could not even be avoided by the exercise of governmental discretion in choosing appellate routes. In light of Carroll, I cannot believe that a perfectly acceptable reading of congressional purpose underpinning the definition of categories of cases directly appealable under 18 U. S. C. § 3731 which excludes statutes applicable only within the District of Columbia would have been turned down by the Court.

Of course, the recent elimination of the direct appeal route removes a great deal of the incentive to continue the stringent standards of construction with respect to this statute that have traditionally prevailed in this Court. Indeed, at this stage of the game, the canon of strict construction produces the ironic result of compelling a relatively greater expenditure of judicial energies in assessing our jurisdiction over the remainder of the criminal cases pending in the district courts of the Nation at the time of the most recent amendment than would be involved in deciding those cases on the merits. Nonetheless, this very Term we have indicated that we intend to adhere to the rules of construction evolved by this Court during the long and tortuous history of this statute. United States v. Weller, 401 U. S. 254 (1971).

The only response we are offered to the reading of congressional purpose I have suggested is that the interests of avoiding inconsistent enforcement of criminal laws argues for exercising jurisdiction over this case because similar statutes in other jurisdictions are under attack on vagueness grounds. See the Court's opinion, at 65-66. Surely those of my Brethren who subscribe to the views on jurisdiction expressed in the opinion of the Court must recognize that we cannot limit the category of appealable cases under this provision of the Act to prosecutions brought under D. C. statutes which are (a) duplicated in other jurisdictions, and (b) under attack on similar federal question grounds in other jurisdictions. The proffered response is, therefore, not truly a reason for concluding we have jurisdiction over the relevant category of cases; rather, it is a reason for exercising our power in this one case to settle Dr. Vuitch's vagueness claim in spite of the absence of the jurisdictional prerequisites which legitimize the exercise of that judicial power.

V

Having concluded that the Government cannot directly appeal the dismissal of the indictments to this Court under the provisions of 18 U. S. C. § 3731, it also follows that we cannot utilize the remand provisions of that statute to reroute the appeal to the Court of Appeals for the District of Columbia Circuit. However, we do have jurisdiction to determine our jurisdiction, and, in the analogous three-judge court situation where an alternative appellate route exists but the statute according this Court direct jurisdiction over the certain appeals includes no remand procedure, this Court has vacated the judgment of the court of original jurisdiction and remanded the case to that court for the entry of a fresh decree from which timely appeal may be taken to the proper appellate tribunal. Rockefeller v. Catholic Medical Center of Brooklyn & Queens, 397 U. S. 820 (1970). The instant case, of course, is a criminal prosecution, and there is a consideration not present in the three-judge court situation: i. e., the additional anxiety caused the defendant by virtue of the Government's erroneous choice of appellate routes. But, while 18 U. S. C. § 3731 cannot empower us to transfer the case, that statute is still relevant as an expression of congressional policy to save the Government's appeal where an erroneous choice of appellate routes is made, even at the expense of additional anxiety to the defendant. Accordingly, I think the proper disposition of this case would be to vacate the judgment of the District Court and remand the case for the entry of a fresh judgment from which the Government could take a timely appeal to the Court of Appeals for the District of Columbia Circuit pursuant to D. C. Code Ann. § 23-105.

VI

Notwithstanding the views on jurisdiction expressed above, and speaking only for myself, and not for those of my Brethren who agree with my discussion of the jurisdictional issue in this case, I have concluded, substantially for the reasons set forth in MR. JUSTICE BLACKMUN'S separate opinion, that I should also reach the merits. Accordingly, I concur in Part II of the Court's opinion and the judgment of the Court.

Notes

[1] The text of 18 U. S. C. § 3731 was as follows:

"An appeal may be taken by and on behalf of the United States from the district courts direct to the Supreme Court of the United States in all criminal cases in the following instances:

"From a decision or judgment setting aside, or dismissing any indictment or information, or any count thereof, where such decision or judgment is based upon the invalidity or construction of the statute upon which the indictment or information is founded.

"From a decision arresting a judgment of conviction for insufficiency of the indictment or information, where such decision is based upon the invalidity or construction of the statute upon which the indictment or information is founded.

"From the decision or judgment sustaining a motion in bar, when the defendant has not been put in jeopardy.

"An appeal may be taken by and on behalf of the United States from the district courts to a court of appeals in all criminal cases, in the following instances:

"From a decision or judgment setting aside, or dismissing any indictment or information, or any count thereof except where a direct appeal to the Supreme Court of the United States is provided by this section.

"From a decision arresting a judgment of conviction except where a direct appeal to the Supreme Court of the United States is provided by this section.

"The appeal in all such cases shall be taken within thirty days after the decision or judgment has been rendered and shall be diligently prosecuted.

"Pending the prosecution and determination of the appeal in the foregoing instances, the defendant shall be admitted to bail on his own recognizance.

"If an appeal shall be taken, pursuant to this section, to the Supreme Court of the United States which, in the opinion of that Court, should have been taken to a court of appeals, the Supreme Court shall remand the case to the court of appeals, which shall then have jurisdiction to hear and determine the same as if the appeal had been taken to that court in the first instance.

"If an appeal shall be taken pursuant to this section to any court of appeals which, in the opinion of such court, should have been taken directly to the Supreme Court of the United States, such court shall certify the case to the Supreme Court of the United States, which shall thereupon have jurisdiction to hear and determine the case to the same extent as if an appeal had been taken directly to that Court."

As noted in United States v. Weller, 401 U. S. 254 (1971), these provisions were amended by § 14 (a) of the Omnibus Crime Control Act of 1970, 84 Stat. 1890. But cases begun in the District Court before the new statute took effect are not affected. See United States v. Weller, supra, at 255 n. 1.

[2] The bill had been amended earlier to require the Government to take an appeal within 30 days. 41 Cong. Rec. 2193-2194.

[3] The Court's opinion characterizes Burroughs as having "held only that the term `district court' in the Criminal Appeals Act did not include the then-existing Supreme Court of the District of Columbia." Ante, at 65. As I read the italicized portion of the above-quoted passage, that is the precise question that the Burroughs Court concluded it did not have to decide, in light of its holding that the Criminal Appeals Act could not, by implication, effect the repeal of § 935 of the District Code.

[4] These explicit references were subsequently omitted by amendment in 1949, 63 Stat. 97, which altered the language of the statute to conform to the changed nomenclature of the federal courts.

[5] This last provision was an amendment to 28 U. S. C. § 225 (1940 ed.); see 56 Stat. 272 and Carroll v. United States, supra, at 398 n. 5.

[6] The focus was on the decision to accord the Government a right of appeal to the courts of appeals where no direct appeal to this Court lay. See H. R. Rep. No. 45, 77th Cong., 1st Sess. (1941); S. Rep. No. 868, 77th Cong., 1st Sess. (1941).

[7] The Government suggests a construction of the Criminal Appeals Act excluding D. C. statutes would require the Court to exclude other criminal statutes of only limited territorial application, e. g., 18 U. S. C. §§ 1111-1112 (punishing homicide "[w]ithin the special maritime and territorial jurisdiction of the United States"); 18 U. S. C. §§ 1151-1165 (regulating offenses within Indian territory). See Brief for the United States 15-16. But I would not construe 18 U. S. C. § 3731 as excluding D. C. criminal cases punishable under D. C. statutes because they are of limited territorial application; rather, the point is that given the existence of a prior right of Government appeal, the risks of disuniformity which Senator Clarke described the statute as intended to cure do not exist.

[8] The Government suggests, in its Supplemental Memorandum for the United States 6-7, that a construction of the 1907 Act excluding statutes applicable only within the District of Columbia from the scope of the first two provisions leads to the "anomalous consequence" that 18 U. S. C. § 3731 would still allow a direct appeal in a D. C. case where the motion-in-bar provision is concerned. E. g., United States v. Sweet, 399 U. S. 517 (1970). The alleged "anomaly" would seem to argue for the conclusion that D. C. cases involving the motion-in-bar provision are not directly appealable here, either. Certainly, the Court's disposition in Sweet would not foreclose that result.

In any event, the purpose Senator Clarke had in mind in offering his limiting amendment with regard to the first two provisions of 18 U. S. C. § 3731 was rather clearly expressed; that he failed to address himself to the motion-in-bar provision—which, after all, received very little attention in the prolonged debates on the floor of the Senate— hardly justifies an expansive reading of the other provisions of the Act.

[9] The Government relies principally on Shapiro v. Thompson, 394 U. S. 618, 625 n. 4 (1969), as supporting its construction of the generic reference to "statutes" in 18 U. S. C. § 3731 to include statutes applicable only within the District of Columbia. Shapiro dealt with 28 U. S. C. § 2282, which requires a three-judge court to hear requests for injunctions against the enforcement of "any Act of Congress" when the ground for the requested relief is the alleged unconstitutionality of the Act. Decisions of such three-judge courts are, under the circumstances set forth in 28 U. S. C. § 1253, directly appealable to this Court. In Shapiro, the Court noted at least one prior instance where the Court had taken jurisdiction over a case involving a statute applicable only within the District and then stated: "Section 2282 requires a three-judge court to hear a challenge to the constitutionality of `any Act of Congress.' We see no reason to make an exception for Acts of Congress pertaining to the District of Columbia." 394 U. S., at 625 n. 4 (emphasis in original).

The Shapiro approach is obviously inappropriate for the present problem. First, despite the Government's assertion to the contrary, see Brief for the United States 15, the phrase "any Act of Congress" is arguably broader than a generic reference to "statutes." Indeed, the Shapiro Court explicitly chose to emphasize the presence of the word "any" in the relevant portion of that statute. Second, while an exercise of jurisdiction in a case where jurisdiction is not challenged is of little precedential value, the Court in Shapiro still chose to take note of such a prior case; in the present context, this Court has never taken jurisdiction of a § 3731 appeal involving a statute applicable only within the District.

Third, and most importantly, Congress at the time of the three-judge court Acts altered the principles of both original and appellate jurisdiction for the substantive categories of litigation involved; the new procedural routes reflect crucial considerations of comity between sovereigns and among the branches of the Federal Government. See generally Currie, The Three-Judge District Court in Constitutional Litigation, 32 U. Chi. L. Rev. 1 (1964). There is no legislative history supporting the notion that the new procedures were narrowed to alleviate particular defects of inconsistent constitutional interpretation due to the absence of any appellate route for the substantive categories of cases to be included within the Act.

In these circumstances, it is fair to conclude that the principle of strict construction applicable to such statutes must yield to the "inert language" of the statute. Cf. Florida Lime Growers v. Jacobsen, 362 U. S. 73, 92 (1960) (Frankfurter, J., dissenting).

Justice Harlan's dissent in Org. for a Better Austin v. Keefe (May 17, 1971)

MR. JUSTICE HARLAN, dissenting.

In deciding this case on the merits, the Court, in my opinion, disregards the express limitation of our appellate jurisdiction to "[f]inal judgments or decrees," 28 U. S. C. § 1257, and does so in a way which undermines the policies behind limiting our review to judgments "rendered by the highest court of a State in which a decision could be had," ibid., and interferes with Illinois' arrangements for the expeditious processing of litigation in its own state courts.

It is plain, and admitted by all, that the "temporary" or "preliminary" injunction entered by the Circuit Court of Cook County and affirmed by the Appellate Court, First District, is not a final judgment. Review of preliminary injunctions is a classic form of interlocutory appeal, which Congress has authorized in limited instances not including review by this Court of state decrees. See 28 U. S. C. §§ 1252, 1253; cf. 28 U. S. C. § 1292 (a) (1). Despite the seemingly absolute provision of the statute, the Court holds that this case is within the judicially created exception for instances in which the affirmance of the interlocutory order by the highest state court decides the merits of the dispute for all practical purposes, leaving the remaining proceedings in the lower courts as nothing more than a formality. See Pope v. Atlantic Coast Line R. Co., 345 U. S. 379, 382 (1953); Construction Laborers' Local 438 v. Curry, 371 U. S. 542, 550-551 (1963); Mills v. Alabama, 384 U. S. 214, 217-218 (1966). The apparent, though unstated, justification for this is the petitioners' representation in this Court that they have no defense to offer other than their First Amendment contentions, which they assert the Illinois courts have decided against them on the merits. Pet. for Cert. 6.

Even assuming that the latter position is correct,[*] this case does not fit into the mold of the cases in which this Court has reviewed orders of state supreme courts affirming the grant of preliminary relief, for here the Illinois Supreme Court has never passed on the merits of petitioners' constitutional contentions. If this case were permitted to return to the trial court for consideration of the merits of petitioners' contentions and the entry of final judgment, petitioners would have an appeal as of right directly to the Illinois Supreme Court if that judgment were adverse to them. Ill. Const., Art. 6, § 5; Ill. Sup. Ct. Rules 301, 302 (a). That court would then have an opportunity to correct the errors, if any, in the lower court judgment; or if it failed to do so we would have the benefit of that court's views on the issues here presented. Such review by "the highest court of a State in which a decision could be had" is particularly important in the context of Illinois procedure, which places primary responsibility for review of constitutional contentions in the State Supreme Court. All appeals from final judgments in cases involving a constitutional question must be taken directly to that court, see Ill. Sup. Ct. Rule 302 (a) (2); consequently the intermediate Appellate Court rarely has occasion to engage in constitutional adjudication.

To be sure, the Illinois Supreme Court, by denying petitioners' motion for leave to appeal from the order of the Appellate Court, had an opportunity to rule on the issue presented by this case and declined to do so. However, Illinois has a strong policy against Supreme Court review of interlocutory orders. Until recently the Supreme Court had no direct appellate jurisdiction over judgments of the Appellate Court on interlocutory appeals, but simply reviewed the issues presented by the subsequent final judgment. 6 C. Nichols, Illinois Civil Practice § 5998 (1962 rev. vol. H. Williams & M. Wingersky). Although interlocutory review is now available in the discretion of the Supreme Court, it is "not favored." Ill. Sup. Ct. Rule 318 (b); see also Ill. Sup. Ct. Rule 315 (a). We have ourselves often made a similar resolution of the competing interests in prompt correction of lower courts' errors on the one hand and in expeditious processing of litigation to final judgment on the other. See R. Stern & E. Gressman, Supreme Court Practice § 4.19 (4th ed. 1969). Under today's decision, Illinois will have to surrender its judgment in these matters if it desires to interpose the State Supreme Court between the subordinate state courts and review by this Court, as the highest-state-court requirement permits it to do. If this Court would respect the final-judgment limitation on our jurisdiction, Illinois would not be put to this choice.

It is, of course, tempting to ignore the proper limitations on our power when the alternative is to delay correction of what the Court today holds was a flagrant error by lower courts. This is particularly true where, as here, a "temporary" injunction has been outstanding for a lengthy period. But the question is not whether we think our intervention in the dispute at this stage would be desirable—although with our overall docket running at about 4,000 cases a Term there is surely much to be said for giving each litigant only one bite at the apple. The policy judgment involved was expressly committed to Congress by Art. III, § 2, of the Constitution, and Congress has spoken in § 1257.

I would respect that congressional judgment and dismiss the writ for lack of jurisdiction.

[*] Settled Illinois law provides that "[i]t is not, of course, the purpose of a temporary injunction to decide controverted facts or the merits of the case," Lonergan v. Crucible Steel Co. of America, 37 Ill. 2d 599, 611, 229 N. E. 2d 536, 542 (1967), but "merely to preserve the last actual peaceable uncontested status which preceded the pending suit." Consumers Digest, Inc. v. Consumer Magazine, Inc., 92 Ill. App. 2d 54, 61, 235 N. E. 2d 421, 425 (App. Ct., 1st Dist., 1968). "It is enough if [the applicant] can show that he raises a fair question as to the existence of the right which he claims and can satisfy the court that matters should be preserved in their present state until such questions can be disposed of." Nestor Johnson Mfg. Co. v. Goldblatt, 371 Ill. 570, 574, 21 N. E. 2d 723, 725 (1939). The granting of a preliminary injunction is committed to the sound discretion of the trial judge, and it is reviewable only for abuse of discretion. Lonergan v. Crucible Steel Co. of America, supra, at 612, 229 N. E. 2d, at 542.

In argument before the Illinois chancellor, petitioners' attorney stated:

"We don't wish to go into lengthy argument on constitutional provisions at this time. We feel that it is only fair that both sides prepare briefs in preparation for a full hearing on the permanent injunction. And, to that end, we just want to point out that these are constitutional questions, on which we feel the law is abundantly clear, and that is a further reason why Your Honor in his discretion, should not see fit to issue a temporary injunction." R. 56.

Justice Harlan's dissent in Rosenbloom v. Metromedia, Inc. (June 7, 1971)

MR. JUSTICE HARLAN, dissenting.

The very facts of this case demonstrate that uncritical acceptance of the Pennsylvania libel law here involved would be inconsistent with those important First and Fourteenth Amendment values we first treated with in an analogous context in New York Times Co. v. Sullivan, 376 U. S. 254 (1964). However, as the plurality opinion implicitly recognizes, only an undiscriminating assessment of those values would lead us to extend the New York Times rule in full force to all purely private libels. My Brother BRENNAN'S opinion would resolve the dilemma by distinguishing those private libels that arise out of events found to be of "public or general concern" from those that do not, and subjecting the former to full-scale application of the New York Times rule.

For the reasons set forth in Part I of my Brother MARSHALL'S dissent, I cannot agree to such a solution. As he so well demonstrates, the principal failing of the plurality opinion is its inadequate appreciation of the limitations imposed by the legal process in accommodating the tension between state libel laws and the federal constitutional protection given to freedom of speech and press.

Once the evident need to balance the values underlying each is perceived, it might seem, purely as an abstract matter, that the most utilitarian approach would be to scrutinize carefully every jury verdict in every libel case, in order to ascertain whether the final judgment leaves fully protected whatever First Amendment values[1] transcend the legitimate state interest in protecting the particular plaintiff who prevailed. This seems to be what is done in the plurality opinion. But we did not embrace this technique in New York Times, supra. Instead, as my Brother MARSHALL observes, we there announced a rule of general application, not ordinarily dependent for its implementation upon a case-by-case examination of trial court verdicts. See also my dissent in Time, Inc. v. Pape, 401 U. S. 279, 293 (1971). Nor do I perceive any developments in the seven years since we decided New York Times, supra, that suggest our original method should now be abandoned. At least where we can discern generally applicable rules that should balance with fair precision the competing interests at stake, such rules should be preferred to the plurality's approach both in order to preserve a measure of order and predictability in the law that must govern the daily conduct of affairs and to avoid subjecting the press to judicial second-guessing of the newsworthiness of each item they print Consequently, I fully concur in Part I of MR. JUSTICE MARSHALL'S dissent.

Further, I largely agree with the alternative proposals of that dissent. I, too, think that, when dealing with private libel, the States should be free to define for themselves the applicable standard of care so long as they do not impose liability without fault; that a showing of actual damage should be a requisite to recovery for libel; and that it is impermissible, given the substantial constitutional values involved, to fail to confine the amount of jury verdicts in such cases within any ascertainable limits. However, my reasons for so concluding are somewhat different than his, and I therefore reach a different result than he does with respect to the tolerable limits of punitive damages.

I

I think we all agree on certain core propositions. First, as a general matter, the States have a perfectly legitimate interest, exercised in a variety of ways, in redressing and preventing careless conduct, no matter who is responsible for it, that inflicts actual, measurable injury upon individual citizens. Secondly, there is no identifiable value worthy of constitutional protection in the publication of falsehoods. Third, although libel law provides that truth is a complete defense, that principle, standing alone, is insufficient to satisfy the constitutional interest in freedom of speech and press. For we have recognized that it is inevitable that there will be "some error in the situation presented in free debate," Time, Inc. v. Hill, 385 U. S. 374, 406 (1967) (opinion of this writer), a process that needs "breathing space," NAACP v. Button, 371 U. S. 415, 433 (1963), to flourish, and that "putting to the pre-existing prejudices of a jury the determination of what is `true' may effectively institute a system of censorship." Time, Inc. v. Hill, supra, at 406.

Moreover, any system that punishes certain speech is likely to induce self-censorship by those who would otherwise exercise their constitutional freedom. Given the constitutionally protected interest in unfettered speech, it requires an identifiable, countervailing state interest, consistent with First Amendment values, to justify a regulatory scheme that produces such results. And, because the presence of such values dictates closer scrutiny of this aspect of state tort law than the Fourteenth Amendment would otherwise command, it may well be that certain rules, impervious to constitutional attack when applied to ordinary human conduct, may have to be altered or abandoned where used to regulate speech. Finally, as determined in New York Times, the constitutional interest in tolerance of falsehood as well as the need to adjust competing societal interests, prohibits, at a minimum, the imposition of liability without fault.

The precise standard of care necessary to achieve these goals is, however, a matter of dispute as is the range of penalties a State may prescribe for a breach of that standard. In analyzing these problems it is necessary to begin with a general analytical framework that defines those competing interests that must be reconciled. My Brother MARSHALL'S opinion, I think, dwells too lightly upon the nature of the legitimate countervailing interests promoted by the State's libel law and, as a result, overstates the case against punitive damages. Because we deal with a set of legal rules that treat truth as a complete defense it strikes, I think, somewhat wide of the mark to treat the State's interest as one of protecting reputations from "unjustified invasion." Post, at 78. By hypothesis, the respondent here was free to reveal any true facts about petitioner's "obscure private life."[2]

Given the defense of truth, it is my judgment that, in order to assure that it promotes purposes consistent with First Amendment values, the legitimate function of libel law must be understood as that of compensating individuals for actual, measurable harm caused by the conduct of others. This can best be demonstrated by postulating a law that subjects publishers to jury verdicts for falsehoods that have done the plaintiff no harm. In my view, such a rule can only serve a purpose antithetical to those of the First Amendment. It penalizes speech, not to redress or avoid the infliction of harm, but only to deter the press from publishing material regarding private behavior that turns out to be false simply because of its falsity. This the First Amendment will not tolerate. Where the State cannot point to any tangible danger, even knowingly erroneous publication is entitled to constitutional protection because of the interest in avoiding an inquiry into the mere truth or falsity of speech. Moreover, such a scheme would impose a burden on speaking not generally placed upon constitutionally unprotected conduct—the payment of private fines for conduct which, although not conformed to established limits of care, causes no harm in fact.

Conversely, I think that where the purpose and effect of the law are to redress actual and measurable injury to private individuals that was reasonably foreseeable as a result of the publication, there is no necessary conflict with the values of freedom of speech. Just as an automobile negligently driven can cost a person his physical and mental well-being and the fruits of his labor, so can a printing press negligently set. While the First Amendment protects the press from the imposition of special liabilities upon it, "[t]o exempt a publisher, because of the nature of his calling, from an imposition generally exacted from other members of the community, would be to extend a protection not required by the constitutional guarantee." Curtis Publishing Co. v. Butts, 388 U. S. 130, 160 (1967) (opinion of this writer). A business "is not immune from regulation because it is an agency of the press. The publisher of a newspaper has no special immunity from the application of general laws. He has no special privilege to invade the rights and liberties of others." Associated Press v. NLRB, 301 U. S. 103, 132-133 (1937). That the damage has been inflicted by words rather than other instrumentalities cannot insulate it from liability. States may legitimately be required to use finer regulatory tools where dealing with "speech," but they are not wholly disabled from exacting compensation for its measurable adverse consequences. If this is not so, it is difficult to understand why governments may, for example, proscribe "misleading" advertising practices or specify what is "true" in the dissemination of consumer credit advertisements.

Nor does this interest in compensating victims of harmful conduct somehow disappear when the damages inflicted are great. So long as the effect of the law of libel is simply to make publishers pay for the harm they cause, and the standard of care required is appropriately adjusted to take account of the special countervailing interests in an open exchange of ideas, the fact that this may involve the payment of substantial sums cannot plausibly be said to raise serious First Amendment problems. If a newspaper refused to pay its bills because to do so would put it out of business, would the First Amendment dictate that this be treated as a partial or complete defense? If an automobile carrying a newsman to the scene of a history-making event ran over a pedestrian, would the size of the verdict, if based upon generally applicable tort law principles, have to be assessed against the probability that it would deter broadcasters from news gathering before it could pass muster under the First Amendment?

However, without foreclosing the possibility that other limiting principles may be surfaced by subsequent experience, I do think that since we are dealing, by hypothesis, with infliction of harm through the exercise of freedom of speech and the press to which the Constitution gives explicit protection, recoverable damages must be limited to those consequences of the publication which are reasonably foreseeable. The usual tort rule seems to be that once some foreseeable injury has been inflicted, the negligent defendant must compensate for all damages he proximately caused in fact, no matter how peculiar were the circumstances of the particular plaintiff involved. W. Prosser, The Law of Torts § 50 (3d ed. 1964). However, our cases establish, I think, that, unless he has knowledge to the contrary, a speaker is entitled to presume that he is addressing an audience that is not especially susceptible to distress at the specter of open, uninhibited, robust speech. Cohen v. California, ante, p. 15. See also Brandenburg v. Ohio, 395 U. S. 444 (1969); Butler v. Michigan, 352 U. S. 380 (1957). Thus, I think the speaker should be free from a duty to compensate for actual harm inflicted by his falsehoods where the defamation would not have caused such harm to a person of average sensibilities unless, of course, the speaker knew that his statements were made concerning an unusually sensitive person. In short, I think the First Amendment does protect generally against the possibility of self-censorship in order to avoid unwitting affronts to the frail and the queasy.

II

Of course, it does not follow that so long as libel law performs the same compensatory function as civil law generally it is necessarily legitimate in all its various applications. The presence of First Amendment values means that the State can be compelled to utilize finer, more discriminating instruments of regulation where necessary to give more careful protection to these countervailing interests. New York Times, supra, and Curtis Publishing Co., supra, established that where the injured party is a "public figure" or a "public official," the interest in freedom of speech dictates that the States forgo their interest in compensating for actual harm, even upon a basis generally applicable to all members of society, unless the plaintiff can show that the injurious publication was false and was made "with `actual malice'—that is, with knowledge that it was false or with reckless disregard of whether it was false or not." New York Times, supra, at 280. Tacitly recognizing that it would unduly sacrifice the operative legitimate state interests to extend this rule to all cases where the injured party is simply a private individual, the plurality opinion would nevertheless apply it where the publication concerned such a person's "involvement in an event of public or general concern." Ante, at 52. I would not overrule New York Times or Curtis Publishing Co. and I do agree, as indicated above, that making liability turn on simple falsity in the purely private libel area is not constitutionally permissible. But I would not construe the Federal Constitution to require that the States adhere to a standard other than that of reasonable care where the plaintiff is an ordinary citizen.

My principal concern with the plurality's view, of course, is that voiced by my Brother MARSHALL. However, even if this objection were not tenable, unlike the plurality, I do think there is a difference, relevant to the interests here involved, between the public and the private plaintiff, as our cases have defined these categories, and that maintaining a constitutional distinction between them is at least as likely to protect true First Amendment concerns as one that eradicates such a line and substitutes for it a distinction between matters we think are of true social significance and those we think are not.

To begin, it does no violence, in my judgment, to the value of freedom of speech and press to impose a duty of reasonable care upon those who would exercise these freedoms. I do not think it can be gainsaid that the States have a substantial interest in encouraging speakers to carefully seek the truth before they communicate, as well as in compensating persons actually harmed by false descriptions of their personal behavior. Additionally, the burden of acting reasonably in taking action that may produce adverse consequences for others is one generally placed upon all in our society. Thus, history itself belies the argument that a speaker must somehow be freed of the ordinary constraints of acting with reasonable care in order to contribute to the public good while, for example, doctors, accountants, and architects have constantly performed within such bounds.

This does not mean that I do not agree with the rule of New York Times, supra, but only that I deem it inapplicable here. That rule was not, I think, born solely of a desire to free speech that would otherwise have been stifled by overly restrictive rules, but also rested upon a determination that the countervailing state interests, described above, were not fully applicable where the subject of the falsehood was a public official or a public figure. For me, it does seem quite clear that the public person has a greater likelihood of securing access to channels of communication sufficient to rebut falsehoods concerning him than do private individuals in this country who do not toil in the public spotlight. Similarly, our willingness to assume that public personalities are more impervious to criticism, and may be held to have run the risk of publicly circulated falsehoods concerning them, does not rest solely upon an empirical assertion of fact, but also upon a belief that, in our political system, the individual speaker is entitled to act upon such an assumption if our institutions are to be held up, as they should be, to constant scrutiny. And, at least as to the "public official," it seems to be universally the case that he is entitled to an absolute immunity for what he may utter in response to the charges of others. Where such factors are present the need to provide monetary compensation for defamation appears a good deal more attenuated. Finally, in light of the plurality opinion's somewhat extravagant delineation of the public interest involved in the dissemination of information about nonpublic persons, it bears emphasizing that a primary rationale for extending the New York Times rule to public figures was the desire to reflect, in the constitutional balance, the fact that "in this country, the distinctions between governmental and private sectors are blurred," Curtis Publishing Co., supra, at 163 (opinion of Warren, C. J.), and to treat constitutional values as specially implicated where important, albeit nonofficial, policy and behavior were the subjects of discussion. At the very least, this tends to diminish the force of any contention that libelous depictions of nonpublic persons are often likely to involve matters of abiding public significance.

I cannot agree that the First Amendment gives special protection to the press from "[t]he very possibility of having to engage in litigation," ante, at 52 (opinion of BRENNAN, J.). Were this assertion tenable, I do not see why the States could ever enforce their libel laws. Cf. my Brother BLACK'S opinion, ante, at 57. Further, it would certainly cast very grave doubts upon the constitutionality of so-called "right-of-reply statutes" advocated by the plurality, ante, at 47 n. 15, and ultimately treat the application of any general law to a publisher or broadcaster as an important First Amendment issue. The notion that such an interest, in the context of a purely private libel, is a significant independent constitutional value is an unfortunate consequence of the plurality's single-minded devotion to the task of preventing self-censorship, regardless of the purposes for which such restraint is induced or the evils its exercise tends to avoid.

It is, then, my judgment that the reasonable care standard adequately serves those First Amendment values that must inform the definition of actionable libel and that those special considerations that made even this standard an insufficiently precise technique when applied to plaintiffs who are "public officials" or "public figures" do not obtain where the litigant is a purely private individual.

III

There remains the problem of punitive damages.[3] No doubt my Brother MARSHALL is correct in asserting that the specter of being forced to pay out substantial punitive damage awards is likely to induce self-censorship. This would probably also be the case where the harm actually caused is likely to be great. But, as I indicated above, this fact in itself would not justify construing the First Amendment to impose an arbitrary limitation on the amount of actual damages recoverable. Thus, as my Brother MARSHALL would apparently agree—since he, too, proposes no limitation on actual damages—one cannot jump from the proposition that fear of substantial punitive damage awards may be an important factor in inducing self-censorship directly to the result that punitive damages cannot be assessed in all private libel cases. A more particularized inquiry into the nature of the competing interests involved is necessary in order to ascertain whether awarding punitive damages must inevitably, in private libel cases, serve only interests that are incompatible with the First Amendment.

At a minimum, even in the purely private libel area, I think the First Amendment should be construed to limit the imposition of punitive damages to those situations where actual malice is proved. This is the typical standard employed in assessing anyone's liability for punitive damages where the underlying aim of the law is to compensate for harm actually caused, see, e. g., 3 L. Frumer et al., Personal Injury § 2.02 (1965); H. Oleck, Damages to Persons and Property § 30 (1955), and no conceivable state interest could justify imposing a harsher standard on the exercise of those freedoms that are given explicit protection by the First Amendment.

The question then arises whether further limitations on this general state power must be imposed in order to serve the particularized goals of the First Amendment. The most compelling rationale for providing punitive damages where actual malice is shown is that such damages assure that deterrent force is added to the jury's verdict. If the speaker's conduct was quite likely to produce substantial harm, but fortuitously did not, simple assessment of actual damages will not fully reflect the social interest in deterring that conduct generally. Further, even if the harm done was great the defendant may have unusually substantial resources that make the award of actual damages a trivial inconvenience of no actual deterrent value. And even where neither of these factors obtains, the State always retains an interest in punishing more severely conduct that, although it causes the same effect, is more morally blameworthy. For example, consider the distinction between manslaughter and first-degree murder.

I find it impossible to say, at least without further judicial experience in this area, that the First Amendment interest in avoiding self-censorship will always outweigh the state interest in vindicating these policies. It seems that a legislative choice is permissible which, for example, seeks to induce, through a reasonable monetary assessment, repression of false material, published with actual malice, that was demonstrably harmful and reasonably thought capable of causing substantial harm, but, in fact, was not so fully injurious to the individual attacked. Similarly, the State surely has a legitimate interest in seeking to assure that its system of compensating victims of negligent behavior also operates upon all as an inducement to avoidance of such conduct. And, these are burdens that are placed on all members of society, thus permitting the press to escape them only if its interest is somehow different in this regard.

However, from the standpoint of the individual plaintiff such damage awards are windfalls. They are, in essence, private fines levied for purposes that may be wholly unrelated to the circumstances of the actual litigant. That fact alone is not, I think, enough to condemn them. The State may, as it often does, use the vehicle of a private lawsuit to serve broader public purposes. It is noteworthy that my Brother MARSHALL does not rest his objection to punitive damages upon these grounds. He fears, instead, the self-censorship that may flow from the unbridled discretion of juries to set the amount of such damages. I agree that where these amounts bear no relationship to the actual harm caused, they then serve essentially as springboards to jury assessment, without reference to the primary legitimating compensatory function of the system, of an infinitely wide range of penalties wholly unpredictable in amount at the time of the publication and that this must be a substantial factor in inducing self-censorship. Further, I find it difficult to fathom why it may be necessary, in order to achieve its justifiable deterrence goals, for the States to permit punitive damages that bear no discernible relationship to the actual harm caused by the publication at issue. A rational determination of the injury a publication might potentially have inflicted should typically proceed from the harm done in fact. And where the compensatory scheme seeks to achieve deterrence as a subsidiary by-product, the desired deterrence, if not precisely measured by actual damages, should be informed by that touchstone if deterrence of falsehood is not to replace compensation for harm as the paramount goal. Finally, while our legal system does often mete out harsher punishment for more culpable acts, it typically begins with a gradation of offenses defined in terms of effects. Compare, for example, larceny with murder. It is not surprising, then, that most States apparently require that punitive damages in most private civil actions bear some reasonable relation to the actual damages awarded, Oleck, at § 275, Pennsylvania included, Weider v. Hoffman, 238 F. Supp. 437, 444-447 (MD Pa. 1965).

However, where the amount of punitive damages awarded bears a reasonable and purposeful relationship to the actual harm done, I cannot agree that the Constitution must be read to prohibit such an award. Indeed, as I understand it, my Brother MARSHALL'S objection to my position[4] is not that the interest in freedom of speech dictates eliminating such judgments, but that this result is compelled by the need to avoid involving courts in an "ad hoc balancing" of "the content of the speech and the surrounding circumstances," post, at 86, 85, much like that undertaken today in Part VI of the plurality opinion, the same technique criticized in my dissent in Time, Inc. v. Pape, supra. I find this argument unpersuasive. First, I do not see why my proposed rule would necessarily require frequent judicial reweighing of the facts underlying each jury verdict. A carefully and properly instructed jury should ordinarily be able to arrive at damage awards that are self-validating. It is others, not I, who have placed upon the federal courts the general duty of reweighing jury verdicts regarding the degree of fault demonstrated in libel actions. Further, to the extent that supervision of jury verdicts would be required it would entail a different process from that undertaken where judges redetermine the degree of fault. The defendant's resources, the actual harm suffered by the plaintiff, and the publication's potential for actual harm are all susceptible of more or less objective measurement. And the overriding principle that deterrence is not to be made a substitute for compensation should serve as a useful mechanism for adjusting the equation. Finally, even if some marginal "ad hoc balancing" becomes necessary, I should think it the duty of this Court at least to attempt to implement such a process before pre-empting, for itself, all state power in this regard.[5]

In sum, given the fact that it seems to reflect the majority rule, that most of our jurisprudence proceeds upon the premise that legislative purposes can be achieved by fitting the punishment to the crime, and since we deal here with a precise constitutional interest that may legitimately require the States to resort to more discriminating regulation within a more circumscribed area of permissible concern, I would hold unconstitutional, in a private libel case, jury authority to award punitive damages which is unconfined by the requirement that these awards bear a reasonable and purposeful relationship to the actual harm done. Conversely, where the jury authority has been exercised within such constraints, and the plaintiff has proved that the speaker acted out of express malice, given the present state of judicial experience, I think it would be an unwarranted intrusion into the legitimate legislative processes of the States and an impermissibly broad construction of the First Amendment to nullify that state action.

Because the Court of Appeals adjudicated this case upon principles wholly unlike those suggested here, I would vacate the judgment below and remand the case for further proceedings consistent with the views expressed herein.

Notes

[1] Of course, for me, this case presents a Fourteenth, not a purely First, Amendment issue, for the question is one of the constitutionality of the applicable Pennsylvania libel laws. However, I have found it convenient, in the course of this opinion, occasionally to speak directly of the First Amendment as a shorthand phrase for identifying those constitutional values of freedom of expression guaranteed to individuals by the Due Process Clause of the Fourteenth Amendment.

[2] I would expressly reserve, for a case properly presenting it, the issue whether the New York Times rule should have any effect on "privacy" litigation. The problem is briefly touched upon in Time, Inc. v. Hill, 385 U. S. 374, 404-405 (1967) (HARLAN, J., concurring and dissenting).

[3] The conclusions I reach in Part III of this opinion are somewhat different from those I embraced four Terms ago in Curtis Publishing Co., supra, at 159-161. Where matters are in flux, however, it is more important to re-think past conclusions than to adhere to them without question and the problem under consideration remains in a state of evolution, as is attested to by all the opinions filed today. Reflection has convinced me that my earlier opinion painted with somewhat too broad a brush and that a more precise balancing of the conflicting interests involved is called for in this delicate area.

[4] Of course, I do not envision that, consistently with my views, the States could only exact some predetermined multiple of the actual damages found. I should think a jury could simply be instructed, along the lines set out in my opinion, on the legitimate uses of the punitive damage award and the necessity for relating any such judgment to the harm actually done.

[5] The plurality opinion states that the "real thrust" of my position is that it "will not `constitutionalize' the factfinding process." Ante, at 53. In fact, I have attempted to demonstrate throughout this opinion that I believe the positions of my Brother BRENNAN, BLACK, and MARSHALL all, in varying degrees, overstate the extent to which libel law is incompatible with the constitutional guarantee of freedom of expression, and have pointed out that I think my views have merit "even if [the objection noted in my Brother MARSHALL'S opinion] were not tenable." Supra, at 69. Moreover, the assertion that an inquiry into whether actual damages were suffered "will involve judges even more deeply in factfinding," ante, at 53, than ascertaining whether "the defendant in fact entertained serious doubts as to the truth of his publication," ante, at 56, or whether the publication involved "an event of public or general concern," ante, at 52, seems to me to carry its own refutation. The former focuses on measurable, objective fact; the latter upon subjective, personal belief. Finally, I cannot see why juries may not typically be entrusted

responsibly to determine whether a publisher was negligent, a function they perform in judging the harmful conduct of most other members of society; or why it should be materially more difficult for judges to oversee such decisions where a speaker, rather than any other actor, is a defendant.

Justice Harlan's opinion in Whitcomb v. Chavis (June 7, 1971)

Separate opinion of MR. JUSTICE HARLAN.

Earlier this Term I remarked on "the evident malaise among the members of the Court" with prior decisions in the field of voter qualifications and reapportionment. Oregon v. Mitchell, 400 U. S. 112, 218 (1970) (separate opinion of this writer).

Today's opinions in this and two other voting cases now decided[1] confirm that diagnosis.

I

Past decisions have held that districting in local governmental units must approach equality of voter population "as far as is practicable," Hadley v. Junior College District, 397 U. S. 50, 56 (1970), and that the "as nearly as is practicable" standard of Wesberry v. Sanders, 376 U. S. 1, 7-8 (1964), for congressional districting forbade a maximum variation of 6%. Kirkpatrick v. Preisler, 394 U. S. 526 (1969). Today the Court sustains a local governmental apportionment scheme with a 12% variation. Abate v. Mundt, post, p. 182.

Other past decisions have suggested that multi-member constituencies would be unconstitutional if they could be shown "under the circumstances of a particular case . . . to minimize or cancel out the voting strength of racial or political elements of the voting population." Fortson v. Dorsey, 379 U. S. 433, 439 (1965); Burns v. Richardson, 384 U. S. 73, 88 (1966). Today the Court holds that a three-judge District Court, which struck down an apportionment scheme for just this reason, "misconceived the Equal Protection Clause." Ante, at 160.

Prior opinions stated that "once the class of voters is chosen and their qualifications specified, we see no constitutional way by which equality of voting power may be evaded." Gray v. Sanders, 372 U. S. 368, 381 (1963); Hadley v. Junior College District, 397 U. S. 50, 59 (1970). Today the Court sustains a provision that gives opponents of school bond issues half again the voting power of proponents. Gordon v. Lance, ante, p. 1.

II

The Court justifies the wondrous results in these cases by relying on different combinations of factors. Abate v. Mundt relies on the need for flexibility in local governmental arrangements, the interest in preserving the integrity of political subdivisions, and the longstanding tradition behind New York's practice in the latter respect. This case finds elementary probability theory too simplistic as a guide to resolution of what is essentially a practical question of political power; the opinion relies on the long history of multi-member districts in this country and the fear that "affirmance of the District Court would spawn endless litigation." Ante, at 157. Gordon v. Lance relies heavily on the "federal analogy" and the prevalence of similar anti-majoritarian elements in the constitutions of the several States.

To my mind the relevance of such considerations as the foregoing is undeniable and their cumulative effect is unanswerable. I can only marvel, therefore, that they were dismissed, singly and in combination, in a line of cases which began with Gray v. Sanders, 372 U. S. 368 (1963), and ended with Hadley v. Junior College District, 397 U. S. 50 (1970).

That line of cases can best be understood, I think, as reflections of deep personal commitments by some members of the Court to the principles of pure majoritarian democracy. This majoritarian strain and its nonconstitutional sources are most clearly revealed in Gray v. Sanders, supra, at 381, where my Brother DOUGLAS, speaking for the Court, said: "The conception of political equality from the Declaration of Independence, to Lincoln's Gettysburg Address, to the Fifteenth, Seventeenth, and Nineteenth Amendments can mean only one thing—one person, one vote." If this philosophy of majoritarianism had been given its head, it would have led to different results in each of the cases decided today, for it is in the very nature of the principle that it regards majority rule as an imperative of social organization, not subject to compromise in furtherance of merely political ends. It is a philosophy which ignores or overcomes the fact that the scheme of the Constitution is one not of majoritarian democracy, but of federal republics, with equality of representation a value subordinate to many others, as both the body of the Constitution and the Fourteenth Amendment itself show on their face. See generally Baker v. Carr, 369 U. S. 186, 297-324 (1962) (Frankfurter, J., dissenting).

III

If majoritarianism is to be rejected as a rule of decision, as the Court implicitly rejects it today, then an alternative principle must be supplied if this earlier line of cases just referred to is still to be regarded as good law. The reapportionment opinions of this Court provide little help. They speak in conclusory terms of "debasement" or "dilution" of the "voting power" or "representation" of citizens without explanation of what these concepts are. The answers are hardly apparent, for as the Court observes today:

"As our system has it, one candidate wins, the others lose. Arguably the losing candidates' supporters are without representation since the men they voted for have been defeated; arguably they have been denied equal protection of the laws since they have no legislative voice of their own. . . . But we have not yet deemed it a denial of equal protection to deny legislative seats to losing candidates, even in those so-called `safe' districts where the same party wins year after year." Ante, at 153.

A coherent and realistic notion of what is meant by "voting power" might have restrained some of the extreme lengths to which this Court has gone in pursuit of the will-o'-the-wisp of "one man, one vote."

An interesting illustration of the light which a not implausible definition of "voting power" can shed on reapportionment doctrine is provided by the theoretical model created by Professor Banzhaf, to which the Court refers, ante, at 144-146.[2] This model uses as a measure of voting power the probability that a given voter will cast a tie-breaking ballot in an election. Two further assumptions are made: first, that the voting habits of all members of the electorate are alike; and second, that each voter is equally likely to vote for either candidate before him. On these assumptions, and taking the voting population in Marion County as roughly 300,000, it can be shown that the probability of an individual voter's casting a decisive vote in a given election is approximately .00146. This provides a standard to which "voting power" of residents in other districts may be compared. See generally Banzhaf, Multi-Member Electoral Districts—Do They Violate the "One Man, One Vote" Principle, 75 Yale L. J. 1309 (1966).

However, Professor Banzhaf's model also reveals that minor variations in assumptions can lead to major variations in results. For instance, if the temper of the electorate changes by one-half of one percent,[3] each individual's voting power is reduced by a factor of approximately 1,000,000. Or if a few of the 300,000 voters are committed—say 15,000 to candidate A and 10,000 to candidate B[4]—the probability of any individual's casting a tie-breaking vote is reduced by a factor on the rough order of 120,000,000,000,000,000,000,000. Obviously in comparison with the astronomical differences in voting power which can result from such minor variations in political characteristics, the effects of the 12% and 28% population variations considered in Abate v. Mundt and in this case are de minimis, and even the extreme deviations from the norm presented in Baker v. Carr, 369 U. S. 186 (1962), and Avery v. Midland County, 390 U. S. 474 (1968), pale into insignificance.[5]

It is not surprising therefore that the Court in this case declines to embrace the measure of voting power suggested by Professor Banzhaf. But it neither suggests an alternative nor considers the consequences of its inability to measure what it purports to be equalizing. See n. 2, supra. Instead it becomes enmeshed in the haze of slogans and numerology which for 10 years has obscured its vision in this field, and finally remands the case "for further proceedings consistent with [its] opinion." Ante, at 163. This inexplicit mandate is at least subject to the interpretation that the court below is to inquire into such matters as "the actual influence of Marion County's delegation in the Indiana Legislature," ante, at 147, and the possibility of "recurring poor performance by Marion County's delegation with respect to Center Township ghetto," ante, at 155, with a view to determining whether "any legislative skirmish affecting the State of Indiana or Marion County in particular would have come out differently had Marion County been subdistricted and its delegation elected from single-member districts." Ante, at 148. If there are less appropriate subjects for federal judicial inquiry, they do not come readily to mind. The suggestion implicit in the Court's opinion that appellees may ultimately prevail if they can make their record in these and other like respects should be recognized for what it is: a manifestation of frustration by a Court that has become trapped in the "political thicket" and is looking for the way out.

This case is nothing short of a complete vindication of Mr. Justice Frankfurter's warning nine years ago "of the mathematical quagmire (apart from divers judicially inappropriate and elusive determinants) into which this Court today catapults the lower courts of the country." Baker v. Carr, 369 U. S. 186, 268 (1962) (dissenting opinion). With all respect, it also bears witness to the morass into which the Court has gotten itself by departing from sound constitutional principle in the electoral field. See the dissenting opinion of Mr. Justice Frankfurter in Baker v. Carr, supra, and my separate opinions in Reynolds v. Sims, 377 U. S. 533, 589 (1964), and in Oregon v. Mitchell, 400 U. S. 112, 152 (1970). I hope the day will come when the Court will frankly recognize the error of its ways in ever having undertaken to restructure state electoral processes.

I would reverse the judgment below and remand the case to the District Court with directions to dismiss the complaint.

Notes

[1] Abate v. Mundt, post, p. 182, Gordon v. Lance, ante, p. 1.

[2] The Court, though stating that it does "not quarrel with plaintiffs' mathematics," nevertheless implies that it may be ignored because "the position remains a theoretical one . . . and does `not take into account any political or other factors which might affect the actual voting power of the residents, which might include party affiliation, race, previous voting characteristics or any other factors which go into the entire political voting situation.' " Ante, at 145, 146. Precisely the same criticism applies, with even greater force, to the "one man, one vote" opinions of this Court. The only relevant difference between the elementary arithmetic on which the Court relies and the elementary probability theory on which Professor Banzhaf relies is that calculations in the latter field cannot be done on one's fingers.

[3] More precisely, the result follows if the second of Professor Banzhaf's assumptions is altered so that the probability of each voter's selecting candidate A over candidate B is 50.5% rather than 50%.

[4] The text assumes that each of the remaining 275,000 voters is equally likely to vote for A or for B.

[5] "There is something fascinating about science. One gets such wholesale returns of conjecture out of such a trifling investment of fact." Mark Twain. Life on the Mississippi 109 (Harper & Row, 1965).

Justice Harlan's concurrence in Bivens v. Six Unknown Fed. Narcotics Agents (June 21, 1971) [Notes omitted]

MR. JUSTICE HARLAN, concurring in the judgment.

My initial view of this case was that the Court of Appeals was correct in dismissing the complaint, but for reasons stated in this opinion I am now persuaded to the contrary. Accordingly, I join in the judgment of reversal.

Petitioner alleged, in his suit in the District Court for the Eastern District of New York, that the defendants, federal agents acting under color of federal law, subjected him to a search and seizure contravening the requirements of the Fourth Amendment. He sought damages in the amount of $15,000 from each of the agents. Federal jurisdiction was claimed, inter alia,[1] under 28 U. S. C. § 1331 (a) which provides:

"The district courts shall have original jurisdiction of all civil actions wherein the matter in controversy exceeds the sum or value of $10,000 exclusive of interest and costs, and arises under the Constitution, laws, or treaties of the United States."

The District Court dismissed the complaint for lack of federal jurisdiction under 28 U. S. C. § 1331 (a) and failure to state a claim for which relief may be granted. 276 F. Supp 12 (EDNY 1967). On appeal, the Court of Appeals concluded, on the basis of this Court's decision in Bell v. Hood, 327 U. S. 678 (1946), that petitioner's claim for damages did "[arise] under the Constitution" within the meaning of 28 U. S. C. § 1331 (a); but the District Court's judgment was affirmed on the ground that the complaint failed to state a claim for which relief can be granted. 409 F. 2d 718 (CA2 1969).

In so concluding, Chief Judge Lumbard's opinion reasoned, in essence, that: (1) the framers of the Fourth Amendment did not appear to contemplate a "wholly new federal cause of action founded directly on the Fourth Amendment," id., at 721, and (2) while the federal courts had power under a general grant of jurisdiction to imply a federal remedy for the enforcement of a constitutional right, they should do so only when the absence of alternative remedies renders the constitutional command a "mere `form of words.' " Id., at 723. The Government takes essentially the same position here. Brief for Respondents 4-5. And two members of the Court add the contention that we lack the constitutional power to accord Bivens a remedy for damages in the absence of congressional action creating "a federal cause of action for damages for an unreasonable search in violation of the Fourth Amendment." Opinion of MR. JUSTICE BLACK, post, at 427; see also opinion of THE CHIEF JUSTICE, post, at 418, 422.

For the reasons set forth below, I am of the opinion that federal courts do have the power to award damages for violation of "constitutionally protected interests" and I agree with the Court that a traditional judicial remedy such as damages is appropriate to the vindication of the personal interests protected by the Fourth Amendment.

I

I turn first to the contention that the constitutional power of federal courts to accord Bivens damages for his claim depends on the passage of a statute creating a "federal cause of action." Although the point is not entirely free of ambiguity,[2] I do not understand either the Government or my dissenting Brothers to maintain that Bivens' contention that he is entitled to be free from the type of official conduct prohibited by the Fourth Amendment depends on a decision by the State in which he resides to accord him a remedy. Such a position would be incompatible with the presumed availability of federal equitable relief, if a proper showing can be made in terms of the ordinary principles governing equitable remedies. See Bell v. Hood, 327 U. S. 678, 684 (1946). However broad a federal court's discretion concerning equitable remedies, it is absolutely clear—at least after Erie R. Co. v. Tompkins, 304 U. S. 64 (1938)—that in a nondiversity suit a federal court's power to grant even equitable relief depends on the presence of a substantive right derived from federal law. Compare Guaranty Trust Co. v. York, 326 U. S. 99, 105-107 (1945), with Holmberg v. Armbrecht, 327 U. S. 392, 395 (1946). See also H. Hart & H. Wechsler, The Federal Courts and the Federal System 818-819 (1953).

Thus the interest which Bivens claims—to be free from official conduct in contravention of the Fourth Amendment—is a federally protected interest. See generally Katz, The Jurisprudence of Remedies: Constitutional Legality and the Law of Torts in Bell v. Hood, 117 U. Pa. L. Rev. 1, 33-34 (1968).[3] Therefore, the question of judicial power to grant Bivens damages is not a problem of the "source" of the "right"; instead, the question is whether the power to authorize damages as a judicial remedy for the vindication of a federal constitutional right is placed by the Constitution itself exclusively in Congress' hands.

II

The contention that the federal courts are powerless to accord a litigant damages for a claimed invasion of his federal constitutional rights until Congress explicitly authorizes the remedy cannot rest on the notion that the decision to grant compensatory relief involves a resolution of policy considerations not susceptible of judicial discernment. Thus, in suits for damages based on violations of federal statutes lacking any express authorization of a damage remedy, this Court has authorized such relief where, in its view, damages are necessary to effectuate the congressional policy underpinning the substantive provisions of the statute. J. I. Case Co. v. Borak, 377 U. S. 426 (1964); Tunstall v. Brotherhood of Locomotive Firemen & Enginemen, 323 U. S. 210, 213 (1944). Cf. Wyandotte Transportation Co. v. United States, 389 U. S. 191, 201-204 (1967).[4]

If it is not the nature of the remedy which is thought to render a judgment as to the appropriateness of damages inherently "legislative," then it must be the nature of the legal interest offered as an occasion for invoking otherwise appropriate judicial relief. But I do not think that the fact that the interest is protected by the Constitution rather than statute or common law justifies the assertion that federal courts are powerless to grant damages in the absence of explicit congressional action authorizing the remedy. Initially, I note that it would be at least anomalous to conclude that the federal judiciary— while competent to choose among the range of traditional judicial remedies to implement statutory and common-law policies, and even to generate substantive rules governing primary behavior in furtherance of broadly formulated policies articulated by statute or Constitution, see Textile Workers v. Lincoln Mills, 353 U. S. 448 (1957); United States v. Standard Oil Co., 332 U. S. 301, 304-311 (1947); Clearfield Trust Co. v. United States, 318 U. S. 363 (1943)—is powerless to accord a damages remedy to vindicate social policies which, by virtue of their inclusion in the Constitution, are aimed predominantly at restraining the Government as an instrument of the popular will.

More importantly, the presumed availability of federal equitable relief against threatened invasions of constitutional interests appears entirely to negate the contention that the status of an interest as constitutionally protected divests federal courts of the power to grant damages absent express congressional authorization. Congress provided specially for the exercise of equitable remedial powers by federal courts, see Act of May 8, 1792, § 2, 1 Stat. 276; C. Wright, Law of Federal Courts 257 (2d ed., 1970), in part because of the limited availability of equitable remedies in state courts in the early days of the Republic. See Guaranty Trust Co. v. York, 326 U. S. 99, 104-105 (1945). And this Court's decisions make clear that, at least absent congressional restrictions, the scope of equitable remedial discretion is to be determined according to the distinctive historical traditions of equity as an institution, Holmberg v. Armbrecht, 327 U. S. 392, 395-396 (1946); Sprague v. Ticonic National Bank, 307 U. S. 161, 165-166 (1939). The reach of a federal district court's "inherent equitable powers," Textile Workers v. Lincoln Mills, 353 U. S. 448, 460 (Burton, J., concurring in result), is broad indeed, e. g., Swann v. Charlotte-Mecklenburg Board of Education, 401 U. S. 1 (1971); nonetheless, the federal judiciary is not empowered to grant equitable relief in the absence of congressional action extending jurisdiction over the subject matter of the suit. See Textile Workers v. Lincoln Mills, supra, at 460 (Burton, J., concurring in result); Katz, 117 U. Pa. L. Rev., at 43.[5]

If explicit congressional authorization is an absolute prerequisite to the power of a federal court to accord compensatory relief regardless of the necessity or appropriateness of damages as a remedy simply because of the status of a legal interest as constitutionally protected, then it seems to me that explicit congressional authorization is similarly prerequisite to the exercise of equitable remedial discretion in favor of constitutionally protected interests. Conversely, if a general grant of jurisdiction to the federal courts by Congress is thought adequate to empower a federal court to grant equitable relief for all areas of subject-matter jurisdiction enumerated therein, see 28 U. S. C. § 1331 (a), then it seems to me that the same statute is sufficient to empower a federal court to grant a traditional remedy at law.[6] Of course, the special historical traditions governing the federal equity system, see Sprague v. Ticonic National Bank, 307 U. S. 161 (1939), might still bear on the comparative appropriateness of granting equitable relief as opposed to money damages. That possibility, however, relates, not to whether the federal courts have the power to afford one type of remedy as opposed to the other, but rather to the criteria which should govern the exercise of our power. To that question, I now pass.

III

The major thrust of the Government's position is that, where Congress has not expressly authorized a particular remedy, a federal court should exercise its power to accord a traditional form of judicial relief at the behest of a litigant, who claims a constitutionally protected interest has been invaded, only where the remedy is "essential," or "indispensable for vindicating constitutional rights." Brief for Respondents 19, 24. While this "essentiality" test is most clearly articulated with respect to damages remedies, apparently the Government believes the same test explains the exercise of equitable remedial powers. Id., at 17-18. It is argued that historically the Court has rarely exercised the power to accord such relief in the absence of an express congressional authorization and that "[i]f Congress had thought that federal officers should be subject to a law different than state law, it would have had no difficulty in saying so, as it did with respect to state officers . . . ." Id., at 20-21; see 42 U. S. C. § 1983. Although conceding that the standard of determining whether a damage remedy should be utilized to effectuate statutory policies is one of "necessity" or "appropriateness," see J. I. Case Co. v. Borak, 377 U. S. 426, 432 (1964); United States v. Standard Oil Co., 332 U. S. 301, 307 (1947), the Government contends that questions concerning congressional discretion to modify judicial remedies relating to constitutionally protected interests warrant a more stringent constraint on the exercise of judicial power with respect to this class of legally protected interests. Brief for Respondents 21-22.

These arguments for a more stringent test to govern the grant of damages in constitutional cases[7] seem to be adequately answered by the point that the judiciary has a particular responsibility to assure the vindication of constitutional interests such as those embraced by the Fourth Amendment. To be sure, "it must be remembered that legislatures are ultimate guardians of the liberties and welfare of the people in quite as great a degree as the courts." Missouri, Kansas & Texas R. Co. v. May, 194 U. S. 267, 270 (1904). But it must also be recognized that the Bill of Rights is particularly intended to vindicate the interests of the individual in the face of the popular will as expressed in legislative majorities; at the very least, it strikes me as no more appropriate to await express congressional authorization of traditional judicial relief with regard to these legal interests than with respect to interests protected by federal statutes.

The question then, is, as I see it, whether compensatory relief is "necessary" or "appropriate" to the vindication of the interest asserted. Cf. J. I. Case Co. v. Borak, supra, at 432; United States v. Standard Oil Co., supra, at 307; Hill, Constitutional Remedies, 69 Col. L. Rev. 1109, 1155 (1969); Katz, 117 U. Pa. L. Rev., at 72. In resolving that question, it seems to me that the range of policy considerations we may take into account is at least as broad as the range of those a legislature would consider with respect to an express statutory authorization of a traditional remedy. In this regard I agree with the Court that the appropriateness of according Bivens compensatory relief does not turn simply on the deterrent effect liability will have on federal official conduct.[8] Damages as a traditional form of compensation for invasion of a legally protected interest may be entirely appropriate even if no substantial deterrent effects on future official lawlessness might be thought to result. Bivens, after all, has invoked judicial processes claiming entitlement to compensation for injuries resulting from allegedly lawless official behavior, if those injuries are properly compensable in money damages. I do not think a court of law—vested with the power to accord a remedy—should deny him his relief simply because he cannot show that future lawless conduct will thereby be deterred.

And I think it is clear that Bivens advances a claim of the sort that, if proved, would be properly compensable in damages. The personal interests protected by the Fourth Amendment are those we attempt to capture by the notion of "privacy"; while the

Court today properly points out that the type of harm which officials can inflict when they invade protected zones of an individual's life are different from the types of harm private citizens inflict on one another, the experience of judges in dealing with private trespass and false imprisonment claims supports the conclusion that courts of law are capable of making the types of judgment concerning causation and magnitude of injury necessary to accord meaningful compensation for invasion of Fourth Amendment rights.[9]

On the other hand, the limitations on state remedies for violation of common-law rights by private citizens argue in favor of a federal damages remedy. The injuries inflicted by officials acting under color of law, while no less compensable in damages than those inflicted by private parties, are substantially different in kind, as the Court's opinion today discusses in detail. See Monroe v. Pape, 365 U. S. 167, 195 (1961) (HARLAN, J., concurring). It seems to me entirely proper that these injuries be compensable according to uniform rules of federal law, especially in light of the very large element of federal law which must in any event control the scope of official defenses to liability. See Wheeldin v. Wheeler, 373 U. S. 647, 652 (1963); Monroe v. Pape, supra, at 194-195 (HARLAN, J., concurring); Howard v. Lyons, 360 U. S. 593 (1959). Certainly, there is very little to be gained from the standpoint of federalism by preserving different rules of liability for federal officers dependent on the State where the injury occurs. Cf. United States v. Standard Oil Co., 332 U. S. 301, 305-311 (1947).

Putting aside the desirability of leaving the problem of federal official liability to the vagaries of common-law actions, it is apparent that some form of damages is the only possible remedy for someone in Bivens' alleged position. It will be a rare case indeed in which an individual in Bivens' position will be able to obviate the harm by securing injunctive relief from any court. However desirable a direct remedy against the Government might be as a substitute for individual official liability, the sovereign still remains immune to suit. Finally, assuming Bivens' innocence of the crime charged, the "exclusionary rule" is simply irrelevant. For people in Bivens' shoes, it is damages or nothing.

The only substantial policy consideration advanced against recognition of a federal cause of action for violation of Fourth Amendment rights by federal officials is the incremental expenditure of judicial resources that will be necessitated by this class of litigation. There is, however, something ultimately self-defeating about this argument. For if, as the Government contends, damages will rarely be realized by plaintiffs in these cases because of jury hostility, the limited resources of the official concerned, etc., then I am not ready to assume that there will be a significant increase in the expenditure of judicial resources on these claims. Few responsible lawyers and plaintiffs are likely to choose the course of litigation if the statistical chances of success are truly de minimis. And I simply cannot agree with my Brother BLACK that the possibility of "frivolous" claims—if defined simply as claims with no legal merit—warrants closing the courthouse doors to people in Bivens' situation. There are other ways, short of that, of coping with frivolous lawsuits.

On the other hand, if—as I believe is the case with respect, at least, to the most flagrant abuses of official power—damages to some degree will be available when the option of litigation is chosen, then the question appears to be how Fourth Amendment interests rank on a scale of social values compared with, for example, the interests of stockholders defrauded by misleading proxies.

See J. I. Case Co. v. Borak, supra. Judicial resources, I am well aware, are increasingly scarce these days. Nonetheless, when we automatically close the courthouse door solely on this basis, we implicitly express a value judgment on the comparative importance of classes of legally protected interests. And current limitations upon the effective functioning of the courts arising from budgetary inadequacies should not be permitted to stand in the way of the recognition of otherwise sound constitutional principles.

Of course, for a variety of reasons, the remedy may not often be sought. See generally Foote, Tort Remedies for Police Violations of Individual Rights, 39 Minn. L. Rev. 493 (1955). And the countervailing interests in efficient law enforcement of course argue for a protective zone with respect to many types of Fourth Amendment violations. Cf. Barr v. Matteo, 360 U. S. 564 (1959) (opinion of HARLAN, J.). But, while I express no view on the immunity defense offered in the instant case, I deem it proper to venture the thought that at the very least such a remedy would be available for the most flagrant and patently unjustified sorts of police conduct. Although litigants may not often choose to seek relief, it is important, in a civilized society, that the judicial branch of the Nation's government stand ready to afford a remedy in these circumstances. It goes without saying that I intimate no view on the merits of petitioner's underlying claim.

For these reasons, I concur in the judgment of the Court.

Justice Harlan's dissent in US v. Harris (June 28, 1971)

MR. JUSTICE HARLAN, with whom MR. JUSTICE DOUGLAS, MR. JUSTICE BRENNAN, and MR. JUSTICE MARSHALL join, dissenting.

This case presents the question of how our decisions in Aguilar v. Texas, 378 U. S. 108 (1964), and Spinelli v. United States, 393 U. S. 410 (1969), apply where magistrates in issuing search warrants are faced with the task of assessing the probable credibility of unidentified informants who purport to describe criminal activity of which they have personal knowledge, and where it does not appear that such informants have previously supplied accurate information to law enforcement officers.

I cannot agree that the affidavit here at issue provided a sufficient basis for an independent determination, by a neutral judicial officer, that probable cause existed. Accordingly, I would affirm the judgment of the Court of Appeals. Five members of this Court, however, for four separately expressed reasons, have concluded that the judgment below must be reversed. Some of the theories employed by those voting to reverse are wholly unlike any of the grounds urged by the Government.

I

Where, as in this case, the affiant states under oath that he has been informed of the existence of certain criminal activity, but has not observed that activity himself, a magistrate in discharging his duty to make an independent assessment of probable cause can properly issue a search warrant only if he concludes that; (a) the knowledge attributed to the informant, if true, would be sufficient to establish probable cause; (b) the affiant is likely relating truthfully what the informer said; and (c) it is reasonably likely that the informer's description of criminal behavior accurately reflects reality.[1]

In the case before us, no one maintains that the magistrate's judgment as to elements (a) and (b) was not properly supported. Plainly the information set forth in the affidavit, if entitled to credit, establishes probable cause. And the magistrate was certainly entitled to rely on the agent's official status, his personal observation of the agent, and the oath administered to him by the magistrate in concluding that the affiant's assertions as to what he had been told by the informer were credible.

The final component of the probable cause equation, here involved, is that it must appear reasonably likely that the informer's claim that criminal conduct has occurred or is occurring is probably accurate. Our cases establish that this element is satisfied only if there is reason to believe both that the informer is a truthful person generally and that he has based his particular conclusions in the matter at hand on reliable data, Aguilar v. Texas, supra; Spinelli v. United States, supra, for it is not reasonable to invade another's premises on the basis of information, even if it appears quite damning when simply taken at face value, unless there is corroboration of its trustworthiness. The fact that the magistrate has determined that the agent probably truthfully reported what the informant conveyed cannot, of course, establish the credibility or reliability of the information itself. More immediately relevant here, our cases have established that where the affiant relies upon the assertions of confidants to establish probable cause, the affidavit must set forth facts which enable the magistrate to judge for himself both the probable credibility of the informant and the reliability of his information, for only if this condition is met can a reviewing court be satisfied that the magistrate has fulfilled his constitutional duty to render an independent determination that probable cause exists. Aguilar v. Texas, 378 U. S. 108 (1964); Spinelli v. United States, 393 U. S. 410 (1969). Cf. Giordenello v. United States, 357 U. S. 480 (1958); Nathanson v. United States, 290 U. S. 41 (1933); Whiteley v. Warden, 401 U. S. 560 (1971).[2]

The parties are in agreement with these principles and have not urged that they be re-examined. Indeed, I think these precepts follow ineluctably from the constitutional command that "no Warrants shall issue, but upon probable cause." Whether, in this case, either of these tests of the trustworthiness of the informer's tip has been met is, however, vigorously disputed.

II

Although the Court of Appeals did not address itself to this contention, respondent claims that the affidavit is insufficient to establish the reliability of the evidence upon which the informant based his conclusions. Of course, most of these data come from alleged direct personal observation of the informant, surely a sufficient basis upon which to predicate a finding of reliability under any test. However, respondent stresses that the allegation of direct observation of the criminal activity does not necessarily purport to embrace a period less than two weeks prior to the issuance of the search warrant. Moreover, the reliability of the source of the information that a purchase was made "within the past two days" is not established and, it is argued, the other information was too stale to support the issuance of a warrant.

This argument is premised upon an overly technical view of the affidavit. The informant is said to have personally bought illegal whiskey from respondent "within the past 2 weeks," which could well include a point in time quite close to the issuance of the warrant. More importantly, the totality of the tip evidently reveals that the informer purported to describe an ongoing operation which he claimed he had personally observed over the course of two years. Giving due deference to the magistrate's determination of probable cause and reading the affidavit "in a commonsense and realistic fashion," United States v. Ventresca, 380 U. S. 102, 108 (1965), I must conclude that the affidavit sets forth sufficient data to permit a magistrate to determine that, if the informer was likely telling the truth, information adequate to support a finding of probable cause was likely obtained in a reliable fashion.

III

I turn, then, to what the parties have treated as the crux of the controversy before us. Respondent contends, and the Court of Appeals so held, that the affidavit does not sufficiently set forth facts and circumstances from which the magistrate might properly have concluded that the informant, in purporting to detail his personal observation, was probably telling the truth. Conversely, the Government principally argues that two factors, singly or in combination, provided a factual basis for the magistrate's judgment that the tip was credible. First, the agent stated that he had "interviewed this person [and] found this person to be a prudent person." Second, the informant described the criminal activity in some detail and from his own personal knowledge.[3]

A

The Government's first contention misconceives the basic thrust of this Court's decisions in the Nathanson, Giordenello, Aguilar, Spinelli, and Whiteley cases, supra. The central proposition common to each of these decisions is that the determination of probable cause is to be made by the magistrate, not the affiant. That the agent-affiant determined the informer to be prudent cannot be a basis for sustaining this warrant unless magistrates are entitled to delegate their responsibilities to law enforcement officials. Nathanson held that an affidavit to the effect that the affiant "has cause to suspect and does believe" that illicit liquor was located on certain premises did not sufficiently apprise the issuing magistrate of the underlying "facts or circumstances" from which "he can find probable cause." 290 U. S., at 47 (emphasis added). In Aguilar, a sworn assertion that the informant was "a credible person" was held insufficient to enable the magistrate to assess that conclusion for himself. Only two Terms ago, we held a warrant constitutionally defective because "[t]hough the affiant swore that his confidant was `reliable,' he offered the magistrate no reason in support of this conclusion." Spinelli v. United States, 393 U. S., at 416. Reading the assertion that the informer in this case was "prudent" in the broadest conceivable commonsense fashion, it does no more than claim he was "credible" or "reliable," i. e., that he was likely telling the truth.[4] Such an assertion, however, is no more than a conclusion which the Constitution requires must be drawn independently by the magistrate. What this portion of the affidavit lacks are any of the underlying "facts or circumstances" that informed the agent's conclusion and whose presentation to the magistrate would enable him to assess the probability that this determination was sufficiently plausible to justify authorizing a search of respondent's premises.

B

Nor do I think this void is filled by the fact that the informant claimed to speak from his personal knowledge.

It is true that in Nathanson the Court was not dealing with the sufficiency of the allegations respecting one or more of the above-described components of probable cause, but merely with a bare overall statement of the affiant that probable cause existed. Further, as the Government notes, our chief, but not sole, emphasis in Aguilar was upon the absence of any evidence communicated by the affiant from which a magistrate could infer that the confidant gathered his evidence from a reliable source. From this, the Government contends that Aguilar's reliability-of-the-informer test is not applicable in full force where, as here, it does seem clear that the sources of the informer's belief, if truthfully reported, were reliable. I think this argument makes too much of the circumstances of our previous cases. The central point of the discussion of probable cause in Aguilar is, as perhaps more precisely emphasized by our explicit twin holdings in Spinelli, see 393 U. S., at 416, that the two elements necessary to establish the informer's trustworthiness—namely, that the tip relayed to the magistrate be both truthful and reliable—are analytically severable. It is not possible to argue that since certain information, if true, would be trustworthy, therefore, it must be true. The possibility remains that the information might have been fabricated. This is why our cases require that there be a reasonable basis for crediting the accuracy of the observation related in the tip. In short, the requirement that the magistrate independently assess the probable credibility of the informant does not vanish where the source of the tip indicates that, if true, it is trustworthy.

This is not to say, however, that I think the fact of asserted personal observation can never play a role in determining whether that observation actually took place. I can perceive at least two ways in which, in circumstances similar to those of this case, that information might be taken to bear upon the informer's credibility, as well as upon the reliability of his sources of information. For example, to the extent that the informant is somehow responsible to the affiant, the fact of asserted personal observation might be of some value to a magistrate in assessing the informer's credibility. In such circumstances, perhaps a magistrate could conclude that where the confidant claimed to speak from personal knowledge it is somewhat less likely that the informant was falsifying his report because, if the search yields no fruit, when called to account he would be unable to explain this away by impugning the veracity or reliability of his sources. However, no such relationship is revealed in this case.

Additionally, it might be of significance that the informant had given a more than ordinarily detailed description of the suspect's criminal activities. Although this would be more probative of the reliability of the information, it might also permissibly lead a magistrate, in an otherwise close case, to credit the accuracy of the account as well. I do not believe, however, that in this instance the relatively meager allegations of this character are, standing alone, enough to satisfy the credibility requirement essential to the sufficiency of this probable-cause affidavit. Reading this aspect of the affidavit in a not unduly circumspect manner, the allegations are of a character that would readily occur to a person prone to fabricate. To hold that this aspect of the affidavit, without more, would enable "a man of reasonable caution," Berger v. New York, 388 U. S. 41, 55 (1967), to conclude that there was adequate reason to believe the informant credible would open the door to the acceptance of little more than florid affidavits as justifying the issuance of search warrants.

C

Some members of the Court would reverse the judgment below on the grounds that the magistrate might properly have credited the informant's assertions because they confessed to the commission of a crime. This rationale is advanced notwithstanding the Government's failure even to suggest it.

Had this argument been pressed upon us, I would find it difficult to accept. First, the analogy to the hearsay exception is quite tenuous. The federal rule, although it is often criticized, is that declarations against penal interest do not fall within this exception. Donnelly v. United States, 228 U. S. 243 (1913). Moreover, because it has been thought that such statements should be relied upon by factfinders only when necessity justifies it, the rule universally requires a showing that the declarant cannot be produced personally before the trier of fact, C. McCormick, Evidence §§ 253, 257 (1954), an element not shown to be present here. See Part V, infra. Finally, we have not found any instance of the application of this rule where the witness declined to reveal to the trier of fact the identity of the declarant, presumably because without this knowledge it cannot be readily assumed that the declarant might have had reason to suspect the use of the statement would do him harm. Thus, while strict rules of evidence certainly do not govern magistrates' assessments of probable cause, it would require a rather extensive relaxation of them to permit reliance on this factor. And these rules cannot be completely relaxed, of course, since the basic thrust of Spinelli, Aguilar, Nathanson, Whiteley, and Giordenello, supra, is to prohibit the issuance of warrants upon mere uncorroborated hearsay. The simple statement by an affiant that an unspecified individual told the affiant that he and another had committed a crime, where offered to prove the complicity of the third party, is little, if any, more than that.

Secondly, the rationale for this exception to the hearsay rule is that the fact that the declaration was against the speaker's self-interest tends to indicate that its substance is accurate. 5 J. Wigmore, Evidence § 1457 (3d ed. 1940). But where the declarant is also a police informant it seems at least as plausible to assume, without further enlightenment either as to the Government's general practice or as to the particular facts of this case, that the declarant-confidant at least believed he would receive absolution from prosecution for his confessed crime in return for his statement. (This, of course, would not be an objection where the declarant is not also the informant. See Spinelli, supra, at 425 (WHITE, J., concurring).) Thus, some showing that the informant did not possess illusions of immunity might well be essential.

Thirdly, the effect of adopting such a rule would be to encourage the Government to prefer as informants participants in criminal enterprises rather than ordinary citizens, a goal the Government specifically eschews in its brief in this case upon the explicit premise that such persons are often less reliable than those who obey the law. Brief for the United States 14.

In short, I am inclined to the view, although I would not decide the question here, that magistrates may not properly predicate a determination that an unnamed confidant is credible upon the bare fact that by giving information he also confessed to having committed a crime. More importantly at this juncture, it seems to me quite clear that no such rule should be injected into our federal jurisprudence in the absence of any representation by the Government that the factual assumptions underlying it do, indeed, comport with reality, and in the face of the Government's apparent explicit assertion, in this very case, that those able to supply information sufficient to establish probable cause under such a new rule would tend to be less reliable than those who cannot. The necessity for this haste to embrace such a speculative theory, without any argument from those who will be affected by it, wholly escapes me.

IV

Finally, it is argued that even if the tip plus the affiant's assertion that the informant was "prudent" did not provide a reasonable basis for the magistrate's conclusion that the confidant was credible, two other factors would have sufficed. First, at some time in the past four or more years, in an abandoned house "under Harris' control," the local constable had located "a sizeable stash of illicit whiskey." While an assertion of "prior events within the affiant's own knowledge . . . indicating that the defendant had previously trafficked in contraband," ante, at 581, admittedly did not appear in the affidavit held insufficient in Spinelli, this hardly distinguishes that case in any purposeful manner. Surely, it cannot seriously be suggested that, once an individual has been convicted of bootlegging, any anonymous phone caller who states he has just personally witnessed another illicit sale (up to four years later) by that individual provides federal agents with probable cause to search the suspect's home. I can only conclude that this argument is a make-weight, intended to avoid the necessity of calling for an outright overruling of Spinelli.

Secondly, the claim is made that a magistrate could conclude the confidant here was credible because the agent had "received numerous information from all types of persons as to [respondent's] activities." To rely on this factor alone, of course, is flatly inconsistent with Spinelli, where we held that "the allegation that Spinelli was `known' to the affiant and to other federal and local law enforcement officers as a gambler and an associate of gamblers is but a bald and unilluminating assertion of suspicion that is entitled to no weight in appraising the magistrate's decision." Spinelli, supra, at 414. In the instant case, the affiant did not purport to "know" respondent was a dealer in illicit whiskey, nor did he identify the source of his information to that effect.

Nevertheless, the contention is advanced that this aspect of Spinelli had "no support in our prior cases, logic, or experience," ante, at 583, and thus should be discarded. However, Nathanson held that "[m]ere affirmance of belief or suspicion is not enough" to establish probable cause for issuance of a warrant to search a private dwelling. 290 U. S., at 47. It is argued that Nathanson "was limited to holding that reputation, standing alone, was insufficient." Ante, at 582. But this is the precise problem here—only the respondent's reputation has been seriously invoked to establish the credibility of the informant, an element of probable cause entirely severable from the requirement that the confidant's source be reliable. See Parts I and III of this opinion.

A narrower view of Nathanson is said to be confirmed by reading Brinegar v. United States, 338 U. S. 160 (1949), to have "held proper the assertion of the searching officer that he had previously arrested the defendant for a similar offense and that the defendant had a reputation for hauling liquor." Ante, at 582. But Brinegar itself was very carefully limited to situations involving the arrest of those driving moving vehicles, 338 U. S., at 174, 176-177, a problem that has typically been treated as sui generis by this Court. Further, the Court in Brinegar specifically held the arrest valid "[w]holly apart from [the agent's] knowledge that [the suspect] bore the general reputation of being engaged in liquor running." Id., at 170. While it is true that Jones v. United States, 362 U. S. 257, 271 (1960), cites the fact that the informant's "story was corroborated by other sources of information," the opinion nowhere suggests that this factor, standing alone, would have been sufficient to enable a magistrate to assess the confidant's reliability. At least equal emphasis was placed upon the informant's previously proved veracity and his tangible proof of actual observation of the illegal activity.

Thus, I conclude that Spinelli and Nathanson, without contradiction, stand for the proposition that the magistrate could not establish the likely veracity of the unidentified informant on the grounds that his story coincided, in unspecified particulars, with rumors circulated by unknown third parties. I am not certain what is meant by the claim that such a rule of law is illogical. It would, indeed, be illogical to argue that the agent could not have relied upon information as to respondent's reputation that he deemed credible and reliable in concluding that the informant had likely told the truth. But it was not the agent's task to determine whether a search warrant should issue. This was the magistrate's responsibility. As to the magistrate, I confess that I do not comprehend, where the issue is whether the confidant is to be believed, how the agent's assertion that he had "received numerous information from all types of persons as to [respondent's] activities," can, as a matter of logic or experience, be accurately described as other than "a bald and unilluminating assertion of suspicion." It is, at best, a conclusory statement that respondent had a deserved reputation as a dealer in illicit whiskey. The Fourth Amendment, I repeat, requires that such conclusions be drawn, from the underlying facts and circumstances, by the magistrate, not the agent.

V

The Government has earnestly protested that the result below, if permitted to stand, will seriously hamper the enforcement of the federal criminal law. It is said that if this affidavit is insufficient to support the issuance of a search warrant, it will be extremely difficult to meet the Fourth Amendment's standards where the informer, although apparently quite credible, has never before given accurate information to law enforcement officers, especially where he, or the agent, is unwilling to have the informant's identity disclosed. It would, indeed, be anomalous if the Fourth Amendment dictated such results, for it surely was never intended as a hindrance to fair, vigorous law enforcement. Further, I think there is much truth in the Government's supporting assertion that the ordinary citizen who has never before reported a crime to the police may, in fact, be more reliable than one who supplies information on a regular basis. "The latter is likely to be someone who is himself involved in criminal activity or is, at least, someone who enjoys the confidence of criminals." Government's Brief 14.[5]

I do not, however, share the Government's concern that a judgment of affirmance would have such a constricting effect on legitimate federal law enforcement. For example, it would seem that such informers could often be brought before the magistrate where he could assess their credibility for himself. We cannot assume that the ordinary law-abiding citizen has qualms about this sort of cooperation with law enforcement officers. And I do not understand the Government to be asserting that effective law enforcement will often dictate that the identity of informants be kept secret from federal magistrates themselves. Moreover, it will always be open to the officer to seek corroboration of the tip.

Beyond these considerations, I do not understand why a federal agent, who has determined a confidant to be "reliable," "credible," or "prudent" cannot lay before the magistrate the grounds upon which he based that judgment. I would not hold that a magistrate's determination that an informer is "prudent" is insufficient to support the issuance of a warrant. To the contrary, I would only insist that this judgment be that of the magistrate, not the law enforcement officer who seeks the warrant. Without violating the confidences of his source, the agent surely could describe for the magistrate such things as the informer's general background, employment, personal attributes that enable him to observe and relate accurately, position in the community, reputation with others, personal connection with the suspect, any circumstances which suggest the probable absence of any motivation to falsify, the apparent motivation for supplying the information, the presence or absence of a criminal record or association with known criminals, and the like.

VI

This affidavit is barren of anything that enabled the magistrate to judge for himself of the credibility of the informant. We should not countenance the issuance of a search warrant by a federal magistrate upon no more evidence than that presented here. A person who has not been shown to possess any of the common attributes of credibility, whose name cannot be disclosed to a magistrate, and whose information has not been corroborated is precisely the sort of informant whose tip should not be the sole basis for the issuance of a warrant, if the constitutional command that "no Warrants shall issue, but upon probable cause" is to be respected. And the assertion that such a person may be believed where he confesses that he is a criminal or where his statements dovetail with other, unspecified rumors carries its own refutation. With all respect, such an analysis bespeaks more a firm hostility to Aguilar, Nathanson, and Spinelli than a careful judgment as to the principles those cases reflect. Despite all its surface detail, this affidavit cannot be sustained without cutting deeply into the core requirement of the Fourth Amendment that search warrants cannot issue except upon the independent finding of a neutral magistrate that probable cause exists.

For these reasons, I dissent.

Notes

[1] Of course where, as here, the affiant provides information in addition to the informant's tip, the magistrate could alternatively find probable cause, without examining the tip, if he can conclude that (a) the affiant is probably telling the truth and (b) the affidavit apart from the tip is sufficiently informative to establish probable cause. See Spinelli v. United States, 393 U. S. 410, 414 (1969). Concededly, this latter element is not present here. Government's Brief 16. Without crediting the tip, the affidavit is insufficient.

[2] Giordenello and Whiteley each involved an arrest warrant rather than a search warrant, but the analysis required to determine the validity of either is basically the same.

[3] The Government makes brief reference to the assertion that the informant's verbal statement to the affiant was "sworn." Government's Brief 13 n. 2. I do not see how this affects the case. Surely there is no reason to suspect that this indicates the confidant anticipated potential perjury proceedings if he were subsequently proved a liar. Nor does that assertion reveal, in any meaningful sense, what sort of relationship this might have reflected or created between the agent and his informer.

[4] The Court of Appeals in reversing respondent's conviction stated that "[t]he allegation that [the informant] is a `prudent person' signifies that he is circumspect in the conduct of his affairs, but reveals nothing about his credibility." 412 F. 2d 796, 797-798. I consider this a too restrictive construction of the affidavit and cannot accept that aspect of the reasoning of the Court of Appeals.

[5] Of course, the magistrate was presented no evidence that this is, in fact, such a case. Indeed, the very allegations in the affidavit to the effect that the informant here had been a frequent purchaser from respondent would suggest that he "is, at least, someone

who enjoys the confidence of criminals." The Government's argument, as I understand it, is that the affidavit in this case is typical of those that can be produced by agents who rely on first-time informers not bound up themselves in criminal activity. As I point out below, if this had been the situation here, and that fact had been communicated to the magistrate, this would be a very different case.

Justice Harlan's dissent in New York Times Co. v. U. S. (June 30, 1971)

MR. JUSTICE HARLAN, with whom THE CHIEF JUSTICE and MR. JUSTICE BLACKMUN join, dissenting.

These cases forcefully call to mind the wise admonition of Mr. Justice Holmes, dissenting in Northern Securities Co. v. United States, 193 U. S. 197, 400-401 (1904):

"Great cases like hard cases make bad law. For great cases are called great, not by reason of their real importance in shaping the law of the future, but because of some accident of immediate overwhelming interest which appeals to the feelings and distorts the judgment. These immediate interests exercise a kind of hydraulic pressure which makes what previously was clear seem doubtful, and before which even well settled principles of law will bend."

With all respect, I consider that the Court has been almost irresponsibly feverish in dealing with these cases.

Both the Court of Appeals for the Second Circuit and the Court of Appeals for the District of Columbia Circuit rendered judgment on June 23. The New York Times' petition for certiorari, its motion for accelerated consideration thereof, and its application for interim relief were filed in this Court on June 24 at about 11 a. m. The application of the United States for interim relief in the Post case was also filed here on June 24 at about 7:15 p. m. This Court's order setting a hearing before us on June 26 at 11 a. m., a course which I joined only to avoid the possibility of even more peremptory action by the Court, was issued less than 24 hours before. The record in the Post case was filed with the Clerk shortly before 1 p. m. on June 25; the record in the Times case did not arrive until 7 or 8 o'clock that same night. The briefs of the parties were received less than two hours before argument on June 26.

This frenzied train of events took place in the name of the presumption against prior restraints created by the First Amendment. Due regard for the extraordinarily important and difficult questions involved in these litigations should have led the Court to shun such a precipitate timetable. In order to decide the merits of these cases properly, some or all of the following questions should have been faced:

1. Whether the Attorney General is authorized to bring these suits in the name of the United States. Compare In re Debs, 158 U. S. 564 (1895), with Youngstown Sheet & Tube Co. v. Sawyer, 343 U. S. 579 (1952). This question involves as well the construction and validity of a singularly opaque statute—the Espionage Act, 18 U. S. C. § 793 (e).

2. Whether the First Amendment permits the federal courts to enjoin publication

of stories which would present a serious threat to national security. See Near v. Minnesota, 283 U. S. 697, 716 (1931) (dictum).

3. Whether the threat to publish highly secret documents is of itself a sufficient implication of national security to justify an injunction on the theory that regardless of the contents of the documents harm enough results simply from the demonstration of such a breach of secrecy.

4. Whether the unauthorized disclosure of any of these particular documents would seriously impair the national security.

5. What weight should be given to the opinion of high officers in the Executive Branch of the Government with respect to questions 3 and 4.

6. Whether the newspapers are entitled to retain and use the documents notwithstanding the seemingly uncontested facts that the documents, or the originals of which they are duplicates, were purloined from the Government's possession and that the newspapers received them with knowledge that they had been feloniously acquired. Cf. Liberty Lobby, Inc. v. Pearson, 129 U. S. App. D. C. 74, 390 F. 2d 489 (1967, amended 1968).

7. Whether the threatened harm to the national security or the Government's possessory interest in the documents justifies the issuance of an injunction against publication in light of—

a. The strong First Amendment policy against prior restraints on publication;

b. The doctrine against enjoining conduct in violation of criminal statutes; and

c. The extent to which the materials at issue have apparently already been otherwise disseminated.

These are difficult questions of fact, of law, and of judgment; the potential consequences of erroneous decision are enormous. The time which has been available to us, to the lower courts,[*] and to the parties has been wholly inadequate for giving these cases the kind of consideration they deserve. It is a reflection on the stability of the judicial process that these great issues— as important as any that have arisen during my time on the Court—should have been decided under the pressures engendered by the torrent of publicity that has attended these litigations from their inception.

Forced as I am to reach the merits of these cases, I dissent from the opinion and judgments of the Court. Within the severe limitations imposed by the time constraints under which I have been required to operate, I can only state my reasons in telescoped form, even though in different circumstances I would have felt constrained to deal with the cases in the fuller sweep indicated above.

It is a sufficient basis for affirming the Court of Appeals for the Second Circuit in the Times litigation to observe that its order must rest on the conclusion that because of the time elements the Government had not been given an adequate opportunity to present its case to the District Court. At the least this conclusion was not an abuse of discretion.

In the Post litigation the Government had more time to prepare; this was apparently the basis for the refusal of the Court of Appeals for the District of Columbia

Circuit on rehearing to conform its judgment to that of the Second Circuit. But I think there is another and more fundamental reason why this judgment cannot stand—a reason which also furnishes an additional ground for not reinstating the judgment of the District Court in the Times litigation, set aside by the Court of Appeals. It is plain to me that the scope of the judicial function in passing upon the activities of the Executive Branch of the Government in the field of foreign affairs is very narrowly restricted. This view is, I think, dictated by the concept of separation of powers upon which our constitutional system rests.

In a speech on the floor of the House of Representatives, Chief Justice John Marshall, then a member of that body, stated:

"The President is the sole organ of the nation in its external relations, and its sole representative with foreign nations." 10 Annals of Cong. 613 (1800).

From that time, shortly after the founding of the Nation, to this, there has been no substantial challenge to this description of the scope of executive power. See United States v. Curtiss-Wright Corp., 299 U. S. 304, 319-321 (1936), collecting authorities.

From this constitutional primacy in the field of foreign affairs, it seems to me that certain conclusions necessarily follow. Some of these were stated concisely by President Washington, declining the request of the House of Representatives for the papers leading up to the negotiation of the Jay Treaty:

"The nature of foreign negotiations requires caution, and their success must often depend on secrecy; and even when brought to a conclusion a full disclosure of all the measures, demands, or eventual concessions which may have been proposed or contemplated would be extremely impolitic; for this might have a pernicious influence on future negotiations, or produce immediate inconveniences, perhaps danger and mischief, in relation to other powers." 1 J. Richardson, Messages and Papers of the Presidents 194-195 (1896).

The power to evaluate the "pernicious influence" of premature disclosure is not, however, lodged in the Executive alone. I agree that, in performance of its duty to protect the values of the First Amendment against political pressures, the judiciary must review the initial Executive determination to the point of satisfying itself that the subject matter of the dispute does lie within the proper compass of the President's foreign relations power. Constitutional considerations forbid "a complete abandonment of judicial control." Cf. United States v. Reynolds, 345 U. S. 1, 8 (1953). Moreover, the judiciary may properly insist that the determination that disclosure of the subject matter would irreparably impair the national security be made by the head of the Executive Department concerned—here the Secretary of State or the Secretary of Defense—after actual personal consideration by that officer. This safeguard is required in the analogous area of executive claims of privilege for secrets of state. See id., at 8 and n. 20; Duncan v. Cammell, Laird & Co., [1942] A. C. 624, 638 (House of Lords).

But in my judgment the judiciary may not properly go beyond these two inquiries and redetermine for itself the probable impact of disclosure on the national security.

"[T]he very nature of executive decisions as to foreign policy is political, not judicial. Such decisions are wholly confided by our Constitution to the political departments of the government, Executive and Legislative. They are delicate, complex, and involve large elements of prophecy. They are and should be undertaken only by those directly responsible to the people whose welfare they advance or imperil. They are decisions of a kind for which the Judiciary has neither aptitude, facilities nor responsibility and which has long been held to belong in the domain of political power not subject to judicial intrusion or inquiry." Chicago & Southern Air Lines v. Waterman Steamship Corp., 333 U. S. 103, 111 (1948) (Jackson, J.).

Even if there is some room for the judiciary to override the executive determination, it is plain that the scope of review must be exceedingly narrow. I can see no indication in the opinions of either the District Court or the Court of Appeals in the Post litigation that the conclusions of the Executive were given even the deference owing to an administrative agency, much less that owing to a co-equal branch of the Government operating within the field of its constitutional prerogative.

Accordingly, I would vacate the judgment of the Court of Appeals for the District of Columbia Circuit on this ground and remand the case for further proceedings in the District Court. Before the commencement of such further proceedings, due opportunity should be afforded the Government for procuring from the Secretary of State or the Secretary of Defense or both an expression of their views on the issue of national security. The ensuing review by the District Court should be in accordance with the views expressed in this opinion. And for the reasons stated above I would affirm the judgment of the Court of Appeals for the Second Circuit.

Pending further hearings in each case conducted under the appropriate ground rules, I would continue the restraints on publication. I cannot believe that the doctrine prohibiting prior restraints reaches to the point of preventing courts from maintaining the status quo long enough to act responsibly in matters of such national importance as those involved here.

Made in the USA
Las Vegas, NV
06 September 2024

94794919R00453